THE OXFORD HANDBOOK OF

COMPARATIVE JUDICIAL BEHAVIOUR

THE OXFORD HANDBOOK OF

COMPARATIVE JUDICIAL BEHAVIOUR

Edited by
LEE EPSTEIN,
GUNNAR GRENDSTAD,
URŠKA ŠADL,
and
KEREN WEINSHALL

OXFORD
UNIVERSITY PRESS

OXFORD
UNIVERSITY PRESS

Great Clarendon Street, Oxford, OX2 6DP,
United Kingdom

Oxford University Press is a department of the University of Oxford.
It furthers the University's objective of excellence in research, scholarship,
and education by publishing worldwide. Oxford is a registered trade mark of
Oxford University Press in the UK and in certain other countries

Published in the United States of America by Oxford University Press
198 Madison Avenue, New York, NY 10016, United States of America

British Library Cataloguing in Publication Data
Data available

Library of Congress Control Number: 2024939888

ISBN 978–0–19–289857–9

DOI: 10.1093/oxfordhb/9780192898579.001.0001

Printed and bound by
CPI Group (UK) Ltd, Croydon, CR0 4YY

FSC www.fsc.org MIX Paper | Supporting responsible forestry FSC® C013604

Contents

PART III DATA, METHODS, AND TECHNOLOGIES

PART IV STAFFING THE COURTS

PART V ADVOCACY, LITIGATION, AND APPELLATE REVIEW

PART VI OPINIONS

PART VII RELATIONS WITHIN, BETWEEN, AND AMONG COURTS

PART VIII JUDICIAL INDEPENDENCE

PART IX COURTS AND SOCIETY

PART X ON THE FRONTIERS OF COMPARATIVE JUDICIAL BEHAVIOUR

Acknowledgements

In December 2022, we held a contributors' conference at the Hebrew University in Jerusalem. The conference would not have been possible without the generous support of Peter and Julie Weil, the Hebrew University Faculty of Law, and Washington University in St Louis. We also thank Ohad Halevy, the conference organizer, for his professionalism.

Compiling the volume was a true team effort. We are grateful to Arnold Zahn, a law student at the University of Southern California (now a lawyer at Sullivan & Cromwell in New York) for his excellent editing skills. We also thank Lisa Butts, our project editor at Oxford. We could not have asked for a better, more attentive editor. Finally, thanks to the Gould School of Law at the University of Southern California for providing research support.

Contributors

Wolfgang Alschner, Hyman Soloway Chair in Business and Trade, Common Law Section, University of Ottawa

Ori Aronson, Associate Professor of Law, Bar-Ilan University

Elliott Ash, Associate Professor of Law, Economics, and Data Science, ETH Zurich

Santiago Basabe-Serrano, Professor of Political Science, Facultad Latinoamericana de Ciencias Sociales, FLACSO ECUADOR

Henrik Litleré Bentsen, Senior Researcher, NORCE Norwegian Research Centre

Eileen Braman, Associate Professor of Political Science, Indiana University

Benjamin Bricker, Associate Professor of Political Science; Associate Dean of the College of Liberal Arts, Southern Illinois University

Michael Burnham, Graduate Student, Political Science and Social Data Analytics, The Pennsylvania State University

Clifford J. Carrubba, Samuel Candler Dobbs Professor of Political Science and Quantitative Theory and Methods, Emory University

Andrea Castagnola, Visiting Professor, Universidad Torcuato Di Tella

Yun-chien Chang, Jack G. Clarke Professor in East Asian Law, Law School, Cornell University

Bao Kham Chau, Visiting Fellow, Cornell Tech

Kevin L. Cope, Associate Professor of Law, University of Virginia

Shai Dothan, Associate Professor of International and Public Law, University of Copenhagen

Björn Dressel, Associate Professor, Crawford School of Public Policy, Australian National University

Christoph Engel, Director, Max-Planck-Institute for Research on Collective Goods, Max-Planck-Institute for Research on Collective Goods

Benjamin G. Engst, Associate Professor, Norwegian University of Science and Technology

Brad Epperly, Associate Professor of Political Science, University of British Columbia

Lee Epstein, Ethan A. H. Shepley Distinguished University Professor, Washington University in St Louis

Jens Frankenreiter, Associate Professor of Law, Washington University in St Louis

Matthew J. Gabel, Professor of Political Science, Washington University in St Louis

Nuno Garoupa, Professor of Law, George Mason University

Tom Ginsburg, Leo Spitz Professor of International Law, University of Chicago

Gunnar Grendstad, Professor of Political Science, Universitetet i Bergen

Thomas Gschwend, Professor of Political Science, Quantitative Methods in the Social Sciences, University of Mannheim

Ivar A. Hartmann, Associate Professor of Law, Insper Institute of Education and Research in São Paulo, Brazil

Courtney Hillebrecht, Professor and Chair, Department of Political Science; Hitchcock Family Chair in Human Rights and Humanitarian Affairs, University of Nebraska-Lincoln

Ran Hirschl, David R. Cameron Distinguished Professor in Law and Politics, University of Toronto

Ching-Fang Hsu, Assistant Professor, Department of Public Policy and Administration, National Chi Nan University

Katalin Kelemen, Associate Professor in Law, Örebro University

Jack Knight, Frederic Cleaveland Distinguished Professor of Law and Political Science, Duke University

Jay N. Krehbiel, Associate Professor of Political Science, West Virginia University

Michael A. Livermore, Professor of Law, University of Virginia

Andrew D. Martin, Chancellor, Professor of Political Science, Law, and Statistics and Data Science, Washington University in St Louis

Alexander Morell, Professor of Private Law, Business Law, and Law and Economics, Department of Law, Goethe University

Daniel Naurin, Professor of Political Science, ARENA Centre for European Studies, University of Oslo

Michael J. Nelson, Professor of Political Science and Affiliate Law Faculty, Pennsylvania State University

Anthony Niblett, Professor and Canada Research Chair in Law, Economics, & Innovation, University of Toronto

C. L. Ostberg, Professor of Political Science, University of the Pacific

Tommaso Pavone, Assistant Professor of European Politics, University of Toronto

Aníbal Pérez-Liñán, Professor of Political Science and Global Affairs, University of Notre Dame

Kevin Quinn, Charles Howard Candler Professor of Law and Professor of Quantitative Theory and Methods, Emory University

Gerald N. Rosenberg, Associate Professor Emeritus and Lecturer in Law, University of Chicago

Urška Šadl, Professor (Part Time), European University Institute

Anne Sanders, Chair for Civil Law, Company Law, the Law of Family Businesses, and Comparative Judicial Studies, Bielefeld University

Alex Schwartz, Senior Lecturer in Public Law, University of Glasgow

Elin Skaar, Research Professor, Chr. Michelsen Institute

Jon Kåre Skiple, Senior Researcher, NORCE Norwegian Research Centre

Russell Smyth, Professor and Deputy Dean Research, Monash Business School, Monash University

Rorie Solberg, Professor of Public Policy, Oregon State University

Jeffrey K. Staton, Professor, Political Science and Senior Associate Dean, James T. Laney School of Graduate Studies, Emory University

Lydia Brashear Tiede, Professor of Political Science, University of Houston

Frans van Dijk, Professor of Empirical Analysis of Legal Systems (Emeritus), Montaigne Centre for Rule of Law and Administration of Justice, Utrecht University

Mila Versteeg, Henry L. and Grace Doherty Charitable Foundation Professor of Law, University of Virginia

Erik Voeten, Peter F. Krogh Professor of Geopolitics and Justice in World Affairs, Georgetown University

Eric N. Waltenburg, Professor of Political Science, Department of Political Science, Purdue University

Keren Weinshall, Edward S. Silver Professor of Law, The Hebrew University of Jerusalem

Diego Werneck Arguelhes, Associate Professor of Law, Insper Institute of Education and Research in São Paulo, Brazil

Matthew E. Wetstein, President, Cabrillo College

Table of Cases

EUROPEAN UNION

Court of Justice of the European Union (CJEU)

European Court of Human Rights (ECtHR)

European Court of Justice (ECJ)

INTERNATIONAL COURT

Inter-American Court of Human Rights

United Kingdom

United States

Table of International Instruments

Table of National Instruments

PART I

FUNDAMENTALS

CHAPTER 1

INTRODUCTION TO THE STUDY OF COMPARATIVE JUDICIAL BEHAVIOUR

LEE EPSTEIN, GUNNAR GRENDSTAD, URŠKA ŠADL, AND KEREN WEINSHALL

1. Introduction

THESE are momentous times for the comparative analysis of judicial behaviour. Once the sole province of US political scientists, the field has transformed into a global research enterprise with scholars drawing on history, economics, and psychology to illuminate *how and why judges make the choices they do and the consequences of their choices for society.*

Virtually no judicial system has escaped systematic and rigorous attention, from Argentina (Muro et al. 2018) and Brazil (Arguelhes and Hartmann 2017) up to Mexico (Staton 2010) and Canada (Alarie and Green 2014); and from China (Liu and Li 2019) and Taiwan (Chen, Huang, and Lin 2015) across the globe to India (Green and Yoon 2017), Israel (Weinshall-Margel 2016), and most of Europe (e.g. Hanretty 2020 (United Kingdom); Grendstad et al. 2020 (Norway); Krehbiel 2016 (Germany); Melcarne 2017 (Italy)), down to South Africa (Sill and Haynie 2010) and Australia (Nielsen and Smyth 2019). Analysis extends from long-standing to developing democracies and authoritarian regimes (Moustafa 2014). Likewise, judges serving on international and transnational courts, long of interest to scholars, are now more than ever the targets of sophisticated theoretical and empirical work (e.g. Gabel et al. 2012; Lupu and Voeten 2012; Cichowski 2016; Frankenreiter 2017; Voeten 2020).

Despite their common interest in explaining the causes and effects of judicial choices, scholars ask substantively different questions, subscribe to manifold theories, apply multiple methodologies, and pursue varied targets of inquiry.

Some draw comparisons over time (e.g. Gabel et al. 2012; Lupu and Voeten 2012; Frankenreiter 2017; Bentsen 2018); others engage in cross-national studies of multiple courts operating during similar eras (e.g. Garoupa and Ginsburg 2015; Voigt, Gutmann, and Feld 2015; Brouard and Honnige 2017; Alarie and Green 2017; Basabe-Serrano 2019; Voeten 2020). The researchers' motivations are equally diverse, from describing features of judging to offering measures of crucial concepts (e.g. judicial independence) to making causal inferences to developing implications for law and public policy.

Perhaps tracing back to these differences and the wide array of publication outlets in multiple languages in multiple disciplines, researchers sometimes lose track of new developments.[1] They may be entirely unaware of studies directly bearing on their research conducted in other corners of the world and in other disciplinary pockets.

The *Oxford Handbook of Comparative Judicial Behaviour* (the *Handbook*) unites scholars from many corners of the world and disciplinary pockets to offer up-to date expert roadmaps of the topics falling under the field's domain, from approaches to judging to staffing the courts to relations among courts and society. Each chapter critically assesses the major contributions to the literature, describes how the literature has developed, and provides promising directions for future research. All in all, the *Handbook* aims to provide an indispensable tool for veterans and newcomers alike.

The *Handbook*'s table of contents reflects these objectives. Rather than zooming in on countries, legal cultures, or regions, the organization is topical, following the research process of scholars and students. With 42 chapters divided into ten sections, we hope to introduce comparative analysis of judicial behaviour and encourage contributions to this growing and exciting field.

We begin, in Section 2, with a discussion of 'comparative judicial behaviour,' emphasizing our inclusive approach to the field. Section 3 surveys the major approaches (theories) which remain guideposts for scholars seeking to develop and answer a range of research questions. Section 4 provides a comprehensive outline of the structure of the *Handbook* and individual chapters. Throughout this introduction, we flag contributions to the field detailed in the *Handbook's* chapters, as well as identify opportunities for advancement.

2. Comparative Judicial Behaviour: State of the Art

Comparative judicial behaviour seeks to illuminate the choices judges make and the consequences of their choices for society. Understanding key terms in this definition—choices, consequences, illuminate, and comparative—opens a window into the field's goals and domains.

2.1 Choices

The modern-day study of judicial behaviour owes its origins to US political scientists working in the mid-twentieth century (Dyevre 2010). At that time, the discipline was in the early stages of the behavioural revolution, grounded in studies of citizens' voting behaviour (notably Campbell et al. 1960). When political scientists turned to the judiciary, they naturally equated the 'choices judges make' with the 'votes judges cast' and, ultimately, the outcomes: to affirm or reverse the lower court's decision, for or against the government, in the 'liberal' or 'conservative' direction, and so on (Pritchett 1948; Schubert 1965; Spaeth 1963).

Contemporary scholars of judicial behaviour have broadened their definition of 'choices' without, however, turning away from judicial votes and case outcomes. Explaining these choices remains a mainstay of the field because the judges' votes and the cases' outcomes, like citizens' voting choices, matter to countless stakeholders.

Helmke's (2002, 2005) path-marking research on the Argentine Supreme Court illustrates the value of 'vote' and 'outcome' studies. She shows that although both the Argentine and the US Constitutions allow judges to 'hold their office during good behaviour', that rule is a parchment guarantee in Argentina: 'good behaviour' does not mean life tenure as understood and practised in the US but tenure for the life of the appointing regime. As Helmke (2002, 292) writes, 'incoming governments in Argentina routinely get rid of their predecessors' judges despite constitutional guarantees'. She (2002, 291) theorized and empirically demonstrated that Argentine judges, fearing for their jobs or even their lives, rationally anticipate the threat and 'strategically defect', that is, vote against the existing regime once it begins losing power.

The government's preferences might figure in outcomes even when the threats are milder. Carrubba and his co-authors show that the European Court of Justice relies on 'observations' (briefs filed by European Union's institutions and member state governments in judicial proceedings) to assess the 'balance of member state preferences regarding the legal issue' (Carrubba, Gabel, and Hankla 2008, 440). The political majority thus has higher chances of winning a legal argument, which seems intuitively sound. If most member states disfavour the Court's ruling, they can potentially form a coalition to override the decision by contrary legislation, thereby rendering the ruling ineffective (see also Martinsen 2015).

On the flipside, when the political branches lack the wherewithal to overturn their high court's decisions or otherwise retaliate against the court and its members—perhaps because of gridlock or disagreement over the 'right' course of action—judges ignore the government and the public. Such is how studies have characterized the US Supreme Court in the 2020s. That Court, the research suggests, has exhibited historic levels of partisan bias, not to mention a strong penchant for judicial supremacy rather than deference (Lemley 2022; Brown and Epstein 2023).

While the above studies focus on the effect of external forces on votes and outcomes, other work is more internal looking. Sen (2015), for example, finds that Black US trial court judges face reversal on appeal more often than their White colleagues, attributing the finding to implicit bias. Blanes i Vidal and Leaver's (2015) study of English courts shows that the judges' 'collegial culture' artificially lowers the reversal rate. Judges 'actively avoid public contradiction of their peers'. These results are akin to findings in the United States, indicating that justices tend to affirm cases coming from the appellate court on which they served (Epstein et al. 2009).

The chapters in the *Handbook* highlight other examples of vote-outcome studies; they remain central to the study of judicial behaviour. Worth reiterating, though, is that the term 'choices' now encompasses more than just votes and outcomes. Examples include:

- whether and how to encourage settlement (Boyd 2013; Sela and Gabay-Egozi 2020)
- which cases to select for 'full-dress treatment' (Sanchez Urribarri et al. 2011; Eisenberg et al. 2012; Arguelhes and Hartmann 2017) and which to avoid (e.g. Epstein, Knight, and Shvetsova 2002; Goelzhauser 2011)
- to whom to assign the opinion of the court (e.g. Alarie and Green 2017)
- how to approach opinion writing, including what sources to cite (e.g. Lupu and Voeten 2012; Frankenreiter 2017; Green and Yoon 2017), whether to dissent (e.g. Tiede 2016; Bentsen 2018), and how to frame opinions for different audiences (e.g. Staton and Vanberg 2008)
- strategies to enhance future job prospects (including promotion and retention) (Ramseyer and Rasmusen 2001; Melcarne 2017; Stiansen 2022) and the judges' reputation and legacy (Posner 1990; Garoupa and Ginsburg 2015)
- ways to keep lower (or national) courts in line (e.g. Sweet and Brunell 1998; Dyevre 2013) and ways to evade backlash from governments (Helmke 2002 2005; Carrubba, Gabel, and Hankla 2008)
- approaches to cement the court's legitimacy and encourage compliance with its decisions (e.g. Vanberg 2005; Krehbiel 2016)
- when to leave the bench (e.g. Massie, Randazzo, and Songer 2014; Pérez-Liñán and Araya 2017) and even when to avoid judicial posts altogether (Basabe-Serrano 2012).

As the choice set expanded so too did the number of topics falling under the rubric of comparative judicial behaviour. To note a few examples: Helmke's (2002, 2005) and Carrubba, Gabel, and Hankla's (2008) studies, recall, embed the judges' choices in their regimes, and now an entire branch of judicial behaviour centres on the courts' relations with elected political actors (e.g. Epstein, Knight, and Shvetsova 2002; Brouard and Hönnige 2017; Engst 2021). Along somewhat different lines, work by Sen (2015) and Blanes i Vidal and Leaver (2015) illustrates the value of embedding courts within their legal system. A large area of inquiry that goes under the name 'The Hierarchy of Justice', explores the interactions between judges on higher (or transnational) and lower (or domestic) courts. Extensive scholarship draws attention to connections between courts and citizens. Some studies explore how judges develop popular rights or incorporate public opinion into their decisions or procedures (see generally Epstein and Knight

2018), perhaps pursuing legitimacy goals; other research focuses on public relations campaigns mounted by courts to generate conditions favourable to the exercise of their power (Staton 2010).

As a final example of subjects under study is a vast literature linking institutions (formal and informal rules) governing judicial selection and retention to judicial decisions. That literature tends to confirm what many constitutional framers seem to understand: if law in books and law in action coincide, institutional arrangements for judicial appointment and tenure can affect the people selected to serve and, ultimately, the choices they, as judges, make (e.g. Driscoll and Nelson 2015; Varol, Pellegrina, and Garoupa 2017; Weinshall and Epstein 2020; Stiansen 2022; Spirig 2023). Work on economic prosperity provides a classic example. The hypothesis, in a nutshell, is that judges with life tenure will more likely enforce contract and property rights, thereby indirectly ensuring economic investment and growth (North and Weingast 1989). Scholars have validated this expectation against contemporaneous cross-national (most famously, La Porta et al. 2004) and even historical data. Looking back to England in the 1700s, Klerman and Mahoney (2005), for example, found that laws providing greater job security to judges increased the value of financial assets.

2.2 Consequences

Klerman and Mahoney's study of eighteenth-century England draws attention to the relationship between institutions (tenure arrangements) and judicial choices, and to the consequence of those choices: economic prosperity. Clever research by Mehmood (2022) runs along similar lines. It shows that a change in Pakistan's method of appointing judges (from presidential selection to appointment by merit commissions) resulted in judges less inclined towards government expropriation, resulting in greater investment in the construction industry.

These examples focus on how institutions governing judicial appointments prompted judicial decisions affecting economic trends. But the formal and informal rules shaping judicial choices are hardly limited to selection mechanisms, and the consequences are not cabined to economics. On almost all comparative analyses, constitutional provisions, statutes, treaties, case law, and the like serve to structure the judges' choices, thereby affecting their decisions and the decisions' impact. Consider studies exploring the relations between judges and external actors. Because constitutional arrangements usually provide a mechanism(s) for the people or their representatives to undo judicial decisions, studies demonstrate that judges can't afford to ignore the possible consequences of rulings against the regime's or the public's preferences (unless the public and its representatives are so divided that they can't retaliate). Carruba et al.'s (2008) analysis of the European Court of Justice it is hardly alone in this category.

Other work on judicial behaviour considers the consequences of internal institutional arrangements like rules that allow the chief justice to set the size and composition of panels (e.g. Indian and Canadian Supreme Courts), norms that permit, if not encourage, dissent (e.g. US and Australian Supreme Courts) (Alarie and Green 2014) or how docket control shapes judicial behaviour (Skiple, McKenzie, and Bentsen 2021). Once again, the idea is to explore how institutions drive judicial choices and, ultimately, the effect of those choices for society or even for the Court.

An example is a court's approach to dissenting opinions. Some courts (e.g. the German Constitutional Court and especially the European Court of Justice) and judges (US Chief Justice Roberts) disfavour dissents. More preferable, they argue, is a norm of consensus because it produces positive consequences: consensus 'contributes to stability in law', reflects a more 'cautious' approach, encourages deliberation, and promotes the court's legitimacy. Studies on international human rights judiciaries tend to support the dissent naysayers: in those courts, separate opinions lower compliance rates (Naurin and Stiansen 2020). Experimental research on domestic courts, however, shows that dissents can boost support for courts because they amount to consolation prizes for people who disagreed with the decision: even losers get representation (Salamone 2018; Bentsen 2019).

Whatever the studies' particulars, a focus on the relationship among institutions, judicial choices, and consequences highlights the importance of comparative analysis. It is one thing to claim that job security frees judges to act on own their own preferences (rather than the government's) or that dissent produces good (or bad) consequences, but quite another to test those assertions. Only by comparing judges in societies with different jurisdictions and audiences and where particular institutions, such as life tenure, exist or not (or where institutional change occurred) is it possible to even begin to determine whether and which rules matter for judicial choice and eventually for society.

2.3 Illumination of Choices and Consequences

The term 'illuminate' refers to the aim of comparative judicial behaviour to make the judges' choices and the consequences of their choices for society intelligible. This term is purposefully broad to convey the different motivations and methods scholars bring to the comparative analysis of judicial behaviour. The goals vary widely, including rich description of features of judging (such as norms governing dissent or the institutions structuring judicial selection and retention), measures of crucial concepts (such as judicial ideology or judicial independence), to causal claims with legal and public policy implications (such as the effect of tenure arrangements on economic prosperity).

These varying motivations lead scholars to different types of data (facts about the world) and methods. Some favour quantitative (numerical) data and the process of data collection, which allows for statistical inference. Others prefer qualitative (non-numerical) data that they can interpret, categorize, and use to identify patterns or understand particular legal phenomena; and still others produce narratives about specific features of the judges' choices. The data can be historical or contemporary, based on legislation, treaties, case law, interviews, secondary archival research, or primary data collection.

The choice of data and methods should be guided by the research questions, theory, and hypotheses—not by a belief that some are per se superior or preferable. None is. In fact, all have led to valuable insights, answered pertinent research questions, and helped solve persistent societal puzzles, as the chapters in this *Handbook* so ably demonstrate.

2.4 Comparative Judicial Behaviour

For the purposes of the *Handbook*, the term 'comparative' is equally wide and inclusive. It ranges from intuitive attempts to make sense of judicial behaviour through contrasts and similarities between courts, legal systems, or institutional characteristics, to sophisticated research agendas falling squarely within a particular comparative school and following a prescribed comparative design. Such an expansive (and for some, unorthodox) definition best reflects the reality of the emerging field united around a common commitment to illuminate judicial choices and their implications for society, while drawing on a range of disciplines, a wealth of motivations, and the gamut of research strategies, data sources, and methods.

This definition of, or approaches to, comparative has at least four advantages. First, it potentially avoids internecine strife inherent in a priori or top-down conceptualizations. Attempts to define the formal features of a comparative study (i.e. what counts as comparative) have long plagued the comparative legal scholarship, leading to idiosyncratic and at times unproductive debates (Siems 2022; Legrand and Munday 2003). There is little need to reproduce them but a pressing need to learn from them.

Second, our definition of comparative is pragmatic, enabling scholars to enrich the debate by capitalizing on their own skill set, know-how, and experience acquired in various disciplines, legal traditions, and approaches. In this sense, the definition encourages interdisciplinary research. Put another way, the contributors to the *Handbook* could independently decide which meaning of the term was the most meaningful to their topics and research questions.

Third, the definition best furthers the double aim of the *Handbook*: to map and review the existing scholarship on the topics of judicial behaviour (such as the relations within, between, and among courts), and to develop new and exciting research agendas for the comparative study of judicial behaviour where currently none exist (examples include Niblett's chapter on AI and judging; Pavone's outline of a comparative agenda to understand the influence of government lawyers on judicial behaviour).

Finally, the definition strives for a geographical rebalancing, indirectly responding to the historical dominance of US-based scholarship—both subject—and methodology-wise. The need for such rebalancing follows Macridis' (1955) early criticism of traditional comparative politics as 'essentially noncomparative' (Sartori 1991, 243), which got second wind in Sartori's (1991, 243) critique of American comparativists' nonsensical focus on (typically one) 'other country'. In Sartori's words, 'a scholar who studies only American presidents is an Americanist, whereas a scholar who studies only the French presidents is a comparativist'.

While the readers will be the final arbiters of the usefulness of the distinction, Sartori's critique has been instructive to the *Handbook* in two respects. On the one hand, it contextualized the tendency to transplant ideas developed in the United States unreflectively to non-American legal and political systems, originating in the tendency to speak of 'comparative courts' when actually speaking of non-American courts and political systems. Because interest in judicial behaviour originated in the United States and developed much earlier there than elsewhere—a fact to which the *Oxford Handbook of U.S. Judicial Behavior* clearly speaks (Epstein and Lindquist 2017)—this tendency is unsurprising. But it has had obvious and even troubling implications: European, Asian, and other scholars adopted influential theories (like the attitudinal or ideological model); and comparative studies adopted crude or misleading (Lasser 2009) assumptions about courts and judicial decision making, as they relied on early comparative law treaties by American scholars (notably Dawson, see Garoupa in Chapter 2).

On the other hand, Sartori's critique highlights the methodological consequences of testing the theories developed in the US context elsewhere: chiefly, the US system became the default benchmark. To be sure, this benchmark occasionally results in implicit comparisons and illuminating studies (see e.g. Hanretty's (2020) analysis of judicial behaviour on the UK Supreme Court). More often, though, studies do not feel the urge to adopt or explicitly follow a clearly defined comparative or cross-national design (Driscoll 2021), with the comparative judicial behaviour literature showing bias towards country-level or court-level research strategy (Garoupa, Gill, and Tiede 2021).

To conclude, the *Handbook* is neither oblivious nor dismissive of weighty scholarly debates about the acceptable aims, methods, and research strategies of comparative analysis of judicial behaviour. Then again, to chart the state of the art as comprehensively as possible and to avoid self-sabotaging quarrels and paralysing navel-gazing, it casts a wide net. Hopefully, the strategy will increase scholarly interest in the exciting field of comparative judicial behaviour.

3. Approaches to Analyse Judicial Behaviour

The study of comparative judicial behaviour is rich, diverse, and stable at its core. In their quest to explain judicial choices, scholars continue to labour within the five key approaches outlined in Table 1.1. The sections to follow flesh them out in greater detail.

Table 1.1 Approaches to analyse judicial behaviour

Approach (disciplinary origins)	Description
Legalism (traditional version: law; institutional version: law, political science)	Traditional version: Judges 'find' the meaning of legal rules through (politically) neutral methods. Law-as-an-Institution: 'Law' (broadly defined) constrains judges from acting on their personal preferences, intuitions, biases, and emotions.
Attitudinal Model (political science, psychology)	Judges' votes reflect their policy preferences towards case facts.
Rational Choice Accounts (economics, political science)	Labour Market Model: Judges are motivated and constrained by (mostly) non-pecuniary costs (e.g. effort, criticism) and benefits (e.g. esteem, influence, self-expression). Strategic Analysis: Judges are strategic actors who realize that their ability to achieve their goals depends on the preferences of other actors, the choices they expect others to make, and the institutional context in which they interact.
Identity Accounts (psychology, sociology)	Judges' biographies, professional backgrounds, personal characteristics, and identities affect their choices.
'Thinking Fast' Judging (psychology, behavioural economics)	Judges rely on heuristics, intuitions, and the like (e.g. 'hunches') to make fast and effortless decisions.

Sources: Adapted from Epstein and Weinshall (2021, 2) and Epstein, Šadl, and Weinshall (2021).

3.1 Legalism

On trial for his life, Socrates refused to appeal to the 'emotions' of judges, believing that the judge 'has sworn that he will judge according to the laws and not according to his own good pleasure' (Jowett 2020).[2] This outlook is often labelled 'legalism'. In its simplest form, legalism holds that law exists independently from judges, free of morals and politics; legal rules are determinate; the legal system is 'complete' (Maitland's 1898 seamless web).

A traditional version of the legalist outlook requires judges to 'find' or discover the meaning of legal rules through politically neutral methods—regardless of careerism, ideology, and emotions, just as Socrates proclaimed. And it engages the scholars (especially of the continental or civil law tradition) in the construction of a rationalized ideal: a systematization of legal sources, including judicial decisions, into a coherent whole.

Legalism continues to permeate theories of judicial behaviour but usually in its weaker or more modern form. The dominant approaches today tend to reject extreme legalistic assertions that law's rationality, neutrality, and objectivity guide the judges' choices. Rather, contemporary accounts—which we label 'law-as-an-institution' approaches—suggest that law 'matters', though with a twist. The idea is that law (broadly defined to include a variety of legal sources, like constitutional provisions, statutes, and past judicial decisions) is one of many institutions that structure judicial behaviour, either by constraining their choices or by shaping shared judicial preferences.

Seen in this way, legal rules cannot fully explain why judges make the choices they do; rather, law is a normative constraint on judges from acting on their personal preferences, intuitions, biases, and emotions. Put another way, judges might have a preferred rule that they would like to establish in a case or a preferred reading of a statute, but they adapt their position to the constraints imposed by law.

To see why, consider the norm of *stare decisis* ('to stand by things decided'). Confronted with a precedent they disfavour judges may nonetheless apply it because *stare decisis* signals respect for the established expectations of a community. To the extent that people act on the belief that others in their community will follow existing laws, courts have an interest in minimizing the disruptive effects of overturning entrenched rules of behaviour. Radical changes of the established rules may prove too disruptive for the members of the community, resulting in inefficacious decisions.

Studies of judicial behaviour have provided evidence of this constraint in action. For example, analyses of US and Canadian Supreme Court decisions demonstrate that various 'jurisprudential regimes' structure how the justices evaluate cases (respectively Richards and Kritzer 2002 and Muttart 2007).

But more work awaits. New studies should inquire how, why, and under what circumstances law shapes judicial decisions in national legal systems and international regimes. Future research could contribute to the on-going debate over how to measure the 'law' and the weight of precedent (thus the actual force of *stare decisis* on judicial choices). Under the institutional understanding, law is not a static formalistic concept but a complex and dynamic institution structuring and constraining judges' thinking. This makes empirically defining law a challenging task, though no doubt one that more cross-country comparisons would aid.

3.2 The Attitudinal Model

Of all the approaches listed in Table 1.1, the attitudinal model likely dominates the field. Developed by US political scientists in the mid-twentieth century (e.g. Schubert 1965), this model holds that judges' votes reflect their political preferences towards the facts raised in disputes—with political preferences usually defined by the judges' ideology or partisan identity (Segal and Spaeth 2002).

The sustained sway of the attitudinal model is a testament to its explanatory power. Political preferences, no matter how measured, drive judicial decisions everywhere—not just in the US Supreme Court. Virtually all studies that measure it, find that partisanship or ideology affect judging. Grendstad, Shaffer, and Waltenburg's (2015) book on the Norwegian Supreme Court demonstrates that justices appointed by social democratic governments are significantly more likely than non-socialist appointees to find for the litigant pursuing a 'public economic interest'. Ideology (as measured by the appointing regime) plays a bigger role in these decisions than almost any other factor considered by Grendstad, Shaffer, and Waltenburg (2015). Hönnige (2009) found that ideology helps predict the votes of judges serving on the French and German Constitutional Courts; and Carroll and Tiede (2012, 85) identify dissent patterns on the Constitutional Court of Chile 'consistent with a general separation between the judges with centre-left and right backgrounds'.

At the same time, though, these and other studies demonstrate the limits of ideological (or partisan) motivations: in none is there even close to a perfect correlation between political preferences and voting. Moreover, moving down the judicial hierarchy, from apex to trial courts, ideology and partisanship carry even less weight (Epstein, Landes, and Posner 2013).

That political preferences do not seem to fully explain the judges' choices—they may not even be especially weighty for many judges—has influenced the study of judicial behaviour in two ways. First, it has prompted scholars to try to isolate the factors that lead to 'attitudinal' voting. The list is now long and includes the process of judicial appointments (e.g. the more political actors involved, the more political the court), agenda-setting (weighty for many, the degree of discretion the court has to decide which cases to hear), the size of the court's docket, and the size of judicial panels (courts with a mandatory docket, high caseload, and small panels tend to be more legalistic) (see Narayan and Smyth 2007; Eisenberg et al. 2012; Robinson 2013; Weinshall, Sommer, and Ritov 2018; Skiple, McKenzie, and Bentsen 2021).

A second result of the realization that political preferences have limited explanatory power has been even more consequential: a quest for other motivations and explanations. That quest, in turn, spurred a new generation of approaches to judicial behaviour, the labour market model and strategic accounts, both of which accommodate preferences beyond the political.

3.3 Rational Choice Accounts

The labour market model and strategic accounts are distinct approaches to judging with a common grounding in rational choice theory. On this theory, judges (or any other actors) make rational decisions when they choose a course of action that they believe satisfies their desires most efficiently. Or as Posner (2011, 3) famously put it, the judge is 'a rational maximizer of his ends in life, his satisfactions ... his "self-interest"'.

The difference between the labour market model and strategic accounts is the flavour of rational choice theory that grounds them (Epstein and Knight 2017). The labour market model considers how individuals act to maximize their preferences, 'given the constraints they happen to face' (Lovett 2006). According to this model judges, just as other workers, are motivated and constrained by costs and benefits both pecuniary and non-pecuniary (Epstein, Landes, and Posner 2013). A judge wanting to earn more might write a novel assuming she has carefully weighed her own costs (e.g. time away from her job) and benefits. In other words, she is the variable and all others, the constants (Elster 1983).

Strategic accounts, in contrast, assume that goal-directed judges (regardless of their goal) operate in interdependent decision-making context; that is, when the judges make decisions, they attend to the preferences and likely actions of other relevant actors (Epstein and Knight 1998). For example, judges who care about the implementation of their decisions will consider the implementers' possible responses in their opinions (Staton and Vanberg 2008).

Although both the labour market model and strategic accounts have shed much light on judicial behaviour, their chief contributions are complementary. The labour market model has expanded the set of relevant motivations, and strategic accounts have introduced the importance of actors beyond the individual judge.

3.3.1 *The Labour Market and Personal Motivations*

The judges' preferences matter in almost all studies of judicial behaviour. Political scientists tend to emphasize ideology and partisanship, whereas strong forms of legalism focus on legal motivations. Without denigrating either, the labour market model draws attention to personal motivations for judicial choice. The idea is that given time constraints, judges seek to maximize their preferences over a set of roughly five personal factors (most of which also have implications for political and legal goals): (i) job satisfaction, or the internal satisfaction of feeling of doing a good job, as well as the more social dimensions of judicial work, such as relations with other judges, clerks, and staff (Baum 1997; Lopes 2019; Swalve 2022); (ii) external satisfactions that come from being a judge, including reputation, prestige, power, influence, and celebrity (Baum 2006; Kureshi 2021); (iii) leisure (Clark, Engst, and Staton 2018; Engel and Weinshall 2020); (iv) salary and income; (v) promotion to a higher or more prestigious office.

Chapter 10 fully fleshes out these specific personal factors, so suffice it here to make two more general points here. First, the factors—really elements in the judge's personal utility function—are not mutually exclusive but rather overlap substantially. Promotion provides an example. This would seem to be an important factor in its own right, influencing the personal utility that judges (and, in fact, many of us) gain from their work (Bell 2006). But promotion also tends to increase job satisfaction, external satisfactions (such as prestige and reputation) and, of course, salary.

Second, because the five personal motivations are rather universal, they lend themselves nicely to comparative analysis. Again, consider promotion. This as an important factor in its own right influencing the personal utility that judges gain from their work. But promotion could also coincide with policy preferences: the higher judges sit in the hierarchy, the more important the cases they hear, and the greater the opportunity to shape the law. Promotion also tends to increase job satisfaction, prestige, and reputation, and, of course, income. For these reasons, it is no surprise that many studies demonstrate a connection between the judges' choices and promotion goals. Ramseyer and Rasmusen (2001), for example, find that Japanese lower court judges tend to defer to the national government because deference improves their chances of 'doing better in their careers'. And Salzberger and Fenn (1999) show that UK judges work to avoid reversal because a lower reversal rate increases the judge's prestige and the likelihood of promotion.

Despite the generalizability of promotion and other personal motivations, most studies focus on US judges. This gap, in turn, suggests numerous opportunities for new research. Comparative work could unpack the mechanisms driving these seemingly universal motivations and their effect on judges in national or international settings. To provide some examples: research comparing the effect of time constraints in courts characterized by *certiorari* (the power to select the cases to decide on the merits) versus the prohibition of *non liquet* (the duty to decide a case on the merits) might reveal that a preference for leisure, say, does not have a linear effect on decisions (e.g. a decision to push litigants to compromise, or formalism); a study of promotion rules may aid in designing a system with tamer effects of career prospects on case outcomes (if that's desirable).

3.3.2 *Strategic Accounts and Interdependent Decision Making*

If the labour market model goes some distance towards layering the one-dimensional portrait of judges as policy maximizers or mechanical legalists, strategic accounts highlight the importance of interdependent decision-making. The idea is that judges must attend to the preferences and likely actions of *other relevant actors* when making decisions if they are to achieve their goals. Those other 'relevant actors' run the gamut, from the judges' colleagues to the ruling regime and the public.

Interesting strands of literature cover these actors, and this work, especially on court–government relations, is likely to mushroom if only because of global conditions. The rise of populism presents opportunities to explore backlash against international and domestic courts in the form of impeachment, jurisdiction stripping, court packing, non-compliance, or even criminal indictment and physical violence—and how backlash might affect the judges' choices (see Voeten 2020). Other research programmes might consider threats to courts from politicians who have taken to social media to express their displeasure with decisions or even threaten judges by name (Krewson, Lassen, and Owens 2018).

New projects, though, need not write on a blank slate. Strategic accounts of court–government relations hypothesize that rational judges will respond to threats with various strategies to preserve their legitimacy, such as avoiding cases that may contribute to further escalation (Epstein and Knight 2018), vague opinions (Staton and Vanberg 2008), and soliciting public support (Staton 2010). A next step for scholars would be to specify the circumstances under which certain strategies might be more effective (Dothan 2015). So doing is likely to help us understand how political threats reduce the ability of courts to develop doctrines, ensure individual protection, reduce arbitrariness, or engage in international cooperation. Comparative analyses of the efficacy of strategies used elsewhere to calm rough political waters would also benefit judges, helping to inform their choices of what cases to hear and decide and how to justify their decisions.

3.4 Identity Approaches

Studies exploring the relationship between the choices judges make and their biographies is old and new. Early research tended to focus on career experience, asking, for example, whether former prosecutors-turned-judges are tougher on criminal defendants (Goldman 1975) or whether judges who were corporate lawyers favoured wealthy and powerful interests (Tate and Sittiwong 1989).

But these days, as the composition of judiciaries throughout the world has become (somewhat) more diverse, the characteristics under analysis have expanded to include the judges' (and, sometimes, the litigants') social categories and personal attributes—especially gender (Boyd, Epstein, and Martin 2010; Voeten 2021), religion (Koev 2019), race (Sen 2015), ethnicity (Schwartz and Murchison 2016), and nationality (Posner and de Figueiredo 2005; Voeten 2008).

Reading across the growing number of articles and books on social identity and social diversity in courts, it seems that their findings have converged—though in distinct ways (see Epstein and Knight 2022). On the one hand, research that characterizes individual judges based on their social identity (e.g. gender, race, nationality) tends to generate results in line with in-group bias: the inclination of individuals to disfavour outsiders. Examples include the tendency of international court judges to favour the appointing government (Posner and de Figueiredo 2005), of Jewish judges to rule for Jewish litigants, and Arab judges for Arab litigants (Shayo and Zussman 2011).

On the other hand, research on the social diversity of collegiate courts (those on which judges sit in panels or *en banc*) suggests that greater heterogeneity leads to better reasoned (more persuasively argued) decisions. For example, studies find that gender- and racially diverse panels more frequently consider alternative views on the questions presented in cases (Haire, Moyer, and Treier 2013).

These are the differences between studies on social identity and on social diversity. Their commonality may be even more important: both can potentially increase our understanding of judicial behaviour. But 'potential' is the operative word. Much more work is needed for the field to reach its full potential in terms of academic consequence and, we might add, policy impact.

One example of a gap squarely implicates 'identity' or more accurately 'identities'. Virtually all existing data studies of judging 'separate out the effects of individual identity attributes' (Page 2017, 142; see also Bonthuys 2015). A Jewish female judge is deconstructed into a Jewish effect and a female effect; a Black male British judge into a Black, a male, and a British effect, and on and on. Many scholars working in the diversity space, however, reject this approach arguing instead that 'the inseparability of attributes ... should give us pause when interpreting data sorted by a single attribute' (Page 2017, 142). Recognizing that individual judges are, like all of us, bundles of identities—identities that intersect and overlap (Crenshaw 1989)—is crucial to advance work in the field.

But the studies need not move in lockstep. One approach is to consider more carefully when one identity over others is likely to be activated because it may be particularly salient to the dispute at hand (Shayo 2009). Comparative research could serve as a method to identify or unpack the most relevant overlap of interaction of personal attributes that affect judicial choices. Likewise, it might be desirable to explicitly account for the intersectionality of identities (Kang et al. 2020). One of the rare examples is a study of US appellate judges modelling the joint effects of gender and race (Collins and Moyer 2008).

3.5 Thinking-Fast Judging

Some findings of the identity studies, like the effect of national identity in judging on international courts, resonate with rational choice accounts. Posner and de Figueiredo (2005, 608) explain that International Court of Justice judges tend to vote for the appointing state:

> Economically, judges may be motivated by material incentives. Judges who defy the wills of their government by holding against it may be penalized. The government may refuse to support them for reappointment and also refuse to give them any other desirable government position after the expiration of their term.

A decades' worth of studies in social psychology (and behavioural economics) offers a competing explanation: people generally rely on mental shortcuts derived from intuition and emotion for effortless fast decisions (Kahneman 2011; Thaler 2015). On this account, judges may not rationally but intuitively side with their own country. Posner and de Figueiredo (2005, 608) concur, offering an alternative explanation:

> Psychologically, if judges identify with their countries, they may find it difficult to maintain impartiality. International Court of Justice judges are … nationals who would normally have strong emotional ties with their country … Even with the best intentions, they may have trouble seeing the dispute from the perspective of any country but that of their native land.

The basic point is that regardless of the judges' goals, irrational factors can complicate their ability to make strategically rational decisions. These human features can distort rational decision-making and find their way into legal interpretation and the legal outcomes that ultimately become the law.

Even so, many judges think they can 'suppress or convert' their intuitions, prejudices, sympathies, and the like into rational decisions. But experiments conducted on thousands of judges suggest that they are just as human on the bench as the rest of us (e.g. Wistrich, Rachlinski, and Guthrie 2015; Spamann and Klöhn 2016). Judges respond more favourably to litigants they like or with whom they sympathize (Wistrich,

Rachlinski, and Guthrie 2015), harbour implicit bias against Black defendants (Rachlinski et al. 2009), and use anchoring and other simplifying heuristics in making numerical estimates (Sonnemans and van Dijk 2012).

This line of research is extremely important. It has real implications for lawyering; and, more relevant here, it presents real opportunities for scholars of comparative judicial behaviour. To the extent that cognitive biases are features of human decision making, research findings should transport to judges working across the globe, regardless of the appointment and tenure arrangements, the type of court, or the legal origin. Experiments on non-US judges and observational data suggest as much (Sonnemans and van Dijk 2012). But far more work is needed, not only to identify the effects of various biases but also to devise legal solutions to promote debiasing.

4. Overview of the *Handbook*

The ten sections of the *Handbook* reflect our understanding of the field of comparative judicial behaviour. The first three offer a foreword to the field's premises, approaches, and methods. The subsequent seven sections explore significant inquiries within the field on how and why judges make the choices they do (Sections 4–8) and how those choices affect society (Section 9). The *Handbook* concludes with a section devoted to the frontiers of comparative judicial behaviour.

To be more specific: the chapters in Section 1 ('Fundamentals') provide overviews designed to identify common trends in courts worldwide. In his chapter on legal traditions and their relation to judicial behaviour, Nuno Garoupa lays out an analytical division between courts in which the emphasis is on single judges—individual recognition judiciaries—and collective judiciaries, which emphasize the institution. The classification relates to the traditional common law–civil law divide but contributes more significant insights in the context of judging. Tom Ginsburg and Mila Versteeg, in Chapter 3, offer a new and fresh take on another classic topic in the analysis of comparative judicial behaviour—the three 'canonical models' of judicial review (associated with the United States, Germany, and France). Briefly, they suggest an alternative classification along three dimensions (access, finality, and concentration), which cut across the canonical models.

In Chapter 4 Ran Hirschl identifies a global movement towards the expansion of judicial power. Hirschl's comparative analysis allows him to categorize the causes for this worldwide phenomenon, among them the proliferation of international tribunals. Chapter 5, by Daniel Naurin and Erik Voeten, investigates the extent to which studies on domestic and international courts are converging into 'one coherent literature'. The answer is that, overall, the division remains but it is mostly driven by US studies of judicial behaviour. Putting those studies aside and solely focusing on comparative and international courts, convergence is indeed occurring.

Section 2 turns to the different approaches to judging. Alexander Morell expands on both the traditional and institutional versions of legalism in Chapter 6. He traces the origins of traditional legalism back to legal positivism, which has evolved distinctively within common law and continental civil law judiciaries. Through a comparative analysis of these divergent trajectories, Morell illuminates fresh insights into the notion of law as a constraining professional norm. Chapter 7 focuses on the attitudinal model. Rorie Solberg and Eric N. Waltenburg conduct a meta-analysis of global attitudinal studies to evaluate the extent of attitudinal voting within various judiciaries and explore institutional and contextual variables that impact attitudinal behaviour. In Chapter 8, Santiago Basabe-Serrano and colleagues bring a comparative perspective to bear on the relationship between the judges' decisions and their personal characteristics—especially their social identities.

A strategic analysis approach is introduced in Chapter 9 by Shai Dothan, who differentiates between the strategies employed by judges and courts and between short-term strategies, which encompass a single judgment and its immediate consequences, and long-term strategies. In Chapter 10, the focus shifts to the labour market model, with Lee Epstein and Jack Knight delving into the significance of five crucial personal motivations shaping judicial choices (job satisfaction, external satisfactions, leisure, salary, and promotion). Finally, in Chapter 11, Eileen Braman introduces the comparative research on 'thinking-fast' judging, showcasing how cognitive shortcomings implicate the ability of judges to make fair and accurate decisions around the world.

Section 3 includes five chapters that address the various data, methods, and technologies employed in the comparative analysis of judicial behaviour. In Chapter 12, Benjamin G. Engst and Thomas Gschwend proceed from the premise that if the study of judicial behaviour is to be truly comparative, scholars need comparable data. One obstacle is that national data sets often are developed for single case studies. They then proceed to detail the procedures and coding of national databases so that observational data can be more easily connected with databases in other countries. In Chapter 13 on experimental research, Christoph Engel discusses the difficult tradeoff where internal validity eliminates alternative explanations while external validity makes the research question relevant. Experimental research on judges must account for judicial decision-making that takes places in a heavily institutionalized context by a rich set of procedural rules.

Wolgang Alschner, in Chapter 14, shows how network analysis reduces the complex interactions of legal actors, legal sources, and decisions, displaying the complexities in more intuitive spiderwebs of ties and nodes. A crucial challenge to network analysis is missing data which is not randomly distributed and can lead to major gaps. In Chapter 15, Bao Kham Chau and Michael A. Livermore discuss how digitalization permits researchers to move from 'small data' doctrinal analysis to computational text analysis techniques of large corpora of legal documents. They survey different tools for analysing legal documents which today are 'born digital'. In the last chapter in this section, Lee Epstein, Andrew D. Martin, and Kevin Quinn appraise strategies for measuring and estimating judges' political preferences. They consider exogeneous measures of partisanship, which can be easily identified but also risk tenuously linking the judge to the label, and endogenous measures of ideology, which are more precise but risk explaining votes by votes.

Sections 4–8 investigate the internal and external forces shaping judges' decision-making (although the distinction may sometime blur). Section 4 focuses on the critical issue of staffing the courts, a major external factor affecting judges' choices. In Chapter 17, Lydia Brashear Tiede maps the comparative variation in judicial selections across 220 courts in 180 countries. She discusses how these selections can have significant implications for judicial behaviour and highlights how different methods of appointing judges have the potential to allow for political manipulation of decisions. In the next chapter, Michal Burnham and Michael J. Nelson examine judicial elections, an atypical and empirically rare procedure of selecting judges. They suggest that judicial elections present researchers with theoretically rich opportunities: if researchers are willing to abandon their 'institutional silos', they can test general theories of elections on elite behaviour, electoral representation, and judicial decision-making.

In Chapter 19, Anibal Pérez-Liñán and Andrea Castagnola tackle the trade-offs between tenure protection on the one side and judicial performance and accountability on the other. Next, they offer and discuss four types of judicial exit: natural exit, strategic retirement, induced departure, and formal removal. Finally, in Chapter 20, Anne Sanders addresses law clerks, the often-forgotten court staff with legal education who support judges in the adjudicative process. Drawing on a unique survey by the Council of Europe, Sanders discusses the wide variation in recruitment, organization, and duties of law clerks.

Section 5 on 'Advocacy, Litigation, and Appellate Review' offers more on the mechanisms that enable and affect external influences on judging. Ching-fang Hsu and Yun-chien Chang survey the literature on lawyering in the private sector, arguing for the use of comparative research designs with cross-country data. Those could bring scholars closer to the gold standard of causal inference. Tommaso Pavone's chapter tackles the impact of government lawyers on judges' choices. The chapter, by developing a typology of government lawyers and formalizing their influence, offers an excellent springboard for a new comparative research agenda. Diego Werneck Arguelhes and Ivar A. Hartmann propose a matrix that ranks courts' agenda-setting powers using two dimensions: the court's power to control its docket and to time its decisions. Courts with high agenda settings power can better respond to external influences. Finally, Jay N. Krehbiel's insightful chapter shows how the design of oral hearings relates to the court's need for public legitimacy, awareness, and support.

Section 6 on opinions underscores the significant strides that law and political science are making to expand their conception of choices with the aim of understanding judicial language and arguments. Katalin Kelemen offers a comparative analysis of judicial dissent, outlining the existing literature, and highlighting the areas and questions for further research. Jens Frankenreiter's in-depth exploration of micro- and macro-level studies presents a compelling argument for methodological advancement that can increase our understanding of the behaviour behind judges' citation practices across jurisdictions. Elliott Ash grapples with an elusive subject: the judicial choice of words, asking how judges decide what to write in their opinions. After a formal presentation of a model explaining judges' language choices and a comprehensive discussion of various measurement methods, Ash sheds light on the factors influencing these choices and their potential ramifications.

Section 7 on relations within, between, and among courts shifts towards internal influences on judges' choices. Henrik Litleré Bentsen and Jon Kåre Skiple examine the effects of leadership in courts. Their review suggests that court leaders in most courts prioritize stability, consensus building, and the preservation of institutional legitimacy over favourable policy outcomes, strategically encouraging decisions that promote these values. Cynthia L. Ostberg and Matthew E. Wetstein's chapter focuses on panel effects in apex courts, specifically comparing courts where chief justices assign panels versus those that operate with rotating panels. As scholars persist in studying panel effects in global courts, Ostberg and Wetstein advocate for greater methodological pluralism and the advancement of new theoretical paradigms tailored to civil law jurisdictions.

Benjamin Bricker, Clifford J. Carrubba, and Matthew J. Gabel conduct a comprehensive review of the scholarship on judicial referrals in the Court of Justice of the European Union, other major international courts, and national courts. They aim to understand the motivations behind judges, national courts, and private litigants soliciting referrals. Björn Dressel focuses on the effects of judge networks, which he broadly interprets as encompassing the interlocking, relatively stable relationships that a judge maintains with peers and other political and social actors on and off the bench. Dressel also discusses the potential and the limitations of a judge-centred relational perspective on the study of judicial decision-making in the Global South and beyond. In the last chapter of this section, Ori Aronson offers a critical comparative assessment of the hierarchy of justice, with a central focus on the institution of appeal. Aronson further highlights the presence of hierarchical inversions and the various contexts in which lower courts and judges can exercise agency, generating information that may not be accessible to higher judicial levels.

Section 8 delves into a central topic that may significantly influences judicial choices and affects the courts' impact on society: judicial independence. Alex Schwartz discuss the many ways in which governments or legislatures may attempt to curb the power or independence of the judiciary. His chapter considers both theory and evidence concerning the factors that might encourage or discourage court curbing. The next two chapters examine judicial independence from different perspectives. Brad Epperly, in Chapter 34, takes a conceptual approach to the topic, arguing that research on judicial independence does not devote sufficient attention 'to the related matter of judicial review,' while Frans van Dijk, in Chapter 35, focuses cross-national measures of judicial independence.

Section 9 of the *Handbook* concentrates on the second half of the judicial behaviour puzzle: how do judges' choices impact society? In Chapter 36, Russel Smyth starts with the fundamental assumption that judicial legitimacy is crucial for ensuring the public's acceptance of court decisions. Recognizing the tug of war between the positivity bias and subjective ideological disagreement theorists in the United States over the nature and causality of diffuse and specific support, Smyth encourages comparativists to replicate studies of legitimacy and study how courts curate their images and how attacks from politicians affect the legitimacy of courts. Elin Skaar unpacks the role of courts in transitional justice, a field where the behaviour of judges has remained almost entirely unexplored despite consensus that criminal trials are vital to re-establishing the rule of law, and hence contribute to transitions to peace and democracy after violent conflict.

In Chapter 38, Courtney Hillebrecht discusses how compliance with judicial decisions is an elusive process that is best understood both as a process and an outcome and where three factors are crucial: the degree of 'wiggle room' in the decisions that judges leave for the stakeholders; the institutional capacity; and the commitment from key actors of stakeholders to overcome collective action challenges. Finally, Gerald N. Rosenberg investigates courts as agents of change, identifying the characteristics of judges and legal systems that influence judges' ability to act 'progressively'. The chapter suggests that judicial decision-making designed to produce progressive social change is highly contextual, varying from country to country, underlining the importance of initial in-depth, country-focused studies as indispensable for comparative research in courts as agents of social change.

The final Section 10 is dedicated to the frontiers of comparative judicial behaviour. While all the chapters in the book explore avenues for advancement, this section specifically focuses on pushing the boundaries and exploring new frontiers in the field. In Chapter 40, Kevin L. Cope develops a broad functional definition of judicial ideology and a typology of judges' positions along the two distinct dimensions of pragmatism versus idealism and legalism versus activism. He argues that third-party expert assessment is a more promising method of measuring judges' ideology than vote counting and proxy models. Jeffrey K. Staton makes a compelling case for collective investment of comparative law and politics in data infrastructure in Chapter 41. Pointing at the prohibitive costs associated with data production for single researchers and small research groups the chapter sketches the terms for a meaningful and mutually rewarding collaboration on vital infrastructure. Anthony Niblett's chapter delves in the brave new literature of artificial intelligence (AI) and judging, from 'robot judges' to the great promise of AI to improve judicial process and outcomes. While the chapter embraces the new developments, it does not shy away from the grimmer prospects and risks associated with the increasing use of AI by judges.

The comparative analysis of judicial behaviour is thriving. Once a small cottage industry dominated by US political scientists, it has grown into a worldwide enterprise.

Still, because many gaps in our knowledge remain, prospects for new projects abound. Each chapter in this *Handbook* flags specific opportunities. But a few of the suggestions are universal, appearing in chapter after chapter. One is the need for more data in service of better description. Good description often starts with case studies that come in many different forms. Description involves conceptualization and measurement, providing the basis for associational arguments because 'descriptive arguments are nested within causal arguments' (Gerring 2012, 723). Another relates to theoretical and empirical gaps in our knowledge of judging on civil law courts, in non-Western countries, and in societies under non-democratic regimes. Third, many authors are keen on the development of new infrastructure to analyse courts and judging (see generally Weinshall and Epstein 2020). We agree. Not only will high-quality common resources advance knowledge and drive discovery, but they also have the potential to bring together diverse scholars interested in comparative law, legal institutions, and judicial behaviour.

Acknowledgements

For research support, we thank Washington University in St Louis, Peter and Julie Weil, and the University of Southern California. We are grateful to Arnold Zahn for excellent editorial assistance. Epstein thanks the National Science Foundation and the John Simon Guggenheim Foundation for supporting her work on judicial behaviour. Weinshall thanks the I-CORE program of the Planning and Budget Committee and the Israeli Science Foundation (grant no. 1821/12). We adapt some of the material in this chapter from our previous work on comparative judicial behaviour especially from Epstein, Šadl, and Weinshall 2021; Epstein and Weinshall 2021.

Notes

1. The list includes some university presses (especially in Asia and Latin America) and various journals in law and political science (both in and out of Europe) that don't always or even usually publish in English (examples relating to judicial behaviour include Weinshall-Margel 2016; Rodrigues et al. 2017; Hartmann et al. 2018; Grendstad, Shaffer, and Waltenburg 2012).
2. Then again, Socrates predicted that his trial would be the equivalent of the trial of a doctor prosecuted by a cook before a jury of children (Cope 1864).

References

Alarie, Benjamin, and Andrew J. Green. 2014. 'Policy Preferences and Expertise in Canadian Tax Adjudication'. *Canadian Tax Journal* 62: 985–1027.

Alarie, Benjamin, and Andrew J. Green. 2017. *Commitment and Cooperation on High Courts: A Cross-Country Examination of Institutional Constraints on Judges*. Oxford: Oxford University Press.

Arguelhes, Diego Werneck, and Ivar A. Hartmann. 2017. 'Timing Control without Docket Control'. *Journal of Law and Courts* 5: 105–40.

Basabe-Serrano, Santiago. 2012. 'Judges Without Robes and Judicial Voting in Contexts of Institutional Instability: The Case of Ecuador's Constitutional Court, 1999–2007'. *Journal of Latin American Studies* 44: 127–61.

Basabe-Serrano, Santiago. 2019. 'The Judges' Academic Background as Determinant of the Quality of Judicial Decisions in Latin American Supreme Courts'. *Justice System Journal* 40: 110–25.

Baum, L. 2006. *Judges and Their Audiences: A Perspective on Judicial Behaviour*. Princeton: Princeton University Press.

Baum, Lawrence 1997. *The Puzzle of Judicial Behaviour*. Ann Arbor: University of Michigan Press.

Bell, John. 2006. *Judiciaries Within Europe: A Comparative Review*. Cambridge: Cambridge University Press.

Bentsen, Henrik Litleré. 2019. 'Dissent, Legitimacy, and Public Support for Court Decisions: Evidence from a Survey-Based Experiment'. *Law & Society Review* 53: 588–610.

Bentsen, Henrik Litleré. 2018. 'Court Leadership, Agenda Transformation, and Judicial Dissent: A European Case of a "Mysterious Demise of Consensual Norms"'. *Journal of Law and Courts* 6: 189–213.

Blanes i Vidal, Jordi, and Clare Leaver. 2015. 'Bias in Open Peer-Review: Evidence from the English Superior Courts'. *Journal of Law, Economics and Organization* 31: 431–71.

Bonthuys, Elsje. 2015. 'Gender and Race in South African Judicial Appointments'. *Feminist Legal Studies* 23: 127–48.

Boyd, Christina L. 2013. 'She'll Settle It?' *Journal of Law & Courts* 1: 193–219.

Boyd, Christina L., Lee Epstein, and Andrew D. Martin. 2010. 'Untangling the Causal Effect of Sex on Judging'. *American Journal of Political Science* 54: 389–411.

Brouard, Sylvain, and Christoph Hönnige. 2017. 'Constitutional Courts as Veto Players: Lessons from the United States, France and Germany'. *European Journal of Political Research* 56: 529–52.

Brown, Rebecca L., and Lee Epstein. 2023. 'Is the U.S. Supreme Court a Reliable Backstop for an Overreaching U.S. President? Maybe, but is an Overreaching (Partisan) Court Worse?' *Presidential Studies Quarterly*, 53 (2):234–55. https://doi.org/10.1111/psq.12831.

Campbell, Angus, Philip E. Converse, Warren E. Miller, and Donald E. Stokes. 1960. *The American Voter*. New York: Wiley.

Carroll, Royce, and Lydia Tiede. 2012. 'Ideological Voting on Chile's Constitutional Tribunal: Dissent Coalitions in the Adjudication of Rights'. *Journal of Human Rights* 11: 85–105.

Carrubba, Clifford J., Matthew Gabel, and Charles Hankla. 2008. 'Judicial Behaviour under Political Constraints: Evidence from the European Court of Justice'. *American Political Science Review* 102: 435–52.

Chen, Kong-Pin, Kuo-Chang Huang, and Chang-Ching Lin. 2015. 'Party Capability versus Court Preference: Why Do the 'Haves' Come Out Ahead?—An Empirical Lesson from the Taiwan Supreme Court'. *Journal of Law, Economics, and Organization* 31 (1): 93–126.

Cichowski, Rachel A. 2016. 'The European Court of Human Rights, Amicus Curiae and Violence against Women'. *Law & Society Review* 50 (4): 890–919.

Clark, Tom S., Benjamin G. Engst, and Jeffrey K. Staton. 2018. 'Estimating the Effect of Leisure on Judicial Performance'. *Journal of Legal Studies* 47: 349–90.

Collins, Todd, and Laura Moyer. 2008. 'Gender, Race, and Intersectionality on the Federal Appellate Bench'. *Political Research Quarterly* 6: 219–27.

Cope, Edward Meredith. 1864. *Plato's Gorgias*. Cambridge: Deighton, Bell.

Crenshaw, Kimberle. 1989. 'Demarginalizing the Intersection of Race and Sex: A Black Feminist Critique of Antidiscrimination Doctrine, Feminist Theory and Antiracist Politics'. *University of Chicago Legal Forum* 1989: 139–67.

Dothan, Shai. 2015. *Reputation and Judicial Tactics: A Theory of National and International Courts*. Cambridge: Cambridge University Press.

Driscoll, Amanda, and Michael J. Nelson. 2015. 'Judicial Selection and the Democratization of Justice: Lessons from the Bolivian Judicial Elections'. *Journal of Law and Courts* 3: 115–48.

Driscoll, Amanda. 2021. 'Comparative Studies of Judicial Behaviour'. In *High Courts in Global Perspective: Evidence, Methodologies, and Findings*, edited by N. Garoupa, R. D. Gill and L. B. Tiede, 275–306. Charlottesville: University of Virginia Press.

Dyevre, Arthur. 2010. 'Unifying the Field of Comparative Judicial Politics: Towards a General Theory of Judicial Behaviour'. European Political Science Review 2 (2): 297–327.

Dyevre, Arthur. 2013. 'Filtered Constitutional Review and the Reconfiguration of Judicial Politics'. *American Journal of Comparative Law* 61: 729–55.

Eisenberg, Theodore Talia Fisher, and Issi Rosen-Zvi. 2012. 'Does the Judge Matter? Exploiting Random Assignment on a Court of Last Resort to Assess Judge and Case Selection Effects'. *Journal of Empirical Legal Studies* 9: 246–90.

Elster, Jon. 1983. *Explaining Technical Change*. Cambridge: Cambridge University Press.

Engel, Christoph, and Keren Weinshall. 2020. 'Manna from Heaven for Judges: Judges' Reaction to a Quasi-Random Reduction in Caseload'. *Journal of Empirical Legal Studies* 17: 725–51.

Engst, Benjamin G. 2021. The Two Faces of Judicial Power. Dynamics of Judicial-Political Bargaining. Palgrave Macmillan.

Epstein, Lee, and Jack Knight. 1998. *The Choices Justices Make*. Washington, D.C.: Congressional Quarterly Press.

Epstein, Lee, Andrew D. Martin, Kevin M. Quinn, and Jeffrey A. Segal. 2009. 'Circuit Effects: How the Norm of Federal Judicial Experience Biases the U.S. Supreme Court'. *University of Pennsylvania Law Review* 157: 101–46.

Epstein, Lee, and Jack Knight. 2017. 'The Economic Analysis of Judicial Behaviour'. In *The Oxford Handbook of U.S. Judicial Behavior*, edited by Lee Epstein and Stefanie A. Lindquist, 320–39. Oxford: Oxford University Press.

Epstein, Lee, and Jack Knight. 2018. Efficacious Judging on Apex Courts. In *Comparative Judicial Review*, edited by Erin F. Delaney and Rosalind Dixon, 272–89. Cheltenham: Edward Elgar.

Epstein, Lee, and Jack Knight. 2022. 'How Social Identity and Social Diversity Affect Judging'. *Leiden Journal of International Law* 35: 897–911.

Epstein, Lee, and Keren Weinshall. 2021. *The Strategic Analysis of Judicial Behaviour: A Comparative Perspective*. Cambridge: Cambridge University Press.

Epstein, Lee, and Stefanie A. Lindquist, eds. 2017. *The Oxford Handbook of U.S. Judicial Behavior*. Oxford: Oxford University Press.

Epstein, Lee, Jack Knight, and Olga Shvetsova. 2002. 'The Role of Constitutional Courts in the Establishment and Maintenance of Democratic Systems of Government'. *Law & Society Review* 35: 117–64.

Epstein, Lee, Urška Šadl, and Keren Weinshall. 2021. 'The Role of Comparative Law in the Analysis of Judicial Behaviour'. *American Journal of Comparative Law* 69: 689–710.

Epstein, Lee, Urška Šadl, and Keren Weinshall. Forthcoming. 'The Comparative Analysis of Judicial Behaviour'. In *Handbook of Comparative Political Institutions*, edited by Adrian Vatter and Rahel Freiburghaus. Cheltenham: Edward Elgar Publishing.

Epstein, Lee, William M. Landes, and Richard A. Posner. 2013. *The Behaviour of Federal Judges: A Theoretical and Empirical Study of Rational Choice*. Cambridge: Harvard University Press.

Frankenreiter, Jens. 2017. 'The Politics of Citations at the ECJ—Policy Preferences of E.U. Member State Governments and the Citation Behaviour of Judges at the European Court of Justice'. *Journal of Empirical Legal Studies* 14: 813–57.

Gabel, Matthew J., Clifford J. Carrubba, Caitlin Ainsley, and Donald M. Beaudette. 2012. 'Of Courts and Commerce'. *Journal of Politics* 74 (4): 1125–37.

Garoupa, Nuno, and Tom Ginsburg. 2015. *Judicial Reputation: A Comparative Theory*. Chicago: University of Chicago Press.

Garoupa, Nuno, Rebecca D. Gill, and Lydia B. Tiede, eds. 2021. *High Courts in Global Perspective: Evidence, Methodologies, and Findings*. Charlottesville: University of Virginia Press.

Gerring, John. 2012. 'Mere Description'. *British Journal of Political Science* 42 (4): 721–46.

Goelzhauser, Greg. 2011. 'Avoiding Constitutional Cases'. *American Political Research* 39: 483–511.

Goldman, Sheldon. 1975. 'Voting Behaviour on the United States Courts of Appeal Revisited'. *American Political Science Review* 69: 491–506.

Green, Andrew, and Albert H. Yoon. 2017. 'Triaging the Law: Developing the Common Law on the Supreme Court of India'. *Journal of Empirical Legal Studies* 14: 683–715.

Grendstad, Gunnar, William R. Shaffer, Jørn Øyrehagen Sunde, and Eric N. Waltenburg. 2020. *Proactive and Powerful. Law Clerks and the Institutionalization of the Norwegian Supreme Court*. The Hague: Eleven International Publishing.

Grendstad, Gunnar, William R. Shaffer, and Eric N. Waltenburg. 2012. 'Ideologi og grunnholdninger hos dommerne i Norges Høyesterett'. *Lov og Rett* 51 (4): 240–53.

Grendstad, Gunnar, William R. Shaffer, and Eric N. Waltenburg. 2015. *Policy Making in an Independent Judiciary: The Norwegian Supreme Court*. Colchester: ECPR Press.

Haire, Susan B., Laura P. Moyer, and Shawn Treier. 2013. 'Diversity, Deliberation, and Judicial Opinion Writing'. *Journal of Law and Courts* 1: 303–30.

Hanretty, Chris. 2020. *A Court of Specialists. Judicial Behaviour on the UK Supreme Court*. Oxford: Oxford University Press.

Hartmann, Ivar, Clara Iglesias Keller, Daniel Chada, Guilherme Vasconcelos, José Luiz Nunes, Letícia Carneiro, Luciano Chaves, Matheus Barreto, Fernando Correia, and Felipe Araújo. 2018. 'O Impacto no Sistema Prisional Brasileiro da Mudança de Entendimento do Supremo Tribunal Federal Sobre Execução da Pena Antes do Trânsito em Julgado No HC 126.292/SP—Um Estudo Empírico Quantitativo'. *Revista de Direito Econômico e Socioambiental* 9: 399–426.

Helmke, Gretchen. 2002. 'The Logic of Strategic Defection: Court-Executive Relations in Argentina Under Dictatorship and Democracy'. *American Political Science Review* 96: 291–303.

Helmke, Gretchen. 2005. *Courts Under Constraints: Judges, Generals, and Presidents in Argentina*. Cambridge: Cambridge University Press.

Hönnige, Christoph. 2009. 'The Electoral Connection: How the Pivotal Judge Affects Oppositional Success at European Constitutional Courts'. *West European Politics* 32: 963–84.

Jowett, Benjamin, trans. 2020. 'The Apology of Socrates'. The Center for Hellenic Studies, Harvard University, Washington, DC. https://chs.harvard.edu/primary-source/plato-the-apology-of-socrates-sb/

Kahneman, Daniel. 2011. *Thinking, Fast and Slow*. New York: Farrar, Straus and Giroux.

Kang, Alice J., Miki Caul Kittilson, Valerie Hoekstra, and Maria C. Escobar-Lemmon. 2020. 'Diverse and Inclusive High Courts: A Global and Intersectional Perspective'. 8 *Politics, Groups, & Identities* 8: 812–21.

Klerman, Daniel, and Paul Mahoney. 2005. 'The Value of Judicial Independence: Evidence from Eighteenth-Century England'. *American Law and Economics Review* 7: 1–27.

Koev, Dan. 2019. 'Not Taking it on Faith: State and Religious Influences on European Court of Human Rights Judges in Freedom of Religion Cases'. *Journal of Human Rights* 18: 184–200.

Krehbiel, Jay N. 2016. 'The Politics of Judicial Procedures: The Role of Public Oral Hearings in the German Constitutional Court'. *American Journal of Political Science* 60: 990–1005.

Krewson, Chris, David Lassen, and Ryan J. Owens. 2018. 'Twitter and the Supreme Court: An Examination of Congressional Tweets about the Supreme Court'. *Justice System Journal* 39: 322–30.

Kureshi, Yasser. 2021. 'When Judges Defy Dictators: An Audience-Based Framework to Explain the Emergence of Judicial Assertiveness against Authoritarian Regimes'. *Comparative Politics* 53: 233–57.

La Porta, Rafael, Florencio López-de-Silanes, Cristian Pop-Eleches, and Andrei Shleifer. 2004. 'Judicial Checks and Balances'. *Journal of Political Economy* 112: 445–70.

Lasser, Mitchel de S. O. 2009. *Judicial Transformations: The Rights Revolution in the Courts of Europe*. Oxford: Oxford University Press.

Legrand, Pierre, and Roderick Munday, eds. 2003. *Comparative Legal Studies: Traditions and Transitions*. Cambridge: Cambridge University Press.

Lemley, Mark A. 2022. 'The Imperial Supreme Court'. *Harvard Law Review* 136: 97–118.

Liu, John Zhuang, and Xueyao Li. 2019. 'Legal Techniques for Rationalizing Biased Judicial Decisions: Evidence from Experiments with Real Judges'. *Journal of Empirical Legal Studies* 16 (3): 630–70.

Lopes, Felipe de Mendonça. 2019. 'Dissent Aversion and Sequential Voting in the Brazilian Supreme Court'. *Journal of Empirical Legal Studies* 16: 933–54.

Lovett, Frank. 2006. 'Rational Choice Theory and Explanation'. *Rationality and Society* 18: 237–72.

Lupu Yonatan, and Erik Voeten. 2012. 'Precedent on International Courts: A Network Analysis of Case Citations by the European Court of Human Rights'. *British Journal of Political Science* 42: 413–29.

Macridis, Roy. 1955. *The Study of Comparative Government*. New York: Random House.

Maitland, Frederic William. 1898. 'A Prologue to a History of English Law'. *Law Quarterly Review* 14: 13–33.

Massie, Tajuana, Kirk A. Randazzo, and Donald R. Songer. 2014. 'The Politics of Judicial Retirement in Canada and the United Kingdom'. *Journal of Law and Courts*, 2: 273–99.

Martinsen, Dorte Sindbjerg. 2015. *An Ever More Powerful Court?: The Political Constraints of Legal Integration in the European Union*. Oxford: Oxford University Press.

Melcarne, Alessandro. 2017. 'Careerism and Judicial Behaviour'. *European Journal of Law and Economics* 44: 241–64.

Mehmood, Sultan. 2022. 'The Impact of Presidential Appointment of Judges: Montesquieu or the Federalists?' *American Economic Journal: Applied Economics* 14: 411–45.

Moustafa, Tamir. 2014. 'Law and Courts in Authoritarian Regimes'. *Annual Review of Law and Social Science* 10: 281–99.

Muro, Sergio, Alejandro Chehtman, Jorge Silva M´endez, and Nelson Amaya Dur´an. 2018. 'Testing Representational Advantage in the Argentine Supreme Court'. *Journal of Law and Courts* 6 (1): 1–23.

Muttart, Daved. 2007. *Empirical Gap in Jurisprudence: A Comprehensive Study of the Supreme Court of Canada*. Toronto: University of Toronto Press.

Narayan, Paresh Kumar, and Russell Smyth. 2007. 'What Explains Dissent on the High Court of Australia? An Empirical Assessment Using a Cointegration and Error Correction Approach'. *Journal of Empirical Legal Studies* 4: 401–25.

Naurin, Daniel, and Øyvind Stiansen. 2020. 'The Dilemma of Dissent: Split Judicial Decisions and Compliance with Judgments from the International Human Rights Judiciary'. *Comparative Political Studies* 53: 959–91.

Nielsen, Ingrid, and Russell Smyth. 2019. 'What the Australian Public Knows about the High Court'. *Federal Law Review* 47: 31–63.

North, Douglass C., and Barry R. Weingast. 1989. 'Constitutions and Commitment: The Evolution of Institutions Governing Public Choice in Seventeenth-Century England'. *The Journal of Economic History* 49: 803–32.

Page, Scott E. 2017. *The Diversity Bonus*. Princeton: Princeton University Press.

Pérez-Liñán, Anibel, and Ignacio Arana Araya. 2017. 'Strategic Retirement in Comparative Perspective: Supreme Court Justices in Presidential Regimes'. *Journal of Law and Courts* 5: 173–98.

Posner, Eric A., and Miguel F. P. de Figueiredo. 2005. 'Is the International Court of Justice Biased?' *Journal of Legal Studies* 34: 599–630.

Posner, Richard A. 1990. *Cardozo: A Study in Reputation*. Chicago: University of Chicago Press.

Posner, Richard A. 2011. *Economic Analysis of Law*. Boston: Aspen Publishing.

Pritchett, C. Herman. 1948. *The Roosevelt Court*. New York: Macmillan.

Rachlinski, Jeffrey J., and Sheri L. Johnson. 2009. 'Does Unconscious Racial Bias Affect Trial Judges?' *Notre Dame Law Review* 84: 1195–246.

Ramseyer, J. Mark, and Eric B. Rasmusen. 2001. 'Why Are Japanese Judges So Conservative in Politically Charged Cases?' *American Political Science Review* 95: 331–44.

Richards, Mark J., and Herbert M. Kritzer. 2002. Jurisprudential Regimes in Supreme Court Decision Making. *American Political Science Review*, 96: 305–20.

Robinson, Nick. 2013. 'Structure Matters: The Impact of Court Structure on the Indian and U.S. Supreme Courts'. *American Journal of Comparative* Law 61: 173–208.

Rodrigues, Maria de Lurdes, Nuno Garoupa, Pedro Magalhães, Conceição Gomes, and Rui Guerra da Fonseca, eds. 2017. *40 Anos de Políticas de Justiça em Portugal*. Coimbra: Almedina.

Salamone, Michael F. 2018. *Perceptions of a Polarized Court: How Division Among Justices Shapes the Supreme Court Public Image*. Philadelphia: Temple University Press.

Salzberger Eli, and Paul Fenn. 1999. 'Judicial Independence: Some Evidence from the English Court of Appeal'. *Journal of Law & Economics* 42: 831–47.

Sanchez Urribarri, Raul A., Susanne Schorpp, Kirk A. Randazzo, and Donald R. Songer. 2011. 'Explaining Changes to Rights Litigation: Testing a Multivariate Model in a Comparative Framework'. *Journal of Politics* 73: 391–405.

Sartori, Giovanni. 1991. 'Comparing and Miscomparing'. *Journal of Theoretical Politics* 3 (3): 243–57.

Schubert, Glendon. 1965. *The Judicial Mind: The Attitudes and Ideologies of Supreme Court Justices, 1946–1963*. Evanston: Northwestern University Press.

Schwartz, Alex, and Melanie Janelle Murchison. 2016. 'Judicial Impartiality and Independence in Divided Societies: An Empirical Analysis of the Constitutional Court of Bosnia-Herzegovina'. *Law & Society Review* 50: 821–55.

Segal, Jeffrey A., and Harold J. Spaeth. 2002. *The Supreme Court and the Attitudinal Model Revisited*. Cambridge: Cambridge University Press.

Sela, Ayelet, and Limor Gabay-Egozi, 2020. 'Judicial Procedural Involvement (JPI): A Metric for Judges' Role in Litigation, Settlement and Access to Justice'. *Journal of Law and Society* 47 (3): 468–98.

Sen, Maya. 2015. 'Is Justice Really Blind? Race and Appellate Review in U.S. Courts'. *Journal of Legal Studies* 44: 187–229.

Shayo, Moses, and Asaf Zussman 2011. 'Judicial Ingroup Bias in the Shadow of Terrorism'. *Quarterly Journal of Economics* 126: 1447–84.

Shayo, Moses. 2009. 'A Model of Social Identity with an Application to Political Economy: Nation, Class and Redistribution'. *American Political Science Review* 103: 147–74.

Sill, Kaitlyn L., and Stacia L. Haynie. 2010. 'Panel Assignment in Appellate Courts: Strategic Behaviour in the South African Supreme Court of Appeal'. *Politikon* 37 (2): 269–85.

Siems, Mathias. 2022. *Comparative Law*. Cambridge: Cambridge University Press.

Skiple, Jon Kåre, Mark Jonathan McKenzie, and Henrik Litleré Bentsen. 2021. 'How Docket Control Shapes Judicial Behaviour: A Comparative Analysis of the Norwegian and Danish Supreme Courts'. *Journal of Law and Courts* 9 (1): 111–36.

Sonnemans, Joep, and Frans van Dijk. 2012. 'Errors in Judicial Decisions: Experimental Results'. *Journal of Law, Economics, and Organization* 28: 687–716.

Spaeth, Harold J. 1963. *Supreme Court Policy Making*. New York: Free Press of Glencoe.

Spamann, Holger, and Lars Klöhn. 2016. 'Justice is Less Blind, and Less Legalistic, Than We Thought: Evidence from an Experiment with Real Judges'. *Journal of Legal Studies* 45: 255–80.

Spirig, Judith. 2023. 'When Issue Salience Affects Adjudication: Evidence from Swiss Asylum Appeal Decisions'. *American Journal of Political Science* 67: 55–70.

Staton, Jeffrey K. 2010. *Judicial Power and Strategic Communication in Mexico*. Cambridge: Cambridge University Press.

Staton, Jeffrey K., and Georg Vanberg. 2008. 'The Value of Vagueness: Delegation, Defiance, and Judicial Opinions'. *American Journal of Political Science* 52: 504–19.

Stiansen, Øyvind. 2022. '(Non)renewable Terms and Judicial Independence in the European Court of Human Rights'. *American Journal of Political Science* 67: 55–70.

Swalve, Tilko. 2022. 'Does Group Familiarity Improve Deliberations in Judicial Teams? Evidence from the German Federal Court of Justice'. *Journal of Empirical Legal Studies* 19: 223–49.

Sweet, Alec Stone, and Thomas L. Brunell. 1998. 'The European Court and the National Courts: A Statistical Analysis of Preliminary References'. *Journal of European Public Policy* 5: 66–97.

Tate, C. Neal, and Panu Sittiwong. 1989. 'Decision Making in the Canadian Supreme Court: Extending the Personal Attributes Model Across Nations'. *Journal of Politics* 51: 900–16.

Thaler, Richard H. 2015. *Misbehaving: The Making of Behavioural Economics*. New York: W. W. Norton.

Tiede, Lydia B. 2016. 'The Political Determinants of Judicial Dissent: Evidence from the Chilean Constitutional Tribunal'. *European Political Science Review* 8: 377–403.

Vanberg, Georg. 2005. *The Politics of Constitutional Review in Germany*. Cambridge: Cambridge University Press.

Varol, Ozan O., Lucia Dalla Pellegrina, and Nuno Garoupa. 2017. 'An Empirical Analysis of Judicial Transformation in Turkey'. *American Journal of Comparative Law* 65: 187–216.

Voeten, Erik. 2008. 'The Impartiality of International Judges: Evidence from the European Court of Human Rights'. *American Political Science Review* 102: 417–33.

Voeten, Erik. 2020. 'Populism and Backlashes against International Courts'. *Perspectives on Politics* 18: 407–22.

Voeten, Erik. 2021. 'Gender and Judging: Evidence from the European Court of Human Rights'. *Journal of European Public Policy* 28: 1453–73.

Voigt, Stefan, Jerg Gutmann, and Lars P. Feld. 2015. 'Economic Growth and Judicial Independence, A Dozen Years On: Cross-Country Evidence Using an Updated Set of Indicators'. *European Journal of Political Economy* 38: 197–211.

Weinshall, Keren, and Lee Epstein. 2020. 'Developing High-Quality Data Infrastructure for Legal Analytics: Introducing the Israeli Supreme Court Database'. *Journal of Empirical Legal Studies* 17: 416–34.

Weinshall, Keren, Udi Sommer, and Ya'acov Ritov. 2018. 'Ideological Influences on Governance and Regulation: The Comparative Case of Supreme Courts'. *Regulation & Governance* 12: 334–52.

Weinshall-Margel, Keren. 2016. *Law and Ideology in Supreme Court Decision-Making: A Comparative and Quantitative Analysis*. Jerusalem: Hebrew University Sacher Press.

Wistrich, Andrew J., Jeffrey J. Rachlinski, and Chris Guthrie. 2015. 'Heart Versus Head: Do Judges Follow the Law or Follow Their Feelings?' *Texas Law Review* 93: 855–923.

CHAPTER 2

LEGAL TRADITIONS AND THEIR RELATION TO JUDICIAL BEHAVIOUR

NUNO GAROUPA

1. Introduction

The sophisticated and elegant theories that prevail nowadays in the study of judicial behaviour (see the review of the literature by Epstein and Weinshall 2021, and chapters in this *Handbook*) are understood as valid or universal to any specific legal tradition. The attitudinal model and the agency-based explanations are developed and structured around individual preferences, incentives, and institutional interactions. Therefore, their prescriptive implications are not conditioned on a certain legal family such as the common law or the civil law traditions (Pargendler 2012; Garoupa and Pargendler 2014). However, in that respect, the common law–civil law distinction has an indirect role to play. It is relevant in the extent to which legal traditions shape or constrain these individual preferences, incentives, and institutional interaction (Garoupa and Ginsburg 2015).

Published in 1968, Dawson's seminal work and masterpiece, *Oracles of the Law*, has influenced generations of comparative law scholars in addressing the relationship between judicial behaviour and legal traditions. The book proclaimed that the differences between the civil law (although making significant distinctions between French and German courts) and the common law (in this perspective, mostly US courts) are at the heart of explaining variations in judicial behaviour.

Dawson's prominent descriptive work seems significantly distant from current trends in the study of judicial behaviour by political scientists and economists. Still, his thesis has played an important role in the field of comparative law. His influential masterpiece implicitly presupposed that legal traditions are an exogenous independent variable that (co)determines judicial behaviour.

Legal traditions are not limited to the distinction between the common law and the civil law. Inevitably, *Oracles of the Law* was a product of its time. The Western-centric perspective has been, by now, widely challenged by multiple comparative law scholars (see e.g. Ruskola 2013; Glenn 2014; Matsubara 2018; Siems 2022; Erie 2023; a general critique by Reimann 2002). Still, the discussion about the common law versus the civil law divide is far from being finished in explaining observable trends in judicial behaviour and court decision-making. Therefore, most of the focus of the present chapter is on this classical divide of common law–civil law, even if many of the observations can be extended, at a methodological level, to broader theorizing and empirical testing of judicial behaviour and legal traditions.

The chapter goes as follows. In section 2, we summarize the fundamental insights from Dawson (1968). In section 3, we turn to Garoupa and Ginsburg (2015) in explaining how different institutional arrangements might shape judicial behaviour within the common law–civil law distinction. In section 4, the empirical literature is summarized. Section 5 concludes the article with a short discussion about possible approaches to integrating judicial politics and comparative law.

2. Oracles of the Law

In his famous lectures, Dawson (1968) suggested that comparisons between courts and across legal systems need to start by defining the object of analysis. He reminded scholars that if one starts with specific language such as 'case law', very soon a comparative analysis of judicial behaviour is highly problematic. For example, civil law countries such as France and Germany formally do not have 'case law'. Therefore, he argued for a functionalist approach. By making use of language originally introduced by Llewellyn, Dawson focused on 'law found in decided cases and created by judges in the process of solving particular disputes' (Dawson 1968, 400–01). Under this functionalist definition of 'case law', there is plenty to be considered and studied in both common law and civil law jurisdictions.

Within courts of civil law, Dawson identified significant distinctions across countries. Concerning French judges, Dawson emphasized the secrecy of deliberations and the role of anonymous decisions. He described the French judicial style in ways that created a specific enduring narrative: legalistic formulas so that all members of court can agree; laconic and neutral forms of expression; restrictive grammar; detached propositions and conflicting terms; sophisticated technical language to hide dissent; no intrusion of personal views; and significant economy of facts and legal terms (parsimony).

More specifically, Dawson explained the absence of separation opinions in French courts as the outcome of an effort to suppress deviant views. This explicit effort by French courts, according to the author, undermines the disclosure of divergent arguments and emphasizes single decisions. Dawson proposed that, in comparison to US judges, the French refusal of precedent is based on a self-serving narrative of judicial restraint that presents precedent as a mechanism to empower the judiciary. Dawson, nevertheless, took the opposite view. While the French reject precedent under the idea that abstaining from reasoned opinion limits the judiciary, this rejection of precedent in fact creates more power but much less transparency. According to him, judges are left with a range of choices from the general language of a code but with no burden of disclosure to the public. Dawson firmly rejected the myth of the neutral interpreter of the code. However, in doing this, he created another myth—that French judges claim to operate as neutral interpreters of the code in order to hide their policy preferences under the veil of secrecy and lack of transparent reasoning.

On the other hand, the *Oracles of the Law* was much less critical of German judges. Dawson praised the systematization efforts by German courts and found the role of precedent appealing in German courts. According to him, while English precedent is excessively dependent on the opaque skills of lawyers, German precedent is part of legal systematization. This is not uncomplicated. Dawson conceded that precedent can have a 'congealing effect' on legal systematization—'denying judges needed power to develop law through judicial decision' (Dawson 1968, 484); that is, judges are too dependent on the past.

According to the author, the binding effect of the decisions by the Federal Constitutional Court (after its creation in the early 1950s) changed the tension between precedent and civil law. German judges have a more liberated judicial style (as compared to French judges) but still a degree of concern about revealing divisions of opinion. In turn, this has generated self-imposed discipline and it has limited personal views and styles. The result is reduced judicial activism compared to American standards. For Dawson, although German legal science is less axiomatic than it used to be, judicial opinions embody legal change. This 'revolution', however, is doctrinal, not a product of the legal realist movement as in US courts.

In summary, Dawson's main insight was that judging in civil law, unlike common law, is about hiding personal preferences and avoiding divisions within collegial courts. Precedents in the common law are a mechanism of individual accountability at odds with the civil law's ideology against empowering the judiciary.

Even if the insights by Dawson have been disputed and challenged by many comparative law scholars (e.g. Reitz 2009 or Nazareno 2022), they have predominated to a large extent in the academic debate for decades (see, among others, Goutal 1976; Soper 1977; Bell 1987; Legrand 1987; Merryman 1988 and 1996; Hohmann 1990; Wells 1994; Koch 2004; Bobek 2013). In fact, the *Oracles of Law* determined judicial stereotypes that have largely prevailed in the last fifty years of scholarship. For example, Ferejohn and Pasquino (2004) build on the narrative that European constitutional courts are more insulated from politics when there is plenty of empirical evidence to the contrary (see the survey by Bagashka and Garoupa 2021). Or consider Farber and Sherry (2009) who, after criticizing the French system for lack of transparency, add:

> the judges are in on the scam, and apparently so are French academics. It is not clear, however, the extent to which the French public—of even French lawyers—know what

> the judges say they are doing and what they are really doing are quite two different things. Nor are they able to evaluate judicial decisions. (Farber and Sherry 2009, 103–04)

Legal economists (Klerman and Mahoney 2007) have critiqued the pervasive influence of Dawson's perspective on the so-called legal origins theory popularized by development economists (La Porta, de Silanes, and Shleifer 2008).

One particular aspect where *Oracles of Law* cannot be ignored is its impact on the theory of dissent in collegial courts. Although diverse scholarship has explored rational choice explanations for asymmetric rates of dissent and concurrence across courts (see a review of the literature by Garoupa and Santos Botelho 2022), the common law–civil law distinction as championed by Dawson is still a popular argument (see Stack 1996 and Jacobson 2005 on the US tradition; Lasser 2009 on explaining how public judicial opinions are formulaic and sparse in French courts; Kelemen 2018 on providing justifications for European diversity).

It is possible that Dawson's famous *Oracles of the Law* seems quite distant from current trends in the study of judicial behaviour by political scientists and economists. Still, his (largely descriptive) thesis has played an important role in the field of comparative law. In the context of modern theories of judicial behaviour, his influential masterpiece implicitly presupposed that legal traditions are an exogenous independent variable that (co)determines judicial behaviour.

3. Comparative Institutional Analysis

Garoupa and Ginsburg (2015) started with a rational choice model that is largely detached from legal traditions. They noted that, in every legal system, judges deal with individual reputation (how different audiences perceive each individual judge) and collective reputation (how the collective of judges, the judiciary, is regarded by other political branches of government and public opinion more generally). However, the authors recognized that the relative degree of importance varies not only across legal families but even within the same legal family. For example, they observed that for the US federal judiciary, individual reputation seems to matter a great deal. In their own description of the US institutional arrangements,

> [t]he Supreme Court is identified with the name of the Chief Justice (such as Warren, Rehnquist, or Roberts) and the great judges of the past are heroes. Newspapers frequently discuss how individual justices vote in particular cases and quote from dissents. Federal judges give talks to the public and write books advancing their views on important issues, and the appointment mechanism includes Senate confirmation hearings in which individual candidates to the federal courts have to expose their views.
>
> (Garoupa and Ginsburg 2015, 28)

Although the United States and the United Kingdom belong to the same common law tradition, the authors remarked that a different pattern prevails in the United Kingdom. They suggest that institutional arrangements in the United Kingdom are not that different from civil law jurisdictions. In their own words,

> the United Kingdom judiciary is more akin to those of France, Japan and Germany, where most people have no idea of the identity of the Chief Justice, much less the other justices of the Supreme Court. Newspapers in these countries very rarely report on dissenting views; justices usually avoid exposure and contact with public opinion in general; and very few judges get to be known by the public in general. If justice is blind, judges are anonymous. In these legal systems, information about individual performance seems to be intentionally underplayed, if not systematically hidden from the general public.
>
> (Garoupa and Ginsburg 2015, 28–29)

These observations are consistent with Posner (1998) who provided a similar conclusion—English judges are significantly different from US judges and more like Continental European judges. However, other authors, such as the legal historian Caenegem, emphasized the opposite viewpoint. In Caenegem (1987), the author suggested that it matters when the legal system is dominated by judges as in the common law or by law professors as in the civil law. Later, in Caenegem (2002), the same author noted that while in England the bench is paramount and the judges have a highly personal role, in Continental European courts are faceless and the judges are described as fungible persons.

In short, according to Garoupa and Ginsburg (2015), in some legal systems collective reputation prevails over individual reputation whereas in other legal systems the reverse occurs; some legal systems pursue individual performance whereas others prefer to limit information about individual performance and rely more on collective assessment. Within each legal family, the balance between individual and collective reputation can vary.

The authors related general trends and inclinations in the balance between collective and individual reputations to the institutional structures of each legal family. Their common law–civil law distinction was thus endogenous to a set of characteristics that explain why judicial behaviour emerges from a different interaction of possible (universal) determinants. In this light, their work was not in contradiction with *Oracles of Law*. It bridged the gap between Dawson's description (mostly based on historical and political evolution) and the modern rational choice theory scholarship (more specifically, the political economy theory provided by the principal–agent model).

The institutional structures discussed by Garoupa and Ginsburg (2015) are:

(a) *Career versus recognition judiciary*—A career system implies judges enter a judicial bureaucracy at earlier stages and thus respond mostly to internal audiences (their superiors); recognition mechanisms presuppose an external audience (mostly politicians and legal professionals) assessing the quality of potential judicial candidates.

(b) *Individual opinions/dissents and concurrences*—Any form of individual opinion reveals information about the specific author; therefore, individual opinions matter in systems based on individual reputation and can be disruptive or dysfunctional in systems based on collective reputation. For example, when individual opinions cannot be recorded for external audiences and public dissent is not allowed, the judiciary is perceived as a homogeneous body, faceless and bureaucratic, in which private discussion and diversity are replaced with formal compromise and uniformity. At the same time, individual opinions are associated with a relatively flat organizational structure, in which superior judges have little control over inferiors. Collective opinions rely on the suppression of individual reputation and promote institutional hierarchical controls to overcome collective action problems in the production of collective reputation.

(c) *Oral proceedings*—Orality provides an opportunity for cultivating individual reputation. 'Oral proceedings allow judges not only to reveal their legal skills, but also their individual positions and make specific contributions to the decision taken by the court. They can also communicate to the specialist audience of lawyers, distinguishing themselves from their colleagues' (Garoupa and Ginsburg 2015, 31).

(d) *Publicity and access to proceedings*—The strategic use of communication techniques with the public and/or specific audiences (such as the legal profession or politicians) reflects reputation priorities. Media relations are of relevance. In an increasingly dense media environment, if the courts do not communicate clearly they can find that publicity may actually harm the reputation of the court as a whole. Furthermore, appearances on radio, television, and social media may encourage individual justices to seek to distinguish themselves, leading to a more incoherent jurisprudence and harming collective reputation.

(e) *Sentencing and procedural discretion*—A generous degree of discretion in sentencing and in procedural rulings emphasizes individual reputation over collective reputation by allowing judges to distinguish themselves from each other. One implication is that differences in sentencing or in procedure can be exacerbated by judges who are purely interested in building individual reputation. At the same time, strict sentencing rules can have very different consequences in a system in which collective reputation prevails as opposed to a system where individual reputation is important. Under collective reputation, rules that enhance uniformity are important. Under individual reputation, strict sentencing guidelines can have perverse consequences. For example, if the degree of judicial discretion is higher regarding procedure than in sentencing, judges might be tempted to use procedure to undermine sentencing rules as a way of maintaining individual reputation.

(f) *Appeals*—The rules and norms of an appeal system impact the nature of the relationship between superior and inferior courts which, in turn, plays an important role in shaping incentives to invest in individual versus collective reputation building. Consider a generous appeal system that essentially allows superior courts to review and evaluate the decisions taken by inferior courts. This arrangement induces compliance by junior judges and favours homogeneity and uniformity in decision-making. An appeal system that effectively internalizes potential conflicts and therefore reduces discrepancies in courts' decisions contributes decisively to collective reputation. Consider, instead, an appeal system that imposes few constraints on junior judges. It gives them more discretion and naturally generates more heterogeneity in decision-making, which favours individual reputation. An appeal system that permits conflicts of jurisdiction and law across courts disfavours collective reputation and pushes toward investment in individual reputation.

(g) *Citations*—The practice of citations in judicial decisions is consistent with recognizing the relevance of individual opinions (an element of individual reputation). The widespread use of citations in Anglo-American jurisprudence promotes individual reputation building, particularly when combined with the institution of individual named opinions. Many legal systems do not cite extensively to other cases. These legal systems treat the law as a collective, uniformly determined product.

(h) *Case selection*—Judicial control of dockets is strategic in enhancing reputation. When courts cannot, in most cases, effectively influence or adjust the cases they adjudicate, collective reputation operates as a type of insurance, since some judges will randomly be assigned cases that are more suited for enhancing individual reputation than others through a mechanism that does not consider different skill levels across the bench. Moreover, the control of dockets can operate at two significant levels: choosing specific cases and establishing standing and justiciability doctrines that narrow or expand the scope of judicial review.

(i) *Branding*—When judges can attach their names to what they do (opinions, doctrines, extrajudicial inquiries, law reform projects), individual reputation matters. Branding has consequences for private sector opportunities after retirement, including lawyering, arbitration and mediation, corporate advisory positions, participation in politics, teaching, and speaking at prestigious conferences. Individual reputation is more important than collective reputation for private sector opportunities after retirement, although a collective reputation for honesty, competence, and transparency could be beneficial from this point of view.

(j) *Size*—The size of a court is instrumental in structuring individual and collective incentives. When there is a larger judiciary, the cost for each judge to engage in individual reputation building is more significant because there is more competition. At the same time, it decreases the cost for each judge to engage in collective reputation building, since the investment required of any individual judge will be smaller. When one has a smaller judiciary, investment in individual reputation and recognition is more attractive. Larger numbers induce uniformity and investment in collective reputation, additional opportunities for horizontal monitoring by other judges, and more possibilities for advancement and promotion. For example, if there are relatively few opportunities for promotion, judges will be less sensitive to pressures from higher levels of the hierarchy, thus less willing to sacrifice elements of individual reputation for the collectivity. 'In contrast, in a large bureaucratic judiciary, there are significant opportunities for advancement and judges will be sensitive to the concerns of their superiors. This design tends to suppress individual variance and lead to greater investments in collective reputation' (Garoupa and Ginsburg 2015, 40–41).

(k) *Discipline*—Regulating rules and enforcing discipline are important because all judges share a collective loss in reputation when one of them breaches conduct. All judicial systems contain mechanisms for judicial discipline. These mechanisms protect the collective reputation against harms caused by judicial misbehaviour. These are obviously implicated when a judge breaks the law or acts corruptly. However, other interventions into less significant wrongs are important. Different legal systems contemplate a distinct set of actions that constitute the basis for potential discipline, the processes used, and the potential sanctions. It is inevitable that if judges can be subjected to discipline for minor actions or based on broad standards, they will be more considerate of the views of their superiors in the judiciary.

(l) *Budget and allocation of resources*—Any judicial system needs resources to operate and reward judges. Resources can be allocated to judges as individuals or as a collective. When resources are allocated to judges as individuals, then individual reputation is a major asset in bargaining over resources within the judicial system. When resources are allocated in a manner that is administratively independent of the individual judge, collective reputation is crucial since only through collective reputation can the judiciary obtain more resources from the government.

This vast list of institutional features shapes judicial behaviour. However, when analysed together, they generate an interdependence of institutional choices. More specifically, Garoupa and Ginsburg (2015) explained why these institutional choices reinforce mechanisms that provide for a distinction between the common law and the civil law when explaining judicial behaviour.

First, the common law tradition and a recognition judiciary are intrinsically related. It is an institutional arrangement that relies on selecting judges because their earlier investments in reputation allow *ex ante* screening for quality and effort. Within this institutional arrangement, judges can be trusted to write high quality individual opinions. 'In contrast, the career system associated with the civil law hires judges at a young age, and therefore cannot trust them to adequately invest in individual reputation without extensive monitoring. Hence there is an implicit logic to anonymous, collective opinions, and less of a culture of citation. Branding is frowned upon' (Garoupa and Ginsburg 2015, 43).

Second, in the same vein, a career system requires many more judges because monitoring output at the lowest level requires an intermediate supervisory level (itself an autonomous body or a different layer of a more hierarchical judicial system). For example, appeal is essential to maintain quality and discourage shirking. Moreover, appeals are *de novo*. They ensure that individual judges do not harm the collective reputation of the judiciary. 'We thus observe much larger judiciaries to accomplish *de novo* review. This reinforces the notion of team rather than individual production, and reduces the amount of effort required by any single judge to produce reputation' (Garoupa and Ginsburg 2015, 44).

Finally, from a comparative perspective, 'judges in recognition systems have a variety of devices to exercise docket control, particularly at the senior levels. This allows the judiciary to control its policy-making role. In contrast, career judges are viewed as relatively low level functionaries without individual discretion' (Garoupa and Ginsburg 2015, 44).

The authors suggested that their characterization is consistent with the stylized description by Merryman and Pérez Perdomo (2018). However, their theory accomplishes the same stylized description without relying on some unspecified ideology of the common law and civil law, but rather a coherent and consistent choice of institutional features. The different understandings of the role of the law described by Merryman and Pérez Perdomo (2018) track the distinction between collective and individual reputation. Hence, the role of a common law–civil law distinction in explaining judicial behaviour results from the delicate balance between collective and individual reputation.

4. Empirical Studies

There is by now a vast empirical literature showing that the myth of the civil law judiciary insulated from politics has little adherence to reality (see e.g. the book edited by Garoupa, Gill, and Teide 2021). This is not to say that judicial decision-making is immune to legal traditions but that explicit judicial politics is not unknown in the civil law world. As more empirical studies are produced, it is likely that the sharp contrast described by *Oracles of the Law* gives away to a more nuanced understanding of how individual preferences (including ideology), demographics (such as gender, age, race, religion, or background), institutional interaction, peer pressure, and other nonlegal determinants explain judicial behaviour in both common law and civil law jurisdictions.

As to testing the common law–civil law distinction, the current state of the art is much less straightforward. For example, Garoupa and Ginsburg (2015) provided several qualitative comparisons to support their thesis. The comparative law literature following *Oracle of the Law* also engaged widely with case studies and qualitative analysis. However, rigorous quantitative studies are difficult to find due to limitations in data availability and, more importantly, comparability across jurisdictions.

Cross-country regression analyses look at how legal families explain certain judicial variables. The legal origins theory suggests that common law courts are more efficient, more independent, and better in legal accuracy and consistency (Djankov, de Silanes, and Shleifer 2003; La Porta et al. 2004). Notwithstanding, Cross and Donelson (2010) found that common law decreases judicial performance measures within European jurisdictions—independence, efficiency, rule of law, impartiality. In his survey of the literature, Voigt (2016) did not mention the distinction between the common law and the civil law in his list of strong predictors for the quality of the judiciary.

At the micro level, international courts are a promising venue because they combine common law and civil law judges. Concerning the European Court of Human Rights, Voeten (2007 and 2008) did not find strong evidence supporting the hypothesis that legal traditions matter in explaining judicial behaviour. Zhang, Liu, and Garoupa (2016) provided substantially different findings concerning the European Court of Justice. The authors detected robust results that common law judges at the European courts behave differently from civil law judges in relation to competition law. They suggested different explanations for why legal traditions could matter in European courts. One is closely related to the legal origins theory and simply reflects general judicial attitudes. A second explanation is about the role of administrative law in different legal traditions—this is not about individual preferences or incentives but about the institutional context of judging. Finally, the authors emphasized that other possible explanatory variables potentially correlated with legal traditions (such as ideology, selection effect on appointment, judicial background in the private sector) were controlled for. Their findings found a cold audience among European law scholars (Nicola 2016). Although the empirical evidence is undisputable concerning judges from different legal traditions in European courts, legal scholars cannot agree on what explains these behavioural differences (Frankenreiter 2019; Wijtvliet and Dyevre 2021).

Another auspicious venue is federal courts in mixed jurisdictions where both legal traditions are represented such as the Canadian Supreme Court. Although there is evidence that English and French-speaking justices approach legal decision-making in different ways (Schertzer 2016), it is not easy to separate legal traditions, in the narrow sense, from other possible explanations (such as representation of linguistic minorities, provincial-specific goals, or political ideology).

From a different perspective, another interesting quantitative study is provided by Anidjar, Katz, and Zamir (2020). In the context of Israel, the authors explore the switch from common law to civil law in contractual doctrines (concerning specific performance as a remedy for breach of contract). They consider judgments for the period 1948–2016. They found documented evidence that the common law–civil law distinction has played a major role in explaining judicial behaviour in Israeli courts.

A promising methodology to test the common law–civil law distinction in shaping judicial behaviour is experimental empirical investigation. For example, Spamann and Klöhn (2016) created a relevant hypothetical to test the extent to which US judges care about precedent over largely irrelevant descriptive attributes of defendants. They concluded that, unexpectedly, individual defendant characteristics are more important than legal precedent, thus indicating that legalism is less prevalent than usually assumed by legal scholarship. A similar approach was pursued by Spamann et al. (2021) to compare judges from common law and civil law jurisdictions (namely, Argentina, Brazil, China, France, Germany, India, and the United States). As in the previous experiment, precedent effect is barely detectable and secondary to irrelevant defendant characteristics and sentence anchors. The authors found important variations in judicial style and written reasons. However, these differences do not seem correlated with the common law–civil law divide.

5. Conclusion

The study of judicial behaviour has changed in the last fifty years. Dawson's *Oracles of the Law* must be read in conjunction with modern theories of judicial behaviour. Together, they highlight the challenge of endogenous judicial institutions. Current literature explores in more detail the role played by contextual variables, including judicial behaviour, in shaping features of legal families. Therefore, *Oracles of Law* can be read as a fundamental inspiration for understanding the complex interaction between courts and judges and the distinct institutions that flourish under the different legal families.

It is important to emphasize that, while the literature recognized decades ago the limitations of excessive focusing on the common law–civil law divide, there is a clear and persistent lag in both theoretical and empirical applications to judicial behaviour in non-Western traditions.

One lesson from this chapter is that universal theories of judicial behaviour must be transparent in establishing their independent variables. First, this is the only way to avoid tautology or circular explanations—that legal families determine judicial behaviour, and judicial behaviour determines features of legal families. Second, the risk of confounding legal families and other possible explanatory variables must be minimized. Third, the inevitable tendency to assign any observable differences across jurisdictions to legal families or traditions (rather than e.g. political determinants as suggested by Garoupa and Grajzl 2020) begs for more and better quantitative analysis.

Acknowledgements

I am grateful to Arnold Zahn and the Jerusalem workshop participants for useful suggestions, and to Madeline Conn for excellent research assistance. Usual disclaimers apply.

References

Anidjar, Leon Yehuda, Ori Katz, and Eyal Zamir. 2020. 'Enforced Performance in Common Law versus Civil Law Systems: An Empirical Study of Legal Transformation'. *American Journal of Comparative Law* 68: 1–54.

Bagashka, Tanya, and Nuno Garoupa. 2021. 'European Constitutional Courts'. In *High Courts in Global Perspective: Evidence, Methodologies, and Findings*, edited by Nuno Garoupa, Rebecca D. Gill, and Lydia Tiede, 186–98. Charlottesville: University of Virginia Press.

Bell, John. 1987. 'Principles and Methods of Judicial Selection in France'. *Southern California Law Review* 61: 1757–94.

Bobek, Michal. 2013. *Comparative Reasoning in European Supreme Courts*. Oxford: Oxford University Press.

Caenegem, Raoul C. Van. 1987. *Judges, Legislators and Professors: Chapters in European Legal History*. Cambridge: Cambridge University Press.

Caenegem, Raoul C. Van. 2002. *European Law in the Past and the Future: Unity and Diversity over Two Millennia*. Cambridge: Cambridge University Press.

Cross, Frank, and Dain C. Donelson. 2010. 'Creating Quality Courts'. *Journal of Empirical Legal Studies* 7: 490–510.

Dawson, John P. 1968. *The Oracles of the Law*. Ann Arbor: University of Michigan Law School.

Djankov, Rafael La Porta, Florencio López de Silanes, and Andrei Shleifer. 2003. 'Courts'. *Quarterly Journal of Economics* 118: 453–517.

Epstein, Lee, and Keren Weinshall. 2021. *The Strategic Analysis of Judicial Behavior, Cambridge Elements in Law, Economics and Politics*. Cambridge: Cambridge University Press.

Erie, Matthew S. 2023. 'Legal Systems Inside Out: American Legal Exceptionalism and China's Dream of Legal Cosmopolitanism'. *University of Pennsylvania Journal of International Law* 44: 731–813.

Farber, Daniel A., and Suzanna Sherry. 2009. *Judgment Calls: Principles and Politics in Constitutional Law*. Oxford University Press.

Ferejohn, John, and Pasquale Pasquino. 2004. 'Constitutional Adjudication: Lessons from Europe'. *Texas Law Review* 82: 1671–704.

Frankenreiter, Jens. 2019. 'Writing Style and Legal Traditions'. In *Law as Data: Computation, Text, and the Future of Legal Analysis*, edited by Michael A. Livermore and Daniel N. Rockmore, 153–91. Santa Fe: Santa Fe Institute Press.

Garoupa, Nuno, and Catarina Santos Botelho. 2022. 'Judicial Dissent in Collegial Courts: Theory and Evidence'. In *Oxford Research Encyclopedia of Politics*, edited by William R. Thompson. Oxford: Oxford University Press. https://oxfordre.com/politics/display/10.1093/acrefore/9780190228637.001.0001/acrefore-9780190228637-e-1990.

Garoupa, Nuno, and Tom Ginsburg. 2015. *Judicial Reputation: A Comparative Theory*. Chicago: University of Chicago Press.

Garoupa, Nuno, and Peter Grajzl. 2020. 'Spurred by Legal Tradition or Contextual Politics? Lessons about Judicial Dissent from Slovenia and Croatia'. *International Review of Law and Economics* 63: article 105912.

Garoupa, Nuno, and Mariana Pargendler. 2014. 'A Law and Economics Perspective on Legal Families'. *European Journal of Legal Studies* 7: 36–60.

Garoupa, Nuno, Rebecca D. Gill, and Lydia B. Tiede. 2021. *High Courts in Global Perspective: Evidence, Methodologies, and Findings*. Charlottesville: University of Virginia Press.

Glenn, H. Patrick. 2014. *Legal Traditions of the World: Sustainable Diversity in Law*, 5th edn. Oxford: Oxford University Press.

Goutal, Jean Louis. 1976. 'Characteristics of Judicial Style in France, Britain and the USA'. *American Journal of Comparative Law* 24: 43–72.

Hohmann, Hanns. 1990. 'The Nature of Common Law and the Comparative Study of Legal Reasoning'. *American Journal of Comparative Law* 38: 143–70.

Jacobson, Arthur J. 2005. 'Publishing Dissent'. *Washington and Lee Law Review* 62: 1607–36.

Kelemen, Katalin. 2018. *Judicial Dissent in European Constitutional Courts: A Comparative and Legal Perspective*. London: Routledge.

Klerman, Daniel, and Paul Mahoney. 2007. 'Legal Origin?' *Journal of Comparative Economics* 35: 278–93.

Koch, Charles H. 2004. 'The Advantages of the Civil Model Judicial Design as the Model for Emerging Legal Systems'. Indiana *Journal of Global Legal Studies* 11: 139–60.

La Porta, Rafael, Florencio López de Silanes, Cristian Pop-Eleches, and Andrei Shleifer. 2004. 'Judicial Checks and Balances'. *Journal of Political Economy* 112: 445–70.

La Porta, Rafael, Florencio López de Silanes, and Andrei Shleifer. 2008. 'The Economic Consequences of Legal Origins'. *Journal of Economic Literature* 46: 285–332.

Lasser, Mitchel. 2009. *Judicial Deliberations: A Comparative Analysis of Judicial Transparency and Legitimacy*. Oxford: Oxford University Press.

Legrand, Pierre. 1987. 'Taking Another Look at French Civil Law'. *Oxford Journal of Legal Studies* 7: 136–44.

Matsubara, Kentaro. 2018. 'East, East, and West: Comparative Law and the Historical Processes of Legal Interaction in China and Japan'. *American Journal of Comparative Law* 66: 769–89.

Merryman, John H. 1988. 'How Other Do It: The French and German Judiciaries'. *Southern California Law Review* 61: 1865–76.

Merryman, John H. 1996. 'The French Deviation'. *American Journal of Comparative Law* 44: 109–19.

Merryman, John H., and Rogelio Pérez-Perdomo. 2018. *The Civil Law Tradition: An Introduction to the Legal Systems of Europe and Latin America*, 4th edn. Stanford: Stanford University Press.

Nazareno, Patricio. 2022. 'Profiling the American Judge: A Comparative Argument about Ideological Conceptions of Judging'. In *Common Law-Civil Law: The Great Divide?*, edited by Nicoletta Bersier, Cristoph Bezemek, and Frederick Schauer, 117–40. Cham: Springer Cham.

Nicola, Fernanda. 2016. 'National Legal Traditions at Work in the Jurisprudence of the Court of Justice of the European Union'. *American Journal of Comparative Law* 64: 865–89.

Pargendler, Mariana. 2012. 'The Rise and Decline of Legal Families'. *American Journal of Comparative Law* 60: 1043–74.

Posner, Richard. 1998. *Law and Legal Theory in England and America*. New York: Oxford University Press.

Reimann, Mathias. 2002. 'The Progress and Failure of Comparative Law in the Second Half of the Twentieth Century'. *American Journal of Comparative Law* 50: 671–700.

Reitz, John C. 2009. 'Toward a Study of the Ecology of Judicial Activism?' *University of Toronto Law Review* 59: 185–96.

Ruskola, Teemu. 2013. *Legal Orientalism: China, the United States, and Modern Law*. Cambridge, MA: Harvard University Press.

Schertzer, Robert. 2016. 'Quebec Justices as Quebec Representatives: National Minority Representation and the Supreme Court of Canada's Federalism Jurisprudence'. *Publius: The Journal of Federalism* 46: 539–67.

Siems, Mathias. 2022. *Comparative Law*, 3rd edn. Cambridge: Cambridge University Press.
Soper, Philip. 1977. 'Metaphors and Models of Law: The Judge as a Priest'. *Michigan Law Review* 75: 1196–213.
Spamann, Holger, and Lars Klöhn. 2016. 'Justice Is Less Blind, and Less Legalistic, than We Thought: Evidence from an Experiment with Real Judges'. *Journal of Legal Studies* 45: 255–80.
Spamann, Holger, Lars Klöhn, Christophe Jamin, Vikramaditya Khanna, John Zhuang Liu, Pavan Mamidi, Alexander Morell, and Ivan Reidel. 2021. 'Judges in the Lab: No Precedent Effects, No Common/Civil Law Differences'. *Journal of Legal Analysis* 13: 110–26.
Stack, Kevin M. 1996. 'The Practice of Dissent in the Supreme Court'. *Yale Law Journal* 105: 2235–60.
Voeten, Erik. 2007. 'The Politics of International Judicial Appointments: Evidence from the European Court of Human Rights'. *International Organization* 67: 669–701.
Voeten, Erik. 2008. 'The Impartiality of International Judges, Evidence from the European Court of Human Rights'. *American Political Science Review* 102: 417–33.
Voigt, Stefan. 2016. 'Determinants of Judicial Efficiency: A Survey'. *European Journal of Law and Economics* 42: 183–208.
Wells, Michael. 1994. 'French and American Judicial Opinions'. *Yale Journal of International Law* 19: 81–34.
Wijtvliet, Wessel, and Arthur Dyevre. 2021. 'Judicial Ideology in Economic Cases: Evidence from the General Court of the European Union'. *European Union Politics* 22: 25–45.
Zhang, Angela H., Jingchen Liu, and Nuno Garoupa. 2016. 'Judging in Europe: Do Legal Traditions Matter?' *Journal of Competition Law and Economics* 14: 144–78.

CHAPTER 3

MODELS OF CONSTITUTIONAL REVIEW

TOM GINSBURG AND MILA VERSTEEG

1. Introduction

Constitutional review[1] is the power of a body, usually a court, to assess whether a law or government action complies with the constitution. Originating in the US constitutional order, it has spread all over the world and is now a ubiquitous feature of government: nearly three-quarters of constitutions in force provide for it, including those of many non-democracies (Ginsburg and Versteeg 2013, 590). There is no doubt that the global spread of constitutional review is important as it has made judges the final arbiters over issues that used to be exclusively political in nature (Tate and Vallinder 1995, 5; Stone Sweet 2000; Hirschl 2004; Sieder, Schjolden, and Angell 2005). Indeed, the institution is a subject of ongoing controversy in some countries.

But not all forms of constitutional review are alike. The sweeping diffusion of the institution belies substantial variation in how constitutional review is structured and exercised. The comparative literature mostly explores variation in constitutional review through the lens of three canonical models, associated with the (i) United States, (ii) Germany, and (iii) France respectively. These were the models on offer during the third wave of democracy, when many countries rewrote constitutions to include the institution. They remain the classical starting point for a comparative account of judicial review.

Relying on models is a useful way to conduct a comparative inquiry. In the constitutional context, we think of a model as any configuration of institutional features that tend to co-occur, either by convention or by internal logic, and that may provide a basis on which other jurisdictions develop institutional designs. But a model is also in part a construction of researchers, who need to decide which feature(s) to emphasize in the process of building one. The canonical models are mainly constructed around two features: (i) whether the body that performs constitutional review is specialized and (ii) whether review is abstract and/or concrete.

In this chapter, we argue that there are alternative dimensions of variation in judicial review that deserve more attention in model building: (i) access, that is, who can bring a constitutional claim; (ii) finality, that is whether a ruling by the highest court is final, and (iii) centralization, that is, whether there is merely one or multiple access points to the institution. Emphasizing these features produces different classifications that cut across the three canonical models. We argue that some of these features may be more relevant to the practice of constitutional review than specialization and abstraction. We do not ultimately argue that one or the other approach is better: our goal is to show that multiple classifications are possible. We further reflect on the increasing importance of supranational review and how it affects each of the dimensions of access, finality, and centralization.

The remainder of this chapter is organized as follows. We will start by discussing the classical triad: the models of judicial review associated with the United States, Germany, and France respectively. We then propose alternative classifications. We next describe how supranational review can influence those dimensions. We conclude by reflecting upon the relative importance of each of these dimensions.

2. The Classical Triad

2.1 The US Model

Constitutional review originates in the American colonies for distinctive historical reasons (Shapiro 1994; Prakash and Yoo 2003). The former colonies had relied on British courts to adjudicate disputes with government; sovereignty lay back with the motherland, and so there were no aesthetic or conceptual barriers to individuals suing the charter governments, which were themselves derivative of imperial power. With the American Revolution of 1776, state governments found themselves subjected to decisions of their own courts for violations of rights. Thus, when the founding fathers gathered at Philadelphia in 1787, judicial review was in the air. Indeed, many have found evidence in the Federalist Papers that the founders expected courts to assess legislation for constitutionality, as they had in the colonies. Alexander Hamilton assumes judicial review in Federalist No 78, and sees no risk from judicial power that inheres in 'the least dangerous branch' (Hamilton 1788).

Whatever their understanding of judicial review as a latent power, the founders made a somewhat fateful decision to omit from the constitutional text any mention of the power of courts to assess legislation for constitutionality. The 1803 case of *Marbury v Madison* became the canonical origin of the power of judges to 'say what the law is' at the federal level, but the textual omission has given rise to what is sometimes called the 'counter-majoritarian difficulty', the uneasy relationship of an unelected court setting aside legislation produced by a democratic majority (Bickel 1962). Still, it was clearly understood that judicial review was a distinct feature of the US constitution that placed the judges at the centre of governance, as confirmed by Alexis de Tocqueville in 1835:

> Whenever a law which the judge holds to be unconstitutional is argued in a tribunal of the United States he may refuse to admit it as a rule; this power is the only one which is peculiar to the American magistrate.... The political power which the Americans have intrusted to their courts of justice is therefore immense, but the evils of this power are considerably diminished by the obligation which has been imposed of attacking the laws through the courts of justice alone.... Within these limits the power vested in the American courts of justice of pronouncing a statute to be unconstitutional forms one of the most powerful barriers which has ever been devised against the tyranny of political assemblies.[2]

We see in this brief passage some core features of what would become known as the US model: decentralization, legalization, and judicialization. The power to 'refuse to admit' a law was seen as inherent in the power of judging, and so extended to any judge in the land—hence, decentralization. This power was moderated somewhat by the institutional passivity of judges, dependent as they were on a litigant bringing a *legal* case—so legalization was a feature of the model. But it was nevertheless an immense power, giving rise to concerns of judicialization that remain a feature of American political discourse to this day (Shapiro 1994).

Tocqueville's comment that the power was 'peculiar to the American magistrate' was mostly true for much of the nineteenth century. Some early constitutions in Latin America mention this power, but for the most part, constitutions were meant to guide the political branches without judicial oversight. It was only with the increasingly complex government in the twentieth century, with deeper penetration into the lives of citizens, that the idea of a judicial check on government authority took off. One way to think about this is that the expansion of legislation itself necessitated more judging, and judicial review spread in popularity.

2.2 The German Model

The spread of legislative power, driven by modernity, encountered a very different legal theory among the civil law nations of Europe. These countries, in either the French or German tradition, tended to see law as formalistic and judges as exercising subordinate power (Merryman and Perez-Perdomo 2007). Their legal theory sat uneasily with the idea of judicialization and so required its own model.

Hans Kelsen was the great innovator, and his idea came from a conceptual jurisprudence confronting a practical problem. The practical problem, for Kelsen, was federalism, which meant that the constitutional order had multiple governments each creating their own law. This necessitated some sort of institution to resolve conflicts. Kelsen thought that an ordinary court, whose job was to implement law passed by a legislature, could not as a matter of legal hierarchy be put in the position of judging that legislation (Kelsen 1928). This led him to propose the creation, in the Constitution of the Austrian First Republic of 1920, of a designated body called the 'Constitutional Court' which would have a discrete task insulated from ordinary judging. That task was constitutional review. Thus was born the so-called centralized model of constitutional review, with a designated body dedicated to the task.

The key features of this new model were concentration, specialization, and a combination of abstract and concrete review. First, the power was limited to a single small group of judges—hence, concentration. Second, those judges were dedicated solely to the task of constitutional interpretation, thus leading to specialization. A strict Montesqueian reading of the separation of powers meant that the constitutional court needed to be separate from the ordinary judicial system, and so was characterized by specialization.

Third, the model was characterized by a mix of abstract and concrete review. In the original Kelsenian formulation, review was abstract: the constitutional court did not resolve concrete legal disputes between private parties. Instead, it answered questions referred to it by a designated set of government officials, either before or after the adoption of a law. But abstraction was not complete, and the centralized model as it developed was compatible with resolving constitutional questions that arose in concrete disputes. The manner in which these were resolved illustrates the distinct theoretical position of the constitutional court as slightly outside of the normal legal hierarchy. When an ordinary judge confronts a question of constitutional interpretation in the course of ordinary litigation, she certifies this question to the constitutional court. Ordinary proceedings are suspended until the constitutional court has ruled on the constitutionality of the question. Once rendered, the constitutional court's judgment is sent back to the referring court, which decided the case on the basis of the ruling.[3] Although arising in the context of actual litigation, the decision-making by the constitutional court had a somewhat abstract quality, relative to the US model. The entire emphasis was on maintaining the conceptual integrity of the legal system, in processes that were really internal to government rather than directly deciding disputes between citizen and state.

The Kelsenian model of constitutional review was soon adopted in other countries, including Czechoslovakia (Constitution Article 54.13 (1920)), Liechtenstein (Constitution Article 104 (1921)), Iraq (Constitution Article 83 (1925)), and Spain (Constitution (1931)). But it was really with the *Grundgesetz* of Germany in 1949 that the centralized model reached its fullest expression. Whereas the Austrian Constitutional Court had focused on disputes related to federalism, in which states needed a boundary adjudicator to protect their respective jurisdictions, the German Constitutional Court combined constitutional review of legislation with a vigorous and robust set of constitutional rights, articulated in aversion to the immediate Nazi past. These could be protected through the ordinary courts, using the Kelsenian device of asking ordinary judges to send the question to the Constitutional Court. But the Basic Law also introduced the device of the constitutional complaint, through which any individual could challenge the constitutionality of a statute or government action, even without a specific case or controversy. This new mechanism played an important role in democratizing access to the Constitutional Court and associating the institution with the protection of rights. It meant that access to constitutional review was even broader than found in the US model, which required strictly legal claims. In addition, the Constitutional Court was given many ancillary powers (Ginsburg 2004), including the ability to decide whether to ban a political party and review a state of emergency. But the concentrated power of final review of legislation in a specialized court is the core definitional attribute of this model.

Constitutional courts of the Kelsenian type were adopted throughout Europe after the Second World War (e.g. in Portugal 1976, Spain 1978, and Belgium 1985) and in the former Soviet bloc after the Cold War in the so-called third wave of constitutional review (Elster 1995; see also Stone Sweet, *The Oxford Handbook of Comparative Constitutional Law*).

2.3 The French Model

A third canonical model originates in the French Fifth Republic, embodied in the constitution of 1958. This document is associated with Charles de Gaulle and his solution to the crisis of French politics. The constitution of the Fourth Republic had been parliamentary, but a fragmented party system meant that there was no real coherence to the political system. De Gaulle wanted to correct this weakness with a strong executive in the so-called semi-presidential model. This constitutional design featured a divided executive, with an elected president who had independent decree-making power, alongside a parliament that would select a Prime Minister. Because the scheme featured two kinds of legislation, there was a need for a boundary adjudicator (Shapiro 2002). The body with this role was the *Conseil Constitutionnel*, a concentrated body that shared with Kelsen's design the features of specialization and abstraction. But unlike the German model, the French *Conseil* was restricted to engaging in review of legislation only before it was promulgated, and it had no concrete jurisdiction whatsoever. Its distinct feature was its limitation to *ex ante* abstract review. Review could be initiated by a small number of political actors, including the President of the Senate, the President of the National Assembly, and the President of the Republic. It was squarely oriented towards protecting the integrity of the boundaries of law-making within the constitutional system rather than protecting the rights of citizens. We can thus define the key features as concentration, pure abstraction (rather than the mixed review which the German-style courts exercised), and discrete jurisdiction. The *Conseil* was one of three top courts, along with the *Cour de Cassation* and the *Conseil d'État*, and unlike the Kelsenian model, was in no sense superior over the others. Further, because the members of the *Conseil* included former presidents of the Republic, it was less specialized in the hands of judges.

The *Conseil* acted with perhaps more independence than had been anticipated, especially after the grand figure of De Gaulle himself faded from the scene (Ackerman

2019). The system changed quite significantly in 1974, when President Valerie Giscard d'Estaing decided to expand standing to include minority groups of legislators. As Stone Sweet (1992) tells it, this meant that political parties could attack legislation before promulgation, even when they had lost in legislative debates. The constitutional council became, in his telling, a third house of the legislature, a function that assumed very great importance when the Socialist party took over in 1981. The constitutional council became a mechanism of constraining the socialists from their more radical plans, leading to what Stone Sweet calls the birth of judicial politics in France.

The French model was adopted in many former French colonies in Africa, including the rule that legislative minorities could bring cases to the constitutional councils. Because many of these countries were one-party states, however, there was not a lot of judicial politics. But in recent years, a vigorous judicial politics seems to be emerging on the African continent, including in some countries utilizing the French model. The constitutional courts and councils are sites of occasional constraint of strong executives.

In France itself, the system changed again in 2008. In this year, perhaps responding to convergence pressures, the system was transformed yet again with the addition of *ex post* review. Citizens now have the ability to bring claims to the constitutional council in ways that were similar to those found in other European countries with designated constitutional courts. While this change represented a shift toward the German model, the presence of the other two high courts means that the shift is incomplete. The French model lacks the supremacy associated with the German model.

2.4 Non-Judicial Variants

Not all countries have embraced judicial review. Several countries have a long tradition of parliamentary sovereignty. Parliamentary sovereignty implies that the people's representatives sitting in the legislature should have primacy over any other authority and so be unconstrained by judicial control. This idea remains the guiding principle in democratic countries like the United Kingdom, New Zealand, and the Netherlands.

This theory is classically associated with Dicey in the United Kingdom but it has resonated also outside of the democratic context. Notably, the idea has long been convenient for communist countries, whose constitutions typically involved no form of constitutional review. And in an age of democratic backsliding, the 'political constitutionalism' (Bellamy 2011) associated with the British tradition has been an attractive theoretical device for those wanting to reduce the power of courts (Halmai 2019).

Another approach resembling parliamentary sovereignty in its pure form is taken by authoritarian communist countries. In 1982, the People's Republic of China adopted a constitution as part of Deng Xiaoping's effort to provide a stronger institutional foundation for the rule of the Chinese Communist Party. This document centred the role of interpreting the Constitution in the Standing Committee of the National People's

Congress (Kellogg and Hand 2008). Under Chinese constitutional theory, the National People's Congress is the highest organ of state power and its Standing Committee can thus engage in the authoritative interpretation of the constitution. It engages in *ex ante* review upon request from certain state organs, and also has a role in delivering authoritative interpretations to courts upon request. This form of review within the legislature does not utilize an adjudicative process, but it was a locus increasingly for debates on the constitutionality of major Chinese legislation during the early 2000s (Zhu 2010; Lin and Ginsburg 2015). During the same period, attempts by some lower courts to claim a power of constitutional review over administrative actions were shut down (Zhu 2010). This means that China has no genuine system of constitutional review outside of the legislative process.

One final variant worth mentioning is the one found in the Constitution of Ethiopia, which features a complex tribal and ethnic structure within a federal system. Constitutional review is performed by the House of Federations, the upper house of the legislature. This body does not have a major role in the ordinary legislative process, but it can be seen as a device to protect the interests of the states from encroachment by the central government (Abebe 2010). As a design matter this certainly warrants some attention for its novelty, although less so from a judicial behaviour perspective: there has not been much activity nor impact on the outputs of government.

3. An Alternative Framing

The conventional way of organizing these models is by legal tradition, with the primary dimensions of variation being whether review is specialized and may be exercised abstractly, as in many civil law countries, or whether it is decentralized and purely legal, as found in common law jurisdictions in which concrete cases are the basis of review by ordinary judges (Capelletti 1989). Specialization and abstraction, then, are the central analytic axes for constructing the classical models.

In this section, we decentre specialization to focus on different institutional features as the basis for categorization. We propose three lenses: (i) breadth of accessibility, (ii) finality of the ruling, and (iii) degree of centralization. These lenses produce different classifications that cut across the classical triad.

3.1 Access

A first dimension along with judicial review varies, which cuts across the three canonical models, is *access*. We can see this, for example, within the German model. The Italian variant of constitutional review had a slightly different system of access from the German (Ferejohn and Pasquino 2012). Whereas in Germany, citizens had a direct channel to the Constitutional Court through the mechanism of a constitutional complaint, in Italy all constitutional claims had to be processed through the court system. A citizen who felt that legislation was unconstitutional had to raise the issue in an ordinary court of law, at which point the judge would toll the case and certify a question to the Constitutional Court for resolution. The Constitutional Court would resolve the legal question of interpretation and send the decision back to the ordinary court, which would in turn implement it in the case of hand. This mechanism focused on concrete cases and preserved the legal character of constitutional review, as well as the concentration of interpretation in a designated constitutional court. It resembles the operation of judicial review in the European Union, where the European Court of Justice (ECJ) hears claims certified from national courts about the status of European Union law.

Judicial review in Latin America centred around the procedural device of the *amparo* (Brewer-Carrias 2014). This device originated in Mexico and was created after De Tocqueville's description of judicial review was translated into Spanish. Jurists first introduced the idea at the state level, and later it was adopted in the Federal Constitution of 1857, eventually spreading throughout the continent. A writ of amparo was a procedural device for rights protection, whereby a litigant could ask for protection in a particular case. The key feature, traditionally, was that the remedy was limited to the particular case, and a positive decision did not result in setting aside of legislation. But over time, the Mexican Supreme Court developed the practice that five writs granted on the same issue would lead to a decision of general effect. As the twentieth century has progressed, new devices for rights protection, such as the *tutela* in Colombia or the constitutional complaint in Brazil, provided for broad access and powerful remedies. In this sense, there has been a great expansion of access to the point that judicial review has become more decentralized even in systems with specialized constitutional courts, because ordinary judges also can accept constitutional questions in the first instance.

In a similar vein, in several South Asian jurisdictions, including India and Pakistan, courts have been greatly expanding access, even allowing themselves to take cases at their own initiative (Galanter 2014; Qazi 2015). Such *suo moto* actions are becoming more prevalent, and sometimes concern major issues of policy.

As these examples show, there is substantial variation in how to access judicial review. In terms of accessibility, one can array systems on a spectrum from most closed to most open. Figure 3.1 depicts this graphically. Most closed are the systems in which only certain governmental institutions can bring claims. The original French design, like that of Kelsen's in Austria, limited access to certain governmental actors, such as the President and Prime Minister. In this conception, review is focused on maintaining the internal integrity of the constitutional order in terms of the allocation of governmental power. When France expanded its jurisdiction to include a minority of legislators, review remained within the governmental sphere but increased in political importance, as legislative politics now could play out through judicial review. This mode of legislative access to review is now found in 35 per cent of all constitutional systems, according to

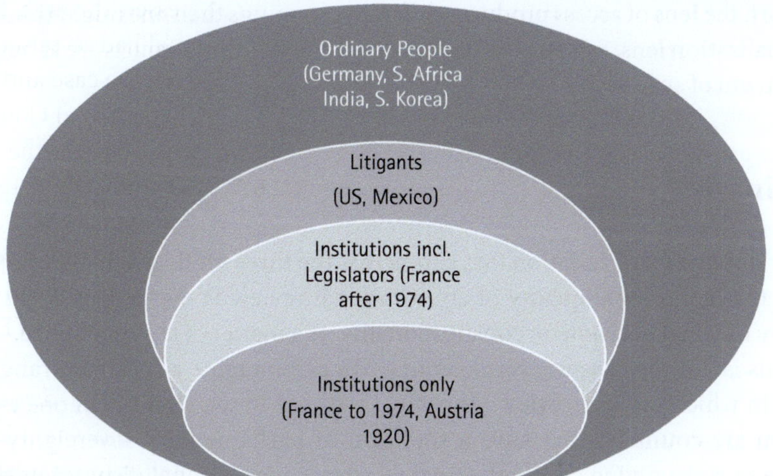

FIGURE 3.1 Classification based on access.

data from the Comparative Constitutions Project (CCP). It is a somewhat more open form of judicial review than one in which only designated governmental actors can bring claim.

Next on the spectrum lie systems in which cases can come up through the ordinary court system. According to CCP data, 25 per cent of all constitutions in force mention the courts as a mode of accessing review. Most countries in the Americas utilize this system of access, since it can be channelled through the ordinary legal process (as in the United States and Caribbean common law jurisdictions) or through special procedural devices like amparo and *tutela* (as in the Latin American countries). On the dimension of access, Mexico and the United States are similar.

Systems with constitutional petitions have the broadest access. These include about 30 per cent of constitutional systems today. The German constitutional complaint, a method provided for by the Basic Law Article 93(1)4a, allows citizens and some entites to raise a claim of violation of rights. Although there are some procedural requirements involved, a complaint does not need to be formulated as a legal claim. Similarly, Section 167 of the South African Constitution allows a person, 'when it is in the interests of justice and with leave of the Constitutional Court', to bring a matter directly to the Constitutional Court, as well as to appeal directly from another court. The Hungarian Constitution in place until 2011 provided access to 'everyone', not even limiting access to citizens. An even broader form of standing is the Indian Supreme Court's adoption of the Public Interest Litigation model, under the leadership of Chief Justice P. N. Bhagwati, through which anyone in the country can bring a complaint with minimal procedural requirements. Under the *suo moto* jurisdiction adopted in India and several other South Asian jurisdictions, even a formal complaint is not required for the courts to take up an issue for resolution and issue orders (Kureshi 2022).

In short, the lens of access produces different groupings than one might think of using the specialization lens. Systems with specialized constitutional courts are at both ends of the spectrum of access.

3.2 Finality

Another dimension of variation that cuts across the three models is finality. Some might say that the definitional quality of constitutional review is that judges at the national level have the final decision on constitutionality, as a matter of law or practice.

But this is not the case in every country. We can imagine a spectrum ranging from systems in which judicial review is not final to those in which it is. On one end of this spectrum are countries that have a tradition of parliamentary sovereignty and that continue to resist giving courts the final word in constitutional disputes, even as they have empowered courts. These countries have seen the emergence of what Gardbaum (2012) calls 'the new constitutional commonwealth model of constitutional review'. The central defining features of this model, according to Gardbaum, are (i) a catalogue of fundamental rights, (ii) entrenched either legally in a constitution or by a statute with political weight, (iii) enforced by courts with the power of constitutional review, that (iv) do not necessarily have the last word in interpretation. It is this last feature, the lack of finality, that really marks the distinctive characteristic of this model, and it has the virtue of putting courts into dialogue with other constitutional actors. The model provided an intellectually satisfying synthesis between traditions of parliamentary sovereignty and demands for rights protection, and received acclaim in the literature. Mark Tushnet (2008) celebrates it as a form of 'weak form review' which avoids the problems of legitimacy that arise from judicial finality. The central feature of these models is that they are dialogic, featuring a back-and-forth between multiple constitutional branches that each bring their own perspectives to constitutional interpretation, and allowing for the overcoming of the counter-majoritarian objection to constitutional review.

One step further on this spectrum are national courts in supranational orders. For example, the Mexican Supreme Court now exists in a legal order that directly incorporates norms from the American Convention of Human Rights, whose authoritative interpreter is the Inter-American Court of Human Rights. The key insight here is that the expansion of supranational review undermines the finality of national constitutional review. This is somewhat counterintuitive, since supranational review is usually justified on the basis of enhancing rights protection, which is also a justification for national judicial empowerment. Yet as an analytic matter, there is no doubt that supranational review reduces the finality of national judges. National high courts can be overturned by supranational courts. At the same time, it is not always obvious that these decisions are final: domestic judges at times resist the supranational legal order (Lustig and Weiler 2018). A notable example is Germany. The German Constitutional Court is, of course, embedded in a broader European supranational order, but it has asserted final authority to interpret the constitution. What is more, the German Constitution makes certain parts of the constitution unamendable; hence one can imagine a theoretical case in which the Court resists supranational interpretations; the legislature amends the constitution to bring it in line with the supranational legal order, and the Constitutional Court strikes down this amendment based on the unamendable 'eternity clause'. For this reason, we note Germany as a contested category on Figure 3.2.

Next on the spectrum are the systems in which judicial review is final, but judicial decisions can be overturned through constitutional amendments. The United States falls in this category, and a number of constitutional amendments have overruled contrary judicial decisions. Indeed, some have suggested that the practice of amending the constitution to overturn certain judicial interpretations is quite common at the state level in the United States (Versteeg and Zackin 2016).

Furthest on the spectrum are the systems in which courts have the power to overturn constitutional amendments. According to the doctrine of unconstitutional constitutional amendments, even a procedurally valid amendment is subject to judicial review for determination as to whether it complies with some deeper standard, such as 'basic structure' (India), 'constitutional custom' (South Korea), an eternity clause (Germany), or some other such norm (Roznai 2016). For systems with a robust doctrine of unconstitutional constitutional amendments, the judiciary is indeed final as a legal matter.

What is important for our purposes is that this dimension again cuts again the three traditional models. That is, there are different degrees of finality within each of the three canonical models.

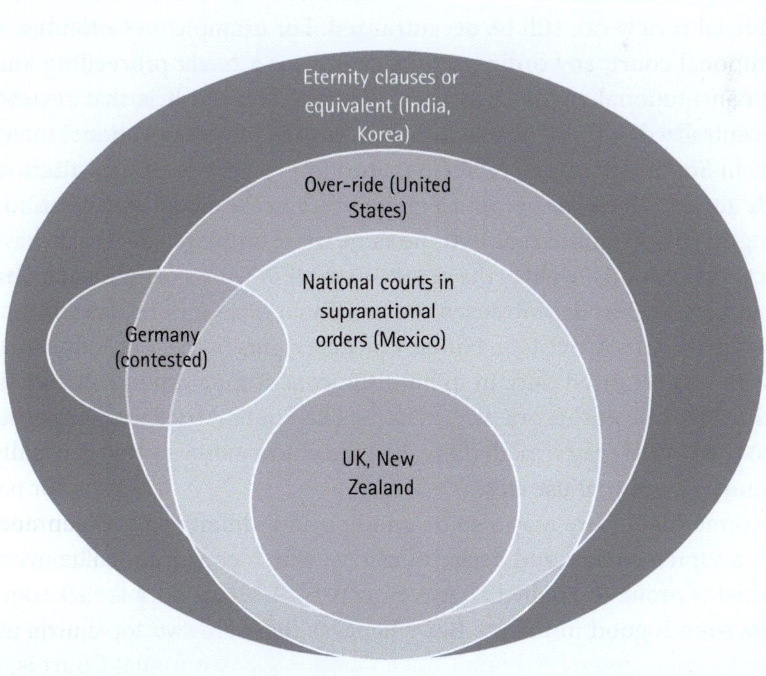

FIGURE 3.2 Classification based on finality.

3.3 Centralization

Another dimension of variation within the three classical models is centralization, or whether there is a single point of access to judicial review powers or whether there are multiple access points. The conventional lens based on legal tradition distinguishes those countries with review by a centralized constitutional court, exclusively devoted to the task from those without such a court, which are presumed to be decentralized. Centralization is closely related to specialization. The classical approach envisions a constitutional court that is both the only body that conducts constitutional review and that is specialized in doing so. Indeed, it is the isolation of the discrete function of constitutional adjudication that is definitional of constitutional courts (Ginsburg and Versteeg 2013). By contrast, supreme courts are typically envisioned as non-specialized courts and as embedded in a system in which lower courts also conduct judicial review.

But the crude distinction between specialized constitutional courts and non-specialized high courts does not truly capture whether constitutional review is centralized or decentralized. First, we observe there are some systems which have centralization without a specialized constitutional court. For example, in Israel, it is only the non-specialized Supreme Court (acting in its capacity as the High Court of Justice) that can exercise judicial review powers, making it dissimilar from systems like the United States where review can be conducted by the lower federal courts.

But perhaps more relevant, in many systems with a centralized constitutional court, judicial review can still be decentralized. For example, in Colombia, which has a constitutional court, any ordinary judge can hear a *tutela* proceeding and evaluate whether constitutional rights have been violated. The result is that review becomes more decentralized with the whole judiciary engaged in constitutional interpretation. Likewise, in South Africa, the 1996 Constitution provides for a Constitutional Court, with wide access, which has become a major voice in the global conversation of how to protect rights (Böckenforde 2022). At the same time, ordinary courts also have the duty to protect constitutional rights. The result is a system with a centralized constitutional court, that nevertheless decentralizes constitutional review, in keeping with a desire of post-apartheid South Africa to maximally protect rights in the wake of apartheid. Open access, with a generalized duty to uphold the constitution among all courts, helps to do just this. Because of this practice, systems like South Africa and Colombia become similar to the United States: in all these, it is the entire judiciary that can hear constitutional claims. Figure 3.3 illustrates.

At the same time, there may also be an important difference between decentralization with a supreme court and decentralization with a constitutional court in that the latter model is prone to conflicts between courts. A broad duty for all courts to protect rights sounds good in theory. But whenever there are two top courts in a system

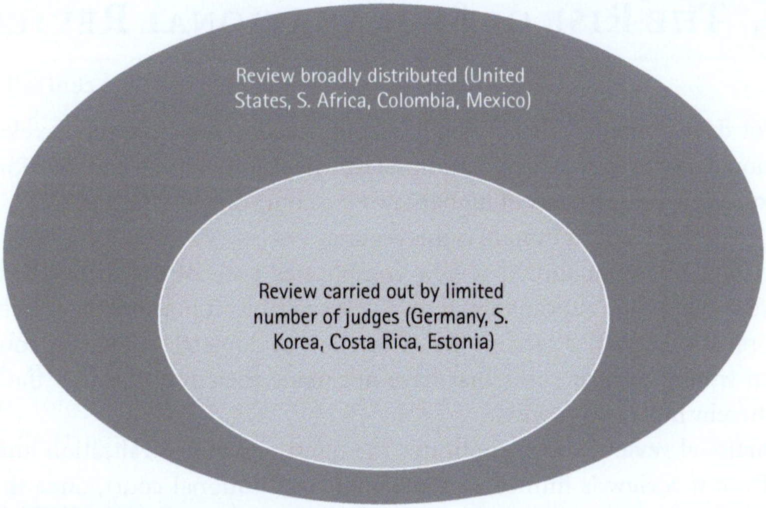

FIGURE 3.3 Classification based on centralization.

of concentrated review, there can be uneasy relations between the two bodies. These often take the form of jurisdictional battles over who has the final word on various legal questions (Garlicki 2007). While a 'pure theory' would suggest that the constitutional court should have the final say on constitutional matters, this has not always played out in practice. Thus, the clean lines implied by models can sometimes break down in messy ways when put into practice.

Whether a system is centralized or decentralized, then, does not neatly track whether the system has a German-style constitutional court or a US-style Supreme Court. A related observation is that this crude distinction likewise does not capture the degree to which the judges that exercise constitutional review are indeed specialized. If constitutional review is conducted by both a constitutional court and ordinary courts, then non-specialized judges decide many constitutional cases. What is more, in some systems without a designated constitutional court, there is specialization. In Costa Rica, there is only one Supreme Court, but it has a special chamber, Sala IV, which exercises constitutional review (Wilson 2009). This is a form of specialized constitutional review within a generalized supreme court, a kind of hybrid model. In Estonia, which alone among former Soviet Republics did not create a separate constitutional court, questions of constitutionality can go to a special constitutional chamber in the Supreme Court, or be heard en banc. In these systems, there is specialization even though there is no specialized constitutional court. We think this means that we should focus on how many judges are capable of exercising constitutional review rather than the question of whether those judges have other tasks.

4. The Rise of Supranational Review

One major development, intensifying in recent decades, has been the development of supranational review, in which national-level decisions about constitutionality are subject to review on the basis of higher law by a court outside the state. Typically, this involves a regional trade or human rights regime.

Any system of supranational review complicates each of the three classifications discussed above. When supranational review is available, it may broaden access. While most supranational courts require the exhaustion of domestic remedies, some bodies have been willing to hear cases that have not made their way through the domestic system, thereby increasing access.

Supranational review also complicates the questions of centralization and specialization. Even if review is limited to a national constitutional court, once there is the possibility of appealing to a court outside the national jurisdiction, the constitutional question will by definition be heard by judges who are not expert in the local system. Their specialization is not in local constitutional law but rather transnational trade or human rights law, and so the traditional picture becomes murkier. At the same time, there are more locations at which review can be carried out, leading to a decentralization of judicial review powers.

But the most dramatic implications are on the issue of finality. Whereas in many systems, the constitutional review body is considered to have the final judicial word, once an international court is in the picture this is no longer the case. A constitutional court decision might itself be a source of violation of the international norms, and thus generate obligations that individuals can enforce supranationally. We thus see how the presence of supranational review, even as a theoretical matter, complicates the traditional models.

One must be careful in delineating which supranational regimes have the power of final *constitutional* review. Under the European Convention of Human Rights, a supranational court interprets a regional treaty and issues judgments against member states on the international plane: the European Court of Human Rights decisions do not have domestic legal effect and so would not count as constitutional review under our definition. The decisions are addressed to member states, and a national constitutional court would still have the final word in interpreting national law. Similarly, the African Court of Human and People's Rights has reviewed constitutional provisions and asked member states to change them, but its decisions do not have direct effect. The picture is murkier in the ECJ, whose decisions have direct effect in the constitutional order (Dulitsky 2015; Huneeus and Madsen 2018). If the ECJ finds that a constitutional provision of a member state is in violation of the European treaties, the direct legal effect of the decision should trump any contrary domestic interpretation. For many years, the German Constitutional Court and the ECJ have engaged in a back and forth about who has the final word in interpreting national constitutional law, with a kind of *détente* in place at this writing.

Direct effect is in place in the Caribbean and Latin American systems. The Caribbean system emerged from an early version of supranational review that was found in the British empire, in which the Judicial Committee of the House of Lords, the Privy Council, served as a court of last result for those members of the British commonwealth that retained its jurisdiction. But in part because of the backlash against a number of Privy Council decisions, Caribbean states created the Caribbean Court of Justice in the CARICOM trade area in 2001 (Helfer 2002). This body has taken over as a collective court for the member states as a court of last resort, including with constitutional jurisdiction, and so can be considered as exercising a form of constitutional review.

The Inter-American Human Rights regime has transformed itself from a system of international law, in which the legal commands operate only among states as such, to one of supranational constitutional review. The crucial steps began with the 2006 case of *Almonacid-Arellano et al v Chile*, which announced a doctrine of 'conventionality control' (Dulitsky 2015).[4] Conventionality control means that the norms of the American Convention and American Declaration, as interpreted by the Inter-American Court, are binding on all the member states and their national courts. This includes not only statutes but national constitutional norms. As when national constitutional courts first had to coordinate with national supreme courts, the doctrine has created some tensions between national courts and the Inter-American Court (Huneeus 2011).

A final development, still only theoretical, is a proposal for an International Court of Constitutional Law (Albert 2023). This idea was pushed by Moncef Marzouki, the first President of Tunisia to serve after the Revolution of 2011. He introduced the idea at the United Nations General Assembly, and created a committee which developed a statute for the Court.[5] But there was little uptake. Recently Richard Albert has called for a revival of the idea, as a way of counteracting democratic backsliding. Albert's view is that such a court should be limited to resolving abstract questions, which would simplify adoption of the proposal as a legal matter. At its most expansive, an international court of constitutional law would transform constitutional review in any state that signed up to the regime. While a proposal like this has not been implemented, it shows has supranational regime can change the finality of domestic constitutional review.

5. Advantages and Disadvantages

The comparative judicial review literature that has emerged around the three classical models has not been particularly normative in character. Our framing allows for some comparative assessment of institutional design, though as always one can only speak of trade-offs and optimization rather than a universal best.

As a start, which of the three dimensions is most important depends on normative considerations. If rights protection is a priority, then broad access is particularly important. There is no doubt that broad access to the institution of judicial review can help generate more rights claims. By contrast, if legal certainty is important to the legal culture, then finality is the key dimension. Finality is also important in settings in which it is important to express the primacy of nation-state vis-à-vis supranational actors. But it raises the spectre of the counter-majoritarian difficulty vis-à-vis national elected authorities. It requires a certain degree of judicial restraint to avoid encroachment into matters seen as lying with the domain of democracy.

It is worth reflecting on the importance of centralization. Centralization of any function in government allows the development of expertise and consistency, but it has potential downsides as well. In our context, all models of constitutional review must grapple with the fact that the institution is embedded in a broader system of politics. This is starkly illustrated by our current era of democratic backsliding. Traditionally, constitutional courts were established to protect the integrity and coherence of constitutional review, as well as the normative hierarchy within a legal system. However, that very concentration means having a good deal of power in a single body, which creates some risk of capture. Perhaps the paradigm case illustrating the risk is the Constitutional Court of Hungary. Scheppele (2003, 2005) once celebrated the constitutional court of Hungary, in a series of articles demonstrating how it assumed a central role in the political system, served as an instrument of Europeanization, and generally helped with Hungary's transformation from communist rule in the 1990s and early 2000s. But this optimistic vision came crashing down with the election of Viktor Orbán in 2010. With a majority in parliament sufficient to pass constitutional amendments, his party replaced the Constitution, voided the entire prior jurisprudence of the Constitutional Court in one swoop, and appointed justices friendly to him. The very centrality of constitutional review meant that this linchpin reform gave him massive leverage over all other bodies in the political system, and the court was transformed into an instrument of consolidating political power rather than a constraint on it.

These stories have been repeated in other places. A major confrontation involving the Polish Constitutional Tribunal played out in 2018, as the Law and Justice Party was able to pack the court, as part of its broader attempt to take over the entire judicial system (Sadurski 2019). The conflict led to direct confrontation between the government of Poland and the European Union, which has sued the country and is penalizing it with fines for violations of the rule of law principle. For our purpose, the interesting point is that the constitutional tribunal, once a guarantor of rights, has become a locus of politicization and back sliding. But it also illustrates the complexities introduced by supranational review, as the ECJ has repeatedly had to rule on the dispute with the European Union.

It does not seem to be obvious that as a general matter, the centralized model is more or less likely to produce a vigorous defence of democracy. In Africa, the Supreme Court of Kenya played the major role and protected the integrity of the country's elections, while constitutional courts in countries such as the Central African Republic have at times stood up against aggrandizing leaders. While more empirical inquiries are needed, these anecdotes suggest that centralized courts are not clearly better at protecting democracy.

We may be entering an era of dissatisfaction with constitutional courts. Some countries are beginning to consider shifting away from the model of a designated constitutional court toward one of review by a single supreme court. Georgia and Armenia have both had discussions to this effect, though neither has yet done away with the constitutional court. Our account has showed that this shift need not entail decentralization of the review function.

6. Conclusion

A model is a configuration of co-occurring institutional features that are adopted and emulated. Early models of constitutional review included that of the United States, a model developed by Hans Kelsen that received its fullest expression in postwar Germany, and a model of pre-promulgation review developed in the French Fifth Republic. As constitutional review has rapidly spread in the last four decades, these models have been adapted and complicated by various constitutional designers and judicial leaders. This introduction of complexity makes it an opportune time to reconsider the classic models.

Our approach to categorizing systems of review has focused on particular institutional features rather than the traditional three models. Once one looks at features like access, finality, and centralization, it becomes apparent that the classical approach has little explanatory power for the actual practice of judicial review. How much explanatory power our proposed classification has is a question for future research. We envision that empirical researchers can quantify these dimensions, explore whether and how they cluster together, and whether they are correlated with particular outcomes.

For the time being, constitutional designers that seek to include some form of constitutional review in their products can jettison legal tradition and instead seek to tailor the system of review to local needs and circumstances.

Notes

1. This chapter uses the terms 'judicial review' and 'constitutional review' interchangeably.
2. Alexis de Tocqueville. 1835 [2012]. *Democracy in America* 183. (Chicago: University of Chicago Press).
3. Austria Constitution, art 89 (1920).
4. Preliminary Objections, Merits, Reparations and Costs, Judgment, Inter-American Court of Human Rights (series C) No 154, para 124 (26 September 2006).
5. Disclosure: one of the present authors (Ginsburg) served on this committee.

References

Abebe, Adem. 2010. 'Towards More Liberal Standing Rules to Enforce Constitutional Rights in Ethiopia'. *African Human Rights Law Journal* 10 (2): 407–31.

Ackerman, Bruce. 2019. *Revolutionary Constitutionalism: Charismatic Leadership and the Rule of Law*. Cambridge: Harvard University Press.

Albert, Richard. 2023. 'Does the World Need an International Constitutional Court?' *Rutgers International Law and Human Rights Journal* 3: 1–25.

Bellamy, Richard. 2011. 'Political Constitutionalism and The Human Rights Act'. *International Journal of Constitutional Law* 9 (1): 86–111.

Bickel, Alexander M. 1962. *The Least Dangerous Branch: The Supreme Court at the Bar of Politics*. New Haven: Yale University Press.

Böckenforde, Markus. 2022. 'Constitutional Review in Africa'. In *Comparative Constitutional Law in Africa*, edited by Rosalind Dixon, Tom Ginsburg, and Adem K. Abebe, 58–107. Cheltenham: Edward Elgar and Co.

Brewer-Carías, Allan R. 2014. *Constitutional Protection of Human Rights in Latin America: A Comparative Study of Amparo Proceedings*. New York: Cambridge University Press.

Cappelletti, Mauro. 1989. *The Judicial Process in Comparative Perspective*. New York: Oxford University Press.

Dulitsky, Ariel E. 2015. 'An Inter-American Constitutional Court? The Invention of the Conventionality Control by the Inter-American Court of Human Rights'. *Texas Law Review* 50: 45–93.

Elster, Jon. 1995. 'Forces and Mechanisms in the Constitution-Making Process'. *Duke Law Journal* 45: 364–96.

Ferejohn, John, and Pasquale Pasquino. 2012. 'Constitutional Adjudication, Italian Style'. In *Comparative Constitutional Design*, edited by Tom Ginsburg, 294–316. New York: Cambridge University Press.

Galanter, Marc. 2014. 'Snakes and Ladders: *Suo Moto* Intervention and the Indian Judiciary'. *FIU Law Review* 10 (1): 69–83.

Gardbaum, Stephen. 2012. *The New Commonwealth Model of Constitutionalism: Theory and Practice*. New York: Cambridge University Press.

Garlicki, Lech. 2007. 'Constitutional Courts versus Supreme Courts'. *International Journal of Constitutional Law* 5 (1) 44–68.

Ginsburg, Tom. 2004. 'Ancillary Powers of Constitutional Courts'. In *Institutions and Public Law*, edited by Tom Ginsburg and Robert A. Kagan, 225–47. Lausanne: Peter Lang Publishing.

Ginsburg, Tom, and Mila Versteeg. 2013. 'Why Do Countries Adopt Constitutional Review?' *Journal of Law, Economics and Organization* 30 (3): 587–622.

Halmai, Gabor. 2019. 'Illiberalism in East Central Europe'. EUI Working Paper 2019/05. Florence: European University Institute.

Hamilton, Alexander. 1788. 'The Federalist No. 78'. In *The Federalist Papers*, edited by Clinton Rossiter, 463–72. New York: Penguin.

Helfer, Larry. 2002. 'Overlegalizing Human Rights: International Relations Theory and the Commonwealth Caribbean Backlash Against Human Rights Regimes'. *Columbia Law Review* 102 (7): 1832–911.

Hirschl, Ran. 2004. *Towards Juristocracy: The Origins and Consequences of the New Constitutionalism*. Cambridge: Harvard University Press

Huneeus, Alexandra. 2011. 'Courts Resisting Courts: Lessons from the Inter-American Court's Struggle to Enforce Human Rights'. *Cornell International Law Journal* 44 (3): 493–533.

Huneeus, Alexandra, and Mikael Rask Madsen. 2018. 'Between Universalism and Regional Law and Politics: A Comparative History of the American, European, and African Human Rights Systems'. *International Journal of Constitutional Law* 16 (1): 136–60.

Kellogg, Thomas E., and Keith Hand. 2008. 'NPCSC: The Vanguard of China's Constitution?' *Jamestown Foundation China Brief* 8 (2). https://jamestown.org/program/npcsc-the-vanguard-of-chinas-constitution/.

Kelsen, Hans. 1928. 'La Garantie Jurisdictionnelle de la Constitution'. *Revue de Droit Public* 45: 197–257.

Kureshi, Yasser. 2022. *Seeking Supremacy: The Pursuit of Judicial Power in Pakistan*. New York: Cambridge University Press.

Lin, Yan, and Tom Ginsburg. 2015. 'Constitutional Interpretation in Lawmaking: China's Invisible Constitutional Enforcement Mechanism'. *American Journal of Comparative Law* 63 (2): 467–92.

Lustig, Doreen, and Joseph H. H. Weiler. 2018. 'Judicial Review in the Contemporary World—Retrospective and Prospective'. *International Journal of Constitutional Law* 16 (2): 315–72.

Merryman, John, and Rogelio Pérez-Perdomo. 2007. *The Civil Law Tradition: An Introduction to the Legal Systems of Europe and Latin America*. Palo Alto: Stanford University Press.

Prakash, Saikrishna B., and John C. Yoo. 2003. 'The Origins of Judicial Review'. *University of Chicago Law Review* 70 (3): 887–982.

Qazi, Asher. 2015. 'Suo Moto: Choosing not to Legislate Chief Justice Chaudhry's Strategic Agenda'. In *The Politics and Jurisprudence of the Chaudhry Court, 2005–2013*, edited by Moeen H. Cheema and Ijaz Shafi Gilani, 281–321. Karachi: Oxford University Press.

Roznai, Yaniv. 2016. *Unconstitutional Constitutional Amendments*. New York: Oxford University Press.

Sadurski, Wojciech. 2019. *Poland's Constitutional Breakdown*. New York: Oxford University Press.

Scheppele, Kim Lane. 2003. 'Constitutional Negotiations: Political Contexts of Judicial Activism in Post-Soviet Europe'. *International Sociology* 18 (1): 219–38.

Scheppele, Kim Lane. 2005. 'Democracy by Judiciary: Or, Why Courts Can be More Democratic than Parliaments'. In *Rethinking The Rule Of Law After Communism*, edited by Adam W. Czarnota et al., 25–60. Budapest: Central European University Press.

Shapiro, Martin. 1994. 'Juridicalization of Politics in the United States'. *International Political Science Review* 15 (2): 101–12.

Shapiro, Martin. 2002. 'The Success of Judicial Review and Democracy'. In *On Law, Politics, and Judicialization*, edited by Martin Shapiro and Alec Stone Sweet, 149–83. Oxford: Oxford University Press.

Sieder, Rachel, Line Schjolden, and Alan Angell. 2005. *The Judicialization of Politics in Latin America*. New York: Palgrave Macmillan.

Stone Sweet, Alec. 1992. *The Birth of Judicial Politics in France*. New York: Oxford University Press.

Stone Sweet, Alec. 2000. *Governing with Judges*. New York: Oxford University Press.

Stone Sweet, Alec. 2012. '"Constitutional Courts."' In *The Oxford Handbook of Comparative Constitutional Law*, edited by Michel Rosenfeld and Andras Sajo, 816–30. Oxford: Oxford University Press.

Tate, C. Neal, and Torbjörn Vallinder. 1995. *The Global Expansion of Judicial Power*. New York: New York University Press.
Tushnet, Mark. 2008. *Weak Courts, Strong Rights: Judicial Review and Social Welfare Rights in Comparative Constitutional Law*. Princeton: Princeton University Press.
Versteeg, Mila, and Emily Zackin. 2016. 'Constitutions Un-Entrenched: Towards an Alternative Theory of Constitutional Design'. *American Political Science Review* 110 (4): 657–74.
Wilson, Bruce M. 2009. 'Institutional Reform and Rights Revolutions in Latin America: The Cases of Cost Rica and Colombia'. *Journal of Politics in Latin America* 1 (2): 59–85.
Zhu, Guobin. 2010. 'Constitutional Review in China: An Unaccomplished Project or a Mirage?' *Suffolk University Law Review* 43: 625–53.

CHAPTER 4

THE GLOBAL EXPANSION OF JUDICIAL POWER

RAN HIRSCHL

1. Introduction

The global expansion of judicial power is one of the most significant developments in late-twentieth and early twenty-first-century government. Not a week goes by without a national high court or international tribunal somewhere in the world releasing a landmark judgment concerning core moral predicaments, the scope of fundamental rights and liberties, key policy-making challenges, and contentious political questions that define and divide entire nations. Scholars have identified this trend as the 'judicialization of politics' (Tate and Vallinder 1995), 'governing with judges' (Stone Sweet 2000), and 'juristocracy' (Hirschl 2004a), conceptualizing judges as 'legislators in robes' (Shepsle 2006), and suggesting that our time may well be defined as the 'Judicial Era' (Delaney and Dixon 2018). Aharon Barak (1993), the former Chief Justice of the Supreme Court of Israel, captured the zeitgeist of this new era: 'nothing falls beyond the purview of judicial review; the world is filled with law; anything and everything is justiciable'.

The global expansion of judicial power is commonly explained by several interconnected developments. The first is the post-Second World War democratization process, in particular the so-called Third Wave of democratization (the late-1970s to mid-1990s) in South Europe, Latin America, Asia, and the former Soviet bloc. By its very nature, establishing a democratic regime involves establishing the separation of powers between the major branches of government, as well as between the central and provincial/regional legislatures. It also entails the codification of a set of procedural rules and decision-making processes to which all political actors must adhere. The persistence and stability of such a system, in turn, requires at least a semi-autonomous, supposedly apolitical judiciary to adjudicate disputes about the scope and nature of the fundamental rules of the political game.

A second development is the spread of so-called global constitutionalism—the worldwide convergence upon a variant of constitutionalism that prioritizes elaborate, constitutionally entrenched catalogues of rights, and the corresponding power of courts to review the constitutionality of laws and regulations, public policies, and political action of various sorts. Constitutions worldwide have become more elaborate than ever, and include a record-high number of rights, most of which are justiciable (Law and Versteeg 2011; Elkins and Ginsburg 2021). The vast majority of national constitutions currently in effect enshrine the practice of judicial review and entrench constitutional interpretation as a judicial function. Equipped with wide, constitutionally entrenched review powers, courts and judges worldwide have embraced their new institutional power. The result has been that 'courts in ever more countries are issuing ever more decisions about seemingly ever more important questions' (Ginsburg 2022).

A third pertinent development is the proliferation of regional and international courts and tribunals in the second half of the twentieth century, particularly in the aftermath of the Cold War. The jurisdiction of these transnational judicial bodies encompasses, *inter alia*, key areas of human rights, trade, economic regulation and cooperation, and individual and regime accountability for serious violations of international norms and standards. Perhaps the most consequential development in that realm, though it is certainly not an outlier, is the establishment and gradual ascent to power of the European Court of Justice (ECJ, the apex court of the European Union) and of the European Court of Human Rights (ECtHR, the apex court with jurisdiction over residents of all signatory party countries to the European Convention of Human Rights). The two organs alone now serve as the apex judicial bodies of a 450 million-person association (the EU) and an 800 million-person alliance (Council of Europe), respectively.

Broad sociological and demographic trends have also contributed to the expansion of judicial power. The modern state—its institutions, administrative and regulatory agencies, and bureaucratic apparatus—relies on laws, regulations, and judicial means for its very functioning (Shapiro and Stone Sweet 2002). Consequently, anything from taxation, welfare, and public works to licensing, immigration, border control, and policing has been heavily juridified. The expansion of the regulatory state to encompass new frontiers such as consumer protection, telecommunication and information technology, banking, anti-trust, and mergers and acquisitions has provided added impetus for the expansion of judicial power. What is more, the sheer volume of human interactions and economic transactions, most of which have significant legal dimensions to them, has grown exponentially as the world's population has more than quadrupled since the early twentieth century (from less than 2 billion in 1900 to approximately 8 billion today). At the same time, modernization has brought about the global spread of legal norms and, importantly, their diffusion into domains such as the family, religion, traditional economy, and other customary forms of human interaction and association. As legal norms and legal authority have become more prominent, so too has the significance of judicial power. Consequently, what has been termed the 'legal complex' (Karpik and Halliday 2011)—the expanded role and place of law, legal institutions, and legal actors in everyday life—has taken hold. Legal jargon permeates the quotidian.

At the same time, a commonly held belief that judicially affirmed rights are self-implementing forces of social change removed from the constraints of political power—the 'myth of rights', as Stuart Scheingold (1974) famously termed it—contrasts the openness of judicial proceedings with the secret bargaining of interest group pluralism, underscoring the integrity and incorruptibility of the judicial process. Under this conception, courts (memorably construed as the 'least dangerous branch' by Hamilton and later Bickel) become an appealing alternative to a messier political process. This trend is aided by canonical post-Second World War constitutional theory that regards judicial review by supposedly independent courts as a pillar of constitutional democracy, as well as by what Charles Epp (1998) has termed the 'support structure for legal mobilization'—a nexus of rights-advocacy organizations, litigation-oriented non-governmental organizations (NGOs), rights-supportive lawyers and law schools, governmental rights-enforcement agencies, and legal aid schemes that help groups and individuals effectively invoke and litigate rights protections.

Certain structural political factors, alongside strategic behaviour by pertinent actors, may further support the expansion of judicial power. The proliferation of federalism and multi-level government more generally poses complex coordination and enforcement challenges and thus requires effective arbitrage, monitoring, and oversight—all functions fulfilled by courts (Cappelletti 1970; Shapiro and Stone Sweet 2002; Friedman and Delaney 2011). Other works point to the concrete political benefits achieved by empowering courts, especially under circumstances of dysfunctional or deadlocked political systems (e.g. Ferejohn 2002) or fragile governing coalitions (Graber 1993), or when employed as a means of insurance or pre-commitment (e.g. Ginsburg 2003). The empowerment of the judiciary may also be a means of 'hegemonic preservation' by threatened elites seeking to entrench their status, worldviews, and preferences (Hirschl 2004a). Likewise, when elected politicians face obstructions in implementing their policy agendas, they may favour the active exercise of constitutional review by a sympathetic judiciary (Hirschl 2004b; Whittington 2005). In a similar vein, powerful apex courts may allow governments to impose a centralizing 'one-rule-fits-all' regime upon enormous and diverse polities (Morton 1995; Goldstein 2001). (Think of the standardizing effect of apex court jurisprudence in the EU.) The creation and empowerment of courts may also have a 'window dressing' effect, in particular, in hybrid or semi-authoritarian regimes seeking to present a façade of constitutional democracy (Ip 2019).

Finally, as should come as no surprise to readers of this volume, the expansion of judicial power cannot be explained without paying close attention to the critical role that courts and judges themselves have played in embracing and further fostering that trend. From canonical accounts of how the US Supreme Court (SCOTUS) established judicial review in *Marbury v Madison* (1803) to the *United Mizrahi Bank* case (1995)—commonly referred to as 'Israel's *Marbury v Madison*'—national apex courts' landmark jurisprudence is frequently credited with (or blamed for) the propagation of judicial review and the expansion of judicial power more generally. Put bluntly, the ever-increasing demand for law, courts, and judges provides the judicial sphere, and the legal profession more generally, with a tremendous opportunity to increase its own influence. In this respect, courts and judges do not behave or reach decisions in a way that is fundamentally different from other branches of government or, for that matter, from any other large institutional apparatus or professional field (understood epistemologically, e.g. by Pierre Bourdieu, or in terms of inter-organization relations and institutional isomorphism associated with Paul DiMaggio and Walter Powell). Like most other institutions, courts and judges are strategic actors (Epstein 2008; Epstein and Weinshall 2021): they seek to maintain or enhance their institutional position vis-à-vis other major national decision-making bodies, or simply to expand the ambit of their political influence, reputation, and profile on a national and (when applicable) international level. Accordingly, apex court rulings, for example, must not only be analysed as acts of professional, apolitical jurisprudence (as doctrinal legalistic explanations of court rulings often suggest), nor as mere reflections of judicial ideology (as 'attitudinal' models of judicial behaviour might suggest). They are also a reflection of courts and judges' own strategic choices (Epstein and Knight 1998, 2000) vis-à-vis other political actors, institutions, and the public.

Naturally, a comprehensive examination of these broad trends falls well beyond the confines of this chapter. Instead, I focus here on three key aspects of the global expansion of judicial power that are most pertinent for the thematic focus of this handbook: (i) the dramatic increase over the last few decades in the number and types of national and transnational courts and tribunals; (ii) the ever-growing significance of courts and judges in determining political and policy-making outcomes worldwide; and (iii) criticism of, resistance to, and occasional backlash against expanded judicial power, at times manifesting in non-compliance with judgments, curtailment of jurisdictional boundaries, tightened political control over judicial appointment processes, and tinkering with judicial independence.

2. The Quantitative Dimension: More Courts with More Powers

The Magna Carta (1215) and the Glorious Revolution (1688) are widely acknowledged milestones in pre-modern development of rights and of judicially enforced limitations on the ruler's powers. With the rise of the modern nation-state in the late-eighteenth century onward, newly founded countries developed legal systems, adopted constitutions, and established courts and tribunals. The Declaration of the Rights of Man and of the Citizen (1789), established by France's National Constituent Assembly during the French Revolution, and the American Bill of Rights (1791) marked the beginning of the modern era in constitutionally protected rights. As indicated earlier, the SCOTUS was the first modern apex court to formally establish the principle of judicial review (*Marbury v Madison* 1803).

Whereas ideals of constitutionalism, rights, and judicial review began to spread globally in the late-nineteenth century and later on in the interwar period, the global expansion of judicial power took off in the aftermath of the Second World War and, in particular, following democratization in Latin America, Asia, and the post-Soviet world (Cappelletti 1988; Lustig and Weiler 2018; Calabresi 2020). Much has been written about the convergence of constitutional supremacy worldwide, resulting in the emergence of a global constitutional order (Law 2005; Law and Versteeg 2011; Möller 2012; Tully et al. 2016). Today, nearly all countries, as well as several regional and transnational political entities, have adopted constitutions that celebrate the polity's aspirations, define the prerogatives of governmental institutions, enshrine a bill of rights, and, importantly for the purpose of this chapter, establish some form of active judicial review that empowers courts to determine the constitutionality of 'ordinary' statutes and decrees.

The figures are striking. Comparative data shows that the average national constitution in force today protects forty-eight rights, an all-time high.[1] This comports with what Law and Versteeg (2011) termed 'rights creep'—the proliferation of new constitutional rights in the post-Second World War period. While some of the newly constitutionalized rights are aspirational or declaratory in nature, the vast majority are justiciable. These rights include classical rights and liberties such as the right to life, freedom of expression, equality before the law, and criminal due process rights; political rights (e.g. freedom of political association, the right to vote and to run for office, and the right to free and fair elections); economic and social rights such as the right to health care, education, housing, welfare, work, food and water; group rights such as the rights of ethnic, linguistic, and Indigenous communities; and collective rights such as the right to the environment.

Due process rights, and in particular the rights of the accused, have proven essential, primarily as they pertain to countless criminal proceedings and also because many of these rights (e.g. right to fair trial, presumption of innocence, inadmissibility of illegally obtained evidence, etc.) are directly enforceable by courts. The open-ended nature of some rights, notably the right to human dignity, and the inevitable clash of some rights with other rights, moral ideals, or social goals, further supported the expansion of judicial power. Furthermore, the growing number and prevalence of economic and social rights (Jung, Hirschl, and Rosevear 2015; Rosevear, Hirschl, and Jung 2019) provided courts with the authority to scrutinize governmental budgetary allocations, as well as social and economic policy priorities more broadly. Additionally, dozens of countries have incorporated international human rights provisions into their own national laws. Other countries (notably Belgium, Finland, Spain, and the United Kingdom) have adopted legislation that grants their courts universal jurisdiction in pursuing and trying alleged perpetrators of war crimes and of crimes against humanity.

To be sure, the rise of 'rights talk' as the vernacular through which nearly every grievance is framed has been the subject of serious criticism. Political theorists and social critics alike have decried the trivializing effect of framing every disagreement in rights terms (e.g. Kundera 1992); the overly adversarial, solipsistic, compromise-impeding, or anti-communitarian nature of clashes of rights (e.g. Waldron 1986; Glendon 1991); the corresponding impoverishment of political discourse (Glendon 1991); the misleading yet prevalent 'myth of rights' (Scheingold 1974); and the limited ability of courts and rights jurisprudence to guarantee real, on-the-ground change (Rosenberg 1991). However, these reservations notwithstanding, the fact remains that the constitutionalization of rights worldwide has contributed considerably to the global expansion of judicial power.

A similar trend is evident with respect to constitutional provisions establishing judicial review. In 1910, for example, less than a quarter of existing constitutions included some judicial review authority. About a hundred years later, in 2008, 158 of 191 (82 per cent) national constitutions explicitly authorized judicial bodies to guard the constitution and its provisions from violations, including by the legislature (Ginsburg 2008; Ginsburg and Versteeg 2014). In 2020, 171 (88 per cent) of the 195 national constitutions in effect that year enshrined the practice of judicial review, and 181 (93 per cent) entrenched constitutional interpretation by courts. Whereas some polities (e.g. the United States, the United Kingdom, Canada, Australia, India, most countries in Latin America, the Scandinavian countries, Japan) subscribe to a diffuse (decentralized or multi-court) model of constitutional review, wherein apex and non-apex courts alike have the ability to exercise constitutional review, others (e.g. Germany, South Korea, South Africa, Chile) subscribe to a centralized model of constitutional review featuring a constitutional court or tribunal with an exclusive authority to review the constitutionality of legislation. Some countries (e.g. Israel, India) allow for direct citizen petitions to courts (including apex courts) challenging the constitutionality of legislation or the compliance of public authorities with basic norms of constitutional and administrative law. In most Latin American countries, variants of the *amparo* procedure, while not having the *erga omnes* effects of a comprehensive constitutional review, allow individuals to petition courts against state acts and omissions or against allegedly unconstitutional statutes. Naturally, the establishment of judicial review and constitutional interpretation in so many countries has effectively positioned courts and judges worldwide as translators of constitutional provisions into guidelines for public life. In many countries, progressive jurisprudence has facilitated public access to constitutional review by expanding standing rights, allowing public interest litigation, and permitting (often proactively soliciting) extensive amicus briefs by interested third parties.

Additionally, approximately a third of national constitutions establish what has been termed 'fourth branch' entities tasked with monitoring key aspects of the separation of powers, accountability, the rule of law, and the democratic process itself. Chapter Nine of South Africa's Constitution, for example, is titled, 'State Institutions Protecting Constitutional Democracy'. Its list of institutions that 'strengthen constitutional democracy' includes the public prosecutor, the Human Rights Commission, the auditor-general, and the Electoral Commission (Tushnet 2021, 1). Other constitutions establish electoral tribunals, state comptroller bureaus, and anti-corruption agencies. These independent judicial or quasi-judicial bodies not only address apparent gaps in the traditional Montesquiean three-branch government matrix and its incompatibility with modern-day democracy, but they also expand the scope of judicial or quasi-judicial oversight of the twenty-first-century state apparatus. The proliferation of electoral management bodies (see e.g. Pal 2016) has had particularly significant implications for the judicialization of politics, discussed in detail in the next section.

Parallel to the propagation of constitutional review, rights provisions, and fourth branch bodies, the proliferation of administrative agencies in the modern welfare state has expanded the scope of administrative review by courts. Drawing upon basic norms from contract law, constitutional law, and especially administrative law, courts increasingly oversee and enforce the application of due process, equal opportunity, transparency, accountability, and reasonableness in public policy-making. It is therefore not surprising that judicialization of this type dominates the justice system itself, from civil procedure to criminal due process, and the expanded purview of the judiciary is particularly noticeable in process-heavy policy areas such as immigration, taxation, or public tenders. But it is also clearly evident in countless other areas, from urban planning and public health, and industrial relations and consumer protection.

The rise of administrative review has been accompanied by the application of legal norms and procedures to almost every decision-making forum in modern rule-of-law polities. In legal theory, the trend has been termed *horizontality* or *vertical effect*—referring to the application to private entities of legal norms originally meant to govern public bodies. Over the last few decades, norms of procedural fairness have become standard not only in inherently juridical private fora (e.g. private arbitration or mediation) but in countless other private and semi-private contexts, from school board elections to sports tournaments, and condominium regulations to corporate governance. Legal rules and procedures have come to dominate matters previously negotiated in an informal or non-judicial fashion (Sieder, Schjolden, and Angell 2005, 5). At the same time, domains such as intellectual property or one's right to her good name (in particular in the information technology age) have been heavily juridified, with the right to property and freedom of expression stretched to govern disputes among private entities. Judicialization of this type is inextricable from law's capture of social relationships and popular culture and its expropriation of social conflicts (Habermas 1986; Teubner 1987). Related aspects of this type of 'juridification' of modern life have also been identified by early legal sociologists—for example, Henry Maine and Émile Durkheim's 'from status to contract' thesis (Durkheim 1964 [1893]; Maine 2000 [1861]); or Max Weber's emphasis on the rise of a formal, unambiguous, and rational-legal system in Western societies (Weber 1978 [1914]).

Meanwhile, a whole gamut of specialized courts and tribunals has emerged at the national, sub-national, and municipal levels. These range from labour courts and industrial tribunals (adjudicating employment, remuneration, and industrial relations disputes), immigration hearing boards (of critical significance in many illegal immigration destination countries in the West), to family and personal status courts, tax courts, traffic courts, and small-claims courts. Within civil society too, specialized quasi-judicial tribunals have proliferated. Professional sports associations, for example, have developed a nexus of semi-autonomous, quasi-judicial tribunals that adjudicate disciplinary infringements by teams and athletes; fan misconduct; disputes concerning transfers of players; enforcement of contracts; salary grievances and arbitration; and increasingly, racism and doping cases. This has been complemented by the rise of regional (e.g. the UEFA Control, Ethics, and Disciplinary Body) and international sports tribunals, capped by the creation (1984) of the Court of Arbitration for Sports (CAS), which has gained stature as the apex judicial authority in the world of sports.

In many countries that do not subscribe to the strict separation of religion and state, religious courts and tribunals adjudicate key personal status matters, including marriage and divorce, child custody, inheritance, and conversion. Occasionally, clashes arise between the religious jurisprudence of such tribunals and constitutional rights provisions protecting freedom of religion, freedom of expression, gender equality, and children's rights. This often leads to landmark apex court rulings on the jurisdictional boundaries of such religious tribunals and, by extension, on the autonomy granted to the religious groups whose special character is protected by these tribunals. Prime examples are the recent rulings of the Supreme Court of India concerning the status of Islamic triple-talaq divorce (*Shayara Bano v Union of India*, 2017), the Supreme Court of Pakistan ruling on blasphemy (*Asia Bibi v The State*, 2018), and the Malaysia Federal Court ruling on conversion and child custody in interfaith marriage (*Indira Gandhi v Pengarah Jabatan Agama Islam Perak & Ors*, 2018).

Judicial power at the international level has grown in parallel with the expansion of judicial power at the national level. To be sure, international treaties, laws of the sea, and embryonic forms of international adjudication existed well before the current judicial era (O'Connell and VanderZee 2014). The Permanent Court of Arbitration (PCA, established 1890) is perhaps the archetype of a significant transnational tribunal established in the late-nineteenth century that continues to be active today. (Readers may recall the PCA's landmark 2016 ruling in the *Philippines v China*, concerning the so-called South China Sea.) However, it was not until the aftermath of the Second World War, and again following the end of the Cold War, that international courts and tribunals began to proliferate. The Nuremberg Trials (1946–1949) and the Tokyo Trial (1946) were symbolic judicial acts that brought to justice those responsible for the greatest political, military, and humanitarian crisis in modern history.[2] The International Court of Justice (ICJ)—the apex judicial arm of the United Nations—was established in 1945 as the successor to the League of Nations' Permanent Court of International Justice. Often referred to as the 'world court', it adjudicates disputes among UN member states and issues advisory opinions on the request of the UN General Assembly, Security Council, and other UN organs.[3]

As mentioned earlier, the ECJ (created 1952) and the ECtHR (created 1958) have emerged as two of the most influential supranational courts. Importantly, both courts have compulsory jurisdiction over their respective constituents. Beginning with the landmark *Van Gend en Loos* ruling (1963), the ECJ held that Community law had 'direct effect' on the member states, which enables European citizens to rely directly on EU law in their national courts. In the *Costa* case (1964), the ECJ established the primacy of Community law over domestic law. In 1991, the ECJ recognized member state's liability for damage caused to individuals by that state's breach of Community law (*Francovich, Bonifaci and others v Italy*). The European project of unification through constitutionalization gained further momentum with the signings of the Maastricht Treaty (1992) and the Lisbon Treaty (2009), which effectively establish a trans-national quasi-constitutional regime in the EU. Outside of Europe, the Inter-American Court of Human Rights (established in 1979), which has jurisdiction over twenty-five countries, essentially emulates the ECtHR model in the Americas. The Andean Tribunal of Justice (1984) aims at applying an ECJ-like model in the Andean Community.

The end of the Cold War marks a turning point in the evolution of international courts. Between 1985 and 2010, the number of international courts more than tripled (Alter 2011, 2016). Among the international courts established during that period are the Central American Court of Justice (1992), the World Trade Organization Appellate Body (1994), the West African Economic and Monetary Union Court of Justice (1995), the International Tribunal for the Law of the Seas (1996), the Caribbean Court of Justice (2001), and the African Court on Human and Peoples' Rights (2006). New international courts also emerged to address problems of restorative justice and severe violations of international human rights norms. These include the International Criminal Tribunal for the former Yugoslavia (1993) and the International Criminal Tribunal for Rwanda (1994). The International Criminal Court (ICC)—which was agreed upon in the Treaty of Rome in 1998 and came into force in 2002— was created as a permanent judicial body with the purpose of investigating and prosecuting genocide, crimes against humanity, war crimes, and other extreme violations of international human rights norms.

Taken as a whole, the picture is clear. Whether the result of democratization, formal constitutionalization, diffusion and globalization, political interests, astute judicial behaviour, or social transformation more broadly, courts and tribunals of all kinds have burgeoned around the world. Judicial power has expanded considerably, and now impacts upon virtually every aspect of modern life, whether public or private, local, national, or international.

3. The Substantive Dimension: 'Everything Is Justiciable'

The expansion of judicial power has key substantive dimensions that are not captured by simply noting the rising number of rights or courts. A quantitative aspect may encompass, for example, the increase in the number of apex courts or international tribunals worldwide over time, or the number of provisions in either national, subnational, or supranational constitutions that assign express judicial review powers to courts and other quasi-judicial entities. A qualitative aspect refers to substantive changes in the scope and nature of judicial involvement in determining salient issues and controversies, be they moral dilemmas, consequential policy issues, or matters of high politics. To be sure, evaluating the scope of that substantive dimension, let alone accurately measuring it, is a tricky business. To begin with, whereas some issues are commonly regarded as salient (e.g. elections results, term limits, or the scope of executive powers), another issue (say, the right to bear arms or the scope of reproductive freedoms including abortion) may be highly salient in one polity (e.g. the United States) but a non-issue in another (e.g. Sweden). Another considerable difficulty in assessing trends in judicial power is the level of analysis; whereas a macro-level analysis points in one direction (taken as a whole, judicial power is undoubtedly on the rise globally), a micro-level analysis focusing on a specific subset of countries or conditions may point in another direction (e.g. in certain countries at certain times, judicial power may well be on the decline). A third challenge in measuring judicialization and judicial power more generally is the multiple definitions and manifestations of these trends (Hamlin and Sala 2018). For example, judicial power may refer to formal, *de jure* power (i.e. judicial authority existing in law) but it also may mean real, *de facto* power (i.e. the actual authority courts possess). Likewise, an assessment of judicial power may focus on concrete judicial outputs, most notably jurisprudence, or it may emphasize the real-life impact of particular rulings, or even underscore the level of enforcement and implementation of court rulings. Along the same lines, judicial power may also mean the quiet power (or 'shadow effect') of law and courts to alter behaviour at the outset, whether in the context of 'bargaining in the shadow of the law' (Mnookin and Kornhauser 1979) or to alter legislation and regulations in anticipation of judicial review (e.g. Pavone and Stiansen 2022).

These methodological difficulties notwithstanding, the central place of law and courts in contemporary politics, culture, and society is undisputed. As early as 1835, Alexis de Tocqueville famously observed in *Democracy in America* that

> there is hardly any political question in the United States that sooner or later does not turn into a judicial question. From that, the obligation that the parties find in their daily polemics to borrow ideas and language from the judicial system. Since most public men are or have formerly been jurists, they make the habits and the turn of ideas that belong to jurists pass into the handling of public affairs ... Thus, judicial language becomes, in a way, the common language; so the spirit of the jurist, born inside the schools and courtrooms, spreads little by little beyond their confines; it infiltrates all of society, so to speak; it descends to the lowest ranks, and the entire people finishes by acquiring a part of the habits and tastes of the magistrate.
>
> (de Tocqueville 2010 [1835])

Nearly two centuries later, America's penchant for high-voltage constitutionalism has not waned. Veneration of the Constitution amounts to a civil religion (see e.g. Levinson 1988). Adversarial legalism abounds (see e.g. Kagan 2003; Barnes and Burke 2020). Lawsuits, litigants, lawyers, judges, and courts frequently headline daily news. Real-life legal dramas are compulsively reported on, from the O. J. Simpson trials to the *Johnny Depp v Amber Heard* courtroom battle. Legal terminology (think indictments, affidavits, testimonies) is ubiquitous. In popular media, law firm and courtroom dramas (think *Suits*) and reality-like series (think *Judge Judy* and her many epigones) are commonplace. America's number of lawyers far exceed that of any other country, and its lawyers-per-capita ratio is second only to Israel. The daily work of the Supreme Court is the object of endless scholarly and popular discussion, and the political frenzy that surrounds new appointments to the SCOTUS is one of a kind. For its part, the SCOTUS has not shied away from making decisions with dramatic political consequences. Examples include *Bush v Gore* (2000), which essentially determined the outcome of the 2000 presidential election; *Citizens United* (2010), which rejected limitations on corporate contributions to campaign financing; *Shelby County v Holder* (2013), which permitted state pre-clearance requirements for voter registration; and *Rucho v Common Cause* (2019), which designated district gerrymandering as a political issue that is not for the courts to address. And, as is well known, the SCOTUS, now staffed with three Trump appointees, released key rulings in 2022 that, *inter alia*, severely limit the right to have an abortion, states' capacity to regulate guns, and the federal government's ability to regulate the environment.

While few polities assign such a central place for courts, law, and judicial power in their political and popular culture, the ever-growing importance of law and courts has become a global phenomenon (see e.g. Guarnieri and Pederzoli 2002; Kapiszewski, Silverstein, and Kagan 2013). The substantive dimension of this trend is most vividly illustrated by what scholars have identified as an all-out judicialization of politics (Tate and Vallinder 1995) and in particular the judicialization of 'mega-politics' or 'pure' politics—the framing of apparently political controversies as predominantly legal or constitutional ones, resulting in their eventual adjudication in the courts (Hirschl 2008).[4] Questions of pure politics include electoral processes and outcomes, restorative justice, regime legitimacy, executive prerogatives, collective identity, and nation building. The judicialization of politics has meant the demise of the 'political question' doctrine (non-justiciability of explicitly political questions) and has marked a transformation in the classical definition of democracy as rule by, for, and of the people.

Early indications that the global expansion of judicial power would encompass expressly political matters emerged in the 1980s and 1990s. The Supreme Court of Canada (SCC), for example, was quick to reject the 'political question' doctrine following the adoption of the Canadian Charter of Rights and Freedoms (1982). In its landmark ruling in *Operation Dismantle* (1985)—a challenge to the constitutionality of US missile testing on Canadian soil—the SCC held unanimously that '[i]f a case raises the question of whether executive or legislative action violated the Constitution, then the question has to be answered by the Court, regardless of the political character of the controversy ... [d]isputes of a political or foreign policy nature may be properly cognizable by the courts'.

In post-communist Europe, newly created courts were quick to jump into the political cauldron. Two paradigmatic examples stand out among many. In 1993, the Constitutional Court of the Czech Republic upheld a law that declared the entire Communist era in the former Czechoslovakia illegal. And in 1995, the Hungarian Constitutional Court tackled an explicitly political question in the *Austerity Package Decisions* (the so-called Bokros cases). The Court drew upon the concepts of reliance interest and legal certainty to strike down twenty-six provisions of a comprehensive economic emergency plan introduced by the government, the major thrust of which was a substantial cut in the government's expenditures on welfare benefits, pension allowances, education, and health care, which had been enacted to reduce Hungary's enormous budget deficit and foreign debt.

Another example of the judicialization of political problems is the establishment of quasi-judicial 'truth commissions' or special tribunals dealing with core issues of transitional justice, especially in the immediate aftermath of serious political violence or other national trauma. Recall, for example, the judicialization of restorative justice in the early years of the post-apartheid era in South Africa: the newly established Constitutional Court not only vetted and certified the new constitution (but not before rejecting a previous version), it also determined the constitutionality of the 'amnesty-for-confession' formula, arguably the most important tenet of the Truth and Reconciliation Commission process (*AZAPO v President of South Africa* 1996). At around the same time, courts both in Latin America and so-called settler society countries (e.g. Australia, Canada, New Zealand, South Africa) grappled with existential questions of restorative justice and the rights of Indigenous populations. The High Court of Australia's landmark ruling in the *Mabo II* case (1992, voiding the legal fiction of *terra nullius* and recognizing the pre-colonial interests of First Nations people within Australia's common law) is a paradigmatic illustration of this line of jurisprudence.

Arguably, the clearest manifestation of the rise of a Judicial Era in the 1990s was the growing reliance on courts to determine the very definition, or *raison d'être*, of the polity as such. A 'textbook' example of this trend is the unprecedented involvement of the Canadian judiciary in dealing with the status of bilingualism and the political future of Quebec, including the SCC's landmark ruling in the *Quebec Secession Reference* (1998)—the first time a democratic country had ever pre-emptively tested the legal terms of its own dissolution. The question of the status of Quebec—the sole uniquely Francophone province in Canada—dominated Canadian politics from the mid-1970s to the mid-2000s. This issue is commonly considered to have been a driving force behind the adoption of the Constitution Act 1982 (which includes the Canadian Charter of Rights and Freedoms)—a major constitutional overhaul that has never been formally ratified by Quebec.

Following the Quebecois secessionist movement's narrow defeat in the 1995 referendum, the federal government asked the SCC to determine whether a hypothetical unilateral secession declaration by the Quebec government would be constitutional. The Court accepted the challenge with open arms and took the liberty to articulate fundamental pillars of the Canadian polity in a way that no other state organ had ever done before. The Court stated that the Canadian Constitution is based on four principles—federalism, democracy, constitutionalism and the rule of law, and the protection of minorities—none of which trumps any other. This articulation was brand new—nowhere in the Canadian Constitution are these principles stated in this way. Hence, even a majority vote (adhering to the fundamental democratic principle of majority rule) would not entitle Quebec to secede unilaterally.

The transfer of the Quebec question 'hot potato' from the political sphere to the SCC bore immediate fruits for those who masterminded that move. Within a few years, an existential predicament that for three decades loomed large over Canadian politics lost momentum, interest, and support within and outside Quebec. At the same time, the ruling helped bolster the status and reputation of the SCC, both nationally and internationally. The *Quebec Secession Reference*, and the jurisprudential framework that it provided for dealing with the constitutionality and legality of secession claims, has been frequently referred in polities facing secessionist challenges, ranging from Catalonia and Scotland to Chechnya, Taiwan, and the former Yugoslavia. It has likewise become a touchstone for scholarly debate about the constitutional law and international law of secession.

Other illustrations of the expansion of judicial power to encompass foundational dilemmas of collective identity and constitutional disharmony (Jacobsohn 2010) include the Supreme Court of India's crucial role in addressing the delicate balance between India's Hindu majority and its large Muslim minority, the role that apex courts in Egypt, Malaysia, and Nigeria have played in determining the applicability of Islamic *Shari'a* law in public life, and the Israeli Supreme Court's grappling with Israel's fundamental (and, according to some, irreconcilable) definition as a 'Jewish and Democratic State'. In other countries, from Turkey to Brazil to Taiwan, apex courts have developed an 'unconstitutional constitutional amendments' doctrine that permits judicial invalidation of constitutional amendments that are deemed discordant or conflicting with core constitutional ideals (see e.g. Roznai 2017). In adjudicating these issues of 'existential' identity, which address the very definition of the polity, courts and judges have knowingly embraced the Dworkinian vision of the judge being responsible for the Herculean task of preserving the 'enduring values' (Dworkin's term) of their respective polities.

In the first decade of the twenty-first century, the trend towards the judicialization of politics has intensified further. In the early 2000s alone, courts in countries as diverse as Bangladesh, Belgium, India, Israel, Spain, Thailand, and Turkey have banned (or come close to banning) popular political parties from participating in national elections. In the same period, constitutional courts in over twenty-five countries were called upon to determine the political future of prominent leaders through impeachment or disqualification trials. Courts ruled on the extension of presidential terms for Colombia's Alvaro Uribe, Uganda's Yoweri Museveni, and Russia's Boris Yeltsin. Former Pakistani prime ministers Benazir Bhutto, Nawaz Sharif, and Pervez Musharraf, South Korean Roh Moo-Hyun, Honduran president Manuel Zelaya, and Philippine president Joseph Estrada—to give a few examples—have all had their political fate determined by courts. To that list one could add corruption indictments against heads of state (e.g. Italy's Silvio Berlusconi, Peru's Alberto Fujimori, or Thailand's Thaksin Shinawatra) and 'political trials', in which prominent opposition candidates and leaders have been disqualified or otherwise removed from the race by a politicized judiciary.

Although the second decade of the twenty-first century saw increasing resistance to the exponential growth of judicial power (a trend discussed in some detail in section 4 of this chapter), the judicialization of politics has continued in most countries. Over the last few years alone, apex courts in the United Kingdom, Pakistan, Colombia, South Africa, and Kenya, to pick just a handful among countless examples, have rendered dramatic rulings that significantly affected the political scene in their respective countries. The UK Supreme Court's landmark decisions in the *Miller I* (2017) and *Miller II* (2019) cases, dealing with the constitutional preconditions for the Brexit process to launch and the constitutionality of the Johnson government's decision to prorogue parliament to avoid unfavourable votes on the Brexit process respectively, positioned the Court as a key actor in what was debatably the most significant political juncture in post-war United Kingdom. The Supreme Court of Pakistan asserted the primacy of its role in Pakistani politics by overriding Prime Minister Imran Khan's decision to dismiss parliament in order to avoid a crucial no-confidence vote (2022), and later by allowing the serious concealment of assets charges against the now ousted Khan to proceed (2023), ultimately leading to his conviction and sentencing to a three-year jail term. A few years earlier, the Court had ousted Prime Minister Nawaz Sharif (2017), and later banned him from politics for life following his conviction for capital and tax evasion (2018).

Yet another example is provided by the role that the Colombian Constitutional Court played in paving the way for the rapid ratification (2016) of the historic agreement between the government and the leftist FARC rebel group, thus ending a fifty-two-year-long conflict that claimed the lives of more than 220,000 and drove at least 7 million Colombians from their homes. The Court ordered the first version of the peace agreement to be approved in a national referendum, in which the accord narrowly failed to acquire the majority of popular support. Upon reaching a revised agreement with the FARC, the government insisted on ratifying the peace agreement in an expedited fashion, believing that the tentative agreement was too fragile to wait for the traditional legislative process to unfold. The Court accepted that claim and held that Colombia's elected lawmakers possessed the requisite 'democratic legitimacy' to approve the deal without the need for a new referendum.

Meanwhile, in South Africa, the Constitutional Court was called upon at several critical junctures during the bitter political struggle over the future of Jacob Zuma, the powerful president of South Africa and leader of the hegemonic African National Congress (ANC) party. In 2021, in what was the final act in the political drama that tore the country for years, the Constitutional Court found Zuma in contempt of court, confirmed his criminal convictions, and sentenced him to a fifteen-month imprisonment. Never before has the Constitutional Court passed a custodial sentence, let alone on a democratically elected former president. And elsewhere in Africa, Kenya's Supreme Court was tasked with the role of scrutinizing and ultimately corroborating the results of the tight and hotly contested 2022 presidential elections in that country. In declaring William Ruto the elected president, the Supreme Court rejected claims by presidential candidate Raila Odinga (backed by outgoing president Uhuru Kenyatta) for massive elections fraud.

At the same time, national and supranational courts in Europe repeatedly address the question at the core of the European integration project; namely, the status of individual member states' constitutional order, tradition, and identity vis-à-vis the emerging pan-European constitutional and political order. The German Federal Constitutional Court landmark rulings in the *Maastricht Case* (1993), *Lisbon Treaty Case* (2009), and more recently in the *European Central Bank Case* (2020) are prime examples of such foundational judgments at the member-state level, as are the ECtHR's momentous decisions in the cases of *Sejdić and Finci v Bosnia and Herzegovina* (2009), *Lautsi v Italy* (2011), and *S.A.S. v France* (2014), and the ECJ rulings in *European Commission v Poland* (2019) and *V.M.A. v Bulgaria* (2021).[5]

In short, despite some methodological challenges in defining and measuring the substantive scope of judicial power, the evidence of its worldwide expansion to encompass areas of considerable moral and political significance is conclusive. National and transnational apex courts and their jurisprudence now regularly address the scope of fundamental rights and liberties, key policy-making challenges, and contentious political questions that define and divide entire nations.

4. Resistance to the Rise of Judicial Power

The expansion of judicial power has generated some criticism and resistance. Within the scholarly realm, critiques of rights talk (discussed earlier) emerged in the 1980s and 1990s. Criticism of excessive judicial power followed, predominantly on democratic grounds. Building on the counter-majoritarian nature of judicial review, critics have stressed the democratic superiority of legislation over jurisprudence (e.g. Waldron 2006), the need to return the constitution to the people (e.g. Tushnet 1999; Kramer 2004), and advanced the claim that 'political constitutionalism' (essentially, the idea that rights are best safeguarded by political channels, legislatures, and the like) is normatively and empirically superior to 'legal constitutionalism' (essentially, the notion that rights are best protected by courts and other judicial means) (e.g. Bellamy 2007). Meanwhile, critics of constitutional universalism argue that unrestrained judicial interpretation of constitutional provisions, as well as the increasingly commonplace judicial reference to foreign jurisprudence, erode a given polity's authentic constitutional tradition, and may amount to constitutional amendment by stealth (see e.g. Dorsen 2005).

Powerful as these scholarly critiques may be, the main resistance to the rise of judicial power has come from the political sphere. The more politically consequential courts become, the greater the likelihood that pertinent political stakeholders will have an interest in affecting judicial outcomes. Struggles over court composition, judicial appointments, the removal of judges, jurisdictional boundaries, scope of remedies, and enforcement and implementation of contested rulings follow, at times culminating in constitutional revision to curtail judicial power or even in an all-out constitutional replacement (e.g. Russia 1993).[6]

With the recent rise of populist parties in many countries, resistance to judicial power has become a hot-button political issue. Populist parties and leaders explicitly denounce global constitutionalism, liberal rights discourse, and what they see as the large-scale usurpation of power by constitutional courts and judges worldwide. Although the emphasis and style of this rhetoric varies, the trend is unified in its disdain for cultural pluralism, minority rights, and the transfer of controversial political issues to the hands of supranational institutions, courts, or central banks. The trend is also characterized by its sense of 'authentic localism' and 'peoplehood', constructed as an alternative to 'open borders', 'elite government', a 'corrupt centre'. At the level of policy, this rhetoric translates into the desire for (and in many instances, exercise of greater control over) the composition and jurisdiction of apex courts and the enactment of laws that limit judicial control over matters such as minority rights, political speech and association, citizenship, and immigration. While the reaction against judicialization often opens policy fronts against supposed welfare abusers or minority groups with special entitlements, this backlash to the global expansion of judicial power is not limited to the political right. Activists on the left have also mounted an anti-globalization critique, often directed at supranational, quasi-constitutional trade agreements and investor rights that are seen as favouring big business and corporate interests at the expense of democratic representation and national, constitutional, and fiscal sovereignty (Streeck 2016).

Recent comparative studies (e.g. Dixon and Landau 2021; Sadurski 2022) on the spread of populism-driven illiberal constitutionalism suggest that the ease with which various constitutional ideas travel across borders both supports the spread of liberal-democratic constitutional values and helps to proliferate strategies for the limitation of these values. Deploying a strategy of 'abusive borrowing', regimes and leaders pursue a form-over-substance strategy aimed to maintain legitimacy through apparent compliance with the formal requirements of democratic constitutionalism, while at the same time substantively subverting the constitutional system to advance an anti-democratic agenda. For example, regimes that are interested in hollowing out the substantive core of, say, apex courts with the power of judicial review, will not disband the judicial system, shut down the constitutional court, or abolish the practice of judicial review altogether. Rather, they 'capture' the institution through the use of court packing, tightened political control of judicial appointments, implementing new mandatory retirement ages for serving judges, curtailing the jurisdictional wings of courts, and threatening harsh reaction to unwelcome acts of judicial activism. Subservient courts, legislatures, and administrative agencies may also engage in this abusive borrowing practice. In so doing, they often rely on a selective or distorted citation of foreign jurisprudence to support the expansion of concepts such as libel, public safety, blasphemy, lèse-majesté, or treason to smear, restrict, or silence legitimate political opposition.

Direct attacks against courts and judicial actors have occurred in Hungary, Poland, Turkey, Israel, and Brazil, to name a few examples. In all these settings, national-populist regimes or leaders have portrayed courts as bastions of ultra-liberalism and cosmopolitanism, and therefore as posing a threat to national values and traditions. These regimes often accuse courts of staging a judicial coup against elected leaders, or simply of unduly prioritizing minority rights, economic and cultural globalization, or the worldviews and policy agendas favoured by urban intelligentsia and business elites. According to this view, constitutional review, ideally a power-diffusing, minority-protecting, and rights-preserving enterprise, is seen as the enemy of ordinary people and the political preferences of the cultural and economic hinterlands.

Much has been written about the development of this dynamic in Hungary and in Poland, where 'constitutional capture' has reached its zenith (Sadurski 2019; Grabowska-Moroz 2022). In 2016, Jaroslaw Kaczyński, founder and chair of the Polish PiS Party, described the Polish Constitutional Tribunal (at the time, still an enclave of liberalism in Poland) as 'the bastion of everything in Poland that is bad' (New York Times Editorial Board 2016). A PiS-orchestrated assault on the Constitutional Tribunal's jurisdiction, composition, and overall independence—indeed an all-out attempt at 'constitutional capture'—ensued. Frequent rows emerge between Poland and Hungary (occasionally joined by the Czech Republic and Slovakia) and the EU over immigration and refugee settlement policies and EU-wide rule-of-law and judicial independence standards, translating into legal clashes between the ECJ, the Venice Commission, and the Polish and Hungarian national judiciaries, now fully controlled by these countries' respective illiberal governments.

A similar backlash, and calls for 'opting out' of global constitutionalism (Hirschl 2018), may also emanate from the other end of the political spectrum, sometimes taking the form of active resistance to what is seen as an enmity by international tribunals towards countries that purport to resent the so-called Washington Consensus (Madsen, Cebulak, and Wiebusch 2018). A prime example is Venezuela's withdrawal (2013) from the Inter-American Court of Human Rights following what Hugo Chavez viewed as biased due-process rights rulings by that body against his country. A similar impulse lies beneath various African nations' (e.g. Burundi, South Africa) criticism of the ICC for alleged disproportional targeting of African leaders by that tribunal. This criticism was preceded by Zimbabwe's withdrawal (2008) from the Southern African Development Community (SADC) Tribunal following that Tribunal's ruling (based mainly on due process rights and on anti-discrimination grounds) against Zimbabwe's policy of expropriating White farmers' land (Nathan 2013).

In Brazil, former President Bolsonaro and his supporters have waged a political war against the country's Federal Supreme Court and the Electoral Superior Court, all while these courts investigate serious allegations against Bolsonaro and his family. The anti-court campaign includes direct attacks on individual judges, as well as the deliberate dissemination of misinformation about the possibility of court-enabled electoral fraud in the 2022 elections.

Meanwhile, in Israel, the investigation, indictment, and trial of Prime Minister Benjamin Netanyahu for various corruption charges have been framed by Netanyahu's supporters as a conspiratorial scheme devised by the country's judicial elite and supposedly left-leaning media to topple the country's elected leader. Consequently, in early 2023 the country was drawn into one of the most significant political and constitutional crises since its establishment, as the Netanyahu-led right-wing governing coalition formed after the November 2022 elections advanced highly controversial legislation aimed at blatant politicization of judicial appointments (including to the Supreme Court), curtailing the Supreme Court's judicial review powers, and creating an 'override clause' that would allow parliament to reenact laws declared unconstitutional by the court. The proposed attempts to tame judicial power also included the politicization of the government ministries' legal counselling, elimination of the seniority principle in appointing chief justice, and of the 'extreme unreasonableness' basis for judicial scrutiny of manifestly unsuitable political appointments or blatantly unreasonable government action or inaction, as well as legislation that shields the prime-minister from suspension while facing criminal charges, and that allows criminally convicted parliament members to serve as ministers in direct defiance of a Supreme Court ruling that forbids the practice. Mass demonstrations and protests against the proposed reforms ensued. In September 2023, in what was described as the most significant case in Israel's constitutional history, the Supreme Court of Israel heard arguments concerning the constitutionality of a July 2023 amendment to Basic Law: Judging and the Judiciary, that practically eliminates the aforementioned reasonableness standard from the arsenal of review grounds available to courts.

Brazen political threats against the country's Attorney General and other members of the country's supposed 'legal elite' have become common. Extreme right-wing members of parliament (some of whom became governing coalition leaders following the November 2022 elections) have suggested on record that they would not abide the Supreme Court's rulings on the proposed reform, that Israel's judicial elite deserves to be assassinated, and have stated their desire to bulldoze the Supreme Court building.

One also encounters softer versions of this same rejectionist discourse. So-called Euro-sceptic parties in many European countries advocate cutting ties with the EU, and frequently blame the ECJ, the ECtHR, and legal elites more generally for over-zealously advancing the European integration project. Former British Prime Minister Theresa May, for example, expressed her support for the United Kingdom opting out of the European Convention on Human Rights on the basis that 'the ECHR can bind the hands of parliament, adds nothing to our prosperity, makes us less secure by preventing the deportation of dangerous foreign nationals—and does nothing to change the attitudes of governments like Russia's when it comes to human rights'. For these reasons, she continued, 'regardless of the EU referendum, if we want to reform human rights laws in this country, it isn't the EU we should leave but the ECHR and the jurisdiction of its court' (May 2016).

Despite this resistance to the expansion of judicial power in certain settings, it should be noted that regimes that express such resistance do not go so far as to blatantly eschew the global constitutional order. Given the amount of energy that goes into subverting the constitutional domain, those who pursue such a project must assume that constitutional institutions, courts, and practices matter a great deal. At the very least, these actors see the importance of formally adhering to standards of democratic constitutionalism while advancing a local version of these norms that depletes them of real content in practice. In a curious way, this too may be seen as an indication of the significance of judicial power, or at least the significance of its façade.

5. Conclusion

As courts have burgeoned globally over the last few decades, so too has their jurisdiction, jurisprudence, impact, and political salience all grown considerably. It is hard to overstate the scope and significance of this trend. While it has not been met with across-the-board support, the global expansion of judicial power carries on.

From epistemological and methodological standpoints, this expansion provides endless opportunities for developing and testing arguments concerning judicial behaviour across time and place. The rise of law, courts, and judges as critical forces in comparative and world politics further suggests that politics and law are becoming increasingly intertwined domains, affecting each other in intricate ways that are seldom acknowledged by doctrinal analyses. Consequently, traditional disciplinary boundaries between the study of law and politics become increasingly difficult to sustain.

Notes

1. The proposed new constitution for Chile (rejected in a national referendum in September 2022), for example, aimed to protect over one hundred different rights—more than any national constitution.
2. The Eichmann Trial (1961) famously solidified the 'trial and punishment' mode of restorative justice in the wake of the horrors of the Second World War.
3. Due to the contentious nature of most ICJ cases, it occasionally runs out of favor with the world's superpowers. In the landmark *Nicaragua Case* (1984), for example, the ICJ accepted claims brought by Nicaragua against the United States for US use of military force against it in contravention of international law norms. In reaction, the United States withdrew from the court's optional compulsory jurisdiction.
4. The phenomenon has distinct manifestations in different regions, e.g. Latin America (Couso, Huneeus, and Sieder 2010; Helmke and Rios-Figueroa 2011; Botero, Brinks, and Gonzalez-Ocantos 2022) and Asia (Dressel 2012).
5. Whether the all-out judicialization of mega-politics has been as significant at the international level as it has been at the national level, and what are the main theoretical differences, if any, between judicialization at the national and international level, are relatively under-explored themes. For initial accounts see Alter and Madsen (2022); Alter, Hafner-Burton, and Helfer (2019); Abebe and Ginsburg (2019).
6. It is hard to overstate the significance of judicial appointments. As is well known, during his single-term presidency, Donald Trump, despite having received fewer overall votes than his opponent, managed to appoint three Supreme Court Justices during his presidency, thereby shaping the course of American constitutional jurisprudence for decades to come.

References

Abebe, Daniel, and Tom Ginsburg. 2019. 'The Dejudicialization of International Politics?' *International Studies Quarterly* 63: 521–30.

Alter, Karen J. 2011. 'The Evolving International Judiciary'. *Annual Review of Law and Social Science* 7: 387–415.

Alter, Karen J. 2016. 'The Evolution of International Law and Courts'. In *The Oxford Handbook of Historical Institutionalism*, edited by Orfeo Fioretos, Tulia G. Falleti, and Adam Sheingate, 590–610. New York: Oxford University Press.

Alter, Karen J., Emilie Hafner-Burton, and Laurence Helfer. 2019. 'Theorizing the Judicialization of International Relations'. *International Studies Quarterly* 63: 449–63.

Alter, Karen J., and Mikael Rask Madsen. 2022. 'The International Adjudication of Mega-Politics'. *Law and Contemporary Problems* 84: 1–28.

Barak, Aharon. 1993. 'Judicial Philosophy and Judicial Activism'. *Iyunei Mishpat* 17: 475–502.

Barnes, Jeb, and Thomas Burke. 2020. 'Untangling the Concept of Adversarial Legalism'. *Annual Review of Law and Social Science* 16: 473–87.

Bellamy, Richard. 2007. *Political Constitutionalism: A Republican Defence of the Constitutionality of Democracy*. Cambridge: Cambridge University Press.

Botero, Sandra, Daniel Brinks, and Ezequiel Gonzalez-Ocantos, eds. 2022. *The Limits of Judicialization. From Progress to Backlash in Latin America*. Cambridge: Cambridge University Press.

Calabresi, Steven. 2020. 'The Global Rise of Judicial Review since 1945'. *Catholic University Law Review* 69: 401–44.

Cappelletti, Mauro. 1970. *Judicial Review in the Contemporary World*. Indianapolis: The Bobbs-Merrill Co.

Cappelletti, Mauro. 1988. 'The Expanding Role of Judicial Review in Modern Societies'. In *The Role of Courts in Society*, edited by Shimon Shetreet, 79–97. Dordrecht, Boston, Lancaster: Martinus Nijhoff Publishers.

Couso, Javier, Alexandra Huneeus, and Rachel Sieder. 2010. *Cultures of Legality. Judicialization and Political Activism in Latin America*. New York: Cambridge University Press.

Delaney, Erin, and Rosalind Dixon, eds. 2018. *Comparative Judicial Review*. Cheltenham: Edward Elgar Publishing.

Dixon, Rosalind, and David Landau. 2021. *Abusive Constitutional Borrowing: Legal Globalization and the Subversion of Liberal Democracy*. Oxford: Oxford University Press.

Dorsen, Norman. 2005. 'The Relevance of Foreign Legal Materials in U.S. Constitutional Cases: A Conversation between Justice Antonin Scalia and Justice Stephen Breyer'. *International Journal of Constitutional Law* 3: 519–41.

Dressel, Björn, ed. 2012. *The Judicialization of Politics in Asia*. New York: Routledge.

Durkheim, Émile. 1964 [1893]. *The Division of Labor in Society*. New York: Free Press.

Elkins, Zachary, and Tom Ginsburg. 2021. 'Characteristics of National Constitutions, Version 3.0'. *Comparative Constitutions Project*, May 20, 2021. https://perma.cc/RZ36-4JW6.

Epp, Charles. 1998. *The Rights Revolution: Lawyers, Activists and Supreme Courts in Comparative Perspective*. Chicago: University of Chicago Press.

Epstein, Lee. 2008. 'The U.S. Supreme Court'. In *The Oxford Handbook of Law and Politics*, edited by Gregory Caldeira, Daniel Kelemen, and Keith Whittington, 487–502. New York: Oxford University Press.

Epstein, Lee, and Jack Knight. 1998. *The Choices Justices Make*. Washington: CQ Press.

Epstein, Lee, and Jack Knight. 2000. 'Toward a Strategic Revolution in Judicial Politics: A Look Back, A Look Ahead'. *Political Research Quarterly* 53: 625–61.

Epstein, Lee, and Weinshall, Keren. 2021. *The Strategic Analysis of Judicial Behavior: A Comparative Perspective*. Cambridge: Cambridge University Press.

Ferejohn, John. 2002. 'Judicializing Politics, Politicizing Law'. *Law and Contemporary Problems* 61: 41–68.

Friedman, Barry, and Erin Delaney. 2011. 'Becoming Supreme: The Federal Foundation of Judicial Supremacy'. *Columbia Law Review* 111: 1137–93.

Ginsburg, Tom. 2003. *Judicial Review in New Democracies: Constitutional Courts in Asian Cases*. Cambridge: Cambridge University Press.

Ginsburg, Tom. 2008. 'The Global Spread of Constitutional Review'. In *The Oxford Handbook of Law and Politics*, edited by Gregory Caldeira, Daniel Kelemen, and Keith Whittington, 81–98. New York: Oxford University Press.

Ginsburg, Tom. 2022. 'The State of the Field'. In *Constitutionalism in Context*, edited by David S. Law, 23–40. Cambridge: Cambridge University Press.

Ginsburg, Tom, and Mila Versteeg. 2014. 'Why Do Countries Adopt Constitutional Review?' *The Journal of Law, Economics, and Organization* 30: 587–622.

Glendon, Mary Ann. 1991. *Rights Talk: The Impoverishment of Political Discourse*. New York: Free Press.

Goldstein, Leslie Friedman, 2001. *Constituting Federal Sovereignty: The European Union in Comparative Context*. Baltimore: Johns Hopkins University Press.

Graber, Mark. 1993. 'The Nonmajoritarian Difficulty: Legislative Deference to the Judiciary'. *Studies in American Political Development* 7: 35–73.

Grabowska-Moroz, Barbara. 2022. 'How Was the 'Rule of Law' Dismantled in Poland and What Does It Mean for the EU?' In *Unión Europea y el reto del Estado de Derecho*, edited by Susana Sanz Caballero, 277–94. Navarra: Aranzadi.

Guarnieri, Carlo, and Patrizia Pederzoli. 2002. *The Power of Judges: A Comparative Study of Courts and Democracy*. New York: Oxford University Press.

Habermas, Jürgen. 1986. 'Law as Medium and Law as Institution'. In *Dilemmas of Law in the Welfare State*, 203–20. Berlin: Walter De Gruyter.

Hamlin, Rebecca, and Gemma Sala. 2018. 'The Judicialization of Politics Disentangled'. In *Oxford Research Encyclopedia of Politics* (May 2018), edited by Gunther Teubner. Oxford: Oxford University Press.

Helmke, Gretchen, and Julio Ríos-Figueroa, eds. 2011. *Courts in Latin America*. New York: Cambridge University Press.

Hirschl, Ran. 2004a. *Towards Juristocracy: The Origins and Consequences of the New Constitutionalism*. Cambridge: Harvard University Press.

Hirschl, Ran. 2004b. 'Constitutional Courts vs. Religious Fundamentalism: Three Middle Eastern Tales'. *Texas Law Review* 82: 1819–60.

Hirschl, Ran. 2008. 'The Judicialization of Mega-Politics and the Rise of Political Courts'. *Annual Review of Political Science* 11: 93–180.

Hirschl, Ran. 2018. 'Opting Out of Global Constitutionalism' *The Law & Ethics of Human Rights* 12: 1–36.

Ip, Eric C. 2019. *Hybrid Constitutionalism: The Politics of Constitutional Review in the Chinese Special Administrative Regions*. New York: Cambridge University Press.

Jacobsohn, Gary. 2010. *Constitutional Identity*. Cambridge: Harvard University Press.

Jung, Courtney, Ran Hirschl, and Evan Rosevear. 2015. 'Economic and Social Rights in National Constitutions'. *American Journal of Comparative Law* 62: 1043–94.

Kagan, Robert A. 2003. *Adversarial Legalism: The American Way of Law*. Cambridge: Harvard University Press.

Kapiszewski, Diana, Gordon Silverstein, and Robert A. Kagan, eds. 2013. *Consequential Courts: Judicial Roles in Global Perspective*. Cambridge: Cambridge University Press.

Karpik, Lucien, and Terrence C. Halliday. 2011. 'The Legal Complex'. *Annual Review of Law and Social Science* 7: 217–36.

Kramer, Larry. 2004. *The People Themselves: Popular Constitutionalism and Judicial Review*. New York: Oxford University Press.

Kundera, Milan. 1992. *Immortality*. Translated by Peter Kussi. London: Faber and Faber Ltd.

Law, David S. 2005. 'Generic Constitutional Law'. *Minnesota Law Review* 89: 652–751.

Law, David S., and Mila Versteeg. 2011. 'The Evolution and Ideology of Global Constitutionalism'. *California Law Review* 99: 1163–254.

Levinson, Sanford. 1988. *Constitutional Faith*. Princeton: Princeton University Press.

Lustig, Doreen, and J. H. H. Weiler. 2018. 'Judicial Review in the Contemporary World—Retrospective and Prospective'. *I-CON, International Journal of Constitutional Law* 16: 315–72.

Madsen, Mikael, Pola Cebulak, and Micha Wiebusch. 2018. 'Backlash Against International Courts: Explaining the Forms and Patterns of Resistance to International Courts'. *International Journal of Law in Context* 14: 197–220.

Maine, Henry S. 2000 [1861]. *Ancient Law*. Washington: Beard Books.

May, Theresa. 2016. 'Home Secretary's Speech on the UK, EU and Our Place in the World'. Address to the Institute of Mechanical Engineers, London, 25 April 2016. https://www.gov.uk/government/speeches/home-secretarys-speech-on-the-uk-eu-and-our-place-in-the-world.

Mnookin, Robert, and Lewis Kornhauser. 1979. 'Bargaining in the Shadow of the Law: The Case of Divorce'. *Yale Law Journal* 88: 950–97.

Möller, Kai. 2012. *The Global Model of Constitutional Rights*. New York: Oxford University Press.

Morton, Frederick L. 1995. 'The Effect of the Charter of Rights on Canadian Federalism'. *Publius: The Journal of Federalism*, 25: 173–88.

Nathan, Laurie. 2013. 'The Disbanding of the SADC Tribunal: A Cautionary Tale'. *Human Rights Quarterly* 35: 870–92.

New York Times, The Editorial Board. 2016. 'Poland's Tragic Turn'. *New York Times*, 21 Dec, 2016. https://www.nytimes.com/2016/12/21/opinion/polands-tragic-turn.html.

O'Connell, Mary Ellen, and Lenore VanderZee. 2014. 'The History of International Adjudication'. In *The Oxford Handbook of International Adjudication*, edited by Cesare P. R. Romano, Karen J. Alter, and Yuval Shany, 62–87. Oxford: Oxford University Press.

Pal, Michael. 2016. 'Electoral Management Bodies as a Fourth Branch of Government'. *Review of Constitutional Studies* 21: 85–113.

Pavone, Tommaso, and Øyvind Stiansen. 2022. 'The Shadow Effect of Courts: Judicial Review and the Politics of Preemptive Reform'. *American Political Science Review* 116: 322–36.

Rosenberg, Gerald N. 1991. *The Hollow Hope. Can Courts Bring about Social Change?* Chicago: University of Chicago Press.

Rosevear, Evan, Ran Hirschl, and Courtney Jung. 2019. 'Justiciable and Aspirational Economic and Social Rights in National Constitutions'. In *The Future of Economic and Social Rights*, edited by Katharine G. Young, 37–65. Cambridge: Cambridge University Press.

Roznai, Yaniv. 2017. *Unconstitutional Constitutional Amendments: The Limits of Amendment Powers*. New York: Oxford University Press.

Sadurski, Wojciech. 2019. *Poland's Constitutional Breakdown*. New York: Oxford University Press.

Sadurski, Wojciech. 2022. *A Pandemic of Populists*. Cambridge: Cambridge University Press.

Scheingold, Stuart. 1974. *The Politics of Rights: Lawyers, Public Policy, and Political Change*. New Haven: Yale University Press.

Shapiro, Martin, and Alec Stone Sweet. 2002. *On Law, Politics, and Judicialization*. New York: Oxford University Press.

Shepsle, Kenneth A. 2006. 'Old Questions and New Answers about Institutions: The Riker Objection Revisited'. In *The Oxford Handbook of Political Economy*, edited by Barry R. Weingast and Donald Wittman, 1031–49. Oxford: Oxford University Press.

Sieder, Rachel, Line Schjolden, and Alan Angell, eds. 2005. *The Judicialization of Politics in Latin America*. New York: Palgrave Macmillan.

Stone Sweet, Alec. 2000. *Governing with Judges: Constitutional Politics in Europe*. Oxford: Oxford University Press.

Streeck, Wolfgang. 2016. *How Will Capitalism End? Essays on a Failing System*. New York: Verso Books.

Tate, C. Neal, and Torbjörn Vallinder, eds. 1995. *The Global Expansion of Judicial Power*. New York: New York University Press.

Teubner, Gunther, ed. 1987. *Juridification of Social Spheres. A Comparative Analysis of the Areas of Labor, Corporate, Antitrust and Social Welfare Law*. Berlin: Walter de Gruyter.

Tocqueville, Alexis de. 2010 [1835]. *Democracy in America*. Edited by Eduardo Nolla. Translated by James T. Schleifer. Indianapolis: Liberty Fund.

Tully, James, Jeffrey L. Dunoff, Anthony F Lang, Mattias Kumm, and Antje Wiener. 2016. 'Introducing Global Integral Constitutionalism'. *Global Constitutionalism: Human Rights, Democracy, and the Rule of Law* 5: 1–15.

Tushnet, Mark. 1999. *Taking the Constitution Away from the Courts*. Princeton: Princeton University Press.

Tushnet, Mark. 2021. *The New Fourth Branch: Institutions for Protecting Constitutional Democracy*. Cambridge: Cambridge University Press.

Waldron, Jeremy. 1986. 'Rights in Conflict'. *Ethics* 99: 503–19.

Waldron, Jeremy. 2006. 'The Core of the Case against Judicial Review'. *Yale Law Journal* 115: 1346–406.

Weber, Max. 1978 [1914]. *Economy and Society: An Outline of Interpretive Sociology*. Berkeley: University of California Press.

Whittington, Keith E. 2005. 'Interpose Your Friendly Hand: Political Supports for the Exercise of Judicial Review by the United States Supreme Court'. *American Political Science Review* 99: 583–96.

Cases cited

Andrea Francovich and Danila Bonifaci and Others v Italian Republic, C-6/90 and C-9/90 ECR (1991).

Asia Bibi v The State, PLD SC 64 (2018).

Austerity Package Decisions ('Bokros Cases'), 43/1995. (VI. 30.) AB (1995).

AZAPO v President of the Republic of South Africa, 1996 (4) SA 562 (CC) (1996).

Bush v Gore, 531 US 98 (2000).
Citizens United v FEC, 130 S Ct 876 (2010).
Costa v ENEL, C-6/64 ECR (1964).
European Commission v Republic of Poland, C-619/18 ECR (2019).
Imran Ahmed Khan Niazi v Mian Muhammad Nawaz Sharif, P.M. Pakistan, U/A 184, Const. P.29/2016 (2018).
Indira Gandhi v Pengarah Jabatan Agama Islam Perak & Ors, 1 MLJ 545 (2018).
Lautsi v Italy, ECHR 30814/06 (2011).
Mabo v Queensland II, 175 CLR 1 (1992).
Marbury v Madison, 5 US 137 (1803).
Nicaragua v United States of America, ICJ 169 (1984).
NV Algemene Transporten Expeditie Onderneming van Gend en Loos v Nederlandse Administratis der Belastingen, C-26/62 ECR (1963).
Operation Dismantle v The Queen, 1 SCR 441, 18 DLR 481 (1985).
R. (Miller) v Prime Minister ('Miller II'), UKSC 41, [2020] AC 373 (2019).
R. (Miller) v Secretary of State for Exiting the European Union ('Miller I'), UKSC 5; 2 WLR 583 (2017).
Re Rejection of the Motion of No-confidence against the Prime Minister (Imran Khan), U/A 184 (3), SMC1/2022 (2022).
Reference re Secession of Quebec, 2 SCR 217 (1998).
Republic of the Philippines v People's Republic of China, PCA Case No. 2013–19 (2016).
Rucho v Common Cause, 139 S Ct 2484 (2019).
S.A.S. v France, EHCR 43835/11 (2014).
Sejdić and Finci v Bosnia and Herzegovina, ECHR 27996/06 & 34836/06 (2009).
Sentencia C-379/16 (*re Constitutionality of Peace Agreement between the Government of Colombia and FARC*) (2016).
Shayara Bano v Union of India And Ors., 9 SCC 1 (2017).
Shelby County v Holder, 133 S Ct 2612 (2013).
United Mizrahi Bank v Migdal Cooperative Village et al., CA 6821/93 [1995] Israel Law Review 1.
Urteil des Zweiten Senats vom 12. Oktober 1993 ('Maastricht Case'), 2 BvR 2134/92, 2159/92 (1993).
Urteil des Zweiten Senats vom 30. Juni 2009 ('Lisbon Treaty Case'), 2 BvE 2/08 (2009).
Urteil des Zweiten Senats vom 5. Mai 2020 ('European Central Bank Case'), 2 BvR 859/15 (2020).
V.M.A. v Stolichna Obshtina, Bulgaria, C-490/20 ECR (2021).

CHAPTER 5

TRANSCENDING THE DOMESTIC–INTERNATIONAL DIVIDE

DANIEL NAURIN AND ERIK VOETEN

1. Introduction

Over the past three decades, international courts have proliferated and have increasingly produced judgments with considerable economic, social, and political consequences. Scholarly studies have boomed in tandem with this growing influence, including noteworthy studies of international judicial behaviour. In 2011, Jeffrey Staton and Will Moore published an influential article urging scholars at the domestic and international level to write 'in one coherent literature' (Staton and Moore 2011). The study of international law and courts had been overly focused on the absence of an international authority that can coerce governments to implement international legal obligations. This led to a sharp separation between the study of international and domestic law and courts, with international law scholars worrying whether international law really is law and domestic scholars largely side-stepping questions of compliance and authority.

In this chapter we first use citation analyses to demonstrate that the studies of international and domestic judicial behaviour still form distinct clusters with relatively few connections. Moreover, the direction of citations mostly goes one way: with international court scholars citing scholarly works in US or comparative judicial behaviour while domestic (in particular, US) scholars mostly ignore the international literature. We argue that this is unfortunate for two broad reasons.

First, in the context of backlashes against the judiciary scholars of domestic judicial behaviour must increasingly confront the reality that the authority of the courts they study cannot be taken for granted. Staton and Moore already pointed out that the anarchic nature of the international system does not justify siloing research on international and national judicial behaviour. A strong national government only helps courts enforce obligations among private actors. A strong government is a mixed blessing for judicial authority when the actor whose behaviour is under review is the same actor responsible for implementing decisions, appointing judges, and setting budgets. Moreover, in many countries the authority and independence of courts is not inherently stable. Domestic and international scholars can learn from each other about how the fragility of judicial authority shapes judicial behaviour. This question has long been central to the study of international courts.

Second, international judges must solve similar problems as domestic judges and they are motivated by similar goals: to enhance the institutional legitimacy of their court, to advance their own careers, to gain respect within their expert community, and to realize policy preferences. Experience, gender, professional background, and other personal factors are likely to shape international judicial behaviour just as much as domestic judicial behaviour. There is thus considerable potential for cross-fertilization. International courts offer unique opportunities for testing general theories with judges from multiple countries operating in a single institutional setting. For example, international court scholars have utilized unique design features of their courts to test whether judicial dissents undermine compliance (Naurin and Stiansen 2020), whether non-renewable terms increase judicial independence (Stiansen 2022), and how gender shapes judicial behaviour across (legal) cultures (Voeten 2021). These are all central questions to the study of judicial behaviour writ large.

Our claim is that more cross-fertilization would be beneficial, not that there are no differences in how the institutional and political environment constrains and incentivizes international compared to domestic judges. Most notably, international judges are subject to the scrutiny of not one but multiple national governments. Just how this affects political control of the judiciary depends on the context. Some strategies of political control may be more complex. National governments must resolve a coordination dilemma among themselves in order to pack a court, override judicial decisions, and reform an institution. Yet there are also circumstances where a subset of powerful governments can each take actions that undermine the institutional legitimacy of a court, affect policy outcomes, and influence careers. The US insistence not to approve new World Trade Organization (WTO) Appellate Body judges single-handedly stifled that institution. Judges cannot solve this by simply catering to US interests because other countries with different interests could take similar actions. Moreover, withdrawal from the jurisdiction of international courts is often a credible threat whereas this is not as easy an option domestically.

Political control over international courts may take different forms but it is too simplistic to assert that international judges are more or less constrained than domestic judges. Instead, we must carefully theorize how particular institutional settings incentivize judges to behave in certain ways. By writing in one literature on judicial behaviour that surpasses the international–domestic divide scholars gain a broader set of institutional variation to work with. In this chapter, we evaluate what we know from the existing literature and how researchers can take these challenges forward.

We first take a bird's-eye picture of the literature on judicial behaviour by means of bibliographic citation analyses. To what extent are scholars studying international and domestic judicial behaviour writing in one coherent literature? Is there any tendency towards convergence over time? Thereafter, we review more closely how the literature on international judicial autonomy has approached the international–domestic divide on two questions that are key in the judicial behaviour literature: how does the (re-) appointment process shape judicial behaviour? How do judges respond to threats to the fragility of their court's authority? We highlight the places where the challenges for international and national judges depart and coincide. Our conclusion returns to the question of how the domestic and international court literatures can learn from each other.

2. Development of the Literature: A Citation Analysis

Consistent with Staton and Moore, we use Cesare Romano's definition of international legal bodies as 'permanent tribunals, created by an international legal instrument, which resort to international law for the resolution of cases, use preexisting rules of procedure that cannot be altered by the parties, and issue legally binding decisions' (Romano 1999. This includes general courts, most notably the International Court of Justice (ICJ); regional integration courts, most notably the Court of Justice of the European Union (CJEU); regional human rights courts, most notably the European Court of Human Rights (ECtHR) and the Inter-American Court of Human Rights (IACtHR); the International Criminal Court (ICC); and the various tribunals that adjudicate disputes over trade and investment, most notably the WTO's Dispute Settlement Understanding and the various arbitral bodies that settle Investor–State Disputes (ISDS). We also follow Staton and Moore in focusing on comparisons with the literature on domestic constitutional and appellate courts rather than lower-level civil or criminal courts.

In order to get a sense of how the literature has evolved we performed a Web of Science (WoB) search of articles published in English language political science journals since 1990 that included terms related to our judicial bodies of interest.[1] We focused on political science articles given that most of the social science work on international courts is published in that discipline.[2] This search yields 3,406 articles. The most cited articles in this collection are two more general articles about the US political system (Stimson, Mackuen, and Erikson 1995; Hetherington 1998) and legal integration and delegation in the European Union (Burley and Mattli 1993; Pollack 1997). The most frequent journals are *Political Research Quarterly*, the *American Journal of Political Science*, and the *Journal of Politics*. Sixty per cent of the corresponding authors reside in the United States. We

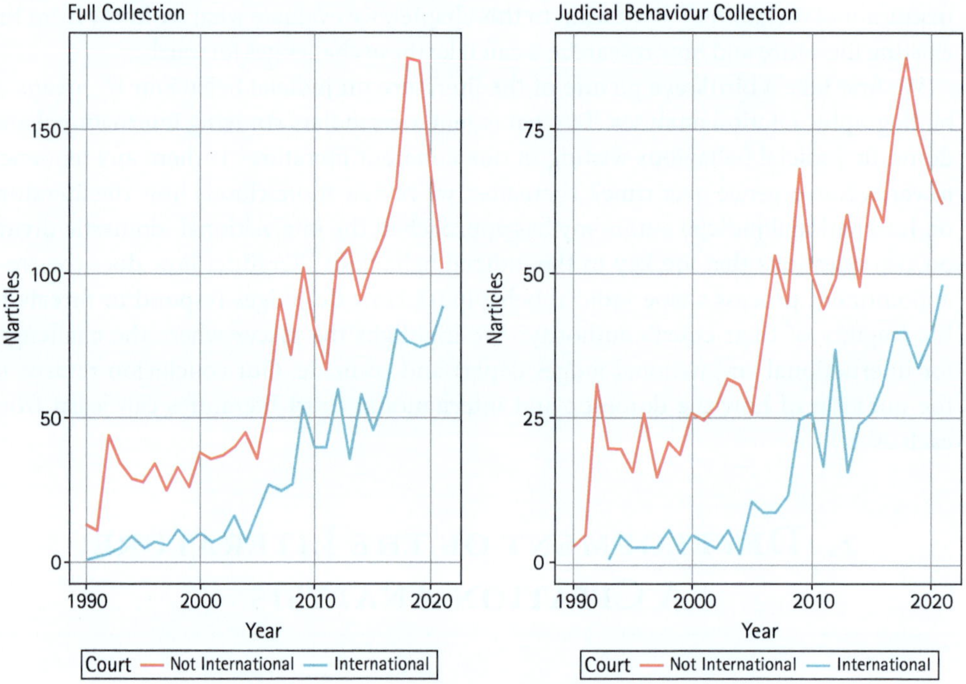

FIGURE 5.1 Political science articles on international and domestic courts.

Note: Based on Web of Science search of keywords, titles, and abstracts in English language political science journals.

refined this collection by also searching for the occurrence of terms in keywords, title, or abstract that are often associated with studies of judicial behaviour, yielding 1,906 articles, 537 of which are about international courts.[3] In this subset, the *Journal of European Public Policy* and *International Organization* are the most common outlets. Within the international court judicial behaviour collection, the most cited articles are several articles on the political constraints on the CJEU (Carrubba, Gabel, and Hankla 2008; Kelemen 2012; Stone Sweet and Brunell 2012; Larsson and Naurin 2016), as well as articles on the ECtHR (Voeten 2007) and the WTO (Busch and Pelc 2010).

Figure 5.1 shows that in both collections the international court literature took off only in the mid-2000s. This also coincides with an increased output in the literature on domestic constitutional courts, perhaps fuelled by an overall greater interest in the judicialization of politics (see Hirschl, *The Oxford Handbook of Political Science*).

To what extent is there one coherent literature on judicial behaviour in domestic constitutional courts and international courts? One way to examine this is through a co-citation analysis, which detects relationships between articles by determining whether a pair of articles are cited together in other articles in the collection (Aria and Cuccurullo 2017). Figure 5.2 plots the co-citation network for the full collection since 2005, which represents the launching point for the international court literature. The network plots fifty nodes that represent articles that are often cited together. The nodes themselves are not necessarily in the collection, but they represent articles that are most often cited

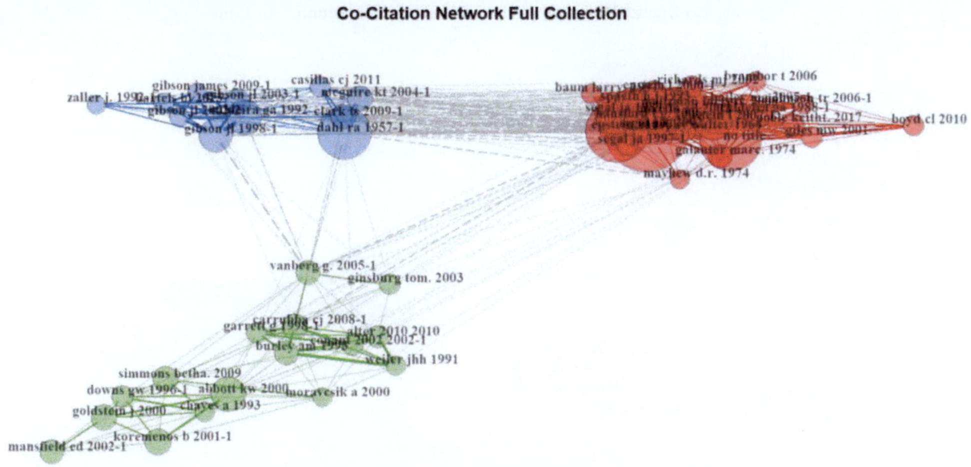

FIGURE 5.2 Co-citation network of full collection since 2005.

Note: Co-citation network plot of fifty nodes from the full collection post 2005 generated using the bibliometrix package in *R*, Fruchterman–Reingold layout. The size of the nodes reflects the frequency of citations.

together in the collection's articles. Several articles published before 2005 are still among the most cited since then.

The red cluster in the network mostly consists of research on the US Supreme Court. The network is very dense. The blue network consists mostly of articles on legitimacy and public opinion, again mostly United States, but also some comparative research (e.g. Gibson, Caldeira, and Baird 1998). There are connections between the blue and red clusters. The green international court cluster is not very densely connected to the other clusters, although it does have some connections via research on comparative constitutionalism (Ginsburg 2003; Vanberg 2005). There are two subnetworks in the international court cluster. First, a set of articles on the CJEU is often cited together. Second, there are several nodes at the top of the picture that represent co-citations to articles that are more general theoretical articles about the role of international law and institutions; that is, articles about international courts often cite articles that offer theoretical justifications for the (ir)relevance of international law and courts (e.g. Chayes and Chayes 1993; Downs, Rocke, and Barsoom 1996).

Figure 5.3 plots the co-citation network for the collection that filters articles that include terms in their abstract or keywords that suggest a study of judicial behaviour. The broad clusters are quite similar to the overall network in Figure 5.2. The international court articles are clearly further removed from the US literature than the comparative court scholarship. In fact, the most cited comparative domestic work is closer to the international court articles, in particular those on the CJEU, than to the US literature. This indicates that the divide between research on US and non-US courts is more significant than the domestic–international divide.

Figure 5.4 plots the co-citation network for the judicial behaviour collection but only among international court articles. The red cluster encompasses European court articles

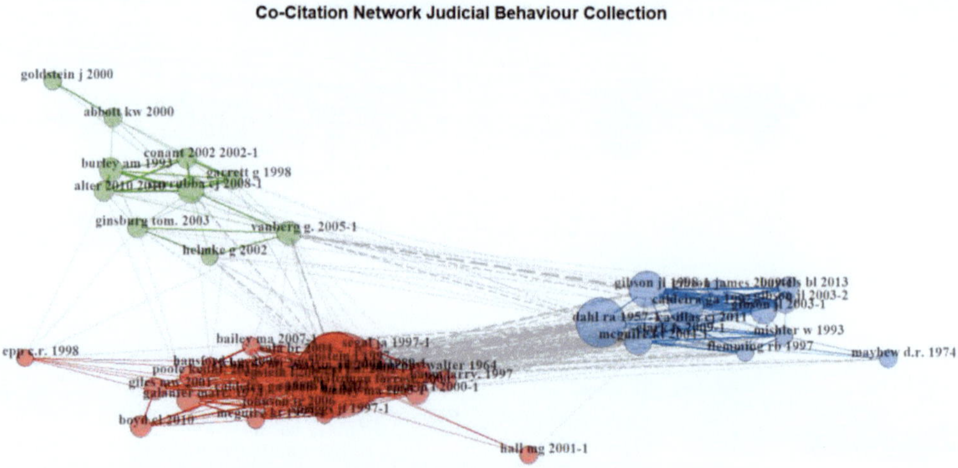

FIGURE 5.3 Co-citation network of judicial behaviour collection since 2005.

Note: Co-citation network plot of forty nodes from the judicial behaviour collection on international courts post 2005 generated using the bibliometrix package in *R*, Fruchterman–Reingold layout.

and is very dense. The blue cluster mostly consists of articles about trade and investment. Nodes that connect both clusters are articles that make more general theoretical arguments about international legalized dispute resolutions, credible commitments theory and the effectiveness of international law (Keohane, Moravcsik, and Slaughter 2000; Moravcsik 2000; Simmons 2009). These nodes again indicate the centrality of general theoretical underpinnings about the relevance of international law. It is notable

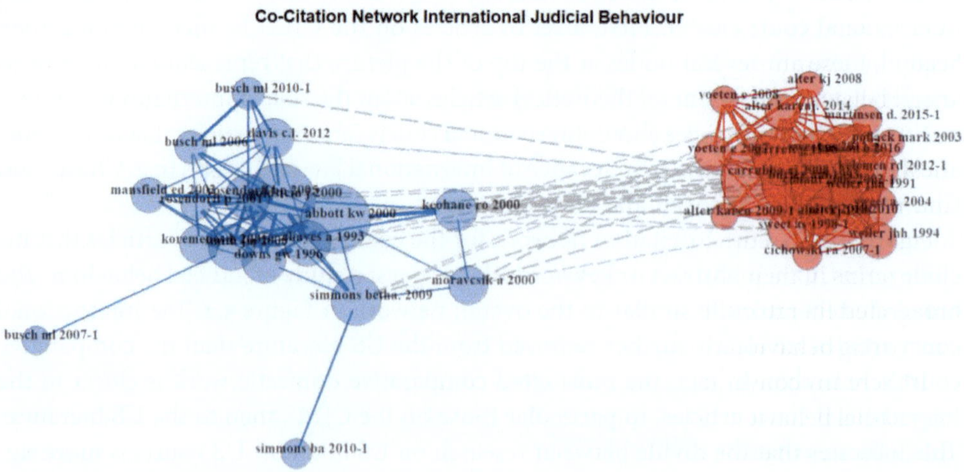

FIGURE 5.4 Co-citation network of international judicial behaviour collection since 2005.

Note: Co-citation network plot of fifty nodes from the judicial behaviour collection post 2005 generated using the bibliometrix package in *R*, Fruchterman–Reingold layout.

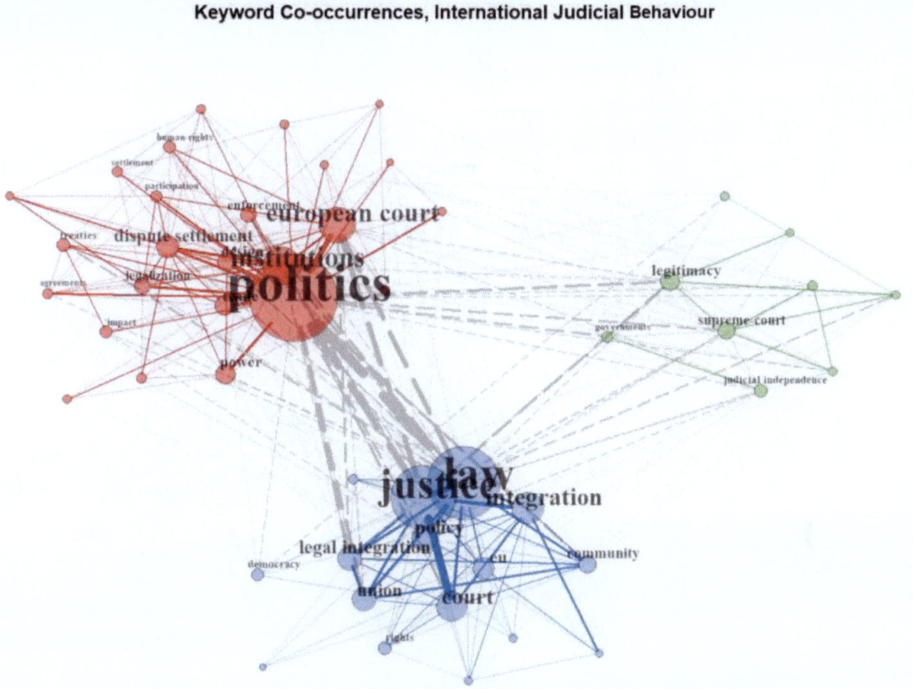

FIGURE 5.5 Keyword co-occurrences in the domestic judicial behaviour network.

Note: Keyword co-occurrences network plot of fifty nodes (thirty labelled) from the international judicial behaviour collection generated using the bibliometrix package in *R*, Fruchterman–Reingold layout.

that there are no domestic court articles among the fifty most important nodes in the international judicial behaviour network.

These network plots suggest that international and domestic judicial behaviour articles tend to deal with somewhat distinct topics. We look at this more systematically by examining keyword co-occurrences in the domestic and international judicial behaviour collections. The resulting network maps tell us something about the substantive focus within each collection. The main implication is that while the domestic literature, as seen in Figure 5.5, is very focused on decision-making, attitudes, and policy, the international court literature, as shown in Figure 5.6, remains more focused on existential themes like justice, democracy, legitimacy, enforcement, and integration. One possibility that the keyword map suggests is that there may be more integrated literatures if we start focusing on subtopics, like judicial selection or judicial voting behaviour.

Is there any convergence over time between the domestic and international literatures on judicial behaviour? We approach that question by examining cross-citations within the collections between international and domestic court articles. Figure 5.7 plots the extent to which international court articles cite domestic court articles in the collection and vice versa. The graphs show a clear pattern. Domestic court articles have not increased their citations of international court articles, despite the rise of such works

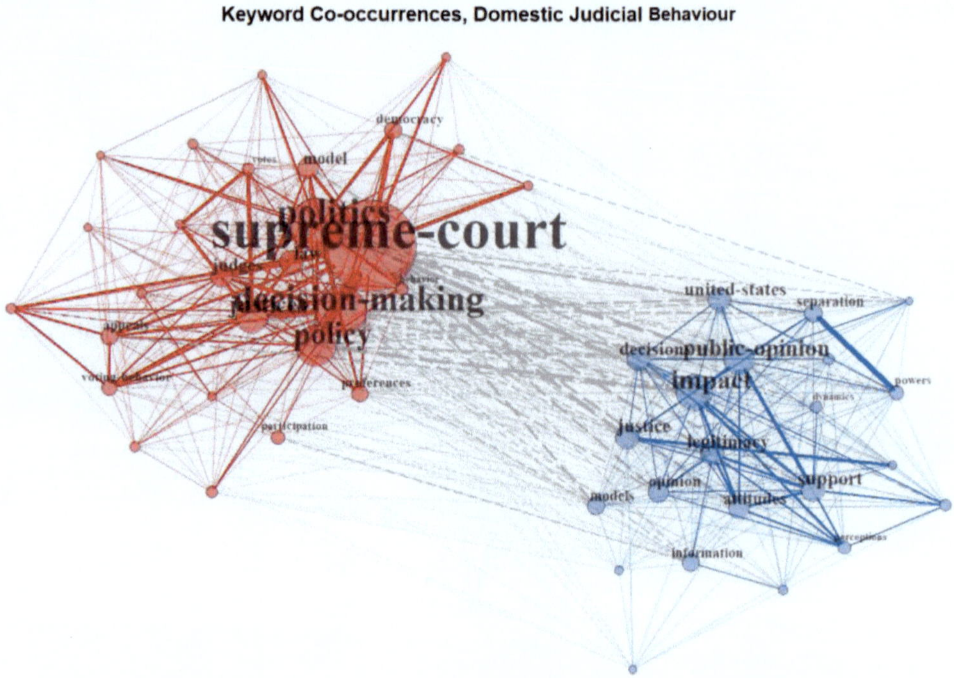

FIGURE 5.6 Keyword co-occurrences in the international judicial behaviour network.

Note: Keyword co-occurrences network plot of fifty nodes (thirty labelled) from the international judicial behaviour collection generated using the bibliometrix package in *R*, Fruchterman–Reingold layout.

that we saw earlier. The most frequently cited international court article in the domestic court literature is a seminal article about the CJEU (Burley and Mattli 1993), perhaps because of its relevance for European constitutional law. The next two are articles on public opinion (Caldeira and Gibson 1995; Gibson and Caldeira 1995). International court articles initially cited domestic and international court articles in roughly similar numbers. However, in more recent years international court articles have started to cite more other international court articles. Note that international court articles on average refer to fewer articles in the collection than domestic court articles. A plausible explanation referred to earlier is that international court articles cite many articles that are not about courts of judicial behaviour per se but that are theoretical articles about the relevance of international law and courts.

Another part of the explanation is probably that some questions are more salient for scholars of international courts, including the structural conditions for judicial autonomy and effectiveness and the struggle for being relevant in an international regime. Theories of international law and international relations are central to the international court literature. It seems that the international court literature is more concerned with existential questions than the domestic court literature. Whereas

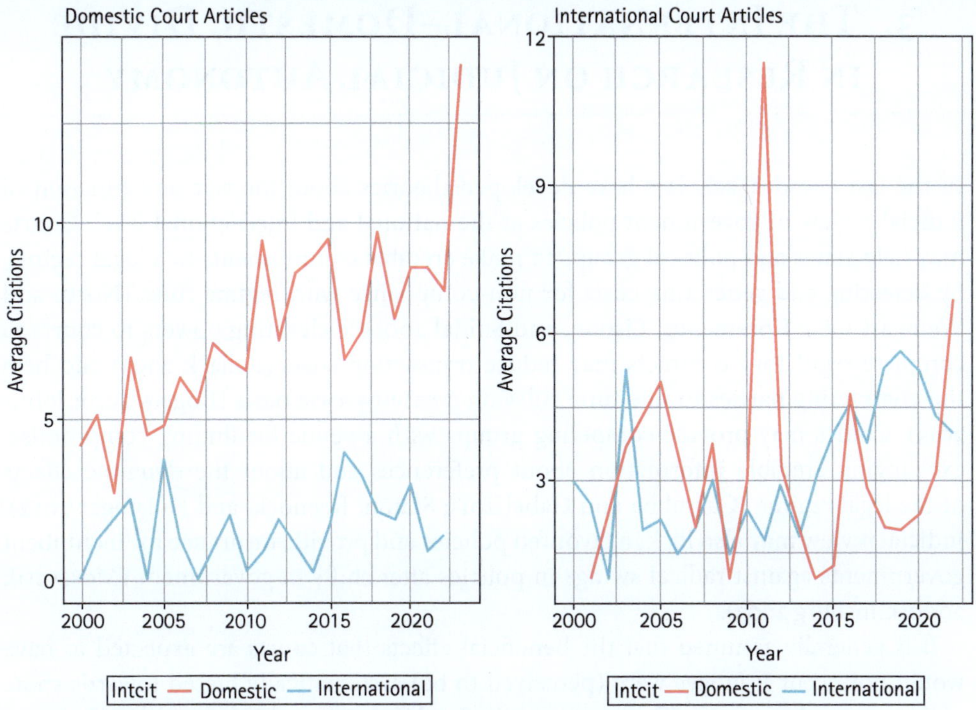

FIGURE 5.7 Cross-citations between the international and domestic court literatures.

Note: Annual citations in the domestic literature (left panel) and international court literature (right panel) to domestic and international court articles.

This citation analysis suggests that the literatures on domestic and international judicial behaviour have not converged in the way hoped for by Staton and Moore. It also suggests that the lack of convergence has as much to do with a division between US- and non-US-focused research as between research on international and domestic courts. Part of the explanation for the persistent divide may be that scholars of domestic judicial behaviour—in particular US courts—already have a large body of work to build on, which means less urgency to look elsewhere for inspiration.

the US literature in particular focuses on judicial decision-making and voting, with many keywords relating to individual judicial behaviour (attitudes, ideology, preferences, voting behaviour, policy), the keyword search in the international literature suggests that it is more focused on integration, enforcement, and other international relations questions.

However, where scholars of international and domestic courts ask similar questions about specific conditions for judicial independence, or about career concerns of judges, gender differences in judging, dissenting opinions, or different aspects of judicial reasoning, there should be more convergence. In the rest of this chapter, we review some of the more specialized themes of research on judicial behaviour and demonstrate how useful integration between research at the international and domestic levels may be accomplished.

3. The International–Domestic Divide in Research on Judicial Autonomy

In the last decades, scholars have developed theories about the role and function of judicial review of government policies at the national and international level. Courts may help states and political groups to make credible commitments to a legal regime, by detecting and generating costs for non-compliance with regime rules (North and Weingast 1989; Koremenos, Lispon, and Snidal 2001). Delegating powers to courts to complete regulatory contracts may reduce transaction costs (Pollack 2003) and help the contracting parties to fine tune rules on a case-by-case basis (Rogers 2001; Johns 2015). Courts may provide competing groups with a venue for finding compromise, exchanging credible information about preferences and about the dynamic effects of the legal regime (Carrubba and Gabel 2015; Staton, Reenock, and Holsinger 2022). Judicial review may also lock in favoured policies and provide insurance for incumbent governments against radical swings in policies after shifts in government (Moravcsik 2000; Ginsburg 2003).

It is generally assumed that the beneficial effects that courts are expected to have would not occur if judges were (perceived to be) systematically biased towards some of the contracting parties. The question of judges' integrity and autonomy in relation to political powerholders is therefore of central importance. In this section we review what the literature has concluded with regards to the independence of international judges; that is, their ability to adjudicate and write opinions according to their own evaluation of the case. To what extent do international courts decide cases independently from the preferences of external actors, in particular state governments? Are the conditions and mechanisms driving international judicial autonomy significantly different from national courts?

We focus first on the formal and informal practices of selection and removal of judges. Who gets to sit on the international bench? What accountability mechanisms exist for those who are selected and how does it affect judicial behaviour? In subsequent sections we turn to questions of how international judges strategically anticipate their political environment in the face of risks of non-compliance, override, or more existential threats to the court's independence and jurisdiction.

4. Selection and Accountability of International Judges

The comparative domestic judicial politics research has found the connection between formal constitutional provisions of judicial independence and judges' *de facto* autonomy weak at best. To the extent that formal provisions matter, these studies point at procedures for selection and removal of judges as the most important (Melton and Ginsberg 2014; Staton, Reenock, and Holsinger 2022). Staton and Moore did not rule out the possibility of generic differences between national and international courts with regards to appointment politics. However, they argued against making assumptions to that effect without convincing empirical evidence to conclude that such differences exist (Staton and Moore 2011, 573). What do we know about how selection and removal procedures and practices impact on international judicial behaviour?

The institutional design of international courts varies widely and so do the rules on appointments of judges (Larsson et al. 2023). For some regional courts the number of judges is proportional to the number of member states (e.g. the ECtHR, CJEU, ATJ), while for courts with larger membership there is selective representation (e.g. the ICJ, WTO Appellate Body). The selection is usually done in two steps, where individual member states nominate a candidate and a collective of states decide on the appointment (Mackenzie et al. 2010). In contrasts to domestic courts (see Tiede Brashear, this volume), the involvement of judicial councils or merit commissions in the appointment procedure is uncommon at the international level. One exception is the so-called Article 255 Committee, which screens EU member states nominations to the CJEU.

Research on national courts has found that the selection of judges is primarily based on two criteria: the professional competence and the political ideology of the candidate (Cameron, Cover, and Segal 1990; Epstein et al. 2006). Professional competence and policy preferences—in particular relating to national sovereignty—is often assumed to permeate selection to international courts as well (Hermansen and Naurin 2019). Nevertheless, there has been some debate around the significance of ideological screening of international judges.

Two types of arguments that question the importance of appointment politics and political ideology for judicial behaviour in international courts have been raised. First, the trustee model, developed by Karen Alter, emphasizes the legitimacy that international judges draw from their professional legal expertise and from the normative ideal of impartial dispute resolution (Alter 2008). Political behaviour is fundamentally different from judicial behaviour, it is argued. In court, influence is obtained through persuasive legal arguments, making legal skills a key asset. Appointing governments are therefore expected to focus less on ideology and more on finding the most competent candidates based on professional legal merits and personal reputation in the legal community.

The trustee model emphasizes an important feature of courts, which is the normative authority derived from ideals of legalism and the rule of law (see Morell, this volume). At the same time, it leaves unanswered the question why political actors sometimes break the norm, choose to politicize courts, and refuse to comply with court orders. Research has shown that governments sometimes appoint international judges who have primarily had careers as diplomats rather than judges (Voeten 2007). Furthermore, it is not clear that selecting judges on the basis of political ideology necessarily contradicts selection on professional competence. The ideal candidate for the job should be a judge that is both competent and able to persuade colleagues on the bench, while at the same time having the right ideological compass from the perspective of the appointer (Hermansen and Naurin 2019).

The second argument for why appointment politics may not be as important for international courts as for national courts focuses on the embeddedness of the former in multilateral institutions where no single government can control the appointment process. The decentralized character of the selection of judges, it is argued, where no single state or group of states can control the ideological composition of the court, makes it a rather futile exercise for governments to engage in, according to this view. States are therefore less likely to bother using their appointment powers to promote policy goals (Alter 2008, 46; Kelemen 2012).

Fragmentation of political power is indeed an important feature of international organizations. The coordination problem that needs to be overcome when a multitude of states must agree on appointments or legal texts is often high. Separation of powers theories of judicial politics predict that judicial power rises with the increase in political fragmentation (Ferejohn and Weingast 1992). At the same time, divided legislators are not unique to international organizations. It is questionable, for example, whether a polarized US Congress is able to coordinate a response to expressions of judicial power better than the EU legislator. Constitutional provisions at the domestic level often provide for several actors to be involved in the appointment process, including judicial councils and executive and legislative institutions. Domestic judges are often replaced consecutively, making it harder to shift the ideology of a court in one strike (Tiede, this volume).

Furthermore, it is unclear why governments would refrain from making use of the influence they may have—even if marginal for a single state—from appointing a judge that is more likely to promote their policy goals. As for many national constitutional courts, there is a correlation between the ideology of appointing governments and the voting behaviour of ECtHR judges (Voeten 2007). This should not be surprising but it remains somewhat controversial among international court scholars.

Elsig and Pollack (2014) show that the WTO Appellate Body appointment process has

> become progressively more politicized over time as member states, responding to earlier and controversial Appellate Body decisions, became far more concerned about judicial activism and more interested in the substantive opinions of Appellate Body candidates, systematically championing candidates whose views on key issues most closely approached their own, and opposing candidates perceived to be activist or biased against their substantive preferences.
>
> (Elsig and Pollack 2014)

This politicization culminated in the United States single-handedly blocking all new Appellate Body appointments until the terms of all Appellate Body members had run out. Since WTO Panel decisions have no legal effect while appeals are pending, this essentially shut down the WTO's dispute settlement process.

There is also some research into the effects of getting national judges on international courts that organize appointments through competitive elections. For example, a country whose national wins a competitive election for an ICC judgeship becomes more likely to reject US advances to sign non-surrender agreements and to adopt domestic legislation that changes the penal code compared to a country whose national just lost this election (Voeten 2014). This suggests that governments care about having a judge on an international court and become less likely to undermine that court.

In sum, the theoretical rationale for downplaying appointment politics in research on international judicial behaviour seems questionable. However, one distinct feature of international courts is the role of 'the national judge', judges that evaluate cases that involve their home government. Their influence may be moderated by procedural rules. For courts with full member state representation, the national judge is not necessarily active in deciding cases from her member state. In the ECtHR, the national judge is always part of the panel that decides cases from her member state. In the CJEU, on the other hand, although a judge may sit on a panel that decides a case from her member state, it is not necessarily the case that she will, and the Reporting Judge who writes the judgment is always from a different member state.

Courts with selective representation may also have specific provisions making sure that a national judge is involved in the case. In the IACtHR, states may appoint an ad hoc judge to join the panel in cases where they are the respondent state, a practice that is similar to party-appointed arbitrators in investor–state dispute settlement (Larsson et al. 2023, 4). Larsson et al. report that in roughly half of all international courts, cases are decided by panels that include a judge from the respondent state.

Existing research shows that the nationality of judges matters. There is evidence across international courts that the national judge is susceptible to home-state bias, in the sense that they are less likely to decide against their member state compared to other judges (Posner and de Figueredo 2005; Voeten 2008; Naurin and Stiansen 2020). Whether that bias is a consequence of a careful screening of judges during the appointment procedure is a different question. A generous interpretation of the behaviour of national judges may be that they have a different—possibly better—understanding of the national law and conditions at stake in their home state. National differences in terms of culture and values may also generate variation in preferences on outcomes.

Stiansen (2022) has studied whether career concerns play a role for the behaviour of the national judge. He analyses the votes of individual ECtHR judges before and after the ratification in 2010 of a reform that changed the tenure of judges from six-year renewable terms to nine-year non-renewable terms. The findings demonstrate that judges became less prone to favour their nominating states after they no longer were eligible for reappointment. The effect was particularly significant among judges who were more likely to rely on the government of their nominating state for future employment opportunities, such as younger judges and judges from domestic courts, diplomacy, and the bureaucracy.

Stiansen's study shows that international judges anticipate and react to a perceived risk of losing their job, from making decisions that contrast with the preferences of their re-appointers. In doing so, he contributes both to general theories of judges' career concerns (Epstein, Landes, and Posner 2013) and to the debate over the political nature of international judicial appointments. Importantly, he also contributes to the domestic literature on US state courts on the link between retention incentives and judicial behaviour (Gray 2019), in particular by demonstrating how the importance of renewable terms as a sanctioning mechanism may depend on political actors' control of judges' career opportunities after their terms have expired.

Dunoff and Pollack (2017) have also theorized and studied the role of renewable terms for international judges. They argue that institutional designers of international courts face a 'judicial trilemma'. Out of three values that creators of international courts may want to promote—independence, accountability, and transparency—they have to forego one. Accountability is understood specifically as judges having renewable terms, with states controlling their reappointments (Dunoff and Pollack 2017, 234). According to the logic of the trilemma, judicial independence and accountability may be compatible only if there is no transparency with regards to votes and opinions of individual judges. If states are unable to monitor in which direction individual judges prefer to take the court's case law, they will not have to fear losing their job based on the substance of the decisions they make.

Dunoff and Pollack do not make any assumptions about judges' motivations for wanting to keep their job—whether it reflects career related concerns or whether they are policy-seekers who want to stay to make a difference to the case law. The key point is that rules and practices governing the removal of judges matter for judicial autonomy—according to the judges' own perceptions[4]—as long as they want to keep their job.[5] It is clear from this research that international judges perceive a potential threat of being ousted for political reasons.

The latter two studies are in many ways exemplary in how they integrate domestic and international literatures. Both Stiansen and Dunoff and Pollack show, unsurprisingly, that personal motivation, such as keeping your job, is an important driver of judicial behaviour in international courts as for domestic courts. More importantly, they also show how the extent to which judges will be constrained by or sheltered from such career related concerns is largely dependent on institutional design.

Overall, although the international context is different in important ways (multiple state principals, national differences between judges) there is little evidence that selection and retention of international judges are driven by different mechanisms compared to the national level, or that judicial behaviour is based on different motivations and incentives.

5. Backlashes against Domestic and International Court Authority

Both domestic and international courts increasingly face challenges from populist leaders who view courts as elitist and unjustifiable constraints on their exercise of power (e.g. Voeten 2019). What is new about these challenges is that they often come from democratically elected leaders in countries that were traditional supporters of international law and had apparently stable rule of law domestically. In some countries, efforts by strong elected leaders to curtail the judiciary were followed by democratic backsliding. But even in the United States and European democracies courts have become increasingly controversial in public debates. Recent public opinion research from Europe suggests that individuals do not really discriminate between international and domestic courts when they form views about whether they think their government should refuse to implement a court decision: all they care about is that the decision itself is undesirable (Madsen et al. 2022).

International judges have long faced challenges related to non-compliance as well as more serious challenges to their authority, including attempts to reform courts, hamstring courts, and (threats of) exit from courts. How have international judges responded to these challenges? And to what extent have studies of international and domestic court backlash engaged with each other?

There is considerable evidence that international judges on several courts have exercised more restraint in their jurisprudence in the anticipation of non-compliance and/or broader backlash. The extent and the form this behaviour takes depends on the specific institutional constraints and incentives for each court. However, the strategies used by international courts are recognizable to and relevant for how domestic courts may navigate challenges to their authority. For example, WTO decisions that extend precedent are less likely to be implemented (Kucik, Peritz, and Puig 2023). There is also evidence that the WTO Appellate Body has responded to political resistance by systematically and subtly modifying precedent in a more restrained direction (Kucik and Puig 2022). The Appellate Body also adopted informal norms against writing public dissents in order to protect Appellate Body members from the political repercussions of their rulings (Pauwelyn and Pelc 2022).

There is evidence that the ECtHR has resorted to similar strategies. The ECtHR has faced both collective and individual state challenges. Collectively, states have met in multiple conferences that were at least partially devoted to the discussion of reforms aimed at curtailing the Court. Eventually these conferences ended with declarations that offered few concrete formal institutional reforms but that nonetheless signalled to the Court that a substantial number of states were interested in a more restrained Court. Many of the practical reforms were ostensibly aimed at reducing the Court's caseload but they also had some limiting effects, such as reducing the time for applications to the court and allowing single judges to declare applications inadmissible. Moreover, the text of the declarations often referred extensively to principles like 'the margin of appreciation' and 'subsidiarity', which clearly signalled a desire that the Court should defer more often to national governments and courts. Individually states, including established democracies, have openly refused to implement certain judgments that were unpopular domestically. For example, the UK government repeatedly refused to implement the 2005 Hirst judgment on prisoner voting rights, including holding a vote in parliament that rejected implementation with an overwhelming majority. The case was finally closed in 2018 when the Council of Europe accepted a very minimal implementation plan that gave about 100 prisoners the right to vote.

The ECtHR evidence is consistent with the idea that international judges are sensitive to threats to the legitimacy of their court, which leads them to balance incentives to exercise restraint towards those who most threaten their court with incentives to maintain other sources of legitimacy, such as perceptions of legalism and impartiality. The ECtHR has adopted procedural approaches to meet both goals. The Court has started to refer more to the margin of appreciation and subsidiarity in its judgments (Madsen, Cebulak, and Wiebusch 2018). Başak Çali argues that the Court is developing a variable geometry approach that gives greater deference to member states that apply ECtHR case law in good faith while developing a 'bad faith jurisprudence' for states that flout established human rights standards; an approach that is greatly helped with references to the subsidiarity principle (Çali 2018).[6] An analysis of all ECtHR judgments through mid-2016 finds that the ECtHR has recently issued fewer violations against established democracies who publicly called for more restraint during multilateral conferences whereas violation rates against non-democracies and less-established democracies have remained steady (Stiansen and Voeten 2020). While the Court rarely explicitly reverses its past case law in a regressive direction, a recent study found that judges more often allege in their dissenting opinions that the Court is in fact walking back previous expansive case law in a more opaque way (Helfer and Voeten 2014).

Similarly, as the ECtHR, the WTO Appellate Body and domestic high courts (Vanberg 2005; Staton 2010; Clark 2011), research from the EU shows substantial evidence that the judges of the CJEU are sensitive to political challenges to its authority. Although this claim was initially controversial (Carrubba, Gabel, and Hankla 2012; Stone Sweet and Brunell 2012), most subsequent empirical studies have found that the Court, in addition to its own legal evaluation of the issues at hand, also takes into account the concerns of EU member states as expressed in their submitted observations to the Court (Carrubba and Gabel 2015; Martinsen 2015; Larsson and Naurin 2016; Larsson et al. 2017; Larsson and Naurin 2019; Hermansen 2020; Ovadek 2021; Schroeder 2023; Schroeder and Lindholm 2023; Stobb and Scalera-Elliott 2023). One study finds that the CJEU is less likely to rule against member states in infringement cases closer to treaty negotiations that may affect the Court's jurisdiction (Castro-Montero et al. 2018), while another study connects shifts in the case law of the Court with regards to citizen rights to shifts in public opinion (Blauberger et al. 2018).

Whether the responsiveness to external social-political preferences is due to concerns for non-compliance, legislative or constitutional override, or other negative reactions to the status of the Court, or whether it reflects an alignment of preferences between judges and appointing member states, or simply the reasonable response from judges working under uncertainty about the broader policy impact of their case law, are questions with which the research on the CJEU—just as the comparative research on judicial autonomy focusing on domestic courts—continues to grapple. The research on the CJEU that is referred to here, without exception, builds on and refers to general theories of judicial behaviour that were developed and tested in other contexts. More generally, the strategies adopted by the WTO Appellate Body, the ECtHR, and the CJEU are not particular to international courts: they could be adopted by domestic courts with fragile authority.

Other areas where scholars of international courts have made important contributions to theories of judicial behaviour include judicial reasoning and opinion writing. Citation analysis from the EctHR (Lupu and Voeten 2012) and the CJEU (Larsson et al. 2017) finds that these courts use references to case law in a strategic manner, by more carefully embedding controversial judgments in previous case law to boost their persuasiveness in the eyes of domestic courts and EU member states. Furthermore, one study uses citation analysis to show that judges at the CJEU are more likely to cite opinions authored by judges appointed by member state governments with similar political ideologies (Frankenreiter 2017).

Scholars have also used linguistic analysis to demonstrate that international courts adjust their wording depending on challenges to compliance and other external threats to their authority. One study shows that the WTO Appellate Body uses more affect-laden words when it adjudicates politically sensitive questions, arguing that such language may increase the chances of compliance (Busch and Pelc 2019). Another study provides evidence that the CJEU varies the certainty of its language depending on whether it restricts member states' autonomy. The Court speaks with greater confidence when expanding the rights associated with EU citizenship compared to when it defers more control to member states in the area of EU citizens' rights (Stobb and Scalera-Elliott 2023).

A further line of research considers the trade-off that courts and other regulatory agencies face when tasked with identifying effective remedies in case of violations of legal rules. Building on Staton and Vanberg's formal work on the value of vagueness in opinion writing (Staton and Vanberg 2008), research on the human rights regimes in Europe (Stiansen 2021) and Latin America (Staton and Romero 2019) have demonstrated how fine tuning the degree of specificity in judicial orders, with regards to what is required of states that have violated their legal obligations, have important effects for the likelihood of compliance and effective policy change.

6. Conclusions

We have argued that the field of judicial behaviour is still not in the process of converging into one coherent literature across national and international courts despite the pleas of Staton and Moore over a decade ago. The broader citation patterns indicate that the divide between research focusing on US courts and courts in other countries and international regimes seems especially hard to overcome. The divisions are not entirely surprising or always unreasonable. The literature on international courts is to some degree, and for good reasons, more focused on the specific structural conditions for judicial autonomy and effectiveness that are generated by the international context and by the fact that many of these courts are relatively new and in need of developing and confirming their authority (Carrubba 2009). Scholars focusing on judicial behaviour in US courts already have a large body of work to build on, and a specific home audience to talk to, and thus fewer incentives to engage in a search for theoretical work or sources for empirical variation outside the usual context.

However, we also show that much of the research on international courts that has been done in the decade after Staton and Moore published their article has in fact integrated work on both domestic and international judicial behaviour. This body of research has demonstrated the usefulness of building on theories from different institutional and social-political contexts, both to better understand judicial behaviour in a specific empirical setting and to contribute to general theory development. The field of judicial behaviour was shaped in very large part by research on the United States. Comparative scholars have added additional case studies that examine existing theories and pose new questions and theories. Some scholarship on international judicial behaviour has tested theories about the effects of reappointment, gender, dissents, and other general factors in settings that span multiple countries. We argue that this scholarship should be considered by the US and comparative literature. Moreover, the international judicial behaviour literature has generated vast knowledge about how the fragility of judicial authority shapes judicial behaviour. Domestic court scholars can learn from this body of literature as concerns over judicial authority gain prominence in numerous settings.

Notes

1. 'International Criminal Court' OR 'international court' OR 'European Court' OR ('WTO' AND 'dispute') OR 'Court of Justice' OR 'Inter-American Court' OR 'Court of Human Rights' OR 'African Court' OR 'ISDS' OR 'investment tribunal' OR ('trade' AND 'dispute') OR ('investment' AND 'dispute') OR 'dispute settlement body' OR 'investor–state disputes' OR 'Supreme Court' OR 'Constitutional Court' OR 'Appellate Court'. We searched for all fields.

2. If we include 'International Relations' this would yield a lot of law journals. Most research on judicial behaviour in international courts is published in journals that are also listed under political science.
3. The precise search terms are: "JUDICIAL|BEHAVIOR|BEHAVIOUR|JUSTICES |DECISION-MAKING|CHOICE|DISSENT|COMPLIANCE|JUDICIAL POLITICS|APP OINTMENT|ACCOUNTABILITY|RESPONSIVENESS|BIAS|IDEOLOGY|ATTITUDIN AL|JUDGES| JUSTICES|LEGITIMACY|INDEPENDENCE|CITATIONS"
4. The research is primarily based on writings by international judges and interviews with current and former judges and court officials at four international courts (CJEU, WTO AB, ECtHR, ICJ).
5. Dunoff and Pollack do not consider rules governing the removal of judges during their term, which may also be relevant for judicial autonomy.
6. Çali (2018) 242.

References

Alter, Karen J. 2008. 'Agents or Trustees? International Courts in Their Political Context'. *European Journal of International Relations* 14 (1): 33–63. https://doi.org/10.1177/1354066107087769.

Aria, Massimo, and Corrado Cuccurullo. 2017. 'Bibliometrix: An R-Tool for Comprehensive Science Mapping Analysis'. *Journal of Informetrics* 11 (4): 959–75. https://doi.org/10.1016/j.joi.2017.08.007.

Blauberger, Michael, Anita Heindlmaier, Dion Kramer, Dorte Sindbjerg Martinsen, Jessica Sampson Thierry, Angelika Schenk, and Benjamin Werner. 2018. 'ECJ Judges Read the Morning Papers. Explaining the Turnaround of European Citizenship Jurisprudence'. *Journal of European Public Policy* 25 (10): 1422–41.

Burley, Anne-Marie, and Walter Mattli. 1993. 'Europe Before the Court: A Political Theory of Legal Integration'. *International Organization* 47 (1): 41–76. https://doi.org/10.1017/S0020818300004707.

Busch, Marc L., and Krzysztof J. Pelc. 2010. 'The Politics of Judicial Economy at the World Trade Organization'. *International Organization* 64 (2): 257–79. https://doi.org/10.1017/S0020818310000020.

Busch, Marc L., and Krzysztof J. Pelc. 2019. 'Words Matter: How WTO Rulings Handle Controversy'. *International Studies Quarterly* 63 (3): 464–76.

Caldeira, Gregory A., and James L. Gibson. 1995. 'The Legitimacy of the Court of Justice in the European Union: Models of Institutional Support'. *The American Political Science Review* 89 (2): 356–76. https://doi.org/10.2307/2082430.

Çali, Basak. 2018. 'Coping with Crisis: Whither the Variable Geometry in the Jurisprudence of the European Court of Human Rights'. *SSRN Scholarly Paper ID 3128198*. https://papers.ssrn.com/abstract=3128198.

Cameron, Charles M., Albert D. Cover, and Jeffrey A. Segal. 1990. 'Senate Voting on Supreme Court Nominees: A Neoinstitutional Model'. *The American Political Science Review* 84 (2): 525–34.

Carrubba, Clifford J., Matthew Gabel, and Charles Hankla. 2008. 'Judicial Behavior under Political Constraints: Evidence from the European Court of Justice'. *The American Political Science Review* 102 (4): 435–52. https://doi.org/10.1017/S0003055408080350.

Carrubba, Clifford James. 2009. 'A Model of the Endogenous Development of Judicial Institutions in Federal and International Systems'. *The Journal of Politics* 71 (1): 55–69.

Carruba, Clifford J., Matthew Gabel, and Charles Hankla. 2012. 'Understanding the Role of the European Court of Justice in European Integration'. *American Political Science Review* 106 (1): 214–23. https://doi.org/10.1017/S0003055412000020.

Carrubba, Clifford J., and Matthew J. Gabel. 2015. *International Courts and the Performance of International Agreements: A General Theory with Evidence from the European Union. Comparative Constitutional Law and Policy*. New York, NY: Cambridge University Press.

Castro-Montero, José Luis, Edwin Alblas, Arthur Dyevre, and Nicolas Lampach. 2018. 'The Court of Justice and Treaty Revision: A Case of Strategic Leniency?' *European Union Politics* 19 (4): 570–96.

Chayes, Abram, and Antonia Handler Chayes. 1993. 'On Compliance'. *International Organization* 47 (2): 175–205. https://doi.org/10.1017/S0020818300027910.

Clark, Thomas S. 2011. *The Limits of Judicial Independence*. Cambridge; New York: Cambridge University Press.

Downs, George W., David M. Rocke, and Peter N. Barsoom. 1996. 'Is the Good News about Compliance Good News about Cooperation?' *International Organization* 50 (3): 379–406. https://doi.org/10.1017/S0020818300033427.

Dunoff, Jeffrey L., and Mark A. Pollack. 2017. 'The Judicial Trilemma'. *The American Journal of International Law* 111 (2): 225–76.

Elsig, Manfred, and Mark A. Pollack. 2014. 'Agents, Trustees, and International Courts: The Politics of Judicial Appointment at the World Trade Organization'. *European Journal of International Relations* 20 (2): 391–415.

Epstein, Lee, William M. Landes, and Richard A. Posner. 2013. *The Behavior of Federal Judges*. Cambridge: Harvard University Press.

Epstein, Lee, René Lindstädt, Jeffrey A. Segal, and Chad Westerland. 2006. 'The Changing Dynamics of Senate Voting on Supreme Court Nominees'. *The Journal of Politics* 68 (2): 296–307.

Ferejohn, John A., and Barry R. Weingast. 1992. 'A Positive Theory of Statutory Interpretation'. *International Review of Law and Economics* 12 (2): 263–79.

Frankenreiter, Jens. 2017. 'The Politics of Citations at the ECJ—Policy Preferences of E.U. Member State Governments and the Citation Behavior of Judges at the European Court of Justice'. *Journal of Empirical Legal Studies* 14 (4): 813–57.

Gibson, James L., and Gregory A. Caldeira. 1995. 'The Legitimacy of Transnational Legal Institutions: Compliance, Support, and the European Court of Justice'. *American Journal of Political Science* 39 (2): 459–89. https://doi.org/10.2307/2111621.

Gibson, James L., Gregory A. Caldeira, and Vanessa A. Baird. 1998. 'On the Legitimacy of National High Courts'. *The American Political Science Review* 92 (2): 343–58.

Ginsburg, Tom. 2003. *Judicial Review in New Democracies: Constitutional Courts in Asian Cases*. Cambridge: Cambridge University Press.

Gray, Thomas R. 2019. 'Executive Influence on State Supreme Court Justices: Strategic Deference in Reappointment States'. *Journal of Law, Economics, & Organization* 35 (2): 422–53.

Helfer, Laurence R., and Erik Voeten. 2014. 'International Courts as Agents of Legal Change: Evidence from LGBT Rights in Europe'. *International Organization* 68 (01): 77–110. https://doi.org/10.1017/S0020818313000398.

Hermansen, Silje Synnøve Lyder. 2020. 'Building Legitimacy: Strategic Case Allocations in the Court of Justice of the European Union'. *Journal of European Public Policy* 27 (8): 1215–35.

Hermansen Synnøve Lyder, Silje, and Daniel Naurin. 2019. 'Will Do? Selecting Judges on the Basis of Policy Preferences or Performance Indicators'. Paper presented at the American Political Science Association Annual Conference, Boston, August 30–September 2.

Hetherington, Marc J. 1998. 'The Political Relevance of Political Trust'. *The American Political Science Review* 92 (4): 791–808.

Johns, Leslie. 2015. *Strengthening International Courts*. Ann Arbor: University of Michigan Press. https://doi.org/10.3998/mpub.7388936.

Kelemen, R. Daniel. 2012. 'The Political Foundations of Judicial Independence in the European Union'. *Journal of European Public Policy* 19 (1): 43–58.

Keohane, Robert O., Andrew Moravcsik, and Anne-Marie Slaughter. 2000. 'Legalized Dispute Resolution: Interstate and Transnational'. *International Organization* 54 (3): 457–88. https://doi.org/10.1162/002081800551299.

Koremenos, Barbara, Charles Lipson, and Duncan Snidal. 2001. 'The Rational Design of International Institutions'. *International Organization* 55 (4): 761–99.

Kucik, Jeffrey, Lauren Peritz, and Sergio Puig. 2023. 'Legalization and Compliance: How Judicial Activity Undercuts the Global Trade Regime'. *British Journal of Political Science* 53 (1): 221–38.

Kucik, Jeffrey, and Sergio Puig. 2022. 'Do International Dispute Bodies Overreach? Reassessing World Trade Organization Dispute Ruling'. *International Studies Quarterly* 66 (4): 1–8.

Larsson, Olof, and Daniel Naurin. 2016. 'Judicial Independence and Political Uncertainty: How the Risk of Override Affects the Court of Justice of the EU'. *International Organization* 70 (2): 377–408. https://doi.org/10.1017/S0020818316000047.

Larsson, Olof, and Daniel Naurin. 2019. 'Split Vision: Multidimensionality in the European Union's Legal Policy Space'. *International Studies Quarterly* 63 (3): 492–506.

Larsson, Olof, Daniel Naurin, Mattias Derlen, and Johan Lindholm. 2017. 'Speaking Law to Power: The Strategic Use of Precedent of the Court of Justice of the European Union'. *Comparative Political Studies* 50 (7): 879–907. https://doi.org/10.1177/0010414016639709.

Larsson, Olof, Theresa Squatrito, Øyvind Stiansen, and Taylor St John. 2023. 'Selection and Appointment in International Adjudication: Insights from Political Science'. *Journal of International Dispute Settlement* 14 (2): 134–48.

Lupu, Yonatan, and Erik Voeten. 2012. 'Precedent in International Courts: A Network Analysis of Case Citations by the European Court of Human Rights'. *British Journal of Political Science* 42 (2): 413–39. https://doi.org/10.1017/S0007123411000433.

Mackenzie, Ruth, Kate Malleson, Penny Martin, and Q. C. Philippe Sands. 2010. *Selecting International Judges: Principle, Process, and Politics*. Oxford: Oxford University Press. https://doi.org/10.1093/acprof:oso/9780199580569.001.0001.

Madsen, Mikael Rask, Pola Cebulak, and Micha Wiebusch. 2018. 'Backlash against International Courts: Explaining the Forms and Patterns of Resistance to International Courts'. *International Journal of Law in Context* 14 (2): 197–220. https://doi.org/10.1017/S1744552318000034.

Madsen, Mikael Rask, Juan A. Mayoral, Anton Strezhnev, and Erik Voeten. 2022. 'Sovereignty, Substance, and Public Support for European Courts' Human Rights Rulings'. *The American Political Science Review* 116 (2): 419–38. https://doi.org/10.1017/S0003055421001143.

Martinsen, Dorte Sindbjerg. 2015. *An Ever More Powerful Court? The Political Constraints of Legal Integration in the European Union*. Oxford: Oxford University Press.

Melton, James, and Tom Ginsburg. 2014. 'Does De Jure Judicial Independence Really Matter? A Reevaluation of Explanations for Judicial Independence'. *Journal of Law and Courts* 2 (2): 187–217.

Moravcsik, Andrew. 2000. 'The Origins of Human Rights Regimes: Democratic Delegation in Postwar Europe'. *International Organization* 54 (2): 217–52.

Naurin, Daniel, and Oyvind Stiansen. 2020. 'The Dilemma of Dissent: Split Judicial Decisions and Compliance With Judgments From the International Human Rights Judiciary'. *Comparative Political Studies* 53 (6): 959–91. https://doi.org/10.1177/0010414019879944.

North, Douglass C., and Barry R. Weingast. 1989. 'Constitutions and Commitment: The Evolution of Institutions Governing Public Choice in Seventeenth-Century England'. *The Journal of Economic History* 49 (4): 803–32.

Ovadek, Michal. 2021. 'Supranationalism, Constrained? Locating the Court of Justice on the EU Integration Dimension'. *European Union Politics* 22 (1): 46–69.

Pauwelyn, Joost, and Krzysztof Pelc. 2022. 'WTO Rulings and the Veil of Anonymity'. *European Journal of International Law* 33 (2): 527–64.

Pollack, M. A. 1997. 'Delegation, Agency, and Agenda Setting in the European Community'. *International Organization* 51 (1): 99+. https://doi.org/10.1162/002081897550311.

Pollack, Mark A. 2003. *The Engines of European Integration: Delegation, Agency, and Agenda Setting in the EU*. Oxford: Oxford University Press.

Posner, Eric A., and Miguel F. P. de Figueiredo. 2005. 'Is the International Court of Justice Biased?' *The Journal of Legal Studies* 34 (2): 599–630.

Rogers, James R. 2001. 'Information and Judicial Review: A Signaling Game of Legislative-Judicial Interaction'. *American Journal of Political Science* 45 (1): 84–99.

Romano, Cesare P. R. 1999. 'The Proliferation of International Judicial Bodies: The Pieces of the Puzzle'. *New York University Journal of International Law & Politics* 31 (4): 709–51.

Schroeder, Philipp. 2023. 'Seizing Opportunities: The Determinants of the CJEU's Deference to National Courts'. *Journal of European Public Policy* 1–24.

Schroeder, Philipp, and Johan Lindholm. 2023. 'From One to Many: Identifying Issues in CJEU Jurisprudence'. *Journal of Law and Courts* 11 (1): 163–86.

Simmons, Beth A. 2009. *Mobilizing for Human Rights: International Law in Domestic Politics. Mobilizing for Human Rights*. New York: Cambridge University Press.

Staton, Jeffrey K. 2010. *Judicial Power and Strategic Communication in Mexico*. New York: Cambridge University Press.

Staton, Jeffrey K., and Will H. Moore. 2011. 'Judicial Power in Domestic and International Politics'. *International Organization* 65 (3): 553–87. https://doi.org/10.1017/S0020818311000130.

Staton, Jeffrey K., Christopher Reenock, and Jordan Holsinger. 2022. *Can Courts Be Bulwarks of Democracy? Judges and the Politics of Prudence*. Cambridge: Cambridge University Press. https://doi.org/10.1017/9781009030939.

Staton, Jeffrey K., and Alexia Romero. 2019. 'Rational Remedies: The Role of Opinion Clarity in the Inter-American Human Rights System'. *International Studies Quarterly* 63 (3): 477–91.

Staton, Jeffrey K., and Georg Vanberg. 2008. 'The Value of Vagueness: Delegation, Defiance, and Judicial Opinions'. *American Journal of Political Science* 52 (3): 504–19.

Stiansen, Oyvind. 2021. 'Directing Compliance? Remedial Approach and Compliance with European Court of Human Rights Judgments'. *British Journal of Political Science* 51 (2): 899–907. https://doi.org/10.1017/S0007123419000292.

Stiansen, Øyvind. 2022. '(Non)Renewable Terms and Judicial Independence in the European Court of Human Rights'. *The Journal of Politics* 84 (2): 992–1006.

Stiansen, Øyvind, and Erik Voeten. 2020. 'Backlash and Judicial Restraint: Evidence from the European Court of Human Rights'. *International Studies Quarterly* 64 (4): 770–84. https://doi.org/10.1093/isq/sqaa047.

Stimson, J. A., M. B. Mackuen, and R. S. Erikson. 1995. 'Dynamic Representation'. *The American Political Science Review* 89 (3): 543–65. https://doi.org/10.2307/2082973.

Stobb, Maureen, and Jamie Scalera-Elliott. 2023. 'Crafting the Language of Borders: The European Court of Justice's Strategic Opinion Writing in Rights Cases'. *Law & Policy*. https://doi.org/10.1111/lapo.12227.

Stone Sweet, Alec, and Thomas Brunell. 2012. 'The European Court of Justice, State Noncompliance, and the Politics of Override'. *The American Political Science Review* 106 (1): 204–13. https://doi.org/10.1017/S0003055412000019.

Vanberg, Georg. 2005. *The Politics of Constitutional Review in Germany. Political Economy of Institutions and Decisions*. Cambridge: Cambridge University Press.

Voeten, Erik. 2007. 'The Politics of International Judicial Appointments: Evidence from the European Court of Human Rights'. *International Organization* 61 (4): 669–701.

Voeten, Erik. 2008. 'The Impartiality of International Judges: Evidence from the European Court of Human Rights'. *The American Political Science Review* 102 (04): 417–33. https://doi.org/10.1017/S0003055408080398.

Voeten, Erik. 2014. 'Does Participation in International Organizations Increase Cooperation?' *Review of International Organizations* 9 (3): 285–308.

Voeten, Erik. 2020. 'Populism and Backlashes against International Courts'. *Perspectives on Politics* 18 (2): 407–22.

Voeten, Erik. 2021. 'Gender and Judging: Evidence from the European Court of Human Rights'. *Journal of European Public Policy* 28 (9): 1453–73. https://doi.org/10.1080/13501763.2020.1786146.

PART II

APPROACHES TO JUDGING

CHAPTER 6

LEGALISM AND PROFESSIONAL NORMS

ALEXANDER MORELL

1. Introduction to Legalism

Epstein, Šadl, and Weinshall (2021, 702) defined legalism in 'its simplest form' to hold that 'the law is "out there", distinct from morals and politics, legal rules are determinate, the legal system is complete'. The elements of this definition can also be found in Shklar (1986, 1, 7, 10, 33–34, 48–49). Segal and Spaeth (2002, 53–85), while starting out with a broader scope, ultimately work with a similar definition. One rare occasion to witness simple legalism from up close is when, in Senate hearings live on TV, Supreme Court nominees commit to deciding solely on the basis of value-free analysis of legal materials (Klein 2017, 2–3). Otherwise, however, dispassionate judges have been likened to the Easter Bunny (Justice Robert Jackson dissenting in US vs. Ballard, 322 U.S. 78 (1944) and the theory that judges pronounce the law as they find it 'out there' to a fairytale (Lord James Reid 1972, 22). The statements by Supreme Court nominees are widely dismissed as 'charade' (Klein 2017, 2), and even authors building their careers on refuting simple legalism admit that no-one actually argues that law is all that determines judicial decision (Segal and Spaeth 1996, 974).

Simple legalism is hard to find in the field. One reason may be that it is a hotchpotch of distinct and partially contradicting theories of law. Of its four claims it draws its first (that the law is 'out there') from the declaratory theory of law according to which judges merely declare what the law says about the case without modifying it (famously found in Montesquieu (1748) 1871, book 11, ch. 6, page 149). The second claim eliminates morals and politics from the set of legal considerations—a position that legalism derives from positivism in its 'hard' variety (Edwards and Livermore 2009, 1901). Implicit in the third and fourth claims of simple legalism (that legal rules are determinate and the legal system is complete) is to view judicial decision-making as a 'mechanistic process' of deduction. In that regard, simple legalism draws from legal formalism of the nineteenth century, which demanded to derive a case's outcome from the facts and the law by means of syllogistic logic (Posner 1986, 181; Leiter 2010b, 111, 114). While a large volume of empirical studies of judicial decision-making have used value-free mechanical application of the law 'as it is' as a benchmark (Edwards and Livermore 2009, 1915; Baum 2010, 5), many legal scholars and practitioners hold more nuanced positions to describe how judges make decisions. The following chapter will highlight some of these nuances and connect them to empirical scholarship on judicial decision-making.

The chapter is comparative in three dimensions. In a comparison between disciplines, it compares the narratives of judicial decision-making between the fields of empirical research and legal scholarship. Here, it will compare how empirical scholars use the term 'legalism' and how it is understood in legal scholarship. In a comparison within legal scholarship, it compares some of these legal narratives, as jurists hold varying views about what the law is and does. In an international comparison that is somewhat limited by the mainly German legal education of the author, it compares such narratives between common law jurisdictions and continental civil law ones. Beyond mere comparison, the chapter will sketch the different implications that empirical findings have for these different views. As a mirror image, the chapter analyses problems that arise for empirical analysis of judicial decision-making. I will close with some suggestions for future research ensuing from the comparative analysis. The chapter does not aspire to be complete on any of these accounts. Instead, it aims at highlighting selected aspects that I hope could inspire the reinterpretation of old findings or inspire studies making interesting new ones.

2. The Declaratory Theory of Law and Formalism

Simple legalism holds that 'the law is "out there"', that 'legal rules are determinate [and] the legal system is complete'. The first claim derives from the declaratory theory of law, which shall be spelled out in the following. The second and the third originate in formalism that I will introduce thereafter. Both approaches to law are closely related.

2.1 The Declaratory Theory of Law

The declaratory theory of law is still actively promoted, albeit its supporters may be more frequent in the United Kingdom and continental Europe than in the United States. Dworkin's ideal of law as a unique right answer (Dworkin 1978) seems to draw from declaratory theory although the constructive aspects of Dworkin's position appear incompatible with the declaratory theory. In Germany few authors seem to explicitly adhere to the declaratory theory but the roots of modern German legal scholarship reach deep into declaratory thinking.

2.1.1 *The Declaratory Theory in the Common Law*

The declaratory theory of law is commonly associated with ancient authors of the eighteenth century. According to William Blackstone ((1765–1779) 1897, 20), when courts change their mind, 'judges do not pretend to make new law, but to vindicate the old one from misrepresentation'. In its more radical take, it indeed claims that the law exists 'out there' and remains unaltered as judges derive their decisions from it. In that variety it links to natural law theory. Beever (2013, 441) claims that the declaratory theory of law in its radical form is a 'fundamental working assumption' for any legal system despite being treated as 'something of a mystical belief'. 'Fulfilling the law is a matter of making the positive law more accurately reflect this abstract enduring law' (Beever 2013, 428–29), he writes. Judges may change the concrete reading of the law but the abstract principles of justice remain unaltered (Beever 2013, 432). More often, however, the declaratory theory is formulated as a norm that should guide judicial behaviour rather than a description of it. In the paragraph cited above, Blackstone wrote:

> he [the judge] being sworn to determine, according to the known laws and customs of the land; not delegated to pronounce a new law, but to maintain and expound the old one. The exception is where the former determination is incorrect much more if it be clearly contrary to divine law. But even in such cases the subsequent judges do not pretend to make a new law but to vindicate the old one from misrepresentation.
>
> (Blackstone (1765–1779) 1897, 20)

The quotation nicely illustrates the understanding that the law is 'out there'. It also shows that this is hardly a descriptive account of what judges do. The judges have sworn to act accordingly. That conveys upon them a duty to abide. Who should ever know whether they do?

2.1.2 *The German 'Historische Rechtsschule' and a Declaratory Theory of Civil Law*

In the times of Blackstone, on the continent, Montesquieu ((1748) 1871, book 11, ch. 6) famously wrote that the judge is 'nothing but the mouth of the law'. However, the declaratory theory of law was not only at the heart of eighteenth century English and French legal thinking but also of the nineteenth century '*Historische Rechtsschule*' (historical school of jurists). A central belief of the *Historische Rechtsschule*, whose most prominent proponents were Friedrich Carl von Savigny and his student Carl Friedrich Puchta, was that the law is latent (i.e. not in explicit rules), manifested in the continuous evolution of systematic meanings of legal institutions and rights (Haferkamp 2004–2023; Rückert 2004–2023; Somek 2010, 343). These legal institutions were thought to originate in the '*Volksgeist*' (spirit of the people), a concept Puchta adopted from Hegel (Haferkamp 2004–2023; Somek 2010, 342). As legal practitioners and scholars explicate legal concepts from the system, they work as the people's legal conscience (Somek 2010, 343). This line of thought resonates with the idea of 'the law' as some abstract and unalterable order of principles and adds the idea of a system that would allow exploring this order by rational conceptual reasoning.

This declaratory approach to law included a limitation to the power of the legislatures, which, at the time in Germany, were absolutist monarchs. Law could not be arbitrarily created by a ruler but had to be derived from prior law by means of technical methods. The legal system created by jurists thus constituted a check to absolutist power (Grechenig and Gelter 2008, 546). Accordingly, Savigny was opposed to the codification of German private law as he thought that such law would be the expression of authoritarian power rather than of the people's will (Savigny 1814). His counterpart, Anton Friedrich Justus Thibaut found this position excessively conservative and a hindrance to any improvement of the people's living conditions. In his mind, laws were to fulfil reasonable purposes (Thibaut 1814). The Savigny–Thibaut controversy (Rückert 2004–2023) parallels that between Blackstone and Bentham (Grechenig and Gelter 2008, 545).

2.2 Formalism

Closely connected to the declaratory theory of law is legal formalism; a current of thought favouring form over substance that Alexis de Tocqueville (1936, 169), Max Weber (1921), and Judith Shklar believed to observe among legal practitioners in very different times and places (Shklar 1986, 14).

2.2.1 *Formalism as Described by US and UK Authors*

Leiter (2010a, 262–63) defines formalism as the belief that judicial decisions flow from axiomatic definitions. According to a wider definition, legal formalists find that legal sources and methods are sufficient to justify legal decisions (Leiter 2010a, 262–63; Weinrib 2010, 327). Dworkin, Bork, and Scalia were counted among influential modern champions of this current (Leiter 2010b, 112). In a tradition going back to Aristotle, formalism attempts to guarantee impartial rational decisions by means of syllogistic deduction (Shklar 1987, 3). To enable logical deduction, formalism relies on the belief that the law exists as a coherent system (Weinrib 2010, 336; Troop 2018, 429). Valid justifications must be coherent with what is known of that system. For formalists, coherence is the 'truth criterion' of legal justification (Weinrib 1988, 969–73). Immanent in the system, they say, is some ethical value that unveils itself in its coherence (Weinrib 1988, 953–55).

Closer inspection reveals two distinct currents of formalism. One, which Troop (2018, 433) calls 'rule formalism', is built around the idea of logically deducing the law from a coherent system of abstract principles. This is what some see as mechanical (Pound 1908; Leiter 2010b, 114, citing Kennedy). In the extreme, authors held the view that the law is completely determinate (Montesquieu (1748) 1871, book 11, ch. 6; Leiter 2010b, 111) and their taste for logical deduction explains why formalists deeply appreciate rules (Scalia 1989, 1176–80). Ultimately, formalists hope that following doctrine faithfully will guarantee objectivity in the application of the law (Millon 1992, 3). However, the system of black-letter law is neither complete nor do judges confine themselves to deducing from 'the law'. In fact, they also complete, amend, and change it. The project of objectivity is likely to fail where the system leaves some discretion to judges and formalist theory provides neither any guidance nor any standard by which to hold judges accountable. On top of that, rule formalism has a hard time explaining how the law came about. In early common law there was no black letter law from which to deduce (Troop 2018, 434) so that it remains unclear how any legal system could have built up legally.

The second current of formalism is concerned with producing a scientific account of law (Leiter 2010a, 263; Troop 2018, 428). Much like a psychological version of the declaratory theory (Troop 2018, 432), it assumes that there is a joint disposition of judges called 'doctrine' (Troop 2018, 429) that causes judges to decide as they do. This doctrine can be represented by a set of rules predicting judicial behaviour—not unlike natural laws allow predicting natural events. Legal scholarship is bound to uncover this set of rules (Troop 2018, 429). Actual court decisions serve to test and refine this representation (Troop 2018, 431). Blackstone provides a classic description of doctrinal formalism when he writes '(t)he law and the opinion of the judge are not always convertible terms, or one and the same thing, since it sometimes may happen, that the judge may mistake the law. But as a rule, the decisions of courts of justice are the evidence of what is common law' (Blackstone (1765–1779) 1897, 20). Doctrinal formalism is not normative but descriptive. It does not say how judges should decide but aims at predicting judicial decisions (Troop 2018, 430).

Dworkin's theory of law has a formalistic touch in its promotion of integrity to guide the judge towards a unique correct decision. Dworkin postulates that there are moral principles binding the law into a coherent whole so that cases must be decided in the spirit that the answer to a case makes the law more coherent (Dworkin 1986, 176, 219, 269–71).

2.2.2 *German Formalism: 'Begriffsjurisprudenz'*

Although Posner (1986, 181–82) wrote that the distinction between formalism and realism only makes sense for the common law, continental legal thinking has produced formalist schools. In Germany, formalism's sister school is pejoratively (Seinecke 2012, 125) called '*Begriffsjurisprudenz*' (conceptual jurisprudence). As the *Historische Rechtsschule* progressed in constructing more and more institutions, rights, and legal concepts, these evolved into a complex and allegedly coherent system from which one could blindly derive judicial decisions without much regard for the individual case. Ultimately, the *Begriffsjurisprudenz* was ridiculed for isolating itself from the (social) reality of its time (Jhering [1884] 1904).

2.3 Empirical Implications of the Declaratory Theory of Law and Formalism

The declaratory theory of law itself is more of a founding myth of law than a description of what judges do. As a norm it does not lend itself to empirical testing. It may structure peoples' expectations regarding judicial behaviour and could be likened to a religious belief. It is also hard to come up with a benchmark that allows measuring the degree of adherence to formalist decision-making. Which cases are easy, that is, those mainly determined by law? Which are hard, that is, leave the judge considerable leeway? Indeed, even if we could agree on the fraction of easy cases among all litigated ones, we would still debate (as Edwards and Livermore 2009, 1898, and Posner 2010, 1180 did in fact) about whether these are many (the system is pretty complete) or few (it is incomplete). Doctrinal formalists, instead, would consider themselves empirical scholars but as there is no way to distinguish 'erroneous' judgments from judgments falsifying prior beliefs about the content of the law, this empiricism strikes me to hold little promise. Ultimately, formalism in its entirety may be best described as a normative theory, too, another foundational narrative, crafted to help judges abstract from their own desires, attitudes, and convictions, to let them focus—in as far as this is possible—on a common consensus or a common good.

The effects of narratives (Shiller 2019) and of religion (Hoffmann 2012; Iyer 2016) on human behaviour by way of shaping beliefs as well as providing group cohesion, values, and social norms have recently begun to be put to some empirical scrutiny. Along similar lines, the effect of beliefs in the declaratory theory of law or in formalism on judicial behaviour may be conducive to empirical study and promise fascinating insights in principle. However, while religious people and atheists may readily state their beliefs in free and tolerant societies, judges may report their professional beliefs less honestly as they could be exposed to strong normative expectations.

3. Realism, *Freirecht*, and the Attitudinal Model

In the earlier decades of the last century, legal realism dealt a blow to the formalist description of judicial decision-making from which it would never fully recover—at least not in the United States and in social science circles. In arguing both that formalistic legal reasoning is neither possible nor even desirable, legal realists deprived rule-formalism of its very foundations. This might be less so for doctrinal formalism.

3.1 Legal Realism

From a theoretical point of view, legal realism argued that the judge is essentially unconstrained when deciding (sufficiently hard) cases. Cases cannot be solved by pure syllogistic deduction (Holmes (1897) 1997, 1000; Pound 1908), because logic is useless for finding a premise (Posner 1986, 182). Instead, premises are found by interpreting the law and interpretation is not logic (Posner 1986, 187). Also, they claimed, there are many legitimate ways to reason from the sources resulting in many conflicting legal rules so that ultimately the judge will find legal support for whatever result she wants to achieve (Leiter 2010a, 253). The sole reason to place rules or precedent into a system is to make law easier to remember and teach (Holmes (1897) 1997, 992). Ultimately, blindly applying 'the law' to cases results in absurd outcomes (Holmes (1897) 1997, 997; Pound 1908) and in superfluous or equally absurd doctrinal distinction (Holmes (1897) 1997, 995). All in all, realist arguments result in the view that judges decide cases by personal preference and rationalize their decisions post hoc using legal arguments to conceal any policy choice that would rather have been openly justified (Holmes (1897) 1997, 1000; Posner 1986, 212).

The realist claim that the only role left for legal scholarship is to predict the outcomes of future cases (Holmes (1897) 1997, 992) is compatible with doctrinal formalism. However, realists believed that such predictions will be more accurate if made with the help of social sciences rather than 'doctrine' (Holmes (1897) 1997, 1002). Legal realists did not deplore that the law is incapable of determining the decisions of cases. Open realism, they hoped, would enable public democratic policy debate (Holmes (1897) 1997, 1000–01) to overcome current conditions and achieve beneficial reform (Grechenig and Gelter 2008, 543).

3.2 *Freirecht*: A German Sister Movement of Legal Realism

Again, similar thoughts evolved in Europe at around the same time. In Germany, Eugen Ehrlich promoted 'free' jurisprudence by which the judge legislates where, as is frequently the case, the judicial decision cannot be derived from the letters of the law (Ehrlich [1903] 1967). Hermann Kantorowicz (1906, 22), writing under the pseudonym Gnaeus Flavius, criticized the methods of the *Begriffsjurisprudenz* in a programmatic text as detaching legal practice from reality and leading to absurd outcomes. Successors of the *Begriffsjurisprudenz* had conceded that the black-letter law was not complete but thought the system of 'law' remained complete because one could induce abstract principles ('*rationes leges*') from which to derive the rules to fill in the voids. Kantorowicz found this procedure inconclusive because particular rules can rely on a multitude of possible principles (1906, 25) thus the law, in parts, was irreducibly indeterminate (1906, 14–15). Judges therefore can and will typically first take a decision and justify it ex post (Kantorowicz 1906, 20–22). Ultimately, according to the proponents of *Freirecht* there is no 'system' of law that could be amended in any coherent way (Kantorowicz 1906, 28). To fill 'gaps' where the law is indeterminate, the judge is to draw from common sense (Kantorowicz 1906, 13) or the 'living law' of the community that was to be identified in a sociological approach (Somek 2010,

343–44). While today the realist perspective is the dominant view in the United States (Balganesh 2015, 1844), the idea of *Freirecht* was less successful (Grechenig and Gelter 2008). In Germany, instead of admitting its fictitious character, formalism survived in remodelled forms. The German '*Wertungsjurisprudenz*', which will be introduced in more detail below is an example of such softened formalism: it claims that although the law does not determine the decision for every case, the judge may and will only base her decision on value judgments derived from the law (Grechenig and Gelter 2008, 554–56).

3.3 Attitudinalism Growing Out of Realist Thought

Legal realism inspired a research program that set out to test some of the predictions realists made about judicial decision-making. This programme is famously called 'attitudinalism' (see Solberg and Waltenburg, this volume). Their behaviouralist turn lead political scientists to concur to the realistic view on judicial decision-making (Clayton and May 1999, 235) and pit its claim that judges decide by their attitudes against simple legalism. In this vein, they provided some empirical support for the realist argument that personal values exert significant influence on judicial decisions.

The '*attitudinal model*' argues that at least in as far as judges are not submitted to judicial review they are unconstrained by the law so that their decisions are direct expressions of their political attitudes and preferences (Segal and Spaeth 1996, 974). Judges' policy preferences then exert the single most important influence on their decisions. That attitudes exert a significant influence on decisions has largely been vindicated with respect to the US Supreme Court (Segal and Cover 1989; Segal et al. 1995; Segal and Spaeth 1996, 2002; Solberg and Lindquist 2006) although the judges' policy preferences have been shown not to be stable but to change over time (Martin and Quinn 2007; Epstein et al. 2007). At the Supreme Court of Israel, attitudes have been shown to influence decisions more strongly than legal considerations in freedom of religion cases (Weinshall-Margel 2011). At the Supreme Court of Canada, attitudinal decision-making has been confirmed; however, the influence was considerably weaker than in the United States (Ostberg and Wetstein 1998; Wetstein and Ostberg 1999; Ostberg, Wetstein, and Ducat 2002). The British Law Lords' position on a one-dimensional policy space did not predict the judges' dissents between 1969 and 2009 any better than assuming the same probability of voting with the majority for every judge (Hanretty 2013; he did, however, find that the judges' votes aligned them on a left–right spectrum with regard to data after 2009, Hanretty 2020, ch. 8).

The attitudinal model explains the variance of judicial decisions but is unable to explain why the law does affect the central tendency of their distribution (Richards and Kritzer 2002; Weinshall-Margel 2011). It also is at odds with the finding that judges do suppress their attitudes more than lay people (Kahan et al. 2016). And it leaves unexplained why judges can submit to an ideology but not to 'the law' although legalism is just another ideology (Shklar 1986, 5; Baum 2010, 22). Attitudinalism was also criticized for over-emphasizing the politics of judicial decision-making and ignoring the impact of the law (Clayton and May 1999, 236) as well as for becoming tautological. If attitudes are all that drives decisions and anything can be an attitude, then attitudes are decisions and cannot explain them (Richards and Kritzer 2002, 307).

3.4 Attitudinalism and the Concept of Law

Ultimately, the empirical literature on attitudinalism may have killed a 'strawman' (Gillman 2001, 475, citing others; Hanretty 2020, 264). Few publishing jurists have defended simple legalism. Historically few judges embraced formalism (Edwards and Livermore 2009, 1915). For a long time already, 'virtually all knowledgeable observers would agree' that judicial decisions are not programmed exclusively by rules (save in easy cases) but that judges exert independent judgment shaped by many factors among which are the law and personality as well as the judges' world views (Gillman 2001; Baum 2010, 5; Livermore 2010, 1188–89; Klein 2017, 2). Scholars may have been eager to kill that strawman because judges may have appeared trying to 'fool the public' by not openly admitting to what extent their decision were driven by private preference (Klein 2017, 3). It is the old reproach that the formal way of making arguments in which judges engage is nothing but a cloak 'behind which a "shameless" liberalism hides' (Shklar 1987, 10, citing Unger). They may have overshot the mark (Klein 2017, 3). Apart from rulings of the US Supreme Court, the attitudinal model is only moderately successful in explaining the data (Edwards and Livermore 2009, 1931; Solberg and Waltenburg, this volume).

What is more, the strawman lives despite the evidence attitudinalism produced. Attitudes influence judicial decisions. However, an increase in the impact of attitudes does not translate one-to-one into a reduction of the impact of law. Law and attitude can in principle both have a lot or little impact if one allows for more complex models of legal decision-making than simple legalism (Bailey and Maltzman 2008, 371; Edwards and Livermore 2009, 1949; Livermore 2010, 1187–88; Klein 2017, 4). Furthermore, attitudes can be law—most obviously if the judge is called upon to make law and implement what she faithfully perceives to be good policy but also if moral principles are supposed to guide legal interpretation in hard cases as Dworkin (1986, 256; also Edwards and Livermore 2009, 1945–47) would claim. Therefore, by claiming that attitudes are extra-legal, attitudinalists take a position in the normative dispute between the many concepts of law—in fact one to which few in the field of law would subscribe (Gillman 2001; Edwards and Livermore 2009, 1948–49; Leiter 2010a, 256; Livermore 2010, 1192; Klein 2017, 19). Describing conclusively what the law is, is hard. Any description of the law must go beyond merely paraphrasing past decisions and therefore involves undetermined interpretation (Bix 2010, 224). That impedes reaching a consensus on what law is (Klein 2017, 10). Even if law could be defined, it remains hard to operationalize not lending itself lightly to quantitative analysis (Edwards and Livermore 2009, 1928; Epstein, Šadl, and Weinshall 2021, 714).

4. Law as a Social Fact

Positivism may be the best shot at providing a definition of law that the empirical social sciences can work with.

4.1 The Positivist Answer to What Is Law

One root of simple legalism that has not yet been discussed is positivism, which rejects the declaratory theory of law as mythical and accepts that judges make law (Troop 2018, 432). Positivists reject any necessary connection of morals and law (Coleman and Leiter 2010, 228). This is not the 'hard positivism' of simple legalism, however. Hard positivism states that all morals are always external to law. Inclusive positivists, their more frequent type, only deny that a norm has to be moral to be law (Coleman and Leiter 2010, 230). They concede that judges may consider morals in their judicial decision especially when the law leaves them discretion or asks them to make law (Klein 2017, 15).

All positivists think that law is defined by the fact of social practice (Coleman and Leiter 2010, 228–30). The law roots in conventions that make the law predictable (Millon 1992, 13). In the positivism of H. L. A. Hart (1994), what is law is decided by 'social rules' (Hart 1994, 54 et seq.) called 'rules of recognition' (Hart 1994, 94), which the legal community follows as a matter of fact (Marmor 1998, 509). Their validity and with it the validity of all lower-ranking rules is identical to the social fact that the rules of recognition are accepted from an internal point of view by the relevant community, in other words by judges (Marmor 1998, 510; Coleman and Leiter 2010, 233).

H. L. A. Hart added what he thought was a general theory of social rules (Hart 1994, 55–58). According to the structured version found in Marmor (1998, 510–11),

> a social rule, say *R*, exists in society *S* if and only if the following conditions obtain:
> 1. There is a regularity of behavior according to *R*, in *S*; namely that most members of *S* regularly conform to it.
> 2. Most members of *S* manifest a normative attitude toward *R*, which Hart called 'acceptance'.
>
> The idea of 'acceptance' consists of basically two components:
> (a) For most members of *S*, the existence of *R* constitutes reasons for action in accordance with *R*.
> (b) The existence of *R* is employed by members of *S* both as grounds for criticizing deviant behavior and as a justification for exerting social pressure on other members of *S* to conform to *R*.

In this definition, Hart's social rule has both a descriptive element (generalized convergent actions) and a normative element (acceptance from an internal point of view). The normative aspect distinguishes social rules from mere habits (Hart 1994, 55–56; also Coleman and Leiter 2010, 232). This two-part structure relates Hart's rule of recognition to modern theories of social norms, some of which also introduce a two-part structure. Cristina Bicchieri (2006) defined and empirically validated a model of social norms that features such a two-part structure too, albeit focusing on agent's normative and descriptive beliefs instead of relying on the relatively vague concept of 'acceptance from an internal point of view'.

In a postscript to his *Concept of Law* published after his death, Hart moved his rules of recognition even closer to the empiricist concept of social norms by clarifying that they are 'conventions' (Hart 1994, 256; see also Marmor 1998, 513). Such conventions in turn have been thoroughly analysed as coordination devices in coordination games. This research reflects on Hart's concept of 'acceptance' that may be completely void of any endorsement. Conventions in a coordination game are simply practiced because others practice them and universal practice is an equilibrium of individually rational behaviour (Marmor 1998, 513–14; Coleman and Leiter 2010, 234–40). In such a model, law would originate in mere coordination, a point Basu (2015) has recently made radically.

Bicchieri's model, in contrast, claims some normative force beyond mere coordination. In her model, a social norm *N* in a situation *S* exists, if agents expect others to behave in accordance with *N* in situations like *S* (first-order descriptive belief) and if the agent expects others to find it wrong not to confirm to *N* in situations like *S* (second-order normative belief). This model resonates with Hart's acceptance from an internal point of view. While Hart demanded that agents themselves take the rule as a reason for action, grounds for critique, and justification for social pressure (Hart 1994, 55–57; also Leiter 2010a, 250), Bicchieri (2006) focuses on the latter aspect and effectively lets her 'second-order normative belief' correspond to fear of social pressure or punishment.

As positivism ultimately reduces law to social facts, it lends itself readily to empirical study.

4.2 Positivism and Principles in Germany: From '*Gesetzespositivismus*' to '*Interessenjurisprudenz*'

In front of the backdrop of the immensely successful hard sciences, legal scholarship in nineteenth-century Germany aimed for a scientific approach to law and found it in treating formal state laws as the 'facts' to be investigated by legal science. This approach stressed the authority of the legislature: whatever it made law was law (Rüthers, Birk, and Fischer 2018, 301). Hans Kelsen's Pure Theory of Law ([1934] 2020) is regarded as the pinnacle of this '*Gesetzespositivismus*' (positivism of laws) (Rüthers, Birk, and Fischer 2018, 302–07). He assumed a strictly hierarchical normative system where every norm can be logically derived from a higher-ranking one until a hypothetical foundational norm that remained unspecified but may simply be understood as the legislature's *de facto* power to make law (Kelsen [1934] 2020, 73–99). In contrast to Hart, Kelsen did not attempt to explain how this power came about. However, soon, legal theory in Germany began to grapple with the problem that the legislature only gave incomplete instructions to his judges (Rüthers, Birk, and Fischer 2018, 344).

Proponents of the *Interessenjurisprudenz*, most prominently Philipp Heck (1914), aimed at retaining the judiciary's submission under the command of the legislature (Grechenig and Gelter 2008, 554), while at the same time acknowledging that formal state laws were at times only incomplete instructions how to decide cases. Interessenjurisprudenz solved this puzzle by claiming that even when the letters of the law did not provide any guidance, the judge was not allowed to follow her own values or preferences. From the law as shaped by the counteracting interests in society (hence the movement's name), the judge had to infer how the legislature would have balanced the parties interests in the relevant case (Grechenig and Gelter 2008, 554; Somek 2010, 344). Influentially, Philipp Heck likened what the judge does to '*denkendem Gehorsam*' (reflecting obedience) of a servant to a master who only provides incomplete instructions (Heck 1914, 16–20). His analogy bears some resemblance with Dworkin's weak discretion, which Dworkin exemplified by the sergeant who is told to select the five most experienced men for a specified mission (Dworkin 1978, 31–33).

What were liberal projects at their origin may have turned into an excuse for conservative judges readily to promote Nazi rule. Shklar (1986, 72) argued that in Germany, '[p]ositivism was only invoked to rationalize [the judiciary's] far greater readiness to comply with Hitler's New Order'. After 1933 Heck and authors like Heinrich Lange who was pursuing a similar programme under the label '*Wertungsjurisprudenz*' (jurisprudence of value judgments) submitted themselves and their theories eagerly to the new command of Nazi rule. The *Wertungsjurisprudenz* of these days argued that where the law had gaps, all value judgments had to be derived from an objective system of values and such values were identified with the Nazi ideology (Rückert 2008, 227).

The complicity in Nazi rule did not, however, discredit '*Wertungsjurisprudenz*' after the war. It was simply recharged by new value judgments (Rückert 2008, 229–36). These values may now be found represented in the black-letter law (Petersen 2001, 8), in the fundamental rights of the constitution (Grechenig and Gelter 2008, 555–56), but could also refer to moral standards outside the codified law (Larenz 1991, 122–27). Today, *Wertungsjurisprudenz* is probably the mainstream in German practical jurisprudence (Petersen 2001, 8; Stürner 2014, 15; Zimmermann 2019, 254). Interestingly, *Wertungs-* and *Interessenjurisprudenz* paved the way for the reception of Dworkin's ideas in Germany because German judges and legal scholars had been used to applying abstract moral principles, which they allegedly found in a coherent corpus of law or in the fundamental rights of the constitution to solve (hard) cases where the black-letter law provided no guidance (Somek 2010, 347).

In contrast to Hart's positivism, the German *Interessen-* and *Wertungsjurisprudenz* remains in the realm of normative narratives. At its inception it seemed to aim at establishing a specific 'rule of recognition' that only what comes from the legislator is law. Later it took a declaratory turn, acknowledging a meta-positive corpus of principles by which to fill 'gaps' in the positive law. Like the declaratory theory and formalism, it asks the judge to suppress his own attitudes and serve the community—here as represented by the legislature. Empirical study of the theories faces the same difficulties and opens the same opportunities as that of the declaratory theory and formalism.

5. Law as Guidance and Constraint of Judicial Behaviour

Starting in the 1990s and in a turn to 'institutions', which the field shared with political science more generally (Weinshall-Margel 2011, 558) students of judicial behaviour have focused on how the law guides and constrains judicial behaviour (Clayton and May 1999, 237).

Hanretty (2020, ch. 9) shows that the single most influential variable predicting the appellants success is lower courts' decisions on the case. The higher court typically agrees with lower courts independently of the politics. This suggests that all courts in the hierarchy reason from a common base, which might be called law. Few other studies have set out to show the law's impact on decision-making so generally. Most authors have treated smaller questions within one of four lines of thought. First and traditionally, legal as well as political science scholars have tried to show the law's constraining effect on judicial behaviour by means of qualitative research, interpreting the reasons of judicial decisions on a particular question (see Gillman 2001, 481 and 490–91 for a brief overview). I leave this traditional branch of the literature aside in the following and focus instead on attempts to demonstrate the impact of law on judicial behaviour by means of quantitative methods. Second, the strategic strand of the quantitative literature sees 'law' as the result of mutual constraint of political actors by the need to coordinate. Third, other authors tried to translate 'the law' into 'legal regimes' (Richards and Kritzer 2002), that is, distinguishable ways of thinking about particular problems one can call 'doctrine'. Fourth, still others turned to the investigation of the effects of specific professional norms like *stare decisis* or the norm of consensus.

5.1 Law's Effect through Coordination

The strategic variant of the institutional take on judicial behaviour uses game theory to identify equilibria that serve as predictions of judicial behaviour. It still assumes that judges follow their attitudes but adds that judges are constrained by other agents following their attitudes (see Dothan, this volume). This may lead to behaviour that looks legally constrained. More specifically, lower court judges pursue their policy goals constrained by the threat of reversal wielded by higher courts. Judges are assumed to be averse to reversal because reversal will spoil the judges' policy goals (Kastellec 2007; Randazzo 2008; Epstein and Weinshall 2021, 17) and may taint their reputation, hurting promotion prospects (Salzberger and Fenn 1999; Choi, Gulati, and Posner 2012; Shepherd 2012). Some studies indeed confirmed the assumption of reversal aversion empirically (Salzberger and Fenn 1999; Randazzo 2008; Choi, Gulati, and Posner 2012; Feess and Sarel 2018; see also overview at Smith 2006, Shepherd 2012; but see section 6.3). For apex courts, strategic interaction arises from the courts' inability to force compliance with their decision (Epstein and Knight 1997; Clayton and May 1999, 238). They can, however, use their public acceptance to discredit non-compliance (Petersen and Chatziathanasiou 2019, 529). The approach is institutionalist, in that 'institutions' determine what combinations of actions result in what degree of goal attainment of agents (Epstein and Waterbury 2020)—typically by serving as a focal point in the grand coordination game.

Baum (2010, 7) called the strategic model of judicial decision-making today's 'standard way of thinking about judicial behavior' and it fared well empirically. It has been confirmed that indeed judges on apex courts in the United States (Lindquist and Corley 2011), France (Franck 2009), Germany (Vanberg 2001), and the EU (Carrubba, Gabel, and Hankla 2008; criticized by Stone Sweet and Brunell 2012; see also Carrubba, Gabel, and Hankla 2012) respond to actions and preferences of other 'players' in the political game. Lower courts seem to act strategically, too: in the United States they respect Supreme Court precedent less when justices supporting it retire (Benjamin and Vanberg 2016).

Ultimately, however, it seems that strategic behaviour by courts depreciates the very capital (apex) courts run their business on, shedding doubt on the stability of equilibria. A court that appears political tends to decline in public regard (Caldeira 1986; Nicholson and Hansford 2014; Gibson and Nelson 2017). The public acceptance that the courts wield to motivate other actors to comply may largely depend on the perception that 'law' is guiding the courts. Also, as courts interact with each other and other political agents infinitely, by the folk theorem, there are multiple equilibria so that much can be rationalized ex post but little can be predicted. The strategic model, despite being institutional, seems to gloss over the impact that law may have in this coordination game rather than measure or explain it. Finally, the strategic model, often, cannot distinguish between motivation by 'law' and by attitudes because the behaviour is typically equivalent (Klein 2017, 11).

5.2 Effects of Doctrine

While in the strategic account of judicial decision-making institutions are often assumed as exogenously given as the rules of the game, other scholars became interested in the emergence of such institutions. This neo-institutionalism defined institutions very broadly. No particular form was required. Instead, the focus shifted on shared cognitive structures. '[I]nformal norms, myths, habits of thought, or background structures and patterns of meaning' could count as 'institutions' (Clayton and May 1999, 240). Neo-institutionalists could agree with attitudinalists that attitudes shaped court decisions but they were interested in how institutions shape such attitudes (Weinshall-Margel 2011, 558). This opened a gate through which the impact of law on decisions could return to the focus of interest in a modified way (Richards and Kritzer 2002, 309–10). Law could be a mindset or at least shape such a mindset and through that mindset affect decisions (Weinshall-Margel 2011, 559).

Such a mindset is, however, hard to conceptualize. Richards and Kritzer (2002) tried to solve the problem by operationalizing the mindset by its effects. Law as a mindset was assumed to determine the weights by which many independent factors influenced the outcome of cases—somewhat like in a regression model (2002, 305–08). Richards and Kritzer (2002, 308) called that mindset 'jurisprudential regime' and connected their work to the strategic model of judicial decision-making by attributing to their jurisprudential regimes the role of coordination devices in the strategic interaction of judges amongst each other and with the world outside the court. This line of thought cautiously opened the research on judicial decision-making, which had largely followed the route of methodological individualism, to elements of more collectivist approaches. It was shown that legal regimes influence judicial decision-making by the United States (Richards and Kritzer 2002) and the Israeli (Weinshall-Margel 2011) Supreme Courts, for instance. However, the approach was criticized for the vagueness of its concepts and that under more galvanized operationalizations, empirical evidence seemed to fade (Lax and Rader 2010).

5.3 Effect of Professional Norms

Neo-institutionalism has also shifted researchers' interest to specific professional norms, which constrain judges. Most importantly, these are the norm of consensus and the rule of *stare decisis*.

Depending on the situation at the court, judges may feel bound by a norm of consensus. Thinking of the declaratory ideal, one may interpret judicial dissent as indication that at least some judges were 'wrong'. Being wrong undermines legitimacy. The desire of judges to maximize legitimacy of the court's decision may result in the mutual expectation to strive for unanimity. This mutual expectation may be called an institution or 'the norm of consensus' (Wittig 2016, 74). Such a norm of consensus has been shown to exist—albeit with declining importance over time. Examples can be found at the US Supreme Court, the US Courts of Appeals (Atkins and Green 1976; Walker, Epstein, and Dixon 1988; Caldeira and Zorn 1998; Epstein, Segal, and Spaeth 2001), the Spanish Constitutional Court (Garoupa, Gomez-Pomar, and Grembi 2013), and—weakly so—at the Australian Supreme Court (Narayan and Smyth 2005). Wittig (2016) provides elegant, albeit indirect, evidence for the impact of a norm of consensus at the German Constitutional Court. She observes that judges dissent more often the closer their departure from the legal profession. She explains this observation by arguing that judges leaving the profession feel bound less by the professional norm of consensus, leaving them more leeway to follow their idiosyncratic attitudes in dissenting opinions.

Another important professional norm is the one of *stare decisis*. It, too, can be rationalized by the strategic model. A court's rulings will only be adhered to if they are accepted. Following precedent may be what the public expects so that following precedent may increase acceptance for the court's rulings (Knight and Epstein 1996, 1022–23). Segal and Spaeth (1996) have famously claimed to have shown empirically that *stare decisis* is without any effect on US Supreme Court Justices. However, their test can be criticized as overly strict (Gillman 2001, 482–83; Bailey and Maltzman 2008, 371) in that they only checked whether dissenters later fall in line with the precedent with which they originally disagreed. Of these originally dissenting justices, 90.8 per cent dissent in the progeny cases to the original precedent, too. Only 9.2 per cent fall in line with the majority from the original precedent. Employing a more reasonable benchmark, Bailey and Maltzman (2008) show that *stare decisis* influences justices more compared to other political actors not bound by the law in the same way. The set-up of their study appears superior to that by Segal and Spaeth in that it measures the constraint imposed by law as delta to a legally non-bound baseline. Their finding is evidence in favour of the existence of a norm of *stare decisis*. For the DC Circuit Court of Appeals, Cross and Tiller (1998) show what they call a whistleblower effect of legal doctrine. Supreme Court precedent (the Chevron test suggesting judicial deference) helps a judge representing the political minority (Republican/Democrat) on a three-judge panel to pull the majority on her side. Panels whose majority would politically prefer to intervene defer in more than 62 per cent of cases, if precedent favours deference and there is a judge from the other political camp on the panel. If the majority favouring intervention encompasses all three judges then the panel only follows the precedent suggesting to defer in 33 per cent of cases. If the majority favours to defer in line with precedent and one judge from the other political camp would prefer intervening, split panels align with their majority's preference even more frequently (84 per cent of the time) than politically homogeneous panels (71 per cent). Knight and Epstein (1996) find that precedent is the most cited type of authority in internal deliberations in courts. Assuming that in internal deliberations judges only cite what they expect to convince their colleagues, this finding provides evidence in favour of an effective rule of *stare decisis*. Bartels (2009) predicts that presumptions of legality or illegality, respectively, or higher degrees of constitutional rights scrutiny, all established by precedent, limit the justices' discretion to follow their ideology. Looking at the introduction of the Grayned test on the regulation of speech, he finds that at least when presumption and degree of constitutional scrutiny point the same way, judges vote with their ideology significantly less than they did before the precedent. This indicates a constraining effect of the precedent introducing a presumption of illegality of content-based regulation of speech.

6. Promising Directions for Future Research

The chapter has shown that, possibly except for Hart's positivism, the roots of simple legalism are normative, not descriptive theories. They tell judges how they are supposed to decide cases and which judicial conduct and arguments are acceptable. They appear designed to help the judge abstract from her own sentiments, preferences, prejudices, and attitudes. In that regard the attitudinal research agenda appears vindicated (somewhat counter to claims by Edwards and Livermore 2009; Livermore 2010). At a minimum, it has shown that the suppression of the judges' idiosyncrasies that judicial founding narratives aspire to induce, does not work quite as well as imagined in judicial pipe-dreams. However, and here Edwards and Livermore (Edwards and Livermore 2009; Livermore 2010) have a point, because attitudinalism turned a pipe dream into an empirical benchmark the attitudinal research agenda does not go beyond showing that life is not fantasy.

6.1 Finding a Realistic Benchmark to Measure the Impact of Legal and Non-Legal Motives

Apart from positivism, legal theories are norms. They cannot be falsified. But degrees of compliance with the law can be measured. For that, a reasonable benchmark is indispensable. The approach by Bailey and Maltzman (2008) to compare the impact of attitudes on judges to that on political actors not bound by law seems to go the right way. Holger Spamann and Lars Klöhn (2016) have made a promising step into this direction, too. They elicited legal scholars' expectations about the effect of a change in precedent on judicial decisions in a vignette experiment and compared these expectations with the decisions of real judges. In another study, Daniel Klerman and Holger Spamann (forthcoming) show that submitting the same case to different standards (by changing the case between treatments so that rules regulating intra-US conflicts of law would submit the case to different state laws) has a smaller effect than legal scholarship would have one expect. Also, Hanretty (2020, ch. 2) has found smart ways to operationalize legal constraints to join them into one model with motives typically treated as non-legal. These may bring badly needed (Klein 2017) improvements of our means to measure genuinely legal influences on judicial decisions.

6.2 Legal Theory as Shaping Judicial Social Norms and Accountability

As alluded to in section 2.3, another interesting route could be to study the effects of endorsing certain narratives (legal 'theories') on beliefs—and through beliefs on behaviour. Wald (1999) expressed the concern that explicitly acknowledging the judge's role as a partisan player may well produce more partisan voting. Social norms transmitted by narratives may be at the root of this conjecture. Modern theories implement social norms as 'beliefs' (i.e. expectations) that either exert some motivating power on agents directly (Bicchieri 2006) or by determining which equilibrium strategy agents play in the vast societal coordination game (Posner 2000; Basu 2015; Nyborg et al. 2016). Beliefs are shaped by narratives (Shiller 2019). Thus, through beliefs, the degree to which judges endorse certain narratives may crucially affect norm-guided behaviour. To this line of research, there may be a promising behavioural twist. Many findings from cognitive and social psychology as well as from behavioural economics may facilitate coordination and cooperation (Basu 2015). These findings may lie at the root of law as a coordination device. The role of shared cognitive processes in behaviour coordinated by norms has largely gone unnoticed in research on judicial behaviour so far. Psychologists and behavioural economists have shown that norms motivate behaviour. It has for instance been found that people are motivated by appeals to morals or norms leading them to act more pro-socially (Dal Bo and Dal Bo 2014; Capraro and Rand 2018). Models of social norms as preferences conditioned on beliefs (Bicchieri 2006) may make valuable contributions to describing how judicial behaviour is linked to 'the law'. These models have largely been confirmed in laboratory experiments (Bicchieri and Xiao 2009; Krupka and Weber 2009; Bicchieri and Chavez 2010; Raihani and McAuliffe 2014; Hauge 2016; Fabbri and Carbonara 2017; Gächter, Gerhards, and Nosenzo 2017; Human and Capraro 2020; Danilov, Khalmetski, and Sliwka 2021). Akerlof and Kranton (2010) have highlighted the role of in-group ideals for norm-abiding behaviour (see also Hogg and Abrams 1988), corresponding to Hart's idea of the rule of recognition as a social convention within 'the relevant community'. A laboratory experiment did indeed show that the more integrated people are by a shared social identity, the stronger the impact of higher order beliefs on behaviour (Morell 2019). It would be fascinating to see what effect social cohesion or disintegration (polarization) of the judiciary has on how attitudes and legally acceptable motives, respectively, impact judicial decisions. Similarly, to group identity, socially conferred roles also shape behaviour. An experiment with lay people found that assuming the role of a neutral 'judge' changes participants' altruistic punishment behaviour to be fairer and more effective (Engel and Zhurakhovska 2017).

6.3 More Attention to Lower Courts

Ultimately, researchers could pay more attention to why and how lower courts follow 'the law'. Apparently they do track higher courts' precedent (Klein 2017, 238). If 'the law' is a vast coordination game, all law must be self-enforcing. The law can only induce shifts from one equilibrium to another. Researchers of judicial behaviour may ask why lower court judges play their role in realizing higher courts or the law maker's policy preferences in this coordination game. The constraint by the threat of reversal may be overstated (see section 5.1). Neither can higher courts review a significant fraction of lower court decisions nor will congress bother micro-monitoring courts and reverse all decisions it disagrees with (Cross and Tiller 1998, 2174; Kim 2011, 556). Although the judges' cost of reversal will probably vary with age (older judges care for promotion less than younger ones so that the loss of reputation by reversal will affect older judges less), reversal rates seem not to vary with age (Higgins and Rubin 1980). Besides, by establishing the facts of cases, lower courts can often attain their policy goals in these cases without deviating from the commands of higher courts. Despite a vast literature on heuristics and biases in evaluating evidence (see Braman, *The Oxford Handbook of US Judicial Behaviour*), it remains largely unexplored whether judges use their discretion in establishing the facts to actively or inadvertently pursue policy goals (but on the impact of ideology (or the lack thereof) on framing the facts, see Braman, this volume; Kahan et al. 2016) and how (legal) institutions could constrain judges in this respect.

7. Conclusion

We know that judges' attitudes impact judicial decisions and that judges act strategically at times. However, we have astonishingly little generalizable knowledge about how, under what conditions, and to what degree the law motivates or constrains judicial decisions. Maybe empirical researchers have not taken the concept of law seriously enough. This chapter has attempted to make some thoughts about the concept of law accessible to empirical researchers. It showed that empirical research on judicial decision making has to take sides in the normative debate of what is law, when claiming that judges follow extra legal motives. The chapter also identified elements of legal theory that lend themselves to empirical operationalization. The idea of social norms, inherent in some forms of positivism, may provide the most promising element of that sort. From their inclination to follow social norms, judges may derive the motivation to control their attitudes, tone down their strategic ambitions, and submit themselves to what they think others think is the law. Thus, judges may be motivated to suppress policy preferences to a greater degree than lay people (Kahan et al. 2016) or non-jurisdictional political actors (Bailey and Maltzman 2008). In that sense, social norms in the judiciary are a resource that may ultimately guarantee the rule of law. Beyond the social norms, to which positivism makes some reference, other theories of law seem to be mainly normative foundational narratives of law. To study the connection between the degree to which judges subscribe to those 'myths' and judicial decisions may be another promising avenue for future research. Finally, the literature has mainly focused on apex courts. Lower courts seem to follow the law, in particular the commands of higher courts, to a considerable degree. However, lower courts establish the facts—often without much scrutiny of higher ones—and in doing that, have a considerable influence on the outcome of the case. It seems that not much effort has been put into investigating in how far 'the law' has managed to channel this source of judicial discretion.

Simple legalism may have been refuted as descriptive theory of judicial behaviour. Judges do not take the facts and the law and deduce by means of formal syllogism the single possible answer to a case. However, the legal narratives from which simple legalism derived remain powerful aspirations rather than a descriptive account of what judges do. That can explain why, at times, legal scholars appear as 'loyal supporters rather than the neutral observers' of courts (Dyevre 2010): with their narratives of how judges decide cases, they may be defending the social norms that may effectively bind judges to the law.

References

Akerlof, George A., and Rachel E. Kranton. 2010. *Identity Economics: How Our Identities Shape Our Work, Wages, and Well-Being*. Princeton: Princeton University Press.

Atkins, Burton M., and Justin J. Green. 1976. 'Consensus on the United States Courts of Appeals: Illusion or Reality?' *American Journal of Political Science* 20 (4): 735–48.

Bailey, Michael A., and Forrest Maltzman. 2008. 'Does Legal Doctrine Matter? Unpacking Law and Policy Preferences on the U.S. Supreme Court'. *The American Political Science Review* 102 (3): 369–84. https://doi.org/10.1017/S0003055408080283.

Balganesh, Shyamkrishna. 2015. 'Foreword: The Constraint of Legal Doctrine'. *University of Pennsylvania Law Review* 163 (7): 1843–58.

Bartels, Brandon L. 2009. 'The Constraining Capacity of Legal Doctrine on the U.S. Supreme Court'. *The American Political Science Review* 103 (3): 474–95. https://doi.org/10.1017/S0003055409990049.

Basu, Kaushik. 2015. 'The Republic of Beliefs: A New Approach to "Law and Economics"'. Policy Research Working Paper 7259.

Baum, Lawrence. 2010. 'Motivation and Judicial Behavior: Expanding the Scope of Inquiry'. In *The Psychology of Judicial Decision Making*, edited by David E. Klein and Gregory Mitchell, 3–25. New York: Oxford University Press.

Beever, Allan. 2013. 'The Declaratory Theory of Law'. *Oxford Journal of Legal Studies* 33 (3): 421–44. https://doi.org/10.1093/ojls/gqt007.

Benjamin, Stuart Minor, and Georg Vanberg. 2016. 'Judicial Retirements and the Staying Power of U.S. Supreme Court Decisions'. *Journal of Empirical Legal Studies* 13 (1): 5–26.

Bicchieri, Cristina. 2006. *The Grammar of Society: The Nature and Dynamics of Social Norms*. Cambridge: Cambridge University Press.

Bicchieri, Cristina, and Alex Chavez. 2010. 'Behaving as Expected: Public Information and Fairness Norms'. *Journal of Behavioral Decision Making* 23 (2): 161–78. https://doi.org/10.1002/bdm.648.

Bicchieri, Cristina, and Erte Xiao. 2009. 'Do the Right Thing: But Only If Others Do So'. *Journal of Behavioral Decision Making* 22 (2): 191–208. https://doi.org/10.1002/bdm.621.

Bix, Brian. 2010. 'Natural Law Theory'. In *A Companion to Philosophy of Law and Legal Theory*, 2nd edn, edited by Dennis Michael Patterson, 211–27. Malden: Wiley-Blackwell.

Blackstone, William. (1765–1779) 1897. *Commentaries on the Laws of England: In One Volume*. St. Paul: West Publishing.
Braman, Eileen. 2017. 'Cognition in the Courts: Analyzing the Use of Experiments to Study Legal Decision-Making'. In *The Oxford Handbook of U.S. Judicial Behaviour*, edited by Lee Epstein and Stephanie A. Lindquist, 483–507. Oxford: Oxford University Press.
Caldeira, Gregory A. 1986. 'Neither the Purse nor the Sword: Dynamics of Public Confidence in the Supreme Court'. *The American Political Science Review* 80 (4): 1209–26.
Caldeira, Gregory A., and Christopher J. W. Zorn. 1998. 'Of Time and Consensual Norms in the Supreme Court'. *The American Journal of Political Science* 42 (3): 874–902.
Capraro, Valerio, and David Rand. 2018. 'Do the Right Thing: Experimental Evidence That Preferences for Moral Behavior, Rather Than Equity or Efficiency Per Se, Drive Human Prosociality'. *Judgment and Decision Making* 13 (1): 99–111.
Carrubba, Clifford J., Matthew Gabel, and Charles Hankla. 2008. 'Judicial Behavior Under Political Constraints: Evidence from the European Court of Justice'. *The American Political Science Review* 102 (4): 435–52. https://doi.org/10.1017/S0003055408080350.
Carrubba, Clifford J., Matthew Gabel, and Charles Hankla. 2012. 'Understanding the Role of the European Court of Justice in European Integration'. *The American Political Science Review* 106 (1): 214–23.
Choi, Stephen J., Mitu Gulati, and Eric A. Posner. 2012. 'What Do Federal District Judges Want? An Analysis of Publications, Citations, and Reversals'. *Journal of Law, Economics, and Organization* 28 (3): 518–49. https://doi.org/10.1093/jleo/ewq020.
Clayton, Cornell, and David A. May. 1999. 'A Political Regimes Approach to the Analysis of Legal Decisions'. *Polity* 32 (2): 233–52.
Coleman, Jules L., and Brian Leiter. 2010. 'Legal Positivism'. In *A Companion to Philosophy of Law and Legal Theory*, 2nd edn, edited by Dennis Michael Patterson, 228–48. Malden: Wiley-Blackwell.
Cross, Frank B., and Emerson H. Tiller. 1998. 'Judicial Partisanship and Obedience to Legal Doctrine: Whistleblowing on the Federal Courts of Appeals'. *Yale Law Journal* 107 (7): 2155–76.
Dal Bo, Ernesto, and Pedro Dal Bo. 2014. 'Do the Right Thing: The Effects of Moral Suasion on Cooperation'. *Journal of Public Economics* 117: 28–38.
Danilov, Anastasia, Kiryl Khalmetski, and Dirk Sliwka. 2021. 'Descriptive Norms and Guilt Aversion'. *Journal of Economic Behavior & Organization* 191: 293–311.
Dworkin, Ronald. 1978. 'No Right Answer'. *New York University Law Review* 53 (1): 1–32.
Dworkin, Ronald. 1986. *Law's Empire*. Cambridge: Belknap Press.
Dyevre, Arthur. 2010. 'Unifying the Field of Comparative Judicial Politics: Towards a General Theory of Judicial Behaviour'. *European Political Science Review* 2 (2): 297–327. https://doi.org/10.1017/S1755773910000044.
Edwards, Harry T., and Michael A. Livermore. 2009. 'Pitfalls of Empirical Studies That Attempt to Understand the Factors Affecting Appellate Decisionmaking'. *Duke Law Journal* 58 (8): 1895–1989.
Ehrlich, Eugen. (1903) 1967. 'Freie Rechtsfindung und Freie Rechtswissenschaft'. In *Recht Und Leben*, edited by Manfred Rehbinder, 170–202. Berlin: Duncker & Humblot.
Engel, Christoph, and Lilia Zhurakhovska. 2017. 'You Are in Charge: Experimentally Testing the Motivating Power of Holding a Judicial Office'. *Journal of Legal Studies* 46:1–50. https://doi.org/10.2139/ssrn.2867696.
Epstein, Lee, and Jack Knight. 1997. *The Choices Justices Make*. New York: Sage.

Epstein, Lee, Andrew D. Martin, Kevin M. Quinn, and Jeffrey A. Segal. 2007. 'Ideological Drift Among Supreme Court Justices: Who, When, and How Important'. *Northwestern University Law Review* 101 (4): 1483–1542.

Epstein, Lee, Urška Šadl, and Keren Weinshall. 2021. 'The Role of Comparative Law in the Analysis of Judicial Behavior'. *American Journal of Comparative Law* 69 (4): 689–719.

Epstein, Lee, Jeffrey A. Segal, and Harold J. Spaeth. 2001. 'The Norm of Consensus on the U.S. Supreme Court'. *American Journal of Political Science* 45 (2): 362–77.

Epstein, Lee, and Nicholas W. Waterbury. 2020. 'Judicial Behavior'. In *Oxford Research Encyclopedia of Politics*, edited by Lee Epstein and Nicholas W. Waterbury. Oxford: Oxford University Press.

Epstein, Lee, and Keren Weinshall. 2021. *The Strategic Analysis of Judicial Behavior: A Comparative Perspective*. Cambridge: Cambridge University Press.

Fabbri, Marco, and Emanuela Carbonara. 2017. 'Social Influence on Third-Party Punishment: An Experiment'. *Journal of Economic Psychology* 62: 204–30. https://doi.org/10.1016/j.joep.2017.07.003.

Feess, Eberhard, and Roee Sarel. 2018. 'Judicial Effort and the Appeals System: Theory and Experiment'. *The Journal of Legal Studies* 47 (2): 269–94.

Franck, Raphael. 2009. 'Judicial Independence Under a Divided Polity: A Study of the Rulings of the French Constitutional Court, 1959–2006'. *Journal of Law, Economics, and Organization* 25 (1): 262–84.

Gächter, Simon, Leonie Gerhards, and Daniele Nosenzo. 2017. 'The Importance of Peers for Compliance with Norms of Fair Sharing'. *European Economic Review* 97: 72–86. https://doi.org/10.1016/j.euroecorev.2017.06.001.

Garoupa, Nuno, Gomez-Pomar, Fernando, and Veronica Grembi. 2013. 'Judging Under Political Pressure: An Empirical Analysis of Constitutional Review Voting in the Spanish Constitutional Court'. *Journal of Law, Economics, and Organization* 29 (3): 513–34.

Gibson, James L., and Michael J. Nelson. 2017. 'Reconsidering Positivity Theory: What Roles Do Politicization, Ideological Disagreement, and Legal Realism Play in Shaping U.S. Supreme Court Legitimacy'. *Journal of Empirical Legal Studies* 14 (3): 592–617.

Gillman, Howard. 2001. 'What's Law Got to Do with It? Judicial Behavioralists Test the "Legal Model" of Judicial Decision Making'. *Law & Social Inquiry* 26 (02): 465–504. https://doi.org/10.1111/j.1747-4469.2001.tb00185.x.

Grechenig, Kristoffel, and Martin Gelter. 2008. 'Divergente Evolution des Rechtsdenkens—Von amerikanischer Rechtsökonomie und deutscher Dogmatik'. *RabelsZ* 72 (3): 513. https://doi.org/10.1628/003372508784937293.

Haferkamp, Hans-Peter. 2004–2023. 'Puchta, Georg Friedrich (1798–1846)'. In *Handwörterbuch zur deutschen Rechtsgeschichte*, 2nd edn, edited by Albrecht Cordes, Hans-Peter Haferkamp, Bernd Kannowski, Heiner Lück, Heinrich de Wall, Dieter Werkmüller, and Ruth Schmidt-Wiegand, 945–46. Berlin: Erich Schmidt Verlag.

Hanretty, Chris. 2013. 'The Decisions and Ideal Points of British Law Lords'. *British Journal of Political Science* 43 (3): 703–16.

Hanretty, Chris. 2020. *A Court of Specialists*. Oxford: Oxford University Press.

Hart, H. L. A. 1994. *The Concept of Law*. Oxford: Clarendon Press.

Hauge, Karen Evelyn. 2016. 'Generosity and Guilt: The Role of Beliefs and Moral Standards of Other'. *Journal of Economic Psychology* 54: 35–43. https://doi.org/10.1016/j.joep.2016.03.001.

Heck, Philipp. 1914. 'Gesetzesauslegung und Interessenjurisprudenz'. *Archiv für die civilistische Praxis* 112 (1): 1–318.

Higgins, Richard S., and Paul H. Rubin. 1980. 'Judicial Discretion'. *Journal of Legal Studies* 9 (1): 129–38.

Hoffmann, Robert. 2012. 'The Experimental Economics of Religion'. *Journal of Economic Surveys* 27 (5): 813–45. https://doi.org/10.1111/j.1467-6419.2011.00716.x.

Hogg, Michael A., and Dominic Abrams. 1988. *Social Identifications: A Social Psychology of Intergroup Relations and Group Processes*. London: Routledge.

Holmes, Oliver Wendell. 1897 [1997]. 'The Path of the Law'. *Harvard Law Review* 110 (5): 991–1009.

Human, Steven J., and Valerio Capraro. 2020. *The Effect of Nudging Personal and Injunctive Norms on the Trade-Off Between Objective Equality and Efficiency*.

Iyer, Sriya. 2016. 'The New Economics of Religion'. *Journal of Economic Literature* 54 (2): 395–441. https://doi.org/10.1257/jel.54.2.395.

Jhering, Rudolph von. (1884) 1904. *Scherz und Ernst in der Jurisprudenz: Eine Weihnachtsgabe für das Juristische Publikum*, 9th edn. Leipzig: Breitkopf und Härtel.

Kahan, Dan M., David Hoffman, Danieli Evans, Neal Devins, Eugene Lucci, and Katherine Cheng. 2016. 'Ideology or Situation Sense: An Experimental Investigation of Motivated Reasoning and Professional Judgment'. *University of Pennsylvania Law Review* 164 (2): 349–440.

Kantorowicz, Hermann. 1906. *Der Kampf um die Rechtswissenschaft*. Heidelberg: C. Winter.

Kastellec, Jonathan P. 2007. 'Panel Composition and Judicial Compliance on the US Courts of Appeals'. *Journal of Law, Economics, and Organization* 23 (2): 421–41. https://doi.org/10.1093/jleo/ewm026.

Kelsen, Hans. (1934) 2020. *Reine Rechtslehre: Einleitung in die Rechtswissenschaftliche Problematik (Studienausgabe Der 1. Auflage 1934)*. Tübingen: Mohr Siebeck GmbH & Co. KG.

Kim, Pauline T. 2011. 'Beyond Principal–Agent Theories: Law and the Judicial Hierarchy'. *Northwestern University Law Review* 105 (2): 535–76.

David Klein. 2017. 'Law in Judicial Decision-Making'. In *The Oxford Handbook of U.S. Judicial Behaviour*, edited by Lee Epstein and Stephanie A. Lindquist, 236–52. Oxford: Oxford University Press.

Klerman, Daniel, and Holger Spamann. Forthcoming. 'Law Matters—Less Than We Thought'. *Journal of Law Economics and Organization*. https://doi.org/10.1093/jleo/ewac008.

Knight, Jack, and Lee Epstein. 1996. 'The Norm of Stare Decisis'. *American Journal of Political Science* 40 (4): 1018–35.

Krupka, Erin, and Roberto A. Weber. 2009. 'The Focusing and Informational Effects of Norms on Pro-Social Behavior'. *Journal of Economic Psychology* 30 (3): 307–20. https://doi.org/10.1016/j.joep.2008.11.005.

Larenz, Karl. 1991. *Methodenlehre der Rechtswissenschaft*, 6th edn. Berlin: Springer-Verlag.

Lax, Jeffrey R., and Kelly T. Rader. 2010. 'Legal Constraints on Supreme Court Decision Making: Do Jurisprudential Regimes Exist?' *The Journal of Politics* 72 (2): 273–84. https://doi.org/10.1017/S0022381609990855.

Leiter, Brian. 2010a. 'American Legal Realism'. In *A Companion to Philosophy of Law and Legal Theory*, 2nd edn, edited by Dennis Michael Patterson, 249–66. Malden: Wiley-Blackwell.

Leiter, Brian. 2010b. 'Legal Formalism and Legal Realism: What Is the Issue?' *Legal Theory* 16 (2): 111–33. https://doi.org/10.1017/S1352325210000121.

Lindquist, Stefanie A., and Pamela C. Corley. 2011. 'The Multiple-Stage Process of Judicial Review: Facial and as-Applied Constitutional Challenges to Legislation Before the U.S. Supreme Court'. *The Journal of Legal Studies* 40 (2): 467–502. https://doi.org/10.1086/661947.

Livermore, Michael A. 2010. 'Realist Lawyers and Realistic Legalists: A Brief Rebuttal to Judge Posner'. *Duke Law Journal* 59 (6): 1187–94.

Marmor, Andrei. 1998. 'Legal Conventionalism'. *Legal Theory* 4 (4): 509–31. https://doi.org/10.1017/S1352325200001129.

Martin, Andrew D., and Kevin M. Quinn. 2007. 'Assessing Preference Change on the US Supreme Court'. *Journal of Law, Economics, and Organization* 23 (2): 365–85. https://doi.org/10.1093/jleo/ewm028.

Millon, David K. 1992. 'Objectivity and Democracy'. *New York University Law Review* 67 (1): 1–66.

Montesquieu, Charles de Secondat. (1748) 1871. *De l'esprit des lois*. Paris. Garnier Frères.

Morell, Alexander. 2019. 'The Short Arm of Guilt—An Experiment on Group Identity and Guilt Aversion'. *Journal of Economic Behavior & Organization* 166: 332–45. https://doi.org/10.1016/j.jebo.2019.06.022.

Narayan, Paresh Kumar, and Russell Smyth. 2005. 'The Consensual Norm on the High Court of Australia: 1904–2001'. *International Political Science Review* 26 (2): 147–68. https://doi.org/10.1177/0192512105050379.

Nicholson, Stephen P., and Thomas G. Hansford. 2014. 'Partisans in Robes: Party Cues and Public Acceptance of Supreme Court Decisions'. *American Journal of Political Science* 58 (3): 620–36. https://doi.org/10.1111/ajps.12091.

Nyborg, Karine, John M. Anderies, Astrid Dannenberg, Therese Lindahl, Caroline Schill, Maja Schlüter, W. Neil Adger, Kenneth J. Arrow, Scott Barrett, Stephen Carpenter et al. 2016. 'Social Norms as Solutions'. *Science* 354 (6308): 42–3. https://doi.org/10.1126/science.aaf8317.

Ostberg, C. L., and Matthew Wetstein. 1998. 'Dimensions of Attitudes Underlying Search and Seizure Decisions of the Supreme Court of Canada'. *Canadian Journal of Political Science* 31 (4): 767–87. https://doi.org/10.1017/S000842390000963X.

Ostberg, C. L., Matthew E. Wetstein, and Craig R. Ducat. 2002. 'Attitudinal Dimensions of Supreme Court Decision Making in Canada: The Lamer Court, 1991–1995'. *Political Research Quarterly* 55 (1): 235–56. https://doi.org/10.2307/3088073.

Petersen, Jens. 2001. *Von der Interessenjurisprudenz zur Wertungsjurisprudenz: Dargestellt an Beispielen aus dem deutschen Privatrecht*. Tübingen: Mohr Siebeck.

Petersen, Niels, and Konstantin Chatziathanasiou. 2019. 'Empirische Verfassungsrechtswissenschaft: Zu Möglichkeiten und Grenzen quantitativer Verfassungsvergleichung und Richterforschung'. *Archiv des öffentlichen Rechts* 144 (4): 501–35.

Posner, Eric A. 2000. *Law and Social Norms*. Cambridge. Harvard University Press.

Posner, Richard A. 1986. 'Legal Formalism, Legal Realism, and the Interpretation of Statutes and the Constitution'. *Case Western Reserve Law Review* 37 (2): 179–217.

Posner, Richard A. 2010. 'Some Realism About Judges: A Reply to Edwards and Livermore'. *Duke Law Journal* 59: 1177–86.

Pound, Roscoe. 1908. 'Mechanical Jurisprudence'. *Columbia Law Review* 8 (8): 605–23.

Raihani, Nichola J., and Katherine McAuliffe. 2014. 'Dictator Game Giving: The Importance of Descriptive Versus Injunctive Norms'. *PloS One* 9 (12): e113826. https://doi.org/10.1371/journal.pone.0113826.

Randazzo, Kirk A. 2008. 'Strategic Anticipation and the Hierarchy of Justice in U.S. District Courts'. *American Politics Research* 36 (5): 669–93. https://doi.org/10.1177/1532673X08317286.

Reid, Lord James. 1972. 'The Judge as Law Maker'. *Journal of the Society of Public Teachers of Law* 12 (1): 22–29.

Richards, Mark J., and Herbert M. Kritzer. 2002. 'Jurisprudential Regimes in Supreme Court Decision Making'. *The American Political Science Review* 96 (02): 305–20. https://doi.org/10.1017/S0003055402000187.

Rückert, Joachim. 2004-2023. 'Historische Rechtsschule'. In *Handwörterbuch zur deutschen Rechtsgeschichte*, 2nd edn, edited by Albrecht Cordes, Hans-Peter Haferkamp, Bernd Kannowski, Heiner Lück, Heinrich de Wall, Dieter Werkmüller, and Ruth Schmidt-Wiegand, 1048–55. Berlin: Erich Schmidt Verlag.

Rückert, Joachim. 2008. 'Vom "Freirecht" zur freien "Wertungsjurisprudenz"—Eine Geschichte voller Legenden'. *Zeitschrift für Rechtsgeschichte Germanistische Abteilung* 125: 199–255.

Rüthers, Bernd, Axel Birk, and Christian Fischer. 2018. *Rechtstheorie: Mit Juristischer Methodenlehre*, 10th edn. Munich: C.H. Beck.

Salzberger, Eli, and Paul Fenn. 1999. 'Judicial Independence: Some Evidence from the English Court of Appeal'. *Journal of Law and Economics* 42: 831–47.

Savigny, Friedrich Carl von. 1814. *Vom Beruf unsrer Zeit für Gesetzgebung und Rechtswissenschaft*. Heidelberg: Mohr und Zimmer.

Scalia, Antonin. 1989. *The Rule of Law as a Law of Rules. The University of Chicago Law Review* 56 (4): 1175–88.

Segal, Jeffrey A., and Albert D. Cover. 1989. 'Ideological Values and the Votes of U.S. Supreme Court Justices'. *The American Political Science Review* 83 (2): 557–65.

Segal, Jeffrey A., Lee Epstein, Charles M. Cameron, and Harold J. Spaeth. 1995. 'Ideological Values and the Votes of U.S. Supreme Court Justices Revisited'. *The Journal of Politics* 57 (2): 812–23.

Segal, Jeffrey A., and Harold J. Spaeth. 1996. 'The Influence of Stare Decisis on the Votes of United States Supreme Court Justices'. *American Journal of Political Science* 40 (4): 971–1003.

Segal, Jeffrey A., and Harold J. Spaeth. 2002. *The Supreme Court and the Attitudinal Model Revisited*. Cambridge: Cambridge University Press.

Seinecke, Ralf. 2012. 'Methode und Zivilrecht beim "Begriffsjuristen" Jhering (1818–1892)'. In *Methodik des Zivilrechts—Von Savigny bis Teubner*, edited by Joachim Rückert and Ralf Seinecke, 123–50. Baden-Baden: Nomos.

Shepherd, Joanna. 2012. 'Measuring Maximizing Judges: Empirical Legal Studies, Public Choice Theory and Judicial Behavior'. *Revista Forumul Judecatorilor* 33 (3): 33–44.

Shiller, Robert J. 2019. *Narrative Economics: How Stories Go Viral & Drive Major Economic Events*. Princeton: Princeton University Press.

Shklar, Judith N. 1986. *Legalism: Law, Morals, and Political Trials*. Cambridge: Harvard University Press.

Shklar, Judith N. 1987. 'Political Theory and the Rule of Law'. In *The Rule of Law: Ideal or Ideology*, edited by Allan C. Hutchinson and Patrick Monahan, 1–16. Toronto: Carswell.

Smith, Joseph L. 2006. 'Patterns and Consequences of Judicial Reversals: Theoretical Considerations and Data from a District Court'. *The Justice System Journal* 27 (1): 28–46.

Solberg, Rorie Spill, and Stefanie A. Lindquist. 2006. 'Activism, Ideology, and Federalism: Judicial Behavior in Constitutional Challenges Before the Rehnquist Court, 1986–2000'. *Journal of Empirical Legal Studies* 3 (2): 237–61.

Somek, Alexander. 2010. 'German Legal Philosophy and Theory in the Nineteenth and Twentieth Centuries'. In *A Companion to Philosophy of Law and Legal Theory*, 2nd edn, edited by Dennis Michael Patterson, 339–49. Malden: Wiley-Blackwell.

Spamann, Holger, and Lars Klöhn. 2016. 'Justice Is Less Blind, and Less Legalistic, Than We Thought: Evidence from an Experiment with Real Judges'. *The Journal of Legal Studies* 45 (2): 255–80.

Stone Sweet, Alec, and Thomas L. Brunell. 2012. 'The European Court of Justice, State Noncompliance, and the Politics of Override'. *The American Political Science Review* 106 (1): 204–13.

Stürner, Rolf. 2014. 'Die Zivilrechtswissenschaft und ihre Methodik—Zu rechtsanwendungsbezogen und zu wenig grundlagenorientiert?' *Archiv für die civilistische Praxis* 214 (1–2): 7–54. https://doi.org/10.1628/000389914X13981553946499.

Thibaut, Anton Friedrich Justus. 1814. *Ueber die Nothwendigkeit eines allgemeinen bürgerlichen Rechts für Deutschland*. Heidelberg: Mohr und Zimmer. https://digi.ub.uni-heidelberg.de/diglit/thibaut1814.

de Tocqueville, Alexis. 1936. De la Democratie en Amerique, Librairie de C. Gosselin, Paris, 169.

Troop, Paul. 2018. 'Why Legal Formalism Is Not a Stupid Thing'. *Ratio Juris* 31 (4): 428–43. https://doi.org/10.1111/raju.12225.

Vanberg, Georg. 2001. 'Legislative-Judicial Relations: A Game-Theoretic Approach to Constitutional Review'. *The American Journal of Political Science* 45 (2): 346–61.

Wald, Patricia M. 1999. 'Last Thoughts'. *Columbia Law Review* 99 (1): 270–72.

Walker, Thomas G., Lee Epstein, and William J. Dixon. 1988. 'On the Mysterious Demise of Consensual Norms in the United States Supreme Court'. *The Journal of Politics* 50 (2): 361–89. https://doi.org/10.2307/2131799.

Weber, Max. 1954. Law in Economy and Society, edited by Max Rheinstein, translated by Edward Shills and Max Rheinstein. Cambridge, MA: Harvard University Press.

Weinrib, Ernest J. 1988. 'Legal Formalism: On the Immanent Rationality of Law'. *Yale Law Journal* 97 (6): 949–1016.

Weinrib, Ernest J. 2010. 'Legal Formalism'. In *A Companion to Philosophy of Law and Legal Theory*, 2nd edn, edited by Dennis Michael Patterson, 327–38. Malden: Wiley-Blackwell.

Weinshall-Margel, Keren. 2011. 'Attitudinal and Neo-Institutional Models of Supreme Court Decision Making: An Empirical and Comparative Perspective from Israel'. *Journal of Empirical Legal Studies* 8 (3): 556–86. https://doi.org/10.1111/j.1740-1461.2011.01220.x.

Wetstein, Matthew E., and C. L. Ostberg. 1999. 'Search and Seizure Cases in the Supreme Court of Canada: Extending an American Model of Judicial Decision Making Across Countries'. *Social Science Quarterly* 80 (4): 757–74.

Wittig, Caroline Elisabeth. 2016. *The Occurrence of Separate Opinions at the Federal Constitutional Court. An Analysis with a Novel Database*. Berlin: Logos.

Zimmermann, Reinhard. 2019. 'Juristische Methodenlehre in Deutschland'. *RabelsZ* 83 (2): 241–87. https://doi.org/10.1628/rabelsz-2019-0021.

CHAPTER 7

ATTITUDINAL JUDGING

Partisanship and Ideology

RORIE SOLBERG AND ERIC N. WALTENBURG

1. Introduction

With the 1941 publication of 'Division of Opinion among Justices of the U.S. Supreme Court', Pritchett ushered in a new understanding of judicial behaviour:[1] the law alone does not determine a case's outcome; a judge's attitudinal preferences matter as well; indeed, preferences matter more. Since then, other 'attitudinalists' (as scholars pursuing this paradigm are known) have used increasingly sophisticated techniques and operationalizations to establish firmly the influence of preferences or attitudes on the work of the occupants of the United States' highest bench (see Epstein and Lindquist 2017; Epstein, Martin, and Quinn in this volume).[2] Not surprisingly, and as an indication of its conceptual power, the 'attitudinal model' (see Segal and Spaeth 1993, 2002) also has influenced studies of courts at other levels in the United States and on courts of other nations. Scholars focused first on systems most similar to the United States (i.e. democratic and common law nations) and then more broadly. This slow, country-by-country application of the attitudinal model has led to a general conclusion—policy preferences sit at the centre of most appellate judicial behaviour. In some sense then, the accumulation of these studies provides a smoking gun; we are less certain, however, regarding who or what pulls the attitudinal trigger.

Indeed, it may be that either intentionally or as the result of subconscious preferences, judges behave as though they are 'single minded seekers of legal policy' (George and Epstein 1992, 325; quoted in Epstein and Knight 1998, 10). Yet attitudinal voting is not always dispositive; reality is more complex. As De Visser notes:

> Finally … constitutional justices will also have ideological and policy preferences. These and other factors (such as their background, education and environment)

> should be borne in mind when studying the behavior of particular judges or the performance of a constitutional court as a body.
>
> (De Visser 2015, 268–669; see also Baum 1997, 2006; Posner 2008; Epstein and Knight 2013)

Goldman (1969) and Songer (1982) show clearly that attitudes are more influential in policy cases.[3] And whether acting according to norms, role conceptions, personal goals, or strategic behaviour, we see judges who ought to disagree converging on unanimous opinions a great deal of the time. Gibson captured this complex reality when he noted that 'judges' decisions are a function of what they prefer to do, tempered by what they think they ought to do, but constrained by what they perceive is feasible to do' (1983, 9). Presumably, the mix of forces that affect a judge's decisional behaviour will vary considerably across different countries and judicial systems. Indeed, as Weinshall points out in her study of the Israeli High Court (2011), the structure and institutional context provide markers for expectations regarding primacy of attitudes. Thus, it is time to step back and take stock of the attitudinal model's application. How have attitudes been operationalized across different judicial systems? Under what conditions do we anticipate a judge's attitudinal preferences to play a major or minor a role in decisional behaviour?

In this chapter, we conduct a 'best evidence synthesis' (Lipsey and Wilson 2001, 8) of the judicial literature, paying close attention to studies that transport the attitudinal model outside the US context. This analysis allows us to assess the degree to which attitudinal voting is present in the decisional behaviour of judges across judicial contexts—common law versus civil law systems, from courts at the top of the judicial hierarchy to courts further down the food chain, supreme courts versus constitutional courts. Here, we attempt both to identify how attitudinal voting has been conceptualized and measured as well as identify the conditions that moderate attitudinal voting, thereby shedding some light on the characteristics of the courts and countries that facilitate attitudinal voting.

As expected, we find variety in the measurement of attitudes and the level of analysis. Conceptually, attitudes have been measured as both an individual and court-level phenomenon. Operationalizations of judicial preferences range from simple nominal identifications using partisanship to more sophisticated scaling metrics (see also Esptein et al. and Cope in this volume). Additionally, regardless of where we look for attitudinal voting, we find it, at least to some degree. Finally, and most importantly, although attitudinal voting is widespread among the world's judges, it is conditional. A variety of factors, both systemic and individual, bear upon the degree to which attitudinal dispositions direct or shape judicial outputs.

While the power of preferences or ideology is well documented for the US Supreme Court, the effect of preferences on judicial behaviour outside the United States is less monolithic. To establish its potency across countries and contexts, we perform a systematic meta-analysis of the literature. Before completing this analysis though, we must first describe the studies comprising this literature to understand their variation, findings, and purpose.

2. Attitudinal Judging

2.1 Conceptualization, Measurement, and Effects

Valid and reliable measurement of attitudes or preferences is no mean feat as there are challenges in simply acquiring the data. An obvious solution is simply to ask, and often elite interviews or scientific survey instruments are employed. Such phenomena as question wording, interviewer effects, and social desirability bias, however, can militate against the authenticity of the soundings taken. And even if these problems can be overcome, when it comes to measuring *judges'* attitudes there is the additional wrinkle that rarely will these individuals report their ideological preferences. As a result, alternative, less direct measures are usually necessary.

2.2 Partisanship

One of the most common operationalizations of judicial attitudes is to associate ideology with party identification. As Kang and Shepard write (in the United States), 'Given that parties organize along ideological lines, the partisan identification of a judge on one hand, and his or her judicial ideology on the other, are closely linked' (2016, 1414). Pinello (1999) shows political party is a valid measure of ideology for US judges. Likewise, partisanship should perform at least as well in parliamentary systems where the parties are sharply defined with regard to their policies. Accordingly, it has been used successfully in analyses examining the outputs of courts in Australia (Smyth 2005; Wood 2009); Belgium (Dalla Pellegrina et al. 2017a); France and Germany (Honnige 2009); Italy (Dalla Pellegrina and Garoupa 2013); Spain (Garoupa et al. 2012, 2011; Lopez-Laborda et al. 2019); Norway (Grendstad et al. 2015); Poland (Kantorowicz and Garoupa 2016); Portugal (Amaral-Garcia et al. 2009); and most extensively Canada (Tate and Sittiwong 1989; Songer and Johnson 2007; Stribopoulos and Yahya 2007; Szmer et al. 2007; Johnson and Songer 2009; Johnson et al. 2011; Hausegger et al. 2013).

Whether as the variable of primary analytical interest or as a control, ideology measured by party has had a significant and theoretically consistent effect on judicial outcomes in most of the studies we examine. Generally these studies find that courts and judges whose partisanship aligns with more conservative or liberal parties decide the way they do because they prefer conservative or liberal outcomes (Segal and Spaeth 1993). The exceptions are rare. For example, Johnson and Songer find that ideology as measured by the party of the appointing prime minister failed to attain statistical significance in a model examining the effect of gender on the voting behaviour of Canadian Supreme Court justices, although gender significantly affected votes in four different substantive areas (2009, 272). At the intermediate appellate court level in Canada, Stribopolous and Yahya find that party (and gender for that matter) has an inconsistent effect. Grendstad, Shaffer, and Waltenburg find no statistical evidence for the effect of ideology as measured by the governing party at the time of appointment on justice's votes in sentencing adjustments and family law cases on the Norwegian Supreme Court (2015, chapter 6). Finally, Schwartz and Murchison show that 'ethno-national affiliation exerts a significant influence on the votes of judges on the Constitutional Court of Bosnia-Herzegovina' (2016, 848). They argue that although political parties closely manage judicial appointments, the deep ethno-national cleavage in Bosnia-Herzegovina organizes the political system.

The use of political party affiliation to measure ideology has several advantages, foremost of which is that it is relatively easy to derive. Judges may have a publicly announced party identification in some form or fashion (e.g. some US states use partisan elections to select judges). Judicial associations, which are tied to political parties, are integral components of some nations' judicial selection bodies. In Spain, the Judicial Council identifies the majority of candidates to fill Supreme Court vacancies. These 'associations are formed according to political views and with informal and subtle, *but undeniable*, links to political parties [emphasis ours]' (Garoupa et al. 2012, 801).

Even where the link between political party and court appointee is less direct, it often can be reasonably inferred, and with it, policy preferences. The basic logic of this inference is that the political actors responsible for elevating a judicial nominee to the bench will seek to place individuals with preferences similar to their own on the court. For example, in describing the Italian appointment process, Dalla Pellegrina and Garoupa write, 'Italian constitutional judges are appointed through a complex institutional arrangement but largely influenced by national political parties. Appointers will select individuals that are ideologically close to their policy preferences' (2013, 562). In a number of studies, Grendstad and his coauthors (2010, 2011a, 2011b, 2015; Skiple et al. 2016) use a similar argument for measuring attitudinal preferences of Norwegian Supreme Court justices. They find that judicial ideology as measured by the nature of the appointing government is statistically secure across different model specifications.

Despite partisanship's great utility and widespread use, it is not without shortcomings. First, as we noted above, its validity relies upon a link resulting from the presence of a political-partisan dimension in the judicial selection and appointment process. This link, however, becomes more tenuous if a judiciary is more professionalized and bureaucratic. To take a seat on the US Supreme Court, for example, there are no formal, professional requirements, and presidents are free to select anyone who meets some perceived minimum threshold. Consequently, political and ideological considerations weigh heavily in the process, with presidents seeking ideologically compatible nominees often from their party. In civil law countries, however, the judiciary is a professional class, more akin to an element of a nation's civil service. As such, the political-partisan connection between the appointer and the appointee is less clear-cut, and alternative attitudinal measures must be sought out. Similarly, even in countries with judicial systems generally considered similar to that of the United States, if partisanship is not embedded in the system, scholars must seek creative solutions that match the characteristics of the system or court under study.

In their study of the decisional behaviour of lower court Italian judges, Ceron and Mainenti (2015) do just that. Competitive, merit exams determine whether an individual is qualified for the bench, and appointment is left to the discretion of the National Judiciary Authority. The Authority is 'organized like a parliament', with ideologically oriented factions or parties (2015, 226). According to Ceron and Mainenti, 'Judges … have strong incentives to align with a faction' (2015, 227). Consequently, Ceron and Mainenti can use the Authority's factional alignments to identify a trial court judge's attitudinal preference. Consistent with their hypotheses, they find 'courts with more left-leaning members … act against right wing parties more frequently. Conversely, courts with more right-leaning members tend to protect right-wing parties' (2015, 236–37).

Weinshall (2011) notes that partisanship is not a factor in selection for the Israel Supreme Court; therefore, she also must look elsewhere to find a characteristic that can illustrate the preferences of the justices. Accordingly, she uses religiosity to distinguish among the jurists and finds this measure is a significant factor, along with the institutional context, to explain votes of Israeli justices.

Second, the identification of a judge's attitudinal preferences with partisanship raises another validity question: some issues that are adjudicated do not break cleanly along traditional partisan cleavages nor should we expect them to. (A similar constraint exists when evaluating measures of ideology, per se.) Hausegger et al. suggest that their measure's failure to attain statistical significance in family law cases 'likely reflects the less clear differences between the two parties in this issue area' (2013, 680). As noted earlier, using the party of the appointing government as a proxy, Grendstad et al. found strong evidence of attitudinal voting in the issue domain of economics but came up empty handed when explaining family law and sentencing adjustments (Grendstad et al. 2015). This may also explain the inconsistent effects of partisanship across issue areas that Stribopolous and Yahya (2007) report.

Third, as nominal level measures, the operationalization of attitudes using partisanship (either of the judge or the appointing authority) is very blunt. A judge or court is conservative or liberal, socialist or non-socialist. The instrumentation does not measure any gradations. Yet surely for each category there can be substantial attitudinal differences across individuals. For example, Justices Souter and Thomas from the US Supreme Court were both appointed by the same US President, and so would receive the same score. Thomas, however, is profoundly more conservative than Souter.[4]

Haussegger et al. include a measure of partisanship that avoids this limitation. Specifically, they use a judge's partisan ties, determined through surveys and interviews, to derive a partisan score, ranging from −2 (major conservative ties) to +2 (major liberal ties) for each judge on the Ontario Court of Appeal. They argue that such a measure 'more accurately captures the judge's connection to a party and its policies (and thus better approximates a judge's policy preferences)' (2013, 677).

The difficulty with the relative bluntness of partisanship as a measure of attitudes is further exacerbated when attempting to use it over time. Ideology linked to nominal party identification remains static as party names endure regardless of the shifts in the ideological winds (e.g. the Prime Minister of the United Kingdom at the time of writing, Rishi Sunak, is equivalent to Margaret Thatcher). Whether the bluntness of the measure is problematic in multiple party systems is necessary to consider, but for comparisons in most common law countries, where typically two or three parties are viable, the measurement suffers from this drawback.

Finally, the nature of a nation's political or party system may militate against the use of partisanship as a proxy for attitudes. As has already been noted, cleavages other than partisan ones may organize a nation's politics, overwhelming parties as distinct platforms for the expression of policy preferences. Ethno-national divisions organize political cleavages in Bosnia-Herzegovina, and they are more closely aligned with voting divisions on that nation's constitutional court than is partisanship (Schwartz and Murchison 2016). In nations with consensual party systems, partisanship may provide little traction in systematically accounting for differences among judges. After all, broad policy coalitions and power sharing among the parties characterize consensual party systems. Consequently, sharp party divisions over policies are unlikely. In majoritarian party systems, on the other hand, competition between the major parties produce distinct policy positions, and this is likely to be reflected among judges in these systems (Liphart 1999; Garoupa and Grembi 2015, 35). Empirically testing this proposition in the context of the Italian Constitutional Court as the nation moved from consensual to majoritarian politics, Garoupa and Grembi find that the effect of political variables (i.e. partisanship) are more pronounced in the majoritarian system (2015, 44).

Despite these analytical weaknesses, the various partisanship-based measures of judicial attitudes generally work well with all the necessary caveats. Employing them, scholars have found that attitudes influence decision-making in a number of judicial systems.

2.3 Ideology

Where partisanship is used as a (blunt) proxy for a judge's attitudes, judicial politics scholars have also devised different measures of ideology per se. They range from the computation of relatively simple decisional averages—for example, a justice who rules in a liberal direction 75 per cent of the time is 'more liberal' than a justice who does so 25 per cent of the time—to sophisticated and computationally demanding dimensional techniques. In this form of the operationalization, the individual justices are presumed to have ideal preference points, while individual cases are effectively stimuli, which vary according to how 'difficult' it is to arrive at a given outcome. Accordingly, cases where only two of nine justices vote in the conservative direction are more 'difficult' to decide conservatively than are cases in which eight of the nine justices vote in the conservative direction. Only justices whose ideal points are at the conservative end of the dimensional continuum would vote conservatively in the former case, whereas all but the justice with the most liberal ideal point would vote conservatively in the latter case. This allows the justices to be ordered along an ideological continuum (for a description of this logic, see Baum 1997, 37–38). In sum, these measures of a justice's attitudes do not rely upon the presence of a link between the attitudinal preferences of the appointer and the judicial appointee, nor do they rely on the presumption that parties are organized along ideological lines with partisan ties made on the basis of attitudinal preferences. They do not depend on the assumption that consistent and identifiable party cleavages map onto all policies. They are not static over time, and they permit the justices to be ordered relative to one another in terms of their ideological dispositions.

Although typically ideology is operationalized at the continuous level, there are some studies that operationalize it nominally. These studies adopt *a priori* expectations about a given court's ideological nature based upon the context of the overall political system. Generally, these measures serve as controls for ideology, rather than the independent variable of interest, and exert some influence on the decisional outcomes. Dotan's (1999) analysis of the differential rates of success of litigants before the Israeli Supreme Court is an excellent example. Dotan claims that the general attitudinal orientation of Israeli Supreme Court justices is to see themselves as the defenders of society's weaker elements (1999, 1063–65). Therefore, the relatively high rate of success of 'have nots' in the Israeli Supreme Court results from 'the ideological propensities of the justices ... as well as institutional considerations in relation to the issue of the legitimacy of the Court' (1999, 1074; see also Haynie 1995). Similarly, Haynie and Sill posit that the South African Supreme Court of Appeal is highly conservative and then use that characteristic as a control in a multivariate model exploring the relative strength of advocates on litigant success. They find 'across all categories of litigants ... the win-loss index of the advocate has a much larger effect than the repeat player status, litigant status, or court ideology' (2007, 447–48).

An important limitation of these country-specific or contextually based measures is they do not provide an avenue for researchers to compare ideology's influence on judicial decision-making across nations. The operationalization's idiosyncrasies make the measure too country, system, or temporally specific. The individual measures do reveal the effect of ideology on those judges but the price is generalizability.

The easiest continuous level measures of ideology to compute and understand are court or judge decisional averages. Conceptually, they are akin to measures of central tendency. That is, they report a most common or typical behavioural outcome, making them particularly useful in analyses exploring rational or expected behaviour. In a study of contextual effects on governmental deference among judiciaries in new democracies, VonDoepp (2008), for example, uses the proportion of times an individual justice on the Namibian Supreme Court voted against the national government to control for the individual justice's anti-government preferences. He found this behavioural history had no bearing on the likelihood of a justice deferring to the government. Rather, he found that foreign justices appointed after 1994, because of their reliance on the national government for work permits, are significantly more deferential.

Wetstein and Ostberg (2005) use the decisional history of three Canadian Supreme Court justices who ascended from associate status to chief to explore whether chief justices engage in unique, strategic behaviour as Court leaders. Specifically, they examine whether becoming chief justice affects the frequency these justices authored a majority opinion, voted in the minority, and wrote a dissent. Because ideology might affect voting behaviour and therefore opinion authorship, Wetstein and Ostberg control for the ideological distance of these three justices from the 'typical' justice (2005, 660). They find distinct behavioural changes for the chief justices.[5] Of greater interest to our purposes here, the ideology measure has the expected effect on both dissenting votes and opinions. Namely, the more distant a justice is from the Court's centre, the more likely the justice is to vote in the minority and write an opinion to that effect (Wetstein and Ostberg 2005, 666).

Where Wetstein and Ostberg (2005) examine the dissenting behaviour of chief justices, Songer et al. (2011) attempt to account systematically for the phenomenon of dissent on the Canadian Supreme Court at an institutional level. Controlling for forces hypothesized to affect the likelihood of a dissent occurring, they find that '[p]olitical factors appear to have the strongest effect with attitudinal differences having the largest impact on dissent' (2011, 403). Of greater consequence here, they also point out that the substantial effect of ideology (measured as the difference in the career liberalism scores between the most and least liberal justice voting) 'is not surprising, given the growing body of literature on the Supreme Court of Canada that has determined that the justices' decisions are attitudinal' (2011, 403).

According to Baum (1997), dimensional-based operationalizations of judicial attitudes constitute the classic behaviouralist approach to the study of courts. He goes on to assert that the voting patterns that dimensional analyses reveal are taken to 'reflect patterns of policy preferences (or as they are usually called attitudes or values)' (1997, 38). Schubert was a pioneer in this methodology (1965), and he 'provided an explicit theoretical framework for the findings from dimensional analysis' (Baum 1997, 37).

Guttman scaling is a form of dimensional analysis that Schubert most fully develops and applies in *The Judicial Mind* (1965), and the application of Guttman scaling procedures to the decisional behaviour of judiciaries beyond the United States has a relatively long history. Indeed, it is used in studies on Australia, Canada, India, and the Philippines as early as 1969. According to Schubert and Danelski, their edited volume was 'the first to focus cross-culturally [i.e. East and West] on this subject' (1969, vii).

Guttman scaling is not the only form of dimensional analysis appearing in that volume. Factor analysis is used to examine systematically the decisional behaviour of the Indian and Japanese judiciaries. More recently, factor analysis has been used to explore the dimensional nature of the Canadian Supreme Court. That dimensional voting occurs on Canada's highest court is well established (see Songer et al. 2011). Ostberg et al. (2002) seek to identify the landscape of that dimensionality. Earlier studies found similar ideological structures in the Canadian and US Supreme Courts. Ostberg et al., however, suggest that this similarity might be a consequence of researchers imposing a dimensional structure on the Canadian Court. Thus, they use exploratory factor analysis to determine if the voting of Canadian justices evinces the same liberal–conservative dimensional pattern as is present in the voting of their US counterparts. In the end, they conclude that the dominant dimensional pattern on the Canadian Court is very similar to the pattern on the US Court (Ostberg et al. 2002, 252).

This is not to say that the dimensional behaviour of Canadian Supreme Court justices is an identical image of their southern neighbours. Pointing out that the Ostberg et al. (2002) study was limited to non-unanimous Charter disputes, Wetstein et al. (2009) replicate the analysis for all non-unanimous decisions during the Lamar natural court in economic, criminal, and civil rights and liberties cases and directly compare the dimensional voting of Canadian and US justices. Although they find that a liberal–conservative divide is 'a central feature of the decision making patterns of the justices of these two high courts' (2009, 780), the Canadian justices' dimensional behaviour is more complex. That is, they do not vote consistently liberal or conservative across all three issues areas; they are far less ideologically constrained than are US justices.[6] Wetstein et al. attribute this lack of ideological consistency on the Canadian Supreme Court to a contextual effect: an emphasis in Canada on composing a bench that is representative in terms of region, language, gender, and legal specialization. As a result, political-partisan forces take a back seat, and polarization of the Court is less likely (2009, 785). They conclude by calling for the development of 'a more sophisticated, generalizable model … in the judicial area to accurately capture decision-making patterns in high courts around the world' (2009, 783).

Ideal point estimation techniques (or item response models) are perhaps the most computationally sophisticated of the dimensional techniques. They derive estimates of the individual justice's ideal points or preferences as well as certain case characteristics. The methodology does so by assuming some latent dimension(s) organize the cases (the items) the justices decide. A justice's vote in each case (the response) is somehow related to his or her preference, while case characteristics help to determine both the dimensional location of a case and the justice's position along that dimension (Martin and Quinn 2002; Hanretty 2012a, 676).

Hanretty has applied this methodology to the decisional behaviour of the Portuguese and Spanish Constitutional Tribunals (2012a), the British Law Lords (2012b), the Estonian Supreme Court (2015), and, with Skiple and Bentsen, the Norwegian Supreme Court (2020). In the case of Portugal and Spain, he found that the justices fall out along a left–right ideological dimension that is consistent with the political nature of their party of appointment. That is, justices appointed by more conservative parties are positioned to the right of justices who are appointees of more liberal parties. Similarly, the cases seem to fall along a left–right dimension. Hanretty notes, however, that this dimensional arrangement must be taken with caution.

> A single latent dimension discriminates much more in cases involving horizontal disputes—and those disputes that would presume to be between left and right—than

> vertical disputes. This does not mean that a second vertical dimension does not also structure judicial decisions.
>
> (Hanretty 2012a, 688–89)

Indeed, for the other courts, the procedure does not reveal a unidimensional ideological cleavage. For Estonian justices, the dominating dimension is the degree to which the justices accept a plaintiff's claim that a right was violated; for the Law Lords, a propensity to dissent; for Norway's justices, deference to public authority.

Dalla Pellagrina and various co-authors use dynamic ideal point estimation to examine the voting patterns of the Spanish Supreme Court and the Catalan Constitutional Court (2017b; 2020). For both courts, they find two dimensions that organize the votes. One is a traditional left/right ideological dimension. On the Catalan Constitutional Court, the second dimension concerns Catalonian sovereignty, and '[j]udicial preferences on [it] affect all types of decisions of the Court, regardless of the nature of the issues that are challenged' (Dalla Pellegrina et al. 2020, 385). The second dimension on the Spanish Supreme Court is dissent aversion. Moral and Tokdemir (2017) use ideal point estimation to examine the effect of justice ideology on decisions to dissolve parties whose ideologies threaten the established political system in Turkey. Like the various Hanretty and Dalla Pellagrina studies, their procedure reveals two dimensions—a left/right ideological dimension and a second dimension that measures activism and restraint. Finally, Weinshall and her colleagues craft individual and court level ideal point measures (2017) and test them on five apex courts—United States, Canada, Philippines, India, and Israel. They find their measures perform well when compared to either the Segal–Cover scores or the Martin–Quinn scores for the US Supreme Court.[7] Beyond providing new measures for these courts, this study offers a methodology for cross-country comparison. Unlike some other studies, they find that attitudinal voting is conditioned by institutional factors.

Analyses using sophisticated measures of ideological voting in other nation's courts suggest that a unidimensional left/right cleavage—which so powerfully captures preferences in the United States (Poole and Rosenthal 1991 (Congress); Martin and Quinn 2002; Spruk and Kovac 2019 (Supreme Court); Shor and McCarty 2011 (state legislatures)—is less accurate elsewhere. Examining expressions of ideology in the decisions of the Slovenian Constitutional Court rather than relying on voting cleavages, Avbelj and Sustersic identify three ideological dimensions—economic, social, and authoritarian. They conclude that judicial 'ideology is a complex multidimensional set of values and convictions' (2019, 154).

A criticism of most of the continuous-level measures discussed to this point is that their use of votes to explore or explain patterns in decisional behaviour introduces endogeneity. Simply put, the use of votes to operationalize attitudes in order to explain votes is tautological (Ostberg and Wetstein 2006, 693; see also Segal and Spaeth 2002).

Consequently, judicial scholars have worked to develop alternative, continuous-level instruments of judicial attitudes that do not rely upon voting outcomes. Perhaps the best known of these measures is the Segal and Cover scores based upon the content analysis of newspaper editorials written in response to an eventual US justice's nomination (1989; Segal et al. 1995).

Weiden uses this measurement technique to examine whether the 'selection culture' of the appointment process affects the degree of ideological voting on a nation's apex court. He posits a theory of 'judicial politicization': selection cultures in which judicial appointment decisions are predicated on ideological and attitudinal factors will result in the selection of justices more likely to decide cases along ideological lines. Deriving ideological scores for US, Canadian, and Australian Supreme Court justices from editorials appearing in each country's newspapers and then using them in models to predict the likelihood of a justice voting to strike down a legislative act, he finds support for his theory. The United States has the most politicized selection process, and its justices 'are more influenced by ideology then either Canadian or Australian justices' (2011, 340).

Ostberg and Wetstein use similar newspaper-based ideology scores to test for the effects of attitudinal voting and case facts on the decisions of the justices of the Canadian High Court in right to counsel and search and seizure cases (2006; Ostberg and Wetstein 1998; Wetstein and Ostberg 1999).[8] The results of their models show that both justices' ideological preferences and the presence of certain case facts[9] go a long way to explaining their votes in these issue domains. Of greater interest is their finding that, in right to counsel cases, case facts resonate differently with the different ideological wings of the Canadian Court. As they put it, 'this finding is critical and adds considerably to the literature on attitudinal behavior, because no scholarship to date has demonstrated that there is differential treatment of factual indicators by justices on opposite sides of the ideological divide' (Ostberg and Wetstein 2006, 696). Ultimately, they conclude that there is 'clear evidence that the full attitudinal model flourishes in the Canadian right to counsel area' and that 'ideology ... plays a prominent role in post-Charter right to counsel cases' (2006, 696).

Songer and Siripurapu (2009) use Ostberg and Wetstein's (1998) ideology measure of Canadian Supreme Court justices to test the effect of attitudinal voting on unanimous decisions. They find that attitudes do not account for these decisions. Instead, the perspectives of the justices regarding such considerations as a case's legal importance and informal norms of collegiality are better predictors of unanimity (Songer and Siripurapu 2009, 88–89).

In a study of Israeli Supreme Court justices, Eisenberg, Fisher, and Rosen-Zvi (2012) caution that studying only discretionary cases for courts that have a docket comprising mandatory and discretionary cases can provide a skewed picture of the role of ideology. Their study of both mandatory and discretionary cases decided between 2006 and 2007 showed that voting patterns, and thus the ideological direction of voting, differed significantly between mandatory and discretionary cases.

3. Meta-Analysis: The Effect Size of Attitudes

To gain some leverage on the magnitude of the effect of attitudes on judicial outputs, we conducted a systematic meta-analysis of the research literature. Not every article we discussed in the preceding qualitative literature review is used in this meta-analysis; only analyses that report quantitative research findings are eligible for inclusion. We also excluded studies that analysed attitudinal voting in the US context. To conduct a systematic meta-analysis, a common effect size statistic must be computed for each study. This requires eligible studies to report measures of the relationship of judicial attitudes with outputs (see Lipsey and Wilson 2001, 12–13). These eligibility criteria resulted in the inclusion of twenty-four research articles, but since the unique quantitative study is our unit of analysis, our total number of observations is sixty-six. Table 7.1 reports the countries, their frequency of inclusion, and their legal system that compose the data for the meta-analysis.

Meta-analysis provides an average effect size measure of the phenomenon of interest across the eligible research studies (Lipsey and Wilson 2001, 146). Because the sixty-six research studies we analyse report their results using different methodologies—ranging

Table 7.1 Countries included in meta-analysis

Country	Number of studies	Legal system
Australia	5	Common Law
Bosnia-Herzegovina	4	Civil Law
Canada	26	Common Law
England	1	Common Law
France	1	Civil
Germany	1	Civil
Israel	6	Mixed
Italy	3	Civil
Namibia	1	Mixed
Norway	8	Mixed
Portugal	1	Civil
South Africa	5	Mixed
Spain	2	Civil
Turkey	2	Civil

from ordinary least squares (OLS) to maximum likelihood estimations—we used Rosenthal and Rubin's r(equivalent) to measure effect size (2003).

The qualitative literature review suggested strong evidence for attitudinal judging, and the meta-analysis provides some confirmation. Any conclusions, however, must be drawn cautiously. First, although statistically significant ($p < 0.000$), the pooled effect size is only 0.08. Substantively, this effect is very small (see Lipsey and Wilson 2001, 147). Second, tests for heterogeneity reveal that the variability among the effect sizes is too great to result only from the expected random sample error associated with each study (see Lipsey and Wilson 2001, 116–17). Indeed, the I^2 statistic indicates that about 63 per cent of the variation in the effect sizes is the result of differences across the studies. This high level of between-study heterogeneity might be the result of some feature of each study that operates as a covariate moderating the effect of attitudes on judicial outputs.

To test this explanation, we performed a subgroup meta-analysis to explore whether the heterogeneity is a function of the different legal systems in our data. Across all three types of legal system—common law, civil law, and mixed—the pooled effect size comfortably attains statistical significance yet is consistently small in magnitude. A test of group-specific differences in the effect sizes indicates that they are statistically indistinct. Only for the studies focusing on the common law systems is heterogeneity substantially reduced ($I^2 = 26\%$). This is likely to be a consequence of more than three-quarters of those studies examining the effect of attitudes on Canadian judicial behaviour.

In sum, the 'best evidence' synthesis shows that attitudes affect judicial outputs. The meta-analysis reveals the magnitude of this effect is statistically the same for common law, civil law, and mixed law legal systems; but the between-study heterogeneity must be addressed before drawing any conclusions. One explanation, of course, is that the differences across the studies are the result of different measurement strategies. We think, however, that another, perhaps more likely explanation is that there are other factors that mitigate or intensify the effect of attitudes on decision-making within the various judicial systems.

4. Lessons from the Literature on Attitudinal Judging

Our literature review and meta-analysis suggest that attitudes are present in the decisional behaviour of justices on apex courts. Often, however, the effect is not constant; it waxes and wanes across systems. Scholars have identified four broad forces that condition attitudes' influence: the selection system; the motivations of the individual justices, particularly audience effects (see Baum 2006); legal-institutional considerations; and the social or cultural context.

4.1 Selection System Effects

Simply put, policy preferences are more central to judicial decision making when politics is more central to the appointment of judges. Political motivations intruding upon the selection system, such as when political actors control the process, generally means justices are more likely to engage in judicial activism than when non-elective actors determine appointments (e.g. Carroll and Tiede 2011, 872). If we think about the most 'political' of selection systems—an elected judiciary—the literature on US state judicial selection and its effect on judicial decision-making provides considerable evidence that an upcoming election influences judicial behaviour. Based upon this proposition, we would expect to find a similar pattern in the Bolivian court system given its recent adoption of judicial elections in 2011 (Driscoll and Nelson 2013).

Of course, non-legal considerations entering into the selection process will affect alignments and voting patterns that organize the broader high court's decisional outputs as well. If partisanship and/or ideological motivations guide the appointers' selection, and there is variation among the policy preferences of the appointing authority, a more ideologically polarized court is likely to result. If, however, considerations such as the racial, regional, or gender representation present on the court enter into the appointing authority's decisional calculus, a different, perhaps more complicated, voting alignment occurs (Diascro and Solberg 2009). As we discussed, this is the finding of Wetstein et al. concerning the dimensional structure of the outputs of the Canadian and US Supreme Courts. Prime ministers must consider regional balance, gender, legal specialization, norms, and requirements of bilingualism—all of which militate against polarization (2009, 785). To be sure, less polarization among judges does not necessarily reduce ideology's primacy in the judicial calculus; however, it is certainly a system characteristic that can vary and influence decision-making.

4.2 Audience Effects

Closely related to the effects of an apex court's selection system are audience effects internal to individual justices. After all, different selection processes result in different judicial constituencies. Justices' recognition of and response to these different audiences presumably would bear upon their behaviour, which in turn could condition the effect of attitudes (see generally Baum 2006). For example, justices dependent upon mass electorates for their seat might be reluctant to pursue policy preferences that are at odds with the position of the median voter (Hall 1992). VonDoepp's (2008) finding that foreign-born justices on the Namibian Supreme Court are more deferential to the government has a similar underlying rationale. These justices depend upon the government for their work permits; consequently, they are less likely to put their judicial career in jeopardy.

It also bears mention that since the selection system helps define the relevant audience(s), it is likely that there is an interaction effect present that may further amplify or mitigate the influence of attitudes. Mandatory retirement or term limits for justices may have a similar effect; justices may be concerned with post-judicial positions or continued work in the legal field. These system characteristics, then, will affect the relevant audience for justices and condition the use of personal preferences (Garoupa and Ginsburg 2011). Garoupa and Ginsburg (2011) recognize the existence of a judicial audience in many countries where a constitutional court, often viewed as a political or politicized court, may compete with the judges of the high regular courts or disagree about the supremacy of the constitutional court. Identifying appropriate audiences and how these various audiences affect the strategic calculations of individual justices and courts and are likely to interfere with the imposition of preferences in decision-making is critical to fully understanding the role of attitudes on judicial behaviour.

4.3 Legal-Institutional

Scholars have identified several legal or institutional forces that affect judicial decision-making. For example, various rules and norms will dictate, to some extent, the behaviour of the judges selected to serve. While it is often noted that life tenure is a core component of judicial independence and aids the imposition of policy preferences when deciding cases, less often is it noted that control of the docket or agenda of a court is also integral to the survival and vitality of a constitutional court (Fontana 2011). Docket control provides leeway for judges to avoid controversial political issues that would enmesh the court in an unwinnable situation—a decision that may crush the court's legitimacy as a neutral arbiter. As Eisenberg, Fisher, and Rosen-Zvi (2012) show, the Israeli Supreme Court justices' votes are significantly different in discretionary cases compared to mandatory cases. The extent of preferential voting may be exacerbated if we only examine one part of a court's docket.

Docket control may affect more than the composition of the docket. A court exercising complete discretion may also alter the ability of various parties to succeed before the judges. Testing Galanter's repeat player hypothesis in Australia, Sheehan and Randazzo (2012) find that once the Australian High Court gained docket control, individuals received a much warmer welcome at the court. While the national government, as would be expected, had the highest success rate over the entire time period, individuals spiked after the justices were provided complete control of their caseload. These findings echo those of Dotan (1999) for the Israeli Supreme Court and Haynie (1995) for the Filipino Supreme Court. The Israeli Supreme Court hears a large range of cases, including routine cases, and has an activist streak that favours the have nots. This activist streak came to the fore as the Israeli Court was better able to reserve its finite decisional resources for those cases that did not have an obvious resolution.

Other institutional rules or norms will likewise condition preferential judicial behaviour. The ability to dissent openly and/or write a dissenting opinion provides more allowance for personal preferences (Garoupa and Ginsburg 2011). Judicial review generally is considered to be critical to the presence of attitudes in judicial decision-making.

After all, judicial review empowers a court to replace a policy preference of, for example, the national legislature with its own. And then there are the effects of different types of judicial review. Abstract review places a judicial body directly into the mix of politics by providing constitutional review prior to a policy's promulgation. Inserting an apex court as a 'negative legislator', as per the Kelsenian model, defies the notion of an apolitical court. Yet concrete review does not necessarily diminish the capacity for preferential behaviour (see Amaral-Garcia et al. 2009, footnote 12 for a definition of the Kelsenian model). As Garoupa and Ginsburg (2011) suggest, the breadth and scope of the review authority, either concrete or abstract, are more influential on the decision making than the presences of the power alone.

4.4 Cultural

Overlaying and shaping these aforementioned forces is the political culture in which a given court is embedded. Dotan (1999) and Haynie's (1995) studies recognize that the philosophy or gestalt of the courts under study (again, Israel and the Philippines respectively) affects the decision-making of the justices. This finding goes beyond the introduction of a legal doctrine providing for implied rights; it is the position of the Court within the individual society. Dotan makes clear that the Israeli Supreme Court is associated with individual rights and protection of minorities and that some of the Court's behaviours are clearly linked to preserving this position. The relative success rate of 'have nots' in the Israeli system is attributed to the cultural position of the Court particularly because, in that system, the respondent is always a governmental entity with a distinct advantage. Haynie examines party capability theory and again finds that the 'have nots' are more advantaged due to the Filipino Supreme Court's legitimacy in a system with governmental institutions that are perceived as corrupt. Likewise, the judges on this court attend to this cultural perception, which in turn affects their decision-making so that the 'haves' do not maintain any advantage. Similarly, Sheehan and Randazzo (2012) find that the 'have nots' in the Australian Supreme Court do not have a distinct disadvantage after this court adopted a doctrine of implied rights. While the change in doctrine is a legal effect, the acceptance and support for the Court's role as a defender of minority interests is a cultural shift with large implications for the discretion of judges. A similar shift was witnessed in the United States during the civil rights era and the Warren Court.

5. Conclusion

Our 'best evidence' synthesis highlighted some of the significant holes in the literature and provides suggestions for future research. First, there are very few truly comparative analyses, which might have provided greater depth to our synthesis. Studies examining more than one court could help identify exactly which institutional rules or cultural norms mitigate or exacerbate preferential voting. Furthermore, the meta-analysis revealed substantial between-study variation that must be identified and accounted for before firm conclusions concerning the effect size of attitudes can be made.

Second, the body of extant literature discussed in the qualitative literature review centred mostly on the established democracies of Europe and North America (see Table 7.2). Consequently, many Asian, South American, African, and Middle Eastern countries have been largely excluded from systematic study. This could be because stable, unbiased, and independent courts are assumed to be a necessary component to the study of attitudinal factors in judicial decision-making. Weinshall (2011) provides a guide for identifying attitudinal voting in countries without an easily discernible ideological divide; identifying a single substantive area of law where there may be differences that proximate ideological division can clearly bear fruit. However scholars choose to approach the problem, it is necessary to study the potential underlying attitudinal

Table 7.2 Countries included in qualitative literature review

Country	Legal system
Australia	Common Law
Belgium	Civil Law
Bosnia-Herzegovina	Civil Law
Canada	Common Law
England	Common Law
Estonia	Civil Law
France	Civil Law
Germany	Civil Law
India	Common Law
Israel	Mixed
Italy	Civil Law
Japan	Civil Law
Namibia	Mixed
Norway	Mixed
Philippines	Mixed
Portugal	Civil Law
Slovenia	Civil Law
South Africa	Mixed
Spain	Civil Law
Turkey	Civil Law
United States	Common Law

factors in judicial decisions in nontraditional or newer democracies. This review of the literature makes one point patently clear: the more extreme stance concerning the role of attitudes of some students of the US Supreme Court is untenable when examining courts comparatively.[10] We cannot simply presume that attitudes are the totality of the explanation, nor can we merely combine the attitudinal model neatly with some conditioning based upon strategic concerns and explain judicial behaviour across countries. Parsimony works well when dealing with a single system; however, we must forgo the beauty of parsimony for complexity as we forge ahead and begin to truly compare constitutional courts.

Third, we contend that the structure of various constitutional courts determines, or at least in large part determines, the latitude of judges—what they can do. In other words, regardless of training, justices will pursue their preferences as much as they can, given the constraints of rules, norms and political culture. As Baum notes, 'the goals on which judges act depend on both their inherent goal orientations and the situations that translate them into operative goal orientations—those configurations of goals that actually affect judicial behavior' (1997, 23). We equate the various situations to the structural rules and norms of the various court systems. Some rules will open the door to judging by outcome or judging based upon good policy, other rules will place a barrier to such judging and given concerns about legal accuracy a more prominent role in judicial decision-making.[11] To this end, scholarship needs to identify the key institutional, cultural, and structural factors that either open the floodgates to preferential voting or reinforce the dam. Ultimately, judicial scholars should seek to derive a set of expectations that can be applied across systems to determine when we should expect to see preferential voting by judges and when we should not be surprised when that innate tendency is suppressed.

Notes

1. Earlier versions of this chapter were presented at the 2015 Annual Meetings of the Law and Society Association, Seattle, WA and the 2021 Annual Meetings of the Pacific Northwest Political Science Association, Portland, OR.
2. Cope, also in this volume, offers a different metric for gauging ideology—the expert opinion.
3. These two scholars focus on the lower federal courts in the United States and define policy cases as cases presenting substantive issues where the judges have significant policy discretion and identify these cases because the final opinion either contains a dissent or reverses the lower court's judgment (see also Ray and Spill 2002).
4. Souter's mean Martin–Quinn score from 1991 to 2000 is −0.556; Thomas's mean score is 3.25. (Higher scores are more conservative.) The average Martin–Quinn score for each justice was computed from data located at https://mqscores.lsa.umich.edu/measures.php (last accessed 11.21.23).
5. They find each of the chief justices wrote more majority opinions, and they dissented less frequently. There was no statistical change, however, in the incidence of authorship of dissenting opinions across all three justices (Wetstein and Ostberg 2005).

6. To be fair, US justices probably do not exhibit the level of ideological constraint that a unidimensional understanding of their behaviour strictly presupposes (Wetstein et al. 2009, 780–81).
7. Their measure also compares well against measures often used to assess the ideology of the Canadian Supreme Court.
8. Technically, the operationalizations of ideology in these studies are not continuous-level measures; they are ordinal scales. For example, in the right to counsel analysis (Ostberg and Wetstein 2006), ideology is measured with scores of −2 (conservative), 0 (moderate), and +2 (liberal).
9. A variety of circumstances associated with warnings and consultation concerning the right to counsel (see Ostberg and Wetstein 2006, 688–89) or the location of a search and the presence of a warrant (see Wetstein and Ostberg 1999, 765–67) matter.
10. It is not tenable in the US context either.
11. We recognize, however, that by studying constitutional courts the caseload of these courts will be dominated by the harder and/or newer questions that could not be resolved elsewhere, and so the deck is stacked toward outcome-based judging. Even in systems where the constitutional court provides rulings before promulgation, this is likely to hold. If the question were simple, the legislature would not refer the law to the court for an advisory opinion before moving forward.

References

Amaral-Garcia, Sofia, Nuno Garoupa, and Veronica Grembi. 2009. 'Judicial Independence and Party Politics in the Kelsenian Constitutional Courts: The Case of Portugal'. *Journal of Empirical Legal Studies* 6 (2): 381–404.

Avbelj, Matev, and Janez Sustersic. 2019. 'Conceptual Framework and Empirical Methodology for Measuring Multidimensional Judicial Ideology'. *DANUBE: Law, Economics, and Social Issues Review* 10 (2): 129–59.

Baum, Lawrence. 1997. *The Puzzle of Judicial Behavior*. Ann Arbor: University of Michigan Press.

Baum, Lawrence. 2006. *Judges and Their Audiences: A Perspective on Judicial Behavior*. Princeton: Princeton University Press.

Carroll, Royce, and Lydia Tiede. 2011. 'Judicial Behavior on the Chilean Constitutional Tribunal'. *Journal of Empirical Legal Studies* 8 (4): 856–77.

Ceron, Andrea, and Marco Mainenti. 2015. 'Toga Party: The Political Basis of Judicial Investigations against MPs in Italy (1983–2013)'. *South European Society and Politics* 20 (2): 223–42.

Dalla Pellegrina, Lucia, and Nuno Garoupa. 2013. 'Choosing Between the Government and the Regions: An Empirical Analysis of the Italian Constitutional Court Decisions'. *European Journal of Political Research* 52: 558–80.

Dalla Pellegrina, Lucia, Jef De Mot, Michael Faure, and Nuno Garoupa. 2017a. 'Litigating Federalism: An Empirical Analysis of Decisions of the Belgian Constitutional Court'. *European Constitutional Law Review* 13: 305–46.

Dalla Pellegrina, Lucia, Nuno Garoupa, and Marian Gili. 2020. 'Estimating Judicial Ideal Points in Bi-Dimensional Courts: Evidence from Catalonia'. *Journal of Empirical Legal Studies* 17 (2): 383–415.

Dalla Pellegrina, Lucia, Nuno Garoupa, and Fernando Gomez-Pomar. 2017b. 'Estimating Judicial Ideal Points in the Spanish Supreme Court: The Case of Administrative Review'. *International Review of Law and Economics* 52: 16–28.

De Visser, Maartje. 2015. *Constitutional Review in Europe*. London: Hart Publishing.

Diascro, Jennifer Segal, and Rorie Spill Solberg. 2009. 'George W. Bush's Legacy on the Federal Bench: Policy in the Face of Diversity'. *Judicature* 92: 289–301.

Dotan, Yoav. 1999. 'Do the "Haves" Still Come Out Ahead? Resource Inequalities in Ideological Courts: The Case of the Israeli High Court of Justice'. *Law and Society Review* 33 (4): 1059–80.

Driscoll, Amanda, and Michael J. Nelson. 2013. 'The Political Origins of Judicial Elections: Evidence from the United States and Bolivia'. *Judicature* 96 (4): 151–60.

Eisenberg, Theodore, Talia Fisher, and Issi Rosen-Zvi. 2012. 'Does the Judge Matter? Exploiting Random Assignment on a Court of Last Resort to Assess Judge and Case Selection Effects'. *Journal of Empirical Legal Studies* 9: 246–90.

Epstein, Lee, and Jack Knight. 1998. *The Choices Justices Make*. Washington: CQ Press.

Epstein, Lee, and Jack Knight. 2013. 'Reconsidering Judicial Preferences'. *Annual Review of Political Science* 16: 11–31.

Epstein, Lee, and Stephanie Lindquist. 2017. *The Oxford Handbook of U.S. Judicial Behavior*. New York: Oxford University Press.

Fontana, David. 2011. 'Docket Control and the Success of Constitutional Courts in Comparative Constitutional Law'. In *Comparative Constitutional Law*, edited by T. Ginsburg and R. Dixon, 624–41. Cheltenham: Edward Elgar.

Garoupa, Nuno, Marian Gili, and Fernando Gomez-Pomar. 2012. 'Political Influence and Career Judges: An Empirical Analysis of Administrative Review by the Spanish Supreme Court'. *Journal of Empirical Legal Studies* 9 (4): 795–826.

Garoupa, Nuno, and Tom Ginsburg. 2011. 'Building Reputation in Constitutional Courts: Political and Judicial Audiences'. *Arizona Journal of International and Comparative Law* 28: 539–68.

Garoupa, Nuno, Fernando Gomez-Pomar, and Veronica Grembi. 2011. 'Judging Under Political Pressure: An Empirical Analysis of Constitutional Review Voting in the Spanish Constitutional Court'. *Journal of Law, Economics, and Organization* 29 (3): 513–34.

Garoupa, Nuno, and Veronica Grembi. 2015. 'Judicial Review and Political Partisanship: Moving from Consensual to Majoritarian Democracy'. *International Review of Law and Economics* 43: 32–45.

George, Tracy E., and Lee Epstein. 1992. 'On the Nature of Supreme Court Decision Making'. *American Political Science Review* 86 (2): 323–37.

Gibson, James L. 1983. 'From Simplicity to Complexity: The Development of Theory in the Study of Judicial Behavior'. *Political Behavior* 5 (1): 7–49.

Goldman, Sheldon. 1969. 'Backgrounds, Attitudes, and the Voting Behavior of Judges: A Comment on Joel Grossman's Social Backgrounds and Judicial Decisions'. *Journal of Politics* 31: 214–22.

Grendstad, Gunnar, William R. Shaffer, and Eric N. Waltenburg. 2010. 'Revealed Preferences of Norwegian Supreme Court Justices'. *Tidsskrift for Rettsvitenskap* 123 (1): 73–101.

Grendstad, Gunnar, William R. Shaffer, and Eric N. Waltenburg. 2011a. 'Judicial behavior on the Norwegian Supreme Court, 1945–2009. Determining the effects of extra-legal forces on the justices' votes: The case of "government friendly" voting'. In *2nd International Conference on Democracy as Idea and Practice. Workshop 4: Constitutional Democracy: How Democratic?* University of Oslo.

Grendstad, Gunnar, William R. Shaffer, and Eric N. Waltenburg. 2011b. 'When Justices Disagree. The Influences of Ideology and Geography on Economic Voting on the Norwegian Supreme Court'. *Retfaerd* 34 (1): 3–22.

Grendstad, Gunnar, William R. Shaffer, and Eric N. Waltenburg. 2015. *Policy Making in an Independent Judiciary: The Norwegian Supreme Court*. Essex: ECPR Press.

Hall, Melinda Gann. 1992. 'Electoral Politics and Strategic Voting in State Supreme Courts'. *Journal of Politics* 54: 427–46.

Hanretty, Chris. 2012a. 'Dissent in Iberia: The Ideal Points of Justices on the Spanish and Portuguese Constitutional Tribunals'. *European Journal of Political Research* 51: 671–92.

Hanretty, Chris. 2012b. 'The Decisions and Ideal Points of British Law Lords'. *British Journal of Political Science* 43: 703–16.

Hanretty, Chris. 2015. 'Judicial Disagreement Need Not Be Political: Dissent on the Estonian Supreme Court'. *Europe-Asia Studies* 67 (6): 970–88.

Hausegger, Lori, Troy Riddell, and Matthew Hennigar. 2013. 'Does Patronage Matter? Connecting Influences on Judicial Appointments with Judicial Decision Making'. *Canadian Journal of Political Science* 46 (3): 665–90.

Haynie, Stacia L. 1995. 'Resource Inequalities and Regional Variation in Litigation Outcomes in the Philippine Supreme Court, 1961-1986'. *Political Research Quarterly* 48 (2): 371–80.

Haynie, Stacia L., and Kaitlyn L. Sill. 2007. 'Experienced Advocates and Litigation Outcomes: Repeat Players in the South African Court of Appeal'. *Political Research Quarterly* 60 (3): 443–53.

Honnige, Christoph. 2009. The Electoral Connection: How the Pivotal Judge Affects Oppositional Success at European Constitutional Courts'. *West European Politics* 32 (5): 963–84.

Johnson, Susan W., and Donald R. Songer. 2009. 'Judge Gender and the Voting Behavior of Justices on Two North American Supreme Courts'. *Justice System Journal* 30 (3): 265–79.

Johnson, Susan W., Donald R. Songer, and Nadia A. Jilani. 2011. Judge Gender, Critical Mass, and Decision Making in the Appellate Courts of Canada'. *Journal of Women, Politics and Policy* 32 (3): 237–60.

Kang, Michael S., and Joanna M. Shepherd. 2016. 'The Long Shadow of *Bush v. Gore*'. *Stanford Law Review* 68: 1411–52.

Kantorowicz, Jaroslaw, and Nuno Garoupa. 2016. 'An Empirical Analysis of Constitutional Review Voting in the Polish Constitutional Tribunal, 2003–2014'. *Constitutional Political Economy* 27: 66–92.

Liphart, Arend. 1999. *Patterns of Democracy: Government Forms and Performance in Thirty-Six Countries*. New Haven: Yale University Press.

Lipsey, Mark W., and David B. Wilson. 2001. *Practical Meta-Analysis*. Edited by L. Bickman and D. J. Rog. Vol. 49. Thousand Oaks: Sage Publications.

Lopez-Laborda, Julio, Fernando Rodrigo, and Eduardo Sanz-Arcega. 2019. 'Consensus and Dissent in the Resolution of Conflicts of Competence by the Spanish Constitutional Court: The Role of Federalism and Ideology'. *European Journal of Law and Economics* 48: 305–30.

Martin, Andrew D., and Kevin M. Quinn. 2002. 'Dynamic Ideal Point Estimation via Markov Chain Monte Carlo for the U.S. Supreme Court, 1953–1999'. *Political Analysis* 10: 134–53.

Moral, Mert, and Efe Tokdemir. 2017. 'Justices "En Garde": Ideological Determinants of the Dissolution of Anti-Establishment Parties'. *International Political Science Review* 38 (3): 264–80.

Ostberg, C. L., and Matthew E. Wetstein. 1998. 'Dimensions of Attitudes Underlying Search and Seizure Decisions of the Supreme Court of Canada'. *Canadian Journal of Political Science* 31 (4): 767–87.

Ostberg, C. L., and Matthew E. Wetstein. 2006. 'The Canadian Supreme Court: Attitudinal Conflict in Right to Counsel Cases'. *Political Science Quarterly* 121 (4): 677–97.

Ostberg, C. L., Matthew E. Wetstein, and Craig R. Ducat. 2002. 'Attitudinal Dimensions of Supreme Court Decision Making in Canada: The Lamer Court, 1991–1995'. *Political Research Quarterly* 55 (1): 235–56.

Pinello, Daniel R. 1999. 'Linking Party to Judicial Ideology: A Meta-Analysis'. *Justice System Journal* 20 (3): 219–54.

Poole, Keith T., and Howard Rosenthal. 1991. 'Patterns of Congressional Voting'. *American Journal of Political Science* 35 (1): 228–78.

Posner, Richard A. 2008. *How Judges Think*. Cambridge: Harvard University Press.

Pritchett, C. Herman. 1941. 'Divisions of Opinion Among Justices of the United States Supreme Court, 1939–1941'. *American Political Science Review* 35 (1): 890–98.

Ray, Leonard, and Rorie L. Spill. 2002. 'The States in Federal Appellate Court: Litigation Trends Over Time'. *The Justice System Journal* 23 (1): 97–108.

Rosenthal, Robert, and Donald B. Rubin. 2003. 'r(equivalent): A Simple Effect Size Indicator'. *Psychological Methods* 8 (4): 492–96.

Schubert, Glendon. 1965. *The Judicial Mind: The Attitudes and Ideologies of Supreme Court Justices, 1946–1963*. Evanston: Northwestern University Press.

Schubert, Glendon, and David J. Danelski, eds. 1969. *Comparative Judicial Behavior: Cross-Cultural Studies of Political Decision-Making in the East and West*. New York: Oxford University Press.

Schwartz, Alex, and Melanie Janelle Murchison. 2016. 'Judicial Impartiality and Independence in Divided Societies: An Empirical Analysis of the Constitutional Court of Bosnia-Herzegovina'. *Law and Society Review* 50 (4): 821–55.

Segal, Jeffrey A., and Albert D. Cover. 1989. 'Ideological Values and the Votes of U.S. Supreme Court Justices'. *American Political Science Review* 83: 557–65.

Segal, Jeffrey A., Lee Epstein, Charles M. Cameron, and Harold J. Spaeth. 1995. 'Ideological Values and the Votes of U.S. Supreme Court Justices Revisited'. *Journal of Politics* 57 (3): 812–23.

Segal, Jeffrey A., and Harold J. Spaeth. 1993. *The Supreme Court and the Attitudinal Model*. New York: Oxford University Press.

Segal, Jeffrey A., and Harold J. Spaeth. 2002. *The Supreme Court and the Attitudinal Model Revisited*. New York: Cambridge University Press.

Sheehan, Reginald S., and Kirk A. Randazzo. 2012. 'Explaining Litigant Success in the High Court of Australia'. *Australian Journal of Political Science* 47 (2): 239–55.

Shor, Boris, and Nolan McCarty. 2011. 'The Ideological Mapping of State Legislatures'. *American Political Science Review* 105 (3): 530–51.

Skiple, Jon Kare, Gunnar Grendstad, William R. Shaffer, and Eric N. Waltenburg. 2016. 'Supreme Court Justices' Economic Behavior: A Multilevel Model Analysis'. *Scandinavian Political Studies* 39 (1): 73–94.

Skiple, Jon Kare, Henrek Litlere Bentsen, and Chris Hanretty. 2020. 'The Government Deference Dimension of Judicial Decision Making: Evidence from the Supreme Court of Norway'. *Scandinavian Political Studies* 43 (4): 264–85.

Smyth, Russel. 2005. 'The Role of Attitudinal, Institutional and Environmental Factors in Explaining Variations in the Dissent Rate on the High Court of Australia'. *Australian Journal of Political Science* 40 (4): 519–40.

Songer, Donald R. 1982. 'Consensual and Nonconsensual Decisions in Unanimous Opinions of the United States Courts of Appeals'. *American Journal of Political Science* 26: 225–39.

Songer, Donald R., and Susan W. Johnson. 2007. 'Judicial Decision Making in the Supreme Court of Canada'. *Canadian Journal of Political Science* 40 (4): 911–34.

Songer, Donald R., and Julia Siripurapu. 2009. 'The Unanimous Decisions of the Supreme Court of Canada as a Test of the Attitudinal Model'. *Canadian Journal of Political Science* 42 (1): 65–92.

Songer, Donald R., John Szmer, and Susan W. Johnson. 2011. 'Explaining Dissent on the Supreme Court of Canada'. *Canadian Journal of Political Science* 44 (2): 389–409.

Spruk, Rok, and Mitja Kovac. 2019. 'Replicating and Extending Martin Quinn Scores'. *International Review of Law and Economics* 60: 1–14.

Stribopoulos, James, and Moin A. Yahya. 2007. 'Does a Judge's Partyof Appointment or Gender Matter to Case Outcomes: An Empirical Study of the Court of Appeal for Ontario'. *Osgoode Hall Law Journal* 45 (2): 315–64.

Szmer, John, Susan W. Johnson, and Tammy A. Sarver. 2007. 'Does the Lawyer Matter? Influencing Outcomes on the Supreme Court of Canada'. *Law and Society Review* 41 (2): 279–303.

Tate, C. Neal, and Panu Sittiwong. 1989. 'Decision Making in the Canadian Supreme Court: Extending the Personal Attributes Model Across Nations'. *Journal of Politics* 51 (4): 900–16.

VonDoepp, Peter. 2008. 'Context-Sensitive Inquiry in Comparative Judicial Research'. *Comparative Political Studies* 41 (11): 1515–40.

Weiden, David L. 2011. 'Judicial Politicization, Ideology, and Activism at the High Courts of the United States, Canada, and Australia'. *Political Research Quarterly* 64 (2): 335–47.

Weinshall-Margel, Keren. 2011. 'Attitudinal and Neo-Institutional Models of Supreme Court Decision Making: An Empirical and Comparative Perspective from Israel'. *Journal of Empirical Legal Studies* 8 (3): 556–86.

Weinshall, Keren, Udi Sommer, and Ya'acov Ritov. 2017. 'Ideological Influences on Governance and Regulation: The Comparative Case of Supreme Courts'. *Regulation and Governance* 12 (3): 334–52.

Wetstein, Matthew E., and C. L. Ostberg. 1999. 'Search and Seizure Cases in the Supreme Court of Canada: Extending an American Model of Judicial Decision Making across Countries'. *Social Science Quarterly* 80 (4): 757–74.

Wetstein, Matthew E., and C. L. Ostberg. 2005. 'Strategic Leadership and Political Change on the Canadian Supreme Court: Analyzing the Transition to Chief Justice'. *Canadian Journal of Political Science* 38 (3): 653–73.

Wetstein, Matthew E., C. L. Ostberg, Donald R. Songer, and Susan W. Johnson. 2009. 'Ideological Consistency and Attitudinal Conflict: A Comparative Analysis of the U.S. and Canadian Supreme Courts'. *Comparative Political Studies* 42 (6): 763–92.

Wood, Rebecca. 2009. 'The Fading Utility of the Australian Legalist Story: Using Social Background Theory to Explain Outcomes on the High Court'. In *Annual Meeting of the Midwest Political Science Association*. Chicago.

CHAPTER 8

BACKGROUNDS, ATTRIBUTES, AND IDENTITIES

SANTIAGO BASABE-SERRANO,
WITH LEE EPSTEIN AND KEREN WEINSHALL

1. Introduction

This chapter explores an important strand of the literature on judicial behaviour, variously described as the analysis of the judges' social backgrounds (Schmidhauser 1962; Ulmer 1973), personal attributes (George and Weaver 2017), biographies (Posner 1995), or identities (Epstein and Weinshall 2021). Whatever the descriptor, the basic idea is that personal characteristics affect judging.

Consideration of personal characteristics and their relation to judicial behaviour is both old and new. Early work traces to the 'legal realists'—a group of US law professors, policymakers, and even judges. Writing at the turn of the twentieth century, the realists speculated that the judges' biographies (especially their social class) influenced their decisions.

Not only does the realists' project continue into the twenty-first century, it has gained steam. Modern-day legal academics and social scientists worldwide are investigating how and why various personal attributes, especially social identities (including gender, religion, race, and nationality), affect judging.

This chapter begins, in section 2, with the realists and then moves to more contemporary studies in section 3. Section 4 discusses mechanisms that can help explain why the judges' personal characteristics influence their decisions. The chapter concludes with thoughts on future research programmes.

2. The Backstory

Linking judges' attributes to their behaviour traces to two intertwined events occurring in the United States in the early 1900s: (i) the rise of corporate influence and, ultimately, business's 'ascendancy in government', including in the courts (Schmidhauser 1959, 6); and (ii) the emergence of legal realism.

Because so much has been written on corporate influence from the perspective of judicial behaviour (see e.g. Epstein and Gulati 2022), suffice it to note here that at the turn of the twentieth century, economic regulation—such as maximum-hour work laws—was met with 'suspicion' from the nation's judges, especially Supreme Court justices (Chafee 1931, 338–39). That pro-business period, known as the 'Lochner era',[1] seemed to end in the 1910s only to return a decade later, when the Court issued a string of decisions favouring employers over unions and overturning laws disfavoured by business (e.g. minimum wage, child labour, and tax laws).

Neither the 'Lochner era' nor the later pro-business decisions went unnoticed by a group of scholars, policy-makers, and even some judges. Known as the legal realists, they tended to reject the 'mechanical theory' of judging, an approach postulating 'absolute legal principles, existing prior to and independent of all judicial decisions and merely discovered and applied by courts' (Haines 1922, 92; see also Morell, this volume). In its stead, the realists accepted the view, encapsulated in Holmes' (1881) famous line, that '[t]he life of the law has not been logic: it has been experience'. Under this view (though perhaps in an extreme version), judges were no different than other humans. Haines (1922, 104–05) explains it this way:

> Just as is the case with other opinions of individuals, judicial opinions necessarily represent in a measure the personal impulses of the judge, in relation to the situation before him, and these impulses are determined by the judge's lifelong series of previous experiences.

As applied to the Court's pro-business posture, the realists speculated that judges would naturally favour business over labour because they came from wealth and privileged 'social positions' (Haines 1922, 116).

Although the realists were interested in using data for policy-making purposes (e.g. improving the bankruptcy and criminal justice systems) (see Kritzer 2009), they conducted very few systematic studies of judicial behaviour. So they never put the posited relationship between social class and pro-business to the test.[2]

But soon enough, this test was applied. The realists' general speculation about the relationship between the judges' biographies and their decisions set the stage for data studies by social scientists, especially US political scientists (for a review of the early data studies, see Grossman 1966). Many of the initial projects focused on party identity (see Spill Solberg and Waltenburg, this volume; and Epstein, Martin, and Quinn, this volume; and e.g. Nagel 1961, Ulmer 1962; Vines 1964). Other work, though, zeroed in on various features of the judges' biographies, including the realists' interest in social class—though the results were mixed. Assuming that 'members of certain Protestant denominations' have a 'higher average income than that of members of other Protestant denominations', Nagel (1962, 337) compared the two types' treatment of criminal defendants. He found no difference among US federal and state high court justices. In contrast, analysing a different outcome variable—the propensity to dissent—and using an alternative measure of social class, Schmidhauser (1962, 203) found that 'justices of humble background had a very strong propensity to dissent ... while the justices of upper middle-class background tended almost equally strongly not to become "great" or frequent dissenters'.

Schmidhauser's study excepted, early research connecting the judges' *prior professional experience* and their decisions proved more promising than the work on social class. Because the early 'careerist' studies are many in number and are summarized in Epstein, Martin, and Knight (2003), we list only few especially noteworthy findings:

- Vines (1964), in a study of federal trial court judges, found a positive relationship between holding state political office and taking a segregationist stance on race relations.
- Nagel (1962) demonstrated that both US and state justices with prosecutorial experience were harsher on criminal defendants.

Despite the variations in these and the many other studies reported in Epstein, Martin, and Knight (2003), the results are fairly uniform: whatever occupational path the authors explored and whether they sought to account for the vote, legal reasoning, or another feature of judicial behaviour, their studies generally unearthed some influence of career experience.

3. Modern-Day Analysis

As even this brief review of the early studies makes clear, systematic work on US courts and judges—mainly by political scientists—dominated the analysis of personal characteristics for much of the twentieth century. Towards the end of the century, political scientists from Canada joined in. While the attitudinal model (widely used in the US context; see Spill Solberg and Woltenburg, this volume) did not appear to travel well up north, Tate and Sittiwong (1989) demonstrated that prior career experience, gender, religion, and regionalism (particularly Quebec vs non-Quebec origins), had a significant impact on how Canadian Supreme Court justices reached their decisions (also see Songer and Johnson 2007).

The twenty-first century has witnessed remarkable growth in the diversity of scholarship work on the influence of judges' personal characteristics. Contemporary research is increasingly global in scope, covering judges serving on domestic and international courts. And these days work is just as likely to draw on economics, law, psychology, and sociology as it is on political science. Last but certainly not least, research on prior professional career experiences, to be sure, continues (see e.g. de Castro 2021, showing that former prosecutors remained tough on criminal defendants even after a change in the law). There is also, relatedly, thought-provoking contemporary work on the judges' academic backgrounds and training (see e.g. Basabe-Serrano 2014, 2019). But many modern-day studies tend to focus less on the judges' professional biographies than on the judges' (and, sometimes, the litigants') social identities (see generally Harris and Sen 2019), reflecting the (somewhat) growing diversity of courts worldwide.

The sections to follow focus on the identities of gender, religion, race, ethnicity, and nationality. These are, of course, distinct (though intersecting) categories but, as we shall see, the research on each has asked similar questions (chiefly, whether a particular identity affects the choices judges make) and has come to comparable conclusions (mostly but not always centring on in-group bias).

3.1 Gender

When the realists and political scientists began drawing links between judges' attributes and the choices they make, the systematic study of social identity (apart from partisanship) was difficult because courts in many countries were quite homogeneous. The judges' gender provides a, if not the, prime example. As Figure 8.1 shows, through the 1970s only about 12 per cent of the 155 countries represented in the data had selected a woman—their first woman—to sit on the country's highest court; in the 1980s, that percentage doubled, such that at least one women had served on about (12.3 + 12.9=) 25 per cent of the countries' courts. By the end of 2010s, only four countries had never appointed a woman to their highest court.

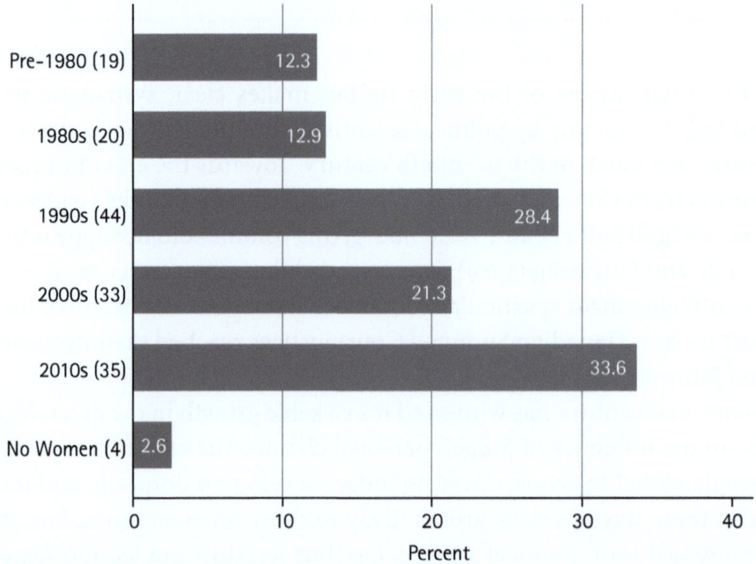

FIGURE 8.1 When the first woman was selected to serve on the highest court in 155 countries. The number in parentheses is the number of countries. For example, before 1980, in only nineteen of the 155 countries (12.3%) did the first woman serve; in the 1980s, twenty countries (12.9%) selected their first woman. Data are from Arrington et al. (2021).

This is not to say that all high courts are now composed of substantial fractions of female judges. To the contrary: the fraction varies considerably. For international courts, Grossman et al.'s (2016) data, running from 1999 to 2015, show that women occupied 47 per cent of the seats on the International Court of Justice but only 14 per cent on the European Court of Justice. Valdini and Shortell's (2016) data for domestic high courts also shows considerable variation, from Latvia's 57 per cent female to under 10 per cent for eleven countries (including Italy, Panama, India, and the United Kingdom). Nonetheless, even low percentages can mask growth in gender diversity over time. In Latin America, for example, the number of female justices 'increased dramatically ... from 3% of all justices in the region's high courts in 1980 to 19% in 2010'. (Arana Araya, Hughes, and Pérez-Liñán 2021, 373).

With increasing gender diversity has come scores of studies mostly aimed at the question typical in the study of personal characteristics: whether the category 'matters'—here, do female judges make different choices than male judges? Perhaps tracing to matters of data and/or methodology, the results of early studies were quite mixed (for a review see Boyd, Epstein, and Martin 2010). But more contemporary work has been rather uniform, with the results fitting comfortably with one of the most central and best documented manifestations of social group identity: in-group bias (or favouritism). More than five decades ago, social scientists noticed the tendency of individuals to favour members of their own group over outsiders (Tajfel 1970; Billig and Tajfel 1973; Tajfel and Turner 1979), and now there is a very substantial literature on the subject across law and the (social) sciences (for a general review, see Hewstone, Rubin, and Willis 2002; for a review with applications to judging, see Epstein, Parker, and Segal 2018). The result is an impressive body of evidence showing that people tend to be more helpful, more willing to allocate resources, and more supportive of policies advocated by members of their own group (and vice versa for the out-group). Moreover, the greater the salience and relevance of the grouping to the task at hand, 'the stronger these intergroup divisions' (Iyengar et al. 2019, 130).

Evidence consistent with in-group bias in courts—'us-against-them' judging—abounds in the gender studies. Contemporary studies have converged on results showing that female judges are more favourable toward plaintiffs (mostly women) in cases of gender-based discrimination and sexual harassment. This holds for courts as diverse as the US intermediate appellate courts (Peresie 2005; Boyd, Epstein, and Martin 2010; Moyer and Tankersley 2012), the European Court of Human Rights (Voeten 2021), and the Supreme Court of Canada (Johnson and Songer 2009). Then there is evidence in the family law context of female judges tending to favour mothers over fathers, whereas male judges support fathers over mothers (Stribopoulos and Yahya 2007). Likewise, in criminal cases involving sex offences (again, with mostly male defendants), female judges favour the state at greater rates than males. Weinshall (2021), for example, finds that female judges on the Israeli Supreme Court, 'were significantly "tougher on crime" when sex offenses were involved, ruling for the state in 80.2% of their decisions, compared to 67.1% of the decisions by men'. Beyond these types of cases—*all salient to gender*—few (or weaker) differences emerge between male and female judges.

But there are certainly exceptions to the in-group findings. Boyd's (2013) analysis of settlements is a prominent example. Analysing 18,000 civil rights and torts cases terminated in US district (trial) courts, she finds that 'the sex of a case's assigned judge matters, with female judges successfully fostering settlement in their cases more often and more quickly than their male colleagues' (193). Boyd attributes the results not to in-group bias but rather to the different management styles adopted by men and women (e.g. women tend to be more oriented toward consensus building).

3.2 Religion

Most studies on gender are relatively new, reflecting the dearth of women on the bench until the late-twentieth century. Religion, in contrast, sometimes figured into early research on social backgrounds and attributes. In comparing Catholic, Jewish, and Protestant US appellate judges, Goldman (1966, 381), for example, found that the Catholics (or, as he noted, 'perhaps [the] upper-class Catholics' who populated the federal bench) were less likely to rule in favour of the government in fiscal cases.

Work on religion continues, with more studies than ever and with many, yet again, reaching results consistent with in-group bias. Take Koev's (2019) study of religious freedom cases in the European Court of Human Rights, which also reports a form of us-against-them judging: the judges are less likely to rule in favour of Muslim applicants. Whether this result reflects bias against adherents of Islam is hard to know, as Koev acknowledges. Nonetheless, 'the strength of the empirical relationship, when paired with the salient and controversial role Muslims (especially Muslim migrants) play in Europe's contemporary political climate, suggests such a bias is plausible' (Koev 2019, 197).

Other studies run along similar lines, though they focus less on religious affiliation than on religious devoutness. Two papers, one on Israel (Weinshall 2021) and the other on the United States (Epstein and Posner 2022), provide examples.

In both countries, interestingly enough, 'devout' justices have increased in number. In 2010, as Figure 8.2 shows, religious Jewish justices (relative to secular Jewish and non-Jewish justices) cast fewer than 25 per cent of the votes in the Israeli Supreme Court; a decade later, the percentage jumped to 41. An increase in religiosity on the US Supreme Court is equally apparent (right panel). Between 2000 and 2020, the percentage of votes cast by Catholic justices, many of whom are devout, doubled, from about 33 to over 66.

To the extent that devoutness affects the judges' decisions, these increases are quite meaningful. Weinshall (2021) reports that religious Jewish justices on the Israeli Court are far less likely to overrule decisions of the rabbinical court than secular Jews, and Epstein and Posner (2022) show that highly devout US justices more frequently rule in favour of religious liberty than the less devout.

These findings square with other studies on judges' affiliation with the Catholic church. Blake (2012), for example, shows that Catholic justices on the US Supreme Court form a distinctive bloc, voting consistently with Catholic theological commitments.

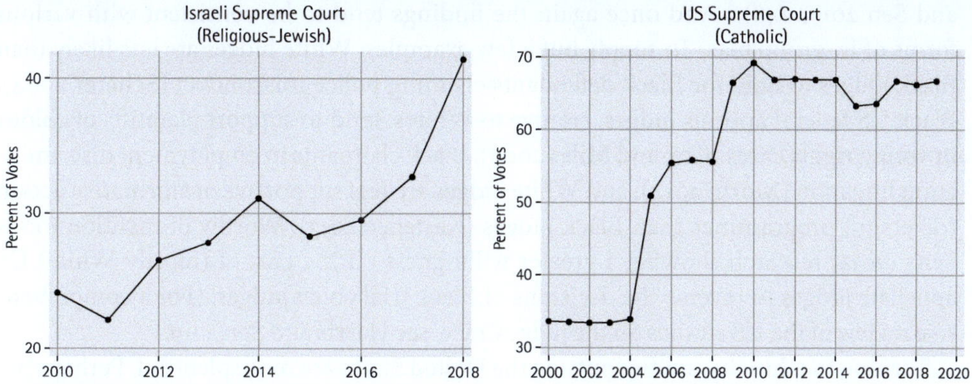

FIGURE 8.2 Percentage of votes cast by religious-Jewish justices on the Israeli Supreme Court (left panel) and by Catholic justices on the US Supreme Court (right panel). Data sources: Israel (Weinshall and Epstein 2020), United States (Epstein and Posner 2022).

Wasserman and Hardy (2013) report that Catholic US justices favour religious organizations more than Protestant justices—by a factor of twelve. And work by Tate and Sittiwong (1989) and Songer and Johnson (2007) highlight distinct differences in the voting patterns of Catholic and Protestant judges on the Canadian Supreme Court.

Other studies reaching similar conclusions are easy enough to summons (see e.g. Songer and Tabrizi 1999). With few exceptions (e.g. Weinshall 2021), though, they are North American based; little is known about the linkage between religion and judging in other societies and regions. Expanding the targets of inquiry into Latin America, in particular, would seem quite important because the Catholic church remains the institution with the greatest credibility and public trust. Studies could compare areas in which the relationship between this sector and judicial choices might be especially salient (abortion, same-sex marriage, and euthanasia) and those where it may be less relevant.

At the same time, it is true that some work on religion, just as some research on gender, reaches results that must reflect explanations other than in-group bias. Take a study of Pakistan and India, showing that Ramadan fasting ritual increases 'Muslim judges' acquittal rates, lowers their appeal and reversal rates, and does not come at the cost of increased recidivism or heightened outgroup bias' (Mehmood, Seror, and Chen 2023, 874). The explanation, the authors suggest, may relate to the ritual itself: because Ramadan fasting is associated with greater reflection, it may prompt judges 'do the right thing' and make 'better' decisions, paying more attention to the facts of the case'.

3.3 Race and Ethnicity

When it comes to race, yet again the vast majority of studies are US based, and (mostly) focus on 'Black judges and how their voting differs from white judges' voting' (Harris and Sen 2019, 248).[3] And once again the findings tend to be consistent with various forms of in-group bias. To supply but a few examples: White judges are less likely than Black judges to hold for Black defendants claiming police misconduct (Scherer 2004); Black US federal appeals judges, relative to Whites, tend to support plaintiffs of colour in voting rights cases (Cox and Miles 2008); Black claimants in employment discrimination litigation (Morin 2014); and White judges are less supportive of affirmative action (diversity) programmes than Black judges (Kastellec 2013). Worthy of mention too is Sen's (2015) research showing a greater willingness on the part of (mostly White) US appellate judges to reverse the decisions of Black trial court judges. (For a comprehensive review of the US studies on the judges' race, see Harris and Sen 2019.)

Turning to ethnicity, studies outside the United States are more plentiful. Perhaps because it is such a salient characteristic in Israel, that country has been a testing ground for work on ethnicity (and religion). Shayo and Zussman's (2011) landmark paper of small claims courts in that country exemplifies both the kinds of questions scholars have asked and the answers their work has produced.

As with work on gender, Shayo and Zussman ask whether the identities of interest—here ethnicity/religion—influences judging. Not only do they demonstrate that these identities matter, the data also provides clear evidence of in-group bias: In small claims courts, Jewish judges systematically favour Jewish litigants, and Arab judges (encompassing both Muslims and Christians) favour Arab litigants (see also Gazal-Ayal and Sulitzeanu-Kenan 2010 reporting similar results in Israeli judges' decisions to detain suspects). Further, when the salience of these identities increases, say, in the aftermath of terrorist attacks, the bias strengthens.

Shayo and Zussman's work focused on a court of first instance. Choi, Harris, and Shen-Bayh (2022), in contrast, consider criminal appeals courts in Kenya but the findings are similar. Not only do the authors show that the judges are 'more likely to grant coethnic appeals than non-coethnic appeals' (1067) but Choi, Harris, and Shen-Bayh are able to trace the mechanism directly to in-group favouritism, demonstrating judges use more 'trust-related terms' when writing for co-ethnics.

3.4 Nationality

Although most early studies on the relation between the judges' backgrounds and their choices focused on US courts, with emphasis on the judges' prior professional careers, there were some notable exceptions. Hensley's (1968) analysis of the International Court of Justice stands out. He hypothesized and demonstrated empirically that the judges would show a 'disposition to favour their own countries' (568)—in other words, he provided evidence of in-group favouritism based on national identity.

Since then numerous empirical studies have confirmed Henley's basic finding, giving little reason to doubt 'that the nationality of the international adjudicator matters' (Titi 2020). Or as three international court judges once put it: 'Of all the influences to which men are subject, none is more powerful, more pervasive, or more subtle, than the tie of allegiance that binds them to the land of their homes and kindred' (quoted in Kuijer 1997, 49). To provide an (extreme) example, an Italian judge on the European Court of Human Rights dissented in 133 judgments concerning alleged Italian violations of the European Convention on Human Rights (Titi 2020).

More generally, in their classic empirical study of judges serving on the International Court of Justice, Posner and de Figueiredo (2005) explored whether the judges are biased toward their home countries, its allies, or even countries that resemble theirs. The researchers' findings are clear: not only do the judges favour their home country but also countries whose wealth level and political systems are like theirs.[4] But why the judges exhibit these biases is unclear. As Posner and de Figueiredo note, it could be because the judges fear reprisal from their home government if they vote against its interests, or it could be a more emotional response: 'if judges identify with their countries, they may find it difficult to maintain impartiality' (608).

These explanations pertain to international courts. But even on domestic courts (ethno-) national affiliation can lead to in-group bias, as a study of the Constitutional Court of Bosnia-Herzegovina uncovered: 'the judges . . . divide predictably along ethno-national lines [and] these divisions cannot be reduced to a residual loyalty to their appointing political parties' (Schwartz and Murchison 2016).

Similarly, Songer and Johnson (2007) discovered that 'regionalism' emerges as one of the most significant factors influencing the decisions of justices on the Canadian Supreme Court. Notably, justices hailing from Quebec exhibit distinct voting patterns: more conservative on personal rights issues, while more liberal in economic matters compared to their counterparts from other regions. These patterns may reflect the unique ethnic subculture of Quebec, where Catholicism has influenced the predominantly French-speaking community, leading to the historical adoption of relatively conservative attitudes and values.

4. Mechanisms Explaining Why Personal Characteristics Affect Judging

Throughout this chapter, we have emphasized that the findings in many studies of personal characteristics are consistent with in-group bias. But not all. Songer and Johnson's (2007) study, as we just mentioned, demonstrates a clear ideological divide between justices from Quebec and those from other regions—a divide that appears unrelated to the origin of litigants or to other regional interests. Another example is Boyd's (2013) work on gender effects, showing that women are more likely to promote settlements than men, all else being equal. The suggestion from these and other studies is that in-group bias is not the only explanation linking identity and judging.

For this reason, several papers explore and compare various explanations that seek to explain why personal characteristics affect judging (see generally Boyd, Epstein, and Martin 2010; Weinshall 2021), though the exact mechanism is not always clear, as acknowledged by Posner and de Figueiredo (2005).

One widely discussed mechanism, commonly known as the 'different voice' theory (Gilligan 1982; Sherry 1986), posits that individuals from diverse origins or backgrounds develop distinct world-views, leading them to hold different perspectives and perceptions concerning moral judgments. This premise suggests that the variations in moral views extend beyond issues directly related to one's own in-group and may manifest across a wide range of judicial decisions. This includes, for example, female judges' tendencies to favour a consensual approach to conflict resolution, as demonstrated in Boyd's 2013 study, or Muslim judges 'forgiving' approach during the month of Ramadan, as shown by Mehmood, Seror, and Chen (2023).

An alternative group of mechanisms falls under the category of 'representational' accounts, all positing that judges act as representatives of their gender, religion, race, ethnicity, class, minority, or other social groups (see e.g. Cook 1981). Accordingly, when deciding cases relevant to their in-group, judges tend to rule in favour of their group's interests.

The in-group bias mechanism can be understood as falling within this approach, or at least seen as having a similar impact on voting. The term 'bias', though, may imply that the behaviour is driven by an unaware or unconscious mechanism, whereas the representational accounts include rationally driven and incentivized decisions to serve one's in-group interests. Conversely, a similar voting pattern can also be explained by differences in information held by individuals belonging to various social categories, an explanation sometimes referred to as the 'informational' approach (see e.g. Gryski, Main, and Dixon 1986). In this context, the 'minority' judge may possess knowledge and information unknown to out-group members, leading to a sincere divergence in their views of the legal conflict and its preferred resolution. In the latter case, the presence of a minority-group judge can influence not only her own vote but also the decisions of her colleagues (as discussed in the diversity studies covered in the next section).

When examining these mechanisms, it is essential to consider the possibility that judges' identities may not significantly influence their decisions or that any effect is marginal. This could be ascribed to the neutral and objective manner in which judges approach their decisions (see Morell, this volume), or it could be linked to peer effects or the influence of court leadership, which may act as a constraint on any personal propensities (see Ostberg and Wetstein, this volume; and Bricker, Carrubba, and Gabel, this volume). Alternatively, the shared professional education and training of judges, along with the consequences of the selection process for appointing them to the bench, could contribute to minimizing the impact of their personal backgrounds. Indeed, the selection process may ultimately override differences in personal backgrounds and lead elite lawyers nominated as judges to adapt the dominant perspective. This perspective is sometimes referred to as the 'organizational' or 'reflecting' approach (e.g.

Steffensmeier and Herbert 1999). Then again, the numerous studies cited in this chapter consistently challenge this viewpoint. The abundance of worldwide data showcasing correlations between personal attributes and judicial decisions underscore the influence of backgrounds, attributes and identities on the choices judges make.

5. What's Next?

Undoubtedly, there is a need for more research that focuses on conceptualizing, identifying, and distinguishing among the possible mechanisms of influence we just discussed.[5] Nonetheless—and regardless of the specific mechanisms at play—scholarly attention should also be given to the normative implications and policy consequences of the attributes' effects. Depending on your perspective, these effects could be seen as offsetting years of 'exclusionary legal processes' (Escobar-Lemmon et al. 2021) or they could be seen as violating a guiding principle of most courts: to treat all parties equally. Either way, a mix of social identities is essential for ensuring socially diverse courts ('teams of judges'), which, in turn, may be crucial for developing innovative, high-quality solutions to the kinds of complex problems that confront contemporary courts. In other words, a 'diversity bonus' may follow for courts with a mix of social identities (Page 2017).[6]

Why? Diversity theorists posit several explanations. Most well suited to courts, we believe, are reasons that emphasize shared information and the requirement of reaching an agreement on a collective decision (for voting strategies of judges, see Epstein and Weinshall 2021).[7] Page, for example, argues that the key to building great teams lies in germane cognitive diversity, which amounts to 'differences in information, knowledge, representations, mental models, and heuristics' that team members bring to the tasks of 'problem-solving, predicting, and innovating' (Page 2017, 14–15). This account aligns closely with the 'informational' mechanism presented earlier, which suggests that minority judges possess information, experience, or expertise that is valuable to their colleagues. To the extent that social category diversity—differences in race, gender, ethnicity, religion, nationality—feeds into people's 'cognitive repertoire', socially diverse groups will perform better.

Although research directly putting ideas about the value of diversity in the courtroom to the test is scant, a handful of results could be seen as consistent with them. Mostly these follow from the 'Collegial Court' studies—a line of inquiry that seeks to assess whether a case's outcome (or a judge's vote) would have been different had a single judge, and not a panel, decided the case. In other words, the key question is whether 'collegial' (or 'panel' or 'peer') effects exist (Kastellec 2007). Often the focus is on the social diversity of the panel, especially its racial (Cox and Miles 200), ethnic (Grossman et al. 2016), or gender (Boyd, Epstein, and Martin 2010) composition. Regardless, the results tend to show that 'minority' judges on a panel can affect the choices of their colleagues in pertinent areas of the law.

Such results are consistent with the social diversity literature. But truth be told, researchers have barely scratched the surface when it comes to using data to suss out diversity 'bonuses' on collegial courts. For this reason, we propose new research programs that explore the possible benefits of diversity on courts—including equity, legitimacy, quality, innovation, and creativity.

Taking equity as an example, one question might be: are the decisions of collegial courts more impartial than those of individual judges? Existing studies tend to answer in the affirmative, suggesting that socially diverse courts may mitigate in-group bias. Recall, for example, the study showing that in family law disputes male judges tend to favour fathers and female judges favour mothers (Stribopoulos and Yahya 2007) The same study, though, reports that 'these effects are dampened on panels that include judges of both genders' (319). Likewise, research on sentencing in the United States finds 'that as the proportion of Black judges increases, white and Black judges are less likely to render incarceration sentences in cases with Black defendants and white judges are more likely to render incarceration sentences in cases with white defendants' (Harris 2023). Both studies, in other words, imply that social diversity can redress inequities caused by in-group bias. But far more work is needed, especially on courts outside the United States.

Equity is but one example. We can imagine equally interesting studies exploring, say, whether diverse courts produce higher-quality decisions or rulings that society is more likely to respect.[8] For, despite its long pedigree, the study of links between the judges' decisions and their biographies, attributes, and identities is still evolving—and evolving in more interesting ways than ever.

Acknowledgements

Thanks to Jack Knight for his valuable insights.

Notes

1. This era was named for a 1905 US Supreme Court decision, *Lochner v New York*, in which the majority struck down a law that prohibited employees of bakeries from working more than ten hours per day and sixty hours per week. The Court claimed that such laws reflected nothing more than government paternalism; they were 'mere meddlesome interferences' with the liberty of contract. In 1937, the Court repudiated this approach.
2. But their conjecture about the justices' backgrounds was later confirmed in a landmark data study by Schmidhauser in 1959 (9): 'Throughout the entire history of the Supreme Court, only a handful of its members were of essentially humble origin .... [They] but were chosen overwhelmingly from the socially-prestigeful and politically influential gentry class or the professionalized upper middle-class.'
3. A far fewer number of studies focus on US Latinx judges. Exceptions include Morin (2014) and Haire and Moyer (2015). For a review, see Harris and Sen (2019).
4. Voeten's (2008, 417) findings are similar: European Court of Human Rights judges tend to favour their home country when it is a party to a dispute. But, in a twist, Voeten shows

that judges 'from former socialist countries are more likely to find violations against their own government and against other former socialist governments, suggesting that they are motivated by rectifying a particular set of injustices'.

5. A unique challenge faced by researchers studying certain European and international courts pertains to acquiring information concerning the judges' personal attributes, such as religion or ethnicity. These details are regarded as private information, and even if researchers manage to acquire them, disseminating the database remains unfeasible.
6. Almost needless to write, many justifications exist for diversity, inclusion, and equity. In the context of courts, see e.g. Grossman (2011) and Haire and Moyer (2015).
7. Two other explanations for the possible influence of minority judges on the decisions of their colleagues are the (i) the voting strategies of judges, and (ii) the very presence of minority judges, which can increase the salience of the minority group (see Grossman et al. 2016; Kastellec 2013).
8. For other ideas running along these lines, see Epstein and Knight (2022).

References

Arana Araya, Ignacio, Melanie M. Hughes, and Aníbal Pérez-Liñán. 2021. 'Judicial Reshuffles and Women Justices in Latin America'. *American Journal of Political Science* 65: 373–88.

Arrington, Nancy, Leeann Bass, Adam Glynn, Jeffrey K. Staton, Brian Delgado and Staffan I. Lindberg. 2021. 'Constitutional Reform and the Gender Diversification of Peak Courts'. *American Political Science Review* 115: 851–68.

Basabe-Serrano, Santiago. 2019. 'Judges' Academic Background as Determinant of the Quality of Judicial Decisions in Latin America'. *Justice System Journal* 40: 110–25.

Basabe-Serrano, Santiago. 2014. 'Determinants of the Quality of Justice in Latin America: Comparative Analysis of the Ecuadorian Case from a Sub-national Perspective'. *Justice System Journal* 35: 104–20.

Billig, Michael, and Henri Tajfel. 1973. 'Social Categorization and Similarity in Intergroup Behaviour'. *European Journal of Social Psychology* 3:27–52.

Blake, William. 2012. 'God Save This Honorable Court: Religion as a Source of Judicial Policy Preferences'. *Political Research Quarterly* 65: 814–26.

Boyd, Christina L. 2013. 'She'll Settle It?' *Journal of Law and* Courts 1: 193–219.

Boyd, Christina L., Lee Epstein, and Andrew D. Martin. 2010. 'Untangling the Causal Effects of Sex on Judging'. *American Journal of Political Science* 54: 389–411.

Chafee, Zechariah Jr. 1931. 'Liberal Trends in the Supreme Court'. *Current History* 35: 338–44.

Choi, Donghyun Danny, J. Andrew Harris, and Fiona Shen-Bayh. 2022. 'Ethnic Bias in Judicial Decision Making: Evidence from Criminal Appeals in Kenya'. *American Political Science Review* 116: 1067–80.

Cook, Beverly B. 1981. 'Will Women Judges Make a Difference in Women's Legal Rights?' In *Women, Power, and Political Systems*, edited by Margherita Rendel, 216–39. London: Croom Helm.

Cox, Adam B., and Thomas J. Miles. 2008. 'Judging the Voting Rights Act'. *Columbia Law Review* 108: 1–54.

de Castro, Samy Alexander. 2021. 'Judicial Attitudes Under Shifting Jurisprudence. Evidence´s from Brazil new drug law of 2006'. *International Review of Law and Economics* 68: 1–15.

Epstein, Lee, and Mitu Gulati. 2022. 'Essay: A Century of Business in the Supreme Court, 1920–2020'. *Minnesota Law Review Headnotes* 107: 49–74.

Epstein, Lee, and Jack Knight. 2022. 'How Social Identity and Social Diversity Affect Judging'. *Leiden Journal of International Law*, 35: 897–911.

Epstein, Lee, and Eric Posner. 2022. 'The Roberts Court and the Transformation of Constitutional Protections for Religion: A Statistical Portrait'. *Supreme Court Review* 2021: 315–47.

Epstein, Lee, and Keren Weinshall. 2021. *The Strategic Analysis of Judicial Behavior: A Comparative Perspective*. Cambridge: Cambridge University Press.

Epstein, Lee, Andrew D. Martin, and Jack Knight. 2003. 'The Norm of Prior Judicial Experience and Its Consequences for Career Diversity on the U.S. Supreme Court'. *California Law Review* 91: 903–66.

Epstein, Lee, Christopher M. Parker, and Jeffrey Segal. 2018. 'Do Justices Defend the Speech They Hate? An Analysis of In-Group Bias on the US Supreme Court'. *Journal of Law and Courts* 6: 237–62.

Escobar-Lemmon, Valerie J. Hoekstra, Alice J. Kang, and Miki Caul Kittilson. 2021. 'Breaking the Judicial Glass Ceiling: The Appointment of Women to High Courts Worldwide'. *Journal of Politics* 83: 662–74.

Gazal-Ayal, Oren, and Kenan-Raanan Sulitzeanu. 2010. 'Let My People Go: Ethnic in-Group Bias in Judicial Decisions-Evidence from a Randomized Natural Experiment'. *Journal of Empirical Legal Studies* 7: 403–28.

George, Tracey E., and Taylor Weaver. 2017. 'The Role of Personal Attributes and Social Backgrounds on Judging'. In *The Oxford Handbook of U.S. Judicial Behavior*, edited by Lee Epstein and Stephane Lindquist, 286–302. Oxford: Oxford University Press.

Gilligan, Carol. 1982. *In a Different Voice: Psychological Theory and Women's Development*. Cambridge, MA: Harvard University Press.

Goldman, Sheldon. 1966. 'Voting Behavior on the United States Courts of Appeals, 1961–1964'. *American Political Science Review* 60: 374–83.

Grossman, Guy, Oren Gazal-Ayal, Samuel D. Pimental, and Jeremy M. Weinstein. 2016. 'Descriptive Representation and Judicial Outcomes in Multiethnic Societies'. *American Journal of Political Science* 60: 44–69.

Grossman, Joel B. 1966. 'Social Backgrounds and Judicial Decision-Making'. *Harvard Law Review* 79: 1551–64.

Gryski, Gerard, Eleanor C. Main, and William J. Dixon. 1986. 'Models of State High Court Decision Making in Sex Discrimination Cases'. *Journal of Politics* 48: 143–55.

Grossman, Nienke. 2011. 'Sex on the Bench: Do Women Judges Matter to the Legitimacy of International Courts'. *Chicago Journal of International Law* 12: 647–84.

Haines, Charles Grove. 1922. 'General Observations on the Effects of Personal Political and Economic Influences in the Decisions of Judges'. *Illinois Law Review* 17: 96–116.

Haire, Susan B., and Laura P. Moyer. 2015. *Diversity Matters: Judicial Policy Making in the U.S. Courts of Appeals*. University of Virginia Press.

Harris, Allison P., and Maya Sen. 2019. 'Bias and Judging'. *Annual Review of Political Science* 22: 241–59.

Harris, Allison. 2023. 'Can Racial Diversity among Judges Affect Sentencing Outcomes?' *American Political Science Review* 117: 1–16.

Hensley, Thomas. 1968. 'National Bias and the International Court of Justice'. *Midwest Journal of Political Science* 12: 568–86.

Hewstone, Miles, Mark Rubin, and Hazel Willis. 2002. 'Intergroup Bias'. *Annual Review of Psychology* 53: 575–604.

Holmes, Oliver Wendell, Jr. 1881. *The Common Law*. Available at: https://www.gutenberg.org/files/2449/2449-h/2449-h.htm

Iyengar, Shanto, Yphtach, Lechkes, Matthew Levendusky, Neil Molhotra, and Sean J. Westwood. 2019. 'The Origins and Consequences of Affective Polarization in the United States'. *Annual Review of Political Science* 22: 129–46.

Johnson, Susan W., and Donald R. Songer. 2009. 'Judge Gender and the Voting Behavior of Justices on Two North American Supreme Courts'. *Justice System Journal* 30: 265–79.

Kastellec, Jonathan P. 2007. 'Panel Composition and Judicial Compliance on the U.S. Courts of Appeals'. *Journal of Law, Economics and Organization* 23: 421–41.

Kastellec, Jonathan P. 2013. 'Racial Diversity and Judicial Influence on Appellate Courts'. *American Journal of Political Science* 57: 167–183.

Koev, Dan. 2019. 'Not Taking It on Faith: State and Religious Influences on European Court of Human Rights Judges in Freedom of Religion Cases'. *Journal of Human Rights* 18: 184–200.

Kritzer, Herbert M. 2009. 'The (Nearly) Forgotten Early Empirical Legal Research'. In *The Oxford Handbook of Empirical Legal Research*, edited by Peter Cane and Herbert M. Kritzer, 875–900. New York: Oxford University Press.

Kuijer, Martin. 1997. 'Voting Behaviour and National Bias in the European Court of Human Rights and the International Court of Justice'. *Leiden Journal of International Law* 10: 49–67.

Lochner v New York. 1905. 198 U.S. 45.

Mehmood, Sultan, Avner Seror, and Daniel L. Chen. 2023. 'Ramadan Fasting Increases Leniency in judges from Pakistan and India'. *Nature Human Behaviour* 7: 874–80.

Morin, Jason L. 2014. 'The Voting Behavior of Minority Judges in the US Courts of Appeals: Does the Race of the Claimant Matter?' *American Politics Research* 43: 34–64.

Moyer, Laura P., and Holley Tankersley. 2012. 'Judicial Innovation and Sexual Harassment Doctrine in the US Courts of Appeals'. *Political Research Quarterly* 65: 784–98.

Nagel, Stuart S. 1961. 'Political Party Affiliation and Judges' Decisions'. *American Political Science Review* 55: 843–50.

Nagel, Stuart S. 1962. 'Judicial Backgrounds and Criminal Cases'. *Journal of Criminal Law and Police Science* 53: 333–39.

Page, Scott E. 2017. *The Diversity Bonus*. Princeton: Princeton University Press.

Peresie, Jennifer L. 2005. 'Female Judges Matter: Gender and Collegial Decisionmaking in the Federal Appellate Courts'. *Yale Law Journal* 114: 1759–1790.

Posner, Eric A., and Miguel F. P. de Figueiredo. 2005. 'Is the International Court of Justice Biased?' *The Journal of Legal Studies* 34: 599–630.

Posner, Richard A. 1995. 'Judicial Biography'. *NYU Law Review* 70: 502–23.

Scherer, Nancy. 2004. 'Blacks on the Bench'. *Political Science Quarterly* 119: 655–75.

Schmidhauser, John R. 1962. 'Stare Decisis, Dissent, and the Background of the Justices of the Supreme Court of the United States'. *University of Toronto Law Journal* 14: 194–212.

Schmidhauser, John R. 1959. 'The Justices of the Supreme Court: A Collective Portrait'. *Midwest Journal of Political Science* 3: 1–57.

Schwartz, Alex, and Melanie Murchison. 2016. 'Judicial Impartiality and Independence in Divided Societies: An Empirical Analysis of the Constitutional Court of Bosnia-Herzegovina'. *Law & Society Review* 50 (4): 822–55.

Sen, Maya. 2015. 'Is Justice Really Blind? Race and Reversal in US Courts'. *Journal of Legal Studies* 44: 187–229.

Shayo, Moses, and Asaf Zussman. 2011. 'Judicial Ingroup Bias in the Shadow of Terrorism'. *Quarterly Journal of Economics* 126: 1447–84.

Sherry, Suzanna. 1986. 'Civic Virtue and the Feminine Voice in Constitutional Adjudication'. *Virginia Law Review* 72: 543–616.

Songer, Donald R., and Susan W. Johnson. 2007. 'Judicial Decision Making in the Supreme Court of Canada: Updating the Personal Attribute Model'. *Canadian Journal of Political Science* 40: 911–34.

Songer, Donald R., and Susan J. Tabrizi. 1999. 'The Religious Right in Court: The Decision Making of Christian Evangelicals in State Supreme Courts'. *Journal of Politics* 61: 507–26.

Steffensmeier, Darrell, and Chris Herbert. 1999. 'Women and Men Policymakers: Does the Judge's Gender Affect the Sentencing of Criminal Defendants?' *Social Forces* 77: 1163–96.

Stribopoulos, James, and Moin A. Yahya. 2007. 'Does a Judge's Party of Appointment or Gender Matter to Case Outcomes: An Empirical Study of the Court of Appeal for Ontario'. *Osgoode Hall Law Journal* 45: 315–63.

Tajfel, Henri and John Turner. 1979. 'An Integrative Theory of Intergroup Conflict'. In *The Social Psychology of Intergroup Relations*, edited by W. G. Austin and S. Worchel, 94–109. Monterey: Brooks/Cole.

Tajfel, Henri. 1970. 'Experiments in Intergroup Discrimination'. *Scientific American* 223: 96–102.

Tate, C. Neal, and Panu Sittiwong. 1989. 'Decision Making in the Canadian Supreme Court: Extending the Personal Attributes Model Across Nations'. *Journal of Politics* 51: 900–16.

Titi, Catharine. 2020. 'Nationality and Representation in the Composition of the International Bench: Lessons from the Practice of International Courts and Tribunals and Policy Options for the Multilateral Investment Court'. https://doi.org/10.2139/ssrn.3519863.

Ulmer, S. Sidney. 1962. 'The Political Party Variable in the Michigan Supreme Court'. *Journal of Public Law* 11: 352–62.

Valdini, Melody, and Christopher Shortell. 2016. 'Women's Representation in the Highest Court: A Comparative Analysis of the Appointment of Female Justices'. *Political Research Quarterly* 69: 865–76.

Vines, Kenneth N. 1964. 'Federal District Judges and Race Relations Cases in the South'. *Journal of Politics* 26: 337–57.

Voeten, Erik. 2008. 'The Impartiality of International Judges: Evidence from the European Court of Human Rights'. *American Political Science Review* 102: 417–33.

Voeten, Erik. 2021. 'Gender and Judging: Evidence from the European Court of Human Rights'. *Journal of European Public Policy* 28: 1453–73.

Wasserman, Lewis M., and James C. Hardy. 2013. 'U.S. Supreme Court Justices' Religious and Party Affiliation'. *British Journal of America Legal Studies* 2: 111–62.

Weinshall, Keren, and Lee Epstein. 2020. 'Developing High-Quality Data Infrastructure for Legal Analytics: Introducing the Israeli Supreme Court Database'. *Journal of Empirical Legal Studies* 17: 416–34.

Weinshall, Keren. 2021. 'Courts and Diversity: Normative Justifications and Their Empirical Implications'. *Law and Ethics of Human Rights* 15: 187–220.

CHAPTER 9

STRATEGIC ANALYSIS

SHAI DOTHAN

1. Introduction

The main premise of strategic analysis of judicial behaviour is that judges have goals and the strategic choices they make in order to reach them are conditioned by the expectations they hold about the actions of other actors involved in the legal process, such as other judges, states, or parliaments. Scholars are free to define what the goals that judges are trying to fulfil are, making strategic analysis a whole field of research rather than a particular argument about judicial motivation (Epstein, Knight, and Martin 2003, 798).

Judges make a variety of choices that could involve an element of strategy. Judicial votes on the final result of a judgement are the most obvious, but judges also make decisions regarding whether they want to write a dissenting or a concurring opinion. They decide what type of reasoning they want to attach to their judgements. They can also make a variety of other choices, such as the decision to issue a writ of certiorari in the US Supreme Court (Epstein and Knight 1998, 58–65). All these choices can involve an element of strategy.

Strategic judicial behaviour can be divided into the strategies of judges and the strategies of courts. A strategic judge is a one who, at least sometimes, makes a decision that is not fully in line with her ideological preferences in the hope of leading to a particular outcome in the case. For example, if the judge thinks that a decision based on her sincerely held beliefs would not be able to secure a majority of the judges, she may compromise on her beliefs and decide to support a decision that is not her first-best option but which may lead to an acceptable judgement (Epstein and Knight 2000, 632).

A strategic court sometimes issues judgements that do not reflect the interests of the court as a whole in the hope of leading to an outcome that is beneficial to the court, given possible interactions with other political bodies. A strategic court could, for example, decide not to issue a certain judgement for fear that it would be overruled by parliament and lead to a result that is unfavourable for the court.

The other distinction that divides different types of judicial behaviour is between short-term strategies and long-term strategies. Short-term strategies are focused on securing a certain result in one specific judgement. Long-term strategies are designed to help the judges or the court reach the results that they want in future cases, even if this means sacrificing the outcome of one or more judgements.

Theories of strategic behaviour are descriptive, not normative, but these theories may have normative implications. They help to provide a better understanding of how courts and judges operate. Based on this understanding, concrete recommendations can be raised to reach certain desired results.

Section 2 explains what judicial strategy is and how it can be established empirically. Section 3 deals with strategic behaviour of judges. Section 4 deals with strategic behaviour of courts. Section 5 elaborates on the normative implications of strategic analysis of judicial behaviour. Section 6 concludes.

2. What Is Judicial Strategy

Before focusing on judicial strategy, it is useful to distinguish it from two other prominent ways to think about the behaviour of judges. The first is the legal model. According to the legal model, judges uphold the law in their judgements without any concern for policy. A natural resistance to this type of model would suggest that the law is too unclear to provide objective guidance to the judges. But the view that judges have a specific understanding about what the law requires from them and they simply follow it in their judgements is both possible and difficult to rule out empirically (Gillman 2001, 485–86). Such a view is opposed to strategic models because it presents judges as oblivious to the outcomes of their behaviour and focused only on their obligation to observe the law.

The second and contending model is the attitudinal model. This model claims that judges have policy preferences and these policy preferences are reflected in their judgements. Attitudinal judges have certain views about what the proper policy is, but they are not trying to get these policies implemented strategically. Instead, they follow these policies tenaciously with no concern for the consequences of their actions.

Strategic judges could be using strategy to reach whatever outcome the researcher specifies. In theory, it is easy to imagine a strategic judge who tries to make sure the law is implemented according to their best understanding of it. But usually, strategic judges have policy preferences, just like attitudinal judges. What sets strategic judges apart from attitudinal judges is that strategic judges care about the outcomes of their actions and they are willing to change their behaviour based on the expected outcomes of their decisions after other actors react to them.

A strategic judge is willing to issue judgements that do not follow her sincerely held policy views in the hope of reaching outcomes she sees as important. But this does not mean that strategic judges would diverge from their policy preferences in every case. There are many situations in which the best way for judges to reach the outcome they want is by issuing a decision that directly follows their policy views. In cases like these, a strategic judge will act sincerely based on her preferences, just like an attitudinal judge. Scholars who are trying to determine if judges in particular circumstances are strategic or attitudinal have to exclude the cases in which the strategic and the attitudinal judge behave in the same way and find ways to focus their empirical investigations on cases in which these two types of judges behave differently (Hettinger, Lindquist, and Martinek 2004, 125–26).

The strategic behaviour of judges implies that their behaviour does not always directly reflect their policy views, for example their views about abortion, gun control, or the welfare system. For scholars interested in describing the policy views of judges, the possibility that strategic choices are involved in the act of judging means there is a need to build a theory about what judges are trying to achieve before their sincerely held policy views can be gleaned from their actions. But this characteristic is not limited to strategic theories. There are other theories that claim that two judges with similar policy views may sometimes behave differently.

One example of such theories is research into judges' role perceptions. A role perception reflects the judges' view about the factors that should determine their behaviour. Judges with the same policy attitudes may have different perceptions about their role that dictate to them a different degree of willingness to follow their own policy attitudes. In other words, a judge with a liberal attitude can either follow it in her judgements if her role perception permits it or decide to ignore her policy views in favour of legal arguments if her role perception counsels against following her policy views. The possibility that a judge's perception of her role as a judge exists and has influence on her decision-making therefore implies that the policy attitudes of judges cannot be discovered solely from their actions without a theory of the perceptions judges hold about their own role (Gibson 1978).

Other theories explain differences in the decisions of judges based on their backgrounds, for example their gender or their professional experience (Grossman and Tanenhaus 1969; Tate 1981; Maučec and Dothan 2022). These theories do not describe judicial behaviour as a result of a rational strategic calculation but rather as an outcome of the attributes of judges as individuals. Background theories should not be viewed as contradicting strategic theories but instead as offering a different perspective on the same problem. They make a direct link between the attributes of the judges and their behaviour without building a theory on what judges are trying to achieve.

3. Strategy of Judges

Judges in a large variety of courts, both national and international, make their most important decisions in panels. The literature in law and political science has realized long ago that judges tend to behave differently when there are other judges sitting with them on a panel. These so-called panel effects are very easy to observe in the Federal Court of

Appeals in the United States. This court issues most of its decisions via panels of three judges. Using the political party of the appointing president of a judge—Democrat or Republican—as a proxy for the ideology of that judge easily reveals a panel effect. Put simply, panels with two Republican appointees and one Democrat appointee decide differently from panels with three Republican judges. The same is true for panels with two Democrats and one Republican compared to panels with three Democrats. If judges were just voting based on their sincere preferences, then panels that are ideologically homogenous and panels with only a majority for an ideological position would decide exactly the same, given that the decision is anyway rendered by a majority vote (Sunstein, Schkade, and Ellman 2004; Sunstein et al. 2006).

The significance of other judges on the panel makes panel composition a crucial element in determining the judicial result not just because the composition of the panel would determine the majority within the panel but because the presence of other judges on the panel shapes the decisions made by their colleagues. Different jurisdictions differ markedly in how panels are constructed. Many times, the most influential strategy is actually in the act of determining the panel itself, since the judicial result can be easily predicted at that point. In the Supreme Court of Canada, the chief justice has full power to determine the size and composition of the panel. This contrasts with the US Supreme Court, which hears cases *en banc*. Other courts fall somewhere in the middle. In the UK Supreme Court, the registrar sets the panels, but the president and deputy president can override that decision. In India, Australia, and Israel, the chief justice or president has discretion about setting panels, but this discretion is limited by formal and informal rules (Alarie and Green 2017, 100–03).

Once it is established that judges influence each other on panels and that strategic behaviour of judges exists, one can question when judicial strategy is likely to occur and what it is designed to serve. The literature provides a variety of answers to these questions, which are addressed in the following section.

3.1 Short-Term Strategy

According to the strategic account, judges may have policy preferences related to the judgements they decide, but they are often willing to change their opinions based on pressure from other judges or to join opinions they do not fully agree with without writing a dissenting opinion (Epstein and Knight 1998, 1–9).[1] The simplest case of a short-term strategy by judges is a form of compromise. By agreeing to join forces with other judges, a binding majority opinion can be reached. The price for that may be that this majority opinion will not reflect the policy preferences of all the judges that agree to join it. At the same time it may prevent a result that some of the judges joining that point of view perceive as inferior.

Even if judges have already secured a majority who share their opinion, they may still be susceptible to pressure from other judges that could lead them to further compromises on their ideology. A judge that is left in a minority can still decide to write a dissenting opinion and use this possibility as a threat to extract concessions from other judges. Depending on the situation, a strong dissenting opinion can increase the chances of appeals on the judgement or of statutory overruling (Fuld 1962, 927; Post 2001, 1353–54). Judges in this situation may therefore also be willing to change their opinion in order to avoid harmful dissents.

The desire to avoid dissent is probably responsible for many of the panel effects observed. Judges tend to compromise on their positions when they face a judge with contrasting policy views and issue opinions that do not suit their sincerely held beliefs. It is also possible, however, that panel effects are caused by judges who are genuinely convinced by the position held by a minority judge. Strategic models do not exclude the possibility that judges may try to stay within the confines of what they consider their legal obligations. A strategic judge who has policy views on issues that involve judicial discretion and is even willing to negotiate a compromise on these views to reach certain outcomes may still recognize legal limits to her discretion. When a judge has a different ideology than that of the majority, she may also be motivated to uncover legal arguments that could convince other judges that they have no choice but to agree with her. Judges whose decisions conform to those of a judge on the panel that is in a political minority may do so because this judge acts as a 'whistleblower' for legal arguments they were unwilling or unable to reveal themselves (Cross and Tiller 1998).

3.2 Long-Term Strategy

A long-term strategy of individual judges is a strategy designed to reach outcomes that exceed the result of a specific judgement. Walter Murphy's book *Elements of Judicial Strategy* is a qualitative study of judges who care about their future influence among their colleagues and not about the case at hand. These are judges who are willing to forgo writing a dissenting opinion despite their ideological reservations from the majority opinion because they want their fellow judges to reciprocate such behaviour in future proceedings. Alternatively, a judge employing a long-term strategy can decide not to reach a compromise with other judges that may affect the ruling and may write a scathing dissent simply in order to preserve the credibility of her threat to write such a dissent in the future if her policy demands are not accepted (Murphy 1964, 90).

The strategies that can be applied to reach long-term goals are varied and complicated and make any empirical proof that such strategies exist difficult to find. Judges can try to boost their position on the court in many different ways. There are several strands of literature that try to present hypotheses on how judges interact while on the bench. One strand looks at how judges form so-called voting blocs—judges who usually vote together. Judges may form a long-term collaboration with specific colleagues that will affect the way they vote and the impact that they have on the court's decisions (Ulmer 1965). Another strand looks at patterns of leadership within the court. Research reveals that some judges write more opinions and tend to convince more judges than others (Walker 1973). A judge can have a uniquely strong impact on her colleagues because of her intellectual and social abilities even without holding a formally superior position on the bench. Judges who are in such a superior position, such as the Chief Justice in the United States Supreme Court, also build their ability to influence other judges through social skills such as the ability to guide others and generate harmonious relations between colleagues (Walker 2003, 252).

In some systems, certain judges have formal powers that others do not have, creating the potential for various strategies to be employed. In the US Supreme Court, the Chief Justice can assign the opinion of the court when they are in the majority, which sometimes leads them to pass on casting a vote in the conference of judges when they doubt they will be in the majority in the hope of still controlling the assignment of opinions (Epstein and Weinshall 2021, 15). In the UK Supreme Court and in the Canadian Supreme Court, there is no formal rule on the assignment of opinions but the unwritten rule is that the presiding judge on the panel assigns the writing of the leading opinion—perhaps based on offers from members of the panel—if they are in the majority. It is not clear what happens if the presiding judge is in the minority (Hanretty 2020, 142–43).

Judges also look beyond the court when they devise their strategies. For example, judges can decide not to dissent in order not to draw attention to a judgement with which they disagree (Posner 2008, 32). Judges may consider all kinds of audiences that they want to impress or curry favour with, in the media, in academia, or among the foreign judiciary, and this can affect their decisions (Baum 2006). When judges care more about their personal prestige than the result of the case, strange behaviours can occur. For example, a judge may choose to support a position that respects human rights knowing that the other judges would leave her in a minority opinion, thus avoiding any threat to national security interests (Dothan 2015, 43–44).

Judges may not care only about lofty ideals or about lobbying for them with various interested parties. Judges may be concerned with much more prosaic things, like minimizing their workload or increasing their earnings (Posner 1993; Schauer 2000). A study of the Brazilian Supreme Court, for example, argues that judges are motivated to decrease their workload and avoid irritating their colleagues by not writing dissenting opinions. The study exploits the sequential voting system of judges in Brazil to show that judges who know already that a majority is formed and they are not going to change the outcome would sometimes simply join the majority and avoid the costs in effort and personal reputation associated with dissenting (de Mendonça Lopes 2019). In the United Kingdom, scholars have found that judges try to avoid reversal of their decisions by the House of Lords because such reversals decrease their chances of getting promoted (Salzberger and Fenn 1999). Judges who engage in such types of behaviour would sometimes not be referred to as strategic because they are not following any policy preference, but these types of judges certainly have goals, and they may attempt to achieve them using sophisticated strategies that take the expected responses of others into account.

4. Strategy of Courts

It is easy to understand how a judge can be strategic. As a human being, she has certain goals and preferences and the ability to make strategic choices in order to promote them. A court is not a rational being and as such it does not have preferences of its own. But making an assumption that the court as a unit tries to reach certain goals strategically can lead to useful hypotheses about judicial behaviour. It is the fact that courts sometimes behave *as if* they are motivated by strategy that justifies recognizing a strategic model for courts, not the fact that courts are operated by human beings who also sometimes employ strategies to get what they want.[2]

4.1 Short-Term Strategy

A short-term strategy by a court is designed to achieve a desired outcome in the aftermath of a specific case. Before such strategies can be explained, one needs to assume that the court has a certain policy preference—a ruling that would be viewed as ideologically ideal, a so-called ideal point. This position may reflect the view of the judge whose views are in the middle-ground position on the panel, known as the median judge who can determine the majority opinion (Hettinger, Lindquist, and Martinek 2004, 127), but it doesn't have to conform to it in every case. If judges are strategic, as the previous section demonstrated, the median judge is not the only judge determining the outcome for the court. It doesn't matter how the ideal point of the court is reached, but it reflects how the court would act if no external pressures existed. A strategic court would deviate from this ideological point in its ruling so that the final outcome after the intervention of other institutions would be as close as possible to this point. The ways in which courts could deviate from their ideal point depend on the institutions and the circumstances surrounding the court. This section considers several possibilities.

The first possibility is the most intuitive. For example, an international court is facing a state that violated international law. The ideal policy point of the court requires the state to take actions that are very demanding and that go against the wishes of the state. If the court demands that the state do exactly what the court wants it to do, the state may well fail to comply completely with the court. But if the court adopts a compromise solution and requires the state to do less than the court's sincere wishes, the state may well comply with the judgement.

Consider this policy line as a demonstration:

demanding	C	S(C)	S	restrained

C = court; S(C)= state compliance point; S = state

Point S(C) represents the most demanding judgement with which the state is willing to comply. If the court requires the state to do more, it would remain at point S, which is the state's preferred position. If the court would like the aftermath of the case to be as close as possible to its preferred point C, it should issue its judgements exactly at point S(C).

The picture gets more complicated when several strategic actors are involved in reacting to the court's judgements. Imagine a court that engages with a legislator and seeks to avoid the possibility of legislative overrule of its judgements. Assume that before parliament makes the decision whether to issue overruling legislation, a legislative committee has to decide whether to legislate in this case.

If the legislative committee is strategic, it will initiate legislation at the parliament when it expects that the policy adopted by the parliament will be better according to the committee's ideology than the policy reflected by the court's relevant judgement. If the policy stretches from liberal to conservative ideological positions, it is possible that the committee would consider ideas that are too conservative to be just as bad as ideas that are too liberal. If that is the case, the committee would not transfer to the parliament even those issues where the court is too liberal, according to its view, if the legislator were to adopt a conservative solution that the committee views as even worse.

What this means is that the committee will have an indifference point—a point that is more liberal than its ideal position but still does not justify suffering a conservative legislation from the parliament. Every decision that is more liberal than the indifference point would, in the eyes of the committee, merit sending the case to parliament, leading to conservative legislation. A strategic court would issue its judgements exactly at this indifference point. This will avoid legislative overruling and lead the final outcome to be as close as possible to the court's genuine policy views.

The following policy line illustrates this situation:[3]

liberal	C	G(L)	G	L	conservative

C = court; G(L) = committee's indifference point; G = committee; L = legislator

This basic policy line can be complicated further by adding other actors that interact with one another strategically. For example, it is possible to consider the possibility of a strategic presidential veto (Eskridge 1991a) or to take into account the policy views of both houses of Congress (Segal and Spaeth 2002, 104).

The two types of strategic situations discussed above—trying to compromise to secure compliance from a reluctant body and trying not to exceed the indifference point of a gatekeeper in order to avoid sending the decision to the wrong body—cover most of the literature on the strategy of courts. But these two options by no means encompass every possible form of strategy that courts can employ. Let us consider two slightly more exotic possibilities.

First, a court may decide to shoot for the moon and land among the stars. If the court requires an extremely demanding judgement, it may be greeted with non-compliance, but it can also push the state or the executive into a better position according to its policy views than the state or the executive were in earlier. Not every case of overreaching leads to backlash. Sometimes strategic actors try to meet the court half way by offering partial compliance with the court's rulings.

This means that national and international courts can sometimes gain from asking a state to do even more than they would actually like the state to do if they could determine state behaviour themselves. The court's hope is that by presenting a more extreme view than its sincere wishes it may achieve a better compromise position from the state that would get as close as possible to its ideal point.

The policy line for this type of strategy looks like this:

demanding	C(S)	C	S(P)C(S)	S(P)C	S	restrained

C(S) = strategic court; C = sincere court; S(P)C(S) = partial compliance by the state to a strategic court; S(P)C = partial compliance by the state to the sincere court; S = state

The last possible strategy to mention here is that of a court that wants to push the legislator to act by presenting it with a decision that the legislator would never be willing to accept. According to this strategy, the court would issue a decision that both the legislator and the court itself view as detrimental to both their policy preferences. The only reason for a court to do such a strange thing is because the legislator has powers that the court doesn't have—it can legislate general statutes. By forcing the legislator to act, the court would reach a result that it cannot reach by itself.

William Eskridge argued that this unique strategy was used by the United States Supreme Court in the case of *Alyeska Pipeline Service Co. v Wilderness Society* (Eskridge 1991a, 625–26).[4] The court made a strategic decision that attorneys' fees for enforcing public rights were not recoverable. This extreme judgement forced Congress to settle the matter of fee shifting in a statute, a result that was probably preferred by the court to the result it could reach in a judicial decision (Eskridge 1991b, 388–89).

To make this strategy more general, it can also be depicted on a policy line:

Liberal	C	L	L(I)	D	conservative

C = the court's ideal point, enactment of a statute; L = legislatures ideal point; L(I) = legislature's indifference point; D = the court's strategic decision

According to this policy line, the court prefers a liberal outcome of enacting a statute that enshrines human rights, but it cannot reach this result on its own. The court has to issue a very conservative decision that passes the legislator's indifference point—the point at which the legislature would rather intervene and create the statute that the court wants to see rather than be left with the disastrously conservative implications of the court's decision.

The four possible strategies examined in this chapter have very different ideas on what courts want to achieve and how they reach their goals. Many more short-term strategies of this kind can be imagined and some may be demonstrated in the work of various courts. What all these strategies have in common is that they are focused on issuing judgements that do not reflect the court's sincerely held preferences and that these judgements can affect the behaviour of other actors and lead to the best result the court can hope for, considering the aftermath of a particular case.

4.2 Long-Term Strategy

Long-term strategies of courts are strategies for writing judgements that will lead to a desired impact not regarding a particular case but in the future. These strategies are attempts to explain the way judgements are reasoned and the decisions they make by assuming that the court's behaviour can be explained by a rational strategy designed to reach certain goals.

Many legal scholars devised plans for how courts ought to behave according to a theory of what constitutes legitimate judicial intervention. John Hart Ely, for example, suggested that courts need to intervene more in cases that concern minorities whose political influence is insufficient (Ely 1980). Theories of strategic behaviour are different: they are not designed to determine how courts ought to behave from the perspective of morality or normative legitimacy. Instead, they are designed to provide a theory that explains why courts behave in the way they do.

Many scholars find it natural to assume that courts wish their judgements to be complied with. This assumption is intuitive because without obtaining compliance, courts cannot shape reality according to their policy preferences. The difference between a long-term and a short-term strategy is that a short-term strategy is focused only on getting compliance with the particular case at hand while a long-term strategy is focused on maximizing the chances of getting compliance in the future. Focusing on improving the chances of compliance in the future implies that a court practising a long-term strategy should be willing to risk a greater chance of non-compliance with the case at hand if for some reason this would lead to a greater chance of compliance in future cases.

Most of the literature called on courts who care about preserving the chances of compliance with their future judgements to practise some form of restraint. The most famous example of this strategy is the 'passive virtues' described by Alexander Bickel (1986)—a recommendation for courts not to demand too much from their governments in the hope that the judgements they issue will be complied with. Variations on the general strategy of restraint were also developed, with some scholars recommending courts to practise more restraint on cases that are particularly salient on the public's agenda so as not to provoke antagonism. According to this strategy, courts can demand more from officials when cases no longer preoccupy the public's attention (Schauer 2006).

Scholars of domestic law may feel a bit uneasy with studies of this kind because they openly admit that non-compliance is a possibility. In a country that respects the rule of law, obedience to judicial decrees is essential and doubting the chances of compliance means the entire legal system doesn't work properly.[5] In the international arena, however, the situation is different. Scholars have no doubt that non-compliance by states to decisions made by international courts is possible, as are a variety of other forms of backlash that states can use against international courts. To avoid non-compliance, international courts need to respect a series of political constraints. If they do that properly, they can hope to optimize their compliance rates (Helfer and Slaughter 1997; Ginsburg 2005; Cogan 2008).

Some scholars add a counterintuitive element to the theory of courts as strategists that strive to improve their compliance record across time. They claim that courts increase their chances of obtaining compliance in the future by deliberately issuing judgements that are demanding and hence less likely to be obeyed. If the court manages to obtain compliance with such a judgement, a signal is sent to the relevant community that compliance with future judgements should be expected (Law 2009, 780–81). My own contribution on this issue argued that national and international courts gain reputation especially as a result of compliance with judgements that are demanding or use discretionary reasoning. Judicial reputation is defined as an expectation of the public that judgements of the court will be complied with. This expectation is likely to increase the incentive of states to comply because acting against the prevalent expectation would signal the state's unwillingness to fulfil its international obligations in the future (Dothan 2015).

The literature regarding international courts recently took another turn. Scholars have realized that explaining judicial behaviour based on the goal of increasing compliance alone misses much of the other missions international courts are tasked with performing. Consequently, new theories have emerged that place an emphasis on the other things courts can contribute to the political bodies that created them, the so-called mandate providers. Contributions include solving disputes, supporting international regimes, and legitimizing international norms, for example (Shany 2012, 244–47).

Long-term strategic courts may manipulate more than their own reputation. They could impact external factors that are useful for them. For example, courts can increase ambiguity in the law because ambiguity helps to makes them essential as a body tasked with resolving disputes (Landes and Posner 1979, 239–40). Courts can also deliberately strengthen weaker parties because if weak parties become stronger, there will be smaller differences in power between the parties affected by the court's judgements. This, in turn, increases the ability of the court to choose which side of the debate to support in their judgements and hence expands judicial discretion (Benvenisti and Downs 2017, 94). As an example of this strategy, scholars have argued that the Israeli Supreme Court deliberately increased the power of parliament to make it a real competitor against the stronger executive (Benvenisti 2001, 817–18). Any type of strategy that improves the court's ability to reach its goals in the future could be counted as a long-term strategy.

Naturally, much of the literature on long-term strategies of judges is theoretical, not empirical. It is difficult to measure the power of a court at a particular point in time and to establish a causal connection between that and the behaviour of the court over a long period. Nevertheless, there are arguments about long-term strategy that combine quantitative insights. For example, the length of judgements may indicate whether judges feel secure in revealing their discretion. Short judgements are an indication that judges fear that their social legitimacy is low and they need to support their judgements with very legalistic and strict reasoning. An early study confirmed that when courts have low public support, such as the judicial system in France after the French Revolution, they opt for very short judgements compared both to later French courts and to courts in the United States and in the United Kingdom (Goutal 1976, 60). Another study showed that judgements of the Israeli Supreme Court became consistently longer from the 1960s to the 2000s (Shachar 2008, 32–33). This finding can be used to support the theory developed by Menachem Mautner that this court became stronger in that period due to the acceptance of its liberal values by elites in Israeli society (Mautner 1993, 126–27).

Another way for courts to defend themselves in times of limited public confidence is to suppress dissent. A single dissent may very well reflect the sincere beliefs of a particular judge, but if judges are strategic, they may decide not to dissent sometimes to comply with the wishes of their colleagues. When dissenting opinions are suppressed on a disproportionally large number of cases compared to other periods, this may indicate that judges are collectively serving the interest of the court as a unit in order to cement its legitimacy. There is historical evidence of judges doing exactly that. For example, under Chief Justice Marshall, the US Supreme Court shifted to unanimous decisions when the status of the court in the public was low (Garoupa and Ginsburg 2009, 243). Under Chief Justice Taft, the US Supreme Court suppressed dissent when the court was under attack from politicians and allowed dissenting opinions again when these attacks abated (Post 2001, 1314–19).

There are also many studies that look at the citation practices of courts and connect them to theories about long-term strategy of the court. A study found, for example, that the Israeli Supreme Court decreased the proportion of references to legislation and increased the proportion of references to scholarly work over the second half of the twentieth century (Shachar 2008, 37–39). This can be interpreted as a sign of the greater confidence the court had in support from the public that allowed it to show its discretion and to avoid anchoring its judgements solely in sources that enjoy significant public legitimacy like legislation. Studies of citations should always be taken with a grain of salt: judges often cite sources that did not shape their thinking to curry favour with their colleagues. At other times, judges would not cite a source that actually affected and even determined the result for strategic reasons and to give the judgement an image that suits the wishes of their audiences.

5. Some Implications of Strategic Behaviour

As mentioned above, the insights that strategic models have on the behaviour of judges are descriptive, not normative. They attempt to explain what is really happening, not what judges ought to do. Nevertheless, the observations of this research have significant normative implications. What scholars think judges are doing should affect the recommendations that they issue for regulating judicial activity.

A simple example can demonstrate this. There is plenty of evidence that judges on international courts are biased in favour of their home state (Posner and Figueiredo 2005; Voeten 2008). A court like the European Court of Human Rights (ECtHR) sits in panels of seven judges called Chambers and in panels of seventeen judges called Grand Chambers. If judges follow their sincerely held policy views, the probability that judges are so evenly divided in these large panels that one judge will determine the result because she is biased towards her home state is very small (Voeten 2008, 426). But if judges are strategic, they do not just vote according to their policy views, they can also influence other judges to join their position. In theory, one committed national judge who is willing to offer future concessions to other judges who are long-term strategists can completely change the result of a case (Dothan 2018). If this scenario happens often, it should affect the procedures used by the court; for example, procedures for judicial selection should be much stricter and give less power to the home states of judges so that every individual judge would be more immune from national bias.

As far as the behaviour of courts as units is concerned, there are also crucial normative implications to the theory about what courts are trying to achieve. A purely descriptive theory that explains that courts seek a particular long-term goal, for example maximizing their chances of getting compliance with their future judgements, is the first step in any plan of action to help such a court succeed. It is also the first step in any plan to restrain the court. Normative decisions can stem from political preferences or from theories about the outcomes of judicial intervention and its legitimacy (Dothan 2020). To execute the policies recommended by these normative decisions, it is crucial to understand the determinants of judicial behaviour (Dothan 2015, 299–301).

6. The Social Embeddedness of Judges and Social Network Analysis

Studies of strategic judicial behaviour could develop in many different and exciting directions. One direction, in particular, looks especially promising—studying the social network in which judges are embedded. Social network analysis is a technique for mapping the social connections of individuals and trying to predict how these connections impact their behaviour. A position in the network can provide a proxy for the policy views of individual judges. Judges can later try to act strategically to fulfil the same policy views.

The predictive power of social network analysis can be much greater than trying to predict the policy views of judges based on who appointed them. First, a social network updates all the time, based on the current choices of the judges or on changes in their environment. Second, the network can provide much more information than any element in a judge's backgrounds about their social preferences that are likely to translate to policy views.

As a first step, networks can be constructed based on the panels judges sit on. If panels are partly chosen by the judges, they provide good evidence about their social connections and preferences. Moreover, if judges worked on the same panels in the past, they may build an ongoing relationship involving mutual compromise and collaboration. A study building a network based on panel participation was conducted in the Israeli Supreme Court (Givati and Rosenberg 2020). Scholars also constructed networks with ties indicating all the appointments of International Centre for Settlement of Investment Disputes (ICSID) arbitrators to the same case (Puig 2014). Another interesting proxy in the literature for the social network of judges is the flow of law clerks between federal courts in the United States (Katz and Stafford 2010). Many more potential proxies for the social connections that could motivate judicial behaviour may still be discovered in the future.

Once the network is established, strategic theories could be devised to hypothesize how the network structure may affect the judges' behaviour. Some theories may view the location of an individual judge in the network as a way to uncover her individual preferences, preferences that the judge would try to achieve strategically. More complicated networks would combine the social positioning of multiple judges with that of the colleagues they have to sit with on a particular panel. In other words, the same judge may behave differently depending on the other judges on her panel and their position relative to each other within the network.

7. Conclusion

When quantitative and anecdotal evidence about the behaviour of courts and of judges is considered, the number of situations in which strategic behaviour seems like a reasonable explanation is considerable. But in many of these situations, judicial behaviour can also be explained more simply; for example, according to the attitudinal or the legal model. Comparative research has revealed a set of factors that can determine whether legalistic or ideological, attitudinal, or strategic, explanations are likely to be more persuasive. Among these factors are the process of judicial appointment (a political process leads to more ideological judges), the size of the court's docket (the higher the caseload, the more legalistic the court), and the size of judicial panels (small panels lead to legalism) (Epstein and Weinshall 2021, 6). In any case, simpler explanations are, as a rule, preferable. Only when these explanations fail should there be recourse to strategic models.

Simpler explanations are also to be preferred within the realm of strategic analysis. When an explanation based on short-term strategy works well, it should be chosen instead of a long-term strategy explanation. The ultimate motivation of the judges or the court is also a matter of choice for the scholar. Part of the reason reading classical judicial behaviour studies is so rewarding is because it can help with forming useful hypotheses about the goals that judges are trying to reach.

Despite its usefulness, learning from theories that were devised to explain the behaviour of other courts should always be done with care. Courts are different from one another. They operate under different sets of political as well as legal constraints. Explanations that work in one court may not apply to another. Therefore, the literature is a great way to think of ideas, but every explanation should be examined based on the information available about every individual court at every particular point in time.

Acknowledgements

This research is funded by the Danish National Research Foundation Grant No. DNRF105 and conducted under the auspices of iCourts, the Danish National Research Foundation's Centre of Excellence for International Courts.

Notes

1. Discussing the case of *Craig v Boren*, 429 US 190 (1976).
2. The importance of thinking through assumptions and checking the behaviour of actors *as if* it is intended to reach a certain goal was clarified by the famous economist Milton Friedman (2007, 154). I have applied this insight to the doctrinal study of the law by scholars (Dothan 2021).
3. This is a simplification of a line used by Jeffrey A. Segal (1997).
4. *Alyeska Pipeline Service Co. v Wilderness Society*, 421 US 240 (1975).
5. But there are scholars who demonstrated that even in the United States the federal government often fails to comply with court orders (Parrillo 2018). The same is true in Israel (Dothan 2015, 184–88).

References

Alarie, Benjamin, and Andrew J. Green. 2017. *Commitment and Cooperation on High Courts: A Cross-Country Examination of Institutional Constraints on Judges*. New York: Oxford University Press

Baum, Lawrence. 2006. *Judges and their Audiences—A Perspective on Judicial Behavior*. Princeton: Princeton University Press.

Benvenisti, Eyal. 2001. 'Judicially Sponsored Checks and Balances'. *Hebrew University Law Review* 31 (4): 797–819 (in Hebrew).

Benvenisti, Eyal, and George W. Downs. 2017. *Between Fragmentation and Democracy*. New York: Cambridge University Press.

Bickel, Alexander M. 1986. *The Least Dangerous Branch—The Supreme Court at the Bar of Politics*, 2nd edn. New Haven: Yale University Press.

Cogan, Jacob Katz. 2008. 'Competition and Control in International Adjudication'. *Virginia Journal of International Law* 48 (2, Winter): 411–50.

Cross, Frank B., and Emerson H. Tiller. 1998. 'Judicial Partisanship and Obedience to Legal Doctrine: Whistleblowing on the Federal Courts of Appeals'. *Yale Law Journal* 107 (7, May): 2155–76.

de Mendonça Lopes, Felipe. 2019. 'Dissent Aversion and Sequential Voting in the Brazilian Supreme Court'. *Journal of Empirical Legal Studies* 16 (4): 933–54.

Dothan, Shai. 2015. *Reputation and Judicial Tactics: A Theory of National and International Courts*. New York: Cambridge University Press.

Dothan, Shai. 2018. 'The Motivations of Individual Judges and How They Act as a Group'. *German Law Journal* 19 (7): 2165–88.

Dothan, Shai. 2020. *International Judicial Review: When Should International Courts Intervene?* New York. Cambridge University Press.

Dothan, Shai. 2021. 'As If: Why Legal Scholarship Needs Assumptions'. *Seton Hall Law Review* 51 (3): 645–68.

Ely, John Hart. 1980. *Democracy and Distrust—A Theory of Judicial Review*. Cambridge: Harvard University Press.

Epstein, Lee, and Jack Knight. 1998. *The Choices Justices Make*. Washington: CQ Press.

Epstein, Lee, and Jack Knight. 2000. 'Toward a Strategic Revolution in Judicial Politics: A Look Back, a Look Ahead'. *Political Research Quarterly* 53 (3): 625–61.

Epstein, Lee, Jack Knight, and Andrew D. Martin. 2003. 'The Political (Science) Context of Judging'. *Saint Louis University Law Journal* 47 (3, Spring): 783–818.

Epstein Lee, and Keren Weinshall. 2021. *The Strategic Analysis of Judicial Behavior*. Cambridge: Cambridge University Press.

Eskridge Jr., William N. 1991a. 'Reneging on History—Playing the Court/Congress/President Civil Rights Game'. *California Law Review* 79 (3, May): 613–84.

Eskridge Jr., William N. 1991b. 'Overriding Supreme Court Statutory Interpretation Decisions'. *Yale Law Journal* 101 (2, November): 331–456.

Friedman, Milton. 2007. 'The Methodology of Positive Economics'. In *The Philosophy of Economics: An Anthology*, 3rd edn., edited by Daniel M. Hausman, 145–78. New York: Cambridge University Press.

Fuld, Stanley H. 1962. 'The Voices of Dissent'. *Columbia Law Review* 62 (6, June): 923–29.

Garoupa, Nuno, and Tom Ginsburg. 2009. 'Reputation, Information and the Organization of the Judiciary'. *Journal of Comparative Law* 4 (2): 228–56.

Gibson, James L. 1978. 'Judges' Role Orientations, Attitudes, and Decisions: An Interactive Model'. *American Political Science Review* 72 (3): 911–24.

Gillman, Howard. 2001. 'What's Law Got to Do with It—Judicial Behavioralists Test the Legal Model of Judicial Decision Making'. *Law & Social Inquiry* 26 (2, Spring): 465–504.

Ginsburg, Tom. 2005. 'Bounded Discretion in International Judicial Lawmaking'. *Virginia Journal of International Law* 45 (3, Spring): 631–74.

Givati, Yehonatan, and Israel Rosenberg. 2020. 'How Would Judges Compose Judicial Panels? Theory and Evidence from the Supreme Court of Israel'. *Journal of Empirical Legal Studies* 17 (2): 317–41.

Goutal, Jean Louis. 1976. 'Characteristics of Judicial Style in France, Britain and the U.S.A'. *American Journal of Comparative Law* 24 (1, Winter): 43–72.

Grossman, Joel B., and Joseph Tanenhaus. 1969. 'Toward a Renascence of Public Law'. In *Frontiers of Judicial Research*, edited by Joel B. Grossman and Joseph Tanenhaus, 3–26. New York: John Wiley and Sons.

Hanretty, Chris. 2020. *A Court of Specialists: Judicial Behavior on the UK Supreme Court*. New York: Oxford University Press.

Helfer, Laurence R., and Anne-Marie Slaughter. 1997. 'Toward a Theory of Effective Supranational Adjudication'. *Yale Law Journal* 107 (2, November): 273–392.

Hettinger, Virginia A., Stefanie A. Lindquist, and Wendy L. Martinek. 2004. 'Comparing Attitudinal and Strategic Accounts of Dissenting Behavior on the US Courts of Appeals'. *American Journal of Political Science* 48 (1): 123–37.

Katz, Daniel M., and Derek K. Stafford. 2010. 'Hustle and Flow: A Social Network Analysis of the American Federal Judiciary'. *Ohio State Law Journal* 71 (3): 457–510.

Landes, William M., and Richard A. Posner. 1979. 'Adjudication as a Private Good'. *Journal of Legal Studies* 8 (2, March): 235–84.

Law, David S. 2009. 'A Theory of Judicial Power and Judicial Review'. *Georgetown Law Journal* 97 (3, March): 723–802.

Maučec, Gregor, and Shai Dothan. 2022. 'The Effects of International Judges' Personal Characteristics on Their Judging'. *Leiden Journal of International Law* 35 (4): 887–95.

Mautner, Menachem. 1993. *The Decline of Formalism and the Rise of Values in Israeli Law*. Tel Aviv: Ma'agalay Da'at Publishing House (in Hebrew).

Murphy, Walter F. 1964. *Elements of Judicial Strategy*. Chicago: University of Chicago Press.

Parrillo, Nicholas R. 2018. 'The Endgame of Administrative Law: Governmental Disobedience and the Judicial Contempt Power'. *Harvard Law Review* 131 (3, January): 685–794.

Posner, Eric A., and Miguel F. P. De Figueiredo. 2005. 'Is the International Court of Justice Biased?' *The Journal of Legal Studies* 34 (2): 599–630.

Posner, Richard A. 1993. 'What Do Judges and Justices Maximize—(The Same Thing Everybody Else Does)'. *Supreme Court Economic Review* 3: 1–42.

Posner, Richard A. 2008. *How Judges Think*. Cambridge: Harvard University Press.

Post, Robert. 2001. 'The Supreme Court Opinion as Institutional Practice: Dissent, Legal Scholarship, and Decisionmaking in the Taft Court'. *Minnesota Law Review* 85 (5, May): 1267–390.

Puig, Sergio. 2014. 'Social Capital in the Arbitration Market'. *European Journal of International Law* 25 (2): 387–424.

Salzberger, Eli, and Paul Fenn. 1999. 'Judicial Independence: Some Evidence from the English Court of Appeal'. *The Journal of Law and Economics* 42 (2): 831–47.

Schauer, Frederick. 2000. 'Incentives, Reputation, and the Inglorious Determinants of Judicial Behavior'. *University of Cincinnati Law Review* 68 (3, Spring): 615–36.

Schauer, Frederick. 2006. 'The Court's Agenda—And the Nation's'. *Harvard Law Review* 120 (1, November): 4–64.

Shachar, Yoram. 2008. 'The Citation Space of the Supreme Court 1950–2004'. *Hapraklit* 50: 29–69 (in Hebrew).

Segal, Jeffrey A. 1997. 'Separation-of-Powers Games in the Positive Theory of Congress and Courts'. *American Political Science Review* 91 (1): 28–44.

Segal, Jeffrey A., and Harold J. Spaeth. 2002. *The Supreme Court and the Attitudinal Model Revisited*. New York: Cambridge University Press.

Shany, Yuval. 2012. 'Assessing the Effectiveness of International Courts: A Goal-Based Approach'. *American Journal of International Law* 106 (2, April): 225–70.

Sunstein, Cass R., David Schkade, and Lisa Michelle Ellman. 2004. 'Ideological Voting on Federal Courts of Appeals: A Preliminary Investigation'. *Virginia Law Review* 90 (1, March): 301–54.

Sunstein, Cass R., David Schkade, Lisa M. Ellman, and Andres Sawicki. 2006. *Are Judges Political? An Empirical Analysis of the Federal Judiciary*. Washington: Brookings Institution Press.

Tate, C. Neal. 1981. 'Personal Attribute Models of the Voting Behavior of U.S. Supreme Court Justices: Liberalism in Civil Liberties and Economics Decisions 1946–1978'. *American Political Science Review* 75 (2): 355–67.

Ulmer, S. Sidney. 1965. 'Toward a Theory of Sub-Group Formation in the United States Supreme Court'. *The Journal of Politics* 27 (1): 133–52.

Voeten, Erik. 2008. 'The Impartiality of International Judges: Evidence from the European Court of Human Rights'. *American Political Science Review* 102 (4): 417–33.

Walker, Thomas G. 1973. 'Behavioral Tendencies in the Three-Judge District Court'. *American Journal of Political Science* 17 (2): 407–13.

Walker, Thomas G. 2003. 'David J. Danelski: Social Psychology and Group Choice'. In *The Pioneers of Judicial Behavior*, edited by Nancy Maveety, 248–69. Ann Arbor: The University of Michigan Press.

CHAPTER 10

HOW PERSONAL MOTIVATIONS AFFECT JUDGES' DECISIONS

LEE EPSTEIN AND JACK KNIGHT

1. Introduction

In the not-so-distant past, social scientists and legal academics approached judging through two (predictably) different lens. To social scientists, especially political scientists, political preferences were the major drivers of judicial decisions. On this account—sometimes called the 'attitudinal model'—judges seek to align the law with their ideological or partisan commitments (Segal and Spaeth 2002). In contrast, legal academics emphasized the importance of 'law'—past decisions, statutes, constitutional provisions, and so on—in explaining the judges' choices.

To contemporary ears, this dichotomy rings false. These days, work by social scientists and legal academics has converged in two ways. First, lawyers and social scientists no longer cling to their own approaches. Studies exploring the role of ideology and partisanship regularly appear in legal publications (Dalla Pellegrina et al. 2017; Devins and Larsen 2021; Sisk and Heise 2022), and research attempting to isolate the effect of law is hardly unknown in social science journals (Richards and Kritzer 2002; Bailey and Maltzman 2008; Bartels and O'Geen 2015; Pang et al. 2017).

Second—and this is even more consequential—neither legal scholars nor social scientists analyse judging solely through the 'law versus politics' dichotomy. They have instead expanded their theoretical toolkit to include four other approaches to judging, in addition to standard legalistic (law) and attitudinal (politics) accounts.

Table 10.1 outlines the approaches, and chapters cited in this volume supply more details (see also Chapter 1).

Here we focus on the labour market model, which emphasizes personal motivations for judicial choice, especially (i) job satisfaction, (ii) external satisfactions, (iii) leisure,

Table 10.1 Six approaches to the study of judicial behaviour

Approach	Description
Legalism (traditional version)[1]	Judges 'find' the meaning of legal rules through politically neutral methods (see Chapter 6)
Attitudinal Model	Judges votes reflect their policy preferences toward case facts (see Chapters 7 and 16)
Identity Accounts	Judges' biographies, personal characteristics, and identities affect their choices (see Chapter 8)
Strategic Analysis	Judges are strategic actors who realize that their ability to achieve their goals depends on the preferences of other actors, the choices they expect others to make, and the institutional context in which they interact (see Chapter 9)
Labor Market Model	Judges are motivated and constrained by (mostly) non-pecuniary costs (e.g. effort, criticism) and benefits (e.g. esteem, influence, self-expression)
'Thinking Fast' Judging	Judges rely on heuristics, intuitions, and the like (e.g. 'hunches') to make fast and effortless decisions (see Chapter 11)

(iv) salary, and (v) promotion. On the one hand, detailing these factors wouldn't seem to be an especially heavy lift. Personal motivations lend themselves nicely to the comparative analysis of judicial behaviour because they are rather universal motivations. Salary is illustrative. Like most of us, judges prefer more salary to less *regardless of where they work*. On the other hand, comparative analysis must consider the context in which they adjudicate because that context could affect how personal motives affect their choices. For example, although most judges aspire to be promoted, the particular structure of the judicial hierarchy and the person(s) making promotion decisions affect the extent to which, and even how, the judges pursue that goal. This becomes clear in the material to come, especially on job satisfaction and, naturally, promotion.

In what follows we provide a brief introduction to the labour market model, with emphasis on the importance of the five key personal motivations (section 2). Next we consider the motivations separately (sections 3–7). For each we identify the relevant literature and offer proposals for new research.

2. The Labour Market Model and Its Emphasis on Personal Motivations

As Table 10.1 suggests, the labour market model and strategic accounts are different approaches to judging but they share a common foundation in rational choice theory.

On this theory, all actors, including judges, make rational decisions when they choose a course of action that they believe satisfies their desires most efficiently. Or as Judge Richard A. Posner (2011, 3) famously put it, the judge is 'a rational maximizer of his ends in life, his satisfactions ... his "self-interest"'.

The difference between the labour market model and strategic accounts is the flavour of rational choice theory that grounds them (Epstein and Knight 2017). Strategic accounts assume that goal-directed judges (regardless of the specific goal) operate in an interdependent decision-making context; that is, when the judges make decisions, they attend to the preferences and likely actions of other relevant actors (Epstein and Knight 1998; Epstein and Weinshall 2021). For example, if judges care about the implementation of their decisions, they will account for the implementers' possible responses (Staton and Vanberg 2008).

The labour market model, in contrast, considers how individuals act to maximize their preferences, 'given the constraints they happen to face' (Lovett 2006, 238). According to this model, judges, just as other workers, are motivated and constrained by costs and benefits both pecuniary and non-pecuniary: costs, such as effort, criticism, and workplace tensions and benefits, such as leisure, influence, self-expression, celebrity, promotion to a higher court, and income (Epstein, Landes, and Posner 2013; Ash and McLeod 2015; Alarie and Green 2017). For example, if a judge wants to earn more money, she might write a novel assuming she has carefully weighed her own costs, like time away from her job, and benefits. In other words, she is the variable and all others, the constants (Elster 1983).

Although both the labour market model and strategic accounts have led to more nuanced understandings of judicial behaviour, their chief contributions are distinct. Strategic accounts introduced the importance of actors beyond the individual judge[2]—including her colleagues, the government, and the public—and now entire literatures are devoted to understanding how these actors influence judicial decisions.[3]

The labour market model's contributions, by contrast, are more internally focused, expanding the set of motivations relevant to judging. Specifically, the labour market model draws attention to personal motivations for judicial choice. The basic idea is that given time constraints, judges seek to maximize their preferences over a set of (roughly) five personal factors.

1. Job Satisfaction, or the internal satisfaction of feeling that one is doing a good job, as well as the more social (or collegial) dimensions of judicial work
2. External Satisfactions that come from being a judge, including reputation, prestige, power, influence, and celebrity
3. Leisure, such that at some point 'the opportunity cost of foregone leisure exceeds the benefits to the judge of additional time spent making decisions' (Drahozal 1998, 476)
4. Salary/Income, in that all else being equal, judges, like most of us, prefer more salary, income, and personal comfort to less
5. Promotion to a 'higher' or more prestigious job or office

Before turning to each motivation, two general notes are in order. One is that these factors—really elements in the judge's personal utility function—are not mutually exclusive; substantial overlaps, in fact, exist. Promotion provides an example. This would seem to be an important factor in its own right, influencing the personal utility that judges (and, in fact, many of us) gain from their work (Bell 2006). But promotion also tends to increase job satisfaction, external satisfactions (such as prestige and reputation), and, of course, salary.

Second, although the labour market model emphasizes personal motivations, it does not denigrate the importance of political and legal motivations. To the contrary: many personal factors are consistent with one or both—as promotion once again illustrates. It takes no great leap to see that the utility judges derive from promotion could be coincident with policy preferences: the higher judges sit in the hierarchy, the more important the cases they hear, and so the greater the opportunity to influence the law.

These overlaps do not go neglected in the sections to follow, which detail the five personal motivations. Our chief goals, though, are to identify literature providing evidence for (or at least consistent with) each and to offer suggestions for new studies.

3. Job Satisfaction

Job satisfaction, recall, is (i) the internal satisfaction of feeling that one is doing a good job, plus (ii) the more social dimensions of judicial work, such as collegial relations with other judges, clerks, and staff (Epstein, Landes, and Posner 2013; see also e.g. Shapiro and Levy 1994; Caldeira 1977; Baum 1997; Drahozal 1998; Gulati and McCauliff 1998; Klein 2002). Both aspects deserve attention, as does literature on 'familiarity', which bears a relationship to studies on collegiality.

3.1 Internal Satisfaction

When it comes to the judges' own internal satisfaction, many scholars imply that this 'pleasure' follows from maximizing political preferences (Landes and Posner 1976; Drahozal 1998; Gulati and McCauliff 1998); that is, judges derive great internal satisfaction from aligning the law with their partisan or ideological commitments.

Fair enough. At the same time, though, politics is hardly the only factor influencing the judges' internal satisfaction. Another is the discretion a judge enjoys. Because many high court judges have broad jurisdiction, are assigned cases randomly, and must justify their decisions, they desire control over their agendas. Macey (1994) provides qualitative evidence indicating that judges design rules to advance this desire. And Cohen (1991, 186), also arguing that 'judicial discretion clearly affects job satisfaction', reports that many US trial judges struck down a law establishing sentencing guidelines, even though the Supreme Court later upheld it in a lopsided 8-1 vote. The reason? The trial judges thought the law would impinge on their discretion to impose sentence. Along somewhat different lines, analyses of the Norwegian and Australian Supreme Courts (Narayan and Smyth 2007; Skiple, Bentsen, and McKenzie 2021) show that discretionary docket control leads to lower caseloads. Lower caseloads, in turn, can enhance job satisfaction by freeing up time for more careful consideration of cases on the court's docket. (Lower caseloads can also increase the judges' time for leisure, as section 4 reports.)

The upshot is that all else being equal, many judges desire more discretion over their docket in part because discretion increases job satisfaction. Worth noting, though, is that increasing judges' job satisfaction through docket control can come at costs to litigants. Studies of US trial judges show that after the Supreme Court restored their discretion over sentencing, racial disparities increased—and those disparities were affected by the judges' party identity: Republican-appointed judges, relative to Democratic appointees, sentenced Black defendants 'to 3 more months than similar non-Black defendants' (Cohen and Yang 2019; see also Yang 2015). Likewise, research demonstrates that on European high courts the more discretion, the higher the likelihood of the judges' ideology and partisanship seeping into their decisions (Dyevre 2010; Grendstad, Shaffer, and Waltenburg 2015; Skiple, Bentsen, and McKenzie 2021).

A comparison of tax cases in the Norwegian Supreme Court (with nearly complete docket control) and the Denmark Supreme Court (mandatory docket) also shores up a cost of discretion. Skiple, Bentsen, and McKenzie (2021) find that discretionary tax dockets decrease the odds of lower-status parties prevailing. The reason is that 'mandatory dockets are completely driven by litigants' decisions to appeal… [T]he less resourceful (the have-nots) or the less experienced litigants (the one-shotters) should be more likely to appeal cases with a low probability of winning than more resourceful (the haves) or more experienced litigants (the repeat players)' (Skiple, Bentsen, and McKenzie 2021, 114–15).

The suggestion here is that however important job satisfaction is for judges, maximizing it by increasing discretion and docket control may work to the detriment of certain kinds of litigants. For this reason, discretion may also carry legitimacy costs. If the legitimacy of courts stems in part from 'impartiality' in their decision-making—that they decide cases based on the facts and law without regard to the identity of the parties—using judicial discretion to (dis)advantage particular parties may ultimately affect the courts' standing in society, which may, in turn, impinge on the judges' job satisfaction.

Offering this hypothesis is one thing; empirically assessing it is quite another. To be sure, Skiple et al. (2021) is an excellent—and explicitly comparative—start, but more targeted tests are necessary to weigh the costs and benefits of maximizing job satisfaction via discretion and docket control.

3.2 Collegiality

Turning to the social dimensions of job satisfaction, judges frequently refer to the importance of collegiality (e.g. Wald 1987; Edwards 2003), which they tend to think of as a 'deliberatively cultivated attitude' among judges who share a 'continuous, open, and intimate relationship' (Coffin 1994, 214). Characteristics of a collegial atmosphere, according to Swalve (2022, 224), are an emphasis on 'collaboration and deliberation, civil and polite exchanges between group members, cohesiveness, and mutual respect' (see also Cross and Tiller 2008; Nash 2022).

Although judges stress the crucial role of collegiality in the decision-making process, scholars often denigrate it. We should not. As most of us know all too well, maintaining good collegial relations is not some abstract, squishy concept; it has a direct effect on the pleasure we derive from our jobs. In the case of judges, good relations with colleagues, law clerks, other staff, and lawyers add to their personal utility, 'while animosities, usually from or toward judicial colleagues and usually resulting from disagreement, subtract from it' (Epstein, Landes, and Posner 2013, 48). It also is likely to be true that '[a] judge seen as violating a court's norm of collegiality might suffer consequences. A judge might be concerned that, if her colleagues perceive her to have acted uncollegially, they may in turn act uncollegially toward her' (Nash 2022).

Linking these ideas about collegiality to actual behaviour has primarily come in studies of dissent aversion: when judges avoid dissenting even if they disagree with the majority. This is a well-documented phenomenon in a range of common law courts, including lower US appellate courts (Epstein, Landes, and Posner 2011), the Canadian Supreme Court (Songer et al. 2012), and the UK Supreme Court (Alarie and Green 2017; Hanretty 2020). But dissent aversion has also been identified in civil law societies. To be sure, some civil law jurisdictions prohibit publication of dissent—though even in those that permit the judges to expose their (minority) views, overall dissent rates tend to be lower among civil law judges in part because they 'have a strong esprit de corps, that is, they tend to place very high value on the reputation of the body to which they belong,' and in part because dissents undermine 'the idea of legal certainty is the "supreme value" of the civil-law system' (Lopes 2019; see also Merryman and Perez-Perdomo 2018). And yet dissent aversion lowers dissent rates even further, as Lopes' (2019) clever study of the Brazilian Supreme Court indicates. He shows that justices who vote after a majority has been formed are significantly less likely to dissent even if they disagree with the inevitable outcome.

In short, research has coalesced around dissent aversion as an empirical regularity. Nonetheless, the studies raise questions about the role of dissent aversion *in the name* of collegiality. One set centres on whether the phenomenon is a direct manifestation of collegial concerns. Lopes (2019, 936) suggests that it is: 'There are collegiality costs [to dissenting], as judges resent criticism—a judge who frequently dissents might become less well-liked, which means that he may find it harder to convince his fellow judges to join his positions.' But dissent aversion (and even collegiality itself) also relates to external satisfactions and leisure goals (Cohen 2002). Along these lines, scholars argue that judges sometimes do not dissent when they disagree with the majority opinion because dissents force other judges on the panel to work harder (e.g. to increase the length of majority opinions in response to the dissent) (Epstein, Landes, and Posner 2013). Future work might consider empirically differentiating these various explanations.

Another set of questions follows from work suggesting a clash between a preference for more docket discretion to maximize job satisfaction and a preference for consensus to maximize collegiality, because it turns out that the more control judges have over their docket, the greater the likelihood of dissent. Bentsen (2018), for example, attributes the rise in dissent on the Norwegian Supreme Court to fundamental changes to the Court's discretionary power, and scholars have suggested much the same in comparisons between the US Supreme Court (high dissent and high discretion) versus the US Courts of Appeals (low dissent and low discretion) (Hall and Windett 2016). The reason is straightforward: judges who control their own dockets also tend to dissent more because they can avoid cases of 'relatively minor legal significance' (Stern, Gressman, and Shapiro 1985). Hence the question emerges: when courts maximize discretion, are they sacrificing collegiality, assuming dissensus is a form of *un*-collegial behaviour?

A third set of questions centres more squarely on whether the benefits of dissent aversion, again, in the name of collegiality, outweigh the costs. Some scholars suggest that dissents, as self-expression, can increase—not detract from—judges' job satisfaction. As Nash (2022, 16) notes, judges may pay 'a psychic cost to joining an opinion with which one disagrees, and it takes time and effort to engage other judges—and possibly then to adjust one's opinion to take account of the opposing arguments'. One US justice put it this way:

> To be able to write an opinion solely for oneself, without the need to accommodate, to any degree whatever, the more-or-less differing views of one's colleagues; to address precisely the points of law that one considers important and no others; to express precisely the degree of quibble, or foreboding, or disbelief, or indication that one believes the majority's disposition should engender—that is indeed an unparalleled pleasure. . . .
>
> (Scalia 1994, 42)

Relatedly, some studies—both normative and positive—suggest that dissents can benefit the courts themselves. Proceeding from literature in social psychology, Swalve, for example, persuasively argues that in civil law societies, 'where workload and the pressure to conform to a group's majority opinion are high', dissenting opinions are vital for the quality of the group's decision-making in part because they protect against 'group think'. (We discuss this study in more detail in the next section.)

Swalve's research pertains to internal deliberations; other work demonstrates the role dissents play in promoting the legitimacy of courts. Salamone (2018) finds that dissents boost (rather than suppress) support for the US Supreme Court because they amount to consolation prizes for Americans who disagreed with the decision: even losers get representation; and Bentsen (2019) shows much the same for the Norwegian Court (see also Hogg and Amarnath 2017, arguing that dissents promote 'transparency as to how a decision was reached by a panel of judges').

Taken collectively, these studies suggest that there may be costs to dissent aversion—for the judges, their court, and even to society. But additional work is needed to make more direct comparisons between the presumed benefits of consensus, such as promoting collegiality, and the costs suggested in Swalve's, Salamone's and Bentsen's research, among others.

The success of such studies—and indeed of any new (and exciting!) empirical research on collegiality—depends on the development of a measure of collegiality.[4] That measure, in turn, could be used as both an input (e.g. do high levels of collegiality lead to more dissent aversion? Does collegiality lead to higher quality decisions?) and as an output (e.g. is a strong *esprit de corps* more common in civil law courts?). Nash (2022) takes a step in this direction, using specific terms in dissents (such as 'respectfully') to assess the degree of collegiality. This is a promising start. To move to the next level, it should be possible, considering technological advances, to take a more holistic look at the judges' work products.

3.3 Familiarity

Perhaps because of the absence of measures of 'collegiality', a growing number of studies explore the effect of 'familiarity' on judicial behaviour—a concept that seems easier to measure. Nelson, Hazelton, and Hinkle (2022), for example, compare the behaviour of US judges who work in the same courthouse and those who do not. In a study of the German Federal Court of Justice, Swalve (2022) asks whether judges who serve together in small panels over months or even years—and so are familiar with one another—produce higher-quality decisions.

How this growing body of literature on 'familiarity' relates to collegiality and, ultimately, job satisfaction is unclear. Swalve (2022) suggests familiarity is a 'necessary antecedent' to collegiality, and some judges agree (see Nash 2022). Maybe. But, for our purposes, a distinction with meaning exists between the two: judges can attempt to foster (or not) collegial relations, but they have little agency over maximizing familiarity. For example, in Nelson, Hazelton, and Hinkle's (2022) research, the judges did not—and, in fact, could not—pick where to work, and in Swalve's study, the judges had no say over their panel mates. Moreover, whereas collegiality almost always implies positive relations, familiarity can breed contempt, as the old saying goes. Being familiar with colleagues, perhaps through more frequent contact, provides judges with more information about their colleagues' capacity—for better or worse (Nelson Hazelton, and Hinkle 2022).

Nonetheless, on the theory that familiarity is (sometimes) a precursor to collegiality and so to job satisfaction, the findings from existing studies bear some consideration. Beginning with Swalve (2022, 225), he makes the theoretical case that familiarity is associated with 'group productivity and higher quality of decision-making' in many workplaces in part because members feel more comfortable sharing information and even disagreeing. Transporting these findings to German judges he hypothesizes that familiarity should improve 'judicial deliberations by encouraging minority dissent and a more extensive debate of different legal viewpoints'—both beneficial especially in civil law societies. The data supports the hypothesis.

Swalve's work may be the most fully theorized of the 'familiarity' studies, but others are equally informative if not necessarily consistent with Swalve's findings. Papers on US courts show that when trial court judges sit (by designation) on appellate court panels, (i) the appellate panel is more likely to affirm trial court decisions (Sayer 2021), (ii) the trial judges are more hesitant to reverse the decisions of their trial court colleagues (Levy 2019), and (iii) future appellate panels are more likely to affirm the decisions of the specific trial court judge (Lemley and Miller 2016). The latter finding is said to reflect familiarity in the form of 'trust and affinity' (479). Finally, Nelson, Hazelton, and Hinkle (2022) find that ideology plays less of a role when appellate panels reverse a trial judge who works in the same courthouse than when contact is less frequent. The suggestion here is that familiarity dampens ideological decision-making—an important finding[5]—though the researchers can't say whether familiarity works for or against particular trial judges based on their interpersonal contact.

Taken collectively, the studies imply that while familiarity has its share of benefits, there are costs as well. Rather than being a precursor to collegiality, familiarity may be the source of workplace frictions and even hostility, thus lowering job satisfaction (i.e. Swalve can't eliminate the possibility that disagreements over the long term lead to a *decline* in collegiality). Then there's the opposite concern brought to light in Levy's (2019) interviews with US trial judges: that their reluctance to reverse decisions of colleagues when they sit on appellate panels has negative implications for the law.

So, where to go from there? Our review of the relevant research uncovers a number of promising directions—most obviously, there's a great need for work that explicitly differentiates job satisfaction and other potential motivations. Return to dissent aversion. How might we distinguish an explanation based on collegiality from an explanation based on leisure? The two represent claims grounded in distinct personal motivations, thus offering different explanations of the same behaviour. But the question itself highlights the conceptual difficulty in studying personal motivations. Specific motivations are hard to discern unless the motivations to be analysed correlate with distinct forms of judicial behaviour. As researchers pursue questions about the role of job satisfaction, they might want to be especially attentive to the ways that we might conceptualize the behavioural implications of the different motivations that fall under the rubric of personal satisfaction.

4. External Satisfactions

Job satisfaction typically relates to the internal dimensions of judging. External satisfactions, as the name suggests, are different. They tend to focus on satisfactions that come from being a judge, including 'reputation, prestige, power, influence, and celebrity' (e.g. Shapiro and Levy 1994; Miceli and Cosgel 1994; Drahozal 1998; Georgakopoulos 2000; Schauer 2000; Whitman 2000; Garoupa and Ginsburg 2015).

Some of these satisfactions are likely to be linked to the policy goal. As Schauer (2000, 633) notes, 'for some judges, judicial reputation might be an instrumental goal' designed to increase power. When judges brand themselves by certain 'substantive or methodological trademarks', they may be attempting not only to develop a reputation but also to exert greater influence on their court—with an eye toward aligning the law with their political commitments. On this account, conservative US Justice Scalia's advocacy of 'originalism' may be the ultimate have-your-cake-and-eat-it-too approach. Under this approach judges search for the 'original public meaning' of words in the constitution—a search that somehow almost always leads them to conservative results.[6]

But the quest for external satisfaction, in the form of building reputations, can be a goal in and of itself, detached from political concerns. Reputation seeking, as Levy (2005, 25) reminds us, is a 'human concern' that academics certainly pursue and judges do too.

How do judges build their reputations? The literature points to two (non-mutually exclusive) ways: become known as a distinctly able judge through craft orientation and cultivate the approval of relevant audiences.

4.1 Craft Orientation

'Able judges' are, on many accounts, judges who are oriented toward 'craft'—or the 'well-reasoned application of [law] to the circumstances of a particular case' (Shapiro and Levy 1994, 1053). Put another way, judges can build reputations as good judges by wisely following the 'law'.

In common law systems that might mean adhering to precedent, though in the formal economics literature debate ensues over the extent to which reputation- or power-seeking judges ought to be followers (apply existing doctrine) or more *avant garde*. Levy (2005) contends that judges motivated by esteem and reputation should be less willing to follow precedent to show that they are more capable than their predecessors. Creating new precedents too can generate citations and other accolades. Landes and Posner (1976, 273), on the other hand, note that if judges mostly fail to follow existing doctrine, the 'precedential value of [their] own decisions would be reduced'.

Landes and Posner also point out that rogue judges—those who feel free to disregard all precedents in their quest for power (or policy)—will be uncommon because appellate review keeps the system in check. Judges who are too innovative run the risk of seeing their decisions overturned, which can harm their reputation. Miceli and Cosgel (1994) explore this trade-off, concluding that judges might deviate from established precedent if they thought other judges would go along (thus enhancing the judges' reputation) but would follow precedent (even if they disagreed with it) if they worried about reversal (see also Posner 1995; Foxall 2004). Similarly, Salzberger and Fenn (1999) provide evidence showing that the lower the reversal rate, the higher the judge's prestige and thus the higher the likelihood of promotion from a court of appeals to the House of Lords in England.

'Following the law' is not the only indication of a craft orientation in service of reputational goals. Corley, Collins, and Calvin (2011) find the lower court judge's prestige is a significant predictor of US Supreme Court 'borrowing' from lower court opinions (and that the ideology of the judge is not) (see also Lindquist and Klein 2006). Bar Niv and Lachman (2010) demonstrate that Israeli judges allocate more time to writing opinions to advance their reputations or chances for promotion, and Choi, Gulati, and Posner (2012) show that US federal district court judges in politically diverse circuits write higher-quality opinions not only to avoid reversal but also to maximize their reputations. Then there's Gulati and McCauliff's (1998) analysis of publication practices on a US appellate court. The researchers come to the seemingly counterintuitive conclusion that judges worry so much about their reputation that they are more—not less—likely to make use of summary opinions in the hardest cases. As Gulati and McCauliff explain it:

> Published opinions in the most difficult and important cases draw attention from lawyers, academics, and other courts. Badly reasoned opinions carry with them the risk of negative attention (in addition to a risk of reversal and disagreement from other circuits). Judges, therefore, have a reputation-driven incentive to tackle difficult issues only when they have the time, resources, and expertise to write a well-reasoned opinion that will withstand external scrutiny and enhance the author's reputation.[7]

These studies imply that judges care about producing top-flight opinions in part to enhance their reputations. Ash and MacLeod (2015) assess and reinforce this suggestion. Not only do they demonstrate that US state court judges are 'motivated to provide high-quality decisions', they also isolate institutions that enable judges to write such decisions. Mostly, judges who face less time pressure because they have discretionary dockets or longer terms of office before they must face the voters produce better opinions.

This is an important study, for when judges produce higher-quality decisions, it's a win for the judges and a win for society. And so understanding the rules that can free judges to pursue reputational goals via excellent opinions is of crucial importance. Ash and MacLeod have produced such an understanding for state judges; we hope others will pursue a similar project for judges outside the United States.

4.2 Audience Cultivation

However important craft orientation, it isn't the only way judges build their reputations. In explaining US Justice Benjamin Cardozo's fame, Posner (1990, 132) demonstrates that Cardozo 'cultivated the good opinion of academics' by regularly referencing their work in his opinions. Cardozo was also far more likely than his colleagues to cite the opinions of other judges, thereby fostering their good will as well. Baum (2006) and Davis (2011) also offer evidence of US justices adjusting their behaviour to conform to the preferences of 'reputation creators' and 'esteem grantors' (Schauer 2000, 629).

The idea of speaking directly to audiences who can make or break the judges' reputation is not limited to the United States' highest court. US federal appellate judges follow public opinion in their states because they care about their home-state reputations (Owens and Wohlfarth 2019), and judges in the fifty US states (most of whom must face the electorate to keep their jobs) deploy social media to increase name recognition and build personal reputations 'as someone the voter can identify with and understand' (Curry and Fix 2019).

Outside the United States there is also a growing literature making use of 'audience-based' approaches (Baum 2006). Kureshi's (2021) analysis of judges in Pakistan (and other authoritarian regimes) is especially instructive. He shows that judges in such societies are willing to take on autocrats when the 'networks, or audiences, from whom judges seek approval, to advance careers and build reputations, grow independent from the regime'.

Kureshi's study and others running along similar lines make clear that audience cultivation isn't only about burnishing the judges' reputation; it's also about building public support. Indeed, a large body of empirical literature falling under the categories of institutional maintenance, legitimacy, and public opinion is consistent with the external satisfaction argument (see, generally, Baum 2006). For self-interested judges, it would be difficult to develop influence, esteem, and prestige if their court or legal system did not enjoy a certain degree of respect. Cultivating and following public opinion are behaviours that follow from this end, and the empirical and historical literatures suggest that justices do just that (McGuire and Stimson 2004; Clark 2009; Friedman 2009; Epstein and Martin 2010). Consider too Sandholtz and Padilla's (2020, 151) analysis showing how international human rights courts, which 'face a tension between the goal of expanding rights and the need to gain legitimacy with domestic constituencies', attend to relevant domestic political contexts.

This last set of studies reinforces a suggestion we made with regard to job satisfaction. An important area for future research would be to distinguish the relative importance of the various motivational claims. For example, the empirical findings of research positing legitimacy as a motivation are quite similar to findings on external satisfactions. But the claimed explanations are different. We could offer a similar observation about the relationship between research on reputation effects and policy goals. The bottom line is that our general understanding of judicial decision-making would benefit from creative studies of the relative importance of the different internal and external motivations.

5. Leisure

A preference for leisure comes to the fore in many economic analyses of judging (e.g. Posner 1993; Macey 1994; Bainbridge and Gulati 2002). The basic idea is that judges, like most of us, value leisure and, at some point, the 'opportunity cost of foregone leisure exceeds the benefits to the judge of additional time spent making decisions' (Drahozal 1998, 475). If so, we would expect judges to engage in behaviours designed to increase or at least protect their leisure time. Exemplary may be the decline in the number of cases the US Supreme Court hears and decides each term, from 140+ in the 1980s to less than half that in the 2020s. Not only do fewer cases free up time for non-judicial work but also for leisure, which may have implications for departures from the bench. In a moment of candour prior to his retirement, Justice Stevens said: 'The fact that the [caseload] has gone down and the work has relaxed a little bit has made it easy for me to hang around' (quoted in Stephan 2009).

In general, though, leisure will be of greater concern for judges with heavier workloads and less staff than the US Supreme Court. In addition to decreasing leisure time, backlogs can decrease respect and thus external satisfaction, not to mention job satisfaction (Cohen 1992; Drahozal 1998). So it is perhaps not surprising that Cohen (1991) reports that trial court judges with heavier dockets were more likely to strike the sentencing guidelines on the theory that the guidelines would discourage plea bargaining and thus increase trials. In another study, Cohen (1992) hypothesized that judges, especially in busy districts, would penalize defendants who opt for a trial over a guilty plea because trials take more time. The data supports the hypothesis. Likewise Taha (2004) demonstrates that the heavier the workload, the less likely judges were to publish their opinions in the sentencing cases. Finally, Epstein, Landes, and Posner (2013) show that busier judges took greater advantage of the Supreme Court's decision in *Ashcroft v Iqbal* (2009), which made it easier for judges to dismiss civil suits. Because this study (like many of the others) controls for the judges' ideology, the findings are difficult to explain without reference to a preference for leisure.

These results on the effect of workload on US courts sit comfortably with an analysis of courts in twenty-two EU countries. Finding a positive relationship between caseload and productivity, the authors note that 'judges sacrifice leisure or the quality of their decisions to achieve a reduction in backlogs' (Deyneli and Mascini 2020). Engel and Weinshall's (2020) study of district courts in Israel reaches a similar conclusion. In districts where additional personnel substantially reduced the judges' caseloads, the judges 'invested more resources in resolving each case' (though whether the added staff also freed up time for leisure is unknown).[8]

Speaking of staff, a growing literature has explored the role of law clerks in judicial decision-making. Because clerks are covered later in the *Handbook*, suffice it to note that clerks have been credited with serving as gatekeepers (Perry 1994), helping to professionalize courts (Grendstad et al. 2020), and, most relevant here, reducing the judges' work by, for example, drafting opinions (including in the United States and the Nordic countries; see Grendstad et al. 2020).[9] Certainly it is possible that the very idea of hiring law clerks reflected a leisure motivation on the judges' part.[10] And yet, ironically, as clerks take on more and more judicial work, they may 'actually attenuate the effect of a judge's increase in leisure incentives' (Clark, Engst, and Staton 2018).

In addition to workload and staff, analyses of leisure focus on the content of opinions. For example, Posner (1995) and Easterbrook (1990) have characterized *stare decisis* as consistent with leisure seeking. Generalist judges 'do not have the time to start anew on each case' (Easterbrook 1990, 782), and so adhering to precedent becomes a time-saving device. Klein and Hume (2003) do not explicitly test this hypothesis but their results are consistent with it. After discovering that circuit judges do not comply with precedent out of fear of reversal, the researchers speculated that the judges' compliance might instead reflect a desire to simplify work:[11]

> Instead of investing the time needed to weigh every detail of each case before them and consider the legal merits of every issue anew, judges might limit their attention to key facts or patterns and simply ask themselves, based on what they have observed in the past, how the case would normally be decided in the federal courts. In fact, it would be very surprising if judges did not do this often.
>
> (Klein and Hume 2003, 602)

Related too is research showing an effect of leisure on the development of doctrine. For example, De Mot, Faure, and Klick (2015) demonstrate US state justices moved from contributory to comparative negligence not 'out of a concern for justice', as some commentators thought, but rather because the justices thought the switch would reduce appeals.

Last but hardly least, we note Clark, Engst, and Staton's (2018) study showing that when a judge's alma mater is in the US's men's collegiate basketball tournament—a big sporting event in the United States—the judge produces lower-quality opinions at a slower rate. These results suggest 'that incentives for leisure influence important normative concerns for swift and high-quality justice'. We're not sure how well this study transports to other societies but the findings are provocative nonetheless.

6. Salary/Income

All else equal, judges, like most of us, prefer more salary, income, and personal comfort to less. The empirical literature provides some evidence that they attempt to maximize these goals by acting in ways consistent with the preferences of their 'bosses' (Baum 1997)—of which the legislative branch is certainly one. Because in many countries elected representatives control raises, court budgets (and so e.g. can augment or reduce the number of staff), and pension plans, it is not unexpected to find some deference to their preferences (e.g. Bergara, Richman, and Spiller 2003; Harvey and Friedman 2006; Segal, Westerland, and Lindquist 2011). But the mechanism is not always clear. It could be that deference is primarily a function of the legislature's power to hold salaries constant or impose other pecuniary sanctions (or rewards), or it could be that the judges are responding to a multitude of other weapons at the legislature's disposal (for a list, see Rosenberg 1992).

Several empirical studies attempt to sort this out. Toma (1991) shows that the US Congress uses the budget to signal its preferences to the Supreme Court, and Toma (1996) provides empirical support for the argument that Congress and the Court 'enter into a contract of budgetary favours in exchange for politically influenced output', with the Chief Justice assuming the role of contract enforcer. Anderson et al.'s (1989) study is equally consistent with a salary motivation. Picking up where Landes and Posner (1976) left off, they ask: what motivates judges to act independently—in this context, to ensure the durability of legislative bargains by interpreting laws in line with the intent of the enacting legislature? The answer they offer, using data from the states, is that legislatures reward judges with higher salaries when they act 'independently'.

It turns out, though, that increased salaries can have salutary effects in their own right. Research shows that higher salaries attract better judicial candidates (Habel et al. 2015), and that salary increases lead to higher-quality decisions (as measured by appeal and reversal rates) (DeAngelo and McCannon 2017)—though both these findings follow from studies of US judges. Much more comparative analysis is needed to establish a stronger link between salary and quality.

Finally and also consistent with a financial motivation is the literature on retirement and retention. Scholars have long suggested that US judges strategically time their retirements to coincide with appointing regimes that share their party affiliation or ideology. Empirical studies tend to support this suggestion (e.g. Spriggs and Wahlbeck 1995), but it does not seem to hold in Canada or the United Kingdom (Massie, Randazzo, and Songer 2014) or in Latin American countries with presidential regimes (Pérez-Liñán and Araya 2017).

What does seem important, both in the United States and in some Latin American countries, is pension eligibility. Even for US Supreme Court justices, eligibility 'raises the annual odds of retirement by an order of magnitude—a huge effect by social science and employment research standards', all else being equal (Stolzenberg and Lindgren 2010, 291; see also Yoon 2006). Pensions may also play a role in explaining why US state judges are motivated to seek re-election. Consider how Hall (1987, 1120), in a study of state supreme court justices, described one of her interviews: '[The justice] expressed a great deal of anxiety over potentially losing his position, for which he would be running again in the upcoming few years. This justice, who seemed particularly satisfied with his office, apparently did not have the necessary years of service to draw a pension if defeated.'

7. Promotion

Promotion would seem to be an important factor influencing the personal utility that judges gain from their work. It could be coincident with policy preferences: the higher judges sit in the hierarchy, the more important the cases they hear, and the greater the opportunity to influence the law. Promotion also tends to increase job satisfaction, prestige, reputation, and, of course, salary.

And yet, at least for US judges scholars tend to dismiss it. They say promotion is such a 'random' (Cooter 1983, 129) or low-probability event that it couldn't possibly drive judicial behaviour. We agree that promotion is not a relevant motivation for most US Supreme Court justices (Schauer 2000; Segal and Spaeth 2002). Arthur Goldberg, in 1965, was the last to leave for 'higher' office—and his departure wasn't voluntary. Of course, some associates might hope to become Chief Justice, but that's truly a rare event.

What of lower court judges? Federal district judges are occasionally promoted to the court of appeals, and court of appeals judges are sometimes promoted to the Supreme Court. But 'occasionally' and 'sometimes' are the operative words; only 11 per cent of all district court and 4 per cent of all appellate judges have been elevated. If a desire for promotion led these judges to alter their behaviour, it would seem they had fallen prey to irrational exuberance, right?

Wrong. The problem is that these percentages are deceiving. The odds of promotion for some judges are substantially higher—for example, about one in five for court of appeals judges desiring appointment to the Supreme Court. That's because these judges possess certain markers (e.g. their age, pedigree, and even circuit) that place them in a genuine promotion pool—and they know it (see Epstein, Landes, and Posner 2013).

Perhaps these relatively high odds help explain the findings of empirical studies, showing that these judges, the 'auditioners', seem motivated by the possibility of promotion to higher-status (and higher-paying) jobs and make choices based on this motivation. Cohen (1991) demonstrates, and Sisk, Heise, and Morris (1998) confirm, that district court judges with a higher chance of promotion were more likely to uphold the politically popular federal sentencing guidelines (see also Taha 2004). In a separate study, Cohen (1992) also finds that judges with promotion potential give higher antitrust fines. Along similar lines, Epstein, Landes, and Posner (2013) show that auditioners, not wanting to appear soft on crime, impose harsher sentences on criminal defendants. Finally, Gaille (1997) demonstrates that the number of articles published by court of appeals judges standing some chance of elevation to the Supreme Court dropped 'precipitously' after the US Senate failed to confirm a prolific nominee (Robert Bork). Gaille concludes (376): 'Rather than the selection process constituting a one-sided choice by the president and Congress, it appears that prospective nominees themselves make important behind-the-scenes decisions that may influence the president's choice and, ultimately, determine the composition of the Court.'

These are studies of the US federal courts. Promotion (and retention) has also figured into research on courts abroad. We've mentioned Salzberger and Fenn's (1999) work on English judges demonstrating that they seek to avoid reversal in part to increase the likelihood of promotion. Along similar lines, Ramseyer and Rasmusen (2001) demonstrate that Japanese lower court judges tend to defer to the national government because deference improves their chances of 'doing better in their careers'.

Still—and despite the generalizability of the promotion motivation—most studies continue to focus on US judges. This gap, in turn, suggests numerous opportunities for contributions by scholars to consider how individual incentives can differ across countries depending on who gets promoted when. In some systems, promotion (or appointment) is a matter of prestige (not money) coming at the end of a distinguished career; in others, promotions can occur far earlier and translate into higher salaries. How to assess the effect of these different incentives falls squarely in the wheelhouse of judicial behaviour scholars.

All these suggestions go to promotion within the judicial system. Melcarne's (2017) study of the Italian Constitutional Court, where judges serve for a non-renewable nine-year term, shows how post-court career concerns can affect the judges' decisions. This too is a fascinating line of research, and one with potentially important implications for countries considering switching from life tenure (even with a retirement age) to set terms. If Melcarne's study is any indication, term limits may come with their own set of drawbacks, but far more work is needed.

8. Conclusion

We end with a few thoughts on future research. First, it would be very helpful if we could find ways of assessing the relative importance of the many empirically supported claims about judicial preferences. The optimal account would be one that explains how judges balance the many motivations. What would be especially interesting is the development of a better understanding of how and why judges act when their motivations conflict with each other. Perhaps this expects too much of our ability to study judicial motivation but a theory of balancing would be a true advancement.

A second proposal is to address the question of the effects of judicial discretion on the litigants themselves. With respect to judicial motivations it would seem especially important to know what motivations are most likely to produce differential treatment among different groups of litigants. To the extent that such treatment undermines judicial impartiality, the relevant motivations would be ones that should be discouraged by judicial rules and practices. And, if it would be possible to conduct comparative studies on the effects in different judicial systems, such studies might lend themselves to institutional reforms. To the extent that impartiality matters for the underlying legitimacy of the courts, this is an issue that should concern all of us.

And this leads to a third recommendation. The legitimacy of courts in particular and the rule of law in general has come under increasing scrutiny in various parts of the world in the last few years. Much of the scrutiny has focused on the behaviour of judges. This gives new urgency to questions related to their motivations. We believe that research, especially comparative studies, on the effects of personal motivations of judges on the basic legitimacy of the courts can offer significant insights into questions of judicial selection and institutional reforms. Developing a better understanding of how and why judges make the decisions that they do is fundamental to these debates.

Acknowledgements

Epstein thanks the John Simon Guggenheim Foundation, the National Science Foundation, the University of Southern California, and Washington University for supporting her work on judicial behaviour. This chapter builds on our previous work on personal motivations, especially Epstein and Knight (2013) and Epstein, Šadl, and Weinshall (2021). We are very grateful to Keren Weinshall and participants at the conference on comparative judicial behaviour for insightful comments.

Notes

1. Under a weaker version of legalism, 'law' (broadly defined) constrains judges from acting on their personal preferences, intuitions, biases, and emotions. See Table 1.1 in Chapter 1.
2. See Chapter 9 of this *Handbook*.
3. See Chapters 29–41 of this *Handbook*.
4. Which itself depends on a conceptual definition of collegiality. For the many possibilities, see Nash (2022).
5. The finding provides partial support for a famous claim made by a federal judge: 'Specifically, it is my contention that collegiality plays an important part in *mitigating* the role of partisan politics and personal ideology by allowing judges of differing perspectives and philosophies to communicate with, listen to, and ultimately influence one another in constructive and law-abiding ways' (Edwards 2003, 1639).
6. Actually, precisely what originalism is—and what variant judges use—is a moving target. As of this writing (March 2023), the *original public meaning* approach dominates but that could change by the time this *Handbook* appears in print. The only constant appears to be the bottom-line results of almost any originalist analysis: conservative decisions.
7. Both the Corley, Collins, and Calvin (2011) and Gulati and McCauliff (1998) studies are also consistent with a preference for leisure, as we discuss below.
8. See also Ponticelli and Alencar (2016) showing that workload ultimately affects firm investment and value.
9. See also Bieri 2016 (on law clerks in Switzerland) and Crichton 2022 (law clerks in Jamaica).
10. Providing some support for this explanation are research findings showing that US judges hire clerks who share their ideological inclinations (Bonica et al. 2017). This is a time

saver for judges because, as Justice Thomas put it, 'I won't hire clerks who have profound disagreements with me. It's like trying to train a pig. It wastes your time, and it aggravates the pig' (quoted in Liptak 2010).

11. See also Bainbridge and Gulati (2002, 84), which shows that in securities litigation, judges engage not in 'complex modes of legal reasoning' but instead 'decision-making heuristics'. Given the judges' high workloads and low expertise in this complex area of law, the use of simplifying strategies makes sense. It reflects a desire to move the cases off their dockets as quickly as possible.

References

Alarie, Benjamin, and Andrew J. Green. 2017. *Commitment and Cooperation on High Courts: A Cross-Country Examination of Institutional Constraints on Judges*. Oxford: Oxford University Press.

Anderson Gary M., William H. Shughart II, and Robert D. Tollison. 1989. 'On the Incentives of Judges to Enforce Legislative Wealth Transfers'. *Journal of Law and Economics* 32: 215–28.

Ash, Elliott, and W. Bentley MacLeod. 2015. 'Intrinsic Motivation in Public Service: Theory and Evidence from State Supreme Courts'. *Journal of Law and Economics* 58: 863–913.

Bailey, Michael A., and Forrest Maltzman. 2008. 'Does Legal Doctrine Matter? Unpacking Law and Policy Preferences on the U.S. Supreme Court'. *American Political Science Review* 102: 369–84.

Bainbridge, Stephen M., and Mitu Gulati. 2002. 'How Do Judges Maximize? (The Same Way Everybody Else Does—Boundedly): Rules of Thumb in Securities Fraud Opinions'. *Emory Law Journal* 51: 83–152.

Bar-Niv, Moshe, and Ran Lachman. 2010. 'Self-Interest in Judges' Time Allocation to Writing Judgments'. Available at SSRN: https://ssrn.com/abstract=1641376.

Bartels, Brandon L., and Andrew J. O'Geen. 2015. 'The Nature of Legal Change on the U.S. Supreme Court: Jurisprudential Regimes Theory and Its Alternatives'. *American Journal of Political Science* 59: 880–95.

Baum, L. 2006. *Judges and Their Audiences: A Perspective on Judicial Behavior*. Princeton: Princeton University Press.

Baum, Lawrence. 1997. *The Puzzle of Judicial Behavior*. Ann Arbor: University of Michigan Press.

Bell, John. 2006. *Judiciaries Within Europe: A Comparative Review*. Cambridge: Cambridge University Press.

Bentsen, Henrik Litleré. 2018. 'Court Leadership, Agenda Transformation, and Judicial Dissent: A European Case of a "Mysterious Demise of Consensual Norms"'. *Journal of Law and Courts* 6: 189–213.

Bentsen, Henrik Litleré. 2019. 'Dissent, Legitimacy, and Public Support for Court Decisions: Evidence from a Survey-Based Experiment'. *Law & Society Review* 53: 588–610.

Bergara, Mario, Barak Richman, and Pablo T. Spiller. 2003. 'Modeling Supreme Court Strategic Decision Making: The Congressional Constraint'. *Legislative Studies Quarterly* 28: 247–80.

Bieri, Peter. 2016. 'Law Clerks In Switzerland—A Solution To Cope With The Caseload?' *International Journal for Court Administration* 7: 29–38.

Bonica, Adam, Adam S. Chilton, Jacob Goldin, Kyle Rozema, and Maya Sen. 2017. 'The Political Ideologies of Law Clerks'. *American Law and Economics Review* 19: 96–128.

Caldeira, Gregory A. 1977. 'Incentives of Trial judges and the Administration of Justice'. *Justice System Journal* 3: 163–80.

Choi, Stephen J., Mitu Gulati, and Eric A. Posner. 2012. 'What Do Federal District Judges Want? An Analysis of Publications, Citations, and Reversals'. *Journal of Law, Economics, & Organization* 28: 518–49.

Clark Tom S. 2009. 'The Separation of Powers, Court Curbing, and Judicial Legitimacy'. *American Journal of Political Science* 53: 971–89.

Clark, Tom S., Benjamin G. Engst, and Jeffrey K. Staton. 2018. 'Estimating the Effect of Leisure on Judicial Performance'. *Journal of Legal Studies* 47: 349–90.

Coffin, Frank M. 1994. *On Appeal: Courts, Lawyering, and Judging*. New York: W.W. Norton.

Cohen, Alma, and Crystal S. Yang. 2019. 'Judicial Politics and Sentencing Decisions'. *American Economic Journal: Economic Policy* 11: 160–91.

Cohen, Jonathan Matthew. 2002. *Inside Appellate Courts*. Ann Arbor: University of Michigan Press.

Cohen, Mark A. 1991. 'Explaining Judicial Behavior or What's "Unconstitutional" about the Sentencing Commission?' *Journal of Law, Economics, and Organization* 7: 183–99.

Cohen, Mark A. 1992. 'The Motives of Judges: Empirical Evidence from Anti-trust Sentencing'. *International Review of Law and Economics* 12: 13–30.

Cooter, Robert D. 1983. The Objectives of Private and Public Judges. *Public Choice* 41: 1071–32.

Corley, Pamela C., Paul M. Collins Jr., and Bryan Calvin. 2011. 'Lower Court Influence on U.S. Supreme Court Opinion Content'. *Journal of Politics* 73: 31–44.

Crichton, Sha-Shana. 2022. 'Using Law Clerks to Improve Efficiency in Jamaican Courts'. *Georgia Journal of International and Comparative Law* 50: 299–356.

Cross, Frank B., and Emerson H. Tiller. 2008. 'Understanding Collegiality on the Court'. *Journal of Constitutional Law* 10: 257–71.

Curry, Todd A., and Michael P. Fix. 2019. 'May It Please the Twitterverse: The Use of Twitter by State High Court Judge'. *Journal of Information Technology & Politics* 16: 379–93.

Dalla Pellegrina, Lucia, Jef De Mot, Michael Faure, and Nuno Garoupa. 2017. 'Litigating Federalism: An Empirical Analysis of Decisions of the Belgian Constitutional Court'. *European Constitutional Law Review* 13: 305–46.

Davis, Richard. 2011. *Justices and Journalists: The U.S. Supreme Court and the Media*. New York: Cambridge University Press.

De Mot, Jef, Michael Faure, and Jonathan Klick. 2015. 'Appellate Caseload and the Switch to Comparative Negligence'. *International Review of Law and Economics* 42: 147–56.

DeAngelo, Gregory, and Bryan C. McCannon. 2017. 'Judicial Compensation and Performance'. *Supreme Court Economic Review* 25: 129–47.

Devins Neal, and Allison Orr Larsen. 2021. 'Weaponizing En Banc'. *NYU Law Review* 96: 1373–437.

Deyneli, Fatih, and Peter Mascini., 2020. 'Utility Maximizing Judges and Judicial Assistants: Testing Rational Choice Theory in 22 EU Countries'. *International Journal for Court Administration* 11: 6.

Drahozal, Christopher R. 1998. 'Judicial Incentives and the Appeals Process'. *SMU Law Review* 51: 469–504.

Dyevre, Arthur. 2010. 'Unifying the Field of Comparative Judicial Politics: Towards a General Theory of Judicial Behaviour'. *European Political Science Review* 2: 297–327.

Easterbrook, Frank H. 1990. 'What's So Special about Judges?' *University of Colorado Law Review* 61: 773–82.

Edwards, Harry T. 2003. 'The Effects of Collegiality on Judicial Decision Making'. *University of Pennsylvania Law Review* 151: 1639–90.

Elster, Jon. 1983. *Explaining Technical Change*. Cambridge: Cambridge University Press.

Engel, Christoph, and Keren Weinshall. 2020. 'Manna from Heaven for Judges: Judges' Reaction to a Quasi-Random Reduction in Caseload'. *Journal of Empirical Legal Studies* 17: 725–51.

Epstein, Lee, and Andrew D. Martin. 2010. 'Does Public Opinion Influence the Supreme Court? Possibly Yes (But We're Not Sure Why)'. *University of Pennsylvania Journal of Constitutional Law* 13: 263–81.

Epstein, Lee, and Jack Knight. 1998. *The Choices Justices Make*. Washington: Congressional Quarterly Press.

Epstein, Lee, and Jack Knight. 2013. 'Reconsidering Judicial Preferences'. *Annual Review of Political Science* 16: 19.1–19.21.

Epstein, Lee, and Jack Knight. 2017. 'The Economic Analysis of Judicial Behavior'. In *The Oxford Handbook of U.S. Judicial Behavior*, edited by Lee Epstein and Stefanie A. Lindquist, 320–40. Oxford, UK: Oxford University Press.

Epstein, Lee, and Keren Weinshall. 2021. *The Strategic Analysis of Judicial Behavior: A Comparative Perspective*. Cambridge: Cambridge University Press.

Epstein, Lee, William M. Landes, and Richard A. Posner. 2011. 'Why (and When) Judges Dissent'. *Journal of Legal Analysis* 3: 101–37.

Epstein, Lee, William M. Landes, and Richard A. Posner. 2013. *The Behavior of Federal Judges: A Theoretical and Empirical Study of Rational Choice*. Cambridge: Harvard University Press.

Epstein, Lee, Urška Šadl, and Keren Weinshall. 2021. 'The Role of Comparative Law in the Analysis of Judicial Behavior'. *American Journal of Comparative Law* 69: 689–710.

Foxall, Gordon R. 2004. 'What Judges Maximize: Toward an Economic Psychology of the Judicial Utility Function'. *Liverpool Law Review* 25: 177–94.

Friedman, Barry. 2009. *The Will of the People: How Public Opinion has Influenced the Supreme Court and Shaped the Meaning of the Constitution*. New York: Farrar, Straus and Giroux.

Gaille, S. Scott. 1997. 'Publishing by United States Court of Appeals Judges: Before and After the Bork Hearings'. *Journal of Legal Studies* 26: 371–76.

Garoupa, Nuno, and Tom Ginsburg. 2015. *Judicial Reputation: A Comparative Theory*. Chicago: University of Chicago Press.

Georgakopoulos, Nicholas L. 2000. 'Discretion in the Career and Recognition Judiciary'. *University of Chicago Law School Roundtable* 7: 205–25.

Grendstad, Gunnar, William R. Shaffer, Jørn Øyrehagen Sunde, and Eric N. Walternburg. 2020. *Proactive and Powerful: Law Clerks and the Institutionalization of the Norwegian Supreme Court*. The Hague: Eleven International Publishing.

Grenstad, Gunnar, William R. Shaffer, and Eric N. Waltenburg. 2015. *Policy Making in an Independent Judiciary: The Norwegian Supreme Court*. Colchester: ECPR Press.

Gulati, Mitu, and C. M. A. McCauliff. 1998. 'On Not Making Law'. *Law and Contemporary Problems* 61: 157–228.

Habel, Philip, Daniel Bennett, Shane A. Gleason, and Scott A. Comparato. 2015. 'The Implications of Salary for the Quality of Nominations to the Federal District Courts, 1964–2012'. *Justice System Journal* 36: 323–40.

Hall, Matthew E. K., and Jason Harold Windett. 2016. 'Discouraging Dissent: The Chief Judge's Influence in State Supreme Courts'. *American Politics Research* 44: 682–709.

Hall, Melinda Gann. 1987. 'Constituent Influence in State Supreme Courts: Conceptual Notes and a Case Study'. *Journal of Politics* 49: 1117–24.

Hanretty, Chris. 2020. *A Court of Specialists: Judicial Behavior on the UK Supreme Court*. Oxford: Oxford University Press.

Harvey, Anna, and Barr Friedman. 2006. 'Pulling Punches: Congressional Constraints on the Supreme Court's Constitutional Rulings, 1987–2000'. *Legislative Studies Quarterly* 31: 533–62.

Hogg, Peter W., and Ravi Amarnath. 2017. 'Why Judges Should Dissent'. *University of Toronto Law Journal* 67: 126–41.

Klein David E. 2002. *Making Law in the United States Courts of Appeals*. Cambridge: Cambridge University Press.

Klein, David E., and Robert J. Hume. 2003. 'Fear of Reversal as an Explanation of Lower Court Compliance'. *Law & Society Review* 37: 579–606.

Kureshi, Yasser. 2021. 'When Judges Defy Dictators: An Audience-Based Framework to Explain the Emergence of Judicial Assertiveness against Authoritarian Regimes'. *Comparative Politics* 53: 233–57.

Landes William M., and Richard A. Posner. 1976. 'Legal Precedent: A Theoretical and Empirical Analysis'. *Journal of Law and Economics* 19: 249–307.

Lemley Mark A., and Shawn P. Miller. 2016. 'If You Cannot Beat 'Em, Join 'Em? How Sitting by Designation Affects Judicial Behavior'. *Texas Law Review* 94: 451–84.

Levy, Gilat. 2005. 'Careerist Judges and the Appeals Process'. *RAND Journal of Economics* 36: 275–97.

Levy, Marin K. 2019. 'Visiting Judges'. *California Law Review* 67: 101–40.

Lindquist Stefanie A., and David E. Klein. 2006. 'The Influence of Jurisprudential Considerations on Supreme Court Decisionmaking: A Study of Conflict Cases'. *Law & Society Review* 40: 135–62.

Liptak, Adam. 2010. 'A Sign of the Court's Polarization: Choice of Clerks'. *New York Times*, September 6.

Lopes, Felipe de Mendonça. 2019. 'Dissent Aversion and Sequential Voting in the Brazilian Supreme Court'. *Journal of Empirical Legal Studies* 16: 933–54.

Lovett, Frank. 2006. 'Rational Choice Theory and Explanation'. *Rationality and Society* 18: 237–72.

Macey Jonathan. 1994. 'Judicial Preferences, Public Choice, and the Rules of Procedure'. *Journal of Legal Studies* 23: 627–46.

Massie, Tajuana, Kirk A. Randazzo, and Donald R. Songer. 2014. 'The Politics of Judicial Retirement in Canada and the United Kingdom'. *Journal of Law and Courts* 2: 273–99.

McGuire Kevin T., and James A. Stimson. 2004. 'The Least Dangerous Branch Revisited: New Evidence on Supreme Court Responsiveness to Public Preferences'. *Journal of Politics* 66: 1018–35.

Melcarne, Alessandro. 2017. 'Careerism and Judicial Behavior'. *European Journal of Law and Economics* 44: 241–64.

Merryman, John Henry, and Rogelio Pérez-Perdomo. 2018. *The Civil Law Tradition: An Introduction to the Legal Systems of Europe and Latin America*. Stanford: Stanford University Press.

Miceli, Thomas J., and Metin M. Coşgel. 1994. 'Reputation and Judicial Decision-Making'. *Journal of Economic Behavior & Organization* 23: 31–51.

Narayan, Paresh Kumar, and Russell Smyth. 2007. 'What Explains Dissent on the High Court of Australia? An Empirical Assessment Using a Cointegration and Error Correction Approach'. *Journal of Empirical Legal Studies* 4: 401–25.

Nash, Jonathan Remy. 2022 'Measuring Judicial Collegiality Through Dissent'. *Buffalo Law Review* 70: 1561–635.
Nelson, Michael J., Morgan L. W. Hazelton, and Rachael K. Hinkle. 2022. 'How Interpersonal Contact Affects Appellate Review'. *Journal of Politics* 84: 573–77.
Owens Ryan J., and Patrick C. Wohlfarth. 2019. 'The Influence of Home-State Reputation and Public Opinion on Federal Circuit Court Judges *Journal of Law and Courts*'. 7: 187–214.
Pang, Xun, Barry Friedman, Andrew D. Martin, and Kevin M. Quinn. 2017. 'Endogenous Jurisprudential Regimes'. *Political Analysis* 20: 417–36.
Pérez-Liñán, Anibel, and Ignacio Arana Araya. 2017. 'Strategic Retirement in Comparative Perspective: Supreme Court Justices in Presidential Regimes'. *Journal of Law and Courts* 5: 173–98.
Perry, H. W., Jr. 1994. *Deciding to Decide: Agenda Setting in the U.S. Supreme Court*. Cambridge: Harvard University Press.
Ponticelli, Jacopo, and Leonardo S. Alencar. 2016. 'Court Enforcement, Bank Loans, and Firm Investment: Evidence from a Bankruptcy Reform in Brazil'. *Quarterly Journal of Economics* 131 (3): 1365–413.
Posner, Richard A. 1990. *Cardozo: A Study in Reputation*. Chicago: University of Chicago Press.
Posner, Richard A. 1993. 'What Do Judges and Justices Maximize? (The Same Thing Everybody Else Does)'. *Supreme Court Economic Review* 3: 1–41.
Posner, Richard A. 1995. *Overcoming Law*. Cambridge: Harvard University Press.
Posner, Richard A. 2011. *Economic Analysis of Law*. N.p.: Aspen Publishing.
Ramseyer, J. Mark, and Eric B. Rasmusen. 2001. 'Why Are Japanese Judges So Conservative in Politically Charged Cases?' *American Political Science Review* 95: 331–44.
Richards, Mark J., and Herbert M. Kritzer. 2002. 'Jurisprudential Regimes in Supreme Court Decision Making'. *American Political Science Review* 96: 305–20.
Rosenberg, Gerald N. 1992. 'Judicial Independence and the Reality of Political Power'. *Review of Politics* 54: 369–98.
Salamone, Michael F. 2018. *Perceptions of a Polarized Court: How Division Among Justices Shapes the Supreme Court's Public Image*. Philadelphia, PA: Temple University Press.
Salzberger Eli, and Paul Fenn. 1999. 'Judicial Independence: Some Evidence from the English Court of Appeal'. *Journal of Law & Economics* 42: 831–47.
Sandholtz, Wayne, and Mariana Rangel Padilla. 2020. 'Law and Politics in the Inter-American System: The Amnesty Cases'. *Journal of Law and Courts* 8: 151–75.
Sayer, Andrew. 2021. 'Affirming the District Judge: An Empirical Analysis of the Effect of District Judges Sitting by Designation on Circuit Court Panels'. *Journal of Empirical Legal Studies* 18: 461–84.
Scalia, Antonin. 1994. 'The Dissenting Opinion'. *Journal of Supreme Court History* 19: 33–44.
Schauer Frederick. 2000. Incentives, Reputation, and the Inglorious Determinants of Judicial Behavior. *University of Cincinnati Law Review* 68: 615–36.
Segal, Jeffrey A., and Harold J. Spaeth. 2002. *The Supreme Court and the Attitudinal Model Revisited*. Cambridge University Press.
Segal, Jeffrey A., Chad Westerland, and Stefanie A. Lindquist. 2011. 'Congress, the Supreme Court, and Judicial Review: Testing a Constitutional Separation of Powers Model'. *American Journal of Political Science* 55: 89–104.
Shapiro, Sidney A., and Richard E. Levy. 1994. 'Judicial Incentives and Indeterminacy in Substantive Review of Administrative Decisions'. *Duke Law Journal* 44: 1051–80.

Sisk, Gregory C., and Heise, Michael. 2022. 'Cracks in the Wall: The Persistent Influence of Ideology in Establishment Clause Decisions'. *Arizona State Law Journal* 54: 625–62.

Sisk, Gregory C., Michael Heise, and Andrew P. Morris. 1998. 'Charting the Influences on the Judicial Mind: An Empirical Study of Judicial Reasoning'. *NYU Law Review* 73: 1377–500.

Skiple, Jon Kåre, and Henrik Litleré Bentsen, and Mark Jonathan McKenzie. 2021. 'How Docket Control Shapes Judicial Behavior: A Comparative Analysis of the Norwegian and Danish Supreme Courts'. *Journal of Law and Courts* 9: 111–36.

Songer, Donald R., et al. 2012. *Law, Ideology, and Collegiality: Judicial Behaviour in the Supreme Court of Canada*. Montreal and Kingston, Canada: McGill-Queen's University Press.

Sprigg, James F., and Paul J. Wahlbeck. 1995. 'Calling It Quits: Retirement on the Federal Courts of Appeals, 1893–1991'. *Political Research Quarterly* 48: 573–97.

Staton, Jeffrey K., and Georg Vanberg. 2008. 'The Value of Vagueness: Delegation, Defiance, and Judicial Opinions'. *American Journal of Political Science* 52: 504–19.

Stephan, Terry. 2009. 'A Justice for All'. *Northwestern Magazine*: 16. At: http://www.northwestern.edu/magazine/spring2009/cover/stevens.html.

Stern, Robert L., Eugene Gressman, and Stephen M. Shapiro. 1985. *Supreme Court Practice*. Washington, D.C.: BNA Books.

Stolzenberg Ross M., and James Lindgren. 2010. 'Retirement and Death in Office of U.S. Supreme Court Justices'. *Demography* 47: 269–98.

Swalve, Tilko. 2022. 'Does Group Familiarity Improve Deliberations in Judicial Teams? Evidence from the German Federal Court of Justice'. *Journal of Empirical Legal Studies* 19: 223–49.

Taha, Ahmed E. 2004. 'Publish or Paris? Evidence of How Judges Allocate Their Time'. *American Law and Economics Review* 6: 1–27.

Toma, Eugenia Froedge. 1991. 'Congressional Influence and the Supreme Court: The Budget as a Signaling Device'. *Journal of Legal Studies* 20: 131–46.

Toma, Eugenia Froedge. 1996. 'A Contractual Model of the Voting of the Supreme Court: The Role of the Chief Justice'. *International Review of Law and Economics* 16: 433–47.

Wald, Patricia M. 1987. 'Some Thoughts on Judging as Gleaned from One Hundred Years of the "Harvard Law Review" and Other Great Books.' *Harvard Law Review* 100: 887–908.

Whitman, Douglas G. 2000. 'Evolution of the Common Law and the Emergence of Compromise'. *Journal of Legal Studies* 29: 753–81.

Yang, Crystal S. 2015. 'Free at Last? Judicial Discretion and Racial Disparities in Federal Sentencing'. *Journal of Legal Studies* 44: 75–111.

Yoon, Albert. 2006. 'Pensions, Politics, and Judicial Tenure, An Empirical Study of Federal Judges, 1869–2002'. *American Law and Economics Review* 8: 143–80.

CHAPTER 11

RESEARCH ON COGNITIVE SHORTCOMINGS IN COMPARATIVE JUDICIAL BEHAVIOUR

EILEEN BRAMAN

1. Introduction

One thing that is true about judges across different institutional and comparative contexts is that they are human, at least until Artificial Intelligence becomes more advanced (see chapter by Niblett this volume). Even then, there are those who would argue that judges should remain human; that the intuitive (Engel 2020) and empathetic features (Lee 2013; Corso 2014) of judging are absolutely necessary for legal institutions where decision-makers arbitrate disputes between parties involving complex individual and societal interests. It is somewhat difficult (and perhaps futile, at this point in our technological development) to argue with such logic. Still, researchers from a growing number of national backgrounds are demonstrating that there is a tension between the 'humanness' of judges and what we require of them as officials who make distributive choices that influence the lives and livelihoods of citizens under a variety of circumstances where the stakes are often substantial.

Judges are charged with different kinds of decisions where we need them to be fair, accurate, and reasoned in their judgments. Indeed, some decision contexts, including those that entail judicial investigation or fact finding, demand that they achieve all three of these important objectives at once. The evidence reviewed in this chapter suggests that judges can fall short of these goals. Often this is through no fault of their own but because they are human, and so subject to the fallibilities we all face in making particular kinds of judgments. But they are also judges and so the institutional power they have to make decisions that influence the lives and fortunes of others demands that we attempt to understand and address cognitive shortcomings that can call distributive choices they make into question.

While some of the decision-making issues that have been identified may be inevitable, others appear to serve different kinds of personal goals that have been characterized as more and less appropriate for judicial officials. If researchers can discover the function particular decision-making strategies serve, perhaps we can design ways to overcome shortcomings. In some instances, taking extra steps reminding jurists to be fair might be enough to prevent biases (Kantorowicz-Reznichenko, Kantorowitz, and Weinshall 2022). Other cognitive shortcomings might require more careful engineering of decision-making situations in line with Jolls and Sunstien's (2006) arguments about 'debiasing through law' or Herbert Simon's vision of optimizing decision-making in particular information and incentive environments (Simon 1956; Gigerenzer 2006).

The next section details how researchers have demonstrated judges can fall short standards of substantive and procedural fairness with findings that they are subject to ideological and in-group biases in their decision-making and that they often consider irrelevant factors in their judgments. The chapter then discusses studies demonstrating that judicial decision-makers are subject to biases that can lead them to inaccurate conclusions in their reasoning. Finally, there is growing evidence that judges may be unaware of the influence of various factors in their judgments. This calls into question their ability to make reasoned decisions that accurately account for the reasons they make the choices that they do. This is significant because legal scholars have argued that in the face of intersubjectivity, where different judges can come to disparate conclusions based on their understanding of the way the law applies to particular circumstances, that the fact that decision-makers can reasonably account for their decisions legitimizes distributive outcomes (see e.g. Powell 2008). If judges cannot accurately report the factors that influence their judgments, it calls such theorized mechanisms of legitimatization into question.

It is important to point out that the evidence in this chapter is about cognitive shortcomings where comparative studies tend to corroborate rather than conflict with one another. Although there is research on any number of cognitive shortcomings in judicial behaviour, the ones discussed here have been established in research across different national contexts. The next section details findings on ideological biases in decision-making (Ferguson, Babcock, and Shane 2008; e.g. Kahan et al. 2012; Kantorowicz-Reznichenko, Kantorowitz, and Weinshall 2022) in-group favouritism (e.g. Shayo and Zussman 2011; Epstein, Parker, and Segal 2018), the consideration of irrelevant evidence in legal judgments (e.g. Sood and Darley 2012; Spamann and Klohn 2016; Liu and Li 2019; Segal, Sood, and Woodson 2019), heuristic biases (Guthrie, Rachlinski, and Wistrich 2000; Harley 2007; Sonnemans and van Dijk 2012), coherence-based reasoning and order effects; (e.g. Holyoak and Simon 1999; Simon 2004; Engel, Timme, and Glöckner 2020); and the justifications legal decision-makers give for their judgments (Cohen 2015; Liu 2018; Lui and Li 2019).

The discussion is anchored by noting how findings in social science challenge the notion that judicial decision-makers are fair, accurate, and reasoned in their judgments. It considers some of the normative implications for the exercise of authority where judicial officials fall short of these ideals. Directions for future research, given the current accumulation of knowledge about various decisional shortcomings, are also suggested as well as how current and future findings may inform strategies to improve judicial decisions in light of some of the normative concerns raised by the growing volume of comparative research on judicial cognition.

2. Fairness in Legal Decision-Making

Judicial officials across comparative contexts are part of adversarial systems where they arbitrate disputes between parties about how legal frameworks apply to specific circumstances where citizens' lives, freedom, and livelihoods are at stake. Litigants present facts and legal arguments to the court with the expectation that jurists will treat them fairly. This commonly involves both substantive and procedural aspects of decision-making.

2.1 Research on Substantive Fairness: Ideological and In-group Biases

Substantively, judges should be neutral between parties and objective in their consideration of evidence and arguments. This aspect of decision-making is important so litigants can have confidence that judgments are based on the application of legal principals to particular facts and circumstances rather than judges' personal biases or their predispositions about the parties or issues involved in litigation.

2.2 Ideological Biases

There is a good deal of social science research demonstrating that judges can fall short of the expectation that they are neutral and objective in their consideration of arguments and litigants. Ideological biases that can influence judicial decision-making have been well established in observational studies across different national contexts (see chapter by Spill and Waltenberg this volume). Somewhat more relevant for this chapter are studies specifying the cognitive mechanisms by with such biases may arrive. Employing the framework of 'motivated reasoning', researchers have theorized and garnered a good deal of experimental evidence that ideological biases can influence decision-makers in the utilization of various norms of legal decision-making (see Sood 2013 for a comprehensive review of such research in the United States).

Braman and Nelson (2007), for instance, find that ideology can play a role in the perception of analogy implicated in the application of legal precedent. Specifically, they demonstrate that lay decision-makers and experimental participants with legal training are more likely to see cases that support the policy outcomes they prefer as similar to cases they are currently considering than identical cases that support outcomes they do not favour. Concerns about such bias in the application of legal doctrine may apply some force in common law systems in Europe, Africa, and Asia where prior judicial pronouncements are commonly used as sources of judicial reasoning. In a similar vein, Ferguson, Babcock, and Shane (2008) find that the policy implications of law can shape the seemingly neutral analyses of law students as to its constitutional soundness. Kahan and colleagues (Kahan et al. 2012) find decision-makers are more likely to punish groups for protests expressing views that are at odds with their own ideological viewpoints than groups who express views that are consistent with their political leanings.

Researchers testing avenues of ideological biases have discovered that particular legal tests and norms of legal decision-making can enable the influence of judicial preferences in legal reasoning. A number of researchers undertaking research on judges in different countries (including Australia, Canada, India, Israel, and Poland) have employed the principle of proportionality as it is utilized in various national and international decision-making contexts to explore how ideological bias can impact judicial decisions (see Kremnitzer, Stiner, and Lang 2020 for review; Kantorowicz-Reznichenko, Kantorowitz, and Weinshall 2022 and Stiner, Netzer, and Sulitzeanu-Kenan 2022 for experiments probing cognitive sources of biases for decision-maker employing different variations of proportionality).

Pointing to decision-making norms that require judges to compartmentalize their thinking so that related preferences they may have are strictly separated, Braman (2006) demonstrates that 'threshold' decision-making in complex cases can be another way for decision-makers to reach outcomes that they favour. This experimental study reveals that law student participants are more likely to dismiss substantive First Amendment claims of litigants on preliminary standing grounds when those litigants express views that are inconsistent to their own on the subject of abortion. There are certainly other instances where the preferences judges have across issues in litigation may influence their judgments. For instance, there also is experimental evidence regarding that judges are not able to separate what they know about settlement discussions from their liability determinations in line with requirements of judicial behaviour (Wistrich, Guthrie and Rachinski 2005).

2.3 In-group Biases

Besides political biases, which can influence a range of decisions that judges make relevant to outcomes, research on another sort of bias implicating the substantive fairness of judicial determinations is becoming quite prominent in comparative research on judicial behaviour: in-group favouritism. In group favouritism is a special kind of group bias that is theorized to be fundamental in the way people think about the social world. People have an almost automatic instinct to categorize others into in-groups and out-groups.

Henri Tajfel (1978) coined the term 'minimal group paradigm' upon discovering that individuals organized the social environment in this way based on rather arbitrary criteria (such as whether they were told they were 'over estimators' or 'under estimators' of dots in random pattern, or whether they had a preference for modern artists Klee or Kandinski). He specifically demonstrated the concept using the type of distributive decisions that judicial officials commonly make. Significantly, besides discovering that it took very little for individuals to favour people that were in their group in allocations, Tajfel also observed that preferences for in-group members motivated to boost group (and thus individual) esteem were not accompanied by out-group animus in his experiments. Subsequent research by scholars like Brewer and Campbell (1976) and Diselhorst and Hou (2014) demonstrate that this basic tendency of favouring in-group members operates across cultural contexts in places like East Africa and China. While discriminatory reactions to members of specific groups (out-group antipathy) may also be deeply ingrained, such reactions are considered more culturally dependent than our innate tendency to favour those who are similar to ourselves (Brewer and Caporael 2006).

Like research on the influence of ideology in decision-making, evidence of in-group biases involves observational and experimental studies around the world. There is a trio of studies from Israel demonstrating in-group bias among Jewish and Arab-Israeli judges in different contexts. The first, by Gazal-Ayel and Sulizenu-Kenan (2010), uses observational data from over 1,200 weekend bail hearings occurring in 2004 involving Arab and Jewish suspects that were assigned to both types of judges randomly. The authors argue that looking at bail judgments which occur in the early stages of defendants' contact with the criminal justice system allows them to investigate biases without the interference of subsequent considerations (such as the quality of representation and the initial detention decision itself) that can influence outcomes across different types of defendants. Controlling for characteristics of the offence and the number of detention days requested by police, they find that Jewish judges are more likely to release Jewish suspects than Arab judges and also more likely to detain Arab suspects than their Arab colleagues. The opposite pattern obtains for Arab judges across each defendant type. In almost 900 decisions to detain, however, they do not find any significant bias in terms of the length of detention different types of judges assign to Jewish and Arab defendants.

A second study by Shayo and Zussman (2011) looks at the decisions of Jewish and Arab judges in small claims matters from transcripts of proceedings that were made available online from 2000 to 2004. Analysing close to 2,000 cases assigned to trial dates where both types of judges were randomly assigned to hear disputes, they find Arab judges are more likely to accept claims from Arab plaintiffs and Jewish judges are more likely to accept claims made by Jewish claimants. They also find a bias in terms of the awards given to plaintiffs by in-group judges and a higher request to award ratio in the 660 cases where they have information about the amount of damages requested by claimants. They provide evidence that these in-group biases are stronger in jurisdictions where deaths from terrorist attacks are higher in the past year compared to jurisdictions where such fatalities are lower.

Using intuitions from research on panel effects involving issues relating to race on the US Courts of Appeal (Cox and Miles 2008; Kastellec 2013), Grossman et al. (2016) demonstrate Arab defendants achieve more favourable outcomes, in terms of both incarceration and the length of sentencing, when there is at least one Arab judge on Israel's appellate district courts, compared to panels with three Jewish judges. They do not find any symmetrical pattern for Jewish defendants. Although these findings do not reveal an in-group bias per se, they do suggest that deliberations limited to in-group members yield substantively different outcomes than those that are more diverse, particularly with regard to out-group members. Their research highlights the importance of descriptive representation for more than just symbolic reasons by signalling that there are *consequential differences in the nature of deliberation* based on the group characteristics of the judges involved.

A pair of studies from researchers in different countries characterize in-group members in terms of their agreement with content of speech where expressive rights are at issue. An observational study of decisions by justices on the US Supreme Court by Epstein, Parker, and Segal (2018) finds that from 1953 to 2014 liberal justices are generally more supportive of free speech. Notwithstanding this difference however, both liberal and conservative justices are more likely to support First Amendment rights where the content of the speech at issue is characterized as ideologically consistent with their policy views, and more likely to vote against free expression where speech is not consistent with their ideology.

In an experimental study with Polish citizens recruited by a survey firm to be representative of that nation's population in terms of age, education, and gender, Kantorowicz-Reznichenko, Kantorowitz, and Weinshall (2022) find that participants are more likely to support a group's right to demonstrate when the claimant group is expressing views closer to their own about abortion rights. They also find that those who are aware of the leanings of the group before they hear about the specifics of the claim are more likely to rate free speech rights as important when their views are close to that group. The authors argue that this demonstrates that bias comes from an affinity toward in-group members rather than antipathy toward out-group members. They also find that participants who are asked to sign a statement saying they will be fair are less likely to demonstrate such bias than those who do not. Asking participants to rate the importance of the right before being told the identity of the group claimant, however, does not have a similar debiasing effect.

In a similar experimental study where the author gave briefs with identical legal arguments to second- and third-year law students concerning whether individuals had standing to challenge a local speech ordinance in the United States, Braman (2006) finds in-group bias in favour of claimants with similar views on abortion. Significantly, findings in that study demonstrate that this in-group bias disappears in the presence of controlling precedent on the standing issue, suggesting legal doctrine can constrain such tendencies. In a qualitive analysis of the reasoning behind those decisions, Braman (2009) finds that law student participants did not seem to be aware any in-group biases in their written justifications for their standing decision. This comports with findings, discussed more fully below, that legal decision-makers may not be cognizant of all the factors relevant in their judgments.

One question this brief survey of research on in-group biases raises is which group memberships are consequential in legal decision-making. In contexts like Israel and the United States, where ethnic and racial identities are salient, it seems obvious that they may be important in legal judgments. But since all individuals, including judges, have multiple identities which could implicate in-group/out-group distinctions it may be worthwhile to think more about what it is about particular identities or the state of mind of decision-makers that trigger such biases. For instance, in a study of tort awards Wistrich, Rachlinski, and Guthrie (2015) discover a bias where Minnesota judges award substantially lower punitive damages to an in-state plaintiff when the defendant also hails from Minnesota (US$1 million), compared to when the defendant is from neighbouring Wisconsin (US$1.75 million).

One may also wonder whether the preference for individuals who share decision-makers' views on issues in expression cases shows just a 'flavour' of the attitudinal biases that have been identified more broadly and often characterized as a consequence of judges' desire to influence policy. Alternatively, perhaps this bias something we need to think about differently, in that, it seems to override decision-makers' ideological tendencies with regard to cases decisions involving expression (Epstein, Parker, and Segal 2018; Kantorowicz-Reznichenko, Kantorowitz, and Weinshall 2022) and court access (Braman 2006). Preferencing the in-group litigant over the ideological case outcome might certainly serve the decision-makers' esteem in the short term, but perhaps at the cost of longer-term doctrinal policy goals. Comparative law and courts scholars could certainly do more to identify and empirically explore such cross-cutting scenarios to identify the conditions under which in-group- versus policy-directed outcomes are obtained. More importantly, we need to update our theories of decision-making to account for such cross-cutting pressures and delve further into their implications.

There have been at least two observational studies where biases *against* in-group members have been observed in judicial sentencing behaviour. Depew, Eren, and Mocan (2017) find a negative in-group bias for Black and White judges looking at the juvenile sentencing behaviour of judges across parishes in Louisiana using an estimation technique matching outcomes for Black and White defendants in terms of incarceration rates and duration. Fishman, Rattner, and Turjeman (2006) find a similar sentencing bias against Arab defendants by Arab judges in northern district courts when cases involve Jewish victims of crime in Israel.

Rather than serving esteem motives, Depew, Eren, and Mocan suggest that biases that are observed against in-group members are an effort to punish them for the violation of societal rules in line with social psychology research on intragroup norm enforcement (Mendoza, Lane, and Amodio 2014). Fishman and his colleagues posit that Arab judges are either trying to prevent potential charges of favouritism by being harsh with in-group members, or alternatively, they are adhering to perceptions members of their own Arab in-group minority are more dangerous than majority group members.

Each of these alternative explanations of negative in-group bias is distinct from esteem motivations posited by research on the minimal group paradigm and perhaps suggest more complex cognitive processing (to punish in-group members or avoid the appearance of favouritism) than Tajfel's original theory contemplates. If we are interested in understanding the range of potential biases toward in-group members in the context of complex societal structures that also can influence group interactions, there must be a way to observe and account for such behaviours. Understanding and explaining these various influences and how they can interact in the minds of decision-makers is likely to prove fertile ground for future research on comparative judicial behaviour.

2.4 Implicit Biases

A third type of bias in legal decision-making that has been the subject of research is implicit bias. This type of cognition is generally considered more culturally determined than esteem serving in-group bias. The general idea is that there are some stereotypes that are so deeply ingrained in particular societal contexts that they become more or less automatic in the minds of individuals who are raised in that environment. This can have particularly damaging effects for members of groups that are disfavoured if judges are unable to overcome such automatic tendencies in their thinking. It may cause them to prefer certain types of litigants over others in adversarial disputes or mete out harsher punishments to individuals based on arbitrary features that individuals cannot control and have no reasonable relationship to civil or criminal culpability.

The fact that implicit biases have been associated with arbitrary characteristics across different national contexts including race (Eisenberg and Johnson 2003; Rachlinski et al. 2009), gender (Levinson and Young 2010; Basfirinci et al. 2019), ethnicity (Kang et al. 2010; Levinson, Bennet, and Hoiki 2017), national origin (Gawronski, Geschke, and Banse 2003), and religion (Levinson, Bennet, and Hoiki 2017) makes them especially problematic for jurists charged with meting out justice in cultural contexts where they exist. Moreover, because they are so pervasive, implicit biases are not necessarily limited to out-group members. Similar to their male colleagues, for example, female judges can harbour implicit biases about the role women in society that can influence their judgments.

Much of the psychological research on implicit bias use rigorously timed computer tasks known as Implicit Attitude Tests (IAT) to demonstrate that individuals have an unconscious preference for certain attributes over others by pairing words associated with different characteristics with positive and negative words and then measuring the response time in microseconds. Obviously, it can be difficult to get judges to take part in such studies. Research that has been done with legally trained populations, however, generally demonstrates that judges and attorneys hold implicit biases to the same extent as do others in society. Rachlinski et al. (2009) find that the percentage of White judges who harbour such preferences (about 80 per cent) is similar to that in the larger population. They also cite a study by Eisenberg and Johnson (2003) demonstrating that capital defence attorneys, a group that has strong ethical reasons to resist such beliefs, show the same propensity for implicit racial bias as citizens generally. Using similar IAT measures, Levinson, Bennet, and Hoiki (2017) find federal district court, federal magistrate, and state court judges hold implicit biases concerning Asians and Jews.

Findings are somewhat contradictory with respect to how implicit biases influence judicial decision-making. Consistent with their hypotheses, in sentencing scenarios involving White-collar crime, Levinson, Bennet, and Hoiki (2017) find federal district court judges give Jewish defendants somewhat longer sentences than Christians, but Asians do not receive longer sentences than Whites; indeed, state court judges treat White defendants significantly more harshly than Asians. Rachlinski et al. (2009) find that when subliminally primed with words about race, implicit biases influence judges' sentencing behaviour regarding Black and White juveniles in a manner consistent with hypotheses predicting that those with bias will treat minority defendants more harshly. When White judges are made consciously aware of the race of the defendant, however, bias is not present. The authors take this as evidence that judges can override implicit biases with cognitive effort; this is good news for those who believe judges have a chronic awareness of potential biases and that they strive to overcome such influences in their decision-making. These authors and others point out, however, that the institutional pressures judges often face to adjudicate a high volume of cases quickly may work to impede such efforts (Marks 2015; Donald, Rachlinski, and Wistrich 2020).

One area where concerns about implicit biases have been raised that seems important across comparative contexts is on immigration courts. Marouf (2011) theorizes that immigration law in the United States has been impacted by biases throughout its history, citing examples of blatant and more nuanced ways preconceptions about national origin have shaped institutions and continue to influence outcomes. In a particularly interesting acknowledgement that implicit biases exist in this context an immigration law judge echoes these sentiments (Marks 2015), noting that judges' unconscious biases may be heightened by institutional choices like housing immigration courts in the agency charged with prosecutorial authority and making judges dependent on its officers for their security from day to day. The author offers a picture of judges struggling to curb improper biases in their decisions, but acknowledges this goal can be impeded by case overloads, the nature of the evidence in immigration proceedings, and the speed in which judges generally hold hearings and make decisions.

The burgeoning research on the role of implicit biases in judicial behaviour emphasizes the importance of jurists recognizing such tendencies in their own thinking. Just as important, court administrators and government actors with the authority to change things need to realize that institutional mechanisms can enable, and perhaps even exaggerate the operation of implicit biases in ways that prevent certain classes of litigants from achieving fair hearings or equitable outcomes compared with others who may be considered more favourably. As these biases are both pervasive and operate largely beneath judges' awareness they are particularly worrying. This is an area where continued research on both cognitive and institutional interventions to reduce such tendencies in comparative judicial behaviour has the potential to make a difference.

2.5 Research on Procedural Fairness: The Consideration of Irrelevant Factors in Decision-Making

In addition to bias that may work to the detriment of particular types of litigants, Tom Tyler (2006) has done a good deal of research on 'procedural fairness', requiring that officials follow specified rules including the consideration of relevant facts and arguments in their decision making. This is important so that affected parties have a fair opportunity to be heard and make their case in light of applicable legal criteria. If irrelevant facts and or circumstances influence judicial decisions without litigants' knowledge, they may not have an adequate chance to speak to those issues. Additionally, such judgments can be called into question as improper under applicable legal frameworks.

Social science research demonstrates that irrelevant factors often influence legal decision-makers. One example is the work by Wistrich, Guthrie, and Rachlinski (2005) mentioned above that shows judges have difficulty disregarding information from settlement negotiations from their thinking about liability. Not only does this demonstrate a failure to compartmentalize thinking as judicial norms require, it demonstrates that information that should not be factored into such determinations can, in fact, play a role in anchoring judicial thinking. Ironically, this shortcoming might work in conflicting ways to the detriment and benefit of particular litigants. For instance, the fact that a defendant makes an offer at all may make it easier for judges to conclude that they are, in fact, somehow responsible for a loss that is in dispute. The fact that offers can anchor liability determinations, however, is likely to work in favour of defendants because it ties awards to amounts that they have already said they are willing to pay, rather than to injuries that claimants have actually incurred.

Sood and Darley (2012) and Kahan et al. (2012) provide experimental evidence of irrelevant factors in speech contexts similar to those in studies of in-group biases mentioned above. Sood and Darley (2012) show that decision-makers' agreement with the content of speech about abortion rights, which should be irrelevant in culpability determinations, influences the degree of 'harm' that decision-makers conclude is caused by defendants charged with identical patterns of disruptive behaviour. Exploiting views on controversial issues like abortion and gay rights, Kahan et al. (2012) show experimental participants are more likely to find protests disruptive and violent when they are ideologically opposed to the group that participants are told is asserting their free speech rights. Although both of these experimental studies involve lay participants, each outlines clear mechanisms whereby decision-makers can be influenced by irrelevant information in the context of legal judgments.

Further, citing several studies tending to show irrelevant factors can influence judges in criminal decision-making (e.g. Sood 2014; Wistrich, Guthrie, and Rachlinski 2015), Segal, Sood, and Woodson (2019) provide observational evidence that the nature of the crime the defendant is charged with can influence judicial determinations of judges on the US Courts of Appeal in search and seizure cases. From a random selection of 495 cases from 1972 to 1986, the authors find 'controlling for search intrusiveness and judicial ideology judges were more likely to uphold the admission of challenged evidence in cases involving more serious crimes' (2019, 572). Wistrich, Rachlinski, and Guthrie (2015) find a similar type of bias in an experiment where judges are more likely to admit challenged searches if the results of those searches yield evidence of guilt with respect to heroin offences compared to searches that find evidence of crime related to marijuana.

Such results are problematic because defendants and their attorneys have no way of countering such bias with arguments they are allowed to make, based on the nature of the search rather than the severity of the offence with which they are charged. Moreover, it is illogical to believe that the propriety of official conduct aligns in such a manner with the characteristics of crimes that officers are investigating. In fact, to the extent there is a relationship between investigative overreach and offence severity, it is very likely to trend in the opposite direction because officers have strong incentives to produce evidence against the most serious offenders.

Also in the context of criminal adjudication, Spamann and Klohn (2016) use an international human rights scenario from Yugoslavia to demonstrate that what judges are told about a defendant's character can influence their decision to affirm lower court convictions. In an experiment with judges on the US Courts of Appeals, the authors informed participants that the defendant in a war crimes case was either a 'nationalist, hateful Serb ... [or] a conciliatory, regretful Croat' (2016, 256) in a fully briefed case. The authors find 87 per cent of judicial participants affirm the conviction for 'aiding and abetting' the crime in the first scenario versus only 41 per cent in the second. Moreover, they find that this tendency persists in the presence of what they define as strong (versus weak) precedent on the question of what sort of behaviour contributes to a 'joint criminal enterprise', going directly to the question of defendant's guilt.

In a similar vein Liu and Li (2019) find Chinese judges also consider irrelevant factors in experiments relating to judgments in civil and criminal cases. They find that character issues are important in judges' determinations about damages in contract disputes, liability in tort, and criminal intent in criminal cases. Moreover, as discussed further in the section about whether judges are aware of various influence decision-making, their study illustrates some very interesting patterns in justifications that judges use to explain the differences in their decisions with legally relevant criteria.

Studies indicating the influence of various irrelevant factors in legal decision-making are normatively important because if judges are not fully aware of the role of such factors in their judgments, litigants have little chance to combat their influence in decisions that influence their freedom and fortunes across comparative judicial contexts.

3. Accuracy in Judicial Reasoning: Heuristic Biases, Coherence Based Reasoning, and Order Effects

Besides neutrality and procedural fairness, accuracy is a goal of judges as they adjudicate cases between adversarial parties. Accuracy here means something distinct from jurists applying the correct precedent or interpretive approach from viable alternatives. Although volumes have been written about such decisions, they often involve subjective assessments about policy outcomes and the proper role of judges in society; these are issues where people can reasonably disagree. But judges, particularly when they act as investigators or fact finders in legal proceedings, often need to reach conclusions about a sequence of events in liability cases, or the course a suspect's behaviour in criminal matters where there is some identifiable, objective answer that has implications for case outcomes. Frequently they must do so in the face of ambiguous or even conflicting evidence.

There are several lines of research in comparative judicial behaviour suggesting cognitive mechanisms that may prevent judges from making accurate judgments. The first, concerning heuristic biases, involves several different ways of thinking that result in errors in decision-making. These patterns of decision-making generally save cognitive resources in reasoning processes; individuals have adopted them to save time and effort in making judgments. However, there is a trade-off: decisions using these tactics can be prone to error.

In a seminal article, Guthrie, Rachlinski, and Wistrich (2000) demonstrate that judges are not immune to heuristic errors in their decision-making. They demonstrate incidents of anchoring, hindsight bias, representativeness bias, ignoring base rates, and availability in the decision-making of federal judges using vignettes designed to simulate simple choices jurists might encounter in litigation. Since then, several law and courts scholars in different comparative contexts have written review essays about how such biases can influence legal decisions (Gigernzer 2006; Peer and Gamliel 2013; Braman 2017).

Harley (2007) specifically reviews research on hindsight bias in legal decision-making. This error is where decision-makers have a higher probability of saying that they predicted events that have subsequently occurred than was the case before they happened. Hindsight bias can have implications for judicial decisions involving foreseeability in negligence cases, or make searches appear more likely to be supported by 'probable cause' where they uncover evidence of criminal wrongdoing (Rachlinski, Guthrie, and Wistrich 2011).

The ability of judges to consider probabilistic evidence and base rates accurately has been implicated by researchers in the Netherlands as resulting in wrongful convictions and unfounded acquittals where decision-makers have or could acquire additional relevant evidence (Sonnemans and van Dijk 2012). These researchers find decision-makers charged with making factual determinations in criminal cases often do not seek out sufficient information before issuing judgments, even in circumstances where that information is available.

There has also been quite a bit of comparative work on anchoring demonstrating that some previously considered quantity can influence subsequent numerical judgments, even when that quantity is totally irrelevant to the estimation task. Anchoring has been found to influence legal decision-makers in a number of comparative contexts, including jury awards. There is research, for instance, on how demand amounts (Chapman and Bornstien 1996) and requests for punitive damages (Hastie, Schkade, and Payne 1999) influence the ultimate awards to plaintiffs. Marti (2000) discusses a 'boomerang effect' against plaintiffs when demands are too high. Anchoring has also been found to affect sentencing decisions of German, Spanish, and Chinese judges (Enough and Mussweiler 2001; Farina, Arce, and Novo 2003; Englich, Mussweiler, and Strack 2006; Xifen and Yong 2018). There is also research that anchoring influences Israeli judges in the consideration of vague legal standards (Feldman, Schurr, and Teichman 2016). Bystranowski et al. (2021) conduct a meta-analysis tending to demonstrate the influence of anchoring in twenty-nine studies involving contexts related to legal decisions.

Dhami and Ayton (2001) find that decision-makers in bail hearings in the United Kingdom are significantly influenced in their decisions by police requests and the amount of time defendants have previously been detained by other bail examiners. They suggest two possible reasons for this bias. First, that this is just a time-saving measure for decision-makers that have a multitude of judgments to make on a given day, which is a version of the adaptive cognitive bias we see in other contexts that might be tempered if decision-makers took more time with considering facts in an individualized manner. An alternative explanation offered by the researchers posits that bail-hearing officers use previously suggested time frames for detention as a way to escape liability for decisions that might be criticized. This is worth noting because it contemplates that decisions attributed to a lack of cognitive capacity might actually be made by decision-makers for other reasons. In such instances, where alternative explanations are plausible, in order to address the issue it would be necessary to figure out which mechanism is at play because distinct solutions would be required to resolve the problem depending on its root cause. Giving decision-makers more time to make judgments may help with cognitive shortcomings caused by case overload, but not with strategic choices to escape accountability. That type of bias may be better addressed by measures to reduce adverse selection in the overall quality of decision-makers making bail determinations.

Another factor that can influence the accuracy of judgments in legal decision-making is how information is presented. Psychological research has determined that the sequence of information can influence how it is processed in the minds of decision-makers. There is a rich literature on order effects in psychology that demonstrates information presented first or last in a sequence can have a disproportionate effect in reasoning these are known as primacy and recency effects, respectively.

Holyoak and Simon (1999) and Simon (2004) have theorized that these tendencies can shape legal decision-making. Specifically, they posit that decision-makers engage in 'coherence-based' reasoning where early information largely shapes the decision-making processes of jurors and judges such that evidence presented first in trials determines the direction and extent of later processing because decision-makers seek to create a consistent narrative to guide their judgments (see also Robbennolt, MacCoun, and Darley 2010; Platt 2012). The theory largely emphasizes primacy effects in the psychological literature and has several important implications, most notably for the order of the presentation of arguments and evidence in civil and criminal trials.

Recent work by comparative courts scholars Engel, Timme, and Glöckner (2020) challenges some of this thinking by demonstrating a number or impactful recency effects in experimental studies involving legal decisions, thus calling much of the logic behind coherence-based reasoning into question. As the psychological literature is replete with both types of order effects, future research may best be directed at uncovering the conditions under which primary and/or recency effects are likely to occur in the minds of decision-makers in such a way as to impair accuracy in judgment.

4. Reasoned Decision-Making: Can Judges Accurately Account for Their Judgments

A final issue raised by research on cognitive shortcomings in legal decision-making is whether or not judges can accurately account for the decisions that they make. Judges are not always required to write legal opinions, but in many circumstances they are. This decision can be the basis for additional recourse if litigants believe that the reasons for a judge's distributive choices are improper or legally incorrect. As such, there is an expectation that judges can explain their reasoning in cases that come before them. If judges cannot accurately account for why they make the judgments they do, then citizens' ability to challenge the grounds of those rulings is severely compromised.

As referenced at the start of this chapter, given that there is a more sophisticated understanding of the intersubjectivity that can exist between judges, where different individuals can come to different conclusions, legal scholars have argued that it is the ability of judges to justify their decisions under applicable legal frameworks that legitimates those choices and the power of judges to make them (Powell 2008). If the explanations judges give for their decisions are not adequately reasoned because those judgments are based on factors of which judges might not even be aware, what happens to this theorized legitimizing mechanism?

The research clearly indicates that there are various factors that influence legal decision-makers across comparative contexts of which they are unaware. As such, we cannot expect that judges can fully account for their judgments in particular cases where these factors may be operating. Several of the studies discussed above specifically indicate decision-makers are not aware of extra-legal factors, such as the nature of plaintiff's speech in standing decisions (Braman 2009, Chapter 4), or the character of the defendant in criminal appeals (Spamann and Klohn 2016). Indeed, several researchers discuss systematic strategies legally trained decision-makers use to rationalize judgments driven by extra-legal or irrelevant factors with doctrinally appropriate criteria (Sood and Darley 2012; Sood 2014; Liu and Li 2019).

Lui and Li (2019), for instance, find that in a commercial real estate case, judges are significantly likely to award greater damages to the plaintiff for failure to deliver occupancy on a specified date when the defendant is someone of low moral character than when the defendant is not described as such. Moreover, judges justify the difference by drawing disparate conclusions about the amount of loss related to the breach, rather than citing defendant's character traits, which was the only factor actually altered across experimental conditions.

In a criminal scenario involving the sale of exotic animals, Chinese judges were more likely to convict (and give significantly longer sentences to) a defendant who was described as a divorced, online gambler than a defendant described as a father caring for his sick daughter, where the alleged criminal conduct, knowingly selling wild animals, was identical. In this instance, judges across treatments differed on the extent to which they felt the defendant was aware of the criminality of his behaviour. Finally, a defendant in a tort case keeping oxygen tanks to care for his mother's lung disease was less likely to be held liable for damages from a fire than when the defendant was alternatively described as using oxygen tanks to produce illegal crystal methamphetamine for sale. Judges justified their decisions by reasoning it was, both, significantly (i) more likely that the meth dealer's conduct caused the fire and (ii) more foreseeable that the conduct would result in grave injury under those experimental conditions. This evidence suggests that judges themselves are not always aware of the influence of irrelevant criteria in their decision-making.

Liu (2018) finds that having decision-makers write their reasons for decisions *before* they make them and instituting a fixed 'deliberation period' prior to making a final decision can reduce bias in judgment in experiments with Chinese judges. Unfortunately, such institutional mechanisms do not exist in most legal systems. The fact that judges are expected to dispose of cases on their dockets quickly does not allow for extended deliberation before judgments, and legal decisions are commonly made before jurists memorialize the logic behind them. The same study finds delegation of decision writing, to law clerks, for example, an institutional mechanism that is quite common across comparative contexts, can accentuate decision-making biases.

Finally, in a very interesting article Cohen (2015) theorizes there may be circumstances where judges 'have reasons not to give reasons'. Specifically, she discusses a variety of cognitive, institutional, and efficiency reasons judges may have not to be forthcoming in every instance in their written opinions in the United States and across Europe (2015,

514–25). With respect to the cognitive shortcomings discussed here, it could be that judges are just not inclined to delve into their own decision-making processes too carefully because they are aware it can lead to uncomfortable truths that challenge their professional self-image as neutral decision-makers.

5. Conclusion and A Way Forward: Understanding the Reasons for Cognitive Shortcomings and Engineering Solutions

This survey of the various ways that comparative judicial research suggests that legal decision-makers can fall short of the goals of neutrality, accuracy, and reasoned decision-making that are so central to the functioning and legitimacy of judicial institutions around the world and that this is somewhat troubling. Some good news is that psychologists have also discovered ways to address some types of bias in decision-making. Several leading scholars undertaking work on judicial behaviour across the world have suggested ways to deal with cognitive shortcomings that have been identified in research (Babcock, Lowenstein, and Issacharoff 1997; Liu 2018; e.g. Donald, Rachlinski, and Wistrich 2020; Kantorowicz-Reznichenko, Kantorowitz, and Weinshall 2022).

Somewhat more sobering is the fact that not all the biases that have been identified have easy resolutions. As discussed earlier, implicit biases that are pervasive and operate under decision-makers' conscious awareness are both troublesome from a normative perspective and extremely difficult to prevent and combat. As Segal, Sood, and Woodson note:

> the growth of empirical research on cognitive biases in judicial decision making, and the dissemination of such information to the bench may hopefully make judges more aware of such influences and therefore better able to guard against them, but 'debiasing' of any kind is notoriously difficult to achieve and efforts to this end are in their infancy in the judicial arena. (2019, fn 113, 566)

Sometimes it seems like offering various solutions suggested by different strands of research in psychology is like throwing darts against a wall and trying to see what hits. For example, Donald, Rachlinski, and Wistrich (2020) suggest no less than ten different strategies to deal with implicit biases including cognitive strategies (like 'consider the opposite' techniques), and changing problematic aspects of judges' decision-making environments. The fact that so many strategies have been identified to curb biases is encouraging; it means we have many options in our cognitive toolbox to address potential problems.

Of course, it is important to acknowledge that training in the tools of legal analysis is itself at least partially aimed at curbing biases and there is evidence that it can be effective to prevent certain types of problems in decision-making. For example, one study in Switzerland found that professional judges were not as prone to a bias discounting witness testimony as lay judges (Zenker et al. 2018; see also Guthrie, Rachlinski, and Wistrich 2000, finding judges not as prone to some types of heuristic biases; Kahan et al. 2015, finding attenuated ideological bias among professional decision makers). Other studies have found, however, that legal training and/or experience can accentuate biases that do not exist in comparison samples (see e.g. Braman and Nelson 2007, finding more motivated reasoning in analogical perceptions among law students than lay decision-makers; Spamann and Klohn (2016, 2023), finding irrelevant character considerations that were relevant among professional judges were not a factor in law students' decision-making).

In their article 'Debiasing Through Law' Jolls and Sunstien (2006) cite seminal work by Herbert Simon on bounded rationality (1956) in discussing how to fashion solutions to biases that occur among litigants involved in consumer protection and corporate litigation. Gigerenzer (2006) uses similar insights to outline how it may be necessary to implement institutional solutions to fix cognitive shortcomings in judicial behaviour. The main insight of such thinking is that where potential problems in judicial reasoning have been identified, to know which strategy to employ, *solutions must be tailored to those particular shortcomings and more importantly to the underlying causes of those deficiencies.*

This highlights the fact that researchers have been much more interested in identifying cognitive shortcomings in legal reasoning than in specifying the reasons why they exist. This is significant because solutions to cognitive deficiencies in decision-making will only be effective to the extent that they address the root causes of those deficits. For instance, some biases are the result of limited cognitive capacities of individuals, others are driven by the various conscious (and unconscious) goals of decision-makers. Identifying which mechanism and what goals are underlying specific shortcomings is vital for engineering effective solutions.

The study by Dhami and Ayton (2001) about the behaviour of bail examiners in the United Kingdom illustrates this point effectively. If examiners are relying on the judgments of previous adjudicators as an anchor to determine current bail and detention determinations due to high caseloads, allowing them additional time to consider relevant factors in defendants' behaviour may result in judgments that are more independently tailored to present circumstances. If their reliance is based on a desire to escape liability for potentially controversial decisions, however, simply allowing them more time will not fix the problem.

Even where effective solutions have been identified, often more could be done to clarify exactly why those measures work to temper deficits in decision-making. For instance, as discussed previously, Kantorowicz-Reznichenko, Kantorowitz, and Weinshall (2022) find that making decision-makers sign an affirmation that they will be fair helps to temper in-group biases in judgments. One could posit two alternative reasons why this works. The first possibility is that the affirmation makes decision-makers more aware of potential biases, and so they expend cognitive effort to prevent that bias from happening. The second possibility is that it makes a different group identity, that of a case adjudicator, relevant and so decision-makers are less likely to treat litigant groups who express views that are similar to their own as in-group members. Each of these avenues is plausible; discovering why the solution works should allow researchers greater insight into addressing similar kinds of in-group biases.

Clearly, comparative judicial scholars have come a long way in identifying the various ways legal decision-makers can fall short of making neutral, accurate, and reasoned judgments. It is also apparent, however, that there is more to do to create effective mechanisms to address cognitive deficiencies that can call the fairness and legitimacy of judicial determinations into question. We should do more to determine where legal training and judicial experience can prevent (and accentuate) potential biases that exist in the general population and more to determine the root causes of cognitive shortcomings in judicial decision making. It may be that some of the problems discussed here are resistant to change across the comparative judicial contexts where they have been identified. In those instances, we may have to reconsider our expectations of judicial authority itself, and what can be reasonably required of legal authorities around the world in light of their limited cognitive capacities and, unavoidably, human nature.

References

Babcock, Linda, George Loewenstein, and Samuel Issacharoff. 1997. 'Creating Convergence: Debiasing Biased Litigants'. *Law & Social Inquiry* 22 (4): 913–25.

Basfirinci, Cigdem, Zuhal Cilingir Uk, Sernur Karaoglu, and Kadriye Onbas. 2019. 'Implicit Occupational Gender Stereotypes: Research among Turkish University Students'. *Gender in Management: An International Journal* 34 (2): 157–84.

Braman, Eileen. 2006. 'Reasoning on the Threshold: Testing the Separability of Preferences in Legal Decision Making'. *The Journal of Politics* 68 (2): 308–21.

Braman, Eileen. 2009. *Law, Politics, and Perception: How Policy Preferences Influence Legal Reasoning*. Charlottesville, VA: University of Virginia Press.

Braman, Eileen. 2017. 'Cognition in the Courts: A Critical Analysis of The Use of Experiments to Study Legal Decision Making'. In *Oxford Handbook of US Judicial Behavior*, edited by Lee Epstein and Stefanie Lindquist, 483–507. New York: Oxford University Press.

Braman, Eileen, and Thomas E. Nelson. 2007. 'Mechanism of Motivated Reasoning? Analogical Perception in Discrimination Disputes'. *American Journal of Political Science* 51 (4): 940–56.

Brewer, Marilynn B., and Linnda R. Caporael. 2006. 'An Evolutionary Perspective on Social Identity: Revisiting Groups'. *Evolution and Social Psychology* 143: 161.

Brewer, Marilynn B., and Donald T. Campbell. 1976. *Ethnocentrism and Intergroup Attitudes: East African Evidence*. New York: Sage.

Bystranowski, Piotr, Bartosz Janik, Maciej Próchnicki, and Paulina Skórska. 2021. 'Anchoring Effect in Legal Decision-Making: A Meta-Analysis'. *Law and Human Behavior* 45 (1): 1.

Chapman, Gretchen B., and Brian H. Bornstein. 1996. 'The More You Ask For, the More You Get: Anchoring in Personal Injury Verdicts'. *Applied Cognitive Psychology* 10 (6): 519–40.

Cohen, Mathilde. 2015. 'When Judges Have Reasons Not to Give Reasons: A Comparative Law Approach'. *Washington & Lee Law Review* 72: 483.

Corso, Lucia. 2014. 'Should Empathy Play Any Role in the Interpretation of Constitutional Rights?' *Ratio Juris* 27 (1): 94–115.

Cox, Adam B., and Thomas J. Miles. 2008. 'Judging the Voting Rights Act'. *Columbia Law Review* 108: 1–54.

Depew, Briggs, Ozkan Eren, and Naci Mocan. 2017. 'Judges, Juveniles, and In-Group Bias'. *The Journal of Law and Economics* 60 (2): 209–39.

Dhami, Mandeep K., and Peter Ayton. 2001. 'Bailing and Jailing the Fast and Frugal Way'. *Journal of Behavioral Decision Making* 14 (2): 141–68.

Distelhorst, Greg, and Yue Hou. 2014. 'In-group Bias in Official Behavior: A National Field Experiment in China'. *Quarterly Journal of Political Science* 9 (2): 203–30.

Donald, Bernice, Jeffrey Rachlinski, and Andrew Wistrich. 2020. 'Getting Explicit About Implicit Bias'. *Judicature* 104: 75.

Eisenberg, Theodore, and Sheri Lynn Johnson. 2003. 'Implicit Racial Attitudes of Death Penalty Lawyers'. *DePaul Law Review* 53: 1539.

Engel, Christoph. 2020. 'Uncertain Judges'. *Journal of Institutional and Theoretical Economics* 176: 44.

Engel, Christoph, Sinica Timme, and Andreas Glöckner. 2020. 'Coherence-Based Reasoning and Order Effects in Legal Judgments'. *Psychology, Public Policy, and Law* 26: 333.

Englich, Birte, Thomas Mussweiler, and Fritz Strack. 2006. 'Playing Dice with Criminal Sentences: The Influence of Irrelevant Anchors on Experts' Judicial Decision Making'. *Personality and Social Psychology Bulletin* 32 (2): 188–200.

Enough, Birte, and Thomas Mussweiler. 2001. 'Sentencing under Uncertainty: Anchoring Effects in the Courtroom 1'. *Journal of Applied Social Psychology* 31 (7): 1535–51.

Epstein, Lee, Christopher M. Parker, and Jeffrey A. Segal. 2018. 'Do Justices Defend the Speech They Hate? An Analysis of In-Group Bias on the U.S. Supreme Court'. *Journal of Law and Courts* 6: 237.

Fariña, Francisca, Ramón Arce, and Mercedes Novo. 2003. 'Anchoring in Judicial Decision Making'. *Psychology in Spain* 7 (1): 56–65.

Feldman, Yuval, Amos Schurr, and Doron Teichman. 2016. 'Anchoring Legal Standards'. *Journal of Empirical Legal Studies* 13 (2): 298–329.

Ferguson, Joshua, Linda Babcock, and Peter M. Shane. 2008. 'Do a Law's Policy Implications Affect Beliefs about Its Constitutionality?'. *Law and Human Behavior* 32: 219–27.

Fishman, Gideon, Arye Rattner, and Hagit Turjeman. 2006. 'Sentencing Outcomes in a Multinational Society: When Judges, Defendants and Victims Can Be Either Arabs or Jews'. *European Journal of Criminology* 3 (1): 69–84.

Gawronski, Bertram, Daniel Geschke, and Rainer Banse. 2003. 'Implicit Bias in Impression Formation: Associations Influence the Construal of Individuating Information'. *European Journal of Social Psychology* 33 (5): 573–89.

Gazal-Ayal, Oren, and Raanan Sulitzeanu-Kenan. 2010. 'Let My People Go: Ethnic In-Group Bias in Judicial Decisions—Evidence from a Randomized Natural Experiment'. *Journal of Empirical Legal Studies* 7 (3): 403–28.

Gigerenzer, Gerd, 2006. 'Heuristics'. In *Heuristics and the Law*, edited by Gerd Gigerenzer and Christoph Engel, 17–44. Boston, MA: MIT Press.

Grossman, Guy, Oren Gazal-Ayal, Samuel D. Pimentel, and Jeremy M. Weinstein. 2016. 'Descriptive Representation and Judicial Outcomes in Multiethnic Societies'. *American Journal of Political Science* 60 (1): 44–69.

Guthrie, Chris, Jeffrey J. Rachlinski, and Andrew J. Wistrich. 2000. 'Inside the Judicial Mind'. *Cornell Law Review* 86: 777.

Harley, Erin M. 2007. 'Hindsight Bias in Legal Decision Making'. *Social Cognition* 25 (1): 48–63.

Hastie, Reid, David A. Schkade, and John W. Payne. 1999. 'Juror Judgments in Civil Cases: Effects of Plaintiff's Requests and Plaintiff's Identity on Punitive Damage Awards'. *Law and Human Behavior* 23: 445–70.

Holyoak, Keith J., and Dan Simon. 1999. 'Bidirectional Reasoning in Decision Making by Constraint Satisfaction'. *Journal of Experimental Psychology: General* 128 (1): 3.

Jolls, Christine, and Cass R. Sunstein. 2006. 'Debiasing through Law'. *The Journal of Legal Studies* 35 (1): 199–242.

Kahan, Dan M., David A. Hoffman, Donald Braman, Danieli Evans, and Jeffrey J. Rachlinski. 2012. 'They Saw a Protest: Cognitive Illiberalism and the Speech Conduct Distinction'. *Stanford Law Review* 64 (4): 851–906.

Kahan, Dan M., David Hoffman, Danieli Evans, Neal Devins, Eugene Lucci, and Katherine Cheng. 2015. 'Ideology or Situation Sense: An Experimental Investigation of Motivated Reasoning and Professional Judgment'. *University of Pennsylvania Law Review* 164: 349.

Kang, Jerry, Nilanjana Dasgupta, Kumar Yogeeswaran, and Gary Blasi. 2010. 'Are Ideal Litigators White? Measuring the Myth of Colorblindness'. *Journal of Empirical Legal Studies* 7 (4): 886–915.

Kantorowicz-Reznichenko, Elena, Jarosław Kantorowicz, and Keren Weinshall. 2022. 'Ideological Bias in Constitutional Judgments: Experimental Analysis and Potential Solutions'. *Journal of Empirical Legal Studies* 19 (3): 716–57.

Kastellec, Jonathan P. 2013. 'Racial Diversity and Judicial Influence on Appellate Courts'. *American Journal of Political Science* 57 (1): 167–83.

Kremnitzer, Mordechai, Talya Steiner, and Andrej Lang, eds. 2020. *Proportionality in Action: Comparative and Empirical Perspectives on the Judicial Practice*. Cambridge: Cambridge University Press.

Lee, Rebecca K. 2013. 'Judging Judges: Empathy as the Litmus Test for Impartiality'. *University of Cincinnati Law Review* 82: 145.

Levinson, Justin D., Mark W. Bennett, and Koichi Hioki. 2017. 'Judging Implicit Bias: A National Empirical Study of Judicial Stereotypes'. *Florida Law Review* 69: 63.

Levinson, Justin D., and Danielle Young. 2010. 'Implicit Gender Bias in the Legal Profession: An Empirical Study'. *Duke Journal of Gender Law. & Policy* 18: 1.

Liu, Zhuang. 2018. 'Does Reason Writing Reduce Decision Bias? Experimental Evidence from Judges in China'. *The Journal of Legal Studies* 47 (1): 83–118.

Liu, John Zhuang, and Xueyao Li. 2019. 'Legal Techniques for Rationalizing Biased Judicial Decisions: Evidence from Experiments with Real Judges'. *Journal of Empirical Legal Studies* 16: 630.

Marks, Dana Leigh. 2015. 'Who, Me: Am I Guilty of Implicit Bias'. *Judges Journal* 54: 20.

Marouf, Fatma E. 2011. 'Implicit Bias and Immigration Courts'. *New England Law Review* 45: 417.

Marti, Mollie Weighner. 2000. *Anchoring Biases and Corrective Processes in Personal Injury Damages Awards*. The University of Iowa.

Mendoza, Saaid A., Sean P. Lane, and David M. Amodio. 2014. 'For Members Only: In-group Punishment of Fairness Norm Violations in the Ultimatum Game'. *Social Psychological and Personality Science* 5 (6): 662–670.

Peer, Eyal, and Eyal Gamliel. 2013. 'Heuristics and Biases in Judicial Decisions'. *Court Review* 49: 114.

Platt, Alexander I. 2012. 'Debiasing Statutory Interpretation'. *Ohio Northern University Law Review* 39: 275.

Powell, H. Jefferson. 2008. *Constitutional Conscience: The Moral Dimensions of Judicial Decision*. Chicago: University of Chicago Press.

Rachlinski, Jeffrey J., Chris Guthrie, and Andrew J. Wistrich. 2011. 'Probable Cause, Probability, and Hindsight'. *Journal of Empirical Legal Studies* 8: 72.

Rachlinski, Jeffrey J., Sheri Lynn Johnson, Andrew J. Wistrich, and Chris Guthrie. 2009. 'Does Unconscious Racial Bias Affect Trial Judges?' *Notre Dame Law Review* 84: 1195.

Rachlinski, Jeffrey J., and Andrew J. Wistrich. 2021. 'Benevolent Sexism in Judges'. *San Diego Law Review* 58: 101.

Robbennolt, Jennifer K., Robert J. MacCoun, and John M. Darley. 2010. 'Multiple Constraint Satisfaction in Judging'. In *The Psychology of Judicial Decision Making*, edited by David Klein and Gregory Mitchell, 27–40. New York: Oxford University Press.

Segal, Jeffrey A., Avani Mehta Sood, and Benjamin Woodson. 2019. 'The 'Murder-Scene Exception'—Myth or Reality? Empirically Testing the Influence of Crime Severity in Federal Search-and-Seizure Cases'. *Virginia Law Review* 105: 543.

Shayo, Moses, and Asaf Zussman. 2011. 'Judicial In-group Bias in the Shadow of Terrorism'. *Quarterly Journal of Economics* 126: 1447

Simon, Dan. 2004. 'A Third View of the Black Box: Cognitive Coherence in Legal Decision Making'. *University of Chicago Law Review* 71: 511.

Simon, Herbert A. 1956. Rational Choice and the Structure of the Environment. *Psychological Review* 63 (2): 129.

Sonnemans, Joep, and Frans van Dijk. 2012. 'Errors in Judicial Decisions: Experimental Results'. *Journal of Law, Economics, and Organization* 28: 687.

Sood, Avani Mehta. 2013. 'Motivated Cognition in Legal Judgments—An Analytic Review'. *Annual Review of Law and Social Science* 9: 307–25.

Sood, Avani Metha. 2014. 'Cognitive Cleansing: Experimental Psychology and the Exclusionary Rule'. *Georgetown Law Journal* 103: 1543.

Sood, Avani Mehta, and John M. Darley. 2012. 'The Plasticity of Harm in the Service of Criminalization Goals'. *California Law Review* 100 (5): 1313–58.

Spamann, Holger, and Lars Klohn. 2016. 'Justice is Less Blind, and Less Legalistic, Than We Thought: Evidence from an Experiment with Real Judges'. *Journal of Legal Studies* 45: 255.

Spamann, Holger, and Lars Klöhn. 2023. 'Can Law Students Replace Judges in Experiments of Judicial Decision-Making?' Available at SSRN 4362199.

Steiner, Talya, Liat Netzer, and Raanan Sulitzeanu-Kenan. 2022. 'Necessity or Balancing: The Protection of Rights Under Different Proportionality Tests—Experimental Evidence'. *International Journal of Constitutional Law* 20 (2): 642–63.

Tajfel, Henri. 1978. *Differentiation Between Social Groups: Studies in the Social Psychology of Intergroup Relations*. London: Academic Press.

Tyler, Tom R. 2006. 'Psychological Perspectives on Legitimacy and Legitimation'. *Annual Review of Psychology* 57: 375–400.

Wistrich, Andrew J., Chris Guthrie, and Jeffrey J. Rachlinski. 2005. 'Can Judges Ignore Inadmissible Information? The Difficulty of Deliberately Disregarding'. *University of Pennsylvania Law Review* 153: 1251–345.

Wistrich, Andrew J., Jeffrey J. Rachlinski, and Chris Guthrie. 2015. 'Heart Versus Head: Do Judges Follow the Law or Follow Their Feelings?' *Texas Law Review* 93: 855.

Xifen, Lin, and Ma Yong. 2018. 'Sentencing Recommendations, Anchoring Effect and Fairness in Criminal Justice—An Empirical Study Based on a Sample of 520 Sentences in K City'. *Social Sciences in China* 39 (3): 149–70.

Zenker, Frank, Christian Dahlman, Rasmus Bååth, and Farhan Sarwar. 2018. 'Reasons Pro et Contra as a Debiasing Technique in Legal Contexts'. *Psychological Reports* 121 (3): 511–26.

PART III

DATA, METHODS, AND TECHNOLOGIES

CHAPTER 12

OBSERVATIONAL DATABASES

BENJAMIN G. ENGST AND THOMAS GSCHWEND

1. Introduction

Why do we need databases in research on comparative judicial behaviour? Databases facilitate the assessment of various key aspects of democracy, such as judicial independence and the judicialization of politics. In order to evaluate competing behavioural models, data of a similar nature but partially different content is necessary. Data comprises 'systematically collected elements of information about the world' (King, Keohane, and Verba 1994, 23) commonly structured in rectangular datasets. Consider the legal model of judicial behaviour which is built on the premise that judges are constrained by constitutional norms and their legal training when making decisions (Parcelle Jr, Curry, and Marshall 2011, 29–32). To assess this model, we need to understand the ways in which opinions are written which requires data on decision characteristics. On the contrary, the attitudinal model assumes that the individual preferences of the judges matter when they make decisions (Parcelle Jr, Curry, and Marshall 2011, 34–39). Data on decision characteristics is essential to the attitudinal model as well but a comprehensive assessment requires identifying the relationship between decision characteristics and characteristics of individual judges, for example, their potential partisan leaning or voting pattern. Databases are helpful tools to establish such relationships and enable scholars and practitioners to link datasets of different content and complexity. Specifically, databases model real-world objects—both entities (e.g. judges, the actor who nominated them, and judicial decisions) and relationships (e.g. 'Chief Justice Roberts' who was 'nominated by President George W. Bush' voted 'with the majority in *Dobbs v Jackson Women's Health*')—and capture structure between them (Foster et al. 2021, 71).

This chapter is no technical guide for computing databases but the research cited here provides a point of departure for scholars eager to develop comprehensive and comparative databases in judicial politics. This is of great importance because courts do not operate in a vacuum. To understand the wider implications of judicial behaviour we require data structures that situate the judiciary within different societies and polities.

In this chapter, we argue that databases in judicial politics are necessary to connect different characteristics to assess competing models of judicial behaviour efficiently. To make this argument we outline the characteristics that we require data to cover in order to assess these behavioural models. The results from an expert survey show that existing data structures already include these characteristics to varying degrees (section 2). However, the data structures are developed for single cases and are seldom comparative in nature. Thus, they do not allow for an analysis of judicial behaviour across countries or regions. Therefore, we continue outlining important features of databases using one of the projects as an example (section 3). This allows us to present ideas on how to develop an international comparative data infrastructure project, the 'Comparative Study of Judicial Behaviour' (CSJB), accounting for the identified features (section 4). The concluding section summarizes our discussion.

2. Datasets and Databases to Study Judicial Behaviour

In this section, we argue that the different models of judicial behaviour require data summarizing different characteristics of the judicial process. An expert survey we conducted shows that there are different data structures that already link multiple of those characteristics. However, databases that allow to study judicial behaviour comparatively across countries or regions are scarce.

The most common models used to explain judicial behaviour are the legal, attitudinal, and strategic model (see part on Approaches to Judging in this volume; Epstein, Sădl, and Weinshall 2022). Each model is built on different premises which is why assessments require different information. The legal model assumes that judges make decisions based on their legal training using jurisprudential methods (Parcelle Jr, Curry, and Marshall 2011, 29–32). Accordingly, judges are constrained by the legal system (George and Epstein 1992). Therefore, if judges wish to incorporate their preferences into their decisions, then they can only do so through the means of decision characteristics; for example, citing certain legal sources to derive at a particular verdict. Decision characteristics are a necessary precondition to contextualize judicial behaviour. Without decisions there is no judicial behaviour. Thus, we argue that a comprehensive assessment of the models of judicial behaviour always requires decision characteristics. The attitudinal model assumes that judges are unconstrained actors who follow their sincere preferences when making decisions (Schubert 1965; Rohde and Spaeth 1976; Segal and Cover 1989; Parcelle Jr, Curry and Marshall 2011, 34–39). It is plausible to assume that attitudes are shaped by a number of formative events, such as judges' age or the places judges were educated. This requires to also collect a number of judges' characteristics in addition to various preference measures in order to assess the attitudinal model. Finally, the strategic model extends upon the attitudinal model adding the assumption that judges are constrained by the decision-making environment (Murphy 1964; Epstein and Knight 1998; Parcelle Jr, Curry, and Marshall 2011, 39–49). Thus, judges account for fellow judges, political, or societal actors as well as the institutional setting when making decisions. These environmental characteristics structure judicial behaviour and constrain judges in voicing their preferences; for example, when judges confront declining public support for their decisions and alter the clarity of writing in their decisions (Staton and Vanberg 2008).

Figure 12.1 visualizes the considerations made. Decision characteristics are necessary to assess the legal model of judicial behaviour (zone 1). These characteristics are also necessary to assess all other models. When individual judicial characteristics are added then assessments of the attitudinal model become possible (zone 2). Finally, analysing the strategic model requires environmental characteristics either coupled with judicial characteristics (zone 3a) or not (zone 3b).

Figure 12.2 highlights examples of data structures that include the different characteristics. The first column indicates the behavioural models that can be studied with the characteristics included in the data. The numbers next to the models speak to the overlapping zones mentioned in Figure 12.1. The examples in Figure 12.2 are from a non-representative expert survey conducted in April 2022 among contributors to this *Handbook* and among scholars that are mentioned in the acknowledgments in Garoupa, Gill, and Tiede (2022, vii).[1] The experts mentioned different datasets and databases and we reviewed the characteristics included in the data. The list makes no claim to be complete. We exclude datasets composed of tailor-made data collected for individual

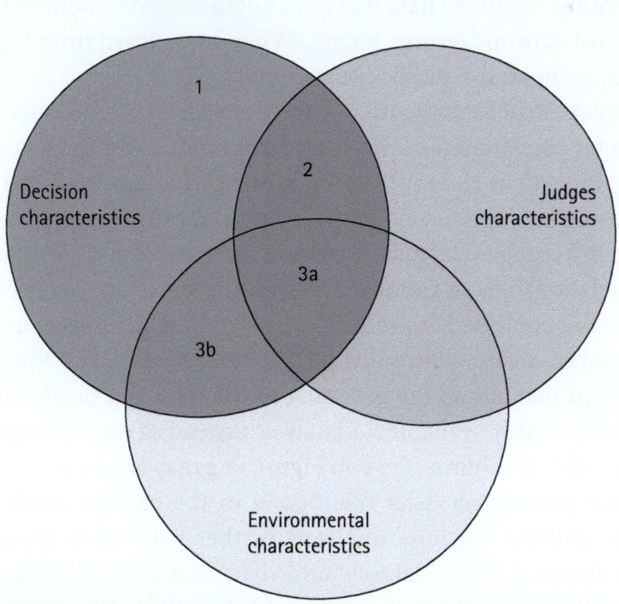

FIGURE 12.1 Overlapping entities necessary to assess judicial behaviour.

Models	Type	Example	Access	Regions	Authors
1 - Legal	Database	PITAD.beta on investment arbitration cases	OA	various countries	Behn et al. 2019
	Datasets	The High Courts Judicial Database	OA*	various countries	Haynie et al. 2007
	Database	European Court of Justice Data	OA	Europe	Carrubba / Gabel 2011
	Datasets	Comparative Constitutional Reasoning Project	OA	various countries	Jakab et al. 2015
	Database	Inter-American Court of Human Rights Project	OA	South America	Loyola Law School
	Database	Websites by courts publishing decisions	OA	various countries	courts
	Database	Proprietary databases such as West Law	CA	various countries	often special publishers
2 - Attitudinal	Datasets /-base	Supreme Court Database	OA	United States	Spaeth et al. 2017
	Datasets /-base	Israeli Supreme Court Database	OA	Israel	Weinshall et al. 2018
	Database	CJEU Database (IUROPA Project)	OA	Europe	Brekke et al. 2023
	Database	Doranoh Database	LA	Norway	Grendstad et al. 2015
	Datasets	UK Supreme Court Data	OA	Great Britain	Hanretty 2020
	Datasets	U.S. Courts of Appeals Databases	OA	United States	Songer et al. 2008
	Datasets	DDL Judicial Data Portal	OA	India	Ash et al. 2021
	Datasets	Swedish Supreme Court Database	OA	Sweden	Lindholm et al. 2023
	Datasets	European Court of Human Rights Database (ECHRdb)	OA	International	Cichowski / Chrun 2017
	Datasets	EEOC Litigation Database	OA	United States	Kim et al. 2013
	Database	Fee Law Project	OA	United States	Lissner et al.
3a - Strategic	Datasets	Inter-American Court of Human Rights Database	OA	South America	Stiansen et al. 2020
	Datasets /-base	Constitutional Court Database	OA	Germany	Engst et al. 2020
	Datasets	European Court of Human Rights Database	OA	International	Stiansen / Voeten 2019
	Dataset	Judicial Review of Congress Database	OA	United States	Whittington 2019
		Comparative Law Project	NP	various countries	Gabel
3b - Strategic	Dataset	Compliance with Human Rights Tribunals Dataset	OA	International	Hillebrecht 2016

Note: Access OA is open access; LA is limited access either requiring registration or contacting the author(s); NP is data not published; CA is commercial access which requires a purchase. * Indicates that data is open access but downloaded files cannot be processed. Source: Non-representative expert survey among judicial politics scholars.

FIGURE 12.2 Examples of data structures to assess models of judicial behaviour.

research projects that address very specific research questions. This includes for example Vanberg's (2005) data on Germany or Staton's (2010) data on Mexico. In line with our argument, we also excluded data that does not include decision characteristics, such as Hamann's (2019) data on German judges. What do we learn from Figure 12.2 on data available to study comparative judicial behaviour?

Overall, most data structures mentioned by the experts include judges' characteristics and are suitable for assessments of the attitudinal model. Among these is the Supreme Court Database (Spaeth et al. 2017), which is one of the most popular data structures in judicial politics. The Supreme Court Database is a prime example of data often not being published in a database format. Databases are flexible and allow for the modelling of entities and relationships to capture the structure between them (Foster et al. 2021, 71). In the originally published Supreme Court Database, entities and relationships are already connected in a case-centred or justice-centred dataset. Only recently an online tool was added that allows the browsing of the data in a flexible database format. Publishing datasets readily available for analysis instead of underlying databases seems not as uncommon as the column 'Type' in Figure 12.2 may indicate.

Comparing the publication dates mentioned in the column 'Author(s)' across the column 'Models' and the 'Regions' uncovers further patterns in the data available to study judicial behaviour. First, datasets and databases that allow for assessments of the legal and attitudinal model are longer established than data structures suitable for analyses of the strategic model. Second, older data structures mostly cover courts in the United States from Courts of Appeal (Songer 2008), certain decisions by Federal Courts (Kim, Martin, and Schlanger 2013) to the Supreme Court (Spaeth et al. 2017; Whittington 2019) as well as popular highest international courts such as the European Court of Justice (Carrubba and Gabel 2011) or the European Court of Human Rights (Cichowski and Chrun 2017). Data on courts from individual countries such as the Supreme Court of the United Kingdom (Hanretty 2020), the German Constitutional Court (Engst et al. 2020), or Indian Courts (Ash et al. 2021) has been published more recently. Moreover, while there are only a few data structures that collect information on various different countries such as the PluriCourts Investment Treaty Arbitration Database (PITAD) (Behn et al. 2019), the High Courts Judicial Database (Haynie et al. 2007), or the Comparative Constitutional Reasoning Project (Jakab, Dyevre, and Itzcovich 2017) most data structures focus on a single international court or national courts, for example the Inter-American Court of Human Rights (Stiansen, Naurin, and Bøyum 2020), the Norwegian (Grendstad, Shaffer, and Waltenburg 2015), or Israeli Supreme Court (Weinshall and Epstein 2020). Finally, participants in our expert survey mostly mentioned European and US courts.

The column 'Access' in Figure 12.2 indicates that the overwhelming majority of data is open access, albeit some projects do not get updated anymore. In this regard, one should note that proprietary databases such as Thomson Reuters *Westlaw* or Germany's equivalent *Juris* provide numerous original legal documents that permit the collection of information for datasets but only as commercial licences. The proprietary databases do not provide ready-to-use data structures for behavioural analyses. Instead, these databases are a collection of documents that allow deriving legal characteristics in raw form. The same holds true for official websites of individual courts that make decisions and legal documents searchable.

In sum, Figure 12.2 shows that data structures that include decision and justice characteristics are well established in judicial politics. Moreover, in recent years scholars tend to add environmental characteristics to such data structures. Thus, data to assess the different models of judicial behaviour is available in open access. Nevertheless, while the available data includes international courts the majority of data does not allow for comparative research across individual countries or regions. This is why in the next section we outline how databases for comparative judicial behaviour can be designed.

3. Developing Comparative Databases

In this section, we identify features essential to the design of databases. To do so we present the Constitutional Court Database (CCDB) (Engst et al. 2020) as an example of a database computed for a single country to assess judicial behaviour. Afterwards we outline how to transfer the features important to the design of the CCDB to a larger international and comparative project.

3.1 Features of a Database for a Single Court

The CCDB is a database recently published that includes decisions, judges, and environmental characteristics on three different layers. The database falls in zone 3a of Figure 12.1. It summarizes information on 2,006 decisions that include 3,284 proceedings initiated by 4,088 plaintiffs who referred 6,790 issues to the German Federal Constitutional Court between 1972 and 2010 (*decision characteristics*). The database also includes information on separate opinions and background information on seventy-six judges who served on the court (*judges characteristics*). Finally, the database includes a layer that allows linking the 301 federal laws referred to the constitutional court to a dataset on Germany's legislative proceedings (*environmental characteristics*). Figure 12.3 visualizes the CCDB. The circles in Figure 12.3 represent the different layers of the database including summary statistics on each layer. The layers reflect on the characteristics we require to assess judicial behaviour in accordance with Figure 12.1. What can we learn from the design of the CCDB?

First, the database consists of twelve different tables similar to rectangular datasets. The tables can be linked through identifiers internal to the databases and each table has at least one of these identifiers; for example, the 2,006 decisions can be linked to the seventy-six judges to compute a dataset that permits identification of the (normally) eight judges that make each of the 2,006 decisions. Instead, of coding the judges' information 2,006 times when creating the initial dataset, it is only necessary to code the judges' information seventy-six times. Obviously, seventy-six entries can be evaluated by the coders much easier than 2,006 entries. When an error is identified for information on a single judge then the correction applies equally to all decisions to which this judge is linked. Therefore, a database *reduces redundancies* in coding information which

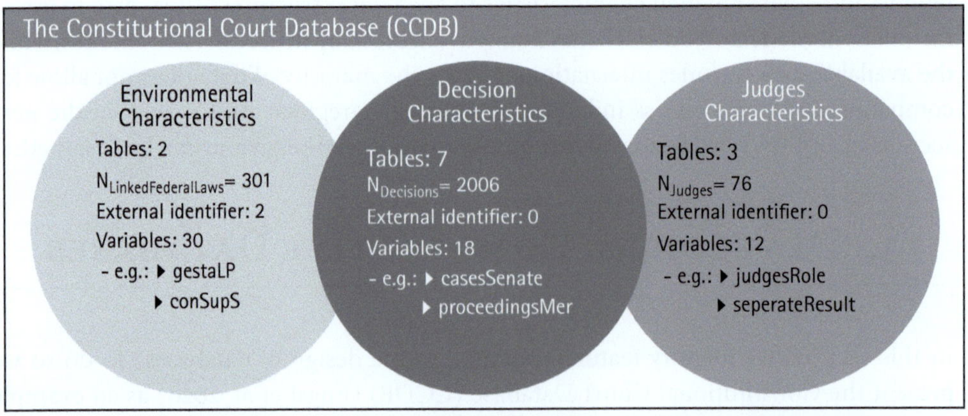

Note: Variable counts only include substantive variables and no technical identifiers. See Engst et al. 2020 for further information on the Constitutional Court Database.

FIGURE 12.3 The Constitutional Court Database as a tool to study judicial behaviour.

makes the data collection less prone to error. If an error on one of the tables is identified it can be corrected easier than when reviewing a long dataset.

Second, a legitimate claim of importance to all data-driven projects is to resist irrational 'data exuberance' (Weinshall and Epstein 2020, 429–30). Reducing redundancies in coding is one way to achieve this. Moreover, linking information across tables in a database allows us to stay focused on essential information of relevance to a data table. It is much easier to answer the question of the characteristics of judges one is interested in when looking at judges independent from decisions or votes. Thus, while the CCDB might appear complex at first sight, Figure 12.3 shows that there are only sixty substantive variables that allow to cover many characteristics necessary to assess judicial behaviour. In our opinion that make the database *parsimonious*. This also makes its future maintenance easier.

Third, the different tables of the CCDB can be linked internally in multiple ways. For instance, the date a decision was published—which is a feature of a table summarizing information on a case—can be linked to a date included in a table summarizing public opinion data on Germany's political parties. This way one can identify the support for a political party, say the Social Democrats (variable conSupS), on the date a decision was made. Equipped with this data scholars can begin to assess how political support influences judicial decision-making. Similar questions have been studied with tailor-made datasets in the past (e.g. Vanberg 2005). Moreover, Figure 12.3 shows that the CCDB also includes external identifiers as part of the environmental characteristics. These identifiers allow links to preexisting data external to the CCDB, for instance to Germany's legislative proceedings. In sum, internal identifiers permit linking data within the CCDB in multiple ways while the external identifiers provide even more opportunities to add or create a number of datasets for a variety of specific research questions. This *flexibility* is a major advantage of databases over single datasets.

Finally, in order for a database to be parsimonious and flexible one has to be clear about the information coded. This is not only a question of the number of variables included in a database but also a question of how to transfer latent judicial concepts into relatable concepts understandable to a wider audience. Take, for example, the complex way in which judges write an opinion and argue a case on the merits. The majority of people are probably not interested in the legal details but a simplifying measure on the merits. In the CCDB the decision on the merits has been coded per proceeding in a trichotomous variable that indicates whether a referred proceeding is not justified, partially justified, or justified on the merits (variable proceedingsMer). Similarly, the German Constitutional Court seldom publishes individual judicial votes which are frequently used in analyses of the attitudinal model in the US context (Epstein and Knight 1998; Martin and Quinn 2002). However, in rare instances, the German judges publish separate opinions (Wittig 2016) and while specific details on those opinions are not included in the CCDB, the results are coded in a trichotomous variable. This variable summarizes whether a separate opinion is written as a concurring, partially dissenting or fully dissenting opinion (variable separateResult). The way the dissenting opinions are coded should be compelling to a wide audience. Therefore, not all information can be coded in a parsimonious database and it is essential to simplify information while being *conceptually clear*.

In sum, databases are powerful tools to account for variables on each characteristic necessary to assess models of judicial behaviour. Databases help to reduce redundancies, permit parsimonious data collection, and provide for high flexibility in dataset production. To enable a large audience to work with databases, scholars need to make sure that the concepts underlying the data collection efforts are clearly specified. The CCDB is an example of a database designed for the German Constitutional Court as a single case, though. Indeed, Figure 12.2 shows that the overwhelming majority of databases are designed for single courts. This is why in the next section we outline how features of the CCDB can be transferred to a comparative project.

3.2 Conceptualizing a Comparative Judicial Behaviour Database

What can we learn from developing the CCDB when conceptualizing other data structures for the analysis of courts (within and) across countries? We identified four features of importance to high-quality data infrastructures: reducing redundancies, parsimony, flexibility, and conceptual clarity. In this section, we outline the implications of these features when designing a comparative judicial behaviour database as part of an international project.

3.2.1 *Reducing Redundancies*

Our first argument concerns the *reduction of redundancies*. As a field, we would benefit if we took advantage of opportunities to systematically learn from each other's expertise on particular courts and judicial systems in order to conceptualize and implement a comparative data infrastructure project. The project could be a driver of novel comparative research particularly *across* courts and legal systems.

It is reasonable to expect that such a data infrastructure can be a game-changer for the questions we aim to answer and for how we conduct comparative judicial research in the future. Currently, such research is often merely equated with studying courts and their decision-making behaviour outside the United States. Recent summaries of the comparative literature by regional specialists highlight that the prevailing research design in the reported studies consists of country-level or court-level case studies (see the respective chapters in Garoupa, Gill, and Tiede 2022).

Driscoll (2022) conducted a content analysis of articles published in top peer-reviewed political science journals between 2000 and 2018 (*American Political Science Review*, *American Journal of Political Science*, *The Journal of Politics*, *British Journal of Political Science*, *Comparative Political Studies*, and the *Journal of Law and Courts*). The analysis provides evidence that only a minority of studies explicitly implement a cross-national design.

Cross-national comparative work encompasses various approaches. There is research that tries to test general theories based on a country-by-country analysis. An example of this is the work by Brouard and Hönnige (2017). The authors utilize veto player theory to derive observable implications that can be tested comparatively. They gather context-specific measures of the positions of institutions (such as the highest court, parliament, government, and president) in the country-specific policy spaces of France, Germany, and the United States to examine how frequently the highest courts are absorbed by veto players. Since their key measures are context-specific, they cannot simply aggregate their data but instead rely on conducting a country-by-country analysis. They select their countries because system design differs greatly (Przeworski and Teune 1970).

In a similar vein, Alarie and Green (2017) adopt a country-by-country analysis of five high courts: the US Supreme Court, the UK Supreme Court (including its predecessor, the House of Lords), the Supreme Court of Canada, the High Court of Australia, and the Indian Supreme Court. The study demonstrates that these courts vary along two dimensions and that the design differences correlate with how the courts decide. While the authors do compile some country-specific measures, their main source of data is the publicly available High Courts Judicial Database (HCJD) assembled by Haynie et al. (2007).

Finally, there is research that pools data for analysis when relevant measures are comparable across different contexts. Take, for instance, Skiple, Bentsen, and McKenzie's (2021) analysis of dissent in tax decisions in the Norwegian and Danish Supreme Courts. Recognizing that courts may respond differently to increasing caseloads by exercising discretionary docket control to varying degrees, the authors employ a most similar design (Przeworski and Teune 1970) and pool the data from both courts. Their aim is to examine whether discretionary dockets are associated with higher dissent and reversal rates compared to mandatory dockets. The data for this analysis is primarily sourced from available databases, namely the Danish Supreme Court Database (McKenzie, Bentsen, and Skiple 2016) and the Norwegian Supreme Court Database (Grendstad, Shaffer, and Waltenburg 2015).

To summarize, even though cross-national comparative work comes in different flavours, one obvious benefit of a comparative database is the provision of data across countries (or courts). Moreover, a second benefit lies in the development of such an infrastructure project. It requires scholars to coordinate their efforts to conceptualize the design of the database. This reduces redundancies (beyond mere technical aspects) by incentivizing scholars to contribute to a common good rather than duplicating each other's data-collection efforts.

3.2.2 *Parsimony*

Our second argument concerns *parsimony*. What does a *parsimonious data collection strategy* imply when developing a comparative database? To enable scholars to eventually use the most common explanatory models of judicial behaviour for their analysis, any data infrastructure should provide information not only on decisions and judge characteristics but also on environmental characteristics. As with children just before their birthday though, the wish lists quickly become quite long. The data of the variables on the wish list has to be not only compiled at some point in time but also needs to get updated to maintain such a project over time.

Thus, scholars involved in designing such an infrastructure project need to resist data exuberance. Less is more! After taking stock of existing resources—for instance the Israeli Supreme Court Database (Weinshall and Epstein 2020), which in many respects is modelled after the US Supreme Court Database—scholars need to define 'core characteristics' that should be collected consistently for all courts and countries included in the comparative database.

Such characteristics describe decisions, judges as well as the environment. They obviously live on different observation levels. While having a master plan is definitely a good thing, scholars are luckily not simply a bunch of Trotskyist internationals. They can allow themselves to change plans—for instance when updating the data across countries and courts. Scholar might therefore distinguish cross-sectional core characteristics, which are only measured once, from longitudinal core characteristics that are repeatedly measured. This allows for the possibility that at some point also new characteristics can make it in the set of 'core characteristics' when starting to update the initial data collection plan. However, relevant characteristics should apply to a large enough subset of cases to allow for a cross-country comparative analysis of those characteristics.

Ideally, one can develop pipelines to automate the updating process for some of these characteristics. The less human judgment is involved in coding decisions, the more reliable is the data collection strategy. The more data can be collected automatically or the fewer characteristics need to get updated, the more room there is to implement ideas for new characteristics that should get coded in subsequent data collection phases. Additionally, alongside the core characteristics, there can be specific characteristics that apply only to a subset of courts or countries.

In summary, each data collection phase to maintain the data infrastructure requires scholars to have a predefined list of characteristics that should be collected. However, it is important to recognize that this list may undergo partial changes when transitioning from one data collection phase to the next.

3.2.3 *Flexibility*

Our third argument concerns *flexibility*. Scholars should leverage the inherent flexibility offered by databases in contrast to standalone datasets. Therefore, in addition to determining what should be collected in a comparative manner and at which level of observation, scholars also need to consider how newly collected data can be systematically integrated with existing data infrastructure projects. Databases offer internal links that enable efficient combination of data stored in separate datasets. When designing a comparative database, scholars should also consider incorporating external links to facilitate the incorporation of specialized information to enhance the richness of the data structure.

By incorporating valid external links, some of the burden of compiling environmental characteristics can be alleviated. By including a time variable for court decisions for instance, scholars could collect their own information to better characterize the political environment in which the respective decisions are published, such as election results or the popularity of the respective government.

Another possibility would be that such time and decision identifiers allow tracking down (potentially using external data) the actual decision text to conduct an analysis of who cites whom among the apex courts and which potentially common other legal sources have been cited. In addition to the decision text itself one could also include accompanying text material such as briefs, press releases, or news reports related to each decision. Moreover, one could also include qualitative interview data, survey marginals but also potentially variables derived from verbatim notes, audio or video files from hearings of the cases, or results from crowd-sourced coding or lab experiments that are related to a decision as well. The sky is the limit.

Likewise, by including court and country identifiers as an external link, for instance, scholars could integrate existing (or newly collected) country-level datasets about institutional characteristics to the analysis. These additional country-level datasets provide valuable information on the system of governance or the legal system.

In summary, by proactively considering how different data sources can be linked to the comparative database through external links and maintaining a flexible data structure also through internal links, the data infrastructure becomes not only highly beneficial to those who conceptualized it but also to a wide range of additional users.

3.2.4 *Conceptual Clarity*

Our fourth argument concerns *conceptual clarity*. This is arguably the most complex feature to address when designing a comparative database. It necessitates consensus among scholars regarding the relevant theoretical concepts to be used, how they should get operationalized into variables, and the methods of measuring them at which appropriate level of observation. Building on the expertise of a diverse group of experts becomes crucial in overcoming challenges related to translating relevant terms and concepts, as well as ensuring that concept specifications are applicable across different countries or legal systems.

It is well known that the meaning of even the most fundamental concepts, such as case outcome, a judge's ideology, or case characteristics, can vary across countries (e.g. Gill and Zorn 2022, 312–18). Consequently, achieving direct comparability of these concepts is not straightforward. This challenge is common in the field of comparative politics. The literature suggests (e.g. van Deth 1998) addressing such challenges by specifying 'functional equivalent' rather than identical concepts. Equivalent concepts are related to other concepts in an analogous way across contexts. This often requires 'increas[ing] the level of abstraction of the concepts' (van Deth 1998, 6) until context-specific differences seem not to matter anymore. This is not a free lunch though, as increasing abstraction could easily lead to concept stretching (Sartori 1970, 1041) such that the functional equivalent concepts lose their analytical power.

Think about how one could conceptualize decision outcomes. The Supreme Court Database, for example, focuses on the ideological direction of a decision, that is, whether an outcome is liberal rather than conservative. Outcomes of decisions in other countries might vary along different substantive dimensions—for instance, more or less European Union integration in the case of the Court of Justice of the European Union (CJEU). By increasing abstraction of the concept 'outcome of a decision' one can avoid any substantive characterization of outcomes that hardly travel across contexts.

An outcome could be simply specified in terms of whether the plaintiff wins, partially wins, or whether the defendant wins. Operationalizing outcomes with regard to those facts we may even end up with a more abstract operationalization, for example plaintiff wins the case or not. Thus, we avoid defining what a 'partial win' implies. This more abstract, yet valid and reliable measurement strategy travels well across different contexts. Another strategy is used by Skiple, Bentsen, and McKenzie (2021). When conceptualizing their non-unanimous decision variable, they distinguish between disagreement about outcome (dissents) and disagreement about the rationales (concurrences). Given that they like to pool the data across different contexts they realize that this can only be done for dissents but not for concurrences. Hence, they only code and analyse dissents as a decision outcome.

Most importantly though, the validity of cross-national measurement strategies must be established rather than assumed. Additionally, the respective coding protocols should minimize the use of human judgment in order to enhance reliability. Reliability is a crucial criterion for defining a reproducible strategy that facilitates the updating of observations within a new time frame in a given context. It is also essential for ensuring that observations from new contexts can be added to the existing infrastructure.

Finally, conceptual clarity is increased by mapping out a precise case selection strategy that defines the criteria for including an observation and determines the appropriate level of observation for each characteristic to be coded. Taking the example of decision outcomes again, we can consider the decision-level outcome or a more refined strategy that examines how the court disposes of each legal issue per case. The latter approach provides more nuanced information that would otherwise be overlooked. However, refined coding strategies are not necessarily superior. They require more effort and potentially more human judgment during the coding process.

Furthermore, if the underlying theory or other variables do not vary across different legal issues within a case, it becomes questionable why one should invest additional coding effort to obtain a more detailed picture.

To summarize, ensuring conceptual clarity is crucial but it can be a challenging task. Designing a comparative database involves establishing case selection criteria, conceptualizations, and coding protocols that are applicable across different contexts. These procedures should be reproducible, allowing others to add new countries and courts in the future or update the existing data for different time periods.

4. An Institutional Proposal for Action: The 'Comparative Study of Judicial Behaviour'

How should we move forward? While it may have been controversial decades ago (e.g. Tate 1989, 1992), by now it seems to be common sense for everyone working on courts comparatively that the field needs to find ways to compile, regularly update, and maintain a high-quality data infrastructure for analysing courts and judicial behaviour within and across countries.

In order to make real progress and allocate our time and resources towards data compilation efficiently, our field needs to change its approach to overcome the dominant data collection strategy known as the 'one-off' approach (e.g. Weinshall and Epstein 2020; Epstein and Weinshall 2021). Currently, scholars often collect data and measures that specifically align with their particular research questions, theories, and chosen institutional and political contexts to test their hypotheses. While this is individually rational—scholars need to use their time and research funds effectively—as a field we would greatly benefit from finding ways to avoid duplicative scholarly efforts. Furthermore, we should also learn from failed attempts to build a database. Why were projects ultimately unsuccessful in accomplishing their intended goals?

How can we establish a high-quality data infrastructure and set it on the right track? We propose looking at how scholars of comparative political behaviour have done this previously. We can learn from them because scholars in this field face similar challenges to those we do when studying judicial behaviour comparatively. Conducting comparable election studies, which involves surveying voters in different electoral systems, poses similar challenges. Implementing the same survey instrument requires case-specific knowledge. Scholars need to understand the political context in which the survey is conducted. They also need to understand the nature of party competition in a country and how its institutional context, such as the electoral system, pre-structures various party strategies and voter behaviour. Additionally, scholars need to have sufficient language proficiency to ensure the comparability of different implementations of the same survey items in different languages. To achieve this, scholars must collaborate and pool their resources and expertise.

We propose the establishment of a collaborative research programme called the Comparative Study of Judicial Behaviour (CSJB) with research teams from around the world. The aim is to create and maintain a high-quality data infrastructure for comparative judicial research, similar to the 'Comparative Study of Electoral Systems' (CSES) (see https://cses.org/ for more information). The CSES is a collaborative programme for election studies that was institutionalized by scholars of comparative political behaviour two decades ago. Participating teams include a common module of survey questions in their post-election studies to measure respondents' voting behaviour and political attitudes during national elections. In addition to individual survey data, the resulting data includes contextual variables that characterize features of, for example, the electoral district, the overall polity, and the electoral system, providing additional context for understanding respondents' voting decisions. All this election-specific and country-specific information is merged with the survey data to create a single, publicly available dataset. Every five years, a new CSES module is designed with a different substantive theme, selected to address relevant questions in comparative political behaviour.

The research design, the required comparative data as well as the study design, for example inclusion criteria, could be developed by a module planning committee, an international committee of scholars of judicial behaviour in political science, law, and neighbouring fields such as sociology and economics. The design is then implemented in each participating country by a scholar or a team of scholars—the country collaborators. Similar to the CSES operations, those country collaborators possess enough case-specific knowledge to organize the data collection within their country. This requires the planning committee to lay out conceptualizations and coding protocols that travel across legal systems and are reproducible (Weinshall and Epstein 2020).

The respective planning committee needs to decide what the first data module should look like, that is which case-level and judge-level data should get collected systematically. Moreover, in addition to case-level and judge-level data the module planning committee should define macro-level characteristics such as features about the court and its internal decision-making processes, as well as characteristics of the legal system together with variables (or at least external identifiers for them) that define the political context (e.g. public opinion data, election results) in which the judicial decisions are made. Such characteristics are on the macro level in the sense that they apply, for instance, to each case-level variable in the same way.

Actively resisting data exuberance is of utmost importance for the committee to motivate scholars participating in this endeavour and to help update already compiled data. Thus, not every characteristic of judges, courts, decisions, and the political context can be included, but whatever characteristic should get coded (at whatever level of observation) requires a detailed coding protocol to make sure that the data are valid and country collaborators can reliably collect (by minimizing human judgment) the data.

Similar to the CSES, the planning committee of the first CSJB module could initially establish a common set of baseline variables and measures that would be expanded and updated in subsequent modules. The sources from which the data is generated are manifold. In addition to the decisions themselves, including accompanying textual material such as briefs, press releases, or news reports, qualitative interview data, survey data, and also potential variables from verbatim notes, audio or video files of hearings on the cases, or results of crowd-sourced coding or laboratory experiments could be included.

While potentially not all variables can be updated, nevertheless a master plan is required that defines which key variables should get updated from one module to the next (or even automatically if such pipelines can be established). Such a plan ensures that the infrastructure is sustainable while not growing too big such that new country teams can still join this collaborative program at a later stage without hesitation. The CSES is meanwhile coordinating its sixth data module.

Why should scholars participate in this comparative infrastructure project? One incentive to participate in the CSJB research programme could be to get access to a (centralized) tech support infrastructure that develops and adapts data collection pipelines to automatically and, thus, reliably code the respective characteristics within a given context. Hand-coding should be avoided as much as possible. This would enable researchers with less knowledge and expertise in automatic data collection strategies (e.g. web-scraping, regular expressions, etc.) and programming expertise to collect more than the required data to further their personal research agenda as well. In addition to defining particular characteristics, the tech support infrastructure could provide tools to automatically use the text of a decision to categorize it depending on the agenda defined by the module's planning committee. The resulting data should be open and accessible. Therefore, it should get deposited along with coding protocols of the macro data to the project's headquarter for data checking and to prepare for its immediate release to the research community. Even if a physical comparative judicial database may not grow as fast as we all would like, it would be nevertheless instrumental that the datasets used in research—as a way of establishing a best-practice norm—become available in various data repositories. If they include external identifiers, such data can be used for new research projects of scholars who might be willing to extend or update existing data.

5. Conclusion

Why do we need databases in research on comparative judicial behaviour? The assessment of common models on judicial behaviour requires knowledge of decisions, judges, and environmental characteristics. Databases allow us to summarize information on all these characteristics in parsimonious and flexible ways without producing redundancies in collected data. An expert survey we conducted shows that while common rectangular datasets were originally used to study the attitudinal model of judicial behaviour, relational databases addressing the strategic model have been published in recent years. However, most existing data structures address single national courts or specific international courts. In order to design an international database for a CSJB, existing comparative projects, such as the CSES, can function as role models.

The development of judicial databases is of major importance to modern research on democracy. Databases allow us to embed courts and judicial action within political systems and societies. Thus, they portray courts as what they are: key institutions in the separation of powers. In order to understand developments within political regimes, open access data on the judiciary is as essential as data on the executive and the legislative branches. Thus, it is important that we as a community are able to engage in large scale comparative data driven projects. Developments that limit the opportunity to analyse data structures (e.g. the French Article 33 LOI n° 2019-222 du 23 mars 2019) eventually hinder scientific progress. After all, databases in judicial politics allow to evaluate the independence of judges, the judicialization of politics as well as the politization of the judiciary and the protection of individual rights as essential features of democracy.

Note

1. We like to thank all participants of our expert survey for their valuable input.

References

Alarie, Benjamin, and Andrew J. Green. 2017. *Commitment and Cooperation on High Courts: A Cross-Country Examination of Institutional Constraints on Judges*. Oxford: Oxford University Press.

Ash, Elliot, Sam Asher, Aditi Bhowmick, Sandeep Bhupatiraju, Daniel Chen, Tanaya Devi, Christoph Goessmann, Paul Novosad, and Bilal Siddiqi. 2021. 'In-group bias in the Indian judiciary: Evidence from 5 million criminal cases'. https://www.devdatalab.org/judicial-data

Behn, Daniel, Malcolm Langford, Ole Kristian Fauchald, Runar Lie, Maxim Usynin, Taylor St John, Laura Letourneau-Tremblay, Tarald Berge, and Tori Loven Kirkebø. 2019. *PITAD Investment Law and Arbitration Database: Version (2019-02-12T09:28:49.184Z)*. Oslo: University of Oslo, Pluricourts Centre of Excellence.

Brouard, Sylvain, and Christoph Hönnige. 2017. 'Constitutional courts as veto players: Lessons from the United States, France and Germany'. *European Journal of Political Research* 56 (3): 529–52.

Carrubba, Clifford J., and Matthew J. Gabel. 2011. *European Court of Justice Data*. https://polisci.emory.edu/home/people/biography/carrubba-clifford.html

Cichowski, Rachel, and Elizabeth Chrun. 2017. *European Court of Human Rights Database (ECHRdb), Version 1.0 Release 2017*. https://depts.washington.edu/echrdb/

Driscoll, Amanda. 2022. Comparative Studies of Judicial Behavior. In *High Courts in Global Perspective: Evidence, Methodologies, and Findings*, edited by Nuno Garoupa, Rebecca D. Gill, and Lydia B. Tiede, 275–306. Charlottesville: University of Virginia Press.

Engst, Benjamin G., Thomas Gschwend, Christoph Hönnige, and Caroline E. Wittig. 2020. *The Constitutional Court Database: Conceptualizing a Relational Database*. https://ccdb.eu/

Epstein, Lee, and Jack Knight. 1998. *The Choices Justices Make*. Washington: CQ Press.

Epstein, Lee, and Keren Weinshall. 2021. *The Strategic Analysis of Judicial Behavior: A Comparative Perspective*. Cambridge: Cambridge University Press.

Epstein, Lee, Urška Sădl, and Keren Weinshall. 2022. 'Symposium: The Role of Comparative Law in the Analysis of Judicial Behavior'. *The American Journal of Comparative Law* 69 (4): 689–719.

Foster, Ian, Rayid Ghani, Ron S. Jarmin, Frauke Kreuter, and Julia Lane. 2021. *Big Data and Social Science. Data Science Methods and Tools for Research and Practice*, 2nd edn. Boca Raton: CRC Press.

Garoupa, Nuno, Rebecca D. Gill, and Lydia B. Tiede. 2022. *High Courts in Global Perspective: Evidence, Methodologies, and Findings*. Charlottesville: University of Virginia Press.

George, Tracey E., and Lee Epstein. 1992. 'On the Nature of Supreme Court Decision Making'. *American Political Science Review* 86 (2): 323–37.

Gill, Rebecca D., and Christopher Zorn. 2022. Overcoming the Barriers to Comparative Judicial Behavior Research. In *High Courts in Global Perspective: Evidence, Methodologies, and Findings*, edited by Nuno Garoupa, Rebecca D. Gill, and Lydia B. Tiede, 307–30. Charlottesville: University of Virginia Press.

Grendstad, Gunnar, William R. Shaffer, and Eric N. Waltenburg. 2015. *Policy Making in an Independent Judiciary: The Norwegian Supreme Court*. Colchester: ECPR Press.

Hamann, Hanjo. 2019. 'The German Federal Courts Dataset 1950–2018: From Paper Archives to Linked Open Data'. *Journal of Empirical Legal Studies* 16 (3): 671–88.

Hanretty, Chris. 2020. *A Court of Specialists: Judicial Behavior on the UK Supreme Court*. Oxford: Oxford University Press.

Haynie, Stacia L., Reginald S. Sheehan, Donald R. Songer, and C. Neal Tate. 2007. *High Courts Judicial Database*. Accessed at the University of South Carolina Judicial Research Initiative. http://www.songerproject.org/national-high-courts.html

Jakab, András, Arthur Dyevre, and Giulio Itzcovich. 2017. *Comparative Constitutional Reasoning*. Cambridge: Cambridge University Press.

Kim, Pauline T., Andrew D. Martin, and Margo Schlanger. 2013. *EEOC Litigation Database*. https://eeoclitigation.wustl.edu/

King, Gary, Robert O. Keohane, and Sidney Verba. 1994. *Designing Social Inquiry: Scientific Inference in Qualitative Research*. Princeton: Princeton University Press.

Martin, Andrew D., and Kevin M. Quinn. 2002. 'Dynamic Ideal Point Estimation via Markov Chain Monte Carlo for the U.S. Supreme Court, 1953–1999'. *Political Analysis* 10 (2): 134–53.

McKenzie, Mark, Henrik Litleré Bentsen, and Jon Kåre Skiple. 2016. 'The Danish Supreme Court Database'. Texas Tech University.

Murphy, Walter F. 1964. *Elements of Judicial Strategy*. Chicago: Chicago University Press.

Parcelle Jr., Richard L., Brett W. Curry, and Bryan W. Marshall. 2011. *Decision Making by the Modern Supreme Court*. Cambridge: Cambridge University Press.

Przeworski, Adam, and Henry Teune. 1970. *The Logic of Comparative Social Inquiry*. New York: Wiley Sons.

Rohde, David W., and Harold J. Spaeth. 1976. *Supreme Court Decision Making*. San Francisco: Freeman.

Sartori, Giovanni. 1970. 'Concept Misformation in Comparative Politics'. *American Political Science Review* 64 (4): 1033–53.

Schubert, Glendon A. 1965. *The Judicial Mind. Attitudes and Ideologies of Supreme Court Justices, 1946–1963*. Evanston: Northwestern University Press.

Segal, Jeffrey A., and Albert D. Cover. 1989. 'Ideological Values and the Votes of U.S. Supreme Court Justices'. *American Political Science Review* 83 (2): 557–65.

Skiple, Jon Kåre, Henrik Litleré Bentsen, and Mark Jonathan McKenzie. 2021. 'How Docket Control Shapes Judicial Behavior: A Comparative Analysis of the Norwegian and Danish Supreme Courts'. *Journal of Law and Courts* 9 (1): 111–36.

Songer, Donald R. 2008. *U.S. Courts of Appeals Databases—Phase II*. http://www.songerproject.org/us-courts-of-appeals-databases.html

Spaeth, Harold J., Lee Epstein, Andrew D. Martin, Jeffrey A. Segal, Theodore J. Ruger, and Sara C. Benesh. 2017. *Supreme Court Database, Version 2017 Release 01*. http://scdb.wustl.edu/

Staton, Jeffrey K. 2010. *Judicial Power and Strategic Communication in Mexico*. Cambridge: Cambridge University Press.

Staton, Jeffrey K., and Georg Vanberg. 2008. 'The Value of Vagueness: Delegation, Defiance, and Judicial Opinions'. *American Journal of Political Science* 52 (3): 504–19.

Stiansen, Øyvind, Daniel Naurin, and Live Standal Bøyum. 2020. 'Law and Politics in the Inter-American Court of Human Rights'. *Journal of Law and Courts* 8 (2): 359–79.

Tate, C. Neal. 1989. 'Scientific Comparative Judicial Politics: An Assessment and a Call to Action'. *Law Courts Newsletter* 7 (1): 1–8.

Tate, C. Neal. 1992. 'The Development of Comparative Judicial Politics'. *Perspectives on Political Science* 21 (3): 138–44.

van Deth, Jan W. 1998. 'Equivalence in Comparative Political Research'. In *Comparative Politics. The Problem of Equivalence*, edited by Jan W. van Deth, 1–19. London: Routledge.

Vanberg, Georg. 2005. *The Politics of Constitutional Review in Germany*. Cambridge: Cambridge University Press.

Weinshall, Keren, and Lee Epstein. 2020. 'Developing High-Quality Data Infrastructure for Legal Analytics: Introducing the Israeli Supreme Court Database'. *Journal of Empirical Legal Studies* 17 (2): 416–34.

Whittington, Keith E. 2019. *Repugnant Laws: Judicial Review of Acts of Congress from the Founding to the Present*. Lawrence: University Press of Kansas.

Wittig, Caroline E. 2016. *The Occurrence of Separate Opinions at the Federal Constitutional Court. An Analysis with a Novel Database*. Berlin: Logos Verlag.

CHAPTER 13

EXPERIMENTS

CHRISTOPH ENGEL

1. Introduction

Experiments are artificial by design. They remove much, sometimes almost all, of the social context. Strictly speaking, what the experiment studies is only an analogue of what the researcher wants to understand. The gap between the experiment and the real-world problem that motivates the endeavour is not a bug; it is the definitional feature. Simplifying the situation is a precondition for excluding confounds. If the experiment is properly designed, alternative explanations are ruled out. If there is a difference between the baseline and the treatment, it must result from the manipulation.

But as has often been argued, everything should be made as simple as possible—but not simpler.[1] For experimental research on judicial decision-making, the resulting trade-off between internal validity (there are no alternative explanations) and external validity (the experimental result is relevant for the research question) is never easy (Lucas 2003; Schram 2005). Extant research is situated on a continuum. At the internal validity end, research starts from the assumption that judicial decision-making is human decision-making. This research hypothesizes that knowledge about human decision-making, in general, is also relevant if these humans happen to be judges. One line of research turns the assumption into a hypothesis and tests real judges on characteristic features of human decision-making that have been robustly documented with convenience samples. The main contribution of this work is the choice of real judges as a non-standard sample.

A second line of research focuses on differences between the standard tasks that have been used to experimentally isolate the behavioural regularity of interest and judicial decision-making. The most basic deviation is motivational. Judges do not decide on behalf of themselves. They decide on behalf of the parties. This feature of the task can be isolated without the necessity of recruiting real judges (Cerrone and Engel 2019).

Actually, the judicial task is heavily institutionally contained. Judicial decision-making is tightly controlled by a rich set of procedural rules. For the most part, judges are also not free how to decide on substance. They have to expressly justify deviations from the existing doctrine. In the common law jurisdictions, they are additionally bound by precedent. Potentially, each of these procedural or substantive constraints has a discernible behavioural effect, as do any of their combinations. If a researcher has reason to believe that an individual constraint has a measurable and sizeable behavioural effect, an experiment can be designed to test the hypothesis. The cumulative effect of multiple constraints is harder to test. In principle, factorial designs are able to test such interactions between impulses. In a factorial design, the experiment manipulates the design in more than one dimension (say gender and education), including their interaction (there is a condition testing female participants who are college educated). But the approach quickly runs into combinatorial explosion. The researcher needs theory, or at least a good guess, to select the combinations of interest.

An alternative research strategy does not start from behavioural theory but from the constraint. Such designs compare the otherwise constant setting, once without and once with the constraint. If the researcher wants to maintain as much experimental control as possible, she will use a hypothetical judicial choice. This makes it possible to tailor the remaining features of the task to the specific intervention of interest, either giving the expected effect its best chance or putting the purported effect to a particularly hard test. The researcher might, for instance, be interested in the effect of warning judges that machine-generated advice about the risk that the defendant recidivates might not be reliable, as mandated by the Supreme Court of Wisconsin.[2] To test the effect, she designs vignettes, and has (mock) judges decide whether they consider the risk of recidivism too high to grant bail. In the baseline, there is no warning, while there is a warning in the treatment (Engel and Grgic-Hlaca 2021). If some rule-making authority has a serious interest in the evaluation of the intervention, she may even collaborate with a researcher and implement a randomized control trial. Then the intervention is tested under real-life conditions. Yet this biggest advantage of the approach is also a major challenge. The authority may, for instance, prematurely lose interest. Then the study may have to be discontinued, possibly even before enough data has been collected to make the analysis meaningful. Moreover, the room for manoeuvre tends to be limited. The design that may be most appealing from an academic perspective, for instance for isolating behavioural channels, may appear too disturbing to the court administration.

Judicial decision-making is a particularly challenging object of study. At court, the parties' well-being is at stake. Just assigning otherwise sufficiently similar cases to manipulated conditions may not be ethically or politically feasible. In the worst of all cases, from the perspective of the empirical researcher, a true control group is out of the question. Then, at most, differently designed interventions may be compared.

Procedural codes worry about impartiality and the perception of impartiality in the population. One safeguard of impartiality is confidentiality. This safeguard becomes particularly relevant if one accepts that judges effectively have leeway, even in continental jurisdictions. Were it to be known which element of procedure has been most important for the disposition of the case, there would be more scope for forum shopping. This concern is imminent if the judicial decision is taken by a panel, a bench of professional judges, or the jury. To contain this risk, the law makes direct observation, let alone manipulation, impossible. Behavioural research must find indirect paths. The classic reaction is studying mock juries, panels of jury-eligible participants on materials that resemble real jury trials (a classic is Hastie et al. 1983). This demonstrates a benefit from experimentation that transcends random assignment to treatment. Shifting from real to hypothetical cases, and real to hypothetical juries, makes social interactions observable that otherwise are purposefully concealed.

A further concern rests on a robust empirical observation. Most individuals rarely, if ever, directly interact with the judicial system. How they, or their relatives or close friends, feel treated on these rare occasions is highly predictive of their willingness to obey the law if enforcement is unlikely (Tyler 2006). Hence there is a pronounced spillover to other areas of life. Randomly exposing individuals to experimental conditions that might trigger such a negative spillover could therefore have a negative externality on potential victims or on society at large. This normatively undesirable effect is a further reason for tweaking the experimental method and shifting from actual to hypothetical cases.

The focus on identification explains why much experimental research investigates judicial behaviour in the abstract, not judicial behaviour embedded in the institutional and cultural setting of one specific jurisdiction, or of several jurisdictions that one wants to compare. This is not to say that experimental methods had nothing to contribute to the agenda of comparative judicial politics; to the contrary. Especially since comparisons of observational data across jurisdictions are fraught with identification problems (as explained in Engel 2021), experimental studies could serve as a welcome complement. The experimental community has not yet been very interested in translating stylized differences between the makeup of the judiciary across jurisdictions into experimental designs. This is why, for the most part, the following survey discusses papers that have studied aspects of judicial decision making in the abstract.

The following survey brackets jury research. There is so much experimental work on the topic that it would require a separate chapter (see only the following surveys and meta-studies Gerbasi et al. 1977; MacCoun 1989; MacCoun 1990; Steblay et al. 1999; Devine et al. 2001; Mitchell et al. 2005, Steblay et al. 2006; Desmarais and Don Read 2011; Wiener et al. 2011; Bornstein et al. 2017; Simon 2019; Hoetger et al. 2022).

2. Experimental Findings

Any survey of experimental research on a topic as broad, and as multifaceted, as judicial decision-making is bound to be incomplete. There is definitely more than can be covered in the following pages. But I hope at least to point interested readers to major areas of interest. The overview starts with work on heuristics and biases and how they play themselves out in the courtroom (i). Political scientists in particular have used experimental methods to isolate the influence of the decision-maker's personal attitudes on the disposition of the case (ii). In the typical court case, relevant information is missing. Often, even the precise scope of the case is unclear. Both induce ambiguity, which triggers predictable behavioural effects (iii). All of the foregoing essentially retests well-established general behavioural effects in a court-related context. An alternative empirical strategy exposes real judges to complete case materials that manipulate a feature of the institutional setting (iv). Courts often decide in panels. The resulting collective decision-making differs from individual decision-making in characteristic ways (v). A rich experimental literature tests the interaction of the court with witnesses (vi). Judicial decision-making is heavily institutionally contained. One may experimentally test how features of this institutional environment affect judicial decision-making (vii). Experiments may finally be used to test how the parties (viii) or the general public (ix) weigh in on judicial decision-making.

2.1 Heuristics and Biases

A rich strand of the literature asks to which degree behavioural regularities that have been robustly documented in other populations matter for judicial decision-making (for an overview see Guthrie et al. 2001; Teichman and Zamir 2014), including specialized panels within their professional area of expertise (Rachlinski et al. 2006).

Judges are subject to anchoring. When faced with a quantitative task, but not having exact numeric information, any number to which they compare the unknown quantity affects their assessment. This effect can be strategically exploited by the parties by throwing in a number that leads to a reduction or increase of the estimate, as serves their cause (Bystranowski et al. 2021). A prosecutor may, for instance, call for a very high sentence, expecting that the judge will correct it downwards but still remain in the neighbourhood of the suggested sentence. Judges are also liable to framing. Whether a decision is presented as a gain or as a loss affects how they evaluate it (Guthrie et al. 2001). The same holds for the way how an expert reports estimates of risk (Scurich and John 2011). Anchoring and framing have been rationalized with salience (Bordalo et al. 2015).

Asylum judges fall prey to the gambler's fallacy. They underestimate the probability of a sequential streak (Chen et al. 2016). In experiments, untrained participants are also inconsistent in the way they translate their qualitative assessment into dollar amounts, for instance about punitive damages, yet the effect does not translate to observational data (Eisenberg et al. 2001).

Judges exhibit hindsight bias. When learning that a possible event has actually happened, they increase the estimated probability that it would have happened (Anderson et al. 1997; Guthrie et al. 2001; Oeberst and Goeckenjan 2016). This is the typical situation in negligence cases. The case is brought as the risk has materialized. Yet whether the defendant has been negligent depends on the ease with which she could have foreseen the damage. Judges neglect the baseline. If the conditional probability of an event is very high, but the unconditional probability (the baseline) is very low, judges tend to come up with an exaggerated assessment (Guthrie et al. 2001). This effect may for instance bias their judgement if an interested party only offers an estimate of the likelihood that a person who has been proven to do X is responsible for harm Y, while neglecting that the unconditional probability that Y obtains is very small. When decision-makers face a portfolio of decisions, evaluations spill over. If there is one severe case, the remaining cases are evaluated more favourably (Kelman et al. 1996).

Judges have a hard time handling probabilities. This leads to miscarriages of justice. Judges do not acquire distributional information when it is available (Sonnemans and Van Dijk 2012).

Judges do not only infer from the emotions of victims how deserving they are (Rose et al. 2006). Emotions also affect how they evaluate the case (Feigenson and Park 2006; Wistrich et al. 2014).

2.2 Personal Attitudes

The foregoing are cognitive limitations. Unless they decide about phenomena that affect society at large, like environmental damage, the case disposition has no direct effect on the judge's personal well-being. Outright selfishness can therefore at most be a minor motive (Posner 1993), for example when preparing for re-election or promotion (Shepherd 2009). The prominent attitudinal model does, however, expect judges to be swayed by ideology (Segal and Spaeth 1993) or, more sophistically, to take into account strategically which decision serves their ideological cause best (Epstein et al. 2001). Experimental evidence qualifies this expectation. Judges decide on behalf of others. In the lab, participants serve their experimental constituency even if they have no personal stake in it, and even if they have to invest a fraction of their experimental endowment. They are motivated to do a good job, even if it has been randomly assigned to them (Engel and Zhurakhovska 2017). In one vignette study, laypersons who have been instructed to decide as judges exhibit ideological bias (Kantorowicz-Reznichenko et al. 2022). In another vignette study, a correlation of some, but not all, political opinions with the proposed decision of the case is observed (Braman 2006). In a further study, professional judges, unlike laypersons, are unaffected by their personal attitude toward salient policy issues (Kahan et al. 2015).

Even if decision-makers are motivated to be impartial, bias may sneak in inadvertently. This has been demonstrated for race (Rachlinski et al. 2008) and ethnicity (Gazal-Ayal and Sulitzeanu-Kenan 2010; Choi, Harris et al. 2022), gender (Kulik et al. 2003; Miller 2019), or ideology (Furgeson et al. 2008). The effect has also been shown in experiments that induced a punishment philosophy (McFatter 1978), or the stereotype that tattoos are typical for criminals, and hence predict guilt (Funk and Todorov 2013). Legal education mitigates the effect of stereotypes but only if the learned rules are simple, rather than judgmental—rules, rather than standards, in the terminology often used in law and economics (Girvan 2016).

In international courts, a further potential for bias results from nationality. If a judge on the bench has the nationality of one of the parties, this may bias the decision in this nation's favor. Random assignment to panels in the appellate body of the World Trade Organization creates quasi-experimental evidence. Overall, there is indeed a bias, but it is driven by the dominance of judges having US nationality (Arias 2019).

2.3 Ambiguity

In the effects listed in the previous section, the bias had a chance due to the characteristic complexity of legal cases, which gives room for motivated reasoning (Norton et al. 2006): a (re)interpretation of the available information such that it conforms with the decision-makers wishes or normative convictions. The literature on judgement and decision-making has characterized the typical task in the courtroom as ambiguous (Simon 2004).[3] Actually, the ambiguity tends to be severe. Judges do not only lack credible information about the base rate of the crime with which the defendant has been charged and the conditional probability of him being guilty, given the available evidence. In most cases, even the state space is not well defined: multiple chains of events might have happened (more on these distinctions from Engel and Goerg 2018). The judge cannot avoid engaging in sense-making (Kunda 1999).

It has been shown (with laypersons) that individuals tend to do so by way of storytelling. They try to combine the pieces of evidence to create a consistent story (Hastie et al. 1983; Pennington and Hastie 1986; Pennington and Hastie 1991). The underlying mental process has been modelled as parallel constraint satisfaction (Simon 1998). In an iterative process (Simon et al. 2001), decision-makers reason bidirectionally: from the evidence to the interpretation but also back from the provisional interpretation to the evidence (Holyoak and Simon 1999), until a coherent interpretation has been forged that meets the probative standard, like preponderance of the evidence or, more strictly, beyond a reasonable doubt (Glöckner and Engel 2013).

This mental mechanism is highly adaptive. It enables decision-makers to make reasonable choices although they know full well that their knowledge and understanding are incomplete. But this human capacity comes at a price. Decision-makers can become partisan, while subjectively believing that they are impartial (Guthrie et al. 2007). This has for instance been shown for experimental participants who have been randomly assigned to represent either plaintiff or defendant (Engel and Glöckner 2013). The effect has been defined as motivated reasoning (Kunda 1990) and has, for instance, been demonstrated for policy preferences regarding discrimination (Braman and Nelson 2007), for example by gender or race. There is also a cognitive downside. As the mental mechanism is constructive, objective information, like numbers, are liable to inadvertent distortion (Hastie 2011; Rachlinski et al. 2015).

2.4 Testing Complete Cases

All of the former is experimental evidence on an individual behavioural effect that one has reason to believe matters for judicial decision-making. In the interest of identification, one removes context and zeroes in on the one behavioural effect of interest. An alternative experimental paradigm exposes real judges to complete materials for a (fictitious) case. That way one, for instance, finds that judges only pay lip service to precedent when *stare decisis* holds (Spamann et al. 2021) and take precedent into account when procedural rules forbid (Liu et al. 2021), while being strongly influenced by clearly irrelevant personal characteristics of the defendant (Spamann and Klöhn 2016).

2.5 Panels

There is a huge literature in political science, some of which is behavioural, on decision-making within panels of multiple judges (see e.g. Songer 1982; Haire et al. 2013). For example, it aims at explaining why the presence of a 'counterjudge' who has been appointed by the president of a different party (Miles and Sunstein 2006), has a different gender (Peresie 2004), or is of a different race (Sommers 2006), tends to lead to more moderate decisions. One explanation is cognitive. The counterjudge alerts the majority of the panel to a concern that they feel unable to overlook (Spitzer and Talley 2013). But relatively little of this evidence is experimental, although group decision-making is a classic topic in experimental economics and social psychology (for a structured overview of this literature see Engel 2010).

An exception is Van Dijk et al. (2014). The authors show that panels commit fewer errors than individual judges; that merely aggregating votes suffices; and that deliberation does not induce new bias but rather improves decision-making if members of the panel decide later cases individually.

2.6 Fact Finding

The courts do not have the luxury of complete information. Usually facts of the case are unknown, and are often additionally contested. Fact-finding is an important part of decision-making in the trial courts. Experiments have tested how likely the courts are to get the facts right. A confession may be the result of coercion rather than the truth. Experimental participants largely ignore the degree of coercion and instead focus on stereotypes. If the defendant comes from the Middle East and is accused of terrorism, even a dubious confession makes him more likely to be held guilty, similarly as an African-American accused of gang violence, while even a seemingly voluntary confession has little effect if nationality and the charge are matched in the opposite direction

(Smalarz et al. 2018). While judges notice that a confession has been coerced, it still creates bias in the disposition of the case (Wallace and Kassin 2012). If defendants retract a confession this has practically no effect on its probative value (Malloy and Lamb 2010).

A rich experimental literature has tested the interaction between the court and eyewitnesses. If they express greater confidence, guilty verdicts are substantially more likely (see the meta-study of Slane and Dodson 2022). Students assuming the role of a judge are overly swayed by hearing (mock) eyewitness identification (Boyce et al. 2008). Safeguards routinely implemented by the courts, like cross-examination, prove largely ineffective (see the review of the experimental literature by Devenport et al. 1997). Novices and even experts are poor at detecting that a witness lies (Nysse-Carris et al. 2011).

A particularly active area of experimental work concerns lineups. A meta-analysis shows that more innocent fillers do a better job of protecting the defendant against false identification (but also increase the number of false negatives) (Juncu and Fitzgerald 2021). If the suspect stands out from the fillers, she is much more likely to be identified, whether innocent or guilty (Fitzgerald et al. 2013). Clear experimental evidence notwithstanding, the courts in the United States continue to assign probative value to eyewitness identifications that result from the police suggesting recognition of the suspect (Wells and Quinlivan 2009).

How an expert presents her findings affects how much the judge relies on it. Qualitative statements carry more weight than quantitative statements, as does a statement summarizing the expert's conclusion. Making limitations explicit has no measurable effect (McQuiston-Surrett and Saks 2009). The way in which a mental health expert informs the court about the risk that a defendant found not guilty for insanity is dangerous affects the decision about her release from hospital (Dolores and Redding 2009). The way DNA evidence is presented dramatically changes how the courts assess its probative value (Koehler 2001). If the expert testifies that she has found supporting evidence, but that it is weak, judicial triers of fact misinterpret this as evidence against the claim (Martire et al. 2013). In another experiment, judges were not sensitive to manipulations of the validity and reliability of expert testimony (Chorn and Kovera 2019).

Participants assuming the role of judges who have been biased against a party as part of the experimental design are less biased when exposed to an adversarial, rather than inquisitorial, procedure (Thibaut et al. 1972). A meta-analysis of experimental studies establishes a small but significant reduction in the likelihood of pre-trial detention if the trier had access to a formal tool to assess the risk of recidivism (Viljoen et al. 2019). But another experiment found an interaction with race: the availability of a risk assessment score helped White but hurt Black defendants (Skeem et al. 2020). Experiments demonstrate that judges have a hard time ignoring inadmissible evidence (Lieberman and Arndt 2000; Wistrich et al. 2004). Judges are not much better than jury members at disregarding potentially biasing information that one of the parties has strategically introduced (Landsman and Rakos 1994).

2.7 Institutional Intervention

Judicial decision-making is institutionally contained. If the legislator expects this to address a normative concern about the carriage of justice, it may redesign elements of the institutional setting. Experiments have tested the impact of multiple of these elements on judicial decision-making, and on case outcomes in particular.

Procedural rules may limit access to information. For instance, lay participants usually do not learn about pre-trial information, whereas the professional judges with whom they interact do. This information gap has been shown to put them at a disadvantage in deliberations within the court (Fujita and Hotta 2010).

Procedural law defines which party is heard at which moment of the trial. In criminal procedure, the defendant traditionally has the last word. This gives the prosecution the opportunity to set an anchor when justifying the charge (Englich et al. 2005). However, when aggregating the ambiguous information of the case to obtain the final judgment, experiments demonstrate a 'recency' effect: the assessment heard last has the strongest effect on the judgment (Engel et al. 2020). A recency effect was also found for the order in which multiple pieces of evidence are presented, but only if the decision-maker re-evaluated the evidence after every new piece (Kerstholt and Jackson 1998). A recency effect was also observed if an eyewitness contradicted the prosecution's suspect (Dahl et al. 2009). Defence attorneys may exploit the recency effect in an attempt at 'stealing thunder': they start their pleading by noting the main incriminating evidence, to later dispel it, and leave the court with a more favourable view (Dolnik et al. 2003).

In multiple respects, courts have discretion. The most salient situation is sentencing. One paper interprets the decision of the US Supreme Court in *Booker* as a natural experiment. In that ruling, the Supreme Court had given the trial courts more leeway to depart from the sentence defined by the guidelines (543 US 220 (2005)). The trial courts immediately seized the opportunity and were more likely to reduce, rather than increase, sentences. Still, the average sentence length approximately stayed constant, as there were a number of very pronounced upward corrections (Hofer 2007). Bushway et al. (2012) exploit the fact that in Maryland, data is available about the true criteria for the state's sentencing guidelines, and the criteria with which the trial judge has been presented. In about 10 per cent of the cases, these criteria did not match; that is, the judge decided on the basis of factually wrong information. Arguing that these errors are random, they find that judges are eager to go along with errors suggesting that the crime has actually been less severe, in particular for violent crime. By contrast, judges tend to use discretion to correct errors suggesting that the crime has actually been more severe, albeit not fully.

Machine learning and the availability of relatively large datasets make it possible to provide trial judges with machine-generated predictions, for example about the risk that the defendant will recidivate. Experimental participants are not easily induced to take this machine-generated advice into account. In the experiment, they only do this if they receive a financial incentive for following the advice. Even a financial incentive for accuracy does not make them rely on the advice (Grgić-Hlača et al. 2019). In Wisconsin, these computer-generated predictions may also be used for sentencing. The Supreme Court of Wisconsin has cleared this practice (881 *N.W.2d* 749 (Wis. 2016)) but has obliged the court administration to add a list of warnings. Experimental subjects largely ignore these warnings. If the warnings are made much more salient and graphic, and if participants are incentivized, warnings have an effect, but it is counterproductive. They follow the machine advice if it has been wrong, while their own prior assessment had been correct (Engel and Grgic-Hlaca 2021).

There have been concerns that the presence of still and video cameras in court might have a chilling effect (Osterreicher 2011). In an experiment, these concerns were not supported. In a criminal case, experimental participants were not more likely to find against defendant (Paddon 1985).

During the pandemic, witnesses frequently had to be heard over video, rather than in person. An experiment shows that audio quality matters. With poor audio, witnesses are rated as less credible, triers had less precise recollections of their statements, and their testimony had less influence on the case disposition (Bild et al. 2021).

A natural experiment in Israel made it possible to identify the effect of a reduction in workload on the way how judges handle cases. It turns out that judges not only use the extra leeway to work harder and more diligently on individual cases; in civil cases the extra work is also to the benefit of plaintiffs, who are more likely to win (Engel and Weinshall Margel 2020). In a lab experiment with law students, time pressure increases the probability that participants follow the law in a straightforward manner, but they are also significantly less confident in the disposition of the case (Sheppard 2011).

For most decisions, judges have to give explicit, often even written reasons. This procedural requirement can potentially have a host of behavioural effects (summarized in Engel 2007). One experiment shows that the requirement may be blunted. Judges may *ex post* rationalize a decision tainted by bias (Liu and Li 2019). Yet if judges are required to spell out their reasons before deciding, a debiasing effect obtains (Liu 2018).

For the most part, trial judges decide under the shadow of appeal. One behavioural channel is self-esteem (the judge does not want to make a mistake) and social esteem (the judge does not want to lose reputation, by seeing her decision reversed). In an experiment, these effects obtain, and lead to higher accuracy (Feess and Sarel 2018).

2.8 Formal and Informal Parties

To a considerable degree, judges are in the hands of the parties and their representatives. To understand error and bias in judicial decision-making, one must therefore understand error and bias in what the court hears from the parties. Experiments show that lawyers tend to be overly convinced by the side they represent (Eigen and Listokin 2012). They also make systematic mistakes in the assessment of the evidence and assign higher subjective probability to events that are described in greater detail (Fox and Birke 2002).

If the police make mistakes, these mistakes are likely to affect the court, directly through hearing the police as witness or indirectly through prosecution. This is why the experimental research about bias in police investigations is relevant. For instance, it has found that police officers tend to be biased against suspects they have themselves arrested (Lidén et al. 2018). Racial bias, to the detriment of Black defendants, has also been documented (Swencionis and Goff 2017).

Experts tasked with informing the court about the severity of mental health limitations are aware of the risk of bias but hold the erroneous belief that it can be overcome with willpower alone (Zapf et al. 2018).

2.9 Public Perception

The judiciary does not have its own enforcement apparatus. This makes the judiciary particularly dependent on public support. Support starts with selection. It is particularly salient for the US Supreme Court. One experiment finds an effect of motivated reasoning (Kunda 1990) on procedural preferences. Those in favour of the candidate wish the Senate hearing to be formal and legalistic. Those opposed to the candidate argue for a more politicized procedure (Badas 2022). A conjoint experiment finds a spillover from the US state to the federal level. Participants from states in which judges are appointed prefer a more legalistic procedure for the selection of Supreme Court justices (Krewson and Owens 2022). Another conjoint experiment demonstrates that the general public essentially sees US Supreme Court justices as ordinary political actors. Information about their political leanings dominates information about judicial competence (Sen 2017). However, yet another experiment finds that information about judicial philosophies also changes public evaluation of a candidate (Krewson and Owens 2021).

Learning that judges have received politically motivated support for their campaigns reduces the perceived legitimacy of the court (Gibson et al. 2011); actually, legitimacy is even reduced if the candidate rejects contributions to her election campaign (Gibson and Caldeira 2012).

Does the general public only care about outcomes or is trust in courts and their perceived legitimacy also influenced by judicial procedure? Experimental evidence is mixed. One study shows a moderating effect of how the procedure is perceived. If judges are seen as using a principled decision-making process, institutional loyalty determines acceptance. If, by contrast, judges are perceived as policy-makers, members of the public only accept the decisions with which they agree on substance (Woodson 2015). In Norway, where the judiciary is perceived less as politicized, public support increases when the judicial decision comes with a dissenting opinion that makes the normative conflict transparent (Bentsen 2019).

A quasi-experiment from Spain shows that the perception of judicial activism can even reduce support for the entire polity: decisions of the European Court of Justice are perceived as a threat to national sovereignty which, in turn, triggers resistance to European integration (Turnbull-Dugarte and Devine 2022). On the other hand, public support for Veterans Treatment Courts in the United States spills over into general support for the legal system. This finding is explained with an effect of procedural justice (Gallagher and Ashford 2021). Support for the judiciary is also increased in participants who are induced to watch a Dutch TV series that makes judicial procedure more transparent (Grimmelikhuijsen and Klijn 2015).

Overall, the effect of the reasons the court gives for a contentious decision had little effect on experimental participants. Priming them with either equality or liberty did not have much effect on them accepting the decision of the US Supreme Court on same-sex marriage. In the experiment, the equality prime reduced declared acceptance of the judicial decision (Cahill and Rapp 2014).

At the opposite end of the spectrum, a court that enjoys high public acceptance, like the German Constitutional Court, has the power to convey legitimacy on political decisions taken by Parliament or government, or to deprive these decisions of legitimacy (Sternberg et al. 2021).

The most important factor for explaining the support of experimental participants for a court ruling is the outcome. The judge's mode of reasoning had no measurable effect on support if they agreed with the outcome. If they disagreed with the outcome, acceptance increased if the ruling expressly acknowledged that the opponent also had a point (Simon and Scurich 2011). This result also holds if experimental participants receive information about the case by a legal expert (Simon and Scurich 2013).

3. Conclusion

Judicial decision-making is definitely not virgin territory. This survey shows how rich the literature is and has only covered experimental research. Should researchers therefore be advised to watch out for alternative topics? Is the expected marginal benefit from new experiments minor? Has the field reached a steady state of normal science? In some dimensions, the answer is probably yes, and this survey may help the next generation of court researchers spot research questions that they may prefer to avoid. In conclusion, I want to sketch areas in which major advances are more likely.

Disciplines have their cultures. Experimental research on judicial decision-making has most intensely engaged with social psychology, and with psychological work on judgment and decision-making. The equally rich literature in behavioural economics has been almost completely neglected, as has the (less rich but still sizeable) literature on experimental political science.

The extant experimental research on judicial decision-making is surprisingly little legal. Judges decide in a tightly controlled institutional context. There is variance in this context over time and across jurisdictions. This variance could be productively translated into stylized facts that are manipulated in the experiment. Related to this, most of the extant experimental research has studied judicial decision-making in the abstract. In many respects (carefully laid out in this volume), judicial decision-making differs across jurisdictions. Some differences are institutional: do professional judges decide, or juries composed of laypersons, or panels composed of professionals and members of the general public? Do individual judges have fixed dockets or are judges randomly assigned to cases? Are judges appointed for life, or do they have fixed tenure, or do they regularly face retention elections? Is the procedure inquisitorial or adversarial? Is there a judge referee, and what are her powers? The list of questions to ask could easily be made much longer, and any such feature of the institutional setting could easily be manipulated experimentally.

Other differences are cultural: in some jurisdictions, judges are appointed or elected at a fairly advanced stage of their careers and the position comes with high social visibility. In other jurisdictions, former law students become judges on completion of their studies, and being a judge essentially feels like working for a branch of the administration. In some jurisdictions, judges are expected to hold political preferences and to act upon them, while in other jurisdictions the legalist culture is pronounced. In some jurisdictions, judicial decision-making is routinely interpreted as an exercise in social engineering, whereas in other jurisdictions, judges are supposed to shy away from attempts at educating the parties. As such, culture can only be measured, not manipulated. But inventive researchers can try to isolate arguable building blocks of cultural differences, and generate causal evidence by randomly giving some participants access to these elements of the social fabric.

Most of the experiments reported in this survey aim to identify a central tendency. Experiments investigate how their sample on average reacts to the manipulation, and they infer the treatment effect in the population. This simplification may prove inappropriate. Different groups of judges may react in characteristically different ways: appointed vs elected; male vs female; Caucasian vs of colour; with or without attorney experience; with or without expertise in the specific field (like medical malpractice, DNA evidence, or antitrust). It may therefore be a promising next step to design experiments that are able to document patterned heterogeneity and the resulting heterogeneous treatment effects.

Finally, no case is the same as the next and, as a practical matter, court cases are only incompletely defined. Traditional experimental methods deliberately eschew this challenge, and purposefully simplify the setting. As machine-learning methods are powerful ways of organizing such rich datasets, next-generation experimental research might introduce controlled manipulations into such more naturalistic settings and might rely on artificial intelligence to organize the resulting data. Such experiments would have only partly *ex ante* defined dependent variables, and would blend theory-driven interventions with pattern-finding.

Experimental research on judicial decision-making is likely to thrive!

Notes

1. The quotation is often attributed to Albert Einstein, but as Kevin Clermont has pointed out to me, a written reference has not been found. It seems this is a piece of oral history (of science).
2. Supreme Court of Wisconsin, 2016 WI 68, *Loomis*.

3. The technical definition of ambiguity qualifies the lack of information: the decision-maker not only lacks information about the realization of a lottery. It is even unclear which outcomes are possible, i.e. the state space is not well defined.

References

Anderson, J. C., M. M. Jennings, D. J. Lowe, and P. M. Reckers. 1997. 'The Mitigation of Hindsight Bias in Judges' Evaluation of Auditor Decisions'. *Auditing* 16 (2): 20–39.

Arias, E. 2019. *Impartiality in International Courts: Evidence from a Natural Experiment at the WTO*. Working paper. https://www.peio.me/wp-content/uploads/2019/01/PEIO12_paper_102.pdf.

Badas, A. 2022. 'Motivated Reasoning and Attitudes Towards Supreme Court Confirmation Hearings. Evidence from Five Nominations and an Experiment'. *Political Research Quarterly* 76: 540–52.

Bentsen, H. L. 2019. 'Dissent, Legitimacy, and Public Support for Court Decisions. Evidence from a Survey-Based Experiment'. *Law and Society Review* 53 (2): 588–610.

Bild, E., A. Redman, E. J. Newman, B. R. Muir, D. Tait, and N. Schwarz. 2021. 'Sound and Credibility in the Virtual Court. Low Audio Quality Leads to Less Favorable Evaluations of Witnesses and Lower Weighting of Evidence'. *Law and Human Behavior* 45 (5): 481–95.

Bordalo, P., N. Gennaioli, and A. Shleifer. 2015. 'Salience Theory of Judicial Decisions'. *Journal of Legal Studies* 44 (S1): S7–33.

Bornstein, B. H., J. M. Golding, J. Neuschatz, C. Kimbrough, K. Reed, C. Magyarics, and K. Luecht. 2017. 'Mock Juror Sampling Issues in Jury Simulation Research. A Meta-Analysis'. *Law and Human Behavior* 41 (1): 13–28.

Boyce, M. A., D. S. Lindsay, and C. Brimacombe. 2008. 'Investigating Investigators. Examining the Impact of Eyewitness Identification Evidence on Student-Investigators'. *Law and Human Behavior* 32 (5): 439–53.

Braman, E. 2006. 'Reasoning on the Threshold. Testing the Separability of Preferences in Legal Decision Making'. *Journal of Politics* 68 (2): 308–21.

Braman, E., and T. E. Nelson. 2007. 'Mechanism of Motivated Reasoning? Analogical Perception in Discrimination Disputes'. *American Journal of Political Science* 51 (4): 940–56.

Bushway, S. D., E. G. Owens, and A. M. Piehl. 2012. 'Sentencing Guidelines and Judicial Discretion. Quasi-Experimental Evidence from Human Calculation Errors'. *Journal of Empirical Legal Studies* 9 (2): 291–319.

Bystranowski, P., B. Janik, M. Próchnicki, and P. Skórska. 2021. 'Anchoring Effect in Legal Decision-Making. A Meta-Analysis'. *Law and Human Behavior* 45 (1): 1–23.

Cahill, C. M., and G. C. Rapp. 2014. 'Does the Public Care How the Supreme Court Reasons. Empirical Evidence from a National Experiment and Normative Concerns in the Case of Same-Sex Marriage'. *North Carolina Law Review* 93: 303–374.

Cerrone, C., and C. Engel. 2019. 'Deciding on Behalf of Others Does Not Mitigate Selfishness: An Experiment'. *Economics Letters* 183: 108616.

Chen, D. L., T. J. Moskowitz, and K. Shue. 2016. 'Decision Making Under the Gambler's Fallacy. Evidence From Asylum Judges, Loan Officers, and Baseball Umpires'. *Quarterly Journal of Economics* 131 (3): 1181–242.

Choi, D. D., J. A. Harris, and F. Shen-Bayh. 2022. 'Ethnic Bias in Judicial Decision Making: Evidence from Criminal Appeals in Kenya'. *American Political Science Review* 116: 1067–80.

Chorn, J. A., and M. B. Kovera. 2019. 'Variations in Reliability and Validity Do Not Influence Judge, Attorney, and Mock Juror Decisions About Psychological Expert Evidence'. *Law and Human Behavior* 43 (6): 542–57.

Dahl, L. C., C. Brimacombe, and D. S. Lindsay. 2009. 'Investigating Investigators. How Presentation Order Influences Participant–Investigators' Interpretations of Eyewitness Identification and Alibi Evidence'. *Law and Human Behavior* 33 (5): 368–80.

Desmarais, S. L., and J. Don Read. 2011. 'After 30 Years, What Do We Know About What Jurors Know? A Meta-Analytic Review of Lay Knowledge Regarding Eyewitness Factors'. *Law and Human Behavior* 35 (3): 200–10.

Devenport, J. L., S. D. Penrod, and B. L. Cutler. 1997. 'Eyewitness Identification Evidence. Evaluation Commonsense Evaluations'. *Psychology, Public Policy, and Law* 3 (2–3): 338–61.

Devine, D. J., L. D. Clayton, B. B. Dunford, R. Seying, and J. Pryce. 2001. 'Jury Decision Making. 45 Years of Empirical Research on Deliberating Groups'. *Psychology, Public Policy, and Law* 7 (3): 622–727.

Dolnik, L., T. I. Case, and K. D. Williams. 2003. 'Stealing Thunder as a Courtroom Tactic Revisited. Processes and Boundaries'. *Law and Human Behavior* 27 (3): 267–87.

Dolores, J. C., and R. E. Redding. 2009. 'The Effects of Different Forms of Risk Communication on Judicial Decision Making'. *International Journal of Forensic Mental Health* 8 (2): 142–46.

Eigen, Z. J., and Y. Listokin. 2012. 'Do Lawyers Really Believe Their Own Hype, and Should They? A Natural Experiment'. *Journal of Legal Studies* 41 (2): 239–67.

Eisenberg, T., J. J. Rachlinski, and M. T. Wells. 2001. 'Reconciling Experimental Incoherence With Real-World Coherence in Punitive Damages'. *Stanford Law Review* 54: 1239–71.

Engel, C. 2007. The Psychological Case for Obliging Judges to Write Reasons. In *The Impact of Court Procedure on the Psychology of Judicial Decision Making*, edited by C. Engel and F. Strack, 71–109. Baden-Baden, Nomos.

Engel, C. 2010. 'The Behaviour of Corporate Actors. A Survey of the Empirical Literature'. *Journal of Institutional Economics* 6: 445–75.

Engel, C. 2021. 'Challenges in the Interdisciplinary Use of Comparative Law'. *American Journal of Comparative Law* 69: 777–97.

Engel, C., and A. Glöckner. 2013. 'Role Induced Bias in Court. An Experiment'. *Journal of Behavioral Decision Making* 26: 272–84.

Engel, C., and S. J. Goerg. 2018. 'If the Worst Comes to the Worst. Dictator Giving when Recipient's Endowments are Risky'. *European Economic Review* 105: 51–70.

Engel, C., and N. Grgić-Hlača. 2021. 'Machine Advice with a Warning about Machine Limitations. Experimentally Testing the Solution Mandated by the Wisconsin Supreme Court'. *Journal of Legal Analysis* 13: 284–40.

Engel, C., S. Timme, and A. Glöckner. 2020. 'Coherence-Based Reasoning and Order Effects in Legal Judgments'. *Psychology, Public Policy, and Law* 26: 333–52.

Engel, C., and K. Weinshall Margel. 2020. 'Manna from Heaven for Judges. Judges' Reaction to a Quasi-Random Reduction in Caseload'. *Journal of Empirical Legal Studies* 17: 722–51.

Engel, C., and L. Zhurakhovska. 2017. 'You Are In Charge. Experimentally Testing the Motivating Power of Holding a Judicial Office'. *Journal of Legal Studies* 46: 1–50.

Englich, B., T. Mussweiler, and F. Strack. 2005. 'The Last Word in Court. A Hidden Disadvantage for the Defense'. *Law and Human Behavior* 29 (6): 705–22.

Epstein, L., J. Knight, and A. D. Martin. 2001. 'The Supreme Court as a Strategic National Policymaker'. *Emory Law Journal* 50: 583–612.

Feess, E., and R. Sarel. 2018. 'Judicial Effort and the Appeals System. Theory and Experiment'. *Journal of Legal Studies* 47 (2): 269–94.

Feigenson, N., and J. Park. 2006. 'Emotions and Attributions of Legal Responsibility and Blame. A Research Review'. *Law and Human Behavior* 30 (2): 143–61.

Fitzgerald, R. J., H. L. Price, C. Oriet, and S. D. Charman. 2013. 'The Effect of Suspect-Filler Similarity on Eyewitness Identification Decisions. A Meta-Analysis'. *Psychology, Public Policy, and Law* 19 (2): 151–64.

Fox, C. R., and R. Birke. 2002. 'Forecasting Trial Outcomes. Lawyers Assign Higher Probability to Possibilities That Are Described in Greater Detail'. *Law and Human Behavior* 26 (2): 159–73.

Fujita, M., and S. Hotta. 2010. 'The Impact of Differential Information Between Lay Participants and Professional Judges on Deliberative Decision-Making'. *International Journal of Law, Crime and Justice* 38 (4): 216–35.

Funk, F., and A. Todorov. 2013. 'Criminal Stereotypes in the Courtroom. Facial Tattoos Affect Guilt and Punishment Differently'. *Psychology, Public Policy, and Law* 19 (4): 466–78.

Furgeson, J. R., L. Babcock, and P. M. Shane. 2008. 'Do a Law's Policy Implications Affect Beliefs About Its Constitutionality? An Experimental Test'. *Law and Human Behavior* 32 (3): 219–27.

Gallagher, J. M., and J. B. Ashford. 2021. 'Perceptions of Legal Legitimacy in Veterans Treatment Courts. A Test of a Modified Version of Procedural Justice Theory'. *Law and Human Behavior* 45 (2): 152–64.

Gazal-Ayal, O., and R. Sulitzeanu-Kenan. 2010. 'Let My People Go. Ethnic in-Group Bias in Judicial Decisions—Evidence From a Randomized Natural Experiment'. *Journal of Empirical Legal Studies* 7 (3): 403–28.

Gerbasi, K. C., M. Zuckerman, and H. T. Reis. 1977. 'Justice Needs a New Blindfold. A Review of Mock Jury Research'. *Psychological Bulletin* 84 (2): 323–45.

Gibson, J. L., and G. A. Caldeira. 2012. 'Campaign Support, Conflicts of Interest, and Judicial Impartiality. Can Recusals Rescue the Legitimacy of Courts?' *Journal of Politics* 74 (1): 18–34.

Gibson, J. L., J. A. Gottfried, M. X. Delli Carpini, and K. H. Jamieson. 2011. 'The Effects of Judicial Campaign Activity on the Legitimacy of Courts. A Survey-Based Experiment'. *Political Research Quarterly* 64 (3): 545–58.

Girvan, E. J. 2016. 'Wise Restraints? Learning Legal Rules, Not Standards, Reduces the Effects of Stereotypes in Legal Decision-Making'. *Psychology, Public Policy, and Law* 22 (1): 31–45.

Glöckner, A., and C. Engel. 2013. 'Can We Trust Intuitive Jurors? Standards of Proof and the Probative Value of Evidence in Coherence Based Reasoning'. *Journal of Empirical Legal Studies* 10: 230–52.

Grgić-Hlača, N., C. Engel, and K. P. Gummadi. 2019. *Human Decision Making with Machine Assistance. An Experiment on Bailing and Jailing.* Proceedings of the ACM on Human–Computer Interaction.

Grimmelikhuijsen, S., and A. Klijn. 2015. 'The Effects of Judicial Transparency on Public Trust. Evidence From a Field Experiment'. *Public Administration* 93 (4): 995–1011.

Guthrie, C., J. J. Rachlinski, and A. J. Wistrich. 2001. 'Inside the Judicial Mind'. *Cornell Law Review* 86: 777–830.

Guthrie, C., J. J. Rachlinski, and A. J. Wistrich. 2007. 'Blinking on the Bench. How Judges Decide Cases'. *Cornell Law Review* 93: 1–43.

Haire, S. B., L. P. Moyer, and S. Treier. 2013. 'Diversity, Deliberation, and Judicial Opinion Writing'. *Journal of Law and Courts* 1 (2): 303–30.

Hastie, R. 2011. 'The Challenge to Produce Useful Legal Numbers'. *Journal of Empirical Legal Studies* 8: 6–20.

Hastie, R., S. Penrod, and N. Pennington. 1983. *Inside the Jury*. Cambridge: Harvard University Press.

Hoetger, L. A., D. J. Devine, E. M. Brank, R. M. Drew, and R. Rees. 2022. 'The Impact of Pretrial Publicity on Mock Juror and Jury Verdicts. A Meta-Analysis'. *Law and Human Behavior* 46: 121–39.

Hofer, P. J. 2007. 'United States v. Booker as a Natural Experiment. Using Empirical Research to Inform the Federal Sentencing Policy Debate'. *Criminology and Public Policy* 6 (3): 433–60.

Holyoak, K. J., and D. Simon. 1999. 'Bidirectional Reasoning in Decision Making by Constraint Satisfaction'. *Journal of Experimental Psychology: General* 128: 1–29.

Juncu, S., and R. J. Fitzgerald. 2021. 'A Meta-Analysis of Lineup Size Effects on Eyewitness Identification'. *Psychology, Public Policy, and Law* 27: 295–315.

Kahan, D. M., D. Hoffman, D. Evans, N. Devins, E. Lucci, and K. Cheng. 2015. 'Ideology or Situation Sense. An Experimental Investigation of Motivated Reasoning and Professional Judgment'. *University of Pennsylvania Law Review* 164: 349–439.

Kantorowicz-Reznichenko, E., J. Kantorowicz, and K. Weinshall. 2022. 'Ideological Bias in Constitutional Judgments. Experimental Analysis and Potential Solutions'. *Journal of Empirical Legal Studies* 19: 716–57.

Kelman, M., Y. Rottenstreich, and A. Tversky. 1996. 'Context-Dependence in Legal Decision Making'. *Journal of Legal Studies* 25 (2): 287–318.

Kerstholt, J. H., and J. L. Jackson. 1998. 'Judicial Decision Making. Order of Evidence Presentation and Availability of Background Information'. *Applied Cognitive Psychology* 12 (5): 445–54.

Koehler, J. J. 2001. 'When Are People Persuaded by DNA Match Statistics?' *Law and Human Behavior* 25 (5): 493–513.

Krewson, C., and R. J. Owens. 2022. 'How State Judicial Selection Methods May Influence Views of US Supreme Court Nominees. Evidence from a Conjoint Experiment'. *Journal of Law and Courts* 10: 189–212.

Krewson, C. N., and R. J. Owens. 2021. 'Public Support for Judicial Philosophies. Evidence from a Conjoint Experiment'. *Journal of Law and Courts* 9 (1): 89–110.

Kulik, C. T., E. L. Perry, and M. B. Pepper. 2003. 'Here Comes the Judge. The Influence of Judge Personal Characteristics on Federal Sexual Harassment Case Outcomes'. *Law and Human Behavior* 27 (1): 69–86.

Kunda, Z. 1990. 'The Case for Motivated Reasoning'. *Psychological Bulletin* 108: 480–98.

Kunda, Z. 1999. *Social Cognition. Making Sense of People*. Cambridge: MIT Press.

Landsman, S., and R. F. Rakos. 1994. 'A Preliminary Inquiry into the Effect of Potentially Biasing Information on Judges and Jurors in Civil Litigation'. *Behavioral Sciences & the Law* 12 (2): 113–26.

Lidén, M., M. Gräns, and P. Juslin. 2018. 'The Presumption of Guilt in Suspect Interrogations. Apprehension as a Trigger of Confirmation Bias and Debiasing Techniques'. *Law and Human Behavior* 42 (4): 336–54.

Lieberman, J. D., and J. Arndt. 2000. 'Understanding the Limits of Limiting Instructions. Social Psychological Explanations for the Failures of Instructions to Disregard Pretrial Publicity and Other Inadmissible Evidence'. *Psychology, Public Policy, and Law* 6 (3): 677–711.

Liu, J. Z., L. Klöhn, and H. Spamann. 2021. 'Precedents and Chinese Judges. An Experiment'. *American Journal of Comparative Law* 69 (1): 93–135.

Liu, J. Z., and X. Li. 2019. 'Legal Techniques for Rationalizing Biased Judicial Decisions. Evidence From Experiments With Real Judges'. *Journal of Empirical Legal Studies* 16 (3): 630–70.

Liu, Z. 2018. 'Does Reason Writing Reduce Decision Bias? Experimental Evidence from Judges in China'. *Journal of Legal Studies* 47 (1): 83–118.

Lucas, J. W. 2003. 'Theory-testing, Generalization, and the Problem of External Validity'. *Sociological Theory* 21 (3): 236–53.

MacCoun, R. J. 1989. 'Experimental Research on Jury Decision-Making'. *Science* 244 (4908): 1046–50.

MacCoun, R. J. 1990. 'Experimental Research on Jury Decision-Making'. *Jurimetrics* 30: 223–33.

Malloy, L. C., and M. E. Lamb. 2010. 'Biases in Judging Victims and Suspects Whose Statements Are Inconsistent'. *Law and Human Behavior* 34 (1): 46–48.

Martire, K. A., R. I. Kemp, I. Watkins, M. A. Sayle, and B. R. Newell. 2013. 'The Expression and Interpretation of Uncertain Forensic Science Evidence. Verbal Equivalence, Evidence Strength, and the Weak Evidence Effect'. *Law and Human Behavior* 37 (3): 197–207.

McFatter, R. M. 1978. 'Sentencing Strategies and Justice. Effects of Punishment Philosophy on Sentencing Decisions'. *Journal of Personality and Social Psychology* 36 (12): 1490–500.

McQuiston-Surrett, D., and M. J. Saks. 2009. 'The Testimony of Forensic Identification Science. What Expert Witnesses Say and What Factfinders Hear'. *Law and Human Behavior* 33 (5): 436–53.

Miles, T. J., and C. R. Sunstein. 2006. 'Do Judges Make Regulatory Policy? An Empirical Investigation of Chevron'. *University of Chicago Law Review* 73: 823–81.

Miller, A. L. 2019. 'Expertise Fails to Attenuate Gendered Biases in Judicial Decision-Making'. *Social Psychological and Personality Science* 10 (2): 227–34.

Mitchell, T. L., R. M. Haw, J. E. Pfeifer, and C. A. Meissner. 2005. 'Racial Bias in Mock Juror Decision-Making. A Meta-Analytic Review of Defendant Treatment'. *Law and Human Behavior* 29 (6): 621–37.

Norton, M. I., S. R. Sommers, J. A. Vandello, and J. M. Darley. 2006. 'Mixed Motives and Racial Bias. The Impact of Legitimate and Illegitimate Criteria on Decision Making'. *Psychology, Public Policy, and Law* 12 (1): 36–55.

Nysse-Carris, K. L., B. L. Bottoms, and J. M. Salerno. 2011. 'Experts' and Novices' Abilities to Detect Children's High-Stakes Lies of Omission'. *Psychology, Public Policy, and Law* 17 (1): 76–98.

Oeberst, A., and I. Goeckenjan. 2016. 'When Being Wise After the Event Results in Injustice. Evidence for Hindsight Bias in Judges' Negligence Assessments'. *Psychology, Public Policy, and Law* 22 (3): 271–79.

Osterreicher, M. H. 2011. 'Cameras in the Courts. The Long Road to the New Federal Experiment'. *Reynolds Court and Media Law Journal* 1: 221–58.

Paddon, A. R. 1985. Television Coverage of Criminal Trials with Cameras and Microphones. A Laboratory Experiment of Audience Effects (Videotape, Photograph, Court, Fair Trial). University of Tennessee. https://www.proquest.com/pagepdf/303422540?accountid=16589.

Pennington, N., and R. Hastie. 1986. 'Evidence Evaluation in Complex Decision Making'. *Journal of Personality and Social Psychology* 51: 242–58.

Pennington, N., and R. Hastie. 1991. 'A Cognitive Theory of Juror Decision Making. The Story Model'. *Cardozo Law Review* 13: 519–57.

Peresie, J. L. 2004. 'Female Judges Matter. Gender and Collegial Decisionmaking in the Federal Appellate Courts'. *Yale Law Journal* 114: 1759–90.

Posner, R. A. 1993. 'What Do Judges and Justices Maximize? (The Same Thing Everybody Else Does)'. *Supreme Court Economic Review* 3: 1–41.

Rachlinski, J. J., C. Guthrie, and A. J. Wistrich. 2006. 'Inside the Bankruptcy Judge's Mind'. *Boston University Law Review* 86: 1227–65.

Rachlinski, J. J., S. L. Johnson, A. J. Wistrich, and C. Guthrie. 2008. 'Does Unconscious Racial Bias Affect Trial Judges'. *Notre Dame Law Review* 84: 1195–246.

Rachlinski, J. J., A. J. Wistrich and C. Guthrie. 2015. 'Can Judges Make Reliable Numeric Judgments. Distorted Damages and Skewed Sentences'. *Indiana Law Journal* 90: 695–739.

Rose, M. R., J. Nadler, and J. Clark. 2006. 'Appropriately Upset? Emotion Norms and Perceptions of Crime Victims'. *Law and Human Behavior* 30 (2): 203–19.

Schram, A. 2005. 'Artificiality. The Tension Between Internal and External Validity in Economic Experiments'. *Journal of Economic Methodology* 12 (2): 225–37.

Scurich, N., and R. S. John. 2011. 'The Effect of Framing Actuarial Risk Probabilities on Involuntary Civil Commitment Decisions'. *Law and Human Behavior* 35 (2): 83–91.

Segal, J. A., and H. J. Spaeth. 1993. *The Supreme Court and the Attitudinal Model*. New York: Cambridge University Press.

Sen, M. 2017. 'How Political Signals Affect Public Support for Judicial Nominations. Evidence from a Conjoint Experiment'. *Political Research Quarterly* 70 (2): 374–93.

Shepherd, J. M. 2009. 'The Influence of Retention Politics on Judges' Voting'. *Journal of Legal Studies* 38: 169–206.

Sheppard, B. 2011. 'Judging Under Pressure. A Behavioral Examination of the Relationship Between Legal Decisionmaking and Time'. *Florida State University Law Review* 39: 931–1001.

Simon, D. 1998. 'A Psychological Model of Judicial Decision Making'. *Rutgers Law Journal* 30: 1–142.

Simon, D. 2004. 'A Third View of the Black Box. Cognitive Coherence in Legal Decision Making'. *University of Chicago Law Review* 71: 511–86.

Simon, D. 2019. 'On Juror Decision Making. An Empathic Inquiry'. *Annual Review of Law and Social Science* 15: 415–35.

Simon, D., L. B. Pham, Q. A. Le, and K. J. Holyoak. 2001. 'The Emergence of Coherence Over the Course of Decision Making'. *Journal of Experimental Psychology: Learning, Memory and Cognition* 27: 1250–60.

Simon, D., and N. Scurich. 2011. 'Lay judgments of judicial decision making'. *Journal of Empirical Legal Studies* 8 (4): 709–27.

Simon, D., and N. Scurich. 2013. 'The Effect of Legal Expert Commentary on Lay Judgments of Judicial Decision Making'. *Journal of Empirical Legal Studies* 10 (4): 797–814.

Skeem, J., N. Scurich, and J. Monahan. 2020. 'Impact of Risk Assessment on Judges' Fairness in Sentencing Relatively Poor Defendants'. *Law and Human Behavior* 44 (1): 51–59.

Slane, C. R., and C. S. Dodson. 2022. 'Eyewitness Confidence and Mock Juror Decisions of Guilt. A Meta-Analytic Review'. *Law and Human Behavior* 46–66 (1): 45.

Smalarz, L., S. Madon, and A. Turosak. 2018. 'Defendant Stereotypicality Moderates the Effect of Confession Evidence on Judgments of Guilt'. *Law and Human Behavior* 42 (4): 355–68.

Sommers, S. R. 2006. 'On Racial Diversity and Group Decision Making. Identifying Multiple Effects of Racial Composition on Jury Deliberations'. *Journal of Personality and Social Psychology* 90 (4): 597–612.

Songer, D. R. 1982. 'Consensual and Nonconsensual Decisions in Unanimous Opinions of the United States Courts of Appeals'. *American Journal of Political Science* 26: 225–39.

Sonnemans, J., and F. Van Dijk. 2012. 'Errors in Judicial Decisions: Experimental Results'. *Journal of Law, Economics, and Organization* 28 (4): 687–716.

Spamann, H., and L. Klöhn. 2016. 'Justice is Less Blind, and Less Legalistic, Than We Thought: Evidence from an Experiment with Real Judges'. *Journal of Legal Studies* 45 (2): 255–80.

Spamann, H., L. Klöhn, C. Jamin, V. Khanna, J. Z. Liu, P. Mamidi, A. Morell, and I. Reidel. 2021. 'Judges in the Lab: No Precedent Effects, No Common/Civil Law Differences'. *Journal of Legal Analysis* 13 (1): 110–26.

Spitzer, M., and E. Talley. 2013. 'Left, Right, and Center. Strategic Information Acquisition and Diversity in Judicial Panels'. *Journal of Law, Economics, & Organization* 29 (3): 638–80.

Steblay, N. M., J. Besirevic, S. M. Fulero, and B. Jimenez-Lorente. 1999. 'The Effects of Pretrial Publicity on Juror Verdicts. A Meta-analytic Review'. *Law and Human Behavior* 23 (2): 219–35.

Steblay, N., H. M. Hosch, S. E. Culhane, and A. McWethy. 2006. 'The Impact on Juror Verdicts of Judicial Instruction to Disregard Inadmissible Evidence: A Meta-Analysis'. *Law and Human Behavior* 30: 469–92.

Sternberg, S., S. Brouard, and C. Hönnige. 2021. 'The Legitimacy-Conferring Capacity of Constitutional Courts: Evidence from a Comparative Survey Experiment'. *European Journal of Political Research* 61 (2022): 973–996.

Swencionis, J. K., and P. A. Goff. 2017. 'The Psychological Science of Racial Bias and Policing'. *Psychology, Public Policy, and Law* 23 (4): 398–409.

Teichman, D., and E. Zamir. 2014. 'Judicial Decision-Making. A Behavioral Perspective'. In *Oxford Handbook of Behavioral Economics and the Law*, edited by E. Zamir and D. Teichman, 664–702. Oxford, Oxford University Press.

Thibaut, J., L. Walker, and E. A. Lind. 1972. 'Adversary Presentation and Bias in Legal Decisionmaking'. *Harvard Law Review* 86: 386–401.

Turnbull-Dugarte, S. J., and D. Devine. 2022. 'Can EU Judicial Intervention Increase Polity Scepticism? Quasi-Experimental Evidence from Spain'. *Journal of European Public Policy* 29 (6): 865–90.

Tyler, T. R. 2006. *Why People Obey the Law*. New Haven: Yale University Press.

Van Dijk, F., J. Sonnemans, and E. Bauw. 2014. 'Judicial Error by Groups and Individuals'. *Journal of Economic Behavior & Organization* 108: 224–35.

Viljoen, J. L., M. R. Jonnson, D. M. Cochrane, L. M. Vargen, and G. M. Vincent. 2019. 'Impact of Risk Assessment Instruments on Rates of Pretrial Detention, Postconviction Placements, and Release. A Systematic Review and Meta-Analysis'. *Law and Human Behavior* 43 (5): 397–420.

Wallace, D. B., and S. M. Kassin. 2012. 'Harmless Error Analysis: How Do Judges Respond to Confession Errors?' *Law and Human Behavior* 36 (2): 151–57.

Wells, G. L., and D. S. Quinlivan. 2009. 'Suggestive Eyewitness Identification Procedures and the Supreme Court's Reliability Test in Light of Eyewitness Science. 30 Years Later'. *Law and Human Behavior* 33 (1): 1–24.

Wiener, R. L., D. A. Krauss, and J. D. Lieberman. 2011. 'Mock Jury Research. Where Do We Go From Here?' *Behavioral Sciences and the Law* 29 (3): 467–79.

Wistrich, A. J., C. Guthrie, and J. J. Rachlinski. 2004. 'Can Judges Ignore Inadmissible Information. The Difficulty of Deliberately Disregarding'. *University of Pennsylvania Law Review* 153: 1251–346.

Wistrich, A. J., J. J. Rachlinski, and C. Guthrie. 2014. 'Heart Versus Head. Do Judges Follow the Law or Follow Their Feelings'. *Texas Law Review* 93: 855–923.

Woodson, B. 2015. 'Politicization and the Two Modes of Evaluating Judicial Decisions'. *Journal of Law and Courts* 3 (2): 193–221.

Zapf, P. A., J. Kukucka, S. M. Kassin, and I. E. Dror. 2018. 'Cognitive Bias in Forensic Mental Health Assessment. Evaluator Beliefs About Its Nature and Scope'. *Psychology, Public Policy, and Law* 24 (1): 1–10.

CHAPTER 14

NETWORK ANALYSIS FOR THE COMPARATIVE STUDY OF JUDICIAL BEHAVIOUR

WOLFGANG ALSCHNER

1. Introduction

Law is full of networks. Lawyers are connected by the law schools that trained them, arbitrators are connected by the cases they sit on, and judicial decisions are connected through the citations that reference them. Network analysis provides the theories, tools, and metrics to study and compare these networks of judicial actors and legal documents. Network analysis is best known for the almost artistic visualizations it produces. Dots connected by lines form colourful spiderwebs or interlaced circles. However, network analysis' most significant contribution to the comparative study of judicial behaviour lies in its intuitive simplicity and compelling simplification. By reducing the complexities of the legal world to a set of simple relations—nodes connected by ties—network analysis elegantly reveals insights, patterns, and structures, which the messiness of the real world otherwise obscures. This simplicity makes network analysis particularly useful for comparative work. It matters little whether network analysis is applied to study common or civil law jurisdictions, German or Canadian judges, social or document relations, citations or co-appointments. The theories and tools of network analysis remain the same, rendering the insights they can produce comparable.

Modern network analysis combines three strands of scholarship that make it useful for a variety of legal research projects. First, part of network analysis has its roots in sociology (Kadushin 2011). The study of how social networks form, how network structures affect individuals, and how individuals use the network, can inform research on the behaviour of legal or judicial actors. Second, modern network analysis also draws on a branch of mathematics known as graph theory (Jackson 2008). As a result, it comes with powerful tools to quantify and model network properties at scale. Third, more recently, network analysis has benefitted from complex, adaptive system research which has shown that diverse, self-organizing natural and social networks share common structural characteristics. (Watts and Strogatz 1998; Albert and Barabási 2002; Lazer et al. 2009) This, in turn, provides concepts and sets expectations to compare legal networks using common baselines.

Network analysis has received increasing attention by legal scholars (Whalen 2016; Puig 2018). In this chapter, I highlight the contributions network analysis can make, in particular, for the comparative study of judicial behaviour. Section 2 introduces basic network analysis concepts, theories, and insights, and explains why network analysis is useful for comparatively investigating courts and tribunals. Section 3 reviews the two main research streams of network analysis in law: social network analysis of legal actors and the network relations of legal documents and citations. Section 4 discusses common challenges in legal network analysis and section 5 sketches out the research frontier.

2. Why Use Network Analysis to Study and Compare Courts?

Network analysis is a useful tool in a legal scholar's method arsenal because (i) it is intuitive making results readily interpretable, (ii) it comes with a set of insightful theories, (iii) its metrics render the empirical study of networks possible and scalable, and, (iv) in combination, these attributes ensure that network analysis produces comparable results in diverse contexts.

2.1 Network Analysis Is Intuitive

Consider the simple network graph in Figure 14.1. It consists of the two elements that make up any network: *nodes*, sometimes called vertices, that are linked via *ties*, sometimes called edges. Together they form *clusters*, groupings of interconnected nodes. These groupings, in turn, are part of a larger structure, the *network*. Figure 14.1 depicts the most basic of networks. More complex networks have *directional* ties, indicating that connections flow in particular directions, or *weighted* ties, varying, for example, based the frequency or intensity of an interaction between two nodes. Moreover, some networks are *bimodal* connecting different types of nodes, for example judges may be linked to the decisions they author, or *multiplex* connecting the same nodes but through different types of ties, for example people who are both friends and colleagues. While networks can thus be rendered more complicated, simple graphs, like in Figure 14.1, help to appreciate the intuitiveness that comes with network analysis.

Inspect Figure 14.1 closely and ask yourself which node is most important in that small network. It could be node B, because it has more connections than any other

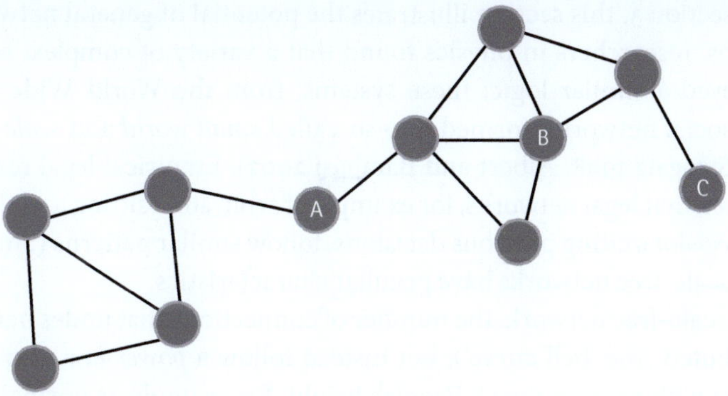

FIGURE 14.1 A simple network.

node in the network. We may imagine B being a leader among a group of friends. Or a particularly important judicial decision that is cited by other decisions in that field of law. Alternatively, one could pick node A. Although node A has few direct ties it connects two otherwise separated groups within the network. Node A functions as a bridge: ideas or information must travel through node A to go from one community to the other. We may think of A as a mediator between opposing camps or as a transition case that is cited when two areas of the law intersect. In fact, these two alternatives represent different ways network analysis assesses the importance, or *centrality*, of nodes. Node B has a high *degree centrality* because it is linked to many other nodes. Node A, in contrast, has a high *betweenness centrality* because it links different parts of the network.

Now consider a different question. Which tie is most likely to form next? Node C is connected to another node in the right-hand-side cluster. However, it is not yet connected to node B. Given that node B already has an extensive network that includes C's connection, C is likely also to connect to node B. Again, our intuition captures core insights, this time from network theory. *Triadic closure* is a common property of networks whereby missing third links in a triad are likely to form. The friends of my friend are more likely also to become my friends. Moreover, the process of *preferential attachment*, common to many networks, suggests that nodes with many existing ties are likely to attract even more. Twitter users with a large pool of followers are likely to gain more followers. Similarly, already important landmark decisions are likely to accumulate even more citations. In short, network analysis is useful because it is intuitive, and its dedicated theories and metrics offer ways to formalize these intuitions.

2.2 Network Analysis Comes with Insightful Theory

Network analysis comes with a set of useful theories that can be applied to study legal and socio-legal networks. Social network analysis, in particular, comes with a wealth of theory derived from law and sociology. Since social network analysis will be discussed in detail in section 3, this section illustrates the potential of general network theory. In the late 1990s, researchers in physics found that a variety of complex, self-organizing systems obeyed a similar logic: these systems, from the World Wide Web to brain neurons to social networks, formed into so-called *small world* and *scale-free* networks (Watts and Strogatz 1998; Albert and Barabási 2002). Empirical legal researchers have since observed that legal networks, for example of arbitrators sitting together on cases or of judicial decisions citing previous decisions, follow similar patterns (Smith 2007; Puig 2014). Such scale-free networks have peculiar characteristics.

First, in a scale-free network, the number of connections that nodes have are not normally distributed (the 'bell curve'), but instead follow a *power law distribution* (an L-shaped curve with smooth dent). People's height, for example, is normally distributed. Few humans are either extremely tall or extremely short; most of us are of intermediate height. Similarly, in a network with normally distributed ties, most nodes would have several connections and few nodes would have no ties or a lot of them. Mediocrity is the rule. In a power law setting, however, most nodes have very few connections and a few nodes have most connections. It is a world of extremes. Power-law structures are common to legal networks, too. In international investment law, most arbitrators sit on very few cases, but a few arbitrator 'superstars' sit on many cases (Puig 2014; Langford, Behn, and Lie 2017). Likewise, across a wide range of domestic and international law jurisdictions, researchers have found that most cases receive few or no citations; meanwhile a small set of landmark judgements attract a large share of references (Fowler et al. 2007; Smith 2007; Lupu and Voeten 2012; Neale 2013; Agnoloni and Pagallo 2015; Pauwelyn 2016; Alschner and Charlotin 2018).

Partly responsible for the scale-free nature of these networks is the process of *preferential attachment*: nodes that already have many connections are likely to attract even more (Barabási 2009). The specific drivers of preferential attachment vary depending on the context. Arbitrators with many appointments may make for safer choices than newcomers. An important case is more likely to be known and thus cited, which in turn further increases its visibility. Attention breeds more attention (Merryman 1954). Whatever the factors at work, scale-free networks share that self-reinforcing dynamic, also known as the richer-get-richer phenomenon, which turns stars into superstars and precedents into landmark decisions. That, in part, helps explain why a small number of academics, judges, law review articles, and decisions tend to shape the law disproportionately. As Pauwelyn put it, in these networks 'minority rules' (Pauwelyn 2016).

The scale-free nature of many networks has important implications. On the one hand, scale-free networks are resilient to change. For example, newcomers to the arbitral appointment market face an uphill struggle as parties prefer to rely on incumbents with proven track record (Puig 2014). Researchers have found, for example, that it will take 2,250 years for gender parity to emerge in the male-dominated community of investment arbitrators, assuming present-day trends were to continue (Bjorklund et al. 2020). Network dynamics further entrenching the most central incumbents are, in part, to blame. At the same time, scale-free networks are vulnerable to targeted disruptions—think of a power grid where the most highly connected nodes fail or a precedential network where a landmark case is overturned. A few central nodes hold the network together. The important role of core connecting nodes links to a second property of such networks—their 'small-world' nature.

Small-world networks are not made up of random connections. They, instead, consist of densely connected node groupings, known as *clusters*, which are in turn connected to other clusters via bridge nodes (Watts and Strogatz 1998). These constellations make small-world networks easily traversable from end to end in just a few steps ('short average path length'). Colloquially, this is known as 'six degrees of separation', based on the idea that people are connected to each other in six relations or less. The implications of small-world structures are profound. Given the high connectivity, ideas or legal change can easily go 'viral' in a small-world network. Bridge nodes and highly connected nodes are of vital importance as gatekeepers and amplifiers of information travelling through the network. Network analysis can thereby reveal possible choke points or identify power brokers. These concepts, in turn, can help study legal processes, such as the diffusion of legal norms, and the development of case law or power dynamics within judiciaries (Sunstein 2000; Katz 2008). Given that many legal networks display small-world characteristics (Smith 2007; Katz 2008; Ridi 2019), network theory can make important contributions to the study of law.

2.3 Network Analysis Provides New and Useful Metrics

Network analysis is also a boon for the empirical study of courts and tribunals because it provides scalable techniques to explore social and normative dynamics in legal networks. In particular, (i) *node* metrics allow measuring the importance of specific actors or cases within a legal network; (ii) *grouping* metrics help dissect the network's structure by identifying clusters; and (iii) *network* metrics enable characterizations of the network as a whole, such as its density or sparsity.

Node metrics. Assessing the role and importance of nodes is among the most widespread uses of network analysis. In the analysis of social networks, they are crucial to identify power brokers or bridge ties, discussed below (Puig 2018). When it comes to legal networks, node metrics enable empirical analysis and scale, clarify, or challenge doctrinal studies (Šadl and Olsen 2017). Since the latter use-case may not be intuitive, consider the question of how to identify a court's most important cases. Although textbooks and scholarly writing routinely describe specific judicial decisions as landmark cases, this label typically results from a qualitative assessment. As Šadl and Olsen point out, such analyses can suffer from blind spots or 'a tendency to succumb to herd behavior' (Šadl and Olsen 2017, 330). Derlén and Lindholm, for example, contrast node metrics derived from legal citations to textbook accounts of leading EU law cases and show that some decisions, like *Bosman*, are underappreciated, while the importance of others, like *van Gend en Loos*, is exaggerated (Derlén and Lindholm 2014). Citation network analysis thus provides a complementary and, at times, corrective perspective and allows us to evaluate the importance of a case quantitatively by situating it in a larger jurisprudential network.

The place of a node in a network is known as its centrality. Centrality comes in different forms and captures different node characteristics (Carmichael et al. 2017). The simplest form of centrality is *degree centrality*, which counts the connections a node has. *Betweenness centrality* evaluates the importance of a node as a 'bridge' node based on the shortest paths that run through it. *Eigenvector centrality* measures consider a node's neighbourhood in evaluating centrality. In directed networks, *authority* scores, for example, assess to what extent a node is referenced by other nodes that in turn are widely connected, while *hub* scores assess whether a node references other nodes that are widely referenced. In citation analysis, high authority scores are a good proxy for landmark cases, whereas cases with high hub scores make for insightful reading to learn about an area of the law because they reference crucial decisions. Centrality measures are found in virtually all legal network studies but are particularly important in citation studies to determine the role and importance of cases as precedents (Fowler et al. 2007; Smith 2007; Neale 2013; Carmichael et al. 2017).

Grouping metrics. So-called community detection algorithms automatically spot clusters within a network. Those measures can be used to group nodes into communities of legal actors or decisions. They reveal cases that are often cited together or arbitrators that often sit on the same panels. Some caution is warranted when applying such grouping metrics. Different equally plausible community detection algorithms exist that can yield different results (van Kuppevelt, van Dijck, and Schaper 2020). Hence, community detection requires careful validation. A selection of validation strategies, such as comparison with existing meta data and comparing techniques, exist and are discussed further in section 4. Scholars have used grouping metrics to identify communities of cases that cite each other with greater frequency. For example, Lupu and Voeten use community detection to show that the European Court of Human Rights' precedents cluster around common legal issues rather than respondent state characteristics suggesting that the choice of precedent is driven by law rather than politics (Lupu and Voeten 2012).

Network metrics. Quantifying network characteristics gives researchers a bird's-eye view of a network. How dense or how sparse is it? What is the average shortest path to traverse it? These high-level network measures can reveal surprising differences among network structures that are particularly useful for comparative purposes. Ridi, for example, found that the network of decisions by the International Court of Justice (ICJ) that are connected by citations is much sparser than the equivalent network of decisions by the World Trade Organization's Appellate Body (Ridi 2019). This, in turn, tells researchers much about the role of precedent and institutional dynamics within the two systems. The Appellate Body deals with a relatively narrow and self-contained set of subject matters, renders decisions typically without dissent, and is supported by an influential secretariat of highly skilled trade lawyers (Mavroidis and Kim 2018; Pelc 2022). The results are decisions firmly rooted and related to prior cases. The ICJ, in contrast, deals with more diverse matters, allows diverging opinion, and lacks a cohesive secretariat that would streamline decisions. As a result, there are fewer opportunities for cross-references and prior cases are cited less often and more ad hoc. In short, networks are mirrors of the legal or socio-legal structures they represent and network measures allow to quantify these characteristics.

2.4 Network Analysis as an Ideal Tool for Comparative Analysis

The intuitions, theories, and metrics of network analysis can be applied to all types of legal networks. That, in turn, facilitates the comparative analysis of judicial behaviour. Network analysis allows us to study similar dynamics in different legal systems, creating new and unprecedented opportunities for comparative legal research. For example, by mapping citation networks in common law and civil law jurisdictions, network analysis can help confirm conventional wisdom or challenge widely held truths on the differences between the two systems. Similarly, by investigating the network of judicial actors, researchers can systematically trace how judicial careers differ across jurisdictions and map how that affects jurisprudence. Network analysis is so attractive to comparative scholars because it initially strips away the myriad differences between legal regimes by reducing the world to nodes and ties. These differences can then be brought in at the end to interpret and make sense of varying network structures. Unsurprisingly, then, recent decades have seen an important growth of scholarship applying network analysis to diverse areas of law.

3. Legal Network Analysis

Scholarship applying network analysis to study law and the courts can be grouped into two camps. One camp studies judicial actors and investigates their social relations drawing on social network analysis. The other camp studies legal document networks. While this can include the links between laws, patents, or treaties (see e.g. Katz and Bommarito 2014; Pauwelyn and Alschner 2015; Boulet, Mazzega, and Bourcier 2018), most work focuses on citation networks investigating the links between judicial decisions through cross-references.

The two camps share many points of connection. They use similar methods to study network structures, and both can shed light on the law's normative evolution. As Dan Katz explains, 'the manner in which doctrine changes cannot be divorced from the manner of self-organized social structure relevant actors confront' (Katz 2008, 981). Differently put, the network of legal actors and of legal documents are deeply linked.

However, there are also important differences between social network analysis and other network studies (Kadushin 2011). First, network analysis of legal actors can leverage and adapt concepts that govern social networks generally to explore and explain network dynamics and formation. While citation networks, on the surface, may resemble social networks, the underlying forces that determine the placement and distribution of nodes and ties are very different. Most importantly, social actors are subject to feedback loops. Individuals shape network structures, but these same structures, in turn, also affect individual behaviour and preferences (Kadushin 2011, 19). Document networks, in contrast, lack such feedback loops because they are time-bound and necessarily directional: a later document can cite an earlier one but a past case cannot cite a future one. It is thus important to discuss the network analysis of legal actors and legal documents separately.

3.1 Network Analysis of Judicial Actors

Social network analysis provides useful concepts that legal scholars have used to study social networks in law. Take *homophily* first. Homophily suggests that individuals with similar characteristics or views tend to connect with each other (Kadushin 2011, 19). Feedback loops further entrench such homophily. As Kadushin explains:

> [I]f people flock together, it appears that there are four processes involved: (1) the same kinds of people come together; (2) people influence one another and in the process become alike; (3) people can end up in the same place; (4) and once they are in the same place, the very place influences them to become alike.
>
> (Kadushin 2011, 20)

Homophily thus produces homogeneity within groups crowding out alternative views and reinforces divisions between groups.

Homophily is also present in legal networks. In a study of the social network of the US law professoriate, Katz et al. found that a small number of institutions (Harvard and Yale) train the majority of US law professors. According to Katz et al., 'individuals with similar intellectual commitments gravitate to the same institution'(Katz et al. 2011, 97). Once there, the views of these individuals are becoming further alike. These elite institutions then become what Katz et al. term 'intellectual super-spreaders': they send their graduates to other universities. The resulting network of law professors is marked by an intellectual homophily that creates a more homogenous intellectual landscape than the diversity of US law schools and of US society would otherwise suggest (Katz et al. 2011). As a byproduct, this network structure entrenches existing hierarchies as the same schools and ideas dominate the legal academy (Kennedy 2007). Social network analysis is thus particularly useful to critical legal scholars interested in revealing power asymmetries embedded in the legal system.

A second social network phenomenon is *influence*: connected actors tend to influence one another and nodes with many connections have more influence than others. Network analysis thereby helps reveal the *social capital* of individuals within a group (Kadushin 2011). Applying these social network insights to the study of investment arbitrators, Puig found that a small set of repeatedly appointed arbitrators form the power brokers of the system (Puig 2014). Katz et al. discovered a similar dynamic in the network of the US judiciary modelled as clerkship connections between judges. They argue that the place of judges in the network mirrors their 'social prestige'. Through the process of preferential attachment, clerks in search of upward mobility opportunity are attracted to judges who are at the centre of the network, which then further enhances the judge's social role (Katz and Stafford 2010, 500–03). Perhaps unsurprisingly then, among the judges with the highest centrality scores in the study were several future appointees to the US Supreme Court.

Beyond the usefulness of these studies for understanding power relations among judicial actors, scholars also highlight the importance of social network structures for the evolution of the law. Katz et al. note that 'the micro-motives of federal jurists and the professional and social interactions between jurists, at least in part, help generate systemic changes in the common law' (Katz 2008, 981). With respect to the professorial network they point out that 'a deep relationship [exists] between the American legal academy and the development of American law' (Katz et al. 2011, 76). Similarly, Puig explains that 'the legal knowledge advanced and preferred by central arbitrators, and with that their political preferences will likely become more dominant' (Puig 2014, 50). Social influence thus translates into normative influence.

A frontier for students of legal networks lies in systematically investigating how the network structure of social actors impacts legal evolution. Two avenues, one empirical and one theoretical, appear particularly fruitful. On the empirical side, scholars could validate whether central actors in academia or the judiciary really use their network position to 'generate systemic changes in the common law' or to render their 'political preferences … more dominant'. Such research is likely to require combining social legal networks with legal document networks to construct bipartite networks—networks with different types of nodes. For example, combining Puig's investment arbitrator network with a network of citations between investment awards could reveal how strongly dominant arbitrators shape precedent in investment arbitration.

On the theoretical side, legal researchers could draw on the rich network diffusion literature to trace how legal innovations travel through legal academia or the judiciary. Sociologists have pointed to the importance of 'weak ties' and 'structural holes' in a network (Granovetter 1973; Burt 2004). These nodes serve to bridge otherwise sparsely connected clusters of the network and are vital conduits for the diffusion of information and new ideas through a network. As a result, these nodes are often agents of change within a network: 'Structural holes are not for satisfying present needs but for creating change and movement' (Kadushin 2011, 66–67). The role of 'structural holes' and 'weak ties' in legal networks can thus shed light on why and how some novel legal concepts go viral while others never catch on.

Network scholars speak of 'structural similarity' when nodes share similar patterns of relationships with other nodes (Kadushin 2011, 49). Studying similar structural patterns across jurisdictions can facilitate comparative legal research. Think of apex court justices occupying similar roles in judiciary networks. For example, Antonin

Scalia began his career as a relative outsider with fringe views on statutory interpretation. His appointment to the US Supreme Court then provided a platform to turn originalism into a mainstream approach of legal reasoning. He thereby shaped both the judiciary network (by inspiring disciples) and the legal network (by affecting the outcome of decisions or choice of precedents). For comparativists, Scalia's path and influence raises interesting general questions that network analysis can help explore. When do outsiders become insiders? And what does it mean for both the judiciary and the law when actors from the network periphery move to its centre? By combining theories of structural similarity with networks of judicial actors and normative change, social network analysis can thus provide an illuminating tool for comparative legal scholars.

3.2 Legal Citation Network Analysis

Most network analysis by legal scholars, however, is dedicated to the study of document networks, first and foremost citation networks. Several reasons explain the popularity of legal citation analysis. Citations are useful (although imperfect) proxies for empirically investigating core normative phenomena. While citing a case is not the same as applying it as part of the legal reasoning process and legal scholars need to be attentive to the difference, citations do provide inroads into the study of precedent, stare decisis, dissent, and normative change or continuity. Moreover, citations are a readily identifiable, explicit references, which makes them easier to detect than indirect or implicit links that may connect cases (such as shared legal principles at issue). Finally, citations typically come in relatively uniform styles making them easier to extract automatically using software.

The body of legal citation scholarship is large and rapidly growing. This summary merely provides an illustrative snapshot into four areas of particular relevance to scholars studying comparative judicial behaviour.

First, researchers have used citation networks to apply network theory to law. After scholars outside of law had noted the propensity of scale-free networks, legal researchers asked whether similar structures pervaded the 'web of law'. Smith, in collaboration with a legal technology provider, investigated the cross-references between more than 4 million cited US cases (state and federal). His research confirmed that the US web of law shared many characteristics with real-world scale-free networks: (i) most cases are cited once, but a few are cited thousands of times ('power law distribution') and (ii) cases are grouped into interconnected clusters making it easier to traverse the network in a few steps ('small world') (Smith 2007). Other scholars have since made similar observations in relation to other legal systems, including Canada, Italy, and in relation to international courts (Neale 2013; Agnoloni and Pagallo 2015; Ridi 2019). This branch of scholarship underscores the promise of applying network theory to law and also demonstrates how insights from fields far removed from law can inform our collective understanding of legal systems.

Second, scholars have also probed different network metrics to map them more accurately to normative questions such as the importance of precedent. Although it is intuitive that more citations of a case roughly correlate with its importance for legal practitioners and scholars, what exact metric best depicts a case's importance is more challenging to establish. First, complicating the exercise is the time-bound nature of citations: more recent cases had less opportunity to accumulate citations than older ones. Some scholars have proposed time-aware metrics to account for that effect either by homing in on recent citations or by normalizing citations based on possible cited opportunities (Tarissan and Nollez-Goldbach 2015; Carmichael et al. 2017). Second, raw citation counts fail to differentiate between cases at the centre of the network and peripheral ones, necessitating network-aware metrics. As noted above, a popular measure to capture the place of a node in a directed citation network is its *authority score* that weighs the number of inward citations by the importance of the citing cases. A decision that is highly cited by other highly cited cases thus scores higher, which helps to identify landmark decisions (Fowler et al. 2007; Fowler and Jeon 2008). These studies have also shown how authority scores can trace the importance of cases over time tracking their rise to prominence or precipitous decline. Another, network-aware measure, is PageRank, the original Google search algorithm, that models how a user would randomly explore a network. Since a user in a directed citation network can only go back in time, PageRank is biased towards giving higher scores to older cases (Derlén and Lindholm 2017). But this property has its use. According to Carmichael at el., it helps to reveal cases of first impression (rather than landmark decisions) where courts first encountered a novel issue (Carmichael et al. 2017).

Third, citation analysis has been used to challenge doctrine or conventional wisdom. Given the amount of information to process, traditional commentary on the importance or influence of cases is necessarily impressionistic. By formalizing the relations between cases and quantifying their relative placement in a citation network, network measures can challenge prevailing accounts. As Šadl and Olsen put it, network analysis 'can provide empirical evidence to validate hunches and prove legal intuitions correct ... yet such methods also provide a necessary means of critically evaluating the research practice of the discipline itself' (Šadl and Olsen 2017, 330). As noted above, Derlén and Lindholm use citation networks to challenge textbook accounts of the EU's landmark cases. They argue that cases with high authority scores, such as *Bosman*, do not receive the attention they deserve in textbooks (Derlén and Lindholm 2014).

Finally, citation analysis can help compare and contrast courts and legal systems. As noted, the density or sparsity of a citation network can tell researchers much of the relative importance of precedent and the institutionalization of a court. Citation analyses can also reveal whether precedent is embedded in argumentation or used ritualistically. Work on the Court of Justice of the European Union, for example, has found that citations are more about form than substance with the Court citing cases without following them (Panagis and Sadl 2010, 7). This has been linked to the Court's institutional structure: multiple languages and standardized translation produce highly stylized texts (McAuliffe 2013). In contrast, the ICJ has been shown actively to integrate cited precedent into its normative reasoning (Alschner and Charlotin 2018). In short, citation networks provide a rich source for the comparative study of judicial behaviour.

4. Challenges of Legal Network Analysis

Researchers applying network analysis to study judicial behaviour comparatively face several challenges relating to (i) data availability, (ii) matching method with legal research question, and (iii) validating insights gained from network analysis.

4.1 Datasets and Missing Data

Network analysis typically requires data in the form of a so-called *link list* or an *adjacency matrix*. At its simplest, a link list consists of two columns where each row indicates the connected nodes. In directed networks, one column is the target column, the other is the source column. An adjacency matrix contains that same information but in a different form: row names and column names indicate nodes and intersecting cells indicate whether a link exists. Network analysis programs like *Visone* or *Gephi* as well as programming languages like *R* can build networks and calculate network measures based on these link lists or adjacency matrices. Researchers can, subsequently, enrich the analysis through additional node or link-related data, for example to weigh connections or colour-code visualizations.

In most settings, however, network data will have to be compiled and curated first. This can raise challenges relating to data access, data extraction, and missing data. Data access is typically a problem when it comes to actor networks as information about the ties that connect individuals need to be compiled laboriously. Moreover, some interpersonal connections may be unknown or would raise ethical concerns if revealed. Networks built on legal documents often face a different hurdle: while judicial documents are often in the public domain in one form or another, it is often difficult to mine them to extract the information relevant for building a document or citation networks. Researchers may thus be compelled to digitize text and collaborate with information extraction experts to extract their variables of interest. The most challenging aspect of network analysis, however, is missing data.

Missing data is a problem for all types of empirical research because missing information is not randomly distributed but often the result of systematic gaps. Some types of actors systematically decline to take part in surveys, some court documents remain systematically unpublished, and some documents are systematically kept outside of the public domain. Although systematically missing data creates biases in all empirical research, the problem is particularly acute in network analysis. Picture a network of your friends and then take yourself out of that network. Once key nodes are missing it becomes impossible to discern what structure holds the network together and all subsequent measurements are off. As a result, care must be taken that researchers reflect on the dangers of missing observations and mitigate it, for example by focusing on parts of the network where information is verifiably complete.

4.2 Matching Network Analysis Concepts with Legal Questions

A second core challenge relates to matching question and method. In a nascent field of scholarship, such as legal network analysis, a methodological orthodoxy has yet to fully emerge (van Kuppevelt, van Dijck, and Schaper 2020). As a result, definite answers to what network analysis method is best suited for what legal research question still need to be found. Nevertheless, some ground truths are beginning to emerge.

First, the choice of method or metric is ultimately dictated by the research question. Writing about legal citation analysis, Hitt, for example, reminds us that '[s]cholars should explicitly decide which theoretical construct... they aim to measure. Analysts must then consider both which type of citations (only deferential or everything) and which level(s) of the hierarchy to analyze based on their theoretical target' (Hitt 2016, 76). According to Hitt, where scholars aim to study the influence of a precedent rather than its overall relevance, they should focus only on cases that follow a precedent and exclude cases that merely reference or even critique it. More generally, scholars need to reflect deeply on their research question and choice of method to be sure the two align.

Second, where scholars investigate social networks of legal actors, they do not have to reinvent the wheel. As noted above, social network scholars have spent decades aligning network methods with the study of specific social phenomena. Unless there is a valid reason to suppose that network dynamics work differently in a particular legal actor network, legal scholars should tap into that existing scholarship.

Third, some methods are more robust than others. Existing scholarship provides profound reflections and useful suggestions on the selection of appropriate node metrics. Although the debate on the appropriateness of specific metrics is far from over, scholars can be expected to make informed decisions about which measure to choose to answer a particular research question. In contrast, on other fronts, network analysis methods are like playing dart in the dark. Node grouping algorithms may provide useful, intuitive groupings or they may not. Telling the difference can be hard because these measures are challenging to validate.

4.3 Validating Insights Gained through Network Analysis

When do researchers know that they picked the correct measure or revealed the correct clusters in a network? Validation of network analysis is difficult for two reasons. First, as noted, there is often no established convention on what metric is best aligned with a research question. Second, the very purpose of network analysis is, at times, to reveal hitherto unknown structures and to challenge conventional wisdom. That, however, implies that known benchmarks cannot be readily used to confirm results.

Van Kuppevelt, van Dijck, and Schaper provide two useful strategies to still engage in a form of validation (van Kuppevelt, van Dijck, and Schaper 2020). First, where there is no consensus on the appropriate method to calculate clusters or centrality, researchers can apply different methods and compare and report on the results. That approach is emerging as standard practice in other fields, such as natural language processing as well, where minor methodological choices can have important consequences (Denny and Spirling 2018). Where results between conceptually similar measures yield similar results, researchers can be more confident about their findings. Second, researchers should wherever possible benchmark their findings against some known data. Clustering algorithms may be compared against meta data on node characteristics and centrality measures could be contrasted against either conventional textbook accounts, expert rankings, or other data, such as click results from search engine users that may also proxy case importance. Finally, political scientists have suggested to use the predictive capacity of a measure to gauge its validity (Fowler and Jeon 2008; Carmichael et al. 2017). The intuition is that a good measure of a case's importance, for example, should be able to accurately forecast future citations to the decision.

5. Networks and Beyond

Legal network analysis is still in its infancy. Many of its theories still wait to be widely applied and many courts and tribunals have yet to be analysed through a network lens. Overcoming the above-described challenges will be key in further popularizing the method. By building readymade datasets of legal networks, establishing conventions for matching methods and legal research questions, and working towards the systemic validation of results, the field will become more accessible to newcomers. In addition, two avenues of research are likely to shape the future of legal network analysis: (i) networks and natural language processing, and (ii) inferential network analysis.

5.1 Networks and Natural Language Processing

Natural language processing investigates text as data (Grimmer and Stewart 2013). Together with machine learning, it allows researchers to process text information in vast quantities automatically. That has repercussions for network analysis on two fronts. First, it becomes easier to create networks from text data through automated information extraction. Indeed, one reason for the growth of scholarship on citation networks is the ability to extract these citations from text automatically. Second, and more interesting for analysis purposes, natural language analysis can enrich the study of networks by generating new node and link characteristics. That is most obvious for legal citation networks.

A frequent critique of citation analysis is that references by themselves tell us little. What matters is *why* the reference was placed and *what* type of relations it describes. Is a citation a mere formality or does it signal actual engagement with precedent? Is a citation used to follow, distinguish, overrule, or critique a prior decision? Natural language analysis can provide insights on these questions. Various methods exist to automatically classify decisions by subject matter or to mine the context of a citation for key words that would indicate how a precedent is used. In the context of the ICJ, for example, Alschner and Charlotin used a text-as-data technique known as *topic modelling* to show that the same cited paragraph was used in support of different legal propositions (Alschner and Charlotin 2018). More challenging is the identification of a citation's treatment (i.e. where it follows, distinguishes, etc.), because such treatment can take various textual guises. Future machine learning models trained on citations with identified treatment could be used to automatically label citations with unknown treatment.

The promise that such additional information holds is immense. Citation networks could be constructed by subject matter, for example allowing researchers to look at citation changes in niche areas of the law. In addition, researchers could, as advocated by Hitt, investigate different treatment categories separately, drawing a line between cases that actually serve as precedent and those cases that are distinguished, overruled, or critiqued (Hitt 2016). Combining network connections between cases with topic similarity connections can furthermore provide a more holistic representation of the case law space with implications for better search and analysis (Dadgostari et al. 2021). Taken together, these natural language processing approaches would move network analysis away from the stylized study of large reference networks and turn it into a tailored tool for mapping specific normative changes or doctrinal disagreements.

5.2 Network Modelling and Inferential Network Analysis

Up to now, this chapter has discussed network analysis as a tool to *describe* existing social structures or citation dynamics. Inferential network analysis, in contrast, is about *explaining* network structure. Why do networks come in the shapes that they do? Inferential work uses models to answer that question (Whalen 2016). These models create counterfactual network structures that can be compared with the actual network to identify factors that determine structure.

Given their different properties, social networks and citation networks require different models. Exponential Random Graph Models (ERGMs) are popular for inferential social network analysis; in contrast, citation networks that by their nature contain only backward-looking directed links can be modelled by Directed Acyclic Graphs

(DAGs) (van Kuppevelt, van Dijck, and Schaper 2020). Each of these models can be implemented in programming environments such as *R*.[1] However, technical barriers to entry remain high as compared to descriptive network analysis.

Nevertheless, network modelling and inferential network analysis promise important insights in exploring the drivers of network formation. In a recent study, Leitão, Lehmann, and Olsen, for example, concluded that a large portion of citations in the European Court of Human Rights can be explained by a preferential attachment model confirming the insight that known dynamics of scale-free networks also underpin the structure of citation networks (Leitão, Lehmann, and Olsen 2019). Overall, such modelling is still in its infancy, in part because it requires dedicated, interdisciplinary collaboration.

6. Conclusion

In summary, network analysis provides a promising set of theories, tools, and metrics to study judicial behaviour comparatively. Whether it is applied to social networks in law or legal document and citation networks, it helps to focus the analysis on structures built on relationships. By reducing the world to nodes and ties, deep insights can be gained about how actor and document networks form and operate and what impacts they have on the law that they help to shape and create.

This contribution suggested a few avenues of how network analyses can help study judicial behaviour across courts and tribunals. Network analysis places actors or documents in their network context and evaluates their importance, roles, and influences. Entire networks themselves can be studied too, widening the comparison from individuals to the institutions or legal fields in which they operate.

This chapter sought to equip scholars with essentials to apply network analysis to their field and research questions. It highlighted core network theory concepts from triadic closure to preferential attachment and introduced the most popular network measures from node metrics, such as degree or betweenness centrality to network metrics such as density. It also discussed obstacles facing scholars applying network analysis to law highlighting challenges relating to (missing) data, methods, and validation. Finally, it concluded by sketching out the research frontier of scholars seeking to combine network analysis with natural language process and move from descriptive to inferential network analysis.

Note

1. See the GGDAG package for DAGS (https://cran.r-project.org/web/packages/ggdag/vignettes/intro-to-ggdag.html) and the ERGM package for ERGMs (https://cran.r-project.org/web/packages/ergm/ergm.pdf).

References

Agnoloni, Tommaso, and Ugo Pagallo. 2015. 'The Case Law of the Italian Constitutional Court, Its Power Laws, and the Web of Scholarly Opinions'. In *Proceedings of the 15th International Conference on Artificial Intelligence and Law*, 151–55. ICAIL '15. New York, NY: Association for Computing Machinery. https://doi.org/10.1145/2746090.2746108.

Albert, Réka, and Albert-László Barabási. 2002. 'Statistical Mechanics of Complex Networks'. *Reviews of Modern Physics* 74 (1): 47–97. https://doi.org/10.1103/RevModPhys.74.47.

Alschner, Wolfgang, and Damien Charlotin. 2018. 'The Growing Complexity of the International Court of Justice's Self-Citation Network'. *European Journal of International Law* 29 (1): 83–112.

Barabási, Albert-László. 2009. 'Scale-Free Networks: A Decade and Beyond'. *Science* 325 (5939): 412–13. https://doi.org/10.1126/science.1173299.

Bjorklund, Andrea K., Daniel Behn, Susan D. Franck, Chiara Giorgetti, Won Kidane, Arnaud de Nanteuil, and Emilia Onyema. 2020. 'The Diversity Deficit in International Investment Arbitration'. *The Journal of World Investment & Trade* 21 (2–3): 410–40. https://doi.org/10.1163/22119000-12340177.

Boulet, Romain, Pierre Mazzega, and Danièle Bourcier. 2018. 'Network Approach to the French System of Legal Codes Part II: The Role of the Weights in a Network'. *Artificial Intelligence and Law* 26 (1): 23–47. https://doi.org/10.1007/s10506-017-9204-y.

Burt, Ronald S. 2004. 'Structural Holes and Good Ideas'. *American Journal of Sociology* 110 (2): 349–99. https://doi.org/10.1086/421787.

Carmichael, Iain, James Wudel, Michael Kim, and James Jushchuk. 2017. 'Examining the Evolution of Legal Precedent through Citation Network Analysis'. *North Carolina Law Review* 96: 44.

Dadgostari, Faraz, Mauricio Guim, Peter A. Beling, Michael A. Livermore, and Daniel N. Rockmore. 2021. 'Modeling Law Search as Prediction'. *Artificial Intelligence and Law* 29 (1): 3–34. https://doi.org/10.1007/s10506-020-09261-5.

Denny, Matthew J., and Arthur Spirling. 2018. 'Text Preprocessing for Unsupervised Learning: Why It Matters, When It Misleads, and What to Do about It'. *Political Analysis* 26 (2): 168–89. https://doi.org/10.1017/pan.2017.44.

Derlén, Mattias, and Johan Lindholm. 2014. 'Goodbye van Gend En Loos, Hello Bosman? Using Network Analysis to Measure the Importance of Individual CJEU Judgments'. *European Law Journal* 20 (5): 667–87. https://doi.org/10.1111/eulj.12077.

Derlén, Mattias, and Johan Lindholm. 2017. 'Is It Good Law? Network Analysis and the CJEU's Internal Market Jurisprudence'. *Journal of International Economic Law* 20 (2): 257–77. https://doi.org/10.1093/jiel/jgx011.

Fowler, James H., and Sangick Jeon. 2008. 'The Authority of Supreme Court Precedent'. *Social Networks* 30 (1): 16–30. https://doi.org/10.1016/j.socnet.2007.05.001.

Fowler, James H., Timothy R. Johnson, James F. Spriggs II, Sangick Jeon, and Paul J. Wahlbeck. 2007. 'Network Analysis and the Law: Measuring the Legal Importance of Precedents at the U.S. Supreme Court'. *Political Analysis* 15 (3): 324–46.

Granovetter, Mark S. 1973. 'The Strength of Weak Ties'. *American Journal of Sociology* 78 (6): 1360–80.

Grimmer, Justin, and Brandon M. Stewart. 2013. 'Text as Data: The Promise and Pitfalls of Automatic Content Analysis Methods for Political Texts'. *Political Analysis* 21 (3): 267–97. https://doi.org/10.1093/pan/mps028.

Hitt, Matthew P. 2016. 'Measuring Precedent in a Judicial Hierarchy'. *Law & Society Review* 50 (1): 57–81.

Jackson, Matthew O. 2008. *Social and Economic Networks*. Princeton: Princeton University Press.

Kadushin, Charles. 2011. *Understanding Social Networks: Theories, Concepts, and Findings*. Oxford: Oxford University Press.

Katz, Daniel M. 2008. 'Social Architecture, Judicial Peer Effects and the "Evolution" of the Law: Toward a Positive Theory of Judicial Social Structure'. *Georgia State University Law Review* 24: 27.

Katz, Daniel M., and Derek K. Stafford. 2010. 'Hustle and Flow: A Social Network Analysis of the American Federal Judiciary'. *Ohio State Law Journal* 71: 457.

Katz, Daniel Martin, and Michael J. Bommarito. 2014. 'Measuring the Complexity of the Law: The United States Code'. *Artificial Intelligence and Law* 22 (4): 337–74. https://doi.org/10.1007/s10506-014-9160-8.

Katz, Daniel, Josha Gubler, Jon Zelner, and Michael Bommarito. 2011. 'Reproduction of Hierarchy? A Social Network Analysis of the American Law Professoriate'. *Journal of Legal Education* 61 (1): 76.

Kennedy, Duncan. 2007. *Legal Education and the Reproduction of Hierarchy: A Polemic Against the System*. New York: NYU Press.

Kuppevelt, Dafne van, Gijs van Dijck, and Marcel Schaper. 2020. 'Purposes and Challenges of Legal Citation Network Analysis on Case Law'. In *Computational Legal Studies*, edited by Ryan Whalen, 265–92. Edward Elgar Publishing. https://doi.org/10.4337/9781788977456.00017.

Langford, Malcolm, Daniel Behn, and Runar Hilleren Lie. 2017. 'The Revolving Door in International Investment Arbitration'. *Journal of International Economic Law* 20 (1): 301–32. https://doi.org/10.1093/jiel/jgx018.

Lazer, David, Alex (Sandy) Pentland, Lada Adamic, Sinan Aral, Albert Laszlo Barabasi, Devon Brewer, Nicholas Christakis, et al. 2009. 'Life in the Network: The Coming Age of Computational Social Science'. *Science (New York, N.Y.)* 323 (5915): 721–23.

Leitão, Jorge C., Sune Lehmann, and Henrik Palmer Olsen. 2019. 'Quantifying Long-Term Impact of Court Decisions'. *Applied Network Science* 4 (1): 3. https://doi.org/10.1007/s41109-018-0110-3.

Lupu, Yonatan, and Erik Voeten. 2012. 'Precedent in International Courts: A Network Analysis of Case Citations by the European Court of Human Rights'. *British Journal of Political Science* 42 (2): 413–39. https://doi.org/10.1017/S0007123411000433.

Mavroidis, Petros, and Evan Kim. 2018. 'Dissenting Opinions in the WTO Appellate Body: Drivers of Their Issuance & Implications for the Institutional Jurisprudence'. *European University Institute, Robert Schuman Centre for Advanced Studies, Global Governance Programme Working Paper No. RSCAS 2018/51*, January. https://scholarship.law.columbia.edu/faculty_scholarship/2287.

McAuliffe, Karen. 2013. 'Precedent at the Court of Justice of the European Union: The Linguistic Aspect'. *Law and Language. Current Legal Issues* 15: 483–92.

Merryman, John Henry. 1954. 'The Authority of Authority: What the California Supreme Court Cited in 1950'. *Stanford Law Review* 6 (4): 613. https://doi.org/10.2307/1226493.

Neale, Thom. 2013. 'Citation Analysis of Canadian Case Law'. *Journal of Open Access to Law* 1: 1–60.

Panagis, Yannis, and Urska Sadl. 2010. 'Making EU (Case) Law: Evidence from a Paragraph-to-Paragraph Network on the Cases Concerning the Citizen-Ship of the European Union'. http://www.karlbranting.net/law-and-big-data-workshop/LawBD-2015_submission_3.pdf.

Pauwelyn, Joost. 2016. 'Minority Rules: Precedent and Participation before the WTO Appellate Body'. In *Establishing Judicial Authority in International Economic Law*, edited by Joanna Jemoelniak, Laura Nielsen, and Henrik Palmer Olsen, 141–72. Cambridge University Press. http://papers.ssrn.com/abstract=2474611.

Pauwelyn, Joost, and Wolfgang Alschner. 2015. 'Forget about the WTO: The Network of Relations between Preferential Trade Agreements (PTAs) and "Double PTAs"'. In *Trade Cooperation*, edited by Andreas Dür and Manfred Elsig, 497–532. Cambridge: Cambridge University Press. https://doi.org/10.1017/CBO9781316018453.024.

Pelc, Krzysztof. 2022. 'Counterfactuals and Contingency in WTO Dispute Settlement History'. *World Trade Review* 21 (3): 301–11. https://doi.org/10.1017/S1474745622000076.

Puig, Sergio. 2014. 'Social Capital in the Arbitration Market'. *European Journal of International Law* 25: 387–424.

Puig, Sergio. 2018. 'Network Analysis and the Sociology of International Law'. In *Research Handbook on the Sociology of International Law*, edited by Moshe Hirsch and Andrew Lang, 319–32. Cheltenham, UK: Edward Elgar Publishing.

Ridi, Niccolò. 2019. 'The Shape and Structure of the 'Usable Past': An Empirical Analysis of the Use of Precedent in International Adjudication'. *Journal of International Dispute Settlement* 10 (2): 200–47. https://doi.org/10.1093/jnlids/idz007.

Šadl, Urška, and Henrik Palmer Olsen. 2017. 'Can Quantitative Methods Complement Doctrinal Legal Studies? Using Citation Network and Corpus Linguistic Analysis to Understand International Courts'. *Leiden Journal of International Law* 30 (2): 327–49. https://doi.org/10.1017/S0922156517000085.

Smith, Thomas A. 2007. 'The Web of Law'. *San Diego Law Review* 44 (2): 309–54.

Sunstein, Cass R. 2000. 'On Academic Fads and Fashions 2001 Survey of Books Relating to the Law: Foreword'. *Michigan Law Review* 99 (6): 1251–64.

Tarissan, Fabien, and Raphaëlle Nollez-Goldbach. 2015. 'Temporal Properties of Legal Decision Networks: A Case Study from the International Criminal Court'. In *28th International Conference on Legal Knowledge and Information Systems (JURIX'2015)*. Braga, Portugal. https://doi.org/10.3233/978-1-61499-609-5-111.

Watts, Duncan J, and Steven H Strogatz. 1998. 'Collective Dynamics of "Small-World" Networks' 393: 3.

Whalen, Ryan. 2016. 'Legal Networks: The Promises and Challenges of Legal Network Analysis'. *Michigan State Law Review*: 539–65.

CHAPTER 15

STUDYING JUDICIAL BEHAVIOUR WITH TEXT ANALYSIS

MICHAEL A. LIVERMORE AND BAO KHAM CHAU

1. Introduction

Traditional legal research methods rely on reading and interpreting legal texts. Even with an army of capable assistants, the amount of data that can be generated in this way is quite limited. Analyses of 'small data' can lead to useful insights, but researchers can now move beyond conventional methods of data collection and analysis. In recent decades, the digitalization of legal texts has enabled empirical legal scholars to use computational text analysis techniques to study large digital corpora of legal documents. These computer-based tools can help researchers study long-standing questions and also open new, previously inaccessible epistemic doors.

As with any act of translation, however, the transformation of legal documents into data capable of quantitative analysis can result in some loss of information. Legal texts, such as judicial opinions, are intrinsically high-dimensional. This means that the number of attributes that might be potentially germane to a research question—that is, the number of dimensions that must be used to fully characterize an object like a legal opinion—is extremely high relative to the number of available observations. Reducing this dimensionality is a prerequisite for many forms of quantitative analysis, but this dimensionality reduction comes at the cost of losing potentially valuable information. The challenge for researchers who use law-as-data techniques is to strike a balance between rich, high-dimension representation of legal texts (which can be impractical to analyse) and low-resolution, simplified representations that are tractable but incomplete.

For the empirical study of judicial behaviour, managing this trade-off is worth the effort. Techniques from the fields of machine learning, natural language processing, and text mining have already been put to productive use to study questions about judicial decision-making around the world—from how the emotional valence of legal briefs predicts the outcomes of cases in the US Supreme Court (Black et al. 2016c) to how private litigants in the People's Republic of China use administrative litigation to seek assistance from the state in their disputes (Liebman et al. 2020). Writing at the turn of the twentieth century, Justice Holmes famously predicted that 'blackletter' study of the law would be supplanted, in his future, by 'statistics' and 'economics' (Holmes 1897). It does not seem outlandish, toward the beginning of the twenty-first century, to update Holmes's forecast. While doctrinal analysis (i.e. blackletter law) and traditional statistical and economic analysis of law likely have a long future ahead of them, recent trends provide ample reason to predict that machine learning and natural language processing will take up a central place in the methodological toolkit used to study the law and legal institutions.

This chapter provides a survey of the exciting new literature that uses computational methods to extract information from legal documents to answer research questions on law and legal institutions. In particular, it discusses how legal scholars use computational tools such as term-frequency vectors and word embedding to translate legal texts into data and subject this data to quantitative analysis. This law-as-data approach supplements traditional modes of analysis and empowers legal scholars to further examine the influence on and consequences of judicial decisions.

2. From Law to Data

An important step in integrating computational text analysis techniques into legal scholarship on judicial behaviour is the conversion of judicial texts into computer-readable data. Traditionally, this conversion was done manually, with dedicated research assistants diligently combing through mountains of documents, hand coding or categorizing them, and entering these categorized documents into some type of digital spreadsheet (Ruger et al. 2004; Johnson et al. 2009). Law and Zaring (2010), for example, worked with their research assistants to code US Supreme Court opinions manually before inputting them into a logistic regression model in their study of the use of legislative history by US Supreme Court Justices.

Manually coding legal documents into machine-readable format, however, is intensive both in terms of time and resources. Additionally, hand coding is subjective in ways that could bias results (Burla et al. 2008; Glazier, Boydstun, and Feezell 2021). These limitations thus narrow the scope of research projects and the size of a corpus that can be analysed.

The advent of more sophisticated computational tools solved some of these problems while presenting new challenges. Now, almost all recent judicial texts do not need to be translated into machine-readable format as they are created in a digital format. In addition, a growing portion of legacy texts has been digitized through optical character recognition (OCR) software and could be subjected to quantitative analysis. In this new digital world, the problem is not caused by the scarcity of high-fidelity data but rather the overabundance of it.

The challenge arises because texts are unstructured data. Structured data, such as spreadsheets containing records of banking transactions or airline reservations, follows a particular format and is easily accessible by both humans and machines. Raw texts, by contrast, are referred to as unstructured because computers do not readily process the complex linguistic arrangements of human languages. Without structures that are comprehensible to the computer, most text amounts to little more than files filled with noise.

In order to apply computational text analysis techniques to judicial texts, it is necessary to transform them into structured data. Translating these unstructured texts to their structural counterparts involves a range of choices and trade-offs particular to the research question at issue. If we merely transform raw texts into ordered sequences of words, for example, the dimensionality of such a representation would be prohibitively high. The average US Supreme Court opinion length on abortion, for example, is about 8,000 words.[1] Even assuming a simple vocabulary size of 10,000 words (Brysbaeret 2016), we would still need a space of $10^{78,062}$ dimensions to represent these documents. Such high dimensionality requires an equally inordinate number of datapoints in order to derive meaningful and accurate insights. Because it is impossible to obtain such a large number of data points, it is crucial to find alternative low-dimensional representations that still preserve information germane to the research question at hand.

3. Representing Legal Texts

This section discusses several of the most common tools used by scholars to translate legal texts into data that can be subject to statistical analysis. We provide a brief introduction to the technique and discuss some of the work that applies the tool to study judicial behaviour. This review is meant to be illustrative rather than exhaustive.

3.1 Length

Perhaps the most straightforward way to represent a text is simply the length of the document. This single figure obviously eliminates all of the semantic content in a document, but nevertheless captures an important characteristic that distinguishes documents based on their basic information content. Large variations in document length denote differences in format: differences in length are what functionally distinguish tweets from books. Smaller variations in document length may be associated with individual style or the depth of analysis in a document.

There is considerable variation in the length of judicial opinions, and some interesting trends between and within institutions. The most extensive study of this feature in the US Supreme Court is Black and Spriggs (2008). That study examines trends in opinion length over time and maps those temporal changes onto the changing role of law clerks over the history of the Court. That paper concludes that increasing reliance on judicial clerks was not responsible for longer opinions or opinions with more footnotes. Leonard and Ross (2016) analyse opinion length at the level of state supreme courts in the United States to examine features at the case and institutional level associated with longer opinions. At the case level, characteristics such as amicus participation are associated with longer opinions. Institutionally, the authors find some systematic differences in the factors associated with opinion length between elected, merit selected, and appointed judges. In terms of the consequences of opinion length, Green and Yoon (2017) found correlations between the opinion lengths of the Supreme Court of India and future citations.

The length of opinions is not the only way to derive useful data from word counts. In an interesting use of length features of documents, Patton and Smith (2017) parse transcripts of oral arguments before the US Supreme Court into separate utterances, the length of which is used to measure the impact of attorney gender on the frequency with which they are interrupted by the justices.

3.2 Readability Scores

Another simple but commonly used metric to represent legal documents is a 'readability score'. Generally, readability scores are intended to capture linguistic sophistication, accessibility to a broader audience, or degree of clarity. The Flesch Kincaid Grade level is a readability score that is broadly familiar. This metric is calculated based on a weighted sum of sentence length (total words divided by total sentences) and word length (total syllables divided by total words). Larger numbers are associated with higher 'grades' and are intended to denote documents that are more difficult to read and understand.

Black et al. (2016a) calculate readability scores of US Supreme Court majority opinions to examine how the Court uses the rhetorical opportunity of written opinions to affect public discourse. The authors hypothesize that the justices will attempt to influence the public by writing more clearly when they anticipate negative reactions to their opinions. The authors calculate a range of different readability scores—which are primarily based on sentence length, word length, and the sophistication of the vocabulary used—and take the first principal component, which explains roughly three-quarters of the variation between the different metrics. They compare this readability score with polling data on participants' preferences concerning the size of government. Overall, the authors find that justices write more clearly when the ideological direction of an opinion conflicts with the sentiment of the public. The same group expanded their study in Black et al. (2016b) to estimate the relationship between readability and several other factors, including the parties to litigation and ideological distance with lower courts. Somewhat in contrast to the findings in Black et al. (2016a), Owens, Wedeking, and Wohlfarth (2013) find that opinions are *less* readable when there is greater ideological distance between the Court and Congress.

Whalen (2015) examines similar data, focusing on broad temporal trends and associations with the justices' ideologies. That paper finds that the Court is trending toward less readable opinions, and also finds a mild correlation between reliability and ideology, with conservative justices issuing opinions that are more difficult to read. Expanding the pool of data to briefs before the Court, Coleman and Phung (2010) find a contrary trend in readability, with briefs becoming somewhat easier to read over time, especially in those sections in which lawyers have more stylistic flexibility.

Beyond the Supreme Court, Budziak, Hitt, and Lempert (2019) examine readability among other stylistic features of opinions in the US appellate courts. In that study, the authors were interested in the degree to which variation in readability and other stylistic features were associated with judge-level and case-level characteristics, rather than strategic factors such as fear of reversal. Generally, the authors find that variation in readability is better explained by judge and case characteristics rather than strategic factors. In the United Kingdom, Scheinert and Tonkin (2021) examine the readability of asylum decisions as a metric of their accessibility.

Researchers have also used readability metrics to make cross-institutional comparisons. Feldman (2019) examines readability in the US state and federal courts. Goelzhauser and Cann (2014) analyze readability in the state courts to explore whether there is a relationship between institutional features at the state level (specifically whether judges are appointed or elected) and opinion readability. And Madden (2021) compared the readability scores between Australian, Canadian, South African, British, and US courts and concluded that factors such as average panel size could explain some variances in readability scores.

3.3 Curated Dictionaries

Both document length and readability metrics are far removed from the meaning of the words in a text. Moving to richer textual representations that are sensitive to content, many researchers have taken advantage of tools that are based on curated dictionaries of terms. The instances of these terms in a text can then be counted to derive supplemental measures of stylistic or content features of texts.

Sentiment analysis is one such approach. In a standard approach to sentiment analysis, a dictionary of positively and negatively valenced words is collected. Words such as 'bad', 'terrible', 'disgusting', and 'annoying' would be categorized as negative, while words such as 'good', 'useful', 'delicious', and 'delightful' would be categorized as positive. These dictionaries can be bespoke for a given task or corpus, but more general sentiment analysis dictionaries are also available. Texts are processed by counting the positive and negative words to determine the overall balance of sentiment. Sentiment is typically expressed as a single number, either based on the percentage of a document's words that have affective content (i.e. are on the list of positive or negative words) or over a one-dimensional space that might range over −1 (all negative words) to 1 (all positive words).

Several papers have applied sentiment analysis to judicial opinions. Examining US Supreme Court cases, Carlson, Livermore, and Rockmore (2016) find that there has been an increase in the usage of negative language over time. Bryan and Ringsmuth (2016) measure the sentiment of US Supreme Court dissents and find that cases with dissents that have more negative language tend to attract more media coverage. Rice and Zorn (2021) develop and examine a 'semi-supervised' alternative method for the construction of specialized sentiment dictionaries and test their approach using US Supreme Court cases. Busch and Pelc (2019) apply sentiment analysis to the rulings of World Trade Organization panels and its Appellate Body, finding that certain types of cases tend to elicit greater amounts of affect (either positively or negatively valenced words, compared to neutral words) and that effect tends to decline as an issue area is litigated over time.

Sentiment is one of many potential dimensions that can be extracted using a dictionary-based approach. The Linguistic Inquiry and Word Count (LIWC) tool has dictionaries for dozens of psychologically meaningful categories (Tausczik and Pennebaker 2010). The ease of use, flexibility, and relatively straightforward interpretability of LIWC has led many scholars of judicial behaviour to take advantage of this tool. For example, Cross and Pennebaker (2014) examine opinions issued during the early years of the Roberts Court for several LIWC expert-generated categories of words, including sentiment, but also certainty and cognitive style. Black et al. (2016c) uses LIWC to measure 'emotional language' in briefs to the US Supreme Court. Owens and Wedeking (2011) examine Supreme Court opinions using LIWC dictionaries that they associate with 'cognitive complexity'. They find substantial inter-justice variability, but also find intra-justice variation based on opinion type (with dissents having less complexity than majority opinions) and subject area (with opinions in criminal procedure cases having less complexity than in other areas). Corely and Wedeking (2014) use the LIWC dictionary for 'certainty' to examine the association between that variable in US Supreme Court opinions and the treatment of those opinions by lower courts. In their study of the relationship between opinion language and judge-level, case-level, and strategic factors, Budziak, Hitt, and Lempert (2019) also use the LIWC tool to characterize opinions in terms of the entire suite of available categories. Boston (2020) focuses on LIWC categories of impartiality, personality, and behavioural inclinations in a separate study of the strategic use of language in the appellate courts.

It is also possible to construct bespoke dictionaries for specific research projects. For example, Hinkle et al. (2012) use an automated program running keyword searches to detect hedging and intensifying language in a study of the effect of ideological distance between US District Court judges and their appellate counterparts on lower court opinions. Varsava (2018) uses bespoke dictionaries to estimate informality, forms of referring to litigants, and use of intensifiers and hedging in the opinions of the 10th Circuit to compare the writing style of the then newly minted Justice Gorsuch to his peers. Smith (2014) develops a dictionary of terms associated with 'legal review' and terms associated with 'factual review' in a study of the relationship between strategic factors and the emphasis that judges place on legal or factual questions in their opinions.

Narenchania (2022) develops a specialized terms list to examine the justifications offered by the Supreme Court for its decision to grant *certiorari*.

3.4 Term-Frequency Vectors

Curated dictionaries generally rely on expert knowledge to construct relevant word lists. This approach has the advantage of leveraging the considerable linguistic knowledge of the expert community and may also facilitate the interpretation of results. However, dictionary-based representations ignore the many terms that are not represented in their word lists and are limited to a fairly circumspect and predetermined set of dimensions.

An alternative to the dictionary approach of counting the appearance of certain selected groups of words is simply to summarize documents over their terms. This is referred to as a 'bag-of-words' or term-frequency vector representation. The bag-of-words approach is one of the most common structural representations in law-as-data research. Under this model, documents are represented as vectors that describe the occurrence of words within a document (DeAngelo and McCannon 2017; Sag 2019). The order of words in a document is ignored, and the dimensions of the bag-of-words representation are dependent on the size of the vocabulary in a corpus.

Term frequency vectors are a specific type of *n*-gram model, where *n* is the length of the sequences of words. Typically, *n* is '1', meaning that only unigrams—that is, one-word 'sequences'—are considered. It is possible to have bigrams (*n* of '2', i.e. two-word sequences) or higher *n*-grams. Under such an approach, documents would be represented as frequencies over all of their unique two-word sequences. The dimensionality would be all of the two-word frequencies in the corpus—a huge expansion over a simple unigram term-frequency vector. Due to this dimensionality explosion, unigrams are typically used, although some bigrams may be included.

The general lack of word order means that term frequency vectors are far from a lossless representation of a text. The meaning of certain words depends on their positions in the sentence and what their neighbouring terms are: for example, whether a word is preceded by the term 'not' can have a large effect on semantic content. A term-frequency vector does not provide sufficient information to determine the meaning of a text but can provide a general impression of subject matter, given the types of words that are used.

Figure 15.1 provides a bag-of-words representation of the U.S. Constitution with term-frequencies for the top fifteen words in the document. (Function words—i.e. those that describe grammatical or structural relations rather than content; e.g. 'of', 'the', 'is', and 'a'—have been removed and all letters have been converted to lowercase.) From this information, it is possible to understand that the document concerns governmental institutions and perhaps even constitutional matters. But it would be impossible to read off the actual process used to adopt legislation, or the content of the Bill of Rights.

A term-frequency vector is a different way of representing documents compared to the returns from LIWC or another curated dictionary. A sentiment analysis returns the

Word	Frequency
shall	180
state	148
united	70
may	31
section	22
president	20
constitution	19
house	19
congress	18
one	17
two	17
person	15
law	14
time	14
office	12

FIGURE 15.1 Term frequency of the top fifteen words in the US Constitution.

count of all affectively loaded words, perhaps distinguishing between words with positive or negative valence. Documents are represented as a single number based on either the total degree of affective language, or the balance of positive, neutral, and negative language. By contrast, a term frequency vector is a list of many numbers, each associated with a term in the document.

Because term-frequency vectors over the entire vocabulary occupy a very high-dimensional space, machine-learning tools can be used to reduce that dimensionality in ways that allow for more useful statistical analysis. We discuss one such tool—topic models—in section 3.7 below. But term 'frequency vectors' need not be over the entire vocabulary of a corpus. For example, many analyses of writing style examine only function words. Several studies of judicial texts use term frequency vectors over function words. Carlson, Livermore, and Rockmore (2016) use this representation—sometimes referred to as a 'stylistic fingerprint'—in a study of US Supreme Court decisions. That analysis finds that there is a 'style of the time' that holds together the writing of contemporaneous justices; they also find that justices' individual writing styles have become less consistent over time (i.e. more intra-justice variability) while the style of the Court has become more consistent (i.e. less inter-justice variability). They associate this with the increasing role played by clerks in drafting opinions. Similarly, Frankenreiter (2019) measured the use of function words to conduct a stylometric analysis of the European Court of Justice and Rosenthal and Yoon (2011) use a similar measure to predict authorship of judicial opinions.

Although term-frequency vectors over function words have been used in several papers on judicial style, there are other measures that can be used to estimate stylistic characteristics of documents. For example, Wahlbeck, Spriggs, and Sigelman (2002) use a more general list of stylistic features (such as the type-token ratio, and the diversity of word length) in their study of the influence of law clerks on the opinions of US Supreme Court Justices Marshall and Powell. Cheruvu (2019) calculates a measure of lexical diversity in a study of whether the European Court of Justice's French language mandate differentially affects the efficacy of judges from different backgrounds. Zubrod et al. (2021) utilized the Automated Integrative Complexity scoring system in an analysis of the complexity of the attorneys' opening and closing statements of attorneys in well-known trials.

One of the benefits of the term-frequency vector representation is that it allows for useful mathematical interpretation. Geometrically, vectors with k components can be understood as related to each other in a k-dimensional space. To represent a colour based off the Red, Green, Blue (RGB) colour scheme, for example, one would need a vector with three components. This vector could be represented in a three-dimensional space, where the values of these components indicate how much red, green, and blue a particular colour should contain. Orange, for instance, would be represented by the vector (255, 69, 0). A metric such as cosine similarity can be used to calculate the difference between vectors in geometric terms. The metric does so by measuring the cosine of the angle between the two vectors. In the RGB example, the cosine similarity metric would yield a higher similarity score for orange (255, 69, 0) and red (255, 0, 0) than orange and blue (0, 0, 255).

Hinkle (2016) uses cosine similarity between term frequency vector representation of opinions in the US appellate courts to calculate their similarity. Oldfather, Bockhorts, and Dimmer (2012) used cosine similarity to explore the responsiveness of the US Court of Appeals for the First Circuit's opinions to briefs filed in that jurisdiction. Alternatively, term-frequency vectors that have been normalized into percentages can be treated as distributions, and a measure such as Kullback–Leibler (KL) divergence can be used to calculate differences in statistical or information-theoretic terms. In their study of writing style on the US Supreme Court, Carlson, Livermore, and Rockmore (2016) use KL divergence as their approach to estimating similarity.

In using the bag-of-words model to transform judicial texts, researchers often perform some preprocessing. Questions to consider include whether (i) the capitalization of the words is important; (ii) function words are needed; (iii) inflected forms of the same word are different words (e.g. whether to stem or lemmatize words); (iv) there should be special consideration for proper nouns and numbers; and (v) it is important to supplement the bag-of-words model with a weighting schedule such as the term frequency–inverse document frequency (tf–idf) scaling scheme.[2] There are no globally accepted preprocessing best practices for text analysis; rather, different datasets and different research questions require different combinations of preprocessing options (Grimmer and Stewart 2013).

3.5 Parsers

Text parsers are software packages that separate a corpus of texts into smaller components based on a set of preprogrammed rules or logics. A text parser usually takes as inputs raw, unstructured texts and breaks them into smaller chunks (i.e. tokens) for analysis. After tokenizing the unstructured texts and transforming them into structured data, a parser can then annotate and categorize them according to some structural or grammatical constraints. A relatively straightforward example of this annotation would be part-of-speech tagging, where the tokens are assigned a grammatical category (e.g. noun, verb, adverb, adjective). Once the texts are tokenized and annotated, parsers could then use customized rules or logics to determine the syntactic relationships between the annotated tokens.

Ashley and Brüninghaus (2009) uses a text parser to extract information from the facts of already decided cases that can be used to predict the outcomes of new cases. To do so, they modified their text parser to identify special adjectives and annotate segments containing these adjectives with specific markers for later analysis. The authors then showed that the modified approach eventually yielded a significantly better prediction than the bag-of-words approach. Despite this advantage, supplementing bag-of-words output with expert knowledge might be overly burdensome. If the current selection of automated parsers does not support such annotations, scholars would have to hand code the semantic structures of the interested languages themselves. Additionally, adding semantic context to the bag-of-words model can further increase the dimensionality of the dataset and make the data unwieldy.

3.6 Anti-Plagiarism Software

Anti-plagiarism software is designed to detect textual and stylistic similarities between two or more corpus of texts and prevent the unauthorized appropriation of ideas, words, or results. Most anti-plagiarism software measures similarities through a combination of keyword, syntactic, and semantic analysis. This approach not only looks for literal textual overlaps, but also considers structural (e.g. part of speech) and conceptual (e.g. passive vs active voice) similarities. In addition to these linguistic features, some anti-plagiarism software also uses stylometric analysis to quantify writing styles (e.g. frequency of interpunction and passive voice) and compare stylistic similarities between documents. These similarity measures enabled scholars to establish authorial fingerprints, which helped them investigate, for example, the extent of William Shakespeare's collaboration with John Fletcher and Christopher Marlowe.

Textual and stylistic similarities could also yield novel insights into the judiciary. Choi and Gulati (2005), for example, used plagiarism software to analyse the authorship of judicial opinions. Similarly, Corley (2008) and Corley, Collins, and Calvin (2011) have also used various plagiarism software programs to track the influence of lower court opinions and parties' briefs on US Supreme Court opinions. Because these off-the-shelf tools are designed for different purposes, researchers using these domain-specific tools should ensure that the tools can be used to answer the research questions at issue.

3.7 Topic Models

A topic model is an unsupervised machine-learning algorithm that identifies latent subject matter categories in corpora of texts (Blei and Lafferty 2007; Blei 2012). Given a textual corpus, a topic model produces topics, which in the technical topic modelling sense are probability distributions over a vocabulary, where each word in the vocabulary is assigned a non-negative weight (such that all weights sum to 1). Each document is in turn summarized as a probability distribution over the topics. The highest-weighted words within a topic provide a sense of the subject matter that the distribution represents. For example, in a study of US Supreme Court opinions, a topic labelled by the authors 'trusts and estates' had the following highly weighted words: 'estate, trust, death, property, descendent, wife, interest' (Livermore, Riddell, and Rockmore 2017). The representation of a given document as a distribution over topics summarizes the document as a weighted mixture. These distributions—both of the topics and the words they comprise—are produced as the best fit to an underlying generative probabilistic model for the observed simple word frequencies.

A primary advantage of topic models over simple term frequency vectors is that they can account for word co-occurrence, which helps to uncover characteristics of context. They also substantially reduce the dimensionality needed to describe documents within a corpus. A given group of documents may contain tens of thousands of unique words. To represent documents as frequency distributions over those words requires vectors with an equal number of components. The number of topics generated by a topic model is much smaller, typically fewer than 500.

The most well-known topic model is the latent Dirichlet allocation (LDA) mixed-membership model (Blei, Ng, and Jordan 2003). The LDA topic model served as the basis for a substantial research paradigm in natural language processing, which has sought to improve on its performance and expand its usefulness. For example, dynamic topic models are intended to detect how themes change over time (Blei and Lafferty 2006), and the structural topic model is optimized to test metadata covariates that are associated with different topics (Roberts et al. 2014).

Topic models have been used extensively in the study of courts and judges. Livermore, Riddell, and Rockmore (2017) combined a topic model with a machine-learning classifier to examine how the contents of US Supreme Court opinions evolve over time, rendering them less court-like as compared to the opinions issued by the US appellate courts. Rice (2019) applied a topic model to the US Supreme Court and argued that this more fine-grained representation could provide a better metric for empirically analysing judicial opinions than traditional dichotomous representations of legal opinions. Rice (2017) also used topic modelling to extract two proxies—topic concentration and topic dissimilarity—and used them to investigate whether and how dissenting opinions at the US Supreme Court shaped the scope of the majority's opinions. Lauderdale and Clark (2014) supplemented the voting data of US Supreme Court Justices with results from a topic model to better describe the political cleavages between justices. In a similar vein, Macey and Mitts (2014) and Fagan (2015) used topic models to describe the inner workings of US courts.

Beyond the United States, Keydar (2020) applied topic modelling on trial transcripts from the International Criminal Tribunal for the former Yugoslavia's Kunarac case to examine trends throughout the proceedings. In a similar fashion, Shen-Bayh (2018) used topic modelling to differentiate between theoretical versus actual jurisdiction of autocratic courts in Africa. Grajzl and Murrell (2021a, 2021b) relied on the results generated by topic modelling techniques to describe how ideas associated with the English financial revolution shaped the sources of law used in the English courts. Dyevre and Lampach (2021) used topic modelling to determine that there is a correlation between more inclusive annulment and referral procedures and greater issue heterogeneity in the decisions of the European Court of Justice. Similarly, Carter, Brown, and Rahmani (2016) used topic models to describe the Australian High Court's judicial workload and analyse the court's legal subject matter over time. Finally, Destrooper (2018) applied topic modelling techniques to texts issued by Cambodian non-governmental organizations (NGOs) and the Extraordinary Chambers in the Courts of Cambodia (ECCC) and found that that there is a correlation between the discursive priorities of Cambodian human rights NGOs and the language used by the ECCC.

3.8 Supervised Machine Learning

Researchers have employed machine-learning algorithms to classify legal observations and predict the outcome of legal cases. There are two main families of machine-learning approaches—supervised and unsupervised—both capable of handling high-dimensionality datasets. In supervised machine learning, the models are trained with datasets that have been labelled by humans. After the models are trained, they can be used to classify new data and predict outcomes. Naive-Bayes classifier and Support Vector Machine (SVM) are two examples of supervised machine learning. Conversely, in unsupervised machine learning, there is no labelled data. Instead, the algorithms are used to analyse and discover patterns without the intervention of humans. The topic modelling approach discussed earlier is an example of unsupervised machine learning.

Many legal scholars have used supervised learning tools to categorize legal texts. Daniels and Rissland (1997) employed a supervised learning algorithm to identify relevant passages within applicable judicial opinions. Gonçalves and Quaresma (2003) explore the use of SVM to classify European Portuguese legal texts and propose ways to reduce the computational complexity of the task. Later work has sought to identify the ideological slant of *amicus curiae* briefs (Evans et al. 2007) and judicial opinions (Hausladen, Schubert, and Ash 2020), to categorize German judicial writings (Urchs, Mitrović, and Granitzer 2020), and to recognize and extract the reasoning of the Supreme Court of Taiwan (Liu and Chen 2019).

In addition to classification, legal scholars have applied machine-learning techniques to predict the outcomes of legal cases (Alschner and Charlotin 2022). One of the earlier precursors to such techniques could be found in the work of Brüninghaus and Ashley (1997). This paper created a rule-based algorithm to predict the outcome of trade secret misappropriation cases. Aletras et al. (2016), Varga et al. (2023), and Aissa et al. (2021) use similar techniques to predict outcomes in the European Court of Human Rights, Slovakian criminal proceedings, and accident cases in Moroccan courts (respectively). A major limitation of all of these studies is that they draw information from the fully published opinions rather than information that was available prior to the decision being issued. Accordingly, they may be better understood as predicting the justifications offered by courts for their decisions, rather than the outcome itself.

Supervised machine learning can also be used as an aid in a broader study of the courts. Rice (2014), for example, uses naive Bayes, maximum entropy, and decision tree classifiers to predict the issue areas of appeals opinions in a study of the relationships between the US Supreme Court's attention to a particular issue and the rise of new legal arguments in the lower federal courts. Livermore, Riddell, and Rockmore (2017) use a simple classifier (logistic regressions) to determine the prediction accuracy of a model trained to distinguish the topic representations of Supreme Court and appellate court opinions.

3.9 Embeddings

To capture word order and other semantic contexts while avoiding the dimension explosion problem, some scholars have turned to a relatively new text representation model called word embedding. Word embeddings is a technique to represent words within a vocabulary as vectors in a relatively low-dimensional space. These vectors are constructed based on a predictive task in which the words in a document are used to predict other words in that document. For example, the word2vec model developed by Google is based on a skip-gram task in which the goal is to use words as inputs to predict their context (i.e. near-neighbour words) as outputs. These predictive tasks are used to train supervised machine-learning models, and in particular artificial neural networks, which contain hidden layers that perform matrix translations on the input layer to project them into an alternative k-dimensional space. The projection is the heart of the embedding and serves as the vector representation of each word. These vectors have been found to encode a substantial amount of semantic information and have been used in sophisticated natural language tasks such as machine translation. Word embeddings have been generalized to represent entire documents as vectors by including additional metadata (here document tags) in the model.

While embeddings are only just beginning to be used in legal scholarship, several projects help demonstrate its promise. Ash and Chen (2019) describes initial results from an embeddings analysis of US appellate courts to describe relationships between embeddings and judge features, such as political party affiliation and law school.

Nyarko and Sanga (2022) use a word-embedding model to compare how legal terms of art (the terms 'reasonable' and 'consent') are used differently by judges and laypersons. Additional projects include Rice, Rhodes, and Nteta (2019), which used word embedding to find racial bias against African-American litigants in over one million US appellate court opinions. Choi, Harris, and Shen-Bayh (2022) study the effects of judge and litigant ethnicity on case outcomes and then use word embedding to analyse written judgments to assess the mechanisms through which judge and litigant ethnicity influence judicial decision making. Ash and Chen (2018) use word embeddings to extract features of the US Supreme Court Justice Kavaneaugh's past judicial rulings to determine his ideological leanings. And Ash, Chen, and Naidu (2022) use word embeddings of judicial opinions in a study of the influence of economics training on the content of judicial opinions.

Word embeddings are also at the heart of generative large language models (LLMs) such as ChatGPT by OpenAI and Bard by Google. LLMs have considerable promise for empirical study of the law, although they raise many important questions concerning interpretability and accuracy. As of the time this writing, LLMs have not yet found their place within the empirical legal scholar's toolkit. But given their substantial power on a wide range of natural language processing tasks, researchers are likely to put them to productive use in the very near future.

4. Conclusion

Computational text analysis techniques empower legal scholars to derive novel insights into the legal system. Computational tools, however, come with their own limitations. These limitations are either the consequences of the software design process or data availability or a combination thereof.

The majority of these tools were developed by English-speaking technologists for the analysis of English texts. This leaves the tools woefully inadequate to evaluate non-English documents. In the field of sentiment analysis, for example, the number of English lexicons dwarfs those for other languages (Lo et al. 2017). Without a readily available labelled sentiment dataset for a specific language, it is difficult to use sentiment analysis techniques for that language. Translation of a non-English language into English is of limited value because the act of translation reduces accuracy (Bakliwal, Arora, and Varma 2012; Perez-Rosas, Banea, and Mihalcea 2012; Franky and Veselovská 2015). In addition to being language specific, these tools are also domain specific (Perry and Benoit 2017). This means that sentiment analysis tools developed for one area (e.g. consumer analysis) might not produce accurate results for another (e.g. legal evaluation).

Another limitation of computational techniques involves bias in underlying data. Computer scientists often describe this phenomenon as 'garbage in, garbage out', which expresses the idea that flawed input inevitably produces flawed output. In tools involving machine learning, for example, biased inputs could cause the machine-learning models to identify erroneous associations and produce undesirable outputs (Chau 2022). For example, Carlson, Livermore, and Rockmore (2020) have found strong evidence that judicial attributes influence publication decisions in the US courts of appeals, raising serious questions about the credibility of a long line of research that uses published opinions to draw inferences concerning the causal effect of judicial attributes and case outcomes.

The continually evolving computational landscape warrants some caution in using state of the art textual processing techniques. Because the outputs of these algorithms can be difficult to interpret, legal scholars should familiarize themselves with these tools before using them. For example, researchers have cautioned that the difficulty of interpreting topic models creates important limitations on their appropriate use (Caspi and Stiglitz 2020; Shadrova 2021).

An important step for the field will be the expanded use of text analysis tools for languages other than English. Although important research has been done on legal systems around the world, the bulk of research using computational techniques to study courts has been in the United States. Comparative computational analysis of law would allow researchers to study factors such as geography, national boundaries, social milieu, and language differences that are held constant in uni-cultural studies. In doing so, they can better understand regional phenomenon and avoid the pitfall of overgeneralizing results that are only applicable to a particular set of circumstances (Epstein, Šadl, and Weinshall 2021).

Notes

1. Adam Feldman. 'Empirical SCOTUS: An Opinion is Worth at Least a Thousand Words' (Corrected). SCOTUSblog. 2 April 2018. https://www.scotusblog.com/2018/04/empirical-scotus-an-opinion-is-worth-at-least-a-thousand-words/.
2. The term frequency–inverse document frequency (tf–idf) scheme is a way to represent texts that reflect how important a word is to a document. The tf–idf value increases proportionally as the number of times a word appears in a document increases and is offset by the number of documents in a corpus that contain that word.

References

Aissa, Haidar, Ahajjam Tarik, Imad Zeroual, and Farhaoui Yousef. 2021. 'Using Machine Learning to Predict Outcomes of Accident Cases in Moroccan Courts'. *Procedia Computer Science* 184: 829–34.

Aletras, Nikolaos, Dimitrios Tsarapatsanis, Daniel Preoţiuc-Pietro, and Vasileios Lampos. 2016. 'Predicting Judicial Decisions of the European Court of Human Rights: A Natural Language Processing Perspective'. *PeerJ Computer Science* 2: e93.

Alschner, Wolfgang, and Damien Charlotin. 2022. 'Data Mining, Text Analytics, and Investor-State Arbitration'. In *International Arbitration and Technology*, edited by Pietro Ortolani, André Janssen, and Pieter Wolters, 135–58. Nijmegen: Kluwer Law International.

Ash, Elliott, and Daniel L. Chen. 2018. 'What Kind of Judge Is Brett Kavanaugh?' *Cardozo Law Review De-Novo* 2018: 70–100.

Ash, Elliott, and Daniel L. Chen. 2019. 'Case Vectors: Spatial Representations of the Law Using Document Embeddings'. In *Law as Data: Computation, Text, and the Future of Legal Analysis*, edited by Michael A. Livermore and Daniel N. Rockmore, 313–37. Santa Fe: Santa Fe Institute Press.

Ash, Elliott, Daniel L. Chen, and Suresh Naidu. 2022. 'Ideas Have Consequences: The Impact of Law and Economics on American Justice'. NBER Working Paper 29788. Cambridge, MA: National Bureau of Economic Research.

Ashley, Kevin D., and Stefanie Brüninghaus. 2009. 'Automatically Classifying Case Texts and Predicting Outcomes'. *Artificial Intelligence and Law* 17 (2): 125–65.

Bakliwal, Akshat, Piyush Arora, and Vasudeva Varma. 2012. 'Hindi Subjective Lexicon: A Lexical Resource for Hindi Adjective Polarity Classification'. In *Proceedings of the Eighth International Conference on Language Resources and Evaluation (LREC '12)*, 1189–96. Istanbul: European Language Resources Association.

Black, Ryan C., and James F. Spriggs. 2008. 'An Empirical Analysis of the Length of US Supreme Court Opinions'. *Houston Law Review* 45: 621–82.

Black, Ryan C., Ryan J. Owens, Justin Wedeking, and Patrick C. Wohlfarth. 2016a. 'The Influence of Public Sentiment on Supreme Court Opinion Clarity'. *Law and Society Review* 50 (3): 703–32.

Black, Ryan C., Ryan J. Owens, Justin Wedeking, and Patrick C. Wohlfarth. 2016b. *U.S. Supreme Court Opinions and Their Audiences*. Cambridge: Cambridge University Press.

Black, Ryan C., Matthew E. K. Hall, Ryan J. Owens, and Eve M. Ringsmuth. 2016c. 'The Role of Emotional Language in Briefs before the US Supreme Court'. *Journal of Law and Courts* 4 (2): 377–407.

Blei, David M., Andrew Y. Ng and Michael I. Jordan. 2003. 'Latent Dirichlet Allocation'. *Journal of Machine Learning Research* 3: 993–1022.

Blei, David M. 2012. 'Probabilistic Topic Models'. *Communications of the ACM* 55 (4): 77–84.

Blei, David M., and John D. Lafferty. 2007. 'A Correlated Topic Model of Science'. *The Annals of Applied Statistics* 1 (1): 17–35.

Blei, David M., and John D. Lafferty. 2006. 'Dynamic Topic Models'. In *Proceedings of the 23rd International Conference on Machine Learning*, 113–20. New York: Association for Computer Machinery.

Boston, Joshua. 2020. 'Strategic Opinion Language on the US Courts of Appeals'. *Journal of Law and Courts* 8 (1): 1–26.

Brüninghaus, Stefanie, and Kevin D. Ashley. 1997. 'Finding Factors: Learning to Classify Case Opinions under Abstract Fact Categories'. In *Proceedings of the 6th International Conference on Artificial Intelligence and Law*, 123–31. New York: Association for Computer Machinery.

Bryan, Amanda C., and Eve M. Ringsmuth. 2016. 'Jeremiad or Weapon of Words? The Power of Emotive Language in Supreme Court Dissents'. *Journal of Law and Courts* 4 (1): 159–85.

Brysbaert, Marc et al. 2016. 'How Many Words Do We Know? Practical Estimates Of Vocabulary Size Dependent on Word Definition, The Degree of Language Input and the Participant's Age'. *Frontiers in Psychology* 7: 1116.

Budziak, Jeffrey, Matthew P. Hitt, and Daniel Lempert. 2019. 'Determinants of Writing Style on the United States Circuit Courts of Appeals'. *Journal of Law and Courts* 7 (1): 1–28.

Burla, Laila, Birte Knierim, Jurgen Barth, Katharina Liewald, Margreet Duetz, and Thomas Abel. 2008. 'From Text to Codings: Intercoder Reliability Assessment in Qualitative Content Analysis'. *Nursing Research* 57 (2): 113–17.

Busch, Marc L., and Krzysztof J. Pelc. 2019. 'Words Matter: How WTO Rulings Handle Controversy'. *International Studies Quarterly* 63 (3): 464–76.

Carlson, Keith, Michael A. Livermore, and Daniel Rockmore. 2016. 'A Quantitative Analysis of Writing Style on the US Supreme Court'. *Washington University Law Review* 93: 1461–510.

Carlson, Keith, Michael A. Livermore, and Daniel N. Rockmore. 2020. 'The Problem of Data Bias in the Pool of Published US Appellate Court Opinions'. *Journal of Empirical Legal Studies* 17 (2): 224–61.

Carter, David J., James Brown, and Adel Rahmani. 2016. 'Reading the High Court at a Distance: Topic Modelling the Legal Subject Matter and Judicial Activity of the High Court of Australia, 1903–2015'. *University of New South Wales Law Journal* 39 (4): 1300–54.

Caspi, Aviv, and Edward H. Stiglitz. 2020. 'Measuring Discourse by Algorithm'. *International Review of Law and Economics* 62: 105863.

Chau, Bao Kham. 2022. 'Governing the Algorithmic Turn: Lyft, Uber, and Disparate Impact'. Center for Legal Court and Technology. https://legaltechcenter.net/files/sites/159/2022/06/Chau_Governing_the_Algorithmic_Turn_Lyft_Uber_and_Disparate_Impact.pdf

Cheruvu, Sivaram. 2019. 'How Do Institutional Constraints Affect Judicial Decision-Making? The European Court of Justice's French Language Mandate'. *European Union Politics* 20 (4): 562–83.

Choi, Donghyun Danny, J. Andrew Harris, and Fiona Shen-Bayh. 2022. 'Ethnic Bias in Judicial Decision Making: Evidence from Criminal Appeals in Kenya'. *American Political Science Review* 2022: 1–14.

Choi, Stephen J., and G. Mitu Gulati. 2005. 'Which Judges Write Their Opinions (and Should We Care)'. *Florida State University Law Review* 32: 1076–122.

Coleman, Brady, and Quy Phung. 2010. 'The Language of Supreme Court Briefs: A LargeScale Quantitative Investigation'. *Journal of Appellate Practice and Process* 11: 75–103.

Corley, Pamela C. 2008. 'The Supreme Court and Opinion Content: The Influence of Parties' Briefs'. *Political Research Quarterly* 61 (3): 468–78.

Corley, Pamela C., Paul M. Collins Jr, and Bryan Calvin. 2011. 'Lower Court Influence on US Supreme Court Opinion Content'. *The Journal of Politics* 73 (1): 31–44.

Corley, Pamela, and Justin Wedeking. 2014. 'The (Dis)advantage of Certainty: The Importance of Certainty in Language'. *Law and Society Review* 48 (1): 35–62.

Cross, Frank B., and James W. Pennebaker. 2014. 'The Language of the Roberts Court'. *Michigan State Law Review* 2014: 853–94.

Daniels, Jody J., and Edwina L. Rissland. 1997. 'Finding Legally Relevant Passages in Case Opinions'. In *Proceedings of the 6th International Conference on Artificial Intelligence and Law*, 39–46. New York: Association for Computer Machinery.

DeAngelo, Gregory, and Bryan C. McCannon. 2017. 'Judicial Compensation and Performance'. *Supreme Court Economic Review* 25 (1): 129–47.

Destrooper, Tine. 2018. 'Accountability for Human Rights Violations in Cambodia: Mapping the Indirect Effects of Transitional Justice Mechanisms'. *Asia-Pacifica Journal on Human Rights and Law* 19: 113–39.

Dyevre, Arthur, and Nicolas Lampach. 2021. 'Issue Attention on International Courts: Evidence from the European Court of Justice'. *The Review of International Organizations* 16 (4): 793–815.

Epstein, Lee, Urška Šadl, and Keren Weinshall. 2021. 'The Role of Comparative Law in the Analysis of Judicial Behavior'. *The American Journal of Comparative Law* 69 (4): 689–719.

Evans, Michael, Wayne McIntosh, Jimmy Lin, and Cynthia Cates. 2007. 'Recounting the Courts? Applying Automated Content Analysis to Enhance Empirical Legal Research'. *Journal of Empirical Legal Studies* 4 (4): 1007–39.

Fagan, Frank. 2015. 'From Policy Confusion to Doctrinal Clarity: Successor Liability from the Perspective of Big Data'. *Virginia Law and Business Review* 9: 391–451.

Feldman, Adam. 2019. 'Opinion Clarity in State and Federal Courts'. In *Law as Data: Computation, Text, and the Future of Legal Analysis*, edited by Michael A. Livermore and Daniel N. Rockmore, 407–30. Santa Fe: Santa Fe Institute Press.

Frankenreiter, J. 2019. 'Writing Style and Legal Traditions'. In *Law as Data: Computation, Text, and the Future of Legal Analysis*, edited by Michael A. Livermore and Daniel N. Rockmore, 153–90. Santa Fe: Santa Fe Institute Press.

Franky, Ondřej Bojar, and Kateřina Veselovská. 2015. 'Resources for Indonesian Sentiment Analysis'. *The Prague Bulletin of Mathematical Linguistics* 103 (1): 21–41.

Glazier, Rebecca A., Amber E. Boydstun, and Jessica T. Feezell. 2021. 'Self-Coding: A Method to Assess Semantic Validity and Bias When Coding Open-Ended Responses'. *Research and Politics* 8 (3): 20531680211031752.

Goelzhauser, Greg, and Damon M. Cann. 2014. 'Judicial Independence and Opinion Clarity on State Supreme Courts'. *State Politics and Policy Quarterly* 14 (2): 123–41.

Gonçalves, Teresa and Paulo Quaresma. 2003. 'A Preliminary Approach to the Multilabel Classification Problem of Portuguese Juridical Documents'. In *Proceedings of the 11th Portuguese Conference on Artificial Intelligence*, 435–44. Berlin: Springer.

Grajzl, Peter, and Peter Murrell. 2021a. 'A Machine-Learning History of English Caselaw and Legal Ideas Prior to the Industrial Revolution I: Generating and Interpreting the Estimates'. *Journal of Institutional Economics* 17 (1): 1–19.

Grajzl, Peter, and Peter Murrell. 2021b. 'A Machine-Learning History of English Caselaw and Legal Ideas Prior to the Industrial Revolution II: Applications'. *Journal of Institutional Economics* 17 (2): 201–16.

Green, Andrew, and Albert H. Yoon. 2017. 'Triaging the Law: Developing the Common Law on the Supreme Court of India'. *Journal of Empirical Legal Studies* 14 (4): 683–715

Grimmer, Justin, and Brandon M. Stewart. 2013. 'Text as Data: The Promise and Pitfalls of Automatic Content Analysis Methods for Political Texts'. *Political Analysis* 21 (3): 267–97.

Hausladen, Carina I., Marcel H. Schubert, and Elliott Ash. 2020. 'Text Classification of Ideological Direction in Judicial Opinions'. *International Review of Law and Economics* 62: 105903.

Hinkle, Rachael K. 2016. 'Strategic Anticipation of En Banc Review in the US Courts of Appeals'. *Law and Society Review* 50 (2): 383–414.

Hinkle, Rachael K., Andrew D. Martin, Jonathan David Shaub, and Emerson H. Tiller. 2012. 'A Positive Theory and Empirical Analysis of Strategic Word Choice in District Court Opinions'. *Journal of Legal Analysis* 4 (2): 407–44.

Holmes, Oliver Wendell. 1897. 'The Path of the Law'. *Harvard Law Review* 10 (8): 457–78.

Johnson, Timothy R., Ryan C. Black, Jerry Goldman, and Sarah A. Treul. 2009. 'Inquiring Minds Want to Know: Do Justices Tip Their Hands with Questions at Oral Argument in the US Supreme Court'. *Washington University Journal of Law and Policy* 29: 241–61.

Keydar, Renana. 2020. 'Listening from Afar: An Algorithmic Analysis of Testimonies from the International Criminal Courts'. *University of Illinois Journal of Law, Technology and Policy* 2020: 55–83.

Lauderdale, Benjamin E., and Tom S. Clark. 2014. 'Scaling Politically Meaningful Dimensions Using Texts and Votes'. *American Journal of Political Science* 58 (3): 754–71.

Law, David S., and David Zaring. 2010. 'Law Versus Ideology: The Supreme Court and the Use of Legislative History'. *William and Mary Law Review* 51: 1653–747.

Leonard, Meghan E., and Joseph V. Ross. 2016. 'Understanding the Length of State Supreme Court Opinions'. *American Politics Research* 44 (4): 710–33.

Liebman, Benjamin L., Margaret E. Roberts, Rachel E. Stern, and Alice Z. Wang. 2020. 'Mass Digitization of Chinese Court Decisions: How to Use Text as Data in the Field of Chinese Law'. *Journal of Law and Courts* 8 (2): 177–201.

Liu, Chao-Lin, and Kuan-Chun Chen. 2019. 'Extracting the Gist of Chinese Judgments of the Supreme Court'. In *Proceedings of the 17th International Conference on Artificial Intelligence and Law*, 73–82. New York: Association for Computer Machinery.

Livermore, Michael A., Allen B. Riddell, and Daniel N. Rockmore. 2017. 'The Supreme Court and the Judicial Genre'. *Arizona Law Review* 59: 837–901.

Lo, Siaw Ling, Erik Cambria, Raymond Chiong, and David Cornforth. 2017. 'Multilingual Sentiment Analysis: From Formal to Informal and Scarce Resource Languages'. *Artificial Intelligence Review* 48 (4): 499–527.

Macey, Jonathan, and Joshua Mitts. 2014. 'Finding Order in the Morass: The Three Real Justifications for Piercing the Corporate Veil'. *Cornell Law Review* 100: 99–156.

Madden, Mike. 2021. 'Stating it Simply: A Comparative Study of the Quantitative Readability of Apex Court Decisions from Australia, Canada, South Africa, the United Kingdom, and the United States'. *North Carolina Journal of Law and Technology* 23: 270.

Narechania, Tejas N. 2022. 'Certiorari in Important Cases'. *Columbia Law Review* 122: 923–1117.

Nyarko, Julian, and Sarath Sanga. 2022. 'A Statistical Test for Legal Interpretation: Theory and Applications'. *The Journal of Law, Economics, and Organization* 38 (2): 539–69.

Oldfather, Chad M., Joseph P. Bockhorst, and Brian P. Dimmer. 2012. 'Triangulating Judicial Responsiveness: Automated Content Analysis, Judicial Opinions, and the Methodology of Legal Scholarship'. *Florida Law Review* 64: 1189–242.

Owens, Ryan J., and Justin P. Wedeking. 2011. 'Justices and Legal Clarity: Analyzing the Complexity of US Supreme Court Opinions'. *Law and Society Review* 45 (4): 1027–61.

Owens, Ryan J., Justin P. Wedeking, and Patrick C. Wohlfarth. 2013. 'How the Supreme Court Alters Opinion Language to Evade Congressional Review'. *The Journal of Law and Courts* 1 (1): 34–59.

Patton, Dana, and Joseph L. Smith. 2017. 'Lawyer, Interrupted: Gender Bias in Oral Arguments at the US Supreme Court'. *Journal of Law and Courts* 5 (2): 337–61.

Perez-Rosas, Veronica, Carmen Banea, and Rada Mihalcea. 2012. 'Learning Sentiment Lexicons in Spanish'. In *Proceedings of the 8th International Conference on Language Resources and Evaluation (LREC '12)*, 3077–81. Istanbul: European Language Resources Association.

Perry, Patrick O., and Kenneth Benoit. 2017. 'Scaling Text with the Class Affinity Model'. *arXiv preprint, arXiv:1710.08963*.

Rice, Douglas. 2014. 'The Impact of Supreme Court Activity on the Judicial Agenda'. *Law and Society Review* 48 (1): 63–90.

Rice, Douglas. 2017. 'Issue Divisions and US Supreme Court Decision Making'. *The Journal of Politics* 79 (1): 210–22.

Rice, Douglas. 2019. 'Measuring the Issue Content of Supreme Court opinions'. *Journal of Law and Courts* 7 (1): 107–27.

Rice, Douglas, Jesse H. Rhodes, and Tatishe Nteta. 2019. 'Racial Bias in Legal Language'. *Research and Politics* 6 (2): 1–7.

Rice, Douglas R., and Christopher Zorn. 2021. 'Corpus-Based Dictionaries for Sentiment Analysis of Specialized Vocabularies'. *Political Science Research and Methods* 9 (1): 20–35.

Roberts, Margaret E., Brandon M. Stewart, Dustin Tingley, Christopher Lucas, Jetson Leder-Luis, Shana Kushner Gadarian, Bethany Albertson, and David G. Rand. 2014. 'Structural Topic Models for Open-Ended Survey Responses'. *American Journal of Political Science* 58 (3): 1064–82.

Rosenthal, Jeffrey S., and Albert H. Yoon. 2011. 'Detecting Multiple Authorship of United States Supreme Court Legal Decisions Using Function Words'. *The Annals of Applied Statistics* 5: 283–308.

Ruger, Theodore W., Pauline T. Kim, Andrew D. Martin, and Kevin M. Quinn. 2004. 'The Supreme Court Forecasting Project: Legal and Political Science Approaches to Predicting Supreme Court Decisionmaking'. *Columbia Law Review* 104: 1150–210.

Sag, Matthew. 2019. 'The New Legal Landscape for Text Mining and Machine Learning'. *Journal of the Copyright Society of the USA* 66: 291–367.

Scheinert, Laura, and Emma L. Tonkin. 2021. 'Towards Ethical Judicial Analytics: Assessing Readability of Immigration and Asylum Decisions in the United Kingdom'. In *Proceedings of the 20th EPIA Conference on Artificial Intelligence*, 53–67. Cham: Springer.

Shadrova, Anna. 2021. 'Topic Models Do Not Model Topics: Epistemological Remarks and Steps Towards Best Practices'. *Journal of Data Mining and Digital Humanities* 2021, https://jdmdh.episciences.org/8608.

Shen-Bayh, Fiona. 2018. 'Autocratic Courts in Africa'. PhD diss., University of California Berkeley.

Smith, Joseph L. 2014. 'Law, Fact, and the Threat of Reversal from Above'. *American Politics Research* 42 (2): 226–56.

Tausczik, Yla R., and James W. Pennebaker. 2010. 'The Psychological Meaning of Words: LIWC and Computerized Text Analysis Methods'. *Journal of Language and Social Psychology* 29 (1): 24–54.

Urchs, Stefanie, Jelena Mitrović, and Michael Granitzer. 2020. 'Towards Classifying Parts of German Legal Writing Styles in German Legal Judgments'. In *2020 10th International Conference on Advanced Computer Information Technologies (ACIT)*, 451–54. London: IEEE.

Varga, Dávid, Zoltán Szoplák, Stanislav Krajci, Pavol Sokol, and Peter Gurský. 2023. 'Analysis and Prediction of Legal Judgements in the Slovak Criminal Proceedings'. In Proceedings of the 28th Conference on Conceptual Structures (ICCS 2023), 201–204.

Varsava, Nina. 2018. 'Elements of Judicial Style: A Quantitative Guide to Neil Gorsuch's Opinion Writing'. *New York University Law Review Online* 93: 75–112.

Wahlbeck, Paul J., James F. Spriggs, and Lee Sigelman. 2002. 'Ghostwriters on the Court? A Stylistic Analysis of US Supreme Court Opinion Drafts'. *American Politics Research* 30 (2): 166–92.

Whalen, Ryan. 2015. 'Judicial Gobbledygook: The Readability of Supreme Court Writing'. *The Yale Law Journal* 125: 200–11.

Zubrod, Alivia, Lucian Gideon Conway III, Kathrene R. Conway, and David Ailanjian. 2021. 'Understanding the Role of Linguistic Complexity in Famous Trial Outcomes'. *Journal of Language and Social Psychology* 40 (3): 354–77.

CHAPTER 16

MEASURING POLITICAL PREFERENCES

LEE EPSTEIN, ANDREW D. MARTIN, AND KEVIN QUINN

1. Introduction

ALMOST all theories of judicial behaviour ascribe a key role to the judges' preferences. In some accounts, personal or institutional preferences move to the fore,[1] but even those approaches leave room for political preferences. The idea is that judges want to align the law with their political commitments—whether ideological or partisan.

Because ideology and partisanship are covered elsewhere,[2] we forego a discussion of the key empirical findings (there are many!), and instead take a deep dive into strategies for measuring and estimating the judges' political preferences. To that end, the chapter consists of two major parts: exogenous measures of political preferences (those that are based on information causally prior to any votes cast or other choices the judges make) and endogenous measures (those that depend on revealed behaviour). Along the way we detail the strengths and weaknesses of the various measures, and offer suggestions for forward movement.

2. Partisan Identity Does Not Equal Ideology

Before turning to the measures of political preferences, we should identify what we're trying to measure. This seems like a reasonable starting point because when it comes to empirically assessing the judges' political preferences, contemporary studies tend to treat political goals, policy goals, partisan goals, and ideological goals as interchangeable.

This move opens the door for researchers to measure ideology—the more common preference of interest—as the judge's (or the appointers') partisan identity. In other words, partisanship becomes a proxy for ideology because under the literature's conceptualization, ideology and party identity are fungible measures of the judges' political preferences.

We question this treatment; party identity and ideology are not the same, especially not in a world where affective polarization—favourable evaluations of co-partisans and negative evaluations of opposing partisans—is on the rise (Westwood et al. 2018; Reiljan 2019; Kekkonen and Yiä-Anttila 2021). Our view is that researchers should decide whether they're interested in partisanship or ideology, and develop their measures accordingly.

Early on in the study of judicial behaviour, scholars did just that (Schubert 1959; Nagel 1961; Ulmer 1962; Vines 1964). Especially compelling was Schmidhauser's 1961 study. Published just a year after *The American Voter*, which demonstrated 'the role of enduring partisan commitments in shaping attitudes toward political objects' (Campbell et al. 1960, 135), Schmidhauser argued that litigation related to the US 'sectional crisis' of 1837–1860 triggered a partisan response: justices affiliating with the Whigs more often favoured the North, and the Democratic justices favoured the South.

Schmidhauser made deft use of qualitative and quantitative evidence to build his case for the importance of partisan (and regional) identity as opposed to ideology. And yet Schubert, in his classic book *The Judicial Mind*, dismissed Schmidhauser's findings in a single sentence: 'The author's conclusion, although stated by him in terms of the political party affiliations of the justices, clearly supports the finding that it was the attitudes of the justices ... that dominated their behavior.' Schubert's response should come as no surprise. Following in the tradition established by the founder of the study of judicial behaviour (Pritchett 1941, 1948), Schubert's goal was to link the justices' *ideology* and their votes.[3] *The Attitudes and Ideologies of Supreme Court Justices* is the subtitle of his book, not *The Partisan Identities of Justices*.

The debate between Schmidhauser and Schubert—two pioneers of judicial behaviour—is instructive because it acknowledges a conceptual difference between ideology and partisanship. In the ensuing decades, however, this difference grew murkier as scholars concentrated on the judges' ideology, not their partisanship, as a driver of judicial behaviour—but they nonetheless sometimes used 'political party' to measure ideology (see Pinello 1999; Peretti 2020). Sunstein et al. (2006, 6) express the conventional view when they write: 'We focus throughout on the political affiliation of the appointing president. But that affiliation is only a proxy for judicial ideology.'

Sunstein et al. (2006) is a study of US appellate courts, but scholars studying courts throughout the world have done much the same, using the judges' party or the party of the appointing regime as a stand-in for ideology. To provide but a few examples:

Belgian Constitutional Court: 'We show that judicial review of federalism is contaminated by *ideological* and strategic aspects that cannot be explained by purely legalistic accounts.' Ideology is proxied through various *partisan* measures (Dalla Pellegrina et al. 2017).

Canadian Supreme Court: 'Absent a more refined measure, we employed an oft-used construct to estimate the preferences of the individual justices: *the party* of the appointing executive/Prime Minister (PM)' (Szmer, Johnson, and Sarver 2007).

French Constitutional Council; German Constitutional Court: We test 'the correlation between the *party affiliation* of the pivotal judge and oppositional success .... In both countries the likelihood of an oppositional victory or defeat varies with the *ideological position* of the pivotal judge' (Hönnige 2009).

Italian Constitutional Court: 'Our work is part of the literature that recognizes that personal ideology (partially) explains the behaviour of constitutional judges.' *Ideology* is measured by whether the judge is a supporter of the right-wing political coalition or the left-wing coalition based on their *political background* (Dalla Pellegrina and Garoupa 2013).

Norwegian Supreme Court: *Ideology* is a significant predictor of the economic votes of the justices. A justice *appointed by a social-democratic government* has a higher probability of voting for the public interest than justices appointed by non-socialist governments (Grendstad, Shaffer, and Waltenburg 2011b, 2015).

Spanish Constitutional Court: 'The level of consensus among [the] justices [is expected] to depend on their *ideology*.' Ideology is measured by whether a majority of justices share the same *political party affiliation* (either the left-wing Spanish Socialist Workers' Party or right-wing Partido Popular) (López-Laborda, Rodrigo, and Sanz-Arcega 2019).

We are in no position to criticize studies using party to proxy ideology; we have made a similar move in our research (e.g. Epstein, Landes, and Posner 2013). Moreover, because various analyses show that party can be 'a dependable yardstick for ideology', equating party and ideology isn't without merit (Pinello 1999).

But a yardstick is one thing; treating party and ideology as fungible is quite another. Truth be told, such treatment would be a serious transgression in research on the citizens' behaviour—and also should be, we believe, in studies of the judges' behaviour.[4] That is because partisanship and ideology are conceptually distinct, and so using partisanship as a proxy for ideology is concerning. To provide an illustration of the difference, in a well-known experiment, Cohen (2003) presented participants with one of two versions of a welfare policy report: one recommending generous benefits and the other more limited benefits. Cohen also manipulated the endorsers of the report: 95 per cent of US congressional Democrats versus 95 per cent of congressional Republicans. It turned out that the effect of the partisan endorser was stronger than the effect of the policy (ideological) content; that is, regardless of the proposal's content, respondents adjudged more favourably the one endorsed by their partisan 'team'. Party trumped policy (see also Hawkins and Nosek 2012; Munro et al. 2013).

Because affective polarization is so pervasive, it is more than ever imperative to separate partisanship and ideology. Assuming party identity is an important form of social identity for judges (Peretti 2020), just as it is for many members of the public (e.g. Iyengar and Westwood 2015; Mason 2015), judges should be equally as susceptible to affective polarization, responding favourably to arguments made by co-partisans and antagonistically to those offered by opposing partisans. Which opens the door to all kinds of compelling research projects if only because partisanship—separate and distinct from ideology—has been mostly ignored as a determinant of judicial behaviour. Does partisan identity have distinct effects on judicial behaviour? Is ideology versus partisanship more influential in certain kinds of disputes? Are particular types of judges more susceptible to ideological or partisan effects? Do different selection systems amplify the effect of party, ideology, or both? And on and on.

Answering many of these questions requires researchers to develop strategies that mirror Cohen's experiment. Of course, we can't ask judges to decide a case with a policy endorsed by one political party and then reverse time and ask them to decide exactly the same case only now the policy is endorsed by another party. Even the usual modus operandi in the political behaviour literature—conducting lab experiments on the influence of party versus policy—is beyond the pale.[5]

Observational studies are feasible, though tricky. If the idea is to mirror Cohen's experiment, one possibility would be to identify cases where the partisan stimuli is clear. Election and voting disputes are reasonable candidates if the political parties vary in their degree of support for, say, expansive voting rules (Lloyd 1995; Peretti 2020). Ditto for policies defended by the government in court, again assuming that governments composed of leftist political parties sometimes take conservative positions and that right-of-centre parties sometimes take liberal positions.

These are just a few possibilities to distinguish party and ideology, but it's the larger point that requires underscoring: the two should be distinguished.

3. Exogenous Measures of Ideology and Partisanship

Measures of political preferences come in roughly two varieties: exogenous measures, which are composed of information causally prior to any votes the judges cast or other choices they make, and endogenous measures, which rely on revealed behaviour. When the goal is to explain the effect of the judges' ideology or partisanship on their votes, scholars tend prefer exogenous measures because explaining votes with measures derived (even in part) from those very same votes involves a degree of circularity. For example, if we classify Judge X as conservative because she casts conservative votes, all we can say is that Judge X's votes predict her votes. But for studies that take the effect of ideology or partisanship as a given and wish to describe how it works—for example, whether liberals or conservatives are most likely to support free expression, whether ideology changes over time—endogenous approaches may be preferable because they are more precise.

In keeping with the conceptual difference between party and ideology, in what directly follows we consider two sets of exogenous approaches: one related to partisanship and the other, to ideology.[6] Section 4 of this chapter turns to the most common contemporary endogenous measures: ideal point estimates.

3.1 Partisanship

For studies theorizing about the role of party identity in judging, there are two obvious measures: the partisanship (i) of the judges and (ii) of their appointers. From what we can gather, the first is not easy to ascertain in many countries (Dalla Pellegrina and Garoupa 2013; Alarie and Green 2017). And even in the United States, where information about the judges' partisanship is fairly readily available, complications can arise (e.g. judges who affiliate with neither major party; judges who switched parties).

For these reasons, scholars often look to the appointers' party. For example, in the United States, the president; in Canada, the prime minister (Alarie and Green 2017); in Germany, the nominating political party (Hönnige 2009). Even when appointment is done by committee, the partisanship of the regime in power has been used to assess the judges' partisan leanings (Grendstad, Shaffer, and Waltenburg 2015).

Whether focusing on judges or appointers, the party-based approach has several nice features. Chief among them is that it produces a reliable measure. Assuming researchers have a list of the party affiliations of every judge (or appointer), no judgment calls are required. On the downside, partisan measures operate under an assumption that often goes untested: that all judges are equally committed to advancing their party's agenda. It seems likely that judges who were elected to office or held high-level positions in a regime could be strongly partisan, but what of judges who had little to do with party politics? Likewise, as Solberg and Waltenburg (this volume) point out, there are questions about whether the 'political partisan connection' makes sense for ordinary court judges in civil law societies (but see Ceron and Mainenti 2015).

These are not fatal flaws. Assuming biographical information is available, studies could attend to the intensity of the judges' party identity. Dalla Pellegrina et al. (2017) follow this path in their study of the Belgian Constitutional Court:

> Judges' political preferences have been assigned as follows. If a judge is a former member of parliament, a preference is associated according to the political party he belonged to ... We followed a different approach when ... aligning, preferences for judges with a legal background. For these judges, we used elements imputing a specific political orientation expressed prior to the judge's appointment to the Court for all judges with a legal background, we also allowed for political neutrality in the interest of empirical robustness.

Dalla Pellegrina et al. (2017) then took the additional step of verifying the judges' political affiliations with local experts.

3.2 Ideology

When it comes to ideology, two exogenous approaches seem plausible, though perhaps are underexploited: expert judgments (the individual judge's ideology) and regime voting patterns (the appointer's ideology).

3.2.1 *Expert Judgments of Judge Ideology*

Expert judgment plays an important role in measuring preferences in many pockets of the social sciences—the study of judicial behaviour not excepted. But the projects on judges are less capacious, relying almost exclusively on some variant of the 'Segal-Cover scores' (Segal and Cover 1989). That approach entails analysing newspaper editorial content ('expert judgments'), written before the judges' appointment, to develop an ideology score for each judge, ranging from, say, 0 (unanimously rated conservative) to 1 (unanimously rated liberal).

Perhaps because editorial scores are one of the few validated exogenous measures of judicial ideology, they make appearances in many studies on US justices (Segal and Cover's initial target), as well as in research on Canadian and Australian justices (Ostberg and Wetstein 2007; Weiden 2011). But the approach is not without its share of drawbacks. One is that the editorial scores are better surrogates for ideology in cases involving civil rights and liberties than in litigation in areas such as federal taxation and intellectual property (see generally Epstein and Mershon 1996). This is hardly surprising. When evaluating the ideology of would-be judges, newspaper editors are far more likely to focus on, say, religion or immigration than on the tax code.

Second, once computed the scores they do not vary over the course of judges' career. That may not matter much for judges who serve for relatively short, non-renewable terms, but it could present a problem in life-tenure countries where judges could (and do) 'evolve' in their thinking, growing more liberal or conservative over time (Epstein et al. 2007b; Alarie and Green 2009). Finally, the approach is best suited to highly visible courts/judges. In the US, for example, scholars have found it nearly impossible to calculate scores for judges serving in the lower federal courts or on state benches because of a dearth of editorials.

For these reasons, we propose an alternative approach: expert surveys. This approach is common in the financial sector (e.g. the World Bank), and it plays a role in various indices of governance (e.g. the BTI Transformation Index) and in many scholarly studies. To provide a few examples, Clinton and Lewis (2008), in an effort to measure US government agency preferences, 'identified experts in bureaucratic politics among academics, journalists, and Washington think tanks.' They sent each expert a list of agencies, and asked:

> I am interested to know which of these agencies have policy views due to law, practice, culture, or tradition that can be characterized as liberal or conservative. For [each agency] does it 'slant Liberal, Neither Consistently, slant Conservative, Don't Know.'

With these responses, along with objective data on the agencies, Clinton and Lewis (2008) used a multi-rater item response model to develop preferences estimates (and measures of uncertainty). Likewise, comparativists studying political parties have long-relied on expert judgments, gathered from surveys, to estimate the parties' positions in political space (Castles and Mair 1984; Ray and Narud 2000; Benoit and Laver 2006; Baker and Green 2011). Finally, it is worth noting that a major scientific project seeking to measure democracy throughout the world (V-Dem)[7] develops its estimates by aggregating expert judgments (about five experts per-country-year observation).

Using experts to rate judges is not unknown in the study of judicial behaviour but the ratings are usually about 'greatness' or 'impact' (e.g. Blaustein and Mersky 1972). A notable exception is Grendstad, Shaffer, and Waltenburg (2011a), in which the researchers asked Norwegian lawyers who had passed the Supreme Court bar to rate the justices along a radical (liberal) to conservative scale. The data resulted in a measure of ideology with acceptable face validity.[8]

As Grendstad, Shaffer, and Waltenburg (2011a) suggest, developed and analysed with care, there seem to be few downsides to applying the expert strategy to measure the judges' ideology.[9] And better still, the upsides are many: the estimates obtained from the surveys could be updated annually and could be developed for less visible judges. So too surveys need not be general; researchers could ask experts about ideology in particular areas of the law, thereby overcoming the problem of the newspapers' focus on highly salient issues.

3.2.2 *Regime Ideology*

Just as some studies use the partisanship of the judges' appointers to measure the judges' partisanship, research also uses the appointers' ideology to proxy the judges. In fact, the state-of-the-art measure for the ideological preferences of US appellate judges (and, for that matter, US trial judges), developed by Giles, Hettinger, and Peppers (2001), exploits an important institutional feature of the appointment process ('senatorial courtesy'), which may constrain the president from nominating a candidate to the lower federal courts who mirrors his ideology. Under courtesy norms, when a senator is of the same party as the president and the vacancy is from the senator's state, the senator can exert considerable influence on the selection of judges. To attend to this norm, Giles, Hettinger, and Peppers (2001) assign the federal judge the ideology of the 'nominating' senator when courtesy is in effect; otherwise the judge receives the score of the nominating president. (To measure the senators' and presidents' ideology, Giles, Hettinger, and Peppers use Lewis et al.'s (2022) NOMINATE scores, which are based on analysis of legislative roll call votes.)

This same approach, adapted to local norms, including norms regarding roll call votes,[10] could be applied beyond the United States to study appointers and regimes; that is because variants on the NOMINATE scaling method, and now the Martin–Quinn dynamic item response model (discussed momentarily) has been used to estimate the ideal points of members of the European Parliament (Hix, Noury, and Roland 2006; Lindstädt, Slapin, and Vander Wielen 2011; Lo 2018) and of legislators in the Czech Republic (Hájek 2020), Britain (Kellermann 2012), Switzerland (Bütikofer and Hug 2010), France (Rosenthal and Voeten 2004), and Germany (Bräuninger, Müller, and Stecker 2016), among others.

4. Endogenous Measures of Ideology: Ideal Point Estimates

Virtually all contemporary endogenous measures of ideology fall into the category of 'ideal point estimates'. Using the judges' votes (or other choices), the goal is to estimate the judges' most preferred position on a dimension(s) of interest. Mostly the authors posit an underlying left (liberal)–right (conservative) continuum and attempt to locate each judge's idea point along that line.

Although contemporary estimation of judicial ideal points can be traced to two authors of this chapter, Martin and Quinn (2002), and was initially applied to US justices, the project has gone global (Voeten 2008; Sánchez, Magaloni, and Magar 2011; Malecki 2012; Hanretty 2013; Dalla Pellegrina, Escresa, and Garoupa 2014; Nery Ferreira and Mueller 2014; Alarie, Green, and Iacobucci 2015; Iaryczower and Katz 2016; Dalla Pellegrina et al. 2017; Gonzalez Bertomeu, Dalla Pellegrina, and Garoupa 2017; Hartmann and Hudson 2017; Yildirim, Kutlar, and Gulener 2017; Frankenreiter 2018; Weinshall, Sommer, and Ritov 2018; Desrieux and Espinosa 2019). To provide a few examples:

Brazilian Supreme Court: Desposato, Ingram, and Lannes (2015) use the Martin–Quinn model to measure the judges' ideologies. The study shows that an increase in the court's policy-making authority created a political cleavage on the court.

Catalan Constitutional Court: Dalla Pellegrina, Garoupa, and Gili (2020) estimate the judges' ideal of points along two dimensions: conservative–progressive and Spanish–Catalan sovereignty. The former affects decisions with significant policy content; the latter affects outcomes regardless of content.

Estonian Supreme Court: After estimating the justices' ideal points, Hanretty (2015) concludes that the recovered dimension does not reflect ideology but rather 'disagreement about the proper scope of constitutional redress'.

Norwegian Supreme Court: Based on their ideal point estimates, Skiple, Littleré Bentsen, and Hanretty (2020) demonstrate that the judges are not divided along left–right lines but instead 'disagree about the appropriate degree of deference' to give to the government.

Turkish Constitutional Court: Applying the Martin–Quinn model, Varol, Dalla Pellegrina, and Garoupa (2017) unearth a conservative ideological shift following a restructuring of the Court.

European Court of Human Rights: Voeten (2007) estimated the ideal points of judges from 1960 to 2006. The results show that activism versus restraint is 'the main dimension of contestation among judges.'

That scholars all over the world are attempting to estimate ideal points in one way or another speaks to the importance of the enterprise. Ideal points have become nearly indispensable for assessing the implications of many accounts of judicial behaviour, characterizing courts (or at least their median judge), studying individual and institutional change over time, and analysing the relations between courts and other relevant actors, among many other pressing projects.

In this section, we briefly explain ideal points and the spatial model that underlies them. Next we turn from the spatial model to the measurement models used to estimate ideal points. We conclude with a discussion of the limitations and challenges of these models—and potential workarounds.

4.1 Ideal Points and Spatial Models of Voting

Ever since Pritchett's groundbreaking work on the 'Roosevelt Court' (the US Supreme Court of the 1930s and 1940s), scholars and other commentators have arrayed judges serving on a collegial court along an ideological continuum. Figure 16.1 below provides an example of the 2021–2022 US Supreme Court.

The horizontal line represents a policy space ordered from left (most 'liberal') to right ('most conservative'). (Here, the line depicts all cases decided by the Court but it could be particular issue area, such as civil rights or criminal procedure.) The vertical lines are the justices' 'most preferred positions', which, in this depiction, is an estimate of each

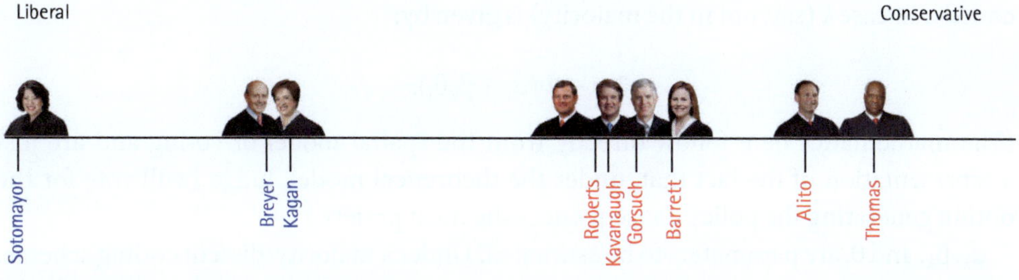

FIGURE 16.1 US Supreme Court Justices, ordered from left to right based on their Martin–Quinn ideal point estimates, 2021–2022 term.

justice's ideal point. If each justice had his or her druthers, the Court's decisions would end up precisely on this point.

All of us have seen these types of figures; they are commonplace worldwide. But underlying them is a general framework: a spatial model of voting. The model that motivates the Martin–Quinn approach to ideal point estimation assumes that judges have a choice between two alternatives (e.g. affirm or reverse the lower court, vote with the majority or not), and that these alternatives have policy consequences that can be represented by points in an issue space. Judges evaluate these policy consequences with utility functions that are single peaked around some ideal policy point specific to each judge. A (trivial) consequence of the model is that a judge is most likely to vote for the alternative closest to her in the policy space.

4.2 From Spatial Models to Measurement Models

To move from spatial models to measurement, most contemporary approaches draw on item response theory (IRT) models. The basic goal is to show a relationship between an attribute, as measured by some instrument, and a response. In educational testing, the trait may be intelligence or ability as measured by answers to questions on a standardized exam. In judging, the trait may be ideology, as measured by votes in cases, to join, say, the majority or not. It is worth emphasizing that IRT models are agnostic about the latent dimension—that is, they won't tell us whether an uncovered pattern is ideology or not. That call is up to the researcher to make. (Ho and Quinn (2010) provide a non-technical introduction to these models.)

The central building block in models of judicial ideal points is that the probability of Judge j voting for the alternative coded 1 (say, voting with the majority in non-unanimous decisions) in case k is given by:

$$\Phi(\alpha_k + \beta_k \theta_j)$$

where $\Phi(\cdot)$ is the standard normal cumulative distribution function, α_k and β_k are deterministic functions of the policy locations of the two alternatives, and θ_j is the ideological location of Judge j's most preferred policy (her ideal point). Because of the dichotomous nature of each judge's decision, the probability that Judge j votes for the alternative coded 0 in case k (say, not in the majority) is given by:

$$1 - \Phi(\alpha_k + \beta_k \theta_j).$$

(The mathematics here follow directly from the spatial model of voting and are just a representation of the fact that, under the theoretical model, Judge j will vote for the option generating the policy consequences she most prefers.)

α_k, β_k, and θ_j are parameters to be estimated. Under a majority/dissent coding scheme, α_k captures the propensity to vote with the majority on case k after accounting for β_k and θ_j. β_k (the discrimination parameter) tells us the extent to which the voting pattern in a given case k is consistent with the dominant pattern unearthed by the model; the higher the (absolute) value of β_k, the better the representation of case k.[11] In Figure 16.1 a 6–3 decision in which the three more liberal justices dissented would be consistent with the model, but a 6–3 decision, with Sotomayor, Kavanaugh, and Thomas dissenting would not be consistent.

For our purposes, the parameter θ_j is of great interest. It represents the judge's location (most preferred position) on the latent dimension for the period under analysis. Looking at Figure 16.1 it seems clear that the dimension is a left–right ideological dimension—if only because the θ_j values are consistent with informed commentary on the justices' behaviour.

Figure 16.1 shows ideal points for the 2021–2022 term of the Court, but they come from a dynamic IRT model, the Martin–Quinn analysis, which allows the estimates to vary by term (or any other time period) and are quite common in studies of judicial behaviour (e.g. Voeten 2008; Alarie, Green, and Iacobucci 2015; Windett, Harden, and Hall 2015; Varol, Dalla Pellegrina, and Garoupa 2017). To generate the dynamic estimates, Martin and Quinn include a Bayesian prior—though many other approaches are possible, including analyses that assume the judges' preferences are stable over the course of their careers (like NOMINATE scores developed for legislators) (e.g. Alarie and Green 2009; Hanretty 2012, 2013; Nery Ferreira and Mueller 2014; Dalla Pellegrina et al. 2017) or that develop estimates separately for each time period of interest (Dalla Pellegrina, Escresa, and Garoupa 2014).

4.3 Advantages . . . and Challenges

This is but a very brief introduction to IRT models designed to estimate judicial ideal points, with emphasis on dynamic Martin–Quinn scores. For readers interested in learning more (including applications), we recommend the original Martin and Quinn article (2002), as well as Martin, Quinn, and Epstein (2005); Alarie and Green (2009); Ho and Quinn (2010); Bailey, Howard, and Randazzo (2017); Gergen et al. (2020). We also note the availability of software packages that simplify the task of analysing item-response models. Martin, Quinn, and Park's (2011) MCMCpack is especially popular. It contains functions to use Bayesian tools to fit many statistical models including an array of measurement models (e.g. a one-dimensional IRT model, a k-dimensional IRT model).

We hope these sources are helpful but for now it is worth stressing that IRT models designed to estimate judicial ideal points are ubiquitous because they have many nice features. Certainly one is that they do not require researchers to determine whether a case or vote is 'liberal' or 'conservative'—almost always a task fraught with difficulty and controversy. More objective binaries are fine (such as, in our example, voted 'with the majority' or 'not with the majority'). Moreover, any dichotomy works as long as the votes are coded consistently within a particular case. In other words, it is perfectly acceptable to code votes in some cases as 'with the majority' or 'not with the majority' and votes in another subset of cases as 'with the chief judge' or 'not with the chief judge', and so on. All such coding will produce *identical* ideal point estimates.

A second excellent property of judicial ideal point estimates is that they allow for comparisons with other actors—including legislators and judges. The exact procedure depends on the comparability of the various estimates. For example, the Judicial Common Space places US justices, lower court judges, presidents, and legislators in the same policy space (Epstein et al. 2007a). Because all but the justices' scores follow from NOMINATE scores, the placements require only a transformation of the justices' (Martin–Quinn) scores to make them comparable. Other strategies are also possible (see e.g. Brouard and Hönnige 2017).

Yet another upside is that dynamic ideal point estimates permit judges to 'evolve'. Although preference change in the form of ideological drift may not be all that interesting for judges serving relatively short, non-renewable terms, it is a phenomenon of note for life-tenured judges (Epstein et al. 2007b; Alarie and Green 2009). Approaches that can generate year-by-year (or actually any other period of interest) allow for assessment of drift over time.

Still, ideal point estimates are not without their share of concerns—though we prefer to think of them as challenges that can be met. The first, and perhaps most obvious, is the circularity issue: Because researchers derive their estimates from votes, deploying, say, the Martin–Quinn scores to study the effect of ideology on votes would amount to using votes to predict votes. One response is that researchers should use them for only certain kinds of projects—typically projects that already assume ideology has an effect on voting. Endogenous scores, for example, have been used in research on ideological drift, which asks whether the judges' ideology changes with time.

Another response to the endogeneity problem is to remove the cases of interest from the data and then estimate the Martin–Quinn (or any other) scores on the remaining cases. Suppose we wanted to study the effect of ideology on votes in religion cases. By purging the religion cases from the data and recalculating the scores, we would avoid the trap of using votes to predict votes.

At one level, this technically resolves the circularity problem, though this problem can be overstated. As Martin and Quinn (2005) write:

> [A]s a practical matter using the full data Martin–Quinn scores when modeling votes in a single issue is perfectly appropriate. While circularity is a technical concern, the resultant measures from purging issues will change very little, and so it is not worth the effort to do so. When modeling votes in a single issue area, circularity is not a practical concern.[12]

A second concern with ideal point estimates is that they (in line with the spatial model) assume that judges vote sincerely for their most preferred outcome. That is, the estimates do not take account of the possibility that judges might vote strategically—for example, by considering the preferences and likely actions of their colleagues or elected actors. Some scholars have attempted to devise workarounds, with Fischman's (2011) effort especially notable. He develops a consensus model that includes the cost of dissent in the judicial utility function (reflecting the 'norm of consensus' on US appellate courts) and shows that it generates more accurate predictions than standard ideal point models. Considering the high rate of consensus on many courts worldwide, Fischman's strategy seems especially promising for the comparative analysis of judicial behaviour. (For another approach to estimating preferences on courts without much or any dissent, see Malecki (2012)).

A third concern centres on dimensionality. Our discussion has highlighted ideal points in a one-dimensional (left–right) space for good reason: The vast majority of studies (and not just US studies) uncover a single dimension usually identified as an ideological or policy pattern, suggesting the plausibility of unidimensionality as a general rule. But exceptions exist, and the same models used to identify ideological voting have been applied to indicators of other dimensions of interest. Such was Dalla Pellegrina et al.'s (2020) study of the Catalan Constitutional Court. The authors used IRT models to estimate the judges' ideal points along two dimensions: conservative–progressive and Spanish–Catalan sovereignty (see also Hartmann and Hudson 2017).

5. Conclusion

We began by noting the ubiquity and substantive importance of the *concept* of political preferences in accounts of judging; and much of the chapter took pains to distinguish the underlying latent *concept* from particular *measures* of that concept. This distinction between a latent concept and the tangible, but imperfect, measures of that concept is vitally important to the social scientific enterprise. Although we are confident that the political preferences of judges will remain important for accounts of judging well into the future, we encourage readers to keep an open mind as to the best ways to measure political preferences in their own applications. We hope that this chapter has clarified the considerations key to that inquiry.

Acknowledgements

For outstanding research assistance we thank Luwei Ying, and for insightful comments we are grateful to Gunnar Grendstad and participants at the conference on comparative judicial behaviour. Epstein thanks the John Simon Guggenheim Foundation, the National Science Foundation, and Washington University for supporting her work on judicial behaviour. Some ideas in this chapter draw on our previous writings, especially Martin, Quinn, and Epstein (2005); Ho and Quinn (2010); Epstein et al. (2012); Gergen et al. (2020).

Notes

1. See Chapter 10.
2. See Chapter 7.
3. Apparently, Schubert had a different take on state judges. Just six years before publishing *The Judicial Mind*, Schubert (1959) explored the effect of partisan stimuli in the form of workers' compensation claims.
4. Here we focus on conceptual differences between party and ideology. But there are other reasons to question party as a proxy for ideology (Epstein et al. 2012). For example, the approach assumes that the judges (or appointers) of one political party are always and uniformly more conservative than another political party. For example, in the United States, all Republican Presidents (or judges) are conservatives and all Democratic Presidents (or judges) are liberal. But data—at least in the United States—tends to show otherwise: 'Presidents of the same political party vary in their ideological preferences. Eisenhower is not Reagan. Indeed, the empirical record demonstrates that the voting propensities of the appointees of some Democratic and Republican presidents do not differ significantly' (Giles, Hettinger, and Peppers 2001). Another (usually untested assumption) is that appointers are motivated to appoint judges who reflect their ideology. But US studies show that appointers may have other goals. To provide but one example, Ronald Reagan's appointment of Sandra Day O'Connor was less about advancing ideological goals than about appealing to female voters (see generally Goldman 1997).
5. Researchers have conducted experiments on judges attending judicial conferences, but almost all the experiments focus on sussing out various cognitive biases; judges are apparently reluctant to provide their partisan affiliation much less participate in political experiments (see e.g. Rachlinski et al. 2009).
6. Campaign contributions made to political parties and candidates is another exogenous measure (Bonica and Sen 2017). It hasn't caught on much in the United States, and we wonder how well it would transport to other countries.
7. Varieties of Democracy: https://www.v-dem.net.
8. This article is in Norwegian. See Appendix B in Grendstad, Shaffer, and Waltenburg (2015) for a summary of the measure in English.
9. For some tips on how to develop and analyse expert surveys, see Curini (2010); Lindstädt, Proksch, and Slapin (2020); Bakker et al. (2014).
10. See Ainsley et al. (2020), cataloguing 'voting procedures for 145 legislative chambers and finding that roll calls are typically discretionary'.
11. β_k can have a negative or positive value. When β_k is large and positive, the ideal points of the judges are highly predictive of their votes in case k with the members of the majority having ideal points to the right of the minority judges.
12. But this response, we hasten to note, does not resolve a related problem as to what causes the justices' votes in the first place. Let's say we're interested in the role of ideology in explaining judges' votes in religion cases. If we exclude religion votes in the calculation of the Martin–Quinn scores, we have eliminated the circularity issue. But that approach begs the question as to what caused the non-religion votes. We can claim that it is ideology, but all we really know is that the same factors that influence the judges' votes in non-religious cases influence their votes in religious cases. Perhaps that's good enough for most applications.

References

Ainsley, Caitlin, Clifford J. Carrubba, Brian F. Crisp, Betul Demirkaya, Matthew J. Gabel, and Dino Hadzic. 2020. 'Roll-Call Vote Selection: Implications for the Study of Legislative Politics'. *American Political Science Review* 114: 691–706.

Alarie, Benjamin, and Andrew Green. 2009. 'Policy Preference Change and Appointments to the Supreme Court of Canada'. *Osgoode Hall Law Journal* 47: 1–46.

Alarie, Benjamin, Andrew Green, and Edward M. Iacobucci. 2015. 'Panel Selection on High Courts'. *University of Toronto Law Journal* 65 (4): 335–81.

Alarie, Benjamin, and Andrew J. Green. 2017. *Commitment and Cooperation on High Courts*. Oxford: Oxford University Press.

Bailey, Michael, Robert M. Howard, and Kirk A. Randazzo. 2017. 'Measuring Ideology on the Courts'. In *Routledge Handbook of Judicial Behavior*, edited by Kirk A. Randazzo. Routledge.

Baker, Andy, and Kenneth F. Green. 2011. 'The Latin American Left's Mandate: Free Market Policies and Issue Voting in New Democracies'. *World Politics* 61: 43–77.

Bakker, Ryan, Erica Edwards, Seth Jolly, Jonathan Polk, Jan Rovny, and Marco Steenbergen. 2014. 'Anchoring the Experts: Using Vignettes to Compare Party Ideology Across Countries'. *Research & Politics* 1.

Benoit, Kenneth, and Michael Laver. 2006. *Party Policy in Modern Democracies*. London: Routledge.

Blaustein, Albert P., and Roy M. Mersky. 1972. 'Rating Supreme Court Justices'. *American Bar Association Journal* 58: 1183–89.

Bonica, Adam, and Maya Sen. 2017. 'A Common-Space Scaling of the American Judiciary and Legal Profession'. *Political Analysis* 21: 114–21.

Brauninger, Thomas, Jochen Müller, and Christian Stecker. 2016. 'Modeling Preferences Using Roll Call Votes in Parliamentary Systems'. *Political Analysis* 24: 189–210.

Brouard, Sylvain, and Christoph Hönnige. 2017. 'Constitutional Courts as Veto Players: Lessons from the United States, France and Germany'. *European Journal of Political Research* 56 (3): 529–52.

Bütikofer, Sarah, and Simon Hug. 2010. 'The Swiss Upper House: "Chambre de Réflexion" or Conservative Renegades?' *Journal of Legislative Studies* 16: 176–94.

Campbell, Angus, Philip E. Converse, Warren E. Miller, and Donald E. Stokes. 1960. *The American Voter*. New York: Wiley.

Castles, Frank, and Peter Mair. 1984. 'Left-Right Political Scales: Some Expert Judgements'. *European Journal of Political Research* 12: 73–88.

Ceron, Andrea, and Marco Mainenti. 2015. 'Toga Party: The Political Basis of Judicial Investigations against MPs in Italy (1983–2013)'. *South European Society and Politics* 20: 223–42.

Clinton, Joshua D., and David E. Lewis. 2008. 'Expert Opinion, Agency Characteristics, and Agency Preferences'. *Political Analysis* 16: 3–20.

Cohen, Geoffrey L. 2003. 'Party Over Policy: The Dominating Impact of Group Influence on Political Beliefs'. *Journal of Personality and Social Psychology* 85 (5): 808–22.

Curini, Luigi. 2010. 'Experts' Political Preferences and Their Impact on Ideological Bias: An Unfolding Analysis based on a Benoit-Laver Expert Survey'. *Party Politics* 16: 299–321.

Dalla Pellegrina, Lucia, and Nuno Garoupa. 2013. 'Choosing Between the Government and the Regions: An Empirical Analysis of the Italian Constitutional Court Decisions'. *European Journal of Political Research* 52: 558–80.

Dalla Pellegrina, Lucia, Laarni Escresa, and Nuno Garoupa. 2014. 'Measuring Judicial Ideal Points in New Democracies: The Case of the Philippines'. *Asian Journal of Law and Society* 1 (1): 125–64.

Dalla Pellegrina, Lucia, Nuno Garoupa, and Marian Gili. 2020. 'Estimating Judicial Ideal Points in Bi-Dimensional Courts: Evidence from Catalonia'. *Journal of Empirical Legal Studies* 17 (2): 383–415.

Dalla Pellegrina, Lucia, Jef De Mot, Michael Faure, and Nuno Garoupa. 2017. 'Litigating Federalism: An Empirical Analysis of Decisions of the Belgian Constitutional Court'. *European Constitutional Law Review* 13: 305–46.

Desposato, Scott W., Matthew C. Ingram, and Osmar P. Lannes, Jr. 2015. 'Power, Composition, and Decision Making: The Behavioral Consequences of Institutional Reform on Brazil's Supremo Tribunal Federal'. *Journal of Law Economics & Organization* 31 (3): 534–67.

Desrieux, Claudine, and Romain Espinosa. 2019. 'Case Selection and Judicial Decision-Making: Evidence from French Labor Courts'. *European Journal of Law and Economics* 47 (1): 57–88.

Epstein, Lee, and Carol Mershon. 1996. 'Measuring Political Preferences'. *American Journal of Political Science* 40: 261–94.

Epstein, Lee, William M. Landes, and Richard A. Posner. 2013. *The Behavior of Federal Judges*. Cambridge: Harvard University Press.

Epstein, Lee, Andrew D. Martin, Jeffrey A. Segal, and Chad Westerland. 2007a. 'The Judicial Common Space'. *Journal of Law Economics & Organization* 23 (2): 303–25.

Epstein, Lee, Andrew D. Martin, Kevin M. Quinn, and Jeffrey A. Segal. 2007b. 'Ideological Drift Among Supreme Court Justices'. *Northwestern University Law Review* 101: 1483–542.

Epstein, Lee, Andrew D. Martin, Kevin M. Quinn, and Jeffrey A. Segal. 2012. 'Ideology and the Study of Judicial Behavior'. In *Ideology, Psychology, and Law*, edited by Jon Hanson, 705–28. Oxford: Oxford University Press.

Fischman, Joshua B. 2011. 'Estimating Preferences of Circuit Judges: A Model of Consensus Voting'. *Journal of Law & Economics* 54 (4): 781–809.

Frankenreiter, Jens. 2018. 'Are Advocates General Political? An Empirical Analysis of the Voting Behavior of the Advocates General at the European Court of Justice'. *Review of Law & Economics* 14: 20160037.

Gergen, Mark P., David A. Carrillo, Benjamin Minhao Chen, and Kevin M. Quinn. 2020. 'Partisan Voting on the California Supreme Court'. *Southern California Law Review* 93: 101–83.

Giles, Micheal W., Virginia A. Hettinger, and Todd Peppers. 2001. 'Picking Federal Judges: A Note on Policy and Partisan Selection Agendas'. *Political Research Quarterly* 54 (3): 623–41.

Goldman, Sheldon. 1997. *Picking Federal Judges*. New Haven: Yale University Press.

Gonzalez Bertomeu, Juan, Lucia Dalla Pellegrina, and Nuno Garoupa. 2017. 'Estimating Judicial Ideal Points in Latin America: The Case of Argentina'. *Review of Law & Economics* 13: 20150040.

Grendstad, Gunnar, William R. Shaffer, and Eric N. Waltenburg. 2011a. 'Ideologi og Grunnholdninger hos Dommerne'. *Lov og Rett* 50 (4): 240–53.

Grendstad, Gunnar, William R. Shaffer, and Eric N. Waltenburg. 2011b. 'When Justices Disagree. The Influences of Ideology and Geography on Economic Voting on the Norwegian Supreme Court'. *Retfaerd* 34: 3–22.

Grendstad, Gunnar, William R. Shaffer, and Eric N. Waltenburg. 2015. *Policy Making in an Independent Judiciary. The Norwegian Supreme Court*. Colchester: ECPSR Press.

Hájek, Lukáš. 2020. 'Dynamic Roll Call Analysis of Parties' Ideological Positions in the Czech Republic'. *Journal of Legislative Studies* 26: 133–57.
Hanretty, Chris. 2012. 'Dissent in Iberia: The Ideal Points of Justices on the Spanish and Portuguese Constitutional Tribunals'. *European Journal of Political Research* 51: 671–92.
Hanretty, Chris. 2013. 'The Decisions and Ideal Points of British Law Lords'. *British Journal of Political Science* 43 (3): 703–16.
Hanretty, Chris. 2015. 'Judicial Disagreement Need Not Be Political: Dissent on the Estonian Supreme Court'. *Europe-Asia Studies* 67 (6): 970–88.
Hartmann, Ivar Alberto, and Alexander Hudson. 2017. 'Can You Bury Ideology? An Empirical Analysis of the Ideal Points of the Ministers of Brazil's Supremo Tribunal Federal'. *A&C-Revista De Direito Administrativo & Constitucional* 17 (68): 43–59.
Hawkins, Carlee Beth, and Brian A. Nosek. 2012. 'Motivated Independence? Implicit Party Identity Predicts Political Judgments Among Self-Proclaimed Independents'. *Personality and Social Psychology Bulletin* 38 (11): 1437–52.
Hix, Simon, Abdul Noury, and Gérard Roland. 2006. 'Dimensions of Politics in the European Parliament'. *American Journal of Political Science* 50: 494–511.
Ho, Daniel E., and Kevin M. Quinn. 2010. '813 How Not to Lie with Judicial Votes: Misconceptions, Measurement, and Models'. *California Law Review* 98: 813–76.
Hönnige, Christoph. 2009. 'The Electoral Connection: How the Pivotal Judge Affects Oppositional Success at European Constitutional Courts'. *West European Politics* 32 (5): 963–84.
Iaryczower, Matias, and Gabriel Katz. 2016. 'More than Politics: Ability and Ideology in the British Appellate Committee'. *Journal of Law Economics & Organization* 32 (1): 61–93.
Iyengar, Shanto, and Sean J. Westwood. 2015. 'Fear and Loathing across Party Lines: New Evidence on Group Polarization'. *American Journal of Political Science* 59 (3): 690–707.
Kekkonen, Arto and Tuomas Yia¨-Anttila. 2021. 'Affective Blocs: Understanding Affective Polarization in Multiparty Systems'. *Electoral Studies* 72: 102367.
Kellermann, Michael. 2012. 'Estimating Ideal Points in the British House of Commons Using Early Day Motions'. *American Journal of Political Science* 56: 757–71.
Lewis, Jeffrey B., Keith Poole, Howard Rosenthal, Adam Boche, Aaron Rudkin, and Luke Sonnet. 2022. 'Voteview: Congressional Roll-Call Votes Database'. https://voteview.com/.
Lindstädt, René, Jonathan. B. Slapin, and Ryan. J. Vander Wielen. 2011. 'Balancing Competing Demands: Position Taking and Election Proximity in the European Parliament'. *Legislative Studies Quarterly* 36: 37–70.
Lindstädt, René, Sven-Oliver Proksch, and Jonathan B. Slapin. 2020. 'When Experts Disagree: Response Aggregation and its Consequences in Expert Surveys'. *Political Science Research and Methods* 8: 580–88.
Lloyd, Randall D. 1995. 'Separating Partisanship from Party in Judicial Research: Reapportionment in the U.S. District Courts'. *American Political Science Review* 89 (2): 413–20.
Lo, James. 2018. 'Dynamic Ideal Point Estimation for the European Parliament, 1980–2009'. *Public Choice* 176: 229–46.
López-Laborda, Julio, Fernando Rodrigo, and Eduardo Sanz-Arcega. 2019. 'Consensus and Dissent in The Resolution of Conflicts of Competence by the Spanish Constitutional Court: The Role of Federalism and Ideology'. *European Journal of Law and Economics* 48: 305–30.
Malecki, Michael. 2012. 'Do ECJ Judges All Speak with the Same Voice? Evidence of Divergent Preferences from the Judgments of Chambers'. *Journal of European Public Policy* 19 (1), SI: 59–75.

Martin, Andrew D., and Kevin M. Quinn. 2002. 'Dynamic Ideal Point Estimation via Markov Chain Monte Carlo for the U.S. Supreme Court, 1953–1999'. *Political Analysis* 10: 134–53.

Martin, Andrew D., and Kevin M. Quinn. 2005. 'Can Ideal Points be Used as Explanatory Variables?' https://mqscores.lsa.umich.edu/media/resnote.pdf.

Martin, Andrew D., Kevin M. Quinn, and Jong Hee Park. 2011. 'MCMCpack: Markov Chain Monte Carlo in *R*'. *Journal of Statistical Software* 42 (9): 1–21.

Martin, Andrew D., Kevin M. Quinn, and Lee Epstein. 2005. 'The Median Justice on the U.S. Supreme Court'. *North Carolina Law Review* 83: 1275–322.

Mason, Lilliana. 2015. '"I Disrespectfully Agree": The Differential Effects of Partisan Sorting on Social and Issue Polarization'. *American Journal of Political Science* 59 (1): 128–45.

Munro, Geoffrey D., Julia Zirpoli, Adam Schuman, and Jeff Taulbee. 2013. 'Third-Party Labels Bias Evaluations of Political Platforms and Candidates'. *Basic and Applied Social Psychology* 35 (2): 151–63.

Nagel, Stuart S. 1961. 'Political Party Affiliation and Judges' Decisions'. *American Political Science Review* 55 (4): 843–50.

Nery Ferreira, Pedro Fernando Almeida, and Bernardo Mueller. 2014. 'How Judges Think in the Brazilian Supreme Court: Estimating Ideal Points and Identifying Dimensions'. *Economia* 15 (3): 275–93.

Ostberg, C. L., and Matthew E. Wetstein. 2007. *Attitudinal Decision Making in the Supreme Court of Canada*. Vancouver: UBC Press.

Peretti, Terri. 2020. *Partisan Supremacy*. Lawrence: University Press of Kansas.

Pinello, Daniel R. 1999. 'Linking Party to Judicial Ideology in American Courts: A Meta-analysis'. *Justice System Journal* 20 (3): 219–54.

Pritchett, C. Herman. 1941. 'Divisions of Opinion among Justices of the U.S. Supreme Court, 1939-1941'. *American Political Science Review* 35 (5): 890–98.

Pritchett, C. Herman. 1948. *The Roosevelt Court*. New York: Macmillan.

Rachlinski, Jeffrey J., Sheri Johnson, Andrew J. Wistrich, and Chris Guthrie. 2009. 'Does Unconscious Racial Bias Affect Trial Judges?' Notre Dame Law Review 84: 1195–246.

Ray, Leonard, and Hanne Marthe Narud. 2000. 'Mapping the Norwegian Political Space: Some Findings from an Expert Survey'. *Party Politics* 6: 225–39.

Reiljan, Andres. 2019. 'Fear and Loathing Across Party Lines (Also) in Europe: Affective Polarisation in European Party Systems'. *European Journal of Political Research* 59: 376–96.

Rosenthal, Howard, and Eric Voeten. 2004. 'Analyzing Roll Calls with Perfect Spatial Voting: France 1946–1958'. *American Journal of Political Science* 48: 620–32.

Sánchez, Arianna, Beatriz Magaloni, and Eric Magar. 2011. 'Legalist versus Interpretativist: The Supreme Court and the Democratic Transition in Mexico'. In *Courts in Latin America*, edited by Gretchen Helmke and Julio Rios-Figueroa. 187–218. Cambridge: Cambridge University Press.

Schmidhauser, John R. 1961. 'Judicial Behavior and the Sectional Crisis of 1837–1860'. *Journal of Politics* 23 (4): 615–40.

Schubert, Glendon. 1959. *Quantitative Analysis of Judicial Behavior*. Glencoe: Free Press.

Segal, Jeffrey A., and Albert D. Cover. 1989. 'Ideological Values and the Votes of U.S. Supreme Court Justices'. *American Political Science Review* 83: 557–65.

Skiple, Jon Kaare, Henrik Littleré Bentsen, and Chris Hanretty. 2020. 'The Government Deference Dimension of Judicial Decision Making: Evidence from the Supreme Court of Norway'. *Scandinavian Political Studies* 43 (4): 264–85.

Solberg, Rorie Spill, and Eric N. Waltenburg. 2023. 'Attitudinal Judging: Partisanship and Ideology'. In *The Oxford Handbook on Comparative Judicial Behaviour*, edited by Lee Epstein, Gunnar Grendstad, Urška Šadl, and Keren Weinshall. Oxford: Oxford University Press.

Sunstein, Cass, David Schkade, Lisa M. Ellman, and Andres Sawicki. 2006. *Are Judges Political?* Washington: Brookings Institution Press.

Szmer, John, Susan W. Johnson, and Tammy A. Sarver. 2007. 'Does the Lawyer Matter? Influencing Outcomes on the Supreme Court of Canada'. *Law & Society Review* 41: 279–304.

Ulmer, S. Sidney. 1962. 'The Political Party Variable in the Michigan Supreme Court'. *Journal of Public Law* 11 (2): 352–62.

Varol, Ozan O., Lucia Dalla Pellegrina, and Nuno Garoupa. 2017. 'An Empirical Analysis of Judicial Transformation in Turkey'. *American Journal of Comparative Law* 65 (1): 187–216.

Vines, Kenneth N. 1964. 'Federal District Judges and Race Relations Cases in the South'. *Journal of Politics* 26 (2): 337.

Voeten, Erik. 2007. 'The Politics of International Judicial Appointments: Evidence from the European Court of Human Rights'. *International Organization* 61 (4): 669–701.

Voeten, Erik. 2008. 'The Impartiality of International Judges: Evidence from the European Court of Human Rights'. *American Political Science Review* 102 (4): 417–33.

Weiden, David L. 2011. 'Judicial Politicization, Ideology, and Activism at the High Courts of the United States, Canada, and Australia'. *Political Research Quarterly* 64: 335–47.

Weinshall, Keren, Udi Sommer, and Ya'acov Ritov. 2018. 'Ideological Influences on Governance and Regulation: The Comparative Case of Supreme Courts'. *Regulation & Governance* 12 (3): 334–52.

Westwood, Sean J., Shanto Iyengar, Stefaan Walgrave, Rafael Leonisio, Luis Miller, and Strijbis Oliver. 2018. 'The Tie that Divides: Cross-National Evidence of the Primacy of Partyism'. *European Journal of Political Research* 57: 333–54.

Windett, Jason H., Jeffrey J. Harden, and Matthew E. K. Hall. 2015. 'Estimating Dynamic Ideal Points for State Supreme Courts'. *Political Analysis* 23 (3): 461–69.

Yildirim, Engin, Aziz Kutlar, and Serdar Gulener. 2017. 'Estimating Judicial Ideal Points of the Justices of the Turkish Constitutional Court between 1962 and 1982'. *Amme Idaresi Dergisi* 50 (4): 1–31.

PART IV

STAFFING THE COURTS

CHAPTER 17

SELECTING JUDGES

LYDIA BRASHEAR TIEDE

1. Introduction

JUDICIAL selection is politically contentious because judges' behaviour may be correlated with their selectors' preferences and judges' decisions often have significant policy implications. Additionally, the manipulation of judicial selection rules has been a favourite tool of autocratic-leaning leaders in countries experiencing democratic regress. As most judges worldwide are not elected, the manner of selection and the identity of those involved in selection have the potential to create openings for political control of the judiciary. This political control, however, is at odds with a normative understanding that judges should be above politics, independent, and make decisions that are bound by case facts and laws. There is no avoiding that judges often make political decisions[1] and judicial selection serves political ends.

Judicial selection can be either designed to curb the ability of one set of political beliefs from dominating a court or judiciary or manipulated to serve more singular interests. The extent that countries design their selection mechanisms to favour one extreme or the other signals their commitment or lack thereof to democratic values and pluralism. When judicial selection is used to serve a singular political motive or support a political party or its beliefs, it undermines the professional, legalistic, and technical nature of judging. On the other hand, suggesting that a judicial selection method can ensure that judges don't make decisions based on their own political or other biases is naïve. Thus, acknowledging that judges may concurrently have great legal skills and biases, courts could serve their purposes better if judicial selection methods prevent one political interest or bias from dominating the court's decision-making and ensure that different types of perspectives are considered.

Policy-makers and citizens are concerned about judicial selection due to the powers that courts possess which may be more minimal, such as courts without the power of judicial review, or quite extensive, such as courts with *a priori* abstract review of legislation held by many constitutional courts. Although Tsebelis (2002) and Dahl (1957) claim that courts are not veto players, the former claiming that courts' preferences are absorbed into those of existing veto players that choose judges in a highly politicized selection process and the latter claiming that judges constitute part of the dominant political elite, courts certainly can and often do veto the policies of strong executives and legislatures under certain conditions. Those conditions are determined in part by judicial selection informing which judges and court compositions face which political actors at any point in time (Brouard and Hönnige 2017). In turn, the delegation of power to judges presents a 'Madisonian dilemma' because unelected judges are provided with power and resources that may be used against those who selected them (see Kiewiet and McCubbins 1991). Elected politicians can counter the potential power that judges and courts hold in society through careful vetting of judicial candidates. In other words, *ex ante* controls over judicial selection provide a means for selecting judges with particular attitudes, skills, or preferences (Brinks and Blass 2018). However, screening and vetting for certain attributes, such as political preferences, over others, such as legal acumen, may result in dangerously biased courts.

Due to the powers that courts hold, many governments reform their judicial selection processes to alter expectations regarding to whom judges should defer. For example, in 2010, the Turkish government amended the constitution, increasing the total number of judges on the Turkish Constitutional Court and increasing those nominated by the elected branches as opposed to the non-elected judiciary which had previously supported the interests of the military (Varol, Pellegrina, and Garoupa 2017). Similar examples of strong executives trying to gain control of judicial appointments have been seen in Hungary in 2011 and Poland in 2017. Argentina altered the selection method for its Supreme Court many times in the 1990s. Bolivia moved to electing constitutional court judges, although later President Evo Morales acknowledged that it was difficult to choose judges through elections (Driscoll and Nelson 2015). Likewise, policy-makers in US states have changed selection methods hundreds of times since the 1800s due to concerns that some branches of government (the executive or legislature) had too much influence over appointments, although often new selection methods did not deliver on their expectations for ensuring judicial independence (Hanssen 2004). Thus, while reforms may be used for political manipulation of the judiciary, there are other times when they are necessary to right historical wrongs or unworkable processes in a changing society.

Judicial selection leads to courts composed of judges with certain attributes which influence how they make decisions individually and collectively. Thus, the enormous amount of variation in judicial selection across countries and courts has significant implications for judicial behaviour but is understudied. Additionally, analysing judicial selection from a comparative perspective provides scholars with fodder for understanding political control of an almost exclusively unelected institution tasked with checking the powers of the elected branches and protecting vulnerable members of society. Judicial selection, specifically of constitutional court judges, also sheds light on constitutional development and constitutionalism within a country. Reform of judicial selection and its influence on policy outcomes shows the capacity of a country to create an institutional environment for achieving economic and social development. However, the manipulation of judicial selection through reforms might aggrandize the power of executives or other important actors or interests leading to democratic backsliding.

To understand the variation in judicial selection, the chapter begins with an analysis of the formal selection mechanisms of over 200 high courts worldwide as of 2022, indicating the most prevalent and innovative forms of selection as well as a discussion of some informal mechanisms. The section that follows then analyses how additional judicial selection rules may improve diversity on the bench. The next section describes how the many variations influence judicial independence and behaviour and how there is an inherent tension between selecting judges with political proclivities to achieve certain political goals and protecting the prestige and professionalism of the court itself. The chapter concludes with avenues for future research.

2. Judicial Selection Mechanisms of the World

2.1 Gender Diversity

There is considerable variation in judicial selection methods worldwide. Several scholars have attempted to capture this variation for high courts (Autheman 2004) and courts in a specific region, such as Latin America (see Ríos-Figueroa 2011; Brinks and Blass 2018; Achury 2019) or state courts in the United States (Hanssen 2004). Capturing such variation across all courts and time periods is a herculean task. Many of the selection methods revealed here have existed for many years, such as that of the US Supreme Court's presidential selection with advice and consent of the Senate, while other methods reflect more recent reforms. Due to the large number of reforms worldwide, this overview, summarized in Table 17.1, categorizes high courts' selection mechanisms appearing predominantly within constitutions as of 2022. High courts refer to supreme courts, supreme administrative courts, or constitutional courts. The table was created using information available from the Constitute Project website (Elkins, Ginsburg, and Melton 2022) and Mavčič (2018).

This method for collecting data has some obvious limitations due to an over-reliance on finding information on judicial selection for high courts from constitutions themselves rather than from formal legislation and organic laws. Additionally, this information was found in articles of the constitution dealing with the courts themselves. However, in some instances, when the executive or legislature nominates or confirms a judge, this is mentioned in other articles dealing with those actors' powers. Despite this, every attempt was made to find selection methods for countries that don't list the method within the constitution itself, but inevitably some may have been missed. Despite these limitations, the overview provided here analyses 218 courts across 179 countries. Of these, ninety-three courts or 43 per cent of the total were Constitutional

Table 17.1 Judicial selection: dominant influences and variations

Dominant influence in selection	Selection variation	Description of selection variation	Number of courts
Executive 46	Executive unilaterally	President/executive or executive branch (such as cabinet or minister of justice) selects alone.	8
	Executive with other	Executive selects with other agreeing. Other could be the head of the senate, chief judge, etc.	7
	Executive with legislature	President selects with legislature confirming.	19
	Non-elected head of state unilaterally	Non-elected head of state selects alone.	12
Legislature 17	Legislature unilaterally	Legislature chooses all judges usually by a supermajority vote.	17
Courts 1	High court with other	High court selects list of judges from which executive chooses and Senate confirms.	1
Mixed system 72	Mixed without judicial council	Mixed system in which different actors select a distinct number of judges. The method may or may not require another institution to confirm selections. A judicial council is not involved at any stage.	59
	Mixed including judicial council as one selector or confirming selection of others	Mixed system in which different actors select a distinct number of judges. One such actor may be a judicial council which selects a portion of judges on the court or confirms the choices of others.	13
Judicial council 76	Judicial council, unilaterally	Judicial council acting alone selects all judges.	17
	Judicial council with legislature	Judicial council selects with legislative confirmation.	9
	Judicial council lists candidates and executive selects	Judicial council selects list of judges and executive or executive branch selects from the council's suggestion.	50
Other 6	Other	Unique or unusual selection methods, such as election of judges.	6

Courts (when a country has both a supreme and constitutional court) and 125 courts or 57 per cent were supreme courts (including supreme administrative courts). See Table 17.1 Appendix available from author for the courts considered to construct Table 17.1.

In Table 17.1, column 1, different selection mechanisms are clustered around five 'dominant influences' including selection dominated by the executive, legislature, courts, a mixed system, or by judicial councils or commissions. A sixth category is for courts that have unusual or not easily classified selection methods. An institution has a dominant influence in selection if it chooses judges unilaterally or initially suggests judicial candidates for further consideration by another institution. Similarly, if the system is predominantly a 'mixed system' in which different judges are chosen by different political actors then this mixed process is the dominant influence in selecting judges. Selecting institutions or methods with 'dominant influences' also possess the first mover advantage in choosing the list of candidates from which other institutions can select or appoint in some cases. In certain circumstances a dominant actor in the selection process may constrain judges' or courts' abilities to veto that actor's policy decisions. In general terms, more veto players in the selection process may ensure the selection of judges who are not hesitant to question or confront elected actors (Moreno, Crisp, and Shugart 2003).

It should be noted that the dominant influence in selection, as used here, is not a measure of the dominant political party in power when selection occurs (such as when the president's party in fact controls the legislature which chooses judges) but simply the institution or process which has the most input or influence in the selection of candidates. Additionally, just because a system is classified as having one dominant actor or process does not mean that other actors are not involved. For example, in mixed systems where different actors choose a specific number of judges, the executive may still be involved with nominating a portion of judges to a court.

The five dominant influences in selection, indicated and described in Table 17.1, column 1, have notable variations providing evidence of the extent that such influences are tempered by other actors or interests. Courts selected with *executive dominance* include four main variations (Table 17.1, column 2). Two executive-dominated subtypes include courts in which the executive, elected or non-elected, chooses all judges unilaterally. These two categories are an extreme example of executive dominance in judicial selection, which may be expected in countries with authoritarian leaders or closed societies but is unexpected in more democratic countries. A third type allows executives to choose judges with the advice of another actor such as a Chief Justice, Minister of Justice, or Cabinet. This selection method is still considered executive dominated because the confirming institution is also within the executive branch. A fourth executive type allows the president or executive to select candidates, and the choices are confirmed by the Senate, such as the system for choosing Supreme Court and other federal judges in the United States. The selection in this situation provides the president with a first mover advantage, although the ultimate dominance of the president in this selection method depends on the composition of the legislature, voting rules for confirming these judges, and the number of vacancies to be filled (see Llanos and Barreiro Lemos 2013). Indeed, presidents supported by 'heterogeneous coalitions' result in presidents nominating compromise candidates perhaps not as aligned with the presidents' political preferences as assumed (Llanos and Barreiro Lemos 2013).

Methods in which the legislature chooses judges or the high court self-selects do not reveal much variation. *Legislative dominant* selection methods allow the legislature to choose all judges to a court, usually by a super majority rule. For example, the National Assembly chooses all Peru's constitutional court judges by a two-thirds majority. *High court-dominant* methods in which the court chooses its own members are quite rare. The only example found was that of the Chilean Supreme Court under reforms in the 1990s and still in place in 2022, which allow the Supreme Court to create a list of candidates to serve as Supreme Court justices from which the president chooses one candidate from the list who is then confirmed by the Senate. Although there is only one Court in this category, sometimes high courts are still involved in selecting some judges sitting on their own court. For example, some Supreme Court justices may be highly involved in proposing and selecting judges when they serve as members on judicial commissions, select chief justices, propose candidates as in the case of supreme courts in Scandinavia (see Ghavanini et al. 2023), or choose some judges unilaterally to constitutional courts in mixed selection systems discussed below. Additionally, high court judges are often involved in the appointment, discipline, and removal of lower court judges, which can impede the judicial independence of those lower court judges as they may feel compelled to follow the preferences of the higher court. For this reason, high court selection is listed separately as a category as it is a prevalent method for choosing lower court judges and any extension of this research to those lower courts would consider this a separate mechanism. More autocratic-leaning leaders seeking to influence judicial selection in a more subtle way could fill the supreme court with loyalists and then allow them to select future judges.

Mixed selection is identified as a dominant category in that it allows several institutions to choose a portion of the court or a specific number of judges, thus institutions of different origins selecting a certain number of judges dominate the selection process. Mixed selection methods may vary in their inclusion or not of a judicial council. Of those mixed systems that do not use a judicial council, some of the various institutions selecting a different number of judges can do so unilaterally or have those choices confirmed by another institution, such as a legislature. The Chilean Constitutional Tribunal is an example of the former in which under the Chilean Constitution with amendments from 2005, the president and Supreme Court each choose three judges unilaterally, and the Senate and chamber of deputies each choose two judges a piece confirming the choice of the other chamber. The Colombian Constitutional Court is an example of the latter in which the President, Supreme Court, and *Consejo de Estado* (i.e. high administrative court) each provide lists of three candidates for each of their open allocated positions and the Senate selects one judge per list by majority vote. In both these situations a judicial council is not involved in any way with selecting judges. Of those courts that use mixed selection with some involvement of a judicial council, the council may be one of many of the selectors choosing a defined portion of the court or the judicial council may confirm the nominations of other institutions as observed in the selection of judges to the Ecuadoran Constitutional Court as of 2022.[2] Despite the use of a judicial council, the above examples are still dominated by mixed selection as under this method different numbers of judges have different selectors.

The final major category of judicial selection involves selection dominated by a *judicial council or commission*. In general terms, a commission of individuals reviews the credentials of candidates and suggests a list of potential and qualified individuals to another political actor (such as a president or governor) vested with appointment authority. According to Garoupa and Ginsberg (2015), judicial councils 'are designed to insulate the functions of appointment, promotion, and discipline of judges from the partisan political process, while ensuring some level of accountability' (102–03). In some US states which use merit commissions to select judges, the governor chooses from a short list of candidates suggested by the commission and later after serving a short time, judges are subject to a non-competitive retention election. Some judicial commissions have unilateral control over selecting judges as well as disciplining them and removing them. Besides unilaterally selecting judges, several countries also have adopted judicial commissions to review judges' credentials prior to appointment by other political branches (usually the president or prime minister) (Hammergren 2002).

In Latin America, a wave of reforms beginning with democratic transitions in the mid-1980s and 1990s led many countries to create judicial commissions for selecting judges. Latin American countries adopted commissions or councils because it was thought that such a method would create a less political court (Hammergren 2007, 104). Additionally, selection of superior court judges by commissions became prevalent after some decolonization efforts in African countries in the 1950s (Smit 2018). Other critical historic junctures such as the fall of the Berlin Wall also led to the adoption of judicial commissions in some countries. One variant allows the judicial commission to choose all judges alone. A second variant has the legislature confirm the choices of the judicial commission and a third variant allows the president to choose from the commission's list of candidates. In theory, the commission dominates the selection process, but this in turn depends on who chooses the members of these judicial commissions. Thus, selection and identity of those judicial commission members who ultimately select justices has become as contentious as their ultimate selection of judges. The 2022/2023 governmental crisis in Israel focuses on this very issue due to government attempts to increase the number of political actors on the Judicial Selection Commission which selects, promotes, and removes judges including those of the Supreme Court (see Lurie 2022).

A sixth category of 'other' captures unusual mechanisms for selecting high court judges. Selection by popular election is included in this category. For example, Bolivia elects its high court judges (see Driscoll and Nelson 2015). Elections provide politicians with an important selection option. As shown in Chapter 20 by Burnham and Nelson in this volume, discussing the election of US state court judges, this method potentially influences judges' behaviour and makes elected courts more responsive to citizens.

Table 17.1 does not include the different selection mechanisms that may be employed to select chief justices, but this variation is worth further investigation. While some courts internally choose their chief justice, other courts allow the executive or government to choose the chief justice in a manner that is distinct from how other judges on the court are chosen. This allows different political actors to influence the judicial behaviour of chief justices in a manner apart from the remaining judges. This may signal the importance of chief judges' leadership roles, as explored in Chapter 31 by Bentsen and Skiple of this volume, depending on the power afforded the chief justice in assigning judges to write opinions, form panels, or issue decisive tie-breaking votes when there is an even number of judges present.

Figures 17.1 and 17.2 examine the prevalence of selection mechanisms by court type, comparing constitutional and supreme courts. The percentages displayed in the figure reflect the portion of a particular selection method used out of both types of courts together (i.e. out of 218 courts). Figure 17.1 shows that the dominant influence in selection varies considerably by court type. The most prevalent method for constitutional courts is some type of mixed selection method in which different institutions choose a specific number of judges, not all of the judges. Sixty-three or 68 per cent of ninety-three constitutional courts in this sample use mixed selection methods. The most prevalent method for supreme courts involves the use of judicial councils or commissions of which sixty-nine or 55 per cent of 125 supreme courts use this method to select judges.

Executive dominated methods are the second most prevalent method of selection for both types of courts, but at a considerably lower percentage than the most prevalent method. Executive dominated selection is used in fifteen of ninety-three or 16 per cent of constitutional courts and thirty-one of 125 or 25 per cent of supreme courts. In many ways it is surprising that there are not more executive-dominated selection systems, but many reforms have attempted to wrest control of courts from the hands of the executive to support ideals of judicial independence from government leaders (see Tiede 2006; Driscoll and Nelson 2015). As discussed below, however, even with reforms, executives have other means of influencing selection even if not named as a dominant influence in the *de jure* selection mechanism.

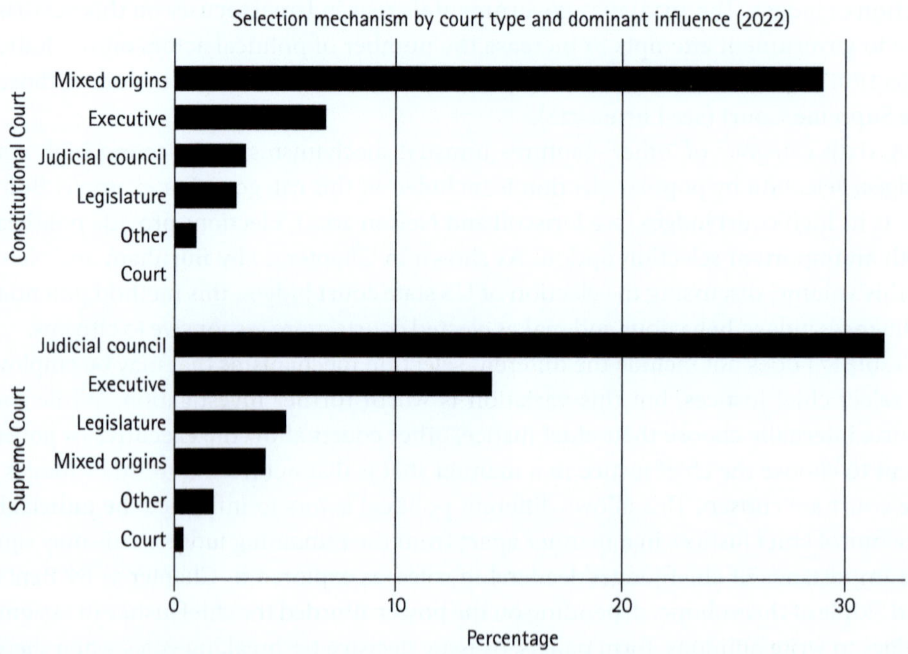

FIGURE 17.1 Selection mechanism by court type and dominant influence, general.

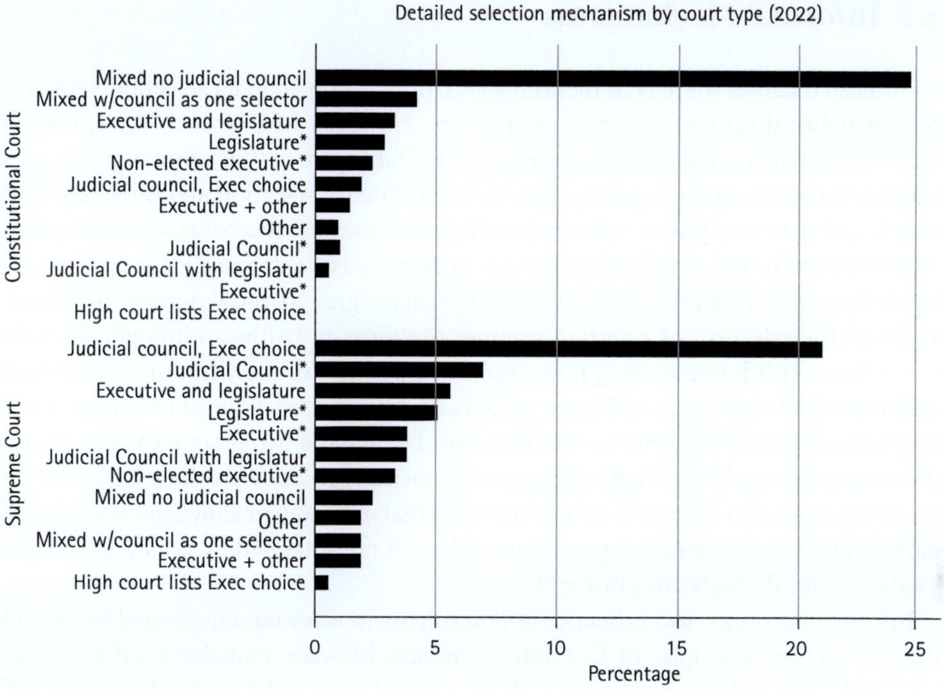

FIGURE 17.2 Detailed selection mechanism by court type.

Note: * Denotes an institutional actor that chooses all judges unilaterally.

Figure 17.2 shows the frequency of twelve specific variations of selection mentioned in Table 17.1. For constitutional courts, selection dominated by judicial councils, the legislatures, or courts is infrequent as is selection dominated by the legislature, courts, or mixed systems for supreme courts. The difference in selection methods by type of court may be due to the function of the court in reviewing legislation or executive decrees and whether a country has both a supreme court and separately named constitutional court. Variation in selection methods may provide a government with different layers of veto points in the selection process across different courts. The prolific use of mixed selection dominated methods for constitutional courts may indicate a concerted effort by policymakers to provide diverse and pluralistic origins for judges especially as the role of judges in these courts is to uphold constitutions, often acting as pseudo-legislatures with broad powers to strike down laws prior to and after legislative approval. For constitutional courts, there are no instances of courts themselves choosing all the judges with executive approval or courts in which the executive chooses all the judges unilaterally. Furthermore, there are few cases in which the judicial council has a large role in choosing judges for constitutional courts either alone or in concert with another actor. For Supreme Courts, there are examples of all twelve types of selection mechanisms, but very few countries in which the high court chooses all the judges alone or in which the executive chooses with an actor other than the legislature or a judicial council.

2.2 Informal Mechanisms

As indicated above, there is tremendous variation in how judicial selection rules allow certain political actors to control the process. However, despite such rules, there are many informal mechanisms, not captured in Table 17.1 or the other figures, which allow other actors, such as political parties, to influence selection and thus may limit a court's ability to veto policy. Informal mechanisms may cause a court to be co-opted by other interests or informally allow for more diversity. For example, in certain instances, legislatures who nominate or confirm judges may agree to allow dominant parties to alternate the selection of a certain number of judges notwithstanding which institution selects. This horse-trading is exemplified by judges of the Chilean Constitutional Tribunal which as of 2022 still had a mixed selection system. Four of ten judges on this court are chosen by the Senate and Congress of which the two main party coalitions of the centre right and centre left have agreed historically to alternate the selection of their preferred judges (El Mercurio 2005). This informal mechanism allows another entry for party politics in the selection procedure although not intended by policy-makers (See Tiede 2022 for the legislative history).

Informal networks also influence appointments in ways not envisioned by the rules themselves. For example, in Colombia, contacts between constitutional court judicial candidates and the selecting (i.e. the Supreme Court and *Consejo de Estado*) or the confirming institution (i.e. the Senate) greatly influence which judges are ultimately selected (see Lamprea 2010; Montoya 2013). Similarly, in Mexico, between 1917 and 1994, Supreme Court judges could choose lower court judges. However, extensive informal rules allowed judges on a rotating basis to hand-pick these judges, resulting in an extensive patronage network (Pozas-Loyo and Ríos-Figueroa 2018). As seen from these examples, informal mechanisms for selection work in concert with formal rules and may undermine the ability to make selection less political.

In summary, the above section has listed and briefly described the main judicial selection methods for supreme and constitutional courts. The comparison of prevalent methods for constitutional and supreme courts highlights that these courts serve very different roles in society and government. Politicians choose different methods for selecting judges to different high courts within a country to influence judicial decision-makers either allowing for only a few branches to dominate the selection or to allow more actors into the process so as to temper any one dominant influence.

3. Judicial Selection Methods and Diversity

The above section draws attention to the different actors who have vetoes in the selection process. Additionally, some governments enact quotas or other constraints on the selection process to ensure that the court is made up of diverse judges who may be overlooked under the mechanisms described above. Diversity also may be improved by staggering judges' terms such that judicial turnover allows different groups of judges to decide cases together at different points in time. However, despite such efforts, diversity may be difficult to establish due to culture and patterns of behaviour related to 'privilege, prejudice, group socialization, and power dynamics' (Smit 2018, 61). As will be discussed below, rules that diversify judges within courts may have implications for judicial behaviour. Such rules also may make political sense in societies that are quite divided or have experienced public backlash about the marginalization of certain groups. To date, these additional diversity safeguards vary by country and court and seek diversity across gender, ethnicity, or language, and sometimes professional or subject matter expertise.

3.1 Gender Diversity

As with the movement to diversify legislatures, some countries want to provide more gender diversity within courts themselves. While this may happen organically as a country's demographics change or some governments make concerted efforts to appoint more women judges or through other constitutional changes (see Arrington et al. 2021), one way to achieve more gender diversity is to require that a certain number or percentage of judges are female. For example, the Central African Republic's 2016 reforms have a minimum quota of 35 per cent women in decision-making bodies such as courts (see Establishing Parity Between Men and Women in Central African Republic, 2016, 3.1 Articles 7 and 8). Specifically, the Constitution uses a mixed selection method in which two judges are magistrates, two attorneys, two law faculty, and one of each of these groups must be female along with three other judges (one appointed by the President, one by the president of the national assembly, and one by the president of the senate), thus ensuring three female judges out of nine. The Ecuador Constitutional Court does not require gender quotas, but the Constitution states that '[i]n the membership of the Court, efforts shall be made to ensure parity between men and women'. The trend in using gender quotas for judicial seats may follow the trend of quotas for legislative seats and become more prevalent in time as countries recognize the benefits of this type of diversification.

Outside quotas, recent literature has established a relationship between selection mechanisms and gender diversity. Valdini and Shortell (2016) show that constitutional court mechanisms in which the selectors themselves are 'sheltered from electoral accountability' allow for the selection of women more infrequently than those selectors that are not sheltered. In contrast, selectors exposed to electoral accountability can claim credit when they choose female judges. This influence of electoral accountability, however, has been observed to influence the selection of the first female justices in OECD but not non-OECD countries (see Escobar-Lemmon et al. 2021). Additionally constitutional reforms, which either increase or decrease the number of actors involved in the selection process, make it more likely that the first woman judge will be appointed to an all-male high court (Arrington et al. 2021). Finally, international norms to include more women in government institutions appear to spur the selection of more women to high courts (see Escobar-Lemmon et al. 2021).

3.2 Ethnic, Linguistic, and Racial Diversity

Some societies provide voice for marginalized groups through opportunities in government institutions or policies which do not preclude them from service. In some cases, judges of different ethnic in- and out-groups serve on collegial courts together (see Von Doepp 2006 regarding ethnicity of judges categorized this way in Malawi and Zambia). Some governments, especially those with historic injustices and problems with inequality more aggressively provide for representation of these voices through more formal legal means. In other words, constitutions or other laws require that positions on the court are held by judges of certain ethnicities or who represent overlooked segments of the population. This mandatory ethnic representation has often come about due to constitutional reforms embedded in peace accords to resolve wars involving significant ethnic conflict.

For example, the General Framework Agreement for Peace in Bosnia and Herzegovina (i.e. the Dayton Accords) changed the ethnic composition of many government institutions including the constitutional court. The intent behind such changes was to provide more equitable representation of ethnic groups in a country that had experienced significant ethnic conflict. For the Bosnia and Herzegovina Constitutional Court, the House of Representatives of the Federation chooses four judges, and the Assembly of the Republika Srpska chooses two judges. The remaining three judges are chosen by the President of the European Court of Human Rights (ECtHR) with consultation with the Presidency. The involvement in appointment of the President of the ECtHR is highly unusual and appears to reflect the volatility of this country's fragmented society as well as a lack of trust in national political actors choosing judges to this important court.

Similarly, building considerations of ethnicity into the selection process due to the resolution of armed conflict and a peace accord also occurred in North Macedonia which has a mixed selection system for choosing constitutional court judges whereby the President and the Judicial Council each choose two judges and the Committee on Election and Appointment affairs chooses five judges. After armed conflict ended between ethnic Albanians and Macedonian security forces in 2001, the government made constitutional changes to several institutions under the Ohrid Agreement. In general, this peace agreement ensured that members of several institutions, including this country's constitutional court, included individuals who represented ethnic minorities especially Albanians, Macedonia's largest minority group. To accommodate the countries' ethnic make-up, the National Assembly by majority vote of all of its representatives confirms six judges chosen by the institutions mentioned above. Then, the Assembly by a majority of 'the total number of representatives belonging to minority communities in Macedonia' confirms the remaining three judges. In this way, the double majority rule ensures that one-third of the Court represents judges approved by minority representatives in Parliament.

Selection of a certain number of judges due to ethno-linguistic characteristics occurs on the Supreme Constitutional Court of Cyprus, the Tanzanian Special Constitutional Court, and the Belgium Constitutional Court. Acknowledgement of the need to diversify also is observed in the selection of judges in Israel, which does not require ethnic quotas but has guidelines that state that judges should 'ideally reflect the country's diversity' (Grossman et al. 2016, 51 citing Zamir, Rubinstein, and Guy-Ron 2001). Additionally, in the United States in recent years, Democratic presidents have attempted to appoint judges with diverse racial, ethnic, and national backgrounds to the federal judiciary.

3.3 Diversity in Professionality of Selectors or in Judges' Professional or Subject Matter Expertise

Most, if not all, countries require that judges meet certain professional and academic requirements prior to being appointed. Additionally, many countries, especially those in which judges have a civil service career, require that judges take proficiency tests. While this is standard in most countries, several countries also specify that a certain number or quota of judges either are appointed by certain organizations, represent certain professional interests, or have had prior experience in non-judicial posts. Some countries allow actors other than the main branches of government and sometimes special interest groups, such as non-governmental organizations, to appoint justices in order to ensure that judges represent or are professionalized in that interest. In Guatemala, Guinea, and Niger, political actors or branches of government choose some constitutional court judges, but these countries also allow universities, attorneys' associations and in the case of Guinea and Niger human rights' organizations to choose judges. These three courts also impose professional requirements, such that some of the judges are professors, teachers, or representatives of human rights' organizations themselves. In an interesting variation on the inclusion of law professors, the Supreme Special Court in Greece requires two law professors to sit on the court when they are deciding issues of constitutionality or conflicts among courts and these two professors are chosen by lots. The Ivory Coast Constitutional Council specifies that judges should be recognized for their expertise and competence in administrative and legal affairs. Croatia's Constitutional Court of thirteen judges selected by two-thirds of parliamentarians favours 'notable' justices, especially those who served previously as judges, public prosecutors, attorneys, and university law professors. These methods ensure that courts have judges with diverse professional expertise.

4. Implications of Selection Methods on Independence and Behaviour

How judges are selected and what interests they represent have significant implications for judicial independence and decision-making for individual judges and those on collegial courts.[3] One way to conceptualize judicial independence is to consider the degree that individual judges or courts are independent from the executive (Tiede 2006). At one extreme, a court completely independent of the executive, if such a court can be envisioned, would be unaccountable and could potentially have no constraints on its decision-making such that it could theoretically make decisions outside of the law. At the other extreme, are judges and courts whose decisions completely reflect the preferences of the executive. Between these two extremes lie different levels of judges' and courts' dependence on the executive which is influenced in turn by the selection method. As noted by Driscoll and Nelson (2015), judicial selection methods, which have over time come to include more participants in the selection process, may 'lessen the grip of the legislative and executive branches on the process, perhaps emboldening judges to participate more actively in the policy-making process' (12) and altering what types of judges are selected in the first place (see Ríos-Figueroa 2011).

Additionally, different types of selection methods which make judges more or less beholden to the desires of the executive or other actors may influence decision-making on collegial courts in which individual judges' decisions are influenced by their own characteristics, loyalties, and preferences and by the characteristics, preferences, and decisions of other judges with whom they make decisions (i.e. panel and voting effects) (see Fischman 2015). In some cases, selection determines the diversity of judicial characteristics and interests impacting court ideology and thus the level of consensus or dissensus on the court (see Boyea 2007 for this proposition on US state courts). What follows is an analysis of the implications of each of the five main selection methods, summarized in Table 17.1, column 1, as well as other diversity and informal rules on judicial independence and decision-making. Several of these implications have not been tested empirically thus providing many areas for future scholarship. Additionally, while the focus is on the theoretical implications of a selection method, 'explicit structural protections' may be only 'parchment barriers to an aggressive executive or legislature unconstrained by voters who value judicial independence' (Cameron 2002, 139).

4.1 Executive Dominant

In general terms, more veto players in the selection process may ensure the selection of judges who are not hesitant to question or confront elected actors. Those chosen by just one actor may decide cases in a manner that is deferential to that selector's preferences. Many studies on attitudinal voting on the US Supreme Court suggest that judges chosen by certain presidents tend to vote with the party line of that president, at least on highly salient cases. Judges may not only show loyalty to the party of the president but specific loyalty to the president that selected them (see Epstein and Posner 2016; Garoupa, Gili, and Pomar 2021a).

Of course, judges and courts may also express deference to the executive under other selection methods if the executive in fact controls other ostensible veto players in the selection process due to autocratic tendencies or high party cohesion. Another way the executive may influence the selection of judges is by choosing the chief justice who may have significant powers. Additionally, the executive may be involved in the selection of members of a judicial commission which chooses judges, thus leaving the chief executive's mark on selection. One way to lessen the impact of the executive in selection and ultimately on judicial decision-making is to require confirmation by the legislature, usually with a supermajority vote. It is thought that the supermajority rule would lead to the appointment of more moderate judges (Moreno, Crisp, and Shugart 2003) even under circumstances of unified government as it is unlikely that all legislators within a supermajority share the same political preferences or party as the president.

4.2 Legislature Dominant

Judicial selection by a legislature should lead to judges who may be beholden or loyal to this institution's preferences if a singular legislative preference can be found. Judicial selection by a legislature should lead to judges with more diverse preferences than selection by an executive, especially if the legislature has a supermajority voting rule for approving judges and no party holds two-thirds of the seats in the legislature. Judges also may reflect more diverse preferences if the legislature is highly fragmented or made up of many different parties. Legislative supermajority rules for choosing judges are thought to lead to judges who act more assertively and impartially and are more independent of the executive. Supermajority rules also may lead to the selection of more moderate judges. For example, referring to the legislative appointment of Peruvian Constitutional Tribunal judges under a two-thirds supermajority rule since 1993, Dargent (2009) argues that 'political negotiation was required to reach an agreement, making it more likely that the candidates elected would be independent ones' (266). Legislative supermajority voting rules to select judges are more likely to lead to the selection of moderate judges in multiparty or highly fragmented party systems as well, but not when the president has a strong hold over the legislature. In theory, legislative dominant selection mechanisms should lead to a court that is more representative of the interests of citizens who selected the legislature through elections, especially when there are many parties represented in the legislature. Judges selected by legislatures may be more considerate of legislation that has been passed by a multi-party legislature perhaps seeing this legislation as approved by compromises and accommodation of the diverse interests that the legislature represents.

4.3 Court Dominant

Although not many courts select all the judges on their own court or other courts, there are still historic and current examples of this method. At first glance, it may seem to provide a way for making courts or the judicial branch independent of political pressure from the legislature or executive. However, this method has its own challenges especially when higher courts are substantially involved in promoting lower court judges to higher posts or demoting or punishing them. In these instances, lower court judges will not be independent from the higher courts involved in their selection and may fear reprisals if they decide cases in a way that is at odds with the higher selecting court. The Magistrates' Association of Chile raised such a concern to the Inter-American Commission of Human Rights about the Supreme Court's influence over lower court judges' selection, demotion, and discipline (González 2017).

4.4 Mixed Selection (Without Singular Dominant Actor)

Mixed judicial selection involves several different judicial actors or combinations of actors nominating or appointing a specific number of judges on a court, but not all members. In other words, the same actors and processes do not select all judges, providing potentially more veto points and different origins for judges working on the same court. Mixed judicial selection is supposed to provide more diversity on the court and with more diversity judges might exhibit different approaches to the law and decision-making. Mixed selection allows for different judges to represent society's pluralism on the court (Venice Commission 2007 citing CDL-STD 1997). The Venice Commission notes that society may be more accepting of courts' decisions if judges represent more of society and a balance of interests in government. The Venice Commission has noted that '[e]ven though constitutional courts largely ensure the regulation of these relationships, it may well be appropriate to ensure in their composition a balanced consideration of each of these authorities or organs' (Venice Commission 2007, 21).

The separate origins of judges selected under mixed selection influence their independence and their propensity to veto laws in some countries. Under mixed selection, particular nominating or selection institutions that vary by number and court, choose constitutional adjudicators that best fit their ideal for such a position. Judges selected tend to vote in line with their selectors because they were selected for their adjudication approach as deemed by their prior jobs as judges, politicians, or academics. Furthermore, selector origin may influence voting to strike down laws more than judges' party associations on courts with this selection mechanism. This phenomenon as well as panel effects based on institutional selector was established on the Chilean and Colombian Constitutional Courts (see Tiede 2020 and 2022 for all types of abstract review cases; but see Garoupa, Gili, and Pomar 2021b for the Spanish Constitutional Court's constitutional review of cases initiated by political actors).

While mixed selection may result in courts that are more independent because each selector rarely chooses the majority of judges on the court and those judges must decide cases collegially, this may not always be the case. For example, mixed selection may result in judges serving the interest of their appointers so closely that they do not exercise the necessary independence and impartiality to determine if a law is constitutional or not (Sadurski 2008, 17). Additionally, mixed selection systems may cause internal fragmentation within a court making it difficult to reach decisions (Ginsburg 2003, 45). However, this fragmentation depends 'not only on institutional interest, but also on the party allegiances and ideological orientations of the appointing bodies' (International IDEA 2017, 11). Disagreements on the court due to overt political differences of judges also may weaken a court's decisions or its reputation (Couso 2004; Keleman 2013). Ultimately, the extent that judges' party associations on mixed selection courts influences their voting depends on whether the selecting branches or institutions themselves represent a majority or supermajority of members associated with one party and seek judges who are party loyalists (see Lamprea 2010; Montoya 2013).

4.5 Judicial Commissions

Using commissions to choose judges rather than appointment by other political actors is thought to result in the selection of more qualified and impartial judges. Advocates of this method suggest it will influence judicial decision-making and perhaps the public's perception of judges and courts. It is hoped that commissions that review judges' credentials prior to appointment enhance the quality of judges and decrease the partisan politics involved in selection (Hanssen 2004). Furthermore, if the judicial commissions themselves include members of civil society or non-traditional actors, then their selections may result in more independent judges as civil society members do not have the power that other political actors do to remove judges (Moreno, Crisp, and Shugart 2003). Whether this method lives up to its praise depends on the qualifications of commission members, their background, and ultimately who appoints them. For Latin American judicial commissions, Hammergren (2007) warns that '[a]s judicial selection bodies, they have made some advances over the prior arrangements, but still have a long way to go in defining what they are looking for in judicial candidates and how they will measure its existence' (117–18). If commission members are chosen themselves by strong political actors or those with strong party affiliations, then judicial selection may not be isolated from political manipulation. Even commissions that seem to be devoid of political actors, such as the one used in the United Kingdom to appoint this country's Supreme Court judges, may not be free of criticism. Delaney (2016) notes that the UK Commission has been criticized for judicial self-selection or a selection method that was overtly isolated from politics. Further study of judicial commissions and their membership is much needed as their use is on the rise across the world, yet some empirical evidence indicates that they do not 'promote judicial independence' (Garoupa and Ginsburg 2015, 137).

4.6 Other Diversity Requirements

Not only do the institutions that select judges influence behaviour and independence but additional selection criteria as to judges' characteristics matter (see George 2008). Several studies have shown how ethnicity, gender, and professional specialization may also influence judicial behaviour, but such studies focus on characteristics of judges within courts that arise either naturally or through more concerted efforts to have more diversity. Fewer studies tie specific selection criteria or quotas for judges based on such characteristics to their behaviour (but see Schwartz and Murchison 2016). The influence of gender on judging has been found to matter in some studies (see Boyd, Epstein, and Martin 2010 on US federal judges), but not always (see George 2001 for the divergence in this research). Additionally, Masengu (2018) notes that some are sceptical about the competence of women judges in Zambia and such scepticism undermines the legitimacy of the courts in which they serve. Additional work, similar to that done on legislatures, might look at how formal and informal quota systems for female judges influence behaviour.

Studies on judges' ethnic backgrounds also show that the ethnicity of judges as well as that of the litigants of the cases they hear matter. Von Doepp (2006) shows how judges of 'out-group' ethnicities are less assertive in their decisions involving government action and Grossman et al. (2016) shows differences related to Arab criminal court judges in Israel. Race also has been shown to influence judicial decision-making (see Scherer 2004 and Kastellec 2013, studying the influence of African-American judges on US courts). One of the few studies which ties selection quotas to behaviour is that of the Constitutional Court of Bosnia and Herzegovina discussed above. Judges on this court divide their votes along 'ethno-national lines' and the divisions are not reduced over time (Schwartz and Murchison 2016).

Selection rules specifying the number of judges that need to have certain substantive specialties or professional requirements are ripe for study. While Hanretty (2020) shows that the legal speciality of judges on the UK Supreme Court influences their decisions, there are few studies that look at how selection that requires certain judges possess professional expertise influences decision-making.

4.7 Other Formal and Informal Rules Influencing Independence and Behaviour

Judicial selection shapes judges and their behaviour, but behaviour also depends on other institutional rules (Keleman 2013). Institutional constraints include decision-making and voting rules within the court. The collegial court provides a forum in which judges' decisions are determined by their own characteristics or biases as well as those of other judges with whom they decide (Fischman 2015). A myriad of studies has shown panel effects based on judges' ideology (see Fischman 2015 for a review), race (Kastellec 2013), ethnicity (Grossman et al. 2016), gender (Boyd, Epstein, and Martin 2010), and selecting institutions (Tiede 2020, 2022).

Because the collegial forum is so important to individual and group decisions, any rules that influence the ability of a judge to vote freely or change the court's composition also influence behaviour. Rules concerning quorums, whether cases can be decided by part of the court or require the full court, tenure, mandatory retirement ages, and rules related to the periodic replenishment of the court, all determine which selected judges must decide cases together. Rules that limit the ability to record judges' dissent also may influence how they vote and what they say (see Keleman 2013). Additionally, voting rules, such as requiring supermajority consensus to overturn laws will influence decisions regardless of who is selected. For example, supermajority rules may cause judges to vote more strategically than sincerely (see Caviedes 2022).

Finally, informal norms and rules which fluctuate over time may influence behaviour. Dressel, Sanchez-Urribarri, and Stroh show that informal networks which influence appointment or selection of judges may 'heighten the likelihood of on-bench conflict' (Dressel, Sanchez-Urribarri, and Stroh 2018 citing Fombad 2014; Sanchez Urribarri 2011). Furthermore, informal connections among judges and 'patronage networks', observed in the Mexican Supreme Court's selection of lower court judges, influence behaviour as they lead to the promotion of loyal judges (Pozas-Loyo and Ríos-Figueroa 2018, 580). While research has shown the need to focus on important informal rules and norms, additional research must be undertaken to determine their influence alone and in conjunction with formal rules on judicial behaviour.

In summary, judicial selection variations and other formal and informal rules have intended and unintended effects on judicial independence and behaviour both for individual judges and courts as a whole. More research should focus on the interaction and sequencing of these rules. With such research, scholars may be able to determine the best combinations of institutions to reach various policy objectives related to the role and purpose of courts.

5. Areas for Further Research

Substantial work has theorized how different selection methods influence judicial independence and judicial behaviour. Less comparative research has been done connecting the institution that selects judges to independence, case outcomes, or decision-making more generally (but see Schwartz and Murchison 2016; Tiede 2020, 2022). Additionally, the use of gender or ethnic quotas are quite under-studied and could complement existing work which notes how the composition of collegial courts with different compositions of judges based on such traits influences the way that judges make decisions. Finally, there are few studies that analyse the mechanisms and their implications related to an institution's choice to select one judge out of several candidates suggested by another institution, such as when a president or legislature selects judges from a list of candidates provided by another institution. Scholars have done little to understand why these institutions choose to appoint one judge out of many with the exception of studies by Montoya (2013) and Lamprea (2010). Understanding these other selection processes may help to refine scholars' understandings about how and why certain characteristics, attributes, or biases of judges matter in their ultimate decisions.

Acknowledgement

Special thanks to Roberto Alas for research assistance.

Notes

1. Judges are generally not selected with 'unknown political beliefs' as most judges are appointed with some kind of party support (Keleman 2013, 6).
2. Since 2008, under the Ecuadorian Constitutional Court's mixed system, the president, Congress, and the Transparency and Social Control Function each propose nine candidates from which the judicial council selects judges after competitive examinations.
3. Several scholars have established that differences in selection method across US state courts influence a wide range of dependent variables (see Boyea 2007; Canes-Wrone, Clark, and Kelly 2014; see also Choi, Gulati, and Posner 2010 on the impact of selection on quality of decisions and how prolific they are).

References

Achury, Susan. 2019. 'The Impact of Formal Authority in Latin America Constitutional Justice'. Unpublished doctoral dissertation on file with the University of Houston.

Arrington, Nancy, Leeann Bass, Adam Glynn, Jeffrey K. Staton, Brian Delgado, and Staffan I. Lindberg. 2021. 'Constitutional Reform and the Gender Diversification of Peak Courts'. *American Political Science Review* 115: 851–68.

Autheman, Violaine. 2004. 'Global Lessons Learned: Constitutional Courts, Judicial Independence, and the Rule of Law'. *IFES Rule of Law White Paper Series* . International Foundation for Electoral Systems, Arlington, Virginia. https://www.ifes.org/.

Boyd, Christina, Lee Epstein, and Andrew Martin. 2010. 'Untangling the Causal Effects of Sex on Judging'. *American Journal of Political Science* 54: 389–411.

Boyea, Brent D. 2007. 'Linking Judicial Selection to Consensus an Analysis of Ideological Diversity'. *American Politics Research* 35 (5): 643–70.

Brinks, Daniel, and Abby Blass. 2018. *The DNA of Constitutional Justice in Latin America: Politics, Governance, and Judicial Design, Comparative Constitutional Policy*. Cambridge: Cambridge University Press.

Brouard, Sylvain, and Christoph Hönnige. 2017. 'Constitutional Courts as Veto Players: Lessons from the United States, France and Germany'. *European Journal of Political Research* 56: 529–52.

Cameron, Charles. 2002. 'Judicial Independence: How Can You Tell It When You See It? And Who Cares?' In *Judicial Independence at the Crossroads: An Interdisciplinary Approach*, edited by Stephen B. Burbank and Barry Friedman, 134. Thousand Oaks: Sage Publications, Inc.

Canes-Wrone, Brandice, Tom S. Clark, and Jason P. Kelly. 2014. 'Judicial Selection and Death Penalty Decisions'. *American Political Science Review* 108: 23–39.

Caviedes, Cristóbal. 2022. 'A Core Case for Supermajority Rules in Constitutional Adjudication'. *International Journal of Constitutional Law* 20 (3): 1162–87.

Choi, Stephen J., G. Mitu Gulati, and Eric A. Posner. 2010. 'Professionals or Politicians: The Uncertain Empirical Case for an Elected rather than Appointed Judiciary'. *Journal of Law, Economics, and Organization* 26 (2): 290–336.

Couso, Javier. 2004. 'The Politics of Judicial Review in Chile in the Era of Democratic Transition, 1990–2002'. In *Democratization and the Judiciary: The Accountability Function of Courts in New Democracies*, edited by Siri Gloppen, Roberto Gargarella, and Elin Skaar, 50–65. London: Frank Cass.

Dahl, Robert. 1957. 'Decision-Making in a Democracy: The Supreme Court as a National Policy-Maker'. *Journal of Public Law* 6: 279–95.

Dargent, Eduardo. 2009. 'Determinants of Judicial Independence: Lessons from Three "Cases" of Constitutional Courts in Peru (1982–2007)'. *Journal of Latin American Studies* 41: 251.

Delaney, Erin. 2016. 'Searching for Constitutional Meaning in Institutional Design: The Debate over Judicial Appointments in the United Kingdom'. *International Journal of Constitutional Law* 14: 752–68.

Dressel, Björn, Raul Sanchez-Urribarri, and Alexander Stroh. 2018. 'Courts and Informal Networks: Towards a Relational Perspective on Judicial Politics outside Western Democracies'. *International Political Science Review* 39 (5): 573–84.

Driscoll, Amanda, and Michael J. Nelson. 2015. 'Judicial Selection and the Democratization of Justice: Lessons from the Bolivian Elections'. *Journal of Law and Courts* 3 (1, Spring): 115–48. doi:10.1086/679017. https://www.constituteproject.org/.

Elkins, Zachary, Tom Ginsburg, and James Melton. 2022. 'Constitute: The World's Constitutions to Read and Search and Compare'. Online at constituteproject.org.

Epstein, Lee, and Posner, Eric. A. 2016. 'Supreme Court Justices' Loyalty to the President'. *The Journal of Legal Studies* 45 (2): 401–36.

Escobar-Lemmon, Maria, Valerie Hoekstra, Alice Kang, and Miki Kittilson. 2021. 'Breaking the Judicial Glass Ceiling: The Appointment of Women to High Courts Worldwide'. *The Journal of Politics* 83 (2): 662–74.

Fischman, Joshua B. 2015. 'Interpreting Circuit Court Voting Patterns: A Social Interactions Framework'. *The Journal of Law, Economics, and Organization* 31 (4): 808–42.

Fombad, Charles M. 2014. 'Appointment of Constitutional Adjudicators in Africa: Some Perspectives on How Different Systems Yield Similar Outcome'. *The Journal of Legal Pluralism and Unofficial Law* 46 (2): 249–75.

Garoupa, Nuno, and Tom Ginsburg. 2015. *Judicial Reputation*. Chicago: University of Chicago Press.

Garoupa, Nuno, Marian Gili, and Fernando Gómez Pomar. 2021a. 'Mixed Judicial Selection and Constitutional Review: Evidence from Spain'. *European Constitutional Law Review* 17: 1–27.

Garoupa, Nuno, Marian Gili, and Fernando Gómez Pomar. 2021b. 'Loyalty to the Party or Loyalty to the Party Leader: Evidence from the Spanish Constitutional Court'. *International Review of Law and Economics* 1. doi:10.1016/j.irle.2021.105999. https://www.sciencedirect.com/science/article/abs/pii/S0144818821000235.

George, Tracey E. 2001. 'Court Fixing'. *Arizona Law Review* 43: 9–62.

George, Tracey E. 2008. 'From Judge to Justice: Social Background Theory and the Supreme Court'. *North Carolina Law Review* 86: 1333–67.

Ghavanini, Anna Wallerman, Gunnar Grendstad, and Johan Karlsson Schaffer. 2023. 'Institutions that Define the Policy-Making Role of Courts: A Comparative Analysis of the Supreme Courts of Scandinavia'. *International Journal of Constitutional Law*, forthcoming. https://academic.oup.com/icon/advance-article/doi/10.1093/icon/moad068/7250119?searchresult=1.

Ginsburg, Tom. 2003. *Judicial Review in New Democracies: Constitutional Courts in Asian Cases*. Cambridge: Cambridge University Press.

González Schmessane, Andrea. 2017. 'Jueces recurren a la Comisión Internacional DDHH en busca de Independencia Judicial'. Emol.com (15 March). https://www.emol.com/noticias/Nacional/2017/03/15/849509/Jueces-recurren-a-la-Comision-Internacional-de-DDHH-en-busca-de-independencia-judicial.html.

Grossman, Guy, Oren Gazal-Ayal, Samuel D. Pimentel, and Jeremy M. Weinstein. 2016. 'Descriptive Representation and Judicial Outcomes in Multiethnic Societies'. *American Journal of Political Science* 60: 44–69.

Hammergren, Linn. 2002. *Do Judicial Councils Further Reform? Lessons from Latin America*. Washington, DC: Carnegie Endowment for Peace.

Hammergren, Linn. 2007. *Envisioning Reform: Improving Judicial Performance in Latin America*. University Park: Pennsylvania State University Press.

Hanretty, Chris. 2020. *A Court of Specialists: Judicial Behavior on the UK Supreme Court*. New York: Oxford University Press.

Hanssen, F. Andrew. 2004. 'Learning About Judicial Independence: Institutional Change in The State Courts'. *Journal of Legal Studies* 33: 431–73.

International IDEA (International Institute for Democracy and Electoral Assistance). 2017. 'Judicial Appointments'. Constitution Building Primers. Stockholm, Sweden: International IDEA.

Kastellec, Jonathan P. 2013. 'Racial Diversity and Judicial Influence on Appellate Courts'. *American Journal of Political Science* 57 (1): 167–83.

Kelemen, Katalina. 2013. 'Dissenting Opinions on Constitutional Courts'. *German Law Journal* 14 (8): 1345–72.

Kiewiet, D. Roderick and Mathew McCubbins. 1991. *The Logic of Delegation: Congressional Parties and the Appropriations Process*. Chicago: The University of Chicago Press.

Lamprea, Everaldo. 2010. 'When Accountability Meets Judicial Independence: A Case Study of the Colombian Constitutional Court's Nominations'. *Global Jurist* 10: 1–38.

Llanos, Mariana, and Leany Barreiro Lemos. 2013. 'Presidential Preferences? The Supreme Federal Tribunal Nomination in Democratic Brazil'. *Latin America Politics & Society* 55 (2): 77–105.

Lurie, Guy. 2022. 'Changing Israel Judicial Appointments only Possible with Broad Consensus - Opinion'. *Jerusalem Post*, 20 December. https://www.jpost.com/opinion/article-725305.

Masengu, Tabeth. 2018. 'One Sauce for the Goose, another for the Gander: Zambian Women Judges and Perceptions of Illegitimacy'. In *Gender, Judging and the Courts in Africa*, edited by J. Jarpa Dawuni, 209–30. London: Routledge.

Mavčič, Arne Marjan. 2018. *Constitutional Review Systems around the World*. Lake Mary: Vandeplas.

El Mercurio. 'Senado aprueba a abogados Bertelsen y Vodanovic para Tribunal Constitucional. en votación Única, los Parlamentarios Votaron en Forma Electrónica por la Dupla que Logró 34 Votos en Favor y Cuatro en Contra de la Bancada PRSD' (8 November 2005). Santiago, Chile.

Montoya, A. 2013. 'Si no Vas al Senado, No te Eligen Magistrado: Instituciones Informales y Criterios de Selección de los Magistrados de la Corte Constitucional Colombiana en el Senado (1992–2009)'. *Colombia Internacional* 79: 155–90.

Moreno, Erica, Brian Crisp, and Matthew Shugart. 2003. 'The Accountability Deficit in Latin America'. In *Democratic Accountability in Latin America*, edited by Mainwaring and C. Welna, 79–131. Cambridge: Cambridge University Press.

Pozas-Loyo, Andrea, and Julio Ríos-Figueroa. 2018. 'Anatomy of an Informal Institution: The "Gentlemen's Pact" and Judicial Selection in Mexico, 1917–1994'. *International Political Science Review* 39 (5): 647–61.

Ríos-Figueroa, Julio. 2011. 'Institutions for Constitutional Justice in Latin America'. In *Courts in Latin America*, edited by G. Helmke and J. Ríos Figueroa, 27–54. New York: Cambridge University Press.

Sadurski, Wojciech. 2008. *Rights before Courts, a Study of Constitutional Courts in Postcommunist States of Central and Eastern Europe*. Dordrecht: Springer.

Sanchez Urribarri Raul. 2011. 'Courts between Democracy and Hybrid Authoritarianism: Evidence from the Venezuelan Supreme Court'. *Law and Social Inquiry* 36 (4): 854–84.

Scherer, Nancy. 2004. 'Blacks on the Bench'. *Political Science Quarterly* 119 (4, Winter): 655–75.

Schwartz, Alex, and Melanie Janelle Murchinson. 2016. 'Judicial Impartiality and Independence in Divided Societies: An Empirical Analysis of the Constitutional Court of Bosnia-Herzegovina'. *Law and Society Review* 50: 821–55.

Smit, Jan van Zyl. 2018. '"Opening up" Commonwealth Judicial Appointments to Diversity? The Growing Role of Commissions in Judicial Selection'. In *Debating Judicial Appointments in an Age of Diversity*, edited by Graham Gee and Erika Rackley, 60–82. London: Routledge.

Tiede, Lydia Brashear. 2006. 'Judicial Independence: Often Cited, Rarely Understood'. *Journal of Contemporary Legal Issues* 15: 129–61.

Tiede, Lydia Brashear. 2020. 'Mixed Judicial Selection and Constitutional Review'. *Comparative Political Studies* 53: 1092–123.

Tiede, Lydia Brashear. 2022. *Judicial Vetoes: Decision-making on Mixed Selection Constitutional Courts*. Cambridge: Cambridge University Press.

Tsebelis, George. 2002. *Veto Players: How Political Institutions Work*. Princeton: Princeton University Press.

Valdini, Melody E., and Christopher Shortell. 2016. 'Women's Representation in the Highest Courts: A Comparative Analysis of the Appointment of Female Justices'. *Political Research Quarterly* 69 (4): 865–76.

Varol, Ozan O., Pellegrina, Lucia, and Garoupa, Nuno. 2017. 'An Empirical Analysis of Judicial Transformation in Turkey'. *The American Journal of Comparative Law* 65 (1): 187–216.

Venice Commission. 1997. 'The Composition of Constitutional Courts—Science and Technique of Democracy'. CDL-STD no. 20.

Venice Commission. 2007. 'Vademecum on Constitutional Justice'. Strasbourg, France.

Von Doepp, Peter. 2006. 'Politics and Judicial Assertiveness in Emerging Democracies: High Court Behavior in Malawi and Zambia'. *Political Research Quarterly* 59: 389–99.

Zamir, Yitzhak, Amnon Rubinstein, and Yoram Guy-Ron. 2001. 'Committee for Evaluating Judges Selection Procedure'. Technical report, Ministry of Justice, Israel.

CHAPTER 18

JUDICIAL ELECTIONS AND JUDICIAL BEHAVIOUR

MICHAEL J. NELSON AND MICHAEL BURNHAM

1. Introduction

Most judges in the United States have a direct connection to the public. Judges in thirty-nine of the fifty US states must win the support of voters to keep their seat on the bench.[1] Worldwide, this is a rarity. Only a handful of countries use judicial elections to staff their courts. Some Swiss cantons and French municipalities elect their judges (Schotland 2001), and some Latin American countries, like Peru, Venezuela, and Costa Rica, elect lower court judges or justices of the peace (Anenson 1997). Japanese judges face uncontestable retention elections at the end of their terms (Ramseyer and Rasmusen 2001). But only Bolivia and the American states use judicial elections to select judges to courts with constitutional jurisdiction (Driscoll and Nelson 2012).

Despite the uniqueness of this institutional arrangement, elections present important (and underused) inferential opportunities for those seeking to understand judicial behaviour. By studying how elections affect judicial *selection* (the ability of someone to become a judge) and judicial *retention* (whether that person can remain on the bench at the end of their term), scholars gain a window into how the broader political environment affects judicial behaviour. In this way, judicial elections provide a unique opportunity to compare judges with other types of elites. Further, because the ability of unelected elites to have immense political power in democratic societies has long been an important normative concern (e.g. Bickel 1986), the study of judicial elections enables scholars to understand how having an independent (and democratic) base of support—the electorate—affects the relationship between the judiciary and other branches of government. Thus, though admittedly rare, judicial elections present theoretically rich opportunities for researchers.

This potential can only be realized if researchers abandon disciplinary silos and use judicial elections as laboratories for testing general theories. On the one hand, the study of elections is a cornerstone of political science. Research on candidate selection, electoral competition, and electoral vulnerability are all foundational areas of research for those who study legislative and executive elections (e.g. Jacobson 2009). Yet judicial scholars have been slow to apply theories and findings from electoral politics to judicial politics. As a result, scholars have not fully leveraged the unique opportunity judicial elections provide researchers to test theories of elections in a different institutional context and, by extension, establish the generalizability of these fundamental theories.

On the other hand, scholars often test and develop theories of judicial behaviour on a subset of judges: appointed judges (Epstein and Knight 1998; Segal and Spaeth 2002). Yet in legislative and executive contexts, evidence abounds that elections affect elite behaviour (e.g. Lazarus 2009; Lim and Snyder, Jr 2021) and the ideological direction of policy-making (Key 1949; Gamm and Kousser 2021). Testing theories of judicial behaviour across selection and retention regimes is therefore important to understand the limitations (and strengths) of prominent theories of judicial behaviour.

The key argument of this chapter is that scholars of judicial behaviour and electoral politics have much to learn from each other. Discussing the effects of judicial elections for judges' on the bench behaviour, the pipeline to the bench, and the public's perceptions of the judiciary, we both summarize the state of our understanding of elected judges and suggest how the broader study of elections might inform future inquiry. Because nearly all studies of elected judges concern the behaviour of US state judges, we focus our attention on the United States but reference opportunities for scholars to expand the inquiry geographically. We conclude by charting some promising paths forward for this area of research. By fusing research on elections and courts, the future of this area of research is bright.

2. Judicial Elections Around the World

Judicial elections—especially for courts with constitutional jurisdiction—are rare world-wide; jurisdictions that employ judicial elections vary widely in the rules and regulations they use to govern these contests. Across the globe, the rarest type of judicial elections are *partisan elections* in which judges publicly affiliate with a political party and compete at the polls against judicial candidates from other parties. While partisan elections were the most common type of judicial elections in the United States in the late 1800s, their use has decreased dramatically (Hanssen 2004). Today, only a handful of states—most notably Texas and Alabama—use partisan judicial elections to select and retain their judges.[2]

A more common approach is to allow multiple candidates to compete against each other but to limit candidates' ability to affiliate with a political party and to advertise their partisan affiliations. These *non-partisan elections* became common in the United States in the first half of the twentieth century as reformers grew worried about party leaders using judgeships as political plums and convinced their states to change from partisan to non-partisan elections (Shugerman 2012). Today, US states like Idaho, Mississippi, and Minnesota use non-partisan elections to staff their courts.

Bolivia, the only other country to use elections to select judges to courts with constitutional jurisdiction, also uses non-partisan elections. Bolivia adopted judicial elections as part of a 2009 constitutional reform. Bolivians elect judges to their major national courts (including their constitutional court). However, though the elections are formally non-partisan—and candidates are prohibited from all campaign activities—there is still some partisan involvement in the electoral process. Unlike the United States, where typically any candidate who gathers enough signatures can appear on the ballot, Bolivian judicial candidates have to be pre-screened by the national legislature before appearing on the ballot (Driscoll and Nelson 2015).[3]

Non-partisan elections are also used to staff local courts. Peruvian law requires justices of the peace to be selected through 'direct and democratic election' (Guerra Cerron 2008, 48), and campaigning is limited (Brandt 1995). Similarly, Barangay justices—who adjudicate low-level communal cases—in the Philippines are also elected to their positions and political parties are expressly forbidden from participating in the electoral process on behalf of a candidate (Brandt 1995).[4]

A final type of judicial election is a *retention election*. In this type of election, only the incumbent's name appears on the ballot, and voters are given a binary, 'yes' or 'no' choice about whether the judge should remain on the bench. Thus, retention elections are only used to decide whether or not a judge already in office should remain on the bench, not to select who should sit on the bench. In the United States, retention elections were pioneered as part of the 'Missouri Plan' of judicial selection in which a commission of laypeople and lawyers would screen judicial applicants before selecting a small list of names to provide to the governor who would, in turn, select the judge; at the end of his term, the judge would face a retention election (Kales 1914; Watson and Downing 1969). These types of elections are the most common type of election used in the United States today, though few judges who face retention elections ever lose office (Aspin 2011).

Outside of the United States, Japan uses retention elections for its Supreme Court. Japanese Supreme Court judges are selected by the cabinet and then face voters in a retention election in the first general election after their appointment (Tadano 2018). However, the odds of losing office are low and, because judges tend to be appointed to the high court late in their career, they are unlikely to face the voters more than once (Law 2009).

3. Judicial Elections and Judicial Decision-Making

The use of judicial elections has been the topic of heated and long-lasting debate among political scientists (cf. Bonneau and Hall 2009; Caufield 2009), legal scholars (Tarr 2012), and advocacy groups (e.g. American Bar Association 2003). Opponents often suggest that judicial elections erode judicial independence by directing judges to pay attention to the public's response to their decisions. To the extent that judges are viewed as impartial arbiters who must occasionally make unpopular decisions in order to protect minority rights, this dependence on public sentiment would harm the ability of judges to perform their unique role in a separation-of-powers system.

On the other hand, political scientists and others who have a more favourable view of judicial elections note that even the decisions of appointed courts tend to be congruent with public opinion (e.g. Marshall 2008). As stated by Hall (2014), appointive methods of judicial retention 'obviate the representative function by disconnecting key mechanisms through which public preferences are translated into judicial votes' (335). And, to the extent that judges are important policy-makers who make major decisions that affect citizens' rights and responsibilities, it may be better for judges to be beholden to public preferences than to act without regard to those affected by their decisions (Bonneau and Hall 2009).

This debate is premised, in large part, on the assumption that judges are doing something unique among political elites when deciding cases. We, by contrast, suggest that judicial behaviour is a class of elite behaviour. Rather than treating judicial behaviour as *sui generis*, judicial behaviour scholars should consider that *any* method of selection and retention has consequences for judicial behaviour and to theorize and model these aspects accordingly.[5]

George and Epstein (1992), for example, differentiate between legal (e.g. doctrines, precedents, and case facts) and extra-legal (e.g. judicial ideology and court legitimacy) influences on judicial behaviour. They propose an integrated model of judicial behaviour that can be expressed mathematically as:

$$Pr(C_i = 1) = \beta_0 + \sum(\beta_g L_{ig}) + \sum(\beta_h P_{ih}) + \sum(\beta_j IN_{ij}) + e_i$$

where C is a conservative outcome, L is a vector of legal constraints, P represents judicial preferences, and IN represents institutional considerations such as judicial legitimacy.[6] These early 'integrated' models of judicial behaviour, originally developed to explain US Supreme Court decision-making, prioritized understanding trade-offs between the constraints of law and a judge's personal characteristics. This is not to say popular influence on judicial behaviour was entirely overlooked. Early work found empirical evidence that judicial behaviour and public opinion were correlated,[7] but this relationship was often considered to be a downstream consequence of regular reappointment (Dahl 1957) or a strategy to maintain court legitimacy (Barnum 1985). Of course, these integrated models were originally developed to explain judicial behaviour in the US Supreme Court, a single court where judges served for life. Perhaps for this reason, the effects of selection and retention mechanisms in general models of judicial behaviour slipped to the background of many studies of judicial choice.

However, most judges around the world do not work in an environment with such minimal retention concerns (Helmke 2002; Tiede 2022).[8] It is therefore helpful to consider a revised integrated model of judicial decision-making which explicitly incorporates variables related to the preferences of those who retain a judge:

$$Pr(C_i = 1) = \beta_0 + \sum(\beta_g L_{ig}) + \sum(\beta_h P_{ih}) + \sum(\beta_j IN_{ij}) + \sum(\beta_m R_{im}) + e_i$$

where the new variable R represents a vector of constraints imposed upon a judge by the entity that retains them. The implication of this revised model is that not only was a key source of constraint missing from the debate between legal and extra-legal models, but that judges are subject to many of the same institutions and incentive structures as many legislators and executives. Put differently, elections introduce a trade-off between the preferences of judges and the preferences of their retention constituency, be it voters, an executive, or a legislature. The existence of this trade-off means there is some expectation that judges act as representatives of their retention constituency. Though judges are not commonly framed as representatives, a representational framework—widely used in other corners of political science—provides a useful theoretical toolkit for scholars wishing to understand when (and how) changes in retention methods (and the accompanying retention constituencies) affect judicial behaviour. Treating judges as representatives in a general model of elite behaviour naturally leads us to questions about when judges prioritize the preferences of voters over their own, and how the preferences of judges differ from their constituents.

There is a strong base of evidence that judges respond to their retention constituencies, be they voters, legislators, or governors. Take, for example, studies of appointed judges in the US states. Shepherd (2009) examines almost all state supreme court decisions between 1995 and 1998, demonstrating that judges facing gubernatorial or legislative reappointment vote strategically to retain their seats. As reappointment approaches, these judges are more likely to vote with litigants from the appointing branch. Similarly, Gray (2017) examines supreme court decisions in states where judges are retained by the legislature, finding that justices appointed by the minority party voted with the preferences of the legislature more frequently than those who could not be reappointed due to mandatory retirement.

Elected judges' behaviour is also affected by their electoral environment. For example, Hall (1992) examined the behaviour of state supreme courts on death penalty cases (see also Hall 1987, 1995; Brace and Hall 1997). Their work showed that justices were more likely to side with the court majority when facing competitive elections, and that single-member districts, prior experience as a representative, and narrow vote margins correlated with voting in line with constituent opinion. Empirical evidence suggests that judges decide cases differently based on whether or not they are retiring (Brace and Boyea 2008; Hall 2014), when a decision was made in an election cycle (Berdejó and Yuchtman 2013), how salient an issue is to the public (Huber and Gordon 2004; Canes-Wrone et al. 2012, 2018; Lim 2013), and the composition of the electorate (Savchak and Barghothi 2007; Shepherd 2009; Lim et al. 2010).

Given the above, retention mechanisms deserve significant scrutiny as a source of judicial behaviour and decision-making. It is emphatically *not* the case that judicial elections induce a responsiveness to the political environment that is absent among appointed judges. Rather, both elections and appointment mechanisms function by focusing the attention of judges to the constituency they must please to maintain their seat on the bench. Those who design judiciaries, therefore, must make value judgments about *to whom* they want courts to respond, rather than to suggest that only elected courts are responsive to the broader political environment.

What are the features of the broader political environment that affect elected judges? In the following sections, we answer this question by discussing research on the relationship between public opinion and the behaviour of elected judges, the effects of different forms of judicial elections, and the competitiveness of the electoral environment.

3.1 Judicial Elections and Public Opinion

The most obvious difference between judicial elections and other forms of retention is the influence of the public. By directly tying judges' continued service on the bench to the electorate, judicial elections naturally suggest the effect of public opinion on judicial behaviour is greater for elected judges than appointed judges.[9] Assessing the relationship between public opinion and judicial behaviour among elected (rather than appointed) judges has been perhaps the most pressing topic for those seeking to understand the consequences of judicial elections for judicial behaviour.

Most studies on this topic have examined judicial behaviour in high-profile criminal cases, especially death penalty cases (e.g. Brace and Hall 1997; Traut and Emmert 1998; Brace and Boyea 2008). Early studies in this vein used this case selection as a research design tactic under the assumption that voters are 'tough on crime' and therefore decisions that uphold death sentences (or reach other similarly punitive outcomes) are congruent with public opinion. Hall (1987), for example, interviewed state supreme court judges who suggested that they would vote against their preferences in some death penalty cases rather than risk an insufficiently punitive vote that could ire voters and be used against them in an upcoming election.

If it is the case that elections make judges particularly wary of constituent preferences, we might expect the effect of public opinion to vary with the electoral cycle. After all, Judge Otto Kraus famously remarked that 'no judge can ignore the political consequences of a decision near election time; that would be like ignoring a crocodile in your bathtub' (quoted in Linde 1987, 2004). There is some evidence that this is the case. Judges that face more electoral pressure or are closer in temporal proximity to an election are more likely to uphold death sentences (Hall 1995; Brace and Hall 1997; Brace and Boyea 2008). No such correlation exists when judges are retiring (Hall 2014). This pattern appears to extend not just to capital cases but criminal cases generally (Huber and Gordon 2004; Berdejó and Yuchtman 2013).

Beyond criminal cases, an emerging trend is that the correlation between judicial decisions and public opinion generally is contingent upon issue salience. There is good evidence that the behaviour of elected judges follows public opinion on hot-button issues such as abortion (Caldarone et al. 2009; Canes-Wrone and Clark 2009; Canes-Wrone et al. 2012). Gibson and Nelson (2021) find the same pattern in their study of inequality-related cases, such as gay rights, class action policies, and election law. But in a study of behaviour in less-salient cases, Canes-Wrone, Clark, and Semet (2018) found no discernible effect of public opinion on state supreme court judicial decisions in most environmental law cases across forty states. However, in instances where environmental cases became the subject of campaign attack ads, judges became more responsive to public opinion on the issue.

For unpopular judicial decisions to have electoral consequences, the public must be aware of them. For this reason, understanding trends in media coverage of state courts and how it ebbs and flows during the electoral cycle is important (Vining, Jr and Wilhelm 2010; Vining and Wilhelm 2011). The bits of research that have been conducted suggest that media coverage of judicial decisions can motivate both judges and voters. For example, the influence of media coverage on judicial decisions has also shown to be more pronounced on elected, rather than appointed judges (Lim 2013). And, voters are more likely to vote in judicial elections when they are salient (Bonneau and Hall 2009).

A natural question that follows from this discussion is to whose preferences are justices most responsive? Within the legislative politics literature, an extensive body of work examines how legislators differentially respond to constituents, interest groups, and donors (e.g. Fenno 1978). The extended party network theory proposed by Bawn et al. (2012) posits that voters have electoral blind spots where it is difficult for them to evaluate policy positions and performance. By mobilizing around these blind spots, interest groups are able to influence legislators disproportionately (Kujala 2020). Applying this theory to judicial politics, we might expect interest groups to have a disproportionately large influence on the decision-making of elected judges. Work by Canes-Wrone and Clark (2009) and Canes-Wrone, Clark, and Kelly (2014) found evidence that interest groups might (indirectly) influence decisions on abortion and the death penalty, but work in this area is still relatively limited. Future research should seek to understand (i) the conditions under which interest groups become involved in judicial elections, (ii) the extent to which voters' judgments of judicial candidates are shaped by this interest group involvement, and (iii) whether judges are more likely to be responsive to the preferences of interest groups (or other elites) than the average citizen.

More specifically, the extended party network theory suggests several testable hypotheses for which congressional election research has provided a template.

Desmarais, La Raja, and Kowal (2015) operationalized these networks via the financial contributions from interest groups to US House candidates. They found that extended party network support both increased the electoral success of candidates and signalled ideological credibility to constituents. Does this relationship between party networks, electoral success, and ideological signalling persist in judicial elections? The potential amplification of ideological signals may have a particularly potent role in nonpartisan judicial elections given the lack of party cues voters typically rely on. Other research has found that party networks are distinct and more polarized than formal party organizations (Koger et al. 2009), and that the talking points and language of these policy groups diffuse the language and text of politicians (Albert 2020). If these networks have a similar influence on judicial elections and decisions, we would expect to see a positive correlation between polarization and network support. Additionally, there may be evidence of ideological diffusion from networks to judges via amicus briefs or organizational platforms. Research by Corley (2008) has provided some groundwork on this question by leveraging plagiarism software to show diffusion from parties to judges. Testing for a similar relationship between interest groups and judges seems to be a natural extension of this work.

3.2 The Effects of Ballot Type

Not all elections are equal. The particulars of an electoral institution shape the incentive structure (and thus the behaviour) of judges. Whether judges run in partisan, nonpartisan, or retention elections is perhaps the most significant feature of how an election is structured. Retention elections, for example, are 'elections in name only' because the rate of incumbent re-election in these races is over 95 percent (Aspin 2011). Likewise, in partisan elections, voters have a heuristic—the party affiliation listed next to each candidate's name—they can rely upon to make a semi-informed decision at the polls. These signals are unavailable to voters in nonpartisan elections.

Evidence suggests that ballot type has several important effects in judicial elections. Non-partisan-elected judges are more responsive to the preferences of the public than judges who face partisan elections (Caldarone et al. 2009; Gibson and Nelson 2021), perhaps because the partisan-elected judges benefit from a party cue listed on the ballot which acts as a form of political cover that can counteract negative campaign information voters have heard about a copartisan judicial candidate. Judges who face nonpartisan elections are more likely to uphold capital sentences (Canes-Wrone et al. 2014) and are more responsive to increased media coverage (Lim, Snyder, Jr., and Strömberg (2015)). Indeed, party cues appear to provide a form of political cover that insulates judges from public scrutiny, although it is unclear to what extent this relationship is causal or a feature of an endogenous relationship between judicial decisions and the types of judges that tend to run and win in partisan elections.

Voters also behave differently in partisan and non-partisan elections (Bonneau and Hall 2009; Bonneau and Cann 2015). For example, Lim, Snyder, Jr., and Strömberg (2015) measure candidate quality via American Bar Association (ABA) ratings and find that it has a larger effect on outcomes in non-partisan elections. In the absence of party cues, voters appear to rely more heavily on indicators of candidate quality to make decisions. This is consistent with the findings of Ash and MacLeod (2021), who find that judges elected by a non-partisan process tend to produce higher-quality judicial opinions. This creates a cross-cutting incentive structure: non-partisan elections may both select higher-quality judges inclined to produce better decisions, but also expose these judges to higher levels of public scrutiny, thus encouraging lower-quality decisions issued with more frequency.

Moving forward, judicial scholars would do well to look at the literature on electoral rules and non-partisan elections to inform their theory building and empirical testing. Consider, for example, the studies of party-centric rather than candidate-centric electoral systems. In party-centric electoral environments, elites can rely on the organization, resources, and support of a political party to aid in their re-election. As a result, elites in these systems can focus on building their party brand because their party's policy successes can translate into personal electoral success (Cox and McCubbins 1993). In candidate-centric systems, by contrast, candidates cannot rely on the resources of a party to steer voters in their direction. Instead, candidates in these electoral systems must build a personal brand, advertising themselves and their positions to encourage voters to select them on election day (e.g. Carey and Shugart 1995). Non-partisan elections, which remove a candidate's party affiliation from the ballot on election day, are one electoral rule that encourages candidate-centric, rather than party-centric behaviour among candidates. As a result, we might expect to see judges in non-partisan electoral systems behaving in ways, such as issuing 'popular' dissenting opinions in order to earn free media coverage and build a popular brand among voters.

Or, as another example, consider the strong literature on non-partisanship in other state- and local-level elections. Schaffner, Streb, and Wright (2001), reviewing this literature, note that the costs of voting in a non-partisan election are higher than the costs of voting in a partisan election. Because less politically sophisticated voters (who often tend to have liberal policy preferences) are also less likely to vote—particularly when the absence of a party cue raises the cost of voting—officials who are elected in non-partisan elections often cater more to the preferences of a more sophisticated electorate (Welch and Bledsoe 1986; Rigby and Wright 2013). Understanding how ballot rules may cull the electorate—and therefore direct judges' responsiveness—is an important topic for those seeking to unravel the effects of electoral rules on judicial behaviour.

3.3 Electoral Competition

Variation across elections of the same ballot type is another important research frontier. While scholars of state politics have devoted a great deal of effort to understanding the effects of increased levels of electoral competition for policy-making (e.g. Barrilleaux 1997; Gamm and Kousser 2021), scholars have typically ignored the judiciary in their attempts to assess the extent of competition in state elections (Hall 2015). Moreover, when scholars have attempted to use measures of competition to explain court-related outcomes, they have been forced to rely upon measures which exclude the judiciary under the unstated assumption that competition for judicial offices mirrors competition for state legislative races, an assumption that remains untested. In studies of judicial decision-making, scholars have used measures of party competition (Brace and Hall 1995), legislative electoral competition (Brace and Hall 1997), and individual-level judicial election returns (Hall 1992, 1995, 2014) to examine the relationship between electoral circumstances and judicial behaviour in death penalty cases.[10] Hall (2015) estimates static measures of electoral competition for twenty state supreme courts in two periods of unequal length: 1980–1999 and 2000–2010, finding that nine states got more competitive in the latter time period, nine states got less competitive, and two states remained stable. However, beyond Hall's effort, scholars lack a consistent, available, reliable, and valid measure of competition in judicial elections. Moreover, we do not know how competition in judicial races mirrors that for legislative offices nor do we know how it affects judicial behaviour.

One plausible theory is that increased electoral competition will make judges pay more attention to public sentiment, becoming less likely to issue salient, unpopular decisions as election day approaches.[11] Moreover, elections in and of themselves may not inspire responsiveness to public opinion. While a few highly salient cases of voter responsiveness to judges' on-the-bench behaviour exist—Rose Bird and her colleagues in California in the 1980s (Culver and Wold 1987) and the Iowa Supreme Court justices after their pro-same-sex marriage ruling (Buller 2012; Harris 2019)—there are some good reasons to expect that the typical judicial election does not present enough of a threat of defeat to motivate a judge to change their behaviour in response to increased electoral competition. After all, studies of state legislators find that the public rarely holds state legislators accountable on election day for poor ideological representation (Rogers 2017). Most state supreme court judges (and most of their decisions) happen outside of the public eye.[12] Thus, future research on judicial elections must account for variation in the *de facto* likelihood that a judge will lose their seat in the next election when trying to estimate the effects of these retention institutions on judges' decision-making.

4. Judicial Elections and Selection Effects

To this point, we have focused primarily on judicial *retention*. But judicial elections also have important consequences for who seeks (and attains) judicial office that may have downstream consequences for judicial behaviour and legal development. We see two major areas in which judicial elections may select particular 'types' of judges that demand additional attention from researchers. First, broader trends in the electoral environment may cause changes in the types of people who seek judicial office and, by extension, are elected to the bench. Finally, the use of elections may (dis)advantage judges with certain demographic traits or prior professional experiences.

4.1 The Burgeoning Extremist Advantage

A first way in which elections outside the courthouse may affect judicial policymaking comes through potential candidates' decisions about whether to run for office. Here, the broader literature on candidate emergence and success in US elections paints a stark picture for the future of state supreme court benches. While the conventional wisdom in state elections had been that ideologically extreme candidates are disadvantaged (Birkhead 2015), recent research challenges this view. In a recent study, for example, Handan-Nader, Myers, and Hall (2022) examine the success of candidates in state legislative elections from 1992 to 2020. Their results demonstrate that the penalty for ideologically extreme candidates has almost vanished during this time period, and ideological extreme candidates may actually be *advantaged* in primary elections. If ideologically extreme candidates are more likely to win primary elections (and appear on a general election ballot) and then do not face a penalty for their extremity among the general electorate, these candidates with views outside the mainstream are becoming more likely to gain state legislative office.

Moreover, extremist candidates are becoming more common in US elections. Thomsen (2014) and Hall (2019) both demonstrate that ideologically moderate candidates are increasingly opting out of the electoral process, ceding the ballot to candidates with extreme policy positions. As moderate candidates become less likely to seek office, they demonstrate, extremist candidates are more likely to achieve electoral success. This, in turn, can fuel partisan and ideological polarization in legislatures.

The emergence of more extreme candidates and their increasing success on election day are important general trends in US elections that may also affect judicial elections. As judicial campaigns continue to be 'nastier, noisier, and costlier' in each successive electoral cycle (Schotland 1985, 75; Keith and Velasco 2022), moderate candidates may decide that their present positions are not worth the hassle (and negative personal experiences) that comes with securing a place on the ballot, raising money, and managing a time-intensive (and often costly) electoral campaign. Here, political scientists' broader understanding of candidate emergence may have lessons for judicial scholars (e.g. Lawless and Fox 2005).

Moreover, because the pool of potential judicial candidates is smaller than for other elective offices (due to the requirement, either *de facto* or *de jure* that candidates must have a law degree to seek judicial office), these trends may be accelerated for judicial offices. Most plausible judicial candidates are successful attorneys, and many successful attorneys are well compensated for their work. In comparison, state judges are not particularly well compensated (especially in some states) (Gibson and Nelson 2021). The relatively low salaries state judges receive (especially compared to the salaries that many successful attorneys can garner) mean that many potential judges would take a financial loss in return for winning a seat on the bench. This financial barrier to office may accelerate the willingness of moderate judicial candidates who would prefer to stay in practice rather enduring a challenging election only to receive a pay cut in return for winning. On the other hand, extremist candidates' calculations may be different, prioritizing the ability to push state policy in accordance with their views over financial compensation.

This, of course, is just a hunch—one that demands empirical testing. Ultimately, it underscores the importance of understanding candidate emergence in judicial elections. Though it may seem far afield for scholars of judicial behaviour, understanding how candidates come to the bench—and how that pool might vary over time—is important to understand trends in judicial decision-making over time. For example, if the trends that Thomsen (2014) and Hall (2019) note to be true of legislative candidates also hold for judicial candidates, then one could expect an increasing level of ideological and partisan polarization on elected courts in coming years.

The importance of candidate emergence has ramification for appointive courts, in the US states and beyond. Substantively, appointive courts are filled by *someone* (or something). That appointing authority is often an executive or legislative body that is elected to office. If the legislators and governors who appoint judges—either to full terms or to interim vacancies—are themselves more extreme, they may become disproportionately likely to appoint candidates with more ideological extreme judges to state benches. Methodologically, scholars often measure judicial ideology using estimates of the preferences of those who appointed judges to office (Giles et al. 2001; Epstein et al. 2007). If the preferences of these appointing authorities becomes more extreme over time, our estimates of the judges they appoint will also become more extreme. To the extent that these increasingly extreme appointing authorities appoint judges who mirror their policy preferences, these indicators will accurately measure an increasingly extreme judiciary. But if these appointing authorities become more extreme but their judicial appointments do not reflect that increasing extremism, then these sorts of ideology measures may become less accurate over time. Thus, it is important for those who study only appointed courts to pay close attention to the electoral environment in which appointing authorities reach their positions.

In short, the broader dynamics of state elections could have important consequences for the composition of state benches; because ideology is a powerful predictor of judges' voting behaviour on both elected and appointed state courts, these trends may affect legal policymaking in the states, as the policies made by state courts become as polarized as the policies made by state legislatures (Grumbach 2023). Yet scholars have not devoted nearly the attention to understanding the ideological dynamics of state electoral selection. This must change.

4.2 Judicial Selection and Judicial Diversity

The selection effects driven by the use of elective, rather than appointive, methods of filling the bench extend beyond the ideological extremism of potential jurists. An important debate in the study of judicial selection has sought to determine whether judicial elections enhance or slow the diversification of the bench. Again, studies have come to varied conclusions with some studies (e.g. Reddick et al. 2009) selecting that judicial elections might inhibit judicial diversity and other studies (e.g. Frederick and Streb 2008) suggesting that female candidates may be *advantaged* in judicial elections. The bulk of the evidence (e.g. Hurwitz and Lanier 2003, 2008) suggests that methods of judicial selection are unrelated to the presence of women or non-White judges on state courts. Studying all state supreme court judges who served between 1990 and 2015, for example, Gibson and Nelson (2021) find neither women nor non-White judges were more likely to win office through judicial appointment than judicial election.

Additionally, this research generally emphasizes demographic diversity, though selection methods may lead to other inequities in the composition of the bench. It is perhaps not surprising that many justices of the South Carolina Supreme Court, whose vacancies are filled through legislative election, are filled by former members of that chamber. These effects may be more broadly felt: individuals who work in large law firms, for example, may both have sympathies for particular types of litigants or legal arguments and have the professional (and financial) networks that will enable them to be competitive judicial election candidates. Similarly, individuals who worked as prosecutors—especially in US Attorney's offices or state attorney generals' offices—may have political connections that make them better able to secure a political appointment than lawyers who work in other areas of practice. Though high-quality evidence on the relationship between prior area of practice and judicial behaviour is less prevalent than the effects of demographic diversity (Boyd et al. 2010; Kastellec 2013; but see Harris and Sen 2019, 2022), understanding how methods of judicial selection may fill the bench with judges with particular types of experiences (which may then affect their decision-making) is a topic of paramount importance.

Understanding the extent to which the use of elections or appointment may enhance the diversity of the bench is important normatively and also in as much as demographic diversity on the bench may enhance institutional legitimacy (Scherer and Curry 2010). But, by focusing on judges' ascriptive characteristics, existing accounts of the effects of judicial elections on the diversity of the bench fail to account for differences among female or non-White judges. The sort of person who is able to navigate the political process to win an elite appointment may differ on a variety of dimensions than the typical person who has the temperament to jump through the hurdles of an election campaign.

For this reason, future research should consider the extent to which methods of judicial selection tilt the composition of the bench with judges whose differences are less visible. A burgeoning literature in the study of judicial behaviour has demonstrated that judges' personalities affect their on-the-bench behaviours (Hall 2018; Black et al. 2019), and psychologists have demonstrated that the personalities of those who seek elected office differ from the general population (Caprara et al. 2003; Scott and Medeiros 2020). In as much as differences in personality both affect who runs for office (rather than who has the political mettle to secure an appointment) *and* also affect judicial behaviour, understanding both how methods of staffing the bench are prone to select judges with particular personality traits is an important topic for future inquiry.

Another topic for future inquiry concerns how variation in electoral rules might affect the composition of the bench. Studies of judicial elections have suggested that a lack of female candidates is a major impediment to women's representation on high courts; when women are on the ballot, they face a slight advantage among voters (Frederick and Streb 2008). However, most of these studies have focused on first-past-the-post systems in which voters select only one candidate at a time. In other electoral contexts, scholars have demonstrated that single-member district elections disadvantage women candidates (Krook 2018). Future research should examine if the same is true in judicial elections.

Further, understanding how selection methods affect judicial quality is another important topic. More generously, this can be framed as a trade-off between decision quality and rendering services to voters. Choi, Gulati, and Posner (2010) found that appointed judges tend to write higher-quality opinions, but elected judges write significantly more opinions. While elected judges are more concerned with providing services to voters, appointed judges seem generally more occupied with legacy and creation of precedent. Ash and MacLeod (2015) present similar findings and argue that judges are 'intrinsically motivated to provide high-quality decisions and that at the margin they prefer quality over quantity' (863). When judges face increased electoral demands the decision quality declines in terms of how well researched opinions are and how frequently opinions are cited in the future. Similarly, using a discontinuity around the implementation of the Missouri Plan, they find that judges produced higher quality work post-Missouri Plan (Ash and MacLeod 2021). Judges shielded from voter influence tend to have better information, are more likely to rule counter to preconceived opinions, and make fewer mistakes than elected counterparts (Iaryczower et al. 2013).

A word of caution is needed, though. Understanding the effects of judicial selection is not as simple as consulting a table to learn whether judges on a particular bench are 'elected' or 'appointed' to office. Judges commonly retire, die, are appointed to other courts, or leave office for other personal or professional reasons in the middle of their terms. In these cases, most states allow a governor or other appointive body to appoint a judge to serve, either until a special election can be held or for the remainder of a term. In practice, this means that many 'elected' judges are actually appointed to office. Because these appointed judges carry an incumbency advantage with them into the next election (Bonneau and Hall 2009; Olson and Stone 2023), the composition of many formally elected courts are actually filled with a majority of judges who were first appointed to that court. In fact, Nelson and Gibson (2020) estimate that nearly a majority of formally elected state supreme court judges who served from 1990 to 2015 were actually initially appointed to office (see also Bratton and Spill 2002).

5. Judicial Elections and Judicial Power

Most of our discussion up to this point has focused on the effects of elections on *judges*, but these elections may also have important consequences for *courts* and their external relationships. A key concern for judicial reformers in the states has been the extent to which elections might damage the legitimacy of the judiciary; by dragging the judiciary into the electoral arena, elections risk equalizing judges with 'ordinary politics' and the 'Washington system' that citizens loathe (Hibbing and Theiss-Morse 1995; Gibson 2012). On the other hand, judicial elections free judges from their dependency on the executive or legislative branch, providing the judiciary with an independent base of political support separate from those whose actions they must review. Indeed, both the adoption of nonpartisan elections in the United States and their introduction in Bolivia were premised on arguments that the use of direct elections would restore faith in distrusted judiciaries (Shugerman 2012; Driscoll and Nelson 2013).

Political scientists have sought to provide some empirical clarity on these points, treating support for elected and appointive courts as an outcome variable to assess whether methods of selection or retention as associated with the public's support for the judicial branch. Cann and Yates (2016) conduct an observational analysis, concluding that judicial elections are associated with a reduction in support for state courts (see also Benesh 2006). On the other hand, Nownes and Glennon (2016) and Nelson (2016) find that public support for elected courts is higher than support for appointive courts.[13] Further, Gibson (2012) studies how rough-and-tumble campaigns for judicial office affect judicial legitimacy and concludes that the benefits of judicial elections for judicial legitimacy outweigh the costs that come from typical campaigning. And, looking at the consequences of these institutions, some research suggests that elected courts may be advantaged compared to appointed courts in their ability to win public support for their controversial decisions (Crabtree and Nelson 2019). Thus, the effect of judicial elections on the public's support for courts is not well understood.

While scholars of US courts have focused on the correlates of judicial legitimacy, scholars of judicial behaviour have devoted much attention to how a court's legitimacy may be an explanatory factor in its interactions with the public and with other branches of government (e.g. Staton 2010; Krehbiel 2016). As an example of how scholars of elected courts might expand their horizons by incorporating the literature on courts outside the United States, many formal theoretic models of interbranch relations assume that elites pay a cost for non-compliance with judicial decisions (Krehbiel 2016) or for attempting to pack courts (Vanberg 2015), and the size of this cost varies according with a court's level of public support (see Driscoll and Nelson 2023a, 2023b). In as much as methods of judicial selection might affect public support for courts, attempts to pack, stack, or ignore the judiciary may be more common according to the method used to select or retain judges (Leonard 2016) or according to the level of public support each court enjoys (Nelson and Driscoll 2023). Similarly, decisions of elected courts may be more difficult to override, just as the US Congress is less likely to override US Supreme Court decisions during periods in which that court has stronger public support (Nelson and Uribe-McGuire 2017). Furthermore, judicial elections may have important separation of powers consequences.

Even elected judges lack the ability to enforce their own decisions, but they can renew their mandate with voters through periodic elections. In this way, judicial elections put courts on more equal footing with the legislative and judicial branches of government in ways that may have important separation-of-powers consequences. Perhaps for this reason, elected judges are more willing to use the power of judicial review (e.g. Langer 2002). Shugerman (2010), for example, charts the use of judicial review in historical perspective as states adopted judicial elections; he finds that state supreme courts became much more likely to use judicial review once state constitutions were amended to make those courts elected, rather than appointed.

Moving forward, scholars should endeavour to integrate findings from studies of interbranch relations into the study of judicial elections. The institutional variation provided by methods of selection and retention provides important variation in the level of support enjoyed by state judiciaries while the federal nature of the system in which these institutions are used provides important consistency in legal rule and procedures that could provide a fertile testing ground both for theories of interbranch relations but also the effect of electoral systems on the balance of power in democratic systems.

6. Conclusion

The increased attention that judicial elections have received over the past three decades from political scientists and legal scholars taught us much about how selection and retention institutions affect the work of courts. There is much work to be done, however, and researchers of all types would do well to expand their theorizing and empirical testing by looking outside the judicial realm for inspiration. Judicial elections provide unique opportunities for testing general theories of elite behaviour, electoral representation, and judicial decision-making, but their potential can only be fully realized if scholars abandon their disciplinary silos.

No institutional choice—be it electing or appointing judges, allowing judges to serve for long or short terms, etc.—is without consequences. It is not the case that judicial elections make judges 'political' while appointed judges act with 'independence'. Rather, methods of judicial retention function to direct judges' responsiveness: judicial elections lead judges to respond to public preferences just as elite reappointment mechanisms lead judges to pay increased attention to the desires of legislators and executives. In this way, there is no 'perfect' way to select or retain judges. Instead, reformers must decide to whom they want courts to respond and design the judiciary accordingly. And, careful empirical scholarship has an important role to play in understanding the consequences of these institutional choices.

We conclude with some additional thoughts about how researchers should move forward. Data availability has been a persistent challenge in the judicial elections literature due to the fact that state court decisions are so numerous and labour-intensive to code. As a result, researchers must often limit the scope of their research to a single issue area for which they can collect and label court decisions. This has had a significant impact on the scope and generalizability of research findings in this area (e.g. Hall and Windett 2013). The bulk of the literature discussed in this review relies on criminal cases, particularly death penalty cases, while some work branches out to other areas such as abortion (Brace et al. 1999) or tort (Tabarrok and Helland 1999) cases. This limitation in the scope of data used makes it challenging to test the boundaries of election influence on decision-making because it focuses so much on the issues that dominate campaigns and therefore are the issue areas where the effects of elections are most likely to be felt (Hall 2015). Questions such as where judicial and constituent beliefs systematically diverge and the relative elasticity of judicial beliefs remain unanswered in large part due to challenges in collecting and annotating data.

We call attention to this well-known shortcoming in the literature because it is ripe for solving. Recent advancements in natural language processing—reviewed in Chapter 16 of this volume—have introduced new tools to social science that excel in semantic-based inference. While previous methods that relied on bag-of-words analysis were able to infer high-level metrics such as topic labels or similarity between documents, contemporary large language models allow for automated labelling of sophisticated and specific concepts with accuracy that is on par, or close to, human levels of performance. These models are increasingly able to do so without large manually labelled training datasets (Rosa et al. 2021). Currently, researchers may limit their analysis to state supreme court cases on capital offences within a certain time period due to resource constraints. Automated labelling with large language models present the opportunity to expand analysis across time and topics without imposing additional resource demands.

Another possible avenue of inquiry is if the representative behaviour of elected judges also influences how judges interact with other political actors such as interest groups and voters (e.g. Baum et al. 2017). Legislative theories of party behaviour and electoral accountability seem directly relevant to this question and could bring new insights to theories of judicial behaviour. Extended party network theory predicts that interest groups will have the most influence on issues and elections that are low salience to voters (Bawn et al. 2012). Given the relative low salience of judicial elections compared to legislators, this would predict that interest groups have relatively more influence over judicial decisions than they do legislators. Whether or not this is empirically true remains unanswered. Further, how do interest groups mobilize around judicial elections and what role do judges themselves play in this dynamic? Are interest groups seeking to instigate change through the courts more likely to fund judicial elections or more likely to bring cases to courts with elected judges? These are all important questions.

Scholars should also examine representation from the other side of the coin: the judge's perspective. Studies of the relationship between public opinion and elite behaviour rely on the assumption that elites know their constituency preferences and can adjust their behaviour accordingly. Yet recent studies of state legislatures (Broockman and Skovron 2018) and congressional staff (Hertel-Fernandez et al. 2019) reveal that elites often systematically misperceive public opinion, believing that their constituency holds more conservative beliefs than public opinion surveys reflect. We have no analogous evidence for judges, despite information that judges update their behaviour when provided with constituency-level, issue-specific information about these preferences (Nelson 2014). This provides some suggestion that judges, too, may not be the best judges of their own constituents, a topic ripe for future inquiry.

It is not lost on us that nearly all the literature we have discussed in this chapter has focused on the United States. On the one hand, this is not particularly surprising because the United States is the country with the most numerous and most high-profile judicial elections. At the same time, the dearth of even descriptive data on judicial elections in other contexts—their prevalence, rates of contestation, and electoral results—is a huge impediment toward our understanding of a clear picture of the operation of these elections across the globe. Just because these elections are most often held to fill seats on low-level or community courts does not mean that these judges or their decisions do not merit our attention.

As we have argued throughout this chapter, despite their relative rarity worldwide, judicial elections have a lot to teach us about judicial behaviour. Scholars are increasingly looking to these institutions to examine the generalizability of theories of both electoral politics and judicial decision-making, and new endeavours on this front are promising. However, for these institutions to be maximally useful to scholars, researchers need to look beyond their comfort zones in their theory building and empirical testing: there is much to be gained from cross-pollination in this regard.

Acknowledgements

We thank Taran Samarth for helpful research assistance and Jim Gibson, Amanda Driscoll, and Jay N. Krehbiel for helpful discussions.

Notes

1. As discussed in the next section, some of these judges are initially elected to the bench; others are initially appointed to the bench and need only run for re-election.
2. For more information on the types of elections and the history of their use in the United States, see Shugerman (2012) and Hanssen (2004).
3. And, in both the United States and Bolivia, voters—through the media or other means—often learn about the partisan affiliation of judges in formally nonpartisan elections; a lack

of partisan affiliation on the printed ballot does not halt politics from the electoral process (Nelson, Caufield and Martin 2013).

4. Other lower-level judges are elected in a handful of other countries, including in Venezuela and Switzerland (Driscoll and Nelson 2012; Kritzer 2015). Similarly, judges of France's commercial courts are also elected (and need not be attorneys) (Kessler 2010). France also elected some lower court judges after the French Revolution: justices of the peace, district judges, and judges *en cassation*. The elections were indirect and limited to citizens with a high enough income (Volcansek and Lafon 1988). However, the processes surrounding these elections are often not professionalized, making information about electoral procedures is hard to come by (Kritzer 2015).
5. Some models of judicial behaviour do this already. As one example, Segal and Spaeth (2002) argue that the influence of justices' ideologies is likely to be particularly prominent at the US Supreme Court because those judges have very minimal (if any) retention considerations: they serve for life and rarely (in the modern era) want to seek another political office.
6. Recent evidence has shown the effects of each to be heterogeneous across justices (Duck-Mayr 2022). We omit that complexity for illustrative purposes but acknowledge it as a fruitful path for future research.
7. For a review, see Epstein and Martin (2010).
8. We focus in this section on judges' retention considerations—how they might need to modify their behaviour to maximize the likelihood they will continue to serve—for two reasons. First, by definition, judges have already survived their selection institution when they reach the bench. Second, where selection and retention constituencies differ, judges tend to respond to their retention constituency (Savchak and Barghothi 2007).
9. Of course, there are other mechanisms through which public opinion might influence judges, such as a downstream effect of judicial appointments by elected officials (Dahl 1957; Mishler and Sheehan 1993) or the need of the courts to maintain popular support in order to secure institutional legitimacy (Caldeira and Gibson 1992).
10. These measures have been used in other judicial contexts. Bonneau and Hall (2009) use the Holbrook–Van Dunk index to assess the relationship between *legislative* electoral competition and participation in *judicial* elections.
11. But, of course, appointed courts may also reflect public opinion (Marshall 2008; Epstein and Martin 2010), illustrating that judicial elections are not a necessary condition for a judicial system that is generally congruent with public opinion (but see Johnson and Strother 2021).
12. In fact, Lax and Phillips (2012) find no evidence that the responsiveness or congruence of state governments to public opinion is greater in states that use judicial elections.
13. Some studies also find null effects for the relationship between selection method and support for courts (Kelleher and Wolak 2007).

References

Albert, Zachary. 2020. 'Partisan Policymaking in the Extended Party Network: The Case of Cap-and-Trade Regulations'. *Political Research Quarterly* 73: 476–91.

American Bar Association. 2003. *Justice in Jeopardy: Report of the American Bar Association Commission on the 21st Century Judiciary*. Saratoga Springs: American Bar Association.

Anenson, T. Leigh. 1997. 'For Whom the Bell Tolls. Judicial Selection by Election in Latin America'. *Southwestern Journal of Law and Trade in the Americas* 4: 261–300.

Ash, Elliott, and W. Bentley MacLeod. 2015. 'Intrinsic Motivation in Public Service: Theory and Evidence from State Supreme Courts'. *Journal of Law & Economics* 58: 863–913.

Ash, Elliott, and W. Bentley MacLeod. 2021. 'Reducing Partisanship in Judicial Elections Can Improve Judge Quality: Evidence from U.S. State Supreme Courts'. *Journal of Public Economics* 201: 104478.

Aspin, Larry. 2011. 'The 2010 Judicial Retention Elections in Perspective: Continuity and Change from 1964 to 2010'. *Judicature* 94: 218–32.

Barnum, David C. 1985. 'The Supreme Court and Public Opinion: Judicial Decisionmaking in the Post New Deal Period'. *Journal of Politics* 47: 652–65.

Barrilleaux, Charles. 1997. 'A Test of the Independent Influences of Electoral Competition and Party Strength in a Model of State Policy-Making'. *American Journal of Political Science* 41: 1462–66.

Baum, Lawrence, David Klein, and Matthew J. Streb. 2017. *The Battle for the Court: Interest Groups, Judicial Elections, and Public Policy*. Charlottesville: University of Virginia Press.

Bawn, Kathleen, Martin Cohen, David Karol, Seth Masket, Hans Noel, and John Zaller. 2012. 'A Theory of Political Parties: Groups, Policy Demands and Nominations in American Politics'. *Perspectives on Politics* 10: 571–97.

Benesh, Sara C. 2006. 'Understanding Public Confidence in American Courts'. *Journal of Politics* 68 (3): 697–707.

Berdejó, Carlos, and Noam Yuchtman. 2013. 'Crime, Punishment, and Politics: An Analysis of Political Cycles in Criminal Sentencing'. *The Review of Economics and Statistics* 95: 741–56.

Bickel, Alexander M. 1986. *The Least Dangerous Branch: The Supreme Court at the Bar of Politics*, 2nd edn. New Haven: Yale University Press.

Birkhead, Nithaniel A. 2015. 'The Role of Ideology in State Legislative Elections'. *Legislative Studies Quarterly* 40: 55–82.

Black, Ryan C., Ryan J. Owens, Justin Wedeking, and Patrick C. Wohlfarth. 2019. *The Conscientious Justice: How Supreme Court Justices' Personalities Influence the Law, the High Court, and the Constitution*. Cambridge: Cambridge University Press.

Bonneau, Chris W., and Damon M. Cann. 2015. *Voters' Verdicts: Citizens, Campaigns, and Institutions in State Supreme Court Elections*. Charlottesville: University of Virginia Press.

Bonneau, Chris W., and Melinda Gann Hall. 2009. *In Defense of Judicial Elections*. London: Routledge.

Boyd, Christina L., Lee Epstein, and Andrew D. Martin. 2010. 'Untangling the Causal Effects of Sex on Judging'. *American Journal of Political Science* 54: 389–411.

Brace, Paul, and Brent D. Boyea. 2008. 'State Public Opinion, the Death Penalty, and the Practice of Electing Judges'. *American Journal of Political Science* 52: 360–72.

Brace, Paul, and Melinda Gann Hall. 1995. 'Studying Courts Comparatively: The View from the American States'. *Political Research Quarterly* 48: 5–29.

Brace, Paul R., and Melinda Gann Hall. 1997. 'The Interplay of Preferences, Case Facts, Context, and Rules in the Politics of Judicial Choice'. *Journal of Politics* 59: 1206–31.

Brace, Paul, Melinda Gann Hall, and Laura Langer. 1999. 'Judicial Choice and the Politics of Abortion: Institutions, Context, and the Autonomy of Courts'. *Albany Law Review* 62: 1265–303.

Brandt, Hans Jürgen. 1995. 'The Justice of the Peace As an Alternative: Experiences with Conciliation in Peru'. In *Judicial Reform in Latin America and the Caribbean*, edited by Malcolm Rowat, Waleed H. Malik, and Maria Dakolias, 92–100. World Bank.

Bratton, Kathleen A., and Rorie Spill. 2002. 'Existing Diversity and Judicial Selection: The Role of the Appointment Method in Establishing Gender Diversity in State Supreme Courts'. *Social Science Quarterly* 30: 115–42.

Broockman, David E., and Christopher Skovron. 2018. 'Bias in Perceptions of Public Opinion among Political Elites'. *American Political Science Review* 112: 542–63.

Buller, Tyler J. 2012. 'Framing the Debate: Understanding Iowa's 2010 Judicial-Retention Election Through a Content Analysis of Letters to the Editor'. *Iowa Law Review* 97: 1745–86.

Caldarone, Richard P., Brandice Canes-Wrone, and Tom S. Clark. 2009. 'Partisan Labels and Democratic Accountability: An Analysis of State Supreme Court Abortion Decisions'. *Journal of Politics* 71: 560–73.

Caldeira, Gregory A., and James L. Gibson. 1992. 'The Etiology of Public Support for the Supreme Court'. *American Journal of Political Science* 36: 635–664.

Canes-Wrone, Brandice, and Tom S. Clark. 2009. 'Judicial Independence and Nonpartisan Elections'. *Wisconsin Law Review* 2009: 21–65.

Canes-Wrone, Brandice, Tom S. Clark, and Jason P. Kelly. 2014. 'Judicial Selection and Death Penalty Decisions'. *American Political Science Review* 108: 23–39.

Canes-Wrone, Brandice, Tom S. Clark, and Jee-Kwang Park. 2012. 'Judicial Independence and Retention Elections'. *Journal of Law, Economics, & Organization* 28: 211–34.

Canes-Wrone, Brandice, Tom S. Clark, and Amy Semet. 2018. 'Judicial Elections, Public Opinion, and Decisions on Lower Salience Issues'. *Journal of Empirical Legal Studies* 15: 672–707.

Cann, Damon M., and Jeff Yates. 2016. *These Estimable Courts*. Oxford: Oxford University Press.

Caprara, GianVittorio, Claudio Barbaranelli, Chiara Consiglio, Laura Picconi, and Philip G. Zimbardo. 2003. 'Personalities of Politicians and Voters: Unique and Synergistic Relationships'. *Journal of Personality and Social Psychology* 84: 849–56.

Carey, John M., and Matthew Soberg Shugart. 1995. 'Incentives to Cultivate a Personal Vote: A Rank Ordering of Electoral Formulas'. *Electoral Studies* 14: 417–39.

Caufield, Rachel Paine. 2009. 'Reconciling the Judicial Ideal and the Democratic Impulse in Judicial Retention Elections'. *Missouri Law Review* 74: 573–604.

Choi, Stephen J., G. Mitu Gulati, and Eric A. Posner. 2010. 'Professionals or Politicians: The Uncertain Empirical Case for an Elected Rather than Appointed Judiciary'. *Journal of Law, Economics, & Organization* 26: 290–336.

Corley, Pamela C. 2008. 'The Supreme Court and Opinion Content: The Influence of Parties' Briefs'. *Political Research Quarterly* 61: 468–78.

Cox, Gary W., and Matthew D. McCubbins. 1993. *Legislative Leviathan: Party Government in the House*. Berkeley: University of California Press.

Crabtree, Charles, and Michael J. Nelson. 2019. 'Judging Judicial Review in the American States'. *State Politics & Policy Quarterly* 19: 287–311.

Culver, John H., and John R. Wold. 1987. 'Rose Bird and the Politics of Judicial Accountability in California'. *Judicature* 70: 78–88.

Dahl, Robert A. 1957. 'Decision-Making in a Democracy: The Supreme Court as a National Policy-Maker'. *Journal of Public Law* 6: 279–95.

Desmarais, Bruce A., Raymond J. La Raja, and Michael S. Kowal. 2015. 'The Fates of Challengers in US House Elections: The Role of Extended Party Networks in Supporting Candidates and Shaping Electoral Outcomes'. *American Journal of Political Science* 59: 194–211.

Driscoll, Amanda, and Michael J. Nelson. 2012. 'The 2011 Judicial Elections in Bolivia'. *Electoral Studies* 31: 628–32.

Driscoll, Amanda, and Michael J. Nelson. 2013. 'The Political Origins of Judicial Elections: Evidence from the United States and Bolivia'. *Judicature* 96: 151–60.

Driscoll, Amanda, and Michael J. Nelson. 2015. 'Judicial Selection and the Democratization of Justice: Lessons from the Bolivian Judicial Elections'. *Journal of Law and Courts* 3: 115–48.

Driscoll, Amanda, and Michael J. Nelson. 2023a. 'The Costs of Court Curbing: Evidence from the United States'. *Journal of Politics* 85: 609–24.

Driscoll, Amanda, and Michael J. Nelson. 2023b. 'Are Courts 'Different?:' Experimental Evidence on the Unique Costs of Attacking Courts'. *Research & Politics*. https://doi.org/10.1177/20531680231188302.

Duck-Mayr, J. Brandon. 2022. 'Explaining Legal Inconsistency'. *Journal of Theoretical Politics* 34: 107–26.

Epstein, Lee, and Jack Knight. 1998. *The Choices Justices Make*. Washington: CQ Press.

Epstein, Lee, and Andrew D. Martin. 2010. 'Does Public Opinion Influence the Supreme Court? Possibly Yes (But We're Not Sure Why)'. *University of Pennsylvania Journal of Constitutional Law* 13: 263–81.

Epstein, Lee, Andrew D. Martin, Jeffrey A. Segal, and Chad Westerland. 2007. 'The Judicial Common Space'. *Journal of Law, Economics, & Organization* 23: 303–25.

Fenno, Richard F. 1978. *Home Style: House Members in Their Districts*. Boston: Little Brown.

Frederick, Brian, and Matthew J. Streb. 2008. 'Women Running for Judge: The Impact of Sex on Candidate Success in State Intermediate Appellate Court Elections'. *Social Science Quarterly* 89: 937–54.

Gamm, Gerald, and Thad Kousser. 2021. 'Life, Literacy, and the Pursuit of Prosperity: Party Competition and Policy Outcomes in 50 States'. *American Political Science Review* 115: 1442–63.

George, Tracey E., and Lee Epstein. 1992. 'On the Nature of Supreme Court Decision Making'. *American Political Science Review* 86: 323–37.

Gibson, James L. 2012. *Electing Judges: The Surprising Effects of Campaigning on Judicial Legitimacy*. University of Chicago Press.

Gibson, James L., and Michael J. Nelson. 2021. *Judging Inequality: State Supreme Courts and the Inequality Crisis*. New York: Russell Sage Foundation.

Giles, Micheal W., Virginia A. Hettinger, and Todd Peppers. 2001. 'Picking Federal Judges: A Note on Policy and Partisan Selection Agendas'. *Political Research Quarterly* 54: 623–41.

Gray, Thomas. 2017. 'The Influence of Legislative Reappointment on State Supreme Court Decision-Making'. *State Politics & Policy Quarterly* 17: 275–98.

Grumbach, Jake. 2023. 'Laboratories of Democratic Backsliding'. *American Political Science Review* 117: 967–84.

Guerra Cerron, Maria Elena. 2008. 'Justice of the Peace in Peru: An Efficient Justice Service'. *Florida Journal of International Law* 20: 65–91.

Hall, Andrew B. 2019. *Who Wants to Run? How the Devaluing of Political Office Drives Polarization*. Chicago: University of Chicago Press.

Hall, Matthew E. K. 2018. *What Justices Want: Goals and Personality on the U.S. Supreme Court*. Cambridge: Cambridge University Press.

Hall, Matthew E. K., and Jason Harold Windett. 2013. 'New Data on State Supreme Court Cases'. *State Politics & Policy Quarterly* 13: 427–445.

Hall, Melinda Gann. 1987. 'Constituent Influence in State Supreme Courts: Conceptual Notes and a Case Study'. *Journal of Politics* 49: 1117–24.

Hall, Melinda Gann. 1992. 'Electoral Politics and Strategic Voting in State Supreme Courts'. *Journal of Politics* 54: 427–46.

Hall, Melinda Gann. 1995. 'Justices as Representatives: Elections and Judicial Politics in the American States'. *American Politics Quarterly* 23: 485–503.

Hall, Melinda Gann. 2014. 'Representation in State Supreme Courts: Evidence from the Terminal Term'. *Political Research Quarterly* 67: 335–46.

Hall, Melinda Gann. 2015. *Attacking Judges: How Campaign Advertising Influences State Supreme Court Elections*. Stanford: Stanford University Press.

Handan-Nader, Cassandra, Andrew C. W. Myers, and Andrew B. Hall. 2022. 'Polarization and State Legislative Elections'. Working Paper. https://stanforddpl.org/papers/handan-nader_myers_hall_polarization_2022/handan-nader_myers_hall_polarization_2022.pdf.

Hanssen, F. Andrew. 2004. 'Learning about Judicial Independence: Institutional Change in State Courts'. *Journal of Legal Studies* 33: 431–73.

Harris, Allison P. 2019. 'Voter Response to Salient Judicial Decisions in Retention Elections'. *Law & Social Inquiry* 44: 170–91.

Harris, Allison P., and Maya Sen. 2019. 'Bias and Judging'. *Annual Review of Political Science* 22: 241–59.

Harris, Allison, and Maya Sen. 2022. 'How Judges' Professional Experience Impacts Case Outcomes: An Examination of Public Defenders and Criminal Sentencing'. Working Paper. https://scholar.harvard.edu/files/msen/files/harris-sen-public-defenders.pdf.

Helmke, Gretchen. 2002. 'The Logic of Strategic Defection: Court–Executive Relations in Argentina Under Dictatorship and Democracy'. *American Political Science Review* 96: 291–303.

Hertel-Fernandez, Alexander, Matto Mildenberger, and Leah C. Stokes. 2019. 'Legislative Staff and Representation in Congress'. *American Political Science Review* 113: 1–18.

Hibbing, John R., and Elizabeth Theiss-Morse. 1995. *Congress as Public Enemy: Public Attitudes Toward American Political Institutions*. New York: Cambridge University Press.

Huber, Gregory A., and Stanford C. Gordon. 2004. 'Accountability and Coercion: Is Justice Blind When it Runs for Office?' *American Journal of Political Science* 48: 247–63.

Hurwitz, Mark S., and Drew Lanier. 2003. 'Explaining Judicial Diversity: The Differential Ability of Women and Minorities to Attain Seats on State Supreme and Appellate Courts'. *State Politics & Policy Quarterly* 3: 329–52.

Hurwitz, Mark S., and Drew Noble Lanier. 2008. 'Diversity in State and Federal Appellate Courts: Change and Continuity Across 20 Years'. *Justice System Journal* 29: 47–70.

Iaryczower, Matias, Garrett Lewis, and Matthew Shum. 2013. 'To Elect or to Appoint? Bias, Information, and Responsiveness of Bureaucrats and Politicians'. *Journal of Public Economics* 97: 230–44.

Jacobson, Gary C. 2009. *The Politics of Congressional Elections*, 7th edn. London: Pearson Longman.

Johnson, Ben, and Logan Strother. 2021. 'The Supreme Court's (Surprising?) Indifference to Public Opinion'. *Political Research Quarterly* 74: 18–34.

Kales, Albert M. 1914. 'Methods of Selecting and Retiring Judges in a Metropolitan District'. *Annals of the American Academy of Political and Social Science* 52: 1–12.

Kastellec, Jonathan P. 2013. 'Racial Diversity and Judicial Influence on Appellate Courts'. *American Journal of Political Science* 57: 167–83.

Keith, Douglas, and Eric Velasco. 2022. *The Politics of Judicial Elections, 2019–20*. New York: Brennan Center for Justice.

Kelleher, Christine A., and Jennifer Wolak. 2007. 'Explaining Public Confidence in the Branches of State Government'. *Political Research Quarterly* 60: 707–21.

Kessler, Amalia D. 2010. 'Marginalization and Myth: The Corporatist Roots of France's Forgotten Elective Judiciary'. *American Journal of Comparative Law* 58: 679–720.

Key, V. O. Jr. 1949. *Southern Politics in State and Nation*. New York: A. Knopf.

Koger, Gregory, Seth Masket, and Hans Noel. 2009. 'Partisan Webs: Information Exchange and Party Networks'. *British Journal of Political Science* 39: 633–53.

Krehbiel, Jay N. 2016. 'The Politics of Judicial Procedures: the Role of Public Oral Hearings in the German Constitutional Court'. *American Journal of Political Science* 60: 900–1005.

Kritzer, Herbert M. 2015. *Justices on the Ballot: Continuity and Change in State Supreme Court Elections*. Cambridge: Cambridge University Press.

Krook, Mona Lena. 2018. 'Electoral Systems and Women's Representation'. In *Oxford Handbook of Electoral Systems*, edited by Erik S. Herron, Robert J. Pekkanen, and Matthew S. Shugart, 174–92. Oxford University Press.

Kujala, Jordan. 2020. 'Donors, Primary Elections, and Polarization in the United States'. *American Journal of Political Science* 64: 587–602.

Langer, Laura. 2002. *Judicial Review in State Supreme Courts: A Comparative Study*. New York State University of New York Press.

Law, David S. 2009. 'The Anatomy of a Conservative Court: Judicial Review in Japan'. *Texas Law Review* 87: 1545–94.

Lawless, Jennifer L., and Richard L. Fox. 2005. *It Takes a Candidate: Why Women Don't Run for Office*. Cambridge: Cambridge University Press.

Lax, Jeffrey R., and Justin H. Phillips. 2012. 'The Democratic Deficit in the States'. *American Journal of Political Science* 56: 148–66.

Lazarus, Jeffrey. 2009. 'Party, Electoral Vulnerability, and Earmarks in the U.S. House of Representatives'. *Journal of Politics* 71: 1050–61.

Leonard, Meghan E. 2016. 'State Legislatures, State High Courts, and Judicial Independence: An Examination of Court-Curbing Legislation in the States'. *Justice System Journal* 37: 53–62.

Lim, Claire S. H. 2013. 'Preferences and Incentives of Appointed and Elected Public Officials: Evidence from State Trial Court Judges'. *American Economic Review* 103: 1360–97.

Lim, Claire S. H., and James M. Snyder, Jr. 2021. 'What Shapes the Quality and Behavior of Government Officials? Institutional Variation in Selection and Retention Methods'. *Annual Review of Economics* 13: 87–109.

Lim, Claire S. H., James J. Snyder, Jr., and David Strömberg. 2010. 'Measuring Media Influence on U.S. State Courts'. Meeting Papers 1193, Society for Economic Dynamics. https://ideas.repec.org/p/red/sed010/1193.html.

Lim, Claire S. H., James M. Snyder, Jr., and David Strömberg. 2015. 'The Judge, The Politician, and the Press: Newspaper Coverage and Criminal Sentencing Across Electoral Systems'. *American Economic Journal: Applied Economics* 7: 103–35.

Linde, Hans A. 1987. 'Elective Judges: Some Comparative Comments'. *Southern California Law Review* 61: 1995–2006.

Marshall, Thomas R. 2008. *Public Opinion and the Rehnquist Court*. New York: State University of New York Press.

Mishler, William, and Reginald S. Sheehan. 1993. 'The Supreme Court as a Countermajoritarian Institution? The Impact of Public Opinion on Supreme Court Decisions'. *American Political Science Review* 87: 87–101.

Nelson, Michael J. 2014. 'Responsive Justice? Retention Elections, Prosecutors, and Public Opinion'. *Journal of Law and Courts* 2: 117–52.

Nelson, Michael J. 2016. 'Judicial Elections and Support for State Courts'. In *Judicial Elections in the 21st Century*, edited by Chris W. Bonneau and Melinda Gann Hall, 217–32. London: Routledge.

Nelson, Michael J., and Amanda Driscoll. 2023. 'Accountability for Court Packing.' *Journal of Law and Courts* 11: 290–311.

Nelson, Michael J., and James L. Gibson. 2020. 'Measuring Subjective Ideological Disagreement with the U.S. Supreme Court'. *Journal of Law and Courts* 8: 75–94.

Nelson, Michael J., and Alicia Uribe-McGuire. 2017. 'Opportunity and Overrides: The Effect of Institutional Public Support on Congressional Overrides of Supreme Court Decisions'. *Political Research Quarterly* 70: 632–43.

Nelson, Michael J., Rachel Paine Caufield, and Andrew D. Martin. 2013. 'OH, MI: A Note On Empirical Examinations of Judicial Elections'. *State Politics & Policy Quarterly* 13: 495–511.

Nownes, Anthony J., and Colin Glennon. 2016. 'An Experimental Investigation of How Judicial Elections Affect Public Faith in the Judicial System'. *Law & Social Inquiry* 41: 37–60.

Olson, Michael P., and Andrew R. Stone. 2023. 'The Incumbency Advantage in Judicial Elections: Evidence from Partisan Trial Court Elections in Six U.S. States'. *Political Behavior* 45: 1333–1354.

Ramseyer, J. Mark, and Eric B. Rasmusen. 2001. 'Why are Japanese Judges So Conservative in Politically Charged Cases?' *American Political Science Review* 95: 331–44.

Reddick, Malia, Michael J. Nelson, and Rachel P. Caufield. 2009. 'Racial and Gender Diversity on State Courts'. *The Judge's Journal* 48: 28–32.

Rigby, E., and G. C. Wright. 2013. 'Political Parties and Representation of the Poor in the American States'. *American Journal of Political Science* 41: 1462–66.

Rogers, Steven. 2017. 'Electoral Accountability for State Legislative Roll Calls and Ideological Representation'. *American Political Science Review* 111: 555–71.

Rosa, Guilherme Moraes, Ruan Chaves Rodrigues, Roberto de Alencar Lotufo, and Rodrigo Nogueira. 2021. 'To Tune or Not To Tune? Zero-shot Models for Legal Case Entailment'. *Proceedings of the Eighteenth International Conference on Artificial Intelligence and Law* June 2021: 295–300.

Savchak, Elisha Carol, and A.J. Barghothi. 2007. 'The Influence of Appointment and Retention Constituencies: Testing Strategies of Judicial Decisionmaking'. *State Politics & Policy Quarterly* 7: 394–415.

Schaffner, Brian F., Matthew Streb, and Gerald Wright. 2001. 'Teams without Uniforms: The Nonpartisan Ballot in State and Local Elections'. *Political Research Quarterly* 54: 7–30.

Scherer, Nancy, and Brett Curry. 2010. 'Does Descriptive Race Representation Enhance Institutional Legitimacy? The Case of the U.S. Courts'. *Journal of Politics* 72: 90–104.

Schotland, Roy A. 1985. 'Elective Judges' Campaign Financing: Are State Judges' Robes the Emperor's Clothes of American Democracy?' *Journal of Law and Politics* 2: 57–167.

Schotland, Roy A. 2001. 'Financing Judicial Elections, 2000: Change and Challenge'. *Law Review of Michigan State University Detroit College of Law* 2001: 849–900.

Scott, Colin, and Mike Medeiros. 2020. 'Personality and Political Careers: What Personality Types are Likely to Run for Office and Get Elected?' *Personality and Individual Differences* 152: 109600.

Segal, Jeffrey A., and Harold J. Spaeth. 2002. *The Supreme Court and the Attitudinal Model Revisited.* Cambridge: Cambridge University Press.

Shepherd, Joanna M. 2009. 'Are Appointed Judges Strategic Too?' *Duke Law Journal* 58: 1589–626.

Shugerman, Jed. 2012. *The People's Courts*. Cambridge: Harvard University Press.

Shugerman, Jed Handelsman. 2010. 'Economic Crisis and the Rise of Judicial Elections and Judicial Review'. *Harvard Law Review* 123: 1061–150.

Staton, Jeffrey K. 2010. *Judicial Power and Strategic Communication in Mexico*. Cambridge: Cambridge University Press.

Tabarrok, Alexander and Eric Helland. 1999. 'Court Politics: The Political Economy of Tort Awards'. *Journal of Law and Economics* 42: 157–88.

Tadano, Masahito. 2018. 'The Role of the Judicial Branch in the Protection of Fundamental Rights in Japan'. In *Contemporary Issues in Human Rights Law: Europe and Asia*, edited by Yumiko Nakanishi, 73–90. Springer.

Tarr, G. Alan. 2012. *Without Fear or Favor: Judicial Independence and Judicial Accountability in the States*. Stanford: Stanford University Press.

Thomsen, Danielle M. 2014. 'Ideological Moderates Won't Run: How Party Fit Matters for Partisan Polarization in Congress'. *Journal of Politics* 76: 786–97.

Tiede, Lydia. 2022. *Judicial Vetoes: Decision-making on Mixed Selection Constitutional Courts*. Cambridge: Cambridge University Press.

Traut, Carol Ann, and Craig F. Emmert. 1998. 'Expanding the Integrated Model of Judicial Decision Making: The California Justices and Capital Punishment'. *Journal of Politics* 60: 1166–80.

Vanberg, Georg. 2015. 'Constitutional Courts in Comparative Perspective: A Theoretical Assessment'. *Annual Review of Political Science* 18: 167–85.

Vining, Jr., Richard L., and Teena Wilhelm. 2010. 'Explaining High-Profile Coverage of State Supreme Court Decisions'. *Social Science Quarterly* 91: 704–23.

Vining, Richard, and Teena Wilhelm. 2011. 'Measuring Case Salience in State Courts of Last Resort'. *Political Research Quarterly* 64: 559–72.

Volcansek, Mary L., and Jacqueline Lucienne Lafon. 1988. *Judicial Selection: The Cross-Evolution of French and American Practices*. Westport: Greenwood Press.

Watson, Richard A., and Rondal G. Downing. 1969. *The Politics of Bench and Bar: Judicial Selection Under the Missouri Non-Partisan Court Plan*. Chichester: John Wiley & Sons.

Welch, Susan, and Timothy Bledsoe. 1986. 'The Partisan Consequences of Nonpartisan Elections and the Changing Nature of Urban Politics'. *American Journal of Political Science* 30: 128–39.

CHAPTER 19

JUDICIAL TENURE AND RETIREMENTS

ANÍBAL PÉREZ-LIÑÁN AND ANDREA CASTAGNOLA

1. Introduction

Are constitutional protections for tenure an effective way of preserving judicial independence? Do models of judicial tenure affect judicial performance? Scholars understand that norms regulating tenure and retirements are crucial 'to secure a steady, upright, and impartial administration of the laws' (as noted by Alexander Hamilton, Hamilton 1788), but they show little agreement when trying to answer those questions.

Albeit strong norms protecting judicial tenure are necessary to secure an independent judiciary, those norms confront two intrinsic trade-offs. The first one is a potential trade-off between tenure protection and judicial performance. Norms allowing judges to retire on their own schedule protect their autonomy, but they do not guarantee that judges will use this prerogative wisely. The second one is the trade-off between tenure protection and accountability. Norms allowing other branches of government to exercise oversight over the judiciary are necessary to secure judicial accountability, but they do not guarantee that politicians will use their powers to dismiss judges wisely.

In the first part of this chapter, we analyse three institutional models for judicial careers: life tenure, mandatory retirement ages, and fixed terms in office. Although life tenure is traditionally considered as the strongest protection for judicial independence, this arrangement creates problems. After reviewing the debate on this issue, we conclude that—at least for high court justices—long fixed terms without reappointment may be a better option than life tenure. In the second part of the chapter, we analyse the political mechanisms that disrupt tenure. We introduce a test to identify four types of exits: natural exits, strategic retirements, formal removals, and induced departures. While removals and induced departures typically undermine judicial independence, we identify two boundary situations: cases of lustration, in which a purge of the judiciary appears to be justified, and extreme cases of judicial instability, in which the effective absence of tenure protections actually induces judicial independence. The conclusions discuss those situations and identify novel lines of research.

2. Institutional Frameworks for Tenure and Retirement

In this section we assess alternative models of judicial tenure and retirement. Scholars agree on the nature of these models, although they outline slightly different taxonomies. Bulmer (2017) compares systems that grant tenure during 'good behaviour' against those that appoint judges for fixed terms in office. Opeskin (2015) introduces a trichotomous distinction between systems of tenure ended by life limits, age limits, and term limits. Lara-Borges, Castagnola, and Pérez-Liñán (2012) compare four models: life tenure, fixed terms with reappointment, fixed terms without re-appointment, and indefinite terms. Despite these nuances, the central concerns of these authors are quite similar.

Life tenure—or more precisely, permanence in office during 'good behaviour'—is considered a core protection for the judiciary. However, the literature has identified several problems that undermine its advantages. Older judges experience declining health, and they may drift away from society's preferences. Moreover, judges may choose the timing of their retirement strategically to facilitate the nomination of like-minded colleagues, raising the stakes for new judicial appointments. Longer tenures also increase the value of each court seat and therefore create incentives for political purges. For this reason, there are some doubts, addressed in the second part of this chapter, on whether life tenure is an effective mechanism to secure judicial independence.

As alternatives to life tenure, mandatory retirement rules and fixed terms also present advantages and disadvantages. Retirement rules set the maximum age for judges and improve court performance. However, rigid rules force the departure of experienced judges and impose discrimination based on age. Moreover, manipulation of retirement ages, as shown later in this chapter, is a common instrument employed by politicians to remove senior judges. Fixed terms in office, in turn, can be designed in ways that strengthen or undermine judicial independence. Short terms with the possibility of re-appointment create incentives for judges with static ambitions to serve the interests of politicians in charge of (re)nomination. In contrast, long terms without reappointment are more likely to produce an independent judiciary without the pitfalls of life-tenure arrangements.

Models of tenure tend to vary across types of courts, with supreme courts and lower courts usually relying on life tenure (or a mandatory retirement age) and separate constitutional courts relying on fixed terms in office. The Comparative Constitutions Project identified clear tenure rules for the supreme court of ninety-one countries in 2020. Of those, 42 per cent explicitly protected life tenure, 27 per cent established ages for mandatory retirement, and only 31 per cent set fixed terms in office (with a majority of the terms longer than six years). For lower courts (data available for forty-seven countries), life tenure is the most frequent system, present in 66 per cent of the cases. In contrast, constitutional courts (data available for sixty-nine countries) typically appoint justices for fixed-terms, with only 9 per cent adopting life tenure.

2.1 Life Tenure and Its Critics

There is a general consensus that life tenure protects judicial independence. Life terms free judges from the need to curry favour with political actors (Brinks and Blass 2018, 27). Judges with life tenure are less susceptible to political pressure, and also less likely to have been selected by the incumbent government (La Porta, López-de-Silanes, Pop-Eleches, and Shleifer 2004). Jackson (2007) underscores that tenure and salary protections granted by the US constitution promote independence not only from the political branches, but also from public opinion. The formal length of tenure is often taken to be a proxy for *de jure* judicial independence (Clark 1975; Feld and Voigt 2003; La Porta, López-de-Silanes, Pop-Eleches, and Shleifer 2004).

Unfortunately, the literature has identified three problems with this arrangement: ageing, strategic retirement, and preference drift. If judges refuse to retire in a timely manner, they will age in office, undermining court performance and drifting away from the preferences of society. Conversely, if they decide to retire in a timely manner, they will choose a convenient political moment to influence the nomination of their successors. Thus, because retirements under life-tenure regimes are rare and controlled by the outgoing judges, politicians operating in weak institutional environments will have strong incentives to purge the courts. This may ultimately undermine the effectiveness of life-tenure regimes where they are most needed.

The effects of ageing have been at the centre of institutional debates about tenure in the US Supreme Court. Garrow (2000) documents at least twenty instances in which Supreme Court justices were mentally or physically impaired prior to the twenty-first century. In several instances, their fellow justices were in the unenviable position of convincing them to resign. In late 1869, acting on behalf of the Court, Justices Chase and Nelson convinced Robert Grier (appointed in 1846) to step down the following year. For about five years, Grier's physical and mental abilities had been visibly in decline. Appointed in 1863, Stephen J. Field served on the US Supreme Court for more than thirty-four years. By the 1890s, 'Field's mental condition was noticeably on decline' (Atkinson 1999, 69). At a private meeting, John Marshall Harlan tactfully reminded Field of Grier's resignation in 1870, but Field abruptly rejected the insinuation. He eventually resigned in 1897. In the 1920s, the Court had to confront the case of Joseph McKenna who, at eighty-one years, 'was no longer capable of sustained mental effort and had shown gross signs of senility for several years' (Bloom 1963, 72). In late 1924, the justices agreed to avoid any decisions in which McKenna's vote was pivotal. After this agreement, Chief Justice Taft convinced McKenna to retire within three months (Atkinson 1999, 69). In 1932, the Court urged Oliver Wendell Holmes (aged ninety) to retire. Holmes graciously agreed to leave after almost three decades on the Court. In contrast, after William O. Douglas suffered a stroke in 1974, he refused to resign. Other Court members decided to postpone any decision in which his vote was pivotal and stopped assigning him any opinions. Douglas finally announced his retirement in late 1975, yet he attempted to participate in some cases before his replacement joined the Court. The other justices simply ignored him.

Franklin Delano Roosevelt justified his 1936 'Court packing plan' based on ageing considerations. Attorney General Homer Cummings had proposed a constitutional amendment for mandatory retirement at the age of seventy. But because the amendment's ratification would be a cumbersome process, Roosevelt introduced a bill allowing the president to nominate an extra justice for each sitting justice over the age of seventy. As the plan failed to gain traction, senators in the Democratic Party introduced several constitutional amendments requiring the retirement of federal justices at the age of seventy-five, but the President failed to support these initiatives. In 1947–1950, the American Bar Association (ABA) debated, and eventually embraced, a proposal to fix the number of Supreme Court members at nine and order mandatory retirements at seventy-five years, as a pre-emptive plan to protect the Court from future political attacks. Congress debated the proposal in 1952–1954, but after the Court decided *Brown v Board of Education* in 1954, the conservative coalition that initially supported the protective measures abandoned the plan (Garrow 2000).

Atkinson (1999, 69) notes that problems of decrepitude observed in the Supreme Court in the nineteenth century were less common in the twentieth century, in part because retirement benefits improved after 1937. Although medical advances in the late twentieth century enhanced health conditions, they also expanded longevity, and justices now serve for long periods (Crowe and Karpowitz 2007). Thus, the empirical debate on the effects of ageing on productivity remains open. Posner (1995, Chapter 8) and Teitelbaum (2006) offer empirical evidence to argue that productivity in the US courts does not really decline until a very advanced age. In contrast, empirical studies of the Australian High Court and Federal Court suggest that judges achieve peak productivity much earlier, between their early sixties and early seventies (Bhattacharya and Smyth 2001; Smyth and Bhattacharya 2003).

While the problem of *ageing* results from judges who refuse to retire voluntarily, the problem of *strategic retirement* results from judges who agree to leave on their own timing. A strand of scholarship on the US Supreme Court argues that retirement-age justices select the moment to leave the bench in time for the president to nominate a like-minded successor. If the president is ideologically close, judges will have an incentive to retire, but if the president is ideologically distant, they will postpone their departure hoping for alteration in power (Calabresi and Lindgren 2006; King 1987; Hagle 1993; Ward 2003; Zorn and Van Winkle 2000). This behaviour is a source of normative concern because it implies that justices reproduce their preferences in the Court (Jackson 2007).

The idea of strategic retirement is contested by some empirical studies analysing the US Supreme Court (Brenner 1999; Squire 1988; Yoon 2006) and by studies of high courts elsewhere (Smyth and Maitra 2005; Kerby and Banfield 2014; Massie, Randazzo, and Songer 2014; Pérez-Liñán and Arana Araya 2017). Brenner (1999) documents that between 1937 and 1998, only two elderly justices in good health retired at a time when the president was ideologically aligned. He concludes strategic retirement is a 'myth'. Bailey and Yoon (2011) argue that strategic retirements, even if they occur, should cancel each other out and thus have limited implications for the US Supreme Court. Adding nuance to the debate, Stolzenberg and Lindgren (2022) find that strategic retirement is stronger among Republican Supreme Court appointees than Democratic appointees. Partisan differences in retirement strategies remains a topic open for exploration.

A third concern with life-tenure regimes involves the potential disconnection of judges from society, as a result of preference drift. Mueller (1996, 1999) warns that lifetime appointments protect the judiciary, but they do not guarantee that the judiciary will act in the interest of the citizens. Secure tenure over long periods potentially leads to a disconnection from society's preferences. However, other scholars argue that judges are unlikely to drift away from society because elected politicians are involved in their nomination and appointment (Dahl 1957) and because Congress can engage in court curbing (Epstein, Knight, and Martin 2001). Burbank similarly dismisses concerns about disconnection from society, noting that the US Supreme Court remains more popular than Congress (Burbank 2006, 1533).

Concerns about performance, strategic retirement, and preference drift are heightened in weak institutional environments where, as explained in the second part of this chapter, powerful politicians have the ability to induce judicial retirements (Pérez-Liñán and Castagnola 2016; Ríos-Figueroa 2006). Helmke and Staton (2011) infer that longer tenures increase the value of a court seat by extending the salary stream, the span of professional prestige, and the opportunities to hear on important cases associated with the position. The greater value of court seats also makes politicians more willing to pay the costs of a purge to appoint their co-partisans. Bulmer (2017) similarly notices that, under life tenure systems, turnover can be slow and vacancies irregular, a situation that raises the stakes of each appointment. Those studies raise serious doubts on whether life tenure rules protect judicial independence in contexts where this protection is most needed. In an empirical study of 192 countries, Melton and Ginsburg (2014) find no significant association between life tenure and *de facto* judicial independence. A study of Latin America similarly documents that justices with life tenure have not served in the high courts any longer than other justices appointed for fixed terms (Lara-Borges, Castagnola, and Pérez-Liñán 2012). However, Hayo and Voigt (2007) find that *de jure* independence generally supports *de facto* independence. Cameron (2002) ultimately admits that formal rules may not guarantee independence, but they provide bright lines and incentives to protect judges.

2.2 Alternatives to Life Tenure: Mandatory Retirement and Fixed Terms

A first institutional solution for the problem of ageing is the establishment of a mandatory retirement age. For instance, an amendment to the Brazilian constitution has established mandatory retirement for justices at the age of 75 (Article 40.II). Mandatory retirement ages, however, are not free of challenges. Next door, the Argentine constitutional reform of 1994 included a similar provision (Article 99.4), but the Supreme Court—ruling in favour of one of their own—declared this clause unconstitutional in the *Fayt* case (1999), arguing procedural flaws in the amendment process, and eventually upheld the norm in the *Schiffrin case* (2017).

Bulmer (2017) notes that a mandatory retirement age is in any case difficult to set. If the retirement age is too high, the arrangement creates problems—such as preference drift and declining intellectual capacity—similar to those under life tenure; if the retirement age is too low, the judges need to move into private practice after leaving office, creating incentives for influence peddling and corruption. Opeskin (2015) agrees that setting parameters is difficult, but concludes that the age at which retirement is compulsory is not nearly as important as the proposition that there must be an age at which retirement is expected. Discussing the Australian case, Blackham (2016) argues instead that mandatory retirement is no longer valid in a modern society. It is discriminatory, deprives the judiciary of skilled adjudicators, and imposes undue expenses to taxpayers.

In the United States, institutional variation across state supreme courts offers an opportunity to test the effects of mandatory retirement. Ash and MacLeod (2020) find that mandatory retirement rules reduce the age of working judges and improve their performance, measured through the number of published opinions and the number of citations. At the same time, Hall (2014) finds that mandatory retirement provisions remove incentives for elected judges to align with voter preferences during their last term in office. Constitutionally unable to impose a mandatory retirement age, the US allows federal judges to opt for 'senior status' after reaching the age of sixty-five and fifteen years of service. Senior judges retain a caseload and salary, but a new vacancy is opened in the court. Some states have adopted this procedure as well.

As a protection for judicial independence, mandatory retirement is similar to service during 'good behaviour'. In both instances, judges are expected to serve until an advanced age, and they do not depend on political parties to retain office. Comparative studies occasionally lump together mandatory retirement and 'good behaviour' protections as 'life tenure' arrangements (Lara-Borges, Castagnola, and Pérez-Liñán 2012). However, mandatory retirement procedures can be more easily manipulated. As discussed in the next section, several governments (e.g. in El Salvador, Hungary, and Poland) have lowered mandatory retirement ages as a way of forcing the exit of senior judges in their high courts.

A second alternative to tenure during 'good behaviour' is the appointment of judges for a fixed term in office. This practice is common for constitutional courts worldwide, but it is rarely adopted for lower-level judges (aside from initial probation periods), and it is less common for high courts of appeals (i.e. supreme tribunals or supreme courts of cassation). Fixed terms can pose important challenges to judicial independence, but they also offer an effective solution to the critical issues identified above.

Opeskin (2015) notes that all provisions relating to tenure, including fixed terms, can be crafted in ways that support a greater or lesser degree of independence. With respect to fixed terms, Ríos-Figueroa (2011) underscores that the key factor is whether the term of judges is longer than the term of those who appoint them. Thus, there is a crucial distinction between short terms (typically lasting four or five years and allowing for re-appointment) and long terms (which usually range between nine and fifteen years and are non-renewable).

Bulmer (2017) and Stiansen (2022) argue that judges serving for short, renewable terms are likely to remain dependent on the appointing authorities. For example, Ecuador's 1998 Constitution established four-year terms for members of the Constitutional Tribunal. Grijalva (2010) offers empirical evidence to argue that justices were sensitive to the needs of legislative parties that controlled nominations and reappointments (constitutional terms were ultimately extended to nine years in 2009). Similarly, the Guatemalan Constitution establishes five-year terms for members of the Constitutional Court and the Supreme Court. Brinks and Blass (2018, 129) surmise that this 'choice of extremely short tenures for both Supreme Court and Constitutional Court justices responds to a perception that, in Guatemala, the coalition of control needed to keep a shorter rein … on people in positions of power'. Rachel Bowen further notices that short terms make corruption more attractive to Guatemalan justices, because 'this law makes potential lame ducks of all of the magistrates. They have incentives to engage in corruption in order to secure their own futures' (Bowen 2017, 177).

In contrast, long terms combined with limits on reappointment will produce a more independent judiciary (Bulmer 2017). In Spain, Constitutional judges serve for nine years without the possibility of immediate re-election. They are required to retire at the age of seventy, with the possibility of a two-year extension. In Germany, judges of the Federal Constitutional Court serve for twelve years without reappointment, and they are required to retire at the age of sixty-eight years. In Mexico, members of the Supreme Court serve for a fifteen-year non-renewable term. These arrangements combine the advantages of life tenure regimes—periods in office that transcend the terms of the politicians who nominated the judges, and that make judges independent of political favours—and minimize their disadvantages in terms of ageing and infirmity.

3. Judicial Tenure Interrupted

Rules about tenure and retirement are effective to protect judicial independence only to the extent that they constrain the behaviour of political actors. Unfortunately, there are multiple situations in which powerful actors are able to circumvent or manipulate formal protections, and therefore find ways to purge the judiciary. Politicians have multiple motivations to force new vacancies in the courts: they seek to appoint judges aligned with their policies, to avoid prosecution in corruption cases, and to secure carte blanche as they undermine the rights of the opposition, among other goals (Pérez-Liñán and Castagnola 2009). There are also situations in which purges appear to be justified from a normative perspective, as when newly democratic regimes engage in the lustration of judges who served the prior dictatorship. Irrespective of their diverse motivations, the strategies followed by politicians to force the exit of judges formally protected by law are equally varied.

Figure 19.1 outlines a typology of judicial exits that allows us to place the interruption of tenure in context. The figure identifies four types of exits—non-political exits, strategic retirements, formal removals, and informally induced departures—based on a three-question test:

1. Are the reasons that motivate the judge's departure (A) political or (B) non-political?
2. In the first case, are political motivations hosted by (A.1) judges or (A.2) politicians?
3. If the latter, are politicians forcing the judge's departure through (A.2.a) formal removal procedures or (A.2.b) informal pressures?

Empirical answers to these questions, as we illustrate below, are often elusive. However, the three nodes in the figure offer an analytical test to summarize the complex literature on judicial exits. The first question is *why* judges exit the court. 'Natural' (non-political) reasons result from health conditions (death in office being the most extreme example), from reaching the end of a fixed term or a mandatory retirement age,

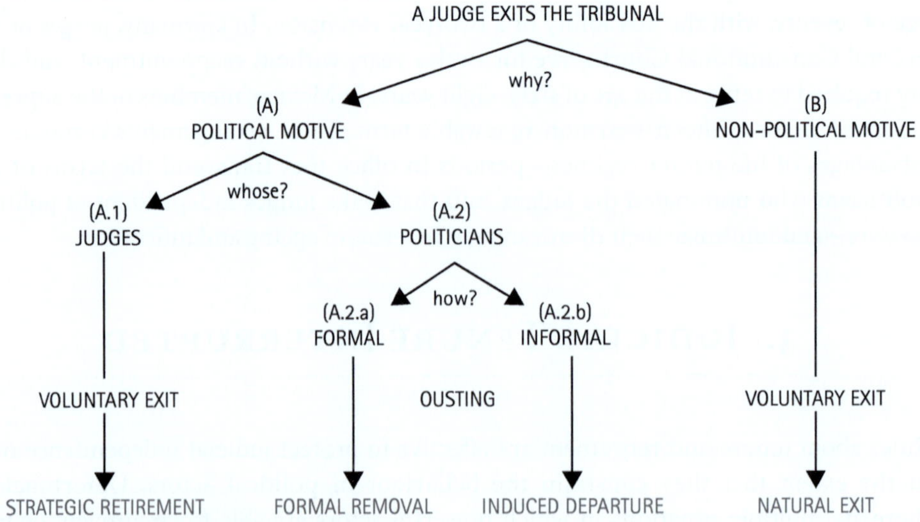

FIGURE 19.1 A typology of judicial exits.

or from personal motivations such as the desire to go back to private practice or work fatigue. As scholars documented in the cases of Argentina and the United States, 'natural' departures follow a uniform distribution (King 1987; Hagle 1993; Ward 2003; Zorn and Van Winkle 2000; Castagnola 2018). Unless judges serve for fixed, concurrent terms, individual exits tend to be randomly scattered over time, as individuals die or decide to retire for reasons unrelated to the political context. In contrast, political reasons account for instances in which judges act strategically or in which politicians seek to displace unsympathetic judges, in order to influence the preferences of the court.

The second question of the test is *whose* political interests motivate the departure. When the decision to quit reflects the judge's own desire, judicial exits are depicted as strategic retirements—a form of voluntary, yet political exit discussed in the first part of this chapter.[1] When political motivations emanate from other actors, judicial exits are depicted by a broad range of labels: purges, induced retirements, lustration, informal interference, (un)constitutional capture, and judicial crises, among others (Llanos et al. 2016; Dressel, Sanchez-Urribarri, and Stroh 2018; Koncewicz 2017; Castagnola 2018; Helmke, Jeong, and Kim 2022). Each label conveys specific nuances about the process forcing judges off the bench, but they all share a common counterfactual assumption: that judges would depart at a later date in the absence of political pressures. Thus, the second question introduces the fundamental distinction between *voluntary* and *involuntary* exits, which is central to this literature. Voluntary exits include strategic retirements (A.1) as well as non-political exits (B). The latter are voluntary to the extent that judges agree to retire for health reasons, decide to stay in office until the end of their lives, or accept the position knowing the duration of their terms in advance. In contrast, involuntary exits are driven by the preferences of outside actors who oust judges from their positions. Involuntary exits have received considerable attention among judicial comparative scholars, and are the focus of this section.

If judicial tenure is protected by law, *how* can political actors displace judges from office? The last question of the test introduces a distinction between formal (A.2.a) and informal (A.2.b) strategies to oust judges. National constitutions and organic laws establish formal mechanisms by which judges can be legally removed from the bench, impeachment being the most common procedure. In addition, politicians employ informal strategies to induce the retirement of judges, including rewards (such as nominations to political office) and intimidation (like smear campaigns or impeachment *threats*). We illustrate formal and informal procedures, and clarify the meaning of the term 'politicians'—used so far with deliberate ambiguity—in the following sections.

Notice that the involuntary path presented in Figure 19.1 does not involve any assumption about the legitimacy of the motivations driving the process. Because formal removals and induced departures are motivated by political reasons—including, perhaps, some politicians' desire to serve the public interest—there is always controversy on whether those exits are justified. Although we are highly suspicious of any ousters along path A.2, we acknowledge that there are circumstances in which removal is appropriate: judicial corruption, abuse of the office, lustration of judges who collaborated with authoritarian regimes, and so on. Unfortunately, there is no consensus in the literature on how to distinguish legitimate from illegitimate removals. Some scholars argue that any debate about the fairness of dismissals must be resolved by analysing the driving political motivations and the context in which the process takes place (Chowdhury 2015; Mollah 2012). Even though politicians' 'true' intentions are unobservable, two operational principles are key to assess the fairness of dismissals: due process and legality. Judicial ousters are questionable when removals do not follow a well-established legal procedure, or when accusers fail to prove that judges violated a 'good behaviour' standard that predated the process. The establishment of systematic criteria to assess involuntary exits is an important area of research that requires further work connecting normative and empirical analysis.

3.1 Who Threatens Judicial Tenure?

It is not surprising that political scientists have focused their attention on path (A), seeking to understand the political drivers of judicial exits. We discussed the literature on strategic retirements briefly in the first part of the chapter. In the following sections, we cover the literature on involuntary retirements, identifying the actors that threaten judicial tenure, as well as the formal and informal mechanisms they use to disrupt it.

Figure 19.1 employs the term 'politicians' as shorthand to identify the set of actors with sufficient political clout to undermine judicial tenure. Even though the executive branch is the most likely source of removals, opposition legislators sometimes lead the charge against sitting judges. Moreover, it is not uncommon that powerful politicians will rely on civil society allies, such as friendly media outlets, to back their attacks against the judiciary. In some contexts, non-state actors such as professional bar associations, powerful oligarchs, and even organized crime have played a prominent role in the process.

Executives: Presidents and prime ministers are the most common initiators of judicial purges. The comparative literature has documented this pattern for national and subnational executives in Latin America (Verner 1984; Pérez-Liñán and Castagnola 2009; Castagnola 2018; Leiras, Tuñón, and Giraudy 2015), and multiple case studies illustrate the role played by executives across regions, regime types, and historical periods. In Ukraine, presidents Yushchenko, Poroshenko, and Zelensky all oversaw attempts to remove Constitutional Court judges with varying degrees of success (Barrett 2021; Cherviatsova 2021). In Zimbabwe, President Mugabe used informal threats and pressures to purge 'disloyal' judges (IBAHRI 2011). In Turkey, Tayyip Erdoğan purged several members of the Turkish Constitutional Court and thousands of judges and prosecutors following the 2016 failed military coup (Perilli 2021). In Bangladesh, the executive invoked martial law to remove Supreme Court members from 1982 to 1986, and retained considerable power over judicial careers in later years (Chowdhury 2015; Mollah 2012).

Legislatures: Legislative bodies play an important role in judicial removals in at least three ways. First, when executives are strong, they may enrol the support of pliant legislatures to legitimize judicial purges. In an extreme example, the German Reichstag granted Chancellor Adolf Hitler emergency powers in 1933 through the Enabling Act, which allowed him to reshape the legal system and allowed the Nazi party to purge the judiciary (Fountaine 2020). Second, when executives are weak, the legislature may be tempted to reshuffle the courts unilaterally. In 1984, the Ecuadorian Congress dismissed all members of the Supreme Court and appointed new ones, triggering a confrontation with President León Febres Cordero. The reluctance of sitting justices to accept this decision resulted in the abnormal situation of having two Supreme Courts operating concomitantly for a brief period. After this episode, Ecuadorian legislators bargained over repeated judicial purges for more than two decades (Basabe-Serrano and Polga-Hecimovich 2017; Basabe-Serrano and Llanos Escobar 2014). Third, when executive-legislative balance is contested, minority presidents who anticipate major confrontations with Congress may purge the courts pre-emptively to secure a supportive constitutional interpretation in the likely case of policy deadlock or presidential impeachment (Helmke 2018; Helmke, Jeong, and Kim 2022).

Judiciary: Occasionally, judicial authorities themselves threaten tenure. In countries with corporatist judicial structures, the Supreme Court exercises control over the judiciary and can disrupt the tenure of lower court judges. For example, after Chile's military coup in 1973, decree-laws 169 and 170 allowed the Chilean Supreme Court to dismiss judicial employees based on poor performance reviews. This framework enabled the Supreme Court to carry out an internal purge by forcing 12 per cent of judicial employees, forty of whom were judges, into retirement (Hilbink 2008).

Non-state actors: In other instances, non-state actors may play a role in the political removal of judges. For example, in post-communist Slovakia, where politicians had traditionally influenced the Chief Justice, prominent oligarchs and judicial associations increasingly gained significant leverage over this position (Kosař and Spáč 2021). Political actors not holding office may also take part in 'irresponsible criticism', defined by Bright (1997) as criticism for the purpose of intimidation or undue influence over the judiciary. In the United States, State Supreme Court justices have suffered this type of attack, like the electoral campaign to 'vote off' (or not re-elect) Justice Robertson from the Mississippi Supreme Court after a contested decision on a criminal case in 1992, or the public campaign by a Republican presidential candidate for the removal of Judge Harold Baer from New York in 1996 (Bright 1997).

3.2 How Political Actors Disrupt Judicial Tenure

Political actors can disrupt judicial tenure by deploying formal institutional powers to remove judges from office (e.g. via impeachment) or by deploying leverage to induce resignations from the bench (e.g. via *threats* of impeachment). In this section, we outline some of the most common mechanisms.

Formal removal: The formal removal of judges requires legal proceedings triggered by political actors in control of other institutions. Formal removals can take place as a result of a parliamentary decision, as in India and Malta; as a result of a judicial disciplinary process, as in the Netherlands and Denmark; or as a result of impeachment, the most common procedure for removing judges in separation-of-powers systems (Bulmer 2017). The conventional impeachment model, inspired by the US Constitution, entails two different proceedings: the lower house of the legislature is responsible for evaluating allegations of wrongdoing or misconduct against a judge. If the house approves the charges, the process moves to the Senate, which conducts the trial and votes to remove the judge. The share of votes required to impeach judges differs across countries, but a two-thirds majority is typically required for conviction.

In the United States, an impeachment process failed to remove the controversial justice Samuel Chase in 1805, and no other Supreme Court justice has been impeached ever since. However, fourteen federal judges serving in lower courts were impeached between 1803 and 2017, and only four of them were acquitted by the Senate (Radnofsky 2017). Argentina was one of the first countries in Latin America where a massive judicial impeachment took place. In 1946, four days after President Juan Perón took office, four of the five justices and the Solicitor General were impeached. The purge secured Perón's control of the Court and opened a recurrent history of judicial purges in Argentina (Helmke 2005; Castagnola 2020). A similar—and more contemporary—episode took place in El Salvador in 2021. Just few weeks after an election in which President Bukele's party captured a two-thirds majority in the legislature, the Assembly impeached all five justices in the Constitutional Chamber of the Supreme Court and the Prosecutor General. Almost every country in Latin America has witnessed the use of impeachment as a politicized tool for removing judges from the bench. In the twenty-first century, cases involving judges from Argentina, Ecuador, El Salvador, Honduras, Paraguay, Peru, and Venezuela have reached the Inter-American Court of Human Rights, prompting a regional jurisprudence about judicial removals.[2]

Even though impeachment is the best-known mechanism for removing judges, executives and legislatures employ many other formal—yet controversial—procedures for ousting judges. For example, in Ukraine President Zelensky revoked the decrees signed by the former president that had appointed two Constitutional Court justices (Barrett 2021; Cherviatsova 2021). In Croatia, the 1990 Constitution established that judges appointed by the newly created State Judicial Council would have life tenure rather than serve for an eight-year term. The previous legislation regulating judicial tenure was abrogated, and thousands of active judges were placed in a constitutional limbo. In the end, some judges remained on the bench while others received a decree terminating their terms or were simply notified to leave due to the 'new situation' (Uzelac 2001).

An alternative means for disrupting judicial tenure has been reducing the mandatory retirement age. In 2012, a new Hungarian Constitution reduced the retirement age for judges from seventy to sixty-two years, forcing about 274 judges into early retirement, including twenty of the seventy-four Supreme Court justices (Halmai 2017). A similar situation occurred in Poland when Parliament passed Law No 17 in July 2017 to lower the age of judges from sixty-seven to sixty-five years for men and sixty years for women, affecting 40 per cent of the members of the Supreme Court (including its

Chief Justice). In both cases, the European Court of Justice ruled against those reforms (Bard and Sledzinska-Simon 2020). In 2021, El Salvador's legislative assembly approved a Judicial Career Act that forced all judges older than sixty years or with three decades of service—a third of the judges in the country—into retirement.

Induced departures: This label describes instances in which judges are persuaded to step down from the bench through selective incentives. Political actors 'persuade' judges by offering positive (e.g. rewards and benefits) or negative inducements (e.g. harassment, physical or verbal attacks, disruptive career transfers, etc.).[3]

Positive incentives encourage early departures through 'friendly' means, avoiding an open confrontation. Judges are amicably convinced by political actors to leave their positions in exchange for benefits. These informal departures often presuppose a 'loyal act' from the judge, since a voluntary resignation allows political leaders to fulfil political agreements or realign forces within the government. For example, in 1993, President Carlos Menem offered Justices Barra and Cavagna the Ministry of Justice and the Argentine ambassadorship to Italy as compensation for stepping off the bench (Castagnola 2018). These two vacancies were part of a larger political agreement package that would allow Menem to run for re-election (Finkel 2004; Helmke 2005).

Informal departures via negative incentives are more frequent—and more coercive. Political actors usually employ three forms of punishment to induce resignations: (i) physical attacks against judges, (ii) rhetorical or verbal attacks against judges, and (iii) infringements on judicial privilege. The first form of punishment constitutes the most extreme one, since it affects the physical integrity of the judge. For instance, in 1985 Honduran President Roberto Suazo Cordova ordered the arrest of Chief Justice Ramón Valladares due to his denunciations of corruption and wrongdoing of the government (Castagnola 2010). Violence may also result in exile, as occurred in Georgia when elected President Saakashvili forced Chief Justice Lado Chanturia into exile in Germany (Trochev 2013; Barrett 2021).

Rhetorical, verbal attacks, or smear campaigns on judges are a very common strategy employed by political actors. These informal strategies are powerful tools for inducing early departures since many judges do not outlast persecutions, moral attrition, and coercion, and end up stepping off the bench. Smear campaigns can target an individual judge or the institution as a whole, and their main goal is to publicly discredit judges in order to wear them out emotionally and psychologically. The most common defamation campaigns involve the participation of bar associations, members of Judicial Councils, or the president (Garoupa and Maldonado 2011). For example, in Pakistan, President Pervez Musharraf requested the resignation of Chief Justice Iftikhar Chaudhry in 2007, following a political confrontation. The justice was physically restrained from leaving the president's office for several hours until he presented his resignation. In Zimbabwe, the Supreme Court consistently ruled against the controversial land reform of President Mugabe in 2000. By December 2000, the ZANU-PF ruling party was promoting political slogans and calling for judges to be killed, and the President described judges as guardians of 'White racist commercial farmers' (IBAHRI 2011). In Bolivia, the extensive defamatory presidential campaign against Justice José A. Rivera Santivañez resulted in his resignation from the bench in 2006 (Castagnola and Pérez-Liñán 2011).

The last form of harassment is not associated with verbal or physical violence, but with a violation of professional rights. Examples of this practice include the transfer of judges to inconvenient locations, or purposefully stagnating their wages to force resignations. For example, in Turkey the forced relocation of politically dissident judges and prosecutors to remote areas of the country often made them resign to their position in protest (Perilli 2021). Even though these strategies involve the (mis)use of legal instruments, they do not qualify as removals because the legal tools employed to harass judges do not authorize politicians to dismiss them.

The use of positive or negative incentives does not guarantee that judges will be persuaded to depart from the bench. In some cases, an incentive will have the intended consequence on some judges but not on others, as occurred in Ukraine in 2007 (Barrett 2021; Cherviatsova 2021). President Yushchenko dismissed three justices from the Constitutional Court in order to guarantee the dissolution of the Parliament. After a political deal, two of those justices (Volodymyr Ivaschenko and Valerii Pshenychnyi) agreed to retire 'voluntarily,' retaining all retirement benefits. A third justice (Suzanna Stanik) did not. Although the Supreme Court sided with the justice and ordered her reinstatement to the Constitutional Court, President Yushchenko annulled the decree which had appointed her as a judge in 2004.

4. Conclusion

This chapter has underscored two trade-offs created by the norms designed to protect judicial tenure. The first one is a potential tension between tenure protections and judicial performance. Norms that guarantee *de jure* life tenure, allowing judges to retire according to their preferences, protect judicial autonomy but create other problems, including an over-aged judicial body, incentives for judges to engage in strategic retirement, and incentives for politicians to disrupt tenure arrangements. These challenges invite further research. For example, more comparative work will be necessary to establish the effect of different tenure regimes on judicial performance, while more work on the US case will be necessary to understand partisan differences in strategic retirement (Stolzenberg and Lindgren 2022).

Although life tenure is traditionally envisaged to be the most secure arrangement to ensure judicial independence, it has proven to be controversial. Long, fixed terms without reappointment are more likely to produce an independent judiciary and to have fewer problems than life tenure arrangements.

The second trade-off involves a tension between tenure protections and accountability. Because, to secure judicial accountability, other branches need to exercise oversight, politicians can exploit accountability mechanisms to undermine judicial careers and capture the courts. Political actors are *de facto* able to circumvent formal protections of tenure to purge the judiciary.

Judicial tenure interruption has become a widespread practice among democracies and non-democracies. Executives, legislatures, judicial authorities, and non-state actors such as bar associations and the mass media play important roles in the ousting of judges. We introduced a three-question test that allows us to identify four types of judicial exits: natural exits, strategic retirements, formal removals, and induced departures. The existing literature exposes a repertoire of tactics used by political actors in different countries. However, important patterns of variation, in the speed of the ousters as well as the type of judges targeted, still call for systematic explanation. Judicial purges have occurred at different paces, abruptly in some cases (e.g. massive judicial impeachments) and gradually in others (i.e. targeting one justice at a time) (Helmke 2005; Chowdhury 2015; Halmai 2017; Barrett 2021; Cherviatsova 2021). In addition, political actors have targeted different types of courts, in different sequences, to capture the judiciary. In top-down capture processes, higher court justices were targeted first to rapidly limit any potential resistance to the actions undertaken by political actors and to generate a facade of legality around the regime (Koncewicz 2018). In bottom-up processes, lower court judges were targeted first to subtly undermine the judiciary as purges escalated into higher courts (Perilli 2021).

While these practices systematically undermine judicial independence, we note two intriguing situations that call for investigation. One is a paradoxical situation in which the repeated violation of tenure protections ultimately induces judicial autonomy. In contexts like Ecuador in the 1990s, where judges anticipate that they will be ousted with every new political realignment, their dominant strategy is to rule sincerely because politicians cannot credibly commit to respect their tenure if political coalitions change (Basabe-Serrano 2012).

The other complex situation corresponds to cases of lustration, in which a purge of the judiciary is justified. The literature does not provide a conclusive test to distinguish undesirable purges from desirable episodes of lustration. We have argued that future analyses of this problem should consider two criteria: due process and legality. Legitimate ousters must follow a well-established legal procedure, and they must prove the violation of 'good behaviour' standards that predate the accusation against the judges.

The two trade-offs addressed in this chapter lead us to conclude that life tenure, the most common tenure arrangement to protect judicial independence, may not be as effective as previously thought. It carries negative side-effects, and there are better institutional alternatives. It is not a self-enforcing rule, and it protects judicial independence only to the extent that political actors are willing to respect it. The literature is full of cases in which tenure protections were parchment barriers, and politicians carried out judicial purges without difficulty. Further research should aim to understand why politicians are able to infringe judicial tenure and whether conventional theories of judicial independence help explain the frequency of tenure violations.

Acknowledgements

We are extremely indebted to Micaela Banchero, Felicitas Barrera, Lucie Kneip, Nicole Kohan, Aldana López, Juan Enrique Torres Barry, and Martina Zanetto for their research assistance for this chapter.

Notes

1. Stolzenberg and Lindgren (2022) refer to strategic retirements as 'politicized departures', but this terminology is ambiguous with respect to the source of political motivation.
2. For instance, *Rico v Argentina*, 2 September 2019; *Constitutional Tribunal (Camba Campos and others) v Ecuador*, 28 August 2013; *Colindres Schonenberg v El Salvador*, 4 February 2019; *López Lone et al. v Honduras*, 5 October 2015; *Ríos Avalos and others v Paraguay*, 19 August 2021; *Constitutional Tribunal v Peru*, 31 January 2001; *Reverón Trujillo v Venezuela*, 30 June 2009; *Chocrón Chocrón v Venezuela*, 25 November 2009.
3. Llanos et al. (2016) study informal interferences in six new democracies: Senegal, Benin, Madagascar, Argentina, Chile, and Paraguay. The authors classify interferences in two categories: direct (rhetorical attacks or the use of physical violence) or subtle (unofficial communications or bribery).

References

Ash, Elliott, and W. Bentley MacLeod. 2020. *Mandatory Retirement for Judges Improved Performance on U.S. State Supreme Courts*. Zurich: Center for Law & Economics, ETH Zurich.

Atkinson, David N. 1999. *Leaving the Bench. Supreme Court Justices at the End*. Kansas: University Press of Kansas.

Bailey, Michael A., and Albert Yoon. 2011. '"While There's a Breath in My Body": The Systemic Effects of Politically Motivated Retirement from the Supreme Court'. *Journal of Theoretical Politics* 23 (3): 293–316. https://doi.org/10.1177/0951629811411751.

Bard, Petra, and Anna Sledzinska-Simon. 2020. 'On the Principle of Irremovability of Judges Beyond Age Discrimination: Commission v. Poland'. *Common Market Law Review* 57 (5): 1555. https://doi.org/10.54648/COLA2020747.

Barrett, Thomas. 2021. 'Oligarchs and Judges: The Political Economy of the Courts in Post-Soviet Unconsolidated Democracies'. *Ideology and Politics* 2 (18): 260–91.

Basabe-Serrano, Santiago. 2012. 'Judges without Robes and Judicial Voting in Contexts of Institutional Instability: The Case of Ecuador's Constitutional Court, 1999–2007'. *Journal of Latin American Studies* 44 (1): 127–61. https://doi.org/10.1017/S0022216X1100112X.

Basabe-Serrano, Santiago, and Santiago Llanos Escobar. 2014. 'La Corte Suprema del Ecuador en el Período Democrático (1979–2013): entre la Inestabilidad Institucional y la Influencia Partidista'. *América Latina Hoy* 67: 15–63.

Basabe-Serrano, Santiago, and John Polga-Hecimovich. 2017. 'Desempeño económico y protesta ciudadana como detonantes de las caídas presidenciales: el caso ecuatoriano'. *Perfiles Latinoamericanos* 50: 129–53. https://doi.org/10.18504/pl2550-007-2017.

Bhattacharya, Mita, and Russell Smyth. 2001. 'Aging and Productivity Among Judges: Some Empirical Evidence from the High Court of Australia'. *Australian Economic Papers* 40 (2): 199–212. https://doi.org/10.1111/1467-8454.00122.

Blackham, Alysia. 2016. 'Judges and Retirement Ages'. *Melbourne University Law Review* 39 (3): 738–92. https://search.informit.org/doi/10.3316/ielapa.194973855471402. https://search.informit.org/doi/full/10.3316/ielapa.194973855471402.

Bloom, Murray Teigh. 1963. 'Unseating Unfit Judges'. *National Civic Review* 52 (2): 70–72, 119.

Bowen, Rachel E. 2017. *The Achilles Heel of Democracy: Judicial Autonomy and the Rule of Law in Central America*. Cambridge: Cambridge University Press.

Brenner, Saul. 1999. 'The Myth that Justices Strategically Retire'. *The Social Science Journal (Fort Collins)* 36 (3): 431–39. https://doi.org/10.1016/S0362-3319 (99)00015-4.

Bright, Stephen B. 1997. 'Political Attacks on the Judiciary: Can Justice Be Done Amid Efforts to Intimidate and Remove Judges from Office for Unpopular Decisions?' *NYU Law Review* 72: 308–36.

Brinks, Daniel M., and Abby Blass. 2018. *The DNA of Constitutional Justice in Latin America: Politics, Governance, and Judicial Design*. New York: Cambridge University Press.

Bulmer, Elliot. 2017. *Judicial Tenure, Removal, Immunity and Accountability*. Stromsborg: International IDEA.

Burbank, Stephen B. 2006. 'Alternative Career Resolution II: Changing the Tenure of Supreme Court Justices'. *University of Pennsylvania Law Review* 154 (6): 1511–50. https://doi.org/10.2307/40041346.

Calabresi, Steven, and James Lindgren. 2006. 'Term Limits for the Supreme Court: Life Tenure Reconsidered'. *Harvard Journal of Law and Public Policy* 29 (3): 769–877.

Cameron, Charles M. 2002. *Judicial Independence at the Crossroads: An Interdisciplinary Approach*. Thousand Oaks: Sage Publications, Inc. https://doi.org/10.4135/9781452229577.

Castagnola, Andrea. 2010. *A Long History of the Political Manipulation of the Supreme Courts in Central America and the Caribbean, 1900–2009*. Centro de Estudios y Programas Interamericanos (CEPI). http://interamericanos.itam.mx/working_papers/24CASTAGNOLA.pdf.

Castagnola, Andrea. 2018. *Manipulating Courts in New Democracies: Forcing Judges Off the Bench in Argentina*. New York: Routledge.

Castagnola, Andrea. 2020. 'La Trampa de la Manipulación Judicial: Un análisis histórico del control político de la Corte Suprema Argentina'. *Revista Uruguaya de Ciencia Política* 29 (1): 49–80. https://www.colibri.udelar.edu.uy/jspui/bitstream/20.500.12008/24622/1/RUCP_Castagnola_2020v.29n.1.pdf.

Castagnola, Andrea, and Aníbal Pérez-Liñán. 2011. 'Bolivia: The Rise (and Fall) of Judicial Review'. In *Courts in Latin America*, edited by Gretchen Helmke and Julio Ríos-Figueroa, 278–305. Cambridge: Cambridge University Press.

Cherviatsova, Alina. 2021. False Dilemma: The President of Ukraine vs the Constitutional Court, *VerfBlog*, https://verfassungsblog.de/falsedilemma/, doi: 10.17176/20210121-144606-0. Last accessed 27 September 2023.

Chowdhury, Yasin Khan. 2015. 'Removal of Judges under 16th Amendment of the Bangladesh Constitution: A Euphemism to Curb on the Judiciary'. *DIU Journal of Humanities and Social Science* 3: 89–102.

Clark, David S. 1975. 'Judicial Protection of the Constitution in Latin America'. *Hastings Constitutional Law Quarterly* 2: 405–42.

Crowe, Justin, and Christopher F. Karpowitz. 2007. 'Where Have You Gone, Sherman Minton? The Decline of the Short-Term Supreme Court Justice'. *Perspectives on Politics* 5 (3): 425–45. https://doi.org/10.1017/S1537592707071472.

Dahl, Robert A. 1957. 'Decision-Making in a Democracy: The Supreme Court as a National Policy-Maker'. *Journal of Public Law* 6: 279.

Dressel, Björn, Raul Sanchez-Urribarri, and Alexander Stroh. 2018. 'Courts and Informal Networks: Towards a Relational Perspective on Judicial Politics outside Western Democracies'. *International Political Science Review* 39 (5): 573–84.

Epstein, Lee, Jack Knight, and Andrew Martin. 2001. 'The Supreme Court as A Strategic National Policymaker'. *Emory Law Journal* 50 (Spring): 583–611.

Feld, Lars P., and Stefan Voigt. 2003. 'Economic Growth and Judicial Independence: Cross-Country Evidence Using a New Set of Indicators'. *European Journal of Political Economy* 19 (3): 497–527. https://doi.org/10.1016/S0176-2680 (03)00017-X.

Finkel, Jodi. 2004. 'Judicial Reform in Argentina in the 1990s: How Electoral Incentives Shape Institutional Change'. *Latin American Research Review* 39 (3): 56–80. https://doi.org/10.1353/lar.2004.0045.

Fountaine, Cynthia. 2020. 'Complicity in the Perversion of Justice: The Role of Lawyers in Eroding the Rule of Law in the Third Reich'. *St. Mary's Journal on Legal Malpractice & Ethics* 10 (2): 201–42.

Garoupa, Nuno, and María A. Maldonado. 2011. 'The Judiciary in Political Transitions: The Critical Role of U.S. Constitutionalism in Latin America'. *Cardozo Journal of International and Comparative Law* 3 (19): 526–76.

Garrow, David J. 2000. 'Mental Decrepitude on the U.S. Supreme Court: The Historical Case for a 28th Amendment'. *The University of Chicago Law Review* 67 (4): 995–1087. https://doi.org/10.2307/1600454.

Grijalva, Agustín. 2010. *Courts and Political Parties: The Politics of Constitutional Review in Ecuador*. Saarbrücken: VDM Verlag Dr. Müller.

Hagle, Timothy. 1993. 'Strategic Retirements: A Political Model of Turnover on the United States Supreme Court'. *Political Behavior* 15 (1): 25–48. https://doi.org/10.1007/BF00993415.

Hall, Melinda Gann. 2014. 'Representation in State Supreme Courts: Evidence from the Terminal Term'. *Political Research Quarterly* 67 (2): 335–46.

Halmai, Gabor. 2017. 'The Early Retirement Age of the Hungarian Judges'. In *EU Law Stories: Contextual and Critical Histories of European Jurisprudence*, edited by Fernanda Nicola and Bill Davies, 471–88. Cambridge: Cambridge University Press.

Hamilton, Alexander. 1788. 'The Federalist No. 78'. In *The Federalist Papers*, edited by Ian Shapiro, 391–97. New York: Yale University Press.

Hayo, Bernd, and Stefan Voigt. 2007. 'Explaining De Facto Judicial Independence'. *International Review of Law and Economics* 27 (3): 269–90. https://doi.org/10.1016/j.irle.2007.07.004.

Helmke, Gretchen. 2005. *Courts under Constraints: Judges, Generals, and Presidents in Argentina*. Cambridge: Cambridge University Press.

Helmke, Gretchen. 2018. *The Puzzle of Purges: Presidential Instability and Judicial Manipulation in Latin America*. Prepared for the conference 'Defending Human Rights in Times of Constitutional Crises' in Chicago, 18–19 May 2018. https://www.gretchenhelmke.com/uploads/7/0/3/2/70329843/helmke_puzzleofpurges_2018.pdf.

Helmke, Gretchen, and Jeffrey K. Staton. 2011. 'The Puzzling Judicial Politics of Latin America'. In *Courts in Latin America*, edited by Gretchen Helmke and Julio Ríos-Figueroa, 306–31. Cambridge: Cambridge University Press.

Helmke, Gretchen, Yeonkyung Jeong, and Jae-Eun C. Kim. 2022. 'Insecure Institutions: A Survivalist Theory of Judicial Manipulation in Latin America'. *Journal of Law and Courts* 10 (2): 265–85. https://doi.org/10.1086/716430. https://www.journals.uchicago.edu/doi/abs/10.1086/716430.

Hilbink, Lisa. 2008. 'Agents of Anti-Politics: Courts in Pinochet's Chile'. In *Rule by Law: The Politics of Courts in Authoritarian Regimes*, edited by Tom Ginsburg and Tamir Moustafa, 102–31. Cambridge: Cambridge University Press.

IBAHRI, International Bar Association's Human Rights Institute. 2011. *Zimbabwe: Time for a New Approach*. London: International Bar Association's Human Rights Institute.

Jackson, Vicki C. 2007. 'Packages of Judicial Independence: The Selection and Tenure of Article III Judges'. *The Georgetown Law Journal* 95 (4): 965.

Kerby, Matthew, and Andrew C. Banfield. 2014. 'The Determinants of Voluntary Judicial Resignation in Australia, Canada, and New Zealand'. *Commonwealth & Comparative Politics* 52 (3): 335–57. https://doi.org/10.1080/14662043.2014.921402.

King, Gary. 1987. 'Presidential Appointments to the Supreme Court: Adding Systematic Explanation to Probabilistic Description'. *American Politics Quarterly* 15 (3): 373–86.

Koncewicz, Tomasz Tadeusz. 2017. 'Farewell to the Separation of Powers—On the Judicial Purge and the Capture in the Heart of Europe'. *VerfBlog* (blog). 19 July 2017. https://verfassungsblog.de/farewell-to-the-separation-of-powers-on-the-judicial-purge-and-the-capture-in-the-heart-of-europe/. Last accessed 27 September 2023.

Koncewicz, Tomasz Tadeusz. 2018. 'The Capture of the Polish Constitutional Tribunal and Beyond: Of Institution(s), Fidelities and the Rule of Law in Flux'. *Review of Central and East European Law* 43: 116–73. https://doi.org/10.1163/15730352-04302002.

Kosař, David, and Samuel Spáč. 2021. 'Post-Communist Chief Justices in Slovakia: From Transmission Belts to Semi-Autonomous Actors?' *Hague Journal on the Rule of Law* 13 (1): 107–42. https://doi.org/https://doi.org/10.1007/s40803-021-00150-w.

La Porta, Rafael, Florencio López-de-Silanes, Cristian Pop-Eleches, and Andrei Shleifer. 2004. 'Judicial Checks and Balances'. *Journal of Political Economy* 112 (2): 445–70. https://doi.org/10.1086/381480.

Lara-Borges, Oswald, Andrea Castagnola, and Anibal Pérez-Liñán. 2012. 'Diseño constitucional y estabilidad judicial en América Latina, 1900–2009.' *Política y Gobierno* 19 (1): 3–40.

Leiras, Marcelo, Guadalupe Tuñón, and Agustina Giraudy. 2015. 'Who Wants an Independent Court? Political Competition and Supreme Court Autonomy in the Argentine Provinces (1984–2008)'. *The Journal of Politics* 77 (1): 175–87.

Llanos, Mariana, Cordula Tibi Weber, Charlotte Heyl, and Alexander Stroh. 2016. 'Informal Interference in the Judiciary in New Democracies: A Comparison of Six African and Latin American Cases'. *Democratization* 23 (7): 1236–53. https://doi.org/10.1080/13510347.2015.1081170.

Massie, Tajuana, Kirk A. Randazzo, and Donald R. Songer. 2014. 'The Politics of Judicial Retirement in Canada and the United Kingdom'. *Journal of Law and Courts* 2 (2) 273–99. https://doi.org/10.1086/677057.

Melton, James, and Tom Ginsburg. 2014. 'Does *De Jure* Judicial Independence Really Matter? A Reevaluation of Explanations for Judicial Independence'. *Journal of Law and Courts* 2 (2): 187–217. https://doi.org/10.1086/676999.

Mollah, Awal Hossain. 2012. 'Independence of Judiciary in Bangladesh: An Overview'. *International Journal of Law and Management* 54 (1): 61–77.

Mueller, Dennis. 1999. 'Fundamental Issues in Constitutional Reform: With Special Reference to Latin America and the United States'. *Constitutional Political Economy* 10 (2): 119–48. https://doi.org/10.1023/A:1009054610479.

Mueller, Dennis C. 1996. *Constitutional Democracy*. New York: Oxford University Press.

Opeskin, Brian. 2015. 'Models of Judicial Tenure: Reconsidering Life Limits, Age Limits and Term Limits for Judges'. *Oxford Journal of Legal Studies* 35 (4): 627–63. https://doi.org/10.1093/ojls/gqu029.

Perilli, Luca. 2021. *Judicial Independence & Access to Justice* (Turkey Tribunal). https://turkeytribunal.org/the-reports/judicial-independence-access-to-justice/.

Posner, Richard A. 1995. *Aging and Old Age*. Chicago: University of Chicago Press.

Pérez-Liñán, Aníbal, and Ignacio Arana Araya. 2017. 'Strategic Retirement in Comparative Perspective: Supreme Court Justices in Presidential Regimes'. *Journal of Law and Courts* 5 (2): 173–97. https://doi.org/10.1086/692962.

Pérez-Liñán, Aníbal, and Andrea Castagnola. 2009. 'Presidential Control of High Courts in Latin America: A Long-term View (1904–2006)'. *Journal of Politics in Latin America* 1 (2): 87–114. https://doi.org/https://doi.org/10.1177%2F1866802X0900100204.

Pérez-Liñán, Aníbal, and Andrea Castagnola. 2016. 'Judicial Instability and Endogenous Constitutional Change: Lessons from Latin America'. *British Journal of Political Science* 46 (2): 395–416. https://doi.org/10.1017/S0007123414000295.

Radnofsky, Barbara A. 2017. *A Citizen's Guide to Impeachment: A Citizen's Guide to Impeachment*. Brooklyn: Melville House.

Ríos-Figueroa, Julio. 2006. 'Judicial Independence and Corruption: An Analysis of Latin America'. *SSRN Electronic Journal*. http://dx.doi.org/10.2139/ssrn.912924. https://ssrn.com/abstract=912924.

Ríos-Figueroa, Julio. 2011. 'Institutions for constitutional justice in Latin America'. In *Courts in Latin America*, edited by Gretchen Helmke and Julio Ríos-Figueroa, 27–54. Cambridge: Cambridge University Press.

Smyth, Russell, and Mita Bhattacharya. 2003. 'How Fast Do Old Judges Slow Down? A Life Cycle Study of Aging and Productivity in the Federal Court of Australia'. *International Review of Law and Economics* 23 (2): 141–64. https://doi.org/10.1016/S0144-8188 (03)00029-2.

Smyth, Russell, and Pushkar Maitra. 2005. 'Determinants of Retirement on the High Court of Australia'. *The Economic Record* 81: 193–203. https://doi.org/10.1111/j.1475-4932.2005.00255.x.

Squire, Peverill. 1988. 'Politics and Personal Factors in Retirement from the United States Supreme Court'. *Political Behavior* 10 (2): 180–90. https://doi.org/10.1007/BF00991413.

Stiansen, Øyvind. 2022. '(Non)renewable Terms and Judicial Independence in the European Court of Human Rights'. *The Journal of Politics* 84 (2): 992–1006. https://doi.org/10.1086/715253. https://www.journals.uchicago.edu/doi/abs/10.1086/715253.

Stolzenberg, Ross M., and James Lindgren. 2022. 'Judges as Party Animals: Retirement Timing by Federal Judges and Party Control of Judicial Appointments'. *American Sociological Review* 87 (4): 675–97. https://doi.org/10.1177/00031224221102072. https://doi.org/10.1177/00031224221102072.

Teitelbaum, Joshua C. 2006. 'Age and Tenure of the Justices and Productivity of the U.S. Supreme Court: Are Term Limits Necessary?' *Florida State University Law Review* 34 (1): 161.

Trochev, Alexei. 2013. 'Fragmentation? Defection? Legitimacy? Explaining Judicial Roles in Post-Communist "Colored Revolutions"'. In *Consequential Courts: Judicial Roles in Global Perspective*, edited by Diana Kapiszewski, Gordon Silverstein, and Robert A. Kagan, 67–92. Cambridge: Cambridge University Press.

Uzelac, Alan. 2001. *Role and Status of Judges in Croatia*. Vienna: Manzsche Verlags.

Verner, Joel G. 1984. 'The Independence of Supreme Courts in Latin America: A Review of the Literature'. *Journal of Latin American Studies* 16 (2): 463–506.

Ward, Artemus. 2003. *Deciding to Leave. The Politics of Retirement from the United States Supreme Court*. New York: State University of New York.

Yoon, Albert. 2006. 'Pensions, Politics, and Judicial Tenure: An Empirical Study of Federal Judges, 1869–2002'. *American Law and Economics Review* 8 (1): 143. https://doi.org/10.1093/aler/ahj003.

Zorn, Christopher, and Steven Van Winkle. 2000. 'A Competing Risks Model of Supreme Court Vacancies, 1789–1992'. *Political Behavior* 22 (2): 145–66. https://doi.org/10.1023/A:1006667601289.

CHAPTER 20

LAW CLERKS

ANNE SANDERS

1. Introduction

JUDGES are not alone in courts but work with staff members with different functions. This chapter focuses on law clerks. A law clerk is understood here as a person with a legal education who supports a judge or panel of judges in their adjudicative work (see CCJE Opinion No. 22 (2019)). Court staff ensuring the administration, security and IT, experts, or court officials who decide small cases in their own right, like the German *Rechtspfleger*, are thus not the subject of this discussion.

Law clerks have a special role because they are legally trained like judges and work on legal issues, but they support judges in their judicial work as an assistant, not a colleague. While law clerks are below judges in the hierarchy of courts, they may become judges and may thus be seen as mentees and future colleagues rather than subordinates. They help overburdened courts cope with their workload and gain unique experiences early in their careers. Their involvement in the decision-making process raises questions about their influence, personal background, and ideology, and how much separation of labour in judicial decision-making is permissible, given that judges' legitimacy and independence in a society governed by the rule of law are protected by special rules of selections and guarantees.

According to the available data, law clerks are employed in courts of all instances all over the world, including most European countries, America, Australia, Asia, and Africa. Moreover, there are also law clerks at international courts such as the European Court of Justice (CJEU), the European Court of Human Rights (ECtHR), the International Criminal Court (ICC), and the International Court of Justice (ICJ). As different as the legal systems in which law clerks are employed are their roles and the terms to describe them. Besides the term *law clerks* (United States, Canada) and *judicial assistants* (United Kingdom), there are, for example, *associates* (Australia, Kiefel 2020), *legal advisors* (ICC, Slovenia), *Wissenschaftliche Mitarbeiter* (Germany, Massing 2016,

Masing 2019), *Gerichtsschreiber* (Switzerland, Lienhard and Bieri 2017), and *référendaire* (Belgium, CJEU).

The widespread and growing employment of law clerks make comparative studies rewarding not only because it provides valuable lessons for policy-makers looking for ways to make courts more effective and improve the training of young lawyers and judges. Comparative research on the organization, career opportunities, duties, and influence of law clerks also allows a unique perspective on the behaviour of judges and courts as organizations. Given the rich and recently available data,[1] this chapter will primarily focus on the variation of law clerks in European countries but will also take into consideration the practices at apex and international courts.

Next, the chapter briefly discusses the present state of research on law clerks. Section 3 highlights different types of law clerks in different court systems. Section 4 discusses the selection of law clerks addressing motives for their employment and the different types of law clerks in different judicial systems. Section 5 discusses the organization of law clerks. Section 6 addresses the duties of law clerks and their involvement in the judicial process through research, contributions in deliberations, and the drafting of decisions. As there are not only noticeable differences between different judicial systems but also between different courts, the discussion will distinguish between law clerks at lower courts, apex courts, and international courts. Section 7 discusses the influence of law clerks. The chapter concludes in section 8 with suggestions for future research.

2. Research on Law Clerks

2.1 United States

The US Supreme Court has hired graduates largely from elite law schools for one year since the late nineteenth century (Peppers 2006; Ward and Weiden 2006, 21–53; Johnson, Stras, and Black 2014). Today, law school graduates may clerk at different state and federal courts (Avery et al. 2001, Peppers, Giles and Tainer-Perkins 2007, 2008, 2014, Battaglini et al. 2020) and are rewarded with impressive career opportunities (Ward 2017, 100, 114–17). Clerking at the US Supreme Court is not only worth a signing bonus of US$400,000 (Black and Owens 2021) but also an excellent stepping stone for a career in academia (McAllister 2021; Wassermann 2021) or a post as a lawyer at the Supreme Court Bar, where former law clerks are apparently especially successful in winning their former bosses' votes (Black and Owens 2021). Law clerks are young graduates who clerk for one year directly after graduation. Since clerking is highly prestigious, especially at the Supreme Court, the positions are usually only open to graduates from the top law schools. However, there are also long-term law clerks, also called central staff attorneys, who are hired for longer periods of time and do not work as closely with judges as do the short-term law clerks (also called elbow clerks) (Pether 2007; Kearney 2014; Molloy 2019; McAllister 2022, 1154–59).

The role and influence of law clerks has been the subject of intense academic discussion and the subject of empirical research (Baier 1973; Ward and Weiden 2006; Avery et al. 2001, 2007; Peppers, Giles, and Tainer-Parkins 2008, 2014; Peppers and Zorn 2008; Swanson and Wasby 2008; Wasby 2005, 2008, 2014; Ward and Wasby 2010; Black and Boyd 2012; Peppers 2012, 2019; Johnson, Stras, and Black 2014; Black et al. 2014; Oldfather and Peppers 2014; Yoon 2014; Kromphardt 2015a, 2015b; Peppers and Cushmann 2015; Ward 2016, 2017). In the United States, there is also a considerable number of short memoirs of former law clerks reflecting their time as a law clerk, often with an understandably nostalgic and grateful perspective (Bartell 1992; Burnett 2010; Epps and Warren 2021; Epps et al. 2021; Katsas 2021; Oldfather 2021; Peppers 2021; Tyler 2021; Conde, Garcia, and Leon 2022).

2.2 Outside the United States

In other countries, there is much less research on the topic. However, research outside the United States is important in order to highlight and understand the diversity of law clerk schemes and judicial systems. Findings from the United States cannot simply be used for the analysis of other systems (see e.g. Mascini and Holvast 2023).

Interest has increased in the last years, with research being conducted in *Europe* (Sanders 2019, 2020), for example in Belgium (Renauld 2019), Czechia (Kosar and Vyhnánek 2020, 140), France (Weber 2019, 280), Germany (Massing 2016, Masing 2019, Sanders 2020),[2] Hungary (Kelemen and Steuer 2019 para 15; Bodnár 2020), Ireland (Coonan 2006), Italy (Bifulco and Paris 2016), Malta (Aigus 2021), Moldova, the Netherlands (Holvast 2017), the Nordic countries (Grendstad et al. 2020a, 2020b), Russia (Dzmitryieva 2021, 2017), Switzerland (Bieri 2016; Lienhard and Bieri 2017, Sanders 2020; Stadelmann 2020), Turkey (Esen 2018, para 15; Abad Andrade 2020, 165), and the United Kingdom.[3] For her work on law clerks (*griffier*) in the Netherlands, Nina Holvast must be considered a pioneer in the field (Holvast 2016, 2017), conducting the first experimental study on the influence of law clerks with Peter Mascini (Holvast and Mascini 2020, Mascini and Holvast 2020) in Europe.

In *America*, there is research on Argentina (Barrera 2009, 76–97), Brazil (de Olivera Gomes, de Aquino Guimaraes, and Akutsu 2016; de Martino 2021), Canada (Herman 1975; McInnes, Bolton, and Derzko 1994; Sossin 1996; Bueckert 2011; Bodwin, Rosenthal, and Yoon 2013; Macfarlane 2013; Martin 2020), Colombia (Vallejo 2020), Costa Rica (Ruiz González 2019, para 8) and Mexico (Pou Gimenéz 2017, 213, 214; Lübbe-Wolff 2022).

In *Australia* (Groves and Smyth 2004, 266; Kiefel 2020), in *Asia* India (Chandrachud 2014; Bhakshar 2021, Israel (Barak 2017) Hong Kong (Law 2015), Japan (Kamiya 2011; Law 2015; Ejima 2017; Kurishima 2017; Ojima and Onishi 2020), South Korea (Shin 2022) Taiwan (Law 2015;Chang 2017), and *Africa* Angola (Disant 2019), Egypt (Haimerl

2014), Kap Verde, Kongo (Disant 2019), Senegal,[4] and South Africa (Ejima 2017), research has also been started.

Law clerks at *international courts* have also been the subject of research: the CJEU (Zhang 2016, 2020; Streho 2017; Kenney 2000; Clay and Mcauliffe 2021), the ECtHR (Cohen 2017), the ICJ (Simma and Ortgies 2019), and the ICC (Sanders, 2020).

Researchers have worked empirically (both quantitatively and qualitatively) using experiments (Holvast and Mascini 2020), text analysis (Mascini and Holvast 2023), shadowing (Holvast 2017), and interviews (Holvast 2017, Sanders 2020), but have also used doctrinal legal analysis, discussing the normative foundations of law clerks' influence. Principal agent theory is also used to understand the relationship of judges and law clerks (Kenney 2000; Peppers and Zorn 2008; Rosenthal and Yoon 2011; Mascini and Holvast 2020, Deyneli and Mascini 2020).

While most studies analyse clerks within one country or one court, research on law clerks is at its early stages with very few *comparative* studies undertaken so far. Comparative studies seem to focus on apex and constitutional courts (Kenney 2000; Young 2007; Law 2015; Holvast 2016; Toader and Safta 2016; Ejima 2017; Disant 2019; Weber 2019, 280; Bhakshar 2021; Sanders 2020; Lübbe-Wolff 2022, 448–76).[5]

3. Goals of Law Clerk Employment and Different Law Clerk Models

A first step of comparative research on law clerks involves an analysis why and how law clerks are employed at different courts and judicial systems.

3.1 Goals of Law Clerk Employment

Despite distinctions between different clerkship schemes in different jurisdiction, a common aim in most jurisdictions and at courts of all instances is the reduction of backlogs and workload for judges, enabling them to concentrate on more complicated cases (Bieri 2016; Holvast 2016 10, 19 n. 97; Uebersax 2018; Sanders, 2020; Crichton 2022). Some papers advocate for more law clerks to reduce backlogs in a judicial system (Bryant 2007; Crichton 2022).

The effects of law clerks on the efficiency of courts is not easy to investigate, however. Engel and Weinshall (2020) have investigated the effects of assistant judges on the work of an Israeli court. They found mainly improved quality rather than quantity and that the effect was short lived. However, de Olivera Gomes, de Aquino Guimaraes, and Akutsu (2016) found a positive relationship between the number of assistants and judges and reduced backlogs in their study on Brazilian state courts.

Law clerks may also be employed in order to improve the quality of judicial work, for example, because they may bring fresh ideas from their education. More specifically, law clerks may be hired to support the use of comparative law in the adjudication (Law 2015 Bodnár 2019, 2020, 217) of apex courts through language skills and knowledge of foreign law. An example is South Korea. In South Africa and Israel, graduates from other countries are hired at the highest courts in order to improve access to foreign legal sources and comparative arguments (Ejima 2017, Constitutional Court of South Africa 2022).

Apart from increasing productivity and reducing backlogs, law clerk schemes may also have an educational goal, as the next section will show.

3.2 Different Law Clerk Models

For a comparative approach it is essential to investigate the differences between the various law clerk schemes in different judicial systems, while not overemphasizing them. To do so, three types of law clerks named here: 'interns', 'seconded judges', and 'scribes' shall be distinguished in order to allow comparisons across borders and courts. These models build on different traditions and also serve distinct purposes within different judicial systems and even courts, even though there are significant overlaps (Holvast 2016, 17–21; Sanders, 2020). In the systems where they are employed, the models can be found in courts of all instances.

3.2.1 *Internship Model*

In the so-called internship model, young graduates serve as law clerks for a short time, usually up to five years, to gain insights 'from behind the bench' (Sanders 2020).[6] Such work has an educational purpose since it prepares for a career outside the clerkship position, but it may also support the court's work. Examples may be found at courts of different instances in the United States, United Kingdom, Canada (Coonan 2006, 179–80), Australia, and India (Chauhan 2012).

The US clerkship with young graduates fresh from legal education served as a model in Ireland (Coonan 2006), South Africa,[7] Norway (Grendstad et al. 2020a, 2020b, 9), and the United Kingdom, where law clerk schemes were introduced at the Court of Appeal for England and Wales, the House of Lords (Paterson 2013, 247–55), and Supreme Court and, quite recently, at the High Court (Briggs 2016). In other countries where law clerk schemes have also been introduced, for example Norway, the US Supreme Court clerk scheme functioned as a model as well (Grendstad et al. 2020a, 2020b). This model may even have effects in the United States: Chandrachud (2014) has made the compelling argument that even though a national clerkship may not be as prestigious in India as one in the United States, it can serve as a stepping stone when applying to US law schools.

For the 'intern' law clerk in the United States, but also in other common law countries with a professional judiciary where lawyers become judges after a successful career, clerking allows an interesting look behind the scenes into a court room to which young lawyers usually do not have access. In the United Kingdom, clerking is described by law clerks in interviews as increasingly popular because it offers the opportunity to witness great advocates in action (Sanders 2020).

In countries with a career judiciary like Austria, Germany, Finland, Slovenia, and Switzerland, working at courts for a short time can be a mandatory part of legal education and qualifying for practice, especially before becoming a judge (Sanders 2020). While serving as a law clerk is no prerequisite to become a judge in most other countries, it is often seen as a common first step. In Germany, a new kind of law clerk scheme has been introduced recently in addition to the mandatory clerkship required to qualify as a judge, prosecutor, or advocate. Promising young graduates are invited to serve as paid intern at courts of first or second instance. The focus of this scheme is less to help overburdened judges but more to interest young lawyers in a future career as judges to fill the ranks increasingly depleted by retiring baby-boomers.

3.2.2 *Seconded Judges*

In judicial systems where judges are appointed soon after completing their legal education, there is a need for young judges to gain experience on the job, especially to qualify for promotion. Thus, in countries like Germany, Slovenia, Spain (Sanders 2020), Japan (Ejima 2017), and Senegal,[8] young judges showing promise for promotion can be seconded to higher courts to support higher ranking judges.[9] In professional systems like the United Kingdom, Ireland, and Norway, where judges are appointed after a successful career, judges assisting other judges are difficult to imagine.

To young judges, clerking at a Supreme or Constitutional Court provides the opportunity to gain valuable experiences but also to network with colleagues and high-ranking judges (Kranenpohl 2010, 89; 2016; Ejima 2017). In Germany, most federal judges have served as clerks at the German supreme courts or the German Federal Constitutional Court. However, young judges do not only learn at higher courts, but also bring valuable experiences and specialized knowledge from lower courts and insights into how the case law of higher courts affects the work of lower courts.

Both interns and seconded judges have in common that they only stay in their position for a short time and pursue educational purposes. They aim at careers elsewhere which may reduce competitiveness. They bring fresh ideas to their position and are highly motivated and often remember their work with important judges and smart young colleagues fondly later. Such short-term schemes make it necessary to train new law clerks repeatedly because law clerks continue their career elsewhere. While this may be seen as a disadvantage, their motivation and experiences as law clerks can influence a whole legal system, as for example in Germany, where former law clerks of the German FCC have increased the understanding of constitutional arguments at lower courts for decades (Lübbe-Wolff 2022, 466).

3.2.3 *Scribes*

While 'interns' and 'seconded judges' only serve for a limited time, up to five years at most, a 'scribe' position offers a lifelong career on its own. This often includes opportunities for advancement and potentially substantial duties in the judicial process (Sanders 2019, 2020).

In some judicial systems, 'scribes' look back on a long tradition and may write the official protocol of court hearings, keep the register, make certain procedural decisions, and might even write court decisions similar to a secretary or notary. Such 'scribes' may be found alongside other law clerks, for example interns. The Belgian *gréffier*, *greffe*, or '*Letrado de la Administracion de Justicia*' (LAJ) in Spain perform duties as 'court notaries', while support in the adjudicative work like research and drafting assistance is provided by other law clerks, as for example the *référendaire* in Belgium and special assistants at the court of cassation in Spain (*Letrados del Gabinete Técnico del Tribunal Supremo*, LGTTS). The South Korean Constitutional Court employs research officers for a longer term (Ejima 2017, para 16; Shin 2022, para 4, 25). In the United States, central staff attorneys also work long term compared to the better known law clerks (Pether 2007; Kearney 2014; Molloy 2019; McAllister 2022, 1154–59). However, the Swiss *Gerichtsschreiber* or *gréffier* (Uebersax 2018, 322–23) and the Dutch *griffiers* (Holvast 2017, 2016, 10, 15–16) not only write official protocols of the hearing but also undertake more substantial duties, like writing memos for judges and drafting judgments. In the Swiss system, the *Gerichtsschreiber* even has an advisory vote and has the opportunity in some cantons, for example Zürich, to give a dissenting opinion.

A 'scribe' position is usually not a life goal, as research in the Netherlands (Holvast 2017, 171), Switzerland, and Slovenia (Sanders 2020) showed. Many leave after only a few years. In interviews, law clerks expressed their wish to become judges later but they were sometimes kept back by family responsibilities, a lack of political connections (Switzerland), or open positions (Slovenia). In interviews, law clerks in different countries mentioned that in the long run, they would miss the lack of responsibility for making the final decisions themselves. In Slovenia, the system was started as stepping stone for future judges. It was extended to fight backlogs but then turned into a long-term career because of a lack of open judgeships (Sanders 2020; for Russia see Dzmitryieva 2021, 143).

3.2.4 *Law Clerks at International Courts*

Law clerks at international courts can appear in all models described below. Some national judiciaries second young judges with language skills to international courts, for example to the CJEU. Most law clerks at international courts are employed on a temporary basis which can be prolonged. Recent graduates are relatively rare. Such law clerks are often highly qualified and well paid but may face a lack of opportunity for advancement at their courts as judges are selected on the national level. While law clerks at the CJEU have great opportunities at the EU commission or law firms, legal advisors at the ICC with their specialization in international criminal law have few other opportunities with comparable attractive pay and interesting work. For such law clerks, the work at the courts becomes in fact a lifetime job, making them 'scribes' according to the model described above.

4. Selection

The way law clerks are selected is closely linked to the different law clerk models discussed in section 3. In systems where clerking is a mandatory step to qualifying as a lawyer, as in Germany, access must be open to all graduates with sufficient qualification. While most law clerks work at lower courts, the selection of law clerks at apex or international courts is of greater interest to researchers (Toader and Safta 2016, 99–103). Such research addresses issues such as access to opportunity, transparency (Zhang 2016, 2020), and (gender) diversity through prestigious clerkships (Mauro 2014; Szmer, Kaheny, and Christensen 2014; Peppers 2019; McAllister 2021; Bhaskar 2021; Fogel, Hoopes and Liu 2022; Badas and Stauffer 2023).

Often, law clerks are selected centrally by the administration of the court through a competition in which candidates' resumes (including the grades earned in their law degrees) and writing samples are scrutinized and candidates are interviewed (see Ejima 2017), as for example in Switzerland. In systems where judges work closely with their personal law clerks (see cabinet system discussed in section 5), judges often select their law clerks personally, as for example at the German FCC (Hiéramente 2020; Hellmann 2021; Lübbe-Wolff 2022), the US Supreme Court and Federal Courts (see Ward 2017, 105), and the CJEU (Zhang 2016, 17; Kenney 2000 593, 605). If judges select law clerks themselves, their personal preferences and possibly biases play a role, for example in relation to gender (Battaglini, Harris, and Patacchini et al. 2020) or the law school the judge attended. However, in other systems, for example in the United Kingdom, all law clerks are selected by a commission for the whole court and then assigned to individual judges on the basis of competence or interest in certain legal fields and assumed personal fit (Sanders 2020).

Selecting one's law clerks may have the advantage of fostering trust of judges in their law clerks (Hellmann 2021). However, such a selection may exclude certain groups of applicants because limited resources of individual judges may encourage them to select law clerks on the basis of personal recommendations, personal connections in judicial administration (e.g. at the German FCC), or only from elite law schools (Peppers 2019; McAllister 2021), thus lacking diversity (Rhinehart 1994; Mauro 2014; Szmer, Kaheny, and Christensen 2014). In the United States it has been argued that judges hire law clerks along ideological lines and that such law clerks influence the decision-making (Baier 1973; Ditslear and Baum 2001; Shapiro 2009; Baum 2014; Bonica et al. 2017, 2019). Stereotypes with respect to class, gender, religion, and ethnic background may very well play a role as well. This limits opportunities of other potentially well-qualified young lawyers at the judiciary, academia, and law firms (for India see Bhaskar 2021). Zhang has shown that *referendaire* of the CJEU come from a very small social group and share similar experiences and educational backgrounds (Zhang 2016, 2020).

5. Organization of Law Clerks within Courts

Before turning to the actual work of law clerks, the differences in their organization within courts shall be addressed. However, in different courts, or even within one court, different models may be used. This part distinguishes between cabinet, pool, and panel systems to simplify the analysis.

5.1 Cabinet

The cabinet system entails that one or more law clerks may be assigned to a judge individually. Two judges may also share one assistant. The number of personal law clerks depends on available resources but may also be limited by the ability of judges to read their work. The number may be as high as ten at the Mexican and Brazilian Apex Courts, five as at the Argentinian Supreme Courte, four as at the US Supreme Court (Kromphardt 2014 or at the German FCC), or just one as at the UK Supreme Court (Lübbe-Wolff 2022, 462–64). The most important point about this approach is, however, that a judge always works with the same law clerk(s). This approach is used for instance at the US Supreme Court, the German FCC (Kranenpohl 2010, 87), the Austrian Constitutional Court, at the CJEU (Kenney 2000, 593, 605), in the United Kingdom (Holvast 2016, 10, 19–20), and at courts in Russia, Poland, and Ukraine.[10] Given that the same term is used at the CJEU (Kenney 2000, 593, 605–12) and by the Consultative Council of European Judges (CCJE), this system is called 'cabinet system'.

5.2 Pool and Panel

The opposite of the cabinet system is the 'pool system'. Here, law clerks form a pool for the court or part of the court and work with different judges. A mixture of the pool and cabinet system is the 'panel system' where law clerks are assigned to one panel or senate of judges. There are also mixtures between cabinet and pool system within one court for different cases, as at the Supreme Court of Slovenia.

5.3 Comparative Perspective on Law Clerk Organization

There is not yet much research on the effects of different organizational models. It seems that systems which follow an intern or seconded judge model are more likely to follow a cabinet or panel system than a pool system. Examples are the United Kingdom and

Germany which follow a cabinet and panel approach with an internship and seconded judge model, respectively. This way, law clerks who serve for a shorter time for educational purposes can be assigned to one specific instructor or—in a panel system—a group of them (Sanders 2020).

Countries following a scribe model, like Switzerland and the Netherlands, but also Belgium, seem to be more likely to follow a pool system. In the United States, short-term law clerks are organized in a cabinet system, while long-term clerks or central staff attorneys are organized in pools (McAllister 2022, 1158). Some law clerks reported a preference for pool systems or at least joint office space to support team work and exchange (Sanders 2020).

Asked in interviews about their preferences, judges who worked in pool systems, pointed out that a pool system allowed them to work with law clerks with different qualities and experiences, but that they were not always compatible with different assistants (Sanders 2020). Judges who worked in cabinet systems, for example at the German FCC and the CJEU, point out how important the trusting working relationship with their assistants was for them (Lübbe-Wolff 2022, 458–59). Lübbe-Wolff explained such a safe place of trust could be important to let off steam in times of stress but that there was a risk that judges working in such isolated teams could be divided into different groups rather than work with their colleagues (Lübbe-Wolff 2022, 459).

Within the close working relationship of a cabinet or even pool, judges may develop into mentors with important influence over their law clerks' future. In both the United Kingdom and at the German FCC, judges follow the careers of and organize regular meetings with their former law clerks just like justices of the US Supreme Court (Peppers and Cushman 2015, 253–341; Ward 2017). However, data from Slovenia and Switzerland, where a pool system is used, shows that much depends on the individual style and temperament of judges. While some judges enjoy serving as mentors, others are more reserved. Judges, who enjoyed mentoring their assistants had often been law clerks themselves before.

It is possible that a cabinet system results in higher influence of law clerks because of a higher degree of trust between judge and assistants (see Holvast 2017, 163–64; Holvast and Mascini 2020). Lübbe-Wolff reports that at some courts a personal assignment to an individual judge could increase the risk of attempts to influence that judge through the law clerk (Lübbe-Wolff 2022, 453). However, while it is possible that the high degree of trust built in a cabinet could increase a law clerk's influence, other aspects may have a neutralizing effect, for example the fact that law clerks in a cabinet system change more often.

It is also possible that cabinet systems lead to higher degree of dependence between law clerks and individual judges. In cabinet systems, the employment of law clerks is often restricted to a specific time—one year at the US Supreme Court or in the United Kingdom—or depends on the term of the judge, like at the German FCC or traditionally the CJEU (Kenney 2000, 593, 605; Zhang 2016, 17). This may not be a problem for a highly paid *référendaire* at the CJEU (Zhang 2016, 20) or the seconded judges at the FCC who go back to their courts. In Ukraine, however, after a change in the law in 2015, law clerks lost their status as civil servants and are now so-called political advisors whose position depend on the respective judge in their cabinet (CCJE Responses 2019. Law clerks reported in personal conversations that this had limited their rights, for example in case of pregnancy. With such dependence there may come a risk of exploitation, possibly including sexual harassment, as happened in Australia in 2020.[11]

6. Duties of Law Clerks

The duties of law clerks and their involvement in judicial decision-making is of particular importance to understand the role of law clerks in a judicial system. Different duties of clerks in the decision-making process can be distinguished not only in different judicial systems, but also in different courts in one judicial system (Ejima 2017) Moreover, there can be differences within one court, depending on the individual judge and law clerk (Sanders 2020). The following discussion can only provide an overview. This part will first address the major duties of law clerks.

Following the judicial decision-making process, six duties can be distinguished.

1. Research
2. Memo writing
3. Presence in hearings
4. Presence in deliberation
5. Drafting of decisions
6. Independent case work

The differences between duties of law clerks at different courts from first instance to apex and international court are addressed under the topics listed above. However, special differences between the work at courts of different levels shall be highlighted under section 6.7.

When performing their duties, law clerks usually operate under ethical obligations and are bound to confidentiality (Jones 1991; Lane 2005; Sorensen 2008; Wilner 2011; Martin 2020; Bischoping 2022; Funk, Boutros, and Kendall 2022).

Before a detailed discussion of different duties it is important to note that in many countries, the work of law clerks is largely left to informal rules. However, there is regulation especially in Central European member states of the Council of Europe, for example Bosnia and Herzegovina. In Croatia, law clerks are mentioned in the constitution. In other countries they are only mentioned in contracts or handbooks. In many European countries, however, the rules securing a judge's impartiality also apply to law clerks (Holvast 2016 10, 25; CCJE Responses 2019; Sanders 2019, 2020).

6.1 Research

Most law clerks undertake research and discuss the case and its legal problems with judges, acting as a kind of 'sounding board'. In this way they may support overburdened judges considerably and improve the quality of decisions. Here, language skills and knowledge of foreign law may be relevant for courts interested in comparative arguments (Law 2015; Bodnár 2020).

6.2 Memo Writing

Law clerks may also be asked to summarize the facts of a case in preparation for oral arguments, sometimes called 'bench memos' (Nesterchuk 2013; Johnson, Stras, and Black 2014; Holvast, 2017). Such memos can be quite short but may also include the relevant law, discuss the main problems of the case, and suggest a decision. They may also serve as the basis for hearings or the judges' deliberation.

6.3 Presence in Hearings

In most countries, law clerks are not present in hearings or they only attend when invited as silent guests like other members of the public (Sanders 2019). At the German FCC for example, law clerks have reserved seats in the audience during public hearings. In some countries, for example Switzerland and the Netherlands, however, law clerks, described as scribes in section 3, have a unique role in hearings, wearing official dress, writing the protocol, and sometimes even asking questions or pointing out issues that have been overlooked (Bieri 2016; Holvast 2017; Sanders 2020).

6.4 Presence in Deliberations

The presence of law clerks in deliberations and the formal and informal rules prescribing their role shall be addressed now. Like writing judgments, deliberations are closely connected to the judicial role. While activities like research, memo writing, and drafting can be undertaken in the 'judicial back-office' of chambers, being present or even speaking in deliberations means that these law clerks become visible to other judges. Thus, the presence or absence of law clerks in deliberations can offer important insights into the role of law clerks in a judicial system (Sanders 2020).

At many apex courts, law clerks are not present in deliberations, such as the German FCC, the German Constitutional Court for the State of North Rhine-Westfalia, the UK Supreme Court, and the CJEU. This way, judges can work intensively on the decision without other people present (Kranenpohl 2010, 89, 94–103; Sanders 2020).

The exclusion of law clerks can be justified by the need to keep the judges' discussion confidential. However, this may also encourage exchange and cooperation between judges across ideological lines, as Lübbe-Wolff suggests (2022, 459). An indirect effect of this custom might be that it forces judges to know their cases inside out because they cannot rely on an assistant to provide additional information (Kranenpohl 2010, 89–91). Leaving law clerks outside the deliberation room could therefore function as an (informal) safeguard (Holvast 2016, 10, 24) to prevent judges from avoiding their responsibilities by passing important duties to their assistants.

This reluctance to include law clerks in deliberations is not limited to the highest courts. Law clerks are not present in deliberations in most member states of the Council of Europe, even if they draft complete judgments (Sanders 2019). In the CCJE Responses 2019, representatives from Azerbaijan, Russia, and Ukraine explained that deliberating the judgment was a task which the law reserved for judges alone.

In other countries, judges may invite law clerks to participate as silent observers (Belgium, Denmark, Austria, the English Court of Appeal). In other systems, law clerks participate in the discussion (Croatia, Netherlands) and may even present their work, as in Slovenia, Bosnia, and Herzegovina (Sanders 2020), and at the apex courts of Turkey, Finland, Sweden, and Korea (Lübbe-Wolff 2022, 473–78). This is also the case in some senates (or panels) of Federal Supreme Courts in Germany where the chairpersons have developed their own rules regarding if and how to include law clerks in the deliberation (Sanders 2020).

In courts in Romania and Switzerland, law clerks have a distinct procedural role in the deliberations. In Romania they are present in deliberations of the High Court of Cassation, and in Switzerland law clerks participate in deliberations in courts at all levels with an advisory vote and sign the judgment together with the judge (Bieri 2016, 31).

However, even if law clerks participate in deliberations, this does not mean that there are no procedural and substantive differences between them and the judges. Informal rules seem to exist in many higher courts, which prescribe the order and extent of speaking. Most of the law clerks in Slovenia and Switzerland explained that judges spoke first and that they only contributed when an important point had been overlooked (Sanders 2020).

6.5 Drafting Decisions

A particularly sensitive issue concerning the interaction of judges and law clerks is their involvement in the drafting process. Different countries have developed different approaches to this issue. In most countries law clerks are involved to different degrees in the drafting of decisions. According to the responses of the CCJE questionnaire 2019, the role of law clerks in the drafting process varies considerably from country to country or even within the same courts. Especially where judges and law clerks work together closely, the involvement in the drafting process may depend on the discretion of the individual judge or judges and the competence and experience of the individual law clerk.

The following sections will discuss different degrees of involvement in the drafting process such as editing support, drafting of the facts of a case, drafting complete judgments for simple cases on the basis of established case law, and—finally—the drafting of all kinds of judgments, including difficult cases at the highest courts (section 6.5.1). Then we will turn to the interaction of law clerk and judge when complete decisions are drafted by a law clerk (section 6.5.2). The section will conclude with a discussion of judicial systems which consider the drafting by judicial assistant as problematic (section 6.5.3).

6.5.1 *Different Degrees of Involvement in the Drafting Process*

Law clerks may just perform editorial functions, helping with the proofreading of decisions, including making suggestions to improve the draft or cross-checking references. This is even possible in some of those countries where law clerks being involved in the drafting process is seen as problematic. In some countries, drafting press releases (e.g. UK Supreme Court, Sanders 2020) is also a duty of law clerks. In Japan, law clerks write highly influential commentaries on the decisions (Kurishima 2017, 178–79).

However, in most countries, law clerks have more extensive duties in drafting. The drafting work of law clerks can be limited to the facts or introduction under close supervision of judges or to cases where the case law is already well established (CCJE Responses 2019). However, in the majority of European countries, at all instances, law clerks draft complete judgments (CCJE Responses 2019; Sanders 2019; Lübbe-Wolff 2022, 467–73).

Judges at the German FCC indicated that they do not allow law clerks to help draft in the most important decisions involving all members of a senate. Drafting support was limited to the chamber decisions of three justices by which the court disposes of the majority of cases. However, this differs from judge to judge, just as does the interaction between judge and law clerk (Hellmann 2021; Lübbe-Wolff 2022, 467–69).

6.5.2 *Interaction of Law Clerk and Judge in the Drafting Process*

The available data in Europe shows different approaches to the interaction of judges and law clerks in the drafting process (CCJE Responses 2019; Sanders 2019). There might be a discussion with the judge before the law clerk starts drafting. The law clerk may also be asked to prepare a memo, first suggesting the outcome of the case, which is then discussed with the judge or with a panel of judges. The discussion can also take place after the law clerk has submitted a complete draft.

In some countries, law clerks prepare the entire document autonomously and then submit it for approval. This process may also be subdivided into different steps, as at the Constitutional Court of North Rhine-Westfalia. Here, a law clerk prepares documents for each step which are then discussed by the judges without the assistant being present (Sanders 2020). In some judicial systems and courts, law clerks work independently, as for example in the Netherlands (Holvast 2017; Mascini and Holvast 2023), Slovenia, and Switzerland. Such law clerks solve upcoming questions themselves or confer with the judge. Major changes in the outcome of a case will be discussed with the judge beforehand. At some courts, the independence of law clerks in the drafting process is especially high (Sanders 2020). At the Japanese Supreme Court (Kurishima 2017, 176; Ojima and Onishi 2020, 215) and the Turkish Constitutional Court, law clerks prepare the case, present it in the deliberation, and draft the judgment. At the Turkish Supreme Court, they are even called *raportör* and perform functions close to those of a judge rapporteur (Lübbe-Wolff 2022, 470). In Switzerland, the law clerk, the *Gerichtsschreiber*, has an advisory vote and signs the draft together with a judge or president (Bieri 2016). In Finland, law clerks may even submit a dissenting opinion if a panel of judges does not follow their suggestions (CCJE Responses 2019; Grendstad et al. 2020a, 2020b, 169; Lübbe-Wolff 2022, 470).

The question if and how law clerks draft differently than judges has been investigated empirically. While US research suggests less confident writing (Choi and Gulati 2005; Posner 2006, 1985, 109; Rosenthal and Yoon 2011), the research on experienced law clerks in the Netherlands points in another direction (Mascini and Holvast 2023). This can be explained by the Dutch scribe model which employs law clerks for longer periods than in the US 'intern' model.

6.5.3 *No Drafting of Law Clerks in Common Law Courts?*

In the United Kingdom and Ireland, a law clerk's drafting is seen as highly unethical (Sanders 2019, 2020). The position seems to be the same in Australia (Groves and Smyth 2004, 266; Kiefel 2020, 49; Lübbe-Wolff 2022, 472). However, a textual analysis of Canadian decisions indicates that law clerks are increasingly involved in the drafting process as well (Bodwin, Rosenthal, and Yoon 2013).

It is tempting to explain such differences with a civil law/common law divide. In England and Wales, and following this tradition, Ireland, each judge used to give and write an individual opinion (Ernst 2016 255–282, 2012. Only quite recently, with the increase of the caseload, judges at the Court of Appeal and the Supreme Court assign the opinion writing to one judge, who takes the 'lead' and with whom the others agree. Nevertheless, opinions still bear the names of individual judges and every judge is free to write independently of the others. Dissenting opinions in the common law world have their origin in this individual decision power (Ernst 2012, 637, 640). Moreover, scholars of comparative law are aware of the more individual writing style of common law judges. This tradition might have established the perception that judges in these two common law countries consider the writing of judgments a personal duty which must not be delegated to a third party.

In civil law countries, judges who work in panels or senates give their decisions jointly (Ernst 2012, 638). Even though the decision is mainly prepared and drafted by the judge rapporteur, the judgment does not appear in his or her name alone but is signed by all. The deliberation process must traditionally be kept secret and therefore, dissenting opinions are not part of the civil law tradition (Ernst 2012, 640). Bearing this approach to judicial decision making and the writing of judgments in mind, this might mean that it is traditionally easier for civil law judges to engage the help of an assistant in the drafting of a judgment. For such judges, the joint discussion process in deliberations and signing of the judgment might be more important. This may also explain the reluctance in many civil law systems to have law clerks participate in deliberations.

However, the civil law/common law divide is not as clear cut. At US courts, especially the US Supreme Court, it seems not unusual that judges delegate the drafting of their decisions to law clerks (Choi and Gulati 2005; Rosenthal and Yoon 2011; Carlson et al. 2016).

6.6 Independent Work on Cases

In some judicial systems law clerks take on an even greater role by holding hearings and deciding certain small cases at first instance themselves, with the approval of the judge. According to the CCJE Responses 2019, in some European countries, law clerks have an independent role in certain first-instance procedures. In Malta and Slovenia, law clerks collect evidence including questioning witnesses. In other countries, law clerks decide procedural issues such as appointing experts or deciding on costs (Sanders 2020).

According to CCJE Responses (Sanders 2019), law clerks may even conduct hearings and decide small civil and criminal cases in Bosnia and Herzegovina, Croatia, Czechia, Finland, Iceland, Slovenia, and Sweden. In Croatia, Bosnia and Herzegovina, and Slovenia, law clerks decide these cases alone or under the supervision of a judge, run the hearing, and ask questions. The practice is popular because it saves judges' time and offers great learning experiences to law clerks (Sanders 2020).

6.7 Duties at Different Courts with a Focus on Apex and International Courts

The duties of law clerks and their interactions with judges vary with the kind of court that employs them. At first instance, law clerks may be involved in writing the protocol in court, summarizing the facts, undertaking research, and preparing questions for oral arguments, as research in the Netherlands (Holvast 2017), Switzerland, and Slovenia (Sanders, 2020) show. In these courts, law clerks and judges are often close in age and may feel more like a team of equals. Law clerks may prepare draft judgments alone or together with the judge, depending on the complexity of the case. The organization of the procedure, including scheduling hearings and presiding over them is, however, left to the judge (Bieri 2016; Sanders 2020).

At Courts of Appeal and Supreme and Constitutional Courts without an automatic right to review, law clerks often serve as 'gate keepers' providing important support in the selection of cases (Toader and Safta 2016). They summarize the facts and relevant law of an application in a memo, ending with a suggestion on whether the case should be accepted for review. In the cert-pool of the US Supreme Court, law clerks undertake such duties and their ability to set the agenda of the court has been discussed (Ward 2017, 107; Narechania 2022). At the German FCC (Kranenpohl 2010, 88–91), the UK

Supreme Court (Nesterchuck 2013, 99, 104; Sanders, 2020), the Russian Constitutional Court (Dzmitryieva 2017), and the apex courts of the Nordic countries (Grendstad et al. 2020b, 24–27, 159–70), law clerks also help sift cases. However, thus far, there has been no argument made that they work in a politically biased way.

At international courts, law clerks may perform the same gate-keeping functions. However, law clerks may be of even higher importance because of language skills and institutional knowledge. At the ECtHR and ICC, law clerks may serve for a long time and know more about the court's case law than new judges selected on the national level. This can give law clerks special responsibilities and influence (Sanders 2020).

7. Influence

In research on law clerks, the interaction of judges and law clerks and their influence on judicial decisions is of special interest. Research suggests that the relationship between judges and law clerks depends not only on the formal positions of law clerk and judge but also on their relative experience, age, and the case at hand. The organization of a court, in particular the organizational systems of law clerks discussed above, may play a role as well (Holvast 2017; Holvast and Mancini 2020; Mascini and Holvast 2020; Sanders 2020).

Research indicates that the relationship of law clerks and judges usually remains hierarchical even if law clerks are present in deliberations or take an important role in the drafting process. After all, judges have been appointed formally and are subject to special rules protecting their independence. Especially in apex and international courts, judges are the courts' face to the public, while law clerks work in the judicial 'back-office'. If a judge's formal position is supported by competence and experience, research indicates that law clerks accept this authority. Law clerks are aware that the judges, not they themselves, decide cases. Moreover, in an intern or seconded judges' system, law clerks are usually younger and less experienced than the judges they serve. However, if law clerks are more experienced than judges, as they may be in scribe systems such as Switzerland, the situation might be more challenging but may also open the opportunity for young judges to learn (Sanders 2020).

A discussion of the influence of law clerks must distinguish two distinct questions. First, do law clerks really have influence? How should this be measured? In the CCJE Responses 2019, responding judges representing their member state assume that judges are not influenced by law clerks. However, in an interview study in scribe systems (Slovenia, Switzerland, and at the ICC), both judges and law clerks assumed that law clerks have some influence (Sanders 2020). First experimental studies in the Netherlands (Holvast and Mancini 2020) indicate that the memo of a law clerk has some effect on guiding a judge's decision. Judges seem to follow law clerks' recommendations more if they know and trust a law clerk and have to cope with a high workload. Judges' views on efficiency or the rule of law seems to be less important in that respect. The organizational models discussed above might play a role as well. Furthermore, the more duties law clerks hold, the stronger their position is likely to be (Holvast 2016, 10, 16; CCJE Response 2019; Sanders 2020; see also CCJE Opinion No. 22 (2019) rec. 4).

The second, normative question is the following: assuming law clerks do have influence, how should this influence be evaluated? Or to put it simply, are influential law clerks a good or a bad thing? After all, law clerks are not the only influence on a judge's decision-making and their employment has many advantages for the training of young lawyers and the support of judges. However, there is the question of the legitimacy of decisions influenced by law clerks. Judges are selected and appointed according to distinct procedural rules and their independence is protected by special guarantees. All this assumes that judges decide their cases and bear the responsibility of their decisions. If Article 6 of the European Convention on Human Rights guarantees the decision by an independent tribunal, it is a tribunal headed by a judge, not a law clerk (CCJE Opinion No. 22 (2019)).

However, there are solutions for these challenges. The problem of legitimacy can be solved with legal reform, as in Switzerland, where the law gives law clerks an advisory vote. Moreover, rules demanding the recusal of judges must apply to law clerks as well, as they do in some countries, for example Switzerland, Slovenia, and the Netherlands (Sanders 2019). Finally, law clerk schemes can be designed carefully in order to protect and support law clerks and judges in their respective roles as supporting assistants and responsible decision-makers.[12]

8. Future Research and Conclusion

In the past, there has not been much research on law clerks outside the United States but this has changed over the last few years. The reasons for the employment of law clerks, their contribution to the judicial process, their organization and influence are investigated increasingly at the national level and in a comparative way. Nevertheless, much more research on their organization, role, and influence remains necessary both at the national level as well as comparatively. This is important to highlight commonalities and differences and to understand the diversity of courts as organizations in different judicial systems and even at different levels within judicial systems. Moreover, the work of law clerks at different international courts needs to be understood better as well.

This discussion started in section 3 with goals for employing law clerks and different law clerk models. The background and career of law clerks in different legal systems and the motives for their employment deserve further research. Such research could offer unique insights into judicial careers between prestigious opportunities of law clerks at apex and international courts and precarious employment in dead-end jobs at lowers courts.

Section 4 discussed the selection of law clerks. It would also be worthwhile to investigate the effects of hiring schemes further, especially in relation to access to opportunity, diversity, and judicial career. The establishment of professional networks through clerking may offer interesting insights into different judiciaries.

Section 5 addressed the organization of law clerks into cabinets and pools. However, little is known yet about the effects of law clerk organization on the efficiency and quality of work and courts as institutions. More needs to be learned about the working relationship of judges and law clerks. For example, do cabinet systems encourage team-building between judges and their law clerks on the one hand, and pool systems team-building only among law clerks and the court administration? Judges in their role as team leaders and mentors in different organizational schemes also deserve attention. Dependence and possible exploitation is an important topic in this context. Such research could expand the understanding of judicial behaviour and maybe also help develop training schemes to support judges in their important personal duties. This may also offer important food for thought for developing guidelines for the employment of law clerks. In this context, it could also be asked if the personal selection of law clerks by judges and the work in cabinet systems deepen ideological differences between judges and influence the polarization within courts (Lübbe-Wolff 2022, 455).

Section 6 addressed the duties of law clerks. In this area, there is special need for more nuanced research at different courts at different levels in different judicial systems and at international courts. The work of drafting and the interaction of judges and law clerks and the differences between their work deserves attention (Devins and Klein 2017; Mascini and Holvast 2023).

Section 7 discussed the influence of law clerks. The influence of law clerks on decision-making at different courts and in different judicial systems should be investigated empirically still further, building on the important work of Holvast and Mascini (2020).

Collecting data on the role and work of law clerks is challenging. Access to interview partners, participants for experimental studies, and data for quantitative research is not easy to get. However, it is highly necessary. Judicial decision-making does not happen in isolation, as if conducted by a monk in a cell, but is influenced by different factors and actors of which law clerks are only one if an important group.

Acknowledgements

I wish to thank my research assistant Elisabeth Faltinat for her invaluable support researching the sources for this chapter. Moreover, my most sincere thanks go to Gunnar Grendstad comments on earlier drafts.

Notes

1. In preparation on its Opinion No. 22 (2019) on judicial assistants, the Consultative Council of European judges of the Council of Europe sent out a questionnaire which was filled out by representatives from Albania, Andorra, Austria, Azerbaijan, Bosnia and Herzegovina, Belgium, Bulgaria, Croatia, Cyprus, the Czech Republic, Denmark, Finland, France, Georgia,

Germany, Iceland, Ireland, Italy, Latvia, Liechtenstein, Lithuania, Luxemburg, Malta, Moldova, Monaco, the Netherlands, Norway, Poland, Romania, Russia, Slovenia, Spain, Sweden, Switzerland, Turkey, Ukraine, and the United Kingdom. The responses are referred to in this text as CCJE Responses 2019. Questionnaire and responses can be reviewed at: https://www.coe.int/en/web/ccje/opinion-no.-22-on-the-role-of-court-clerks-and-legal-assistants-within-the-courts-and-their-relationships-with-judges, accessed 31 May 2023. For a summary, see Sanders 2019. CCJE members who usually fill out such questionnaires are high-ranking judges selected by their member state. While the information they provide is usually accurate, this is not always the case. The data must thus be treated with care. The author of this chapter has used CCJE data and data collected through interviews in Germany, Slovenia, Switzerland, the United Kingdom, the Court of Justice of the European Union (CJEU), the European Court of Justice (ECtHR), and at the International Criminal Court (ICC).

2. The focus in research is on the Federal Constitutional Court (FCC): Kranenpohl 2010, 126–28, 246–49; Zuck 2015; Hellmann 2021; Masing 2021; Lübbe-Wolff 2022. See for the constitutional courts of the Länder Quaas 2022; an outdated but broader perspective provides Bichelmeir 1971.
3. In the United Kingdom, research is focused on the Supreme Court: see Darbeyshire 2011; Paterson 2013, ch. 6; Nesterchuk 2013; Arnold 2014; Hanretty 2020, 16. For magistrate's clerks, see Samuels 1974; Astor 1986.
4. See for the relevant law: http://conseilconstitutionnel.sn/la-loi-organique-n2016-23-du-14-juillet-2016-relative-au-conseil-constitutionnel/, accessed 29 May 2023.
5. For someone who reads German, Lübbe-Wolff offers a goldmine of information on law clerks at constitutional courts.
6. Ejima (2017) would describe this as Model A, where law clerks are hired from outside the judiciary.
7. See for the clerkship programme, which hires foreign and local lawyers as judicial assistants, https://www.concourt.org.za/index.php/law-researchers/about-law-clerks, accessed 8 August 2020.
8. See the law on the constitutional court n° 2016-23 du 14 juillet 2016, http://conseilconstitutionnel.sn/la-loi-organique-n2016-23-du-14-juillet-2016-relative-au-conseil-constitutionnel/, accessed 2 December 2023.
9. Ejima (2017) describes this as Model B, where law clerks are hired from within the judiciary https://oxcon.ouplaw.com/display/10.1093/law-mpeccol/law-mpeccol-e575?prd=MPECCOL, accessed 2 December 2023.
10. For a list of European countries and their respective organizational approach, see Sanders 2020.
11. https://theconversation.com/high-court-apologises-for-dyson-heydons-sexual-harassment-of-six-associates-141215, accessed 29 May 2023. See on workplace challenges of the judiciary in the United States McKeown (2021).
12. See for recommendations CCJE Opinion No. 22 (2019).

References

Abad Andrade, Maria. 2020. *Verfassungsgerichtliche Entscheidungsfindung und ihre Folgen: Das Türkische Verfassungsgericht zwischen Mehrheitslogik und Konsensverfahren*. Baden-Baden: Nomos.

Aigus, Martina, 2021. 'The Role of the Judicial Assistant in Civil Proceedings'. Bachelor's dissertation, University of Malta.

Arnold, William. 2014. 'The Supreme Court of the United Kingdom (UKSC), an Exploration of the Roles if Judicial Officers and Court Administrators and How the Relationship between Them May Be Improved and Enhanced: A Case Study'. *International Journal for Court Administration* 6 (2): 19–25.

Astor, Hilary. 1986. 'The Unrepresented Defendant Revisited: A Consideration of the Role of the Clerk in Magistrates' Courts'. *Journal of Law and Society* 13 (2): 225–40.

Avery, Christopher, Christine Jolls, Richard Posner, and Alvin Roth. 2001. 'The Market for Federal Judicial Law Clerks'. *University of Chicago Law Review* 68 (3): 793–90.

Avery, Christopher, Christine Jolls, Richard Posner, and Alvin Roth. 2007. 'The New Market for Federal Judicial Law Clerks'. *University of Chicago Law Review* 74 (2): 447–86.

Badas, Alex, and Katalyn E. Stauffer. 2023. 'Gender and Ambition Among Potential Law Clerks'. *Journal of Law and Courts* 11 (1): 116–40.

Baier, Paul. 1973. 'The Law Clerks: Profile of an Institution'. *Vanderbilt Law Review* 26 (November): 1125–17.

Barrera, López Leticia. 2009. 'Performing the Court: Forms and Practices of Legal Knowledge-making in Argentina'. PhD diss., Cornell University.

Bartell, Laura. 1992. 'Rubin: Practitioner, Professor, and Judge: A Splendid Relationship—Judge and Law Clerk'. *Louisiana Law Review* 52 (1992): 1429–40.

Battaglini, Marco, Jorgen Harris, and Eleonora Patacchini. 2020. 'Professional Interactions and Hiring Decisions: Evidence from the Federal Judiciary'. *National Bureau of Economic Research*, Working Paper 26726. https://www.nber.org/papers/w26726, accessed 3 December 2023.

Baum, Lawrence. 2014. 'Hiring Supreme Court Law Clerks: Probing the Ideological Linkage between Judges and Justices'. *Marquette Law Review* 98 (1): 333–60.

Bhakshar, Anurag. 2021. 'Law Clerks and Access to Judges: A Comparative Reflection on the Recruitment Process of Law Clerks in India'. *Comparative Constitutional Law & Administrative Law Journal* 6 (1): 58–88.

Bifulco, Raffaele, and Davide Paris. 2016. 'Der italienische Verfassungsgerichtshof'. In *Verfassungsgerichtsbarkeit in Europa: Institutionen, Ius Publicum Europaeum, Band VI*, edited by Aemin von Bogdandy, Christoph Grabenwarter, and Peter Huber, § 100: 271–356. Heidelberg: C. F. Müller.

Bichelmeir, Jürgen. 1971. *Der juristische Hilfsarbeiter an den obersten deutschen Gerichten*. Cologne: Heymann.

Bieri, Peter. 2016. 'Law Clerks in Switzerland: A Solution to Cope with the Caseload'. *International Journal for Court Administration* 7 (2): 29–38. http://doi.org/10.18352/ijca.201.

Bischoping, Gregory. 2022. 'Reconceiving Ethics for Judicial Law Clerks'. *St. Mary's Journal on Legal Malpractice & Ethics* 12 (1): 58–92.

Black, Ryan, and Christina Boyd. 2012. 'The Role of Law Clerks in the U.S. Supreme Court's Agenda-setting Process'. *American Politics Research* 40 (1): 147–73.

Black, Ryan, Christina Boyd, and Amanda Bryan. 2014. 'Revisiting the Influence of Law Clerks on the U.S. Supreme Court's Agenda-setting Process'. *Marquette Law Review* 98 (1): 75–109.

Black, Ryan, and Ryan Owens. 2021. 'Trends: The Influence of Personalized Knowledge at the Supreme Court: How (Some) Former Law Clerks Have the Inside Track'. *Political Research Quarterly* 74 (4): 795–807.

Bodnár, Eszter. 2020. 'The Use of Comparative Law in the Practice of the Hungarian Constitutional Court: An Empirical Analysis (1990–2019)'. *Hungarian Journal of Legal Studies* 6 (1): 1–22.

Bodnár, Eszter. 2019. 'The Invisible Factors behind Using Comparative Law in Constitutional Adjudication'. *Romanian Journal of Comparative Law* 10 (1): 201–27.

Bodwin, Kelly, Jeffrey Rosenthal, and Albert Yoon. 2013. 'Opinion Writing and Authorship on the Supreme Court of Canada'. *University of Toronto Law Journal* 63 (2): 159–92.

Bonica, Adam, Adam Chilton, Jacob Goldin, Kyle Rozema, and Maya Sen. 2019. 'Legal Rasputins? Law Clerk Influence on Voting at the US Supreme Court'. *The Journal of Law, Economics, and Organization* 35 (1): 1–36.

Bonica, Adam, Adam Chilton, Jacob Goldin, Kyle Rozema, and Maya Sen. 2017. 'The Political Ideologies of Law Clerks'. *American Law and Economics Review* 19 (1): 96–128.

Briggs, Michael. 2016. 'Civil Courts Structure Review: Final Report'. Judiciary of England and Wales, July 2016. https://www.judiciary.uk/wp-content/uploads/2016/07/civil-courts-structure-review-final-report-jul-16-final-1.pdf, accessed 3 December 2023.

Bryan, Christopher. 2007. 'The Role of Law Clerks in Reducing Judicial Backlog'. *Colorado Lawyer* 36 (5): 91–93.

Bueckert, Melanie. 2011. 'Legal Research in Canada's Provincial Appellate Courts'. *Manitoba Law Journal* 35 (1): 181–20.

Burnett, Donald. 2010. 'Law Clerking: My Favorite Year'. *Advocate* 53 (3): 26–28.

Carlson, Keith, Michael A. Livermore, and Daniel Rockmore. 2016. 'A Quantitative Analysis of Writing Style on the U.S. Supreme Court'. *Washington University Law Review* 93 (6): 1461–96.

Chandrachud, Abhinav. 2014. 'From Hyderabad to Harvard: How US Law Schools Make it Worthwhile to Clerk on India's Supreme Court'. *International Journal of the Legal Profession* 21 (1): 73–101.

Chang Wen-Chen. 2017. 'The Constitutional Court of Taiwan'. In *Comparative Constitutional Reasoning*, edited by András Jakab, Arthur Dyevre, and Giulio Itzcovich, 641–78. Cambridge: Cambridge University Press.

Chauhan, Sidharth. 2012. 'Clerkships in the Indian Supreme Court: Some Reflections and Suggestions'. *Critical Twenties*. 17 April. https://www.criticaltwenties.in/lawthejudiciary/clerkships-in-the-indian-supreme-court-some-reflections-and-suggestions, accessed 3 December 2023.

Choi, Stephen, and Gulati G. Mitu 2005. 'Which Judges Write Their Opinions (and Should We Care)'. *Florida State University Law Review* 32 (4): 1077–122.

Clay, Edward, and Karen Mcauliffe. 2021. 'Reconceptualising the Third Space of Legal Translation: A Study of the Court of Justice of the European Union'. *Comparative Legilinguistics* 45 (1): 93–126.

Cohen, Mathilde. 2017. 'Judges or Hostages? Sitting at the Court of Justice of the European Union and the European Court of Human Rights'. In *EU Law Stories. Contextual and Critical Histories of European Jurisprudence*, edited by Fernanda Nicola and Bill Davies, 58–80. Cambridge: Cambridge University Press.

Conde, Djenab, Angie Garcia, and Noel Leon. 2022. 'COVID Clerkship: Holding Space for Justice'. *Litigation* 48 (3): 38–40.

Consultative Council of European Judges (CCJE). Responses to questionnaire sent out in preparation of Opinion No. 22 (2019) on 'the role of judicial assistants'. Reports were completed by representatives from Albania, Andorra, Austria, Azerbaijan, Bosnia and

Herzegovina, Belgium, Bulgaria, Croatia, Cyprus, the Czech Republic, Denmark, Finland, France, Georgia, Germany, Iceland, Ireland, Italy, Latvia, Liechtenstein, Lithuania, Luxemburg, Malta, Moldova, Monaco, the Netherlands, Norway, Poland, Romania, Russia, Slovenia, Spain, Sweden, Switzerland, Turkey, Ukraine, and the United Kingdom. This data is referred to in this text as CCJE Responses 2019. The questionnaire and responses can be reviewed at: https://www.coe.int/en/web/ccje/opinion-no.-22-on-the-role-of-court-clerks-and-legal-assistants-within-the-courts-and-their-relationships-with-judges, accessed 31 May 2023.

Consultative Council of European Judges (CCJE). Opinion No. 22 (2019) on the role of judicial assistants, https://www.coe.int/en/web/ccje/ccje-opinions-and-magna-carta, accessed 31 May 2023.

Coonan, Genevieve. 2006. 'The Role of Judicial Research Assistants in Supporting the Decision-making Role of the Irish Judiciary'. *Judicial Studies Institute Journal* 6 (1): 171–96.

Constitutional Court of South Africa. 2022. 'About Law Clerks'. https://www.concourt.org.za/index.php/law-researchers/about-law-clerks, accessed 12 October 2022.

Crichton, Sha-Shana. 2022. 'Using Law Clerks to Improve Efficiency in Jamaican Courts'. *Georgia Journal of International and Comparative Law* 50 (2): 301–31.

Darbyshire, Penny. 2011. *Sitting in Judgment. The Working Lives of Judges*. Oxford: Hart Publishing.

de Olivera Gomes, Adalmir, Tomas de Aquino Guimaraes, and Luiz Akutsu. 2016. 'The Relationship between Judicial Staff and Court Performance: Evidence from Brazilian State Courts'. *International Journal for Court Administration* 8 (1): 12–19.

de Martino, Fabio Nunes. 2021. 'The Judicial Branch Seen from the Inside: The Performance of Judicial Assistants as Invisible Characters in the Brazilian Decision-Making Process'. PhD diss., Fluminense Federal University.

Devins Neil, and David Klein. 2017. 'The Vanishing Common Law Judge?' *University of Pennsylvania Law Review* 595 (165): 621–22.

Deyneli, Fatih, and Peter Mascini. 2020. 'Utility Maximizing Judges and Judicial Assistants: Testing Rational Choice Theory in 22 EU Countries'. *International Journal for Court Administration* 11 (3): 1–15.

Disant, Mathieu. 2019. 'Synthèse générale des travaux'. In Association des Cours Constitutionnelles Francophones (ACCF), Bulletin no. 13, April 2019, Actes de la conférence organisée pour le 20e anniversaire de l'ACCPUF, November 2017, 107–18.

Ditslear, Corey, and Lawrence Baum. 2001. 'Selection of Law Clerks and Polarization in the U.S. Supreme Court'. *Journal of Politics* 63 (3): 869–85.

Dzmitryieva, Aryna. 2017. 'Case Selection in the Russian Constitutional Court: The Role of Legal Assistants'. *Laws* 6 (3): 1–23.

Dzmitryieva, Aryna. 2021. 'Becoming a Judge in Russia: An Analysis of Judicial Biographies'. *Europe-Asia Studies* 73 (1): 131–56.

Ejima, Akiko. 2017. 'Clerks of Constitutional Courts and Supreme Courts'. In *Max Planck Encyclopedia of Comparative Constitutional Law* (MPECCoL), edited by Rainer Grote, Frauke Lachmann, and Rudiger Wolfrum, last updated December 2017. https://oxcon.ouplaw.com/display/10.1093/law-mpeccol/law-mpeccol-e575?rskey=AderCB&result=1&prd=MPECCOL, accessed 3 December 2023.

Engel, Christoph, and Keren Weinshall. 2020. 'Manna from Heaven for Judges—Judges' Reaction to a Quasi-Random Reduction in Caseload'. *Journal of Empirical Legal Studies* 17 (4): 641–897. https://doi.org/10.1111/jels.12265.

Epps, Willie, and Jonathan Warren. 2021. 'The Who, What, When, Where, Why, and How of Clerking: Told by a Federal Judge and His Former Law Clerk'. *University of Missouri-Kansas City Law Review* 90 (2): 295–312.

Ernst, Wolfgang. 2012. 'Abstimmen über Rechtserkenntnis'. *Juristenzeitung* 67 (12): 637–648.

Ernst, Wolfgang. 2016. *Rechtserkenntnis durch Richtermehrheiten*. Tübingen: Mohr Siebeck.

Esen, Selin. 2018. 'Constitutional Court of Turkey (Anayasa Mahkemesi)'. In *Max Planck Encyclopedia of Comparative Constitutional Law* (MPECCoL), edited by Rainer Grote, Frauke Lachmann, and Rudiger Wolfrum, last updated January 2018. https://oxcon.oup law.com/display/10.1093/law-mpeccol/law-mpeccol-e540?rskey=lKvMUa&result=1&prd= MPECCOL, accessed 3 December 2023.

Fogel, Jeremy, Mary Hoopes, and Liu Goodwin. 2022. 'Law Clerk Selection and Diversity: Insights from Fifty Sitting Judges of the Federal Courts of Appeal'. *Harvard Law Review*, forthcoming. Available at SSRN: https://ssrn.com/abstract=4290102 or http://dx.doi.org/ 10.2139/ssrn.4290102, accessed 3 December 2023.

Funk, Markus, Andrew Boutros, and Virginia Kendall. 2022. 'Betraying the Bench: Could the SCOTUS Leaker Face Criminal Charges?' *Bloomberg Law* 11 May. https://news.bloomberg law.com/us-law-week/betraying-the-bench-could-the-scotus-leaker-face-criminal-char ges, accessed 3 December 2023.

Grendstad, Gunnar, William Shaffer, Jørn Øyrehagen Sunde, and Eric N. Waltenburg. 2020a. 'From Backlogs to Quality Assurance. The Development of Law Clerk Units at Norwegian Courts'. *International Journal for Court Administration* 11 (3): 1–17.

Grendstad, Gunnar, William Shaffer, Jørn Øyrehagen Sunde, and Eric N. Waltenburg. 2020b. *Proactive and Powerful: Law Clerks and the Institutionalization of the Norwegian Supreme Court*. The Hague: Eleven International Publishing.

Groves, Matthew, and Russell Smyth. 2004. 'A Century of Judicial Style: Changing Patterns in Judgment Writing on the High Court 1903–2001'. *Federal Law Review* 32 (2): 255–80.

Haimerl, Maria. 2014. 'Agent der Neuen oder der Alten Ordnung? Die politische Rolle des ägyptischen Verfassungsgerichts nach der ägyptischen Revolution 2011'. Working Paper 12/ 2014. Center for North African and Middle Eastern Politics, Freie Universität Berlin.

Hanretty, Chris. 2020. A *Court of Specialists. Judicial Behavior on the UK Supreme Court*. New York: Oxford University Press.

Hellmann, Vanessa. 2021. 'Blick in die Box: Zur Arbeit der wissenschaftlichen Mitarbeiterinnen am Bundesverfassungsgericht'. In *Reform des Bundesverfassungsgerichts*, edited by Thomas Gawron, Oliver Lembcke, and Robert von Ooyen, 100–17. Berlin: Ducker & Humboldt.

Herman, Michael John. 1975. 'Law Clerking at the Supreme Court of Canada'. *Osgoode Hall Law Journal* 13 (2): 279–92.

Hiéramente, Mayeul. 2020. 'Der "Dritte Senat" des Bundesverfassungsgerichts: Zur Rolle der Wissenschaftlichen Mitarbeiter'. *Zeitschrift für Rechtspolitik* 2020 (2): 56–58.

Holvast, Nina. 2016. 'The Power of the Judicial Assistant/Law Clerk: Looking Behind the Scenes at Courts in The United States, England and Wales, and the Netherlands'. *International Journal for Court Administration* 7 (2): 10–18. http://doi.org/10.18352/ijca.200.

Holvast, Nina. 2017. *In the Shadow of the Judge: The Involvement of Judicial Assistants in Dutch District Courts*. The Hague: Eleven International Publishing.

Holvast, Nina and Mascini, Peter. 2020. "Is the Judge or the Clerk Making the Decision? Measuring the Influence of Judicial Assistants via an Experimental Survey among Dutch District Court Judges." *International Journal for Court Administration* 11 (3): 1–19. https:// doi.org/10.36745/ijca.358.

Johnson, Timothy, David Stras, and Ryan Black. 2014. 'Advice from the Bench (Memo): Clerk Influence on Supreme Court Oral Arguments'. *Marquette Law Review* 98 (1): 21–42.

Jones, John. 1991. 'Some Ethical Considerations for Judicial Clerks'. *Georgetown Journal of Legal Ethics* 4 (4): 771–90.

Kamiya, Masako. 2011. '"Chōsakan": Research Judges Toiling at the Stone Fortress'. *Washington University Law Review* 88 (6): 1601–29.

Katsas, Gregory. 2021. 'Justice Thomas Joins the Supreme Court'. *Harvard Journal of Law & Public Policy Per Curiam* 2021 (1): 1–9.

Kearney, Joseph. 2014. 'A Truth about Career Law Clerk'. *Marquette Law Review* 98 (1): 13–20.

Kelemen, Katalin, and Max Steuer. 2019. 'Constitutional Court of Hungary'. In *Max Planck Encyclopedia of Comparative Constitutional Law* (MPECCoL), edited by Rainer Grote, Frauke Lachmann, and Rudiger Wolfrum, last updated July 2019. https://oxcon.ouplaw.com/display/10.1093/law-mpeccol/law-mpeccol-e802?rskey=GqYV4e&result=1&prd=MPECCOL, accessed 3 December 2023.

Kenney, Sally. 2000. 'Beyond Principals and Agents, Seeing Courts as Organizations by Comparing Référendaires at the European Court of Justice and Law Clerks at the US Supreme Court'. *Comparative Political Studies* 33 (5): 593–625. https://doi.org/10.1177/0010414000033005002.

Kiefel, Susan. 2020. 'An Australian Perspective on Collective Judging'. In *Counting Votes and Weighing Opinions: Collective Judging in Comparative Perspective*, edited by Birke Häcker and Wolfgang Ernst, 47–56. Cambridge: Intersentia Publishing.

Kosař, David, and Vyhnánek, Ladislav. 2020. 'The Constitutional Court of Czechia'. In *The Max Planck Handbook in European Public Law*, Vol. 3, edited by Armin von Bogdandy, Peter Huber and Christoph Grabenwarter, 120–81. Oxford: OxfordUniversity Press.

Kranenpohl, Uwe. 2010. *Hinter dem Schleier des Beratungsgeheimnisses*. Wiesbaden: VS Verlag.

Kranenpohl, Uwe. 2016. 'Decision Making at the German Federal Constitutional Court.' In *Constitutional Courts in Comparison: The US Supreme Court and the German Federal Constitutional Court*, edited by Ralf Rogowski and Thomas Gawron, 146–64. New York: Berghahn Books.

Kromphardt, Christopher. 2014. 'Fielding an Excellent Team: Law Clerk Selection and Chambers Structure at the U.S. Supreme Court'. *Marquette Law Review* 98 (1): 289–311.

Kromphardt, Christopher David. 2015a. 'How Law Clerks Influence Information at the U.S. Supreme Court'. PhD dissertation, University of Alabama.

Kromphardt, Christopher. 2015b. 'US Supreme Court Law Clerks as Information Sources'. *Journal of Law and Courts* 3 (2): 277–304.

Kurishima, Tomoaki. 2017. 'Die Janusköpfigkeit des OGH als Revisions- und Verfassungsgericht. Gegenwartsprobleme und Zukunftsperspektiven'. *Zeitschrift für Japanisches Recht* 22 (44): 143–98.

Lane, David. 2005. 'Bush v. Gore, Vanity Fair, and a Supreme Court Law Clerk's Duty of Confidentiality'. *Georgetown Journal of Legal Ethics* 18 (3): 863–80.

Law, David. 2015 'Judicial Comparativism and Judicial Diplomacy'. *University of Pennsylvania Law Review* 163: 927–1033.

Lienhard, Andreas, and Peter Bieri. 2017. 'Gerichtsschreiberjustiz'. *Justice-Justiz-Giustizia* (4): 2–6.

Lübbe-Wolf, Gertrude. 2022. *Beratungskulturen: Wie Verfassungsgerichte arbeiten, und wovon es abhängt, ob sie integrieren oder polarisieren*. Berlin: Konrad-Adenauer-Stiftung e.V.

Macfarlane, Emmett. 2013. *Governing from the Bench: The Supreme Court of Canada and the Judicial Role*. Vancouver: UBC Press.

Martin, Andrew Flavelle. 2020. 'Legal Ethics and Judicial Law Clerks: A New Doctrinal Account'. *University of New Brunswick Law Journal* 71: 248–74.

Mascini, Peter, and Nina Holvast. 2020. 'Explaining Judicial Assistants' Influence on Adjudication with Principal–Agent Theory and Contextual Factors'. *International Journal for Court Administration* 11 (3): 1–18.

Mascini, Peter, and Holvast Nina. 2023. 'Does Delegation of Drafting Duties to Law Clerks Result in Judgments that Show Lack of Confidence in Terms of Writing Style? A Stylometric Analysis'. *Journal of Law and Courts*, forthcoming. doi: 10.1017/jlc.2023.10, accessed 3 December 2023.

Masing, Johannes. 2019. 'Entscheidung in unterschiedlichen Spruchkörpern: Einblicke in die innere Verfassung des Bundesverfassungsgerichts'. In *Verfassungsentwicklung II. Verfassungsentwicklung durch Verfassungsgerichte (Deutsch-Japanisches Verfassungsgespräch 2017)*, edited by Matthias Jestaedt and Hidemi Suzuki, 177–93. Tübingen: Mohr Siebeck.

Masing, Johannes. 2021. 'Das Bundesverfassungsgericht'. In *Handbuch des Verfassungsrechts. Darstellung in transnationaler Perspektive*, edited by Matthias Herdegen, Johannes Masing, Ralf Poscher, and Klaus Ferdinand Gärditz, § 15. Munich: C. H. Beck.

Massing, Otwin. 2016. 'The Legal Assistants at the German Federal Constitutional Court: A Black Box of Research?' In *Constitutional Courts in Comparison: The US Supreme Court and the German Federal Constitutional Court*, edited by Ralf Rogowski and Thomas Gawron, 180–87. New York: Berghahn Books.

Mauro, Tony. 2014. 'Diversity and Supreme Court Law Clerks'. *Marquette Law Review* 98 (1): 361–66.

McAlister, Merritt. 2021. 'Crocker: The Clerkship–Academia Continuum'. *Judicateur* 105 (5): 5–7.

McAlister, Merritt. 2022. 'Rebuilding the Federal Circuit Courts'. *Northwestern University Law Review* 116 (5): 1138–224.

McInnes, Mitchell, Janet Bolton, and Natalie Derzko. 1994. 'Clerking at the Supreme Court of Canada'. *Alberta Law Review* 33 (1): 58–79.

McKeown, M. Margaret. 2021. 'The Judiciary Steps up to the Workplace Challenge'. *Northwestern University Law Review Online* 116: 275–305.

Molloy, Donald. 2019. 'Designated Hitters, Pinch Hitters, and Bat Boys: Judges Dealing with Judgment and Inexperience, Career Clerks or Term Clerks'. *Law and Contemporary Problems* 82 (2): 133–56.

Nesterchuk, Tetyana. 2013. 'The View from Behind the Bench: The Role of Judicial Assistants in the UK Supreme Court'. In *Judge and Jurist: Essays in Memory of Lord Rodger of Earlsferry*, edited by Andrew Burrows, David Johnston, and Reinhard Zimmermann, 98–110. Oxford: Oxford University Press. https://doi.org/10.1093/acprof:oso/9780199677344.003.0011.

Narechania, Tejas. 2022. 'Certiorari in Important Cases'. *Columbia Law Review* 122 (4): 923–1018.

Ojima, Akira, and Naoki Onishi. 2020. 'Collective Judging by Collegiate Courts in Japan'. In *Counting Votes and Weighing Opinions: Collective Judging in Comparative Perspective*, edited by Birke Häcker and Wolfgang Ernst, 207–24. Cambridge: Intersentia Publishing.

Oldfather, Chad. 2021. 'A Job for a Year, an Example for a Lifetime: Clerking for Judge Jane Richards Roth'. In *Of Courtiers and Princes: Stories of Lower Court Clerks and their Judges*, edited by Todd Peppers, 288–304. Charlottesville: University of Virginia Press.

Oldfather Chad, and Todd C. Peppers. 2014. 'Judicial Assistants or Junior Judges: The Hiring, Utilization and Influence of Law Clerks'. *Marquette Law Review* 98 (1): 1–12.

Paterson, Alan. 2013. *Final Judgment: The Last Law Lords and the Supreme Court*. Oxford: Hart Publishing.

Peppers, Todd. 2006. *Courtiers of the Marble Palace: The Rise and Influence of the Supreme Court Law Clerk*. Standford: Stanford University Press.

Peppers, Todd. 2012. 'Of Leakers and Legal Briefers: The Modern Supreme Court Law Clerk'. *Charleston Law Review* 7 (1): 95–110.

Peppers, Todd. 2019. '"The Best and the Brightest" Clerks: Why the Justices Should Look Beyond Harvard and Yale'. *The National Law Journal*, 23 September. https://www.law.com/nationallawjournal/2019/09/23/the-best-and-the-brightest-clerks-why-the-justices-should-look-beyond-harvard-and-yale/?slreturn=20220912080156, accessed 3 December 2023.

Peppers, Todd, ed. 2021. *Of Courtiers and Princes: Stories of Lower Court Clerks and Their Judges*. Charlottesville: University of Virginia Press.

Peppers, Todd, and Clare Cushman, eds. 2015. *Of Courtiers and Kings: More Stories of Supreme Court Law Clerks and Their Justices (Constitutionalism and Democracy)*. Charlottesville: University of Virginia Press.

Peppers, Todd, Michael Giles, and Bridget Tainer-Parkins. 2007. 'The Hiring and Utilization of Federal District Court Law Clerks'. Available at SSRN https://papers.ssrn.com/sol3/papers.cfm?abstract_id=1022623 (accessed 30 December 2023).

Peppers, Todd, Michael Giles, and Bridget Tainer-Parkins. 2008. 'Inside Judicial Chambers: How Federal District Court Judges Select and Use their Law Clerks'. *Albany Law Review* 71 (2): 623–46.

Peppers, Todd, Michael Giles, and Bridget Tainer-Parkins. 2014. 'Surgeons or Scribes: The Role of United States Court of Appeals Law clerks in Appellate Triage'. *Marquette Law Review* 98 (1): 313–32.

Peppers, Todd, and Christopher Zorn. 2008. 'Law Clerk Influence on Supreme Court Decision Making: An Empirical Assessment'. *DePaul Law Review* 58 (1): 51–78.

Pether, Penelope. 2007. 'Sorcerers, Not Apprentices: How Judicial Clerks and Staff Attorneys Impoverish U.S. Law'. *Arizona State Law Journal* 39 (1): 1–68.

Posner, Richard A. 1985. *The Federal Courts: Crisis and Reform*. Cambridge: Harvard University Press.

Posner, Richard A. 2006. 'The Courthouse Mice'. *The New Republic*, 5–12 June : 32

Pou Giménez, Francisca. 2017. Changing the Channel: Broadcasting Deliberations in the Mexican Supreme Court. In *Justices and Journalists: The Global Perspective*, edited by Richard Davis and David Taras, 209–34. Cambridge: Cambridge University Press.

Quaas, Michael. 2022. 'Der wissenschaftliche Mitarbeiter beim Bundesverfassungsgericht und den Verfassungsgerichten der Länder im Rahmen einer Verfassungsbeschwerde'. *Das Deutsche Verwaltungsblatt* 2022 (16): 937–47.

Renauld, Bernadette. 2019. 'La collaboration entre le juge rapporteur et son assistant en Belgique'. *l'ACCPUF* 13 (April): 33–35.

Rhinehart, Lynn. 1994. 'Is There Gender Bias in the Judicial Law Clerk Selection Process'. *Georgetown Law Journal* 83 (2): 575–604.

Rosenthal, Jeffrey, and Albert H. Yoon. 2011. 'Judicial Ghostwriting: Authorship on the Supreme Court'. *Cornell Law Review* 96 (6): 1307–44.

Ruiz González, Ana María. 2019. 'Supreme Court of Justice of Costa Rica (Corte Suprema de Justicia de Costa Rica)', (last updated July 2016). In Max Planck Encyclopedia of Comparative Constitutional Law (MPECCoL), edited by Rainer Grote, Frauke Lachmann, and Rudiger Wolfrum, https://oxcon.ouplaw.com/display/10.1093/law-mpeccol/law-mpeccol-e525?rskey=D3dJRu&result=1&prd=MPECCOL, accessed 3 December 2023.

Samuels, Alec. 1974. 'Magistrates' Clerk'. *Journal of Criminal Law* 38 (2): 169–84.
Sanders, Anne. 2020 'Judicial Assistants in Europe—A Comparative Analysis'. *International Journal for Court Administration* 11 (3): 1–18.
Sanders, Anne. 2019. 'Summary of the responses to the questionnaire for the preparation of the CCJE Opinion No. 22 (2019) on "The role of court clerks and legal assistants within the courts and their relationships with judges"'. Consultative Council of European Judges Working Document (CCJE(2019)2Prov4). https://rm.coe.int/summary-of-the-responses-to-the-questionnaire-for-the-preparation-of-0/168093f579, accessed 31 May 2023.
Shapiro, Carolyn. 2009. 'The Law Clerk Proxy Wars: Secrecy, Accountability, and Ideology in the Supreme Court'. *Florida State University Law Review* 37 (1): 101–36.
Shin, Yoon Jin. 2022. 'Constitutional Court of Korea'. In *Max Planck Encyclopedia of Comparative Constitutional Law* (MPECCoL), edited by Rainer Grote, Frauke Lachmann, and Rudiger Wolfrum, last updated June 2022. https://oxcon.ouplaw.com/display/10.1093/law-mpeccol/law-mpeccol-e536?rskey=WTOjDl&result=1&prd=MPECCOL, accessed 3 December 2023.
Simma, Bruno, and Jan Ortgies. 2019. 'Deliberation and Drafting: International Court of Justice (ICJ)'. In *Max Planck Encyclopedia of International Procedural Law*, edited by H. Ruiz Fabri, last updated January 2019. https://opil.ouplaw.com/view/10.1093/law-mpeipro/e3399.013.3399/law-mpeipro-e3399, accessed 3 December 2023.
Sorenson, Charles. 2008. 'Are Law Clerks Fair Game: Invading Judicial Confidentiality'. *Valparaiso University Law Review* 43 (1): 1–8.
Sossin, Lorne. 1996. 'The Sounds of Silence: Law Clerks, Policy Making, and the Supreme Court of Canada'. *University of British Columbia Law Review* 30 (2): 279–308.
Stadelmann, Thomas. 2020. 'Collective Judging at the Swiss Supreme Court'. In *Collective Judging in Comparative Perspective: Counting Votes and Weighing Opinions*, edited by Birke Häcker and Wolfgang Ernst, 181–193. Cambridge: Intersentia.
Streho, Imola. 2017. 'The Référendaires, the Chambers, Staffing and Recruitment Matters'. In *The New EU Judiciary: An Analysis of Current Judicial Reforms*, edited by Emmanuel Guinchard and Marie-Pierre Granger, 213–20. Alphen aan den Rijn: Wolters Kluwer.
Swanson, Rick, and Stephen Wasby. 2008. 'Good Stewards: Law Clerk Influence in State High Courts'. *The Justice System Journal* 29 (1): 24–46.
Szmer, John, Erin Kaheny, and Robert Christensen. 2014. 'Taking a Dip in the Supreme Court Clerk Pool: Gender-Based Discrepancies in Clerk Selection'. *Marquette Law Review* 98 (1): 261–88.
Toader, Tudorel, and Marieta Safta. 2016. 'Judges and Assistant Magistrates within Constitutional Courts. *Constitutional News* 2016 (2), 93–109. doi:10.47743/rdc-2016-2-006.
Tyler, Amanda. 2021. 'Lessons Learned from Justice Ruth Bader Ginsburg'. *Columbia Law Review* 121 (Special Issue): 741–58.
Uebersax, Peter. 2018. 'Art. 24'. In *Basler Kommentar zum Bundesgerichtsgesetz*, edited by Marcel Alekander Niggli, Peter Uebersax, Hans Wiprächtiger, and Lorenz Kneubühler, 195–216. Basel: Schulhess.
Vallejo, Gonzalez. 2020. 'Hercules in the Colombian Constitutional Court'. *Baltic Journal of Law and Politics* 13 (1): 1–23.
Ward, Artemus. 2016. 'Junior Varsity Judges? Law Clerks in the Decisional Process of the U.S. Supreme Court'. In *Constitutional Courts in Comparison: The US Supreme Court and the German Federal Constitutional Court*, edited by Ralf Rogowski and Thomas Gawron, 165–79. New York: Berghahn.

Ward, Artemus. 2017. 'Law Clerks'. In *The Oxford Handbook of US Judicial Behavior*, edited by Lee Epstein, Gunnar Grendstad, Urška Šadl, and Keren Weinshall, 100–25. Oxford: Oxford University Press.

Ward, Artemus, and Stephen L. Wasby. 2010. 'Get a Life: On Interviewing Law Clerks'. *Justice System Journal* 31 (2): 125–43.

Ward, Artemus, and David L. Weiden. 2006. *Sorcerers' Apprentices: 100 Years of Law Clerks at the United States Supreme Court*. New York: New York University Press.

Wasby, Stephan. 2005. 'A Judicial Secretary's Many Roles: Working with an Appellate Judge and Clerks'. *Journal of Appellate Practice and Process* 7 (1): 151–66.

Wasby, Stephan. 2008. 'Clerking for an Appellate Judge: A Close Look'. *Seton Hall Circuit Review* 5 (1): 54–55.

Wasby, Stephen. 2014. 'The World of Law Clerks: Tasks, Utilization, Reliance, and Influence'. *Marquette Law Review* 98 (1): 111–13.

Wassermann, Howard. 2021. 'Academic Feeder Judges: Are Clerkships the Key to Academia?' *Judicature* 105 (1): 61–74.

Weber, Ruth Katharina. 2019. *Der Begründungsstil von Conseil constitutionnel und Bundesverfassungsgericht. Eine vergleichende Analyse der Spruchpraxis*. Tübingen: Mohr Siebeck.

Wilner, Joshua. 2011. 'To Be or Not to Be? Some Legal Ethics for Judicial Law Clerks'. *Canadian Bar Review* 89 (3): 611–42.

Yoon, Albert. 2014. 'Law Clerks and the Institutional Design of the Federal Judiciary'. *Marquette Law Review* 98 (1): 131–50.

Young, Katharine. 2007. 'Open Chambers: High Court Associates and Supreme Court Clerks Compared'. *Melbourne University Law Review* 31 (2): 646–67.

Zhang, Angela Huyue. 2016. 'The Faceless Court'. *University of Pennsylvania Journal of International Law* 38 (1): 71–135.

Zhang, Angela Huyue. 2020. 'The Faceless Court'. Verfassungsblog, 3 June 2020. https://verfassungsblog.de/the-faceless-court/, accessed 3 December 2023.

Zuck, Rüdiger. 2015. 'Die Wissenschaftlichen Mitarbeiter des Bundesverfassungsgerichts'. In *Das Bundesverfassungsgericht im politischen System*, edited by Robert van Ooyen and Martin Möllers, 443–57. Wiesbaden: Springer VS.

PART V

ADVOCACY, LITIGATION, AND APPELLATE REVIEW

CHAPTER 21

LAWYERING IN THE PRIVATE SECTOR

CHING-FANG HSU AND YUN-CHIEN CHANG

1. Introduction

While judicial behaviour is an established and well-recognized independent research field and has attracted attention from both legal scholars and political scientists, the study of behaviours by lawyers appears to be tangential to the study of judicial behaviours and has attracted legal scholars' interests only.

Some lawyers work in or for the government (like prosecutors), whereas others work in the private sector. Due to division of labour, this chapter focuses on private sector lawyering and only includes studies that investigate lawyers' role in courts and alternative dispute resolution mechanisms. Some important topics, due to word limitation, are not covered in this chapter. One such topic is why and to what extent lawyers undertake pro bono and low bono work, which we discuss in a recent work (Hsu, Chiang, and Chang 2024). Other important aspects of lawyering include, for instance, the lawyer–client relationship (e.g. Kritzer 1984; Mather 2003) and lawyers' ethics (e.g. Levin and Mather 2012). Corporate lawyers, of course, also play a key role in non-litigation scenarios such as making deals. Bates, Lv, and Neyland (2022), for instance, find that law firms representing issuers have a material impact on economic outcomes in the initial public offering process. Chang and Lin (2024, forthcoming) find that lawyer representation in trespass lawsuits is associated with a higher percentage of post-litigation bargaining and conjecture that attorneys shield the two parties from engaging with each other, thus preventing mutual animosity from arising.

The uncontroversial classic in the field of private sector legal behaviour is Marc Galanter's 1974 'have' versus 'have-not' framework (Galanter 1974). We group many follow-up studies under this framework in the second section of this chapter. While section 2 is about how well-represented clients gain an edge in courts and other forums, section 3 takes a step back and looks into how the interests of clients are aligned with those of attorneys. The economic literature calls this the principal–agent problem, and a number of studies discuss how the arrangement of attorney fees, the driver of attorneys' (short-term) incentives, changes the dynamics between clients and private sector lawyers. Section 3 also touches on the two-way selection between private sector lawyers and their clients. Lawyers encourage their clients to pursue a claim, drop a claim, settle, or fight all the way to the supreme court, or discourage them from doing so. Potential litigants shop for attorneys they like and may be deterred by the prospect of negative returns from pursuing their claims further. Sections 2 and 3 are 'comparative' in the sense that many referenced studies use non-US and non-UK data. We discuss these works as if research findings derived from any country could be mixed and compared, regardless of the different institutional background. Section 4, drawing on the comparative research design proposed by Ran Hirschl (2007), demonstrates how studies on the behaviours of private sector lawyers could benefit from a true—and careful—comparative research design that investigates the effect of lawyering with data from two or more countries. For us, this is the future of the studies of lawyer behaviour. Section 5 concludes.

2. Galanter's Party Capability Theory

In 1974, Galanter published 'Why the "Haves" Come Out Ahead: Speculations on the Limits of Legal Change', which analyses the distributive effects of legal processes. He divided litigants into two types, the one-shotters (usually the 'have-nots', who have only infrequent engagements with the courts) and the repeat players (generally the 'haves', who anticipate multiple lawsuits over time). The repeat players have tangible and intangible resources to pursue long-term interests, and with repetitive interactions with the legal system, repeat players are likely to produce rules that reinforce their advantages. This framework sets out a research agenda to study the structural advantages that the repeat players may enjoy in the legal system (e.g. Boyd 2015). In particular, lawyers are perceived as critical resources that contribute to a party's capability in the legal process. Lawyers play a pivotal role in shaping litigation outcomes, inducing redistribution, and hence facilitating equality through law.

Section 2.1 reviews whether representation by lawyers affects litigation outcomes. Section 2.2 summarizes the attorney effects outside of trials, including settlement and non-court fora. Section 2.3 inquires about the mechanism by which representation by lawyers affects these outcomes, especially in the court context.

2.1 Judicial Outcomes

Since Galanter (1974), scholars have further empirically tested lawyers' role in influencing judicial outcomes (for a recent review, see Yoon 2017, 270–72). In the United States, scholars have found evidence both at the level of the Supreme Court and the

Court of Appeals that lawyers do matter in affecting case outcomes (McGuire 1995; Haire, Lindquist, and Hartley 1999; Johnson 2001; Black and Owens 2016; Nelson and Epstein 2022). In recent decades, a new development has been the emergence of an elite supreme court bar, in which a small group of lawyers dominate the representation before the US Supreme Court (Lazarus 2008; Bhatia 2012; Perry Jr. 2020) (a similar elite bar also emerged in the field of patent law, see Gugliuzza 2019, 2020). Between 2013 and 2019, out of the 465 cases with oral arguments, nine law firms were in charge of 157 cases, almost one-third of the total, and the top twenty lawyers handled more than half the total number of cases. The trend is in stark contrast to the practice in the 1980s, when the majority of lawyers appearing before the bench were first-timers, only 20 per cent of whom had made more than one appearance. The elite bar has become a group of identifiable repeat players in front of the US Supreme Court (Perry Jr. 2020).

Lawyers' efficacy in litigation, most notably at the highest level of the judicial system, is not limited to the United States. In other similar systems, scholars have investigated the party capability theory with data from the Canadian Supreme Court (Szmer, Johnson, and Sarver 2007), the High Court of Australia (Smyth 2000), the South African Supreme Court (Haynie and Sill 2007), the Israeli High Court of Justice (Dotan 1999), the Philippine Supreme Court (Haynie 1994, 1995), and the Singaporean Supreme Court (Chesterman 2020). This line of research has found general support that good legal behaviour by lawyers is a critical resource. For example, in Israel, when 'have-nots' are represented by legal counsel, the 'haves' did not come out ahead. In fact, despite the activist nature of the Israeli High Court of Justice, representation by lawyers is still a deciding factor for success (Dotan 1999).

While the 'haves' retain good lawyers or seek legal advice, the 'have nots' may appear *pro se* or can only afford less capable attorneys (Huang, Lin, and Chen 2014). Good lawyers, as compared to less capable colleagues, have at least two important measurements: lawyers' previous success and litigation experience. Using the South African appellate court to test the two, scholars have found that previous *successes* of advocates are a better predictor of litigation outcomes than the advocates' experience, and a far better predictor than litigant status and court ideology (Haynie and Sill 2007). But in Canada, litigation experience (measured by the average of all team members), along with litigation team size, exerts significant impact on the Canadian Supreme Court's decisions (Szmer, Johnson, and Sarver 2007, 293–95).

Another interesting variable is the ranking of lawyers—being Senior Counsel (formerly called Queen's Counsel) or not—and studies show that this is not a strong indicator of a favourable case outcome. In Canada, the designation of Queen's Counsel is not associated with a significant effect on the Canadian Supreme Court's decisions (Szmer, Johnson, and Sarver 2007, 294). In Singapore, Senior Counsel only outperform their opponents when they represent defendants/respondents but not plaintiffs/appellants, though the sample size in the study is quite small (Chesterman 2020, 31). Simply put, Queen's Counsels (or Senior Counsels) do not necessarily outperform other lawyers. In a related vein, using English data between 1996 and 2010, Hanretty (2016) finds no significant effect of having better-ranked counsel on case outcomes, at least for tax cases in the appellate courts. More specifically, representation by better-ranked lawyers might have a positive effect *only if* better-ranked lawyers receive cases that are substantially more difficult to win. Yet the fact that better-ranked lawyers do receive substantially more difficult cases suggests that consumers of legal representation are sophisticated enough to ascertain the difficulty of a case *ex ante*, and select a lawyer on this basis.

Lawyers in civil law jurisdictions also serve as critical resources that boost litigants' capability in the legal process. Scholars have found evidence in Taiwan (Chen, Huang, and Lin 2015), China (He and Su 2013), Norway (Bjørnebekk et al. 2020), and Argentina (Muro et al. 2018) that representational advantage plays a critical role in attaining a favourable case outcome. At the Taiwanese Supreme Court, a party of higher status is able to mobilize superior legal representation that enhances the chance of success (Chen, Huang, and Lin 2015). Nonetheless, Chen, Huang, and Lin (2015) note that the party capability theory is insufficient to tell the whole story—Taiwanese judges' identification of themselves as part of government also leads them to strongly favour governmental litigants. In Argentina, scholars further use the Supreme Court's docket control to assess the role of legal counsel. Representational advantage does play a significant role as legal counsel has the ability to fulfil certain formal requirements. This is a crucial function because a large proportion of appeals were rejected on formal grounds, not on merits. In the courts in Shanghai, China, legal representation contributes to a party's chance of winning, although the disparity between one-shotters and repeat players seems to result from not only resource disparity but also the institutional nature of Chinese law and courts (He and Su 2013, 133–34).

In the literature of private lawyering, government is still a powerful actor aligning with capable counsel. Legal counsel is one of the determinant resources in litigation irrespective of the public versus private nature of litigants. More specifically, how private legal counsel contribute to the government's prevailing advantage in courts differs from case to case. For example, in Shanghai, China, the government has an overwhelming advantage in that it is so much more likely to be represented professionally than organization litigants and the majority of individual litigants. In fact, Chinese government agencies or state-owned enterprises are the biggest winners in courts—their win rate over private litigants is overwhelming. In cases against farmers, the government's win rate was 100 per cent, and 91.7 per cent and 94.1 per cent for cases against unknown individuals and companies, respectively. Legal representation matters but the disparity also points to the government's immense dominance (He and Su 2013, 133–34).

Lawyers also play a mediating function to reinforce the government's advantage. For example, the Israeli government enjoys extremely high success rates in litigation that reaches final judicial disposition. Dotan (1999, 1075) attributes the success to the Israeli government's 'special institutional position' and its strategy of high case settlement rates but also notes that lawyers are the key factor helping the have-nots to reach success in settlements; that is, the small number of government lawyers (about ten lawyers from the High Court of Justice Department) repeatedly represent in over 80 per cent of the petitions and settle in the vast majority of cases that reach the court. It might be the settlements that strongly served the have-nots, and later allowed the government lawyers to win the remaining cases that went to court (Dotan 1999, 1076). Huang, Chen, and Lin (2010) also find that criminal defendants represented by public defenders, as compared to those represented by legal aid attorneys, tend to have higher conviction rates but shorter sentences if they are convicted. The institutional characters for the two types of counsel and the pecuniary incentives they face explain the results. It is also interesting to observe the performance of lawyers who used to work in the office of solicitor general (OSG) in the United States; that is, to investigate whether the government's advantage would extend *through* lawyers even after they enter private practice. Black and Owens (2016) analysed all 7,993 lawyers who appeared in the 3,336 oral arguments at the Supreme Court between 1979 and 2014 and found very limited evidence to suggest a difference between former OSG lawyers and non-OSG lawyers.

Finally, a caveat is in order. Since the causal revolution, scholars have advanced rigorous research designs to identify and re-examine causal relationships in the study of behaviours by private sector lawyers. Greiner and Pattanayak (2011, 2175–84) point out that most of the dozens of studies before theirs are 'unworthy of credence' due to the lack of causal inference frameworks.[1] Greiner and Pattanayak (2011, 2125) use data from a real-world randomized experiment on legal representation, but 'could come to no firm conclusion regarding a use-of-representation effect on the win rate'. Later, Greiner, Pattanayak, and Hennessy (2013), using randomized controlled trials in the real world, find that full representation by attorneys leads to better outcomes for clients as compared to those who receive only limited legal assistance. Not all works cited and discussed in this chapter may stand the rigorous test of causal inference research designs, so readers beware! Still, we discuss works that show correlations, especially those from outside of the United States and the United Kingdom, where empirical studies on lawyering are hard to come by. We will return to the issues of causal inference below.

2.2 Settlement and Non-Court Fora

Trials and adjudications are the final stage of disputes and are the tip of the dispute iceberg. Lawyers also affect whether cases enter trial. That is, lawyers could be instrumental in settlement decisions. There are two paradigmatic theories that explain why parties do not settle: divergent expectation theory (e.g. Landes 1971; Gould 1973; Posner 1973; Priest and Klein 1984) and asymmetric information theory (e.g. Bebchuk 1984; Reinganum and Wilde 1986; Spier 1992; Shavell 1996; Spier 2007; Klerman, Lee, and Liu 2018). Clearly, lawyers play an important role under both theories: represented parties are more likely than *pro se* parties to form a good estimate of how the court will rule, and with attorneys' help in the discovery process, parties are more likely to overcome their informational disadvantage. Hence, economic theories would predict that, other things being equal, represented parties are more likely to settle disputes than *pro se* parties. Huang (2008, 217), however, finds that attorney representation is negatively associated with settlement rates—represented parties settle less frequently as compared to pro se ones—and contends that it is due to the 'representation selection': 'a party's initial decision to litigate the case [leads] to him or her retaining counsel'.

A separate line of inquiry looks into how lawyers may make a difference in front of a different audience.[2] Gilad (2010) looks into British ombudsmen and finds a different logic of private lawyering. The ombudsman setting is interesting because of three characteristics: the cost is lower, the procedures are inquisitorial, and no formal precedents are at work, all working in favour of one-shotters and in less need of professional legal counsel. Two findings are worthy of note. Larger and more experienced firms do not necessarily fare better than smaller firms. Relatedly, complainants represented by professionals with relevant experience and expertise are not more successful than those who are not. In fact, the adjudicators tend to be cautious when handling professionally represented cases precisely because professionals have the capacity and attempt to use favourable decisions to constrain the adjudicators' discretion in the future. The inquisitorial procedures also offset the legal professionals' advantages in providing pertinent information. Therefore, 'professional representation was perceived as superfluous and even harmful for complainants' (Gilad 2010, 303). This study provides intriguing paths as to how lawyers may play an effective role in non-judge, non-court legal arenas.

2.3 Mechanisms of Lawyers' Effect

As the importance of legal counselling has been established, the logical next question is, what is it in lawyers that makes a difference in courts? That is, why does legal representation have its effect? This is the question of mechanism.

The existing works offer competing (though plausibly complementary) stories. The first plausible explanation of lawyers' influence is that lawyers provide credible information to courts and therefore affect the probability of litigation success (McGuire 1995; Johnson 2001; Black and Owens 2016).[3] Put differently, the haves and have-nots fare differently in court not because judges discriminate against the poor but because judges need credible information in rendering decisions, and (experienced) attorneys, as compared to parties themselves or inexperienced attorneys, provide more credible information to courts (McGuire 1995; Johnson 2001), particularly through hearings and oral arguments (Krehbiel, Chapter 27 of this *Handbook*). Thus, experienced attorneys (often retained by the rich) are associated with higher win rates.[4]

The second explanation is that certain characteristics of lawyer expertise, such as experience and specialization, correlate with case outcomes (Haire, Lindquist, and Hartley 1999; Nelson and Epstein 2022).[5] In particular, with frequent appearance in oral arguments before the bench, veteran lawyers become the actual repeat players bringing favourable outcomes irrespective of whether they represent the 'haves' or the 'have-nots' (McGuire 1995). Following the second channel of lawyer effects, two types of knowledge, specialized versus general legal knowledge, may be usefully distinguished, and it may be specialized knowledge, rather than general legal knowledge, which makes a difference. Kritzer (1998) finds evidence that non-lawyers with specialized knowledge and experience with a given forum or case type can be more effective in some circumstances than generalist lawyers with no prior experience. However, another study on immigration courts shows that specialized knowledge does not necessarily matter. Miller, Keith, and Holmes (2015) find that generalist lawyers with strong overall legal skills and experience perform better in trial than low-skilled lawyers with specialized knowledge.

Under the second paradigm, Sandefur (2015) conceptualizes legal expertise as a combination of *substantive expertise* and *relational expertise*. The former refers to professional training and knowledge of formal law, procedural rules, and legal documents, while the latter can be understood as insider knowledge of how to navigate the human relationship that exists in a given litigation context. Surprisingly, Sandefur (2015) finds that substantive knowledge explains little of lawyers' advantage as compared to *pro se* laypeople. By contrast, lawyers' impact appears in navigating simple procedures and assisting courts in following their own rules. In fact, legal representation functions as a signal of the merit of the case, and courts tend to give greater credence to arguments offered by lawyers who appear repeatedly before them than those by unknown lawyers—not to mention those by *pro se* parties. Here, the two explanations converge.

Relatedly, some scholars contrast lawyers and *non*-lawyers to identify the element of effective representation. Following Sandefur (2015), Carpenter, Mark, and Shanahan (2017) propose the concept of 'strategic expertise', which differentiates lawyers and non-lawyers: lawyers make choices in their work by connecting formal rules and training with the informal relationships they navigate in the course of that work. Using data from over 5,000 unemployment insurance appeal hearings in the United States, they found that non-lawyers can, indeed, help people through their experience with common court procedures and basic substantive legal concepts, and yet non-lawyers are not equipped to challenge judges on contested issues of substantive or procedural law in individual cases or advance novel legal claims. An interesting distinction is the source of knowledge: non-lawyers heavily rely on judges to provide essential knowledge about procedures and substantive law, while lawyers only see judges as their audience to be persuaded.

Finally, lawyers may affect case outcomes by manipulating the judicial process. Morrison, Pang, and Zytnick (2022) find that in the US bankruptcy courts, certain law firms exploit the transparency of the assignment of trustees to cases to increase their clients' probability of being assigned to favourable trustees, eventually getting more favourable court adjudications.

Overall, the mechanism with which clients may obtain effective legal representation is still incomplete.[6] This line of empirical research, therefore, leaves us with an open question and requires further investigation.

3. Attorney Fees and Case Selection

Attorneys are clients' agents, and attorneys' incentives do not always align with those of clients. Attorneys may charge fixed, hourly, contingent, or conditional fees, and according to standard economic theory, different fee schemes induce different attorney behaviours. In the law and economics literature, the different incentive schemes of hourly fees vis-à-vis contingent fees and their effect on settlement decisions, time spent on a case, and other issues have been analysed in detail (e.g. Danzon 1983; Miller 1987; Miceli and Segerson 1991; Thomason 1991; Dana and Spier 1993; Miceli 1994; Watts 1994; Cumming 2001; Deffains and Desrieux 2015). There are also empirical studies on the practice of contingent fee attorneys (e.g. Kritzer 1997; Kritzer and Krishnan 1999; Helland and Tabarrok 2003; Kritzer 2004). Conditional fees, a new form of attorney fee, have also been studied (Emons and Garoupa 2006; Hyde 2006). Chang and Tu (2020) study what drives attorneys who charge fixed fees to select cases.

A natural extension of this topic is to examine how clients (the principals) try to put attorneys in check, and how clients attempt to find the attorneys that best suit them (which, presumably, ameliorates the need for intensive monitoring). For instance, Chang and Tu (2020) find that the most prevalent concern for clients is to find attorneys who will listen to their stories.

Another important issue is how lawyers affect case selection. Put differently, lawyers encounter (potential) clients and have to decide whether to take the case, and, if so, whether to settle the dispute or bring it to courts. This is a principal–agent setting. Attorneys may try to convince clients to settle because settlement makes more financial sense for the attorneys, not for the clients. Attorneys may refuse to be an agent, even though bringing a dispute to courts has positive expected value for the principal.

It has been common sense since Priest and Klein (1984) that litigated cases are not a representative sample of all disputes (see also Eisenberg 1990; but cf. Helland, Klerman, and Lee 2018). It stands to reason that lawyers are a critical filter in selecting disputes to bring to courts. In a legal system where the plaintiff attorneys often charge contingent fees, like the United States, lawyers routinely turn away more than half of all potential clients (Hyman, Black, and Silver 2015, 1596–98), while in a legal system where plaintiff attorneys almost always charge fixed fees, like Taiwan, lawyers turn away only 10 per cent of potential clients (Chang and Tu 2020, 156).

These aforementioned studies estimate the extent to which lawyers filter out disputes from lawyers' angles—that is, the data is from surveying lawyers. The studies on paths to justice or legal consciousness provide data from disputants' angles. These studies often produce a 'dispute pyramid' or a flowchart that shows what percentage of 'justiciable problems' are brought by a relevant party to lawyers for legal advice and eventually brought to courts. By calculating the gap between the two steps (seeking legal advice and bringing litigation), a rough estimate of what can be called the 'lawyer filtering rate' can be reached. Table 21.1 summarizes the lawyer filtering rate in civil law, common law, and mixed jurisdictions, which range from nearly 25 per cent to almost 90 per cent.

Table 21.1 Lawyer filtering rate

Jurisdiction	Seeking legal advice, per 1000 disputes	Going to court, per 1000 disputes	Estimated lawyer filtering rate
	(1)	(2)	(3)=[(1)-(2)]/(1)
Taiwan†	61	47	23%
Japan†	87	21	76%
The Netherlands*	441	57	87%
Scotland	294	50	83%
England and Wales	303	91	70%
The U.S.	103	50	51%

Sources: Taiwan (Lin et al. 2016, 107); Japan (Murayama 2009, 274); Scotland (Genn and Paterson 2001, 162); the Netherlands (Velthoven and Voert 2008, 245); the U.S. (Miller and Sarat 1980–1981, 544); England and Wales (Genn 1999, 154).

Notes: †In Japan and Taiwan, the dispute pyramid shows the percentage of people seeking legal advice and that of people going to court. Not all litigants have sought legal advice, though. In other jurisdictions, the data sources show the percentage of people going to court *after* seeking legal advice.

* 44.1% of people sought advice, but not necessarily from lawyers.

Because the survey questions, definitions of terms, and methods are not exactly the same across countries, Table 21.1 is only an approximation of the selection effects of lawyers. This suggests fertile ground for future comparative research regarding how selective attorneys are in bringing disputes to courts. Ideally, future research could also control for merits of the case and the amount at stake, in addition to case types.

4. Toward Comparative Lawyering Behaviours

This *Handbook* is titled *Comparative Judicial Behaviour*, but so far this chapter has been barely comparative, other than reviewing empirical legal studies around the world.[7] That is, the current paradigm in the social-scientific study of the behaviour of private sector lawyers is still largely confined within national borders. While large, federalist nations tend to have internal variations in institutional environments, they appear to have been rarely exploited to study lawyers' behaviours.

A future research agenda for comparative lawyering behaviours is to conduct cross-country comparison to tease out the factors driving certain lawyer behaviours. Nonetheless, it is notoriously difficult to undertake causal inference in comparative law (Spamann 2009, 2015; Engel 2022). Hirschl (2007), in the comparative constitutional context, has advanced five research designs that help researchers stay close to the gold standard of causal inference. These designs are: the most similar cases, the most different cases, prototypical cases, the most difficult cases, and outlier cases.

Many comparative studies—what Zweigert and Kötz (1998) call 'national comparative law'—have been implicitly conducted with the logic of the most similar cases, as scholars in the common law jurisdictions tend to make comparisons among the Commonwealth countries and the United States, and East Asian countries look to German jurisprudence for inspiration and guidance. With social science lenses, the most similar cases attempt to identify one key institutional difference while holding other factors equal or similar. The difference in the key institutional feature is used to explain variation in outcomes (such as whether lawyers undertake *pro bono* work). One of us has compared the civil procedure reforms in Taiwan, Japan, and Germany around 2000 and examined why the reform in Japan failed to make an impact while the reform in Germany has been a success (Chang 2024). One explanation is that lawyers in Japan did not comply with the new discovery stipulation, and courts did not force them to do so, either. Due to the lack of case-level data, Chang was unable to dig deeper. Future studies like this with more detailed data may tease out not only what institutional factors affect lawyering behaviours but also how lawyering behaviours affect (or do not affect) institutions.

Under the most different cases design, the key institutional feature is similar, while other variables are different, so that researchers can examine whether the key institutional feature is critical in leading to certain outcomes. Chang and Hubbard (2021) use debt collection cases to test whether cases with clear facts and only monetary payments at issue would, as theories predict, lead to high settlement rates. The key institutional feature, the nature of debt collection cases, is similar in US federal circuit courts and ordinary courts in Taiwan, while lawyering practices in the United States and Taiwan are different in many aspects. For instance, attorneys in Taiwan mostly charge fixed (flat) fees in civil cases, while plaintiff attorneys in the United States often charge contingent or conditional fees and defendant attorneys often charge by the hour. In both countries, however, Chang and Hubbard (2021) find that debt collection cases show very similar patterns—very low settlement rates and very high default judgment rates. The finding of Chang and Hubbard (2021) not only challenges prior theories but also shows that lawyering practices do not influence how debt collection cases play out. Future studies that focus on the potential effects of lawyering would of course benefit from a more direct research design.

Under the design of prototypical cases, researchers compare the prototype countries to test existing theories. Chang and Klerman (2022) compare settlement rates in twenty-one of the world's top twenty-five economies, among them the prototypical countries such as the United States, the United Kingdom, France, Germany, and Japan. This study exemplifies the difficulty of conducting comparisons on the practice of law in different jurisdictions. While it is feasible to ascertain whether the contingent fee is prohibited and whether fee shifting is required (Reimann 2012), it is almost impossible to figure out how often hourly, flat, and contingent fees are used in each country. In a study on settlement rates, it is ideal if each country has publicized case-level data and recorded whether parties are represented in each case and what kind of fee arrangement is used. Nonetheless, only Taiwan has this type of data available. Chang and Klerman (2022) find that the settlement rate in, say, France is much lower than that in the United States and the United Kingdom, but without solid evidence of what percentage of litigants is represented by attorneys and how prevalent contingent fees are in represented cases, it is difficult to test theories regarding, say, whether legal representation affects settlement (Huang 2008). Chang and Klerman (2022) attempt to tease out, for instance, whether the discovery (or evidence disclosure) rule affects settlement (Huang 2009) but find it hard to come to a conclusion, partly because it is unclear how well litigation practices in various countries track their own laws on the books.

Using the design of the most difficult cases, scholars pick countries that are the least likely to identify relationships between an institutional feature and a certain outcome. Association between the feature and the outcome provides a *prima facie* case for the existence of such a relationship. In this spirit, Chang et al. (2017) conduct a comparative study on the relationship between non-pecuniary damages and pecuniary damages in the United States and Taiwan. In both countries, there is a debate as to whether pain and suffering damages or punitive damages (both non-pecuniary) have a rational relation with pecuniary damages (see e.g. Viscusi 1988, 1996; Eisenberg et al. 1997, 2006, 2010; Sunstein et al. 2002; Hersch and Viscusi 2004; Eisenberg and Wells 2006; Del Rossi and Viscusi 2010; Rachlinski 2016). For those who believe in the story of run-away juries, in or outside of medical malpractice cases, the United States is the most difficult case to establish the relationship between a more-or-less formulaic assessment of pecuniary damages and a completely discretionary assessment of non-pecuniary damages. Chang et al. (2017) show that, in the US state courts, be it bench trials or jury trials, in medical malpractice cases or car accident cases, after taking logarithmic values of the amount of damages, there are linear relationships in all four scenarios. In addition, in Taiwan, bench trials in medical malpractice cases and car accident cases also lead to a log-linear relationship. This type of research is particularly useful in the national comparative law setting. Suppose that policy-makers in a country are pondering whether to reform civil procedural law in response to criticisms that non-pecuniary damages are unpredictable. Unfortunately, the data infrastructure in that hypothetical country is insufficient to allow an empirical study of its own system. For that hypothetical country, empirical studies on the United States would be the most difficult case—if US juries could decide on non-pecuniary damages 'rationally', surely professional judges in the hypothetical country could be at least as good. While Chang et al. (2017) offer a better example for comparative judicial behaviours, future studies on comparative judicial behaviours would certainly benefit from such a design. For instance, if scholars could find that in a country where wealth is highly unequal and the civil procedure system is highly adversarial, and yet the haves and have-nots are equally likely to prevail, it would be a good study with the most difficult cases design.

Under the fifth research design, outlier cases, researchers pick a prevalent phenomenon that cannot be explained by existing theories to challenge the current paradigmatic theories and try to build new theories that can explain both the phenomenon in the outlier country and that in the countries on which the paradigmatic theories were built. Hsu, Chiang, and Chang (2024) note the well-documented phenomenon in Taiwan that corporate lawyers and successful solo practitioners are actively involved in *pro bono* projects but refuse to participate in the well institutionalized legal aid cases and use it to challenge the current studies on pro bono, which focus too much on corporate law firms in developed common law countries. As paradigmatic theories in judicial and lawyering behaviours are often developed against the institutional backgrounds in developed common law countries, developing and/or civil law countries are likely outliers.[8] Comparative lawyering studies that include these outlier countries thus would be fertile ground for developing more comprehensive theories.

5. Conclusion

This chapter selectively reviews the literature on lawyering in the private sector, in particular whether lawyers affect litigants' decisions to abandon their claims and settle and whether attorney representation affects adjudication outcomes, and, if so, why. As a part of a handbook with a comparative emphasis, this chapter draws on many studies conducted outside the United States and the United Kingdom, and, more importantly, attempts to compare the findings in a framework that brings us closer to making causal inference.

Acknowledgements

We thank Courtney Hillebrecht, Urška Šadl, Keren Weinshall, Matthew Wetstein, and participants in the *Oxford Handbook of Comparative Judicial Behaviour* Conference for helpful comments. Hsin-yi Han and Kuan-Ting Chen provided invaluable research assistance. Contribution: Hsu, 60 per cent; Chang, 40 per cent.

Notes

1 In the study of attorney effects in criminal cases, random assignments of public defenders in Abrams and Yoon (2007) and between public defenders and appointed counsel in Anderson and Heaton (2012) and Huang, Chen, and Lin (2010) avoid the selection effect. These studies fall into the domain of government lawyering.

2 Another interesting study looks at lawyers' performance in front of juries. Wood et al. (2011) examine the relationship between jurors' perception of attorneys and their verdicts. For the prosecution or plaintiff, positive perceptions of attorneys' sincerity, evidence presentation, and closing statements are significantly associated with favourable outcomes. Prior studies (Weld and Danzig 1940; Pyszczynski et al. 1981) note the framing effect of opening statements, whose effect is not significant for the plaintiffs studied by Wood et al. (2011). In contrast, the opening statement of defendants' attorneys makes an impact. Another

interesting result is that lawyer attitudes also have varying impacts. For plaintiffs' attorneys and prosecution, sincerity is negatively associated with the case result, but for defendants' attorneys, more aggression results in less favourable outcomes.

3 In the government lawyering context, for instance, the Office of the Solicitor General enjoys a built-in advantage (Black and Owens 2013; Feldman 2016).

4 Note that Black and Owens (2016) find that the Supreme Court does not tend to favour attorneys who have worked in the OSG.

5 Lin, Chang, and Chen (2018) show that in Taiwan, more experienced plaintiff attorneys in torts cases claim a higher amount of pain and suffering damages. Chang et al. (2015) and Chang et al. (2017) show that a higher amount of claimed pain and suffering damages, after controlling for observable case characteristics, still positively correlate with the amount of adjudicated pain and suffering damages. Hence, attorney experience may affect case outcomes indirectly.

6 Chen, Halberstam, and Yu (2017), in a working paper, find that in the US Supreme Court, the masculinity and femininity of the leading counsel's voice may affect case outcomes.

7 As Epstein, Sadl, and Weinshall (2021, 701) observe, in the legal literature, 'comparative' was often treated as coterminous with 'foreign'.

8 Another example is Lin and Chang (2018), who study the changes in corporate charters in stock exchanges in Shanghai, Shenzhen, Hong Kong, and Taiwan and find results opposite to predictions by theories developed in the US context.

References

Abrams, David S., and Albert H. Yoon. 2007. 'The Luck of the Draw: Using Random Case Assignment to Investigate Attorney Ability'. *The University of Chicago Law Review* 74 (4): 1145–77.

Anderson, James M., and Paul Heaton. 2012. 'How Much Difference Does the Lawyer Make? The Effect of Defense Counsel on Murder Case Outcomes'. *The Yale Law Journal* 122: 154–217.

Bates, Thomas W., Jin Roc Lv, and Jordan Neyland. 2022. 'Do Lawyers Matter in Initial Public Offerings?' http://dx.doi.org/10.2139/ssrn.4274529.

Bebchuk, Lucian Arye. 1984. 'Litigation and Settlement Under Imperfect Information'. *RAND Journal of Economics* 15 (3): 404–15.

Bhatia, Kedar S. 2012. 'Top Supreme Court Advocates of the Twenty-First Century'. *Journal of Law* 2: 561–82.

Bjørnebekk, Olav Laug, Gunnar Grendstad, William R. Scaffer, and Eric N. Waltenburg. 2020. 'Case Inertia and a Better Lawyer Secure Victory in Court'. *Retfærd* 43: 51–70.

Black, Ryan C., and Ryan J. Owens. 2013. 'A Built-In Advantage: The Office of the Solicitor General and the U.S. Supreme Court'. *Political Research Quarterly* 66 (2): 454–66.

Black, Ryan C., and Ryan J. Owens. 2016. 'The Success of Former Solicitors General in Private Practice: Costly and Unnecessary'. *Michigan State Law Review* 2016: 325–68.

Boyd, Christina L. 2015. 'Litigant Status and Trial Court Appeal Mobilization'. *Law & Policy* 37 (4): 294–323.

Carpenter, Anna E., Alyx Mark, and Colleen F. Shanahan. 2017. 'Trial and Error: Lawyers and Nonlawyer Advocates'. *Law & Social Inquiry* 42 (4): 1023–57.

Chang, Yun-chien. 2024. 'Comparative Law as Double Causal Reasoning: Using Empirical Studies on How Civil Procedural Law Reform Affects Settlement Rates as Examples'. *Academia Sinica Law Journal* (34): 81–152.

Chang, Yun-chien, Theodore Eisenberg, Han-wei Ho, and Martin T. Wells. 2015. 'Pain and Suffering Damages in Wrongful Death Cases: An Empirical Study'. *Journal of Empirical Legal Studies* 12 (1): 128–60.

Chang, Yun-chien, Theodore Eisenberg, Tsung Hsien Li, and Martin T. Wells. 2017. 'Pain and Suffering Damages in Personal Injury Cases: An Empirical Study'. *Journal of Empirical Legal Studies* 14: 199–237.

Chang, Yun-chien, and William H. J. Hubbard. 2021. 'New Empirical Tests for Classic Litigation Selection Models: Evidence from a Low Settlement Environment'. *American Law and Economics Review* 23 (2): 348–94.

Chang, Yun-chien, and Daniel Klerman. 2022. 'Settlement Around the World: Settlement Rates in the Largest Economies'. *Journal of Legal Analysis* 14 (1): 80–175.

Chang, Yun-chien, and Chang-ching Lin. 2024. 'Do Parties Negotiate After Trespass Litigation? An Empirical Study of Coasean Bargaining'. Journal of Law and Empirical Analysis 1 (1): 1–19.

Chang, Yun-chien, and Su-hao Tu. 2020. 'Two-way Selections Between Flat-fee Attorneys and Litigants: Theoretical and Empirical Analyses'. *European Journal of Law and Economics* 49: 131–64.

Chen, Daniel L., Yosh Halberstam, and Alan Yu. 2017. 'Covering: Mutable Characteristics and Perceptions of Voice in the US Supreme Court'. http://dx.doi.org/10.2139/ssrn.2816241.

Chen, Kong-Pin, Kuo-Chang Huang, and Chang-Ching Lin. 2015. 'Party Capability versus Court Preference: Why Do the "Haves" Come Out Ahead?—An Empirical Lesson from the Taiwan Supreme Court'. *Journal of Law, Economics & Organization* 31: 93–126.

Chesterman, Simon. 2020. 'Do Better Lawyers Win More Often? Measures of Advocate Quality and Their Impact in Singapore's Supreme Court'. *Asian Journal of Comparative Law* 15 (2): 250–80.

Cumming, Douglas J. 2001. 'Settlement Disputes: Evidence from a Legal Practice Perspective'. *European Journal of Law and Economics* 11 (3): 249–80.

Dana, James D., and Kathryn E. Spier. 1993. 'Expertise and Contingent Fees: The Role of Asymmetric Information in Attorney Compensation'. *Journal of Law, Economics, & Organization* 9 (2): 349–67.

Danzon, Patricia Munch. 1983. 'Contingent Fees for Personal Injury Litigation'. *The Bell Journal of Economics* 14 (1): 213–24.

Deffains, Bruno, and Claudine Desrieux. 2015. 'To Litigate or Not to Litigate? The Impacts of Third-party Financing on Litigation'. *International Review of Law and Economics* 43: 178–89.

Del Rossi, Alison F., and W. Kip Viscusi. 2010. 'The Changing Landscape of Blockbuster Punitive Damages Awards'. *American Law and Economics Review* 12: 116–61.

Dotan, Yoav. 1999. 'Do the "Haves" Still Come Out Ahead? Resource Inequalities in Ideological Courts: The Case of the Israeli High Court of Justice'. *Law & Society Review* 33 (4): 1059–80.

Eisenberg, Theodore. 1990. 'Testing the Selection Effect: A New Theoretical Framework with Empirical Tests'. *The Journal of Legal Studies* 19 (2): 337–58.

Eisenberg, Theodore, and Martin T. Wells. 2006. 'The Significant Association Between Punitive and Compensatory Damages in Blockbuster Cases: A Methodological Primer'. *Journal of Empirical Legal Studies* 3: 175–95.

Eisenberg, Theodore, Michael Heise, Nicole L. Waters, and Martin T. Wells. 2010. 'The Decision to Award Punitive Damages: An Empirical Study'. *Journal of Legal Analysis* 2 (2): 577–620.

Eisenberg, Theodore, John Goerdt, Brian Ostrom, David Rottman, and Martin T. Wells. 1997. 'The Predictability of Punitive Damages'. *The Journal of Legal Studies* 26 (S2): 623–61.

Eisenberg, Theodore, Paula L. Hannaford-Agor, Michael Heise, Neil LaFountain, G. Thomas Munsterman, Brian Ostrom, and Martin T. Wells. 2006. 'Juries, Judges, and Punitive Damages: Empirical Analyses Using the Civil Justice Survey of State Courts 1992, 1996, and 2001 Data'. *Journal of Empirical Legal Studies* 3 (2): 263–95.

Emons, Winand, and Nuno Garoupa. 2006. 'US-style Contingent Fees and UK-style Conditional Fees: Agency Problems and the Supply of Legal Services'. *Managerial and Decision Economics* 27 (5): 379–85.

Engel, Christoph. 2022. 'Challenges in the Interdisciplinary Use of Comparative Law'. *American Journal of Comparative Law* 69 (4): 777–97.

Epstein, Lee, Urska Sadl, and Keren Weinshall. 2021. 'The Role of Comparative Law in the Analysis of Judicial Behavior'. *American Journal of Comparative Law* 69: 689–719.

Feldman, Adam. 2016. 'Who Wins in the Supreme Court: An Examination of Attorney and Law Firm Influence'. *Marquette Law Review* 100: 429–60.

Galanter, Marc. 1974. 'Why the "Haves" Come Out Ahead: Speculations on the Limits of Legal Change'. *Law and Society Review* 9: 95–160.

Genn, Hazel. 1999. *Paths to Justice: What People Do and Think About Going to Law*. Oxford: Hart.

Genn, Hazel, and Alan Paterson. 2001. *Paths to Justice Scotland: What People in Scotland Think and Do About Going to Law*. Oxford: Hart.

Gilad, Sharon. 2010. 'Why the "Haves" Do Not Necessarily Come Out Ahead in Informal Dispute Resolution'. *Law & Policy* 32 (3): 283–312.

Gould, John P. 1973. 'The Economics of Legal Conflicts'. *The Journal of Legal Studies* 2 (2): 279–300.

Greiner, D. James, Cassandra W. Pattanayak, and Jonathan P. Hennessy. 2013. 'The Limits of Unbundled Legal Assistance: A Randomized Study in a Massachusetts District Court and Prospects for the Future'. *Harvard Law Review* 126: 903–89.

Greiner, James, and Cassandra Wolos Pattanayak. 2011. 'Randomized Evaluation in Legal Assistance: What Difference Does Representation (Offer and Actual Use) Make'. *Yale Law Journal* 121: 2118–215.

Gugliuzza, Paul R. 2019. 'Elite Patent Law'. *Iowa Law Review* 104: 2481–510.

Gugliuzza, Paul R. 2020. 'The Supreme Court Bar at the Bar of Patents'. *Notre Dame Law Review* 95: 1233–80.

Haire, Susan Brodie, Stefanie A. Lindquist, and Roger Hartley. 1999. 'Attorney Expertise, Litigant Success, and Judicial Decisionmaking in the U.S. Courts of Appeals'. *Law & Society Review* 33 (3): 667–85.

Hanretty, Chris. 2016. 'Lawyer Rankings Either Do Not Matter for Litigation Outcomes or Are Redundant'. *International Journal of the Legal Profession* 23 (2): 185–205.

Haynie, Stacia L. 1994. 'Resource Inequalities and Litigation Outcomes in the Philippine Supreme Court'. *The Journal of Politics* 56 (3): 752–72.

Haynie, Stacia L. 1995. 'Resource Inequalities and Regional Variation in Litigation Outcomes in the Philippine Supreme Court, 1961–1986'. *Political Research Quarterly* 48 (2): 371–80.

Haynie, Stacia L., and Kaitlyn L. Sill. 2007. 'Experienced Advocates and Litigation Outcomes: Repeat Players in the South African Supreme Court of Appeal'. *Political Research Quarterly* 60 (3): 443–453.

He, Xin, and Yang Su. 2013. Do the "Haves" Come Out Ahead in Shanghai Courts? *Journal of Empirical Legal Studies* 10 (1): 120–45.

Helland, Eric, Daniel Klerman, and Yoon-Ho Alex Lee. 2018. 'Maybe There's No Bias in the Selection of Disputes for Litigation'. *Journal of Institutional and Theoretical Economics* 174 (1): 143–70.

Helland, Eric, and Alexander Tabarrok. 2003. 'Contingency Fees, Settlement Delay, and Low-Quality Litigation: Empirical Evidence from Two Datasets'. *Journal of Law, Economics & Organization* 19 (2): 517–42.
Hersch, Joni, and W. Kip Viscusi. 2004. 'Punitive Damages: How Judges and Juries Perform'. *The Journal of Legal Studies* 33: 1–36.
Hirschl, Ran. 2007. 'On the Blurred Methodological Matrix of Comparative Constitutional Law'. In *The Migration of Constitutional Ideas*, edited by Sujit Choudhry, 39–66. Cambridge: Cambridge University Press.
Hsu, Ching-fang, Ivan Kan-hsueh Chiang, and Yun-chien Chang. 2024. 'Lawyers' Legal Aid Participation: A Qualitative and Quantitative Analysis'. *Journal of Empirical Legal Studies* 21 (2): 337–74.
Huang, Kuo-Chang. 2008. 'How Legal Representation Affects Case Outcome: An Empirical Perspective from Taiwan'. *Journal of Empirical Legal Studies* 51 (2): 197–238.
Huang, Kuo-Chang. 2009. 'Does Discovery Promote Settlement? An Empirical Answer'. *Journal of Empirical Legal Studies* 6 (2): 241–78.
Huang, Kuo-Chang, Kong-Pin Chen, and Chang-Ching Lin. 2010. 'Does the Type of Criminal Defense Counsel Affect Case Outcomes? A Natural Experiment in Taiwan'. *International Review of Law and Economics* 30 (2): 113–27.
Huang, Kuo-Chang, Chang-Ching Lin, and Kong-Pin Chen. 2014. 'Do Rich and Poor Behave Similarly in Seeking Legal Advice? Lessons from Taiwan in Comparative Perspective'. *Law & Society Review* 48 (1): 193–223.
Hyde, Charles E. 2006. 'Conditional Versus Contingent Fees: Litigation Expenditure Incentives'. *International Review of Law and Economics* 26 (2): 180–94.
Hyman, David A., Bernard Black, and Charles Silver. 2015. 'The Economics of Plaintiff-side Personal Injury Practice'. *University of Illinois Law Review* 2015: 1563–603.
Johnson, Timothy R. 2001. 'Information, Oral Arguments, and Supreme Court Decision Making'. *American Politics Research* 29 (4): 331–51.
Klerman, Daniel, Yoon-Ho Alex Lee, and Lawrence Liu. 2018. 'Litigation and Selection with Correlated Two-Sided Incomplete Information'. *American Law and Economics Review* 20 (2): 382–459.
Kritzer, Herbert M. 1984. 'The Dimensions of Lawyer-Client Relations: Notes Toward a Theory and a Field Study'. *American Bar Foundation Research Journal* 9 (2): 409–25.
Kritzer, Herbert M. 1997. 'The Wages of Risk: The Returns of Contingency Fee Legal Practice'. *DePaul Law Review* 47: 267–319.
Kritzer, Herbert M. 1998. *Legal Advocacy: Lawyers and Nonlawyers at Work*. Ann Arbor: University of Michigan Press.
Kritzer, Herbert M. 2004. *Risks, Reputations and Rewards: Contingency Fee Legal Practice in the United States*. Palo Alto: Stanford University Press.
Kritzer, Herbert M., and Jayanth Krishnan. 1999. 'Lawyers Seeking Clients, Clients Seeking Lawyers: Sources of Contingency Fee Cases and Their Implications for Case Handling'. *Law & Policy* 21 (4): 347–75.
Landes, William M. 1971. 'An Economic Analysis of the Courts'. *Journal of Law & Economics* 14 (1): 61–107.
Lazarus, Richard J. 2008. 'Advocacy Matters Before and Within the Supreme Court: Transforming the Court by Transforming the Bar'. *Georgetown Law Review* 96: 1487–564.
Levin, Leslie C., and Lynn Mather, eds. 2012. *Lawyers in Practice: Ethical Decision Making in Context*. Chicago: University of Chicago Press.

Lin, Chang-ching, Yun-chien Chang, and Kong-pin Chen. 2018. 'Knowledge in Youth Is Wisdom in Age: An Empirical Study of Attorney Experience in Torts Litigation'. *International Review of Law & Economics* 63 (105913): 1–12.

Lin, Chang-Ching, Kong-Pin Chen, Kuo-Chang Huang, and Ya-Ting Yu. 2016. 'The Research Design and Methodology of the 2011 Civil Justice Survey in Taiwan'. *Survey Research—Method and Application* 36: 87–123.

Lin, Yu-Hsin, and Yun-chien Chang. 2018. 'An Empirical Study of Corporate Default Rules and Menus in China, Hong Kong and Taiwan'. *Journal of Empirical Legal Studies* 15 (4): 875–915.

Mather, Lynn. 2003. 'What Do Clients Want? What Do Lawyers Do?' *Emory Law Journal* 52: 1065–86.

McGuire, Kevin T. 1995. 'Repeat Players in the Supreme Court: The Role of Experienced Lawyers in Litigation Success'. *The Journal of Politics* 57: 187–96.

Miceli, Thomas J. 1994. 'Do Contingent Fees Promote Excessive Litigation?' *The Journal of Legal Studies* 23 (1): 211–24.

Miceli, Thomas J., and Kathleen Segerson. 1991. 'Contingent Fees for Lawyers: The Impact on Litigation and Accident Prevention'. *The Journal of Legal Studies* 20 (2): 381–99.

Miller, Banks, Linda Camp Keith, and Jennifer S. Holmes. 2015. 'Leveling the Odds: The Effect of Quality Legal Representation in Cases of Asymmetrical Capability'. *Law & Society Review* 49: 209–39.

Miller, Geoffrey P. 1987. 'Some Agency Problems in Settlement'. *The Journal of Legal Studies* 16 (1): 189–215.

Miller, Richard E., and Austin Sarat. 1980–1981. 'Grievances, Claims, and Disputes: Assessing the Adversary Culture'. *Law & Society Review* 15 (3): 525–66.

Morrison, Edward R., Belisa Pang, and Jonathon Zytnick. 2022. 'Manipulating Random Assignment: Evidence from Consumer Bankruptcies in the Nation's Largest Cities'. *American Law and Economics Review*.

Murayama, Masayuki. 2009. 'Japanese Disputing Behavior Reconsidered'. In *Empirical Studies of Judicial Systems*, edited by Kuo-Chang Huang, 261–98. Taipei: Institutum Iurisprudentiae, Academia Sinica.

Muro, Sergio, Alejandro Chehtman, Jorge Silva Méndez, and Nelson Amaya Durán. 2018. 'Testing Representational Advantage in the Argentine Supreme Court'. *Journal of Law and Courts* 6 (1): 1–23.

Nelson, Michael J., and Lee Epstein. 2022. 'Human Capital in Court: The Role of Attorney Experience in U.S. Supreme Court Litigation'. *Journal of Law and Courts* 10 (1): 61–85.

Perry Jr., H. W. 2020. 'The Elitification of the US Supreme Court and Appellate Lawyering'. *South Carolina Law Review* 72: 245–304.

Posner, Richard A. 1973. 'An Economic Approach to Legal Procedure and Judicial Administration'. *The Journal of Legal Studies* 2: 399–458.

Priest, George L., and Benjamin Klein. 1984. 'The Selection of Disputes for Litigation'. *The Journal of Legal Studies* 13 (1): 1–56.

Pyszczynski, Tom A., Jeff Greenberg, Dave Mack, and Lawrence Wrightsman. 1981. 'Opening Statements in a Jury Trial: The Effect of Promising More Than the Evidence Can Show'. *Journal of Applied Social Psychology* 11: 434–44.

Rachlinski, Jeffrey J. 2016. 'Does Empirical Legal Studies Shed More Heat Than Light? The Case of Civil Damage Awards'. *Ratio Juris* 29 (4): 556–71.

Reimann, Mathias, ed. 2012. *Cost and Fee Allocation in Civil Procedure*. Berlin: Springer.

Reinganum, Jennifer F., and Louis L. Wilde. 1986. 'Settlement, Litigation, and the Allocation of Litigation Costs'. *RAND Journal of Economics* 17 (4): 557–66.

Sandefur, Rebecca L. 2015. 'Elements of Professional Expertise: Understanding Relational and Substantive Expertise through Lawyers' Impact'. *American Sociological Review* 80 (5): 909–33.

Shavell, Steven. 1996. 'Any Frequency of Plaintiff Victory at Trial Is Possible'. *The Journal of Legal Studies* 25 (2): 493–501.

Smyth, Russell. 2000. 'The "Haves" and the "Have Nots": An Empirical Study of the Rational Actor and Party Capability Hypotheses in the High Court 1948–99'. *Australian Journal of Political Science* 35 (2): 255–74.

Spier, Kathryn E. 1992. 'The Dynamics of Pretrial Negotiation'. *Review of Economic Studies* 59: 93–108.

Spier, Kathryn E. 'Litigation'. In *Handbook of Law and Economics: Volume 1*, edited by A. Mitchell Polinsky and Steven Shavell, 259–342. Amsterdam: Elsevier.

Spamann, Holger. 2009. 'Large-sample, Quantitative Research Designs for Comparative Law?' *American Journal of Comparative Law* 57 (4): 797–810.

Spamann, Holger. 2015. 'Empirical Comparative Law'. *Annual Review of Law and Social Science* 11: 131–53.

Sunstein, Cass R., Reid Hastie, John W. Payne, David A. Schkade, and Kip W. Viscusi. 2002. *Punitive Damages: How Juries Decide*. Chicago: University of Chicago Press.

Szmer, John, Susan W. Johnson, and Tammy A. Sarver. 2007. 'Does the Lawyer Matter? Influencing Outcomes on the Supreme Court of Canada'. *Law & Society Review* 41 (2): 279–303.

Thomason, Terry. 1991. 'Are Attorneys Paid What They're Worth? Contingent Fees and the Settlement Process'. *The Journal of Legal Studies* 20 (1): 187–223.

Velthoven, Ben C. J. van, and Marijke ter Voert. 2008. 'Paths to Justice in the Netherlands'. In *Legal Aid in the Global Era* 231–55. Glasgow: Centre for Professional Legal Studies, University of Strathclyde. https://wrlc-gulaw.primo.exlibrisgroup.com/discovery/fulldisplay?context=L&vid=01WRLC_GUNIVLAW:01WRLC_GUNIVLAW&search_scope=MyInst_and_CI&tab=Everything&docid=alma991001518749704113

Viscusi, W. Kip. 1996. 'Pain and Suffering: Damages in Search of a Sounder Rationale'. *Michigan Law and Policy Review* 1: 141–78.

Viscusi, W. Kip. 1988. 'Pain and Suffering in Product Liability Cases: Systematic Compensation or Capricious Awards?' *International Review of Law and Economics* 8 (2): 203–20.

Watts, Alison. 1994. 'Bargaining Through an Expert Attorney'. *Journal of Law, Economics & Organization* 10 (1): 168–86.

Weld, H. P., and E. R. Danzig. 1940. 'A Study of the Way in Which a Verdict Is Reached by a Jury'. *American Journal of Psychology* 53: 518–36.

Wood, Steve M., Lorie L. Sicafuse, Monica K. Miller, and Julianna C. Chomos. 2011. 'The Influence of Jurors' Perceptions of Attorneys and Their Performance on Verdict'. *Jury Expert* 23: 23–34.

Yoon, Albert. 2017. 'The Legal Profession and the Market for Lawyers'. In *The Oxford Handbook of Law and Economics: Volume 3: Public Law and Legal Institutions*, edited by Francesco Parisi, 259–79. Oxford: Oxford University Press.

Zweigert, Konrad, and Hein Kötz. 1998. *Introduction to Comparative Law*, 3rd edn. Oxford: Oxford University Press.

CHAPTER 22

AGENDAS, DECISIONS, AND AUTONOMY

How Government Lawyers Shape Judicial Behaviour

TOMMASO PAVONE

1. Introduction: A Research Blind Spot

THERE is arguably no professional class as well-represented in government than lawyers. In the United States, lawyers account for 39 per cent of the seats in the House and 56 per cent of the seats in the Senate, making them 100 times more likely to be elected than the average citizen[1] and raising concerns that attorneys have 'colonized' the state (Miller 2002, 3). In Brazil and most of Latin America, 'even the legislators elected from the [w]orker's [p]art[ies] tend to be lawyers' (Carnes and Lupu 2015, 6). In Europe, 22 per cent of cabinet ministers are lawyers, far outnumbering the 3 per cent of ministers drawn from all other professions.[2] Although reliable figures for autocracies are difficult to come by, even revolutionary regimes intent on purging lawyers from their ranks soon realized that they are useful after all (Hendley 1996, 168–70; Komaiko and Que 2009, 35–36).

No wonder, for lawyers perform all manner of government service. They craft legislation as legally trained policy-makers (Hain and Piereson 1975); they advise the executive as to what regulatory actions to take and how best to legally justify them (Casey and Kenny 2022); they defend the government's interests and represent it in court (Salokar 1994);[3] they open prosecutions in the state's name (Langer and Sklansky 2017). As they advise, defend, enforce, and gatekeep while on public employ, government lawyers mould the state and the degree to which the government is constrained by the rule of law and democratic accountability. In other words, government lawyers are crucial agents of institutional change and political development.[4]

Yet for all their influence, 'government lawyers' are not yet objects of a coherent and comparative agenda. Even as studies of private attorneys and the legal profession proliferated into an influential subfield of socio-legal research (e.g. Abel and Lewis 1988, 1989, 1995; Abel et al. 2020, 2022; Pavone 2022), no self-conscious research programme on government lawyers exists. This blind spot is not because studies of government lawyers do not exist—they do, and we will engage several exemplars throughout this chapter. Rather, it is because these studies have yet to be put into conversation with one another and integrated in the burgeoning literature on comparative judicial behaviour.

In this chapter, I sketch the contours of what a comparative research agenda on government lawyers and judicial behaviour might look like, and I defend the value of this agenda. My goal is to illuminate and empirically substantiate the diversity of ways that government attorneys can impact the judiciary. Because 'government lawyer' is such an amorphous and encompassing term, I limit my attention to those legal professionals employed by the state who either regularly appear in court or occupy sufficiently powerful executive positions to directly shape judicial independence. I thus focus on three types of government lawyers: public prosecutors, government litigators, and executive branch attorneys. While government attorneys can influence courts in multiple ways, I tie each type of government lawyer to the outcome of interest for the study of judicial behaviour—the shaping of judicial agendas, decisions, and autonomy—over which they tend to exert the greatest influence, linking each outcome to a specific mechanism of influence.

The rest of this chapter conceptualizes and illustrates a tripartite politics of government lawyers. I first spotlight recent research tracing how public prosecutors shape judges' agendas and the courts' capacity to enforce public law by strategically withholding or prioritizing particular lawsuits. I refer to this as a *politics of discretion*. Next, I highlight studies demonstrating how government litigators can wield their institutional position as intermediaries and repeat players to influence judges' decisions—so long as their credibility as litigators is not hampered by overt politicization. I refer to this as a *politics of positionality*. Finally, I chronicle a burgeoning literature on executive branch attorneys who weaponize their legal training not so much to steer governments towards legality but rather to undermine judicial independence and advance democratic backsliding. I call this *power politics, lawyer-style*. Taken together, these dynamic yet hitherto fragmented studies highlight the pressing need to synthesize disparate strands of research on government lawyers and place them in conversation with studies of comparative judicial behaviour.

2. Government Lawyers and Judicial Behaviour: Three Politics

To conceptualize how government lawyers influence judicial behaviour, we must first define what a 'government lawyer' is. This task turns out to be unexpectedly challenging.

We might be tempted to proceed negatively by defining government lawyers in opposition to private lawyers. Yet the boundaries between public and private in the legal field are increasingly porous. Sometimes, private lawyers are summoned to play public roles. For instance, US big law firms are regularly hired by debtor governments shaken by economic crises to manage sovereign debt restructuring and secure bailouts—as Cleary Gottlieb did in Latin America and Eastern Europe during the Washington consensus era, in Greece during the European sovereign debt crisis, and in Iraq following the US invasion (Dezelay and Garth 2002, 50, 204; Meager, Price, and Yap 2016; Hinrichsen 2021, 101). While we might associate private lawyers playing public roles with common law, neoliberal, or developing countries lacking state capacity, in fact these boundary-blurring actors are far more ubiquitous, even in developed civil law states.[5] In Denmark, for instance, the government delegates legal representation to a private law firm that represents it before the national courts.[6] Elsewhere, boundary crossings and revolving doors increasingly muddy the public–private distinction, as when government officials join corporate law firms, advise and lobby governments for favoured policies, and sometimes return to government. This revolving door has become common even in the prototypical centralized and (seemingly) autonomous civil law state of France, to the point that the French have coined a word to describe it: *pantouflage* (Vauchez and France 2021).

To cut through this complexity, I define a government lawyer as a person with legal training pursuing a career as a state civil servant (such as prosecutors or lawyers in state legal services) or occupying a position in government (such as attorneys general, offices of legal counsel, and sometimes even presidents and prime ministers themselves). This definition excludes private attorneys hired on temporary contracts as government legal counsel, although it may include lawyers who have left private practice to join the public sector. The definition also encompasses both nominally apolitical lawyers pursuing careers in a state civil service as well as more political lawyers whose public employ hinges on the fate of a particular governing coalition; for simplicity, I refer to both as 'government lawyers'.

How might these government lawyers shape judicial behaviour? A helpful way to think through this question is to consider how government lawyers might influence the litigation process and shape the broader institutional environment in which judges make decisions. Vis-à-vis the litigation process, government lawyers can shape the cases that judges get and do not get—that is, judicial *agendas*—as well as how judges adjudicate and resolve those cases, namely judicial *decisions*. Vis-à-vis the broader judicial institutional environment, government lawyers can mould the degree of executive interference in judicial affairs and the degree to which the judiciary is politicized: that is, judicial *autonomy*. Let us conceptualize each of these modes of influence in turn.

The first opportunity for lawyer influence is inherent in a fundamental way that judiciaries differ from legislatures and executives: courts are reactive institutions that largely depend upon others for their agendas. Because judges 'have no self-starting mechanisms', they can only make decisions if a public or private party brings a case to court (Horowitz 1977, 53). Judges might send signals to prospective litigants to incentivize them to bring some cases over others, but at the end of the day this choice lies with the parties (Pavone and Stiansen 2022). In other words, courts' substantive agenda—or whether judges even get to have an agenda at all—depends a great deal on lawyers. This agenda-setting capacity is especially evident when it comes to law enforcement, where government lawyers enjoy sometimes unfettered prosecutorial discretion in deciding whether and when to lodge cases under criminal or international law. By prioritizing certain cases or strategically withholding prosecutions—what political scientists call 'forbearance' (Holland 2016; Kelemen and Pavone 2023)—government lawyers can direct or starve judges' very capacity to decide on fundamental social, economic, and political issues (Brinks 2007). I call this a *politics of discretion.*

Once a case makes it onto a court's agenda, government lawyers tend to benefit from significant advantages as litigants. These advantages are all tied to the unique institutional position that government lawyers occupy. First, government lawyers usually do not have to worry about mobilizing the financial resources and human capital necessary to sustain a litigation campaign—at least not to the same extent as private attorneys.[7] Combined with the fact that many lawsuits target the state, government lawyers can become prototypical 'repeat players' (as opposed to 'one shotters'; see Galanter (1974)). Being a repeat player enables government lawyers to develop tacit knowledge of court procedures and judicial personalities ('process expertise'), as well as the ability to forge a credible reputation and build trust with judges (Kritzer 1998, 194). Finally, government lawyers can provide important political signals and information to judges because of their political embeddedness (Michelson 2007). This boundary-blurring position—part court insider, part government insider—can bolster government attorneys' capacity to secure favourable rulings in court. I thus refer to this as a *politics of positionality.*

Government lawyers can also shape the institutional environment in which judges are embedded without ever stepping into the courtroom. This mode of influence is particularly evident if we consider the role of lawyers at the helm of the executive branch. These lawyers can serve as legal advisors to presidents and prime ministers, such as attorneys in offices of legal counsel, or as chief executives themselves, what Kim Scheppele (2019) calls 'lawyers-in-chief'. Although executive branch lawyers were often presumed to carry forth their commitment to political liberalism—and thus serve as a constraint on executive action (Halliday and Karpik 1997; Halliday, Karpik, and Feeley 2007)—increasingly it is apparent that these attorneys can threaten judicial prerogatives and independence. They can do so by curtailing courts' jurisdiction—as when the US office of legal counsel in the Bush Administration promoted the view that the US judiciary should not try terrorism cases (Bruff 2009). Executive attorneys can also devise and justify frontal attacks and court curbing—as when Hungarian Prime Minister Viktor Orbán devised policies to pack the Constitutional Court with loyalists and assert government control over judicial appointments (Scheppele 2018). By eroding judicial independence and propelling repertoires of 'autocratic legalism', executive lawyers can profoundly affect judicial behaviour via what we may call *lawyer-style power politics.* While most judges may conform or be forced into quiescence, some may respond via protest and activism (Matthes 2022).

Table 22.1 Government lawyers and judicial behaviour: Three politics of influence

	Actors types of government-employed lawyers		Mechanisms of influence over judicial behaviour		Outcomes impact on judicial behaviour
Politics of discretion	***prosecutors:*** lawyers in law enforcement offices	→	***discretion:*** forbearance and prioritization in enforcement	→	shape judicial ***agendas***
Politics of positionality	***litigators:*** lawyers representing governments in court	→	***positionality:*** institutional reputation and repeat-player advantage	→	influence judicial ***decisions***
Power politics, lawyer-style	***executives:*** lawyers at the helm of the executive branch	→	***power:*** 'autocratic legalist' reforms	→	erode judicial ***autonomy***

Table 22.1 summarizes the predominant ways in which three types of government lawyers—prosecutors, litigators, and executives—can influence judicial behaviour. It captures a conceptual framework that parses three political processes into actors, mechanisms,[8] and outcomes of interest. To be sure, these processes are neither comparatively exhaustive nor mutually exclusive: government lawyers can influence judicial behaviour in a multiplicity of ways, sometimes simultaneously. But for clarity, it is helpful to consider the primary modes of government lawyer influence and tie each mode to the type of lawyer best situated to exercise it. First, in a politics of discretion, lawyers (especially prosecutors occupying law enforcement positions) wield their discretion to prioritize particular cases or forbear from enforcement, thus shaping courts' agendas. Second, in a politics of positionality, lawyers (primarily attorneys in government litigators) leverage their favoured institutional position and advantages as repeat-players to influence judicial decisions. Finally, in power politics, lawyer-style, attorneys (particularly those the helm of the executive branch) weaponize state power to devise autocratic legalist reforms that erode judicial autonomy. Let us consider each politics in turn.

3. Prosecutors and Judicial Agendas: The Politics of Discretion

In distinguishing courts from other branches of government, scholars and policymakers routinely quote Alexander Hamilton's *Federalist 78*: courts have 'neither force nor will, but merely judgement', having 'no influence over either the sword or the purse' (Hamilton 1788). But we should add something else: that courts do not control their own agendas. Courts are designed as reactive institutions which depend on other social and political actors for their cases and their capacity to shape policy. Although informally judges can signal their desire to adjudicate certain kinds of controversies to prospective litigants, courts have no direct control over this crucial pre-litigation phase (Pavone and Stiansen 2022).

It follows that by wielding their discretion in the pre-litigation phase, lawyers can mould judicial agendas. And as the overwhelming repeat-players in certain fields of law—such as administrative, criminal, constitutional, and international law—government lawyers' influence over judicial agenda-setting can be extraordinary. In particular, they can wage a *politics of discretion* via two strategies: selecting which cases to prioritize and vigorously push, and selecting which cases to drop and subtract from courts' attention. The impact of this politics is maximized when courts are seldom solicited and the government has exclusive standing—since it increases judges' dependence on the cases that government attorneys choose to bring—and when courts lack discretionary dockets—since it forces judges to pronounce themselves in all cases brought.

Yet even when judges are regularly solicited and boast a discretionary docket, their agendas can depend on government lawyers to a surprising extent. Consider the instructive example of the US Supreme Court's agenda and the influence of the lawyers in the Solicitor General's (SG) office. Since 1925, the Supreme Court can select which subset of cases to adjudicate (by 'granting cert' via a writ of *certiorari*); today, the Court selects only eighty or so cases a year from a pool of thousands of petitions (Kastellec and Liu 2023, 3–4). SG attorneys—who coordinate the federal government's litigation strategy and represent the government before the Court—are uniquely effective in pushing favoured cases past this onerous filter. As the justices confide, 'the Court look[s] at the solicitor general as fulfilling part of their own screening function'; by being very selective in bringing petitions, SG lawyers can 'convinc[e] [the justices] that refusal to decide the issue now would be disastrous' (quoted in Perry (1994, 280)). So while the Court only grants cert in 3 per cent of petitions, when the SG petitions to hear a case the justices abide 70 per cent of the time (Chandler 2011, 728; more on the SG's privileged relationship *vis* the Court in the next section). This discrepancy is dizzying even for seasoned Supreme Court attorneys: when Paul Clement left the SG's office in 2008 to return to private practice, his success rate in cert petitions plunged from 72.3 per cent to 23.2 per cent.[9] As Kritzer (1994, 690) cleverly concludes, when scouting a 'needle in the haystack' of what drives the Court's agenda, 'some needles are much larger than others (e.g. when the needle bears the imprimatur of the Solicitor General)'.

To some extent, private attorneys can wage a politics of discretion too—by strategically pushing clients to settle some cases in the shadow of the courts (Mnookin and Kornhauser 1979). But in some legal fields, government lawyers are the *sole* actor with authority to bring suit. The prototypical exemplar is that of criminal law and government attorneys in law enforcement positions. For instance, national prosecutors usually have exclusive discretion to indict persons or businesses and take them to court for violating criminal law (Haynie and Dover 1994). Here, the common law adversarial system maximizes prosecutors' discretion: beyond their enforcement monopoly, it grants them 'essentially unchecked discretion' to overcharge defendants to obtain guilty verdicts and avoid trial (prosecutors succeed 95 per cent of the time in the United States) while relegating judges to a deferential and passive role in the few cases that do make it to trial.[10] In the inquisitorial system of civil law countries like Italy and Germany, prosecutors' discretion is actually more constrained: plea bargaining is limited, prosecutions are nearly compulsory, and judges assume a more proactive role as fact-finders who scrutinize prosecutors.[11] At the supranational level, prosecutorial discretion is usually encompassing on paper (albeit politically constrained in practice): nine regional organizations—such as the African Union, the Andean Community, and the European Free Trade Area—empower international secretariats with sole discretion to bring member states to court when they violate regional or international law (Alter 2014, 112–60). And in 1998, the creation of the International Criminal Court (ICC) established an international prosecutor with discretion to initiate proceedings against individuals for genocide, crimes against humanity, and war crimes (Brubacher 2004).

Recently, a vibrant comparative literature has revealed a politics of prosecutorial discretion that is particularly consequential to judicial agenda-setting: the politics of *forbearance*, or the 'intentional and revocable under-enforcement of the law' (Holland 2016: 232). Forbearance is significant for courts because if taken too far, it can starve judges of their supervisory function and preclude them from enforcing the law against powerful political actors, like corrupt politicians or states violating international law (Pavone and Stiansen 2022). An emergent finding of this research is that government lawyers in enforcement positions usually adopt forbearance when they are insufficiently insulated from political interference—that is, when 'politicians [can] make decisions to halt enforcement', even when lawyers 'perform their jobs' (Holland 2016, 240). Government lawyers' liminal position—part government agent, part agent for the public interest—opens the door to politics and strategic behaviour.

At the national level, a politics of discretion is usually driven by an electoral calculus. That is, government lawyers may be pressured by powerful politicians (such as ministers of justice or mayors) to under-enforce the law against political allies and electoral constituencies that said politicians value for re-election (or, conversely, to target opponents or disfavoured groups). In Guatemala, prosecutors began to uncover networks of political corruption beginning in 2015; the President and the Congress quickly united to attack the lawyers leading the investigations, quashing them before they could reach the courts (Freeman 2023). In Chile, Peru, Colombia, and Brazil, mayors facing large working-class constituencies routinely interfere with government lawyers to block prosecutions of squatters, street vendors, and informal workers—especially in the lead-up to elections (Holland 2017; Feierherd 2020). In some US states where prosecutors are elected, district attorneys in cities like San Francisco and Philadelphia actively campaign on the promise to under-enforce unpopular drug and immigration laws (Holland 2016, 245; Sawyer 2020). In Italy and Germany, where small business owners are a powerful constituency for centre-right parties, governments engage in 'organizational sabotage' by cutting staff and resources allocated for prosecuting tax evasion (Dewey and Di Carlo 2021).

In short, political meddling can effectively reduce government lawyers' institutional autonomy and prosecutorial capacity. As a result, in Latin American countries like Brazil, prosecutors often depend on citizens and non-governmental organizations to gather evidence of illegality to pursue enforcement against powerful state actors like the police (Brinks 2007). The takeaway is that even well-resourced and independent judiciaries may be starved of opportunities to supervise government agents and enforce the law against certain electoral constituencies. Figure 22.1 visualizes this politics: given a certain number of detected violations of the law, it distinguishes a process of normal attrition at the investigation and litigation stages from forbearance for favoured groups and over-enforcement against disfavoured groups.

A discretionary politics of forbearance can also arise and reshape judicial behaviour at the supranational level and in the field of international law. Its logic, however, is not electoral since international policy-makers are not directly elected by voters. Instead, supranational forbearance is more likely to arise when international executives face cross-pressures between their duty to enforce the law against noncompliant states and their desire to work cooperatively with national governments to advance common policies. Eight of nine such international executives in regional organizations like the European Union and the East African Community 'double-hat' as policy-makers and prosecutors. As national governments respond to a cross-national backlash against international institutions by reasserting control over transnational policy-making

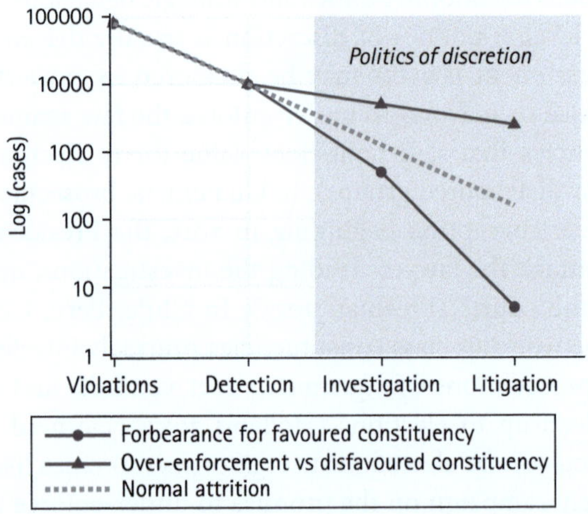

FIGURE 22.1 Visualizing a politics of prosecutorial discretion: normal attrition, overenforcement, and forbearance.

Notes: Draws from Holland (2016, 243) figure 6.

(Voeten 2022), these international executives may sacrifice their role as prosecutors to safeguard their role as policy agenda-setters (Kelemen and Pavone 2023).

In my research with R. Daniel Kelemen, we trace the rise of this politics of forbearance in the European Union's (EU) executive: the European Commission. The Commission not only is almost akin to a pan-European government, it is also the sole EU institution capable of bringing national governments before the European Court of Justice (ECJ) for violating European law (via what are known as 'infringement cases'). We show that when José Manuel Barroso—the former Portuguese Prime Minister—became Commission President in 2004, he spearheaded internal reforms to gain political control over prosecutorial decisions hitherto made by the independent-minded lawyers in the Commission's Legal Service (LS). By politicizing the LS (Leino-Sandberg 2021, 137–96) and reining in prosecutions against member governments, Barroso successfully rekindled intergovernmental support for his policy agenda. Yet as one lawyer confided, this 'very heavy political interference' to 'drop' enforcement cases and 'remain on good terms with the member governments' (quoted in Kelemen and Pavone 2023, 809) deprived the ECJ of opportunities to supervise and sanction non-compliance, even as some governments like Hungary and Poland began systematically to flout fundamental EU rules (Scheppele 2023). Figure 22.2 visualizes this decline in enforcement cases lodged before the ECJ by the Commission following the politicization of the LS: cases brought by the LS plummeted from comprising 49 per cent of the Court's docket in 2004 to a mere 8 per cent by 2014.[12]

The takeaway from this burgeoning research agenda is that in certain legal fields like criminal law and international law, government lawyers have an extraordinary first-mover advantage: how they move, and whether they even choose to move, frames courts' agendas. To the extent that prosecutors submit to political pressures to prioritize

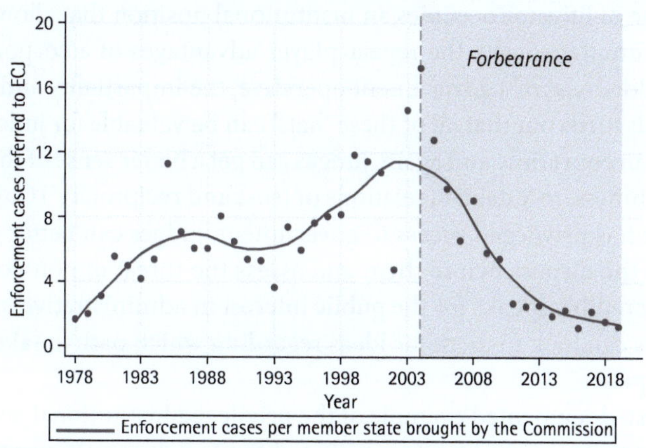

FIGURE 22.2 The European Commission's Legal Service (LS) referred member states to the ECJ far less often following its politicization post-2004.

Notes: Draws from Kelemen ... Pavone (2023, 6), figure 1.

certain cases or forbear from bringing some violations to courts' attention, government lawyers effectively warp judges' supervisory and law enforcement functions.

4. Litigators and Judicial Decisions: The Politics of Positionality

When government lawyers enter a courtroom—particularly in administrative and constitutional disputes—they tend to do so from a decidedly privileged institutional position. After all, their 'client'—the state (or the government; more on this ambiguity in a second)—usually possesses the economic prowess to fund repeated and often protracted litigation campaigns. Government lawyers thus have the opportunity to accrue 'human capital in court', becoming known personalities capable of dexterously forging a favourable rapport with their judicial interlocutors (Epstein and Nelson 2022). This capacity can be limited for lawyers representing private litigants whose engagement with the court system tends to be ephemeral and who may lack the money to sustain litigation. The state's capacity to absorb the costs of litigation also enables government lawyers to litigate with an eye to obtaining policy changes that may only concretize in the long-run: to 'play for rules', and not just 'play for cases' (Galanter 1974, 99–100).

Impressive though the foregoing advantages may be, they are not unique to government attorneys: they also apply to lawyers representing multinational corporations. The final ace up government lawyers' sleeve, however, is uniquely their own: it lies, once again, in their very political embeddedness. Government lawyers can supply judges with credible political signals regarding the government's preferences and policy intentions. And if they play their cards right, government lawyers can simultaneously cultivate a reputation for impartiality as representatives of the public interest.

No other type of litigator occupies an institutional position that allows them to wear so many hats simultaneously: the repeat-player advantages of a corporate lawyer, the political embeddedness of a government operative, the impartiality and public spirit of a civil servant. It turns out that all of these 'hats' can be valuable for judges too. When a lawyer appears in court time and again, judges can get a better sense of their abilities and their trustworthiness, to 'establish relations of trust and reciprocity' (Galanter 1974, 99). When a lawyer has privileged access to government, judges can better glean the political salience of the dispute before them and assess the threat of non-compliance. And when a lawyer credibly speaks for the public interest in administrative or constitutional disputes, judges can look to them for ideas regarding which path to take in pursuit of a common enterprise.

By far the best-documented example of the privileged institutional position or 'built-in advantage' of government litigators is that of the few dozen attorneys serving in the US Solicitor General's (SG) office (Black and Owens 2012, 454; Caplan 1987, 3–6). Since the 1970s, lawyers from the SG office have comprised 13 per cent of all lawyers before the Court and have appeared in approximately 30 per cent of all cases argued (Johnson, Wahlbeck, and Spriggs II 2006, 105–07; Epstein and Nelson 2022, 69). When SGs address the justices to argue a case, they do so with an average experience of thirty-four prior appearances under their belt (their assistants do so with an average experience of fifteen prior Supreme Court lawsuits). By contrast, the average private lawyer before the Court has only appeared in that forum once before (Johnson, Wahlbeck, and Spriggs II 2006, 105–07). Regularly arguing cases before the nation's highest court endows the SG with unique professional prestige: as Rex Lee, the former SG under President Reagan, put it, 'I was very much hoping that I would be picked [as SG] because that is ... probably the creamiest lawyering job in the country' (quoted in Salokar 1994, 33).

US Supreme Court justices rely heavily on the Solicitor General—and not just at the agenda-setting stage, as we saw previously. First, justices know that as a repeat-player, the SG will be able to speak their language, as it were. One justice described the SG's 'process expertise' (Kritzer 1998, 194) to H. W. Perry (1994, 132) as follows: 'the Solicitor General also knows all the catchwords, and they just know how to write them in a brief'. Second, justices rely on SG lawyers for political signals about what the government wants, how much it wants it, and what it is willing (and unwilling) to tolerate. As Thomas Merrill—deputy SG under Presidents Reagan and Bush—confided, justices 'look to the solicitor general for guidance ... for signals about the political atmosphere, "for what's do-able"' (quoted in Bailey, Kamoie, and Maltzman 2005, 74). In this way, the justices treat the SG as a political operative, an emissary of the government and President. Yet justices *also* treat the SG as one of their own, as a state civil servant representing the public interest, earning the SG the nickname of 'the tenth justice' (Caplan 1987). As Justice Powell illustrated during deliberations in one case, 'the importance of this case—and the interest of the government—justify giving the Solicitor General 15 minutes [for oral argument] ... he may be more helpful than the more partisan counsel' (quoted in Johnson, Wahlbeck, and Spriggs II 2006, 101–02). Supreme Court clerks and justices have confided in scholarly interviews that they expect the SG to 'play as an honest broker of the facts' who serves as a 'surrogate' for the Court (quoted in Black and Owens 2011, 766; Perry 1994, 75–76). As one justice put it, 'we jokingly referred to the SG's petition as the answer sheet' (quoted in Perry 1994, 133) and there is striking historical evidence that in salient cases—such as the *Brown v Board of Education* desegregation cases—the Court effectively 'adopted the position' articulated by the SG (Gillman, Graber, and Whittington 2013, 594).

There is also consistent quantitative evidence that lawyers representing the federal government—particularly those in the SG office—do deliver 'answer sheets' to the Supreme Court. As Figure 22.3 shows, government lawyers are almost twice as likely to sway the Court in their favour (with a 65–75 per cent win rate) than lawyers representing individuals (with a 30–40 per cent win rate) (Songer, Sheehan, and Haire 1999, 821). Government lawyers in the SG office have the greatest advantage, as demonstrated by research revealing that justices informally assign significantly higher grades to their oral arguments than those by private attorneys (Johnson, Wahlbeck, and Spriggs II 2006, 107–08). Sophisticated econometric analyses confirm that that 'OSG attorneys ... are

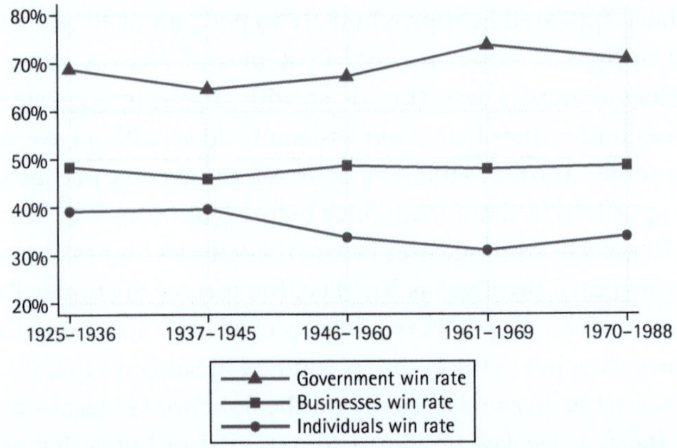

FIGURE 22.3 US government lawyers win at higher rates than lawyers representing private litigants.

Notes: Draws from Songer et al. (1999, 821), table 3.

more likely to win their cases' compared to 'nearly identical non-OSG lawyers in nearly identical cases' (Black and Owens 2012, 454).

At the same time, research on the SG office suggests that government lawyers' influence is conditional on their capacity to cultivate a reputation for institutional independence. This reputation is bolstered, for instance, when government attorneys argue in favour of a position that counters the partisan or ideological orientation of the sitting government. For instance, when an SG appointed by a Republican President argues in favour of a liberal outcome, their probability of securing the justices' support rises by fifteen percentage points from 68 per cent to 83 per cent (Bailey, Kamoie, and Maltzman 2005, 81). Conversely, historical and econometric studies suggest that when the Reagan Administration and its pugnacious Attorney General, Edwin Meese, began pressing the SG office to push 'agenda cases' towing the party line, the SG's credibility as a litigator was hampered (Caplan 1987; Salokar 1994, 72). Once Reagan and Meese made overtly partisan appointments to the SG office, government attorneys lost some of their capacity to double-hat not only as political operatives but also as disinterested surrogates of the Court. Consequently, their litigation success rate plunged by 12 per cent, despite the increasingly conservative orientation of the Supreme Court.[13]

The US experience suggests two comparative insights regarding when a politics of positionality is most likely to sway judicial decisions: when (i) the government is sufficiently resourceful to forge an elite group of repeat-players as its litigators; and (ii) when government attorneys can cultivate a credible reputation of institutional independence to double-hat as political emissaries and representatives of the public interest. To the extent that a government lacks the resources and organizational capacity to nurture human capital, or that it wields government lawyers as overtly partisan actors, then its attorneys are less likely to sway judicial decisions.

One example indicating that the US experience generalizes beyond the American context is that of government lawyers in the EU. In the EU, the European Commission employs an elite group of about 150 lawyers in its Legal Service (LS) tasked with representing the European executive before the ECJ. Like the SG office, the LS has 'far more resources' than any other body of EU-employed legal counsel, and is thus 'the single most frequent litigator before the Court of Justice, and the prototypical repeat player on the European legal stage' (Hofmann 2013, 9; Leino-Sandberg 2021, 152). The Director of the LS is arguably the EU's most influential lawyer, just as the SG is arguably the most influential litigator in the United States.[14] Since many LS lawyers served as clerks for ECJ judges, they possess unique knowledge of the 'inner workings of the [European] Court' (Leino-Sandberg 2021, 174). Like the SG's office, the Commission has historically cultivated a 'special rapport' with the ECJ: the Court trusts that the LS will work 'in the service of the European interest' (Leino-Sandberg 2021, xi, 140–41) and will ensure that 'the general interest of the Community takes precedence at all times'.[15] At the same time, the ECJ looks to the Commission for signals of what is politically feasible given the latter's involvement in the EU's intergovernmental politics. Hence, just as the US Supreme Court treats the SG's observations as something of an 'answer sheet', so too does the ECJ develop its case law with an eye to the arguments of the Commission LS. For instance, recent archival work traces how the ECJ's ground-breaking decisions holding that EU law has primacy over conflicting national law and can be directly invoked by private litigants before national courts were devised by LS lawyers and then appropriated by the Court (Rasmussen 2012; Boerger and Rasmussen 2014).

Quantitative evidence confirms that the ECJ follows the Commission's LS to a remarkable degree. Not only does ECJ decision-making closely reflect the pro-EU bias in the LS' briefs (see Figure 22.4) but the LS wins the vast majority of the cases it argues before the Court. In cases lodged by Commission lawyers against member states for violations of EU law, the ECJ consistently sides with the LS 90 per cent of the time

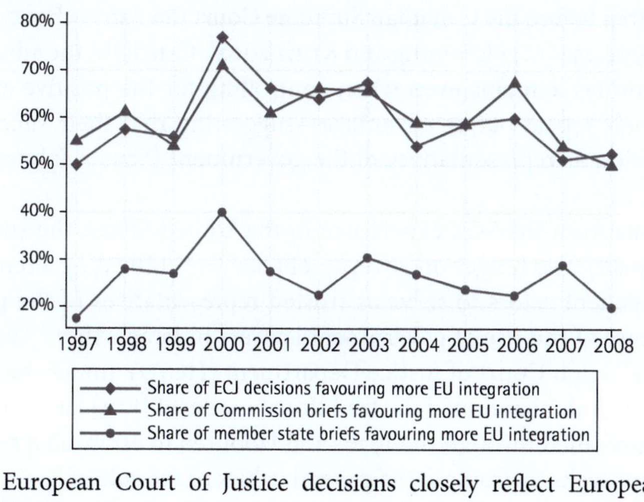

FIGURE 22.4 European Court of Justice decisions closely reflect European Commission lawyers' pro-EU briefs.

Notes: Draws from Larsson and Naurin (2016, 395), figure 2.

(Kelemen and Pavone 2023, 797). Where the LS intervenes in disputes lodged by private parties and referred to the ECJ by national courts (known as 'preliminary reference' cases), the Court sides with the LS just under 80 per cent of the time (Stone Sweet and Brunell 2012, 211). And when 'the Commission favors the plaintiff [in a case], the Court listens': a plaintiff supported by the LS is approximately twice as likely to win compared to a plaintiff that is not supported by the LS (Stone Sweet and Brunell 2012, 210). Private attorneys do not come close to replicating the success rate of the EU's 'government' lawyers: attorneys representing individuals prevail in one-third to one-half of the cases they argue before the ECJ, whereas attorneys representing businesses prevail one-quarter to two-fifths of the time (Hermansen, Pavone, and Boulaziz 2023).

We can identify scope conditions to the foregoing findings that open fruitful pathways for comparative research. These conditions hinge on the variegated capacity of governments to mobilize the resources necessary to employ specialized teams of litigators, to cultivate the human capital necessary to boost these legal units' prestige, and to forbear from excessive partisan politicization. When it comes to resources and human capital, a revealing comparison is offered by the divergent success of government litigators in South Africa and Canada. In post-apartheid South Africa, the fledgling democratic state initially lacked resources and depended on a rotating cast of private attorneys to represent it in court (Haynie and Sill 2007, 446–47). Once funds were appropriated to employ government litigators in 2007—by creating the office of the Chief Litigation Officer (OCLO)—the office struggled to recruit high-profile attorneys and remains a low-prestige post for South African lawyers (Klaaren 2016). Unsurprisingly, statistical analyses find that the South African 'government [is] unable to consistently prevail in litigation outcomes', and its advocates are no more likely to sway judges than lawyers representing private parties (Haynie and Sill 2007, 448–50). Conversely, in Canada, where the resource-rich Attorney General's office employs an elite unit of attorneys to represent it in court, government litigators historically prevail far more often before the Canadian Supreme Court than any other type of advocate (McCormick 1994, 152–67; Flemming and Krutz 2002). Crucially, the advantage of these 'government gorillas' remains even when controlling for the positive effect of lawyer experience—their repeat-player advantage—suggesting that their success inheres in their very position as representatives of the government (Szmer, Johnson, and Sarver 2007, 296–98).

Yet, as we saw from the SG's experience in the United States, the success of a politics of positionality also hinges on government lawyers cultivating a reputation as sufficiently independent actors to serve as trusted representatives of the public interest. Consider the case of the rise of government lawyers in Israel. There, career lawyers in the 'prestig[ous]' High Court of Justice Department (HCJD), under the supervision of the Attorney General, 'abandoned the traditional model of [just] lawyering for the government' that prevailed through the 1970s and laboured to establish a reputation as an 'organ that [also] seeks to promote the general values of the rule of law' and is 'accountable' to the Israeli Supreme Court (Dotan 2014, 63, 75, 87). This institutional double-hatting paid off: the Supreme Court—soon presided over by Aharon Barak, himself the former Attorney General—began treating 'the cooperation of the department' as essential, and the HCJD as a 'natural ally in its struggle to enhance its influence over society' (Dotan 2014, 82, 85). Unsurprisingly, then, by the 1990s HCJD lawyers grew significantly more successful in defending the government before the Court (boasting a 58.5 per cent win rate) compared to other government attorneys, such as those representing municipalities (with a 45.8 per cent win rate) (Dotan 2014, 106–08). Of course, recently the Israeli government has made the choice to renounce a politics of positionality supportive of the Court and shift to lawyer-style power politics targeting the Court, a U-turn with explosive consequences, as we will soon see.

In short, a politics of positionality is a strategic balancing act: given a government with enough resources to nurture human capital and endow lawyers with a repeat-player advantage, the most successful attorneys also leverage their political embeddedness as the government's agents while simultaneously wielding their judicial embeddedness to serve as the court's trustees. Too much of the former and their credibility in court is compromised; too much of the latter and their loyalty in government is scrutinized, jeopardizing their career. But when the right balance is struck, no party can match the capacity of government lawyers to come out ahead in court.

5. Executives and Judicial Autonomy: Power Politics, Lawyer-Style

Across the world, executive power is making an unlikely resurgence. I say 'unlikely' because it was fashionable in the 1990s and early 2000s to presume that globalization and the post-Cold War spread of liberal democracy[16] would go hand in hand with the 'disaggregation' of executive power and the rise of judicial power (Slaughter 2004, 35). Given these political developments, lawyers would 'enthusiastically suppor[t] efforts to delegate power to the judiciary' (Hirschl 2004, 63). After all, 'the fight by lawyers for judicial autonomy' in countries like France, Germany, and the United States suggested that lawyers would be inclined to cultivate political liberalism and support a 'moderate state' (Halliday, Karpik, and Feeley 2007, 4). For our purposes, the implication is that the more lawyers can achieve positions of executive influence, the more moderate the government and the greater its deference to an autonomous judiciary.

We certainly know of cases that fit the foregoing narrative, such as the critical support that the Israeli Attorney General's office offered the Supreme Court in the 1980s and 1990s in its assertive exercise of judicial review (Dotan 2014). But what is most striking about the post-Cold War era has been the rise of executive branch attorneys who weaponize their legal training and power to cow judges into obeisance and undermine democratic checks and balances. As we will see, even government lawyers in Israel are now mobilizing to disempower the very court they helped empower in the past.

As the world experienced a 'democratic recession' (Diamond 2015, Levitsky and Way 2019) and the share of the population living in autocratizing states spiked from 5 per cent in 2011 to 36 per cent in 2021 (V-Dem 2002, 7), we have witnessed the rise of a cadre of 'autocratic legalists'—attorneys with both feet planted in the executive branch who seek to dismantle liberal democracy by law (Scheppele 2018). Some of these government lawyers are even 'lawyers-in-chief'—chief executives like Vladimir Putin in Russia and Viktor Orbán in Hungary, who are 'deeply trained as lawyers and their governing styles reflect their legal education' (Scheppele 2019, 362). Elsewhere from Turkey, Venezuela, Brazil, and most recently Israel, wannabe-autocrats deploy executive branch attorneys to devise a modular script for capturing institutions that can check what the government does, which is to say to go after the courts (Corrales 2015; Lieblich and Shinar 2023).

Figure 22.5 visualizes the worrying trend 'buried within the general phenomenon of democratic decline': the increasing government attacks on courts and the correlated decline in their independence (Scheppele 2018, 545). But even Figure 22.5 does not capture the whole story: it traces public speeches and rhetorical affronts that are easiest

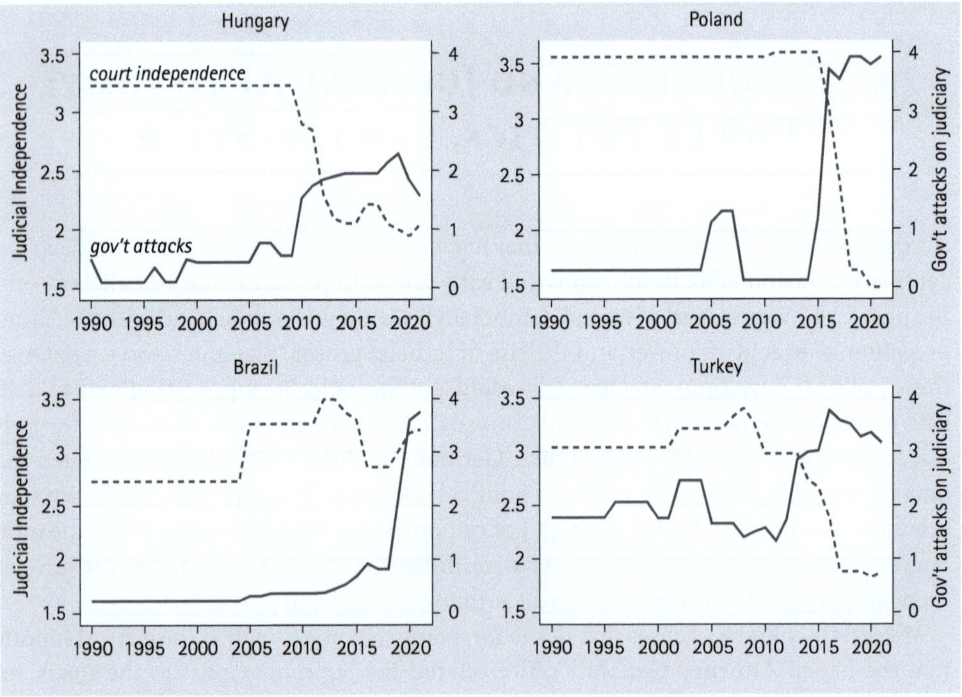

FIGURE 22.5 Judicial independence eroded in tandem with rising government attacks on the courts in Hungary, Poland, Brazil, and Turkey.

Notes: Data is from Varieties of Democracy (V-DEM), version 12. For judicial independence, I use the high court independence variable. The government attacks variable is reverse-coded for ease of interpretation, such that both variables range from 0 (low) to 4 (high). See Coppedge et al. (2022).

Source: Coppedge et al. 2022. 'VDem [Country–Year/Country–Date] Dataset v12'. Varieties of Democracy (V-Dem) Project. Available at: https://doi.org/10.23696/vdemds22.

to perceive and measure. In addition to these 'informal' court-curbing tools that non-lawyers may be better equipped to use,[17] autocratic legalists engage in a form of *lawyer-style power politics*: they mobilize their legal training to weaponize the law and make it appear like the executive is reforming the judiciary to make it more efficient or responsive. By the time coercion comes into play and rule *by* law supplants the rule *of* law (Ginsburg and Moustafa 2008), the courts may be co-opted to such an extent that they no longer serve as a forum to challenge the government.

For instance, autocratic legalists might expand a high court's jurisdiction to flood it with new cases—and then justify packing the court with executive-appointed (loyalist) judges. This strategy makes it appear as if high courts are being strengthened by improving their accessibly and efficiency, when in reality the judiciary's leadership is being co-opted. Upon taking power in 2010, Hungarian Prime Minister and lawyer-in-chief Viktor Orbán pushed through a new constitution that expanded the Constitutional Court's jurisdiction to include constitutional complaints (borrowing from the much-admired German constitutional system). To respond to the rising caseload, the new constitution also expanded the Court from eleven judges to fifteen—enabling the Orbán government to pack the Court with loyalists. To make it clear that the newly packed Court should not follow its previously autonomous (and much-admired) predecessor by taking rights seriously, the Orbán government amended the Constitution in 2013 to nullify the previous twenty years of the Court's case law (Kelemen and Orenstein 2016, 551–53).

Poland during the eight-year rule of the Law and Justice (PiS) party offers another example of autocratic legalism as embodied in the government's top lawyer: Zbigniew Ziobro. Following PiS' electoral victory in 2015, Ziobro was appointed Minister of Justice. Ziobro used his executive post to secure a majority of the seats in the National Council of the Judiciary, appointing more than a dozen new members 'who [owed] him everything'. Then in 2016 the PiS parliamentary majority pushed through legislation that made Ziobro not just the top government lawyer but also the chief prosecutor (Prosecutor General). This allowed him to manipulate criminal proceedings in the name of 'efficiency', force all court presidents to 'report to him',[18] and prosecute judges who 'mishandle' cases involving his personal or party interests.[19] Then in 2017, new PiS legislation empowered Ziobro to fire and appoint court presidents within six months, a power he weaponized to replace the leadership of one-fifth (158 out of 730) of all Polish courts, solidifying Ziobro's grips over judges' careers (Sadurski 2019, 115–16). Having Ziobro consolidate executive power over the judiciary was particularly efficacious because he was a former member of the Legal Affairs Committee of the European Parliament: once EU officials noticed the reforms and debated whether to respond, Ziobro knew which EU legal arguments to spin into a 'rhetoric of inaction' (Emmons and Pavone 2021).

Executive branch attorneys figure prominently in power politics well beyond Hungary and Poland: from Venezuelan President Hugo Chavez's creation of a new Supreme Court in 1999 and its legislative packing in 2005 (Corrales 2015, 43–44), to the design of a constitutional referendum in 2010 that enabled Turkish President Recep

Erdoğan's to solidify political control of the Constitutional Court (Keck 2022, 145), to Brazilian prosecutors developing a legal discourse that was weaponized post-2019 by President Jair Bolsonaro to justify 'act[ing] beyond the existing law' in response to 'existential threats' (De Sá e Silva 2020, 110), to Israeli Justice Minister Yariv Levin's selective use of comparative constitutional law in 2023 to propose judicial reforms drastically curbing the Supreme Court's judicial review powers and enabling the Parliamentary override of Court decisions by simple majority (Jaffe-Hoffman 2023; Lieblich and Shinar 2023). Across the world, lawyers in the executive branch are emerging as a fierce adversary of autonomous judges.

In many instances, lawyer-style power politics succeed in engineering judicial quiescence. As Figure 22.5 makes clear, judicial independence is at best on life support in countries like Hungary and Turkey. In Venezuela, out of 45,474 decisions rendered by the Supreme Court after it was packed by the Chavez regime, not once did its judges rule against the government (Corrales 2015, 44). Even the newly-elected democratic government in Poland is having to grapple with a captured Polish Constitutional Tribunal long habituated to doing PiS' bidding. For instance, in response to a court action spearheaded by Minister Ziobro, in 2021 the Tribunal declared some provisions of the European Convention on Human Rights[20] (and later the primacy of EU law)[21] to be unconstitutional, blunting judges and civil society's attempts to mobilize European law to promote a democratic transition. Installing loyalists in high places often does the trick. Other times, handing begrudging judges a 'carrot' can help reward quiescence and make the 'stick' easier to bear. When in 2012 the Orbán government lowered the judicial retirement age to forcibly retire half of lower court presidents, it promised to pay those judges a year's salary to stay retired instead of heeding EU calls to return to their posts (Halmai 2017, 482–83).[22] Most judges took the deal.

On occasion, however, autocratic legalism can proceed so brusquely that it triggers rare forms of judicial behaviour: namely, 'off-bench mobilization', protests, and coalition-building with social movement activists (Bakiner 2016). In the leadup to Poland's October 2023 election that saw the democratic opposition defeat PiS at the ballot box, many judges became activists by 'protesting on the streets, spreading information through social media and the websites of their associations and are reaching out to the European Commission and European Parliament' (Matthes 2022, 468). European judicial associations like *Magistrats européens pour la démocratie et les libertés* (MENDEL) also mobilized to put pressure on national and EU politicians to defend their colleagues, including by challenging the disbursement of EU funds to Poland in a lawsuit before the ECJ (Shipley 2022). In Israel, proposed reforms to gut the Supreme Court's judicial review powers provoked massive protests and general strikes that brought together a cross-cutting coalition of jurists, labour unions, business interests, opposition party activists, and everyday citizens. The protests were so large and sustained that they attracted widespread international attention (Estrin and Khalid 2023; Weinrib and Weinrib 2023) and forced Justice Minister Levin and Prime Minister Benjamin Netanyahu reluctantly to pause and then abandon some of the planned reforms, as protesters continued to gather in the streets until the sudden outbreak of the

Israel-Hamas war in October 2023 (Freedman 2023). The Polish and Israeli examples suggest that judges need a cross-cutting and unified political opposition at their side to stand any chance of blocking or reversing an executive takeover of the courts. At the same time, judges may be uniquely placed to legitimate popular opposition, institutionalize its tactics, and attract an international audience.[23]

Still, judges rarely abandon their commitment to 'apoliticism' in dramatic fashion, even when faced with the spectre of autocracy (Hilbink 2007). Armed with government attorneys unencumbered by a commitment to political liberalism, executive aggrandizers often get their way when they target the courts. Our understanding of judicial behaviour would thus be greatly enriched by structured comparisons of clashes between autocratic legalists and the courts, to identify when these clashes push judges into rare off-bench resistance and when they instead manufacture judges' deference.

6. Conclusion: Fertile Next Steps

No scholar of comparative judicial behaviour can ignore the potentially enormous influence that government lawyers wield over the courts. Government lawyers can in some instances determine the contours of courts' agendas; they are often the most successful architects of judges' decisions; and they can wield their executive power to curtail judicial autonomy and induce quiescence. Government lawyers also cannot be vapourized as mere emissaries of their governments, under the presumption that 'the government' speaks through them. As actors who repeatedly find themselves in court, government attorneys can sometimes carve a surprising amount of bureaucratic autonomy for themselves; as legal professionals, they have a distinctly legalistic style of governance that distinguishes them from other executive actors, even when they aid and abet executive power politics. Government lawyers are powerful agents in their own right—neither interchangeable with private attorneys nor subsumable with other government officials.

By tracing three distinct politics waged by government lawyers—a politics of discretion, a politics of positionality, and lawyer-style power politics—I have sought to identify three non-exhaustive mechanisms of influence over judicial behaviour. Examples illustrating these mechanisms are abundant, only a fraction of which have been mentioned here. What remains scarce is a coherent attempt to synthesize the study of these politics with the study of comparative judicial politics. Yet, if we care about where judges' agendas come from; if we care about why judges rule the way they do; if we care about the political environment that constrains or enables judicial review, then government lawyers must be placed at the heart of our conversation.

Taking government lawyers seriously has benefits beyond explaining the microfoundations of judicial decision-making. It also forces scholars of comparative law and politics to embed courts in a broader political constellation of actors and processes.

By shadowing these liminal intermediaries as they shuttle back and forth between governments, courts, and society, we can unearth the myriad ways that judicial behaviour *in court* is entangled in a broader politics *outside court.* If we are interested in how elections or intergovernmental politics shape opportunities for judicial review; if we ponder whether state capacity and bureaucratic autonomy may undergird the rise of judicial power; if we are curious about the forces that are undermining judicial independence and eroding liberal democracy, then following the footsteps of government attorneys is an excellent place to start.

To be sure, government lawyers are not all-powerful. They can be starved of resources or fired from their posts when they stray too far; they can tarnish their credibility and trustworthiness in the eyes of judges; they can interfere too brusquely in courts' affairs and trigger rare forms of judicial resistance. Having recognized their potentially enormous influence over judicial agendas, decisions, and autonomy, comparativists are uniquely placed to illuminate which political conditions tend to amplify and constrain government attorneys' influence over the courts. Much fertile terrain remains to be treaded on this front. To borrow from Marx, we might well say that government lawyers make their own judiciaries, but they do not make them as they please.[24] Therein lies the social science puzzle.

Notes

1 Lawyers only make up 0.4 per cent of the adult US population, by contrast. These figures are for the 115th Congress (Bonica 2020, 253).

2 This figure surveys cabinet ministers across fourteen European countries from the 1940s to the 1980s (Thiebault 1991, 22).

3 Rebecca Mae Salokar. 1994. *The Solicitor General: The Politics of Law*. Philadelphia: Temple University Press.

4 Here, I borrow from Fukuyama's (2014, 23–39) definition of political development, which centres on the evolution and entanglement of three institutions: the state (especially the executive), the rule of law (especially the judiciary and the legal profession), and mechanisms of accountability (especially democratic elections).

5 On a classic comparison of the development of the legal profession in a common law state and a civil law state, see Rueschemeyer (1973).

6 Many thanks to Urška Šadl for raising this important example.

7 On the importance of resource mobilization for litigation campaigns, see Epp (1998).

8 By mechanisms, I follow the definition provided by Beach and Pedersen (2019, 99–100), namely a set of entities, or actors, engaging in activities.

9 Compare the cert petition success rate of Clement as non-SG attorney to when he served as SG in Feldman and Kappner (2016, 820, 828). Black and Owens (2016) also find that former SGs are no more likely to obtain the Court's support compared to attorneys with similar levels of experience.

10 For instance, American judges are highly dependent on and deferential to prosecutors' evidence and charging decisions (Ross 2006; Johnson and Hernandez 2021, 75).

11 Prosecutors are not allowed to overcharge, and plea bargains cannot be used to avoid trial (Ma 2002).

12 That is, 259 out of 531 new cases in 2004, versus fifty-two of 622 new cases in 2014 (Kelemen and Pavone 2023).

13 This decline in litigation success occurred in particular after Rex Lee was criticized for being insufficiently loyal as SG to the Reagan administration, and was replaced by the more obedient Charles Fried (Wohlfarth 2009, 227–28, 231, 234).

14 Probably the most influential director of the LS is Michel Gaudet, who built up the service and established its unparalleled influence over the ECJ from 1958 to 1967 (Bailleux 2013).

15 Case C-432/04, *Commission of the European Communities v Edith Cresson* [2006], ECLI:EU:C:2006:455, para 71.

16 This belief was epitomized in Francis Fukuyama's (1992) 'end of history' thesis.

17 On 'informal' vs 'formal' court-curbing by the executive, see Aydin-Cakir (2023).

18 These quotations are from President of the Polish Supreme Court Małgorzata Maria Gersdorf, describing Ziobro's role in the rise of autocratic legalism in Poland, as quoted in Sadurski (2019, 96).

19 For instance, Ziobro's Prosecutor General office opened criminal proceedings against Krakow judge Pilarczyk for her conduct in a dispute involving Ziobro's late father; see Sadurski (2019, 119).

20 Specifically, the Tribunal ruled Article 6 of the ECHR on the right to a fair trial to be unconstitutional, after the European Court of Human Rights invoked Article 6 to hold that the Tribunal was violating citizens' right to a fair trial because it is politically captured (Ploszka 2022).

21 The Tribunal ruled unconstitutional Article 19(1) of the Treaty on European Union (guaranteeing effective legal and judicial protection), after the European Court of Justice invoked the article to hold that the government's judicial reforms violated EU law (Bard and Bodnar 2021).

22 The PiS Ministry of Justice in Poland copied this strategy to lower the judicial retirement age a few years later (Sadurski 2019, 121).

23 On the importance of these strategies to the success of resistances to democratic backsliding, see Gamboa (2022).

24 Here, I riff off Marx's (1852) famous phrase that 'men make their own history, but they do not make it as they please'.

References

Abel, Richard, and Philip Lewis. 1988. *Lawyers in Society: The Civil Law World*. Berkeley: University of California Press.

Abel, Richard, and Philip Lewis. 1989. *Lawyers in Society: Comparative Theories*. Berkeley: University of California Press.

Abel, Richard, and Philip Lewis. 1995. *Lawyers in Society: An Overview*. Berkeley: University of California Press.

Abel, Richard, Ole Hammerslev, Hilary Sommerlad, and Ulrike Schultz. 2020. *Lawyers in 21st-Century Societies: National Reports*. London: Bloomsbury.

Abel, Richard, Ole Hammerslev, Hilary Sommerlad, and Ulrike Schultz. 2022. *Lawyers in 21st-Century Societies: Comparisons and Theories*. London: Bloomsbury.

Alter, Karen. 2014. *The New Terrain of International Law: Courts, Politics, Rights*. Princeton: Princeton University Press.

Aydin-Cakir, Aylin. 2023. 'The Varying Effect of Court-Curbing: Evidence from Hungary and Poland'. *Journal of European Public Policy* 1–27.

Bailey, Michael, Brian Kamoie, and Forrest Maltzman. 2005. 'Signals from the Tenth Justice: The Political Role of the Solicitor General in Supreme Court Decision Making'. *American Journal of Political Science* 49 (1): 72–85.

Bailleux, Julie. 2013. 'Michel Gaudet, a Law Entrepreneur'. *Common Market Law Review* 50 (2): 359–67.

Bakiner, Onur. 2016. 'Judges Discover Politics: Sources of Judges' Off-Bench Mobilization in Turkey'. *Journal of Law and Courts* 4 (1): 131–57.

Bard, Petra, and Adam Bodnar. 2021. 'The End of an Era: The Polish Constitutional Court's Judgment on the Primacy of EU Law and its Effects on Mutual Trust'. *CEPS Policy Insights No. 2021-15*: 1–7. Available at: https://www.ceps.eu/wp-content/uploads/2021/10/PI2021-15_The-end-of-an-era_The-Polish-Constitutional-Courts-judgment-on-the-primacy-of-EU-law-and-its-effects-on-mutual-trust.pdf.

Beach, Derek and Rasmus Brun Pedersen. 2019. *Process-tracing Methods: Foundations and Guidelines*. Ann Arbor: University of Michigan Press.

Black, Ryan, and Ryan Owens. 2011. 'Solicitor General influence and agenda setting on the US Supreme Court.' *Political Research Quarterly* 64 (4): 765–78.

Black, Ryan, and Ryan Owens. 2012. 'A Built-In Advantage: The Office of the Solicitor General and the U.S. Supreme Court'. *Political Research Quarterly* 66 (2): 454–66.

Black, Ryan, and Ryan Owens. 2016. 'The Success of Former Solicitors General in Private Practice: Costly and Unnecessary?' *Michigan State Law Review*: 325–65.

Boerger, Anne, and Morten Rasmussen. 2014. 'Transforming European Law: The Establishment of the Constitutional Discourse from 1950 to 1993'. *European Constitutional Law Review* 10 (2): 199–225.

Bonica, Adam. 2020. 'Why Are There So Many Lawyers in Congress?' *Legislative Studies Quarterly* 45 (2): 253–89.

Brinks, Daniel. 2007. *The Judicial Response to Police Killings in Latin America: Inequality and the Rule of Law*. Cambridge: Cambridge University Press.

Brubacher, Matthew. 2004. 'Prosecutorial Discretion within the International Criminal Court'. *Journal of International Criminal Justice* 2: 71–95.

Bruff, Harold. 2009. *Bad Advice: Bush's Lawyers in the War on Terror*. Lawrence: University Press of Kansas.

Caplan, Lincoln. 1987. *The Tenth Justice: The Solicitor General and the Rule of Law*. New York: Knopf.

Carnes, Nicholas, and Noam Lupu. 2015. 'Rethinking the Comparative Perspective on Class and Representation: Evidence from Latin America'. *American Journal of Political Science* 59 (1): 1–18.

Casey, Conor, and David Kenny. 2022. 'The Gatekeepers: Executive Lawyers and the Executive Power in Comparative Constitutional Law'. *International Journal of Constitutional Law* 20 (2): 664–95.

Chandler, Adam. 2011. 'The Solicitor General of the United States: Tenth Justice or Zealous Advocate?' *Yale Law Journal* 121: 725–37.

Coppedge, Michael, John Gerring, Carl Henrik Knutsen, Staffan Lindberg, Svend-Erik Skaaning, Jan Teorell, David Altman et al. 2022. 'VDem [Country–Year/Country–Date]

Dataset v12'. Varieties of Democracy (V-Dem) Project. Available at: https://doi.org/10.23696/vdemds22.

Corrales, Javier. 2015. 'The Authoritarian Resurgence: Autocratic legalism in Venezuela'. *Journal of Democracy* 26 (2): 37–51.

De Sá e Silva, Fabio. 2020. 'From Car Wash to Bolsonaro: Law and Lawyers in Brazil's Illiberal Turn (2014–2018)'. *Journal of Law and Society* 47: 90–110.

Dewey, Matias, and Donato Di Carlo. 2021. 'Governing through Non-Enforcement: Regulatory Forbearance as Industrial Policy in Advanced Economies'. *Regulation and Governance* 16 (3): 930–50.

Dezelay, Yves, and Bryant Garth. 2002. *The Internationalization of the Palace Wars: Lawyers, Economists, and the Contest to Transform Latin American States*. Chicago: University of Chicago Press.

Diamond, Larry. 2015. 'Facing up to the Democratic Recession'. *Journal of Democracy* 26 (1): 141–55.

Dotan, Yoav. 2014. *Lawyering for the Rule of Law: Government Lawyers and the Rise of Judicial Power in Israel*. Cambridge: Cambridge University Press.

Epp, Charles. 1998. *The Rights Revolution: Lawyers, Activists, and Supreme Courts in Comparative Perspective*. Chicago: University of Chicago Press.

Epstein, Lee, and Michael Nelson. 2022. 'Human Capital in Court: The Role of Attorney Experience in Supreme Court Litigation'. *Journal of Law & Courts* 10 (1): 61–85.

Emmons, Cassandra, and Tommaso Pavone. 2021. 'The Rhetoric of Inaction: Failing to Fail Forward in the EU's Rule of Law Crisis'. *Journal of European Public Policy* 28 (1): 1611–29.

Estrin, Daniel, and Asma Khalid. 2023. 'Biden Expresses Concern for Israel Judicial Overhaul Plan'. *National Public Radio*, 2 April, available at: https://www.npr.org/2023/04/02/1167665451/biden-expresses-concern-for-israel-judicial-overhaul-plan

Feierherd, German. 2020. 'Courting Informal Workers: Exclusion, Forbearance, and the Left'. *American Journal of Political Science* 66 (2): 418–33.

Feldman, Adam, and Alexander Kappner. 2016. 'Finding Certainty in Cert: An Empirical Analysis of the Factors Involved in Supreme Court Certiorari Decisions from 2001–2015'. *Villanova Law Review* 61: 795–842.

Flemming, Roy, and Glen Krutz. 2002. 'Repeat Litigators and Agenda Setting on the Supreme Court of Canada'. *Canadian Journal of Political Science* 35 (4): 811–33.

Freedman, Eliyahu. 2023. 'Israel Protesters Vow to Continue Until Judicial "Reform" Gone'. *Al Jazeera*, 28 March, available at: https://www.aljazeera.com/news/2023/3/28/israel-protesters-vow-to-continue-until-judicial-reform-gone.

Freeman, Will. 2023. *Ending Impunity: The Prosecution of Grand Corruption in Latin America*. PhD. Dissertation, Princeton University.

Fukuyama, Francis. 1992. *The End of History and the Last Man*. New York: Simon … Schuster.

Fukuyama, Francis. 2014. *Political Order and Political Decay: From the Industrial Revolution to the Globalization of Democracy*. New York: Farrar, Straus, and Giroux.

Galanter, Marc. 1974. 'Why the "Haves" Come out Ahead: Speculations on the Limits of Legal Change'. *Law … Society Review* 9 (1): 95–160.

Gamboa, Laura. 2022. *Resisting Backsliding: Opposition Strategies Against the Erosion of Democracy*. Cambridge: Cambridge University Press.

Gillman, Howard, Graber, Mark, and Keith Whittington. 2013. *American Constitutionalism, Vol II: Rights and Liberties*. Oxford: Oxford University Press.

Ginsburg, Tom, and Tamir Moustafa. 2008. *Rule by Law: The Politics of Courts in Authoritarian Regimes*. Cambridge: Cambridge University Press.

Hain, Paul, and James Piereson. 1975. 'Lawyers and Politics Revisited: Structural Advantages of Lawyer-Politicians'. *American Journal of Political Science* 19 (1): 41–51.

Halliday, Terence, and Lucien Karpik. 1997. *Lawyers and the Rise of Western Political Liberalism*. Oxford: Oxford University Press.

Halliday, Terence, Lucien Karpik, and Malcolm Feeley. 2007. *Fighting for Political Freedom*. London: Bloomsbury.

Halmai, Gabor. 2017. 'The Early Retirement Age of the Hungarian Judges'. In *EU Law Stories*, edited by Fernanda Nicola and Bill Davies, 471–88. New York: Cambridge University Press.

Hamilton, Alexander. 1788. 'Federalist No. 78'. Available at: https://guides.loc.gov/federalist-papers/text-71-80#s-lg-box-wrapper-25493470.

Haynie, Stacia, and Ernest Dover. 1994. 'Prosecutorial Discretion and Press Coverage: The Decision to Try a Case'. *American Politics Quarterly* 22 (3): 370–81.

Haynie, Stacia, and Kaitlyn Sill. 2007. 'Experienced Advocates and Litigation Outcomes: Repeat Players in the South African Supreme Court of Appeal'. *Political Research Quarterly* 60 (3): 443–53.

Hendley, Kathryn. 1996. *Trying to Make Law Matter: Legal Reform and Labor Law in the Soviet Union*. Ann Arbor: University of Michigan Press.

Hermansen, Silje, Tommaso Pavone, and Louisa Boulaziz. 2023. 'Leveling and Spotlighting: How International Courts Refract Private Litigation to Build Institutional Legitimacy'. Paper on file with author.

Hilbink, Lisa. 2007. *Judges Beyond Politics in Democracy and Dictatorship: Lessons from Chile*. Cambridge: Cambridge University Press.

Hinrichsen, Simon. 2021. 'The Iraq Sovereign Debt Restructuring'. *Capital Markets Journal* 16 (1): 95–114.

Hirschl, Ran. 2004. *Towards Juristocracy: The Origins and Consequences of the New Constitutionalism*. Cambridge: Harvard University Press.

Hofmann, Andreas. 2013. 'Strategies of the Repeat Player: The European Commission between Courtroom and Legislature'. PhD thesis, University of Cologne.

Holland, Alisha. 2016. 'Forbearance'. *American Political Science Review* 110 (2): 232–46.

Holland, Alisha. 2017. *Forbearance as Redistribution: The Politics of Informal Welfare in Latin America*. Cambridge: Cambridge University Press.

Horowitz, Donald. 1977. *The Courts and Social Policy*. Washington: Brookings Institution Press.

Jaffe-Hoffman, Maayan. 2023. 'Is Judicial Reform Dangerous for Israeli Democracy?' *Jerusalem Post*, 10 February.

Johnson, Brian, and Raquel Hernandez. 2021. 'Prosecutors and Plea Bargaining'. In *The Oxford Handbook of Prosecutors and Prosecution*, edited by Ronald F. Wright, Kay L. Levine, and Russell M. Gold, 75–100. Oxford: Oxford University Press.

Johnson, Timothy, Paul Wahlbeck, and James Spriggs II. 2006. 'The Influence of Oral Arguments on the US Supreme Court'. *American Political Science Review* 100 (1): 99–113.

Kastellec, Jonathan, and Huchen Liu. 2023. 'The Revolving Door in Judicial Politics: Former Clerks and Agenda Setting on the U.S. Supreme Court'. *American Politics Research* 51 (1): 3–22.

Keck, Thomas. 2022. 'Court-Packing and Democratic Erosion'. In *Democratic Resilience*, edited by Robert Lieberman, Suzanne Mettler, and Kenneth Roberts. Cambridge: Cambridge University Press: 141–68.

Kelemen, R. Daniel, and Mitchell Orenstein. 2016. 'Europe's Autocracy Problem'. *Foreign Affairs*, 7 January.

Kelemen, R. Daniel, and Tommaso Pavone. 2023. 'Where Have the Guardians Gone? Law Enforcement and the Politics of Supranational Forbearance in the European Union'. *World Politics* 75 (4): 779–825.

Klaaren, Jonathan. 2016. 'Civil Government Lawyers in South Africa'. *New York Law School Law Review* 60: 417–29.

Komaiko, Richard, and Beibei Que. 2009. *Lawyers in Modern China*. Amherst: Cambria Press.

Kritzer, Herbert. 1994. 'Interpretation and Validity Assessment in Qualitative Research: The Case of H.W. Perry's Deciding to Decide'. *Law ... Social Inquiry* 19 (3): 687–724.

Kritzer, Herbert M. 1998. *Legal Advocacy: Lawyers and Nonlawyers at Work*. Ann Arbor: University of Michigan Press.

Langer, Maximo, and David Sklansky, 2017. *Prosecutors and Democracy: A Cross-National Study*. Cambridge: Cambridge University Press.

Larsson, Olof, and Daniel Naurin. 2016. 'Judicial independence and political uncertainty: how the risk of override affects the Court of Justice of the EU.' *International Organization* 70 (2): 377–408.

Leino-Sandberg, Päivi. 2021. *The Politics of Legal Expertise in EU Policy-Making*. Cambridge: Cambridge University Press.

Levitsky, Steven, and Lucan Way. 2019. *How Democracies Die*. Portland: Broadway Books.

Lieblich, Eliav, and Adam Shinar. 2023. 'The End of Israeli Democracy? Netanyahu's Latest Reforms Come Straight from the Autocrat's Playbook'. *Foreign Affairs*, 8 February.

Ma, Ye. 2002. 'Prosecutorial Discretion and Plea Bargaining in the United States, France, Germany, and Italy'. *International Criminal Justice Review* 12: 22–52.

Marx, Karl. 1852. *The Eighteenth Brumaire of Louis Bonaparte*, ch 1. Available at: https://www.marxists.org/archive/marx/works/1852/18th-brumaire/ch01.html.

Matthes, Claudia-Y. 2022. 'Judges as Activists: How Polish Judges Mobilise to Defend the Rule of Law'. *East European Politics* 38 (3): 468–87.

McCormick, Peter. 1994. *Canada's Courts*. Toronto: James Lorimer.

Meager, Lizzie, Edward Price, and Brian Yap. 2016. 'How to Jump-Start Sovereign Debt'. *International Financial Law Review* 35: 23–26.

Michelson, Ethan. 2007. 'Lawyers, Political Embeddedness, and Institutional Continuity in China's Transition from Socialism'. *American Journal of Sociology* 113 (2): 352–414.

Miller, Mark. 2002. *The High Priests of American Politics: The Role of Lawyers in American Political Institutions*. Knoxville: University of Tennessee Press.

Mnookin, Robert, and Lewis Kornhauser. 1979. 'Bargaining in the Shadow of the Law: The Case of Divorce'. *Yale Law Journal* 88 (5): 950–97.

Pavone, Tommaso. 2022. *The Ghostwriters: Lawyers and the Politics behind the Judicial Construction of Europe*. Cambridge: Cambridge University Press.

Pavone, Tommaso, and Øyvind Stiansen. 2022. 'The Shadow Effect of Courts'. *American Political Science Review* 116 (1): 322–36.

Perry, H.W. 1994. *Deciding to Decide: Agenda Setting in the United States Supreme Court*. Cambridge: Harvard University Press.

Ploszka, Adam. 2022. 'It Never Rains but it Pours'. *Hague Journal on the Rule of Law* 15 (1): 1–24.

Rasmussen, Morten. 2012. 'Establishing a Constitutional Practice of European law: The History of the Legal Service of the European Executive, 1952–65'. *Contemporary European History* 21 (3): 375–97.

Ross, Jacqueline. 2006. 'The Entrenched Position of Plea Bargains in United States Legal Practice'. *American Journal of Comparative Law* 54: 717–32.

Rueschemeyer, Dietrich. 1973. *Lawyers and their Society: A Comparative Study of the Legal Profession in Germany and in the United States*. Cambridge: Harvard University Press.

Sadurski, Wojciech. 2019. *Poland's Constitutional Breakdown*. Oxford: Oxford University Press.

Salokar, Rebecca. 1994. *The Solicitor General: The Politics of Law*. Philadelphia: Temple University Press.

Sawyer, Logan. 2020. 'Reform Prosecutors and the Separation of Powers'. *Oklahoma Law Review* 72: 603–34.

Scheppele, Kim Lane. 2018. 'Autocratic Legalism'. *University of Chicago Law Review* 85 (2): 545–84.

Scheppele, Kim Lane. 2019. 'The Legal Complex and Lawyers-in-Chief'. In *The Legal Process and the Promise of Justice: Studies Inspired by the Work of Malcolm Feeley*, Rosann Greenspan, Hadar Aviram, and Jonathan Simon, 361–84. Cambridge: Cambridge University Press.

Scheppele, Kim Lane. 2023. 'The Treaties Without a Guardian'. *Columbia Journal of European Law* 29 (2): 93–18.

Shipley, Trajan. 2022. 'European Judges v Council: The European Judiciary Stands up for the Rule of Law'. *EU Law Live*, 30 August.

Slaughter, Anne-Marie. 2004. *A New World Order*. Princeton: Princeton University Press.

Songer, Donald, Reginald Sheehan, and Susan Haire. 1999. 'Do the "Haves" Come out Ahead over Time?' *Law... Society Review* 33 (4): 811–32.

Stone Sweet, Alec, and Thomas Brunell. 2012. 'The European Court of Justice, State Noncompliance, and the Politics of Override'. *American Political Science Review* 106 (1): 204–13.

Szmer, John, Susan Johnson, and Tammy Sarver. 2007. 'Does the Lawyer Matter? Influencing Outcomes on the Supreme Court of Canada'. *Law... Society Review* 41 (2): 279–304.

Thiebault, Jean-Louis. 1991. 'The Social Background of Western European Cabinet Ministers'. In *The Profession of Government Minister in Western Europe*, edited by Jean Blondel and Jean-Louis Thiebault, 19–30. New York: St. Martin's Press.

V-Dem. 2022. *Democracy Report 2022: Autocratization Changing Nature?* Gothenberg: V-Dem Institute.

Vauchez, Antoine, and Pierre France. 2021. *The Neoliberal Republic: Corporate Lawyers, Statecraft, and the Making of Public-Private France*. Ithaca: Cornell University Press.

Voeten, Erik. 2022. 'Is the Public Backlash against Globalization a Backlash against Legalization and Judicialization?' *International Studies Review* 24 (2): 1–17.

Weinrib, Lorraine, and Ernest Weinrib. 2023. 'Statement by Canadian Law Professors and Jurists on the Proposed Legal Reforms in Israel'. *Verfassungsblog*, 10 February.

Wohlfarth, Patrick. 2009. 'The Tenth Justice? Consequences of Politicization of the Solicitor General's Office'. *Journal of Politics* 71 (1): 224–37.

CHAPTER 23

AGENDA SETTING

DIEGO WERNECK ARGUELHES AND
IVAR A. HARTMANN

1. Introduction and Definitions

In the underground floor of the UK Supreme Court, there is a small museum on the institution's history, role, and rules and practices of operation. Among the set of text boxes on display on the walls, there is one titled 'Case Selection'. The plaque describes the procedures by which plaintiffs in the appeal courts of Scotland, Wales, England, and Northern Ireland can apply for permission to bring a case to the UK Supreme Court. The plaque also asserts that, apart from a few exceptions regarding Scotland, the UK justice system operates on the assumption that the Supreme Court should largely 'determine its own workload': parties decide if and when they will appeal to the court, but it is the court, not the parties, that chooses what it will decide.

In this chapter, our focus is on agenda-setting, the mechanisms whereby courts decide what to decide. These institutional features are very consequential for courts, as they can shape both their power, standing, and role in the political community, and the behaviour of their individual judges. Much work needs to be done both on organizing information about the circumstances of case selection in different countries, and on consolidating the concepts and categories useful for court analysis and comparison. While information on case selection mechanisms in most countries is still insufficient to build a fully comprehensive comparative map, we present an overview of key aspects in which these institutions differ and existing empirical findings on how they are employed and why they matter for judicial behaviour.

To readers familiar with the now vast literature discussing the US Supreme Court's *writ of certiorari*—a procedure by which the court discretionarily accepts or refuses to hear an appeal against a lower court decision—case selection is a topic of evident public interest and concern about the functioning of courts. From this perspective, it might seem obvious that a twenty-first-century court, the UK Supreme Court, should explain to the public the general procedures by which it selects the cases it will decide. Moreover, to lawyers operating within the US legal system, it is hardly controversial that an apex court should possess the power to decide what it will decide—a system that UK judge Lord Bingham famously compared to 'dining à la carte'.[1] But this uncontroversial status quo in the United States was built over time, after decades of sustained inquiry and debate by journalists, social scientists, and lawyers. This general clarity over the basic rules and procedures of case selection has been characteristic of the US Supreme Court for a few decades now, and the *certiorari* mechanism has spawned a consolidated body of literature in law and in the social sciences. However, it is a relatively recent accomplishment in the country's history—and an even more exceptional feature in comparative terms.[2]

From a global, comparative perspective, both things—a court with the discretionary power to decide what it will decide, and this fact being publicly acknowledged and uncontroversial—are far from the norm. For decades, while it flourished in the US literature, the issues of agenda-setting and case selection were largely absent from the global conversation on courts. In the field of comparative constitutional law, discussions on courts focused primarily on powers, competences, and structures employed by judges to decide the merit of cases. Courts would be compared on how they deployed their decision-making powers in a certain jurisdiction and how they reasoned in deciding comparable issues.[3] Indeed, while our comparative knowledge advanced on patterns of judicial decision-making, little to no attention has been paid to what was not decided (see e.g. Rosenfeld and Sajo 2012).

Specialized constitutional courts typically do not have the formal, discretionary power to decide what will enter their docket (Comella 2004). Whatever they do to adjust the timing of their decisions, they typically do not do it as openly as their 'Supreme Court' counterparts. Observers of those systems might recognize that screening mechanisms might give courts some leeway in avoiding certain cases, but this possibility is generally under-theorized.

The idea that apex courts might avoid deciding certain issues at certain times, whatever the means they have to do so, and whatever their underlying motivations, is gaining traction in the legal literature on apex courts globally (see e.g. Dixon and Issacharoff 2016). This is a recent development, though, yet to be incorporated in standard comparisons between constitutional courts. When the issue of timing control and case selection finds its way into comparative discussions of constitutional courts, it is usually indirectly, not as a topic of comparison and analysis in itself. For example, a recent volume comparing European constitutional courts' institutional design and decision-making procedures in detail does not include any systematic discussion of how different courts select cases for decision, only of different techniques to deal with the temporal effects of legal decisions (de Visser 2015). However, the author notes that those courts end up deciding on the merits only a small fraction of the petitions they receive. Although the official justification for such screening would be to avoid too large an influx of cases, 'it may at the same time enable these courts to eschew potentially disruptive confrontations' with other national courts (de Visser 2015, 386).

In contrast, a recent volume comparing apex courts in mostly common law or hybrid jurisdictions openly discusses docket control and case selection mechanisms (Alarie and Green 2017). In a specific chapter, the book discusses both the mechanisms by which judges decide what to decide and potential explanations for those uses. The apparent correlation between 'constitutional court / Supreme Court' models and the 'discretionary/mandatory jurisdiction' features might explain, in part, the dearth of scholarly analysis and comparisons involving case selection in apex courts beyond the US Supreme Court. While it has more limited implications than it would seem at first glance (as we discuss in section 2), this conventional distinction arguably shaped different patterns of attention to case selection mechanisms across the globe.

Moreover, until very recently, comparative constitutional scholarship tended to focus on a limited set of Western democracies—the United States, France, Germany, the United Kingdom, what Hirschl (2014) labelled the 'World Series' syndrome. In this scenario, case selection in apex courts could more plausibly remain at the background, as a question of institutional detail. After all, most countries in the list of 'usual suspects' of comparative legal research had decades of case law on a common set of issues that draw the attention of lawyers across democracies—such as reproductive rights, federalism, equality, civil rights, and the right to vote. In these debates, comparative scholars focused on those 'usual suspects' did not need to explain why certain topics were largely absent from the jurisprudence of constitutional courts in recent democracies. Consider, for example, that for nearly two decades since its transition from military rule in the late 1980s, a democracy as large as Brazil did not have an 'abortion case', an 'affirmative action case', or even a 'transitional justice case' to contribute to comparative debates on constitutional adjudication.[4] Such long judicial silences in recent democracies is meaningful, but cannot be explained without attention to (and comparison of) case selection mechanisms (as we discuss in section 3).

One additional problem is that, in many jurisdictions, case selection is a delicate topic for the legal community. In Brazil, for example, even framing the question in terms of how judges 'select' or 'choose' cases for decision might not sit well with domestic lawyers and courts. Consider social media posts by the Brazilian Supreme Court's (STF) official accounts, with 'fact-checking' claims on the court's procedures. In 2021, the Court's official TikTok account posted a video explaining to the public that it is incorrect to say that the judges choose what they will decide, and that the STF's jurisdiction is determined by law, not by judicial choice.[5] Those assertions, however, run contrary to two decades of studies showing that, as practical matter, the STF has wide latitude to decide when and what to decide, by several different informal and indirect means (e.g. Oliveira 2005; Arguelhes and Hartmann 2017). Furthermore, even as a formal legal matter, in 2005 the STF gained the formal power to discretionarily refuse to accept in its docket a kind of appeal (*Recurso Extraordinário*) that represents more than 80 per cent of its workload (Garoupa and Oliveira 2012).

The UK Supreme Court's openness about the idea that an apex court should decide what to decide—a new court choosing to discuss this issue even with its most casual visitors—is a sign of the times. But such candour is still exceptional, just as in the US

Supreme Court's case. Eisenberg et al. (2013) consider case selection mechanisms and patterns to be a 'hidden dimension' of the Israeli Supreme Court, and their remark would surely be applicable to most apex courts. As access to justice and to constitutional review has expanded across the globe, many courts have undergone reforms to adjust their limited number of judges to ever-expanding workloads. While public debates on judicial backlogs and workloads are pervasive across jurisdictions, such reforms are not simply about the efficiency of judicial institutions. Empowering courts to select what they will decide, prioritizing certain issues and cases and avoiding others, by whatever mechanism, allows them to be less 'reactive and backward-looking institutions', focused in solving specific disputes, and more 'proactive and forward-looking ones', focused on developing the law in certain directions (Grenstad et al. 2020).

The chapter is divided as follows. In section 2, we contrast the agenda-setting powers and practice of the Supreme Court of the United States (SCOTUS) and the Brazilian STF to illustrate decision-making elements that shape multiple possible arrangements of docket control and timing control. This section shows why the study of agenda-setting needs to move beyond discussions of mandatory versus discretionary jurisdiction. In section 3, we discuss empirical studies on different courts in varying jurisdictions to show how a more nuanced framework can make better sense of diverse judicial agenda-setting experiences across the globe. In section 4, we relate our proposed framework to existing theories of how agenda-setting influences judicial behaviour and vice versa. Lastly, in section 5, we point to relevant, open questions in the study of how courts decide what to decide.

2. Agenda-Setting Systems and Mechanisms

The debate about agenda-setting powers and institutional design is often oversimplified by the dichotomy between mandatory jurisdiction and discretionary jurisdiction. In this section, we use a description of basic aspects about formal rules and practice at the SCOTUS and the Brazilian STF to tease out the realities of agenda-setting that do not conform to the traditional binary framework. Our goal is to propose a framework that enhances the understanding of how courts decide what to decide, without obscuring judicial prerogatives with significant practical impact.

Following Caldeira and Wright (1988), and Epstein, Segal, and Victor (2002) we define 'agenda-setting' as the manner in which 'branches of government go about the task of determining which of the issues on the "public" agenda [they will] place on their "institutional agenda"'. *Judicial* agenda-setting is, in this substantive, broad sense, equivalent to 'case selection'. Both expressions refer to the processes by which a court chooses which lawsuits it will decide at a given point in time. Such processes find institutional expression in different specific rules and practices governing how courts decide and announce (i) *which* cases they will formally decide (docket control mechanisms), as well as (ii) *when* they will include such cases for the consideration and decision of their judges (timing control mechanisms). Accordingly, courts select cases and set their agenda whenever they accept or refuse to hear a case, as well as when they exercise different levels of discretion on the exact date—and sometimes the year, the legislature, the current mandate of the chief executive, the decade, and so on—in which that case will be heard and decided.

This two-pronged prerogative is a decisive building block of the authority of apex courts. Cases provide opportunities for judges to exercise power. More precisely, cases are necessary conditions for any exercise of judicial power. Courts typically decide issues brought to them; with very few exceptions, their jurisdiction needs to be triggered by external actors.[6] Because of this limitation, the agenda of any court is first determined exogenously, and the rules governing how a court's jurisdiction can be triggered are the first determinants of the judges' agenda.

Courts can influence the profile of cases brought to it in the first place. First, by signalling. This can happen at an institutional level, whereby the court gradually indicates to litigants, through case selection and merit rulings, what types of issues it is eager to decide. This, in turn, causes litigants to bring more petitions about such issues to the court. In the U.S., 'one politically salient decision results in .74 additional cases' entering the court's docket five years down the line as 'signals in particular policy areas lead to greater attention to those policy areas on the agenda of the Supreme Court' (Baird 2004, 762). Judges can also express individual preferences to potential litigants. When they believe it will help them advance a precedent they favour, judges will sometimes signal litigants in order to stimulate them to bring a lawsuit with a specific challenge (Jacobi 2008). Second, a court or panel's composition can produce case selection effects, as this reveals information on the ideologies and legal views of potential decision-makers and shapes litigants' choices on what cases to pursue and what cases to settle out of court (Desrieux and Espinosa 2019).

By and large, however, before they can choose what to decide, courts are themselves chosen by litigants who bring cases to them—without which judicial agenda-setting cannot take place at all. The wider and less costly the possibilities of triggering a court's jurisdiction, the less influence each potential litigant will have in determining which issues will be brought to the court's consideration. However, litigants' decision whether to bring a case to the court, and of which kind, is not exogenous from judicial decision-making, including previous decisions to decide or not a certain type of case, involving a certain topic. Beim et al. (2017) call this the 'downstream consequences' of judicial decisions: when selecting for decision a case 'x', what will this mean in terms of future litigation brought to the court? Which kinds of legal issues and litigants will case 'x' encourage to appear before the court? We will return to these questions below. Access to courts in itself, however, is beyond the scope of this chapter (see Chang, this volume) We focus here on what happens after litigants ask a court to consider and decide a certain issue or case.

Scholarship on the US Supreme Court has benefited from detailed, consolidated information on the internal process by which cases are selected for inclusion in the court's docket via *certiorari* petitions. While the content of the judges' discussion and voting on each of such petitions is formally secret, the structure of the procedure itself is public, and its details and practices are well known. Litigants submit *certiorari* petitions providing the reasons why they believe their case should merit decision by the Court. Since 1972, petitions are then sent to the 'cert pool', formed by clerks taken from almost all the Justices' chambers. A randomly assigned law clerk writes a memo, which is distributed to the Justices, analysing the petition with a recommendation to grant or deny *certiorari*. Then, from the existing set of petitions, the Chief Justice selects some for consideration by the court at a specific conference date; other Justices can add petitions to this selection, but no petition can be removed. The rest of the petitions are summarily dismissed.

Clerks are a key part of these agenda-setting mechanisms. While the role of judicial bureaucracy is an understudied aspects of case selection in a comparative perspective, some studies have already pointed to its potential for judicial politics research. At the Russian Constitutional Court, for example, legal assistants, organized under a body called 'the Secretariat', appear to have a relevant role in case selection (Dzmitryieva 2017). In their study of case selection and the rise of clerks in the Norwegian Supreme Court, Grenstad et al. (2020, 159) observe that clerks participate in 'gatekeeping' (screening appeals for case selection) in all Nordic countries (Norway, Iceland, Finland, Sweden, and Denmark).

In the US Supreme Court, conferences take place regularly throughout the year, except in the recess period between late June and late September, and petitions are usually considered up to roughly a month after the submission of briefs. In conference, Justices discuss and vote on each petition (beginning with the one who included that case in the discussion, and following on in order of seniority). Voting is discretionary, and the judges are not required to present formal reasons for their decision to grant or deny. Any case who obtains at least four favourable votes (the famous 'Rule of Four') is then included in the court's docket for a decision on the merits.

From that moment on, 99 per cent of granted petitions follow a predictable schedule (Epstein et al. 2015). They will be scheduled for argument in at least three months, and the court's decision will be issued within three months after oral arguments—occasionally in up to six months, but almost always in the same term when the case was argued.

The US Supreme Court has formal, absolute discretion to decide not to hear a case. But it is constrained, in practice, in its capacity to decide when to decide the cases it selects. The most it can do is adjust timing within each judicial term, as only rarely cases are re-argued or decided in the following term (Epstein et al. 2015). Presumably, deviating from these patterns would raise eyebrows and draw public criticism. The range of things the US Supreme Court can do regarding timing is very narrow, even if, within this range, judicial discretion is near absolute. In terms of docket control, it is a court with near absolute discretion, but in terms of timing control its margin of appreciation is considerably limited. It can select some judgments to be issued closer to the end of the judicial year, just before the recess (Epstein et al. 2015), and there have been instances in which the court scheduled a case for re-argument in the following judicial year (fifty-four times, according to Blackman and Shapiro 2016). But such leeway seems very limited when compared to the case of the Taiwanese Constitutional Court, for example, which can take years to decide cases in its docket (Su and Ho 2014).

Moreover, there is a single procedure (*certiorari*) accounting for most of the court's docket and case selection. All the information on this procedure is public, relatively stable over time, and relatively well-known by the professional and scholarly communities and the specialized press. The fact that Justices, lawyers, and scholars would agree on a description of the court's docket control prerogatives in practice illustrates. Finally, *certiorari* operates basically as a collegial enterprise: while judges individually vote and propose petitions to be accepted, the court's decision is taken collectively by a sub-majority of at least four out of nine judges.

To consider possible variations in case selection mechanisms, contrast the arrangement described above (wide docket control autonomy combined with narrow timing control autonomy) with the STF (which has little perceived docket control autonomy, but wide *de facto* timing control autonomy). Although it is a 'Supreme Court', not a 'Constitutional Court', the STF formally combines expansive mandatory jurisdiction with some limited discretionary pockets. It can formally refuse to hear a case by a two-thirds majority of its judges, and can only do so in a specific kind of appeal, but this procedure encompasses around 80 per cent of its workload (amounting to dozens of thousands of cases per year). All abstract review lawsuits, however, are in principle a matter of mandatory jurisdiction. Yet the Court has absolute discretion, in practice, to decide when a given case will be decided.

Many cases can be decided by individual judges, mostly by their own criteria, including cases involving the exercise of judicial review (Arguelhes and Ribeiro 2018); they can be selected for collective decision either in a synchronous or an asynchronous procedure, each with their own rules. Once cleared for decision by the case reporter in a synchronous procedure, they can wait in line for years until being finally discussed in a given court session, but they sometimes also simply linger in the docket without a decision (see e.g. Oliveira 2005; Arguelhes and Hartmann 2017). Just like in the US Court, judges do not need to provide reasons for any such agenda-setting decisions. Furthermore, since there is no enforceable (not even informally) deadline or time frame for any decision, some cases remain in a judge's chambers for years.

Moreover, even in the absence of enforceable deadlines for the judges, the STF hears cases through dozens of different procedures, each with their own rules regarding timing. Most of the details by which the judges select and promote cases for decision are still unknown not just to the public but also by scholars and the specialized press. This is largely because most of the action happens either at the individual level, since agenda-setting powers are spread within the court (Arguelhes and Hartmann 2017; Arguelhes and Ribeiro 2018), or as informal interactions and calculations between the judges. There is significant variation within each chamber, and only recently scholarship has delved into the different informal practices adopted by the judges and the institution in this regard (see Esteves 2022). In the STF, then, it is often hard for the public to ascribe responsibility for a delayed decision on a case.

Considering these two brief sketches of apex courts in the United States and Brazil, we can see that timing control and docket control are two independent dimensions of agenda-setting. This point has become clear to scholars in recent decades (Fontana 2011), as well as in reform proposals. For example, Faiz (2016) argues for constitutional reform to increase the docket control discretion of the Indonesian Constitutional Court, while at the same time expressing concern with the possibility of excessive leeway in the time afforded to the court for rulings on the merits.

Once we factor in the complexity of the arrangements described above, neither the STF nor SCOTUS can be taken as representative. Case selection mechanisms vary widely across courts. The Mexican Supreme Court, for example, seems to have little control over the timing of its decisions, and might be thus drawn to disputes it would be more prudent to avoid (Magar et al. 2010). The Colombian Constitutional Court has limited docket control regarding abstract review lawsuits, but it has 'complete docket control over the flow of *tutelas*' (individual complaints regarding violation of fundamental rights): they are screened by a randomly selected panel of two judges, who must both agree for a *tutela* to be selected (Cepeda Espinosa and Landau 2017, 13). In Norway, cases are discretionarily selected by the court's 'Appeal Selection Committee' (ASC), a panel of three judges (out of the court's twenty judges). When the ASC analyses an appeal, a single vote by one of the judges is enough to send a case for decision by a 'Grand Chamber' of eleven judges, or (more rarely) by the court *en banc*; if all judges agree the case is not relevant, however, the appeal is dismissed (although in some cases involving procedural questions the ASC can issue a decision on the merits) (Grenstad et al. 2020).

According to a standard view, European constitutional courts typically lack comparable leeway both to choose cases and to remain silent on a given case for long periods of time (Comella 2004; Lavie 2017). The SCOTUS itself, however, is different from other apex courts in common law systems. While the SCOTUS' docket is almost entirely discretionary, in Canada this kind of jurisdiction amounts to 20 per cent of the docket (Alarie and Green 2017). The Israeli Supreme Court has both substantive mandatory and appellate jurisdiction and a set of complex rules by which individual judges may decide to hear or not a case in certain conditions, while panels of judges decide other cases (Eisenberg et al. 2011).

Even considering the potential complexities above, the brief contrast between the SCOTUS and the STF allows us to see how the simple distinction between 'mandatory jurisdiction' and 'discretionary jurisdiction' is insufficient. It refers only to the formal question of docket control: will the court accept to include the case in its docket? In this sense, it has limited descriptive ability, leaving out a host of other elements relevant for agenda-setting and case selection. For example, an account of the tenure of four Chief Justices of the Constitutional Court of Indonesia between 2003 and 2015 suggests the individual leadership of two of them was decisive in shaping court agenda-setting styles and allowing it to navigate hostile political settings (Hendrianto 2016). If we focus just on the formal question of accepting or not a case into the docket, we risk missing most of the action.

If we want to ask, answer, and compare research questions about agenda-setting across countries, both the specific question of the nature of the court's jurisdiction and the rule-centred, formal perspective are too limiting. Consider instead the following framework for organizing and comparing information on how different apex courts set their agenda:

(1) *Docket control* (How does the court decide which cases will be included in its docket? Does the court have mandatory jurisdiction, discretionary jurisdiction, or a combination of both?)
(2) *Timing control* (How does the court decide when to decide a case? Does the court have a formal rule or informal practice establishing a deadline to decide a case in its docket?)
(3) *Types of rulings and dismissals* (Does the court have the power to summarily dismiss a case in its docket, without a full decision on the merits?)
(4) *Internal allocation of agenda-setting powers* (How are decisions on (1), (2), and (3) made—by individual judges, by a panel, by the chief justice, by the full court, or by a combination of such actors? What is the level of direct engagement of the judges with these procedures—how much is done by court staff and bureaucracy and how much is done by judges themselves?)

Topics 1 and 2 involve *what* a court can do to set its agenda; docket control is but a mechanism for this broader dimension of judicial design and decision-making (Fontana 2011). Topics 3 and 4 involve *how* a court exercises the broader powers it has to set its agenda. All four topics can be answered by looking at a court's formal, official rules of operation, or by considering informal practices and how the court actually operates—and these different approaches will yield very different results when it comes to comparing agenda-setting mechanisms. Consider Table 23.1.

We use 'limited' and 'expansive', and 'significant' and 'relevant', because each quadrant represents a global assessment of a court's powers that expresses a continuum. Specific questions about these powers could be asked in ways that would entail a binary answer (does the court have mandatory or discretionary jurisdiction?), but varying answers about the same court, regarding different procedures, areas of law, and types of competences, when combined, point to a classification framework that cannot be merely binary. For example, the Canadian and Israeli Supreme Courts both combine relevant mandatory jurisdiction in some cases and procedures, while not in others, and they differ in the relevant weight of such different kinds of procedures in their total workload (Alarie and Green 2017). Therefore, to place specific courts in the cells, we would have to ask the relevant questions as many times as necessary regarding all specific mechanisms by which the courts control their docket and set the timing of their decisions. The purpose of Table 23.1, then, is not to force the continuum into a binary

Table 23.1 Dimensions and models of agenda-setting in courts

		'Timing control': Power to select when a case will be decided	
		Limited Strict deadlines and time frame for issuing decisions	Expansive Generous (or non-existent) deadlines and time frame for issuing decisions
'Docket control': Power to select if a case will be decided	Limited No relevant discretion in including or not a case in the docket	(1)	(2)
	Expansive Significant discretion in including or not a case in the docket	(3)	(4)

framework but rather to make explicit the dimensions at stake, with potentially different implications for judicial behaviour.

Moreover, Table 23.1 shows how courts would be placed differently in the two dimensions depending on whether we consider just the formal rules and procedures, or the actual operation of the court. Consider the case of Brazil. Both *de jure* and *de facto*, the STF should be placed on the 'expansive' column regarding timing control. There are simply no enforceable deadlines—even in the few procedures where there is a deadline, there is no formal remedy to force the court to apply it. The court and its individual judges can remain silent on a given case for months or years.

Regarding the 'docket control' dimension, however, *de jure* and *de facto* perspectives lead to different results. If we consider just the formal rules, since 2005 the Court has enjoyed formal discretion over a large share of its docket—two-thirds of the judges can decide not to hear an appeal that lacks 'general repercussion'. The decision is final, and can in principle be made by means of a simple 'yes' or 'no' vote, with no further justification by the court. However, in terms of how the court actually operates, STF judges rarely consider that a case lacks 'general repercussion', and they do not even publicly present themselves and the court as having this kind of power. In spite of the rules, the court *de facto* operates as if it did not have the power to simply refuse to include a case in its docket.

Finally, recall that Table 23.1 focuses on *what* courts can do to set their agenda—they choose what they will decide, and/or they choose when to decide what they must decide (topics 1 and 2). It does not explicitly account for *how* the relevant powers to answer those two questions are allocated internally (topics 3 and 4). The US Supreme Court's famous 'rule of four' is not the norm in comparative terms. It is not necessarily the case that the full court participates in agenda-setting decisions (either regarding docket control or timing control).[7] For example, as we mentioned, panels of two judges of the Colombian Constitutional Court exercise docket control over *tutelas* (both judges must vote to hear a case, for it to be included in the court's docket) (Cepeda Espinosa, and Landau 2017). In Brazil, each case reporter freely decides if and when a case is ready for decision by a panel or by the full court; the Chief Justice discretionarily decides if and when cases in the docket who have been cleared by the reporters will be included for decision in a plenary session; and each individual judge can ask for more time to study a case and, in practice, force the case to be decided at a much later date (Arguelhes and Hartmann 2017). These are just two examples of agenda-setting mechanisms in which the full court does not participate, or in which each individual judge has sufficient power to shape the agenda.

3. Implications of Agenda-Setting to Courts: Institutional Perspectives

In section 2, we laid out a framework for analysing agenda-setting designs and practices. Any general description, however, needs to come to terms with the particularities of courts embedded in vastly diverse political and social contexts. In this section, we discuss the promises and limitations of agenda-setting theory in building accounts of the practices by courts in varying jurisdictions.

Scholarship on judicial review has long recognized that choosing which cases to hear is consequential not just for the litigants, but for the court and its judges as well. At a most basic level, docket control shapes judicial workload, with implications for the overall cost and efficiency of judicial institutions, as well as (depending on the gap between workload and human resources) for the professional well-being of individual judges and their staff. More than efficiency, however, is at stake: workload shapes the possible roles a court can play in the legal system, and even regarding the other branches of government (Grenstad et al. 2020).

Many decades ago, writing on the US Supreme Court, Bickel (1986) developed the argument that, considering its 'counter-majoritarian' character, judicial review should be exercised only when the underlying questions and their implications had been adequately debated in society. The court should display 'passive virtues' to avoid deciding issues that were not yet ripe, so as to give social actors, politicians, and lower courts enough time to work on all sides and implications of such controversies. Also from a normative point of view, Comella (2004) argued that whether a court should stay silent is contingent on whether the same question could be be answered by other courts. In the case of specialized constitutional courts, it is often the case that, if the court avoids an issue or case, the relevant constitutional controversy will remain unanswered in the legal system (assuming that, in those systems, ordinary judges and lower courts cannot adjudicate matters of constitutional review).

Bickel's and Comella's arguments focused on when a court *should* stay silent, building on normative assumptions on the court's role in a democracy. They were less interested in the actual consequences, for the court, for mistakenly selecting an issue for decision at the wrong time, and more focused on what *should* happen to the court's legitimacy if it wrongly decides to decide or if it wrongly remains silent. In the last two decades, however, the field has moved precisely towards investigating the expected practical consequences of agenda-setting for courts. Deciding not to decide can be framed as a purely instrumental issue, as judges postpone decisions on 'contentious issues that might threaten a court's institutional viability [as] a way of engaging various external actors to create and secure institutional support' (Delaney 2016, 4; see also Fontana 2011).

Not deciding a case, however, is costly in itself. First, there is the opportunity cost of not having the chance to influence policy (Epstein et al. 2001). Second, there is the missed opportunity of exercising, legitimizing, and consolidating its powers in a democracy. The less a court decides, the more public perceptions of legitimacy can diminish over time (Owen and Simon 2012). What courts decide—however they decide to decide, and if they get to freely select cases at all—is a key part of the process of building constitutional power, since different cases raise different incentives for governments to retaliate, ignore, or comply with judicial decisions (Ginsburg 2003).

A first comparative attempt to understand the institutional implications of case selection for courts, from an empirical point of view, came from US judicial behaviour scholars. In a pioneering piece, Epstein et al. (2001) built a strategic model to understand the role of courts in democracies, based on the interaction between a constitutional court and the political branches—an interaction that 'begins with the CC deciding whether to take a case involving a particular policy issue and, if it accepts the case, where to place the policy' (2001, 127–28). The paper applies the model to the Russian Constitutional Court in the 1990s, testing the prediction that the court would avoid deciding cases on some topics (most notably Separation of Powers and Federalism) in periods in which there were no 'tolerance intervals' between the court and the other branches of government on such issues.

In building their analysis, the authors raised a key question: does the court have the power to avoid selecting 'undesirable' cases? Because the Russian Constitutional Court enjoyed broad discretion, due to several different features, to select the cases it would hear, the paper answers the question in the affirmative. Recent studies show that this discretion has been cloaked by 'the secrecy of case selection proceedings' combined with a carefully tailored narrative of 'focus on purely legalistic considerations [which] helps the Court to overcome political partisanship' (Dzmitryieva 2017, 12).

Comella (2004) presented an initial framework for comparing agenda-setting mechanisms across legal systems, by distinguishing between a 'Supreme Court model' (courts that choose what to decide) and a 'Constitutional Court model' (courts that do not have such a power). Beyond noting this typical divergence between two kinds of apex courts, Comella's work made the key move of connecting mechanisms for case selection (or their absence) and judicial legitimacy. However, his work focused on *established* courts in consolidated democracies. At the same time, in the same vein as Epstein et al. (2001), Ginsburg (2003) was drawing our attention to how case selection might be useful for new courts building their authority in a new democracy; his work, however, did not explicitly discuss if and how such courts could decide what to decide in the first place. A decade later, Fontana (2011) tied those two strands. His argument connected a very specific feature of institutional design in courts—docket control, the power by which a court decides which incoming petitions it will accept to hear—and the broader challenge of consolidating judicial authority in new democracies.

Hodžić (2016) claims the track record of constitutional courts in transitional regimes in Central and Eastern Europe includes few rulings on subjects that place these institutions 'at risk of attack by the political elites, [while] also endanger[ing] their legitimacy and acceptance in the polity at large'. The same dynamics are at play when international courts try to build legitimacy and foster support from governments in different countries. Jackson (2022) argues that the European Court of Human Rights unsuccessfully attempted avoidance by issuing rulings that proactively carve out the sensitive issue and refuse to discuss it. Instead, the court could protect its stability better by embracing docket control, exercising strategic avoidance, and deciding not to decide at all certain salient cases (Jackson 2022).

Recent comparative studies have documented a host of different strategies of avoidance and their limitations in specific contexts. For example, a court striving to consolidate its position vis-à-vis the other branches can also avoid politically sensitive rulings by modulating the effects of its rulings through "remedial grace periods", which give legislators enough time to remedy the unconstitutionality declared by the court. Lau (2016) uses extensive qualitative data to show that the Constitutional Court of South Africa has benefited from this timing control method as it struggled to consolidate its authority in a young democracy. Pereira (2022) claims traditional theories of agenda-setting fail to account for courts in Latin American countries such as Argentina, Brazil, Colombia, Costa Rica, and Peru, where judges have no initial 'reservoir of public support to protect themselves from political attacks' (Pereira 2022, 702). In this setting, judges behave as 'equilibrists' as they balance in their agenda cases where it is useful to face and decide the more sensitive issues—and where avoidance would deny an opportunity for the court to increase public support—and cases where deciding not to decide enables them to avoid a clash with government (Pereira 2022, 705).

4. Agenda-Setting and Individual Judicial Behaviour

Agenda-setting and mechanisms of case selection can be both the dependent variable and the independent variable in judicial behaviour studies. In the first scenario, the relevant questions involve explaining why judges choose cases the way they do, within the existing rules and constraints of a given court. In the second one, researchers use the existing rules and constraints regarding case selection to explain judicial behaviour. We discuss the two strands of studies in this section.

4.1 How Judicial Behaviour Shapes Agenda-Setting

How do judges choose which cases they will decide? Once again, studies on the US Supreme Court led the way in answering this question. On the one hand, that Court is exceptional in many ways, since case selection is a formal, discretionary decision in which the full court participates. On the other hand, even in courts with no discretion over their dockets, we inevitably find judges prioritizing some cases over others, postponing decision times, and finding ways of deciding a case focusing on non-core or procedural issues that allow them to avoid discussing the substantive controversies at stake. Alarie and Green' (2017, 157) provide an useful starting point by distinguishing four types of theories to explain how judges shape their agenda: workload, cue, ideology, and sophisticated ideology (or strategic) theories of judicial behaviour in case selection.

For the first group, judges prioritize the adequate management of their workloads. Assuming that courts have a limited capacity to deal with cases within the relevant time period, we can expect judges to accept to hear a smaller proportion of the cases they receive, as the absolute number of petitions increase. In the US case, there is evidence that workload influences strategic behaviour within judicial panels, as judges contemplate whether to write an opinion when they are not formally required to do so (Epstein, Landes, and Posner 2013).

Assessing the impact of workload for each individual justice, however, requires a detailed description of internal court proceedings, at the level of the judge's chambers. While the court as an institution might be limited in its capacity to produce rulings, it is not necessarily the case that the individual *judge* is affected by changes in workload. This depends on how much each judge delegates to clerks and other court staff the costs of dealing with new, incoming cases, as well as writing opinions. Moreover, in courts that face mass litigation and dozens of thousands of cases per year, technology can make individual judges and their chambers less affected by increases in the docket's size, as it becomes possible to use 'templates' to deal with repeat cases involving similar issues (Soucek 2012; Hartmann and Chada 2017).

In this perspective, we should note that workload is relevant in explaining not just which cases, but how many cases judges decide—and how those things change over time. For example, scholars have explored a combination of factors—from judicial to congressional behaviour—to explain the fact that the US Supreme court has decided fewer cases each year (Heise, Wells, and Chutkow 2020). In Canada, the docket has shrunk similarly (Alarie and Green 2017, 163–64). In the United Kingdom, in contrast, the Supreme Court seems to have accepted an increasing number of cases in the last decade (Robinson, 2013; Alarie and Green 2017, 166). In India, the Supreme Court's massive workload has been explained more as a product of judicial choice over time, than as the inevitable result of expansive access to constitutional appeals (Chowdhury 2012, 354).

Owens and Simon posit that ideological divergence between judges is a key variable in understanding case selection: the more dissimilar the judges are to one another, the harder it is for them to agree on agenda-setting decisions, and the harder it is for them to predict potential outcomes of selected cases; therefore, they should select fewer cases for decision (Owens and Simon 2012). But Alarie and Green (2017) observe that, because ideological cohesion is higher in the Canadian Supreme Court, and because it is harder for judges to predict the panel composition that will decide a given case, they should be willing to select more cases.

One additional possibility in explaining this variation involves how efficiently the court believes it can fulfil other goals, like correcting errors made by lower courts, and how much it can adjust its own internal workings for this task, by expanding the number of panels or delegating powers to individual judges (Clark and Kastellec 2013). A theoretical model of high court docket control proves that the effects of increased or decreased agenda-setting power will vary depending on the quality of lower courts (Clark and Strauss 2010, 264).

This brings us to 'cue theories', which consider that judges have limited resources analyse to analyse petitions to be selected for consideration in the first place. In such a scenario, judges would use properties of the case or the litigants to assess which lawsuits will provide them with better use of their attention—that is, a legal or political controversy worthy of the court's time. The criteria for what counts as 'better' varies, and studies have included areas of law (Muro et al. 2016, for example, present evidence that legal subject is a predictor of how the Argentinian Supreme Court handles case selection), the ideological composition of the lower courts (Black and Owens 2012), the presence of relevant government actors (like state governments, the federal government), the status or other visible resources of litigants (Black and Boyd 2012), and the type number of other societal actors intervening in the process through *amicus curiae* or comparable mechanisms. More recently, Liu and Kastellec (2023) show that former SCOTUS clerks litigating before the court exert influence on the cert stage. Studies on the United States, Canada, and Israel have shown, for example, that the government is typically successful in being heard (Alarie and Green 2017, 172), although results concerning the status of litigants are less evident outside the United States (Flemming and Krutz 2002).

The third kind of theory is ideological—what Alarie and Green label 'simple ideological voting' or 'error correction'. Judges would select cases based on their views on how wrong they believe the lower court decision is. This theory fits best in the context of courts that basically hear appeals; that is, courts that decide on rulings previously made by other judges.

An experiment using randomized panels shows ideology does accurately predict case selection decisions at the US Supreme Court (Hall 2009). Policy preferences also play a role in court workload fluctuations. Scott (2006) attempts to 'link the factors that determine the likelihood of the acceptance of an individual case with the factors that influence the overall size of the Court's docket' and finds it is not a set of exogenous factors such as lower court rulings that are controlling, but rather the Justices' own preferences. Black and Owens' (2009) research helps to improve our understanding of how ideology operates by showing its limitations. A complex causal model shows that 'legal considerations limit justices' abilities to maximize their policy goals' (2009, 1063).

A more recent study argues that *certiorari* grant data indicates justices in fact do not favour their policy preferences over the law (Johnson 2018).

Courts who receive abstract review cases, however, have no existing baseline of lower court decisions to 'correct'; if they avoid deciding a case, the underlying issue will most likely be left undecided (Comella 2004). Still, the same underlying idea seems applicable, with adjustments: the baseline is not an existing judicial decision but the legal status quo itself. Judges are ideological in case selection, in this broader sense, when the decision on whether the case should be heard or decided on the merits correlates with the judge's decision on the merits. In this sense, for example, when it comes to abstract review, we could expect a judge who believes that the challenge to an existing statute is unfounded to vote not to hear the case (or not to select it for consideration on the merits), since that judge is satisfied with the existing status quo (and does not consider the statute to be unconstitutional).

The last group of theories sees judges as strategic or 'sophisticated ideological' selectors of cases. The starting point is that 'there is a problem at the core of the error correction view of how judges decide which appeals to hear' (Alarie and Green 2017, 181): the best way for a judge to advance his interests in shaping the law in a particular direction involves avoiding cases in which he or she will not able to secure a majority for their preferred outcome. Beyond his own preferences, then, a judge would consider the likelihood of a majority of his colleagues expressing similar preferences regarding the merits of the case.

Benesh, Brenner, and Spaeth (2002) describe two types of behaviour in case selection decisions. Though lower court conflict, case salience, and the presence of the solicitor general are better predictors of whether an appeal will be granted *certiorari*, such factors might be less controlling when a justice wants to pick a case for review predominantly as a means to consolidate their preferred position. If they are confident to have a majority in the ruling on the merits that will follow afterwards, this justice might perform an 'aggressive grant'. On the contrary, if they fear a majority of peers will use that case to introduce or consolidate a position with which they disagree, the justice will perform a 'defensive denial' and vote for the court to refuse the case.

Institutional design, as well as the stability of voting blocs and ideological coalitions within the court, heavily shape a judge's capacity to engage in such predictions (Caldeira, Wright, and Zorn 1999; Alarie and Green 2017, 182–83). This might help explain the lack of evidence for sophisticated ideological voting in the Canadian Supreme Court: the unpredictable panel decision-making structure makes it much harder for an individual judge to correctly predict which of their colleagues will decide a case in the future, if they select it now for a decision on the merits (Flemming and Krutz 2002).

Another factor judges take into account is public opinion. For merit rulings, public opinion is a factor that explains the content of merit rulings even in non-salient cases (Unah and Hancock 2006; Casillas, Enns, and Wohlfarth 2011). An unpopular ruling, however, is a more significant threat at a time when the court enjoys weak public support. Bryan (2020) tests such a hypothesis for the US Supreme Court *certiorari* decisions and finds that 'when support is low, the effect of public opinion can be as strong or stronger than the canonical legal and institutional variables that we have long believed govern the Court's decision-making almost exclusively'. Public attention also influences case selection. Montgomery (2019) innovatively uses Twitter data to measure public attention and finds that it influences the attention of the attorney general and *amici curiae*, which in turn hold sway over certiorari decisions. Perhaps more importantly, public attention affects the time spent deliberating on whether to admit an appeal.

4.2 How Agenda-Setting Shapes Judicial Behaviour

As we discussed above, agenda-setting can be both the dependent and the independent variable in empirical studies of judicial behaviour. While studies of the first kind (how and why judges select cases the way they do? How and why do they behave in certain ways when deciding what to decide?) are widely acknowledged, the field of judicial behaviour has been built around certain assumptions on how specific mechanisms for case selection might be relevant in understanding judicial behaviour *on the merits*. Such assumptions about agenda-setting are decisive even when the studies do not focus explicitly on agenda-setting mechanisms.

This is the case of the influential 'attitudinal model' of judicial behaviour in the US Supreme Court, first developed by Harold Spaeth and Jeffrey Segal in the 1970s, and consolidated in a series of works by these and other authors in the following decades (Segal and Spaeth, 2002). In their original formulation, Spaeth and Segal do not exclude the possibility that, in principle, legal considerations could be relevant in explaining judicial behaviour. In building a theory to explain judicial behaviour in the US Supreme Court (specifically, to explain votes on the *merits* of the cases), however, they focus on the specific institutional setting in which those judges act and decide, and then ask whether legal considerations could play a relevant role in this specific decisional context.

In their reconstruction, two sets of elements in the Supreme Court's design are decisive. The first one, judicial independence (job stability and life tenure), eliminates any incentives for judges to consider the preferences of any actors outside the court. Judicial independence would make it unnecessary, in their view, to account for the possibility of strategic behaviour (since judges would have no incentive to deviate from their sincere, ideal positions in each case).

The second set of elements centres precisely on how cases arrive and are selected for decision in the Supreme Court—that is, on agenda-setting. Litigating a case all the way to the highest court in the country is expensive, and appeals would not be filed unless the respective parties believe they have some chance of winning on the merits. This means that the Supreme Court can choose between cases that have already been self-selected in important ways: the legal issues involved are typically complex and difficult enough to admit several different equally reasonable technical answers. The court is choosing its way into a pool of cases for which there is no obvious, uncontroversial legal solution.

Consider the implications of this line of reasoning for judicial behaviour in systems beyond the US Supreme Court. As a court transitions to a system of more discretion in docket control, we expect judges' docket profile preferences to command more influence. In Canada, the introduction of formal discretionary docket control translated into the Supreme Court's ability to permanently increase the share of human rights litigation, in addition to whatever effects were produced by the adoption of the Charter of Rights and Freedoms or by the support structure for rights litigants (Sanchez Urribarri et al. 2011).

In contrast, in high courts that do not get to choose their cases as freely as the US one, and/or that sit at the apex of systems in which hiring a lawyer and filling appeals is relatively cheaper, the 'selection effects' at play will be very different. Litigants might bring less controversial cases before the court. Consequently, as 'easy' cases become more represented in the court's docket, judges will face cases for which existing laws provide an uncontroversial answer; therefore, contrary to the scenario described in the 'attitudinal model' studies, legal variables might have comparably higher explanatory power, potentially impacting on dissenting behaviour, among other dimensions of judicial behaviour.

After a constitutional reform in Mexico, the Supreme Court faced a new docket profile which it could not reasonably shape, as procedural rules left justices no agenda-setting prerogatives. Magar, Magaloni, and Sanchez (2010) examine data from rulings between 1995 and 2007 and conclude that sometime after the reform, 'the legal dimension had clearly overshadowed the policy dimension in Court rulings'. The authors believe this might 'reflect strategic behaviour by justices attempting to shield the bench from political battles that they cannot avoid precisely because they lack control of their agenda' (Magar, Magaloni, and Sanchez 2010, 19).

In Israel, Eisenberg et al. (2011) found that dissent rates are lower in mandatory jurisdiction cases (considering that in discretionary jurisdiction cases individual judges influence docket control in non-random ways). A recent comparative analysis of Norway and Denmark reveals a similar phenomenon. In their comparison of the two apex courts, Skiple, Bentsen, and McKenzie (2021) observe that discretionary dockets are correlated with higher rates of dissent and reversal of lower court decisions. In his empirical study of the Norwegian Supreme Court, Bentsen (2018) shows that the increasing frequency of dissent since the 1990s can be explained in terms of reforms that gave the court the discretionary power to select its agenda (which the judges have then used to select more controversial cases, mostly involving fundamental rights).

When judges decide cases that have been selected through discretionary docket control, then, judicial ideologies find more intense expression in decisions. Such results are consistent with Segal and Spaeth's argument on selection effects and judicial behaviour. Moreover, Skiple, Bentsen, and McKenzie (2021) note that mandatory jurisdiction tends to make it more likely that 'low status' litigants will have their cases decided by the court—which can in itself affect judicial behaviour.

5. Open Questions and Research Frontiers

From the previous sections, we can extract to two elements of judicial agenda-setting that are still understudied. First, the development of a public, visible, and convincing discourse by the court of its inability to decide the cases it does not wish to decide. Second, the role of clerks in docket control. These elements, which we discuss below, highlight potential paths for future agenda-setting studies.

In this chapter, we treated docket control and timing control as different paths to achieve a single goal: agenda-setting or case selection, by which a court decides if and when it will face a relevant case or legal issue. As we discussed, however, the very idea that courts 'choose' what to decide is in itself controversial in many countries. While the formal distinction between discretionary and mandatory jurisdiction is less problematic for lawyers, informal docket control mechanisms and timing control are more elusive phenomena in many legal communities.

Studies of younger or transitional courts helped to uncover the relevance of an element of agenda-setting that often goes unnoticed. Agenda-setting is decisive for courts building their power (Epstein et al. 2001; Ginsburg 2003; Fontana 2011). However, as a court gradually consolidates a prerogative to decide what to decide (for example, by establishing an interpretation of procedural rules whereby it can refuse to rule on the merits of controversial requests), this might create new problems. A court that is openly seen as free to decide whatever it wants might frustrate powerful political actors both when it decides and when it doesn't, since judges would bear full responsibility for the timing of all of their decisions. Whether they avoid or select a case, this will be publicly perceived as a judicial choice. In this sense, it is arguably useful for courts in consolidating democracies to have full control over their agenda, but without appearing as having such freedom to choose. A clear and consistent public narrative— sponsored by members of the court itself—about the court's legal inability to decide certain issues can increase the costs of retaliation by political actors.

Judicial ability to convincingly state, in admission decisions, that a politically salient case could not be decided due to procedural reasons is therefore crucial. It helps judges maintain plausible deniability. In most cases when the court does not wish to rule on a case, we would expect it to prefer that the public believed a ruling on the merits was not legally possible. In order to maintain the flexibility to admit cases when convenient while also claiming to be bound by strict docket control limitations, judges need to cultivate some level of ambiguity about case selection rules (Delaney 2016). This explains one apparent disconnect mentioned earlier: in some countries, Supreme or Constitutional Court judges can thus proactively argue they have little or no docket control power even as lawyers and scholars know that this is not accurate from a descriptive standpoint. Looking beyond the mere outcome of merits and admission decisions and into precedent-citing patterns might enable a more accurate understanding of such case circumstances (see Frankenreiter, this volume).

The benefits a court can derive from a specific agenda-setting framework are often contingent on the success of certain narratives in the public debate. This underlines the relevance of analysing and understanding the descriptions judges and courts establish in public discourse about their perceived roles and alleged limitations in docket control prerogatives. If public opinion accepts an interpretation that judges are severely constrained in their ability to decide what to decide, then strategic avoidance can be an effective and safe option for the court. The Federal Constitutional Court of Germany, for example, uses goal-oriented press releases to create an image of docket diversity but also to take the lead in communicating with the public about salient cases (Meyer 2022). Courts also make strategic use of hearings—their publicity, timing, and length, for instance, as a means of 'curating the court's image' and stimulating the Justice's preferred view of how relevant, complex, or out of bounds a case might be that is in their docket (see Krehbiel, this volume).

These considerations on the potential usefulness, for courts, to appear as *not* having relevant agenda-setting mechanisms bring us back to the formal/informal dimension we discussed in section 3. Whatever the formal case selection rules, judges in all jurisdictions often have ways for avoiding unwanted cases or issues by disposing of cases just on procedural issues; they can decide a case simply by saying that, according to existing rules and procedures, that particular lawsuit or appeal should not have reached the court—or that the underlying question is now 'moot'. This, and not explicitly discretionary docket control, is what Bickel had in mind in describing the Supreme Court's 'passive virtues' (1986); it is also something that Comella (2004) recognizes that even specialized constitutional courts can do, although at a higher legitimacy cost. Such strategies, however, are heavily contingent on the internal perspective of a specific legal system. Mapping and comparing them across different countries is a key enterprise in expanding our comparative understanding of agenda-setting mechanisms. Have courts in older democracies gone further in developing a widely accepted discourse regarding their docket control and timing control limitations? Are there similar milestones for courts in transitional regimes as they establish a dialogue with the public? How has the digitalization of the public sphere impacted courts' ability and fluency to communicate their reasons and alleged legal grounds for how they shape their dockets? This is a promising point in a comparative agenda-setting research agenda that intrinsically connects with studies on courts and public opinion (see Smyth, this volume).

Finally, we emphasized in this chapter the need to go beyond the *what* and compare the *how*, focusing on the specific internal rules by which the power to select cases (either through docket control, or through timing control) is allocated within different courts. Decision-making power is not necessarily allocated to a majority of a judicial body, and individual judges or a sub-majority of a court decide even the highest profile cases in some countries; the same is true of agenda-setting powers, as they are not necessarily exercised through a majority or collective decision.[8] Moreover, understanding the internal workings of courts requires us to account for the bureaucratic structures that enable both decision-making over a very large mandatory docket and/or and the filtering of cases for full consideration by the court (once again, the examples of Brazil and Norway, respectively, come to mind.) As a growing body of clerks and other specialized staff become decisive for the operation of docket control and case selection mechanisms in many courts (as Grenstad et al. 2020 have shown to be the case in Norway), they become potentially relevant variables in explaining both the development of agenda-setting mechanisms and their impact on the observable behaviour of judges.

Acknowledgements

We would like to thank Ana Laura Barbosa, Luiz Gomes Esteves, Gunnar Grendstad, Urška Šadl, and participants in the Handbook Contributors' Conference at the Hebrew University, Jerusalem (December 2022) for helpful discussion on previous versions of this chapter, and Helena Funari for excellent research assistance.

Notes

1. Judge Lady Brenda Hale, 'Should the Law Lords have left the House of Lords?', Michael Ryle Lecture (2018) at 1: 'We hear civil and criminal appeals from England, Wales and Northern Ireland, and civil appeals from Scotland. Cases can only come to us with the permission, either of the court from which they come, or from us. Usually the lower court leaves the decision to us. As Lord Bingham put it, we "dine a la carte".' (Available at: https://www.supremecourt.uk/docs/speech-181114.pdf).
2. See e.g. Michael Heise, Martin Wells, and Dawn Chutkow. 2020. 'Does Docket Size Matter? Revisiting Empirical Accounts of the Supreme Court's Incredibly Shrinking Docket'. *Notre Dame Law Review* 95 at 1572 (observing that 'the *Supreme Court Case Selections Act* of 1988 resulted in the removal of virtually all of the Court's remaining mandatory jurisdiction', which, 'in turn, afforded the Justices almost total freedom in selecting the appeals that they wanted to hear and decide'). In contrast, see Lavie (2017, 28) (observing that SCOTUS-style 'unfettered discretionary review is by no means a universal standard', as 'European legal systems typically embrace the idea of a single constitutional court with narrow discretion to dismiss cases').
3. In some judicial behaviour studies, 'agenda-setting' is defined so as to include individual judicial strategies to influence the content of a ruling on the merits, once the court has already decided to decide that case or issue. For example, Bonneau et al.'s (2007) ideological 'agenda control' model shows that the majority opinion does not always coincide with the median Justice's ideal point and instead reflects the preferences of the majority opinion writer. This understanding of 'agenda-setting' is not our main focus in this chapter. Note that this is not the same as using case selection mechanisms, *before* a decision on the merits, to explain how judges behave when deciding on the merits (which we discuss in section 4.2).
4. The Brazilian Supreme Court (STF) only decided cases directly involving those issues in the late 2000s.

5. The video can be found at: https://www.tiktok.com/@stfoficial/video/7122211805916613893?is_copy_url=1&is_from_webapp=v1. The post is accompanied by the text: 'O STF escolhe os casos que vai julgar? O que você acha? Confere aqui a resposta'. ('Does the STF choose the cases it will decide? What do you think? Check out the answer here').
6. In Brazil, for example, a judge (even in the Supreme Court) can issue an unsolicited ('*ex officio*') writ of *habeas corpus*, independently from any ongoing procedures, if he or she becomes aware of a person being unjustly detained by authorities. This is a very narrow exception and one that is rarely used at the court. A more frequent exception is judges spontaneously bringing legal *issues* (not cases) to discussion and formal decision in session, if they consider them urgent and connected to the case at hand—'*Questões de Ordem*'.
7. As we mentioned, however, *certiorari* selection in the US Supreme Court is not limited to the 'rule of four', since most petitions will only be analysed by court staff, without direct engagement or decision from the judges.
8. In Brazil, for example, reform proposals have been made concerning agenda-setting. In the last decade, scholarship has documented and ultimately 'unveiled' the STF's powers to remain silent for years or decades on the issues it wants to avoid—not through docket control, but by timing control mechanisms. This has sparked scholarly and political debates on how to organize and make accountable the court's timing control powers (see, e.g. Barbosa 2023, comparing alternative models and proposal a 'meta-decision'—a procedure by which the court explicitly decides when it will decide a given case in its docket).

References

Alarie, Benjamin, and Andrew Green. 2017. *Commitment and Cooperation on High Courts A Cross-Country Examination of Institutional Constraints on Judges*. Oxford: Oxford University Press.

Arguelhes, Diego W., and Leandro M. Ribiero. 2018. '"The Court, it is I"? Individual Judicial Powers in the Brazilian Supreme Court and Their Implications for Constitutional Theory'. *Global Constitutionalism* 7 (2): 236–62.

Arguelhes, Diego W., and Ivar A. Hartmann. 2017. 'Timing Control without Docket Control: How Individual Judges Shape the Brazilian Supreme Court's Agenda'. *Journal of Law and Courts* 5 (1): 105–40.

Barbosa, Ana Laura. 2023. 'Meta-Voto: A solução para a pauta de julgamentos do STF?' *Revista Direito & Práxis* 14 (2): 691–719.

Baird, Vanessa A. 2004. 'The Effect of Politically Salient Decisions on the U.S. Supreme Court's Agenda'. *The Journal of Politics* 66 (3): 755–72.

Beim, Deborah, Tom S. Clark, and John W. Patty. 2017. 'Why Do Courts Delay?' *Journal of Law and Courts* 5 (2): 199–241.

Benesh, Sara C., Saul Brenner, and Harold J. Spaeth. 2002. 'Aggressive Grants by Affirm-Minded Justices'. *American Politics Research* 30 (3): 219–34.

Bentsen, Henrik L. 2018. 'Court Leadership, Agenda Transformation, and Judicial Dissent: A European Case of a "Mysterious Demise of Consensual Norms"'. *Journal of Law and Courts* 6 (1): 189–213.

Bickel, Alexander. 1986 [1962]. *The Least Dangerous Branch: The Supreme Court at the Bar of Politics*. New Haven: Yale University Press.

Black, Ryan C., and Ryan J. Owens. 2009. 'Agenda Setting in the Supreme Court: The Collision of Policy and Jurisprudence'. *Journal of Politics* 71 (3): 1062–75. https://doi.org/10.1017/S0022381609090884.

Black, Ryan C., and Ryan J. Owens. 2012. 'Consider the Source (and the Message): Supreme Court Justices and Strategic Audits of Lower Court Decisions'. *Political Research Quarterly* 65 (2): 385–95.

Black, Ryan C., and Cristina L. Boyd. 2012. 'US Supreme Court Agenda Setting and the Role of Litigant Status.' *The Journal of Law, Economics, and Organization* 28 (2): 286–312.

Blackman, Josh, and Ilya Shapiro. 2016. 'Only eight Justices? So what', *Wall Street Journal*, 23 February 2016. Available at https://www.wsj.com/articles/only-eight-justices-so-what-1456272088. Accessed 24 January 2024.

Bonneau, Chris W., Thomas H. Hammond, Forrest Maltzman, and Paul J. Wahlbeck. 2007. 'Agenda Control, the Median Justice, and the Majority Opinion on the U.S. Supreme Court'. *American Journal of Political Science* 51 (4): 890–905. https://doi.org/10.1111/j.1540-5907.2007.00287.x.

Bryan, Amanda C. 2020. 'Public Opinion and Setting the Agenda on the U.S. Supreme Court'. *American Politics Research* 48 (3): 377–90. https://doi.org/10.1177/1532673X18822312.

Caldeira, Gregory A., John R. Wright, and Christopher J. W. Zorn. 1999. 'Sophisticated Voting and Gate-Keeping in the Supreme Court'. *Journal of Law, Economics, & Organization* 15 (3): 549–72.

Caldeira, Gregory A., and John R. Wright. 1988. 'Organized Interests and Agenda Setting in the U.S. Supreme Court'. *American Political Science Review* 82 (4): 1109–27.

Casillas, Christopher J., Peter K. Enns, and Patrick C. Wohlfarth. 2011. 'How Public Opinion Constrains the U.S. Supreme Court'. *American Journal of Political Science* 55 (1): 74–88.

Chowdhury, Rishad Ahmed. 2012. 'Missing the Wood for the Trees: The Unseen Crisis in the Supreme Court'. *National University of Juridical Studies Law Review* 5: 351–77.

Clark, Tom S., and Aaron B. Strauss. 2010. 'The Implications of High Court Docket Control for Resource Allocation and Legal Efficiency'. *Journal of Theoretical Politics* 22 (2): 247–68. https://doi.org/10.1177/0951629809359036.

Clark, Tom S., and Jonathan P. Kastellect. 2013. 'The Supreme Court and Percolation in the Lower Courts: An Optimal Stopping Model.' *Journal of Politics* 75 (1): 150–68.

Cepeda Espinosa, José Manuel, and David Landau. 2017. *Colombian Constitutional Law: Leading Cases*. Oxford: Oxford University Press.

Comella, Victor Ferreres. 2004. 'The Consequences of Centralizing Constitutional Review in a Special Court: Some Thoughts on Judicial Activism'. *Texas Law Review* 82.

Delaney, Erin F. 2016. 'Analyzing Avoidance: Judicial Strategy in Comparative Perspective'. *Duke Law Journal* 66 (1): 1–67.

De Vrisse, Maartje. 2015. *Constitutional Review in Europe: A Comparative Analysis*. London: Bloomsbury.

Desrieux, Claudine, and Romain Espinosa. 2019. 'Case Selection and Judicial Decision-Making: Evidence from French Labor Courts'. *European Journal of Law and Economics* 47 (1): 57–88. https://doi.org/10.1007/s10657-018-9594-7.

Dixon, Rosalind, and Samuel Issacharoff. 2016. 'Living to Fight Another Day: Judicial Deferral in Defense of Democracy'. *Wisconsin Law Review* 73 (4): 683–731.

Dzmitryieva, Aryna. 2017. 'Case Selection in the Russian Constitutional Court: The Role of Legal Assistants'. *Laws* 6 (4): 12. https://doi.org/10.3390/laws6030012.

Eisenberg, Theodore, Talia Fisher, and Issi Rosen-Zvi. 2011. 'Israel's Supreme Court Appellate Jurisdiction: An Empirical Study'. *Cornell Law Review* 96 (4): 693–726.

Eisenberg, T., T. Fisher, and I. Rosen-Zvi. 2013. Group Decision Making on Appellate Panels: Presiding Justice and Opinion Justice Influence in the Israel Supreme Court. *Psychology, Public Policy, and Law* 19 (3): 282–96.

Epstein, Lee, William M. Landes, and Richard A. Posner. 2013. *The Behavior of Federal Judges: A Theoretical and Empirical Study of Rational Choice*. Cambridge: Harvard University Press.

Epstein, Lee, Jack Knight, and Olga Shvetsova. 2001. 'The Role of Constitutional Courts in the Establishment and Maintenance of Democratic Systems of Government'. *Law & Society Review* 35 (1): 117–64.

Epstein, Lee, William M. Landes, and Richard Posner. 2015. 'The Best for Last: The Timing of U.S. Supreme Court Decisions'. *Duke Law Journal* 64: 991–1022.

Epstein, Lee, Jeffrey A. Segal, and Jennifer Nicoll Victor. 2002. 'Dynamic Agenda-Setting on the United States Supreme Court: an empirical assessment'. *Harvard Journal on Legislation* 39: 395–433.

Esteves, Luiz Fernando Gomes (2022). 'A Construção da Pauta do Supremo: Quem, o quê e como'. PhD Dissertation (Law), University of São Paulo, Brazil.

Faiz, Pan Mohamad. 2016. 'A Prospect and Challenges for Adopting Constitutional Complaint and Constitutional Question in the Indonesian Constitutional Court'. *Constitutional Review* 2 (1): 103–28.

Fontana, D. 2011. 'Docket Control and the Success of Constitutional Courts'. In *Comparative Constitutional Law*, edited by T. Ginsburg and R. Dixon, 624–41. Cheltenham: Edward Elgar.

Flemming, Roy B., and Glen S. Krutz. 2002. 'Selecting Appeals for Judicial Review in Canada: A Replication and Multivariate Test of American Hypotheses'. *Journal of Politics* 64 (1): 232–48. https://doi.org/10.1111/1468-2508.00126.

Hall, Matthew. 2009. 'Experimental Justice'. *American Politics Research* 37 (2): 195–226. https://doi.org/10.1177/1532673x08324887.

Ginsburg, Tom. 2003. *Judicial Review in New Democracies*. Cambridge: Cambridge University Press.

Grenstad, Gunnar, et al. 2020. *Proactive and Powerful: Law Clerks and the Institutionalization of the Norwegian Supreme Court*. The Netherlands: Eleven International Publishing.

Hartmann, Ivar A. M., and Daniel M. Chada. 2017. 'A razão sem condições de qualidade'. In *A razão e o voto. Diálogos constitucional com Luís Roberto Barroso*, edited by Oscar Vilhena Vieira and Rubens Glezer, 169–96. São Paulo: FGV Direito SP.

Hendrianto, Stefanus. 2016. 'The Rise and Fall of the Heroic Chief Justices: Constitutional Politics and Judicial Leadership in Indonesia'. *Washington International Law Journal* 25 (3): 489–564.

Heise, Michael, Martin T. Wells, and Dawn M. Chutkow. 2020. 'Does Docket Size Matter? Revisiting Empirical Accounts of the Supreme Court's Incredibly Shrinking Docket'. *Notre Dame Law Review* 95: 1565–92.

Hirschl, Ran. 2014. *Comparative Matters: The Renaissance of Comparative Constitutional Law*. Oxford: Oxford University Press.

Hodžić, Edin. 2016. 'Examining the Role of Constitutional Courts in Post-Yugoslav Transitions: Conceptual Framework and Methodological Issues'. Analitika – Center for Social Research Working Paper series (01/2016). Sarajevo: Analitika.

Jackson, Miles. 2022. 'Judicial Avoidance at the European Court of Human Rights: Institutional Authority, the Procedural Turn, and Docket Control'. *International Journal of Constitutional Law* 20 (1): 112–40. https://doi.org/10.1093/icon/moac003.

Jacobi, Tonja. 2008. 'The Judicial Signaling Game: How Judges Shape Their Dockets'. *Supreme Court Economic Review* 16 (1): 1–38. https://doi.org/10.1086/655878.

Johnson, Ben. 2018. 'The (Surprisingly Small) Role of Policy Preferences in Supreme Court Agenda-Setting', in *Essays on Supreme Court Agenda-Setting*. PhD Dissertation (Politics), Princeton University. Available at https://dataspace.princeton.edu/handle/88435/dsp01th83m202t. Accessed on 22 January 2024.

Lau, Holning. 2016. 'Comparative Perspectives on Strategic Remedial Delays'. *Tulane Law Review* 91 (2): 259–324. http://heinonline.org/HOL/Page?handle=hein.journals/tulr91&start_page=259&collection=journals&id=285.

Lavie, Shay. 2017. 'Discretionary Review and Undesired Cases'. *European Journal of Law and Economics* 44 (2): 265–85. https://doi.org/10.1007/s10657-015-9522-z.

Liu, Huchen, and Jonathan P. Kastellec. 2023. 'The Revolving Door in Judicial Politics: Former Clerks and Agenda Setting on the U.S. Supreme Court'. *American Politics Research* 51 (1): 3–22.

Magar, Eric, Beatriz Magaloni, and Arianna Sanchez. 2010. 'No Self-Control: Decentralized Agenda Power and the Dimensional Structure of the Mexican Supreme Court'. APSA 2010 Annual Meeting Paper. https://papers.ssrn.com/sol3/papers.cfm?abstract_id=1642431.

Meyer, Philipp. 2022. 'Transparency and Strategic Promotion: How Court Press Releases Facilitate Judicial Agenda-Building in Germany'. *Public Relations Review* 48 (4): 102228. https://doi.org/10.1016/j.pubrev.2022.102228.

Montgomery, Matthew. 2019. 'Public Attention and Certiorari: The Impact of Public Attention on Supreme Court Petitions'. PhD Dissertation (Political Science), Georgia State University. Available at: https://doi.org/https://doi.org/10.57709/14263116. Accessed 22 January 2024.

Muro, Sergio, Alejandro Chehtman, Jorge Silva Méndez, and Nelson Amaya Durán. 2016. 'Dismissing Appeals on Formal Grounds: The Case of the Argentine Supreme Court'. *The Latin American and Iberian Journal of Law and Economics* 2 (1): 1–38.

Oliveira, Vanessa E. 2005. 'Judiciário e privatizações no Brasil: Existe uma judicialização da política?' *Dados* 48 (3): 559–87.

Garoupa, Nuno, and Maria Angela Jardim de Santa Cruz Oliveira. 2012. 'Stare Decisis and Certiorari Arrive to Brazil: A Comparative Law and Economics Approach'. *Emory International Law Review* 26 (2): 555–98.

Owens, Ryan J., and David A. Simon. 2012. 'Explaining the Supreme Court's shrinking docket.' *William & Mary Law Review* 53 (4): 1219–85.

Pereira, Gabriel. 2022. 'Judges as Equilibrists: Explaining Judicial Activism in Latin America'. *International Journal of Constitutional Law* 20 (2): 696–732.

Robinson, Nick. 2013. 'Structure Matters: The Impact of Court Structure on the Indian and U.S. Supreme Courts'. *The American Journal of Comparative Law* 61 (1): 173–208.

Rosenfeld, Michel, and A. Sajo, eds. 2012. *The Oxford Handbook of Comparative Constitutional Law*. Oxford: Oxford University Press.

Sanchez Urribarri, Raul A., Susanne Schorpp, Kirk A. Randazzo, and Donald R. Songer. 2011. 'Explaining Changes to Rights Litigation: Testing a Multivariate Model in a Comparative Framework'. *Journal of Politics* 73 (2): 391–405. https://doi.org/10.1017/S0022381611000156.

Segal, Jeffrey A., and Harold J. Spaeth. 2002. *The Supreme Court and the Attitudinal Model Revisited*. New York: Cambridge University Press.

Scott, Kevin M. 2006. 'Shaping the Supreme Court's Federal Certiorari Docket'. *Justice System Journal* 27 (2): 191–207.

Soucek, Brian. 2012. 'Copy-Paste Precedent'. *The Journal of Appellate Practice and Process* 13 (2): 153–71.

Skiple, J., H. Bentsen, and M. McKenzie. 2021. 'How Docket Control Shapes Judicial Behavior: A Comparative Analysis of the Norwegian and Danish Supreme Courts'. *Journal of Law and Courts* 9 (1): 111–36.

Unah, Isaac, and Angie Marie Hancock. 2006. 'U.S. Supreme Court Decision Making, Case Salience, and the Attitudinal Model'. *Law and Policy* 28 (3): 295–320. https://doi.org/10.1111/j.1467-9930.2006.00228.x.

Yen-tu, Su, and Han-wei Ho. 2014. 'Judging, Sooner or Later: A Study of Decision Timing in Taiwan's Constitutional Court. Available at SSRN: https://papers.ssrn.com/sol3/papers.cfm?abstract_id=2467934.

CHAPTER 24

THE FORM AND FUNCTION OF ORAL ARGUMENTS IN HIGH COURTS

JAY N. KREHBIEL

1. Introduction

PERHAPS no part of the judicial process leaves as indelible of an image as oral arguments.[1] From the procession of judges into the courtroom, often clad in their regalia, to the presentations of litigants' arguments, oral arguments can appear on the surface to be a finely choreographed event. Consider the case of the Austrian Constitutional Court (*Verfassungsgerichtshof*). With an announcement, those present stand as the Court's fourteen members—in their black and purple robes—enter the courtroom one by one led by Court's president and vice-president. The media take photos of the assembled justices, everyone is seated, and the Court's president begins the proceedings. The impact of the process is not lost on courts, with the German Constitutional Court recognizing the impact of hearings on its public image when it stated the following in its 2021 Annual Report: 'Among citizens, the Justices are perhaps best known for the scarlet robes and white jabots they wear for oral hearings . . . .' (German Constitutional Court 2021). But while such finely manicured appearances can matter in their own right, it is the politics behind these processes that has increasingly come into focus for scholars.

While scholars have long recognized the import of oral arguments in the United States, particularly at the Supreme Court (e.g. Johnson, Wahlbeck, and Spriggs 2006; Black, Johnson, and Wedeking 2012), it is only in more recent years that scholars have begun to pay similar attention to the procedure from a comparative perspective. Much like the broader comparative judicial politics literature, this development has come by two broad paths. First, scholars have come to apply the insights of the Supreme Court literature to other high courts (e.g. Szmer, Johnson, and Sarver 2007; Jacobi, Robinson, and Leslie forthcoming). Second, scholars have diverged from that US-focused literature to leverage the unique features of those contexts (e.g. Krehbiel 2016; Bentsen et al. 2021). Combined, this small but growing comparative literature has brought a part of the judicial process that was once viewed as perfunctory into the broader conversation of judicial politics.

In this chapter, I evaluate the state of comparative research on oral arguments and highlight avenues for further developing this line of research. To do so, this chapter focuses on apex courts, such as supreme and constitutional courts. While this necessarily precludes extensive discussion here on the many important functions—and research thereon—of lower courts, considering high courts reflects the focus of much of the research both on oral arguments and the broader 'new wave' of comparative judicial politics highlighted throughout this volume. This emphasis on high courts stems from a few of their features. For one, within the judiciary high courts are typically the most engaged in functions such as constitutional review or electoral disputes that bring the judiciary into direct contact with the other branches of government. For another, by virtue of being at the apex of the judicial hierarchy, the decisions of high courts carry outsized influence and impact throughout a legal system. As I note later in the chapter, however, the reflection of the focus on high courts onto research on oral arguments has left us with a scarcity of systematic social science and socio-legal research on the processes of appellate and lower courts.

While emphasizing the role and dynamics of oral arguments at high courts, the chapter does not focus on specific courts or countries but rather on three broad questions facing scholars interested in studying oral arguments. The purpose of this approach is threefold. First, it speaks to the growing trend within judicial politics to look beyond geographic or domestic/international divides and instead emphasize the major theoretical questions confronting scholars of all courts (Staton and Moore 2011). In so doing, the chapter emphasizes both hearings' form—*how* courts hold hearings—and function—*why* courts hold hearings. Second, this approach allows for a more comprehensive—and critical—view of the empirical and theoretical scope of the literature, thereby connecting works both on high-profile and lesser studied courts. Third, it provides a roadmap of where scholars have been and helps identify opportunities for further theoretical and empirical innovation. As a whole, the chapter's goal is to apprise scholars of both the current state of research on oral arguments and identify possible directions for future work to pursue as scholars of this topic engage with the big theoretical and empirical questions in judicial politics.

The chapter is organized around three themes in the literature on oral arguments. First, I consider why courts opt to hold oral arguments when they do, as many courts only hold hearings in a limited number of cases. Second, the chapter examines the content and conduct of the hearings themselves. The third section then reviews the literature on the effects—both legal and political—of oral hearings. The chapter then concludes with a brief discussion on potential avenues for further research.

2. Why Hold an Oral Hearing?

While oral hearings often occupy a prominent place for many when conjuring the image of a court, they are in fact something of the exception rather than the rule for many of the world's courts. For example, the German Constitutional Court held only five oral hearings in 2018 while receiving nearly 6,000 new proceedings (German Constitutional Court 2018). Similarly, the Grand Chamber of the European Court of Human Rights granted thirteen oral hearings in 2017 amidst a caseload that produced nineteen judgments that year (European Court of Human Rights 2021). And these are numbers just for the most significant parts of these courts' dockets, as each receives thousands of applications each year with the overwhelming majority resolved exclusively through written briefs without ever receiving a hearing. Even the US Supreme Court, whose oral arguments are some of the most closely watched and studied, has increasingly taken to using its 'shadow docket' to resolve some cases—including some quite salient ones—without a hearing (Baude 2015; Vladeck 2019).

For some courts, the use of hearings is strictly regulated by statute, constitutions, norms, or a combination thereof. The French Constitutional Council, for instance, was precluded from holding hearings until reforms in 2008, while on the other end of the spectrum the UK Supreme Court makes extensive use of hearings. Notably, however, for many courts their discretion is considerable—albeit not unlimited—over which cases are granted a hearing. For example, the South Korean Constitutional Court's use of hearings is governed by the Constitutional Court Act, which states in Article 30 paragraph 1:

> The adjudication on impeachment, dissolution of a political party, or competence dispute shall be conducted through oral arguments ... The adjudication on the constitutionality of statutes or constitutional complaint shall be conducted through written review. Provided, that, if it is deemed necessary, the Full Bench may hold oral arguments, and hear the statements of parties, interested persons, and persons for reference.

Similar language formalizing the instances in which a hearing is required or optional can be found in the rule of many other courts. This includes international courts like the Court of Justice of the European Union (CJEU), whose rules of procedure (Article 76) state:

> On a proposal from the Judge-Rapporteur and after hearing the Advocate General, the Court may decide not to hold a hearing if it considers, on reading the written leadings or observations lodged during the written part of the procedure, that it has sufficient information to give a ruling.

And even when statutory language seems like it should make hearings a regular occurrence, courts may interpret the law in ways that make the procedure exceedingly rare. For example, Chen, Huang, and Lin (2015) note that, despite the Taiwan Code of Civil Procedure stating that the Taiwan Supreme Court should, in principle, hold hearings in all merit cases, it had only done so twice in the eight years since the law's passage. As a result, for many high courts—both national and international—oral hearings are by and large a discretionary procedure rather than a mandated one.[2] Such limited use of hearings is illustrated in Figure 24.1, which shows the number of hearings held each year from 2016 to 2020 by three courts: the European Court of Human Rights, the German Constitutional Court, and the Czech Constitutional Court.

That so few cases at many of the world's apex courts receive a hearing carries a number of significant implications. For one, if hearings are meant to provide a critical connection between litigants and courts, then the selectivity of courts in granting hearings necessarily means some will be denied the opportunity to present their case in person to the court. While this may be of limited impact in many cases, it does raise the potential for the miscarriage of justice. For example, in *Selmani and Others v the former Yugoslav Republic of Macedonia*, the European Court of Human Rights ruled that the North Macedonian Constitutional Court had violated a litigant's rights by, among other things, failing to justify the Court's refusal to hold an oral hearing before rejecting the litigants' application. For another, discretion over such a time-consuming procedure may allow courts to dispose of cases more efficiently, thereby helping to alleviate backlogs that can, among other things, undermine public confidence in the courts. What determines, then, whether or not a court holds a hearing presents a central

FIGURE 24.1 The annual number of hearings held by each court from 2016 to 2020. Data collected from respective court websites.

research question to the study of hearings. I consider here three of the most prominent explanations for the procedure's use.

2.1 Information

Perhaps the most commonly posited explanation for the use of oral hearings is that they provide judges an opportunity to obtain additional information relevant to a case. By allowing litigants to plead their case and, perhaps more importantly, judges to pose questions and demand clarifications of arguments, oral hearings are thought to serve a critical informational function (Johnson, Wahlbeck, and Spriggs 2006). Importantly, such information can relate not only to the legal merits of a case but also the potential social, political, or economic consequences of a court's decision (Johnson 2004).

It is logical, then, that courts with discretionary hearings may look to use them when confronted with an informational shortfall. Indeed, this consideration is often reflected in the justifications courts themselves provide for holding a hearing. In its description of its decision process, the Austrian *Verfassungsgerichtshof* describes the decision to hold a hearing as being a reflection of the Court's need 'to obtain further clarification of the facts' (Austrian Constitutional Court 2022). Similarly, interviews with judges at the constitutional courts of Albania and Germany indicate an emphasis on the need for information when deciding to grant a hearing.

Scholars have similarly recognized the connection between a court's need for information and its likelihood of incurring the costs of holding a hearing. Rosas (2014), for instance, notes that the CJEU may reconsider the need for a hearing 'if the Court considers that it lacks sufficient information' (603). Studying hearings at Brazil's Supreme Federal Court, Guimarães (2020) depicts hearings as at least having the purpose of informing the Court, although the extent to which they do so can vary based in part on the parties presenting the information. In one of the few quantitative empirical studies on the connection between information and the use of hearings, Grundmanns (2022) contends that external actors—particularly interest groups—can signal to courts the informational need for a hearing. Studying the context of the German Constitutional Court, he finds that the Court's likelihood of granting a hearing was influenced not only by the complexity of a case but also the presence of these external actors providing information through written briefs. Taken together, these studies seem to suggest some informational component to judges' calculus, although the extent of that influence in many respects remains unanswered.

2.2 Legitimacy

A second rationale for holding a hearing is that it will increase the perceived legitimacy—both among the litigants and the general public—of a court's decision (Cann and Goelzhauser 2024). By providing litigants their 'day in court', holding a hearing may encourage those who lose a case to accept the judgment as having been fairly reached (Tyler and Rasinski 1991; Tyler 1994). Importantly, judges are keenly aware of this consequence of hearings. Haynie (2005), for example, interviewed a number of South African judges and advocates, one of whom conveyed the role of oral hearings as stemming, at least in part, from being 'important from the client's point of view' because it will 'give the individual the perception that he or she has had their day in court' (480). The use of hearings, then, may correspond to the desire—or need—for a court to legitimate the judicial process.

Similarly, courts may use hearings in particularly salient cases to demonstrate to the public that both sides are being thoughtfully and carefully heard before a decision is reached. In such instances, the significance of a case is concomitant with the need for legitimacy, as it is in these cases in particular that a court would want to avoid the appearance of bias.[3] The public nature of hearings contributes significantly to this function, with high courts typically obliged to hold hearings in public unless there are extenuating circumstances such as the need to protect national security (Venice Commission 2010). While actual deliberations still take place behind closed doors with no public record or access, the presence of a court's judges in the courtroom asking questions of litigants can present the image of thoughtful consideration of both sides.

The implication of this legitimacy-focused account for holding hearings is that courts are more willing to do so in salient cases. Vanberg (2005), for example, notes the German Constitutional Court's use of hearings corresponds with a case's salience, which Krehbiel (2016) similarly finds in his analyses of the German Court's use of the procedure. In an in-depth study of the Argentine Supreme Court's use of hearings in high-profile environmental law cases, Barrera (2013) relates the legitimizing goal of the procedure, with one judge describing it as a critical tool in the Court's pursuit of 'real legitimacy' (333). At an institutional level, the extent of a court's discretion over hearings may be lower in proceedings likely to be salient. At the European Court of Justice, hearings are integral to the Court's recently created 'urgent' procedures designed to expedite important, time-sensitive cases (Rosas 2014). While consistent with the legitimizing logic, however, studies have primarily taken the influence of case salience as a given rather than an empirical question.

2.3 Public Awareness and Publicity

While the need for information and legitimacy tends to be the focus of how courts often present the use of hearings, a third potential explanation is the desire to increase public awareness of specific cases. Where they are the exception rather than the norm, hearings often generate significant media coverage that raises the public profile of a case. In many instances, the opening remarks of a hearing are recorded by news media and replayed in evening broadcasts while newspapers run stories on the hearing. Indeed, it is often a court's media relations team that handles the logistical aspects of hearings, such as providing the media with formal credentials and offering reporters with a summary of the case at issue. This is all done with the intent of not only curating the court's image but also ensuring that the case reaches the broader public.

Beyond its normative appeal, such increased public awareness can serve a strategic purpose for courts. Without the ability to directly enforce their decisions, courts are reliant on the willingness of others—particularly executives and legislatures—to ensure the proper execution of their orders. When these external actors would rather not do so, however, scholars have identified the public as a critical source of pressure for compliance (Gibson, Caldeira, and Baird 1998). Because fulfilling this function requires citizens to be aware of a court's action in the first place (Vanberg 2001, 2005), courts may have an incentive to selectively promote the public profile of cases they see as potentially generating conflict with other political branches (Staton 2006, 2010). With their ability to generate significant media coverage, oral hearings may be a tool particularly well suited to addressing this need for public awareness.

While Vanberg (2001, 2005) first linked the value of public awareness with hearings, Krehbiel (2016) provides an explicit theoretical and empirical account of this potential role for the procedure. In his account, Krehbiel (2016) contends that courts can strategically use hearings when they are confronting potential resistance from the government and a hearing is likely to be effective at promoting public awareness. Building on Vanberg's analyses of the German Constitutional Court, the article reveals a clear relationship between the risk of noncompliance and the likelihood of a hearing. Similarly, Grundmanns (2022) finds that external actors, like interest groups, can factor into a court's consideration for how effective and needed a hearing might be to generate awareness.

In a related study, König (2022) argues that courts use hearings to control the narrative surrounding potentially contentious cases, particularly those involving laws passed by populist governments. The novelty of this argument is that it emphasizes the role of public relations, in part through the media reports and images produced by public hearings, in projecting and protecting judicial power, and then connects this logic with the growing threat to judicial power posed by populist governments. Taken together, these studies indicate that there may be more to the use of hearings beyond the traditional accounts often afforded to them.

2.4 Further Research

Despite the growing breadth of research on oral arguments, much remains to be studied systematically with regard to why courts grant some cases a hearing and not others. Besides Krehbiel's (2016) article and the ongoing work of Grundmanns and König, accounts for why a case is or is not granted a hearing tend either to be only suggestive or limited in scope to a specific case or court. As such, we have little by way of quantitative examinations of when hearings are held, or for that matter even carefully structured tests of the standard received wisdom of the role played by the need for information and legitimacy. The end result is that when it comes to the question of 'why do courts hold hearings' we at once appear to be sure of the answer and are yet to truly put that answer up for proper scrutiny.

As such, there are a number of potential avenues for future research. There remain opportunities for evaluating the impact of informational and legitimacy needs on the use of hearings. While it is widely presumed that salience matters, for example, this largely remains untested. As such, we have little insight into either the extent to which these factors matter or the case aspects that might condition their importance. Moreover, institutional factors, such as the presence and extent of clerks at a court or norms regarding third-party engagement in cases through amicus briefs or other forms of participation, remain under-studied in the context of hearings. As several other chapters in this volume have highlighted the importance of factors such as agenda setting and the attorneys involved in the case, future work might similarly benefit from linking our knowledge of these considerations to the use of hearings. To put it simply, there is precious little work with oral hearings as a dependent variable.

Beyond examining the use of hearings at individual courts, scholars might also consider examining the variation across courts with respect to their level of discretion over hearings. If hearings are an important aspect of the judicial process, as scholars and jurists generally think is the case, then understanding why they are the norm in some contexts and the exception in others may grant valuable insights into both the judicial process itself and the relationship between courts, litigants, and the public. This line of inquiry may be all the more worthwhile when considering the role political institutions frequently have in setting those rules in courts' organic legislation. If it is the case that hearings have implications for judicial power, then the political actors setting a court's rules might be mindful of this when doing so. A change to the Czech Constitutional Court's rules, for instance, led to a drastic decrease in the number of hearings held by the Court. Such changes, as well as the initial rules for hearings, are ripe for study in the tradition of research on the political design of courts.

3. What Happens During Oral Hearings?

As arguably the most high-profile judicial activity, the conduct and content of oral hearings have long been the subject of scholarly study. This tradition is particularly robust in the United States, where scholars have seemingly parsed and studied effectively every utterance from each Supreme Court justice. Yet interest in how hearings play out is far from limited to the context of the US Supreme Court, as scholars increasingly leverage the variation afforded by engaging in comparative studies and consider the influence of differing political cultures, institutions, and traditions on the procedure. In this part of the chapter, I examine the insights scholars have gleaned into the conduct of hearings and suggest how future work might further our understanding of how hearings work in comparative context.

3.1 Length of Hearing

Just as many courts hold discretion over which cases are granted a hearing, so too do courts often have control over the amount of time dedicated to an oral hearing. Unlike the US Supreme Court and Circuit or the Canadian Supreme Court (Szmer, Johnson, and Sarver 2007), courts like UK Supreme Court and South African Constitutional Court consequently hold hearings of quite variable length from less than an hour to multiple days.[4] For example, one case at the Norwegian Supreme Court was granted nearly eight days of oral arguments (Bentsen et al. 2021), whereas the Australian High Court generally has no time limit (Bennett 2001).

Explanations for this variation connect directly to the rationale for holding hearings in the first place. In particular, courts' need for information appears a clear explanation for holding longer (or shorter) hearings. Recognizing the connection between case complexity and time granted for a hearing, Bentsen et al. (2021) use the case of the Norwegian Supreme Court to model the influence of the need for information on hearing length explicitly. Their examination of an oral hearing's length not only demonstrates its relationship with case complexity but it also validates a new measure of case complexity that can serve as a prototype for scholars to use when examining case characteristics at similarly structured courts.

Alternatively, the salience of a case—and therefore a court's need to present itself as thorough and unbiased—may call for longer hearings. For example, in its landmark and highly publicized *Bosnian Genocide* decision, the International Court of Justice allowed for nine weeks of oral arguments (Rose 2008). Such additional time can promote a court's image of impartiality by demonstrating its willingness to hear all sides of a case and take in as much testimony and information as it can before rendering a decision. While appealing theoretically, however, there is little systematic research examining such a relationship between the length of hearings and the need to promote a court's legitimacy; in fact, besides Bentsen et al. (2021) there is surprisingly little empirical research at all on the variation in the length of hearings either at a particular court or across judicial contexts.

3.2 Participation of Judges

Regardless of the path by which a court comes to hold a hearing or how long it lasts, a central component of oral arguments is the participation of the judges hearing the case. If, for instance, the primary function and goal of hearings is to provide information, then the willingness of judges to ask questions of litigants and further conversations over the questions at stake in a case is of particular importance. And for scholars, judges' contributions to oral arguments are often the only insight into judges' thinking available before a court issues its decision. As such, the quality and quantity of such participation takes on a prominent role in the literature on oral hearings.

Much of the literature on judges' contributions to oral arguments stems from work on the US Supreme Court. What and how much a justice speaks during oral arguments has been used, for example, to measure case salience (Black, Sorenson, and Johnson 2013), predict coalition formations on the Court (Black, Johnson, and Wedeking 2012), and ultimately predict justices' votes (Johnson, Black, and Wedeking 2009). Indeed, effectively every utterance by the justices is parsed for its content as Supreme Court scholars look for insights into the justices' behaviour, with different justices and eras of the Court evaluated based on how much justices speak at oral arguments (Johnson and Black 2017).

While such an approach has greatly expanded our understanding of the US Supreme Court, for a few reasons attempts to replicate this approach have been limited in comparative research. For one, the convention in some courts is for judges not to speak during oral hearings and instead solely listen to the arguments as they are presented. This is the case, for example, at the Italian Constitutional Court, where 'as a rule, the judges only listen and do not pose questions to the lawyers, who present their arguments without interruption' (Italian Constitutional Court 2019, 42). Similarly, at the International Court of Justice, 'questions from the bench are very much the exception rather than the rule' (Rose 2008, 49). In such instances, there simply is little to no information for scholars to work from when it comes to judges' contributions to oral arguments.

Where judges do regularly speak during oral arguments, systematic research into what that participation looks like is sparse. One exception, though, is a growing literature on this topic that has developed examining the case of the High Court of Australia (e.g. Tutton, Mack, and Roach Anleu 2018; Loughland 2019). In one of the few thorough studies of oral arguments outside the US context, Jacobi, Robinson, and Leslie (2023) empirically examine twenty-six years of oral arguments at the High Court. Among their findings, they present evidence of justices becoming more active as their tenure on the Court progresses and that the Chief Justice appears to exert particular influence on discussions at oral arguments. Interestingly, their findings mirror many of those found by scholars of the US Supreme Court, suggesting that at least some dynamics of oral arguments might travel well across contexts.

One such aspect of oral arguments that has garnered the interest of comparative scholars is the frequency and source of interruptions during oral arguments. With previous research on the US Supreme Court identifying interruptions as being a function of factors like judges' ideology (Johnson, Black, and Wedeking 2009) and gender (Feldman and Gill 2019), recent research on other high courts has looked for similar patterns. For example, scholars have found conflicting evidence of a gender bias when it comes to judges being interrupted (Loughland 2019; Jacobi, Robinson, and Leslie 2020), as past evidence from the US context had revealed that female judges tend to be interrupted at higher rates than their male counterparts. Such studies are particularly valuable in helping to establish the extent to which US-based arguments can be generalized to other cases, something future research would do well to build on.

3.3 Further Research

With considerable variation both within and across courts, there is ample opportunity for further comparative research into how oral arguments are conducted. Theories for why certain judges speak more than others, for example, are grounded primarily in the common law tradition, particularly in the United States. Yet with civil law dominant in most of the world, it is not immediately clear whether the same patterns would occur in such contexts as norms of participation and the expected role of judges is quite different (Cohen 2014). This may be particularly relevant in settings where court presidents or chief justices have less of a dominant role in proceedings, as this may produce opportunities for other members of the courts—and other motivating factors—to drive the conversation with litigants. For example, for many courts a single judge will be assigned the role of 'rapporteur' or reporting judge, who is charged with taking the lead in a case; one might expect these judges to be particularly influential in oral hearings. While descriptive studies of judges' speaking rates are certainly useful in assessing the generalizability of extant accounts and garnering insights into the behaviour of judges on a particular court, theoretical innovations derived from considering the impact of institutional and contextual variation may be a fruitful path to broadening our understanding of how judges use hearings in the judicial process. One example of such work is Meland, Westrheim, and Grenstad (2022), who analysed oral arguments for two oral hearings sessions at the Norwegian Supreme Court. Their analyses provide insights into important aspects such as which judges spoke (they find that the presiding judge spoke the most), the frequency and length of dialogue between judges and attorneys, and ultimately the linkage between such dialogue and case outcomes.

Beyond the question of how much individual judges speak, taking a comparative perspective allows scholars to consider variation in the amount of judges' contributions within and across courts. With many courts having norms of limited judicial participation in hearings and others known for having judges speak for a substantial portion of the proceedings, a natural question for scholars of judicial institutions is why we observe such variation. It could be, for example, that those courts with more robust third-party involvement, such as through amicus briefs, have less need to demand clarification of arguments and therefore are more prone to have judges who listen rather than talk. Alternatively, institutional features like the provision of a robust corps of law clerks could address the court's informational needs such that judges have fewer questions to ask of litigants (Grenstad et al. 2020a, 2020b), while a lack of such support might place even greater emphasis on hearings' informational role (Haynie and Sill 2007). By considering such institutional-level differences, scholars may be able to improve their understanding of why courts conduct hearings as they do.

In addition to such an expansion of studies on judges' behaviour during hearings, important empirical and theoretical questions remain regarding the participation of other actors in oral arguments. While a substantial literature in the US context has revealed the considerable influence brought to bear by the Solicitor General when they choose to become involved in a case and speak before the Supreme Court (Wohlfarth 2009; Black and Owens 2011), comparative research on the effect government officials can have by addressing a court in hearings remains underexamined. Moreover, hearings often include the testimony of experts and other third parties along with the arguments of litigants. Such involvement has clear implications for the information-gathering function of hearings, and may further drive judges' conversations with litigants as they respond to the information they are receiving. In that vein, observing the extent to which a court requests or invites the participation of such third parties may serve as another useful measure of case complexity akin to that of Bentsen et al. (2021).

There are similarly opportunities for further work on the structure and length of hearings. Besides the work of Bentsen et al. (2021), there is little systematic work examining the variation in the length of hearings. This is, in many respects, a missed opportunity as the time allotted to hearings presents another source of variation from which scholars can glean insights into the workings of courts from a comparative perspective. It is the president of the South African Constitutional Court, for example, who determines the length of hearings at that court (Haynie 2005), while at others like the Irish Supreme Court this decision is made by the parties to the case along with the managing judge (Bentsen et al. 2021). Such differences are far from trivial, as court presidents have regularly been shown at times to have different considerations than other judges, particularly with respect to protecting the integrity and legitimacy of their institution (Cheruvu and Krehbiel 2022). Differences in how this power over hearings is distributed, then, may reveal another potential institutional tool available to courts to address concerns beyond the need for information in complex cases. For instance, one consequence of a hearing might be procedural delays that result in courts taking a longer time to render a decision. Critically, such delays might be strategic, for instance to push a case beyond an election date such that a new government might come into office (Krehbiel 2021). More broadly, future work ought to consider the agenda setting power hearings provide, as other contributions to this volume demonstrate the substantial impact such authority brings.

While the organization and conduct of hearings tend to be largely unchanging within a given court, the onset of the COVID-19 pandemic brought about profound changes to means by which many courts held their hearings. With in-person hearings either discouraged or prohibited as a result of pandemic-related restrictions, many courts turned to remote hearings as an alternative. For example, the US Supreme Court shifted its oral arguments to be conducted over the telephone, which scholars noted resulted in marked changes in justices' participation (Jacobi et al. 2020; Johnson et al. 2021). Other courts like the German Constitutional Court, by contrast, were more likely to respond to pandemic restrictions by simply cancelling oral arguments and leaving them for a future date. Considering the potential implications of hearings for judicial decision-making and legitimacy, how courts have responded to these unprecedented conditions may provide some indication into how they value hearings and are able to adapt to changing conditions.

4. What Impact Do Oral Hearings Have?

Perhaps the most substantively significant question in the study of oral arguments is also its simplest one: do they matter? The answer to this question has been subject to considerable debate, as scholars and practitioners alike have both defended hearings as a highly influential part of the judicial process and characterized it as a performative act with little substantive impact (Walker and Epstein 1993; Segal and Spaeth 2002; Johnson, Wahlbeck, and Spriggs 2006). In answering this question, both in the US and comparative contexts, scholars have focused particularly on the role lawyers play by effectively—or ineffectively—presenting their arguments and the political implications of the procedure itself. In this third and final section of the chapter, I consider the evidence of such effects and suggest avenues for scholars to pursue moving forward in the pursuit of understanding the broader impacts of hearings.

4.1 Persuasion and Attorney Efficacy

One means by which oral arguments could potentially influence judicial decisions is by providing litigants with an opportunity to persuade judges of their position. Recognizing this potential, scholars have taken particular interest in evaluating the characteristics that make some litigants more successful than others at persuading justices. Building on the argument of Galanter (1974) regarding repeat players, one line of argumentation is that more experienced attorneys fare better in oral arguments than more novice counterparts (McGuire 1995; Johnson, Wahlbeck, and Spriggs 2006). With such experience—particularly experience succeeding in previous cases (Haynie and Sill 2007)—lawyers are thought to be seen as more capable of constructing arguments more effectively tailored to convince justices. This effect is most clearly demonstrated empirically in the work of Johnson, Wahlbeck and Spriggs (2006), who use the notes of US Supreme Court Justice Blackmun on the quality of lawyers' arguments to demonstrate the impact of hearings on decision making. Importantly from a comparative perspective, Galanter's repeat player theory and its derivatives have been tested extensively beyond the American context, with studies examining the relative advantage of 'haves' over 'have-nots' in courts such as the South African Supreme Court of Appeals (Haynie and Sill 2007), Canadian Supreme Court (Szmer, Johnson, and Sarver 2007), the UK Law Lords (Hanretty 2014), Taiwan's Supreme Court (Chen, Huang, and Lin 2015), the

Norwegian Supreme Court (Bjørnebekk et al. 2020), the Israeli High Court of Justice (Yoav 1999), and the Australian High Court (Smyth 2000), among others. Indeed, perhaps no single argument related to oral arguments has been subject to as widespread of empirical and theoretical study as that linking the experience of litigators with case outcomes.

One extension of the repeat player logic has been to consider the relative advantage government lawyers have over private litigants. Examining the US Solicitor General, a number of studies have demonstrated the high win rate of this ultimate repeat player (Bailey, Kamoie, and Maltzman 2005; Black and Owens 2012). Much like research on the effect of lawyers' experience, comparative studies consistently find that governments win at higher rates than any other type of litigant (McCormick 1993; Dotan 2013). Although many of these studies do not explicitly take oral arguments into account, as governments may be particularly successful for several reasons, they do raise the possibility that hearings present an opportunity for government officials to exercise their relative advantage over private litigants.

Other characteristics beyond experience may similarly influence an attorney's likelihood of persuading high court justices. One such factor may be gender, because a broad body of research has identified gender effects throughout the judicial process (Feldman and Gill 2019; Gleason and Ivy 2021). Extending these arguments to the context of oral arguments, scholars have similarly sought to evaluate whether female attorneys fare more poorly than their male counterparts in persuading justices. Interestingly, findings in this respect have varied across contexts, with studies of the US Supreme Court finding limited evidence of such a disadvantage (e.g. Szmer, Sarver, and Kaheny 2010) while others have found a clear gender bias at the High Court of Australia (Smyth and Mishra 2014). One possible explanation for such divergent results, as the authors note, is that the High Court is more persuadable—and therefore more susceptible to such biases—than the US Supreme Court, due its less politicized nature. Extending this literature, for example, to consider differences in speaking norms for judges during hearings might similarly reveal insights into the extent and nature of gender's effect on attorney's ability to successfully persuade judges.

The informational function of oral arguments may also influence judges' decisions. As judges take in new information and details provided by counsel during a hearing, they may in turn alter the lines of argument used to justify a ruling. Johnson (2004), for instance, finds that Supreme Court decisions often reflect the information provided in hearings. Similarly, courts may use the information gleaned from hearings to more effectively assess the political environment surrounding a case and the likely political response to its decision (Ringsmuth, Bryan, and Johnson 2013). While intuitive, however, accounts such as these have yet to be systematically tested in a comparative context.

4.2 Political Impact of Hearings

Importantly, the impact of hearings is not necessarily limited to the opportunity they present for persuading or informing judges. Rather, holding an oral hearing has the potential to have significant political consequences, particularly with respect to a court's relationship with the litigants of a case and the broader public. Returning to accounts of why courts hold hearings, two specific mechanisms for this appear.

With respect to the parties of a case, a hearing may increase their likelihood of accepting a court's decision even if it is not in their favour. Following the procedural legitimacy logic (Tyler and Rasinski 1991; Tyler 2006), having their 'day in court' may make litigants view the final decision as more legitimate than they otherwise might. Such an effect may be particularly important in politically contentious cases, including those directly involving political actors, as such procedural legitimacy may help shield a court from political backlash. While recent experimental evidence from the context of international courts raises doubts about the impact of procedures on citizens' support and acceptance of decisions with which they disagree (Madsen et al. 2022), the specific influence of oral hearings remains an open empirical question well-suited to the experimental methods increasingly used in comparative judicial politics (e.g. Braman 2021; Dinas and Gonzalez-Ocantos 2021).

The capacity of hearings to increase media coverage and public awareness of a case similarly has potential political consequences. For courts that rely on public support to ensure the efficacy of their decisions, such awareness is critical (Vanberg 2001; Staton 2006; Krehbiel 2016). As both Vanberg (2005) and Krehbiel (2016) note, hearings are indeed likely to generate greater media attention that can filter down to the public.[5] With greater public awareness, according to these accounts, comes greater latitude for a court to invalidate government policy with the expectation of compliance. That is, courts are more likely to rule against government policies in cases granted a hearing, especially when the topic at issue in the case is amenable to media coverage and the court faces a potentially resistant government (Krehbiel 2016; König 2022). Such findings suggest that hearings may serve not only to improve the quality of judicial decisions but also have the effect of strengthening the efficacy of courts in the face of potential political resistance to judicial power.

4.3 Further Research

Even with growing interest from scholars, several important questions—both theoretical and empirical—remain under-studied. Consider the influence of attorneys' characteristics, which is perhaps one of the most extensively studied comparative research questions. In addition to examining the effect of gender and experience, contextual factors like race or religion may be relevant in certain contexts. Moreover, it is noteworthy that most of this work has examined common law systems—the United States, Australia, United Kingdom—and thus may be leaving unconsidered the potential influence of civil law traditions on the efficacy of lawyers' arguments at high courts. As such systems are also often ones with limited use of hearings, the impact of those arguing before the court may be particularly important for understanding whether the procedure is used for informational purposes or more for legitimizing and publicizing a case. For example, one might consider the impact of attorney quality on the likelihood of a dissenting opinion in collegial courts where dissents are infrequent.

Similarly, much is left to be studied when it comes to the influence of government representatives during oral hearings. In addition to solicitor general (or equivalent) offices, a comparative perspective brings into focus other legal actors, such as ombudsmen, and differing approaches to how government agencies and ministries are represented in hearings. Examining, for instance, the win rate of ombudsmen in individual rights cases may provide insights into the efficacy of such offices and invite scholars to further consider how cross-national differences in the structure of these offices might affect their efficacy. Alternatively, broadening one's conception of 'government' to account for coalition governmental arrangements might allow scholars to consider the efficacy of government officials from different parties and ministries. König's (2022) finding that the Austrian Constitutional Court is responsive to the presence of a populist party in government and Schroeder's (2022) research demonstrating the German Constitutional Court's ability to make inferences about the credibility of information based in part on the partisanship of its source, for example, suggests that courts may not treat all governments—or constituent parties in a government—the same.

The impact of hearings on public sentiment towards courts and their decisions similarly has particular potential for further comparative research. While citizens of countries with a strong tradition of oral arguments may be likely to ascribe greater legitimacy to decisions reached with the benefit of an oral hearing, this may not necessarily always be the case in contexts without such a tradition. More nuanced theoretical developments await study as well, such as the case characteristics that might make hearings more or less effective at legitimizing a decision. Decisions striking down a law or prominent legal precedent, for example, might particularly benefit from greater acceptance after a hearing. Engaging with such questions would not only expand the scope of extant arguments but would also create opportunities for examining the impact of hearings in settings beyond those that have so far received the lion's share of scholars' attention.

5. Conclusion

While still in many respects developing, comparative research on oral arguments and hearings is growing to produce valuable insights into the decision-making and public standing of courts around the globe. With the firm basis of an expansive literature on the US Supreme Court, comparative scholars have already covered considerable ground in understanding why courts hold hearings, how courts conduct hearings, and the impact of hearings. Notably, these studies have revealed the extent to which US-based arguments are generalizable, with some revealing trends that travel well across contexts and others demonstrating the insights one can glean only by looking at the institutional variation gained from a comparative perspective. In particular, detaching from the US context has revealed the value gained from examining oral arguments as 'exceptional' events rather than perfunctory facets of the judicial decision-making process.

For example, the lessons learned from a diversity of contexts including Norway and the European Court of Human Rights are born at least in part from efforts to conceptualize hearings as they are used by such courts. Indeed, this is a point, albeit in a more generalized form, that is evident through this volume, particularly in the other chapters examining facets of advocacy, litigation, and appellate review.

Importantly, the body of research discussed in this chapter continues to expand as scholars recognize new contexts and ways in which hearings are significant. With this in mind, I conclude by suggesting additional directions for future research into oral hearings and arguments. Considering the outsized attention hearings often receive in citizens' familiarity with courts, much remains to be examined about how the procedure affects and frames those attitudes. For instance, oral arguments may be an opportunity for justices to float ideas not only to their colleagues but also to the public. In doing so, they can effectively 'test run' potential outcomes, which media sources often pick up on as key takeaways or themes of the hearings. This suggests that hearings may have a further purpose for courts, namely testing the waters of public opinion on possible outcomes in key decisions. Similarly, hearings may elicit reactions from political elites that can inform a court about the political environment in which it is likely to be issuing its decision. To this end, work could consider how justices' statements and questions in hearings filter into media coverage and politicians' statements, as well as public familiarity with issues and expectations for how a court might rule.

While much of the literature on oral hearings originates in work on the US Supreme Court, scholars are increasingly leveraging a comparative perspective to gain new insights. Naturally, there remains much to do in this respect, as variation in institutional structure and norms presents opportunities for expanding research beyond questions based on the US context. For example, the organization of high courts varies considerably, with many constitutional and supreme courts issuing many, if not most, of their decisions in panels rather than *en banc*. This division of judicial labour may present a methodological opportunity to examine the factors that influence the use of hearings, as one might for instance compare similar cases across panels to evaluate how considerations beyond the specific facts of a case impact a panel's willingness to hold a hearing. Along similar lines, the growing research on the impact of gender diversification (e.g. Valdini and Shortell 2016; Arrington et al. 2021) increases the opportunities for scholars to evaluate how the presence of women on high court benches—particularly in leadership positions—might affect the content of hearings and their impact on decisions. In short, a comparative approach opens the door for research into a range of topics, including those aspects of hearings that are hard to study at the US Supreme Court because of the slow rate of change in the institution and its membership.

More generally, the insights provided by the other chapters in this volume, such as those on agenda setting and attorneys (both government and private), speak to the potential value of linking core concepts in our theoretical accounts of judicial behaviour. That is, these topics, oral arguments included, do not exist in a vacuum but rather in the interconnected thing we call judicial behaviour. Thus, when considering a facet of the judicial process such as oral arguments, it is vital to recognize that it does not operate in isolation but rather is itself a function of that broader process. Scholars of comparative judicial behaviour—in its most interdisciplinary form—stand to benefit from synthesizing accounts of these varied aspects of behaviour together. As such, I close this chapter by encouraging readers to see this chapter not only as 'about' oral hearings but also as part of the broader conversation set forth by the other contributions to this volume.

Notes

1. Throughout the chapter I will use the terms 'oral arguments' and 'oral hearings' interchangeably.
2. Exceptions are often provided requiring hearings for the most sensitive of cases such as attempts to ban political parties or challenges brought by political institutions.
3. Indeed, many of the cases most likely to be especially contentious, such as abstract review applications, often are required to include an oral hearing.
4. It is worth noting that the US Supreme Court has, in part as a consequence of the procedural changes wrought by the COVID-19 pandemic, begun allowing for more variable hearing lengths.
5. Krehbiel (2016) conducts an analysis of German media coverage of Constitutional Court decisions illustrating this relationship.

References

Arrington, Nancy, Leeann Bass, Adam Glynn, Jeffrey K. Staton, Brian Delgado, and Staffan I. Lindberg. 2021. 'Constitutional Reform and the Gender Diversification of Peak Courts'. *American Political Science Review* 115 (3): 851–68.

Austrian Constitutional Court. 2022. 'Annual Report'. Austrian Constitutional Court.

Bailey, Michael A., Brian Kamoie, and Forrest Maltzman. 2005. 'Signals from the Tenth Justice: The Political Role of the Solicitor General in Supreme Court Decision Making'. *American Journal of Political Science* 49 (1): 72–85.

Barrera, Leticia. 2013. 'Performing the Court: Public Hearings and the Politics of Judicial Transparency in Argentina'. *PoLAR: Political and Legal Anthropology Review* 36 (2): 326–40.

Baude, William. 2015. 'Foreword: The Supreme Court's Shadow Docket'. *NYU Journal of Law & Liberty* 9 (1): 1–47.

Bennett, David. 2001. 'Argument before the Court'. In *The Oxford Companion to the High Court of Australia*, edited by Michael Cooper, Tony Blackshield, and George Williams, 31–32. Oxford: Oxford University Press.

Bentsen, Henrik L., Gunnar Grendstad, William R. Shaffer, and Eric N. Waltenburg. 2021. 'A High Court Plays the Accordion: Validating Ex Ante Case Complexity on Oral Arguments'. *Justice System Journal* 42 (2): 130–49.

Bjørnebekk, Olav Laug, Gunnar Grenstad, William R. Shaffer, and Eric N. Waltenburg. 2020. 'Case Inertia and a Better Lawyer Secure Victory in Court'. *Reffærd* 43 (2): 51–70.

Black, Ryan C., Timothy R. Johnson, and Justin Wedeking. 2012. *Oral Arguments and Coalition Formation on the US Supreme Court: A Deliberate Dialogue*. Ann Arbor: University of Michigan Press.

Black, Ryan C., and Ryan J. Owens. 2011. 'Solicitor General Influence and Agenda Setting on the US Supreme Court'. *Political Research Quarterly* 64 (4): 765–78.

Black, Ryan C., and Ryan J. Owens. 2012. *The Solicitor General and the United States Supreme Court: Executive Branch Influence and Judicial Decisions*. Cambridge: Cambridge University Press.

Black, Ryan C., Maron W. Sorenson, and Timothy R. Johnson. 2013. 'Toward an Actor-Based Measure of Supreme Court Case Salience: Information-Seeking and Engagement During Oral Arguments'. *Political Research Quarterly* 66 (4): 804–18.

Braman, Eileen. 2021. 'Thinking about Government Authority: Constitutional Rules and Political Context in Citizens' Assessments of Judicial, Legislative, and Executive Action'. *American Journal of Political Science* 65 (2): 389–404.

Cann, Damon, and Greg Goelzhauser. 2024. 'The Impact of Oral Argument Attendance'. *Journal of Law and Courts* 12 (1): 132–43.

Chen, Kong-Pin, Kuo-Chang Huang, and Chang-Ching Lin. 2015. 'Party Capability Versus Court Preference: Why Do the 'Haves' Come Out Ahead?—an Empirical Lesson from the Taiwan Supreme Court'. *The Journal of Law, Economics, & Organization* 31 (1): 93–126.

Cheruvu, Sivaram, and Jay N. Krehbiel. 2022. 'Delegation, Compliance, and Judicial Decision Making in the Court of Justice of the European Union'. *Journal of Law and Courts* 10 (1): 113–38.

Cohen, Mathilde. 2014. 'Ex Ante Versus Ex Post Deliberations: Two Models of Judicial Deliberations in Courts of Last Resort'. *The American Journal of Comparative Law* 62 (4): 951–1008.

Dinas, Elias, and Ezequiel Gonzalez-Ocantos. 2021. 'Defending the European Court of Human Rights: Experimental Evidence from Britain'. *European Journal of Political Research* 60 (2): 397–417.

Dotan, Yoav. 2013. *Lawyering for the Rule of Law: Government Lawyers and the Rise of Judicial Power in Israel, Vol. 9*. Cambridge: Cambridge University Press.

European Court of Human Rights. 2021. 'Annual Report'. Strasbourg: European Court of Human Rights.

Feldman, Adam, and Rebecca D. Gill. 2019. 'Power Dynamics in Supreme Court Oral Arguments: The Relationship between Gender and Justice-to-Justice Interruptions'. *Justice System Journal* 40 (3): 173–95.

Galanter, Marc. 1974. 'Why the Haves Come Out Ahead: Speculations on the Limits of Legal Change'. *Law & Society Review* 9: 95.

German Constitutional Court. 2018. 'Annual Report'. German Constitutional Court.

German Constitutional Court. 2021. 'Annual Report'. German Constitutional Court.

Gibson, James L., Gregory A. Caldeira, and Vanessa A. Baird. 1998. 'On the Legitimacy of National High Courts'. *American Political Science Review* 92 (2): 343–58.

Gleason, Shane A., and Diana K. Ivy. 2021. 'As She Was Saying: The Role of Gender and Narratives in Oral Argument Amicus Success'. *Justice System Journal* 42 (3–4): 416–33.

Grendstad, Gunnar, William R. Shaffer, Jørn Øyrehagen Sunde, and Eric N. Waltenburg. 2020a. *Proactive and Powerful: Law Clerks and the Institutionalization of the Norwegian Supreme Court*. The Hague: Eleven International Publishing.

Grendstad, Gunnar, William R. Shaffer, Jørn Øyrehagen Sunde, and Eric N. Waltenburg. 2020b. 'From Backlogs to Quality Assurance. The Development of Law Clerk Units at Norwegian Courts'. *International Journal for Court Administration* 11 (1): 1–17.

Grundmanns, David. 2022. 'The Impact of External Actors on Judicial Decision-Making: Evidence from the German Federal Constitutional Court'. Working Paper.

Guimarães, Lívia Gil. 2020. 'Participação Social No STF: Repensando oPapel Das Audiências públicas'. *Revista Direito e Práxis* 11: 236–71.

Hanretty, Chris. 2014. 'Haves and Have-Nots before the Law Lords'. *Political Studies* 62 (3): 686–97.

Haynie, Stacia L. 2005. 'Oral Advocacy and Judicial Decision-Making in the South African Appellate Courts'. *South African Journal on Human Rights* 21 (3): 473–89.

Haynie, Stacia L., and Kaitlyn L. Sill. 2007. 'Experienced Advocates and Litigation Outcomes: Repeat Players in the South African Supreme Court of Appeal'. *Political Research Quarterly* 60 (3): 443–53.

Italian Constitutional Court. 2019. 'Annual Report'. Italian Constitutional Court.

Jacobi, Tonja, Timothy R. Johnson, Eve M. Ringsmuth, and Matthew Sag. 2020. 'Oral Argument in the Time of COVID: The Chief Plays Calvinball'. *Southern California Interdisciplinary Law Journal* 30: 399.

Jacobi, Tonja, Zoe Robinson, and Patrick Leslie. 2023. 'Comparative Exceptionalism? Strategy and Ideology in the High Court of Australia'. *The American Journal of Comparative Law* 71 (3): 568–617.

Jacobi, Tonja, Zoë Robinson, and Patrick Leslie. 2020. 'Querying the Gender Dynamics of Interruptions at Australian Oral Argument'. *University of New South Wales Law Journal Forum* 1: 1–19.

Johnson, Timothy R. 2004. *Oral Arguments and Decision Making on the United States Supreme Court*. New York: SUNY Press.

Johnson, Timothy R., and Ryan C. Black. 2017. 'The Roberts Court and Oral Arguments: A First Decade Retrospective'. *Washington University Journal of Law & Policy* 54: 137.

Johnson, Timothy R., Ryan C. Black, and Justin Wedeking. 2009. 'Pardon the Interruption: An Empirical Analysis of Supreme Court Justices' Behavior During Oral Arguments'. *Loyola Law Review* 55: 331.

Johnson, Timothy R., Maron W. Sorenson, Maggie Cleary, and Katie Szarkowicz. 2021. 'COVID-19 and Supreme Court Oral Argument: The Curious Case of Justice Clarence Thomas'. *Journal of Appellate Practice & Process* 21: 113.

Johnson, Timothy R., Paul J. Wahlbeck, and James F. Spriggs. 2006. 'The Influence of Oral Arguments on the US Supreme Court'. *American Political Science Review* 100 (1): 99–113.

König, Jasmin. 2022. 'Do High Courts Change Their Communication When Facing Populists? Evidence from Austria'. Working Paper.

Krehbiel, Jay N. 2016. 'The Politics of Judicial Procedures: The Role of Public Oral Hearings in the German Constitutional Court'. *American Journal of Political Science* 60 (4): 990–1005.

Krehbiel, Jay N. 2021. 'Strategic Delay and the Use of Incompatibility Rulings at the German Constitutional Court'. *The Journal of Politics* 83 (3): 821–33.

Loughland, Amelia. 2019. 'Female Judges, Interrupted: A Study of Interruption Behaviour During Oral Argument in the High Court of Australia'. *Melbourne University Law Review* 43: 822.

Madsen, Mikael Rask, Juan A. Mayoral, Anton Strezhnev, and Erik Voeten. 2022. 'Sovereignty, Substance, and Public Support for European Courts' Human Rights Rulings'. *American Political Science Review* 116 (2): 419–38.

McCormick, Peter. 1993. 'Party Capability Theory and Appellate Success in the Supreme Court of Canada, 1949–1992'. *Canadian Journal of Political Science/Revue Canadienne de Science Politique* 26 (3): 523–40.

McGuire, Kevin T. 1995. 'Repeat Players in the Supreme Court: The Role of Experienced Lawyers in Litigation Success'. *The Journal of Politics* 57 (1): 187–96.

Meland, Ida Marie Støp, Welat Akman Westrheim, and Gunnar Grendstad. 2022. 'Spørsmål Og Dialog i Muntlige Forhandlinger i Norges høyesterett'. *Lov Og Rett*, no. 2: 117–28.

Ringsmuth, Eve M., Amanda C. Bryan, and Timothy R. Johnson. 2013. 'Voting Fluidity and Oral Argument on the US Supreme Court'. *Political Research Quarterly* 66 (2): 429–40.

Rosas, Allan. 2014. 'Oral Hearings before the European Court of Justice'. *Maastricht Journal of European and Comparative Law* 21 (4): 596–610.

Rose, Cecily. 2008. 'Questioning the Silence of the Bench: Reflections on Oral Proceedings at the International Court of Justice'. *Journal of Transnational Law & Policy* 18: 47.

Schroeder, Philipp. 2022. 'Pushing Boundaries: How Lawmakers Shape Judicial Decision-Making'. *Comparative Political Studies* 55 (14): 247–49.

Segal, Jeffrey A., and Harold J. Spaeth. 2002. *The Supreme Court and the Attitudinal Model Revisited*. Cambridge: Cambridge University Press.

Smyth, Russell. 2000. 'The "Haves" and the "Have Nots": An Empirical Study of the Rational Actor and Party Capability Hypotheses in the High Court 1948–99'. *Australian Journal of Political Science* 35 (2): 255–74.

Smyth, Russell, and Vinod Mishra. 2014. 'Barrister Gender and Litigant Success in the High Court of Australia'. *Australian Journal of Political Science* 49 (1): 1–21.

Staton, Jeffrey K. 2006. 'Constitutional Review and the Selective Promotion of Case Results'. *American Journal of Political Science* 50 (1): 98–112.

Staton, Jeffrey K. 2010. *Judicial Power and Strategic Communication in Mexico*. New York: Cambridge University Press.

Staton, Jeffrey K., and Will H. Moore. 2011. 'Judicial Power in Domestic and International Politics'. *International Organization* 65 (3): 553–87.

Szmer, John J., Tammy A. Sarver, and Erin B. Kaheny. 2010. 'Have We Come a Long Way, Baby? The Influence of Attorney Gender on Supreme Court Decision Making'. *Politics & Gender* 6 (1): 1–36.

Szmer, John, Susan W. Johnson, and Tammy A. Sarver. 2007. 'Does the Lawyer Matter? Influencing Outcomes on the Supreme Court of Canada'. *Law & Society Review* 41 (2): 279–304.

Tutton, Jordan, Kathy Mack, and Sharyn Roach Anleu. 2018. 'Judicial Demeanor: Oral Argument in the High Court of Australia'. *Justice System Journal* 39 (3): 273–99.

Tyler, Tom R. 1994. 'Governing and Diversity: The Effect of Fair Decisionmaking Procedures on the Legitimacy of Government'. *Law & Society Review* 28: 809.

Tyler, Tom R. 2006. 'Psychological Perspectives on Legitimacy and Legitimation'. *Annual Review of Psychology* 57: 375.

Tyler, Tom R., and Kenneth Rasinski. 1991. 'Procedural Justice, Institutional Legitimacy, and the Acceptance of Unpopular US Supreme Court Decisions: A Reply to Gibson'. *Law and Society Review* 25 (3): 621–30.

Valdini, Melody E., and Christopher Shortell. 2016. 'Women's Representation in the Highest Court: A Comparative Analysis of the Appointment of Female Justices'. *Political Research Quarterly* 69 (4): 865–76.

Vanberg, Georg. 2001. 'Legislative-Judicial Relations: A Game-Theoretic Approach to Constitutional Review'. *American Journal of Political Science* 45 (2): 346–61.

Vanberg, Georg. 2005. *The Politics of Constitutional Review in Germany*. New York: Cambridge University Press.

Venice Commission. 2010. 'Study on Individual Access to Constitutional Justice'. Venice Commission.

Vladeck, Stephen I. 2019. 'The Solicitor General and the Shadow Docket'. *Harvard Law Review* 133: 123.

Walker, Thomas G., and Lee Epstein. 1993. *The Supreme Court of the United States: An Introduction*. New York: St. Martin's Press.

Wohlfarth, Patrick C. 2009. 'The Tenth Justice? Consequences of Politicization in the Solicitor General's Office'. *The Journal of Politics* 71 (1): 224–37.

Yoav, Dotan. 1999. 'Do the Haves Still Come Out Ahead-Resource Inequalities in Ideological Courts: The Case of the Israeli High Court of Justice'. *Law & Society Review* 33: 1059.

PART VI

OPINIONS

CHAPTER 25

DISSENTS AND OTHER SEPARATE OPINIONS

KATALIN KELEMEN

1. Introduction

Disagreement between judges on concrete legal questions, which seems to emerge inevitably from time to time in the long life of any judicial body, has long interested legal scholars and political scientists, and occasionally other social scientists. Dissent in courts has always existed. However, not all courts have been allowed to reveal it. This naturally limited, but did not entirely exclude, the possibility of researching judicial dissent in countries where separate opinions are banned.

When looking at it from a comparative perspective, we promptly find that concealing (and preventing) judicial dissent has been a traditional aspiration of the civil law systems since the Enlightenment. Montesquieu's famous words about the judge being just the 'mouth of the law' still echo in the civil law tradition today. It seems that continental European judges, even when allowed to write separately, are more reluctant to do so than their colleagues in common law jurisdictions, even though the latter also show a considerable degree of variety when it comes to dissent. In any case, the common law tradition, with its tradition of oral procedure and practice of delivering personal judicial opinions, has been the natural habitat of dissenting and other separate opinions (Kelemen 2018, 52).

It is unsurprising, therefore, that most research on dissents and other separate opinions emerges from the common law countries, primarily carried out by scholars of judicial politics in the United States. However, judicial politics has also started to flourish in Europe in recent decades. We now have analyses of the practice of dissenting opinions in relation to some, but not all, European courts, especially constitutional courts, operating either at the national or regional level. There are, however, still very few comparative studies on this matter that carry out a quantitative analysis looking for possible causal patterns (Garoupa et al. 2021). As this chapter will show, rather than a distinction between the civil law and the common law tradition, we can notice a difference between the United States and the rest of the Western legal tradition, including other common law countries. Still, the availability of research on judicial dissent varies among jurisdictions to a great extent, and in any case, each court must be examined in its specific legal and political context.

The chapter first offers a definition of the terminology, and then it presents the research findings on dissents and other separate opinions. In doing so, it first addresses the primary methodological challenges and examines the two main research questions that have captivated scholars studying judicial dissent. Subsequently, the following section takes a comparative approach, examining several studies conducted in different parts of the world, to shed light on dissent and other separate opinions.

2. Definitions

By 'dissent' we mean disagreement in opinion. Naturally, dissent can only exist when decisions are made by multiple actors. Therefore, it can only exist in a court if it is a collegial body or a judicial panel to decide. The terms 'judicial dissent' and 'dissenting opinion' can be used interchangeably. However, the distinction lies in the fact that the former refers to the phenomenon of judges being in disagreement with each other, whereas the latter refers to its product, a separate opinion.

It is also important to clarify that the term 'separate opinion' is broader in scope than 'dissenting opinion', which can be used in a narrower or broader sense. In the broad sense, 'dissenting opinion' is synonymous with 'separate opinion'. A dissenter, however, may disagree with the majority only in part. She or he may agree with the outcome of the case but provide different reasons for reaching that conclusion. In this case, his or her separate opinion is technically referred to as a 'concurring opinion'. On the other hand, a dissenting opinion in the narrow sense disagrees with the majority not only on the reasoning but also on the ruling itself. A dissenting judge would have decided the case differently. Conversely, a concurring judge would have simply written the judgment differently, without altering the outcome of the case. Thus, a concurring opinion either presents an alternative reasoning for the decision, adds further arguments (supplementary reasoning), or aims to provide a clearer explanation of the opinion of the court (explanatory opinion) (Kelemen 2018, 5).

When we look at other languages, we often find that they put the dissenting or separate opinion in a different light. For instance, the Spanish term *voto particular* signifies an extraordinary opinion, meant to be used exceptionally. The German term *Minderheitsvotum* literally means 'minority vote', highlighting the significance of majority rule in judicial decision-making. The European Court of Human Rights (ECtHR) employs the French term *opinion individuelle*, emphasizing the personal character of a separate opinion. However, the finest curiosity among the foreign expressions is the Portuguese *voto de vencido*, which translates to 'vote of the loser' (Panizza 1998, 115).

This implies that the dissenter is a loser in the sense that he or she was unable to convince his or her colleagues.

While not commonly used in that manner, the term 'dissent' can also be meant in a broader sense, which includes differences of opinion between judges who are not part of the same panel. Judicial dissent can indeed arise between different chambers within the same court or between different courts. Such disagreements are not uncommon, particularly in large jurisdictions like the United States. The appellate system itself, inherent in any modern court system, allows for the possibility of disagreement. When the reversal of a lower court's judgment is based solely on legal interpretation rather than new factual evidence presented during the appeal process, the nature of disagreement between the superior and inferior courts does not differ substantially from other forms of judicial dissent (Llewellyn et al. 1988, 992). However, this chapter will only examine dissents within the context of judicial panels, so in the traditional sense.

3. Research on Dissent and Other Separate Opinions

For a long time, research on the practice of dissenting opinions in Europe was very limited. However, this has changed in recent decades. It is worth noting that scholars' interest in separate opinions is not necessarily dependent on their actual existence in the judicial practice of their respective countries. In Italy, for example, even though no court is allowed to publish dissent, legal scholars have consistently demonstrated interest in this matter. The debate surrounding the permissibility of publishing separate opinions has notably emerged in relation to and within the constitutional court (Kelemen 2018, 96; Tega 2018). Although the Italian legislature has never approved any such proposal, Italian legal scholars have made a significant contribution to the European legal literature on judicial dissent (Panizza 1998). But we may find writings discussing the possibility of allowing dissenting opinions also in Belgium (Nelissen 2011; De Jaegere 2019) and France (Mastor 2022).

In legal research, separate opinions may play a double role. On the one hand, they can be in and of themselves the object of research aiming to analyse court practice and judicial behaviour. On the other hand, for researchers who study any legal problem, they may serve as a useful source of arguments and possible solutions (Kelemen 2013). The first type of research can take two forms: doctrinal research, which focuses on normative and theoretical inquiries, and empirical research, which measures dissent rates and looks for correlations with various factors associated with judicial decision-making. The latter approach has been more prevalent in political science than among legal scholars, especially in Europe, where familiarity with empirical methods in legal scholarship is not as widespread.

As regards doctrinal legal research, it is more common for separate opinions to be utilized as tools rather than being the primary focus of research. Separate opinions can be considered as (non-binding) sources of law themselves. They contribute to legal scholarship by providing alternative arguments in relation to specific legal questions. When scholars comment on judgments, they typically include separate opinions in their analysis. In some cases, concurring opinions may even shed light on intriguing facts concerning the internal dynamics of the court in a particular case.[1] Moreover, they frequently aim to provide a clearer explanation of the opinion of the court or specific aspects of it, as majority opinions—usually resulting from compromise—may employ deliberately vague or narrow language. A majority judgment is prone to represent the opinion of everyone, but it may end up representing the opinion of no-one fully (Alder 2000, 242).

The use of quantitative and qualitative empirical methods has, however, a long tradition in US legal scholarship and is an emerging trend in Europe and Latin America as well. While in the US legal and political science are strongly intertwined when it comes to research on courts, the same cannot be said about Europe, where collaboration between legal scholars and political scientists is more limited.

3.1 Methodological Challenges

The most important challenge for researchers who want study the opinion-writing practice of judges is the secrecy of deliberation, a fundamental principle of judicial decision-making. Judicial panels deliberate behind closed doors in all democratic legal systems. A complete publicity would entail undue popular pressures on judges and endanger the court's independence (Kelemen 2018, 166).

From a comparative perspective, the US Supreme Court follows a rather unique practice. On the famous 'Opinion Day', the Court announces the decisions it has reached. In this occasion, every judge reads, paraphrases, or summarizes his or her opinion (Abraham 1998, 240). Consequently, it is no secret which judges approved the ruling and which ones remained in the minority. The identity of the opinion-writer judge is also public, with the notable exception of *per curiam* opinions that are unsigned and amount to 15 to 25 per cent of all judgments (Abraham 1998, 201). The judgment is usually written as the 'opinion of the Court', unless there is a tie, but it is authored by one judge who delivers the decision in the name of the majority.

In the civil law tradition, on the other hand, secrecy of deliberation typically extends to the voting. Every judge must sign the decision and, as a rule, the result of the voting is not made public. Dissenting and concurring opinions, where they exist, are perceived as an exception to the rule. In the European practice, the identity of judges remaining in the minority is revealed only if they write a dissenting opinion. If they decide not to write separately even though in the minority, the public will never know who voted against the decision (Kelemen 2018, 167).

In courts where the result of the voting is not public, it is not possible to compile complete statistics on the voting behaviour of judges, let alone in courts where dissenting opinions are banned (De Jaegere 2019). A researcher can only analyse the number and content of published separate opinions. Only the judges themselves know how many times they remained in the minority with their opinions. In common law supreme courts, instead, where as a rule the result of the voting is public, it is possible to undertake a thorough analysis of the judges' voting behaviour.[2] The most important difference, however, between a common law and civil law judge is that the former cannot vote against the judgment without stating his or her reasons for it, even if only in the form of joining a fellow judge's opinion.

A civil law judge, if allowed to write separately, has four options when remaining in minority: (i) voting with the majority anyway, as a sign of respect and loyalty towards the majority and the court's authority, or the 'withheld dissent' option; (ii) voting against the majority, without writing separately and remaining silent about his or her dissent in the eyes of the public, or the 'silent dissenter' option; (iii) voting against the judgment, without writing separately but joining the separate opinion of another judge, or the 'concurring dissent' option; and, finally, (iv) voting against the majority and writing separately, or the 'full dissent' option (Kelemen 2018, 175). The fact that for judges it is a right and not a duty to write a dissenting or concurring opinion (with the remarkable exception of Greece)[3] leaves space for strategic behaviour. Judges are supposed to vote according to their conscience, but the lower dissent rates in European courts seem to suggest that sometimes their loyalty towards the institution supersedes their conscience. Alternatively, or in addition, it might also suggest that they work harder to reach an agreement than their American colleagues. In any event, it is a demonstration of loyalty and respect.

3.2 The Role of Political Ideology in Judicial Decision-Making

The primary research question regarding the practice of judicial dissent is the extent to which judges are influenced by their own political views when making decisions. Separate opinions have proven to be an excellent resource for researchers in investigating this question. Typically employing quantitative methods, these studies' focus aim to discern insights into individual judges' ideological background and party alignment. They look for correlations between voting patterns on the bench and factors such as the political party which appointed the judge or the career path (professional background) of the judge before appointment to the bench. This line of research explores dissent variations to identify potential political alignments and dynamics.

When it comes to research on constitutional courts, one of the methodological lines that seem to emerge in the last couple of decades to explore how different procedural questions impact court outcomes is ideal point estimations (Bagashka and Garoupa

2021, 186). This method is directly related to dissent and separate opinions, as ideal point estimations model each judge's vote in a particular case as function of his or her ideal point plus characteristics of the case. For example, Hanretty (2012) used this technique in his study comparing the Spanish Tribunal Constitutional with its Portuguese counterpart and found that Spanish constitutional judges' votes tend to reflect the political preferences of the nominating party. Similarly, Voeten (2007) studied dissents in the ECtHR to estimate the ideal points of judges and found that the expansion of the European Union (EU) was an important driving force behind the Court's activism. In particular, he showed that aspiring EU members and governments more favourably disposed toward European integration appointed more activist judges.

Another method is to measure the relation of distance between the constitutional court and the political opposition in Germany and France, analysing the results of cases of abstract review (Hönnige 2009). In relation to the German court, where separate opinions are available, he brought the analysis to the micro level, finding support for the hypothesis that constitutional judges have political preferences when adjudicating constitutional questions. In other words, he found that constitutional judges are policy-seekers just as the justices of the US Supreme Court are.[4]

However, majority judgments and separate opinions alone do not offer a sufficient picture of the judges' opinion-writing practice. There are other sources of information that may contribute to such an investigation. In the United States, for example, despite the duty of confidentiality, law clerks have sometimes served as a source of information for journalists and researchers.[5] Moreover, judges themselves at times reveal important facts in scholarly articles or interviews given to researchers or journalists. Therefore, oral history is also an important source when studying judicial dissent.

3.3 Judicial Dissent and the Doctrine of Binding Precedent

Even if it is a more significant concern for common law jurisdictions than other legal traditions, another research question related to judicial dissent and other separate opinions is the relationship between dissenting opinions and the value of precedents. This relationship holds greater significance for legal scholars than for political scientists.

There are two main questions that arise. First, what precedential value can a separate opinion have? Second, does a judgment accompanied by a dissenting opinion have the same precedential value as a unanimous decision? In particular, what if the reasons underlying a decision are not supported by the majority of the judges? As regards the first question, there is consensus among lawyers: separate opinions do not have any precedential value. They are not binding for anybody. It does not mean, however, that they cannot have an impact or even be adopted fully in a future case. They certainly may have a persuasive effect. In the United States, Balkin and Levinson (1998) studied dissenting opinions that have become part of the canons of constitutional law, and found that 'canonical' dissents were mainly authored by Justices Holmes, Brandeis, and Harlan.

The proliferation of dissenting opinions, especially in the United States, has emphasized the second, more difficult question. The phenomenon of the so-called plurality opinions, opinions shared by the majority only as regards the outcome of the case but not the reasoning, puts a serious challenge on a legal system built on the rule of precedent. Several legal scholars in the common law jurisdictions have discussed and analysed the precedential value of plurality opinions. In US legal scholarship, according to the classical theory, an opinion of the court which is not clearly shared by the majority in its entirety is not a binding precedent, and its authority is limited to the outcome of the case (Novak 1980). Some explained the phenomenon of plurality opinions by the fact that the Supreme Court has been increasingly engaging in substantive reasoning, which arose as a reaction to legal formalism during the Lochner era ('Plurality Decisions and Judicial Decisionmaking' 1981).

4. Dissent and Other Separate Opinions from a Comparative Perspective

Dissenting and other separate opinions have spread gradually in the Western legal tradition, being first 'institutionalized' in the United States as an adaptation of the heritage of English common law to local needs and circumstances. Separate opinions then spread to Germany and Spain where they upheld and renewed judicial traditions, and finally arrived in East-Central Europe in the context of the transition from socialism to constitutional democracy. In each legal system, dissenting opinions grew out of different needs and were embedded in different surroundings. Examples of disclosure of judicial dissent, even if few and isolated, were nonetheless present even in the long history of the civil law tradition. This comparative history has also been object of research, especially in Italy and France (Gorla 1965; Panizza 1998; Di Martino 2016; Mastor 2022).

Comparative research has shown that the publication of dissent is today no longer limited to the practice of common law judges. It has become a relatively widespread practice even in many continental European countries. However, interestingly, it still represents an exception for judges of ordinary courts, while today most European constitutional courts publish separate opinions (Kelemen 2018). While there is a growing literature on judicial dissent in constitutional courts and ordinary courts with judicial review powers—such as the common law supreme courts and, for example, the Brazilian (Lopes 2019) and the Norwegian Supreme Courts (Sunde 2012; Bentsen 2014, 2018)—the practice of dissenting opinions in ordinary courts in continental Europe remains largely unexplored. Among the Nordic countries, all of which have a decentralized system of judicial review, as of today we can only find empirical research on this matter in Norway, and more recently in Sweden (Derlén and Lindholm 2016).

4.1 *Seriatim* Opinions in the Common Law Tradition

The roots of today's dissenting and other separate opinions can be found in medieval England where legal disputes, if argued before a panel of judges, were decided separately by each member of the panel. This practice of delivering judicial opinions '*seriatim*' (separately) was a natural consequence of the orality of English court procedure. Judicial opinions were necessarily delivered separately, as they were announced orally at the end of the trial by the single judges (Kirby 2007). This principle also aimed to ensure that judges did everything in public so that their behaviour could be monitored (Posner 2010). The judges' opinions were written down by a clerk, rather than by the judges, in order to be collected and published in the Reports. In this practice of *seriatim* opinions, judgments could be identified as a majority, dissenting or concurring opinion only after all judges expressed their judgment. Only in the seventeenth century did majority voting become the preferred mode of decision-making in England (Alder 2000, 233).

4.2 The Practice of the 'Opinion of the Court'

The English practice of *seriatim* opinions was quickly rationalized and adapted to the local political reality in the United States. It is here that the institution of dissenting opinion as such was born. Historical research explains that for a short period after its creation in 1789, the US Supreme Court followed the practice of the English King's Bench (ZoBell 1958). The turning point was marked by the appointment of John Marshall as Chief Justice in 1801. The objective of the new Chief Justice was to consolidate the prestige and authority of the Supreme Court and to bring its position to a level equal to the other two branches of government. Establishing the power of judicial review and the discontinuance of the practice of *seriatim* opinions were the main achievements of Chief Justice Marshall. The new decision-making practice made it possible for the Court to speak with one voice and to assert itself more forcefully in the US legal system, especially against the Congress and the President. Thus, research in comparative legal history has shown that separate opinions represent a compromise between the English practice of writing *seriatim* opinions and that of apparently unanimous judgments, which was the practice in continental Europe (Kelemen 2018). Today's US practice represents a half-way solution between these two opposite positions. It allows the judges to express themselves freely, and at the same time it ensures that the court shows unity through the 'opinion of the court' shared by at least a majority of the judges. In this way, the *ratio decidendi* to be followed as binding precedent is to be found in one opinion and not to be deduced from more individual judgments. It makes the job of those who have to apply and interpret the decision much easier.

4.3 The Practice of the Common Law Supreme Courts

There is much more written about the decision-making process of the court of last instance in the United States than in other common law countries, including the United Kingdom. It might be simply due to the fact that legal literature is more abundant in the United States in general (Samuel 2023, 188). The US Supreme Court, since the 1940s in particular, has received much attention by researchers and the general public. Also, being a rather complex and large court system, in the US legal system there is a greater variety of judicial decisions and of decision-making processes. Indeed, US studies are not limited to the federal court system but often also include state courts.

However, scholarly writings on judicial dissent on other common law supreme courts are not missing. There is a relatively abundant literature on the practice of the Supreme Court of Canada (Songer et al. 2011; Dawood 2013; Vitale 2014). In the United Kingdom, such research emerged also as a result of personal writings and judicial notebooks of the judges having become available. Blom-Cooper and Drewry (1972) authored the first important work on the practice of the Appellate Committee of the House of Lords, followed by Paterson's valuable contribution (Paterson 1983), offering an insight into the Law Lords' decision-making. The behaviour of the justices sitting on the new UK Supreme Court that replaced the Appellate Committee of the House of Lords in 2009 continues to arouse the interest of researchers (Paterson 2013; Hanretty 2020). This new Court appears to be far more accessible and transparent than the House of Lords ever was, making research on judicial behaviour more feasible.

Notwithstanding this trend in the United Kingdom, a comparison of descriptive statistical data on dissent rates reveals a significant difference between the highest courts of the United States and the United Kingdom. Empirical research found that in the period 1990–2007, there were one or more separate opinions in 62 per cent of the cases in the US Supreme Court (Epstein et al. 2011), peaking at 78 per cent in 1952 and 1972 (Alder 2000, 238). In the United Kingdom, the average dissent rate between 1966 and 1999 was 9.3 per cent (Alder 2000, 243), while on the new Supreme Court 157 of 674 decisions have been non-unanimous in the first eight years of its existence (Hanretty 2020, 172). Even in comparison with other common law supreme courts, the percentage of unanimous decisions (not excluding decisions that contain separate concurring opinions) is significantly lower in the United States: 43 per cent until the mid-2000s, compared to 81 per cent in the United Kingdom, 76 per cent in Canada, and 59 per cent in Australia (Hanretty 2020, 173).

There is also less romantic rhetoric around dissenting opinions in the United Kingdom than in the United States. Alder (2000, 241) suggests that this might be influenced by the fact that the legislative process in the United States is less responsive to change than in the United Kingdom. Di Martino argues that the style of the English justices is different from that of their American colleagues mainly due to their different conception of the law, and their more formalist-positivist approach may lie behind the lower dissent rate as well (Di Martino 2016, 197).

Research into the practice of separate opinions has also shown that, unlike in the US Supreme Court, it is rare that judicial opinions in the UK's highest court directly engage which each other (Alder 2000, 243), and that the phenomenon of the so-called canonical dissents is also uniquely American, unknown in the United Kingdom or other common law jurisdictions (Di Martino 2016, 461). Some English dissenting opinions, especially in the 1960s and 1970s, did have an impact on legal development as they expressed the conflict taking place within the House of Lords between the more formalist and the more progressive Law Lords, but they did not become the majority opinion in later cases, as happened to some classic dissents of Justice Harlan or Justice Holmes in the United States (White 1995). However, even in the United States, the canonization of dissenting opinions has taken place gradually. It is either the result of a long public deliberation process or a dissent is first supported by legal doctrine and is vindicated by the court (Di Martino 2016, 464).

Concluding, while legal tradition certainly plays a role in the judicial process, there are significant differences within the common law tradition as regards the practice of judicial dissent. According to Reynolds, who explored and compared disagreement and dissent on the UK and US Supreme Courts, it is presumably ascribable to at least two factors. First, the US Supreme Court has the power of striking down statutory law. Second, its members are appointed through a very political process. These two features of the US Supreme Court contributed to its dividedness to a great extent (Reynold 2013, 125). There are, however, no large-*N* empirical studies that would further explore variations in the practice of separate opinions within the common law tradition.

4.4 Judicial Dissent in the Civil Law Tradition

In continental Europe, under the dominant influence of the French and German legal cultures, judgments are typically delivered in the name of the people, the republic, or the monarch. They are seemingly unanimous decisions. In most civil law systems, there is no possibility for the judge to dissent publicly from her colleagues (Kelemen 2018). The right to write separately is today mostly a privilege of judges sitting on constitutional courts. Only five of the twenty constitutional or quasi-constitutional courts[6] in Western and East-Central Europe are not allowed to publish dissent, while ordinary judges can write separately in nine countries (Raffaelli 2012). Interestingly, those ordinary courts that have the power of judicial review (quite exceptional in continental Europe, only four systems) also have the possibility to publish dissenting opinions. There are actually just a handful (six) legal systems that belong to the civil law tradition and allow for the publication of dissent while not granting the power of judicial review to their ordinary judges.[7] Second, there seems to be a difference between Western and East-Central Europe. In Western Europe, only Portugal and Spain allow the publication of dissent in ordinary courts, while in East-Central Europe it is more common. These findings should be subject to further comparative research to understand the reasons behind them.

Comparative research showed that European judges are more reluctant to write separately than common law judges (Kelemen 2018). Even when they have the possibility to do so, they show considerable loyalty towards their colleagues and the court as an institution. However, constitutional courts are different from ordinary courts in a number of ways. Therefore, the examination of the practice of dissenting opinions in ordinary courts, where allowed, could bring to different conclusions and would certainly greatly contribute to a better understanding of the judicial function in the civil law tradition. While there is a growing literature on the practice of separate opinions in constitutional courts, empirical research on the use of dissenting opinions in ordinary courts in European civil law jurisdictions is still missing, not only comparatively but even at the country level.

4.5 Dissent and Other Separate Opinions in Constitutional Courts

Constitutional courts are *sui generis* institutions, since they merge judicial (dispute resolution) and political (law-making) functions (Cappelletti 1971). This explains why disagreement and dissent on constitutional courts has drawn more scholarly interest in civil law jurisdictions, where ordinary judges typically do not have the power of judicial review. In comparative legal research, it is common practice to involve both constitutional courts and supreme courts in the comparison as they have the final word on constitutional issues. It is, however, important to bear in mind that constitutional courts differ from supreme courts in several aspects. As Ferreres Comella (2009, 58) pointed out, constitutional courts have a 'dialogic disadvantage' compared to common law supreme courts, which—being courts of last instance, unlike constitutional courts—have at least one other judicial opinion on the matter available to them. In centralized systems of judicial review instead there is no variety of judicial voices on constitutional issues and the time for debate is shortened. In such a context, separate opinions play an important role in enriching the constitutional debate and may help the evolution of constitutional law. Laffranque (2004) claimed that separate opinions may provide instructive commentaries, which can be especially valuable for a legal system in transition. In such systems, interpretive gaps are frequent, and an established interpretation of new rules may not have emerged. In fact, this may be a potential explanation for the introduction of dissenting opinions in the formerly socialist countries of Central and Eastern Europe.

The first constitutional court to allow the publication of dissent was the German Federal Constitutional Court in 1970. This has immediately arisen the interest of legal scholars even beyond German borders (Amram 1957; Cohn 1957). Constitutional courts, including the German Federal Constitutional Court, are institutions that often have had to face transitional issues and, in the period immediately following their establishment, could not rely on an established body of domestic case law. Moreover, as newly created institutions, in their first years of existence, they often struggled with asserting their own authority and legitimacy (Teitel 1997). Separate opinions have been discussed in literature in this context as well, examining how the publication of dissenting opinions can be seen as a way to ensure transparency in the decision-making processes of the new court, thereby enhancing its credibility and legitimacy. Sólyom (2003, 135) argued that on the one hand, a lack of confidence in the legislative power increased the need for judicial review, and on the other hand, mistrust in a new institution composed of members appointed by politicians increased the need for transparency. In times when the court's authority and legitimacy are still weak, the publication of seemingly unanimous opinions can serve to protect the newly established court. Consequently, as explained by Rasmussen (2009), in a transitional period, a ban on dissenting opinions would serve exactly the same goal as permitting dissents. Kelemen (2018, 83) showed that this apparent contradiction was solved in different ways by different countries. In Germany and in Lithuania, for example, the publication of dissent was not allowed in the first period of the respective courts' existence on the ground that it might compromise the authority of the newly established institution. In both countries it took approximately two decades to acknowledge that the constitutional court's authority was sufficiently established to introduce dissenting opinions. Other countries (Spain, Portugal, and Central and Eastern European countries with the exception of Lithuania and Romania), on the other hand, allowed constitutional judges to publish their dissent from the very beginning. In the latter case, it is difficult to examine whether dissenting opinions had a negative effect on the court's authority, since in these jurisdictions the institution of dissenting opinion has 'grown up' together with the constitutional court itself.

There is a growing amount of empirical research on the practice of separate opinions in constitutional courts, even though large-*N* comparative studies are still missing. In the paragraphs that follow, a brief review of a few works that focus on three selected European constitutional courts is provided.

The German Federal Constitutional Court: Wittig (2016) created a database of decisions of the German Federal Constitutional Court and found that German constitutional judges are highly determined by their expectations regarding their career after retiring from the Court. In particular, judges leaving the law community are more likely to deliver separate opinions. She also showed that in the vast majority of cases German constitutional judges do not write separate opinions, but when they do so, they deliver considerably more full dissents than partial dissents or concurrences. A further important finding of Wittig is that it is the amount of questions a case raises that causes a potential for dissent rather than controversial topics. More recently, Klatt (2023) also offered an empirical analysis of the German Court's practice of separate opinions.

The Spanish Constitutional Court: The already mentioned study by Hanretty (2012) found that Spanish constitutional judges' votes tend to reflect the political preferences of the nominating party. Another study by Garoupa, Gomez-Pomar, and Grembi (2013) found, moreover, that political influence in the voting behaviour of Spanish constitutional judges is maximal when national party interests are directly involved. In other cases, they could be willing to sacrifice mere ideological goals to satisfy alternative goals, such as strengthening the legitimacy of the Court and increasing its prestige in front of other courts.

The Hungarian Constitutional Court: Kelemen (2018, 134) studied the practice of dissents and other separate opinions on the Hungarian Constitutional Court in its early period, between the Court's establishment in 1990 until the 2010 constitutional amendment, which made it possible for the government to unilaterally nominate new judges. Based on both quantitative and qualitative data, she examined trends, motivations, judicial styles, what separate opinions reveal about the relationships among the members of the Court, and the impact of certain trailblazing separate opinions on the Court's case-law. Pócza, Dobos, and Gyulai (2019) studied dissenting coalitions at the Hungarian Constitutional Court in the first three decades of its history, between 1990 and 2018, using network analysis. Specifically, they analysed the networks made up of dissents that aimed at constraining the legislature to the same extent and in the same manner. Their results showed that polarization based on political background had been present on the Court already before the 2010 reform, since the late 1990s.

4.6 Dissent and Other Separate Opinions in International Courts

The practice of separate opinions has been studied also in relation to international courts that allow for the publication of dissent. Merrill (1988, 38) claimed as early as the 1980s that dissenting opinions are especially useful, even necessary, in the field of international law, as international courts apply a body of law that consists of treaties, principles and general rules that are mainly developed through case law. If the law is developed mainly by judges, the argument goes, every opinion expressed contributes to this development. Another peculiarity of international courts is their composition. Their members come from different jurisdictions and, consequently, have different legal cultural backgrounds. One consequence of this is that while the voting patterns of judges in the national courts are usually analysed to place the judges along a liberal–conservative continuum, studies on the voting behaviour of international judges most often focus on national bias.

The practice of the various international courts, however, differs considerably. The Court of Justice of the European Union (CJEU) does not allow the publication of separate opinions at all. But this has not impeded scholars and judges from discussing the possibility of lifting this ban (Laffranque 2004; Rasmussen 2009; Skouris 2019). According to many, this secrecy is to be blamed, for example, for the poor quality of the CJEU's reasoning in many judgments (Rasmussen and Rasmussen 2013). When it comes to other international courts, such as the Inter-American Court of Human Rights (IACtHR), the ECtHR, and the International Court of Justice (ICJ), an analysis of the voting behaviour of their judges is made possible by the presence of a large number of separate opinions.

In relation to the IACtHR, for example, Resende (2019) explored whether individual opinions really matter to the Court's decision-making process and found that notwithstanding the significant number of separate opinions, the IACtHR tends to isolate the *ratio decidendi* from past individual opinions, which are therefore not an explicit part of the Inter-American precedent. Jain (2017) claims that international criminal law, for much of its history, has been characterized by dissents and studied the nature and functions of dissents at international criminal tribunals, focusing on radical dissents. Indeed, the practice of judicial dissent attracted the attention of a number of students of international criminal justice. Mistry (2015), for example, discussed the practice of judicial dissent through the lens of five prominent examples of dissenting opinions.

The ECtHR has been object of several quantitative analyses that revealed an interesting difference in the voting pattern of *ex officio* and ad hoc judges,[8] finding that the latter have a considerably higher national bias than the former (Kuijer 1997; Bruinsma and De Blois 1997; Bruinsma 2006). This may be explained by the fact that often ad hoc judges are potential future candidates to the Court. As Kuijer (1997, 52) explains, voting against one's home state might place one's nomination at risk. In addition, the ad hoc judge is nominated when the state party is already familiar with the content of the complaint, which may play a role in the choice. Bruinsma (2008) provides a further explanation. He claims that ad hoc judges are less exposed to 'collegial' group pressure than *ex officio* judges, since they sit on the bench only for that particular case. Consequently, they do not feel much solidarity with the other members of the adjudicating panel. Moreover, Bruinsma and De Blois (1997, 183) claim that the role of the ad hoc judge is similar to the role of separate opinions: they may not be significant to the outcome of the case but they are significant with respect to the legitimation of the court.

Besides the individual judges' national bias, separate opinions enabled researchers to examine, among other things, the 'coalitions' formed between members of the ECtHR in relation to specific legal issues (Bruinsma 2006), the relevance of the judges' previous career path, and the peculiarities in the behaviour of judges nominated by the new member states (Flauss 1998). Voeten (2008, 430), for example, found that judges from former socialist countries were harsher on other former socialist countries than they were on countries without a socialist heritage. There have also been attempts to estimate the judicial ideology of ECtHR judges along an activism–restraint dimension, with different methods (Bruinsma and De Blois 1997; Voeten 2007). While White and Boussiakou (2009) examined the judges' interpretation of the doctrine of margin of appreciation, Voeten (2007) looked at judicial appointments and used ideal points estimation. White and Boussiakou labelled the belief that states' margin of appreciation should be broad as judicial self-restraint, while the conviction that states have less room to invoke national interests was labelled as judicial activism. They concluded that it was not possible to find any patterns in the judges' decision-making and that it is judicial temperament which determines the extent to which a judge writes separately. Voeten (2007) used a different proxy to measure judicial activism. He claimed that, in the specific context of the ECtHR, an activist judge is more likely to rule in favour of the applicant, and thus against a government. While there seems to be no correlation between the degree of activism of the judge and the level of domestic human rights protection, he found that governments use judicial appointments to signal their human rights commitments to interested parties, especially the EU. Governments more favourably disposed towards European integration are more likely to appoint activist judges. Voeten suggested that the EU has been the driving force behind the increased activism of the ECtHR, even if there is still no formal relationship between them. Moreover, Bruinsma (2006) found a correlation between a judge's previous career path and his or her judicial ideology, claiming that academics become the most activist judges, while judges appointed from the domestic ordinary courts are more inclined to self-restraint.

5. Conclusion

As regards the practice of judicial dissent from a comparative perspective, rather than a distinction between the civil law and the common law tradition, we can notice a difference between the United States and the rest of the Western legal tradition, including other common law countries. A very high dissent rate, the phenomenon of 'canonization' of dissents, and the frequent use of non-legal (social, political, moral) arguments are unique to the US practice.

As we could see, ordinary judges in most civil law jurisdictions are not permitted to write separate opinions. This makes researching judicial behaviour in these courts arduous. Although an increasing number of civil law jurisdictions now allow their ordinary judges to write separately, there is still a lack of empirical analysis on how this possibility is used in practice. As a result, our understanding of how (ordinary) judges make their decisions in civil law jurisdictions remains rather limited. On the other hand, there is a substantial body of literature on judicial dissent in constitutional courts, including comparative studies. However, there is a scarcity of large-scale comparative studies on this subject, with most empirical comparative works focusing on examining two or three courts.

From a methodological perspective, the combination of quantitative analysis and the collection of oral history through interviews with judges provides valuable insights into the judicial process and how judges make their decisions. In addition to calculating dissent rates and analysing the voting behaviour of individual judges, quantitative data can uncover various correlations. For instance, it enables us to examine the ideologies of individual judges and determine which types of cases trigger more dissent.

In any case, it is necessary to examine each court within its specific legal and political context. The internal organization of courts varies considerably across legal systems, even within the same legal tradition. This includes variations in the distribution of workload between judges and other court personnel, such as law clerks and other figures. These factors, along with the broader socio-political context in which the courts operate, can pose serious challenges for comparative analysis.

NOTES

1 See, for example, a dissenting opinion of the Dutch judge Martens on the ECtHR in the case *Borger v Belgium*, app. no. 12005/86, 30 October 1991, suggesting that a given formulation of a maxim in a previous judgment was attributable to the British judge presiding over the case.

2 It is also true, however, that a common law judge can also decide to withhold his or her dissent. Thus, the percentage of dissenting opinions is not necessarily a true reflection of all the occasions in which one judge disagrees with the majority in the common law courts either (Newman 1984).

3 In Greece, Article 93(3) of the Constitution provides that 'publication of the dissenting opinion shall be compulsory'. However, Greek separate opinions are published anonymously in order to avoid putting the individual judges in the spotlight. Article 35(1) of Act no 184/1975 (Raffaelli 2012).

4 In 77 per cent of the cases with separate opinions examined by Hönnige the dissenting opinion was delivered by a judge nominated by the losing political party. At the same time, in the examined cases, no judge ever dissented if the party which had nominated him won the case (Hönnige 2009, 979).

5 This was the case for example in relation to the *Bush v Gore* (2000) judgment.

6 'Quasi-constitutional courts' are the Estonian Supreme Court's Constitutional Chamber and the Greek Special Highest Court.

7 Remarkably, the Czech Republic allows administrative courts but not ordinary courts to publish dissent.

8 As a rule, every court panel composed to hear against a state must include *ex officio* the judge nominated by that state. If that judge is unable to sit, an ad hoc member is chosen by the President of the Court from a list submitted by the member state concerned. Article 26(4) of the European Convention on Human Rights.

REFERENCES

Abraham, Henry J. 1998. *The Judicial Process: An Introductory Analysis of the Courts of the United States, England, and France*, 7th edn. New York: Oxford University Press.

Alder, John. 2000. 'Dissents in Courts of Last Resort: Tragic Choices?' *Oxford Journal of Legal Studies* 20 (2): 221–46.

Amram, Philip W. 1957. 'The Dissenting Opinion Comes to the German Courts'. *The American Journal of Comparative Law* 6 (1): 108–11.

Balkin, J. M., and Sanford Levinson. 1998. 'The Canons of Constitutional Law'. *Harvard Law Review* 111 (4): 963–1024.

Bentsen, Henrik Litleré. 2014. 'Dissenting Opinions in the Norwegian Supreme Court'. *Tidsskrift for samfunnsforskning* 55 (1): 3–22.

Bentsen, Henrik Litleré. 2018. 'Court Leadership, Agenda Transformation, and Judicial Dissent: A European Case of a "Mysterious Demise of Consensual Norms"'. *Journal of Law and Courts* 6 (1): 189–213. https://doi.org/10.1086/695555

Blom-Cooper, Louis, and Gavin Drewry. 1972. *Final Appeal: A Study of the House of Lords in Its Judicial Capacity*. Oxford: Clarendon Press.

Bruinsma, Fred J. 2006. 'Judicial Identities in the European Court of Human Rights'. In *Multilevel Governance in Enforcement and Adjudication*, edited by Aukje A.H. van Hoek, 203-40. Antwerpen: Intersentia.

Bruinsma, Fred J. 2008. 'The Room at the Top: Separate Opinions in the Grand Chambers of the ECHR (1998–2006)'. *Ancilla Iuris*, 32–43.

Bruinsma, Fred J., and Matthijs De Blois. 1997. 'Rules of Law from Westport to Wladiwostok. Separate Opinions in the European Court of Human Rights'. *Netherlands Quarterly of Human Rights* 15 (2): 175–86.

Cappelletti, Mauro. 1971. *Judicial Review in the Contemporary World. Judicial Review in the Contemporary World*. Indianapolis: Bobbs-Merrill.

Cohn, E. J. 1957. 'Dissenting Opinions in German Law'. *The International and Comparative Law Quarterly* 6 (3): 540–43.

Dawood, Yasmin. 2013. 'Democracy and Dissent: Reconsidering the Judicial Review of the Political Sphere'. *Supreme Court Law Review* 63: 59–87.

De Jaegere, Josephine. 2019. *Judicial Review and Strategic Behaviour: An Empirical Case Law Analysis of the Belgian Constitutional Court. Judicial Review and Strategic Behaviour*. Cambridge: Intersentia.

Derlén, Mattias, and Johan Lindholm. 2016. 'Judiciell aktivism eller prejudikatbildning? en empirisk granskning av Högsta domstolen'. *Svensk Juristtidning* 2: 143–58.

Di Martino, Alessandra. 2016. *Le opinioni dissenzienti dei giudici costituzionali: uno studio comparativo. Pubblicazioni del Dipartimento di scienze giuridiche, Università degli studi di Roma La Sapienza 104*. Naples: Jovene.

Epstein, Lee, William M. Landes, and Richard A. Posner. 2011. 'Why (And When) Judges Dissent: A Theoretical and Empirical Analysis'. *The Journal of Legal Analysis* 3 (1): 101–37.

Ferreres Comella, Víctor. 2009. *Constitutional Courts and Democratic Values: A European Perspective*. New Haven: Yale University Press.

Flauss, Jean-François. 1998. 'Les Juges Des Pays d'Europe Centrale et Oriéntale à La Cour Européenne Des Droits de l'homme: Vues de l'extérieur'. In *Mélanges En Hommage à Louis Edmond Pettiti*, 343–79. Brussels: Bruylant. https://www.stradalex.com/fr/sl_rev_utu/toc/jt_1999_9-fr/doc/jt1999_9p175_2

Garoupa, Nuno, Rebecca D. Gill, and Lydia B. Tiede. 2021. 'Constitutional Courts in Europe: Quantitative Approaches'. In *High Courts in Global Perspective*, edited by Nuno Garoupa, Rebecca D. Gill, and Lydia B. Tiede, 186-98. Charlottesville: University of Virginia Press.

Garoupa, Nuno, Fernando Gomez-Pomar, and Veronica Grembi. 2013. 'Judging under Political Pressure: An Empirical Analysis of Constitutional Review Voting in the Spanish Constitutional Court'. *Journal of Law, Economics, & Organization* 29 (3): 513–34.

Gorla, G. 1965. *La struttura della decisione giudiziale in diritto italiano e nella 'common law': Riflessi di tale struttura sull'interpretazione della sentenza, sui 'Reports' e sul Dissenting*. Milan: UTET.

Hanretty, Chris. 2012. 'Dissent in Iberia: The Ideal Points of Justices on the Spanish and Portuguese Constitutional Tribunals: Dissent in Iberia'. *European Journal of Political Research* 51 (5): 671–92.

Hanretty, Chris. 2020. *A Court of Specialists: Judicial Behavior on the UK Supreme Court. A Court of Specialists*. New York: Oxford University Press.

Hönnige, Christoph. 2009. 'The Electoral Connection: How the Pivotal Judge Affects Oppositional Success at European Constitutional Courts'. *West European Politics* 32 (5): 963–84.

Jain, Neha. 2017. 'Radical Dissents in International Criminal Trials'. *European Journal of International Law* 28 (4): 1163–86.

Kelemen, Katalin. 2013. 'Dissenting Opinions in Constitutional Courts'. *German Law Journal* 14 (8): 1345–71.

Kelemen, Katalin. 2018. *Judicial Dissent in European Constitutional Courts: A Comparative and Legal Perspective*. Abingdon: Routledge.

Kirby, Michael. 2007. 'Judicial Dissent—Common Law and Civil Law Traditions'. *Law Quarterly Review* 123 (July): 379–400.

Klatt, Matthias K. 2023. *Das Sondervotum beim Bundesverfassungsgericht. Veröffentlichungen zum Verfahrensrecht, Band 191*. Tübingen: Mohr Siebeck.

Kuijer, Martin. 1997. 'Voting Behaviour and National Bias in the European Court of Human Rights and the International Court of Justice'. *Leiden Journal of International Law* 10 (1): 49–67.

Laffranque, Julia. 2004. 'Dissenting Opinion in the European Court of Justice. Estonia's Possible Contribution to the Democratisation of the European Union Juridical System'. *Juridica International* 9: 14–23.

Llewellyn, Karl N., Paul Gewirtz, and Michael Ansaldi. 1988. 'The Case Law System in America'. *Columbia Law Review* 88 (5): 989–1020.

Lopes, Felipe de Mendonca. 2019. 'Dissent Aversion and Sequential Voting in the Brazilian Supreme Court'. *Journal of Empirical Legal Studies* 16 (4): 933–54.

Mastor, Wanda. 2022. 'Opinions Séparées et Interprétations Concurrentes de La Constitution'. *Revue Des Droits de l'homme* 21: 1–14. https://journals.openedition.org/revdh/13695

Merrills, J. G. 1988. *The Development of International Law by the European Court of Human Rights. Melland Schill Monographs in International Law*. Manchester: Manchester University Press.

Mistry, Hemi. 2015. 'The Paradox of Dissent: Judicial Dissent and the Projects of International Criminal Justice'. *Journal of International Criminal Justice* 13 (3): 449–74.

Nelissen, Bart. 2011. 'Judicial Loyalty Through Dissent or Why the Timing Is Perfect for Belgium to Embrace Separate Opinions'. *Electronic Journal of Comparative Law* 15 (1): 1–14.

Newman, Jon O. 1984. 'Between Legal Realism and Neutral Principles: The Legitimacy of Institutional Values'. *California Law Review* 72 (2): 200–216.

Novak, Linda. 1980. 'The Precedential Value of Supreme Court Plurality Decisions'. *Columbia Law Review* 80 (4): 756–81.

Panizza, Saulle. 1998. *L'introduzione dell'opinione dissenziente nel sistema di giustizia costituzionale*. Turin: Giappichelli.

Paterson, Alan. 1983. *The Law Lords*. London: Palgrave Macmillan.

Paterson, Alan. 2013. *Final Judgment: The Last Law Lords and the Supreme Court*. Oxford: Hart.

'Plurality Decisions and Judicial Decisionmaking'. 1981. *Harvard Law Review* 94 (5): 1127–47. https://www.jstor.org/stable/1340692

Pócza, Kálmán, Gábor Dobos, and Attila Gyulai. 2019. 'Dissenting Coalitions at the Hungarian Constitutional Court 1990–2018'. In *The Role of Courts in Contemporary Legal Orders*, edited by Martin Belov, 359–70. The Hague: Eleven International Publishing.

Posner, Richard A. 2010. *How Judges Think*. Cambridge: Harvard University Press.

Raffaelli, Rosa. 2012. 'Dissenting Opinions in the Supreme Courts of the Member States'. European Parliament, Directorate-General for Internal Policies. https://www.europarl.europa.eu/document/activities/cont/201304/20130423ATT64963/20130423ATT64963EN.pdf

Rasmussen, Hjalte. 2009. 'Legal Opinion about the European Court of Justice's Competence Transgressions, Poor Reasonings and the Complete Non-Transparency of Willensbildung'. Unpublished paper. http://curis.ku.dk/ws/files/18105617/Doc

Rasmussen, Hjalte, and Louise Nan Rasmussen. 2013. 'Comment on Katalin Kelemen—Activist EU Court "Feeds" on the Existing Ban on Dissenting Opinions: Lifting the Ban Is Likely to Improve the Quality of EU Judgments'. *German Law Journal* 14 (8): 1373–86.

Resende, Ranieri Lima. 2019. 'Deliberation and Decision-Making Process in the Inter-American Court of Human Rights: Do Individual Opinions Matter?' *Northwestern University Journal of International Human Rights* 17 (1): 25–50.

Reynold, Frederic. 2013. *Disagreement and Dissent in Judicial Decision-Making*. London: Wildy, Simmonds & Hill.

Samuel, Geoffrey. 2023. 'Common Law'. In *Elgar Encyclopedia of Comparative Law*, edited by Jan M. Smits, Jaakko Husa, Catherine Valcke, and Madalena Narciso, 317–26. Edward Elgar Publishing Limited.

Skouris, Vassilios. 2019. 'Judging at the Court of the Justice of the European Union: Is There a Need for Dissenting Opinions?' In *An Ever-Changing Union? Perspectives on the Future of EU Law in Honour of Allan Rosas*, edited by Koen Lenaerts et al., 99–109. Oxford: Hart Publishing.

Solyom, Laszlo. 2003. 'The Role of Constitutional Courts in the Transition to Democracy: With Special Reference to Hungary'. *International Sociology* 18 (1): 133–61.

Songer, Donald R., John Szmer, and Susan W. Johnson. 2011. 'Explaining Dissent on the Supreme Court of Canada'. *Canadian Journal of Political Science* 44 (2): 389–409.

Sunde, Jorn Oyrehagen. 2012. 'Dissenting Votes in the Norwegian Supreme Court 1965–2009: A Legal Cultural Analysis'. *Rechtskultur: Zeitschrift Für Europäische Rechtsgeschichte*, 1: 59–73.

Tanya Bagashka, and Nuno Garoupa. 2021. 'Constitutional Courts in Europe: Quantitative Approaches'. In *High Courts in Global Perspective: Evidence, Methodologies, and Findings*, edited by Nuno Garoupa, Rebecca D. Gill, and Lydia B. Tiede, 186–98. Charlottesville: University of Virginia Press.

Tega, Diletta. 2018. 'Collegiality Over Personality. The Refusal of Separate Opinions in Italy'. SSRN Electronic Journal. https://doi.org/10.2139/ssrn.3325457

Teitel, Ruti. 1997. 'Transitional Jurisprudence: The Role of Law in Political Transformation'. *The Yale Law Journal* 106 (7): 2009–80.

Vitale, David. 2014. 'The Value of Dissent in Constitutional Adjudication: A Context-Specific Analysis'. *Review of Constitutional Studies* 19 (1): 83–108.

Voeten, Erik. 2007. 'The Politics of International Judicial Appointments: Evidence from the European Court of Human Rights'. *International Organization* 61: 669–701.

Voeten, Erik. 2008. 'The Impartiality of International Judges: Evidence from the European Court of Human Rights'. *The American Political Science Review* 102 (4): 417–33.

White, G. Edward. 1995. 'The Canonization of Holmes and Brandeis: Epistemology and Judicial Reputations'. *New York University Law Review* 70: 576–621.

White, Robin C. A., and Iris Boussiakou. 2009. 'Separate Opinions in the European Court of Human Rights'. *Human Rights Law Review* 9 (1): 37–60.

Wittig, Caroline Elisabeth. 2016. *The Occurrence of Separate Opinions at the Federal Constitutional Court: An Analysis with a Novel Database*. Berlin: Logos Verlag Berlin.

ZoBell, Karl M. 1958. 'Division of Opinion in the Supreme Court: A History of Judicial Disintegration'. *The Cornell Law Quarterly* 44: 186–214.

CHAPTER 26

STUDYING JUDICIAL CITATIONS AND CITATION DATA

JENS FRANKENREITER

1. Introduction

REFERENCES to prior case law and other legal materials play a crucial role in justifying judicial decisions in many jurisdictions worldwide. Numerous empirical and normative questions surround the use of such citations. Do courts in different jurisdictions differ in their use of legal authorities in a way that reflects fundamental features of their respective legal systems? Specifically, do courts in common law jurisdictions cite differently than those in civil law jurisdictions? Does judges' use of citations indicate that they are constrained in their decision-making, or do they strategically employ these references to increase their decisions' legitimacy or advance specific policy goals? Finally, to what extent do judges cite authorities from other jurisdictions, and should they do so? Over the years, scholars have attempted to address these and related questions using various methodological approaches. This chapter surveys one group of such studies, namely those that employ quantitative methods.

The chapter has three interconnected goals. First, it aims to provide an overview of major existing quantitative studies and the insights they have generated.[1] Second, it offers readers who contemplate becoming producers of such research a roadmap for gathering, processing, and analysing quantitative information on citations. Finally, it describes what the author perceives as the most significant opportunities for advancement in this literature, including the need to overcome a range of methodological challenges that have bedevilled existing research in this area.

The chapter's focus on quantitative research implies that it largely ignores the contributions of qualitative research and related work to the literature on citations in judicial opinions. This focus should not be interpreted as downplaying the importance of such work. The rationale for concentrating on quantitative research lies in the distinct approaches it employs for data collection, analysis, and reporting. Given this chapter's emphasis on common research strategies and methodological questions in the quantitative literature, a detailed examination of qualitative research would not be as beneficial in this context.

Conversely, this chapter casts a wide net regarding the topics of quantitative studies included in the survey. Researchers often use quantitative information on citations to answer questions that are only indirectly concerned with courts' citation practices. Examples include investigations into the influence of precedent over time, studies of the relationship between judge characteristics and opinion content, and analyses that describe certain structural features of citation networks. The broad approach taken here stems from a desire to avoid deciding which studies are sufficiently related to citation practices to warrant inclusion. Simultaneously, the chapter critically discusses the contributions that each stream of literature can make to a comparative understanding of judicial behaviour.

This chapter proceeds as follows. Section 2 explores the various motivations that drive researchers to study citation data. This section also discusses questions related to obtaining information on citations and representing them in a quantitative format. Section 3 surveys existing uses of citation data, with a focus on highlighting the differences between studies that focus on large-scale descriptions of citation patterns and those that explore the determinants of citations in or to individual cases. Section 4 discusses the potential of this work to contribute to a comparative understanding of judge behaviour and reflects on important methodological challenges. Section 5 concludes with reflections on areas of advancement.

2. Citation Data

Much of this chapter revolves around the gathering and use of citation data. Citation data, as understood here, is a form of metadata that captures the references made by judges in their opinions to prior legal authorities, including statutes, regulations, and other case law. This data is the raw material required by all quantitative investigations of courts' use of references.

2.1 Citation Data as a Measure for Various Legal Phenomena

Citation data can be used to construct measures for various phenomena of interest. First and foremost, citation data can be used to measure the frequency and types of references made by judges in their opinions, shedding light on how they rely on different legal authorities to justify their decisions. For example, scholars can use citation data to identify how frequently judges rely on precedent when deciding cases and to examine the prevalence of specific types of legal authorities cited in opinions, such as statutes, regulations, or other case law (e.g. Merryman 1954, 1977). Another example of this use of citation data are studies analysing the factors that lead judges to include more references to legal sources in their opinions (Lupu and Fowler 2013).

Second, citation data can also serve as an indicator of the ongoing relevance and importance of a particular legal authority. Scholars use citation data in this way when they analyse the frequency with which a specific case is cited by other judges in subsequent cases, which can provide insight into the level of authority and influence of the original opinion at a given point in time (Landes and Posner 1976).

Third, researchers can use citation data to develop measures for the relatedness of cases. For example, they can determine whether a later case cites an earlier one (or whether they are part of a 'subgraph' in the network of cases connected through citations), or they can identify clusters of cases that are frequently cited together (Bommarito et al. 2010a, 2010b). Finally, citation data can also be used as quantifiable information about opinion content (Arnold et al. 2023). The idea behind this use of citation data is related to the last one: if two cases cite the same legal sources (or if they are frequently cited together), they might share a legal principle or issue.

2.2 Data Sources

Regardless of how citation data is utilized in a study, all quantitative research using this data requires researchers to obtain information on citations in legal opinions and represent that information in a quantitative format. As a first step, researchers need to identify a method for obtaining citation information. Citation data can be gathered in several ways, each with its own advantages and disadvantages, which may make a particular method more or less suitable for a specific research project.

Early studies often relied on researchers or assistants manually reading and extracting citations from the opinion text (e.g. Merryman 1954). The most significant advantage of this approach is that it allows researchers to obtain the specific information they require for their work. Most importantly, researchers can deploy a coding scheme that distinguishes between different types of citations, such as instances where an opinion favourably cites a previous decision and cases in which the former distinguishes or overrules the latter. However, due to the cost of manually coding citation data, research relying on this data gathering method will inevitably be limited in scale.

At least in principle, it now seems possible to automate this process by creating algorithms that identify citations in the text of an opinion and extract the relevant information. Indeed, some researchers have reported promising first steps in that direction (e.g. Clark and Lauderdale 2012). However, one primary challenge to developing such algorithms is that citation practices vary between different courts. As a result, it seems unlikely that researchers can create algorithms capable of reliably extracting citations across multiple jurisdictions.

In practice, most research in recent years has relied on citation data assembled outside the academy, primarily from commercial and court-run legal databases. Many projects in the United States depend on data from Shepard's Citations, a legal service that lists all judgments citing a particular case (e.g. Hansford and Spriggs 2006; Cross 2012). Research on citations in the case law of the Court of Justice of the European Union (CJEU) often takes advantage of the fact that official case law databases include information on which previous decisions (and other EU law materials) are referenced in the opinion text (e.g. Frankenreiter 2017a). Similarly, researchers interested in the European Courts of Human Rights (ECtHR) often obtain citation data from the official court database maintained by this institution (Voeten 2010). The most significant advantage of this approach is that it enables researchers to access citation data for large numbers of opinions at a relatively low cost, often essential for studying citations at scale. However, these databases may not always report information on citations with the ideal level of granularity for the research project. For instance, official EU law databases generally only report whether another decision is referenced in an opinion but do not provide any information on whether the opinion cites the previous case approvingly or not.

2.3 Data Structure(s)

Citation data can take on a variety of formats. In its most basic (unaggregated) form, citation data reports whether individual judicial opinions (or parts of opinions) reference other judicial opinions or legal sources (e.g. a particular section in a legislative code) or not. More comprehensive representations also include information on the nature of the reference, for example, whether an opinion approvingly cites an earlier decision. Individual judicial opinions can appear in such a dataset both as opinions that cite other sources and as opinions to which later opinions refer. This is typically the case in studies investigating how courts cite their own case law. However, such an overlap between citing and cited opinions is not a necessary feature of citation data, as demonstrated by studies that analyse circumstances under which circuit court judges are more likely to refer to decisions by the US Supreme Court (Boyd and Spriggs 2009).

Alternatively, researchers might gather or obtain data that reports aggregated citation information. Such aggregated data could come in the form of a dataset reporting the number of citations in the text of individual opinions, the number of citations to those opinions, or the number of references to judgments authored by individual judges.

2.4 Special Features of Unaggregated Citation Data

Unaggregated citation data has several notable features. Perhaps the most important of these features is what can be called its inherent network structure. This structure allows citation data to be easily represented as a network where individual opinions, along with other legal sources referenced in these opinions, constitute the nodes and citations form the edges. Another approach is to construct a network where courts or judicial systems serve as nodes, with edges indicating the frequency of citations between them. Due to this inherent structure, employing network analysis techniques to study citation data becomes a straightforward and intuitive approach.

However, the inherent network structure of citation data can also pose challenges, even when the data is not explicitly represented as a network. For instance, in research that analyses the likelihood of a citation based on characteristics of both the citing and the cited opinion, this structure can result in correlated error terms that necessitate specific techniques to avoid biased or overconfident results. Section 4.2 discusses this challenge in greater detail.

Additionally, when considering the individual (citing or cited) opinion as the unit of observation, unaggregated citation data can be comparatively high-dimensional. For instance, in a dataset reporting cross-citations between 1,000 decisions by the same court, each document would be represented in a space of 1,000 dimensions. As with other types of high-dimensional data, this fact poses challenges for researchers seeking to employ traditional quantitative techniques (e.g. regression analysis) to study certain features of judicial opinions using (unaggregated) citation data (see also Frankenreiter and Livermore 2020).[2]

Consequently, many applications require researchers to reduce the data's dimensionality as a first step. There are various ways to achieve this goal. Relatively straightforward options include calculating the total number of (outward) citations in or the number of (inward) references to an opinion. Network analysis techniques provide researchers with more sophisticated options. For example, several studies use network analysis to obtain measures for the centrality of cases in a citation network, which are subsequently used as variables in regressions and other quantitative analyses (Fowler et al. 2007; Fowler and Jeon 2008; Lupu and Voeten 2012; Lupu and Fowler 2013). Additionally, researchers can achieve dimensionality reduction by using methods from the field of machine learning. One noteworthy example of this approach is Clark and Lauderdale (2012), further described in Section 3.5. In general, whether a particular approach to dimensionality reduction is appropriate depends on the research question and is highly context-specific. Moreover, while dimensionality reduction allows researchers to employ familiar statistical tools to answer their research questions, it necessarily entails a loss of information.

As an alternative to dimensionality reduction, researchers can also attempt to use network analysis to answer research questions directly.[3] Different from the approach described above, in which network analysis is used to generate one or a small number of variables that are subsequently used in tests employing traditional quantitative techniques, such applications use network analysis tools as the primary analytic step. Section 3.3 describes several examples of research that follow this approach.

3. Uses of Citation Data

As mentioned earlier, researchers utilize citation data in various contexts, such as describing legal authorities used in court opinions, testing hypotheses about judge behaviour, and understanding properties of citation networks. This section offers an overview of these and other streams of work and discusses their primary methodological approaches.

3.1 Describing and Comparing Citation Patterns

One important stream of research uses citation data to describe and compare courts' citation practices. Most studies in this group adopt what can be called a macro perspective, aggregating information at the court level and largely ignoring potential sources of heterogeneity in a court's citation practice. While much of this research is descriptive in nature, several more recent studies also use regression analysis and similar techniques to explore the relationship between various court- or country-level factors and the frequency of citations.

Research in this category dates back to at least the early 1950s, when Merryman (1954) reported data on the citation practices of the California Supreme Court in 1950. Twenty years later, Merryman (1977) followed up on this study with more extensive data covering additional periods. After these early studies, researchers shifted their focus away from merely describing citation patterns. However, numerous studies still report how often courts cite different legal materials as part of other investigations. For example, Landes and Posner (1976) collect information on how often the US Supreme Court and the federal courts of appeals cite different courts at various points in time in the context of a study of decision influence. Cross et al. (2010), as part of an investigation into the drivers of citation decisions, describe the development of the US Supreme Court's practice of citing its own prior decisions over time and case categories; they also report how citation rates have differed between individual opinion authors throughout the court's history.

Siems (2010) is among the first contributions to provide quantitative data on citation patterns in domestic courts outside the United States. His study counts citations in opinions of the German Federal Supreme Court and the Court of Appeal of England and Wales, documenting important differences between the two courts. At the international level, Jacob (2014) developed a taxonomy of different uses of citations in the opinions of the CJEU and counted how often each occurred in a series of fifty-two decisions decided in 2010.

While the previously discussed research focuses primarily on courts' practice of citing opinions from within their own jurisdiction, another line of inquiry that has garnered significant interest is the study of cross-citations, or citations to legal materials—in particular, court decisions—from other jurisdictions. This research sheds light on how judges engage with authorities from other jurisdictions and the factors that influence such citations, offering valuable insights into how courts incorporate and interact with legal materials from beyond their own jurisdiction. This research not only provides a unique perspective on the global landscape of legal systems and their interdependence but also has the potential to contribute important context to the ongoing, heated normative debate regarding whether courts should cite legal sources from other jurisdictions.

Researchers have investigated cross-citations in various jurisdictions around the world. Early contributions in this area are Smithey (2001), who compares rates of cross-citations in decisions of the high courts of Canada and South Africa, and Örücü (2007), who studies cross-citations in the decisions of UK courts. A prominent example of work focusing on cross-citations in the case law of federal courts in the United States is Zaring (2006), who documents the numbers and types of citations to foreign legal sources over sixty years of federal courts of appeals decisions. At the international level, Voeten (2010) describes cross-citations in the case law of the ECtHR.

Recent work in this field often adopts an explicitly comparative approach, examining cross-citations between courts of different jurisdictions. For instance, Gelter and Siems (2012, 2014) examine cross-citations between ten European supreme courts. Groppi and Ponthoreau (2013) undertake an analysis of cross-citations between various constitutional courts. Law (2015) investigates cross-citations in the case law of the highest courts in Taiwan, Japan, and South Korea, and Ng and Jacobson (2017) conduct a similar study for courts in Hong Kong, Malaysia, and Singapore. Hoadley et al. (2021) analyse cross-citations between the apex courts in twenty-six common law countries, and d'Andrea et al. (2021) describe cross-citations between the apex courts of all EU member states. Notably, the latter study also enriches the analysis by grouping courts into different categories according to their tendency to cite foreign case law.

A related body of literature investigates patterns of cross-citations between state courts in the United States. Notable examples of this work include Friedman et al. (1981) and Harris (1982), both of whom describe how patterns of cross-citations between state courts have evolved over time.

While most of this work is primarily descriptive in nature, some studies use regression analysis and similar tools to identify the factors that predict cross-citations between courts from different jurisdictions. Examples of this work at the international level are Gelter and Siems (2013) and Siems (2023). Within the United States, Caldeira (1985, 1988), Denniston (2014), and Hinkle and Nelson (2016) analyse the predictors of citations between state court systems.

3.2 Testing the Drivers of Judges' Citation Decisions

A second notable segment of the literature uses citation data to explore potential personal motivations for judges' decisions about when and which decisions to cite. Methodologically, studies in this segment differ from most studies in the previous group. The majority of them adopt a micro perspective: they focus on citations in individual opinions (or groups of opinions), measuring the extent to which citation patterns differ between different opinions by the same court or within the same court system. At the same time, research in this group relies more on regression analysis and similar quantitative techniques to address their respective research questions.

Although most studies in this group investigate judges' decisions to cite, the motivation behind many of these studies extends beyond merely enhancing our understanding of judges' citation behaviour. Instead, numerous studies are driven by a desire to test more comprehensive models of judicial behaviour. As an early influential contribution aptly put it, citation data is viewed as 'a window into the behavior of judges' (Choi and Gulati 2008).

In fact, the study of citation behaviour can provide valuable opportunities for researchers to generate insights into judges' behaviour that are beyond the reach of other work in this area. While there exists a large stream of literature that studies judges' behaviour through a quantitative lens, most of this research has traditionally relied on studying judges' voting behaviour. For example, studies might analyse whether circuit court judges appointed by Democratic or Republican presidents are more likely to side with the plaintiffs in appeals proceedings in various legal areas (Sunstein et al. 2006; Epstein et al. 2013).

One way the analysis of citation data can advance this field is by offering a means to quantitatively measure specific aspects of an opinion's content that elude studies focused exclusively on judicial votes (Choi and Gulati 2008; Niblett and Yoon 2016). Judicial votes and case outcomes often serve as poor proxies for a case's legal reasoning and the rule articulated in an opinion (Cross 2012). In this context, studying citation behaviour can provide insights into how judges' personal characteristics and case circumstances influence those parts of a decision that are relevant for future cases. This opportunity remains relevant despite recent developments in natural language processing (see Frankenreiter and Livermore 2020) because currently available tools still sometimes struggle to extract substantive meaning from text (Frankenreiter and Nyarko 2023).

A second reason why the study of citation patterns can yield insights unattainable by studying judges' votes is related to data availability. For many courts in jurisdictions outside the United States, information on the voting behaviour of individual judges is not publicly available. In some institutions, there is even a strong norm against judges disclosing whether they were in favour of a decision in which they partook. However, the court might still publish information on the judge responsible for drafting the opinion. In such circumstances, opinions can serve as a measure of judge behaviour that can be more confidently attributed to the individual judge (Frankenreiter 2017a).

Similar to other research, citation data has been used to study various aspects of judicial behaviour. Political scientists typically differentiate between three fundamental models of judicial behaviour: the legal, attitudinal, and strategic models. Evidence suggests that all three models can help explain the citation behaviour of judges around the world.

The attitudinal model posits that judges' personal policy preferences, often referred to as judge ideology, are the main driver of judicial decisions. Most research on the role of judge ideology in citation behaviour investigates whether judges are more likely to cite decisions authored by judges with a similar ideological background. One of the early studies in this area is Johnson (1986), who compiled a dataset of all citations in Supreme Court opinions to a randomly selected sample of twenty-seven decisions by the same court. In this dataset, there appeared to be no unusual accumulation of instances where justices cited other justices with a similar ideological voting record. Over twenty years later, Choi and Gulati (2008) conducted what seems to be the first large-scale study in this field. Focusing on outside-circuit citations in 3,072 circuit court opinions written between 2009 and 2010, they found that most opinions tend to cite more decisions authored by judges appointed by a president from the same party. Later, Anthony Niblett and Albert Yoon demonstrated that these effects are not limited to technically non-binding out-of-circuit precedent: Niblett and Yoon (2016) showed that the ideological tilt of Supreme Court decisions cited by unanimous circuit court panels differs systematically with the composition of the circuit court panels. For divided panels, Niblett and Yoon (2015) demonstrated that the majority opinion and the dissent differ sharply in the precedent they cite, and that both the majority and the minority author tend to cite opinions authored by judges with a similar ideological background to themselves.

Research on the relationship between judge ideology and citations is not limited to courts in the United States. However, while most research on US judges in this area operationalizes judge ideology as a measure of where a judge stands on a conservative–liberal scale, this measure might be less relevant in other contexts. For example, most work on international courts uses some measure of expansionist views of international legal frameworks as the variable for judge ideology. For the ECtHR, Voeten (2010) demonstrated that ECtHR judges with higher levels of judicial activism (which he considers indicative of a 'more universalist approach to human rights') are more likely to cite external sources (international courts such as the CJEU and the International Court of Justice, and domestic courts in important non-European common law jurisdictions, including US courts) than other judges. In the context of the CJEU, Frankenreiter (2017a) uncovered evidence of a relationship between EU member state governments' preferences regarding European integration (member state governments are responsible for appointing judges to the CJEU) and the judges' citation behaviour.

Similar to the attitudinal model, the strategic model also attributes importance to judges' personal preferences but focuses more on the consequences that different actions could have for the decision-maker due to the reactions of others. In particular, researchers in this field have often focused on evidence that lower court judges are motivated by a desire to avoid reversal, for example by adjusting their decision behaviour to the ideological preferences of their superiors (e.g. Randazzo 2008). Analogously, some studies have used citation data to investigate whether the nature of the material cited in an opinion changes with the political preferences of judges higher up the judicial hierarchy. For instance, Boyd and Spriggs (2009) examined whether district court judges consider appellate courts' ideological compositions when deciding which Supreme Court precedent to cite, but they did not find supporting evidence. In contrast, Abramowicz and Tiller (2009) discovered that district court judges' decisions on whether to include references to legislative history in their opinions are influenced more by ideological similarities between legislators and higher-level judges than by the relationship between legislators and the district court judges themselves. Similarly, Hinkle (2016) documented that the propensity of circuit court judges to negatively limit precedent depends on the court's ideological makeup as a whole, suggesting that judges anticipate *en banc* review in cases of decisions that go against the preferences of the court's majority.

Other studies focus not on the ideological leanings of the cited material but investigate the circumstances under which judges invest more heavily in supporting their opinions by referring to precedent. Unlike other studies in this area, these studies often do not primarily aim to examine judges' efforts to avoid reversal; consequently, they frequently investigate decision-making at apex courts. An early example of such work is Harris (1985), who found that state supreme courts cite more in seemingly complicated cases in which judges might want to ensure their decisions are perceived as legitimate. Cross et al. (2010) conducted a similar investigation for the US Supreme Court, documenting that various measures of case complexity and collegial interaction are determinative of citation counts. Lupu and Fowler (2013) demonstrated that Supreme Court justices' opinions cite more and more important precedents when more justices write and join concurring opinions, which they interpret as suggesting that the option for other justices to write separate opinions provides a significant motivation for the majority opinion writers to ground decisions in precedent.

As with studies in the attitudinalist tradition, researchers have adapted this work to other settings. Lupu and Voeten's (2012) research closely resembles that of Lupu and Fowler (2013) but focuses on the context of ECtHR decisions. For the CJEU, Derlén and Lindholm (2015) demonstrate that citations to precedent vary systematically with several factors, including the number of observations submitted by member states to the court. Larsson et al. (2017) also uncovered evidence for the strategic use of citations in this court's case law.

Compared to the robust streams of literature that test predictions derived from the attitudinal and strategic models of judge behaviour using citation data, research attempting to find quantitative evidence for legal motivations in judges' decisions is relatively scarce. This scarcity is primarily because many empirical strategies that researchers use to obtain credible estimates for the effect of attitudinal or strategic considerations do not lend themselves to testing legal motivations. In particular, as all judges apply the same law, it is usually impossible to draw inferences about legal factors in judges' decisions from comparisons between the behaviour of individual judges.

Walsh (1997) tries to overcome this challenge by studying characteristics of courts that cite more (and more broadly) than others, as well as features of decisions that appear as 'central' in the network of citations. Relatedly, Cross et al. (2010) attempt to draw inferences about legal factors in judges' citation decisions by investigating the circumstances under which US Supreme Court opinions include more references to prior decisions. Hinkle (2015) takes a different approach, comparing the influence of ideology on the use of precedent at various circuit courts. This setup allows her to study whether ideology plays a more significant role in judges' decisions to cite persuasive precedent than in decisions to cite binding precedent, which she interprets as evidence of the constraining effect of the law.

Studying citations in judicial opinions has also enabled researchers to investigate questions entirely beyond the scope of research that uses judicial votes. Specifically, a newer stream of research has begun to explore how factors such as social interactions between judges and in-group favouritism affect judges' citation decisions (Blanes I Vidal and Leaver 2013; Hinkle and Nelson 2018).

3.3 Studying Citation Networks

A third significant stream of research, which has gained particular prominence in recent years, involves describing and analysing network-theoretical properties of citation networks. Similar to the research outlined in Section 3.1, most studies in this area primarily have a descriptive focus. When a hypothesis testing framework is adopted, the hypotheses tested generally concern features of the citation network rather than the influence of external factors on citation patterns.

The idea of modelling citations in judicial opinions as a network first emerged in the context of improving legal information retrieval systems (Marx 1970). It took several decades for researchers to incorporate these methods into their toolboxes. Post and Eisen (2000) serves as an early example of work that, while not explicitly using the language of network analysis, models citations in decisions of the US Supreme Court as a complex system. Attempting to demonstrate that legal doctrine possesses a 'fractal structure', they reveal that both inward and outward citation distributions fit a power law. Smith (2007), who explicitly describes judicial citations as a network, presents similar findings in his effort to show that the structure of the citation network closely resembles that of the Internet. Bommarito et al. (2011) analyse features of the network consisting of citations in decisions of the US Tax Court to different sections of the Internal Revenue Code. In recent years, several researchers, including those from other disciplines, have followed up with similar high-level analyses of network-theoretical features of judicial citation networks (e.g. Adusumilli et al. 2022).

Besides describing the structural features of citation networks, this literature suggests that network analysis can assist researchers with two specific tasks: identifying important cases and detecting clusters of related decisions. Fowler et al. (2007) and Fowler and Jeon (2008) are among the pioneering contributions that propose using network analysis to derive measures of legal importance for cases. They demonstrate that eigenvector centrality measures correlate with legal experts' assessments of case importance and can predict the future number of inward citations. Bommarito et al. (2010a, 2010b) discuss various approaches for detecting clusters of related cases.

Although the use of network analysis to study judicial citations seems to have originated in the United States, similar methods have been extensively applied to investigate citation networks of international courts and domestic courts in other countries. In the international context, the CJEU's citation network has received particularly thorough scholarly examination (e.g. Derlén et al. 2013; Derlén and Lindholm 2012, 2017; Mirshahvala et al. 2012; Šadl and Hink 2014; Šadl and Olsen 2017). Researchers have also studied citations in decisions of the International Court of Justice (Alschner and Charlotin 2018), the International Criminal Court (Manley 2016; Tarissan and Nollez-Goldbach 2016), the Appellate Body of the World Trade Organization (Pauwelyn 2015), and in investment arbitration proceedings (Lie 2022). In the domestic context, studies have utilized data from Austria (Moser and Strembeck 2019), Brazil (Correia et al. 2019), Germany (Milz et al. 2021), Italy (Agnoloni and Pagallo 2016), and the Netherlands (van Kuppevelt et al. 2020).

3.4 Other Research Questions Related to Citations

Numerous papers have tackled other research questions related to citations in legal opinions. Methodologically, most of the literature described in this section occupies a middle ground between the literature streams described in sections 3.1 and 3.2. While some papers employ more descriptive approaches to analyse large-scale patterns in citation practices, others concentrate on factors that predict the number of citations in or to individual decisions.

Landes and Posner (1976) initiated a series of papers investigating the determinants of decision influence. While their paper mainly aims to document the decreasing citation numbers to judgments over time, later contributions have examined various potential determinants of decision influence. A significant part of this literature focuses on how the treatment of precedent by the authoring court or other courts in subsequent decisions can affect the future influence of a decision (Hansford and Spriggs 2006, 2014; Kassow et al. 2012; Masood et al. 2017). Broughman and Wildiss (2017) use a similar approach to measure the impact of legislative, as opposed to judicial, overrulings on continuing citations to cases.

Other studies concentrate on the effects of case attributes (Cross 2010; Black and Spriggs 2013; Szmer et al. 2020), features of opinion text (Nelson and Hinkle 2018; Varsava 2018), and judge characteristics (Bhattacharya and Smyth 2001; Gleason et al. 2021) on the number of inward citations to (groups of) decisions. Many studies in this group use the number of inward citations as a proxy for opinion influence. An exception is Lauderdale and Clark (2012), who developed an alternative measure for influence based on a 'genealogical model'.

A related stream of literature utilizes inward citations to rank judges and courts, primarily by their influence or prestige. This literature dates back to Mott (1936), who proposed using citations to state court decisions to assess the relative prominence of different state court systems. Kosma (1998) provides the first large-scale investigation into the influence of Supreme Court justices (measured by the number of citations) over extended periods. Landes et al. (1998) conduct a similar analysis for judges in the federal courts of appeals. Klein and Morrisroe (1999) tackle the same question using an alternative measure for citations that includes only those mentioning a judge's name. Choi and Gulati (2004) propose using citations as one of several measures to evaluate potential candidates for open seats on the Supreme Court, while Choi et al. (2009) develop similar measures for state high courts and their judges. Finally, Choi and Gulati (2007) use outward citations in opinions to measure judges' bias.

3.5 Citation Data in Other Contexts

While much of the research described so far examines questions that are at least loosely related to citations, citation data has also been used in work that investigates seemingly unrelated topics. For instance, Lauderdale and Clark (2012, 2016) construct measures for the substantive similarity of US Supreme Court cases from citation data. These measures are then used to explore the role of judicial preferences in judicial behaviour unrelated to citations.

Others use citation data as a proxy for opinion content. One example is Cross (2012), who constructs a measure for the ideological valence of a sample of US Supreme Court opinions by counting the number of times they are positively or negatively cited by opinions that support liberal and conservative case outcomes. Clark and Lauderdale (2010) combine citation data with scaling techniques to obtain estimates for the ideological valence of US Supreme Court opinions, which they use to test various theories of opinion writing and strategic behaviour. Similarly, Arnold et al. (2023) propose a scaling model that allows them to estimate the position of decisions by lower courts in Germany on a latent dimension.

4. Citation Data and the Comparative Study of Judicial Behaviour

Section 3 highlighted the diverse ways in which data on citations in judicial decisions has been utilized in quantitative research on courts and legal systems. This section connects this discussion to the general topic of this *Handbook* by exploring what this research has contributed and can contribute to a comparative understanding of judicial behaviour. Additionally, it identifies a significant methodological challenge faced by some of the most relevant work in this area.

4.1 General Observations

At a general level, not every stream of literature discussed above appears equally suited to contribute to a comparative understanding of judicial behaviour. This is because some of the questions asked in this literature are unrelated to judicial behaviour, do not lend themselves easily to a comparative perspective, or both. For instance, research using citation data to rank judges in a specific jurisdiction according to their influence (Section 3.4) does not aim to uncover insights into the behaviour of judges or the functioning of the legal system that could be readily compared across jurisdictions.

Similarly, studies analysing network-theoretical features of citation networks (Section 3.3) seem not to have made significant contributions to a comparative understanding of judicial behaviour. The main reason lies in the limited scope of research questions addressed with these methods. As Section 3.3 demonstrates, much of the existing research in this category falls into one of three categories: (i) identifying central decisions in the citation network, (ii) investigating the existence of clusters of related cases, or (iii) describing high-level properties of the citation network. None of these questions directly relate to judicial behaviour, and the first two questions are unlikely to produce results that can be easily compared across courts in different jurisdictions.

Some researchers argue that specific high-level properties of citation networks allow us to learn about the 'fractal structure of systems of legal doctrine and legal argument' (Post and Eisen 2000) or about whether courts follow a 'conscious approach vis-à-vis case law' (Derlén and Lindholm 2017). These claims suggest that the study of citation networks has the potential to yield insights into aspects of judge behaviour that could be compared across jurisdictions.

However, we currently lack a theory about how features of legal systems that are of interest to the legal discourse (e.g. the use of precedent by judges) manifest themselves in measurable qualities of citation networks. In the absence of such a theory, it is of limited value to the legal discourse to report that citation networks observed in different contexts share certain network-theoretic features, for example, that the distribution of the numbers of inward citations follows a power law. While such a finding might be intriguing from the perspective of a social physics researcher interested in documenting statistical commonalities in various types of social phenomena, absent more work in this area, it remains unclear what this result implies for our comparative understanding of judicial behaviour (Frankenreiter 2017b).

In contrast, studies following the methodological approaches described in the first and second groups above (Sections 3.1 and 3.2) hold greater potential for generating insights that can contribute to a comparative understanding of judicial behaviour. Note, however, that the insights generated by both groups of studies differ in their nature.

Research that investigates citation practices and patterns across various courts and jurisdictions and would therefore fall into the first group holds significant potential for yielding valuable insights into comparative judicial behaviour. By examining how courts from diverse legal systems use and engage with citations, scholars can identify similarities and discrepancies in how judges process and rely on legal materials, both from within their jurisdiction and beyond. Furthermore, understanding the factors that drive cross-citations between jurisdictions can shed light on the complexities of legal interdependence and the role of transnational influences in shaping judicial decision-making. Consequently, this strand of literature advances our knowledge of citation practices and serves as a rich source of information for comparative analysis of judge behaviour across legal systems.

However, research in this group does not seem well-positioned to answer questions about judges' motivations in using citations, primarily due to the 'macro' perspective which most of these studies adopt. Of course, any observed differences in citation usage between courts and legal systems may indicate underlying differences in judicial philosophies, legal traditions, and interpretative approaches. However, legal systems vary on so many dimensions that it is usually futile to attribute any observed variation to specific differences in the legal systems.

Studies belonging to the second group (Section 4.2) are arguably better suited to generate comparative insights into the drivers of judges' decisions to cite. This research often uses traditional quantitative techniques, in particular regression analysis, to analyse the determinants of judges' citation decisions at a micro-level, often at the level of individual opinions. The view that such studies are best positioned to analyse judges' decisions on whether and what sources to cite is corroborated by the fact that this stream of literature has produced the most insights into the role of judicial ideology, strategic motives, and legal considerations in these decisions.

One potential challenge in using such studies for comparative insights is their incremental nature. Most often, individual studies in this group will only investigate the behaviour of judges in one specific setting. Even within this setting, the insights from such studies will usually be limited to particular aspects of judge behaviour.[4] It might take a long time to generate the results necessary to understand whether judges in different jurisdictions act similarly. This situation is further complicated because the institutional setting in which judges operate will often differ between jurisdictions. Hence, it will sometimes be impossible to repeat a study conducted in one jurisdiction in another jurisdiction.

Nevertheless, this type of research has considerable potential to further our comparative understanding of judicial behaviour. To illustrate this potential, consider the literature that analyses the relationship between judicial ideology and judges' citation behaviour. This literature originated in the United States, where researchers documented that the citation behaviour of Democratic-appointed judges differed in predictable ways from that of their Republican-appointed counterparts (Choi and Gulati 2008; Niblett and Yoon 2015). The absence of a similar left–right divide permeating many legal issues made it impossible for researchers interested in the behaviour of judges at the ECtHR and CJEU to directly replicate those studies in these settings. Against this background, researchers developed different, context-appropriate measures of judicial ideology. Using these measures, they were able to document that citation behaviour at these courts is also influenced by ideology (Voeten 2010; Frankenreiter 2017a). Similarly, Lupu and Voeten (2012) demonstrated that judges at the ECtHR use citations strategically, similar to what can be observed for judges at the US Supreme Court (Lupu and Fowler 2013). These are but two examples of comparative insights that micro-level studies using citation data can generate.

4.2 Using Traditional Quantitative Techniques to Study Citation Data

The previous subsection argued that studies that use traditional quantitative tools to analyse the determinants of citations at a micro level (typically, at the level of individual decisions) are particularly well suited to generate comparative insights into questions relating to judicial behaviour. However, there are methodological challenges associated with these tools that warrant further attention.[5] This issue, which has largely gone unnoticed in the literature studying citations in the legal context, relates to the complex nature of citation networks. The likelihood of a reference to a previous decision might be influenced by whether other opinions have cited this decision in the past. Additionally, decision-level factors at both the level of the citing and the cited decision might impact the likelihood of a citation (Schmid et al. 2021). As is described in more detail below, this fact creates severe issues for the validity of the statistical estimators traditionally used in such studies.

Micro-level studies that use citation data to investigate questions about judges' citation behaviour typically adopt one of two general approaches to constructing the datasets they use in their analysis. Most studies treat individual decisions (or groups of decisions) as the unit of analysis and aggregate information on inward or outward citations at that level. Subsequently, they analyse this data with tools such as regression analysis. Several more recent studies (e.g. Hinkle 2015, 2016; Frankenreiter 2017a) adopt a different approach, analysing the determinants of citations at the dyadic level. In other words, their models treat every citing opinion–cited decision pair as an individual observation.

The problem with both approaches is that the tools used in the analysis (in particular, regression analysis) generally assume that individual observations are independent of each other. The assumption that individual observations are independent and identically distributed (i.i.d.) is crucial in traditional statistical techniques as it allows for the use of parametric models and the calculation of estimated standard errors and confidence intervals. Researchers often apply techniques such as clustered standard errors that can remedy violations of the independence assumption that are related to the influence of group-level factors. However, such remedies are generally insufficient to deal with the complex dependencies that can exist in citation networks. As a result, researchers using regression analysis and similar tools to analyse citation data risk producing overconfident or biased results (Schmid et al. 2021).

The problem described here is not unique to citation data in the legal context, and several potential solutions have been proposed in the literature. The so-called Quadratic Assignment Procedure (QAP) allows for the generation of alternative hypothesis tests that take into account the unique dependencies in datasets generated based on citation data. Exponential Random Graph Models (ERGMs) enable researchers to account explicitly for certain complex features of citation networks in their statistical models (see

Schmid et al. 2021). However, these techniques have so far not been widely used in the literature studying citations in judicial opinions.[6]

To illustrate this problem, this section reports the results from a series of simulations that demonstrate how the complex nature of citation networks can lead to overconfident results in studies that rely on traditional quantitative techniques to analyse citation data.[7] These simulations mimic a simple study that seeks to find out whether one group of decisions in a network is cited more often than another group. A real-world example could ask whether a judge's party affiliation impacts their likelihood of being cited in subsequent decisions. The main findings from these simulations show that traditional quantitative techniques can produce misleading results due to their inability to account for the complex dependencies within citation networks, emphasizing the need for alternative methods such as QAP and ERGMs.

In these simulations, I simulate the emergence of a network of decisions and citations between them. Ten decisions are of type A, ten of type B, and the remaining eighty are of type o.[8] I assume that decisions of type A and type B have a higher than normal probability of citing previous decisions of the same type. By contrast, I assume that decisions of type o cite decisions of type A and B with the same probability (for the sake of simplicity, the model does not allow for citations between decisions of type o). The primary quantity of interest is whether there is a significant difference in the number of citations to decisions of type A and B in decisions of type o.

Because of the nature of the data-generating process, an appropriate statistical test for differences in the number of inward citations in decisions of type A and B should reject the null hypothesis under the usual significance standard of .05 roughly 5 per cent of the time. In fact, this is the approximate result that I obtain under the basic model. However, when I modify the data-generating processes to include an element of 'transitivity', one of the complex features that can occur in citation networks (Schmid et al. 2021), the same statistical tests produce severely overconfident results.

In each simulation, I complete the following steps to construct the citation network. The starting point is a 'network' consisting of one decision of type A and one of type B, without any citation between them. Subsequently, I grow the network over eighty-nine rounds. In each of the first nine rounds, two new decisions are created (again, one of type A and one of type B). New decisions cannot cite each other, but every new decision has the same non-zero probability p_{same_type} of citing a previous decision of the same type and a non-zero probability p_{basis} of citing a previous decision of the opposite type. After the first nine rounds are completed, the network consists of twenty decisions, ten of type A and ten of type B. In each of the remaining eighty rounds, one new decision of type o is created. In the basic simulation model, every decision of type o cites every decision type A or B with probability p_{basis}. In versions of the simulation that allow for transitivity, the probability of a reference in decision i of type o to a decision k of type A or B is increased ($p_{transitivity}$ instead of p_{basis}, with $p_{transitivity} > p_{basis}$) if i also cites a more recent decision j of type A or B which references k. Because of the nature of the data-generating process

I impose, the network has some of the essential features of citation networks. In particular, it is directed and acyclic.

I then use regression analysis to analyse whether decisions of type A receive significantly higher or lower numbers of inward citations from decisions of type 0 than decisions of type B. For this, I aggregate the simulated citation data at the decision level by counting, for every decision of type A or B, the number of inward citations from decisions of type 0. I fit Poisson and ordinary least squares (OLS) models to this data, with an indicator for whether a decision is of type B and the round in which the decision was created as the independent variables.[9] Finally, I record whether the coefficient of the indicator variable (together with the associated p-value) suggests a rejection of the null hypothesis. In other words, I test whether the statistical test produces evidence against the hypothesis that there is no difference in the expected number of inward citations between decisions of type A and B.

Note that no version of the data-generating process described above (whether it includes an element of transitivity or not) is biased in favour of one or the other group of decisions. Accordingly, if traditional quantitative techniques could generate reliable hypothesis tests in the face of the complex nature of citation data, one would expect the rate of statistically significant results to remain constant across these simulations.

Tables 26.1 and 26.2 report the rate of rejections of the null hypothesis in simulations using different values for p_{basis} and $p_{transitivity}$ (p_{same_type} is set to 0.25). For each combination of values, the data-generation process was repeated 1,000 times. The first column

Table 26.1 Rejection rates, Poisson regressions

	$p_{transitivity}$					
	p_{basis}	.1	.2	.3	.4	.5
p_{basis} .01	.034	.052	.100	.136	.140	.178
.02	.043	.047	.091	.115	.172	.190
.03	.038	.059	.082	.110	.157	.203
.04	.037	.050	.078	.124	.170	.198
.05	.034	.046	.073	.115	.141	.172
.06	.044	.042	.064	.099	.148	.207
.07	.029	.044	.062	.115	.162	.213
.08	.051	.049	.071	.088	.144	.179
.09	.035	.043	.053	.077	.143	.175
.1	.030	.044	.057	.084	.133	.186

Notes: This table reports rejection rates (p-value < .05) in 1,000 Poisson regressions regressing the number of inward citations on an indicator variable for whether a decision is of type A. Control variable: Round in which decision was created.

Table 26.2 Rejection rates, OLS regressions

		$p_{transitivity}$				
	p_{basis}	.1	.2	.3	.4	.5
p_{basis} .01	.047	.065	.121	.155	.144	.161
.02	.054	.068	.111	.116	.151	.155
.03	.050	.075	.083	.081	.125	.146
.04	.050	.045	.073	.097	.121	.110
.05	.039	.051	.075	.100	.091	.100
.06	.047	.051	.063	.088	.092	.119
.07	.051	.050	.069	.101	.102	.100
.08	.061	.047	.077	.079	.085	.089
.09	.046	.054	.059	.064	.089	.083
.1	.049	.050	.068	.074	.074	.085

Notes: This table reports rejection rates (*p*-value < .05) in 1,000 OLS regressions regressing the logarithmic version of the number of inward citations (+1) on an indicator variable for whether a decision is of type A. Control variable: Round in which decision was created. Results based on robust Huber–White standard errors.

($p_{transitivity} = 0$) displays the results from the basic model without transitivity. It can be seen that the null hypothesis in Poisson regressions is rejected at rates slightly below .05, indicating that the statistical test yields conservative results in this setting. The rejection rates for OLS regressions hover around .05, potentially suggesting that this model fits the data better.

Importantly, for both models, the rate of rejections increases substantially if the data-generation process includes an element of transitivity. In individual scenarios, the rejection rate lies more than two times higher than the expected level of .05. What is the underlying problem? As described above, in a citation network that features elements of transitivity, inward citation counts for individual decisions are not independent of each other. Instead, in the presence of transitivity, a higher citation count for decision *j* will also increase the expected citation for decision *k*, violating the i.i.d. assumption that underlies most of the most commonly used statistical models.

As a result, it seems reasonable to assume that researchers should proceed with caution when using traditional statistical models to investigate the determinants of the numbers and the nature of inward or outward citations at a micro level, lest they risk producing overconfident results. Given the limitations of traditional quantitative models, the incorporation of innovative techniques like QAP and EGRMs appears overdue.

5. Conclusion and Outlook

This chapter has offered an overview of the current state of quantitative research on citations in legal opinions, focusing on the strengths and weaknesses of macro-level studies describing and comparing citation patterns and micro-level analyses of judges' citation decisions. While micro-level studies seem particularly well-suited for generating comparative insights into judicial behaviour, they often face methodological challenges due to the complex nature of citation networks. Specifically, applying regression analysis and similar tools that assume independence and identically distributed observations may result in biased or overconfident findings when used with citation data. In light of these challenges, this chapter has highlighted the need for methodological advancements in this area. Alternative methods such as QAP and ERGMs can address complex dependencies in citation networks. However, these techniques have yet to gain widespread adoption in the literature on citations in judicial opinions.

Beyond overcoming the limitations of traditional quantitative techniques in micro-level studies of judicial behaviour, there are additional opportunities for advancement in the study of citations in legal opinions. First, researchers can conduct more studies that explicitly compare the use of citations across different legal systems, thereby documenting similarities and differences in citation practices among jurisdictions. While existing work adopting this approach primarily focuses on cross-citations, examining general citation patterns can provide valuable context for discussions on judicial decision-making in different jurisdictions, including for questions about the role of precedent in common and civil law systems.

Second, researchers can explore new ways to deploy network-theoretical methods to study comparative citation behaviour. Such work could involve developing theories that connect measurable characteristics of citation networks to relevant features of legal systems. It could also involve using network-theoretical features to classify legal systems into clusters or categories based on the similarity or dissimilarity of their citation networks. The latter approach could test, for example, whether traditional assumptions about the functioning of different legal systems around the world (e.g. the existence of several legal families with distinct decision-making approaches) are reflected in such classifications. Notably, this approach may work without an underlying theory as validating it could simply involve deploying it within legal systems for which researchers assume the ground truth is known.

All in all, this chapter underscores the importance of methodological advancement and new research directions in the quantitative study of citations in legal opinions. This includes embracing alternative techniques such as QAP and ERGMs, conducting research that explicitly compares citation patterns across jurisdictions, and developing theories that connect citation networks to relevant features of legal systems. Pursuing these opportunities can bolster the credibility of research investigating citation behaviour and contribute to a more nuanced understanding of the factors that influence both the use of citations in legal systems across the globe and judicial behaviour more generally.

Acknowledgement

I am grateful to Danielle Hoyer for outstanding research assistance.

Notes

1. The literature review focuses on studies published in English due to their widespread accessibility. However, it is worth noting that there exists substantial and valuable research in other languages that could offer additional perspectives on this topic.
2. Because of the high-dimensional nature of citation data, the quantitative study of such data is sometimes considered part of the emerging field of computational legal studies (Frankenreiter and Livermore 2020; van Kuppevelt et al. 2020).
3. Alternatively, unaggregated citation data could also be used in conjunction with machine-learning algorithms, which are better equipped than regression analysis and similar techniques to deal with high-dimensional data. However, to date, such applications are rare or non-existent.
4. Notably, none of the micro-level studies surveyed in Section 3.2 simultaneously investigated the conduct of judges in more than one country/legal system.
5. Note that this challenge may also be relevant for studies that use traditional quantitative techniques to analyse predictors of decisions at the court or country level.
6. A notable exception is Siems (2023).
7. The code for these simulations is available at https://www.jensfrankenreiter.com/studying-judicial-citations.
8. The size of the groups does not affect substantively affect the results I present below.
9. The choice of estimator does not substantially affect my results. Similar patterns can be observed, for example, when *t*-tests or Mann–Whitney U tests are used to test for differences in the mean (median) of the distributions obtained from the simulations.

References

Abramowicz, Michael, and Emerson H. Tiller. 2009. 'Citation to Legislative History: Empirical Evidence on Positive Political and Contextual Theories of Judicial Decision Making'. *Journal of Legal Studies* 38: 419–43.

Adusumilli, Keerthi, Bradford Brown, Joey Harrison, Matthew Koehler, Jason Kutarnia, Shaun Michel, Max Olivier, et al. 2022. 'The Structure and Dynamics of Modern United States Federal Case Law'. *Frontiers in Physics* 9: 695219.

Agnoloni, Tomasso, and Ugo Pagallo. 2016. 'The Case Law of the Italian Constitutional Court between Network Theory and Philosophy of Information'. *Informatica e diritto* 25: 139–51.

Alschner, Wolfgang, and Damien Charlotin. 2018. 'The Growing Complexity of the International Court of Justice's Self-Citation Network'. *European Journal of International Law* 29: 83–112.

Arnold, Christian, Benjamin G. Engst, and Thomas Gschwend. 2023. 'Scaling Court Decisions with Citation Networks'. *Journal of Law and Courts* 11: 25–44.

Bhattacharya, Mita, and Russell Smyth. 2001. 'The Determinants of Judicial Prestige and Influence: Some Empirical Evidence from the High Court of Australia'. *Journal of Legal Studies* 30: 223–52.

Black, Ryan C., and James F. Spriggs II. 2013. 'The Citation and Depreciation of U.S. Supreme Court Precedent'. Journal of Empirical Legal Studies 10: 325–58.

Blanes I Vidal, Jordi, and Clare Leaver. 2013. 'Social Interactions and the Content of Legal Opinions'. *Journal of Law, Economics, and Organization* 29: 78–114.

Bommarito II, Michael J., Daniel Martin Katz, Jonathan L. Zelner, and James H. Fowler. 2010a. 'Distance measures for dynamic citation networks'. *Physica A* 389: 4201–08.

Bommarito II, Michael J., Daniel M. Katz, and Jonathan L. Zelner. 2010b. 'On the Stability of Community Detection Algorithms on Longitudinal Citation Data'. *Procedia Social and Behavioral Sciences* 4: 26–37.

Bommarito II, Michael J., Daniel Martin Katz, and Jillian Isaacs-See. 2011. 'An Empirical Survey of the Population of U.S. Tax Court Written Decisions'. 30 *Virginia Tax Review* 30: 523–57.

Boyd, Christina L., and James F. Spriggs II. 2009. 'An Examination of Strategic Anticipation of Appellate Court Preferences by Federal District Court Judges'. *Washington University Journal of Law & Policy* 29: 37–81.

Broughman, Brian J., and Deborah A. Wildiss. 2017. 'After the Override: An Empirical Analysis of Shadow Precedent'. *Journal of Legal Studies* 46: 51–92.

Caldeira, Gregory A. 1985. 'The Transmission of Legal Precedent: A Study of State Supreme Courts'. *American Political Science Review* 79: 178–94.

Caldeira, Gregory A. 1988. 'Legal Precedent: Structures of Communication between State Supreme Courts'. *Social Networks* 10: 29–55.

Choi, Stephen J., and G. Mitu Gulati. 2007. 'Ranking Judges According to Citation Bias (as a Means to Reduce Bias)'. *Notre Dame Law Review* 82: 1279.

Choi, Stephen J., and G. Mitu Gulati. 2004. 'Choosing the Next Supreme Court Justice: An Empirical Ranking of Judge Performance'. *Southern California Law Review* 78: 23.

Choi, Stephen J., and G. Mitu Gulati. 2008. 'Bias in Judicial Citations: A Window into the Behavior of Judges?' *Journal of Legal Studies* 37: 87–129.

Choi, Stephen J., Mitu Gulati, and Eric A. Posner. 2009. 'Judicial Evaluations and Information Forcing: Ranking State High Courts and Their Judges'. *Duke Law Journal* 58: 1313–81.

Clark, Tom S., and Benjamin Lauderdale. 2010. 'Locating Supreme Court opinions in doctrine space'. *American Journal of Political Science* 54: 871–90.

Clark, Tom S., and Benjamin E. Lauderdale. 2012. 'The Genealogy of Law'. *Political Analysis* 20: 329–50.

Correia, Fernando A., José Luiz Nunes, Guilherme F. C. F. de Almeida, Alexandre A. A. Almeida, and Hélio Lopes. 2019. 'An Exploratory Analysis of Precedent Relevance in the Brazilian Supreme Court Rulings'. *Proceedings of the ACM Symposium on Document Engineering 2019—DocEng '19* (2019).

Cross, Frank B. 2010. 'Determinants of Citations to Supreme Court Opinions (And the Remarkable Influence of Justice Scalia)'. *Supreme Court Economic Review* 18: 177–202.

Cross, Frank B. 2012. 'The Ideology of Supreme Court Opinions and Citations'. *Iowa Law Review* 97: 693–751

Cross, Frank B., James F. Spriggs II, Timothy R. Johnson, and Paul J. Wahlbeck. 2010. 'Citations in the U.S. Supreme Court: An Empirical Study of Their Use and Significance'. *University of Illinois Law Review* 2010: 489–575.

D'Andrea, Sabrina, Nikita Divissenko, Maria Fanou, Anna Krisztián, Jaka Kukavica, Nastazja Potocka-Sionek, and Mathias Siems. 2021. 'Asymmetric Cross-Citations in Private Law: An Empirical Study of 28 Supreme Courts in the EU'. *Maastricht Journal of European and Comparative Law* 28: 498–534.

Denniston, Mark W. 2014. *Dialogue among State Supreme Courts: Advancing State Constitutionalism*. El Paso: LFB Scholarly Publishing.

Derlén, Mattias, Johan Lindholm, Martin Rosvall, and Atieh Mirshahvalad. 2013. 'Coherence out of Chaos: Mapping European Union Law by Running Randomly Through the Maze of CJEU Case Law'. *Europarättslig Tidskrift* 2013: 517.

Derlén, Mattias, and Johan Lindholm. 2012. 'The Court of Justice and the Ankara Agreement: Exploring the Empirical Approach'. *Europarättslig Tidskrift* 2012: 462–81.

Derlén, Mattias, and Johan Lindholm. 2015. 'Characteristics of Precedent: The Case Law of the European Court of Justice in Three Dimensions'. *German Law Journal* 16: 1073.

Derlén, Mattias, and Johan Lindholm. 2017. 'Peek-A-Boo, It's a Case Law System: Comparing the European Court of Justice and the United States Supreme Court from a Network Perspective'. *German Law Journal* 18: 647–86.

Epstein, Lee, William M. Landes, and Richard A. Posner. 2013. *The Behavior of Federal Judges: A Theoretical and Empirical Study of Rational Choice*. Cambridge: Harvard University Press.

Fowler, James H., and Sangick Jeon. 2008. 'The Authority of Supreme Court Precedent'. *Social Networks* 30: 16–30.

Fowler, James H., Timothy R. Johnson, James F. Spriggs II, Sangick Jeon, and Paul J. Wahlbeck. 2007. 'Network Analysis and the Law: Measuring the Legal Importance of Precedents at the U.S. Supreme Court'. *Political Analysis* 15: 324–46.

Frankenreiter, Jens. 2017a. 'The Politics of Citations at the ECJ—Policy Preferences of EU Member State Governments and the Citation Behavior of Judges at the European Court of Justice'. *Journal of Empirical Legal Studies* 14: 813–57.

Frankenreiter, Jens. 2017b. 'Network Analysis and the Use of Precedent in the Case Law of the CJEU—A Reply to Derlén and Lindholm'. *German Law Journal* 18: 687–93.

Frankenreiter, Jens, and Michael A. Livermore. 2020. 'Computational Methods in Legal Analysis'. *Annual Review of Law and Social Science* 16: 39–57.

Frankenreiter, Jens, and Julian Nyarko. 2023. 'Natural Language Processing in Legal Tech'. In *Legal Tech and the Future of Civil Justice*, edited by David Freeman Engstrom, 70–90. Cambridge: Cambridge University Press.

Friedman, Lawrence M., Robert A. Kagan, Bliss Cartwright, and Stanton Wheeler. 1981. 'State Supreme Courts: A Century of Style and Citation'. *Stanford Law Review* 33: 773–818.

Gelter, Martin, and Mathias Siems. 2012. 'Networks, Dialogue or One-Way Traffic? An Empirical Analysis of Cross-Citations Between Ten of Europe's Highest Courts'. *Utrecht Law Review* 8: 88–99.

Gelter, Martin, and Mathias M. Siems. 2013. 'Language, Legal Origins, and Culture Before the Courts: Cross-Citations Between Supreme Courts in Europe'. *Supreme Court Economic Review* 21: 215–69.

Gelter, Martin, and Mathias M. Siems. 2014. 'Citations to Foreign Courts—Illegitimate and Superfluous, or Unavoidable? Evidence from Europe'. *American Journal of Comparative Law* 62: 35–85.

Gleason, Shane E., Scott A. Comparato, and Chrstine M. Bailey. 2021. 'Walking on Broken Glass. Justice Gender in State Supreme Court Citations'. In *Open Judicial Politics*, edited by Rorie Spill Solberg and Eric Waltenburg, 113–32.

Groppi, Tania, and Marie-Claire Ponthoreau, eds. 2013. *The Use of Foreign Precedents by Constitutional Judges*. Oxford: Hart Publishing.

Hansford, Thomas G., and James F. Spriggs II. 2006. *The Politics of Precedent on the U.S. Supreme Court*. Princeton: Princeton University Press.

Hansford, Thomas G., and James F. Spriggs II. 2014. 'Attention to Precedent in a Judicial Hierarchy'. Paper presented at the Annual Meeting of the Southern Political Science Association, New Orleans, LA.

Harris, Peter. 1982. 'Structural Change in the Communication of Precedent among State Supreme Courts, 1870–1970'. *Social Networks* 4: 201–12.

Harris, Peter. 1985. 'Difficult Cases and the Display of Authority'. *Journal of Law, Economics, & Organization* 1: 209–21.

Hinkle, Rachael K. 2015. 'Legal Constraint in the U.S. Courts of Appeals'. *Journal of Politics* 77: 721–35.

Hinkle, Rachael K. 2016. 'Strategic Anticipation of En Banc Review in the U.S. Courts of Appeals'. *Law and Society Review* 50: 383–414.

Hinkle, Rachael K., and Michael J. Nelson. 2016. 'The Transmission of Legal Precedent among State Supreme Courts in the Twenty-First Century'. *State Politics & Policy Quarterly* 16: 391–410.

Hinkle, Rachael K., and Michael J. Nelson. 2018. 'The Intergroup Foundations of Policy Influence'. *Political Research Quarterly* 771: 729–42.

Hoadley, Daniel et al. 2021. 'A Global Community of Courts? Modelling the Use of Persuasive Authority as a Complex Network'. *Frontiers in Physics* 9: 665719.

Jacob, Marc. 2014. *Precedents and Case-based Reasoning in the European Court of Justice: Unfinished Business*. Cambridge: Cambridge University Press. 2014.

Johnson, Charles A. 1986. 'Follow-Up Citations in the U. S. Supreme Court'. *Western Political Quarterly* 39: 538–47.

Kassow, Benjamin, Donald R. Songer, and Michael P. Fix. 2012. 'The Influence of Precedent on State Supreme Courts'. *Political Research Quarterly* 65: 372–84.

Klein, David, and Darby Morrisroe. 1999. 'The Prestige and Influence of Individual Judges on the U.S. Courts of Appeals'. *Journal of Legal Studies* 28: 371–91.

Kosma, Montgomery N. 1998. 'Measuring the Influence of Supreme Court Justices'. *Journal of Legal Studies* 27: 333–72.

Landes, William M., Lawrence Lessig, and Michael E. Solimine. 1998. 'Judicial Influence: A Citation Analysis of Federal Courts of Appeals Judges'. *Journal of Legal Studies* 27: 319–32.

Landes, William M., and Richard A. Posner. 1976. 'Legal Precedent: A Theoretical and Empirical Analysis'. *Journal of Law and Economics* 19: 249–307.

Larsson Olof, Daniel Naurin, Mattias Derlén, and Johan Lindholm. 2017. 'Speaking law to power: The strategic use of precedent of the Court of Justice of the European Union'. *Comparative Political Studies* 50: 879–907

Lauderdale, Benjamin E., and Tom S. Clark. 2012. 'The Supreme Court's Many Median Justices'. *American Political Science Review* 106: 847–66.

Lauderdale, Benjamin E., and Tom S. Clark. 2016. 'Estimating Vote-Specific Preferences from Roll-Call Data Using Conditional Autoregressive Priors'. *Journal of Politics* 78: 1153–69.

Law, David S. 2015. 'Judicial Comparativism and Judicial Diplomacy'. *University of Pennsylvania Law Review* 163: 927–1036.

Lie, Runar Hilleren. 2022. 'The Influencers of International Investment Law: A Computational Study of ISDS Actors' Changing Behavior'. *German Law Journal* 23: 350–75.

Lupu, Yonatan, and James H. Fowler. 2013. 'Strategic Citations to Precedent on the U.S. Supreme Court'. *The Journal of Legal Studies* 38 (1): 151–86.

Lupu, Yonatan, and Eric Voeten. 2012. 'Precedent in international courts: A network analysis of case citations by the European Court of Human Rights'. *British Journal of Political Science* 42: 413–39.

Manley, Stewart. 2016. 'Referencing Patterns at the International Criminal Court'. *European Journal of International Law* 27: 191–214.

Masood, Ali S., Benjamin J. Kassow, and Donald R. Songer. 2017. 'Supreme Court Precedent in a Judicial Hierarchy'. *American Politics Research* 45: 403–43.

Marx, Stephen M. 1970. 'Citation Networks in the Law'. *Jurimetrics Journal* 10: 121–37.

Merryman, John H. 1954. 'The Authority of Authority: What the California Supreme Court Cited in 1950'. *Stanford Law Review* 6: 613–73.

Merryman, John Henry. 1977. 'Toward a Theory of Citations: An Empirical Study of the Citation Practice of the California Supreme Court in 1950, 1960, and 1970'. *Southern California Law Review* 50: 381–428.

Milz, Tobias, Michael Granitzer, and Jelena Mitrovic. 2021. 'Analysis of a German Legal Citation Network'. In *Proceedings of the 13th International Joint Conference on Knowledge Discovery, Knowledge Engineering and Knowledge Management (IC3K 2021)—Volume 1: KDIR*, Valletta, Malta, 147–54.

Mirshahvalad, Atieh, Johan Lindholm, Mattias Derlén, and Martin Rosvall. 2012. 'Significant Communities in Large Sparse Networks'. *PLoS One* 7: e33721.

Moser, Markus, and Mark Strembeck. 2019. 'An Analysis of Three Legal Citation Networks Derived from Austrian Supreme Court Decisions'. In *Proceedings of the 4th International Conference on Complexity, Future Information Systems and Risk (COMPLEXIS 2019)*, Heraklion, Crete, Greece, 85–92.

Mott, Rodney L. 1936. 'Judicial Influence'. *American Political Science Review* 30: 295–315.

Nelson, Michael J., and Rachael K. Hinkle. 2018. Crafting the Law: How Opinion Content Influences Legal Development. *Justice System Journal* 39: 97–122.

Ng, Kwai Hang, and Brynna Jacobson. 2017. 'How Global Is the Common Law? A Comparative Study of Asian Common Law Systems—Hong Kong, Malaysia, and Singapore'. *Asian Journal of Comparative Law* 12: 209–32.

Niblett, Anthony, and Albert H. Yoon. 2015. 'Judicial Disharmony: A Study of Dissent'. *International Review of Law and Economics* 42: 60–71.

Niblett, Anthony and Albert H. Yoon. 2016. 'Friendly Precedent'. *William & Mary Law Review* 57: 1789–823.

Örücü, Esin. 2007. 'Comparative Law in Practice: The Courts and the Legislator'. In *Comparative Law: A Handbook*, edited by Esin Örücü and David Nelken, 411–34. Oxford: Hart Publishing.

Pauwelyn, Joost. 2015. 'Minority Rules: Precedent and Participation Before the WTO Appellate Body'. In *Establishing Judicial Authority in International Economic Law*, edited by Joanna Jemielniak, Laura Nielsen, and Henrik Palmer Olsen, 141–72. Cambridge: Cambridge University Press.

Post, David G., and Michael B. Eisen. 2000. 'How Long is the Coastline of the Law? Thoughts on the Fractal Nature of Legal Systems'. *Journal of Legal Studies* 29: 545–84.

Randazzo, Kirk A. 2008. 'Strategic Anticipation and the Hierarchy of Justice in U.S. District Courts'. *American Politics Research* 36: 669–93.

Šadl, Urška, and Sigrid Hink. 2014. 'Precedent in the Sui Generis Legal Order: A Mine Run Approach'. *European Law Journal* 20: 544–67.

Šadl, Urška, and Henrik Palmer Olsen. 2017. 'Can Quantitative Methods Complement Doctrinal Legal Studies? Using Citation Network and Corpus Linguistic Analysis to Understand International Courts'. *Leiden Journal of International Law* 30: 327–49.

Schmid, Christian S., Ted Hsuan Yun Chen, and Bruce A. Desmarais. 2021. 'Generative Dynamics of Supreme Court Citations: Analysis with a New Statistical Network Model'. *Political Analysis* 30: 515–34.

Siems, Mathias. 2010. 'Citation Patterns of the German Federal Supreme Court and the Court of Appeals of England and Wales'. *King's Law Journal* 21: 152–71.

Siems, Mathias. 2023. 'A Network Analysis of Judicial Cross-Citations in Europe'. *Law & Social Inquiry* 48 (3): 881–905.

Smith Thomas A. 2007. 'The Web of Law'. *San Diego Law Review* 44 (2007): 309–54.

Smithey, Shannon Ishiyama. 2001. 'A Tool, not a Master. The Use of Foreign Case Law in Canada and South Africa'. *Comparative Political Studies* 34: 1188–211.

Sunstein, Cass R., David Schkade, Lisa M. Ellman, and Andres Sawicki. 2006. *Are Judges Political? An Empirical Analysis of the Federal Judiciary*. Washington: Brookings Institution Press.

Szmer, John, Robert K. Christensen, and Samuel Grubbs. 2020. 'What Influences the Influence of U.S. Courts of Appeals Decisions?' *European Journal of Law & Economics* 49 (1): 55–81.

Tarissan, Fabien, and Raphaëlle Nollez-Goldbach. 2016. 'Analysing the First Case of the International Criminal Court from a Network-Science Perspective'. *Journal of Complex Networks* 4: 616–34.

van Kuppevelt, Dafne, Gijs van Dijk, and Marcel Schaper. 2020. 'Purposes and Challenges of Legal Citation Network Analysis on Case Law'. In *Computational Legal Studies. The Promises and challenge of Data-Driven Research*, edited by Ryan Whalen, 265–92. Cheltenham: Edward Elgar Publishing.

Varsava, Nina. 2018. *The Form and Function of Legal Precedent.*

Voeten, Erik. 2010. 'Borrowing and Nonborrowing among International Courts'. *Journal of Legal Studies* 39: 547–76.

Walsh, David J. 1997. 'On the Meaning and Pattern of Legal Citations: Evidence from State Wrongful Discharge Precedent Cases'. *Law & Society Review* 31: 337–61.

Zaring, David. 2006. 'The Use of Foreign Decisions by Federal Courts: An Empirical Analysis'. *Journal of Empirical Legal Studies* 3: 297–331.

CHAPTER 27

JUDGE LANGUAGE CHOICES

ELLIOTT ASH

1. Introduction

LAW is a linguistic enterprise (Posner 1995, 2009), with legislation, regulations, judicial opinions, and contracts composed as plain text. In particular, in common law systems, what judges write becomes law, in the sense that parties can rely on those writings as informing or predicting how future judges will decide. The language choices made by judges are socially important and a valuable target of social science study.

This chapter seeks to understand judge language choices from four angles. First, I propose a model of judge language choices with a minimal set of relevant institutional and behavioural features. That model will help organize the discussion around measurement, determinants, and consequences.

Second, I discuss and review the problem of measurement of judge language choices—what a judge decides to write in an opinion. The set of measurable dimensions is many, potentially infinite, so a first question for researchers is what dimensions to try to measure. And then a second question is how to do it. I discuss the different approaches, based on computational linguistics, to identify and measure dimensions of judge language. Most of those approaches are indirect, for example proxying for discussion of criminal law by mentions of the word 'crime'; or proxying for conservative ideology by the use of phrases that are distinctive of Republican-appointed judges. I will highlight the limitations of measuring judge language choices.

The third angle is on the determinants or causes of judge language choice. How do judges decide what to write in their opinions? Starting with a given dimension of language, we would like to use empirical social science methods to produce evidence on that type of question. I will review the body of work that has produced some of that evidence. I will then highlight the limitations of most of that evidence. The most important problem is the same as most empirical social science research: the difficulty of producing broadly applicable causal evidence in the absence of natural or field experiments. But the use of text-based measurements produces its own problems for econometric inference.

Fourth and finally, I will discuss the even harder problem of producing empirical evidence on the consequences of judge language choices. Those choices must have some effect, given that judicial opinions constitute formal legal precedent, and given the intense, costly bargaining by judges and other legal actors over how things are written. But teasing that out causally is difficult because judicial texts are confounded with, and a response to, many other factors. Some of these factors are observed, such as the main direction of a judicial ruling, but many are unobserved. That could include subsequent monitoring activities by judges, for example, or even unmeasured language dimensions of the original text.

2. A Model of Judge Language Choice

This section presents the problem of analysing judge language choices on a general, theoretical level.

2.1 Setup

I consider the problem of a judge deciding what to write in a judicial opinion. I focus on the single-author case, although in many real-world contexts judges would decide in teams of judges, or with the help of clerks. The judge is indexed by j, with personal characteristics $X_j \in \mathbf{R}^{n_j}$ (e.g. political party, age). The judge takes the case k he works on, with characteristics $X_k \in \mathbf{R}^{n_k}$ (e.g. area of law, industrial sector), as given. That is consistent with the rule in many courts where cases are randomly assigned to judges, and judges cannot influence what cases they work on. The judge works in a court and legal environment l, with institutional characteristics $X_l \in \mathbf{R}^{n_k}$ (e.g. judge selection rule, mandatory retirement age), also taken as given. The concatenation of these variables can be written as $\boldsymbol{X}_{jkl} = (X_j, X_k, X_l)$.

The outcome of interest is a language choice $\boldsymbol{W}$, with the realized choice indexed as $\boldsymbol{W}_k$ or $\boldsymbol{W}_{jkl}$. The range of $\boldsymbol{W}$ could be quite general. It could be something simple like number of words written, or something subtle like the use of originalist arguments. Characterizing $\boldsymbol{W}$ is a complicated issue on its own. Another subtlety is that W can reflect information that a judge intended to communicate, or what was actually written, or what was interpreted by a reader. Those items might not be the same.

For now, I treat all of these variables as observed by the researcher. But later on, I will discuss the implications when some variables are not observed. Notationally, that will be indicated by O (for observed) and U (for unobserved), for example (X_k^O, X_k^U) for observed and unobserved aspects of case k.

The most general formulation of the judge's problem is to say that the judge chooses the opinion text $\boldsymbol{W}$ to maximize a utility function $u(\boldsymbol{W})$. If that function includes costs and/or time budget constraints, we can write observed language features as

$$\boldsymbol{W}_{jkl} = \boldsymbol{W}^*(\boldsymbol{X}_{jkl}) = \arg\max_{\boldsymbol{W}} u(\boldsymbol{W} \mid \boldsymbol{X}_{jkl})$$

We can make the problem more tractable and ensure an interior solution with some additional inoffensive assumptions. Let's say that the language choice is non-negative, $\boldsymbol{W} \in \mathbf{R}_+^{n_W}$, and $u(\cdot)$ is increasing and strictly concave in $\boldsymbol{W}$. We can then assume some time cost $T(\boldsymbol{W} \mid \boldsymbol{X}_{jkl})$, positive and increasing in $\boldsymbol{W}$. If we assume a positive, finite time budget $\overline{T}_{jl}$, and then we can write

$$\boldsymbol{W}_{jkl} = \boldsymbol{W}^*(\boldsymbol{X}_{jkl}) = \arg\max_{W} u(\boldsymbol{W} \mid \boldsymbol{X}_{jkl}).$$
$$\text{s.t. } T(\boldsymbol{W} \mid \boldsymbol{X}_{jkl}) \le \overline{T}_{jl}.$$

But judges can usually decide how much time they spend on cases (Ash and MacLeod 2015). They will spend more time on cases that they care about more—that is, the cases which can give more utility. So a better model would be

$$\boldsymbol{W}_{jkl} = \boldsymbol{W}^*(\boldsymbol{X}_{jkl}) = \arg\max_{W} u(\boldsymbol{W} \mid \boldsymbol{X}_{jkl}) - T(\boldsymbol{W} \mid \boldsymbol{X}_{jkl})$$

where $T(\cdot)$ is weakly convex in W. That again ensures an interior solution on W for some dimensions.

2.2 Language Choice Responses to Inputs

The selected language w_{jkl} satisfies the standard first-order conditions for this type of optimization problem. For further simplicity, assume that the time cost of writing is separable between the language choice and the case characteristics: $T(\boldsymbol{W} \mid \boldsymbol{X}_{jkl}) = T_W(\boldsymbol{W}) + T_X(\boldsymbol{X}_{jkl})$. Then, for each dimension of language w, we have

$$\frac{\partial u(\boldsymbol{W} \mid \boldsymbol{X}_{jkl})}{\partial W_w} = \frac{\partial T(W)}{\partial W_w}$$

If we further assume linear time costs, $T_W(\boldsymbol{W}) = \gamma_1 W_1 + \ldots + \gamma_{n_W} W_{n_w}$, with all γ_i strictly positive, we can write

$$\frac{\partial u(\boldsymbol{W} \mid \boldsymbol{X}_{jkl})}{\partial W_w} = \gamma_w$$

Under the assumptions so far, we can say that a language dimension w will decrease as the time cost γ_w increases. That could already be empirically relevant, as technological changes might affect writing costs. For example, if W_w is the number of previous cases cited, that might increase when the cost γ_w decreases with the introduction of legal search engines like WestLaw.

We cannot say much more without strong assumptions on the relevant functional forms. Let's make that leap. Now assume a log-linear functional form for $u(\cdot)$:

$$u(\boldsymbol{W} \mid \boldsymbol{X}_{jkl}) = \sum_x \sum_w \alpha_{xw} X_x \log(W_w)$$

that is, every dimension of the environmental inputs are potentially linearly related to the log of each language feature W_w. Then the First Order Conditions (FOC) for each language dimension w gives

$$\sum_x \frac{\alpha_{xw} X_x}{W_w} = \gamma_w$$

or

$$W_w^* = \frac{1}{\gamma_w} \sum_x \alpha_{xw} X_x$$

This expression tells us that a language choice on w could increase or decrease with each relevant input x, depending on the parameter α_{xw}, measuring the effect of input x on the marginal utility from language dimension w.

More specifically, we can start to analyse the effects of judge, case, and court characteristics on judge language choices. Let's take a single dimension of the inputs, i, and increase it by one. The effect on writing choices is given by

$$\frac{\partial W_w^*}{\partial X_x} = \frac{\alpha_{xw}}{\gamma_w} \tag{1}$$

That is the structural quantity estimated by well-identified regressions with language choices as the outcome and some judge, case, or environmental variable as the treatment. We will return to that problem in Section 4.1.

2.3 Consequences of Judge Language Choices

A second important set of questions are on the impacts of judge language choices. There could be many such outcomes, for example whether a decision is appealed by the parties, reversed on appeal, or cited by later judges. Those outcomes could also depend on the same case inputs discussed earlier. We can write $Y(\boldsymbol{W} \mid \boldsymbol{X}_{jkl})$. If we assume that Y

is not an argument in $u(\cdot)$, we can summarize the effect of changing a language dimension W_w on Y as the partial derivative,

$$\frac{\partial Y(W \mid \boldsymbol{X}_{jkl})}{\partial W_w}$$

In the linear models characterizing most empirical research designs, we might assume

$$Y(\boldsymbol{W},\boldsymbol{X}) = \beta_0 + \sum_x \beta_x X_x + \sum_w \beta_w W_w + \sum_x \sum_w \beta_{xw} X_x W_w \tag{2}$$

Then we would have

$$\frac{\partial Y(\boldsymbol{W} \mid \boldsymbol{X}_{jkl})}{\partial W_w} = \beta_w + \sum_x \beta_{xw} X_x$$

as the predicted effect of increasing the language dimension w by one unit for judge/case jkl. As with the determinants, whether regressions actually do capture this structural quantity requires strong empirical identification assumptions, which I discuss in Section 4.2.

An assumption worth additional discussion now is whether Y is an argument in $u(\cdot)$. That is, do judges care about the impacts of their writing choices? While many judge writing choices might be based only on a case at hand and the relevant law, it is clear that some, probably most, choices do depend on future impacts. At a minimum, judges care about whether a case is appealed or reversed. But they often care about many other impacts of their decisions, including the precedential effect on future judges (Posner 2008). So assuming that Y is excluded from $u(\cdot)$ is almost always unrealistic.

As an alternative, let the vector of potential impacts $\boldsymbol{Y} \in \mathrm{R}^{n_Y}$ be an argument in the judge utility function: $u(\boldsymbol{W} \mid \boldsymbol{X}_{jkl}, \boldsymbol{Y}(\boldsymbol{W}))$. For simplicity, assume that **Y** is a vector of outcomes that are linearly related to **X** and **W**, as above:

$$Y_y(\boldsymbol{W},\boldsymbol{X}) = \beta_{y0} + \sum_x \beta_{yx} X_{yx} + \sum_w \beta_{yw} W_w + \sum_x \sum_w \beta_{yxw} X_x W_w$$

Further, assume that judges attach a separable linear value to each Y_y, given by μ_y. Then, using the log-linear utility specification from above, we can write

$$\begin{aligned} \boldsymbol{W}^*(\boldsymbol{X}_{jkl}) &= \arg\max_{\boldsymbol{w}} \sum_x \sum_w \alpha_{xw} X_x \log(W_w) - \sum_w \gamma_w W_w + \sum_y \mu_y Y_y(\boldsymbol{W},\boldsymbol{X}) \\ &= \arg\max_{\boldsymbol{W}} \sum_x \sum_w \alpha_{xw} X_x \log(W_w) - \sum_w \gamma_w W_w \\ &\quad + \sum_y \mu_y \left(\beta_{y0} + \sum_x \beta_{yx} X_{yx} + \sum_w \beta_{yw} W_w + \sum_x \sum_w \beta_{yxw} X_x W_w \right) \end{aligned}$$

As above, the FOCs for each language dimension w give

$$\sum_x \frac{\alpha_{xw} X_x}{W_w} = \gamma_w - \mu_y \left(\beta_{yw} + \sum_x \beta_{yxw} X_x \right)$$

which simplifies to

$$W_w^* = \frac{\mu_y \beta_{yw}}{\gamma_w} + \frac{1}{\gamma_w} \sum_x (\alpha_{xw} + \mu_y \beta_{yxw}) X_x$$

Now, the estimated effect on writing choice w of a change in input variable x is given by

$$\frac{\partial W_w^*}{\partial X_x} = \frac{\alpha_{xw} + \mu_y \beta_{yxw}}{\gamma_w} \qquad (3)$$

This expression is comparable to Eq. (1) and gives the quantity estimated by well-identified regressions using an exogenous perturbation to X_x. As can be seen, (3) differs from (1) in the potential influence of the expected impacts of a language choice. Disentangling these structural components of empirical estimates is a major design challenge and not usually possible.

3. Measuring Judge Language Choices

In the abstract, we can think of 'judge language choice' as the cognitive and manual process of judicial opinion writing. We cannot usually observe this process directly, except in special circumstances like controlled lab experiments where at least the words typed (if not the process of thinking) can be recorded (e.g. Spamann et al. 2021). Hence, in observational studies, measurements of judge language choices must be constructed from the outputs of that process—judicial opinions.

To relate to the model notation, we don't observe W_k (for case k) directly. Instead, we observe some plain-text document(s) D_k. The measurement approaches that I discuss in this section can all be thought of as building a text feature extractor, or codebook function (Egami et al. 2022), $W(D)$, which transform unstructured, plain-text documents to more structured, interpretable choice vectors.

That is still quite abstract, however, as language is not a well-defined set of potential actions, as one might have in a consumer's choice of what available goods to buy on the market. That is, a judge has to broadly decide what facts, ideas, and arguments to commit to the page, in what order, and with what stylistic flourishes. Language choices have some constraints and costs, but they are also generative and arbitrarily complex. The set of measurable dimensions is infinite, so a paramount question for researchers is what dimensions to try to measure.

The language dimension of interest will depend on the substantive research question that a researcher is interested in. But that is not a trivial task, as it might be for more standard questions like measuring the direction of a ruling. Some dimensions of language that might be articulated might themselves be controversial or difficult to define. For example, is there an 'originalist' dimension of judge language choice? One might argue that this is a concept, rather than language.

Even when one is settled on a language choice in theory, there is a just as difficult problem of measuring it in practice. Most interesting dimensions of language are not directly measurable. The empirical literature analysing judicial opinion text has produced a number of creative, if imperfect, solutions to this problem.

There is a rich literature on measuring various dimensions of judge language. We review these different dimensions here. An important existing source on this topic is Frankenreiter and Livermore (2020), a recent review of computational methods in legal analysis. Frankenreiter and Livermore have a broader domain focus—on law, generally—while I focus on judges. For a more detailed discussion of text-analysis methodologies, see Livermore and Chau, this volume and the review chapter by Ash and Hansen (2023). This chapter will also leave out discussion of an important 'writing' choice, that of which legal authorities to cite; see Frankenreiter, this volume.

As we will see, there isn't a single approach to converting documents to data points. There isn't much consensus yet on which methods are preferred overall or in which circumstances. At the moment, the choice of measurement method will depend heavily on the research question—for example, influence of ideology, precedent, etc.

There are also no good answers to very difficult measurement problems. One problem is that opinion texts are written not just by judges but also by clerks (Sanders, this volume). Another problem is that the message intended by a judge might not be the same message that is understood by lawyers and other judges.

3.1 Writing Style

A first, conceptually simple decision that judges make in their opinions is how much to write. In a very early comparative study of judicial opinions, Goutal (1976) notes that '[a] Common Law case is sometimes forty or eighty pages long; a fifteen-line French case is nothing unusual' (p. 56). Goutal also remarks how American opinions are much shorter than British opinions.

More recently, computational approaches have put such comparisons on a more statistical footing. Black and Spriggs (2008), for example, analyse the length of US Supreme Court opinions. Ash and MacLeod (2015) use opinion length as a measure of judge effort. A longer opinion is a rough proxy for the amount of time that a judge puts into an opinion, so it could be a sign that they care more about the issue (see also Leonard and Ross 2016).

Beyond the volume of text, there are other aspects of writing on which judges decide. These include word and sentence length, for example, or combined readability scores that assess overall text sophistication (Law and Zaring 2009; Goelzhauser and Cann 2014; Whalen 2015; Feldman 2019; Potter 2019). Owens and Wedeking (2011) use a set of linguistic indicators for cognitive complexity to compare Supreme Court justices. Along these lines, Friedrich, Luzzatto, and Ash (2020) compute the entropy of the frequency distribution across words in a document, to proxy for the complexity or diversity of language used.

Concerning word choice, there are a number of judge writing decisions that are more about the style of writing, rather than the content. For example, Carlson, Livermore, and Rockmore (2015) analyse the frequency distribution over function words (e.g. 'such', 'as') as a measurement of judge style, to understand the role of clerks at the court (see also Wahlbeck, Spriggs, and Sigelman 2002; Choi and Gulati 2004; Frankenreiter 2019). These stylometric signatures can be used to de-anonymize judges (Rosenthal and Yoon 2011; Li et al. 2012).

A handful of papers have analysed judge writing style along some more interpretable dimensions, such as sentiment. Hinkle et al. (2012) study the use of hedging and intensifying language in opinions by district court judges. Carlson, Livermore, and Rockmore (2015) document an increase in negatively toned language in the US Supreme Court over time. Sternberg (2018) produces measures of vagueness in German and French court opinions using word embeddings, finding that vague language is used strategically by courts in response to public support and support by the legislature.

3.2 Legal Topics and Reasoning

The next choice for a judge writing an opinion is what are the broad topics or legal matters to focus on. For example, does a judge focus on the facts or the law? This decision could be important because, *inter alia*, legal issues are easier to appeal than factual ones. Natural language processing (NLP) papers on detecting fact sections include Smith (2014) and Cao, Ash, and Chen (2020).

An early cross-country comparative study of patterns of legal reasoning is provided in Goutal (1976). Through a close reading of opinions in the United States, the United Kingdom, and France, Goutal identifies a number of persistent qualitative differences. According to the close reading, French and common law judges differ in their use of deduction, induction, analogy, reasoning by example, syllogism, and reasoning by contradiction.

More general measures of legal reasoning have taken automated approaches to detecting legal issues or legal topics in written opinions. Some early and later practical work uses pattern matching or text classifiers to identify a pre-specified set of topics (Brüninghaus and Ashley 1997; Daniels and Rissland 1997; Thompson 2001; Gonçalves and Quaresma 2005; Rice 2014). A more recent line of literature learns topics inductively from the corpus using unsupervised topic models. For example, Macey and Mitts (2014) use a topic model to analyse reasoning in corporate law cases. More general descriptive explorations of topic coverage include Rice (2017), Carlson, Livermore, and Rockmore (2020), and Rice (2019).

A smaller set of papers has worked on distinguishing different types of reasoning by judges. For example, Choi (2020) shows how much judges use different modes of statutory interpretation in dealing with tax cases. Mainali et al. (2020) use a classifier to distinguish deontological from consequentialist reasoning in legal text.

3.3 Document Similarity

Another strand of literature uses document similarity to analyse the sources of judicial language. Text algorithms can be used to detect shared language or shared sequences across judicial opinions. For example, some papers track the borrowing of language between judicial opinions (Corley 2008; Corley, Collins Jr, and Calvin 2011; Li et al. 2023), showing that judges borrow from party briefs, from lower court cases, and from higher court cases. Another set of papers use style comparisons to assess whether clerks wrote an opinion rather than the judge (Wahlbeck, Spriggs, and Sigelman 2002; Choi and Gulati 2004; Carlson, Livermore, and Rockmore 2015; Frankenreiter 2019).

One unusual entry in this literature, Livermore, Riddell, and Rockmore (2017), compares Supreme Court opinions to other types of text to consider its similarity to law versus other genres. Chen, Parthasarathy, and Verma (2018) combine the citation network with shared n-grams to extract persuasive 'meme' phrases that judges tend to borrow when citing a case. These results give insight into what ideas judges are most receptive to.

3.4 Political and Social Attitudes

A set of papers in law, economics, and political science have tried to use text to analyse politics and other attitudes in judicial opinion text (Bonica and Sen 2021; Epstein, Martin, and Quinn, this volume). An early work on political features of opinions is Evans et al. (2007). Lauderdale and Clark (2014) combine both text features and voting on the US Supreme Court to rank judges by their ideology. Dumas (2019) uses a machine learning model to predict political affiliation of judges based on the language in judicial opinions. Hausladen, Schubert, and Ash (2020) use a supervised learning approach to detect language associated with more conservative, versus more liberal, rulings in US Circuit Court decisions.

Ash, Chen, and Ornaghi (2024) provide a method, based on word embeddings, to measure gender attitudes among US Circuit judges. A related descriptive paper by Rice, Rhodes, and Nteta (2019) uses word embeddings to explore racial bias in judicial language. Ash, Chen, and Galletta (2022) provide a text-analysis method for measuring expressed judge sentiment toward a broader range of social groups. Other work using sentiment analysis includes Carlson, Livermore, and Rockmore (2015), Busch and Pelc (2019), and Rice and Zorn (2021). Klingenstein, Hitchcock, and DeDeo (2014) explore the attitudes of judges toward violence in an archive of London criminal cases dating back to the eighteenth century.

In the realm of policy preferences, Rockmore et al. (2018) explore how constitutional commitments vary over time and across countries. Ash, Chen, and Naidu (2020) use word embeddings to construct a measure of economics reasoning in judicial opinions.

3.5 Unexamined Aspects of Judge Language Choice

In the future, it could be interesting to explore further aspects of judge language choices that have not yet been studied. From a comparative perspective, one basic choice that has not been analysed is the *specific language* used. In Switzerland, for example, judges could use German, French, or Italian. That language choice could have both legal and political implications.

As another example, when and how do judges tell stories? Narratives are the target of a rich literature and the relevance of narratives feels self-evident. Yet there is little empirical social science evidence on what drives the narratives used by judges and what are their subsequent impacts (e.g. Brooks and Gewirtz 1996; Posner 1997, 2009; Shiller 2017).

Further, it could be worthwhile to try to understand the mental model—the worldview—instantiated by judge writings. This may be achievable by NLP technologies in information extraction, which read through corpora and extract entity-verb pairs. For example, Ash et al. (2020) extract these pairs to measure obligations and entitlements for workers and firms in labour union contracts. A more sophisticated version of this approach, from Ash, Gauthier, and Widmer (2024), identifies agents and patients, and the verbs connecting them.

4. Empirical Analysis of Judge Language Choices

The papers described in the previous section can be divided up into four groups. First, there are methods papers that try to measure a judge language choice, provide summary statistics, and sometimes validate it. Second, there are descriptive papers that show relationships between judge languages and other variables, such as judge identity characteristics, case type, or changes over time, but without making any strong causal interpretation. Almost all the papers fit into these first two categories. The third (less frequent) type of paper seeks to document causal determinants of language. Fourth (and least frequently), there are papers seeking to document causal consequences of language. From a social science perspective, convincing causal evidence is the most difficult to produce, but also the most valuable. That is the focus of this section.

4.1 Determinants of Judge Language Choices

There are many interesting open questions to ask about what drives judge language choices. Those could include changes in judge characteristics X_j, case characteristics X_k, and the legal or institutional environment X_l. For example, does judge gender influence (part of X_j) his or her writing style? Or does the gender of the judge in the lower court (part of X_k). Or is there an effect on how judges are selected or retained (part of X_l)?

There are relatively few papers addressing such questions with causal answers. Differences between judges of different political parties, or differences over time, are purely descriptive. Ash, Chen, and Ornaghi (2024) provide several analyses on the determinants of their measure of gender slant—which is a measure of the use of traditional gender stereotypes. Intuitively, women judges use fewer stereotypes, as do judges from later cohorts. Both of those comparisons are descriptive, however, as gender and age are not exogenously assigned.

There are a few examples of causal papers looking at the determinants. As mentioned, Hinkle et al. (2012) look at the use of hedging and intensifying language in opinions by district court judges. They show that such language depending on how their own ideology compares with that of judges at the courts of appeals.

Ash, Chen, and Ornaghi (2024) provide one causal analysis for the determinants of gender attitudes, looking at the effect of having more daughters, relative to sons. Conditional on the number of children, the number of daughters is randomly assigned. They show that having more daughters causally reduces the use of gender stereotypes.

Ash, Chen, and Naidu (2020) analyse a potent source of policy ideas in the US judiciary—law and economics—and in particular the impact of the Manne Program—a popular, controversial economics training course for federal judges operating in the late twentieth century. They show that the Manne Program increased the use of economics reasoning by attending judges. This change in reasoning brings changes in decision-making, such as more conservative decisions on regulatory appeals and, perhaps more surprisingly, harsher criminal sentencing by district judges.

The previous empirical work on judges is somewhat limited in scope, given the demanding institutional requirements to make reasonable causal inferences on the determinants of judge language choices. For example, random assignment of cases to judges is needed for all these papers to work. If judges could influence the set of cases they work on, then differences in the observed language could be due to selection of judge types to case types, rather than the judge's choices over what to write.

With the assumption on random assignment of cases, that can be verified institutionally and statistically. But other assumptions cannot be verified easily or at all. For example, the text written in an opinion is not just the product of a judge's choices. Opinion drafting is often delegated to clerks, for example. And there could also be interactions between judges that is not observed by the researcher.

A final empirical problem comes from how text is measured. For example, consider that a researcher measures economics reasoning and shows that it increases after an economics course. It could be that the course had no effect on economics reasoning, but rather had an effect on some other language dimension that is correlated with economics reasoning, such as economics style, which the measure picks up. That is a very difficult problem without an easy answer.

Beyond these empirical challenges, most questions about the determinants of judge language choices are still unanswered. Language choices could be interesting outcomes for other issues explored in this volume, including legal traditions (see Garoupa, this volume), peer effects (Ostberg and Wetstein, this volume), elections (Burnham and Nelson, this volume), tenure/retirement rules (Perez-Linan and Castagnola, this volume), clerks (Sanders, this volume), partisan ideology (Spill and Waltenburg, this volume), personal motivations (Epstein and Knight, this volume), and the introduction of artificial intelligence (see Niblett, this volume). While there are established empirical methods for these types of questions, those are often not available in most empirical contexts. And there are many other research questions for which natural experiments are not available.

4.2 Consequences of Judge Language Choices

Another interesting set of empirical questions are those on the effects of judge language choices. It is clear that judge language choices—as opposed to the direction of the ruling—have some additional legal or policy impact. Opinions are legal precedent, and lawyers and judges invest a lot of time and effort into shaping the language of opinions. Estimating those effects causally is extremely difficult.

Take the example from Ash, Chen, and Ornaghi (2024) on the effects of judge language choices about gender. That paper provides a measure of gender attitudes by judges based on the use of gender stereotypes, measured by word embedding associations. In the empirical analysis, the paper shows that judges who use more gender stereotypes tend to make decisions against women's rights and tend to reverse decisions by female colleagues.

One way of framing this result is that the judge language had an impact on decisions and treatment of colleagues. But that is arguably the wrong framing, as the gender-stereotyped language is more a measure of personal attitudes, rather than having an effect itself. Many potential empirical analyses of text will have this limitation. And it could be that the personal characteristic that the text-based measurement is proxying for—such as gender attitudes—is confounded with other personal characteristics that are driving an outcome, for example, general conservatism in the case of gender attitudes.

A more direct example of the effect of language on outcomes is the paper by Ash, Galletta, and Chen (2022), who measure expressed judge sentiment in judicial opinions. That paper uses random assignment of judges, who differ in their average sentiment, to instrument for the realized level of sentiment in the written opinions. They find that cases with exogenously more positive sentiment are more likely to be reversed but also more likely to be cited by future judges.

The strong causal assumption in papers like this one is that judges with a given language choice (e.g. higher sentiment) affect the outcome (e.g. probability that an opinion is appealed or cited) only through the measured language dimension. That is unrealistic, as judges with different language choices in their opinions are different in many other ways, such as how they tend to rule in a case, which would affect relevant outcomes like appeal. Besides the way they rule, there could be confounding variables with a given language choice that are also composed of language. When looking at sentiment, for example, it could be that partisan language, or discussing crimes, is correlated and driving the observed outcome.

These problems are quite fundamental. In the context of natural experiments, it could be they cannot be solved. Good evidence on the causal effects of language choices would be best achieved with controlled lab or field experiments. Ideally, one could randomize whether some parts of an opinion were published, or whether different versions of the opinion's reasoning were published. On this point, controlled experiments like Spamann et al. (2021), which show what information judges use in a hypothetical case, are extremely valuable and productive. Those approaches should be further explored as feasible (Engel, this volume).

5. Conclusion

In the case of the judiciary, language is important because it becomes legal precedent and therefore can have real-world policy consequences. Measuring judge language choice is therefore scientifically valuable, along with the second steps of empirically analysing its causal determinants and impacts. However, the existing tools for measuring and empirically identifying language as treatment or outcome are still quite limited, and there are important theoretical challenges as well (Cope, this volume). Relatively little is known about this socially important yet empirically elusive phenomenon.

There are a number of promising future directions and opportunities in the analysis of judge language choices. First, the NLP literature has recently been developing sophisticated deep learning-based tools that extract context-sensitive information from documents. These models allow each word to interact with each other even at a distance (Ash and Hansen 2023), giving much more subtle measures of content and intent. They can solve natural language inference tasks, and for example detect whether sentences within or across documents agree or disagree. At the level of broader corpora, we can now perform subtle comparisons of questions and claims (Stammbach and Ash 2020; Stammbach, Zhang, and Ash 2023).

From a comparative law perspective, there is an especially notable gap in terms of data (Engst and Gschwend, this volume; Staton, this volume). In the recent literature there are few papers outside of the United States, besides a few papers on the European Court of Human Rights (e.g. Aletras et al. 2016). I hope that is addressed as new corpora become available and the research community expands globally.

Finally, scholarship should not just be limited to analysis of *written* language in judicial opinions. An important feature of judging involves verbal communication, for example in hearings (Krehbiel, this volume). There is some early exciting work on audio and other non-text communication. For example, Patton and Smith (2017) analyse interruptions of attorneys by judges, and show gender bias there. Dietrich, Enos, and Sen (2019) show that a measure of emotionality in judge speech audio predicts their votes. Future work could look at other aspects of communication, such as facial expressions and gestures.

References

Aletras, Nikolaos, Dimitrios Tsarapatsanis, Daniel Preoţiuc-Pietro, and Vasileios Lampos. 2016. 'Predicting Judicial Decisions of the European Court of Human Rights: A Natural Language Processing Perspective'. *PeerJ Computer Science* 2 (10): e93. https://doi.org/10.7717/peerj-cs.93.

Ash, Elliott, Daniel Chen, and Suresh Naidu. 2020. 'Ideas Have Consequences: The Impact of Law and Economics on American Justice'. *Center for Law & Economics Working Paper Series 4*. https://www.research-collection.ethz.ch/handle/20.500.11850/376884

Ash, Elliott, Daniel Chen, and Arianna Ornaghi. 2024. 'Gender Attitudes in the Judiciary: Evidence from US Circuit Courts'. *American Economic Journal: Applied Economics* 16 (1): 314–50.

Ash, Elliott, Daniel Chen, and Sergio Galletta. 2022. 'Measuring Judicial Sentiment: Methods and Application to US Circuit Courts'. *Economica* 89 (354): 362–76.

Ash, Elliott, Germain Gauthier, and Philine Widmer. 2024. "Relatio: Text semantics capture political and economic narratives." *Political Analysis* 32 (1): 115–32.

Ash, Elliott, and Stephen Hansen. 2023. 'Text Algorithms in Economics'. *Annual Review of Economics* 15: 659–88.

Ash, Elliott, Jeff Jacobs, Bentley MacLeod, Suresh Naidu, and Dominik Stammbach. 2020. 'Unsupervised Extraction of Workplace Rights and Duties from Collective Bargaining Agreements'. In *2nd International Workshop on Mining and Learning in the Legal Domain (MLLD-2020)(virtual)*, 766–74.

Ash, Elliott, and W. Bentley MacLeod. 2015. 'Intrinsic Motivation in Public Service: Theory and Evidence from State Supreme Courts'. *Journal of Law and Economics* 58 (4): 863–913.

Black, Ryan C., and James F. Spriggs. 2008. 'An Empirical Analysis of the Length of US Supreme Court Opinions'. *Houston Law Review* 45: 621.

Bonica, Adam, and Maya Sen. 2021. 'Estimating Judicial Ideology'. *Journal of Economic Perspectives* 35 (1): 97–118.

Brooks, Peter, and Paul Gewirtz. 1996. *Law's Stories: Narrative and Rhetoric in the Law*. New Haven: Yale University Press.

Brüninghaus, Stefanie, and Kevin D. Ashley. 1997. 'Using Machine Learning for Assigning Indices to Textual Cases'. In *International Conference on Case-Based Reasoning*, 303–14. Berlin Heidelberg: Springer.

Busch, Marc L., and Krzysztof J. Pelc. 2019. 'Words Matter: How WTO Rulings Handle Controversy'. *International Studies Quarterly* 63 (3): 464–76.

Cao, Yu, Elliott Ash, and Daniel Chen. 2020. 'Automated Fact-Value Distinction in Court Opinions'. *European Journal of Law and Economics* 50: 451–67. https://doi.org/10.2139/ssrn.3202438.

Carlson, Keith, Michael A. Livermore, and Daniel Rockmore. 2015. 'A Quantitative Analysis of Writing Style on the US Supreme Court'. *Washington University Law Review* 93 (6): 1461.

Carlson, Keith, Michael A. Livermore, and Daniel N. Rockmore. 2020. 'The Problem of Data Bias in the Pool of Published US Appellate Court Opinions'. *Journal of Empirical Legal Studies* 17 (2): 224–61.

Chen, Daniel L., Adithya Parthasarathy, and Shivam Verma. 2018. 'The Genealogy of Ideology: Identifying Persuasive Memes and Predicting Agreement in the U.S. Courts of Appeals'. Proceedings of the ACM Conference on AI and the Law.

Choi, Jonathan H. 2020. 'An Empirical Study of Statutory Interpretation in Tax Law'. *New York University Law Review* 95: 363.

Choi, Stephen J., and G. Mitu Gulati. 2004. 'Which Judges Write Their Opinions (and Should We Care)'. *Florida State University Law Review* 32: 1077.

Corley, Pamela C. 2008. 'The Supreme Court and Opinion Content: The Influence of Parties' Briefs'. *Political Research Quarterly* 61 (3): 468–78.

Corley, Pamela C., Paul M Collins Jr, and Bryan Calvin. 2011. 'Lower Court Influence on US Supreme Court Opinion Content'. *Journal of Politics* 73 (1): 31–44.

Daniels, Jody J., and Edwina L. Rissland. 1997. 'Finding Legally Relevant Passages in Case Opinions'. In *Proceedings of the 6th International Conference on Artificial Intelligence and Law*, 39–46.

Dietrich, Bryce J., Ryan D. Enos, and Maya Sen. 2019. 'Emotional Arousal Predicts Voting on the U.S. Supreme Court'. *Political Analysis* 27 (2): 237–43. https://doi.org/10.1017/pan.2018.47.

Dumas, M. 2019. 'Detecting Ideology in Judicial Language'. In *Law as Data: Computation, Text, and the Future of Legal Analysis*, edited by Michael Livermore and Dan Rockmore, 383–405. Santa Fe: Santa Fe Institute Press.

Egami, Naoki, Christian J. Fong, Justin Grimmer, Margaret E. Roberts, and Brandon M. Stewart. 2022. 'How to Make Causal Inferences Using Texts'. *Science Advances* 8 (42): eabg2652.

Evans, Michael, Wayne McIntosh, Jimmy Lin, and Cynthia Cates. 2007. 'Recounting the Courts? Applying Automated Content Analysis to Enhance Empirical Legal Research'. *Journal of Empirical Legal Studies* 4 (4): 1007–39.

Feldman, Adam. 2019. 'Opinion Clarity in State and Federal Courts'. In *Law as Data: Computation, Text, and the Future of Legal Analysis*, edited by Michael Livermore and Dan Rockmore, 407–30. Santa Fe: Santa Fe Institute Press.

Frankenreiter, Jens. 2019. 'Writing Style and Legal Traditions'. In *Law as Data: Computation, Text, and the Future of Legal Analysis*, edited by Michael Livermore and Dan Rockmore, 153–90. Santa Fe: Santa Fe Institute Press.

Frankenreiter, Jens, and Michael A. Livermore. 2020. 'Computational Methods in Legal Analysis'. *Annual Review of Law and Social Science* 16: 39–57.

Friedrich, Roland, Mauro Luzzatto, and Elliott Ash. 2020. 'Entropy in Legal Language'. In *2nd Workshop on Natural Legal Language Processing (NLLP, collocated with KDD 2020)*. Proceedings of the Natural Legal Language Processing Workshop 2020 co-located with the

26th ACM SIGKDD International Conference on Knowledge Discovery & Data Mining (KDD 2020). Vol. 2645. CEUR-WS, 2020.

Goelzhauser, Greg, and Damon M. Cann. 2014. 'Judicial Independence and Opinion Clarity on State Supreme Courts'. *State Politics & Policy Quarterly* 14 (2): 123–41.

Gonçalves, Teresa, and Paulo Quaresma. 2005. 'Is Linguistic Information Relevant for the Classification of Legal Texts?' In *Proceedings of the 10th International Conference on Artificial Intelligence and Law*, June 6, 168–76.

Goutal, Jean Louis. 1976. 'Characteristics of Judicial Style in France, Britain and the USA'. *American Journal of Comparative Law* 24: 43.

Hausladen, Carina I., Marcel H. Schubert, and Elliott Ash. 2020. 'Text Classification of Ideological Direction in Judicial Opinions'. *International Review of Law and Economics*, 62, 105903.

Hinkle, Rachael K., Andrew D. Martin, Jonathan David Shaub, and Emerson H. Tiller. 2012. 'A Positive Theory and Empirical Analysis of Strategic Word Choice in District Court Opinions'. *Journal of Legal Analysis* 4 (2): 407–44.

Klingenstein, Sara, Tim Hitchcock, and Simon DeDeo. 2014. 'The Civilizing Process in London's Old Bailey'. *Proceedings of the National Academy of Sciences of the United States of America* 111 (26): 9419–24.

Lauderdale, Benjamin, and Tom S. Clark. 2014. 'Scaling Politically Meaningful Dimensions Using Texts and Votes'. *American Journal of Political Science* 58 (3): 754–71.

Law, David S., and David Zaring. 2009. 'Law Versus Ideology: The Supreme Court and the Use of Legislative History'. *William & Mary Law Review* 51: 1653.

Leonard, Meghan E., and Joseph V. Ross. 2016. 'Understanding the Length of State Supreme Court Opinions'. *American Politics Research* 44 (4): 710–33.

Li, William, Pablo Azar, David Larochelle, and Phil Hill. 2012. 'Using Algorithmic Attribution Techniques to Determine Authorship in Unsigned Judicial Opinions'. *Stanford Technology Law Review* 16: 503.

Li, Zhiyu, Benjamin Minhao Chen, David Cai, and Elliott Ash. 2023. "Detecting the influence of the Chinese guiding cases: a text reuse approach." *Artificial Intelligence and Law*, pp. 1–24.

Livermore, Michael A., Allen B. Riddell, and Daniel N. Rockmore. 2017. 'The Supreme Court and the Judicial Genre'. *Arizona Law Review* 59: 837.

Macey, Jonathan R., and Joshua Mitts. 2014. 'Finding order in the morass: The Three Justifications for Piercing the Corporate Veil'. *Cornell Law Review* 100: 99.

Mainali, Nischal, Liam Meier, Elliott Ash, and Daniel Chen. 2020. 'Automated Classification of Modes of Moral Reasoning in Judicial Decisions'. In *Computational Legal Studies*, edited by Ryan Wahlenm, 77–94. Cheltenham: Edward Elgar Publishing.

Owens, Ryan J., and Justin P. Wedeking. 2011. 'Justices and Legal Clarity: Analyzing the Complexity of US Supreme Court Opinions'. *Law & Society Review* 45 (4): 1027–61.

Patton, Dana, and Joseph L. Smith. 2017. 'Lawyer, Interrupted: Gender Bias in Oral Arguments at the US Supreme Court'. *Journal of Law and Courts* 5 (2): 337–61.

Posner, Richard. 2008. *How Judges Think*. Cambridge: Harvard University Press.

Posner, Richard A. 1995. 'Judges' Writing Styles (and Do They Matter?)'. *The University of Chicago Law Review* 62 (4): 1421–49.

Posner, Richard A. 1997. 'Legal Narratology'[Review of Law's Stories: Narrative and Rhetoric in the Law, by P. Brooks & P. Gewirtz]. *The University of Chicago Law Review 64* (2): 737–47.

Posner, Richard A. 2009. *Law and Literature*. Cambridge: Harvard University Press.

Potter, Rachel Augustine. 2019. 'Bending the Rules: Procedural politicking in the bureaucracy'. Chicago: University of Chicago Press.

Rice, Douglas. 2014. 'The Impact of Supreme Court Activity on the Judicial Agenda'. *Law & Society Review* 48 (1): 63–90.

Rice, Douglas. 2019. 'Measuring the Issue Content of Supreme Court Opinions'. *Journal of Law and Courts* 7 (1): 107–27.

Rice, Douglas R. 2017. 'Issue Divisions and US Supreme Court Decision Making'. *The Journal of Politics* 79 (1): 210–22.

Rice, Douglas R., and Christopher Zorn. 2021. 'Corpus-Based Dictionaries for Sentiment Analysis of Specialized Vocabularies'. *Political Science Research and Methods* 9 (1): 20–35.

Rice, Douglas, Jesse H. Rhodes, and Tatishe Nteta. 2019. 'Racial Bias in Legal Language'. *Research & Politics* 6 (2): 2053168019848930.

Rockmore, Daniel N., Chen Fang, Nicholas J. Foti, Tom Ginsburg, and David C. Krakauer. 2018. 'The Cultural Evolution of National Constitutions'. *Journal of the Association for Information Science and Technology* 69 (3): 483–94.

Rosenthal, Jeffrey S., and Albert H. Yoon. 2011. 'Detecting Multiple Authorship of United States Supreme Court Legal Decisions Using Function Words'. *The Annals of Applied Statistics* 5 (1): 283–308.

Shiller, Robert J. 2017. 'Narrative Economics'. *American Economic Review* 107 (4): 967–1004.

Smith, Joseph L. 2014. 'Law, Fact, and the Threat of Reversal from Above'. *American Politics Research* 42 (2): 226–56.

Spamann, Holger, Lars Klöhn, Christophe Jamin, Vikramaditya Khanna, John Zhuang Liu, Pavan Mamidi, Alexander Morell, and Ivan Reidel. 2021. 'Judges in the Lab: No Precedent Effects, No Common/Civil Law Differences'. *Journal of Legal Analysis* 13 (1): 110–26.

Stammbach, Dominik, and Elliott Ash. 2020. 'E-FEVER: Explanations and Summaries for Automated Fact Checking'. In *Proceedings of the 2020 Truth and Trust Online Conference (TTO 2020)*, 32–43.

Stammbach, Dominik, Boya Zhang, and Elliott Ash. 2023. 'The Choice of Textual Knowledge Base in Automated Claim Checking'. *ACM Journal of Data and Information Quality* 15 (1): 1–22.

Sternberg, Sebastian. 2018. 'Why Do Courts Craft Vague Decisions? Evidence from a Comparative Study of Court Rulings in Germany and France Using Quantitative Text Analysis'. University of Mannheim, Working Paper. https://Sebastiansternberg.Github.Io/Pdf/Sternberg_Value_of_Vagueness_CELSE18.Pdf.

Thompson, Paul. 2001. 'Automatic Categorization of Case Law'. In *Proceedings of the 8th International Conference on Artificial Intelligence and Law*, 70–77.

Wahlbeck, Paul J., James F. Spriggs, and Lee Sigelman. 2002. 'Ghostwriters on the Court? A Stylistic Analysis of US Supreme Court Opinion Drafts'. *American Politics Research* 30 (2): 166–92.

Whalen, Ryan. 2015. 'Judicial Gobbledygook: The Readability of Supreme Court Writing'. *Yale Law Journal Forum* 125: 200.

PART VII

RELATIONS WITHIN, BETWEEN, AND AMONG COURTS

CHAPTER 28

LEADERSHIP IN COURTS

HENRIK LITLERÉ BENTSEN AND JON KÅRE SKIPLE

1. Introduction

The significance of high court leaders throughout the world is often emphasized in scholarly literature. The prime example is the position of Chief Justice in the United States, which is widely recognized by scholars and observers as immensely important in determining the direction of the law and by extension public policy (e.g. Cross and Lindquist 2006; Danelski and Ward 2016). But the importance of court leadership is not only recognized as important in established democracies. In newly established constitutional regimes, court leaders have been described as guardians of the constitution personified and as central figures in the furthering and maintaining of judicial legitimacy (e.g. Scheppele 2006).

When it comes to leadership of courts, chief justices and court presidents often come to mind. This is only natural as they are handed the responsibility of representing the court in the broader political system and in public. However, while chief justices and court presidents are formal leaders of courts, all members of a court may be considered, in a broader sense, to be judicial leaders. Associate court justices, too, hold a prominent public position at the top of the judicial system. In many courts, including both apex courts and lower courts, associate justices hold important leadership responsibilities, such as authoring the majority opinion or serving in panels as a presiding justice with the responsibility of managing the processing of the case. This chapter therefore takes a broad perspective on leadership in the courts.

In this chapter, we provide an overview of the current state of judicial behaviour literature on the leadership of courts. We first discuss the various theoretical perspectives used to study court leadership and provide an overview of the courts and countries that have been studied. Following this, we outline the main findings and debates in extant literature, emphasizing those that are covered in comparative literature. These include the influence of court leaders on consensus formation, their powers as 'first among equals' on the bench, the balancing act of strategically pursuing personal policy goals without sacrificing organizational needs, collegial relations, or public discontent and institutional legitimacy, and the role of powerful yet vulnerable court leaders in hybrid regimes. Finally, we conclude by summarizing the main insights drawn from the literature and make suggestions for future research.

2. Theoretical Foundations: Judicial Leadership from the Perspective of Judicial Behaviour Theory

Studies of court leadership from the perspective of judicial behaviour originated in the United States, more specifically on the Chief Justice of the US Supreme Court. Traditionally, the chief justice was studied in judicial biographies focusing on the man and not necessarily the office (Danelski and Ward 2016, 4). While these studies provided insights into the workings and personalities of the individual chief justices and the functioning of the Supreme Court under their leadership, they were the results of historical methods and not the systematic application of social science methods. However, with the emergence of the field of judicial politics, which can be attributed to the Behavioural revolution of the 1960s and the advancements in quantitative and statistical methodologies, scholars shifted their attention towards scrutinizing the voting patterns exhibited by individual justices and investigating the underlying processes that influenced the formulation of judicial decisions.

2.1 Describing Leadership Styles

Using social psychology concepts of leadership, Danelski was the first political scientist to study how chief justices carry out or fail to fulfil their duties of marshalling the court (Danelski and Ward 2016). Danelski's early work focused on the importance of the managerial and administrative role of the chief justice. In his research on what he called the 'task' and 'social' leadership responsibilities of the chief justice, Danelski made the case that to ensure the Court's orderly operation, chief justices must simultaneously ensure that the court is efficiently administered and maintain the social and personal ties between the justices.

While the concepts of task and social leadership contain overlapping elements, the primary difference between the two leadership styles is that task leaders concentrate on the court's decisional process while social leaders focus on maintaining social cohesion and a collegial working environment. Successful task leaders may become the Court's leading intellectual voices.[1] These justices are some of the most effective members when it comes to opinion writing, frequently win internal arguments in conferences, and are generally well-esteemed by their colleagues. Social leaders, on the other hand, are more concerned with their co-workers' emotional needs and attempt to create a supportive environment so that the Court can function as a unified and effective team.

Danelski's concepts (and similar ones) have often been used in more descriptive analyses to identify which judges emerge as either task or social leaders. For example, it has been assumed that a social leader will to a greater extent produce unanimity as a presiding justice or in instances where they write the leading judgment, while a task leader will perhaps more frequently write dissents or concurrences in order to have their views thoroughly presented (Hunter and Rackley 2018). Others also contend that successful task leaders will more often find themselves in the majority (Ostberg et al. 2004). By examining the extent to which judges either produce unanimity or dissents, or find themselves in the majority or not, one may be able to identify successful task or social leaders in the courts.

2.2 Explaining Leadership Behaviour

While the study of leadership roles has benefited greatly from Danelski's concepts of task and social leadership, other models of judicial behaviour have informed extant research aimed at explaining leadership behaviour. According to the simplest (i.e. legal) model, supreme courts can be thought of as a judicial body where judges decide cases by applying fair and impartial standards of law. Alternative judicial behaviour theories, however, argue that a variety of extra-legal considerations, including the justices' personal backgrounds and policy preferences, have an impact on decisional outcomes (e.g. Baum 1997; see also Solberg and Waltenburg, this volume, and Basabe-Serrano, this volume). The most famous of these is the attitudinal model, which claims that judges have policy preferences, and that these policy preferences are sincerely reflected in their judgments (Segal and Spaeth 2002).

In addition, strategic factors may influence how justices pursue the goals of legal policy (see Dothan, this volume). According to the strategic model, justices make strategic decisions to write majority opinions that result in a legal doctrine that is more compatible with their preferred alternatives. As such, a strategic judge may occasionally render decisions that deviate from her personal preference with the intention of achieving a specific outcome in a given case (e.g. Epstein and Knight 1998; Maltzman et al. 2000). For instance, if a judge perceives that a sincere decision would fail to obtain majority support from fellow judges, they may opt to compromise and endorse an alternative decision that is not their primary choice but may result in an acceptable judgment.

Similarly, a strategic court may issue judgments that do not align with the collective interests of the court itself, aiming to secure an outcome that is advantageous considering potential interactions with other political bodies. For example, a strategic court may choose not to deliver a particular judgment due to apprehensions that it could be overturned by the parliament, resulting in an unfavourable outcome for the court. Other examples include the necessity to avoid congressional court curbing and to maintain public support (e.g. Clark 2009; Ura and Wohlfarth 2010; Casillas et al. 2011).

The role of the chief justice has primarily been examined within this final theoretical framework, emphasizing strategic considerations that arise under collegial courts. Political scientists have focused on the ways the chief justice may strategically utilize the special powers of his position to influence the development of legal policy, particularly his capacity to designate authorship for the Court's opinion when he votes with the majority on the merits (e.g. Maltzman et al. 2000; Johnson et al. 2005). Simply put, this literature views the chief as a regular justice with exceptional institutional prerogatives. This means that, like the other justices, the chief is driven by a mix of his personal preferences and taste in legal reasoning, but also has tools at his disposal to further those interests that other justices do not typically have (e.g. Ura and Flink 2016).

However, while court leaders may use the tools at their disposal to advance personal policy goals, systematic empirical investigations of the chief justice's behaviour also show that the chief's power to affect legal policy is 'conditioned' and 'limited ... by the prevailing political and institutional background of the Court' (Maltzman et al. 2000, 55). Historical evidence suggests that chief justices play a special role in the Court's ongoing efforts to establish, promote, and maintain judicial independence. Chief justices may thus utilize their formal and unofficial authority to make decisions that are driven by concerns about the legitimacy and institutional integrity of the court rather than by considerations of public policy or the law (e.g. Ura and Flink 2016).

Accordingly, while strategic considerations and institutional norms may be seen as constraints on judicial leadership, it might be more appropriate to see them as distinct goals that are of particular importance to leaders of courts (e.g. Baum 1997; see also Morell, this volume). As we will see in section 5 of this chapter, whether and how these goals influence court leaders have been the focus of several studies, ranging from the empirical assessments of the strategic allocation of cases by court presidents to more historical accounts of the behaviour of court leaders in times when courts have been under pressure, or in instances where court leaders have been central (or a threat to) establishing judicial power in hybrid regimes.[2]

3. Breath of Coverage

Judicial behaviour studies of court leadership have predominantly focused on US Courts. Many of the seminal studies in the literature have focused on the United States Supreme Court (Maltzman and Wahlbeck 1996, 2004; Maltzman et al. 2000; Lax and Cameron 2007; Lax and Rader 2015; Ura and Flink 2016). Several studies also exist for the US state supreme courts (Hall and Windett 2016; Gray and Miller 2021). Within the North American context, there are also studies of court leadership in the Supreme Court of Canada (Ostberg et al. 2004; Wetstein and Ostberg 2005).

Outside the North American context, a handful of studies exist for courts in the common law world, including Australia (Smyth and Narayan 2004), the United Kingdom (Alarie and Green 2017; Hunter and Rackley 2018), and Israel (Eisenberg et al. 2013; Givati and Rosenberg 2020). Some studies have examined leadership in specific countries in Western Europe; for example, Norway (Grendstad et al. 2015; Bentsen 2018; Nie et al. 2022). In addition, several studies exist that examine the role of chief justices in hybrid regimes—contexts where the standard theories of judicial behaviour are not necessarily applicable. These include studies of court leadership in Central and Eastern Europe (e.g. Scheppele 2006; Kosař 2017; Blisa and Kosař 2018; Trochev 2018; Kosař and Spáč 2021), Asia (Ghias 2010; Hendrianto 2016), and Africa (Hausegger and Haynie 2003; Leakey 2012).

Finally, there are some related studies of court leadership in international courts, such as the Court of Justice of the European Union (CJEU) (Hermansen 2020).

4. Data and Measurement Issues

Empirically assessing the influence of court leadership is difficult—some have even regarded this task impossible (Hall and Windett 2016, 685). The availability of data on decisional processes internal to the court is one reason for this. It is, for example, difficult to examine the social leadership skills of court leaders without having had access to internal processes normally performed behind closed doors (Hunter and Rackley 2018). Consequently, studies investigating the influence of leadership style and the personalities of court leaders often rely on aggregate and time series data where evidence of a leadership effect is inferred from the influence of dummy variable predictors when controlling for other factors. Some scholars have devised indirect means of getting at the relative influence of key players in the court's deliberations by using data from the US Supreme Court's internal memoranda (e.g. Maltzman et al. 2000). However, such data is often not available for other courts.

Sample size is another reason why it might be difficult to statistically distinguish between the influence of leadership and other factors explaining the outcome of interest. For example, while many previous works have suggested the leadership style of Chief Justice Stone was the primary culprit in the collapse of consensual decision-making norms in the US Supreme Court (e.g. Walker et al. 1988), others have emphasized more institutionally oriented explanations, including giving the Court the ability to select its cases and a change in the underlying composition of cases decided by the Court (Calderia and Zorn 1998; Hendershot et al. 2013). Yet distinguishing these explanations can be difficult because there are so few total chief justices against which to gauge leadership outcomes. To increase sample size, scholars have shifted their focus onto US state courts or to other high courts outside the US context where different institutional settings can provide a richer source of data (e.g. Brace and Hall 1990; Eisenberg et al. 2013; Hall and Windett 2016).

5. Main Findings and Controversies

Our focus in this section is to highlight important findings and debates in the comparative judicial behaviour literature regarding the behaviour and influence of court leadership. Specifically, we focus on studies, both quantitative and qualitative, that engage in some respect with the theoretical aspects of judicial decision-making as described above.

5.1 Do Chief Justices Use Their (In)Formal Powers to Promote Consensus?

The majority of judicial behaviour studies of court leaders focus on their desire for and ability to influence consensus. The expectation that chief justices will value consensus more is well established in the literature on judicial behaviour (e.g. Walker et al. 1988; Ura and Flink 2016). The reasons why a chief justice may be particularly interested in promoting consensus include not only their concerns for their legacy and perceptions as a leader on the court but could also be for institutional rationales such as 'produc[ing] decisions motivated by concerns for the legitimacy and institutional integrity of the judiciary rather than public policy or law' (Ura and Flink 2016, 187). In the United States, there are numerous historical examples of justices—such as Chief Justice Warren in *Brown v Board of Education*—foregoing perhaps their preferred legal policy as a means to achieve consensus (Ura and Flink 2016). Similar accounts of Chief Justices in other countries forging consensus can be found for example in Australia, where Sir Owen Dixon worked hard to maintain consensus on the High Court while he was Chief Justice (Smyth and Narayan 2004).

Several studies from the United States argue that if chief justices seek to promote consensus, they are indeed able to do so (e.g. Walker et al. 1988; Haynie 1992; Corley et al. 2013; Ura and Flink 2016). Chief justices possess some unique institutional advantages, such as priority in vote order or opinion assignment, which they may utilize to set the agenda and establish the level of a congenial work environment (e.g. Hendershot et al. 2013). Studies of consensus rates in the US Supreme Court have found that chiefs use these advantages to promote different consensual norms over time and that the overall rate of consensus has tended to shift correspondingly (e.g. Calderia and Zorn 1998).

Chief justices appear able to influence consensus rates also in high courts outside the US context. Using Danelski's concepts of task and social leadership, leadership style has been found to relate to consensus on the high courts in Canada (Ostberg, Wetstein, and Ducat 2004). In Australia, Smyth and Narayan (2004) examined nearly 100 years of court cases over eleven chief justice in the Australian High Court. They found significant effects in dissent rates based on changes in chief justices on the Court, suggesting that leadership style matters. However, they caution that their findings did not include other causal factors such as the types of cases arriving at the Court.

However, although the impact of chief justices on consensus norms is frequently associated with their leadership style, scholarly discourse remains divided on the magnitude of the influence exerted by leadership style compared to other explanatory factors. For example, as already noted, scholars disagree on the extent to which the apparent demise of consensual norms in the US Supreme Court in the early 1940s was a result of the leadership of Chief Justice Harlan Fish Stone (Hendershot et al. 2013; e.g. Walker et al. 1988).

The limited influence of court leaders on consensus norms is also observable within the European context. For instance, a noteworthy illustration of the leadership effect on consensus can be found in the Norwegian Supreme Court (Bentsen 2018). During the 1990s, the Norwegian Supreme Court witnessed a significant increase in rate of dissent, growing from approximately 8 per cent in 1990 to a peak of 29 per cent in 1999. This increase coincided with substantial transformations in court leadership, composition of justices, discretionary power, and agenda. Bentsen (2018) examines the relative influence of these factors and shows that although the change in leadership to the somewhat controversial Chief Justice Carsten Smith did influence the rise in dissent, the predominant reason for the rise in dissent relates to changes to the Court's discretionary docket and agenda during the Smith court.

Alarie and Green (2017) find further evidence that the chief justice only has a partial influence on dissent and consensus rates. Comparing the influence of several competing factors (including ideological differences, case complexity, workload, panel size, and leadership) on dissent rates in the Supreme Courts of Australia, Canada, and the United Kingdom, they conclude that judicial leadership may offer at best a partial explanation for the changing dissent rates in these countries. Specifically, they find that while leadership seems to influence the relatively low disagreement rates in the UK Supreme Court, changing rates in dissent in Australia and Canada do not appear related to the identity of the chief justice.

It can be difficult to distinguish and measure the relative influence of leadership and other potential explanations in the highest courts because there are so few total chief justices against which to gauge leadership outcomes. To overcome these difficulties, scholars have turned to studies of lower courts where there is richer data on chief justices and where comparisons between courts with different characteristics provide a more nuanced entry into the effects of leadership.

Seminal studies by Brace and Hall (1990), Hall and Brace (1989) demonstrate that chief judges in the US state courts can indeed use their formal powers to influence consensus. However, other studies also show that whether chief justices can make effective use of the assignment tool to promote consensus is conditioned on institutional factors and member resources. In a comprehensive study of US state supreme courts, Hall and Windett (2016) show that the chief judge's opinion assignment power has little or no relationship with dissension (or consensus) in state courts with more time, staff, docket control, and electoral insulation. In state courts with fewer member resources, the chief's powers appear to play a significantly larger role in discouraging dissent. On this basis, it is reasonable to assume that the extent to which chief justices can promote consensus should vary between courts not just within the United States but also between courts in different judicial and political systems.

Not all US state supreme court studies have found significant effects of being a chief justice. Gray and Miller (2021) draw on the Hall and Windett data and then expand that data over a sixteen-year time period to determine whether leadership by the chief justice affects consensus as defined by unanimity, rates of dissent, *per curiam* opinions, and pivotal cases.[3] Although they could not completely reject the possibility that a chief justice's leadership has some effect on consensus, their view is that if there is any, it is very minimal at best. The authors are, however, careful not to claim their findings apply to other types of courts such as the US Supreme Court.

Some authors also hypothesize that the gender of the chief justice influence consensus formation, but the literature provides divergent results regarding this effect. According to Leonard and Ross' (2020) study of US state supreme court decisions in three policy areas (employment discrimination, search and seizure, and environmental law), women chief justices are no more likely than their male counterparts to build consensus. This finding reflects the results of a study surveying US state supreme court justices (Norris 2022), which finds that 'female justices do not believe consensus formation is a primary responsibility of the state chief justice' (Norris 2022, 146). Yet Norris is also careful to point out that his findings are based off those justices who responded to the survey and not necessarily the entire universe of state supreme court justices.

Recent studies have examined how judicial decision-making is influenced by the different leadership styles between men and women that are more generalizable than the idiosyncratic leadership styles of individual chief justices. For instance, Boyd (2013) shows that female district court judges are more adept than their male counterparts at negotiating agreements and reaching compromises. Furthermore, Leonard and Ross (2020) found that women majority opinion authors appear to increase consensus in employment discrimination and search and seizure cases (though not environmental cases). Consequently, Leonard and Ross argue that the positive effects of women on collegiality come from being in the position of the majority opinion writer, not necessarily the chief justice. A study of the Supreme Court of Norway also finds that it takes more time to decide a case with the presence of a female leader, suggesting that this is a likely result of female leaders' predisposition to promote a more democratic and consensus-driven decision-making environment (Nie et al. 2022).

In a broad sense, court leaders seem to possess only a limited capacity to exert influence on consensus. Various scholarly investigations further indicate that the extent to which court leaders can shape consensus is subject to moderation by institutional and collegial factors. Consequently, it is reasonable to anticipate that the opportunities available to a court leader to foster consensus may vary across different courts and legal systems. Simultaneously, it often proves arduous to establish a causal relationship between leadership and its effects, primarily due to the scarcity of observations or challenges associated with controlling for other factors. In this regard, there exist prospects for enhancing research designs, such as exploring the impact of leadership in courts where cases are heard by rotating panels.

5.2 Do Court Leaders Use Their (In)Formal Powers to Gain Support for Their Personal Policy Preferences, or Are Other Goals More Important?

The US chief justice's power to assign majority opinions provides an indispensable agenda-setting tool for the chief. However, scholars disagree on what factors guide the chief's use of his assignment powers. According to the attitudinal model (Segal and Spaeth 2002), the chief justice will use the assignment procedure to advance his or her policy views by seeking out opinion authors whose policy views are most similar to their own. Several of the early studies of judicial decision-making suggest that ideological goals are central to chief justice's assignments (e.g. Murphy 1964; Ulmer 1970; Rohde and Spaeth 1976).

There is also support for this hypothesis outside the US context. Hausegger and Haynie (2003) compare the use of panel assignments in the Supreme Court of Canada in the post-charter years and the Appellate Division of the apartheid-era Republic of South Africa. By comparing these two countries, one with a long, stable democratic tradition and one authoritarian regime, they argue that if judges exhibit similar behaviours we can have greater confidence in the underlying assertions of judicial behaviour theory. More specifically, they hypothesize and test whether justices that are closer to the chief justice's policy preferences are more likely to be selected for cases involving issues salient to the public, the government, and the judges themselves. Their results suggest that individual chief justices are indeed similarly motivated when considering the use of their power to assign like-minded judges to panels. Similar to the findings from the US context, both Canadian and South African chief justices are more likely to assign judges closer to themselves in more salient cases.

While policy goals may be a central motivation, others propose that chief justices will promote alternative goals. The chief is often argued to 'seek the equitable and harmonious functioning of the Court as a small organization' (Maltzman and Wahlbeck 2004, 552). This theory contends that the chief justice aims to evenly distribute the workload of the Court among the justices, to assign cases to the most efficient justices, and to promote specialization by assigning similar cases to the same justice. Maltzman and Wahlbeck (1996) used data from the Rehnquist Court's first four years to provide empirical evidence for the claim that organizational needs—rather than ideological objectives—are a better way to explain the chief justice's assignment decisions.

In an influential study of the relative influence of these multiple goals, Maltzman and Wahlbeck (2004) found that chief justices on the US Supreme Court are more likely to assign majority opinions to those justices with whom they are ideologically aligned, but that they also take into consideration the organizational needs of the Court. They also show that more narrow initial coalitions force the chief to temper his pursuit of policy gain in favour of promoting a more stable majority coalition. Thus, the chief appears to exercise his power of assignment seeking favourable policy gains only in cases where it matters the most. For less significant matters, regardless of whether cases are legally or politically less salient, the chief also restrains his desire for policy gain.

The strategic use of assignment powers to advance organizational needs is also found in international courts. In a study of case allocation in the CJEU, Hermansen (2020) argues that the president seeks to build the court's legitimacy already at the case management stage by strategically allocating cases to select judges. The CJEU relies on a 'judge-rapporteur' to prepare cases and to draft the final judgment. The rapporteur is designated before the decisional panel's first meeting and remains the same throughout the process. Although dissenting opinions are not allowed, the identity of the decision-makers is disclosed. Given that justices to the CJEU are appointed by member states, the mere identity of the judge-rapporteur can lead to suspicions of bias among governments that are parties to a case. Hermansen argues that the president is cognizant of these suspicions and demonstrates that the president strategically allocates cases where member states have expressed opposing opinions to judges whose governments occupy a moderate position. Furthermore, similar to the existing literature, case saliency appears to matter. The effect of the president's strategic case allocation decreases once the Court has established its case law. This is because politics are the most salient when legal uncertainty is high.

The above literature focuses on court leaders' strategic assignment of leadership and author responsibilities in given cases. But how would (chief) justices compose judicial panels if they could? There is little research that examines this exact issue. This is only natural, given that few courts designate powers to compose panels to a given justice or a chief justice. In the United States, for example, the federal courts of appeal typically hear cases in three-judge panels, but these are randomly configured (Epstein et al. 2011, 110). However, there are instances in which high court justices may compose their own panels and where the chief justice has the mandate to do so.

Givati and Rosenberg (2020) investigate this question by focusing on the Supreme Court of Israel. The Supreme Court of Israel functions as both an appellant court and a High Court of Justice. In its capacity as the High Court of Justice, the Supreme Court typically hears cases that are filed against the government. In these cases, the Supreme Court serves as a court of first instance and the way these cases are handled is crucial for examining how judges would compose judicial panels. Every week, a different justice is assigned to be the Justice on Duty, and he or she receives every High Court of Justice case that is filed that week. If the Justice on Duty decides to reject the case, he or she writes the opinion and chooses two other justices to form the official panel of the case. Givati and Rosenberg investigate how the Justice on Duty composes his or her panel from three theoretical perspectives: the random selection of justices; the professional selection of justices, whereby the Justice on Duty selects justices who are known as experts in the subject matter of these cases; and the strategic selection of justices, where the Justice on Duty selects justices who are more likely to agree with his or her decision to reject the case. Testing the validity of these three theories, their findings are consistent with the strategic selection theory. They thereby proceed to investigate how panels are composed for cases that are granted a three-justice court hearing. Under the law, the chief justice can compose these panels. By comparing the chief justice's choice of panel members as Justice on Duty before he or she became chief justice, with the choice of panel members after becoming chief justice, they find evidence that the chief justice also engages in strategic panel composition.

5.3 Do Opinion Authors or Presiding Justices Influence Deliberations and Case Outcomes?

While chief justices and court presidents are formal leaders of courts, all members of a court may be considered, in a broader sense, to be judicial leaders. In most courts, associate justices take on various leadership roles, for example by being designated as majority opinion authors or by acting as presiding justice. As often stated in the literature, the chief justice's power to designate leadership responsibilities and opinion authorship on specific cases provides an indispensable agenda-setting tool for the chief. But how significant is the influence of presiding justices and opinion authors during case deliberations and for the policy outcome of a case? While it might seem clear that the opinion author should wield some extra influence on the decisional process and the outcome of the case, the extent to which the author shapes the content of the final legal policy is subject to debate (e.g. Carrubba et al. 2012).

For example, assuming that policy preferences are the dominant factor influencing decisional content and outcomes on Supreme Courts, other theories (often termed 'monopoly' theories) contend that the content and policy outcome of the final opinion is instead placed precisely at the ideal point of the median justice (either of the court as a whole or the majority) or directly on the opinion author (Lax and Rader 2015). In such a scenario, opinion authorship should have little influence over the votes and decisions of other justices. However, Lax and Cameron (2007) contend that in addition to policy content, opinions have a second dimension that offers the author some negotiating power. Justices are ultimately driven by a concern for judicial policy but the policy impact of an opinion also depends on its persuasiveness, clarity, and craftsmanship—its legal quality. Hence, even though the policy outcome may be the ultimate concern of the justices, they are also induced to care about legal quality.

To examine the relative influence of opinion authorship and the 'monopoly' theories, Lax and Rader (2015) analyse the extent to which justices switch their votes from the initial conference to the final merits of the case. In the Court's deliberations of a case, the justices cast two votes, one during the initial conference and one on the final merits of the case. Between these two votes, a justice is assigned to write the majority opinion. They argue that vote switching can be used to detect the power of opinion authors over opinion content. The results of their study show that opinion authorship does matter as authors have disproportionate influence over opinion content, and by extension so do chief justices who assign the opinion author. The result of this study thus demonstrates that 'collegial interaction on the Supreme Court is not just noise leading to a predetermined end or merely grit for Court watchers' (Lax and Rader 2015, 661).

There is also evidence outside the US context that leadership roles in cases influence decisional outcomes and voting patterns. In a study of appellate panels on the Supreme Court of Israel, Eisenberg and Rosen-Zvi (2013) compare justices' voting patterns in cases in which they presided and wrote opinions with their voting patterns when they did not preside or write opinions. The Israeli Supreme Court panels include a presiding judge, who by law is the most senior justice on the panel. Eisenberg and Rosen-Zvi hypothesize that the presiding justice might be influential due to experience as reflected by greater seniority, due to presiding status in a case, and due to authority to assign responsibility for writing the opinion in a case. Presiding justices may also specialize in a substantive legal area, generating additional deference from colleagues. By examining differences in voting for a defendant in criminal cases, they find that voting patterns varied significantly with presiding and non-presiding status. Their main finding is that a justice is 4.5 per cent more likely to vote in his or her preferred direction when the justice presides compared with when the justice does not preside. The results overall suggest that when justices are not presiding, they tend to defer to the position of the presiding justice on the panel.

5.4 Do Court Leaders Behave Differently Than Other Justices in Response to External Constraints?

It is well established in the literature that court leaders, being the leader and public face of the court, may be more likely than their colleagues to be cognizant of the institution's legitimacy. As a result, court leaders may behave differently when the court is facing increased institutional constraint or heightened public discontent. As the public face of the institution, they may also more than other justices feel the need to devote time and energy to promote and defend judicial legitimacy in the public.

In a study of the US Supreme Court, Li (2020) examines the opinion assignment process when the chief justice is in majority. Li suggests that the chief is also attentive to the Court's institutional legitimacy when assigning majority opinions, hypothesizing that when the Court faces lower levels of legitimacy, chiefs are less inclined to assign opinions to their ideological allies (or more likely to assign opinions to ideologically distant colleagues) and thus trade policy gains for legitimacy enhancement. Li examines three separate indicators measuring the legitimacy of the court at any given time: (i) when the Court is institutionally constrained by ideologically incongruent elected branches; (ii) when Congress explicitly signals public dissatisfaction with the Court by proposing court-curbing bills attempted at curtailing judicial legitimacy; and (iii) when the public loses confidence in the Court as a legitimate institution (i.e. shows less diffuse support for the Court). The results of Li's study show that when the Court is ideologically at odds with Congress and the President, chief justices will more often designate majority opinion authorship to more ideologically distant colleagues. In addition, the results show that the effect of ideological distance is greatly moderated by the public's support for the Court. Hence, the chief justices prioritize institutional legitimacy over policy when the Court is dealing with declining public confidence.

The finding that chief justices' behaviour is influenced by public opinion is supported by a study by Badas (2021), who hypothesizes that the chief justice will be influenced by public opinion to a greater extent than the associate justices because the goal of maintaining the Court's legitimacy is more salient for the chief justice. Using the public mood indicator developed by Stimson (1998), Badas compares the extent to which the chief justice, in comparison to the associate justices, cast votes for a liberal case outcome when the public mood is either more liberal or more conservative. The results of this study indicate that the chief justice is influenced by public mood to a greater extent than the associate justices. Crucially, the size of the effect of public mood is comparable to the effect size found in studies of other external factors influencing the Supreme Court's decision-making, including court-curbing legislation, amicus briefs, and oral arguments, suggesting that public opinion has a relatively strong influence on the behaviour of chief justices.

Outside the US context, few empirical studies exist that examine the influence of external constraints and public opinion on the behaviour of court leaders. There is, however, some evidence suggesting that aspiring chief justices on the Supreme Court of Norway will adjust their behaviour towards the government when seeking to gain the position of chief justice (Grendstad et al. 2015). In Norway, the government possesses the power to appoint chief justices. Given that justices on the Supreme Court aspiring to become chief justices are dependent on the government to acquire that position, they might seek to adjust their behaviour strategically in cases where the government is a party. Then, once they are selected as chief, the new occupant of the seat can begin to vote sincerely. Grendstad and colleagues test this hypothesis by comparing the justices' votes as aspirant chief justices before their elevation with their votes cast as chiefs after elevation. The results of their comparison suggest that the justices changed their voting behaviour. Before elevation, the aspirant chiefs cast 70 per cent of their votes for the government party. After elevation, the chiefs cast 40 per cent of their votes for the government party (Grendstad et al. 2015, 155).

That justices change their behaviour after being elevated to chief justices is also evident in the Canadian Supreme Court. Using Danelski's concepts of task and social leadership, Wetstein and Ostberg (2005) compared the behaviour of the three justices Dickson, Lamer, and McLachlin before and after becoming chief justice. They find that while Dickson and Lamer seemed to maintain their status as task leaders after being elevated to the office of the chief justice, Justice McLachlin underwent a major transformation in her dissenting behaviour and became the most important social leader in her Court. They further argue that the fact that Justice McLachlin chose to become a social leader can be seen as a strategic inter-institutional move in a period in time when the Canadian Supreme Court faced increasing scrutiny and criticism from the media, academia, and the broader political community for its activist rulings.

5.5 The Role of Court Leaders in Hybrid Regimes

Court leaders in hybrid regimes can be powerful figures, even masters of their judiciaries (Kosař 2017), yet they are also vulnerable to political pressure and blatant interference (Trochev and Ellett 2014; Blisa and Kosař 2018). The emerging literature on court leaders in hybrid regimes sheds light on the intricate dynamics at play when court leaders are confronted with the formidable challenge of wielding judicial power and safeguarding autonomy within 'unpredictable and frequently hostile environments' (Trochev and Ellett 2014, 70). Scholars in this field thus contribute to a deeper understanding of the complex interplay between court leaders, their political contexts, and the exercise of judicial authority.

In an effort to enhance our understanding of court presidents from a comparative perspective, Blisa and Kosař (2018) have developed the Court President Power Index (CPPI), which examines the powers vested in court presidents across seven interconnected dimensions: judicial careers, administrative, jurisprudential, financial, ambassadorial, media, and ancillary powers. Applying the CPPI to thirteen European jurisdictions (eleven countries and two supranational courts), including hybrid regimes and established democracies, Blisa and Kosař find considerable variation in the power associated with court leadership not only between Western and Eastern Europe but also within each region.[4]

Sitting atop the CPPI, with extensive powers on all but the media dimension, are Russian court presidents. They represent the type of court president that Blisa and Kosař label the 'Boss'. Not only do these court presidents have significant jurisprudential and administrative powers through such measures as case and opinion assignment but they also exercise extensive powers over rank-and-file judges' careers and lives. At the other end of the CCPI are court presidents in Germany, the Netherlands, and Romania. They are labelled 'first among equals', whose influence mainly runs through their leadership skills. Yet, as Blisa and Kosař note, the extent to which court presidents are able to exploit the various powers vested in their position depends on several conditions, including terms of office and the political environment in which they operate.

Two case studies examining the role of court leaders in countries transitioning from communism to EU membership, namely Czechia and Slovakia, shed light on the delicate nature of judicial institutions within hybrid regimes (Kosař 2017; Kosař and Spáč 2021). Following the collapse of communism, Slovakia, like many other Central European (CE) nations, implemented a judicial council model of judicial administration in order to safeguard the judiciary from undue interference by the executive branch of government. Nevertheless, Kosař and Spáč (2021) argue that the turnover of the Slovakian chief justices indicates that the process remains politicized. Their research reveals that no chief justice has managed to secure consecutive terms after their initial five-year tenure due to a lack of executive support. This demonstrates that the formally influential position of the Slovakian Chief Justice retains strategic importance for Slovakian politicians.

In Czechia, Kosař's (2017) case study demonstrates the potential pitfalls of granting excessive power to court presidents with regard to judicial independence. Unlike Slovakia and other CE countries, Czechia has opted to maintain a judicial administration model where the Minister of Justice possesses the formal authority to nominate judges, who are subsequently appointed by the President. However, in practice, most Ministers of Justice have delegated the task of selecting new judges to influential court presidents. In Czechia, court presidents have managed at times to gain the upper hand of Ministers of Justice due to informational asymmetries between the two positions, a much higher turnover of Minister of Justice than court presidents, and a political environment where the political cost of dismissing courts presidents is high. On one hand, strong court presidents preserve the independence of the courts in relation to other branches of government. On the other hand, their authority poses a threat to internal judicial independence, specifically the autonomy of individual judges in relation to the Chief Justice.

A key question in newly established constitutional regimes is how court leaders can contribute to the building of strong institutions and empower their courts under difficult political circumstances. Scheppele's (2006) comparative case study of the early days of the Hungarian and Russian constitutional courts shows how their first court presidents were able to rule against the wishes of political elites and protect the courts from political attacks, as long as they followed a script in which they acted as judicial personalities who used legal power in the service of constitutional aggression. Similarly, when the Indonesian Constitutional Court was established in 2003, it started from scratch without sufficient funding and an office building, yet only a few years later the court had struck down many government policies and even aggressively confronted the government when it did not comply with the court's decisions. According to Hendrianto (2016), the quick rise in judicial power was only possible due to the heroic leadership of Chief Justice Jimly Asshidiqie, who was able to broaden the court's power significantly through jurisprudential development and internal consensus building.

The studies mentioned above emphasize the capacity of court leaders to wield judicial power given specific circumstances. However, the literature also reveals the diverse strategies employed by hybrid regimes to blatantly interfere with the judiciary (Trochev and Ellett 2014), including removing court leaders they perceive as unfavourable through measures like refraining from renewing their terms, altering eligibility criteria, and reducing mandatory retirement ages (Scheppele 2006; Hendrianto 2016; Blisa and Kosař 2018).

While numerous court leaders are allies of the ruling elite (Solomon 2007), and their ability to protect judicial autonomy varies considerably (Leakey 2012), effective leadership can also be a key factor in explaining successful resistance against blatant attacks on the judiciary. Such resistance also takes form of actions outside the courtroom (Trochev and Ellett 2014). Troche and Ellet's (2014) study further suggests that the extent to which judges successfully engage in off-bench strategies to protect their judicial autonomy is influenced by the strength and breadth of their social networks. A prominent example is the mobilization against the removal of Chief Justice Iftikhar Chaudry during the

Musharraf regime in Pakistan in 2007, where lawyers and judges lobbied international allies and engaged in sustained street protests that endured for a duration of two years. These concerted efforts culminated in the successful reinstatement of Chief Justice Chaudry in 2009 (Ghias 2010).

6. Conclusions and Directions for Future Research

As our overview shows, there exists a quite substantial body of comparative judicial behaviour literature on court leadership. This extant literature explores numerous crucial questions concerning the influence court leaders exert over other judges, including their ability to generate consensus or advance their own preferences. Additionally, it investigates the degree to which court leaders behave differently from other judges, either due to having different goals and objectives or from being more responsive to institutional and external pressures from political actors or public opinion. As such, a central theme in the extant literature revolves around whether court leaders can be described by traditional attitudinal (rational choice) models or if other more strategic or institutional models better explain their behaviour.

Based on the literature, we believe it is safe to say that court leaders, in comparison to regular judges, exhibit a heightened sensitivity to both institutional and strategic considerations. While court leaders do pursue their own policy goals, their approach is marked by strategic calculations, often leading them to forgo personal goals in favour of securing a more stable majority coalition. They are also strategic when utilizing their assignment powers, using these powers particularly in cases that are of significant importance or characterized by legal uncertainty. Furthermore, court leaders demonstrate a greater inclination towards fostering consensus, recognizing its significance in bolstering the public perception and standing of the court. They display a notable awareness of public opinion and prioritize the preservation of institutional legitimacy over advancing specific policy agendas, particularly when the court's public confidence is on the decline. This recognition underscores their understanding of the importance of maintaining public trust in the judiciary.

It is important to emphasize that most investigation of court leadership has predominantly focused on North America and Europe, while other regions such as Asia, South America, Africa, and the Middle East have received only limited scholarly attention. This could be because the study of judicial behaviour is challenging in hybrid regimes, where the neat vertical or horizontal separation of powers that serves as the conceptual foundation for political scientists studying law and courts is disrupted (Trochev and Ellett 2014). Nonetheless, several of the studies included in our overview reveal valuable insights that can be derived from examining the operational strategies employed by court leaders in hybrid regimes.

To advance our understanding of court leadership, future research should examine and compare the behaviour and influence of court leaders across diverse institutional and political contexts. Given that the actions of court leaders appear profoundly shaped by strategic calculations and institutional factors, a comprehensive analysis of their behaviour under varying settings holds great significance. By undertaking such investigations, scholars can shed light on how different institutional arrangements and political settings affect the decision-making processes, strategies, and overall influence of court leaders. Such a comparative approach will enable a more nuanced comprehension of the complexities inherent in court leadership and its interactions with the broader socio-political environment.

A potential concrete avenue for future comparative research lies in examining the appointment processes of court leaders. Notably, there exist significant variations across courts regarding the appointment of court leaders. In many countries, the responsibility for appointing court leaders lies with the government or the incumbent president. However, in other nations, such as Denmark, the selection of a new chief justice is entirely entrusted to the sitting justices themselves (Ghavanini et al. 2023). Exploring these divergent appointment procedures across countries presents a valuable opportunity for comparative research. By closely examining these varied procedures, researchers can uncover valuable insights regarding the potential ramifications of different appointment systems on court leadership as well as the subsequent effects on the court leader's prospects for exerting influence within the court and in relation to other branches of state power. Such a comparative analysis holds significant potential for enhancing our understanding of court leadership and its multifaceted implications.

Finally, in the extant scholarship, the primary emphasis in the investigation of court leaders has been on chief justices. However, due to the inherent challenges associated with empirically measuring the impact of these leaders on diverse judicial outcomes, it is advisable for future studies to take a broader approach to the study of court leadership. This approach should encompass not only the role of chief justices but also other key positions within the judiciary, such as presiding justices and opinion authors. Moreover, it is essential for scholars to delve deeper into exploring the influence of different types of leadership within courts where cases are adjudicated by panels and where the assignment of cases to panels is randomized. These institutional features enable causal research designs that allow for a more intricate analysis of the influence of court leaders' characteristics and backgrounds on various outcomes, including the ability to foster consensus among panel members or the evolution of legal doctrines.

Notes

1. Task leadership is also sometimes termed 'jurisprudential' leadership, which 'refers to the influence of a given judge on the decisions or jurisprudence of the Court, in a specific area or more generally' (Hunter and Rackley 2018, 193).

2. Hybrid regimes are countries that contain both democratic and authoritarian elements (e.g. Levitsky and Way 2010).
3. Their primary method uses a 'RIFLE technique developed by Berry and Fowler (2021) … to leverage … leader fixed effects to assess the portion of the data variation nominally explained by leadership … and then compares that to the "explanatory power" that could be obtained through random permutations of fictitious leader fixed effects' (Gray and Miller 2021, 321).
4. These jurisdictions are the Court of Justice of the European Union, the European Court of Human Rights, Czechia, France, Germany, Ireland, Italy, the Netherlands, Poland, Romania, Slovakia, Slovenia, and Russia.

References

Alarie, Benjamin, and Andrew J. Green. 2017. *Commitment and Cooperation on High Courts: A Cross-Country Examination of Institutional Constraints on Judges*. Oxford: Oxford University Press.

Badas, Alex. 2021. 'The Chief Justice and Judicial Legitimacy Evidence from the Influence of Public Opinion'. *Justice System Journal* 42 (2): 150–63.

Baum, Lawrence. 1997. *The Puzzle of Judicial Behavior*. Ann Arbor: University of Michigan Press.

Bentsen, Henrik Litleré. 2018. 'Court Leadership, Agenda Transformation, and Judicial Dissent: A European Case of a "Mysterious Demise of Consensual Norms"'. *Journal of Law and Courts* 6 (1): 189–213.

Berry, Christopher R., and Anthony Fowler. 2021. 'Leadership or Luck? Randomization Inference for Leader Effects in Politics, Business, and Sports'. *Science Advances* 7 (4): eabe3404.

Blisa, Adam, and David Kosař. 2018. 'Court Presidents: The Missing Piece in the Puzzle of Judicial Governance'. *German Law Journal* 19 (7): 2031–76.

Boyd, Christina L. 2013. 'She'll Settle It?' *Journal of Law and Courts* 1 (2): 193–219.

Brace, Paul, and Melinda Gann Hall. 1990. 'Neo-Institutionalism and Dissent in State Supreme Courts'. *The Journal of Politics* 52 (1): 54–70.

Calderia, Gregory A., and Christopher J. W. Zorn. 1998. 'Of Time and Consensual Norms in the Supreme Court'. *American Journal of Political Science* 42 (3): 874–902.

Carrubba, Cliff, Barry Friedman, Andrew D. Martin, and Georg Vanberg. 2012. 'Who Controls the Content of Supreme Court Opinions?' *American Journal of Political Science* 56 (2): 400–12.

Casillas, Christopher J., Peter K. Enns, and Patrick C. Wohlfarth. 2011. 'How Public Opinion Constrains the U.S. Supreme Court'. *American Journal of Political Science* 55 (1): 74–88.

Clark, Tom S. 2009. 'The Separation of Powers, Court Curbing, and Judicial Legitimacy'. *American Journal of Political Science* 53 (4): 971–89.

Corley, Pamela C., Amy Steigerwalt, and Artemus Ward. 2013. *The Puzzle of Unanimity: Consensus on the United States Supreme Court*. Stanford: Stanford University Press.

Cross, Frank B., and Stefanie Lindquist. 2006. 'The Decisional Significance of the Chief Justice'. *University of Pennsylvania Law Review* 154 (6): 1665–707.

Danelski, David J., and Artemus Ward. 2016. *The Chief Justice: Appointment and Influence*. Ann Arbor: University of Michigan Press.

Eisenberg, Theodore, Talia Fisher, and Issi Rosen-Zvi. 2013. 'Group Decision Making on Appellate Panels: Presiding Justice and Opinion Justice Influence in the Israel Supreme Court'. *Psychology, Public Policy, and Law* 19 (3): 282–96.

Epstein, Lee, and Jack Knight. 1998. *The Choices Justices Make*. Washington: CQ Press.

Epstein, Lee, William M. Landes, and Richard A. Posner. 2011. 'Why (And When) Judges Dissent: A Theoretical and Empirical Analysis'. *Journal of Legal Analysis* 3 (1): 101–37.

Ghavanini, Anna W., Gunnar Grendstad, and Johan K. Schaffer. 2023 'Institutions That Define the Policy-Making Role of Courts: A Comparative Analysis of the Supreme Courts of Scandinavia'. *International Journal of Constitutional Law* 21 (3): 770–97.

Ghias, Shoaib A. 2010. 'Miscarriage of Chief Justice: Judicial Power and the Legal Complex in Pakistan under Musharraf'. *Law & Social Inquiry* 35 (4): 985–1022.

Givati, Yehonatan, and Israel Rosenberg. 2020. 'How Would Judges Compose Judicial Panels? Theory and Evidence from the Supreme Court of Israel'. *Journal of Empirical Legal Studies* 17 (2): 317–41.

Gray, Thomas, and Banks Miller. 2021. 'Swineherds and Hogs on Ice: Leadership Impacts for State Chief Judges'. *American Politics Research* 49 (3): 319–27.

Grendstad, Gunnar, Eric N. Waltenburg, and William R. Shaffer. 2015. *Policy Making in an Independent Judiciary. The Norwegian Supreme Court*. Colchester: ECPR Press.

Hall, Matthew, and Jason Harold Windett. 2016. 'Discouraging Dissent: The Chief Judge's Influence in State Supreme Courts'. *American Politics Research* 44 (4): 682–709.

Hall, Melinda Gann, and Paul Brace. 1989. 'Order in the Courts: A Neo-Institutional Approach to Judicial Consensus'. *Western Political Quarterly* 42 (3): 391–407.

Hausegger, Lori, and Stacia Haynie. 2003. 'Judicial Decisionmaking and the Use of Panels in the Canadian Supreme Court and the South African Appellate Division'. *Law & Society Review* 37 (3): 635–57.

Haynie, Stacia L. 1992. 'Leadership and Consensus on the U.S. Supreme Court'. *The Journal of Politics* 54 (4): 1158–69.

Hendershot, Marcus E., Mark S. Hurwitz, Drew Noble Lanier, and Richard L. Pacelle. 2013. 'Dissensual Decision Making: Revisiting the Demise of Consensual Norms within the U.S. Supreme Court'. *Political Research Quarterly* 66 (2): 467–81.

Hendrianto, Stefanus. 2016. 'The Rise and Fall of Heroic Chief Justices: Constitutional Politics and Judicial Leadership in Indonesia'. *Washington International Law Journal* 25: 489.

Hermansen, Silje Synnøve Lyder. 2020. 'Building Legitimacy: Strategic Case Allocations in the Court of Justice of the European Union'. *Journal of European Public Policy* 27 (8): 1215–35.

Hunter, Rosemary, and Erika Rackley. 2018. 'Judicial Leadership on the UK Supreme Court'. *Legal Studies* 38 (2): 191–220.

Johnson, Timothy R., James F. Spriggs II, and Paul J. Wahlbeck. 2005. 'Passing and Strategic Voting on the U.S. Supreme Court'. *Law & Society Review* 39 (2): 349–78.

Kosař, David. 2017. 'Politics of Judicial Independence and Judicial Accountability in Czechia: Bargaining in the Shadow of the Law between Court Presidents and the Ministry of Justice'. *European Constitutional Law Review* 13 (1): 96–123.

Kosař, David, and Samuel Spáč. 2021. 'Post-Communist Chief Justices in Slovakia: From Transmission Belts to Semi-Autonomous Actors?' *Hague Journal on the Rule of Law* 13 (1): 107–142. https://doi.org/10.1007/s40803-021-00150-w

Lax, Jeffrey R., and Charles M. Cameron. 2007. 'Bargaining and Opinion Assignment on the US Supreme Court'. *The Journal of Law, Economics, and Organization* 23 (2): 276–302.

Lax, Jeffrey R., and Kelly Rader. 2015. 'Bargaining Power in the Supreme Court: Evidence from Opinion Assignment and Vote Switching'. *The Journal of Politics* 77 (3): 648–63.

Leakey, Kyela. 2012. 'The Role of the Chief Justice in Commonwealth Africa: A Comparative Study of South Africa, Ghana and Kenya'. Thesis. Queen Mary University of London. https://qmro.qmul.ac.uk/xmlui/handle/123456789/8835

Leonard, Meghan E., and Joseph V. Ross. 2020. 'Gender Diversity, Women's Leadership, and Consensus in State Supreme Courts'. *Journal of Women, Politics & Policy* 41 (3): 278–302.

Levitsky, Steven, and Lucan A. Way. 2010. *Competitive Authoritarianism: Hybrid Regimes After the Cold War*. Cambridge: Cambridge University Press.

Li, Siyu. 2020. 'A Separation-of-Powers Model of U.S. Chief Justice Opinion Assignment'. *Justice System Journal* 41 (1): 3–21.

Maltzman, Forrest, James F. Spriggs, and Paul J. Wahlbeck. 2000. *Crafting Law on the Supreme Court: The Collegial Game*. Cambridge: Cambridge University Press.

Maltzman, Forrest, and Paul J. Wahlbeck. 1996. 'May It Please the Chief? Opinion Assignments in the Rehnquist Court'. *American Journal of Political Science* 40 (2): 421–43.

Maltzman, Forrest, and Paul J. Wahlbeck. 2004. 'A Conditional Model of Opinion Assignment on the Supreme Court'. *Political Research Quarterly* 57 (4): 551–63.

Murphy, Walter F. 1964. *The Elements of Judicial Strategy*. Chicago: University of Chicago Press.

Nie, Mintao, Gunnar Grendstad, William R. Shaffer, and Eric N. Waltenburg. 2022. 'The Impact of Female Leadership in Collegial Courts on Time to Render Merits Decisions: Evidence from the Norwegian Supreme Court'. *Justice System Journal* 43 (3): 353–72.

Norris, Mikel. 2022. 'Beyond Consensus: Gender, Chief Justices, and Leadership on State Supreme Courts'. *Journal of Women, Politics & Policy* 43 (2): 134–51.

Ostberg, C. L., Matthew E. Wetstein, and Craig R. Ducat. 2004. 'Leaders, Followers, and Outsiders: Task and Social Leadership on the Canadian Supreme Court in the Early "Nineties"'. *Polity* 36 (3): 505–28.

Rohde, David W., and Harold J. Spaeth. 1976. *Supreme Court Decision Making*. New York: W. H. Freeman.

Scheppele, Kim Lane. 2006. 'Guardians of the Constitution: Constitutional Court Presidents and the Struggle for the Rule of Law in Post-Soviet Europe'. *University of Pennsylvania Law Review* 154 (6): 1757–851.

Segal, Jeffrey Allan, and Harold J. Spaeth. 2002. *The Supreme Court and the Attitudinal Model Revisited*. Cambridge: Cambridge University Press.

Smyth, Russell, and Paresh Kumar Narayan. 2004. 'Hail to the Chief! Leadership and Structural Change in the Level of Consensus on the High Court of Australia'. *Journal of Empirical Legal Studies* 1 (2): 399–427.

Solomon, Peter H. 2007. 'Informal Practices in Russian Justice: Probing the Limits of Post-Soviet Reform'. In *Russia, Europe, and the Rule of Law*, edited by Ferdinand J. M. Feldbrugge, 79–91. Leiden: Brill Nijhoff. https://brill.com/display/book/edcoll/9789047411642/Bej.9789004155336.i-226_006.xml

Stimson, James A. 1998. *Public Opinion in America: Moods, Cycles, and Swings*, 2nd edn. London: Routledge & CRC Press.

Trochev, Alexei. 2018. 'Patronal Politics, Judicial Networks and Collective Judicial Autonomy in Post-Soviet Ukraine'. *International Political Science Review* 39 (5): 662–78.

Trochev, Alexei, and Rachel Ellett. 2014. 'Judges and Their Allies: Rethinking Judicial Autonomy through the Prism of Off-Bench Resistance'. *Journal of Law and Courts* 2 (1): 67–91.

Ulmer, S. Sidney. 1970. 'Dissent Behavior and the Social Background of Supreme Court Justices'. *The Journal of Politics* 32 (3): 580–98.

Ura, Joseph Daniel, and Carla M. Flink. 2016. 'Managing the Supreme Court: The Chief Justice, Management, and Consensus'. *Journal of Public Administration Research and Theory* 26 (2): 185–96.

Ura, Joseph Daniel, and Patrick C. Wohlfarth. 2010. '" An Appeal to the People": Public Opinion and Congressional Support for the Supreme Court'. *The Journal of Politics* 72 (4): 939–56.

Walker, Thomas G., Lee Epstein, and William J. Dixon. 1988. 'On the Mysterious Demise of Consensual Norms in the United States Supreme Court'. *The Journal of Politics* 50 (2): 361–89.

Wetstein, Matthew E., and C. L. Ostberg. 2005. 'Strategic Leadership and Political Change on the Canadian Supreme Court: Analyzing the Transition to Chief Justice'. *Canadian Journal of Political Science/Revue canadienne de science politique* 38 (3): 653–73.

CHAPTER 29

PANEL EFFECTS ON COURTS AROUND THE WORLD

C. L. OSTBERG AND MATTHEW E. WETSTEIN

1. Introduction

One of the most important insights regarding appellate courts that sit in smaller panels is that panel composition influences case outcomes. This finding prompted scholars to apply myriad theories and methodologies to document when, how, and why panel effects occur on appellate courts around the globe. Scholars in this area are interested in exploring how judges in panels influence each other and how they are influenced by other actors in the judicial system. With few exceptions (see Alarie and Green 2017; Garoupa, Gill, and Tiede 2021), researchers have explored this phenomenon within a single country, yet over time they have begun embracing more sophisticated interdisciplinary models that borrow from a variety of disciplines, such as political science, psychology, law, and economics to understand panel effects on different level courts. Panel scholars have primarily focused on unpacking two distinct lines of inquiry. First, what factors influence chief justices in courts where they control the size and composition of panels, and second, how do judges in smaller panels influence each other horizontally and/or vertically in the judicial hierarchy? While studies examining the first line of inquiry tend to study apex courts outside the US context, those focusing on the second primarily examine panel effects in the US Courts of Appeals, although scholarship on other appellate courts is on the rise.

In this chapter, we limit our review to studies conducted over the past twenty-five years or so, and thus do not provide a full encyclopaedic account or geographic coverage of all panel research. Moreover, we focus primarily on empirical studies using quantitative or qualitative data to examine how panels operate rather than addressing normative concerns. Given these constraints, our survey may overrepresent US Courts of Appeals research, yet in truth, this is where the bulk of the research to date has occurred.

In Table 29.1 we provide a survey of some of the constitutional and high courts outside the United States where panel research exists.

The chapter proceeds by briefly discussing major theories explaining panel effects, followed by a summary of some important attitudinal, institutional, and strategic studies conducted in the US Courts of Appeals. It then examines scholarship conducted on Supreme Courts where chief justices have power of panel assignment, and those that operate in rotating panels. The chapter closes by discussing gaps in the literature and calls for continuing methodological and theoretical pluralism and an increase in the study of this phenomenon in more courts around the world.

2. Core Theories for Studying Panel Effects on Courts

Scholars studying panel effects rely on a variety of theoretical paradigms to help inform their understanding of small group activity, most notably the attitudinal, strategic, and institutional approaches. Traditional legal scholars and judges themselves often contend that judges simply use legal reasoning, rely on precedent, and apply laws to facts in an effort to make good law (see Murphy 1964; Epstein and Knight 1998; Edwards 2003). Yet, scholarship beginning with Pritchett (1941, 1948) and Schubert (1965, 1974), launched a behavioural revolution showing that policy preferences in the US Supreme Court play a critical role in explaining case outcomes (for examples see Rohde and Spaeth 1976; Segal and Spaeth 1993, 2002; Spaeth and Segal 1999; Wahlbeck, Spriggs II, and Maltzman 1999). Despite these findings, an extensive debate emerged over whether attitudinal theory explains behaviour on panels in the US Courts of Appeals and appellate courts in other nations, where judges operate under vastly different institutional structures. Although attitudes *do* matter in smaller panels, such as the US Courts of Appeals, and in the Supreme Court of Canada and Norway, it might surprise some to realize it plays a far more muted and nuanced role in these settings (see Ostberg and Wetstein 2007; Skiple et al. 2016; Wetstein and Ostberg 2017; Skiple, Littlere Bentsen, and Hanretty 2020).

A second line of theoretical inquiry initiated by Murphy (1964) and Epstein and Knight (1998) shows that since US Supreme Court Justices work in a small nine-member group, rational choice theory or sophisticated strategic behaviour plays an important role in shaping how judges operate at all stages of the decision-making process (see also Caldeira, Wright, and Zorn 1999; Maltzman, Spriggs II, and Wahlbeck 2000). Since the rulings of appellate court judges are subject to possible review and reversal by courts above and they review decisions from below, the literature is rife with increasingly complex models exploring when, how, and why panel judges engage in strategic behaviour with each other and in reference to other actors in the judicial hierarchy. The research findings vary, but some have shown that judges decide not to dissent (to avoid conflict) or dissent (to send a signal to others), or they may alternatively author a consenting opinion to advance a particular argument.

Table 29.1 Selected countries with Constitutional or Supreme Courts and panel composition power

Country	Size of court	Panel sizes and when they are used
Albania	9	Three members for case selection
Austria	14	Minimum of five for motions and dismissals
Australia	7	Three-, five-, and seven-member panels
Belgium	12	Seven with regional/language representation
Bosnia/Herzegovina	9	Three members on requests for interim and admin. issues
Brazil	11	Five members in criminal cases, single members in easy cases
Canada	9	Five, seven, and nine (five typical for Quebec and criminal cases); three for case selection
Czechia	15	Four three-member panels with President and Vice-Presidents not permanent
Croatia	35	Six members on constitutional complaints, three for dismissal and electoral cases
France	9	Three-member panels on limited cases re: electoral issues
Germany	16	Two eight-member panels (Senates)
Hungary	15	Five members on residual competence
India	31	Panels consist largely of two or three members; thirteen is largest panel
Israel	15	Mostly three members; larger panels in extraordinary cases
Kosovo	9	Three members for case selection
Latvia	7	Three members for case selection
Luxembourg	9	Five-member panels
Poland	15	Five- and three-member panels
Portugal	13	Mainly thirteen, but five-member panels on residual competence
Serbia	15	Two seven-member 'Grand Chambers' + President; three for dismissals and procedural decisions
Slovakia	13	Three-member panels for residual competence
Slovenia	9	Three members for case selection and privacy of petitioners
Spain	12	Two six-member panels appointed by the full court
United Kingdom	12	Five, seven, and nine members
United States	9	None; four members for case selection
US Court of Appeals	varies	Three-member panels with avenue for full circuit review

Sources: Alarie and Green (2017); Kelemen (2018); de Mendonca Lopes (2019); Garoupa et al. (2021).

A third line of inquiry has used increasingly sophisticated psychological theories pertaining to group cohesion to help explore more systematically *when* and *how* institutional and circuit court norms structure the internal deliberative process on US Appellate Courts (see Hettinger, Lindquist, and Martinek 2006; Sunstein et al. 2006; Kim 2009; Hinkle, Nelson, and Hazelton 2020). For example, judges who want to operate in a satisfactory work environment may reduce their dissents in order to limit tension and conflict with others to make it more psychologically and socially satisfying for everyone. To date, these three theoretical paradigms lie at the heart of panel scholarship conducted both in the United States and abroad.

Studies involving these three dominant theories *initially* focused on the application of one theory at the expense of others, and could typically be grouped into two distinct overarching but interrelated categories. The first explored the *internal deliberative dynamics*, or the horizontal exchange between panel judges (Kim 2009). These studies tend to examine attitudinal/background traits and institutional norms and rules that impact decision-making. Scholarship relying on *strategic theories*, in turn, suggest judges consider both panel colleagues and actors above and below them in the judicial hierarchy when deciding cases (Kim 2009). Strategic studies often deploy theories from psychology and economics. Over time, scholars realized that different theories worked interactively to collectively explain appellate courts panel activity (see Kim 2009; Epstein, Landes, and Posner 2013; Fischman 2015; Skiple, et al. 2016; Hinkle, Nelson, and Hazelton 2020). We argue another wrinkle in the complexity of panel activity is that there is an ebb and flow to the impact these theories have on different kinds of panels, depending on the court level examined, the appointment process, the institutional rules constraining judges, and the issues studied. In short, context matters. Future scholars should also consider that what explains panel activity in one era may change over time as judicial values shift in line with changing values in society at large (see Wetstein and Ostberg 2017). The changing impact of theories on panel effects points to the complexity of judicial behaviour, which is illustrated in the studies that are covered in the following pages. Our discussion of the literature is organized into three broad categories: (i) attitudinal and background factors that shape the internal deliberative process; (ii) institutional norms of collegiality and acquiescence; and (iii) external strategic considerations.

3. Application of Theories to Examine Panel Effects

3.1 Attitudinal/Trait Theories Explaining Internal Deliberative Panel Dynamics

Most scholarship on panel effects has been on the US Courts of Appeals, where judges sit in rotating panels of three judges. Given the dominance of the attitudinal model in the US Supreme Court, it is not surprising that early scholarship emphasized the ideological composition or partisanship of a panel as driving case outcomes in these settings (for examples see Songer and Haire 1992; Revesz 1997; Cross and Tiller 1998; Songer, Sheehan, and Haire 2000; Hettinger, Lindquist, and Martinek 2006; Miles and Sunstein 2006; Sunstein et al. 2006; Epstein, Landes, and Posner 2013; Spitzer and Talley 2013; Beim Hirsch, and Kastellec 2014). Early research by Revesz (1997) found the presence of a Democrat or a Republican affected the outcome in salient environmental cases. Cross and Tiller (1998, 2175) studied the same court and found that Republican controlled panels tended to defer to conservative agencies while Democratic ones deferred to liberal ones in administrative cases. A seminal study by Hettinger, Lindquist, and Martinek (2006), in turn, showed that greater ideological disagreement on US appellate panels predicts both dissenting and concurring opinions, even when contrasted with strategic explanations. In a comprehensive study of ideology done that same year, Sunstein et al. (2006) found the presence of one Republican counterjudge on a panel produced 10 per cent fewer liberal rulings, while a Democratic one triggered 5 per cent more liberal rulings across most of the twenty-three issue areas studied. They also found that panels of *all* like-minded judge produced collective preference opinions, and this 'group polarization' effect existed precisely because there was no internal threat of dissent. A research update by Epstein, Landes, and Posner (2013) found similar counterjudge trends, although both sets of scholars acknowledge the magnitude of the panel effects varies by issue area. Overall, these scholars, along with a host of others, have shown that partisanship critically influences how panels operate in the US Court of Appeals (see also Songer and Sheehan 1990; Songer and Haire 1992; Sunstein, Schkade, and Ellman 2004).

Aside from policy preferences, scholars have examined if other personal attributes impact panel voting in US Court of Appeals, most notably gender and race (see Farhang and Wawro 2004; Peresie 2005; Boyd, Epstein, and Martin 2010; Kastellec 2013; Haire and Moyer 2015). This research has produced somewhat *mixed results* outside the civil rights area, which is partly attributed to scholars using different methodologies, types of cases, and time periods of analysis. Initial scholarship by Gottschall (1983) found that race and gender *did not* garner voting differences among Carter appointees in discrimination, prisoner, and criminal cases. Songer, Davis, and Haire (1994), in turn, also found *no* difference between male and female voting across all circuit courts in criminal search and seizure or obscenity cases over a ten-year period, but *did* find women were more liberal than men in employment discrimination cases (see also Peresie 2005). More recent scholarship documents relatively consistent gender differences in civil rights and liberties cases. For example, Farhang and Wawro (2004) showed the presence of one female increases the likelihood of a liberal vote by males on the panel in employment discrimination cases, but race did not matter. Boyd, Epstein, and Martin (2010) found similar effects in sex discrimination cases (see also Peresie 2005), but not in any of the *other* twelve issues studied. They also found that minority judges tended to vote for discrimination claimants and tended to influence the behaviour of their white male colleagues. Kastellec (2013), in turn, using a matching method found the presence of a minority judge increases rulings favouring affirmative action programmes in voting rights cases (see also Cox and Miles 2008 for race effects). Yet Johnson and Schulman (1989) and Karpowitz, Mendelberg, and Shaker (2012) showed the presence of a lone female on a panel had little influence, but signs of a gender gap did appear once two women where on a panel, suggesting the strength of majority voices over a solo female voice.

More recently, Haire and Moyer (2015) used the multidimensional nature of identity, interviews, and oral histories to find greater heterogeneity in terms of gender and race effects in the deliberative process of certain cases in appellate courts. Although race and ethnicity effects are modest at the individual level, their impact is significant across certain salient issues, such as employment discrimination, where African-American judges are more likely to favour the claimant than White or Latino judges. Moreover, females vote at significantly greater rates for the plaintiff in sex discrimination cases than males. Although they found the presence of a single female/minority judge did not change how male colleagues voted, the presence of two such colleagues significantly influences the lone white male on a panel (see Johnson and Schulman 1989; Karpowitz, Mendelberg, and Shaker 2012). Moreover, when White males are not in the majority, greater attention is paid to the diversity of issues covered in the opinions, and females write longer, more detailed opinions. Despite the mixed findings, some highlights have emerged. Most notably, gender and race matter the most in discrimination cases, shaping the contours of how opinions are written, and in panel votes when women and minorities are in the majority. Yet disagreement remains over the degree to which the presence of a token non-White member of a panel matters to the content and outcome of cases. Obviously, more systematic studies are needed to examine the impact of these intersectional forces in the United States and elsewhere.

3.2 Institutional Norms Shaping the Deliberative Dynamics: Conformity and Collegiality

A second line of inquiry has examined the extent to which dissent aversion, collegial norms, and collective behaviour guide the internal deliberative judicial process. Since judges work in small groups and seek to optimize their workload, it makes sense that conformity plays a critical role in resolving cases. A discussion of how legalistic norms and the norm of consensus can influence judicial behaviour can be found in Morell's (2023) chapter in this volume. As his work indicates, scholars have developed different explanations for why collegial behaviour exists, but he advocates for greater attention to the significance of precedents as a guiding force (Morell 2023). Still others, like Edwards (1998, 2003), argue that US Courts of Appeals judges change their initial views through the intellectual exchange of ideas in the deliberative process (see Caminker 1999; Wald 1999; Kim 2009; Spitzer and Talley 2013 for similar arguments). A host of scholars have shown norms of consensus play a key role in affecting both *minority* and *majority* judges on panels. Interviews with US Appellate judges by Howard (1981) and Cohen (2002) indicate that judges place a high value on collegial relationships. Scholarship by Posner (2008) in turn asserts that since these judges do not engage in much collaborative deliberation, any panel effects are likely to be a result of dissent aversion (avoiding the cost of writing dissents, time pressures, workload concerns, and potential harm to collegial relations).

Expanding on Posner's (2008) findings, Epstein, Landes, and Posner (2013) used an economic labour theory to evaluate both the intensity of a panel member's policy preferences coupled with dissent aversion to assess when and why a judge might dissent. They found dissent aversion in the Courts of Appeals occurs for a variety of reasons relating to workload pressures, concerns about impaired collegiality due to frequency of dissents, salience of a case, the ideological composition of the court, the likelihood a dissent will influence future law, and the degree the court adheres to precedent (see also Caminker 1999; Cameron, Segal, and Songer 2000; Hettinger, Lindquist, and Martinek 2006; Sunstein et al. 2006; Kastellec 2007; Carrubba and Clark 2012 for other similar arguments). This finding supports and contradicts earlier work by Hettinger, Lindquist, and Martinek (2006, 112) that showed horizontal dissent suppression was not due to workload or efficiency concerns but rather due to norms of collegiality and a pressing desire to ensure the court's legitimacy.

To account for collegial norms, Fischman (2011) used an econometric consensus model that determines the cost of dissent while also exploiting the random panel composition in both unanimous and non-unanimous cases to isolate the impact of judicial preferences in asylum cases. He determined that around half the cases would be decided differently if assigned to a different panel of judges, and thus concluded a colleague's vote and not a judge's characteristic, like party, race, and gender, help explain how judges vote in small groups (Fischman 2011 at 804). Fischman (2015) subsequently applied his 'endogenous consensus model' to re-examine eleven prior panel studies and found that a colleague's votes in a particular direction increased the probability of a judge voting similarly by 40 per cent. For Fischman, the bottom line is that norms of consensus are stronger in US Appellate Courts than any individual judge traits, like party, gender, and race, although he acknowledges judicial attributes cannot entirely be discounted. Although Fischmann's (2011, 2015) consensus paradigm fails to measure possible latent legal considerations that might explain consensus, such as case facts that are easy to reach agreement on, his approach provides insights into panel effects where individual traits are not readily observable, such as in many European courts.

Some scholars have contemplated how institutional norms influence panel *majorities* (see Kim 2009; Epstein, Landes, and Posner 2013). In their examination of the 1995–2008 Sunstein data on appellate courts, Epstein, Landes, and Posner (2013, 192–93) found that judges in the ideological majority sometimes change their vote to align with the minority judge. They speculated that while it may be due to a desire not to provoke dissent, it could alternatively signify a 'wobbler' effect. In short, they argue that in mixed panels, if one or both majority members hold weak ideological views, one or both are likely to acquiesce to the views of a strong ideological minority judge, although they left it to future researchers to test this theory. Epstein, Landes, and Posner

(2013) also tested other *group effects*, such as the relationship between the district court ruling and judge votes in different panel compositions, and concluded that district court rulings do dampen, to some extent, the effects of the ideological composition of appellate court panels (Epstein, Landes, and Posner 2013, 193). They also found that a judge's voting behaviour was influenced by the ideological composition of the larger circuit in which a judge resides (2013, 185–90). Ultimately, future work needs to pay careful attention to individual-level forces, small group dynamics, and circuit-level factors that push or pull appellate judges toward consensus (or not). Moreover, these similar factors deserve wider consideration and application in appellate courts outside the United States.

3.3 External Strategic Considerations of Panel Effects

As we have foreshadowed above, an extensive line of research has examined whether judges who sit in panels act strategically in relation to judges either above or below them in the hierarchy. Not surprisingly, scholars have reached different conclusions regarding if, when, and why strategic activity occurs on panels since they have used different sample sizes, methodologies, cases studies, and most importantly because it is difficult to disentangle strategic considerations from other competing explanations for panel effects. In regards to strategic behaviour related to *courts below*, a study by Haire, Lindquist, and Songer (2003) showed that circuit courts overturn district court cases based on judicial policy preferences in civil rights and liberties disputes. Yet scholarship by Hettinger, Lindquist, and Martinek (2006, 111–14) determined that reversal of lower court rulings was not attitudinal but more reflective of 'bounded objectivity', which includes institutional roles (the presence of a chief or district judge), case facts (the number of amicus filings or issues raised), and circuit norms (ambiguous lower court signals and collegial norms). Even so, they found that if there was collective attitudinal disagreement among the circuit court judges, it increased the likelihood of a reversal. So, horizontal disagreement between the judges also influences vertical disagreement between the different level courts (Hettinger, Lindquist, and Martinek 2006, 121). These findings point to the complexity in unpacking panel effects in intermediate-level courts that have courts above and below them in the hierarchy.

The bulk of the research in the strategic area focuses on whether US Court of Appeals judges alter their voting on different types of panels because they *fear or seek potential review* from above by either the full court (en banc review) or a higher-level court (see Van Winkle 1997; Cross and Tiller 1998; Klein and Hume 2003; Hettinger, Lindquist, and Martinek 2006; Kastellec 2007; Clark 2009; Kim 2009; Westerland et al. 2010; Beim, Hirsch, and Kastellec 2016). Research in this area has yielded mixed results, partly because some have looked at dissent activity on mixed panels while others have focused on relations in the judicial hierarchy. An early study of search and seizure cases between 1992 and 1993 by Van Winkle (1997) showed that judges used dissents to signal strategically for an en banc review when a panel's ruling conflicted with the circuits' preferences.

One year later, Cross and Tiller (1998) developed the 'whistleblower theory' indicating that when a minority judge's preferences align with the higher court's legal doctrine (take, for instance, following the *Chevron* principle), the majority judges are twice as likely to acquiesce to the legal doctrine fearing higher court review if they dissent. Conversely, they might take a cognitive shortcut to build consensus by threatening dissent when discussing a case, and thus avoid blowing the whistle by dissenting (see also Linkous and Tiller 2009). Kim (2009), in turn, showed that whistle-blowing sometimes results in en banc review but not Supreme Court review, at least in Title 7 sex discrimination cases between 1995 and 2002.

In light of these findings, Kastellec (2007) empirically demonstrated that more sophisticated whistleblower models are needed that utilize a fact-based approach while simultaneously considering ideological distances between panel members and the Supreme Court along with panel member views on precedent. He argued that introducing this complexity would increase the likelihood of determining when whistleblower activity occurs (see also Kastellec 2011 for a similar argument). Beim, Hirsch, and Kastellec (2014) found that whistleblowing is most effective for triggering review when it is rarely used and that beyond a certain point it becomes counterproductive. The conclusion to be drawn is that if the whistle of dissent is blown too frequently, the noise becomes too commonplace and loses its power with a higher court.

The work above has been supported by Hinkle, Nelson, and Hazelton (2020), who used a complex hybrid model to document the ideological alignment a judge has with the lower court along with the panel distance from the reviewing bodies in order to help explain dissents and higher court review. Their research shows that it is important for a panel judge to know where she sits vis-à-vis the lower court ruling *and* the full en banc circuit when thinking about casting a dissenting vote. Hinkle, Nelson, and Hazelton (2020, 295) concluded, like Kastellec (2007, 2011) and Beim, Hirsch, and Kastellec (2014), that hierarchical alignments between judges and across court levels, which lie outside a judge's control, largely explain the complex nature of panel effects. The implication is that an individual judge's attributes may matter less than prior studies have suggested, and panel effects are driven far more by hierarchical alignment across court levels and within a given circuit. Readers should note that this body of scholarship also aligns with notions of sophisticated voting and *certiorari* decision-making at the US Supreme Court level (see Caldeira, Wright, and Zorn 1999; Brenner and Kohl 1989).

Some scholars examining strategic behaviour on US Appellate Courts have moved *beyond* vote outcomes to explore panel effects at the *opinion writing stage* (see Bowie, Songer, and Szmer 2014; Hazelton, Hinkle, and Seon Jeon 2016; Hinkle 2016; 2017). Work by Bowie, Songer, and Szmer (2014) empirically demonstrated that more divergent panels take longer to craft final rulings, suggesting they may be spending more time debating and negotiating over how to write content. Hinkle (2017) used ideological distance measures to show that circuit judges strategically shift the types of precedent they cite when writing opinions for different types of ideological panels in search and seizure cases handed down between 1953 and 2010. The citations authors used matched their ideological preferences only when issuing unified panel rulings, while a more diverse panel dampened ideologically driven citations in an effort to accommodate or anticipate requests for opinion revisions. Ultimately, Hinkle (2017) argued that a combination of strategic, deliberative, and institutional factors produces panel effects at the opinion writing stage. Not surprisingly, models of judicial behaviour that invoke complexity over simplicity tend to carry the day when it comes to explaining panel effects like dissent activity or dissent aversion. Clearly, more research assessing panel effects outside of the narrow confines of case outcomes is needed in the future.

4. Panel Effects on Supreme Courts and Other International Courts

Since scholarship has shown panel composition matters to case outcome, more researchers are exploring how panels are formed. A fundamental question that has emerged in the literature is: Do chief justices or others act strategically and/or politically when striking panels? While scholars have shown strategic activity does occur on high courts, such as Canada, South Africa, Israel, and Norway, the findings are not conclusive on either side of the debate.

4.1 Canadian Supreme Court

In the Canadian context, numerous judicial interviews have revealed that chief justices construct panels based on regional considerations, workload, and case salience rather than political motivations (see Baar 1988; Greene et al. 1998; Songer et al. 2012). Yet descriptive research of early *Charter of Rights* cases by Heard (1991, 304–05) found the chief justice created panels predisposed to favour a Charter claim, and the Charter claimant subsequently won at a much higher rate. Likewise, a statistical study by Hausegger and Haynie (2003, 655) showed that the first two Post-Charter chief justices created panels that were ideologically closer to them in salient Charter cases, yet they did not abuse this power. Although subsequent work by Ostberg and Wetstein (2007, 212) did not focus on panel effects, their study of panel size and assignment led them to infer that the first three Post-Charter chiefs did not overtly abuse their panel assignment in the civil rights and liberties cases, yet in a prior study they did find chiefs acted strategically by significantly lowering their own dissent rates to control their own courts (Wetstein and Ostberg 2005).

Despite the debate over the political nature of panel assignment, most scholars agree that Canadian chief justices strike larger-sized panels in high-profile Charter cases, especially during the McLachlin tenure (see Alarie, Green, and Iacobucci 2015; Hausegger, Hennigar, and Riddell 2015; McCormick 2015; Hausegger 2021). Research by Songer et al.

(2012) showed that chiefs constructed smaller panels when the law is clear or when dealing with Quebec Civil law (requiring a three-judge Quebec majority), rather than for ideological reasons. Alarie, Green, and Iacobucci (2015; see also Greene et al. 1998, 117) indicated that while chief justices could in theory construct panels based on their preferences, in practice the effects are small, and there is some evidence that chief justice McLachlin assigned more seven- and five-member panels mirroring the Court's median ideological position (Alarie, Green, and Iacobucci 2015, 349–55). In Canada, anyway, while there is some question over whether ideology plays a critical role in panel and opinion assignments, agreement exists that chiefs form larger panels for the most important cases.

4.2 South African Supreme Court

In the South African context, Hausegger and Haynie (2003) found that during the apartheid era (1950 to 1990), chief justices did strategically assign judges to panels based on their ideology, seniority, and issues in cases. Unlike the Canadian context, South African chiefs were more likely to assign senior judges to panels, and construct more ideologically similar judge panels on a regular basis (outside civil rights cases), possibly because they had a larger pool of judges to choose from and could construct smaller panel sizes (pool = eighteen by 1990; panels ranged typically from three to five judges). Their statistical findings reinforced prior speculation by scholars that South African chiefs manipulated panel assignments for ideological reasons or to ensure a government win (Ellmann 1992; Hausegger and Haynie 2003, citing earlier work by Forsyth 1985).

While earlier studies of the South African Court uncovered panel manipulation by the chief, a follow-up study of the South African Supreme Court by Sill and Haynie (2010) provides a more nuanced understanding of panel assignment by chiefs over a thirty-year period. Their study revealed that chiefs did not create panels based on policy preferences of individual judges but rather repeatedly created panels based on the minimum number of like-minded judges needed to achieve favourable outcomes. Thus, the chief justices, especially after the 1994 constitutional change, used strategy to construct panels that built a minimum winning coalition, versus creating all like-minded panels, especially in salient cases. The implication is that unanimity was not the strategic goal but rather the aim was to produce a majority win in a certain ideological direction.

4.3 Israel Supreme Court

Israel's Supreme Court presents fertile ground for testing panel effects, since many cases are decided by three-judge panels that are established in theory by the chief justice. Research by Eisenberg, Fisher, and Rosen-Zvi (2013) applied 'role responsibility theory' and evidence from social and organizational psychology to assess the impact that the presiding justice and opinion writer had on voting behaviour of panel members in mandatory criminal law cases. Although the chief justice has the power to create the three-judge panels hearing most cases on the fifteen-member Israeli High Court, in practice they discovered the Calendar Clerk (an experienced lawyer) selects most panels. This is interesting, especially since prior research by Gross and Schachar (1998) and Eisenberg, Fisher, and Rosen-Zvi (2012) indicated that several non-random factors, such as seniority, specialization, and workload, influenced panel assignments in Israel. Eisenberg, Fisher, and Rosen-Zvi (2013) also found that justices were statistically more likely to vote according to their own voting preferences when they served as a *presiding justice* than when serving as mere panel members, and colleagues were 50 per cent more likely to *rule for the defendant* when a particular justice served as a panel member versus a presiding judge (Eisenberg, Fisher, and Rosen-Zvi 2013). Although there was some evidence of opinion effects on a justices' voting behaviour, given the non-random assignments of panels they did not reach any conclusions on this front. Ultimately, this study joins a growing body of research showing that institutional features, such as seniority and opinion writing, aside from individual judicial panel traits, affect the voting behaviour of judges in panels.

More recent scholarship by Givati and Rosenberg (2020) on the Israel Supreme Court showed that in certain cases where individual justices are allowed to compose three-judge panels to assess review rejections, they do so strategically. Although the chief has the power to create all three-judge decision panels heard by the fifteen-member Israeli high court, a unique procedure allows the weekly Justice on Duty to have the power to select the two other panel participants to assess whether to reject review by the High Court of Justices. Their study showed a high variance in panel composition over a two-year period indicating that these justices selected panels strategically based on ideological agreement rather than based on random assignment or professional expertise. These findings, in turn, triggered the Supreme Court to immediately issue new rules that took away panel composition discretion in High Court of Justice cases (Givati and Rosenberg 2020). Irrespective of the changes made to the unique High Court of Justices rejection procedure, Givati and Rosenberg's (2020) research indicates when chiefs have the power to strike panels in Israel, they do so in a strategic manner, leading them to argue for the implementation of random panel assignment on appellate courts.

Just as background traits have been found to have significance for US Appellate Court justices, scholars have found these factors also play a significant role in the Supreme Court of Israel. For example, Weinshall-Margel (2011) found that the religious or secular orientation of Israeli Supreme Court judges serves as a good predictor of ideological voting in religious freedom cases. Indeed, even when controlling for case facts and legal changes, religious values have a 'significant, though not overpowering' impact on their judgments (Weinshall-Margel 2011, 581). Earlier work by Bogoch and Don-Yechiya (1999) also documented gender effects in Israeli courts. These studies reinforce that comparative panel scholars must consider factors like race, gender, and religion as possible drivers of dissent and ideological rulings in key issue areas.

4.4 British Courts

The example of Britain and the analysis of judgments by the Law Lords provides clear evidence of panel effects (see Robertson 1998). Using both logistic regression and multidimensional scaling methods, Robertson (1998, 70) concluded that a 'good prediction can be made of case resolution by knowing who is on the panel' hearing the appeal. In fact, his model of panel compositions across various areas of law from 1986 to 1995 suggests that knowing which Law Lord was on the appeal panel could correctly predict 97 per cent of criminal and constitutional appeals, 91 per cent of tax cases, 87 per cent of civil cases, and 83 per cent of public law cases (Robertson 1998, 50–55). Subsequent scholarship by Hanretty (2012) indicated that it may be wrong to attribute attitudinal decision-making to individual Law Lords. His analysis of patterns of voting indicated that the Law Lords do not fit well into a single ideological dimension, and thus cautioned individuals to not make too much of panel effects based on individual political views (Hanretty 2012, 201, 701). Instead, his model reflects a propensity to dissent and not a propensity to cast liberal or conservative votes per se (Hanretty 2012, 712). Having said this, Hanretty's analysis may be tied to an assumption that panel effects play out in a one-dimensional ideological space. Robertson's earlier analysis suggested that panel effects might play out across multiple issue dimensions, and even Hanretty (2012, 716) conceded that the new UK Supreme Court might devolve into higher levels of ideological discord, so further multidimensional studies of conflict in United Kingdom panels are warranted.

4.5 Studies of Multiple High Courts

The recent comparative work by Alarie and Green (2017, 110–12) introduces a novel approach for studying how panel effects might vary across national high courts. They constructed a mathematical 'gaming prospect ratio' (GPR) to tease out how often a case might be decided differently if a chief justice created different sized panels for cases. Studying the percentages across multiple courts, they determined that Canadian cases might have been decided differently about 20 per cent of the time with different size panels, and the effect was larger in Australia's High Court (30 per cent) and the US Supreme Court (34 per cent). The United Kingdom and India had GPR measures at 100 per cent because they are composed of large numbers of judges that decide cases in small panels (Alarie and Green 2017, 110–11; see also Parikh 2021). Even though these chiefs wield this important power, they believe that Australian and Canadian chief justices resisted temptations to game the system and tended to assign larger panel sizes in important cases. Even so, their regression models explaining dissents suggests that panel size is significant in explaining split panels in Canada, the United Kingdom, and the United States, indicating that size matters (see Alarie and Green 2017, 295–314). Thus, it behooves researchers to consider panel size as a potential variable, especially when panels range across three, five, and seven members.

4.6 European International Courts

In his normative paper on European International Courts, law scholar Shai Dothan (2018) examines whether justices siting in large and diverse panels, such as the International Court of Justice or the European Court of Human Rights, might try to form strategic coalitions with those from other states in order to obtain their preferred case outcome. This assertion stems, in part, from the fact that previous empirical scholarship has conclusively shown that individual judges sitting on these courts *do* systematically favour their own state (see Posner and de Figueiredo 2005; Voeten 2008). As such, it makes sense to ponder whether coalitions emerge among like-minded judges from different states on these courts. In light of this possibility and the fact that 'home country' bias exists, Dothan (2018) argued these institutions ought to push for greater self-governance in the selection process of their judges to ensure more judicial independence. Given the variations in the appointment processes in these institutions, he suggested that future scholars need to apply strategic models, while also considering legal and institutional differences, to examine the internal group dynamics and coalition building efforts that might occur between these judges. He also argues that future scholars need to critically examine the impact other critical actors in these institutions might have, such as the large professional staff or repeat litigators, because they may also shape the direction of case outcomes in these courts (for work documenting the significance of repeat litigators, see Galanter 1974, 2003).

5. Panel Effects on Supreme and Constitutional Courts with Rotating Panel Assignments

There is a growing body of scholarship examining panel effects on constitutional and high courts that sit in rotating panels, where a designated set of justices decide cases as a group across a given term or year. In the European context, studying panel effects has been complicated by a myriad of institutional and procedural factors that make such studies difficult. Yet Kelemen (2013, 2018) has noted that most constitutional courts in both Western and East-Central Europe do operate in smaller panel sizes to decide the admissibility of constitutional complaints or assessing residual constitutional matters (see Table 29.1 for a list of representative courts). While many courts work in smaller-size panels, she argued that most constitutional courts assess parliamentary laws and treaties in the full plenary session, and some courts, such as Albania, Bulgaria, Italy, Latvia, Lithuania, Luxembourg, Macedonia, Montenegro, Slovakia, and Romania (since 1997) do not engage in any panel activity (Kelemen

2018, 17–28). The point here is that panel designation can vary from court to court and often the smaller panels decide cases of lower political salience, making studies of this sort more difficult.

Studies of panel effects on these courts have also been hampered by the civil law traditions requiring most courts to issue collective judgements (see Skiple et al. 2016, 74). For example, courts in France, Italy, Belgium, Austria, and the European Court of Justice issue collective judgments, yet the jurisdictions of Germany, Spain, Portugal, and most European Constitutional Courts *do* allow dissent activity (see Garoupa, Gill, and Tiede 2021). For those European courts that do embrace the publicity of dissent, Kelemen (2018) points out that many of these courts do not publicly identify the rapporteur judge (who is usually assigned by the President in a majority of Constitutional courts). Moreover, since most rapporteurs have expertise on the topic and have control over the facts and materials in specific cases, Keleman (2018) argues that low dissent rates continue and might be due to the fact that other judges lack key information and face workload pressures (see also Dyevre 2013 for similar commentary on difficulty of measuring policy preferences in these courts). Other complications to studying panel effects in these courts stem from the lack of comprehensive datasets, and reluctance by many political scientists to recognize extra-legal influences on voting behaviour. Despite these difficulties, as these courts become more influential in their policy making role and comprehensive datasets emerge, scholars have begun conducting more empirical studies on these courts, including efforts to study panel composition in several different institutional settings (see Skiple et al. 2016, 74).

5.1 Norwegian Supreme Court

The Norwegian Supreme Court has become fertile ground for exploring the applicability of various theoretical models. In a longitudinal study of this Court, where judges typically sit in two quasi-randomized parallel rotating panels of five justices, Skiple et al. (2016) developed a complex multilevel model to examine the impact of three categories of variables, namely individual attitudes and traits, institutional panel level factors, and legal case facts on judicial voting in economic cases from 1963 to 2021. Their model demonstrated that panel and case-level factors more readily explained judicial voting than a justice's raw policy preference. In terms of panel effects, they found that gender matters. A panel of majority women were able to significantly sway the whole panel to side with the private party over the government (decrease by 43 per cent). Moreover, the presence of a dissenting judge significantly reduced the likelihood that the panel will vote for the government. In a more recent study, Skiple, Littlere Bentsen, and Hanretty (2020) used a hierarchical item response model to examine dissenting behaviour in five-, eleven-, or nineteen-judge panels in all non-unanimous cases over a twenty-year period. They found that unlike the US left–right spectrum, the biggest predictor of Norwegian disagreement pertains to governmental deference, with justices who have academic backgrounds less likely to defer to governmental authority than career lawyers or judges. Additionally, the change from a ministerial to merit-based appointment process did not matter much, partly because appointments have never been overly political. These findings suggest that in Norway, like Canada, judicial attitudes and values play a much more muted and diminished role than in the United States. This knowledge shifts the discussion, for comparativists anyway, away from the wholesale acceptance of the attitudinal model as the decisive theory for explaining high court behaviour around the world.

5.2 Brazilian Supreme Court

Brazil presents a unique feature for the study of possible panel effects. The Brazilian Supreme Court issues decisions ranging from one justice (in 'easy' cases) to five-member panels (in criminal cases) and full court membership (in constitutional cases). Even so, any justice has the power to stop the voting at the merit stage by issuing a 'vista' request. According to de Mendonca Lopes (2019) this formal request allows a Brazilian justice, who is uncertain how to vote, the ability to examine complex cases for an additional thirty days before voting. Yet, according to Arguelhes and Hartman (2017), the formal thirty-day deadline was rarely met across a thirty-year study. Their research shows that the vista request is used at various phases of the agenda process, and its application has increased in number and duration since the mid-1990s. Their study also provided evidence that some justices might use the vista power strategically to postpone an unpopular vote to a more suitable time when the court composition or the external political context is more favourable. Clearly, more scholarship needs to be done to examine the degree and extent of this individualistic strategic power of agenda control.

Scholarship by de Mendonca Lopes (2019) examined whether dissent aversion identified by Garoupa, Gili, and Gomez-Pomar (2012) in the Spanish civil law tradition, where justices face unanimity pressure, also plays out in the Brazilian Supreme Court. He found once the pivotal sixth conference vote in the majority is cast, the remaining justices on a full eleven-justice panel tend to suppress dissents. This suppression occurs despite a rotating practice of which justice votes first, second, and so on. This finding aligns with the contention from Garoupa, Gili, and Gomez-Pomar (2012) that norms within civil law courts mask far higher disagreement levels, setting them apart from the overt patterns of disagreement seen in common law courts. Their study also showed that the full panel of eleven justices mattered from year to year in dissent rates, with justices serving on more politically oriented homogeneous full courts issuing lower dissents across all regression models. This lends credence to the argument that political conflict specified in the attitudinal model matters to some degree in the Brazilian high court, but it might be masked by civil law traditions promoting consensus.

6. Conclusion: Gaps in the Literature and Suggestions for the Future

In our overview of the research on appellate courts around the world to date, there are several observations that are worth revisiting. First, there has been extensive research conducted on panel effects in the US Courts of Appeals over the past several decades. Over time, scholars have developed increasingly sophisticated methods to analyse such effects. Moreover, scholars have come to embrace, to a greater and lesser degree, the fact that legal, ideological/trait, and strategic theories combined with psychological and economic considerations collectively help explain this complex multifaceted phenomenon. Future scholars need to work at untangling the *relative* impact of each of these theoretical paradigms to help understand how different panel compositions shape decisions. In other words, more research needs to assess *why* panel effects occur, and if and when different theories become more salient in the decision-making process. For example, tax or regulatory cases, which are far more technical, might make acquiescence or the deliberative process more important, while these approaches might be less relevant in search and seizure or discrimination disputes, where ideology and attitudinal forces are more prominent (Ostberg and Wetstein 2007; Hinkle, Nelson, and Hazelton 2020). In salient cases, where strong ideological differences emerge, attitudinal and strategic considerations are likely to play a more decisive role in panel splits. Future research needs to continue to explore how traits, such as race and gender, may impact different types of cases. As more women and minorities sit on appellate courts, new insights may appear, especially at the intersection of race, gender, religion, and ideology. On another level, scholarship needs to move beyond the regional US Appellate Courts, to explore panel effects on the US Court of Appeal for the Federal Circuit, bankruptcy courts, or other specialized courts that sit in panels, such as the US Court of Appeals for Veterans Claims.

The review of the literature also shows a continuing paucity of published research on panel effects in courts outside the United States. As mentioned before, the research to date has been largely country specific, and applies theories developed in the United States to different cultural settings. The fact that this body of research is growing is a promising trend. The lack of sustained research on panel effects outside the United States stems partly from the considerable time, money, and effort needed to build databases where courts sit in smaller panel sizes. However, as more information becomes available in some countries, this bodes well for making future panel scholarship more feasible. Even today, there remains a reluctance in many countries to recognize studies outside the traditional legal framework, although efforts to overcome this barrier are making headway in places like Brazil, Canada, India, Norway, and Israel.

One overarching consideration that future panel scholars need to unpack when studying courts outside the US context is that judges may have different incentives in other cultural settings. For example, civil law judges work in vastly different institutions and follow different cultural norms than common law judges. Thus, as some have argued, it might make sense for scholars to develop new theories that capture the unique institutional features and background traits of judges serving on civil courts, such as in the European and Latin American context. Additionally, political culture matters. Judges in corrupt political settings may face existential threats to their livelihood and independence that are far different from say, the United States or Canadian settings, resulting in different implications of whether and how panel effects materialize.

A second overarching consideration is the need to develop more systemic comparative studies of panel effects similar to the one conducted by Alarie and Green (2017). Such an effort makes more sense as efforts are made to build more comprehensive datasets outside the United States. Moreover, the examination of panel effects and the biases of home-state judges in transnational tribunals is also worthy of further consideration (see Posner and de Figueiredo 2005; Voeten 2008; Garoupa and Ginsburg 2015; Dothan 2018; Carrubba and Fjelstul 2021). While such studies might forgo some important cultural considerations, such work could provide important insights into critical similarities and differences in how panels operate in different institutional settings. These insights become important for a variety of reasons. First, they help scholars gain a better understanding of how judicial selection and institutional structures impact how panels operate in different countries. This, in turn, can help countries seeking more democratic judicial systems identify different strategies for creating better panel structures. Systematic comparative studies can also help current democratic systems featuring smaller panels develop institutional safeguards to ensure they operate more efficiently and impartially. This, in turn, allows judicial systems to remain strong, independent, and deliver more widely accepted rulings. This effort remains critical in an increasingly interdependent world that Tate and Valinder (1995) noted has triggered an increase in the judicialization of politics around the globe.

For scholars who came of age when the attitudinal model dominated the literature, it is heartening to see panel scholars recognizing that myriad theories collectively shape the complex, nuanced, and multifaceted nature of panel effects. One reason scholars need to apply multiple theories to improve the understanding of this phenomenon is that the small cadre of judges hearing cases change, courts decide newer or refined issues over time, new laws materialize, and societal values evolve. The reputation of courts and judges can also wax and wane (see Garoupa and Ginsburg 2015). We believe that different theoretical paradigms will also provide intersecting levels of explanation in different case types and across different courts. In essence, theoretical explanations work both in concert and in a disparate manner in courts around the world. Their relative impact are also likely to change over time. This underscores both the beauty and challenge of studying this sub-field of judicial behaviour as we try to unpack what Baum (1997) aptly labelled the continuing 'puzzle or mystery of judicial behavior'. Through theoretical and methodological humility, and a broader field of vision in courts across the globe, we can all benefit from new insights in the ever-changing puzzle of panel effects on appellate courts.

References

Alarie, Benjamin and Andrew J. Green. 2017. *Commitment and Cooperation on High Courts: A Cross-Country Examination of Institutional Constraints on Judges*. New York: Oxford University Press.

Alarie, Benjamin, Andrew Green, and Edward M. Iacobucci. 2015. 'Panel Selection on High Courts'. *University of Toronto Law Journal* 65 (4 Fall): 335–81.

Arguelhes, Diego Werneck, and Ivar A. Hartmann. 2017. 'Timing Control without Docket Control: How Individual Justices Shape the Brazilian Supreme Court's Agenda'. *Journal of Law and Courts* 5 (1 Spring): 105–40.

Baar, Carl. 1988. 'The Courts in Canada'. In *The Political Role of Law Courts in Modern Democracies*, edited by J. L. Waltman and K. M. Holland, ch. 4. London: Palgrave MacMillan.

Baum, Lawrence. 1997. *The Puzzle of Judicial Behavior*. Ann Arbor: University of Michigan Press.

Beim, Deborah, Alexander V. Hirsch, and Johnathan P. Kastellec. 2014. 'Whistleblowing and Compliance in the Judicial Hierarchy'. *American Journal of Political Science* 58 (4 October): 904–18.

Beim, Deborah, Alexander V. Hirsch, and Johnathan P. Kastellec. 2016. 'Signaling and Counter-signaling in the Judicial Hierarchy: An Empirical Analysis of En Banc Review'. *American Journal of Political Science* 60 (2): 490–508.

Bogoch, Bryna, and Rachelle Don-Yechiya. 1999. *The Gender of Justice: Bias Against Women in Israeli Courts*. Jerusalem: The Jerusalem Institute for Israeli Studies (Hebrew).

Bowie, Jennifer Barnes, Donald R. Songer, and John Szmer. 2014. *The View from the Bench and Chambers: Examining Judicial Process and Decision Making on the U.S. Courts of Appeals*. Charlottesville: University of Virginia Press.

Boyd, Christina L., Lee Epstein, and Andrew D. Martin. 2010. 'Untangling the Causal Effects of Sex on Judging'. *American Journal of Political Science* 54 (2): 389–411.

Brenner, Saul, and J. F. Krohl. 1989. 'Strategies in Certiorari Voting on the U.S.'. Supreme Court. *Journal of Politics* 51 (4): 828–40

Caldeira, Gregory A., John R. Wright, and Christopher J. W. Zorn. 1999. 'Sophisticated Voting and Gate-Keeping in the Supreme Court'. *Journal of Law, Economics & Organization* 15 (3): 549–72.

Cameron, Charles M., Jeffrey A. Segal, and Donald R. Songer. 2000. 'Strategic Auditing in a Political Hierarchy: An Informational Model of the Supreme Court's Certiorari Decisions'. *American Political Science Review* 94 (1): 101–16.

Caminker, Evan H. 1999. 'Sincere and Strategic Voting Norms on Multimember Courts'. *Michigan Law Review* 97 (8): 2297–380.

Carrubba Clifford J., and Tom S. Clark. 2012. 'Rule Creation in a Political Hierarchy'. *American Political Science Review* 106 (3): 622–43.

Carrubba, Clifford J., and Joshua C. Fjelstul. 2021. 'International Courts: The CJEU and the ECtHR'. In *High Courts in Global Perspective: Evidence, Methodologies, and Findings*, edited by Nuno Garoupa, Rebecca D. Gill, and Lydia B. Tiede, ch. 9. Charlottesville: University of Virginia Press.

Clark, Tom S. 2009. 'A Principal Agent Theory of En Banc Review'. *The Journal of Law, Economics & Organization* 25 (1): 55–79.

Cohen, Johnathan M. 2002. *Inside Appellate Courts*. Ann Arbor: University of Michigan Press.

Cox, Adam B., and Thomas J. Miles. 2008. 'Judging the Voting Rights Act'. *Columbia Law Review* 108 (1): 1–54.

Cross, Frank B., and Emerson H. Tiller. 1998. 'Judicial Partisanship and Obedience to Legal Doctrine: Whistleblowing on the Federal Courts of Appeals'. *Yale Law Journal* 107 (7): 2155–76.

de Mendonca Lopes, Felipe. 2019. 'Dissent Aversion and Sequential Voting in the Brazilian Supreme Court'. *Journal of Empirical Legal Studies* 16 (4): 933–54.

Dothan, Shai. 2018. 'The Motivations of Individual Judges and How They Act as a Group'. *German Law Journal* 19 (7): 2165–88.

Dyevre, Arthur. 2013. 'European Integration and National Courts: Defending Sovereignty under Institutional Constraints'. *European Constitutional Law Review* 9 (1): 139–68.

Edwards, Harry T. 1998. 'Collegiality and Decision Making on the D.C. Circuit'. *Virginia Law Review* 84 (7): 1335–70.

Edwards, Harry T. 2003. 'The Effects of Collegiality on Judicial Decision Making'. *University of Pennsylvania Law Review* (151): 1639–90.

Eisenberg, Theodore, Talia Fisher, and Issi Rosen-Zvi. 2013. 'Group Decision Making on Appellate Courts: Presiding Justice and Opinion Justice Influence in the Israel Supreme Court'. *Psychology, Public Policy, & Law* 19 (3): 282–96.

Eisenberg, Theodore, Talia Fisher, and Issi Rosen-Zvi. 2012. 'Does the Judge Matter? Exploiting Random Assignment on a Court of Last Resort to Assess Judge and Case Selection Effects'. *Journal of Empirical Legal Studies* 9: 246–90.

Ellmann, Stephen. 1992. *In a Time of Trouble: Law and Liberty in South Africa's State of Emergency*. Oxford: Clarendon Press.

Epstein, Lee, and Jack Knight. 1998. *The Choices Justices Make*. Washington: Congressional Quarterly Press.

Epstein, Lee, William M. Landes, and Richard A. Posner. 2013. *The Behavior of Federal Judges: A Theoretical and Empirical Study of Rational Choice*. Cambridge: Harvard University Press.

Farhang, Sean, and Gregory Wawro. 2004. 'Institutional Dynamics on the U.S. Court of Appeals: Minority Representation Under Panel Decision Making'. *The Journal of Law, Economics & Organization* 20 (2): 299–330.

Fischman, Joshua B. 2011. 'Estimating Preferences of Circuit Judges: A Model of Consensus Voting'. *Journal of Law & Economics* 54 (4 November): 781–810.

Fischman, Joshua B. 2015. 'Interpreting Circuit Court Voting Patterns: A Social Interactions Framework'. *The Journal of Law, Economics & Organization* 31 (4): 808–42.

Forsyth, Christopher. 1985. *In Danger for their Talents*. Cape Town: Juta Press.

Galanter, Marc. 1974. 'Why the "Haves" Come Out Ahead: Speculations on the Limits of Legal Change'. *Law and Society Review* 9: 95–160.

Galanter, Marc. 2003. 'Why the "Haves" Come Out Ahead: Speculations on the Limits of Legal Change'. In *Litigation: Do the 'Haves' Still Come Out Ahead*, edited by Herbert Kritzer and Susan Silbey, 13–81. Stanford: Stanford University Press.

Garoupa, Nuno, Marian Gili, and Fernando Gomez-Pomar. 2012. 'Political Influence and Career Judges: An Empirical Analysis of Administrative Review by the Spanish Supreme Court'. *Journal of Empirical Legal Studies* 9 (4): 795–826.

Garoupa, Nuno, and Tom Ginsburg. 2015. *Judicial Reputation: A Comparative Theory*. Chicago: University of Chicago Press.

Garoupa, Nuno, Rebecca D. Gill, and Lydia B. Tiede, eds. 2021. *High Courts in Global Perspective: Evidence, Methodologies, and Findings*. Charlottesville: University of Virginia Press.

Givati, Yehonatan, and Israel Rosenberg. 2020. 'How Would Judges Compose Judicial Panels? Theory and Evidence from the Supreme Court of Israel'. *Journal of Empirical Legal Studies* 17 (2 June): 317–41.

Gottschall, Jon. 1983. 'Carter's Judicial Appointments: The Influence of Affirmative Action and Merit Selection on Voting on the U.S. Courts of Appeals'. *Judicature* 67: 165–73.

Greene, Ian, Carl Baar, Peter McCormick, George Szablowski, and Martin Thomas. 1998. *Final Appeal: Decision Making in Canadian Courts of Appeal*. Toronto: James Lorimer.

Gross, M., and Y. Schacher. 1998. 'How Are Supreme Court Panels Selected: A Quantitative Analysis'. *Hebrew University Law Review* 29: 567–85.

Haire, Susan B., Stefanie A. Lindquist, and Donald R. Songer. 2003. 'Appellate Court Supervision in the Federal Judiciary: A Hierarchical Perspective'. *Law & Society Review* 37: 143–68.

Haire, Susan B., and Laura P. Moyer. 2015. *Diversity Matters: Judicial Policy Making in the U.S. Courts of Appeals*. Charlottesville: University of Virginia Press.

Hanretty, Chris. 2012. 'The Decisions and Ideal Points of British Law Lords'. *British Journal of Political Science* 43 (3 July): 703–16.

Hausegger, Lori. 2021. 'Examining the Empirical Study of the Supreme Court of Canada'. In *High Courts in Global Perspective: Evidence, Methodologies, and Findings*, edited by Nuno Garoupa, Rebecca D. Gill, and Lydia B. Tiede, ch. 5. Charlottesville: University of Virginia Press.

Hausegger, Lori, and Stacia Haynie. 2003. 'Judicial Decisionmaking and the Use of Panels in the Canadian Supreme Court and the South African Appellate Division'. *Law & Society Review* 37 (3): 635–57.

Hausegger, Lori, Matthew Hennigar, and Troy Riddell. 2015. *Canadian Courts: Law, Politics, and Process*. Oxford: Oxford University Press.

Hazelton, Morgan L. W., Rachael K. Hinkle, and Jee Seon Jeon. 2016. 'Sound the Alarm? Judicial Decisions Regarding Publication and Dissent'. *American Politics Research* 44 (4): 649–81.

Heard, Andrew D. 1991. 'The Charter in the Supreme Court of Canada: The Importance of Which Judges Hear an Appeal'. *Canadian Journal of Political Science* 24 (2 June): 289–307.

Hettinger, Virginia, Stefanie A. Lindquist, and Wendy L. Martinek. 2006. *Judging on a Collegial Court: Influences on Federal Appellate Decision Making*. Charlottesville: University of Virginia Press.

Hinkle, Rachael K. 2016. 'Strategic Anticipation of En Banc Review in the U.S. Courts of Appeals'. *Law & Society Review* 50 (2): 383–414.

Hinkle, Rachael K. 2017. 'Panel Effects and Opinion Crafting in the U.S. Courts of Appeals'. *Journal of Law and Courts* 5 (2): 313–36.

Hinkle, Rachael K., Michael J. Nelson, and Morgan L. W. Hazelton. 2020. 'Deferring, Deliberating, or Dodging Review: Explaining Counter-judge Success in the U.S. Courts of Appeals'. *Journal of Law and Courts* 8 (2): 277–300.

Howard, J. Woodford. 1981. *Courts of Appeals in the Federal Judicial System: A Study of the Second, Fifth, and District of Columbia Circuits*. Princeton, Princeton University Press.

Johnson, Richard A., and Gary I. Schulman. 1989. 'Gender Role Composition and Role Entrapment in Decision Making Groups'. *Gender & Society* 3 (3): 355–72.

Karpowitz, Christopher F., Tali Mendelberg, and Lee Shaker. 2012. 'Gender Inequality in Deliberative Participation'. *American Political Science Review* 106 (3): 533–47.

Kastellec, Johnathan P. 2007. 'Panel Composition and Judicial Compliance on the U.S. Courts of Appeals'. *The Journal of Law, Economics, & Organization* 23 (2): 421–41.

Kastellec, Johnathan P. 2011. 'Panel Composition and Voting on the U.S. Courts of Appeals over Time'. *Political Research Quarterly* 64 (2): 377–91.

Kastellec, Johnathan P. 2013. 'Racial Diversity and Judicial Influence on Appellate Courts'. *American Journal of Political Science* 57 (1 January): 167–83.

Kelemen, Katalin. 2013. Dissenting Opinions in Constitutional Courts. *German Law Journal* 14 (8): 1345–71.

Kelemen, Katalin. 2018. *Judicial Dissent in European Constitutional Courts: A Comparative and Legal Perspective*. New York: Routledge.

Kim, Pauline T. 2009. 'Deliberation and Strategy on the United States Courts of Appeals: An Empirical Exploration of Panel Effects'. *University of Pennsylvania Law Review* 157 (5): 1319–81.
Klein, David E., and Robert J. Hume. 2003. 'Fear of Reversal as an Explanation for Lower Court Compliance'. *Law & Society Review* 37: 579–606.
Linkous, Derek J., and Emerson H. Tiller. 2009. 'Panel Effects, Whistleblowing Theory and the Role of Legal Doctrine'. *University of Pennsylvania Law Review* 158: 83–92.
Maltzman, Forrest, James F. Spriggs II, and Paul J. Wahlbeck. 2000. *Crafting Law on the Supreme Court: The Collegial Game*. New York: Cambridge University Press.
McCormick, Peter J. 2015. *The End of the Charter Revolution: Looking Back from the New Normal*. Toronto: University of Toronto Press.
Miles, Thomas J., and Cass R. Sunstein. 2006. 'Do Judges Make Regulatory Policy? An Empirical Investigation of *Chevron*'. *University of Chicago Law Review* 73: 823–82.
Morell, Alexander. 2023. 'Legalism and Professional Norms'. In *The Oxford Handbook of Comparative Judicial Behaviour*, edited by Lee Epstein, Gunnar Grendstad, Urška Šadl, and Keren Weinshall, ch. 6. Oxford: Oxford University Press.
Murphy, Walter. 1964. *Elements of Judicial Strategy*. Chicago: University of Chicago Press.
Ostberg, C. L., and Matthew E. Wetstein. 2007. *Attitudinal Decision Making in the Supreme Court of Canada*. Vancouver: UBC Press.
Parikh, Sunita. 2021. 'Empirical Studies of Judicial Behavior and Decision Making on Indian Courts'. In *High Courts in Global Perspective: Evidence, Methodologies, and Findings*, edited by Nuno Garoupa, Rebecca D. Gill, and Lydia B. Tiede, ch. 8. Charlottesville: University of Virginia Press.
Peresie, Jennifer L. 2005. 'Female Judges Matter: Gender and Collegial Decisionmaking in the Federal Appellate Courts'. *Yale Law Journal* 114 (7 May): 1759–90.
Posner, Eric, and Miguel F. P. de Figueiredo. 2005. 'Is the International Court of Justice Biased?' *The Journal of Legal Studies* 34 (2): 599–630.
Posner, Richard A. 2008. *How Judges Think*. Cambridge: Harvard University Press.
Pritchett, C. Herman. 1941. 'Divisions of Opinion among Justices of the U.S. Supreme Court, 1939–1941'. *American Political Science Review* 35 (Oct.): 890–98.
Pritchett, C. Herman. 1948. *The Roosevelt Court: A Study in Judicial Politics and Values, 1937–1947*. New York: MacMillan.
Revesz, Richard. 1997. 'Environmental Regulation, Ideology, and the DC Circuit'. *Virginia Law Review* 83: 1717–72.
Robertson, David. 1998. *Judicial Discretion in the House of Lords*. Oxford: Oxford University Press.
Rohde, David W., and Harold J. Spaeth. 1976. *Supreme Court Decision Making*. San Francisco, CA: Freeman.
Schubert, Glendon. 1965. *The Judicial Mind: Attitudes and Ideologies of Supreme Court Justices, 1946–1963*. Evanston: Northwestern University Press.
Schubert, Glendon. 1974. *The Judicial Mind Revisited*. New York: Oxford University Press.
Segal, Jeffrey, and Harold J. Spaeth. 1993. *The Supreme Court and the Attitudinal Model*. Cambridge: Cambridge University Press.
Segal, Jeffrey, and Harold J. Spaeth. 2002. *The Supreme Court and the Attitudinal Model*. Cambridge: Cambridge University Press.
Sill, Kaitlyn L., and Stacia L. Haynie. 2010. 'Panel Assignment in Appellate Courts: Strategic Behaviour in the South African Supreme Court of Appeal'. *Politikon* 37 (2–3 December): 269–85.
Skiple, Jon Kåre, Henrik Littlere Bentsen, and Chris Hanretty. 2020. 'The Government Deference Dimension of Judicial Decision Making: Evidence from the Supreme Court of Norway'. *Scandinavian Political Studies* 43 (4): 264–85.

Skiple, Jon Kåre, Gunnar Grendstad, William R. Shaffer, and Eric N. Waltenburg. 2016. 'Supreme Court Justices' Economic Behaviour: A Multilevel Model Analysis'. *Scandinavian Political Studies* 39 (1): 73–94.

Songer, Donald R., and Reginald S. Sheehan. 1990. 'Supreme Court Impact on Compliance and Outcomes: *Miranda* and *New York Times* in the United States Courts of Appeals'. *Western Political Quarterly* 43: 297–316.

Songer, Donald R., and Susan B. Haire. 1992. 'Integrating Alternative Approaches to the Study of Judicial Voting: Obscenity Cases in the U.S. Courts of Appeals'. *American Journal of Political Science* 36: 963–82.

Songer, Donald R., Sue Davis, and Susan B. Haire. 1994. 'A Reappraisal of Diversification in the Federal Courts: Gender Effects in the Courts of Appeals'. *Journal of Politics* 56: 425–39.

Songer, Donald R., Reginald S. Sheehan, and Susan B. Haire. 2000. *Continuity and Change on the United States Courts of Appeals*. Ann Arbor: University of Michigan Press.

Songer, Donald R., Susan W. Johnson, C. L. Ostberg, and Matthew E. Wetstein. 2012. *Law, Ideology, and Collegiality: Judicial Behaviour in the Supreme Court of Canada*. Montreal: McGill-Queen's Press.

Spaeth, Harold J., and Jeffrey Segal. 1999. *Majority Rule or Minority Will: Adherence to Precedent on the U.S. Supreme Court*. Cambridge: Cambridge University Press.

Spitzer, Matthew, and Eric Talley. 2013. 'Left, Right, and Center: Strategic Information Acquisition and Diversity in Judicial Panels'. *Journal of Law, Economics & Organization* 29 (3): 638–80.

Sunstein, Cass R., David Schkade, and Lisa M. Ellman. 2004. 'Ideological Voting on Federal Courts of Appeals: A Preliminary Investigation'. *Virginia Law Review* 90 (1): 301–54.

Sunstein, Cass R., David Schkade, Lisa M. Ellman, and Andres Sawicki. 2006. *Are Judges Political? An Empirical Analysis of the Federal Judiciary*. Washington, DC: Brookings Institution.

Tate, C. Neal, and Torbjorn Vallinder. 1995. *The Global Expansion of Judicial Power*. New York: NYU Press.

Van Winkle, Steven R. 1997. 'Dissent as a Signal: Evidence from the U.S. Courts of Appeals'. Paper presented at the Annual Meeting of the American Political Sciences Association, Washington, DC.

Voeten, Erik. 2008. 'The Impartiality of International Judges: Evidence from the European Court of Human Rights'. *American Political Science Review* 102 (4): 417–33.

Wahlbeck, Paul J., James F. Spriggs, II, and Forrest Maltzman. 1999. 'The Politics of Dissents and Concurrences on the U.S.'. Supreme Court. *American Politics Quarterly* 27 (4): 488–514.

Wald, Patricia M. 1999. 'A Response to Tiller and Cross'. *Columbia Law Review* 99 (1 Jan.): 235–61.

Weinshall-Margel, Keren. 2011. 'Attitudinal and Neo-Institutional Models of Supreme Court Decision Making: An Empirical and Comparative Perspective from Israel'. *Journal of Empirical Legal Studies* 8 (3): 556–86.

Westerland, Chad, Jeffrey A. Segal, Lee Epstein, Charles M. Cameron, and Scott Comporato. 2010. 'Strategic Defiance and Compliance in the U.S. Courts of Appeals'. *American Journal of Political Science* 54 (4): 891–905.

Wetstein, Matthew E., and C. L. Ostberg. 2005. 'Strategic Leadership and Political Change on the Canadian Supreme Court: Analyzing the Transition to Chief Justice'. *Canadian Journal of Political Science* 38 (3): 653–73.

Wetstein, Matthew E., and C. L. Ostberg. 2017. *Value Change in the Supreme Court of Canada*. Toronto: University of Toronto Press.

CHAPTER 30

REFERRALS

BENJAMIN BRICKER, MATTHEW J. GABEL, AND CLIFFORD J. CARRUBBA

1. Introduction

WHETHER working alone in a trial court or deliberating with other judges in a collegial court, judges in modern judicial systems function within a larger interactive network. An increasingly important—and increasingly studied—aspect of modern judicial networks is the ability of one court to call upon another court for definitive interpretations of law. This process, known as a referral, is perhaps most widely known from the European Union, where referrals from national courts have constituted a significant share of cases decided by the Court of Justice of the European Union (CJEU) since the 1970s. The EU's referral procedure, called the preliminary reference, has been a vital link between the member state judicial systems and the Court of Justice, helping to drive the Europeanization of law and the judicialization of EU governance in the process (Kelemen 2011; Krommendijk 2021). Though referrals from member state judiciaries to the CJEU are by far the most prominent form of referral in the legal and political science literature, referral and reference processes occur in judicial systems around the world, both national and international.

In this chapter we discuss and review the scholarship on judicial referrals, with referrals broadly defined as any request from one court to another court for a definitive interpretation of law. The scholarship on referrals has grown tremendously in the twenty-first century, with most of that scholarly work focusing on the CJEU and its preliminary reference procedure. Within this growing area of study there are several major areas of research: (i) why national courts and judges file references; (ii) why and how private litigants seek out CJEU referrals; and (iii) how the CJEU uses and participates in the preliminary reference system. We also examine the scholarship focusing on other international courts, as well as the less-developed literature examining how national legal systems employ referral processes. After a brief overview of referrals, we begin by examining the major questions posed in the CJEU preliminary reference literature, the most developed literature and research on referrals. Some of these questions and accompanying literatures are better developed than others, though many areas have seen a proliferation of research questions and answers over the past two decades. We conclude with some thoughts on the scholarship on referrals in other major international courts and national court systems. Along the way, we try to point out new and unexplored questions that are ripe for future research.

2. Referrals: An Overview and Definition

As noted above, we define a referral as a request from one court to another court for a definitive interpretation of law prior to the ultimate ruling in the case. Referrals processes occur in a variety of courts and sometimes have different names. But, regardless of name, they operate as a functionally equivalent set of procedures in which an extant case is interrupted to obtain a legal answer from another court. In the international or supranational context, this means that a national court is empowered to refer a question of international law or of the compatibility of domestic and international law to the international court. In domestic court contexts the referral procedure allows a lower court to refer a question of law to another court, generally a superior court, but it need not always work in this manner. In the United States, for example, federal court judges can ask a state's highest court to answer a question of state law that arises in a federal case through a process known as 'certification' (Cochran 2013, 159). And, in many European countries, referrals are sent by ordinary judges to the national constitutional court, which often is not a part of the regular judiciary. As a general rule, the referral process stays the court proceedings until the reference is answered. However, the receiving court usually is not obliged to answer the referral request (Cochran 2013; Krommendijk 2021). Proponents of referrals point to the benefits to efficiency and uniformity in law gained by the process. However, the process also represents an important exception to the general rule that only final decisions from one court can be examined by another court. It is important to note that the referral process is different than an appeals process in that an appeal is a party-driven decision taken generally after a final ruling by a lower court. Referrals are not directly party-driven but instead are made at the discretion of the judge overseeing the case.

3. Referrals and the Court of Justice of the European Union

The CJEU has the most prominent, and most studied, system of judicial referrals. In fact, the preliminary reference system is often described as one of the most significant developments in the creation of a common and integrated Europe (Burley and Mattli 1993; Dyevre and Lampach 2019). Much of the EU's legal development has not occurred in the EU parliament or even the EU Council but rather through the written decisions of its court in Luxembourg, and many of the CJEU's most important decisions have occurred via the preliminary reference (Alter 1996).[1] It is through the reference process that national judges at any level can question the validity of national laws by asking the CJEU whether national laws are compatible with the European legal and institutional order.

Given its importance in the advancement of the EU system, the preliminary reference procedure has long been a cornerstone of various theories surrounding both the development of the power of the CJEU and also the power of the EU more broadly. Located in Article 267 of the Treaty on the Functioning of the European Union (TFEU), the preliminary reference procedure states that if an issue of EU law is raised in a member state court, that court can refer the question to the CJEU if the member state court 'considers that a decision on the question [of EU law] is necessary to enable it to give judgment'. If the case is accepted, the CJEU will then provide a preliminary ruling answering the question of EU law. The national court is then expected to apply that rule in resolving the pending case.

Though it may not appear so at first glance, there is a considerable amount of discretion built into the referral process. First, though it is the parties in a legal case that request a preliminary reference to the CJEU, it is national courts and national judges that must ultimately make the decision to initiate the referral process, or not.[2] Thus, national judges hold a strategic and potentially powerful position within the creation of EU law and the European legal order. Second, the CJEU is empowered to answer the question of law posed by the national court, but it does not have the power to either overturn the decisions of national courts or solve the case for national courts (Dyevre et al. 2022). Upon receiving the CJEU's answer to its referred question, the national court is then empowered to provide a final decision for the substantive legal case. At the same time, the CJEU holds the power to dismiss any referrals it receives from national courts, which provides the CJEU with a certain amount of power to select preferred cases.

Though this referral process is discretionary for most national courts, Article 267 (TFEU) also mandates that a question of EU law must be referred to the CJEU when 'such question is raised in a case pending before a court or tribunal of a Member State against whose decisions there is no judicial remedy under national law'. This should mean that national peak courts—notably, supreme courts and constitutional courts—must refer cases to the CJEU when they determine that EU law is pivotal to the court's final judgment. However, the reality is that national peak courts also have a great deal of discretion to determine whether or not to submit a reference to the CJEU (Broberg and Fenger 2021). Notably, there is no procedure to contest a decision by a peak court not to refer a question to the CJEU. And, as many scholars have noted, for many years the attitude of national constitutional courts toward CJEU referrals could be characterized somewhere between hesitant and downright distrustful (Claes 2015; Lacchi 2015;

Serrano 2015). Many prominent constitutional courts, including those in Italy and Germany, did not make a reference until the 2010s.

At first glance, then, the referral process appears to provide both national courts and the CJEU with the potential for mutual advantage. However, the terms of Article 267 also provide incentives for resourceful parties (and their attorneys) to introduce issues of EU law into litigation, and for the CJEU to encourage member state courts to refer cases (Pavone 2022). Accordingly, scholarly work has focused a great deal on precisely how, why, and under what conditions national courts, attorneys, and the CJEU are incentivized to use the preliminary ruling process. The past two decades, in particular, have seen a proliferation of studies offering a thorough and sophisticated examination of multiple facets of the preliminary reference process.

3.1 Early Work: The Judicial Empowerment Thesis and Beyond

Looking back on the rise of the European Union and the CJEU, it is clear that the preliminary reference process has been a key feature driving the development of both European integration and the power of the CJEU as an institution (e.g. Tridimas 2015). The expansive use of the reference process has also fundamentally changed the legal and political landscape of the EU as a whole, turning what might otherwise be an obscure supranational court in Luxembourg into one of the main drivers of European economic, legal, and social development.

When examining the development of the preliminary reference, one fundamental question is precisely *why* national courts would ever want to make a reference. For some scholars, the answer is simply procedural: under certain circumstances Article 267 (ex 234) both encourages and demands national judges to refer questions of EU law to the CJEU. The treaty-backed principle of EU law supremacy provides even further impetus to refer such questions to the CJEU, the clear interpreter of EU law (e.g. Claes 2006, 43). However, it is easy to see that national judges could view the process of referring legal questions to the CJEU as an intrusion on their power over decision-making in individual cases. Apart from legal process, then, why would national judges ever participate in this referral process?

First introduced by Weiler (1991), the 'judicial empowerment thesis' proposed the first sophisticated reason why national courts engaged in the preliminary reference process. Weiler's theory posits a two-way interaction of mutual advantage between the national courts and the CJEU. At one end, the CJEU has been able to utilize the preliminary reference procedure to attract cases concerning EU law that the court needs to expand both its own authority within Europe and the larger authority of the EU as an institution. At the other end, national courts have been able to use the preliminary reference procedure to bolster their institutional standing and institutional power within their national political systems. According to Weiler (1991, 2426), the procedure should be particularly beneficial to *lower* national courts, which gain through the preliminary reference a 'de facto judicial review of legislation'—a power long denied to most European lower courts. The source of this *de facto* judicial review power arises from the answer the CJEU provides to the national court's referral. In its answer, the CJEU will often suggest whether the national law or policy in question violates EU law. If it does violate EU law, the national court is then empowered to overturn the national law.

Other theories that developed around the same time as the judicial empowerment thesis also focused on the self-interest of courts as drivers of the reference process, but examined the reference procedure as a particular source of empowerment for lower national courts. Courts at all levels could, after the Treaty of Rome, become a part of the development of the larger European legal order simply by sending a reference for a preliminary ruling on a matter of European law. Burley and Mattli (1993, 64), for example, described the '"heady" taste of power' that lower national courts gained through the referral process as a key reason why the CJEU was able to gain and grow to rely on an ever-increasing stream of references. When combined with the important judicial legitimacy the CJEU gained through those references, we can see the genesis of a symbiotic relationship of mutual advantage between national courts and the CJEU.[3] Ordinary courts of all stripes could gain power by utilizing the reference process. Yet just as important is the reciprocal power the CJEU could gain by accepting references and, in the course of answering referrals, advance the European legal order and ultimately their own institutional power.

Karen Alter's 'inter-court competition' thesis emphasized the possibility that preliminary references can create specific advantages for lower national courts in their relationship to the domestic high courts that otherwise hold a monopoly on interpretive power. As Alter (1996, 466) notes, lower national courts 'found few costs and numerous benefits' to making referrals to the CJEU and applying EU law. Specifically, lower national courts could circumvent unwanted doctrines and deviate from the established jurisprudence of their superior courts by referring cases to the CJEU. Lower courts, then, could become the drivers of EU legal integration and gain power via-a-vis their superior courts in the process (Alter 1996, 2001).

Several questions arise with both the judicial empowerment and the inter-court competition theories. One concerns the accuracy of the assumption that lower courts have the time, the willingness, and the drive or capacity to create lots of preliminary references (see Wind 2010; Pavone 2022). Separately, it is not clear why the CJEU would want as many preliminary references as possible, even at the cost of receiving poorly drafted or ill-conceived questions. Another issue concerns the assumption implicit in these theories that national courts have acted in a uniform manner to both refer cases to the CJEU and increase the Europeanization of law—a point noted early on by Golub (1996). Perhaps some national judges seek Europeanization, but others do not. Perhaps some national court systems are more attuned to the supposed drive for Europeanization than others (Wind 2010; Golub 1996). Additionally, it is uncertain the extent to which lower courts would actually want to create jurisprudential problems for their superior courts. As Alter later notes, however, the best way to conceive of the national court–CJEU relationship may not be one in which direct competition between these two levels of national courts leads to lower courts referring more cases. Instead, this inter-court competition might best be thought of as the avenue through which the CJEU established its supremacy doctrine (the idea that EU law is supreme to national law) in national legal orders (Alter 2010, 12). With a solid base but a host of questions raised by these theories, scholars have taken to both refine and expand the conclusions we can draw from the national court–CJEU relationship.

3.2 Today: Judicial Empowerment Thesis Re-examined

The idea of judicial empowerment and inter-court competition through the preliminary reference procedure is intuitively plausible. National courts, and particularly lower courts, could see institutional value in the referral process. Yet, national courts and judges at all levels could have cross-cutting reasons not to engage with the CJEU and European law. Similarly, the interests of the CJEU could have changed over the years, leading to different dynamics today. These reasons to engage or not engage could centre on legal or jurisprudential factors, but they could also involve concerns about non-compliance with rulings. It is important to note here that many 'empowerment' theories assume compliance with rulings is a non-issue. Those assumptions could be challenged at several steps in the reference process (Carrubba and Gabel 2015, 68).

While not questioning the basis for the theory, Pavone and Kelemen (2019) assert that some ideas within the 'judicial empowerment' framework have eroded over time while others have evolved. Instead of lower national courts continuing to lead the charge of Europeanization, Kelemen and Pavone posit that an institutional evolution has occurred in the reference process: national high courts increasingly seek out and obtain dialogue with the CJEU on the pace and tenor of European integration. In doing so, high courts have now come to dominate the preliminary reference process. In some ways, the CJEU should welcome and encourage this change. As the Union developed from the initial six founding member states in the 1950s to the present twenty-eight member states, the number of possible referring courts has grown exponentially. With that growth comes the risk that too many lower courts will refer cases, which could ultimately lead to legal conflict and jurisprudential chaos (Pavone and Kelemen 2019). Thus, the attractiveness of referrals from high courts that sit at the apex of the legal and jurisprudential order in their respective countries. Referrals from high courts could enable the CJEU to transmit its thoughts on Europeanization to the national court systems in a better way than has been previously possible. At the same time, high courts see the benefit of being the main interlocutors with the CJEU—namely, that they regain control over lower courts and the direction and pace of the Europeanization process.

Others are more critical of the theoretical underpinnings of judicial empowerment. Dyevre, Glavina, and Atanasova (2020) question several key assumptions built into the judicial empowerment and inter-court competition theses. The first is the assumption that the referral process favours lower national courts. Given that peak courts generally focus only on questions of law (and not questions of fact), and that the preliminary reference system is one in which courts only send up questions of EU law for resolution, peak courts may be better placed to initiate successful referrals. More recent data on referrals supports the idea that lower court judges did pioneer the preliminary reference to the CJEU, and were the dominant referring force in the early years of the CJEU's existence (Pavone and Kelemen 2019; Dyevre et al. 2020). However, peak national courts have steadily caught up to the lower courts, with peak courts now accounting for nearly 40 per cent of references to the CJEU (Dyevre et al. 2020). Ultimately, this data shows that high courts have become the preferred interlocutors with the CJEU, which suggests that a major tenet of the judicial empowerment thesis—that lower courts' self-interest in power can uniformly explain the rise of the preliminary reference—is no longer true.

Further reflection produces another apparent weakness in the foundation of the judicial empowerment thesis. As Pavone (2018, 309) notes, one of the bases of the thesis is the large number of references that lower national courts make each year. Yet, there are countless more lower courts than there are appeals and peak courts in the European court systems, so—to the extent it is even of consequence—lower courts sending more references in the aggregate should ultimately be a rather unremarkable finding. What might be of more consequence is the propensity of the various levels of courts to send references. In fact, peak courts are the most likely group to send a repeat referral to the CJEU (Pavone 2018, 311; 2022), and when examining referral rates over the past fifteen to twenty years domestic high courts have become at least the equal of lower ordinary courts in terms of the number of references filed (Pavone and Keleman 2019; Dyevre et al. 2020).

3.3 Why Do National Courts and National Judges File Preliminary References?

Early theories explaining the development of the preliminary reference process focused on the mutual benefits afforded to both national courts and the CJEU. Later theories have sought to develop more fully—and sometimes to question—the premises underlying this idea of mutual benefit. In asking the question of why national courts file preliminary references, scholars have offered two different tracks for analysis. One primary track in the literature has focused at a broader level of theory and data analysis, asking what factors cause *national court systems* to refer (or not refer) cases to the CJEU (e.g. Stone Sweet and Brunell 1998a; Carrubba and Murrah 2005; Wind et al. 2009; Vink et al. 2009; Broberg and Fenger 2013; Hornuf and Voigt 2015; Dyevre et al. 2020; Dyevre et al. 2022). Another track focuses more on micro-level causes and micro-level data, examining what might cause certain *individual judges* within national legal systems to refer more (or fewer) cases to the CJEU (Mayoral et al. 2014; Pavone and Kelemen 2019; Alter 2001; Dyevre et al. 2022; Krehbiel and Cheruvu 2022). A new and evolving understanding of the referral process also has meant a new examination of the role of *parties* and *lawyers* in influencing the submission of preliminary references (e.g. Pavone 2022).

3.3.1 *National-Level Examinations*

The member states of the European Union provide an excellent testing ground for comparative theories of judicial behaviour. With differing legal traditions, legal rules, trade policies, and levels of economic development, the EU contains a diversity of factors that might influence reference behaviour and EU integration. And there is a wide degree of difference among members states. A Belgian court is ten times more likely to call on the CJEU for a preliminary reference than a court in Portugal (Hornuf and Voigt 2015). Early on, this geographic discrepancy in CJEU reference rates was noted as perhaps the 'most important puzzle' for CJEU scholars to face (Stone Sweet and Brunell 1998b, 73). Accordingly, scholars have sought to explain what institutional or structural factors might contribute to referral activity.

As noted above, some member state courts, such as Germany, Austria, and Belgium, traditionally submitted many referrals, while other court systems, like Ireland, Portugal, and Spain, submitted relatively few. What factors might contribute to these varying reference rates? Given that the original impetus for the EU (beginning with the European Economic Community (EEC) and the European Community (EC)) was the creation of a common market for free trade, levels of transnational economic activity have long been examined as a factor influencing referral rates. Over time, a general consensus has developed concerning the importance of several key variables. One factor generally acknowledged to be important to referral rates is the national level of intra-EU trade (Stone Sweet and Brunell 1998a; Carrubba and Murrah 2005, Hornuf and Voigt 2015; cf. Vink et al. 2009).

Stone Sweet and Brunell (1998a) were among the first to examine the theory of EU trade systematically. Similar to Burley and Mattli (1993), their theory begins with the private actors that initiate legal cases. Specifically, they focus on transnational private economic groups and organizations as they should have the greatest interest in challenging local legal rules that stifle transnational trade. It is these actors that were well-placed to rely on the European common market rules and principles in the cases they bring to national courts. National courts then saw their own opportunity in these transnational trade cases to develop their own institutional power via the preliminary reference. Examining preliminary references from 1961 to 1992, Stone Sweet and Brunell find confirmation of the transnational trade thesis, though their results have been questioned for not normalizing their trade data to account for the varying sizes of each EU country and for using ordinary least squares (OLS) regression (Pitarakis and Tridimas 2003; Hornuf and Voigt 2015). Re-examination of the idea using negative binomial regression, a more proper estimator for the count data utilized, also found support for the intra-EU trade hypothesis (Carrubba and Murrah 2005). However, Vink et al. (2009) suggest that population size may be a better proxy for the concept of trade, and analysis by Wind, Martinsen, and Rotger (2009) found no effect of intra-EU trade on referral rates when several additional factors are included in the analysis. Hornuf and Voigt (2015) re-examined the trade theory of referral activity and found solid support for the argument that total gross domestic product (GDP) per country does influence the number of preliminary references, which seems to confirm the theory that the larger the national economy is the more disputes that should arise.

Additionally, there is strong evidence showing that various aspects of legal doctrine and legal culture have influenced national court preliminary reference rates. The concept of legal doctrine or culture has taken various forms, including monism vs dualism, national litigiousness, and forms of constitutional review. Though the monist–dualist split within the EC legal order had long been mentioned in EU law textbooks as a potential divide in acceptance of European law (e.g. Bermann et al. 2002), the thought that judges from monist legal traditions would refer more cases was first explicated in a formal manner by Alter (1996). She proposed that judges in monist legal systems, where international law does not need to be directly translated into national law to be applicable in the national legal order, should be more accustomed to using international law in their decisions, and so should also be more likely to use the CJEU's preliminary reference system to obtain rulings on treaty matters.

However, Carrubba and Murrah's (2005) later work found this relationship to work in exactly the opposite direction: judges from monist systems refer cases less often than judges in the dualist systems. The reason could be that judges in monist legal systems are used to interacting with international law, which means they should be less likely to need to submit a preliminary reference to the CJEU. Instead, dualist judges should need to submit more CJEU references, perhaps because disputes over EU law arise with greater frequency in dualist states. This negative relationship between monist states and CJEU referrals has been confirmed several times in more recent studies (e.g. Vink et al. 2009; Hornuf and Voigt 2015). Similarly, institutional judicial review rules also appear strongly connected to national referral rates. Countries that have adopted the Kelsenian constitutional court model refer more cases than those court systems that have adopted a different set of judicial review rules, while those countries in which lower court can exercise concrete judicial review have lower referral rates (Carrubba and Murrah 2005; Vink et al. 2009; Hornuf and Voigt 2015).

The CJEU is a European endeavour. Public support for the EU project, for more European integration, should then play a critical role in influencing the submission of cases to the CJEU (Carrubba and Murrah 2005; Vink et al. 2009), yet this general claim raises a host of new questions. To what extent do national courts consider public opinion on policies when making referral decisions? Do national courts or the CJEU consider non-compliance issues in the preliminary reference process? And how might the public influence the decisions of national judges and the CJEU? New research examines several of the concepts described above (Krehbiel and Cheruvu 2022). Their theory makes the decision to refer conditional on the relative costs of non-compliance within their own national environment. Additionally, the national court must weigh the relative level of public support for national governments or the EU to handle a given policy area, with that calculus possibly determining whether or not to refer. This strategy is different than many previous works focusing on references in that its theory and data are focused at the level of the case, yet it is also similar to other works focusing more on the strategic dynamic many national and international courts face (see e.g. Carruba et al. 2008). The findings here ultimately bring up a larger issue of the role of the CJEU as an actor that can drive European integration on its own (Carrubba and Gabel 2015), and the ability of national courts to dictate the terms of EU integration.

Could the geographic location of courts and judges contribute to their likelihood of engaging in dialogue with the CJEU? In other words, might a court from Frankfurt or Milan be more likely to refer than a court from Memmingen or Cortona? Here, advances in geographic information systems (GIS) technology have greatly aided the ability of researchers to provide compelling answers to why some courts and judges utilize the reference process. In fact, there are patterns of referral behaviour that are the product of both structural and institutional factors as well as court-level and individual-level factors. On an institutional level, more decentralized judicial systems like Germany allow for more referral activity to arise from lower-level courts. This pattern is likely due to the relatively greater autonomy that lower-level judges have in decentralized systems, as opposed to more centralized legal systems like France (Kelemen and Pavone 2018). At the same time, there are interesting sub-national patterns uncovered through GIS analysis. One intuitive yet still important result is that the greatest number of cases are filed where there are the greatest number of people and the largest amount of trade (Kelemen and Pavone 2018; Dyevre and Lampach 2021). And in the regions with large trade and manufacturing industries, more references are centred on EU trade and competition laws (Kelemen and Pavone 2018, 390). Looking across the entire EU, most references come from regions that contain national capitals (Vienna, Berlin, Athens, etc.), as well as areas that include national peak courts—including constitutional courts (Dyevre and Lampach 2021).

3.3.2 *Why Do National Judges Not File?*

The common assumption is that national courts send referrals to the CJEU, the CJEU then rules in an expansionary manner, and those rules are then transmitted to member states through national court rulings and increased EU legislation (Stone Sweet and Brunell 1998a; Fligstein and Stone Sweet 2002, 1223). In other words, the assumption is that national courts *always* want to file more cases, and they always want more European integration (Alter 2001). Recent work has begun to question this assumption, answering important questions and proposing new questions along the way.

Wind (2010) and co-authors (2009) first prominently challenged the assumption that national judges will always want to file references, pointing to Sweden and Denmark in particular as member states in which the judicial empowerment and inter-court competition theories do not hold. Courts at all levels in these countries have shown reluctance to send preliminary references or otherwise engage with the CJEU. Why is this the case? Wind's findings point to the combination of majoritarian democratic principles and the lack of a judicial review tradition in these countries that has led the judges in these countries not to engage with the CJEU. Similar reasoning also helps explain why judges in the United Kingdom were reluctant to engage with the CJEU (Wind et al. 2009).

And yet some of the Danish and Swedish judges also note their belief in an implicit understanding that the Ministry of Justice, the career bureaucracy from which many judges are appointed, should take the lead in determining whether or not a legal issue needs to be referred to the CJEU—and their default answer is 'not'. The results from these earlier interviews also provide an interesting backdrop to the more recent comparative work on whether judicial independence levels and democratic backsliding contribute to the willingness of high courts to engage in dialogue with the CJEU (Mayoral and Wind 2021).

One promising direction for current and future research arises from Wind's use of interview data with national judges, which suggests there could be systematic factors within national court systems that lead individual judges to choose not to refer cases. In fact, the reality is that referring questions to the CJEU is still a rare event, and most judges will never submit a reference during their entire careers (Glavina 2020). And as with many rare events, it is hard to assess the motivations for making referrals. Judges might refer because they need clarification on the law. Alternatively, referrals might occur to obtain political cover for preferred decisions. Recent research has begun to examine further at the micro-level the motivations of individual judges and how they navigate the process of referring questions.

One main reason for this reticence to engage is an uncomfortableness with EU law and a lack of understanding for CJEU procedures. Simply put, many judges—particularly lower court judges—feel uncomfortable engaging with EU law and the CJEU. Interviews with Italian ordinary court judges make clear that many national judges do not believe they have sufficient training in EU law principles to make competent preliminary references (Pavone 2018, 315–17). Familiarity with the laws of the EU is not a given; in fact, judges who do not believe they have adequate knowledge of EU law are less likely to report that they know when to refer a legal issue to the CJEU (Mayoral et al. 2014).

Another overriding reason not to engage with the CJEU comes from the everyday workload pressures ordinary court judges encounter as part of their job. Again, interviews with national court judges make clear that the day-to-day demands of judging—including case management and writing final decisions—play a role in whether or not judges will file a reference. Leijon and Glavina (2022) interview fifty-five judges in three countries: Sweden, Croatia, and Slovenia. They find different reasons motivate the passivity or inaction of the Swedish and Eastern European judges. While the Swedish judges generally report not referring out of a concern that referring cases is rarely necessary, the Croatian and Slovenia judges report not referring due to a lack of knowledge about the process and because they fear punishment by their judicial supervisors for not meeting production targets for resolving cases. These motivations for not referring accord with Pavone's (2018) research indicating that many Italian judges do not refer cases because they do not understand the process and because the referral will take time away from managing their busy caseloads.

The reality of these interviews also undercuts key aspects of the judicial empowerment thesis, notably the desire of ordinary judges to engage with EU law. Most recently, Pavone's (2022) comprehensive study of reference activity, which includes 134 judicial interviews, points out that—contrary to his expectations—most lower court judges express a mix of fear and trepidation about initiating a referral to the CJEU. Further examination of judicial motivations at the individual level should lead to a more complete understanding of the process of referral submission.

3.4 Interactive Relationships Between National Courts and the CJEU

Any accounting of the preliminary reference process—or any referral process—that we have seen necessarily hinges on the understanding that there are (at least) two actors that must be considered: the referring court and the court that receives the reference. What is the exact nature of this interactive relationship between national judges and the CJEU in the reference process? Nyikos' (2006) study of preliminary reference behaviour was perhaps the first to examine this set of questions systematically. When national courts submit a referral to the CJEU, they must include a reasoned description of the legal issue, including a description of the facts and the competing legal arguments that may require CJEU resolution. This process permits national courts at least some and perhaps a great deal of discretion in terms of framing the issue. Examining this dynamic relationship has taken several forms.

Notably, the referring court can, through the wording of its question, suggest a possible path toward the resolution of the question it poses—what Nyikos (2006, 530) calls a 'preemptive opinion'. This behaviour does not happen in all cases—Nyikos finds these pre-emptive opinions occur in roughly 40 per cent of the cases she studies. What leads national court judges to provide these suggested outcomes? More complex issues often lead the referring court to include a suggested outcome, as well as cases involving equal treatment. Additionally, there is a recursive effect in preliminary references, in which courts that send more preliminary references to the CJEU also send more 'pre-emptive opinions'.

Thus, there is considerable evidence that national courts can act strategically, framing possible solutions to the issues they refer. Yet there are many ways to frame issues. In fact, national courts can frame their referred question in a manner that either supports EU law and EU integration or that supports member state autonomy and national legal compatibility with EU law principles (Leijon 2021). The first type of framing supports the logic of EU integration and judicial empowerment along the lines of Alter (1996), Burley and Mattli (1993), and Weiler's (1991) work, while the second frame supports the logic of national legal sovereignty and national court resistance to EU integration. Thus, one intriguing question is whether the referring national courts support either the logic of European integration or national autonomy—or whether they take a neutral stance.

Recent studies examining legal framing point to several interesting answers. First, supporting EU integration is the most common frame used by national courts when referring cases, while empowering national legal sovereignty is the least likely frame. However, there are many referred cases that do not fit neatly into either frame: in fact, many judges try to balance the competing demands in their written submissions. Often this balance is adopted in cases of high domestic political importance, and in cases of low political importance at the EU level (Leijon 2021, 522). Additionally, lower courts are much more likely to express support for EU integration in their submissions than high courts. This could reflect greater support for EU integration, or it could represent a strategic manoeuvre: many lower court judges might think there is greater likelihood of acceptance by the CJEU if they adopt that frame.

These answers also bring up interesting questions for the future. Perhaps most prominent, are there national or sub-national differences in the way courts frame cases? To put in another way, would a Polish court today be more likely to frame its reference in a way that protects the national legal order? Would a Dutch judge today be more likely to seek EU integration? Also, some national court systems are split into specializations, while others are not. Are there differences that cut across countries that either have adopted or have not adopted specialist courts?

Just as national courts can engage in framing, the CJEU also may be able to frame—or reframe—issues strategically by rephrasing or 'reformulating' the question presented to them in the preliminary reference (Sadl and Wallerman 2019). There are myriad reasons why the CJEU might reformulate preliminary questions, though the court seems most likely to substantively reframe the issue when the referring national court fails to engage with European law and CJEU case law in its referral (Sadl and Wallerman 2019, 426). Reformulating questions can also be used to narrow down the scope of disputes on EU law and to defuse conflicts in general (Sadl and Wallerman 2019; Broberg and Fenger 2021). Still, most reformulations are not substantive in nature, but instead are stylistic rephrasings designed to ensure that the question can be translated in all of the EU member state languages (Krommendijk 2021, 129).

As intimated above, the process of referrals can be thought of as part of an ongoing 'dialogue' between national court judges and the judges on the CJEU. Rephrasings can be a way to subtly change the future course of the dialogue. Yet the answer provided by the CJEU is not really the end of the dialogue. There remains a critical third step: the translation of the CJEU's answer into the substantive decision by the national court. And recent research has indicated that more than one type of judicial dialogue may be occurring—particularly in the third step. Examining the Swedish judiciary, Bogojevic (2017) finds four types of responses by national judges: (i) to accept the decision and implement it as is; (ii) to question the validity of the CJEU's ruling in its final decision; (iii) an interruption in the dialogue that occurs when the law under review has been changed in the interim by parliament; and (iv) when the national court receives the CJEU's ruling and simply ignores it. And here lies a promising area for future research. As Wind and others have shown (2009, 2010), the Scandinavian judiciaries behave differently than other courts in the EU legal system. Could these dialogues be replicated in other countries, or might there be even more ways in which national courts can expand the judicial dialogue in the transmission of the CJEU's answer. Additionally, Bogojevic's fourth category illustrates the real occurrence of 'non-compliance' with CJEU rulings by national courts. Thus, this line of inquiry has future value for separation of powers scholars and those who examine the strategic nature of court interactions.

Examining the written text of the referral, the CJEU's response, and the national court's subsequent actions is one way to examine the interactive relationship between courts in the reference process. Another avenue is to observe how national judges respond to the CJEU's referral feedback, both positive and negative. Dyevre, Lampach, and Glavina (2022) examine the relationship between referring courts and referral courts, particularly the question of whether and how referring courts and judges might learn from unsuccessful referrals. The reality today is that the CJEU is no longer in a position where it needs to seek out national court references. In its early years the CJEU was very hesitant to reject referrals or issue 'reasoned orders' that procedurally dismiss the reference (Broberg and Fenger 2021; Dyevre et al. 2022). In fact, the CJEU regularly rejects scores of references every year—and courts submitting a reference for the first time are much more likely to be rejected than others. Courts from the newer member states also have a much higher proportion of their cases rejected when compared to more established member states (Dyevre et al. 2022, 98). In this environment, might there be a chilling effect from receiving a procedural dismissal order from the CJEU (Bobek 2008, 1616)?

Perhaps counterintuitively, referring courts that received a reasoned order from the CJEU rejecting their referral are in fact more likely to try again and submit another preliminary reference than those courts that were successful in their initial preliminary reference (Dyevre et al. 2022, 102). Further, those courts experiencing CJEU rejection the first time are more likely to have their next reference accepted, thus suggesting that referring courts generally try to learn and improve the quality of their work the next time.

3.5 Litigants and Lawyers

Much of the focus of preliminary references centres on the judicial network and judicial dialogue involved. However, the main avenue for private individuals and groups to assert EU legal rights comes from the preliminary reference procedure. Thus, it is also important to consider the actions of a third set of actors—the parties and lawyers who file the lawsuits. Early on, Burley and Mattli (1993, 54) described interest groups as one of the key players that would try to drive European integration by challenging parochial laws in the local courts. Stone Sweet and Brunell (1998a) also noted the self-interests of private litigants as drivers of EU cases, but it was Alter and Vargas (2000) who first developed a comprehensive theory and logic for when and why organized interests will turn to the courts to advance EU law. Primary among their conclusions is that narrow but well-organized interest groups often mount effective EU litigation strategies, while stronger and well-connected interest groups rarely sought a European litigation strategy (2000, 477). Cichowski's (2004, 2007) examination of the CJEU's gender equality cases concluded that the court's case law in that area effectively mobilized and empowered social actors, solidifying rights while also removing the issue from national government influence.

Conant (2002) also examined the role of interest groups and other private and public actors in the development of EU law. Her thesis largely begins with the CJEU developing new rights and obligations through case law, but it relies critically on the organized interests that then must mobilize to either support or resist the development of CJEU case law within the member states (Conant 2002, 9). This mobilization of interests serves largely as a way for national governments to engage in the policy process, seeking compromise among these organized groups in the application of CJEU case law. Unlike other scholars, her conclusions are more sanguine about the benefits of organized interests. Many of the main beneficiaries of the CJEU's reference process are well-connected and well-funded commercial and social interests (Chalmers 2000; Conant 2002, 89).

The varying conclusions above also raise a host of questions for scholars today. Interest groups may seek CJEU review via the preliminary reference, but the national judge supervising the case still must agree and write the referral. Additionally, the group must secure an attorney knowledgeable enough about EU law to be able to make a compelling argument about why a reference is needed. The group must also secure the funding to move the lawsuit up to Luxembourg. A multi-country study of referral locations across the EU found that regions and cities with larger commercial trade centres saw more references to the CJEU (Dyevre and Lampach 2021)—with more evidence suggesting free movement of goods references occur more often in regions with higher trade and industry (Kelemen and Pavone 2016, 2018). This might point to the validity of Conant's earlier concerns about private interest participation, though it could also simply be a consequence of the long-standing history of the EU as a free-trade area and the importance the CJEU has placed on free trade. An area for future research could try to examine the 'hot spots' of reference activity for evidence of repeat players, and particularly repeat economic and commercial interests in the reference process.

There remains one additional variable or factor to consider: the attorneys who are charged with filing the court cases in national courts and making arguments in favour of preliminary references. Long overlooked, recent work has focused on uncovering the hidden actors helping to drive preliminary references—the 'Euro-lawyers' (Pavone 2022). Pavone argues that more than any other set of actors (including national court judges), it was a group of lawyers that drove European political development through use of legal argumentation in national court cases that would bring issues to the attention of the CJEU. Ultimately, examining the work of these Euro-lawyers also forces a re-examination of many key theories of referral activity that place national court judges as the primary actors, strategic or not, driving the creation of the European order. Future work examining these specialist lawyers and the arguments they make should give even greater appreciation for the role of attorneys in shaping the direction of the law.

3.6 How Does the CJEU View and Use the Preliminary Reference System?

The flip side to the question of how national courts interact with the referral system is how the CJEU itself views referrals and uses the preliminary reference process.

The traditional view was that the CJEU sought out preliminary references from national courts because it needed cases, both to develop EU law and to build institutional power. In the legal orientation of European law, the CJEU has had an interest in developing both the supremacy doctrine and the direct effect doctrine as a way to develop the court's own power. The theory of direct effects holds that EU law can provide rights to individuals living with the EU and that member state governments and courts must uphold rights that have direct effects. Yet, as Bermann et al. (2002, 353) note, the concept of direct effect is 'the cornerstone of supranationalism', albeit one that 'depends utterly on the preliminary reference procedure'. The direct effect doctrine has no real-world value if member state courts do not abide by the concept. Thus, the CJEU has a real interest in ensuring a pipeline of preliminary references from national courts that the CJEU takes seriously.

Though this might have been particularly true in the early days of the CJEU when the court had little institutional legitimacy (Alter 1996), today the CJEU has no shortage of cases. In fact, the average time to resolve a preliminary reference is now around fifteen months (Broberg and Fenger 2021, 5)—not an extraordinary length of time when compared to other courts, but still an indication of the backlog of cases that can develop in Luxembourg. To help manage the rising tide of cases, the CJEU has increasingly turned to adjudicating orders (AOs) to resolve questions. An AO is a final order from the court declaring that the issue referred has either been answered substantively already or where the answer is beyond reasonable doubt. Since 2000, when the court's rules of procedure were amended to improve the AO process, AOs account for between 5 and 10 per cent of the court's responses to national court referrals (Brekke et al. 2023). An increase in AOs is often seen after the court sees a sudden rise in referrals based on a new legal issue coming to the fore. Similarly, AOs often appear when the CJEU is trying to foreclose further discussion with national courts on a specific issue, suggesting the CJEU uses them in part to both establish order and assert its own authority as a final decision-maker in the area.

4. Other Courts

The referral process is most widely known from its use in the CJEU. As seen throughout this chapter, a vast literature has developed to examine the preliminary reference process at the CJEU, including questions of which courts refer, which countries or regions refer, and whether the court itself seeks out specific cases, and if so why. However, the CJEU's referral process is itself derived from the referral processes previously adopted in several national judiciaries of the EU member states, particularly post-Second World War Italy and (West) Germany (Hausmaninger 1997; Pavone 2022). In those countries, national judges were given the power to send questions concerning the constitutionality of laws they were reviewing in their specific case to the new national constitutional courts. Subsequently, this national court–constitutional court referral process has been adopted by nearly all continental European countries.

And the European referral system is not alone. Many African and Latin American courts have some ability to issue referrals (Bulto 2011). US law contains a general rule giving appellate courts jurisdiction only over 'final decisions' of lower courts. However, nearly all federal courts have the ability to certify questions of state law that arise in a federal case to a state supreme court (Nash 2003; Cochran 2013). The process of certification allows courts to ask for definitive interpretations of law, which is functionally identical to a referral. There is no federal law requiring certification of state law questions, but nearly all states have adopted state laws permitting federal courts in their states to certify these types of questions—only North Carolina lacks such a law. And many states permit state supreme courts to receive certifications from state courts when lower courts have produced conflicting rulings. Separately, federal courts can also utilize the interlocutory appeal process to ask superior federal courts to rule on certain questions of law. Interlocutory appeals are limited to specific unanswered issues of civil law central to the case about which there exists substantial grounds for difference of opinion about the outcome, and whose outcome could help determine the final ruling in the case (Lammon 2018).[4]

Despite the large growth in the literature examining the preliminary reference procedure at the CJEU, there is still relatively little work examining the referrals process within national judicial systems. This is an important deficit because the literature that has developed for the CJEU's reference process may be of limited value to help explain non-CJEU behaviour. Notably, the CJEU is an international court, not a domestic court, and the pathways by which a case enters the CJEU's docket are often quite distinct from those seen in the national court systems (Carrubba and Gabel 2015). In the European context, examination of the processes of constitutional court referrals represents an untapped reservoir of potentially insightful answers on referral activity. Different theories are likely to be needed to help explain judicial referrals at the national level—and different data, as well.

Thus, one area in need of comprehensive research is the set of factors and influences that lead to national courts submitting references to their national constitutional court, as well as the factors leading US courts to request certified questions and interlocutory appeals. The referral activity of other international and supranational courts also presents both challenges and possibilities for future research. Though the bulk of research has focused on the CJEU, nine other supranational courts also permit national court referrals (Baudenbacher 2005; Alter 2012; Alter et al. 2013).[5] Yet to date, few scholars have focused on these courts. Works by Helfer and Alter (2017) and Alter and Helfer (2009) on the Andean Tribunal of Justice (ATJ) stand out as key exceptions. Most of the ATJ's cases arise from their preliminary reference procedure, yet Alter and Helfer's findings also show that referral patterns from national court judges under the Andean Tribunal's aegis differ from those seen with the CJEU. Notably, most referrals from national judges are passive and narrow in scope, and most referrals come from a small handful of courts. And most referrals to the ATJ involve intellectual property issues arising from domestic administrative actors (Alter and Helfer 2009, 875). In short, the Andean court has not made itself into a major actor in the region, at least in part because they do not receive a stream of interesting and challenging cases from national courts.

5. Conclusions

Research on referral activity has expanded dramatically in the twenty-first century. As the above discussion points out, most of this research has focused on the preliminary reference process at the CJEU. With its roots in the judicial empowerment thesis, the main focus of research has generally been on the symbiotic interests of national court judges and the CJEU in the referral process. And scholars have made notable inroads into understanding the interests of national courts and judges in the referral decision, as well as the CJEU's involvement in the referral process—including its response to those preliminary references. As research has evolved, some of the key tenets of judicial empowerment have been questioned. Notably, recent work using judicial interviews calls into question the basis for believing that the typical national lower court judge has the desire and legal training to effectively interact with the CJEU. Those that do have this training are more likely to feel confident about the reference process, though. Recent work also shows that peak courts have overtaken lower courts as the main interlocutors with the CJEU. As more is known about the referral process new questions develop. And new research areas become apparent.

Perhaps most notably, research on referrals overwhelmingly focuses on the CJEU's preliminary reference process. This is understandable given the importance of the reference process to the EU's political development, and the importance of the CJEU as a theoretical and observational point for judicial politics and international relations scholars. Yet the CJEU is but one of several supranational and international courts that utilize the referral process. Many national constitutional courts in Europe have a similar mechanism to accept referrals from their national ordinary courts, and many US state and federal courts participate in referral processes. To date, little systematic research has been done outside of the CJEU preliminary references. This represents a key limitation on our broader understanding of judicial referrals. Yet it also presents important future opportunities for researchers to better understand the broader logic and nature of referrals.

Notes

1. For example, *Costa v ENEL* and *van Gend & Loos* both arose through the preliminary reference process.
2. The *acte clair* doctrine states that it is acceptable for national courts not to make a preliminary reference if the judge believes the EU law question raised has already been settled by the CJEU. However, it is worth noting that because the CJEU has determined that it alone can rule on a possible breach of EU law, if member state courts do not use the Article 267 process despite having questions that fall within the article's purview, then the member state could be in violation of the EU treaties and be subject to infringement proceedings (Wind 2010).
3. Burley and Mattli (1993) also incorporate into their theory the motivations of the private litigants who drive the creation of these lawsuits.
4. Other exceptions to the finality rule also include a limited discretionary ability to appeal class certification questions and other collateral orders before a final decision, but these are largely party-driven appeals, not judge-driven referrals.

5. One such court is the European Free Trade Area (EFTA) Court, though the EFTA Court's decisions are not necessarily binding on the referring court (Baudenbacher 2005).

References

Alter, Karen. 1996. 'The European Court's Political Power'. *West European Politics* 19 (3): 458–87.

Alter, Karen. 2001. *Establishing the Supremacy of European Law: The Making of an International Rule of Law in Europe*. Oxford: Oxford University Press.

Alter, Karen. 2010. *The European Court's Political Power*. New York: Oxford University Press.

Alter, Karen. 2012. 'The Global Spread of European Style International Courts'. *West European Politics* 35 (1): 135–54.

Alter, Karen, and Laurence Helfer. 2009. *Transplanting International Courts*. New York: Oxford University Press.

Alter, Karen, and Jeanette Vargas. 2000. 'Explaining Variation in the Use of European Litigation Strategies: European Community Law and British Gender Equality Policy'. *Comparative Political Studies* 33 (4): 452–82.

Alter, Karen, Laurence Helfer, and Jacqueline McAllister. 2013. 'A New International Human Rights Court for West Africa: The ECOWAS Community Court of Justice'. *The American Journal of International Law* 107 (4): 737–79.

Baudenbacher, Carl. 2005. 'The EFTA Court Ten Years On'. In *The EFTA Court: Ten Years On*, edited by Carl Baudenbacher, Per Tresselt, and Thorgeir Orlygsson, 13–54. Oxford: Hart Publishing.

Bermann, George, Roger Goebel, William Davey, and Eleanor Fox. 2002. *Cases and Materials on European Law*, 2nd edn. St. Paul: West.

Bogojevic, Sanja. 2017. 'Judicial Dialogue Unpacked: Twenty Years of Preliminary References on Environmental Matters Initiated by the Swedish Judiciary'. *Journal of Environmental Law* 29 (2): 263–83.

Bobek, Michal. 2008. 'Learning to Talk: Preliminary Rulings, the Courts of the New Member States, and the Court of Justice'. *Common Market Law Review* 45 (6): 1611–43.

Brekke, Stein, Daniel Naurin, Urška Šadl, and Lucía López-Zurita. 2023. 'That's an Order! How the Quest for Efficiency Is Transforming Judicial Cooperation in Europe'. *Journal of Common Market Studies* 61 (1): 58–75. doi:10.1111/jcms.13346.

Broberg, Morten, and Niels Fenger. 2021. *Preliminary References to the European Court of Justice*. Oxford: Oxford University Press.

Broberg, Morten, and Niels Fenger. 2013. 'Variations in Member States' Preliminary References to the Court of Justice—Are Structural Factors (Part of) the Explanation?' *European Law Journal* 19 (4): 488–501.

Bulto, Takele. 2011. 'Judicial Referral of Constitutional Disputes in Ethiopia: From Practice to Theory'. *African Journal of International and Comparative Law* 19 (1): 99–123.

Burley, Anne-Marie, and Walter Mattli. 1993. 'Europe Before the Court'. *International Organization* 47 (1): 41–76.

Carrubba, Clifford J., and Matthew J. Gabel. 2015. *International Courts and the Performance of International Agreements: A General Theory with Evidence from the European Union*. New York: Cambridge University Press.

Carrubba, Clifford J., Mathew J. Gabel, and Charles Hankla. 2008. 'Judicial Behavior under Political Constraints: Evidence from the European Court of Justice'. *American Political Science Review* 102 (4): 435–52.

Carrubba, Clifford J., and Lacey Murrah. 2005. 'Legal Integration and Use of the Preliminary Ruling Process in the European Union'. *International Organization* 59 (2): 399–418.

Chalmers, Damian. 2000. 'The Positioning of EU Judicial Politics within the United Kingdom'. *West European Politics* 23: 169.

Cichowski, Rachel. 2004. 'Women's Rights, the European Court, and Supranational Constitutionalism'. *Law & Society Review* 38 (3): 489–512.

Cichowski, Rachel. 2007. *The European Court and Civil Society*. New York: Cambridge University Press.

Claes, Monica. 2006. *The National Courts' Mandate in the European Constitution*. Oxford: Hart Publishing.

Claes, Monica. 2015. 'Luxembourg, Here We Come? Constitutional Courts and the Preliminary Reference Procedure'. *German Law Journal* 16 (6): 1331–43.

Cochran, Rebecca. 2013. 'Federal Court Certification of Questions of State Law to State Courts: A Theoretical and Empirical Study'. *Journal of Legislation* 29 (2): 157–231.

Conant, Lisa. 2002. *Justice Contained*. Ithaca: Cornell University Press.

Dyevre. Arthur, Nicolas Lampach, and Monika Glavina. 2022. 'Chilling or Learning? The Effect of Negative Feedback on Interjudicial Cooperation in Nonhierarchical Referral Regimes'. *Journal of Law and Courts* 10: 87–112.

Dyevre, Arthur, Monika Glavina, and Angelina Atanasova. 2020. 'Who Refers Most? Institutional Incentives and Judicial Participation in the Preliminary Ruling System'. *Journal of European Public Policy*, 27 (6): 912–30.

Dyevre, Arthur, and Nicolas Lampach. 2021. 'Subnational Disparities in EU Law Use: Exploring the GEOCOURT Dataset'. *Journal of European Public Policy* 28 (4): 615–31.

Dyevre, Arthur, and Nicolas Lampach. 2019. 'Choosing for Europe: Judicial Incentives and Legal Integration in the European Union'. *European Journal of Law and Economics* 50: 65–86.

Fligstein, Neil, and Alec Stone Sweet. 2002. 'Constructing Polities and Markets: An Institutionalist Account of European Integration'. *American Journal of Sociology* 107 (5): 1206–43.

Glavina, Monika. 2020. 'To Refer or Not to Refer, That is the (Preliminary) Question. Exploring Factors which Influence the Participation of National Judges in the Preliminary Ruling Procedure'. *Croatian Yearbook of European Law and Policy* 16: 26–59.

Golub, Jonathan. 1996. 'The Politics of Judicial Discretion'. *West European Politics* 19 (2): 360–85.

Hausmaninger, Herbert. 1997. 'Judicial Referral of Constitutional Questions in Austria, Germany, and Russia'. *Tulane European & Civil Law Forum* 12 (1): 25–38.

Helfer, Lawrence, and Karen Alter. 2017. ". 'The Andean Tribunal of Justice and its Interlocutors: Understanding Preliminary Reference Patterns in the Andean Community'. *NYU Journal of International Law & Politics* 41: 871–930.

Hornuf, Lars, and Stefan Voigt. 2015. 'Analyzing Preliminary References as the Powerbase of the European Court of Justice'. *European Journal of Law and Economics* 39 (2): 287–311.

Kelemen, R. Daniel. 2011. *Eurolegalism*. Cambridge: Harvard University Press.

Kelemen, R. Daniel, and Tommaso Pavone. 2016. 'Mapping European Law'. *Journal of European Public Policy* 23 (8): 1118–38.

Kelemen, R. Daniel, and Tommaso Pavone. 2018. 'The Political Geography of European Legal Integration: Visualizing Institutional Change in the European Union'. *World Politics* 70 (3): 358–97.

Krehbiel, Jay, and Sivaram Cheruvu. 2022. 'Can International Courts Enhance Domestic Judicial Review? Separation of Powers and the European Court of Justice'. *Journal of Politics* 84 (1): 259–75.

Krommendijk, Jasper. 2021. *National Courts and Preliminary References to the Court of Justice*. Cheltenham: Edward Elgar Publishing.

Lacchi, Cielia. 2015. 'Review by Constitutional Courts of the Obligation of National Courts of Last Instance to Refer a Preliminary Question to the Court of Justice of the EU'. *German Law Journal* 16 (6): 1663–700.

Lammon, Bryan. 2018. 'Finality, Appealability, and the Scope of Interlocutory Review'. *Washington Law Review* 93: 1809–52.

Leijon, Karin. 2021. 'National Courts and Preliminary References: Supporting Legal Integration, Protecting National Autonomy or Balancing Conflicting Demands?' *West European Politics* 44 (3): 510–30.

Leijon, Karin, and Monika Glavina. 2022. 'Why Passive? Exploring National Judges' Motives for Not Requesting Preliminary Rulings'. *Maastricht Journal of European and Comparative Law* 29: 263–85.

Mayoral, Juan, and Marlene Wind. 2021. 'Unleashed Dialogue or Captured by Politics? The Impact of Judicial Independence on National Higher Courts' Cooperation with the CJEU'. *Journal of European Public Policy* 29 (9): 1433–53.

Mayoral, Juan, Urszula Jaremba, and Tobias Nowak. 2014. 'Creating EU Law Judges'. *Journal of European Public Policy* 21 (8): 1120–41.

Nash, Jonathan Remy. 2003. 'Examining the Power of Federal Courts to Certify Questions of State Law'. *Cornell Law Review* 88 (6): 1672–749.

Nyikos, Stacy. 2006. 'Strategic Interaction Among Courts within the Preliminary Reference Process—Stage 1: National Court Preemptive Opinions'. *European Journal of Political Research* 45: 527–50.

Pavone, Tommaso. 2018. 'Revisiting Judicial Empowerment in the European Union'. *Journal of Law and Courts* 6 (2): 303–31.

Pavone, Tommaso. 2022. *The Ghostwriters*. New York: Cambridge University Press.

Pavone, Tommaso, and R. Daniel Kelemen. 2019. 'The Evolving Judicial Politics of European Integration: The European Court of Justice and National Courts Revisited'. *European Law Journal* 25 (4): 352–73.

Pitarakis, Jean-Yves, and George Tridimas. 2003. 'Joint Dynamics of Legal and Economic Integration in the European Union'. *European Journal of Law and Economics* 16: 357–68.

Šadl, Urška, and Anna Wallerman. 2019. '"The Referring Court Asks, in Essence": Is Reformulation of Preliminary Questions by the Court of Justice a Decision Writing Fixture or a Decision-Making Approach?' *European Law Journal* 25: 416–33.

Serrano, Miryam Rodriguez-Izquierdo. 2015. 'The Spanish Constitutional Court and Fundamental Rights Adjudication After the First Preliminary Reference'. *German Law Journal* 16 (6): 1509–28.

Stone Sweet, Alec, and Thomas Brunell. 1998a. 'Constructing a Supranational Constitution: Dispute Resolution and Governance in the European Community.' *American Political Science Review* 92 (1): 63–81.

Stone Sweet, Alec, and Thomas Brunell. 1998b. 'The European Court and the National Courts'. *Journal of European Public Policy* 5 (1): 66–97.

Tridimas, Takis. 2015. 'The ECJ and the National Courts: Dialogue, Cooperation, and Instability'. In *The Oxford Handbook of European Union Law*, edited by Damian Chalmers and Anthony Arnull, 403–30. Oxford: Oxford University Press.

Vink, Maarten, Monica Claes, and Christine Arnold. 2009. 'Explaining the Use of Preliminary References by Domestic Courts in EU Member States: A Mixed-Method Comparative Analysis'. http://aei.pitt.edu/33155/

Weiler, J. H. H. 1991. 'The Transformation of Europe'. *Yale Law Journal* 100 (8): 2403–83.

Wind, Marlene. 2010. 'The Nordics, the EU, and the Reluctance towards Supranational Judicial Review'. *Journal of Common Market Studies* 48 (4): 1039–63.

Wind, Marlene, Dorte Martinsen, and Gabriel Rotger. 2009. 'The Uneven Legal Push for Europe'. *European Union Politics* 10 (1): 63–88.

CHAPTER 31

JUDGE NETWORKS

BJÖRN DRESSEL

1. Introduction

This chapter describes judge networks, defined as the interlocking, relatively stable relationships that a judge maintains with peers and other political and social actors on and off the bench. Relational networks, which can be formal but mostly informal, are often thought to influence judicial behaviour. This is illustrated in the United States in how the Federalist Society, a network of conservative and libertarian judges, lawyers, and law professors, may influence appointments, and even decisions, on the US Supreme Court itself (Scherer and Miller 2009; Salamone 2014; Lynch 2022).

Emerging alongside these public concerns is a growing academic literature on the role of judicial networks, which acknowledges that judges do not operate in isolation. Not only do they regularly interact with each other on the bench (Maltzman et al. 2000) but many have been acquainted with each other professionally and socially for years (Baum 2006). They increasingly communicate with colleagues at home and abroad by citing each other or when they exchange perspectives, judicial philosophies, and even staff (Slaughter 2004; Katz and Stafford 2010). Meanwhile, debates among scholars studying the three traditional jurisprudential models—the legal, the attitudinal, and the strategic—have also begun to generate interest in social networks. Strategic models seek to account for a host of contextual, extra-legal influences and constraints on judicial behaviour. Over the last two decades, however, attitudinal and legal models have also slowly begun to accept the relevance of political and social (rather than simply ideological) considerations as potential influences on judges (Segal and Spaeth 2002; Baum 2010).

Nevertheless, current studies of the role of networks in judicial decision-making have been limited both empirically and theoretically. The work on judicial networks (for a good overview see Box-Steffensmeier et al. 2016) has focused almost exclusively on the institutionalized context in the West, particularly the US Supreme Court. Supported by an emphasis on predictive models and the application of formal network theory, studies of judicial networks have been limited to formal networks. Their focus on the structures of the networks themselves tells us little about how judges themselves are shaped and defined by their relationships. Meanwhile, the question of how to link judges' presence within networks to the dominant models of judicial decision-making—whether legal, attitudinal, or strategic—remains theoretically underdeveloped, even as the relational aspect that underpins the network perspective often coexists uneasily with models that emphasize characteristics of individual judges or sophisticated rational-strategic behaviour.

The terms 'judicial networks' and 'judge networks' are often used interchangeably in the literature. However, there is a useful distinction to be drawn between questions asked about the structure and nature of networks, which can be fruitfully addressed by the formal tools of network theory (see chapter by Alschner in this volume) and asking questions about how a judge is embedded within particular networks that influence their opinions, judgments, and subsequent behaviour. Thus, this chapter will use 'judicial networks' to refer to previous formal studies and 'judge networks' to refer to my proposals to evaluate the influence of networks, often informal, on judges' self-perceptions and behaviour. This includes decision-making, which is broadly defined as encompassing activities on the bench from deciding cases, case management, appointments, and reform. I seek to answer two fundamental groups of questions, considering not just the West but the global situation:

(1) How is a judge's network formed and sustained and how do judges relate to each other? In other words, which networks matter most for a judge and why? What influences the ties between judges and other social actors?
(2) How does a judge's network affect judicial decision-making—broadly defined as encompassing activities on the bench from deciding cases, to case management, appointments, and reform? That is, what are theoretically plausible mechanisms by which a judge's networks might influence judicial decisions, and to what effect?

In formulating answers to these questions, I advance a distinct relational perspective on how judges behave that embeds them in a variety of often overlapping social relations and networks, many of which exist outside the courtroom. Putting the judge at the centre of a web of unique social networks draws attention to relational 'ties that bind'. In doing so, I seek to move beyond the attitudinal emphasis on the personal attributes of a judge or the strategic emphasis on goals and incentives.

Instead, the emphasis on social ties suggests that personal networks can be constitutive of how judges construct their role and engage with the law. Following Baum (2006), I argue that the way in which a judge—as a person and not just as a rational actor or legal machine—positions themselves within their social environment and constructs their social identity is a factor to understand their behaviour. A focus on the ties constructed within networks points to cognitive shortcuts and facilitates ideational, personalistic, or material network exchanges that have direct consequences for judicial behaviour. This creates informal relational dynamics that have barely been discussed in popular models of judicial behaviour.

The chapter starts with a survey of the recent literature on judicial networks to draw out the types and relational bases of judges' networks. It proceeds with a discussion on how material, ideational, and personal ties influence their decision-making in areas of appointments, case decisions, and reform. The chapter concludes with a discussion on the limits and the potential of the relational network perspective to improve our understanding of how judges behave, noting some of the methodological challenges.

2. Nodes, Networks, and Relationships

Why do judges decide cases as they do? What forces might be influencing their decisions? Such questions are at the centre of the judicial politics scholarship that has emerged from studies of how judges *ought* to decide cases (Friedman 2006). As illustrated in recent comparative judicial politics debates, growing attention has been directed to relational and network-based aspects of how judges work—even as their alignment with and contribution to existing models of judicial behaviour is far from settled. How this debate has evolved and what inquiry on relationship-based behaviour might entail, particularly for case decisions, will be discussed with a focus on judge networks.

2.1 From Nodes to Networks

Despite an early interest in the role of small group behaviour in the US Supreme Court (Snyder 1958; Ulmer 1965), scholars of judicial politics have been slow to adopt relational perspectives. This should not be surprising: the primary purpose of early studies of judicial behaviour was to explain the behaviour of *individual* judges, which is why the dominant models of judicial behaviour were the legal, the attitudinal, and the strategic.

Legalistic accounts assume that in making a decision, judges draw on precedent and legal norms so that law and legal mechanisms constrain each judge's actions (Segal 2008; Leiter 2010; Bailey and Maltzman 2011). Thus, there is minimal engagement with group dynamics or personal relations. The legal model emphasizes the pressures that the formal legal environment exerts on judges. Similarly, even as it views judges as largely unconstrained by law (and may thus consider a host of extra-judicial influences), the attitudinal model has traditionally failed to engage with relational dynamics (Segal and Spaeth 2002, 1993). This is partly because in the United States, where the model emerged, it is narrowly focused on ideological and policy preferences along party lines and its methodology gives priority to the positions of individual judges rather than capturing how judges interact on the bench.

The dominant rational-strategic models are less narrowly focused. They share the notion of judicial preferences. These models also acknowledge that judges must take into account the preferences of other political and institutional actors, which may divert them from their preferred outcome in order to secure the most acceptable outcome (Epstein and Knight 1998; Spiller and Gely 2010). Because this view suggests that strategic decision-making by judges is interdependent, it implies that judging occurs within a complex institutional framework, which may incorporate colleagues on a collegial court, elected legislative and executive officials, and the public (Kornhauser and Sager 1986; Clayton and Gillman 1999; Epstein and Weinshall 2021). That reality has also led scholars ultimately to question the singular focus on legal preferences and suggests that judges may pursue strategic goals well beyond legal policy, such as personal standing with public and legal audiences (Baum 2006; Ginsburg and Garoupa 2015), career considerations and balance of workload and leisure (Posner 2008), or tending to collegial relations on the bench (Friedman 2006). This gradually makes room for relational considerations, although as part of wider institutional constraints on given individual preferences.

It is not surprising that such debates among the behavioural models have also gradually opened a path to applying network perspectives and methodology to the study of how judges operate. Over the last two decades, all jurisprudential models have increasingly incorporated ideas from each other and converged in acknowledging the relevance of political and social considerations in the areas of preference formation or engagement with the law that has further encouraged research on a host of extra-legal factors (Dyevre 2010). There is also a general recognition that law and judicial processes together form a complex, adaptive system akin to a network (Katz et al. 2011, 2008). Combined with a judiciary awash with network data, this understanding has provoked increasing empirical work on *judicial networks*, as illustrated in a body of literature in areas of citation, prestige, and *amicus curiae* networks (Box-Steffensmeier et al. 2016).

These varied contributions share a concern with structural patterns—the configurations of social networks—and how these patterns affect judicial actors and outcomes. Scholarly work on citation networks has used social network analysis to map connections between judicial opinions, as measured by references and citations, to trace on which previous cases and opinions judges have based their opinions. This highlights the influence of an opinion within the judiciary (Caldeira 1985; Post and Eisen 2000; Fowler and Jeon 2008; Bommarito II et al. 2010; Lupu and Voeten 2012; Hinkle and Nelson 2016). Similarly, to evaluate the social status and reputational esteem of individual judges, scholars have used network analysis to trace the movements of clerks to illustrate pathways of peer effects based on esteem or prestige (Katz and Stafford 2010), and they have drawn attention to elite lawyers (McGuire 1993; Flemming and Krutz 2002), as well as law professors (Katz et al. 2011) to clarify the context in which judges operate. Using network analysis to trace connections between signatories of 'friend of the court' legal briefs, scholarly work on *amicus curiae* networks has allowed for a comprehensive mapping of how non-judges engage with the courts and provided novel insights into the influence of social networks over time (Collins 2008; Box-Steffensmeier et al. 2013; Christenson and Box-Steffensmeier 2017).

The corpus of work on judicial networks has provided a stimulus for the empirical study of judicial behaviour and politics. These studies have sought to clarify reliance on legal, ideological, or political preferences in judicial decision-making as part of the analysis of citation networks; have helped to refine the strategic model through scholarly work on prestige networks; or have drawn attention to the ebb and flow of special-interest influence on courts. They have also stimulated broader theoretical and empirical scholarly efforts on how networks relate to a host of other outcomes of interest to scholars of judicial politics, such as support for judicial reform (Ingram 2016b, 2016a), facilitation of transnational dialogue between judges, compliance with court rulings, and support by advocacy networks for domestic and international courts (Claes and De Visser 2012; Dallara and Piana 2015; Dothan 2018). In addition, they have spurred reflections on the more problematic effects of networks in supporting ingrained clientelism and corruption in the judiciary (Gomez 2011; Basabe-Serrano 2015; Pozas-Loyo and Rios-Figuero 2018).

While these contributions have considerably advanced the understanding of networks among judges and their effects on aspects of judicial behaviour, the current emphasis on the formal structure of judicial networks has also limited the scope for the empirical and theoretical investigation of judge networks. The traditional focus on Western judiciaries has meant an overreliance on formal rather than informal networks, thus ignoring networks that matter in less institutionalized settings. More importantly, a formalist perspective tells reveals little about what holds a network together (e.g. its linking properties) or how judges navigate the relational setting in which they find themselves embedded and to what effect. The result is a very limited, static, and often an *a priori* understanding of a judge network.

The shortcomings in the current debate are even more evident in judicial dynamics beyond the United States or Europe. As studies of comparative judicial politics in the Global South and post-Soviet states have made clear, judges have to contend with a host of informal networks that are only minimally institutionalized and often operate in the shadows of formal institutions where there is little transparency and accountability, as evident in the widespread corruption or clientelist networks within the judiciary (Dressel et al. 2018; Gloppen 2013). Hybrid settings where formal and informal practices are closely intertwined stimulate interest in a broader view of a judge's networks, including the type of actors (e.g. not just legal peers but wider social circles). Moreover, they invite reflections on the relational ties themselves (e.g. not just professional, but also friendship, ethnic, and with clients) and how the relational bond comes to affect judicial behaviour and institutional performance.

2.2 Bringing Relationships Back In

A distinct line of inquiry about judicial politics has emerged that focuses on the relationship-based behaviour of judges. Drawing on psychological theories of self-presentation, scholars have argued that judges are concerned with how others assess their performance, which illuminates how social 'audiences,' particularly those of legal peers, help shape judicial behaviour in established settings (Baum 2006; Ginsburg and Garoupa 2015). Others working on courts in the Global South have shown how a wide set of relational ties and personal networks influence judges in Africa, Asia, and Latin America (see e.g. Trochev and Ellett 2014; Dressel 2018; Pozas-Loyo and Rios-Figuero 2018). These studies explore relational dynamics to explain variations in judicial autonomy, diffusion of ideas, patronage appointments, and even decisions of judges (Staton 2010; Helmke and Rios-Figueroa 2011; Ingram 2016a; Brinks et al. 2020).

These studies recognize how relationships animate judicial behaviour in less institutionalized settings (but also in more institutionalized ones). These relationships may be formal and informal or actively created or born into and can shape how judges engage directly with the law or provide pathways for transmitting ideational, material, or even affective exchanges. In doing so, judicial behaviour moves beyond personally motivated self-presentation (i.e. the desire to impress certain audiences) to acknowledge how a judge situated in a social environment marked by personal relations shapes judicial identity through socialization to norms and values, as well as identifying practices through which judges interpret the law and the judicial process.

Relational sociology may offer the closest theoretical foundation for empirical observations because it treats institutions as having been constructed of a variety of interlocking social and cultural networks that determine what happens in a given institutional space (Mohr and White 2008, 488; Fuhse 2015). Relational sociologists have long criticized what they call substantialist approaches that try to analyse the social world through attributes and properties of discrete units instead of drawing attention to the relational origin of social processes and contingent social and historical ties that constitute the very units that substantialist approaches focus on (see Emirbayer 1997).

Challenging the notion that social action within an institutional setting can refer to a single individual's will or inherent attributes alone (a common assumption in rational accounts), relational sociology views agential behaviour as interdependent and thus relational. Actors become what they are and how they act because of where they are situated in transactional networks. This angle urges empirical research to move beyond the character of the individual (the node) or the formal effects of network structure (centralization, density, path length) to show how social actors are defined by their relationships, which shift and change over time.[1] A network perspective anchored in the linking properties thus becomes central. These social relationships can become 'conduits of information and meaning, incubators of cultural identities and roles, ... "bridges" between institutional domains that convey and construct culture' (Conti 2022, 13). Similarly, where these networks operate becomes a symbolic terrain with its own networks, hierarchical relationships, expertise, and rules (Dezalay and Garth 1996).

What does all this imply for the study of how judges behave? The new relational studies of comparative judicial politics (Dressel et al. 2017) view judicial institutions in terms of human relations and exchanges. It means spotlighting judges and their relationships as both professionals and human beings—that is, looking at each judge's own networks. Focusing the analysis on the network of a single judge offers a complement to the study of judicial behaviour. Drawing attention to the groups and actors linked via a judge network provides a contextual understanding of how judges may construct their judicial identities and understanding of the law. Similarly, illustrating how a judge navigates the relational context, including when and how each uses personal networks, opens up a dynamic view of judicial decision-making in areas such as appointments, deciding on cases, or broader areas of reform and legitimacy of the court.

3. Judge Networks: Exploring the Concept

Inspired by the relational perspective, I define a judge's network as the interlocking, relatively stable relationships a judge maintains with peers and other political and social actors on and off the bench. To advance understanding of how a judge network comes to influence judicial behaviour, I seek to answer three questions: (i) What types of relational ties, and by extension networks, matter to a judge? (ii) How can we systematically map and study the relational ties between judges and other social actors? (iii) Most importantly, how do relational dynamics affect judicial decision-making? Let us consider some preliminary observations.

3.1 Network Types and Ties

There are innumerable types of networks—the groups or systems of social interaction and personal relationships adapted to social circumstances (Granovetter 1973). As Borgatti and Ofem (2010) noted, networks can be based on relational similarities (e.g. membership, attributes), social relations (friendship, kinship) and mental relations (cognitive, affective), or transactions and the flow of information, beliefs, or material resources. Network ties are often thought to form 'paths' or 'pipelines' along which flow resources like information, beliefs, and money (Grosser and Borgatti 2013, 1).

Anecdotal and empirical evidence suggests that the types of networks most relevant for a judge are those based on friendship; recruitment to judicial positions; political interests (partisan or ideological); patronage and clientelism; and those based on cultural, regional, or religious ties. Networks generally form through repetitive interaction (socialization in law school, shared years on the bench, membership in legal associations). They might differ in whether they are formal (alumni associations, legal fraternities and sororities) or informal (friendships, clients). Nevertheless, even in more formal networks, the relationship dynamics are often guided by informality.

Similarly, the ties between actors in these networks can be characterized by differences in intrapersonal dynamics or combinations thereof, such as reciprocity, self-presentation, individual benefit, ideational affinities, or authority and loyalty. A friendship network may be dominated by aspects of self-presentation or ideational affinities. On the other hand, career development networks might be motivated by reciprocity or individual benefits. Meanwhile, networks based on patronage and clientelism might be characterized primarily by authority and loyalty, often reinforced by shared regional, cultural, or kinship ties. Formal network theory suggests that the more overlapping ties between actors or groups, the stronger the ties and the network itself.

In short, rather than thinking of *a* judge network, a single judge is embedded in a variety of social networks—some professional, some personal—that are sustained by very different relational ties and activated or drawn upon in a variety of areas. Some networks might be drawn upon when judges decide to protect institutional independence or influence decisions within a collegial court. Others may shape case management or how careers progress on and off the bench, even after retirement. Table 31.1 is a preliminary outline to illustrate how the relational dimension might be demonstrated.

It should be clear that despite the centrality of professional peer networks, judges are like any other human beings who are part of overlapping social networks. Due to personal circumstances, they may move in and out of these networks over time. However, the ability to do so will greatly depend on the ties themselves, whether these are owned (e.g. joining an association) or unowned (e.g. being a member of a specific community).[2] Because the relational bases for the network are not equal, they affect how judges behave to varying degrees. Friendship or kinship networks might be expected to bind more forcefully than professional or political ties, but whether friendship networks would have a similar relevance to judicial behaviour would depend more heavily on the context (e.g. a case involving a family member).

Table 31.1 Network influences on judges

Type of network	Characteristics of relational ties	Relevant outcomes in terms of judicial behaviour
Professional/recruitment	Professional-outcome oriented; individual benefit	Judicial appointments
Friendship-based	Shared experiences; self-presentation; reciprocal; emotive	Judicial decision-making; case management
Ideational	Shared ideas; reciprocity	On-bench factional voting; internal reform dynamics
Political	Ideological; partisan	On-bench voting; on-bench pursuit of policy preferences
Sociocultural	Primordial loyalties based on regional, religious, or cultural traits	On-bench voting; nepotism in appointments; court legitimacy
Patronage/clientelism	Exchange-focused, dyadic, contingent, asymmetric, iterated, hierarchical	Delivery of judicial decisions in exchange for rewards; case management; appointments etc.

3.2 Mapping a Judge Network: Heuristic Dimensions

Given such empirical complexities, is it even possible to study a judge network systematically? Drawing on earlier work (Dressel et al. 2017), I suggest a three-dimensional heuristic that may help map and systematize the study of judge networks. Focusing on the relational ties rather than the network structure, it draws attention to the arena in which the relations are established, how transparent these relational ties are, and what holds the relationship together and sustains the network.

3.2.1 *Arena Where Relations Are Established*

Perhaps the best way to start thinking about a judge network from a relational perspective is to think in terms of concentric circles of social spaces in which relationships are established and maintained—on-bench, off-bench, or between benches. *On-bench* relations are established in the professional space of each court. These include relationships with judicial peers on a collegial court, judicial clerks who provide direct counsel to the judge, and the general administrative staff associated with the entire court. By contrast, *off-bench* relations include those relations that a judge maintains with a host of actors outside judicial settings, whether private (e.g. friends, family), political (e.g. executive, legislative, prosecutors' office, bar associations), or those in the shadows (e.g. clientelist, corrupt). *Between-bench*, meanwhile, refers to the type of relationships that a judge maintains with judicial peers in other specialized or subordinate courts and their staff domestically as well as with judicial peers in courts of other jurisdictions. This includes membership in a loose international court association, formal exchanges with partner courts, or joint training exercises. In short, it is with judges engaging in various social spaces that relational networks are constituted as well as ultimately observed.

3.2.2 *Degree of Transparency*

Not all judge networks operate in the same way. Some relationships operate in the open, others in secret. A publicly visible, formal membership of judges (e.g. law school, alumni associations, former political party, or law firm associations) marks one end of the spectrum, while at the other end are informal, relational ties anchored in clientelist or corrupt networks deliberately kept in the dark. At times, relations and networks may be public knowledge (at least within the small legal community) but judges and other relevant actors may deny their membership or even the existence of the network. Similarly, it might take time for newcomers to understand fully and 'see' established relational ties and networks within an organization even when they are obvious to those with more experience of the court. And while rules on judicial conduct deliberately seek to delineate the type of relations and their transparency, anecdotal evidence suggests that they are often ineffective—whether because they are circumvented or because judges might not be fully aware of their own relational but informal entanglements. Thus, in studying judge networks, it is important to capture the dimension of transparency in the relations that a judge maintains on and off the bench.

3.2.3 *What Holds a Relationship Together*

Finally, and perhaps most difficult to capture, is the mode of bonding—the social adhesive that sustains relationships (and by extension the network itself). The bonding may be a result of shared professional beliefs, ideological convictions, or primordial and affective attachments such as friendship, kinship, or loyalty. Different modes can overlap and reinforce but also be at odds with each other. Some are the direct results of birth (community affiliation), and others are shaped by socialization and active engagement (professional, educational). What is clear is that bonding power is contextual and judges may not always be in full control of the relational bonds that tie them to others. It is important to situate this dimension carefully in the historical-social context to assess the solidity and capacity of a judge network.

A judge network should be visualized in terms of relationships that unfold in different spatial locations—some in the open and others secret—that are held together by very different relational bonds. Focusing on a given judge, these personal networks are activated at different times depending on the circumstances and the goals pursued (see Figure 31.1).

The basic idea conveyed here is simple: judges are more than professional actors. As a human being, a judge is embedded in numerous relationships and, by extension, networks, whether or not there are ethical and other institutional rules to guide their social interactions. Judges are never totally isolated. They are always influenced to varying

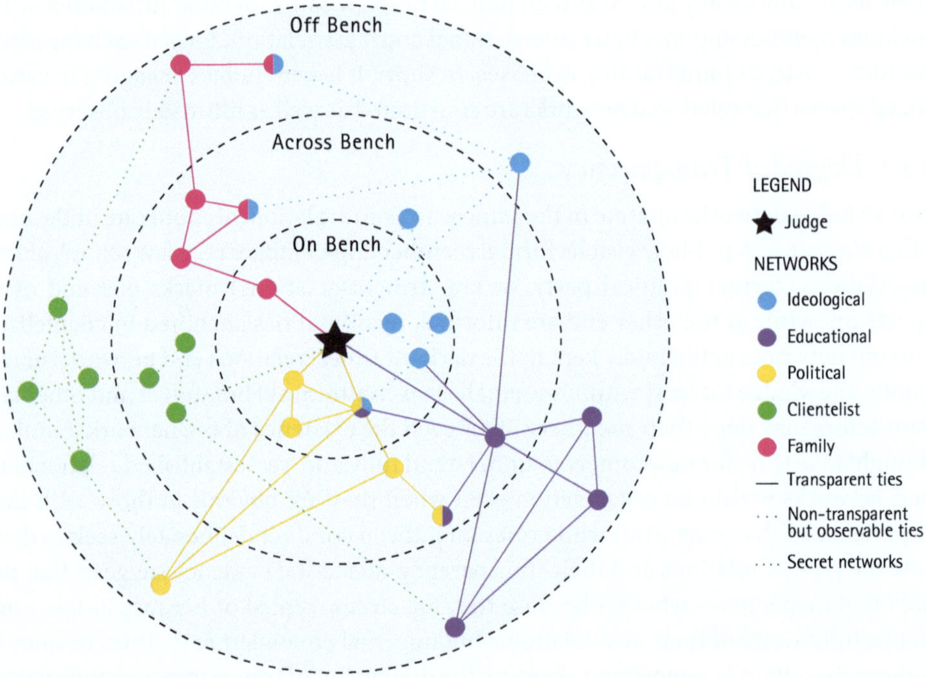

FIGURE 31.1 A hypothetical judge's network.

Note: dotted lines mark non-transparent ties (but observable); dotted boxes and lines mark secret networks.

degrees by relational bonds, including some formed over many years and carried along when a judge moves through the complex institutional tapestry. Whether belonging to such networks is good or bad for judicial behaviour and how courts perform is not immediately clear (although arguably judge networks that are anchored in clientelist or corrupt exchanges might be at odds with how judges as professionals might be expected to behave).

What is clear from the emerging empirical literature is that personal networks function as important social conduits for the flow of ideas and resources. Therefore, they might also function as incubators of judicial identity and the meaning a judge applies to work on the bench. As highlighted in the empirical literature, it is possible to identify three ideal-type relational channels for exerting influence on judicial decision-making:

- **Ideational:** This captures the relational ties based on shared ideas, whether legal, political, or ideological. Ideational networks not only help to transmit ideas onto the bench but they also shape how judges give meaning to their role and to legal concepts and principles. As becomes obvious in patterns of factional voting or of dissents, ideational bonds carry considerable weight in the day-to-day activities of a judge. They are often formed and reinforced by educational or political networks in which a judge has been socialized, whether at home or abroad.
- **Affective/Emotive**: This captures the personal emotive connections and deep primordial ties that constrain a judge, not because of ideas and commitments but rather because of a personal sense of loyalty or obligation to another actor, whether political (e.g. the executive, former political colleagues) or private (friendship, clan-based). Perhaps the most common expression of this bond is the patron–client relationship, although broader loyalty effects to the appointer, dynamics of seniority, or friendship on the bench might also fall into this relational dynamic.
- **Material:** This captures the exchange-oriented relational dynamic that is often at the heart of corrupt or clientelist networks. Such relations are not based on ideational or personal conviction. They are transactional and based on material exchanges, such as when a judge exchanges votes for money, appointments, or other personal rewards.

Arguably, these ideal types are best understood as heuristics. Depending on the circumstances, relational pathways might at times overlap. Similarly, it is not always easy to identify networks and pathways because many operate in the shadows of formal institutions. There is little doubt that methodological challenges remain, particularly as far as data collection is concerned. A relational perspective requires a long-term historical and contextual view that explores how relationships and judge networks have formed over time, how they have influenced judicial identities within an institutional context, how laws and legal principles are interpreted, and how well judicial actors adhere to rule of law principles in their work (Hilbink 2012). From this vantage point, the relational perspective is best suited for qualitative explanation rather than quantitative prediction as it highlights the importance of processes between actors, their interdependence, and their mutual participation in social phenomena (Dépelteau 2018).

Such considerations aside, however, the purpose of this chapter is to identify the conceptual dimensions of this line of inquiry. The heuristic provided is meant as a starting point to systematically describe the relational realities of judges as human beings and draw attention to how judge networks come to influence a judge's behaviour. The next section illustrates how this perspective might further the understanding of the dynamics of judicial decision-making.

4. Judge Networks in Action

The academic and journalistic literature suggests several areas where judge networks have influenced how judges work and judicial institutions perform. Briefly discussed are a few areas of scholarly relevance highlighted in the comparative judicial politics literature: appointments and career, judicial decision-making and independence, and legitimacy and reform.

4.1 Appointments and Careers

One key area for the study of courts is the question of who become judges as well as their professional trajectories in terms of promotions, demotions, dismissal, and other tenure decisions. Anecdotal evidence, journalistic reports, and academic work suggest that personal relationships and broad informal judge networks can be critical to the selection of judges, which can coexist (or even be at odds) with existing rules devised to govern these processes. For instance, a judge's networks has proved to be critical when the executive makes the final decisions about appointments to the bench (Malleson and Russell 2006; Scribner 2004). In Asia, even where judicial commissions are charged with preparing shortlists or there is a multitrack appointment process, judges have been known to draw on their personal networks to seek to influence selections (Chua et al. 2012; Dressel 2018). When there is little transparency and much executive discretion, as is often the case for appointments to regional or international courts, judge networks might even function as cognitive shortcuts for executive appointments (Stroh and Kisakaye forthcoming).

Similarly, personal relationships and judge networks play out forcefully when judges are promoted. This has far-reaching consequences for judicial independence, professionalism, and institutional performance, particularly in patronage-based settings where families or political and ethnic networks permeate judicial institutions (see e.g. Pozas-Loyo and Rios-Figuero 2018). Judge networks that are anchored in political ties also influence the politicization of the bench, such as when the court becomes dominated by a single network (Dressel and Tonsakulrungruang 2019) or 'loyal' high court judges are elevated to critical positions, such as chief justice (Sanchez Urribarri 2012). Judge networks might also heighten the risk of intra-court and on-bench conflict should judges split into intransigent opposing camps more concerned about networks of friends and patrons than about enforcing accountability (Fombad 2014). Some informal judge networks may even transform into party-like formal groupings, as has been reported with judge groupings in Turkey that actively vie for promotions and positions (Shambayati 2015).

Thus, while the activation of a personal network for purposes of appointment or promotion might be seen as legitimate lobbying on behalf of a judge, it raises judicial integrity issues when they regularly bypass formal channels to replace meritocratic advancement. However, there is also evidence that judge networks, anchored in commitments to greater professionalization within and outside the judiciary can function as checks and balances, such as supporting institutional reform efforts or meritocratic practices (Ingram 2012).

4.2 Judicial Decision-Making and Independence

Closely linked to appointments and promotions is the role of judge networks in judicial decision-making. Informal interference with the courts by political actors has long been acknowledged (Russell 2001; Llanos et al. 2014; Kosař 2017). Scholars concerned with the politicization of the courts have scrutinized personal and associational relations between politicians and judges and the consequent dangers for judicial deference and partisan decisions in political cases (Sanchez Urribarri 2011; Popova 2012; Basabe-Serrano 2015). Some studies have illuminated the role of judge networks in on-bench factions, which may be indicative of loyalty to the appointer (Epstein and Posner 2016; Leslie et al. 2021; Dressel et al. 2023; Dressel and Inoue 2018).

Friendship, educational, and ideational ties might also influence the case decisions judges make, help diffuse ideas on the bench, or create reform coalitions within the judiciary (Ingram 2016b, Dressel and Inoue 2018, Posner 1995). Where judges are primarily recruited from the legal profession (e.g., the bar), studies have shown how continuous professional ties between judges and lawyers have directly influenced case management and outcomes of judicial decisions based on professional ties and friendship (Kureshi 2022). Such dynamics differ from corruption-based judge networks, where judicial decisions are traded for monetary rewards, as is common in many less institutionalized settings, where the 'price' of obtaining a judgement might be known to parties, often via lawyers who act as brokers in the network (Butt and Lindsey 2010, Gloppen 2013).

In sum, a judge's complex relational world often constitutes how each judge assumes a professional role and applies the law. Personal networks provide a socializing milieu in which identities, ideas, and loyalties form that have direct consequences for judicial decision-making. At times, judge networks have promoted networks of judges; at other times, they have directly eroded judicial independence and integrity. The role of each judge's networks is highly contextual. The breadth and depth of the legal complex, the exposure to training and ideas beyond the country's border, and how power is concentrated within the political system all help shape the parameters in which judge networks operate on the bench (Dressel et al. 2018).

4.3 Legitimacy and Judicial Reform

Judge networks also affect the legitimacy of the court as well as judicial reform. The perception of a bench dominated by political or ethnic judge networks alone often calls into question the public legitimacy of a court, particularly in polarized or multi-ethnic settings (Stroh 2018; Brett 2022). Similarly, with judges facing political backlash, interference, and threats, judge networks have become critical in encouraging alliances between judges and societal actors in defence of the judiciary (Trochev and Ellett 2014; Kosar and Sipulova 2020). In particular, regional and international courts have seen judges rely on their networks to engage in public diplomacy, sometimes actively creating support networks to help make their rulings enforceable (Dothan 2018; Squatrito 2021). Deliberate efforts to create regional judge networks have not only facilitated exchange and connections between judges but have also functioned as a domestic signal of the credibility of newly established courts, as shown in the wider network of Asian constitutional courts (De Visser 2016).

Meanwhile, some transitional settings have clarified the role of judge networks in judicial reform. Considering the ambiguous stance of some judges on judicial reform and new institutional structures, chief justices would often rely on personal support networks within and outside the court to push for much-needed reform (Widner 2001; Crouch 2019). Studies have shown how close contacts among judges in Mexican subnational courts shape their own subjective, non-material commitments to reform, including empirical evidence of how ideational networks can shape the introduction of institutional changes, such as judicial councils, and new legal and jurisprudential practices (see Ingram 2016b). With areas of legal reform imposing new demands on the judiciary (e.g. environmental governance, sexual and gender-based crimes, etc.), it is common to find domestic or regional networks of judges at the forefront in the dissemination of new ideas and practices, often with direct support from international organizations (Armytage 2011).

In general, the importance of judge networks is recognized in a variety of areas of interest to current scholars of judicial politics, as is the usefulness of a complementary relational perspective on judicial behaviour.

5. Conclusion

In highlighting the role of judge networks, this chapter has drawn attention to an understudied aspect of comparative judicial politics scholarship: how judges as human beings are embedded in society and how that is carried over into judicial behaviour. Judge networks reflect the 'ties that bind' that are at the centre of a judge's personal social network. The concept moves beyond the characteristics of individual judges and rational-strategic assumptions to suggest how a judge's networks can become constitutive for identity and preference formation. This informs how a judge constructs a professional role and engages with the law. Revealing judges as fluid and dynamic social entities that are interconnected, judge networks offer a complementary perspective to the literature on judicial networks, which has emphasized the structure of the network itself over the actors and their links.

Emerging scholarship has taken on these challenges and has opened promising new avenues for future research. In the United States, it was shown that frequent interpersonal contact and collegiality among appellate judges have diminished the role of ideology in judicial decision-making and affected various aspects of judicial behaviour (Hazelton et al. 2023). Macro-level studies have systematically mapped networks of 'judicial families' and informal 'gentlemen's pacts' over time to trace how nepotism in judicial appointments has undermined judicial independence and legitimacy (Pozas-Loyo and Rios-Figuero 2018; Castagnola and Gonzales-Ocanto 2021). Other studies have explored the informal role of judge networks in the broader political context, including how courts facilitate or resist trends of constitutional regression and democratic backsliding (Dressel et al. 2023; Kosar and Sipulova 2020) or have drawn attention to the spatial-relational aspect of actors in facilitating judicial corruption (Wang and Liu 2021). With a growing interest in transnational networks of judges and their role in the spread of ideas and practices (Dallara and Piana 2015), scholarly debates highlight an exciting new 'relational turn' in comparative judicial politics scholarship that moves beyond the traditional focus on the structural configurations of social networks to a judge-centred, spatial-relational analysis of judicial behaviour and performance.

The continued study of judge networks will certainly not be easy. Many judges are hesitant to discuss personal networks, far less admit the extent to which these influence their work. As a result, data collection will require considerable creativity that combines qualitative fieldwork, interviews, archival research, and the systematic analysis of newspapers and other sources. Collecting relational data can be daunting. However, judges are often part of a relatively small group whose members share a personal, academic, and professional background. In many places, they create formal associations as well as informal groups. Thus, data collection would need to rely on ethnographic or anthropological work to capture the backgrounds of judges or map the types of social circles that a judge maintains and is engaged with. There is also the challenge of how to account for the influence of overlapping relational ties and how to parse out their influence on individual behaviour. This would be highly contextual and formal network analysis could be used to complement careful qualitative inference, as illustrated in some of the newly emerging scholarship highlighted above.

In summary, using judge networks as a conceptual lens can enhance both theory development and empirical analysis. Complementing existing scholarly work on structural configurations of social networks and how they affect judicial actors and outcomes, this contribution suggests a judge-centred perspective that draws attention to the type of relational ties that a judge maintains, their spatial location, and the mode of transparency. Despite considerable debate about how best to analyse judicial behaviour, few models have engaged with relational, emotive, or simply informal aspects that shape the work of judges. However, in many diverse judicial settings, ignoring such factors can have far-reaching consequences. This is particularly true for the Global South, where formal and informal practices are often closely interwoven, and judges have to navigate contexts dominated by personal relationships and networks. There is much value to be learned by deepening our understanding of how judges' relational networks influence their behaviour.

Notes

1. For a good summary of these debates in terms of macro-social change, see Erikson and Occhiuto 2017.
2. See for the differentiation between 'owned' and 'unowned', see Jackson and Nexon (1999, 302)

References

Armytage, Livingston. 2011. 'Judicial Reform in Asia. Case Study of ADB's Experience: 1990–2007'. *Hague Journal on the Rule of Law* 3: 70–105.

Bailey, Michael A., and Forrest Maltzman. 2011. *The Constrained Court: Law, Politics and the Decisions Justices Make*. Princeton: Princeton University Press.

Basabe-Serrano, Santiago. 2015. 'Informal Institutions and Judicial Independence in Paraguay, 1954–2011'. *Law & Policy* 37 (4): 350–78.

Baum, Lawrence. 2006. *Judges and their Audiences: A Perspective on Judicial Behaviour*. Princeton: Princeton University Press.

Baum, Lawrence. 2010. 'Motivation and Judicial Behaviour: Expanding the Scope of Inquiry'. In *The Psychology of Judicial Decision Making*, edited by David E. Klein and Gregory Mitchell, 3–26. Oxford: Oxford University Press.

Bommarito II, Michael J., Daniel M. Katz, and Jon Zelner. 2010. 'Distance Measures for Dynamic Citation Networks'. *Physica A* 389: 4201–08.

Borgatti, S. P., and B. Ofem. 2010. 'Overview: Social Network Theory and Analysis'. In *Social Network Theory and Educational Change*, edited by A. J. Daly, 17–30. Cambridge: Harvard Education Press.

Box-Steffensmeier, Janet M., Dino P. Christenson, and Matthew P. Hitt. 2013. 'Quality Over Quantity: Amici Influence and Judicial Decision Making'. *The American Political Science Review* 107 (3): 446–60.

Box-Steffensmeier, Janet M., Dino P. Christenson, and Claire Levitt. 2016. 'Judicial Networks'. In *The Oxford Handbook of Political Networks*, edited by Alexander H. Montgomery Jennifer Nicoll Victor, and Mark Lubell, 491–515. Oxford: Oxford.

Brett, Peter. 2022. 'The New Politics of Judicial Appointments in Southern Africa'. *Law & Social Inquiry* 1–31.

Brinks, Daniel, Steven Levitsky, and Maria Victoria Murillo. 2020. *The Politics of Institutional Weakness in Latin America*. Cambridge: Cambridge University Press.

Butt, Simon, and T. I. M. Lindsey. 2010. 'Judicial Mafia the Courts and State Illegality in Indonesia'. In *The State and Illegality in Indonesia*, edited by Edward Aspinall and Gerry van Klinken, 189–214. Leiden: Brill.

Caldeira, Gregory A. 1985. 'The Transmission of Legal Precedent: A Study of State Supreme Courts'. *American Political Science Review* 79 (1): 178–94.

Castagnola, Andrea, and Ezequiel A. Gonzales-Ocantos. 2021. 'Argentina's "Judicial Family": Mapping Family Connections in the Argentine Provincial Federal Judiciary (Conference Paper)'. Informality and Courts: Comparative Perspectives, Onati, 21–22 July 2022.

Christenson, Dino P., and Janet M. Box-Steffensmeier. 2017. 'Why Amicus Curiae Cosigners Come and Go: A Dynamic Model of Interest Group Networks'. In *Complex Networks & Their Applications V. COMPLEX NETWORKS 2016, Studies in Computational Intelligence*, edited by Cherifi, H., Gaito, S., Quattrociocchi, W., and Sala, A., vol. 693, 349–60.

Chua, Yvonne T., Booma B. Cruz, Ma. Gisela Ordenes-Cascolan, Luz Rimban, Jennifer Santiago, and Ellen Tordessillas. 2012. 'Political Economy Analysis of Judicial Appointments in the Philippines'. *VERA Files*. https://verafiles.org/articles/jbc-partly-to-blame-for-problems-in-judiciary

Claes, Monica, and Maartje De Visser. 2012. 'Are You Networked Yet? On Dialogues in European Judicial Networks'. *Utrecht Law Review* 8 (2): 100–14.

Clayton, Cornell W., and Howard Gillman, eds. 1999. *The Supreme Court in American Politics. New Institutional Interpretations*. Lawrence: University Press of Kansas.

Collins, P. M. 2008. *Friends of the Supreme Court: Interest Groups and Judicial Decision Making*. Oxford: Oxford University Press.

Conti, Joseph A. 2022. 'Relational Sociology and Comparative Law'. *The American Journal of Comparative Law* 69 (4): 636–63.

Crouch, Melissa, ed. 2019. *The Politics of Court Reform. Judicial Change and Legal Culture in Indonesia*. Cambridge: Cambridge University Press.

Dallara, Cristina, and Dianiela Piana. 2015. *Networking the Rule of Law. How Change Agents Reshape Judicial Governance in the EU*. London: Routledge.

De Visser, Maartje. 2016. 'We All Stand Together: The Role of the Association of Asian Constitutional Courts and Equivalent Institutions in Promoting Constitutionalism'. *Asian Journal of Law and Society* 3 (1): 105–34.

Dépelteau, François. 2018. 'Relational Thinking in Sociology: Relevance, Concurrence and Dissonance'. In *The Palgrave Handbook of Relational Sociology*, edited by François Dépelteau, 3–33. London: Palgrave Macmillan.

Dezalay, Yves, and Bryant Garth. 1996. *Dealing in Virtue: International Commercial Arbitration and the Construction of a Transnational Legal Order*. Chicago: Chicago University Press.

Dothan, Shai. 2018. 'Social Networks and the Enforcement of International Law'. In *Research Handbook on the Sociology of International Law*, edited by Moshe Hirsch and Andrew Lang, 333–46. Cheltenham: Edward Elgar.

Dressel, Björn, Tomoo Inoue, and Cristina Bonoan. 2023. 'Justices and Political Loyalties: An Empirical Investigation of the Supreme Court of the Philippines, 1987–2020'. *Law and Social Inquiry* 1–25.

Dressel, Björn. 2018. 'The Informal Dimension of Constitutional Politics in Asia: Insights from the Philippines and Indonesia'. In *Constitutional Courts in Asia*, edited by Albert H. Y. Chen and Andrew Harding, 60–86. Cambridge: Cambridge University Press.

Dressel, Björn, and Tomoo Inoue. 2018. ". 'Informal Networks and Judicial Decisions: Insights from the Philippines Supreme Court, 1986–2015'. *International Political Science Review* 39 (5): 616–33.

Dressel, Björn, Raul Sanchez Urribarri, and Alexander Stroh. 2017. 'The Informal Dimension of Judicial Politics: A Relational Perspective'. *Annual Review of Law and Social Science* 13: 413–30.

Dressel, Björn, Raul Sanchez Urribarri, and Alexander Stroh. 2018. 'Courts and Informal Networks: Towards a Relational Perspective on Judicial Politics beyond Western Democracies'. *International Political Science Review* 39 (5): 573–84.

Dressel, Björn, and Khemthong Tonsakulrungruang. 2019. 'Coloured Judgement? The Work of the Thai Constitutional Court, 1998–2016'. *Journal of Contemporary Asia* 49 (1): 1–23.

Dyevre, Arthur. 2010. 'Unifying the Field of Comparative Judicial Politics: Towards a General Theory of Judicial Behaviour'. *European Political Science Review* 2 (2): 297–327.

Emirbayer, Mustafa. 1997. 'Manifesto for a Relational Sociology'. *American Journal of Sociology* 103 (2): 281–317. doi:10.1086/231209.

Epstein, Lee, and Jack Knight. 1998. *The Choices Justices Make*. Washington: CQ Press.

Epstein, Lee, and Eric A. Posner. 2016. 'Supreme Court Justices' Loyalty to the President'. *The Journal of Legal Studies* 45 (2): 401–36.

Epstein, Lee, and Keren Weinshall. 2021. *The Strategic Analysis of Judicial Behaviour, Cambridge Elements. Law, Economics, and Politics*. Cambridge: Cambridge University Press.

Erikson, Emily, and Nicholas Occhiuto. 2017. 'Social Networks and Macrosocial Change'. *Annual Reviews of Sociology* 43: 229–48.

Flemming, Roy B., and Glen S. Krutz. 2002. 'Repeat Litigators and Agenda Setting on the Supreme Court of Canada'. *Canadian Journal of Political Science / Revue canadienne de science politique* 35 (4): 811–33.

Fombad, Charles M. 2014. 'Appointment of Constitutional Adjudicators in Africa: Some Perspectives on How Different Systems Yield Similar Outcome'. *The Journal of Legal Pluralism and Unofficial Law* 46 (2): 249–75.

Fowler, James H., and Sangick Jeon. 2008. 'The Authority of Supreme Court precedent'. *Social Networks* 30 (1): 16–30.

Friedman, Lawrence M. 2006. 'Judging the Judges: Some Remarks on the Way Judges Think and the Way Judges Act'. In *Norms and the Law*, edited by John N. Drobak, 139–60. Cambridge: Cambridge University Press.

Fuhse, Jan. 2015. 'Theorizing Social Networks: The Relational Sociology of and around Harrison White'. *International Review of Sociology* 25 (1): 15–44.

Ginsburg, Tom, and Nuno Garoupa. 2015. *Judicial Reputation. A Comparative Theory*. Chicago: University of Chicago Press.

Gloppen, Siri. 2013. 'Courts, Corruption and Judicial Independence'. In *Corruption, Grabbing and Development*, edited by Tina Soreide and Aled Williams, 68–82. Cheltenham: Edward Elgar.

Gomez, Manuel A. 2011. 'Greasing the Squeaky Wheel of Justice: Lawyers, Social Networks and Dispute Processing in Venezuela'. In *Lawyers and the Rule of Law in an Era of Globalization*, edited by Yves Dezalay and Bryant Garth, 19–38. Abingdon: Routledge.

Granovetter, Mark. 1973. 'The Strength of Weak Ties'. *American Journal of Sociology* 78 (6): 1360–80.

Grosser, Travis J., and Stephen P. Borgatti. 2013. 'Network Theory/Social Network Analysis'. In *Theory in Social and Cultural Anthropology: An Encyclopedia*, edited by R. Jon McGee and Richard L. Warms, 595–97. Thousand Oaks: Sage.

Hazelton L. W., Morgan, Rachael K. Hinkle, and Michael J. Nelson. 2023. *The Elevator Effect. Contact and Collegiality in the American Judiciary*. Oxford: Oxford University Press.

Helmke, Gretchen, and Julio Rios-Figueroa. 2011. *Courts in Latin America*. Cambridge: Cambridge University Press.

Hilbink, Lisa. 2012. 'The Origins of Positive Judicial Independence'. *World Politics* 64 (4): 587–621.

Hinkle, Rachael K., and Michael J. Nelson. 2016. 'The Transmission of Legal Precedent among State Supreme Courts in the Twenty-First Century'. *State Politics & Policy Quarterly* 16 (4): 391–410.

Ingram, Matthew C. 2012. 'Crafting Courts in New Democracies: Ideology and Judicial Council Reforms in Three Mexican States'. *Comparative Politics* 44 (4): 439–58.

Ingram, Matthew C. 2016a. *Crafting Courts in New Democracies: The Politics of Subnational Judicial Reform in Brazil and Mexico*. Cambridge: Cambridge University Press.

Ingram, Matthew C. 2016b. 'Networked Justice: Judges, The Diffusion of Ideas, and Legal Reform Movements in Mexico'. *Journal of Latin American Studies* 48 (4): 739–68.

Jackson, Patrick Thaddeus, and Daniel H. Nexon. 1999. 'Relations Before States: Substance, Process and the Study of World Politics'. *European Journal of International Relations* 5 (3): 291–332.

Katz, Daniel M., Joshua R. Gubler, Jon Zelner, Michael J. Bommarito II, Eric Provins, and Eitan Ingall. 2011. 'Reproduction of Hierarchy? A Social Network Analysis of the American Law Professoriate'. *Journal of Legal Education* 61 (1): 76–103.

Katz, Daniel M., and Derek K. Stafford. 2010. 'Hustle and Flow: A Social Network Analysis of the American Federal Judiciary'. *Ohio State Law Journal* 71 (3): 467–510.

Katz, Daniel M., Derek K. Stafford, and E. A. Provins. 2008. 'Social Architecture, Judicial Peer Effects and the "Evolution" of the Law: Toward a Positive Theory of Judicial Social Structure'. *Georgia State Law Review* 24 (4): 975–1000.

Kornhauser, Lewis A., and Lawrence G. Sager. 1986. 'Unpacking the Court'. *The Yale Law Journal* 96 (1): 82–117.

Kosař, David. 2017. 'Politics of Judicial Independence and Judicial Accountability in Czechia: Bargaining in the Shadow of the Law between Court Presidents and the Ministry of Justice'. *European Constitutional Law Review* 13 (1): 96–123. doi:10.1017/S1574019616000419.

Kosar, David, and Katarina Sipulova. 2020. 'How to Fight Court-Packing'. *Constitutional Studies* 6 (1): 133–64.

Kureshi, Yasser. 2022. *Seeking Supremacy: The Pursuit of Judicial Power in Pakistan, Cambridge Studies in Law and Society*. Cambridge: Cambridge University Press.

Leiter, Brian. 2010. 'Legal Formalism and Legal Realism: What Is the Issue?' *Legal Theory* 16 (2): 111–33.

Leslie, Patrick, Zoe Robinson, and Russell Smyth. 2021. *Personal or Political Patronage? Judicial Appointments and Justice Loyalty in the High Court of Australia. Australian Journal of Political Science* 56 (4): 445–63.

Llanos, Mariana, Cordula; Tibi Weber, Charlotte Heyl, and Alexander Stroh. 2014. 'Informal Interference in the Judiciary in New Democracies: A Comparison of Six African and Latin American Cases'. *Democratization* 23 (7): 1236–53.

Lupu, Yonatan, and Erik Voeten. 2012. 'Precedent in International Courts: A Network Analysis of Case Citations by the European Court of Human Rights'. *British Journal of Political Science* 42 (2): 413–39.

Lynch, Peter S. K. 2022. 'The Influence of the Federalist Society on Judicial Politics and Law in the United States'. PhD Thesis, Political Science, University of Kentucky.

Malleson, Kate, and Peter H. Russell, eds. 2006. *Appointing Judges in an Age of Judicial Power: Critical Perspectives from around the World*. Toronto: University of Toronto Press.

Maltzman, Forrest, James F. Spriggs II, and Paul J. Wahlbeck. 2000. *Crafting Law on the Supreme Court. The Collegial Game*. New York: Cambridge University Press.

McGuire, Kevin T. 1993. 'Repeat Players in the Supreme Court: The Role of Experienced Lawyers in Litigation Success'. *Journal of Politics* 57 (1): 187–96.

Mohr, John W., and Harrison C. White. 2008. 'How to Model and Institution'. *Theory and Society* 37 (5): 485–512.

Popova, Maria. 2012. *Politicized Justice in Emerging Democracies: A Study of Courts in Russia and Ukraine*. Cambridge: Cambridge University Press.

Posner, Daniel N. 1995. *Overcoming Law*. Cambridge: Harvard University Press.

Posner, Richard A. 2008. *How Judges Think*. Cambridge: Harvard University Press.

Post, David G., and Michael B. Eisen. 2000. 'How Long is the Coastline of the Law? Thoughts on the Fractal Nature of Legal Systems'. *The Journal of Legal Studies* 29 (S1): 545–84.

Pozas-Loyo, Andrea, and Julio Rios-Figuero. 2018. 'Anatomy of an Informal Institution: The 'Gentlemen's Pact' and Judicial Selection in Mexico, 1917–1994'. *International Political Science Review* 39 (5): 647–61.

Russell, Peter H. 2001. 'Toward a General Theory of Judicial Independence'. In *Judicial Independence in the Age of Democracy: Critical Perspectives from around*, edited by Peter H. Russel and David M O'Brian, 1–22. Charlottesville: University Press of Virginia.

Salamone, Michael F. 2014. 'Community and Persuasion: The Influence of the Federalist Society on the Supreme Court'. APSA 2014 Annual Meeting Paper, Washington, DC.

Sanchez Urribarri, Raul. 2012. 'Politicization of the Latin American Judiciary via Informal Connections'. In *Legitimacy, Legal Development & Change: Law & Modernization Reconsidered*, edited by David K. Linnan, 307–22. Abingdon: Ashgate.

Sanchez Urribarri, Raul. 2011. 'Courts between Democracy and Hybrid Authoritarianism: Evidence from the Venezuelan Supreme Court'. *Law & Social Inquiry* 36 (4): 854–84.

Scherer, Nancy, and Banks Miller. 2009. 'The Federalist Society's Influence on the Federal Judiciary'. *Political Research Quarterly* 62 (2): 366–78.

Scribner, Druscilla. 2004. *Limiting Presidential Power: Supreme Court-Executive Relations in Argentina and Chile*. San Diego: University of California.

Segal, Jeffrey A. 2008. 'Judicial Behaviour'. In *The Oxford Handbook of Law and Politics*, edited by Keith E. Whittington, Daniel R. Kelemen, and Gregory A. Caldeira, 19–34. Oxford: Oxford University Press.

Segal, Jeffrey A., and Harold J. Spaeth. 1993. *The Supreme Court and the Attitudinal Model*. New York: Cambridge University Press.

Segal, Jeffrey A., and Harold J. Spaeth. 2002. *The Supreme Court and the Attitudinal Model Revisited*. Cambridge: Cambridge University Press.

Shambayati, Hootan. 2015. 'From Informal Networks to Judicial Parties: The Turkish Case'. Informal Networks in Non-Western Judiciaries workshop in Canberra, Canberra, 26 March 2015.

Slaughter, Anne Marie. 2004. *A New World Order*. Washington: Brookings Institution.

Snyder, Eloise C. 1958. 'The Supreme Court as a Small Group'. *Social Forces* 36 (3): 232–38.
Spiller, Pablo, and Rafael Gely. 2010. 'Strategic Judicial Decision-Making'. In *The Oxford Handbook of Law and Politics*, edited by Keith E. Whittington, Daniel R. Kelemen, and Gregory A. Caldeira, 35–43. Oxford: Oxford University Press.
Squatrito, Theresa. 2021. 'Judicial Diplomacy: International Courts and Legitimation'. *Review of International Studies* 47 (1): 64–84.
Staton, Jeffrey K. 2010. *Judicial Power and Strategic Communication in Mexico*. Cambridge: Cambridge University Press.
Stroh, Alexander. 2018. 'Sustaining and Jeopardizing a Credible Arbiter: Judicial Networks in Benin's Consolidating Democracy'. *International Political Science Review* 39 (5): 600–15.
Stroh, Alexander, and Diana Kisakaye. forthcoming. 'Informality and Multilevel Appointment Processes in African Regional Courts'. In *Informality and Courts: Comparative Perspectives*, edited by Björn Dressel, Alexander Stroh and Raul Sanchez-Urribarri. Edinburgh: Edinburgh University Press.
Trochev, Alexei, and Rachel Ellett. 2014. 'Judges and their Allies'. *Journal of Law and Courts* 2 (1): 67–91.
Ulmer, Sydney S. 1965. 'Toward a Theory of Sub-group Formation in the United States Supreme Court'. *The Journal of Politics* 27 (1): 133–52.
Wang, Juan, and Sida Liu. 2021. 'Institutional Proximity and Judicial Corruption: A Spatial Approach'. *Governance* 35 (2): 633–49.
Widner, Jennifer A. 2001. *Building the Rule of Law*. New York: W.W. Norton & Company, Inc.

CHAPTER 32

HIERARCHIES OF JUSTICE

ORI ARONSON

1. Introduction

A fundamental tension lies at the core of the judicial function, between independence and hierarchy: in systems committed to the rule of law, judges are expected to exercise their authority according to the law alone, and without regard to external pressures or to non-case specific considerations. At the same time, most judges operate within a rigidly vertical organizational structure and belong to a traditional professional community which rewards seniority and longevity. They are thus steeped in hierarchical dynamics—institutional and social—that impose diverse constraints on a judge's capacity to decide purely on her own understanding of the law.

Hierarchy in adjudication therefore differs from hierarchies in other branches of state power: hierarchical executive bodies—cabinets, ministries, agencies, municipalities, militaries, police forces—reflect in their structure the location of political legitimacy with the top-most principal, which is then devolved to its multiple agents for purposes of administrative expediency. This means that any act of an agent within a public organization—high-level manger and street-level bureaucrat alike—is perceived as if it were signed off by the organization's principal, who can instruct the agent on the decision to be taken, decide to revoke or replace it, and is ultimately publicly (and sometimes legally) accountable for it.

Judicial power works differently: it is located, in its entirety, with each judge and each court individually. The validity of a trial court's decision is not contingent upon higher court approval, an appellate court cannot instruct the trial court on how to decide a pending case, nor can it choose to revoke or replace the trial court's decision, unless asked to do so by a losing party. Hierarchy in adjudication thus requires explanation: if it is not a mere organizational means for effectuating principal mandates, and given the immense social costs of appeal, why is it such a ubiquitous institutional phenomenon (Shapiro 1981), and what purposes does it serve? Several functional explanations have been suggested in the literature, which I explore below. Each provides useful insights into the hierarchical logic that permeates adjudication, and each invites challenge and critique.

The purpose of the chapter is to provide a critical comparative assessment of hierarchy in adjudication and to suggest the contours of possible new avenues for its exploration. Due to the universal prevalence of hierarchies in justice, which take a broadly similar structural shape in many jurisdictions, most of the discussion is relatively general in character, while taking account of notable divergences in institutional and procedural culture. It is informed both by contextualized studies of judicial hierarchies worldwide, and by generalizable analyses—theoretical, modelled, empirical—of human and organizational behaviour.

After pointing to the diverse ways in which hierarchy permeates adjudication, I turn to a more focused inquiry into the dominant functional explanations for, and theorizations of, appeal—the central structural means for sustaining hierarchies of justice worldwide (for clarity and brevity, the analysis uses a bare-bones two-tier model of judicial hierarchy). A subsequent section delves further into one of the central institutional features of appeal—the case selection mechanism—and shows how it can serve different purposes and interests in judicial and party behaviour. This is followed by a review of the evidence of hierarchical inversions: the myriad contexts in which lower courts and judges can exert agency and produce information that is not available to upper judicial levels.

The deconstructive evaluation of appeal leads to a concluding reconstructive segment on the possibility of recasting judicial systems as non-hierarchical learning networks. In such a model, 'high' courts turn into networked junctures that collect, analyse, and disseminate normative information among the diverse units within the court system, rather than instructing them on proper behaviour. More of a call to further inquiry than a fully theorized model, this section is meant to open up avenues for future analyses of hierarchies of justice.

2. Faces of Hierarchy

A hierarchical logic is exhibited in diverse contexts in the design and operation of the judicial process and in the drivers of judicial behaviour. It is important to point to these various instances to demonstrate both hierarchy's prevalence in the judicial experience and its often informal character.

2.1 Appeal

The most structurally evident hierarchical feature of judicial systems worldwide, appeal is the process by which one court openly reviews the decisions of another court, normally with the capacity to overturn the initial court's decision. While distinct in certain procedural aspects, appeal's corollaries in civil law judicial traditions—*cassation*, *revision*—follow the same basic structure (Nichols Pugh 1975; Geeroms 2002). It is, in essence, a temporal process: one court decides *after* the other, the latter having the literal and normative last word. Entrusted with the power to cancel the earlier court's decision, appellate courts are often dubbed 'high' or 'supreme', while trial courts are often referred to as 'lower' or 'inferior'. A vertical imaginary is therefore imbued into the logic of adjudication—often also visualized through the imagery of a pyramid—with some courts and judges located above others. Decision-making in this hierarchy runs bottom up: the appellate court's capacity to decide is contingent on the trial court's arrival at a decision (and, normally, on a party's choice to seek appeal).

2.2 Precedent

Appeal and precedent should be distinguished. The power of appellate review, nominally, allows one court to overturn a specific past decision of another court. The power to set precedent, on the other hand, allows one court to instruct other courts on their future decisions; it is, in essence, a legislative power—central to the understanding of the appellate function in common law systems, in gradually receding contrast to the civil law tradition (Nichols Pugh 1975; Fon and Parisi 2006; Shoenberger 2009). While the power to set precedent, in systems in which it is recognized, is often formally located with appellate courts, the coupling is a matter of contingent institutional design. At the same time, as will be detailed below, to the extent that trial judges care about appellate court affirmance, they may seek to align their decisions with their understanding of an upper court's attitudes, granting it effective precedential power even without formal authorization (Caminker 1994).

Still, effective precedent may also emanate from other units within a judicial system, not necessarily higher courts. Most notably, the norm of (horizontal) *stare decisis*—the commitment of a court to its own previous decisions—reflects a sense of the court as a continuous institutional entity, with a methodological unity that transcends its individual judges. Another common law tradition gradually entering adjudication in civil law jurisdictions (Camarena González 2016), *stare decisis* can be explained as a conservative ideological project of tying the present to the past (Hathaway 2001), or as an information-building project with multiple members adding elements to a shared script and saving the costs of regularly restating the law (Bueno de Mesquita and Stephenson 2006). At any rate, it establishes a hierarchal sensibility among past, present, and future courts and judges, which may invoke critiques both functional (risk of epistemic cascades) and moral (the justness of binding the future) (Baude 2019).

A precedential effect may also emanate from content- or person-specific conditions that transcend formal jurisdictional lines. Consider, for example, the deference generalist courts may award the decisions of specialized courts within the same system, regardless of their formal station in the court hierarchy. The command of the Federal Circuit—a mid-level appellate court—over patent law in the United States is a familiar example (Baum 1994; Dreyfuss 2013; Gugliuzza 2013). Similarly, trial judges of exceptional expertise or prominence (intellectual, political, or other) may have an outsized influence on the behaviour of other judges, even ones formally superior or senior to them. This can benefit generalist panels that may enjoy the input of a uniquely versed colleague (Vermeule 2008, 123–62), as in the *rapporteur* system of the German Constitutional Court (Damle 2005), but it may also lead to intellectual lethargy on part of over-reliant judges (Wasserman and Slack 2021).

2.3 Seniority

A combination of formal organizational rules and informal traditionalist norms, seniority often plays a central role in structuring power relations among judges within a court or on a panel. In many jurisdictions, such as Canada (McCormick 2013), France (Lafon 1991), India (Chandrachud 2012; Shukla 2015), Israel (Shinar et al. 2020), Italy (Guarnieri 2004), Nigeria (Dawuni and Kang 2015), multiple states in the United States and its federal system (Fife et al. 2021; Wilhelm et al. 2023), seniority is determinative, either formally or informally, in the promotion of judges and in their selection to leadership positions as chief judges and chief justices. In many judicial panels, the most senior judge serves as the presiding judge—in charge of conducting oral arguments, deciding procedural issues and interim motions, and assigning writing duties among the panel members. And in systems with civil law traditions, senior judges sometimes shadow, train, and evaluate junior ones (Guarnieri 2004, Garoupa and Ginsburg 2009).

Hierarchy here is premised, ostensibly, on the mere passage of time, with the implied assumption that longer-serving judges develop better skills warranting of precedence, with mandatory retirement rules (or, in their absence, the great equalizer) ensuring that all judges, in due course, get to enjoy a position of seniority over their peers. Equal access to seniority however requires a system of staggered and fixed judicial terms in which appointment to collegial courts is done in regular intervals and for defined periods of time, and panels are constructed in a way that ensures equal distribution of membership (Porat 2021). Otherwise, appointing bodies may manipulate seniority effects by, for example, strategically placing relatively young judges on relatively ageing courts, or cynically satisfying diversity concerns with older judges who would remain relatively junior by retirement.

2.4 Organization and Leadership

In their judicial capacity, all judges within a single court normally have the same decisional power—their orders are all enforceable by the same agents and through the same procedures, and their votes on panels have equal weight (Waldron 2014). Judges however often also carry out leadership and administrative tasks, which could grant them effective power over their peers—while not in a purely decisional sense, still in ways that may deeply affect the professional judicial experience (Bentsen and Skiple 2023). Thus, most notably, many courts are presided over by chief judges, who are often members of the court's judicial bench that also control to some degree their peers' case dockets, panel membership, opinion writing assignments, administrative roles, and performance reviews (Langer et al. 2003; Ramseyer and Rasmusen 2006; Scheppele 2006; Chandrachud 2012; Eisenberg et al. 2013; Cohen 2017)—powers that have been shown to be exploited strategically, in various jurisdictions (Hausegger and Haynie 2003; Maltzman and Wahlbeck 2004; Chutkow 2014; Levy 2017; Givati and Rosenberg 2023). In some systems, upper court judges also affect, and sometimes govern, judicial selection and promotion, impacting the extent of what Rios-Figueroa (2019) terms 'internal judicial independence'. Finally, judicial leadership positions may affect colleagues' decision-making behaviour. This has been exhibited in the tendency—and capacity—of chief judges to promote consensus in their court in order to bolster its legitimacy and improve internal working relations (Bentsen and Skiple 2023). On specific panels, the positions of presiding judges have been shown to have an outsize effect on the votes of other panel members (Eisenberg et al. 2013).

2.5 Extra-Systemic

Hierarchies often extend beyond the boundaries of the state's judicial system. This limits the capacity of law-makers and institutional designers to fully control the impact of hierarchical forces on judicial behaviour. Further, it often requires one system's judges to consider not only the possibility of review by extra-systemic judicial forums but also the reviewing court's distinct legal concepts and categories (and vice versa). Thus, in federated countries, federal courts may have the power to review compliance of state courts with national norms—constitutional, regulatory, and other. This often formally takes the shape of an added appellate level, as in the jurisdiction of high federal courts in the United States, Australia, or (more broadly) Canada, but it may also realign hierarchy differently, as when a US district court hears a *habeas* petition challenging the ruling of a state supreme court—ostensibly locating a lower court of one system above the highest court of another. More conspicuously, countries with religious or tribal courts—either state run or community based—may authorize a civil court to review such traditional tribunals' decisions for compliance with the constitution or other general laws, by direct review or (more commonly) through courts' powers under arbitration laws (Grossman 2007). Here the difference between the *nomoi* of the reviewed and the reviewing courts is often uniquely pronounced.

Several international jurisdictions, such as the European Union, the European Community, and the Organization of American States, employ supra-national tribunals with the power to review national courts' decisions for compliance with international commitments (Court of Justice of the European Union (CJEU), European Court of Human Rights (ECtHR), Inter-American Court of Rights (IACtHR)). While this broadly resembles intra-state hierarchies of appellate justice, the dynamics of mediating between national and international forums are often reciprocal, combining various measures of competition, contestation, coordination, and co-dependence (Huneeus 2011; Kunz 2019).

Extra-national hierarchies may also develop through informal networks of power and influence. The judicial method of comparative law itself may reflect acceptance, submission, replication, or affinity of certain judges to those presiding in other countries (Slaughter 1994). It may also be the result of expansionist projects of economies seeking to project their normative imaginaries beyond their borders and bring communities under their ideological fold (Kennedy 2006). Over time and in different contexts, the global influence of different courts—measured by such metrics as citation frequencies—may vary, providing a telling story of the ebbs and flows in global legal consciousnesses and centres of normative power (Aft 2011).

The many faces of judicial hierarchy reflect the richness and complexity of incentives and constraints that affect judicial behaviour through political, institutional, and interpersonal power dynamics. The remainder of the discussion, however, will be dedicated primarily to the most formal hierarchical feature of adjudication: the process and structure of appeal. This is the context on which the lion's share of judicial behaviour analyses has focused (often in more or less principled conjunction with the notion of precedent). Future research is necessary to develop a multidimensional model of the pressures of hierarchy that operate in adjudication.

3. Explaining Hierarchy (Appeal)

Hierarchy in adjudication differs from hierarchies in other branches of state power: hierarchical executive bodies—cabinets, ministries, agencies, municipalities, militaries, police forces—reflect in their structure the location of political legitimacy with the topmost principal, which is then devolved to its multiple agents (be it the initial design or the result of centralizing processes). This means that any act of an agent within a public organization—high-level manger and street-level bureaucrat alike—is perceived as if it were signed off by the organization's principal, who can instruct the agent on the decision to be taken, decide to revoke or replace it, and is ultimately publicly (and sometimes legally) accountable for it.

Judicial power works differently: it is presumably located, in its entirety, with each judge and each court individually. The validity of a trial court's decision is not contingent upon appellate court approval, the appellate court cannot instruct the trial court on how to decide a pending case, nor is it held accountable for the trial court's decision. This means that hierarchy in adjudication requires explanation: why is appeal such a ubiquitous institutional phenomenon, and what purposes does it serve? I review below briefly the main justifications of appeal. These will underly the subsequent discussion on theories of appeal and its impact on judicial behaviour.

3.1 Error Correction and Reduction (Systemic Accuracy)

Appeal is most commonly understood as a mechanism for correcting lower court errors, primarily in law and marginally in fact as well (Shavell 1995; Badawi and Baker 2015). This rationale reflects a goal of enhancing systemic accuracy, i.e., the overall correctness level of case outcomes within a system. It assumes a greater capacity by appellate courts and judges to reach correct results, in comparison to trial courts and judges. Four main reasons underlie this assumption: (i) *information*: appeal takes place after trial, which arguably means that appellate judges have a structural information advantage over trial judges—they have at their disposal all the information gathered and produced during trial, as well as the reasoned decisions of the trial judge (and, where applicable, the unreasoned decisions of the jury), new materials produced for appeal, and in addition the fact that the losing party chose to appeal (Daughety and Reinganum 2000); (ii) *case selection effects*: appeal relies on parties' choice to seek review of a trial court's decision, adding a screening stage that marks suspect decisions for the appellate court to consider; (iii) *judicial selection effects*: appellate benches are smaller than those of trial courts, allowing for selecting, nominating, and appointing processes to be more selective, arguably producing on average courts of superior judicial quality; (iv) *group decision-making*: in contrast to the common single-judge bench of trial courts, in many jurisdictions courts of appeal sit in panels, arguably enhancing the court's capacity to arrive at better results through deliberation, breadth of knowledge, and averaging out of extremes (Kornhauser and Sager 1993).

The error-correction rationale however calls for questioning. To begin with, it assumes the contested premise that there is a decipherable truth in questions decided by courts, let alone in legal questions normally presented on appeal. One can commit to varying levels of scepticism and relativism in this regard, but some differences between trial and appellate courts—for example, in the interpretation of abstract legal notions such as 'equal protection', 'negligence', 'due process', or 'unconscionability'—obviously also reflect differences in policy and ideology, rather than a mere advantage in access to the truth. And in the review of factual determinations, trial judges, who examine live witnesses and are exposed to the full breadth of the litigation, often have a better and more nuanced understanding of the dispute and its underlying facts (Frank 1949, 222–24).

Further, while handing parties the power to select cases for appeal draws on their access to unique information about the case (Cameron and Kornhauser 2012) and produces a unique incentive to appeal when they sense a mistake (Iossa and Palumbo 2007), it also casts doubt on the centrality of error correction as a systemic mission for courts: given the essential divergence between private and public interest in appeal (Shavell 1997), it is likely that many trial court errors go unappealed, leaving them intact and diminishing the overall accuracy of the judicial system. Indeed, in some contexts other values instruct the pre-emption of review, for example when prosecutors are legally barred from appealing exculpating verdicts, even if wrongly decided (Poulin 2008).

3.2 Fairness

The main non-consequentialist justification for appeal is that it is morally just to allow losing parties the possibility to have their detrimental decision reviewed by another decision-maker; a second bite at the apple. The procedural justness of appeal lies in its assurance that people are not subjected to completely random, arbitrary, capricious, or discriminatory adjudication by any single judge but retain the right that another judge would re-decide their case. This limits the subjugation of the single litigant to the single judge, in furtherance of people's dignity and autonomy.

Still, in most systems of appeal, parties are bound by the result of the ultimate appeal—they do not get to choose which of the decisions of the different courts made in their case will prevail. Given that randomness, arbitrariness, capriciousness, and discrimination can take place at the appeal level as well (although these effects are mitigated by the panel formation), the assurance of fairness inherent in two rounds of adjudication seems limited, and indeed it is not regularly understood to be required under constitutional guarantees of due process (Resnik 1984); although some jurisdictions, like South Africa, New Zealand, and Israel, do have constitutional guarantees of a right of appeal (Marshall 2011). Litigants may nonetheless *perceive* the possibility of appeal as procedurally just (Tyler 1988). Some jurisdictions accordingly allow only defendants in criminal cases to appeal convictions and sentences while barring the state from challenging acquittals or lenient punishments (Djukić 2018).

3.3 Judicial Incentives

Hierarchies produce economies of power, status, and effort that are likely to exhibit in agent behaviour. Given the complex set of purposes that underlie judicial hierarchy, and the complex set of mechanics that operate it, how would hierarchy impact judicial behaviour, on both upper and lower courts?

Rational choice models of judicial behaviour normally assign judges some combination of preferences to maximize their capacity to affect the law's content (for legal, ideological, or institutional reasons) as well as their sense of esteem, credibility, and importance, while minimizing the private costs incurred in terms of time, effort, and relationships (Posner 2010; Kastellec 2017). A judge's organizational location within a hierarchy can impact how she pursues these preferences, and hence be exploited to incentivize socially desired judicial behaviour.

3.3.1 *Lower Court Effort*

Appeal is a means of regulating trial judge behaviour (Drahozal 1998; Shavell 2006). To the extent that a system has accepted criteria for proper judicial behaviour, these can be transmitted and enforced in diverse ways: (i) formal rules and orders, directed at judges' intrinsic commitment to following them; (ii) informal norms, inculcated through professional and institutional socialization; (iii) positive incentives, such as promotion and reputational prizes (e.g., citation); and (iv) negative incentives, such as impeachment and reputational sanctions (e.g. disregard).

Appeal applies to all four. It can operate as a direct order to the trial judge to behave in a certain way. It can instil a sense of duty or commitment to the legal order, performed through hierarchy (Cross 2005). It can be used to signal judicial excellence, for example through low measures of appealed decisions or high rates of affirmance. And it can incur emotional and reputational costs, if trial judges mind being reversed (Klein and Hume 2003) or the legal community takes reversals as evidence of poor performance (Levy 2005). Beyond the impact of the possibility of reversal on trial judge effort, appeal is also a hierarchical station in the judicial apparatus, which trial judges are expected to strive toward, seeking the economic, policy, and status benefits of promotion (Posner 1993; Epstein 2016, 2047). Appeal therefore provides not only a judge's 'performance review' but it is also a club which judges are expected to want to join—a motivation empirically demonstrated in diverse jurisdictions such as the United States (Budziak 2013; Epstein et al. 2013, 337–83; Black and Owens 2016), Japan (Ramseyer and Rasmusen 2001, 2006), Germany (Schneider 2005), and Slovenia (Dimitrova-Grajzl et al. 2012).

The possibility of appeal introduces an institutionalized (potential) audience to trial court opinions—the appellate court (Baum 2008, 108–14). Appeal means that an unknown share of a judge's opinions will be read and reviewed by senior professionals, with specific focus on the quality their legal reasoning. In many cases, appellate judges would be the only viable and impartial readers of the trial judge's reasoning, while parties and external audiences would often be mostly interested in outcomes alone. To the extent that judges care about the reception of their opinions by professional audiences, appeal can therefore serve an incentive for clear, rational, and exhaustive reasoning—fundamentals of procedural justice (Cohen 2018).

At the same time, the availability of appeal may engender moral hazard for trial judges, who are concerned more with ultimate case accuracy than with reputation: resource-constrained judges may be incentivized to invest insufficient resources in deciding accurately knowing that a mistaken decision is likely to be corrected on appeal, they can diminish their effort in each individual case in order to cope better with the overall caseload. Appeal may thus lead to suboptimal trial court effort, resulting in lower ultimate systemic accuracy (Chopard et al. 2018).

The prospect of appeal may also lead trial judges to reason strategically rather than truthfully: if they seek to avoid review, they may frame their decision in a manner less amenable to appellate review—for example by grounding it in multiple alternative legal theories or by tying it to a fact-intensive analysis. Conversely, trial judges may sometimes seek to encourage appeal, for example in order to push for a re-examination of a standing precedent or the establishment of precedent where none yet exists. One way to do so is to commit an intentional error—to openly contradict a prevailing norm (governing precedent, clear statutory language), making appeal more likely.

Finally, writing 'for' the appellate court may sometimes come in conflict with the parties' immediate interests, for example whey would benefit from a clear and concise resolution of a case or from a less detailed assessment of their moral culpabilities. Indeed, the proliferation of means and methods for Judicial Conflict Resolution in diverse jurisdictions—empowering trial judges to end disputes without judgment on legal merits—is an effective limitation on the capacity of hierarchical review to instruct their behaviour (Alberstein 2023).

3.3.2 *Upper Court Effort*

Ostensibly, upper court judges have less institutional accountability than lower court ones, since they are not subject (at all, or to a similar extent) to review by yet a higher instance ('We are not final because we are infallible, but we are infallible only because we are final' (*Brown v Allen*, 1953)). Still, upper court judges may care about the effectuation of their decisions—a fact that is heavily reliant on lower court compliance (Masood and Bowie 2023). The interest in the actual impact of upper court decisions can be driven by different motives: a professional mission to improve the law and sustain the rule of law; an institutional interest in bolstering the efficacy of judicial power; an ideological project to affect the content of future judicial behaviour; or a personal interest in power, influence, and prestige.

Regardless of motive, dependence on lower court compliance for the consequential success of upper court adjudication means that lower court judges are a significant audience for upper court decisions. This means that efficacy-driven appellate judges would have reason to draft relatively clear opinions amenable to relatively easy application. Clear appellate opinions also provide useful signals to future parties about the likelihood of success in future appeals on similar topics—curbing docket costs for appellate courts.

3.4 Legitimacy

As we saw, the three central rationales for appeal—accuracy, fairness, effort—have significant limitations that raise the question whether the social costs of operating a system of appeal are worth its benefits. What may explain its prevalence nonetheless is the possible benefit the judicial system gets from projecting its apparent preoccupation with accuracy, fairness, and effort; in other words, the legitimating effect of appeal. Embedding within the judicial system an error-correction mechanism sends two legitimating messages to its constituents: first, that objective notions of truth and correctness are relevant to law and attainable through adjudication, and that courts have an institutionally established method for accessing them; second, and somewhat in contrast, that judges are fallible human beings who operate within a rational bureaucracy, rather than mystical repositories of legal knowledge accessible only to the initiated.

Similarly, as procedural judice literature has shown that people perceive a process as more just if an option of appeal is provided (Tyler 1988), establishing a broad right of appeal from most judicial decisions is likely to bolster constituents' trust in the judicial system. In a system deeply concerned with public trust for its viability as a co-equal branch of government, appeal can thus be central to legitimation, regardless of whether it leads to overall better judicial results.

3.5 Uniformity

Bringing together all of the previous rationales, it is clear how appeal has become attached to the principle of precedent: appeal is a mechanism that inhibits difference in adjudication. Drawing on a rule-of-law sensibility, appeal treats divergences from accepted norms and doctrines as correctable errors, it casts access to centralizing agents a matter of right, it colours reversals not as mere disagreements but rather as penalties, and through these elements projects an image of systemic rationality and retains an elitist power structure. Locating the legislative power of precedent with appellate courts therefore complements their institutional logic, and places uniformity as the organizing principle of court systems, performed through hierarchy.

4. Theorizing Hierarchy

The literature has framed and modelled judicial hierarchy in different ways, some explanatory, some prescriptive, some critical. The following is a brief account of central framings, from which behavioural insights can then be drawn.

4.1 Governance: Principal–Agent

An understating of trial courts as inferior institutional units whose purpose is to effectuate appellate court policy lends itself neatly to a principal–agent framing (Songer et al. 1994; George and Yoon 2003; Haire et al. 2003). This is a top-down conception of appeal in which normative power draws from the top of the pyramid. Lower courts, in this framing, serve the functional purpose of applying centralized legal power in specific cases, making it accessible to local communities, and gathering the facts that would be the basis for new high court norms. The orders of the principal in this model take the shape of precedential, forward-looking statements of the law by courts of appeals that lower courts are expected to follow in future cases (Kastellec 2011; Kim 2011).

Modelling judicial hierarchy as a case of agency relations calls for an understanding of the high court–low court nexus as a strategic game: lower courts may have distinct perceptions of the proper role and method of judging, as well as distinct policy preferences and attitudes regarding proper outcomes in specific cases or in classes of cases. These preferences and attitudes may come into conflict with those of higher courts—and an agency problem ensues (McNollgast 1995; Spitzer and Talley 2000; Badawi and Baker 2015). As Cameron and Kornhauser (2012) explain, these kinds of tensions are more likely when courts assume the capacity to determine the content of a legal standard. In such cases of 'law creation', the challenge for the higher court is not merely in effectively transmitting its orders to lower courts (Smith and Todd 2015) but also in checking divergences from its ideological or theoretical paradigms of adjudication.

Extending the principal–agent paradigm, Caminker (1994) suggested that trial courts ought to decide contested legal questions in approximation to how they predict the appellate court would decide them. This goes beyond the expectation from trial courts to apply *previous* appellate court signals, calling upon them to consider likely *future* appellate court decisions. This is meant to preclude unnecessary appeals while fulfilling a strict hierarchical logic that places appellate discretion above that of the trial courts.

4.2 Hegemony: Controlling Divergent Forces

The perspective of Critical Legal Studies portrays appeal as a pacifying mechanism, used to keep disadvantaged classes of litigants at bay by producing the mere impression that judicial error is possible, identifiable, and amendable. In other words, appeal is hierarchical not only as institutional design but also as a matter of ideology. If indeed litigation is structurally slated to benefit repeat players and better-resourced parties (Galanter 1974), then appeal—presented as a guard against bias—turns out to entrench these effects. Appeal is costly both to pursue and to defend against, which means that advantaged parties have more access to it, can more reliably threaten to seek it, and can buy the other party's right to it if they wish to avoid it.

Appeal is also hegemonic in the stricter sense of the implied class disparities between trial and appellate judges. Relative to trial judges, appellate judges are few, select, and better paid, they enjoy greater visibility, are located in urban centres, and have the power to sanction other judges. Trial judges, on the other hand, are a larger, less selective, more diverse, and more dispersed group, and the scope of their decisions (and hence often the cost of the errors) is normally smaller (Aronson 2010)—features that allow them to be more reflective of diverse constituencies and more experimental in their adjudicatory practices. Appeal can thus be seen as a mechanism of keeping the experimental pluralism of lower courts in check, making sure they don't go too far beyond what is acceptable with the judicial elites.

This critique of appeal casts it, therefore, as a means of retaining ultimate power over law's development and its driving ideologies (Spitzer and Talley 2000) with a stable elite. It coheres with historical aetiologies of judicial hierarchies as modes of control, and of appeal as a modern form of the pardoning power located with political leaders (Shapiro 1980).

5. Activating Hierarchy: The Selection Puzzle

The different understandings of the role of hierarchy in adjudication lend themselves to different models of selection of cases for appellate review. For example, hierarchy as an error-correction mechanism ostensibly requires a system that would target likely lower court mistakes, while a system focused on uniformity would arguably seek to review cases that exhibit conflict or divergence. In practice, selection of cases for appeal is often premised on a limited set of individual party interests, mediated to some extent by systemic screening norms. These norms can grant more or less discretion to either the losing party or the courts in deciding whether an appeal will be pursued—with varying behaviour effects.

5.1 Court Side: Discretionary Appeal vs Appeal as of Right

Like adjudication in general, hierarchies of justice are most commonly activated not by judicial agents but rather through statutory determinations of jurisdiction, which are operated by interested parties pursuing additional rounds of litigation. Once an interest in appeal is expressed, a fundamental choice has to be made between allowing any party access to higher court review (appeal as of right), or letting the system choose which decisions to review (discretionary appeal). Systems vary broadly in this structural choice, employing different selection rules for different types of cases and courts. At the constitutional level, for example, European systems of centralized judicial review are often accompanied by broad access to the constitutional forum, compared to the extremely discretionary docket of the US Supreme Court's *certiorari* rule (Delaney 2016; Lavie 2017). Similar divergences exist in other appellate jurisdictions, such as the broad discretion granted to high courts in Australia and New Zealand, compared to the more limited capacity of the Israeli or the Indian courts to control their dockets (Alarie and Green 2017, 155–57, 167).

Note that under both rules, strategic parties are the ones who select the cases for appeal—the discretionary system merely adds judges as another screening mechanism. Neither system is therefore fully committed to selecting for review only decisions with high social error cost: while parties can be incentivized to select socially valuable cases for appeal, they normally cannot be forced to do so. And since parties' interest in appeal is not necessarily concerned with correcting errors or settling precedent, appellate courts under either rule have to contend with a share of appeals that do not maximize the error-correction function of appeal, nor the norm-setting role of adjudication.

Judges concerned with either caseload management or policy-making could therefore be expected to prefer a discretionary appeal rule over appeal as of right. This would arguably let them summarily dismiss appeals that are either unworthy of concerted judicial effort or are likely to impose exceptional costs if heard and decided on the merits—what Lavie (2017) terms 'perverse outcome cases'. At the same time, they can engage in their own agenda setting, methodically picking cases suitable for fashioning precedent (Kastellec and Lax 2008) while controlling workload (Alarie and Green 2017, 158–68). The matter is however more complicated: discretionary appeal grants parties a relatively cheap avenue for an *initial* review of their case by a higher court. This means, first, that a discretionary system of appeal is likely to garner more initial submissions than one that grants a general right of appeal, given the disparate costs of each option for losing parties.

Second, and more importantly, while discretion whether to allow appeal is usually not supposed to account for the correctness of the decision an appeal from which is sought, this is in fact often the case. As Eisenberg, Fisher, and Rosen-Zvi (2011) have shown in a study of the Israeli Supreme Court, while the doctrines pertaining to granting discretionary appeal usually are not premised on the correctness of the decision, discretionary appeals are more likely to succeed than appeals as of right; a similar effect has been exhibited in the past in the United States (Boucher and Segal 1995). A likely explanation to this finding is that judicial screening of cases for appeal accounts for perceived correctness rather than error cost or precedential value (Kastellec and Lax 2008; Givati and Rosenberg 2023). Another explanation is that discretionary appeals that manage to proceed to a merits determination require substantial party investment, which then also enhances their likelihood of success. In another study, a transition from appeal as of right to discretionary appeal on the Taiwan Supreme Court did not prove to change the behaviour of the Court's justices, who remained focused on error correction rather than legal development (Eisenberg and Huang 2012).

The complex set of empirical and behavioural elements that underlie parties' behaviour has led Shavell (2010) to suggest that the choice between discretionary and as-of-right appeal should be placed with losing parties rather than system designers and interested judges. This ought to allow parties to exploit their unique information to differentiate between appeals with high and low chances and stakes.

5.2 Hierarchies of Selection: Lower vs Higher Court Discretion

In systems where appeal requires judicial leave, the authority to grant leave may be located, in principle, either with the lower court whose decision would be put under review, or with the court of appeal that would be tasked with considering the appeal. More commonly, the latter norm is adopted, allowing appellate courts to decide whether to entertain discretionary appeals. This lets judges set their own court's agenda (from among the cases in which leave of appeal is sought by parties). Higher court selection can be justified by the assumption of epistemic superiority and institutional awareness of these courts compared to inferior courts—the hope that they are better positioned to identify cases warranting of appellate review and settlement. At the same time, letting an appeal court choose its own cases may of course introduce such considerations as pushing (or avoiding) certain ideological projects or mitigating docket loads.

In contrast, certain jurisdictions, like the United Kingdom and South Africa, authorize some lower courts to permit appeal of their own decisions (Alarie and Green 2017, 155). This significantly diffuses the selection process, and exploits case-specific judicial knowledge to single out decisions that could benefit from appellate review. Of course, the power to choose which of one's decisions are to be reviewed on appeal may also skew incentives: on the one hand, it may lead reversal-wary judges to deny leave to appeal their decisions; on the other hand, it may induce the moral hazard of judges cutting their personal investment in high-quality decision-making, knowing that they can send hard cases up the ladder for review by a higher court.

Between higher and lower court discretionary appeal, one can locate procedures of issue certification: contexts in which one court requires the input of another court in order to complete the task under its original jurisdiction. Consider for example the authority of the European Court of Justice to provide a preliminary ruling on EU law for the court of a member states that finds it 'necessary to enable it to give judgment' (Article 267 of the EU Lisbon Treaty). Or, similarly, the power of the German Federal Constitutional Court to provide *Lander* courts with decisions on questions of constitutionality deemed necessary to conclude a litigation (Section 100 of German Basic Law). In such cases, the lower court has the initial discretion whether to frame the question as one necessitating higher court 'pre-ruling', or to interpret the dispute in a way that would avoid certification. At the same time, the court to which a question is certified can usually decline jurisdiction—devising in essence an inter-court dialogue about the activation of hierarchy.

5.3 Party Side: Discretionary vs Mandatory Appeal

In Hohfeldian terms, the design choice of discretionary appeal vs appeal as of right means either granting judges power over the access to appeal, or imposing upon them the duty to entertain appeal. A corollary, if less frequent, choice may also pertain to the parties themselves: normally, the losing party gets to choose whether an appellate court would consider her case, in either a discretionary or as-of-right capacity. This means that losing parties may choose not to seek review at all—they have the power to determine whether appeal will take place. As noted, this locates the decision with an agent not necessarily—indeed, usually necessarily not—interested in the public benefits of appeal such as systemic error reduction and judicial incentives. Sometimes, however, certain decisions are put to mandatory review by a higher court—in effect mandating the losing party to litigate an appeal. Thus, for example, in some jurisdictions, verdicts of capital punishment or ones that impose harsh sentences on minors—in other words, decisions of obviously high error costs—invoke automatic appellate review (Golden 2001; Shannan 2021).

6. Inverting Hierarchy

Hierarchy is everywhere in the administration of justice. It can however be upended, both in practice and in theory. Indeed, any structural formulation of adjudication as a principal–agent scenario expresses the understanding that an agency 'problem' inheres hierarchies of justice. While this is mostly framed as a systemic bug to be minimized, can the structural differentiation between higher and lower courts be framed as a feature to be optimized, if not maximized? An inversion of the fundamental judicial pyramid can be traced in the diverse strategies that lower-court judges may exploit to avoid or disregard upper court review. Tracing these strategies reveals a murkier institutional reality than the one gleaned from pyramidal depictions of judicial systems. Further, it can be a basis for a reconceptualization of lower court agency itself, as well as of the possible role of higher courts in the judicial hierarchy.

6.1 Strategies of Inversion

Lower court judges have multiple avenues for avoidance or circumvention of higher court review (Baum 1978; Westerland et al. 2010). *Ex ante*, trial judges have significant leeway in defining the contested issues in trial and in framing their decisions as ones of fact or of law. As appeals are normally directed at legal determinations, trial judges can contextualize their normative holdings with case-specific findings and conditions. Of course, appellate judges bent on reviewing a given decision can use similar interpretive means to recast determinations as ones of legal creation or application, and thus open them up for review. The availability of these options is however derived from the wording of the trial court's decision—and is thus contingent upon the skill and effort of the lower court judge.

Ex post, lower court judges have the similar interpretive leeway in applying higher court decrees to future decisions (Reynolds and Denning 2000). Both when the high court corrects a specific legal error in a certain case and remands for re-adjudication under the corrected norm, and when it sets a general precedent for a class of future cases, trial judges are the ones entrusted with effectuating the high court's mandate. They can thus selectively cite, distinguish, or interpret it to more closely satisfy their understanding of the legal issue or their competing policy preferences (Baum 1978, 1994).

But trial judges can also be more openly critical of high court mandates: first, they can apply them under protest—explicitly stating that they submit to the higher court's authority out of professional or institutional commitment, but that they object to the content of the norm they are asked to apply. Beyond the virtue signalling benefits a trial judge accrues through such acts of defiance, they can also, over time, work to destabilize existing precedents as well as institutional power structures (McNollgast 1995). Second, in a more extreme but not necessarily more risky strategy, a trial judge could openly disregard a high court order or strike down a standing precedent. These would formally be judicial errors, but ones that are nonetheless binding unless reversed on appeal—the occurrence of which is, as discussed above, fully contingent on the losing party's personal interest calculus. Similar to compliance under protest, 'intentional error' can serve to disrupt existing precedents and power structures over time by surfacing disagreement and flagging points of internal contention among the judicial cadre. But it may also be exploited strategically to encourage appeal—for example due to a change in higher court makeup that could lead to a reconsideration of an existing precedent (Reddick and Benesh 2000).

The combined constitutional assurances of judicial independence, open justice, and full reasoning thus mean that judges have the unique capacity to dissent openly to higher court mandates, without direct and immediate material consequences; although these may sometimes appear over time as promotion sanctions for 'troublemakers'—relevant, by definition, only to judges interested in and amenable for promotion. In this, the divergence of judicial hierarchies from other bureaucratic hierarchies is most conspicuous, and the tension inherent in hierarchies of justice becomes most visible.

6.2 Structures of Inversion

Beyond the capacity of individual lower court judges to assert independence and defy, in specific cases, the top-down logic of judicial hierarchy, the structure of court systems itself can be analysed from a bottom-up perspective. This perspective points to the capacity of lower courts to produce unique and valuable normative—and not merely factual—knowledge, inaccessible to higher courts from their centralized positions (Levinson 1993; Kreimer 1997; Kim et al. 2009; Aronson 2010; Kim 2011; Gewirtzman 2012; Eyer 2013; Frost 2015). Judicial power may sometimes drive up the hierarchical chain, leading appellate courts to fashion opinions that learn from, correspond with, or are influenced by lower court behaviour and opinions, consciously or otherwise (Murphy 1959; Corley et al. 2011; Bruhl 2014; Beim 2017; Lavie 2017; Mate 2021; Schmidt 2022).

Indeed, trial courts are uniquely positioned to serve as legal innovators due to a combination of institutional traits: multiplicity, localism, systemic pluralism, relative invisibility, contextualized discretion, and relatively low errors costs. Lower court levels are usually diffuse in their organizational and spatial structures into local units of adjudication in towns, cities, and districts. This enables, and sometimes compels, trial court judges to exercise judicial discretion in context, considering the distinct characteristics, sensibilities, economic structures, and cultural paradigms of local communities and markets. Given the sheer number of trial judges, the different communities within which they operate, and the amount of discretionary decisions they make, the overall systemic output of trial court levels will necessarily have the quality of diversity, both in the kinds of cases decided, but also in the ways shared questions of law are treated: for example, interpretations of constitutional rights, standards of care in private law, or levels of culpability in criminal law (Kim 2007).

In addition, a bottom-up perspective to adjudication stresses that its lived experience is located mostly in the trial level, from both the demand and the supply sides. From the demand side, the interaction of most of courts' constituents with the judicial system starts and ends at the trial court level. Only few cases result in reasoned judgment, and only a fraction of those arrive on appeal. From the supply side, the bulk of litigation takes place in the lower courts. The content and character of most high court adjudication is contingent on the choices, behaviour, and performance of lower court judges, which often includes diverse managerial elements unfamiliar in appellate levels (Sarat 1977; Resnik 1982). A realist account of adjudicated law would therefore necessarily focus much of its attention to lower court behaviour—and legal education would likely benefit form a similar tilt as well.

7. Conclusion: Recasting Hierarchy and the Judicial Network

Hierarchy is ubiquitous in adjudication, just as it is mysterious: it seems central to most systems' understanding of the rule of law, but puts individual adjudicators in tension with a strict notion of independence. It is fundamental to people's and systems' sense of fairness, but when broken down to its various justifications and explanations it invokes diverse critiques and qualifications, which taken together may ultimately question its value as an institutional staple of modern judiciaries. It is structured in strict and regimented mechanisms, but is susceptible to diverse modes of manipulation and resistance. It is focused on improving judicial accuracy by superior agents but may inhibit access to valuable information located with institutionally inferior ones. Given this equivocal assessment, where should the study of judicial hierarchies proceed?

A promising avenue for further exploration is the application of social network analysis (Scott 2012) to judicial systems (Katz et al. 2008; Gelter and Siems 2012; Shomade and Hartley 2012), reconceiving courts of appeals as communicative junctures rather than command-and-control units. Relieved of assumptions of institutional necessity, and cognizant of the complex set of motivations and expectations attached to judicial hierarchies, such a theoretical move could reconstruct inter-court relationships as more than mere binary, vertical power plays. If we take seriously the capacity of lower courts to produce valuable normative information—through experimenting in doctrinal innovation, identifying social pathologies, flagging legal inconsistencies, and reflecting local knowledge and sensibilities—the court system can be reimagined as a discursive learning network (Box-Steffensmeier et al. 2016). In such a framework, appeals would become the method of communicative mediation among system nodes, facilitating deliberation rather than terminating it. The institutional structure would then also better correspond to the rich informal elements of inter-judicial relationship and interactions (Dressel 2023).

Reimagining the purpose of appeal as a communicative juncture in a network of judicial information producers could serve the as a basis of a re-evaluation of prevalent norms of appellate operation. Thus, understanding appeal as a mechanism for identifying, analysing, and disseminating unique trial court information means that selection of cases for appeal has to focus on their diverse and informative value, rather than their accuracy. This can justify augmenting the loser selection rule with some form of random selection of cases, or a flagging mechanism by trial courts. Similarly, if appeals courts take the form of deliberation enhancers rather than ultimate deciders, panel composition norms can be rethought, for example by extending the use of two-member panels, or by differentiating appellate panel sizes according to the structure and complexity of the debate reflected in the decisions of lower courts. Norms of appellate review and remand could also be redrawn, with the aim of enhancing lower court engagement with other courts' contribution, rather than ironing out discrepancies.

The networked recasting of judicial systems thus 'flattens' judicial hierarchies without losing the value of centralized units of adjudication. These are recast as repositories of normative information, that collect, analyse, and disseminate it continuously. Such a process could diminish the short-term levels of systemic accuracy, for the long-term benefit of an effective judicial learning system. In the long run, learning from 'mistakes' could be more valuable than eliminating them.

References

Aft, A. B. 2011. 'Respect My Authority: Analyzing Claims of Diminished U.S. Supreme Court Influence Abroad'. *Indiana Journal of Global Legal Studies* 18 (1): 421–54.

Alarie, B., and A. J. Green. 2017. *Commitment and Cooperation on High Courts* (Vol. 1). Oxford: Oxford University Press. https://doi.org/10.1093/oso/9780199397594.001.0001.

Alberstein, M. 2023. 'Comparative Judicial Conflict Resolution (JCR)'. In *Comparative and Transnational Dispute Resolution*, edited by S. Ali, 83–100. London: Routledge. https://doi.org/10.4324/9780429354625-8.

Aronson, O. 2010. 'Inferiorizing Judicial Review: Popular Constitutionalism in Trial Courts'. *University of Michigan Journal of Law Reform* 43, 972–1041.

Badawi, A. B., and S. Baker. 2015. 'Appellate Lawmaking in a Judicial Hierarchy'. *The Journal of Law and Economics* 58 (1): 139–72. https://doi.org/10.1086/682905.

Baude, W. 2019. 'Precedent and Discretion'. In *The Supreme Court Review*, edited by D. A. Strauss, G. R. Stone, J. Driver, and W. Baude, 313–34. Chicago: University of Chicago Press.

Baum, L. 1978. 'Lower-Court Response to Supreme Court Decisions: Reconsidering a Negative Picture'. *The Justice System Journal* 3 (3): 208–19.

Baum, L. 1994. 'Specialization and Authority Acceptance: The Supreme Court and Lower Federal Courts'. *Political Research Quarterly* 47 (3): 693. https://doi.org/10.2307/448849.

Baum, L. 2008. *Judges and Their Audiences: A Perspective on Judicial Behavior*. Princeton: Princeton University Press.

Beim, D. 2017. 'Learning in the Judicial Hierarchy'. *The Journal of Politics* 79 (2): 591–604. https://doi.org/10.1086/688442.

Bentsen, H. L., and J. K. Skiple. 2023. 'Leadership in Courts'. In *The Oxford Handbook of Comparative Judicial Behaviour*, edited by L. Epstein, G. Grendstad, U. Sadl, and K. Weinshall. Oxford: Oxford University Press. https://www.comparativejudicialbehavior.org/s/31Bentsen-ksy9.pdf

Black, R. C., and R. J. Owens. 2016. 'Courting the President: How Circuit Court Judges Alter Their Behavior for Promotion to the Supreme Court'. *American Journal of Political Science* 60 (1): 30–43. http://www.jstor.org/stable/24583049.

Boucher, R. L., and J. A. Segal. 1995. 'Supreme Court Justices as Strategic Decision Makers: Aggressive Grants and Defensive Denials on the Vinson Court'. *The Journal of Politics* 57 (3): 824–37. https://doi.org/10.2307/2960195.

Box-Steffensmeier, J. M., D. P. Christenson, and C. Leavitt. 2016. 'Judicial Networks'. In *The Oxford Handbook of Political Networks*, edited by J. N. Victor, A. H. Montgomery, and M. Lubell 491–514. Oxford: Oxford University Press. https://doi.org/10.1093/oxfordhb/9780190228217.013.20.

Brown v Allen 1953. 344 U.S. 443.

Bruhl, A.-A. P. 2014. 'Following Lower-Court Precedent'. *The University of Chicago Law Review* 81 (3): 851–927.

Budziak, J. 2013. 'Blind Justice or Blind Ambition? The Influence of Promotion on Decision Making in the U.S. Courts of Appeals'. *Justice System Journal* 34 (3): 295–320. https://doi.org/10.1080/0098261X.2013.10768042.

Bueno de Mesquita, E., and M. Stephenson. 2006. 'Informative Precedent and Intrajudicial Communication'. In *Institutional Games and the U.S. Supreme Court*, edited by J. R. Rogers, R. B. Flemming, and J. R. Bon, 205–29. Charlottesville: University of Virginia Press.

Camarena González, R. 2016. 'From Jurisprudence Constante to Stare Decisis: The Migration of the Doctrine of Precedent to Civil Law Constitutionalism'. *Transnational Legal Theory* 7 (2): 257–86. https://doi.org/10.1080/20414005.2016.1205871.

Cameron, C. M., and Kornhauser, L. A. 2012. 'Appeals Mechanisms, Litigant Selection, and the Structure of Judicial Hierarchies'. In *Institutional Games and the U.S. Supreme Court*, edited by J. R. Rogers, R. B. Flemming, and J. R. Bond, 173–204. Charlottesville: University of Virginia Press.

Caminker, E. H. 1994. 'Precedent and Prediction: The Forward-Looking Aspects of Inferior Court Decisionmaking'. *Texas Law Review* 73 (1): 1–82.

Chandrachud, A. 2012. 'Supreme Court's Seniority Norm: Historical Origins'. *Economic and Political Weekly* 47 (8): 26–30. https://www.jstor.org/stable/41419894.

Chopard, B., E. Fain, and L. Roussey. 2018. 'Does the Appeals Process Reduce the Occurrence of Legal Errors?' *Review of Law and Economics* 14 (2): 1–18. https://doi.org/10.1515/rle-2014-0038.

Chutkow, D. M. 2014. 'The Chief Justice as Executive'. *Journal of Law and Courts* 2 (2): 301–25. https://doi.org/10.1086/677172.

Cohen, M. 2017. 'Judges or Hostages?' In *EU Law Stories*, edited by F. Nicola and B. Davies, 58–80. Cambridge: Cambridge University Press. https://doi.org/10.1017/9781316340479.004

Cohen, M. 2018. 'When Judges Have Reasons Not to Give Reasons: A Comparative Law Approach'. *Washington and Lee Law Review* 72, 483–571.

Corley, P. C., P. M. Collins, and B. Calvin. 2011. 'Lower Court Influence on U.S. Supreme Court Opinion Content'. *Journal of Politics* 73 (1): 31–44. https://doi.org/10.1017/S0022381610000848.

Cross, F. 2005. 'Appellate Court Adherence to Precedent'. *Journal of Empirical Legal Studies* 2 (2): 369–405. https://doi.org/10.1111/j.1740-1461.2005.00054.x.

Damle, S. V. 2005. 'Specialize the Judge, Not the Court: A Lesson from the German Constitutional Court'. *Virginia Law Review* 91 (5): 1267–311.

Daughety, A. F., and Reinganum, J. F. 2000. 'Appealing Judgments'. *The RAND Journal of Economics* 31 (3): 502–25.

Dawuni, J., and A. Kang. 2015. 'Her Ladyship Chief Justice: The Rise of Female Leaders in the Judiciary in Africa'. *Africa Today* 62 (2): 45–69.

Delaney, E. F. 2016. 'Analyzing Avoidance: Judicial Strategy in Comparative Perspective'. *Duke Law Journal* 66 (1): 1–67.

Dimitrova-Grajzl, V., P. Grajzl, K. Zajc, and J. Sustersic. 2012. 'Judicial Incentives and Performance at Lower Courts: Evidence from Slovenian Judge-Level Data'. *Review of Law & Economics* 8 (1): 215–52. https://doi.org/10.1515/1555-5879.1610.

Djukić, D. 2018. 'The Right to Appeal in Comparative Perspective'. *The Journal of Appellate Practice and Process* 19 (2): 187–222.

Drahozal, C. R. 1998. 'Judicial Incentives and the Appeals Process'. *Southern Methodist University Law Review* 51 (3): 469–503. https://scholar.smu.edu/smulr/vol51/iss3/2http://digitalrepository.smu.edu.

Dressel, B. 2023. 'Judge Networks'. In *The Oxford Handbook of Comparative Judicial Behaviour*, edited by L. Epstein, G. Grendstad, U. Sadl, and K. Weinshall. Oxford: Oxford University Press. https://www.comparativejudicialbehavior.org/s/34Dressel.pdf

Dreyfuss, R. C. 2013. 'Percolation, Uniformity, and Coherent Adjudication: The Federal Circuit Experience'. *Southern Methodist University Law Review* 66 (3): 505–40. http://www.theatlantic.com/business/archive/2012/07/why-there-are-too-many-patents-in-.

Eisenberg, T., T. Fisher, and I. Rosen-Zvi. 2011. 'Israel's Supreme Court Appellate Jurisdiction: An Empirical Study'. *Cornell Law Review* 96 (4): 693–725.

Eisenberg, T., T. Fisher, and I. Rosen-Zvi. 2013. 'Group Decision Making on Appellate Panels: Presiding Justice and Opinion Justice Influence in the Israel Supreme Court'. *Psychology, Public Policy, and Law* 19 (3): 282–96. https://doi.org/10.1037/a0033565.

Eisenberg, T., and K.-C. Huang. 2012. 'The Effect of Rules Shifting Supreme Court Jurisdiction F=from Mandatory to Discretionary—An Empirical Lesson from Taiwan'. *International Review of Law and Economics* 32 (1): 3–18. https://doi.org/10.1016/j.irle.2011.12.005.

Epstein, L. 2016. 'Some Thoughts on the Study of Judicial Behavior'. *William & Mary Law Review* 57 (6): 2017–73. https://scholarship.law.wm.edu/wmlr.

Epstein, L., W. M. Landes, and R. A. Posner. 2013. *The Behavior of Federal Judges*. Cambridge: Harvard University Press. https://doi.org/10.4159/harvard.9780674067325.

Eyer, K. 2013. 'Lower Court Popular Constitutionalism'. *The Yale Law Journal Online* 123, 197–218.

Fife, M., G. Goelzhauser, and S. T. Loertscher. 2021. 'Selecting Chief Justices by Peer Vote'. *State Politics & Policy Quarterly* 21 (2): 165–94. https://doi.org/10.1177/1532440020945285.

Fon, V., and F. Parisi. 2006. 'Judicial Precedents in Civil Law Systems: A Dynamic Analysis'. *International Review of Law and Economics* 26 (4): 519–35. https://doi.org/10.1016/j.irle.2007.01.005.

Frank, J. 1949. *Courts on Trial*. Princeton: Princeton University Press.

Frost, A. 2015. 'Inferiority Complex: Should State Courts Follow Lower Federal Court Precedent on the Meaning of Federal Law?' *Vanderbilt Law Review* 68 (1): 53–103. http://ssrn.com/abstract=2564091.

Galanter, M. 1974. 'Why the "Haves" Come out Ahead: Speculations on the Limits of Legal Change'. *Law & Society Review* 9 (1): 95–160. https://doi.org/10.2307/3053023.

Geeroms, S. M. F. 2002. 'Comparative Law and Legal Translation: Why the Terms Cassation, Revision and Appeal Should Not Be Translated'. *American Journal of Comparative Law* 50 (1): 201–28.

Garoupa, N., and T. Ginsburg 2009. 'Judicial Audiences and Reputation: Perspectives from Comparative Law Comparative Law'. *Columbia Journal of Transnational Law* 47 (3): 451–90. https://scholarship.law.tamu.edu/facscholar/516.

Gelter, M., and M. Siems. 2012. 'Networks, Dialogue or One-Way Traffic? An Empirical Analysis of Cross-Citations Between Ten of Europe's Highest Courts'. *Utrecht Law Review* 8 (2): 88. https://doi.org/10.18352/ulr.196.

George, T. E., and A. H. Yoon. 2003. 'The Federal Court System: a Principal–Agent Perspective'. *St. Louis University Law Journal* 47: 819–34.

Gewirtzman, D. 2012. 'Lower Court Constitutionalism: Circuit Court Discretion in a Complex Adaptive System'. *American University Law Review* 61: 457–522.

Givati, Y., and I. Rosenberg. 2023. 'Why Do Judges Grant Rehearing Requests? Evidence from the Supreme Court of Israel'. *Journal of Institutional and Theoretical Economics* 179 (1): 6. https://doi.org/10.1628/jite-2023-0011.

Golden, S. L. 2001. 'Constitutionality of the Federal Death Penalty Act: Is the Lack of Mandatory Appeal Really Meaningful Appeal?' *Temple Law Review* 74 (2): 429–68.

Grossman, M. C. 2007. 'Is This Arbitration: Religious Tribunals, Judicial Review, and Due Process'. *Columbia Law Review* 107 (1): 169–209.

Guarnieri, C. 2004. 'Appointment and Career of Judges in Continental Europe: the Rise of Judicial Self-Government'. *Legal Studies* 24 (1-2): 169–87. https://doi-org.ezp-prod1.hul.harvard.edu/10.1111/j.1748-121X.2004.tb00246.x.

Gugliuzza, P. R. 2013. 'The Federal Circuit as a Federal Court'. *William & Mary Law Review* 54 (6): 1791–864.

Haire, S. B., D. R. Songer, and S. A. Lindquist. 2003. 'Appellate Court Supervision in the Federal Judiciary: A Hierarchical Perspective'. *Law & Society Review* 37 (1): 143–68.

Hathaway, O. A. 2001. 'Path Dependence in the Law: The Course and Pattern of Legal Change in a Common Law System'. *Iowa Law Review* 86, 601–65.

Hausegger, L., and S. Haynie. 2003. 'Judicial Decisionmaking and the Use of Panels in the Canadian Supreme Court and the South African Appellate Division'. *Law & Society Review* 37 (3): 635–57. https://doi.org/10.1111/1540-5893.3703006.

Huneeus, A. 2011. 'Courts Resisting Courts: Lessons from the InterAmerican Court's Struggle to Enforce Human Rights. *Cornell International Law Journal* 44 (3): 493–533.

Iossa, E., and G. Palumbo. 2007. Information Provision and Monitoring of the Decision-Maker in the Presence of an Appeal Process'. *Journal of Institutional and Theoretical Economics* 163 (4): 657–82.

Kastellec, J. P. 2011. 'Hierarchical and Collegial Politics on the U.S. Courts of Appeals'. *Journal of Politics* 73 (2): 345–61. https://doi.org/10.1017/S0022381611000314.

Kastellec, J. P. 2017. 'The Judicial Hierarchy'. In *The Oxford Research Encyclopedia of Politics*. Oxford: Oxford University Press. https://doi.org/10.1093/acrefore/9780190228637.013.99.

Kastellec, J. P., and J. R. Lax. 2008. 'Case Selection and the Study of Judicial Politics'. *Journal of Empirical Legal Studies* 5 (3): 407–46. https://doi.org/10.1111/j.1740-1461.2008.00129.x.

Katz, D. M., D. K. Stafford, and E. Provins. 2008. 'Social Architecture, Judicial Peer Effects and the Evolution of the Law: Toward a Positive Theory of Judicial Social Structure'. *Georgia State University Law Review* 24 (4): 977–1001.

Kennedy, D. 2006. 'Three Globalizations of Law and Legal Thought: 1850–2000'. In *The New Law and Economic Development*, D. M. Trubeck and A. Santos, 19–73. Cambridge: Cambridge University Press. https://doi.org/10.1017/CBO9780511754425.002.

Kim, P. T. 2007. 'Lower Court Discretion'. *New York University Law Review* 82, 383–442.

Kim, P. T. 2011. 'Beyond Principal–Agent Theories: Law and the Judicial Hierarchy'. *Northwestern University Law Review* 105 (2): 535–75.

Kim, P. T., M. Schlanger, C.L. Boyd, and A. D. Martin. 2009. 'How Should We Study District Judge Decision-Making'. *Washington University Journal of Law & Policy* 29 (1): 83–112.

Klein, D. E., and R. J. Hume. 2003. 'Fear of Reversal as an Explanation of Lower Court Compliance'. *Law & Society Review* 37 (3): 579–606.

Kornhauser, L. A., and L. G. Sager. 1993. 'The One and the Many: Adjudication in Collegial Courts'. *California Law Review* 81 (1): 1–60.

Kreimer, S. F. 1997. 'Exploring the Dark Matter of Judicial Review: A Constitutional Census of the 1990s'. *William & Mary Bill of Rights Journal* 5, 427–526.

Kunz, R. 2019. 'Judging International Judgments Anew? The Human Rights Courts before Domestic Courts'. *European Journal of International Law* 30 (4): 1129–63. https://doi.org/10.1093/ejil/chz063.

Lafon, J. L. 1991. 'The Judicial Career in France: Theory and Practice under the Fifth Republic'. *Judicature* 75 (2): 97–106.

Langer, L., J. McMullen, and N. P. Ray. 2003. 'Recruitment of Chief Justices on State Supreme Courts: A Choice between Institutional and Personal Goals'. *The Journal of Politics* 65 (3): 655–75. https://doi.org/10.1111/1468-2508.00206.

Lavie, S. 2017. 'Discretionary Review and Undesired Cases'. *European Journal of Law and Economics* 44 (2): 265–85. https://doi.org/10.1007/s10657-015-9522-z.

Levinson, S. V. 1993. 'On Positivism and Potted Plants: "Inferior" Judges and the Task of Constitutional Interpretation'. *Connecticut Law Review* 25 (3): 843–52.

Levy, G. 2005. 'Careerist Judges and the Appeals Process'. *Journal of Economics* 36 (2): 275–97.

Levy, M. K. 2017. 'Panel Assignments in the Federal Courts of Appeals'. *Cornell Law Review* 103 (1): 65–116.

Maltzman, F., and P. J. Wahlbeck. 2004. 'A Conditional Model of Opinion Assignment on the Supreme Court'. *Political Research Quarterly* 57 (4): 551–63. https://doi.org/10.1177/106591290405700404.

Marshall, P. D. 2011. 'A Comparative Analysis of the Right to Appeal'. *Due Journal of Comparative & International Law* 22 (1): 1–45.

Masood, A. S., and J. Bowie 2023. 'Hierarchical Interactions and Compliance in Comparative Courts'. *Political Research Quarterly* 76 (4): 1906–1919. https://doi.org/10.1177/10659129231183915.

Mate, M. 2021. 'Inverted Judicial Guardianship'. *Stanford Journal of Civil Rights & Civil Liberties* 17 (1): 53–132. https://perma.cc/WP8A-SVXN.

McCormick, P. 2013. 'Choosing the Chief: Duality, Seniority, and Beyond'. *Journal of Canadian Studies* 47 (1): 5–35.

McNollgast. 1995. 'Politics and the Courts: a Positive Theory of Judicial Doctrine and the Rule of Law'. *Southern California Law Review* 68, 1631–83.

Murphy, W. F. 1959. 'Lower Court Checks on Supreme Court Power'. *Source: The American Political Science Review* 53 (4): 1017–31.

Nichols Pugh, N. 1975. 'The Structure and Role of Courts of Appeal in Civil Law Systems'. *Louisiana Law Review* 35 (5): 1163–202.

Porat, I. 2021. 'Solving One-Side Polarization: Supreme Court Polarization and Politicization in Israel and the U.S.'. *Law and Ethics of Human Rights* 15 (2): 221–58. https://doi.org/10.1515/lehr-2021-2026.

Posner, R. A. 1993. 'What Do Judges and Justices Maximize? (The Same Thing Everybody Else Does)'. *Supreme Court Economic Review* 3, 1–41. https://www.jstor.org/stable/1147064?seq=1&cid=pdf-.

Posner, R. A. 2010. *How Judges Think*. Cambridge: Harvard University Press. https://doi.org/10.2307/j.ctvjk2w91.

Poulin, A. B. 2008. 'Government Appeals in Criminal Cases: The Myth of Asymmetry. *University of Cincinnati Law Review* 1 (1): 1–62.

Ramseyer, J. M., and E. B Rasmusen. 2001. 'Why Are Japanese Judges So Conservative in Politically Charged Cases?' *American Political Science Review* 95 (2): 331–44. https://doi.org/10.1017/S0003055401002040.

Ramseyer, J. M., and E. B Rasmusen. 2006. 'The Case for Managed Judges: Learning from Japan after the Political Upheaval of 1993'. *University of Pennsylvania Law Review* 154 (6): 1879–930. https://doi.org/10.2307/40041354.

Reddick, M., and S. C. Benesh. 2000. 'Norm Violation by the Lower Courts in the Treatment of Supreme Court Precedent: A Research Framework'. *The Justice System Journal* 21 (2): 117–42.

Resnik, J. 1982. 'Managerial Judges'. *Harvard Law Review* 96 (2): 374. https://doi.org/10.2307/1340797.

Resnik, J. 1984. 'Tiers'. *Southern California Law Review* 57, 837–1035.

Reynolds, G. H., and B. P. Denning. 2000. 'Lower Court Readings of Lopez, or What If the Supreme Court Held a Constitutional Revolution and Nobody Came'. *Wisconsin Law Review* 2000 (2): 369–402.

Ríos-Figueroa, J. 2019. 'Independence in Judicial Hierarchies: Civil Law Systems'. In *Research Handbook on Law and Courts*, S. M. Sterett and L. D. Walker, 105–13. Cheltenham: Cheltenham: Edward Elgar Publishing.

Sarat, A. 1977. 'Judging in Trial Courts: An Exploratory Study'. *The Journal of Politics* 39 (2): 368–98. https://doi.org/10.2307/2130056.

Scheppele, K. L. 2006. 'Guardians of the Constitution: Constitutional Court Presidents and the Struggle for the Rule of Law in Post-Soviet Europe'. *University of Pennsylvania Law Review* 154 (6): 1757–851. https://doi.org/10.2307/40041352.

Schmidt, T. P. 2022. 'Judicial Minimalism in the Lower Courts'. *Virginia Law Review* 108 (4): 829–913.

Schneider, M. R. 2005. 'Judicial Career Incentives and Court Performance: An Empirical Study of the German Labour Courts of Appeal'. *European Journal of Law and Economics* 20, 127–44.

Scott, J. 2012. *What is Social Network Analysis?* London: Bloomsbury Academic.

Shannan, T. G. 2021. '"Are We There Yet?" No.: the Numbers that Support Adopting Automatic Appeals in Juvenile Delinquency Proceedings'. *Cornell Law Review* 106 (6): 1629–87.

Shapiro, M. 1980. 'Appeal'. *Law & Society Review* 14 (3): 629–62.

Shapiro, M. 1981. *Courts: A Comparative and Political Analysis*. Chicago: University of Chicago Press.
Shavell, S. 1995. 'The Appeals Process as a Means of Error Correction'. *The Journal of Legal Studies* 24 (2): 379–426.
Shavell, S. 1997. 'The Fundamental Divergence Between the Private and the Social Motive to Use the Legal System'. *Journal of Legal Studies* 26, 575–612.
Shavell, S. 2006. 'The Appeals Process and Adjudicator Incentives'. *Journal of Legal Studies* 35 (1): 1–29. https://doi.org/10.1086/500095.
Shavell, S. 2010. 'On the Design of the Appeals Process: The Optimal Use of Discretionary Review versus Direct Appeal'. *The Journal of Legal Studies* 39 (1): 63–108. https://doi.org/10.1086/605094.
Shinar, A., B. Medina, and G. Stopler. 2020. 'From Promise to Retrenchment: On the Changing Landscape of Israeli Constitutionalism'. *International Journal of Constitutional Law* 18 (3): 714–29. https://doi.org/10.1093/icon/moaa058.
Shoenberger, A. 2009. 'Changes in the European Civil Law Systems: Infiltration of the Anglo-American Case Law System of Precedent into the Civil Law System'. *Loyola Law Review* 55 (1): 5–22.
Shomade, S. A., and R. E. Hartley. 2012. 'The Application of Network Analysis to the Study of Trial Courts'. *Justice System Journal* 31 (2): 144–63.
Shukla, O. P. B. 2015. 'Towards Reforming the Judiciary—The NJAC'. *The Indian Journal of Political Science* 76 (1): 25–28.
Slaughter, A.-M. 1994. 'A Typology of Transjudicial Communication'. *University of Richmond Law Review* 29, 99–137.
Smith, J. L., and J. A. Todd. 2015. 'Rules, Standards, and Lower Court Decisions'. *Journal of Law and Courts* 3 (2): 259–75. https://doi.org/10.1086/681544.
Songer, D. R., J. A. Segal, and C. M. Cameron. 1994. 'The Hierarchy of Justice: Testing a Principal–Agent Model of Supreme Court-Circuit Court Interactions'. *American Journal of Political Science* 38 (3): 673–96.
Spitzer, M., and E. Talley. 2000. 'Judicial Auditing'. *Journal of Legal Studies* 29 (2 Part I): 649. https://doi.org/10.1086/468088.
Tyler, T. R. 1988. 'What is Procedural Justice? Criteria used by Citizens to Assess the Fairness of Legal Procedures'. *Law & Society Review* 22 (1): 103. https://doi.org/10.2307/3053563.
Vermeule, A. 2008. *Law and the Limits of Reason*. Oxford: Oxford University Press. https://doi.org/10.1093/acprof:oso/9780195383768.001.0001.
Waldron, J. (2014. 'Five to Four: Why Do Bare Majorities Rule on Courts?' *The Yale Law Journal* 123, 1692–730.
Wasserman, M. F., and J. D. Slack. 2021. 'Can There Be Too Much Specialization? Specialization in Specialized Courts'. *Northwestern University Law Review* 115 (5): 1405–504.
Westerland, C., J. A. Segal, L. Epstein, C. M. Cameron, and S. Comparato. 2010. 'Strategic Defiance and Compliance in the U.S.'. Courts of Appeals. *American Journal of Political Science* 54 (4): 891–905. https://doi.org/10.1111/j.1540-5907.2010.00465.x.
Wilhelm, T., R. L. Vining, and D. Hughes. 2023. 'Chief Justice Selection Rules and Judicial Ideology'. *State Politics & Policy Quarterly* 1–16. https://doi.org/10.1017/spq.2023.8.

PART VIII

JUDICIAL INDEPENDENCE

CHAPTER 33

THREATS TO JUDICIAL INDEPENDENCE

ALEX SCHWARTZ

1. Introduction

Although most of the world's constitutions profess to guarantee judicial independence, the extent to which judges are actually willing and able to rule against the preferences of governments and legislators varies considerably (Melton and Ginsburg 2014). Courts that might seem powerful and independent as a matter of formal constitutional law can, in practice, turn out to be little more than rubber stamps for the policies of governing elites; courts that do attempt to check the power of governments and legislatures can, nevertheless, be defied; and courts that might have once been independent and powerful can be reined in—manipulated, captured, or debilitated—by the political branches.

The last of these scenarios—sometimes called 'court curbing'—is the focus of this chapter. Court curbing can take many forms. Those directed at the appointment and tenure of judges (e.g. 'court packing', 'court purging', and targeted impeachments) aim to produce a bench more inclined to favour the preferences of governing elites (see Kosař and Šipulová 2023). Other forms—those with a view to punishing or rewarding judges for their decisions—target the governance, professional discipline, or the resources of the judiciary (Cross and Nelson 2000). Still other forms hinder the efficacy or authority of judicial decisions by tampering with a court's jurisdiction, remedial powers, or decision-making procedures (Ura and Wohlfarth 2022).[1] As recent events in places such as Poland show (see Sadurski 2019), various types of court-curbing policies can be combined to undermine the independence or power of the judiciary on multiple fronts.

These are matters of both practical and scholarly concern. Court curbing may prefigure attacks on other values or institutions that people care about—human rights, the integrity of elections, the freedom of the press, etc. Indeed, in extreme cases, court curbing may be an early step in a process of democratic backsliding that culminates in the consolidation of an authoritarian regime (see Ginsburg and Huq 2020; Staton, Reenock, and Holsinger 2022). Court curbing is also an important topic for the study of judicial behaviour; the research in this field suggests not only that judicial decisions can provoke court curbing but also that the threat of court curbing will motivate judges to strategically constrain their own decisions (see Epstein and Weinshall 2021).

The chapter now proceeds in three sections. Section 2 reviews theory and evidence concerning the factors that might encourage attacks on independent judicial power (ideological polarization, political 'self-defence', 'position taking', and populism). Section 3 considers factors that might discourage threats to independent judicial power (constitutional impediments, veto players and political fragmentation, political competition, and public support for the judiciary). Section 4 concludes by highlighting some promising pathways for future research in this area.

2. What Motivates Court Curbing?

At the outset of any discussion of the factors that might motivate (or discourage) legislative or executive threats to independent judicial power, it is helpful to conceptualize the decision to pursue court-curbing policies as a rational calculus of expected costs and benefits (Epstein, Knight, and Shvetsova 2001; Whittington 2003). On one side of the calculus, judicial decisions that frustrate the goals or preferences of incumbents create costs that incentivize court curbing. On the other side, incumbents may derive some positive benefits from maintaining an independent and powerful judiciary (Stone Sweet 2000; Whittington 2005) and, furthermore, court curbing itself may be a costly move—for example, because it provokes a negative public reaction. As Epstein, Knight, and Shvetsova (2001) explain, this hypothetical calculus yields a notional 'tolerance interval', a policy space within which the political branches are prepared to acquiesce to unwelcome judicial decisions because the expected costs of attacking the court (or the expected benefits of acquiescence) outweigh the expected benefits of curtailing independent judicial power (or the expected costs of acquiescence).

It should be noted that this calculus depends in part on the method of court curbing in question. Although some methods of court curbing, such as jurisdiction stripping, might be tailored to respond to specific judicial decisions, most methods of court curbing (e.g. court packing, court purging, resource punishment, and changes to a court's decision-making procedures) have broader consequences beyond an individual decision or policy area. Thus, as Keith Wittington explains, court curbing is often a 'blunt instrument' with implications for the 'judiciary's institutional integrity, not just the outcome of a particular case' (2003, 449). The calculus of court curbing therefore concerns the 'basket of policy outcomes' associated with independent judicial power; 'the crucial question', as Whittington puts it, 'is the value of that basket as a whole' (2003, 449). This insight should not distract us from the possibility that the preferences of incumbents in some matters (particularly when regime survival is at stake) may be so intense that a single court decision can effectively decide the calculus of court curbing one way or another.

This very abstract model of a rational calculus does not tell us which specific factors encourage (or discourage) court curbing. These factors probably vary in importance by context and it would be surprising if a single theory could account for all cases. Nevertheless, the research in this area suggests a set of variables that may have explanatory power across diverse contexts.

2.1 Ideological Polarization

As the generic model outlined above suggests, court curbing may be provoked by judicial decisions that frustrate the policy objectives or preferences of incumbents. One important variable in this equation is the ideological distance between judges and governing elites. There is a vast empirical literature, drawing on evidence from diverse contexts around the world, to show that judicial decisions can be influenced significantly by judges' political ideologies, partisan loyalties, or group affiliations (see e.g. Segal and Spaeth 2002; Weinshall-Margel 2011; Hanretty 2020; Schwartz and Murchison 2016; Dressell and Inoue 2022). If judges are systematically influenced by preferences that deviate from those of governments and legislatures, then the potential costs of independent judicial power (from the perspective of the political branches) may begin to bite. Thus, ideological polarization as between courts and the political branches should increase the chances, other things being equal, that incumbents will be sufficiently provoked to engage in court curbing. Several studies of court curbing in the United States lend empirical support to this conjecture, although those that concern congressional override of court decisions (e.g. Eskridge 1991; Hettinger and Zorn 2005) probably outnumber those that concern efforts to curb the power or independence of the courts (e.g. Leonard 2016; Mark and Zilis 2018).

In theory, ideological divergence between courts and the political branches would not even arise if the latter had perfect information about the ideology of prospective judicial appointees, complete control over those appointments, and unified preferences of their own; in such conditions, the political branches could coordinate to ensure that the bench consists entirely of ideologically convergent judges. But these conditions are demanding and often do not obtain (see Epstein and Weinshall 2021, 20–22). For one thing, appointing authorities may be mistaken about (or only partially aware of) the ideological disposition of their appointees. Consequently, they may appoint judges who turn out to be less ideologically convergent or loyal than expected, especially if unexpected legal controversies arise after appointments have been made. Furthermore, judicial tenure is often significantly longer than the turnover of legislative majorities and governments, leaving ample scope for a lag between the election of new political majorities and the appointment of new judicial majorities. Moreover, in many countries, power over judicial appointments is shared with (or even ceded altogether to) special independent appointment bodies or 'judicial councils' (see Spáč 2018). In sum, gaps in political control over judicial appointments at time t_1 increase the potential for ideological divergence at time t_2, which in turn increases the chances of court curbing at time t_3.

Ideologically motivated court curbing need not be retaliatory; it can also be a pre-emptive strike against a bench that is expected to be ideologically at odds with the objectives of a new government. As Holgado and Urribarri (2023) explain, this is what occurred in Argentina shortly after the election of President Carlos Menem. Apparently believing that 'his economic reform could only be successful if the three branches of government reached an ideological agreement', Menem and his allies in the legislature passed new legislation to expand the Supreme Court, from five justices to nine, thereby allowing for six new ideologically friendly justices to be appointed (Holgado and Urribari 2023, 360). True to the intentions of this plan, the newly created majority on the Supreme Court upheld a series of executive decrees that expedited Menem's agenda for economic reform.

2.2 Political 'Self-Defence'

Court curbing may also be driven by factors that have less to do with ideological disagreement and more to do with the political survival of politicians or regimes clinging to power. In such cases, attacks on independent judicial power would be driven by a logic of 'political self-defence'. A 'survivalist theory' along these lines has been developed and tested as an explanation for executive court curbing in Latin America (Helmke 2017; Helmke, Jeong, and Kim 2022). As Helmke, Jeong, and Kim explain, 'from the standpoint of an embattled incumbent president, the decision over whether to constrain the court no longer simply revolves around the desire to set (or legitimate) policy writ large but instead becomes primarily about how the court can help her to survive in office' (2022, 269). The idea here is that courts can get caught in the crossfire of conflict between a strong executive and a hostile legislature. Presidents may well be strong, in formal constitutional terms, but this only raises the stakes of the office and incentivizes them further to manipulate the judiciary; once under presidential control, the courts can help presidents expand or preserve their powers, limit the strength of the opposition, and shore up public support (Helmke 2017). Consistent with these expectations, Helmke (2017) and Helmke, Jeong, and Kim (2022) find that presidents who have reason to fear being ousted by the legislature are more likely to engage in court curbing (at least in Latin America).

2.3 Position Taking

Politicians may also have motives to propose court-curbing policies apart from any realistic prospect of those policies being enacted. Based on research on court-curbing bills in the United States Congress, Tom Clark (2010, 2009) argues that legislators primarily propose court curbing as a form of 'position taking'—that is to say, incumbents use court-curbing bills to signal to constituents that they are on the 'right' side of an issue or to galvanize supporters. Clark's argument helps to make sense of an important puzzle about court curbing in the United States: why, given that congressional court curbing bills are almost never enacted (and most fail to even reach the stage of a committee), do members of Congress bother to introduce them with considerable frequency? If court curbing was motivated only by the desire to curb ideologically divergent courts, such blatantly futile efforts would seem like an irrational waste of time and political capital. The answer to this puzzle, Clark argues, is that 'members of Congress have an interest in position taking in order to create a public record to which they can point to demonstrate they have taken some action to secure the goals of their constituents' (Clark 2009, 974). He further explains, '[i]t does not matter whether those actions lead directly to policy changes, because constituents may not hold their members of Congress accountable for policy outcomes but rather blame Congress as an institution for failed policy initiatives' (Clark 2009, 974). Consistent with this explanation, Clark finds that, after controlling for ideological distance between the judiciary and the Congress, higher periods of public discontent with the Supreme Court predict a greater frequency of court-curbing bills and that the ideological direction of these bills tends to reflect the prevailing public mood (liberal or conservative), both at the state level and in the aggregate (2011, ch. 4). Subsequent research by Moyer and Key (2018) finds that this logic of 'position taking' also explains congressional court-curbing bills targeting the jurisdiction of the lower federal courts, particularly the 9th Circuit.

2.4 Populism

Another possible factor in court curbing—and one that is a matter of recent public and scholarly concern—is 'populism' (see Tushnet and Bugarič 2021). Populism is a disputed term in social science; there are competing perspectives on what it is and how to study it (see Mansbridge and Macedo 2019). Nevertheless, several perspectives converge (albeit for different reasons) on the idea that populism is a threat to independent judicial power and there is some rough evidence to suggest that populist governments may be especially prone to engage in court curbing (Voeten 2020).

One influential perspective treats populism as a fundamentally majoritarian, illiberal, or anti-pluralist ideology inherently hostile to constitutional constraints (Mudde 2004; Jan-Werner Müller 2016). According to Cass Mudde for example, populism is opposed to constitutionalism because it 'rejects all limitations on the expression of the general will, most notably the constitutional protection of minorities and the independence (from politics, and therefore from democratic control) of key state institutions (e.g. the judiciary, the central bank)' (Mudde 2004, 561). Thus, the apparent connection between populists and attacks on courts might be understood to reflect a sincere ideological predisposition or worldview; courts are attacked because they are counter-majoritarian institutions at odds with the will of 'the People'. Another perspective equates populism with the distinctive mobilization strategy of 'political outsiders' who, in seeking to unseat the political establishment, build a 'plebiscitarian' or 'personalistic' connection with voters (Levitsky and Loxton 2013; Barr 2019). From this perspective, Levitsky and Loxton argue that populist leaders, being outsiders and lacking the will or political experience needed to broker compromise, are especially likely to find themselves in conflict with courts and other 'institutions of horizontal accountability' controlled by their opponents (2013, 108). Thus, the election of a populist leader is likely to trigger 'a showdown between an outsider with a mandate to sweep away the existing elite and regime institutions and an elite that views those institutions as its last bastion of defence' (Levitsky and Loxton 2013, 112). According to a third perspective, populism is a simply a discursive frame—a highly adaptable way of presenting issues or policies in terms of a conflict between a virtuous people and a corrupt elite (Aslanidis 2016; Bonikowski 2016; Norris 2020). From this perspective, we need not assume anything about the sincere beliefs or 'outsider' status of politicians to appreciate a connection between populist rhetoric and court curbing. By definition, judges are 'elites' and, in nearly all cases, they are unelected. Thus, politicians who (for whatever reason) seek to curb independent judicial power will be attracted to populist rhetoric because it offers such a potent way to undercut the legitimacy of the courts and defend court-curbing policies against opposition (Schwartz, forthcoming).

3. What Discourages Court Curbing?

3.1 Constitutional Impediments

One might naturally expect that constitutional protections for judicial independence would tend to prevent or discourage court curbing; when governments or legislators threaten independent judicial power, such protections might help to identify the threat and mobilize opposition. The evidence for this intuitive conjecture is mixed. In a quantitative study relying on cross-national panel data, Hayo and Voigt (2019) find at best a weak positive correlation between *de jure* constitutional protections for judicial independence and *de facto* judicial independence (cf Hayo and Voigt 2007). Relying on different data and methods, Melton and Ginsburg (2014) find that the relationship between constitutional text and *de facto* judicial independence is a tenuous and complicated one: to the extent that constitutional protections do make a systematic difference for *de facto* judicial independence, this effect is apparent only when constitutions combine procedural protections for the selection *and* removal of judges, and even then it is confined, for the most part, to authoritarian (as opposed to democratic) contexts.

These findings do not speak directly to the effect of constitutional impediments on court curbing per se, but they are at least suggestive: if constitutional impediments did deter court curbing, one would expect greater levels of *de jure* judicial independence to be associated with greater levels of *de facto* judicial independence. Nevertheless, given the many challenges of measuring both *de facto* and *de jure* judicial independence, we should be cautious about coming to any firm conclusion on this question. Arguably, the most we can say at this point is that, whatever the deterrent effect of constitutional law, it is probably mediated by other factors—for example, by regime type and the presence (or absence) of other checks on executive power (Melton and Ginsburg 2014), by the ease of constitutional amendment (Tsebelis 2022), and by the extent to which political power is fragmented or unified (Carrubba et al. 2015).

3.2 Veto Players and Political Fragmentation

Even if constitutional protections for judicial independence fail to systematically impede court curbing, other institutional factors may have an indirect deterrent effect. One of these has already been implied: the flipside of Helmke's research (2017), showing that presidential systems may tend to encourage court curbing, is that parliamentary systems may discourage attacks on the judiciary because the associated concentration of executive and legislative power would tend to decrease the chances of the judiciary being caught in the cross-fire of an interbranch conflict. Others have proposed a simpler, more intuitive expectation that runs in exactly the other direction, namely that the fragmentation of power should make it more difficult and less likely, all else equal, for court curbing policies to be enacted. On this view, institutions that create multiple veto players (such as presidential systems, bicameral legislatures, federalism, or consociational power sharing) raise the transaction and coordination costs of enacting court-curbing policies (Ferejohn 2002; Tsebelis 2002; Schwartz 2018). In such circumstances, the costs of court curbing may simply be too steep to make an attack on the courts a viable move. Of course, the expectation that institutional veto players will tend to insulate courts from attack only makes sense if we assume that the relevant veto points are not all controlled by the same leader or political party. Thus, the practical dispersion or division of political power within and across institutions is arguably more important than formal veto points within the institutional setup (see Ferejohn 2002), even if veto points tend to amplify the costs of court curbing (see Tsebelis 2002).

These conjectures about veto players and political fragmentation are indeed intuitive, and there is some empirical evidence to support them. Rebecca Bill Chavez (2004) argues that the ebbs and flows of executive subordination of the judiciary in Argentina can be explained by diachronic variation in party discipline and fluctuation between unified and divided government (see also Iaryczower, Spiller, and Tommasi 2002). Similarly, Ríos-Figueroa (2007) finds that the Mexican Supreme Court was significantly more likely to rule against the interests of incumbents during periods of greater political fragmentation (periods when the ruling party lacked monolithic control over the executive and/or both houses of Congress), which suggests that the Supreme Court was less constrained by the threat of court curbing during these periods. In a similar vein, Trochev (2013) argues that the assertiveness of courts in deciding electoral disputes against incumbents in Georgia, Kyrgyzstan, and Ukraine is at least partly explained by political fragmentation in those countries. There is also some evidence to suggest that veto points and political fragmentation interact with constitutional protections for judicial independence in important ways: checks on executive power may increase the extent to which *de jure* protections of judicial independence enhance *de facto* judicial independence (Melton and Ginsburg 2014) and *de jure* judicial independence may enhance *de facto* judicial independence under conditions of low political fragmentation, when court curbing is a more viable threat (Carrubba et al. 2015).

3.3 Political Competition

There is a veritable subgenre of the judicial politics literature focused on the relationship between political competition and judicial independence. According to the most influential theory in this area, competitive elections incentivize the creation and maintenance of an independent judiciary (Ginsburg 2003; Stephenson 2003; Ramseyer 1994). The central idea here is that politicians who have reason to think they may lose power also have reason to invest in (and to preserve) judicial independence as a kind of insurance against future electoral loss; whatever the costs that independent judicial power may impose on incumbents, these are thought to be offset by the expected benefit of saddling opponents with comparable constraints should the tables be turned.

According to this insurance logic, political competition should tend to discourage court curbing. But much of the empirical evidence for this theory focuses on how political competition encourages judicial empowerment, as opposed to how it discourages court curbing (Ginsburg 2003; Hirschl 2004; Finkel 2008; Ginsburg and Versteeg 2014). Although the insurance logic is similar in both instances, it is important to distinguish between them. As Vanberg (2015) explains, 'even if a coalition at the founding moment favors the creation of a court, this does not imply that the same coalition is willing to comply with adverse decisions and to maintain the authority of the court on an ongoing basis, once the founding moment passes' (169).

Indeed, when scholars have brought court curbing into clearer focus in this area, it is often to complicate the insurance logic. For example, Leiras, Tuñón, and Giraudy (2015) conceptualize political competition in terms of two distinct dimensions. On the one hand, political competition may manifest as political fragmentation which, as we saw above, is expected to make court curbing more difficult and therefore less likely. On the other hand, political competition may manifest as electoral turnover which, according to the 'insurance theory', is expected to raise the value of independent judicial power and so also make court curbing less likely. But, with respect to the Argentine provincial supreme courts, Leiras, Tuñón, and Giraudy show that the effect of these different manifestations of political competition on court curbing is reciprocally dependent: the anticipation of electoral turnover reduces the risk of a politically-motivated termination of judicial tenure (e.g. 'resignations under threats of impeachment or other kinds of pressure') only when political power is otherwise concentrated, while political fragmentation reduces the risk of a politically motivated termination of judicial tenure only when there is no expectation of electoral turnover (Leiras, Tuñón, and Giraudy 2015, 183–84).

Epperly (2019) further complicates the insurance theory by extending it to autocratic contexts. He distinguishes between *de jure* threats to judicial independence (i.e. changes to constitutional rules) and *de facto* threats to judicial independence (i.e. extra-legal pressure on judicial behaviour). He theorizes that the effects of political competition with respect to these two types will vary as between democratic and autocratic contexts. Although the insurance logic applies to both contexts—because even autocrats can worry about losing power—the incentives to pursue *de jure* as opposed to *de facto* court curbing diverge depending on regime type. In democratic contexts, governments should prefer to undermine judicial independence through formal *de jure* changes because such efforts can at least be presented as lawful and are therefore less likely to provoke negative media attention and opposition. Conversely, in autocratic contexts, *de facto* attacks on judicial independence should be the path of least resistance. Epperly provides empirical support for these conjectures in the form a case study of recent court curbing in Hungary—illustrating how a lack of political competition in a democratic context encourages an aggressive but nevertheless legal attack on independent judicial power. He also presents quantitative cross-national evidence to show that increases in electoral competition are associated with increases in *de jure* judicial independence (and decreases with the opposite) in democratic contexts, but that there is no such effect in autocracies. Conversely, with respect to changes in *de facto* independence, Epperly finds that the effect of political competition is significant for autocracies *but not* for democracies (2019, ch. 4; cf Staton, Reenock, and Holsinger 2022, ch. 3).

Still other studies invert the logic of the insurance theory as applied to threats to independent judicial power. In an argument that foreshadows Helmke, Jeong, and Kim's 'survivalist theory of court curbing', Popova (2012) argues that political competition has 'the exact opposite effect on judicial independence' in emerging democracies that it is thought to have in consolidated democracies (3); in emerging democracies, because electoral contests are more of a zero-sum game, 'political competition makes dependent courts more useful and more attractive to vulnerable incumbents' (3). She tests this theory against quantitative data from judicial decisions in Russia and Ukraine, finding that greater political competition in the latter is associated with a greater likelihood of judicial decisions favouring government-affiliated litigants (Popova 2012, chs 4 and 5), and she marshals qualitative evidence to demonstrate that informal practices of pressuring the courts (e.g. 'telephone justice'), although common to both countries, were more extensively applied in Ukraine than in Russia (2012, chs 5 and 7). These practices do not necessarily amount to court curbing, at least not in the sense that scholars normally use the term; they are relatively routinized inheritances from the Soviet era (as opposed to irregular efforts to undermine or break the status quo of independent judicial power). Nonetheless, as Popova explains, these informal pressure tactics allow incumbents to co-opt the judiciary into their contest for power.

Along similar lines, Aydin (2013) argues that political competition should increase the incentives to curb independent judicial power in the context of developing democracies: 'in developing democracies—which are characterized by high levels of corruption, weak party systems and high electoral volatility—the immediate short-term benefits that incumbents may obtain from interfering in judicial decisions may be higher than the long-term benefits that may be gained from high levels of judicial independence' (2013, 107). Furthermore, Aydin contends, the costs of court curbing in such contexts will be relatively lower because there is less reason to fear a negative public reaction (the judiciary is less trusted, the media is less free, citizens are less engaged, etc.). Consistent with this expectation, Aydin's cross-national quantitative analysis finds that the marginal effect of political competition on *de facto* judicial independence varies across advanced and developing democracies—it is positive and significant for those countries with relatively high levels of democratization, and it is negative and significant for counties with relatively low levels of democratization (Aydin, 2013, 125).

3.4 Public Support for the Judiciary

As Aydin's argument illustrates, public support for the judiciary is often expected to insulate judges from court-curbing attacks, at least in consolidated democracies where political elites need to worry about winning popular elections (see Vanberg 2015). This expectation presumes that the judiciary enjoys some institutional legitimacy (also known as 'diffuse support') that is relatively robust to fluctuating levels of public (dis-)satisfaction with recent judicial decisions (also known as 'specific support') (see Caldeira and Gibson 1992). Thus, court curbing is thought to be a potentially costly endeavour for incumbents, even in the wake of unpopular judicial decisions, because it may provoke some voters (i.e. those who regard the targeted court as a legitimate institution) to turn against the offending politicians. Would-be court curbers are predicted to restrain themselves accordingly.

There is some empirical support for this perspective. Courts around the world have been found to enjoy high levels of public esteem relative to the political branches (Gibson, Caldeira, and Baird 1998). The US Supreme Court—the focus of much of the research in this area—does appear to be (or have been) the beneficiary of various legitimating beliefs, even if those beliefs are under ever increasing strain; there is some evidence to show that, despite political polarization, widespread commitments to broader democratic and constitutional values underpin public support for the US Supreme Court (Caldeira and Gibson 1992; Mondak and Smithey 1997; Gibson and Nelson 2015) and many Americans regard the US Supreme Court, despite its politicization, as a distinctly 'principled' institution (Gibson and Caldeira 2011). In the context of Latin America, Helmke (2017) finds that those courts that have enjoyed relatively high levels of public trust have also been significantly less likely to be attacked by the political branches (145–47). She also notes anecdotal evidence to suggest that court curbing, when it has occurred in Latin America, tends to be a popular policy (Helmke 2017, 134–35).

These findings provide some indirect evidence to suggest that public support for courts may deter court curbing. But direct evidence of the mechanism that underlies the deterrent effect—the supposed electoral risk that accompanies court curbing—is wanting. The paucity of evidence may be understandable, even if the underlying theory is correct, because court curbing may only happen when incumbents correctly discern that courts can be attacked without provoking a public backlash or significant electoral losses. Thus, we would observe courts with relatively low levels of public support being attacked but we would never (or only rarely) get the chance to see what happens when courts with relatively high levels of public support are attacked.

In any case, a parallel body of research questions the extent to which voting publics are likely to punish incumbent court curbers. As was noted above, Aydin (2013) argues that the threat of public backlash is only a reliable deterrent of court curbing in the context of advanced democracies, where a free media and an active civil society can help mobilize a public backlash. But even in so-called consolidated democracies, where courts seem to enjoy considerable 'diffuse support', there are reasons to doubt the extent to which voters will be sufficiently incensed by court curbing to vote against their usual ideological or partisan preferences. With respect to the United States, Clark and Kastellec (2015) find in survey experiments that 'individuals are less likely to support court-curbing measures when informed that elites from the opposite party have proposed them than when such measures are endorsed by either a neutral source or members of their own party' (507). In a similar vein, and using similar methods, Bartels and Johnston (2020) find that (i) general disagreement with Supreme Court decisions 'exhibits a consistently significant and substantively meaningful effect on support for broadly targeted Court-curbing' (121); (ii) that disagreement with specific court decisions also increases support for court curbing, particularly when court curbing is narrowly tailored to respond to the decisions in question (163–64); and (iii) that the effect of disagreement on support for court curbing is amplified significantly by partisan polarization (204–05; see also Bartels and Johnston 2013; Driscoll and Nelson 2023). Research beyond the United States has yielded similar results. Bartels and Kramon (2020) find evidence from across Africa to suggest that diffuse support for judicial power depends on partisan alignment with the president: 'presidential co-partisans are *less* supportive of horizontal judicial power over the president and *more* supportive of vertical power over the people' (Bartels and Kramon 2020, 145). Similarly, Bartels, Horowitz, and Kramon (2021) find that changes in diffuse support for judicial power in Kenya are influenced significantly by partisan-based perspectives on the outcome of judicial decisions; following two Supreme Court decisions—the first annulling the re-election of President Uhuru and the second confirming his re-election—they find diminished support for judicial power among partisan 'losers' and increased support for judicial power among partisan 'winners' (Bartels, Horowitz, and Kramon 2021). They also find that professed commitments to abstract principles of the rule of law and democratic values do not dampen (and may even amplify) partisanship-driven changes in support for judicial power. These findings are consistent with other research suggesting that voters are often prepared to trade democratic principles for partisan interests (Graham and Svolik 2020).

In sum, there are good reasons to think that public opinion may not be such a reliable shield against court curbing. It should be noted, however, that public opinion might deter court curbing even if court curbers are unlikely to pay a significant electoral price for attacking the independence or power of the judiciary. What matters, as far as deterrence is concerned, is that risk-averse incumbents *believe* (rightly or wrongly) that they are likely to pay such a price.

4. Conclusion

As this chapter has shown, there is now a rich body of scholarship concerning threats to independent judicial power. Researchers from around the world have collected and analysed data from diverse contexts and identified several factors that may help to explain the incidence and intensity of court curbing. There are also many outstanding questions to be explored, including when and why some factors matter and how different factors might mediate or interact with one another.

One path for further research is to investigate how the causes and consequences of court curbing might vary according to the method of court curbing in question. So far, albeit with some important exceptions (e.g. Epperly 2019; Bartels and Johnston 2020; Ura and Wohlfarth 2022), the literature tends to lump all threats to independent judicial power together. But there is good reason to think that the factors that encourage or discourage some types of court curbing may be very different from those that influence the occurrence of other types. For example, public support for courts may be more of a deterrent with respect to those types of court curbing that are more obviously interpreted as flagrant attacks on judicial independence (say, major changes to the process of judicial appointment) than those that are narrowly targeted at a specific domain of judicial power (e.g. jurisdiction stripping) or those that can be presented as merely efficiency-driven reforms. Indeed, there is some evidence from the United States to suggest that jurisdiction stripping may even be associated with *greater* public support for the judiciary (Ura and Wohlfarth 2022). It would be productive to extend this line of inquiry beyond the United States.

The varying effects of different types of court curbing on judicial behaviour also warrant further research. There is considerable evidence to show that judges behave strategically to avoid court curbing, constraining their decisions so as not to provoke reprisals from the political branches (e.g. Iaryczower, Spiller, and Tommasi 2002; Ríos-Figueroa 2007; Segal, Westerland, and Lindquist 2011). To take but one example, Helmke (2005) shows (with evidence from decisions of the Argentine Supreme Court) that the threat of future removal may induce judges to rule against incumbents when it becomes apparent that the current government is losing power; by ruling against the current government, judges signal their compatibility with the incoming government and thus mitigate the danger of being removed when power changes hands. The threat of removal at work in Helmke's example is a threat with potential professional and personal consequences; it goes to a judge's career and livelihood. But judges may be much less concerned about other threats to their independence and power (say, changes to a court's remedial powers). Scholars of judicial behaviour can take the field forward by identifying which threats are most likely to induce strategic judicial behaviour and under what conditions.

Such questions might be explored with the help of the Varieties of Democracy (or 'V-Dem') Project's dataset.[2] Amongst many other things, the V-Dem Project provides cross-national estimates of the incidence of several varieties of court curbing ('court packing', 'court purging', and reforms that limit judicial power), as well as estimates of the incidence of government statements attacking the integrity of the judiciary. These data are still underexploited (but see Staton, Reenock, and Holsinger 2022) and scholars should take advantage of them to test more nuanced theories that distinguish between different types of court curbing.

Another promising path for future research is to investigate the ideational factors that motivate or constrain threats to independent judicial power. Scholars of judicial politics often acknowledge that court curbing might be influenced one way or another by values and informal norms, but they have tended to favour rational-strategic (as opposed to ideational) explanations. This emphasis is understandable; rational-strategic explanations often generalize well across contexts, whereas ideational explanations tend to be more idiographic. But ideational factors are likely to interact with rational-strategic factors in important ways that should not be neglected. For example, one of the blind spots in the existing scholarship on how political competition influences judicial independence is the assumption that rival politicians and political parties in a given context are similarly positioned with respect to the costs and benefits of independent judicial power. But the putative insurance value of judicial independence is likely to vary with the ideology of competitors. The logic of judicial independence as political insurance would, for example, apply very differently to a party with illiberal preferences than to a competitor party intent on positioning itself as the liberal or establishment choice. The latter would have every reason to worry about what its opponents might do if left unchecked by independent judicial power, while the former would have much less reason to fear its opponents and may even aspire to wield power autocratically.

A third promising topic for further investigation, closely related to ideational factors, is the role that discourse plays in threats to judicial independence and judicial power. In many other fields of inquiry, scholars have found that the way in which ideas are communicated or 'framed' is an important element in accounting for institutional or policy change (see Schmidt 2008; and Chong and Druckman 2007). Thus far, scholars of judicial politics have not paid comparable attention to the discursive tactics that are used to promote or defend court-curbing policies (but see Nelsen and Gibson 2019; and Staton, Reenock, and Holsinger 2022). Indeed, the field often treats these attacks as if they were effectively epiphenomenal, rather than an important part of why the associated efforts succeed or fail. But surely, court-curbing policies (like all policies) depend on, and are conditioned by, the discourse of persuading and mobilizing potential supporters and countering the criticism of opponents. What is more, the scholarship often treats public support for the judiciary as if it were exogenous to court curbing—a reservoir of sentiment that is part of the background to court curbing—rather than something that can be shaped by those intent on curbing the courts (but see Magalhães and Garoupa 2023). Just as judges may take steps to shore up their public support (Staton 2010), aspiring court curbers may actively attempt to manufacture public hostility to the judiciary. The various discursive tactics that legitimate court curbing (or delegitimate critics) deserve to be studied just as much as the causal factors that explain the underlying motives. This is an area where advances in computational methods will make it possible to study the relevant discourse in ever more rigorous and sophisticated ways (see generally Grimmer, Roberts, and Stewart 2022).

Notes

1. Court-curbing policies can also be analysed in terms of how broad or narrowly tailored they are (Bartels and Johnston 2020), according to whether they are directed to controlling judges *ex ante* or *ex post* appointment (Brinks and Blass 2017), according to whether, as a matter of law, they are formally constitutional or extra-constitutional (Aydin-Cakir 2023), or according to whether they are policy driven or directed at the preservation of a particular regime (Holgado and Urribarri 2023).
2. https://v-dem.net/, accessed 27 November 2023.

References

Aslanidis, Paris. 2016. 'Is Populism an Ideology? A Refutation and a New Perspective'. *Political Studies* 64 (1_suppl): 88–104.

Aydin-Cakir, Aylin. 2023. 'The Varying Effect of Court-Curbing: Evidence from Hungary and Poland'. *Journal of European Public Policy* 30: 1–27.

Aydın, Aylin. 2013. 'Judicial Independence across Democratic Regimes: Understanding the Varying Impact of Political Competition'. *Law & Society Review* 47 (1): 105–34.

Bartels, Brandon L., and Christopher D. Johnston. 2013. 'On the Ideological Foundations of Supreme Court Legitimacy in the American Public'. *American Journal of Political Science* 57 (1): 184–99.

Bartels, Brandon L., and Christopher D. Johnston. 2020. *Curbing the Court: Why the Public Constrains Judicial Independence*. Cambridge: Cambridge University Press.

Bartels, Brandon L., and Eric Kramon. 2020. 'Does Public Support for Judicial Power Depend on Who Is in Political Power? Testing a Theory of Partisan Alignment in Africa'. *American Political Science Review* 114 (1): 144–63.

Bartels, Brandon L., Jeremy Horowitz, and Eric Kramon. 2021. 'Can Democratic Principles Protect High Courts from Partisan Backlash? Public Reactions to the Kenyan Supreme Court's Role in the 2017 Election Crisis'. *American Journal of Political Science* 67 (3): 790–807.

Barr, Robert R. 2019. 'Populism as a Political Strategy'. In *Routledge Handbook of Global Populism*, edited by Carlos de la Torre, 44–56. London: Routledge Taylor & Francis Group.

Bonikowski, Bart. 2016. 'Three Lessons of Contemporary Populism in Europe and the United States'. *The Brown Journal of World Affairs* 23 (1): 9–24.

Brinks, Daniel M., and Abby Blass. 2017. 'Rethinking Judicial Empowerment: The New Foundations of Constitutional Justice'. *International Journal of Constitutional Law* 15 (2): 296–331.

Caldeira, Gregory A., and James L. Gibson. 1992. 'The Etiology of Public Support for the Supreme Court'. *American Journal of Political Science* 36: 635–64.

Carrubba, Clifford J., Matthew Gabel, Gretchen Helmke, Andrew D. Martin, and Jeffrey K. Staton. 2015. 'When Parchment Barriers Matter: De Jure Judicial Independence and the Concentration of Power'. Manuscript (on file with authors).

Chavez, Rebecca Bill. 2004. *The Rule of Law in Nascent Democracies: Judicial Politics in Argentina*. Stanford: Stanford University Press.

Chong, Dennis, and James N. Druckman. 2007. 'Framing Theory'. *Annual Review of Political Science* 10: 103–26.

Clark, Tom S. 2009. 'The Separation of Powers, Court Curbing, and Judicial Legitimacy'. *American Journal of Political Science* 53 (4): 971–89.

Clark, Tom S. 2010. *The Limits of Judicial Independence*. Cambridge: Cambridge University Press.

Clark, Tom S., and John Kastellec. 2015. 'Source Cues and Public Support for the Supreme Court'. *American Politics Research* 43 (3): 504–35.

Cross, Frank B., and Blake J. Nelson. 2000. 'Strategic Institutional Effects on Supreme Court Decisionmaking'. *Northwestern University Law Review* 95: 1437.

Dressel, Björn, and Tomoo Inoue. 2022. 'Politics and the Federal Court of Malaysia, 1960–2018: An Empirical Investigation'. *Asian Journal of Law and Society* 9 (1): 26–58.

Driscoll, Amanda, and Michael J. Nelson. 2023. 'The Costs of Court Curbing: Evidence from the United States'. *The Journal of Politics* 85 (2): 609–24.

Epperly, Brad. 2019. *The Political Foundations of Judicial Independence in Dictatorship and Democracy*. Oxford: Oxford University Press.

Epstein, Lee, and Keren Weinshall. 2021. *The Strategic Analysis of Judicial Behavior: A Comparative Perspective*. Cambridge: Cambridge University Press.

Epstein, Lee, Jack Knight, and Olga Shvetsova. 2001. 'The Role of Constitutional Courts in the Establishment and Maintenance of Democratic Systems of Government'. *Law and Society Review* 35: 117–64.

Eskridge Jr, William N. 1991. 'Overriding Supreme Court Statutory Interpretation Decisions'. *Yale Law Journal* 101: 331–455.

Ferejohn, John. 2002. 'Judicializing Politics, Politicizing Law'. *Law and Contemporary Problems* 65 (3): 41–68.

Finkel, Jodi S. 2008. *Judicial Reform as Political Insurance: Argentina, Peru, and Mexico in the 1990s*. Notre Dame: University of Notre Dame Press.

Gibson, James L., and Gregory A. Caldeira. 2011. 'Has Legal Realism Damaged the Legitimacy of the US Supreme Court?' *Law & Society Review* 45 (1): 195–219.

Gibson, James L., and Michael J. Nelson. 2015. 'Is the US Supreme Court's Legitimacy Grounded in Performance Satisfaction and Ideology?' *American Journal of Political Science* 59 (1): 162–74.

Gibson, James L., Gregory A. Caldeira, and Vanessa A. Baird. 1998. 'On the Legitimacy of National High Courts'. *American Political Science Review* 92 (2): 343–358.

Ginsburg, Tom. 2003. *Judicial Review in New Democracies: Constitutional Courts in Asian Cases*. Cambridge: Cambridge University Press.

Ginsburg, Tom, and Aziz Z. Huq. 2020. *How to Save a Constitutional Democracy*. Chicago: University of Chicago Press.

Ginsburg, Tom, and Mila Versteeg. 2014. 'Why Do Countries Adopt Constitutional Review?'. *The Journal of Law, Economics, & Organization* 30 (3): 587–622.

Graham, Matthew H., and Milan W. Svolik. 2020. 'Democracy in America? Partisanship, Polarization, and the Robustness of Support for Democracy in the United States'. *American Political Science Review* 114 (2): 392–409.

Grimmer, Justin, Margaret E. Roberts, and Brandon M. Stewart. 2022. *Text as Data: A New Framework for Machine Learning and the Social Sciences*. Princeton: Princeton University Press.

Hanretty, Chris. 2020. *A Court of Specialists: Judicial Behavior on the UK Supreme Court*. Oxford: Oxford University Press.

Hayo, Bernd, and Stefan Voigt. 2007. 'Explaining De Facto Judicial Independence'. *International Review of Law and Economics* 27: 269–90.

Hayo, Bernd, and Stefan Voigt. 2019. 'The Long-Term Relationship between De Jure and De Facto Judicial Independence'. *Economics Letters* 183: 108603.

Helmke, Gretchen, Yeonkyung Jeong, and Jae-Eun C. Kim. 2022. 'Insecure Institutions: A Survivalist Theory of Judicial Manipulation in Latin America'. *Journal of Law and Courts* 10 (2): 265–85.

Helmke, Gretchen. 2005. *Courts under Constraints: Judges, Generals, and Presidents in Argentina*. Cambridge: Cambridge University Press.

Helmke, Gretchen. 2017. *Institutions on the Edge: The Origins and Consequences of Inter-Branch Crises in Latin America*. Cambridge: Cambridge University Press.

Hettinger, Virginia A., and Christopher Zorn. 2005. 'Explaining the Incidence and Timing of Congressional Responses to the US Supreme Court'. *Legislative Studies Quarterly* 30 (1): 5–28.

Hirschl, Ran. 2004. *Towards Juristocracy: The Origins and Consequences of the New Constitutionalism*. Cambridge: Harvard University Press.

Holgado, Benjamin Garcia, and Raúl Sánchez Urribarri. 2023. 'Court-Packing and Democratic Decay: A Necessary Relationship?'. *Global Constitutionalism* 12 (2), 350–77.

Iaryczower, Matías, Pablo T. Spiller, and Mariano Tommasi. 2002. 'Judicial Independence in Unstable Environments, Argentina 1935–1998'. *American Journal of Political Science* 46: 699–716.

Kosař, David, and Katarína Šipulová. 2023. 'Comparative Court-Packing'. *International Journal of Constitutional Law* 21 (1): 80–126.

Leiras, Marcelo, Guadalupe Tuñón, and Agustina Giraudy. 2015. 'Who Wants an Independent Court? Political Competition and Supreme Court Autonomy in the Argentine Provinces (1984–2008)'. *The Journal of Politics* 77 (1): 175–87.

Leonard, M. E. 2016. 'State Legislatures, State High Courts, and Judicial Independence: An Examination of Court-Curbing Legislation in the States'. *Justice System Journal* 37 (1): 53–62.

Levitsky, Steven, and James Loxton. 2013. 'Populism and Competitive Authoritarianism in the Andes'. *Democratization* 20 (1): 107–36.

Magalhães, P. C., and Nuno Garoupa. 2023. 'Populist governments, judicial independence, and public trust in the courts'. *Journal of European Public Policy*, 1–28. https://doi.org/10.1080/13501763.2023.2235386.

Mansbridge, Jane, and Stephen Macedo. 2019. 'Populism and Democratic Theory'. Annual Review of Law and Social Science 5: 59–77.

Mark, Alyx, and Michael A. Zilis. 2018. 'Restraining the Court: Assessing Accounts of Congressional Attempts to Limit Supreme Court Authority'. *Legislative Studies Quarterly* 43 (1): 141–69.
Melton, James, and Tom Ginsburg. 2014. 'Does De Jure Judicial Independence Really Matter? A Re-evaluation of Explanations for Judicial Independence'. *Journal of Law and Courts* 2: 187.
Mondak, Jeffery J., and Shannon Ishiyama Smithey. 1997. 'The Dynamics of Public Support for the Supreme Court'. *The Journal of Politics* 59 (4): 1114–42.
Moyer, Laura P., and Ellen M. Key. 2018. 'Political Opportunism, Position Taking, and Court-Curbing Legislation'. *Justice System Journal* 39 (2): 155–70.
Mudde, Cas. 2004. 'The Populist Zeitgeist'. Government and Opposition 39 (4): 541–63.
Müller, Jan-Werner. 2016. *What Is Populism?* Pittsburgh: University of Pennsylvania Press.
Nelson, Michael J., and James L. Gibson. 2019. 'How Does Hyperpoliticized Rhetoric Affect the US Supreme Court's Legitimacy?' *The Journal of Politics* 81 (4): 1512–16.
Norris, Pippa. 2020. 'Measuring Populism Worldwide'. *Party Politics* 26 (6): 697–717.
Popova, Maria. 2012. *Politicized Justice in Emerging Democracies: A Study of Courts in Russia and Ukraine*. Cambridge: Cambridge University Press.
Ramseyer, J. Mark. 1994. 'The Puzzling (In)Dependence of Courts: A Comparative Approach'. *The Journal of Legal Studies* 23 (2): 721–47.
Ríos-Figueroa, Julio. 2007. 'Fragmentation of Power and the Emergence of an Effective Judiciary in Mexico, 1994–2002'. *Latin American Politics and Society* 49 (1): 31–57.
Sadurski, Wojciech. 2019. *Poland's Constitutional Breakdown*. Oxford: Oxford University Press.
Schwartz, Alex, and Melanie Janelle Murchison. 2016. 'Judicial Impartiality and Independence in Divided Societies: An Empirical Analysis of the Constitutional Court of Bosnia-Herzegovina'. *Law & Society Review* 50 (4): 821–55.
Schwartz, Alex. 2018. 'Judicial Power and Consociational Federation: The Bosnian Example'. *Federal Law Review* 46 (4): 631–44.
Schwartz, Alex. forthcoming. *Populist Court Curbing*. Cambridge: Cambridge University Press.
Schmidt, Vivien A. 2008. 'Discursive Institutionalism: The Explanatory Power of Ideas and Discourse'. *Annual Review of Political Science* 11: 303–26.
Segal, Jeffrey A., and Harold J. Spaeth. 2002. *The Supreme Court and the Attitudinal Model Revisited*. Cambridge: Cambridge University Press.
Segal, Jeffrey A., Chad Westerland, and Stefanie A. Lindquist. 2011. 'Congress, the Supreme Court, and Judicial Review: Testing a Constitutional Separation of Powers Model'. *American Journal of Political Science* 55 (1): 89–104.
Spáč, Samuel. 2018. 'Recruiting European Judges in the Age of Judicial Self-Government'. *German Law Journal* 19 (7): 2077–104.
Staton, Jeffrey K. 2010. *Judicial Power and Strategic Communication in Mexico*. Cambridge: Cambridge University Press.
Staton, Jeffrey K., Christopher Reenock, and Jordan Holsinger. 2022. *Can Courts be Bulwarks of Democracy? Judges and the Politics of Prudence*. Cambridge: Cambridge University Press.
Stephenson, Matthew C. 2003. '"When the Devil Turns… ": The Political Foundations of Independent Judicial Review'. *The Journal of Legal Studies* 32 (1): 59–89.
Sweet, Alec Stone. 2000. *Governing with Judges: Constitutional Politics in Europe*. Oxford: Oxford University Press.
Trochev, Alexei. 2013. 'Fragmentation? Defection? Legitimacy? Explaining Judicial Roles in Post-Communist "Colored Revolutions"'. In *Consequential Courts: Judicial Roles in Global*

Perspective, edited by Diana Kapiszewski, Gordon Silverstein, and Robert A. Kagan, 67–92. Cambridge: Cambridge University Press.

Tsebelis, George. 2022. 'Constitutional Rigidity Matters: A Veto Players Approach'. *British Journal of Political Science* 52 (1): 280–99.

Tsebelis, George. 2002. *Veto Players: How Political Institutions Work*. Princeton: Princeton University Press.

Tushnet, Mark V., and Bojan Bugarič. 2021. *Power to the People: Constitutionalism in the Age of Populism*. Oxford: Oxford University Press.

Ura, Joseph Daniel, and Patrick C. Wohlfarth. 2022. 'Greater Public Confidence in the US Supreme Court Predicts More Jurisdiction Stripping'. *Political Science Research and Methods* 10 (4): 831–39.

Vanberg, Georg. 2015. 'Constitutional Courts in Comparative Perspective: A Theoretical Assessment'. *Annual Review of Political Science* 18: 167–85.

Voeten, Erik. 2020. 'Populism and Backlashes against International Courts'. Perspectives on Politics 18 (2): 407–22.

Whittington, Keith E. 2005. '"Interpose Your Friendly Hand": Political Supports for the Exercise of Judicial Review by the United States Supreme Court'. *American Political Science Review* 99 (4): 583–96.

Whittington, Keith E. 2003. 'Legislative Sanctions and the Strategic Environment of Judicial Review'. *International Journal of Constitutional Law* 1: 446–474.

Weinshall-Margel, Keren. 2011. 'Attitudinal and Neo-Institutional Models of Supreme Court Decision Making: An Empirical and Comparative Perspective from Israel'. *Journal of Empirical Legal Studies* 8 (3): 556–86.

CHAPTER 34

DEVELOPING JUDICIAL INDEPENDENCE

BRAD EPPERLY

1. Introduction

Judicial behaviour—the subject of this *Handbook*—occurs in the context of judicial–executive and judicial–legislative relationships. While the study of such behaviour is vital, this chapter focuses not on judicial behaviour per se but rather on the development of judicial independence, because an institutional environment enabling independent courts is a necessary precursor to any discussion of judicial behaviour being meaningfully determined by factors other than the preferences of the political branches. The last twenty years have seen significant attention to the question of judicial independence among comparativists studying law and politics, with many arguing that the question of 'why independent courts?' is *the* central question for comparative law and courts research (Vanberg 2015; Epperly 2019; Krehbiel 2022). In this chapter, I discuss advances that have been made in answering this question before identifying a number of challenges that remain in tackling this central puzzle. I then argue that work on the development of judicial independence does not pay enough attention to the related matter of judicial review, which is in fact critical for nearly every answer to the central question. Finally, I discuss the two most popular measures of judicial independence, and how they are—or are not—effective after considering the critical import of judicial review in our explanations of judicial independence.

The fact that political scientists are increasingly paying attention to the question of judicial independence is evidenced by the fact that overviews of the topic are numerous. In recent years, the *Annual Review of Political Science* has featured two exemplary pieces on the question, the first by Helmke and Rosenbluth (2009), the second by Vanberg (2015). Such synthetic accounts have not been limited to the *Annual Review*, however, with scholars offering general discussions of the question of judicial independence elsewhere (Ríos-Figueroa and Staton 2014; Epperly and Lineberger 2017; Staton 2017), as well as examining the role of judicial independence in accounts of law and courts in specific contexts, such as autocratic regimes (Moustafa and Ginsburg 2008; Moustafa 2014). Recognizing these contributions, and wanting to neither reinvent the wheel nor repeat myself (or others), this chapter's review section focuses specifically on recent developments, focusing on work published after 2014. Similarly, I refrain from offering readers any detailed summaries of popular explanations for judicial independence, and proceed assuming they have previously encountered important existing accounts, such as insurance or public support-based theories.[1]

This chapter proceeds as follows. In section 2, I discuss recent research examining the development of judicial independence, first assessing advances in the insurance model, then work critical of its electoral argument, and finally alternative explanations to competition-based accounts. In section 3, I identify a number of challenges remaining for comparative law and courts research on independence, including challenges at the conceptual and theoretical levels regarding the relevant actors in question, the parameters of their expected utility calculations, and what threats they face. In section 4, I present an argument for the need to explicitly integrate the question of judicial review into our accounts of independence. Such a move is critical because despite almost all existing theories explaining the development of (and variation in) independence being predicated on the power and exercise of judicial review, few take into account the fact that review conditions the benefits of (in)dependent courts. Building on this, in section 5 I assess how existing measures of *de facto* independence handle the question of judicial review, and show how failure to adequately do so leads to measures lacking face validity.

2. Recent Advances in Explaining Independence

As much recent work on judicial independence in the comparative law and courts literature could be dichotomized into what engages (supportive or critical) the insurance model and what offers non-electoral explanations, this section follows suit. First, I discuss recent research advancing or challenging the insurance model. I then discuss work focusing on other factors explaining independent courts.

2.1 The Insurance Model

In 2003, Ginsburg (2003) and Stephenson (2003) each published an important early work stressing the critical role electoral competition plays in determining judicial independence, with the former popularizing the term 'insurance model'; the subsequent decade saw the insurance model applied to a host of new cases and, far more rarely, tested quantitatively and cross-nationally. While these years saw much attention to the insurance model, and its widespread application to different country cases, there was little corresponding development of the model, either with regards to its causal logics or scope conditions. Put differently: while many leveraged this electoral account to better understand the development of judicial independence in a wide variety of democratic countries, there was minimal attention to how these applications of the insurance model might allow us to refine or reformulate its logics or insights. Since 2014, this has not been the case. Rather than case studies of the insurance model applied to one or a handful of countries, work has expanded the scope of the insurance model, and, to a lesser degree, attempted to make advances in the theoretical framework itself.

In classic insurance accounts, the thing being insured against is policy change. A promising area of advancement is the realization, however, that independent courts can offer different kinds of insurance. Building on the argument that independent courts also provide personal insurance to leaders (Epperly 2013), Dixon and Ginsburg (2017) introduce a typology of risks that leaders might want to insure against. Beyond offering insurance to their policies and persons, independent courts also offer insurance to power; that is, more independent courts are more able to ensure access to the political arena, inhibiting partisan lockout and electoral manipulation. Dixon and Ginsburg's conceptual insight has already found its way into empirical work. In an article investigating what leads to investigations of former executives, Bahry and Kim (2021) demonstrate that more independent courts are a strong predictor of a safe post-tenure fate. Similarly, while critical of the contention that electoral competition leads to more independence, Helmke, Jeong, and Kim (2022) offer persuasive evidence supporting the idea that more independent judiciaries provide more personal insurance for executives.

An exciting new development in the insurance framework is offered by Krehbiel (2022). Taking seriously the framework's electoral logic, he teases out the implication that competition affects not only political actors' preferences regarding the behavioural independence of courts but also induces those in power to engage in institutional change so that those independent courts are more able to affect policy. Looking at the establishment of panel systems, Krehbiel argues that incumbents in highly competitive electoral environments (where better insurance policies are more desirable) are more likely to create panel systems on high courts, because doing so expands their caseload capacity, thereby allowing them more influence and thus more effective political insurance. Beyond its specific insights regarding panels, Krehbiel's piece has two further, important implications. First, unlike most work on *de jure* changes, it does not restrict itself to constitutional change but also assesses statutes, where much action occurs.[2] Second, the piece is an important early example of scientific development of the sort suggesting work on insurance is entering a mature stage of inquiry: rather than examining whether competition/insurance matters, Krehbiel uses the insurance model to build a further theoretical insight. In other words, if we take the insurance model seriously, what *else* can we learn about courts? In Krehbiel's case, it is better understanding when panel systems develop; let us hope this is the first of many pieces teasing out theoretical implications and empirical insights from the insurance model.

Perhaps the most significant advance to the insurance model of the past few years has been its extension beyond democracies. While early proponents dismissed the model's applicability to autocracies (Moustafa and Ginsburg 2008), competitive authoritarianism research demonstrates that there are autocratic contexts where elections—while neither free nor fair—matter. The insight that meaningful elections are not restricted to democracies has important implications for the study of independence. Although meaningful elections are far more common in democracies, in those competitive authoritarian regimes where they are present the insurance model's electoral logic should also obtain: if (i) autocrats do in fact worry about electoral defeat, and if (ii) courts are able to offer insurance in non-democratic regimes. Both (i) and (ii) can be answered in the affirmative: scholars of competitive authoritarianism demonstrate autocrats do worry about defeat, and there is evidence that courts provide insurance in both democracies and autocracies (Epperly 2013). I develop and test this theoretical insight, as well as a number of its empirical implications (Epperly 2017), finding substantial evidence of the insurance model's traction outside the democratic context. I further expand on this argument (Epperly 2019), formalizing the expected utility calculation faced by executives in democracies and dictatorships, arguing that the logic of the insurance model implies that the incentivizing effects of elections should be *more* salient in autocratic regimes. Building on the personal insurance argument discussed above, I show that the personal downside risks associated with losing office are greater for autocrats, and their need to buy insurance (in the form of an independent judiciary) is greater.

If expanding the insurance model's scope conditions to autocracies is arguably its most important recent development, it is probably also its most challenged. Building on the work of Popova (2010, 2012) and Aydın (2013),[3] research in this vein focuses not on how electoral competition induces executives to seek future insurance and bolster independence but rather how in unconsolidated or non-democratic states it induces them to weaken independence, using courts as tools to tilt the electoral playing field in their favour. A compelling recent example is Helmke, Jeong, and Kim (2022), who argue that political crises in Latin American presidential systems prompt executives to gut judicial independence. While the authors analyse both democratic and non-democratic polities without explicitly examining differential relationships based on regime type, their findings illustrate possible limitations to the insurance model outside the context of consolidated democracies.

2.2 Beyond the Insurance Model

While the insurance model might be the dominant explanation for independence (VonDoepp and Ellett 2011), it is hardly the only one. Recent work in comparative law and courts builds on three alternative (not necessarily competing or mutually exclusive) explanations developed prior to or in parallel with insurance accounts.

The first focuses on the role that courts play in providing information to political actors. As a general framework, this account is associated with Carrubba's (2009) work on the development of judicial power in federal states and international organizations, where courts play an information clearinghouse role. Building on Svolik's (2012) distinction between the problems of authoritarian control and power sharing, recent work on courts in autocracies focuses on the role independent courts play in ameliorating the latter problem. Sievert (2018) offers the best example to date, theorizing under what conditions the increased information more independent courts provide autocrats outweigh their costs. Particularly interested in the context of civil conflict, she contends that courts are uniquely placed to provide information on potential challengers, their resolve, and the likely cost of policy concessions.

While information is one benefit courts can offer, control of bureaucracies is another (Halliday 2004; McNollgast 2007). Of course, noting a benefit independent courts offer does not tell us when such a benefit will be viewed as important enough to induce judicial empowerment. In a new piece, Bertoli, Garcia, and Garoupa (2022) do just that. Looking at sub-national administrative courts in Mexico, they argue these courts are particularly attractive tools for new incumbents to constrain opposition-allied bureaucracies. Here, it is the need to buy insurance against recalcitrant bureaucrats today, rather than losing office in the future, that is key. Empirically, they find state-level electoral competitiveness unable to predict the expansion of administrative courts, and that it is those newly in power, rather than those facing electoral defeat, that establish these courts.[4]

The role of public support for courts, and the constraining effects it has on attempts to undermine judicial independence, is a major explanatory framework (Vanberg 2005; Staton 2010). While no recent work directly tests the role of public support in ensuring independence, a number of experimental papers test when the public might support courts that are under attack. Their conclusions are sobering. In a series of vignette and conjoint experiments, Driscoll and Nelson (2023) find little evidence for any meaningful electoral punishment for court curbing in the United States, corroborating prior research showing partisans disinclined to punish their side's attacks on democratic institutions and norms (Graham and Svolik 2020). These findings suggest public support models have more stringent scope conditions than previously thought:[5] those contexts of low to moderate polarization and/or partisanship, where there already exists enough support for/trust in courts for attacks on them to alienate co-partisans and independents (Engst and Gschwend n.d.).

I briefly summarize recent work in these three areas to illustrate the wide analytical breadth of current scholarship of the non-insurance variety. Drawing on various earlier perspectives explaining why independent courts might be beneficial, these recent works go further, laying out the conditions under which those benefits are likely to outweigh the known costs of independent courts. By and large, these theories are in no way mutually exclusive, either with each other or with insurance accounts. There need be no primary, let alone singular, answer to the puzzle of developing independence: information does not preclude insurance, nor does a need to monitor and sanction bureaucrats undermine an argument concerning autocrats use of independent courts to credibly commit to securing the property rights of foreign investors (Moustafa 2007;

Ma 2020; Chen and Wang 2021). Indeed, that last coupling shows it is quite the contrary: executives seeking to signal to investors their commitment to respecting property rights might also want to inform them of the tools they have to deal with recalcitrant state agents. The challenge of when each possible explanation might hold is but one challenge confronting comparative law and courts scholars going forward; it is to these challenges that I now turn.

3. Challenges to Explaining Independence

Naturally, challenges remain to improving our understanding of the development of judicial independence. While integrating disparate explanations into a grand narrative of independence is likely to be impossible (and probably ill-advised, regardless), our understanding of under what conditions each explanation is more relevant is not. Unanswered fundamental questions present further challenges; an example is an adequate account of the relationship between *de jure* and *de facto* independence. To date, despite no compelling answer explaining the (lack of) relationship between parchment barriers and actually existing independence, I nonetheless suspect that there must be some contexts in which *de jure* rules matter; finding out what those contexts might be is vital. A second example is the under-theorized and under-studied role of other powerful actors in developing independence. Beyond executives and legislatures, it seems likely that there are circumstances under which powerful private actors like economic elites, foreign actors like supranational institutions, or even judges themselves might be critical in developing and bolstering independent judiciaries. A third fundamental question that has received scant attention is the fact that many of the alleged benefits of independent courts—from political insurance to information to oversight—can be provided by other institutional arrangements. Given this, work on *when* actors choose independence as the solution to their problems is necessary.

While fully tackling even one of these challenges is far beyond the scope of this chapter, identifying some steps forward when dealing with these and other challenges is not. As such, in the rest of this section, I focus on three issues of conceptual clarity that all research on judicial independence can improve upon, and discuss how doing so will improve our collective attempts to understand the development of independence.

3.1 The Relevant Actors

Although some work on independence clearly conceptualizes and specifies the relevant actors, much, probably most, does so in only a cursory or ambiguous manner. This is most easily observed in work speaking about 'courts' generally, without specifying the precise type of courts that are of interest, leaving the reader to wonder whether it's a constitutional court, ordinary courts, specialized tribunals, or the judicial branch writ large. But this is not simply a matter of researchers vaguely speaking of 'courts' or 'executives' and leaving the reader unsure of the author's referent; more crucially, such vagueness inhibits better theorizing regarding the relationship between independence and its potential determinants.

Perhaps most fundamental is the question of who is doing the empowering. Even looking only at insurance accounts, references are made to political parties, non-partisan political actors,[6] and individual executives. Clearly articulating which actors are central in establishing, deepening, or curtailing independence is vital because different actors should have different preferences and beliefs. While in some cases it might make no difference whether it is an individual or a party as a collective actor that is deciding among strategies, in others it might be key.[7] In autocratic contexts, for example, the form of autocratic regime might be relevant: while Epperly (2019) argues that the risks of being out of office are greater for autocrats, that these risks *also* vary for leaders in military and dominant-party regimes (Escribà-Folch 2013) is ignored. Likewise, though the risk of civil conflict is vital in Sievert's (2018) explanation for independence in autocracies, the variation in conflict risk among forms of autocracy (Fjelde 2010) plays no role in her theorizing or empirics.

Similarly, despite the fact that comparativists have long examined how presidential and parliamentary systems affect incentives, constraints, and strategies, to date these distinctions rarely play an explicit role in theories explaining variation in independence.[8] One recent exception is Helmke, Jeong, and Kim's (2022) superb piece on Latin American presidents manipulating their high courts to stave off extra-electoral challenges. Here, the authors tie the incentive to manipulate the court specifically to the nature of presidential power, in particular the interaction between popularly elected presidents and legislatures, each able to claim a democratic mandate, and the latter sometimes able to force removal of the former, often conditional on the expansiveness of the constitutional powers afforded to the presidency. Yet this recent piece is the exception, not the rule: other work is silent on whether the executive in question is a prime minister or a president has relevance, despite the fact that presidents are often untethered to any long-standing political party, with all the implications this scenario has for preferences, time horizons, and potential access to non-judicial mechanisms for achieving similar benefits to those provided by independent courts.

The lack of clarity regarding who is doing the empowering produces three problems. First, it can mean under- or improperly theorized relationships, leading us to gloss over or ignore important factors that might condition our accounts. Second, it leads to worse empirics. If the form of the executive, nature of the autocratic regime, or the very court(s) in question matter, ignoring this means our empirical results—be they quantitative or qualitative—are likely to be flawed. Third, it hinders comparison across research and building a cohesive body of knowledge. When key actors remain unspecified, it is difficult for research to inform other work, and simply assuming different authors are speaking of a similar underlying logic, or even phenomenon of interest, is problematic at best and actively harmful at worst.

3.2 The Expected Utility Calculation

Rationalist explanations of judicial independence all share a unifying feature: recognition that since independent courts impose costs on political actors, all explanations must identify benefits provided by independence that can outweigh these costs. Therefore, implicit in all (and explicit in some) is an expected utility calculation on the part of the political actor(s) tolerating, bolstering, or attacking judicial independence: assessing the relative costs and benefits of (in)dependent courts, these actors pursue a policy to maximize their preferences. While this is obvious, less so in most independence research is the nature of the implicit calculation being made. At the theoretical level, most independence research makes reference to the costs and benefits of independent courts, yet in fact specifies neither. Although I illustrate these problems below with reference to the insurance model of independence, this insight applies to all rationalist explanations of independence; regardless of whether the benefit is post-tenure protection, lack of electoral backlash, or credibly signalling to foreign investors, political actors pursuing independence do so when they decide that adopting a strategy that does so will maximize their preferences.

Take work in the insurance vein as an example: from its first articulation to now, work almost universally leaves the parameters of the model undefined, and empirically treats most as constants (e.g. Stephenson 2003; Epperly 2017).[9] What, then, are the parameters in the insurance model, exactly? First are the *costs* imposed by an independent court. As noted above, these costs—constraints on incumbents' policy-making discretion—are critical in all explanations of independence because they are what produce the fundamental puzzle of independence. Second are the *benefits* provided by an independent court: Constraints on future incumbents. Like costs, these are fundamental to the explanation as they are the solution to the puzzle of independence. To explain variation requires some other parameter. In the insurance model, this is the *demand for insurance*, which in effect identifies when the benefits outweigh the costs. As noted, in existing work the costs and benefits provided by courts are treated as constant, and what is assessed is purported to be this demand for insurance: when high, executives pursue a strategy of establishing or respecting independence, whereas when low they decline to purchase insurance against being out office. While empirical work uses different measures for this demand, in all instances it is operationalized by the competitiveness of the electoral environment.

While most of the above is straightforward, clearly articulating these parameters can lead us to identify failures in our theorizing more easily and when our concepts are not being properly operationalized. The reader may have already identified one such failure above: the demand for insurance is not simply a function of the *likelihood* of downside risk but also its *severity* if it occurs. Think back to classic policy insurance accounts. Here, the likelihood of the risk is a function of the probability of political opponents gaining power. But that probability says nothing about the severity of this risk: a centre-right party losing power to a centre-left coalition is less worried about its policies facing wholesale reversal than one facing the prospect of losing power to a Marxist government advocating for widespread appropriation of private property and the nationalization of industry.[10] At the same time, a centre-right executive pondering whether to purchase insurance in the form of judicial independence will assess the demand differentially based on whether their Marxist opponents are a fringe group or a credible electoral threat.

Unfortunately, existing insurance work conflates these two aspects of the demand for insurance, and empirically holds the severity of downside risk constant, focusing solely on variation in the likelihood of losing office. This example of a recurring failure in insurance accounts highlights one of the major benefits of carefully articulating the expected utility models underlying our rationalist explanations for independence: the severity of the risk is not the same, and recognizing this leads to the obvious insight that the severity of policy reversals is dependent on the ideological distance between those in and out of power. Such an insight flows from clearly specifying the parameters, and its testable empirical implications illustrate the benefits of this clarity: whether those in power should be likely to purchase policy insurance is not a function of electoral competitiveness *or* ideological distance but the combination of both. A clearer articulation of what matters for the insurance model at the conceptual and theoretical level can thus offer substantial benefits for both theory and empirics. And while I use the insurance account as an example, the benefits of clarity extend to other explanations for independence, which also suffer from leaving key aspects of the underlying expected utility calculation under-theorized and/or under-specified.[11]

3.3 The Nature of the Threat

An astute reviewer once objected to insurance accounts saying political competition induces independence, pointing out it is not political competition that induces independence but *electoral* competition. This was not merely a semantic quibble or call for increased specificity: political competition, after all, can take a variety of different forms (one of which is electoral), and we should not assume each has similar effects on any given outcome, including judicial independence. In autocratic regimes, for example, political competition more often includes actors seeking to overthrow the regime, not just replace the government (they may or may not engage in armed struggle). It also often includes regime insiders who are very much a *political* threat, despite offering no *electoral* challenge to those in power.

Thinking carefully about the nature of the threat posed to those in power means more accurately capturing how dealing with that threat affects independence. Even if one concludes that an insurance explanation holds in autocratic regimes, it does not follow that empowering courts to insure against the downside risk of losing power in an election means such courts offer protection against those aiming to imprison, exile, or kill incumbents. Such risks—eminently political though they are—are extra-legal, and there is no reason to think an independent court able to inhibit politicized prosecution provides similar protection from coups, be they conducted by regime insiders or opposition groups. Indeed, pointing out that independent courts cannot insure against such threats is a non-sequitur, and in no way damning: insurance models seek to identify one factor that might lead those in power to pay the costs associated with independent courts. If the threat a given actor faces is not electoral, it is hardly a puzzle as to why they would not pay the price to ameliorate the risks associated with losing elections!

I stress the insurance model above only because I know it best, not because the insight that specifying the nature of the threat will lead to better research on the development of judicial independence is restricted to insurance accounts. Returning to Helmke, Jeong, and Kim's (2022) recent article should help illustrate the general applicability of this insight.[12] The authors focus on the role that 'political insecurity' plays in incentivizing presidents to manipulate courts. To do so, they expand the scope of the threat that presidents face. Theirs is not a story of Latin American presidents responding to the threat of losing office via elections but precisely the opposite: how these presidents, soon after taking office, respond to non-electoral threats, specifically 'legislatures invoking constitutional mechanisms to remove them, by protesters taking to the streets, or by some combination of both'. Helmke, Jeong, and Kim seem (to this reader) to structure their account as one that turns the insurance logic on its head, suggesting a competing account. Such a framing is unfortunate (and not only because their empirics are not able to reach such a conclusion) because it undercuts one of the most promising aspects of their important piece: highlighting a specific set of conditions under which presidential systems are problematic when it comes to judicial independence. That set of conditions consists of two political threats beyond 'normal' electoral competition; while it might be the case that these non-electoral threats deactivate the impetus electoral competition provides, they need not. I look forward to seeing an increasing amount of work on such divergent threats, and the conditions under which they incentivize actors to develop (or destabilize) independence, and the increasing recognition that what many see as competing explanations can be complementary.

Zooming out, one might say that an implicit theme of this section is that while comparative law and courts research on judicial independence is no longer in its infancy, it remains in an early stage of development. This is likely to be why much of it is still debates like 'competition: good or bad' rather than scholars carefully articulating the conditions under which competition is beneficial for independence, and those where it is inimical. It is likely also to be why there has been little in the way of sustained theoretical progress within any given explanatory model. I *think* that our area of research is rapidly maturing; I *hope* that more cogently articulating our theories in (at least) the three ways I outline above will speed the pace.

4. Judicial Independence and Judicial Review

In the previous section, I observe that rationalist accounts of independence share one commonality: a recognition that independent courts impose a cost on those in power, and thus any compelling explanation to the puzzle of why develop an independent judiciary must identify some number of benefits independent courts provide that outweigh their costs. Building on this observation, this section elucidates a second commonality: the importance of and explanations for independent courts—at least for comparative law and courts scholars—inextricably intertwine the twin issues of the independence of courts and the review powers they exercise. Properly recognizing the importance of courts in (and for) the study of politics requires recognizing that independence is important only in as much as courts have and wield judicial review, and that for review to be meaningful, courts must, practically by definition, be independent. Rather than thinking of these as separate and distinct concepts, they are fundamentally the same phenomenon in almost all comparative law and courts research; while some legal scholars might have interest in the *descriptive* question of whether or not courts face undue pressure, for *explanatory* comparative law and courts research courts are an object of interest because of their political role.[13]

Be it from a position of significant autonomy and power, or from one of dependence on those in power, it is this political role that is viewed as an object of interest, either as an outcome to be explained or as a key explanatory factor for other outcomes of interest. I do not labour under the misapprehension that this observation amounts to a novel insight; rather, I think that an understanding of independent courts as having policy-making influence and constraining political actors is implicit in nearly all recent comparative law and courts research. Despite this fact, however, even in research that explicitly links independence and review, each are presented as distinct concepts, even when they implicitly overlap. Making this linkage explicit is the contribution of this section; the implications of this linkage for empirical work using cross-national measures of judicial independence is the focus of the next.

Explicitly linking these two sides of the courts coin is important because both are needed to answer the central theoretical puzzle of studying courts comparatively: 'What explains the (growing) power and influence of the judiciary in democratic politics?' (Vanberg 2015, 168). Like others, Vanberg seemingly distinguishes between the two, using phrases (and section headings) like 'judicial independence and authority' and 'judicial authority and autonomy'. In application, however, his discussions of the various explanations for explaining politically salient courts integrate the two sides of the coin: independent courts are those exercising review, and review is exercised by independent courts. This is similar to the distinction between judicial autonomy and judicial influence that Ríos-Figueroa and Staton (2014) lay out, or between autonomy and power discussed by Epperly and Sievert (2019). For each pair of authors, judicial autonomy requires that judges be the authors of their own opinion, whereas influence (or power) requires that their decisions be respected and enforced by other state actors; courts are thus independent when each of these two sub-components exist. In his review of attempts to answer the central puzzle of the comparative law and courts literature, Vanberg groups theoretical accounts into two categories: endogenous explanations that identify the direct or indirect benefits of judicial review, and exogenous explanations focused on constraints that force policy-makers to respect judicial autonomy and power (even if they would otherwise prefer not to, for it offers no direct or indirect benefit). What unifies these explanations of how courts constrain executives and legislatures is that they require courts to be able to check policy. Absent this ability, any theorized benefits provided or costs imposed by independent courts dissipate.

Of course, one *can* imagine a discussion of judicial autonomy and power with courts lacking judicial review. In such a world, courts would have varying degrees of autonomy, from telephone justice-style dependent legal orders to legal orders where those in power rarely consider influencing ordinary court proceedings. And, naturally, the influence or power these courts have might similarly vary. One could, therefore, meaningfully have a discussion on, for example, the relative independence of courts in Prussia, France, and Russia in 1820 (or 1920, with country names appropriately updated), and in such a discussion the matter of judicial review would not appear. Yet such a discussion, while of historical interest, is not relevant for comparative law and courts research, for three reasons.

The first is that this is simply not what the scholarly political science (and political science-adjacent) literature on courts aims to do: when explaining the *political* role of the judiciary, we are by definition explaining its role as a policy-maker, and as such explaining its role in blocking, modifying, or mandating policies passed by the legislature and/or their enforcement by the executive (Stone Sweet 2000); that is, its power of judicial review.

The second reason—the global expansion of judicial power—is related to the first. That is, the goal of explaining the political role of the judiciary stems from the massive increase in the judiciary's importance in the post-Second World War era, which saw the widespread adoption of judicial review. If Stone Sweet and others are correct in their contention that, to paraphrase, 'courts are different now', then a discussion of independence that takes as its starting point an ideal-typical pre-Kelsenian judiciary faithfully and apolitically enforcing the content of a civil code requiring no interpretation is far from the correct discussion to be having.

The third reason involves the particular judicial object of interest that is usually the focus for scholars. While on rare occasion comparative political science work on courts focuses on specialized or low-level courts, such occasions are very much the exception. Instead, most comparative work examines high courts, defined as either the court of last resort or the body with constitutional review powers (Melton and Ginsburg 2014). Both theoretical and practical reasons have been offered. On the theoretical side, scholars argue that apex courts affect the entire judicial branch: whether dependent or independent, they set the tone for lower and/or ordinary courts, providing a floor/

ceiling effect that has implications throughout the judiciary (Ramseyer and Rasmusen 2007). On the practical level, doing so allows for a functional comparison across time and space, comparing like to like, rather than the diverse variety of courts found in any given country, many of which lack comparisons elsewhere. At its core, an apex court—whether US style or with original and sole constitutional jurisdiction like European constitutional courts—is deciding cases of high salience, rarely focused on settling questions of fact (with some explicitly forbidden from considering such questions), but instead questions of constitutional or statutory interpretation, and in doing so exercising a policy-making role.

In both sections 2 and 3, I discuss a number of frameworks for explaining the development of independence, including insurance, credible commitment, and public support models. A reader familiar with this literature will need little convincing that these explanations are predicated on the behaviour of courts that not only possess meaningful judicial review powers but as important regularly wield them. In insurance models, after all, it is precisely the ability and willingness of courts to block executive action that offers those in power the insurance against threats once they leave office;[14] this holds true regardless of whether those threats are political, personal, or policy related. Similarly, in credible commitment models from Landes and Posner (1975) to Chen and Wang (2021), it is the ability of courts to review and reject policies that make them attractive as they allow those in power to make binding commitments to interest groups or foreign investors. In fact, the causal logic of Moustafa's (2007) credible commitment framework implies that courts need not only be able and willing to review and reject state action but instead that they must do so with some regularity; if they do not, the signal that the development of independent courts seeks to convey to foreign investors would be uninformative. It is only by (i) exercising review powers and visibly constraining the executive from doing something that (ii) foreign investors know the executive would otherwise prefer to do that courts can (iii) signal the executive's credible commitment to respecting property rights. Similarly, in the causal logic of blame avoidance models (Salzberger 1993; Hirschl 2000), a court needs to be more than just able to strike down state policy, it must in fact actually do so with some frequency, and the public must be able to recognize this. If courts do not use judicial review to usurp the policy-making purview of the legislature or the enforcement powers of the executive, they can hardly be leveraged to avoid blame for unpopular policies.

Put simply, the comparative law and courts literature conceptualizes judicial review as an important component of judicial independence. Even more importantly, the theoretical accounts offered for explaining the power of courts and the respect for their independence—questions central to the subfield—in fact *require* the power of judicial review: if Hamilton was correct in Federalist 78 that courts are 'the bulwarks of a limited Constitution against legislative encroachments', then such courts must be active in pushing back against legislative encroachments. Judicial review is precisely how they do so. In other words, absent judicial review, our conceptualization of judicial independence is incomplete, and our theories of the development of independence fall apart.

5. Judicial Review and Measures of Judicial Independence

If the power of judicial review is baked into all our explanations for the central puzzle of our subfield, then our measures of independence, so vital for quantitative work, must also take seriously the issue of the power of—and decision to wield—judicial review. In this section, I discuss how the Latent Judicial Independence (LJI) and V-Dem measures address this, and present evidence suggesting that the latter routinely ignores the issue of judicial review, despite seeming on first glance to take seriously its importance.

While it was over a decade ago that Rios-Figueroa and Staton first circulated their (ultimately 2014) review of measures of judicial independence, the piece's assessment of the slate of options researchers have for conducting quantitative analyses of independence has been made obsolete. Not through any fault of the authors' cogent analysis (and, indeed, their theoretical and conceptual insights are as relevant as ever) but because in the intervening decade new measures have been introduced and have seen widespread adoption due to their improvements on both measurement and coverage. These are Linzer and Staton's (2015) LJI (Latent Judicial Independence) measure and measures from the Varieties of Democracy project, specifically high court independence and compliance with the high court. While the details of each are discussed at length by their authors, summarizing briefly each uses item-response theory (IRT) models to create point estimates (with uncertainty) of judicial independence in each included country each covered year. The original LJI measure draws on eight existing measures of and proxies for judicial independence.[15] As not all measures are available for the entire panel of interest, the IRT model is designed to borrow strength, using overlapping agreement between measures when available to weight which measures are available in what years in a better manner. The V-Dem high court independence and compliance with the high court measures are also produced by an IRT model, but rather than utilize existing measures of or proxies for independence in their IRT model, V-Dem uses surveys of country and topic experts, using their answers as inputs for the IRT estimates for each country-year. Coverage of the V-Dem data begins in 1789 for many—but obviously not all—countries and is updated regularly. While the V-Dem measures have not been used as extensively as the (earlier released) LJI measure, they have seen increasing attention in the last few years (e.g. Epperly 2019; Krehbiel 2022; Powell and Rothkopf 2022).

As the construct validity of the LJI measure is addressed at length in its presentation (Linzer and Staton 2015), here I focus primarily on the V-Dem high court independence and compliance with high court measures, which have to date received minimal attention at the conceptual level. Country experts are asked the following question regarding the independence of the country's high court, and asked to rate it always/usually/about half the time/seldom/never:

> *Question*: When the high court in the judicial system is ruling in cases that are salient to the government, how often would you say that it makes decisions that merely reflect government wishes regardless of its sincere view of the legal record?
>
> *Clarification*: We are seeking to identify autonomous judicial decision-making and its absence. Decisions certainly can reflect government wishes without "merely reflecting" those wishes, *i.e.* a court can be autonomous when its decisions support the government's position. This is because a court can be fairly persuaded that the government's position is meritorious. By "merely reflect the wishes of the government" we mean that the court's own view of the record, its sincere evaluation of the record, is irrelevant to the outcome. The court simply adopts the government's position regardless of its sincere view of the record.

When it comes to compliance with the high court, respondents are asked (with the same five answers): '*Question*: How often would you say the government complies with important decisions of the high court with which it disagrees?'

Given the V-Dem project is a political science undertaking, and its intended users are primarily political scientists, it is fair to assess the degree to which the conceptualization of V-Dem's high court measures tracks to what is known by and relevant for comparative law and courts scholars. At first glance, it would appear that these two V-Dem measures accurately capture the general consensus of what is meant by judicial independence in the literature. First, high court independence tracks the ability of courts to rule free of undue governmental influence, with judges the authors of their own opinions. Second, compliance tracks the degree to which rulings are respected by governments who disagree with them. In effect, these two measures capture the two aspects of judicial independence discussed above: autonomy and power/influence.

Closer inspection, however, suggests that there is major variation in *which* courts are being assessed and *what* expert reviewers are assessing when it comes to a court's independence. As noted, assessments of 'high courts' in systems with separate constitutional courts can examine those constitutional courts, or the highest appellate court. Despite not explicitly including constitutional review powers in its conception of high court independence, the V-Dem measure (usually) assesses the constitutional court in those countries that have one. For example, of the high courts that V-Dem assesses in the twenty-seven European Union member states, three-quarters are constitutional courts rather than apex supreme courts (with or without judicial review powers). This is not surprising, as most European states have adopted a model of constitutional review in which a court-like body separate from ordinary courts is empowered to assess whether legislation and state behaviour are in accordance with the constitution. It, however, illustrates clearly that the V-Dem measure aims to assesses the degree to which constitutional courts are autonomous and powerful, rather than the apex court of the ordinary judiciary.

This is, of course, of great import when considering the relationship between independence and review: judicial review is baked into the functioning of constitutional courts in a way it is not for courts of last resort. The latter spend significant amounts of time deciding cases where the government has little or no direct interest, whereas the former's task is largely assessing the constitutionality of state policy. This is not to say governments, or parts thereof, might not have indirect interests in the outcome of ordinary cases, but governments by definition have direct interests in the outcomes of cases to which they are parties. Therefore, when such cases comprise the overwhelming majority rather than a minority of cases a court hears, the court has far more ability to be powerful. And its autonomy, when present, is of a far more meaningful sort. The German Federal Constitutional Court (FCC) offers a prime example. Over 80 per cent of cases the FCC hears are constitutional complaints, almost all of which directly involve state action. Roughly two-thirds of the remaining cases it hears are preliminary injunctions (the overwhelming majority of which are against state action) or the specific judicial review of statutes (which obviously all involve state action). The Supreme Court of Ireland, a court of last resort with judicial review powers, serves as an excellent counterpoint: the vast majority of the cases it hears in any given year involve criminal and civil appeals, with no review of government policy or any direct interests of the state.[16]

Beyond variation in what courts are being assessed, V-Dem scores suggest that expert respondents in some countries assess the presence and use of judicial review in deciding the degree of independence, and that in other countries courts with zero ability to engage in judicial or constitutional review are assessed. As Stone Sweet (2000) and others have noted, the establishment of constitutional orders that guarantee individual rights demand an adjudicator of rights disputes; this in effect demands the creation of a constitutional court or similar body with the powers of judicial review, a fact which fundamentally altered democratic legal orders in and beyond Europe. And, indeed, in some countries there are visible improvements in V-Dem high court scores after the introduction of the 'new constitutionalism' in post-war Europe. In others, however, we see no effect: despite increasing demand for political courts with autonomy and power in new constitutional orders, we see no changes in measures reflecting these new circumstances.[17] In other words, in some cases the establishment of judicial review affects the data, while in (many if not most) others it does not.[18]

A brief examination of the Danish case illustrates a number of the issues arising from the way in which the V-Dem high court independence and compliance scores do not include judicial review, despite prioritizing the assessment of courts whose primary role is judicial review (an apt priority, given law and courts theories regarding independence require review). While chosen to best illustrate the problems with the data and a failure explicitly to include judicial review in their conceptualization of independence, examining Denmark is nevertheless a fair endeavour when it comes to the validity of the V-Dem data: it is a well-established and stable state, with the (nominally) same organ serving as the high court for centuries. Additionally, Denmark has long been a consolidated democracy, and is a country for which information is readily available.[19] Perhaps most important, the country is an exemplar of independence in the V-Dem data, one of only two countries to score top-five in both high court independence and compliance measures.

Figure 34.1[20] plots the V-Dem high court independence (solid grey) and compliance with high court decisions (dashed black) measures for Denmark for the full time period (1789–2017) covered by a recent V-Dem release, after normalizing the V-Dem IRT scores to a 0–1 interval.[21] Figure 34.1 illustrates three problems with how V-Dem conceptualizes judicial independence that the coding for Denmark demonstrates to the careful reader. The first of these is simply that it is clear from the data that expert respondents are conceptualizing judicial independence in vastly different ways, a problem observed for a variety of different cross-national perception-based measures. This can be seen best when looking at the scores for the first sixty years of time covered by the data. Prior to 1849, Denmark was an absolute monarchy, and the Supreme Court was formally an instrument of and chaired by the sovereign. While it is the case that the King rarely overturned acts of the Supreme Court, he nonetheless had the power to do so, and it did not go entirely unused; more critically, even after the King *de facto* left decisions to the Court (while remaining *de jure* chairman of the court), he did so with the caveat of excepting those cases that involved 'the question of the legality of the administration's conduct' (Guard, Skat Rørdam, and Jensen 2022).[22]

That is, the Court operated 'independently' (i) at the discretion of the King, and (ii) in those cases that did not involve any evaluation of the legality of the state's conduct. In other words, the Court operated in a manner similar to the ideal-typical operation of judiciaries in modern autocracies, whereby courts are allowed to be independent as long as that independence does not involve any credible commitment to independence, and as long as the autocrat is able to ensure disputes involving his or her interests remain outside the purview of such 'independent' courts (Ríos-Figueroa and Aguilar 2018). The compliance measure is similarly befuddling, as it goes without saying that the King would be likely to 'comply' with a Court whose rulings he oversees and which cannot affect his own behaviour. That the Court is scored as exceptional with regards to its independence and compliance by itself illustrates a failure to conceptualize independence

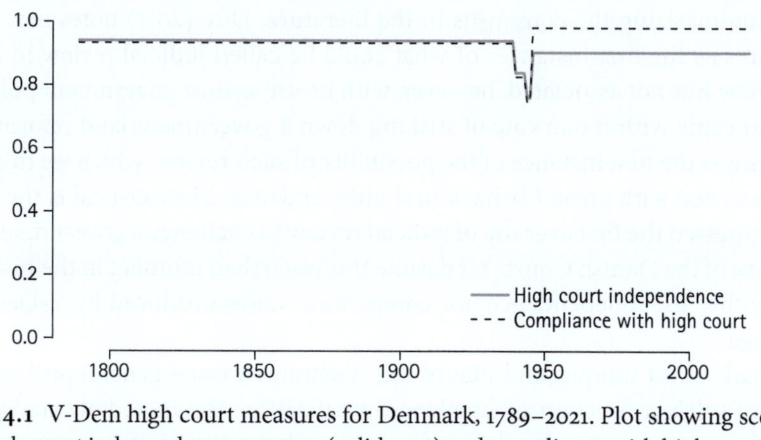

FIGURE 34.1 V-Dem high court measures for Denmark, 1789–2021. Plot showing scores of the V-Dem high court independence measure (solid grey) and compliance with high court decisions measures (dashed black) in Denmark over time.

adequately or consistently, but this fact is all the more apparent if one considers the Danish Court in the 1789–1939 period is, according to V-Dem, the third most independent court of the last 230 years of political history, surpassed only by the high court of the colony of New South Wales and the contemporary Australian court.[23]

Figure 34.1 illustrates a second problem: significant events that should affect the behavioural independence of the court are not captured in the conceptualization of independence employed by country coders. Further, the high levels of agreement among country coders in the Danish case, as evidenced by its exceptionally high score, demonstrates that this is not the problem of an idiosyncratic coding decision, but systematic misconceptualization of independence, with all the implications such systematic errors entail. Two important events that one would expect to affect independence and compliance produce no change in the Denmark time series visualized above. In 1849 and 1953, new constitutions were adopted. 1849's was incredibly important, ending absolute rule and establishing a constitutional monarchy with a bicameral parliament. Given it ended absolutism, and that multiple principals compounds the agency problem and increases agent discretion (Ward and Filatotchev 2010), one would expect an increase in independence; there is even greater reason to expect the 1849 constitution's removal of the King from his role on the Supreme Court would increase independence. The constitution adopted in 1953 was a typical post-war European document in that it established constitutionally guaranteed individual rights that were enforceable via law. As Tate and Vallinder (1997), Stone Sweet (2000), and Hirschl (2004) all argue, the establishment of judicially enforceable rights is associated with, or in fact sufficient for, large increases in the autonomy and power of the judiciary. As such, it is puzzling that it is only the end of German occupation in 1945, and not also the adoption of a new constitutional order eight years later, that is associated with increasing scores after the Second World War.

The third problem Figure 34.1 highlights involves the lack of any changes in *de facto* independence and compliance on those occasions where the Danish Supreme Court threatened or actually engaged in judicial review and the striking down of government policy. Summarizing the consensus in the literature, Duy (2015) notes that it was the 1910s that saw the first instances of what could be called judicial review in Denmark. Such review was not associated, however, with its *use* against government policy. While the Court came within one vote of striking down a government land reform policy in 1920, this was the first instance of the possibility of such review, which we might expect to be associated with greater behavioural independence. More critical is the year 1999, which witnessed the first ever use of judicial review to challenge a government policy in the history of the Danish Court. Yet despite this watershed moment in the history of the court, neither the independence nor compliance scores produced by V-Dem observe any change.

Denmark is not unique, and Figure 34.1 illustrates a more general problem, related to but not solely a function of (mis)conceptualization: the incredibly static nature of the V-Dem measures, despite aiming to capture a behavioural phenomenon which—if any one of the numerous theories forwarded by comparative law and courts scholars

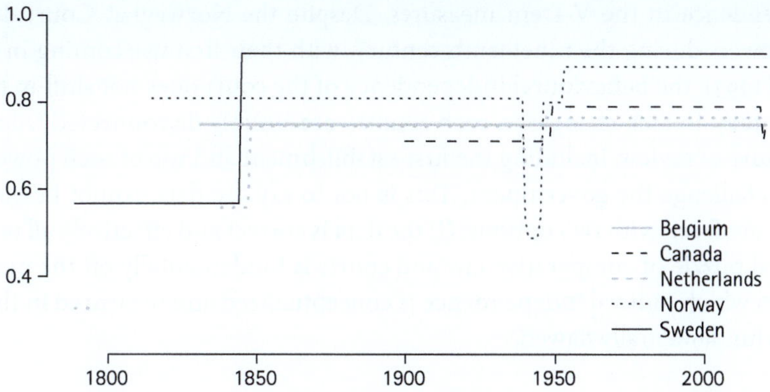

FIGURE 34.2 V-Dem high court independence for five countries, 1789–2021. Plot showing scores of the V-Dem high court independence measure in Belgium (solid grey), Canada (dashed black), the Netherlands (dashed grey), Norway (dotted black), and Sweden (solid black).

is even partially correct—should be expected to fluctuate over time. Figure 34.2 further illustrates this, plotting high court independence scores for five long-consolidated democracies. While the exact ranges differ, in each country save Canada we see zero change for an entire century. Sweden's court is a paragon of stability, observing no change from 1845 to 2021, despite judicial review being constitutionalized during this time period. From 1815 until the Nazi occupation 125 years later, Norway sees no change in its judicial independence, despite large changes in its domestic political environment (both *de jure* and *de facto*). Similarly, from 1848 to the Nazi occupation the Netherlands sees no change. Curiously, despite being occupied by the Germans in both the First and Second World Wars, according to V-Dem Belgium's court (unlike its neighbours') remained unaffected, and has never in its history witnessed any change in its level of behavioural independence—this despite V-Dem changing which Belgian judicial body was considered the high court during this period.[24] The only change in high court independence in Canada from 1841 to 2020 occurred in 1949, when appeals to the Privy Council were abolished and the Supreme Court of Canada became the court of last resort. That this is where we observe a change is most curious, given that (i) V-Dem codes the Canadian high court as 'NA' from 1841 to 1899; (ii) confederation occurred in 1867, which saw not only the creation of the Canadian state but also the Supreme Court of Canada; and (iii) 1982 saw the adoption of the Charter of Rights and Freedoms, which expanded the Court's autonomy and power (Manfredi 2004).

Such incredibly static measures make empirical estimation of the causes and consequences of *de facto* independence effectively impossible. They also fail to comport with what we know about the nature of judicial independence and review. With a small number of exceptions, judicial review of government policy scarcely existed until after the Second World War; law and courts explanations for judicial independence, however, require review as part of their causal logics. And yet each country listed in Figure 34.2 demonstrates that changing review powers play no role in the assessment of independence in the V-Dem measures. Despite the Norwegian Court developing review powers during the nineteenth century, with their first use coming in the 1860s (Slagstad 1995), the behavioural independence of the court does not shift in the subsequent century. In fact, changes in each country are entirely disconnected from changes in the nature of review, including the first establishment and use of such powers to successfully challenge the government. This is not to say the data cannot be correct, but rather we are faced with two options: (i) the data is correct and effectively all research on the central puzzle of comparative law and courts is fundamentally off the mark, or (ii) the way in which judicial independence is conceptualized and measured in the V-Dem project is fundamentally flawed.

5.1 The LJI (Latent Judicial Independence) Measure

In its original formulation, Linzer and Staton's (2015) IRT model of independence relied on eight measures analysed by Ríos-Figueroa and Staton (2014); in recent years, the LJI measure has been updated to include the two V-Dem measures among its components. As such, any of the systematic concept measurement issues in the V-Dem measure are included in the updated LJI measure. Due to (i) how the LJI measure was designed not to require full component coverage for each country-year, and (ii) the fact that the V-Dem measure project has asked coders to code every year going back centuries, this means the V-Dem components are likely to have significant leverage in the IRT model.

This is, in fact, what one observes in many cases. Figure 34.3 consists of two plots of the LJI measure for three of the countries shown in Figures 34.1 and 34.2. Subplot (a) on the left shows the original LJI measures for Belgium, Canada, and Denmark. These generally track with what we know about high courts in the twentieth century: the post-war era saw the expansion (slow in some places, rapid in others) of judicial power. The story is well known: the widespread adoption of judicially enforceable rights in post-war constitutionalism meant the judicialization of politics. This phenomenon was aided in EU member states by the establishment of the doctrines of direct and indirect effect by *Van Gend en Loos* and *Von Colson and Kamann* in 1963 and 1984, respectively, as these doctrines significantly empower domestic courts in the EU vis-à-vis their governments.

Subplot (b) on the right of Figure 34.3 show revised LJI scores, which include the high court independence and compliance with high court decisions measures from the V-Dem project (Staton et al. 2019). Comparing these lines to those in the left plot is instructive: the temporal variation captured by the eight-component IRT model disappears, and estimates look far more akin to the V-Dem scores on their own. Now, although here Belgium's judicial independence is not perfectly constant for the entirety of the twentieth century, its marked improvement from about 1980–1995 disappears (and the country's updated LJI score is, interestingly, almost identical to

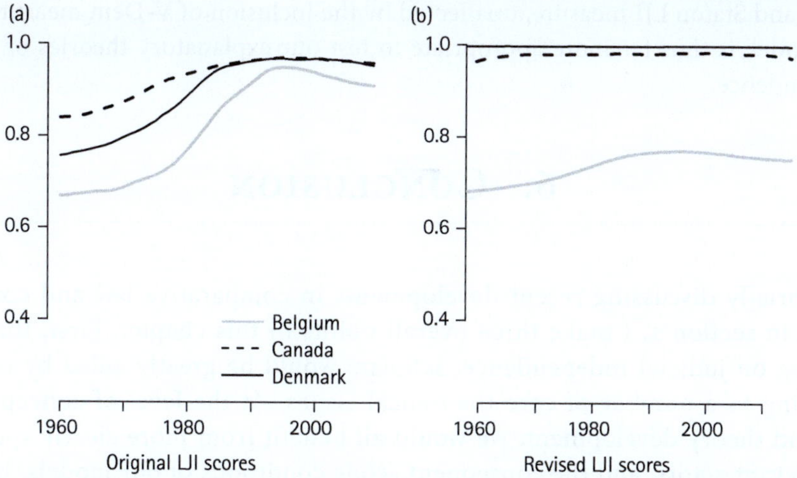

FIGURE 34.3 Original and updated LJI scores for three countries. Two plots showing LJI estimates for Belgium (solid grey), Canada (dashed black), and Denmark (solid black). Subplot (a) on the left shows scores from the original IRT measure based on eight measures of *de facto* independence. Subplot (b) on the right shows revised scores when those eight measures are augmented with the V-Dem high court independence and compliance measures.

that of Hungary after Orbán put the screws to the Constitutional Court post-2010). The inclusion of the V-Dem measures also largely removes the importance of judicial review in considering independence, and subplot (b) looks far more like Figure 34.2 than the original LJI scores: the Canadian court, using and wielding review a century before the one time its Scandinavian counterpart did so, is now always surpassed by the Danish court.

Put simply, the inclusion of the V-Dem components radically alters LJI scores. Whether or not a given scholar will think this is appropriate depends on the conceptualization of judicial independence they rely upon.[25] Two facts remain clear, however, and both are a function of including the V-Dem measures. First, the updated LJI measure fails to capture the global expansion of judicial power, the new constitutionalism, and juristocracy. Second, the importance of judicial review is attenuated in estimating independence scores in the updated LJI measure, as is evidenced by the exceptionally high score for Denmark. Whether or not any given comparative law and courts scholar thinks the nature of courts was meaningfully changed in the post-war era is unimportant; what is important is that any scholar who thinks the evidence shows such a change should be aware that the V-Dem measures, as well as the updated LJI measure, erase this change. Perhaps more importantly, in as much as our theories explaining the development of judicial independence are conceptually founded on courts able and willing to wield judicial review powers, using these measures to test models of judicial independence empirically is highly problematic. Using the original

Linzer and Staton LJI measure, unaffected by the inclusion of V-Dem measures in its IRT model, is thus far more appropriate to test our explanatory theories of judicial independence.

6. Conclusion

After briefly discussing recent developments in comparative law and courts research in section 2, I make three overall points in this chapter. First, that when working on judicial independence, scholars would be greatly aided by carefully attending to a number of core theoretical issues. At the level of conceptualization and theory development, we would all benefit from more clearly specifying the relevant actors, and the consequent scope conditions of our models. In doing so, explicitly laying out the nature of the expected utility model implicit in our theories would allow not only for improved theory development but also ensure our empirics don't go astray. Finally, as all rationalist accounts of the development of judicial independence focus on some threat to those in power than independent courts can help with, we ought to be more precise in specifying the nature of the threat, and its implications for the preferences, beliefs, and strategies of those empowering courts.

My second overall point flows from the first. While all rationalist accounts share a focus on the benefits independent courts can provide, they also share a commonality in their answers to the central puzzle of the literature. That is, all our theories of independence are predicated on these courts possessing—and wielding—the power of judicial review. I show how this is true for insurance, credible commitment, and blame avoidance models, among others. Similarly, the causal necessity of judicial review applies to our theories that explain the development of independence regardless of regime type, with review being as critical for Epperly (2019) as it is for Ginsburg (2003), and as critical for Moustafa (2007) as it is for Landes and Posner (1975).

I suspect my third point will be more contentious than my first and second. If, however, we take seriously the insight that judicial review is critical for our theories of independence, then we must also seriously examine the degree to which measures of independence include—or ignore—a court's ability *and* willingness to wield review. I do not intend to suggest that the brief discussion in section 5 is conclusive. Rather, I hope that this assertion of problems with popular measures of judicial independence is able to spark a conversation, and increases attention to the linkages (or lack thereof) between our concepts and measures, as well as issues of construct validity. While I am not comfortable asserting that the V-Dem measure's seeming inability to track existing knowledge on judicial autonomy and power means we should always refrain from using it, I am comfortable suggesting that, if it cannot get it right when it comes to stable Western democracies whose legal systems are closely linked with one another, then we should be even more cautious when it comes to the less easy cases.

Acknowledgements

Many thanks to participants of the Comparative Judicial Behavior Workshop at Hebrew University and the 2022 annual meeting of the European Political Science Association, with extra thanks to Benjamin Engst, Silje Synnøve Lyder Hermansen, Jay Krehbiel, Jeffrey K. Staton, and Geoff Sigalet.

Notes

1. If, for example, a reader is unfamiliar with explanations of independence highlighting the critical role of public support for the high court, I would encourage them to first consult Vanberg's (2015) excellent overview, and then—if appropriate—core works on the subject, including Vanberg (2005) and Staton (2010).
2. For a discussion of the importance of including statutory change when examining *de jure* independence, see Epperly and Lineberger (2017).
3. But see Epperly (2018), which shows how Aydın's substantive conclusions reverse after properly coding democracy.
4. While such a finding is consistent with the need to constrain inherited bureaucracies, the authors don't directly test this, or measure how loyal an inherited bureaucracy is to those formerly in power. As such, the results are equally supportive of any proposed reason for why parties new to power might develop judicial independence.
5. Epperly (2019) highlights a further limitation of public support models: they are predicated on sufficient levels of electoral competition, such that there exists a viable alternative political party able to capitalize on any attacks on the court (as well as a media free enough to shine a spotlight on them). If this is correct, then public support models are in some sense subsumed by insurance models, in as much as public support is only able to constrain in those circumstances in which the need for insurance also obtains.
6. These actors are often particularly relevant during constitution drafting.
7. Thinking back to the different forms of insurance (Dixon and Ginsburg 2017) is instructive. For a party, political insurance that decreases the risk of being locked out of power is likely a more salient purchase than individual personal insurance against politicized justice.
8. While it is the case some empirical models include covariates capturing this, these are treated as control variables—warranting at best a few sentences justifying their inclusion—not well-developed aspects of the theoretical story itself.
9. A partial exception to this rule are strategic pressure accounts that flip the relationship, as both Popova (2010) and Aydın (2013) contend the benefits of dependent courts are greater in less democratic regimes; in recent work I take a similar tack, theorizing that the benefits accrue differentially between autocratic and democratic regimes (Epperly 2019). While this is a step forward, it is but a small one, as it leaves any differential costs and benefits

unmeasured, assumes they are constant *within* regime type, and crudely proxies for these differences with a regime dummy or democracy score.

10. A possible response to this is that the benefit of an insurance policy captures the variation in this severity. But such is incorrect: the benefit is the insurance payout, or put more correctly the anticipated benefit is the likelihood of the insurance policy paying out. The above policy insurance example makes this clear: the severity of policy risk (e.g. expropriation and nationalization) is independent from whether courts are effective brakes on policy change.
11. I am not suggesting that all work needs to formalize this but rather that being explicit about each parameter improves individual research and the literature as a whole.
12. Alternatively, compare the nature of the threat identified in credible commitment accounts of independence (the need for better economic performance), and how it remains underspecified in both its original (Moustafa 2007) and more recent (Chen and Wang 2021) formulations.
13. There are, of course, important descriptive questions focused solely on whether courts are independent, with no reference to review powers. It makes sense, for example, to ask whether or not judges made decisions independently before the global expansion of judicial power created courts with review powers throughout the democratic world. Such a question is not, however, core in the comparative law and courts literature, and not what contemporary political science research on courts—as either outcome or explanatory variable of interest—seeks to understand.
14. One articulation of the insurance model might not require judicial review. In my personal insurance account (Epperly 2017, 2019), independent courts are less prone to engage in politicized prosecution. As this generally involves non-apex courts, and is not directly related to policy matters requiring review, we can imagine independent courts lacking review still being of some utility to executives (I thank Jeffrey K. Staton for this point). There are two reasons I am unpersuaded this is an issue in all but edge cases, however. First, because prosecutions of former leaders rarely stay with courts of first instance, as their seriousness invites continued appeal. Second, because the empirical implication would be that independent, review-less courts should be ubiquitous, because they provide clear benefits and impose no cost. The world does not corroborate this implication, however, with only a handful of democracies having what are generally considered independent judiciaries that either do not have or do not wield review powers.
15. An updated version also includes these two measures from the V-Dem project, extending LJI's temporal coverage to 1900. To assess key differences between these datasets, I first rely on Linzer and Staton's original eight-item measure of latent judicial independence.
16. Excepting, naturally, that the role of prosecutors in criminal cases involves state interests, albeit in a fundamentally different—and far weaker—way than does judicial review of legislation or executive action.
17. Then there are those instances which seemingly make no sense. In France, the Constitutional Council established in 1958 under the 5th Republic is observed to have less independence than any French high court under the 3rd or 4th Republics, despite the fact that V-Dem codes identifies the French high court from 1900 to 1958 as 'NA.'
18. Similarly, despite the common argument that EU membership and the (in)direct effects of the Court of Justice have empowered national courts, making them more independent of their domestic governments, such is typically not reflected in the V-Dem data.

19. Denmark is also less than 100 kilometres from the University of Gothenburg, where the V-Dem project is based, with a language mutually intelligible with Swedish.
20. Analyses are conducted using version 12 (full country-year) of the V-Dem data.
21. As the original scores range from approximately −3 to 3, I create an interval score treating the highest observed score for each measure as 1 and the lowest as 0. This produces a more intuitive measure, and allows for direct comparison with LJI scores.
22. Original Danish: 'I 1791 overlod kongen afgørelsen i enhver retssag til Højesterets suveræne bestemmelse bortset fra spørgsmålet om lovligheden af forvaltningens handlemåde'.
23. While V-Dem codes New South Wales as Australia from 1823 to 1900, this is incorrect. Australian federation occurred in 1901, with Tasmania, South Australia, New Zealand, Victoria, Queensland, and the Northern Territory established as separate colonies between 1825 and 1863. Also noteworthy is the fact that for the entirety of its existence, decisions of the Supreme Court of New South Wales were subject to appeal to the UK Privy Council, meaning it wasn't really either a constitutional or an apex court.
24. Pre-1984, V-Dem codes the Court of Cassation, then shifts to the Court of Arbitration (renamed the Constitutional Court in 2007). While this shift makes sense given the Court of Arbitration/Constitutional Court has review power, a change of organ to a body with significantly different powers curiously has no effect on behavioural independence scores. Similarly, major changes to its jurisdiction in 1988 and 2003 have no effect.
25. As Hirschl (2011) emphasizes, inattention to the Nordic cases in comparative constitutional law is curious and unfortunate, as the extreme weakness of judicial review in the region has implications for understanding the relationship between judicial review, democracy, human rights, and the rule of law.

References

Aydın, Aylin. 2013. 'Judicial Independence across Democratic Regimes: Understanding the Varying Impact of Political Competition'. *Law & Society Review* 47 (1): 105–34.

Bahry, Donna, and Young Hun Kim. 2021. 'Executive Turnover and the Investigation of Former Leaders in New Democracies'. *Political Research Quarterly* 74 (1): 199–211.

Bertoli, Paola, Adriana G. Garcia, and Nuno Garoupa. 2022. 'Testing an Application of the Political Insurance Model: The Case of the Mexican State-Level Administrative Courts'. *Journal of Economic Behavior & Organization* 195: 272–87.

Carrubba, Clifford James. 2009. 'A Model of the Endogenous Development of Judicial Institutions in Federal and International Systems'. *The Journal of Politics* 71 (1): 55–69.

Dixon, Rosalind, and Tom Ginsburg. 2017. 'The Forms and Limits of Constitutions as Political Insurance'. *International Journal of Constitutional Law* 15 (4): 988–1012.

Driscoll, Amanda, and Michael J. Nelson. 2023. 'The Costs of Court Curbing: Evidence from the United States'. *The Journal of Politics* 85 (2): 609–24.

Duy, Iris Nguyên. 2015. 'New Trends in Scandinavian Constitutional Review'. *Scandinavian Studies in Law* 61: 11–48.

Engst, Benjamin G., and Thomas Gschwend. n.d. 'Attitudes on Judicial Independence A Discrete Choice Experiment in Nine European Countries'. working paper, https://www.sowi.uni-mannheim.de/media/Lehrstuehle/sowi/Gschwend/Articel/202006_DCE-EU__1_.pdf

Epperly, Brad. 2013. 'The Provision of Insurance? Judicial Independence and the Post-Tenure Fate of Leaders'. *Journal of Law and Courts* 1 (2): 247–78.

Epperly, Brad. 2017. 'Political Competition and de Facto Judicial Independence in Nondemocracies'. *European Journal of Political Research* 56 (2): 279–300.

Epperly, Brad. 2018. '(Re) Examining the Insurance Model of Judicial Independence across Democracies'. *Journal of Law and Courts* 6 (2): 405–19.

Epperly, Brad. 2019. *The Political Foundations of Judicial Independence in Dictatorship and Democracy*. Oxford: Oxford University Press.

Epperly, Brad, and Monica Lineberger. 2017. 'Strategic Behavior of Comparative Courts'. In *Routledge Handbook of Judicial Behavior*, edited by Robert Howard and Kirk Randazzo, 370–88. London: Routledge.

Epperly, Brad, and Jacqueline Sievert. 2019. 'Conflict and Courts: Civil War and Judicial Independence across Democracies'. *Political Research Quarterly* 72 (3): 700–13.

Escribà-Folch, Abel. 2013. 'Accountable for What? Regime Types, Performance, and the Fate of Outgoing Dictators, 1946–2004'. *Democratization* 20 (1): 160–85.

Fjelde, Hanne. 2010. 'Generals, Dictators, and Kings: Authoritarian Regimes and Civil Conflict, 1973–2004'. *Conflict Management and Peace Science* 27 (3): 195–218.

Ginsburg, Tom. 2003. *Judicial Review in New Democracies: Constitutional Courts in Asian Cases*. Cambridge: Cambridge University Press.

Graham, Matthew H., and Milan W. Svolik. 2020. 'Democracy in America? Partisanship, Polarization, and the Robustness of Support for Democracy in the United States'. *American Political Science Review* 114 (2): 392–409.

Guard, Peter, Julie Skat Rørdam, and Torben Jensen. 2022. 'Højesteret'. *Lex DK*. https://denstoredanske.lex.dk/Højesteret.

Chen, Guorong, and Zhiyuan Wang. 2021. 'Climbing to the Top? How Globalized Competition for Capital Affects Judicial Independence'. *Studies in Comparative International Development* 56: 511–35.

Halliday, Simon. 2004. *Judicial Review and Compliance with Administrative Law*. Oxford: Hart Publishing.

Helmke, Gretchen, Yeonkyung Jeong, and Jae-Eun C. Kim. 2022. 'Insecure Institutions: A Survivalist Theory of Judicial Manipulation in Latin America'. *Journal of Law and Courts* 10 (2): 265–85.

Helmke, Gretchen, and Frances Rosenbluth. 2009. 'Regimes and the Rule of Law: Judicial Independence in Comparative Perspective'. *Annual Review of Political Science* 12: 345–66.

Hirschl, Ran. 2000. 'The Political Origins of Judicial Empowerment through Constitutionalization: Lessons from Four Constitutional Revolutions'. *Law & Social Inquiry* 25 (1): 91–149.

Hirschl, Ran. 2004. 'The Political Origins of the New Constitutionalism'. *Indiana Journal of Global Legal Studies* 11 (1): 71–108.

Hirschl, Ran. 2011. 'The Nordic Counternarrative: Democracy, Human Development, and Judicial Review'. *International Journal of Constitutional Law* 9 (2): 449–69.

Krehbiel, Jay. 2022. 'The Politics of Panel Systems: Political Insurance and the Organization of High Courts'. *European Political Science*: 1–15.

Landes, William M., and Richard A. Posner. 1975. 'The Independent Judiciary in an Interest-Group Perspective'. *The Journal of Law and Economics* 18 (3): 875–901.

Linzer, Drew A., and Jeffrey K. Staton. 2015. 'A Global Measure of Judicial Independence, 1948–2012'. *Journal of Law and Courts* 3 (2): 223–56.

Ma, David K. 2020. 'Explaining Judicial Authority in Dominant-Party Democracies: The Case of the Constitutional Court of South Africa'. *Comparative Politics* 52 (4): 625–46.

Manfredi, Christopher P. 2004. 'Judicial Power and the Charter: Reflections on the Activism Debate'. *Univeristy of New Brunswick Law Journal* 53: 185.

McNollgast. 2007. 'The Political Economy of Law: Decision-Making by Judicial, Legislative, Executive and Administrative Agencies'. In *Law and Economics Handbook*, edited by A. Mitchell Polinsky and Stephen Shavel. Amsterdam: North Holland.

Melton, James, and Tom Ginsburg. 2014. 'Does de Jure Judicial Independence Really Matter? A Reevaluation of Explanations for Judicial Independence'. *Journal of Law and Courts* 2 (2): 187–217.

Moustafa, Tamir. 2007. *The Struggle for Constitutional Power: Law, Politics, and Economic Development in Egypt*. Cambridge: Cambridge University Press.

Moustafa, Tamir. 2014. 'Law and Courts in Authoritarian Regimes'. *Annual Review of Law and Social Science* 10:281–99.

Moustafa, Tamir, and Tom Ginsburg. 2008. 'Introduction: The Functions of Courts in Authoritarian Politics'. *Rule by Law: The Politics of Courts in Authoritarian Regimes* 1:27.

Popova, Maria. 2010. 'Political Competition as an Obstacle to Judicial Independence: Evidence from Russia and Ukraine'. *Comparative Political Studies* 43 (10): 1202–29.

Popova, Maria. 2012. *Politicized Justice in Emerging Democracies: A Study of Courts in Russia and Ukraine*. Cambridge: Cambridge University Press.

Powell, Emilia Justyna, and Ilana Rothkopf. 2022. 'Domestic Constitutional Oversight and International Courts: Islamic Law States'. *Journal of Law and Courts* 10 (2): 319–52.

Ramseyer, Mark, and Eric Rasmusen. 2007. 'Political Uncertainty's Effect on Judicial Recruitment and Retention: Japan in the 1990s'. *Journal of Comparative Economics* 35 (2): 329–45.

Ríos-Figueroa, Julio, and Paloma Aguilar. 2018. 'Justice Institutions in Autocracies: A Framework for Analysis'. *Democratization* 25 (1): 1–18.

Ríos-Figueroa, Julio, and Jeffrey K. Staton. 2014. 'An Evaluation of Cross-National Measures of Judicial Independence'. *The Journal of Law, Economics, & Organization* 30 (1): 104–37.

Salzberger, Eli M. 1993. 'A Positive Analysis of the Doctrine of Separation of Powers, or: Why Do We Have an Independent Judiciary?' *International Review of Law and Economics* 13 (4): 349–79.

Sievert, Jacqueline. 2018. 'The Case for Courts: Resolving Information Problems in Authoritarian Regimes'. *Journal of Peace Research* 55 (6): 774–86.

Slagstad, Rune. 1995. 'The Breakthrough of Judicial Review in the Norwegian System'. In *Constitutional Justice Under Old Constitutions*, edited by Eivind Smith, 81–112. The Hague: Kluwer Law International.

Staton, Jeffrey K. 2010. *Judicial Power and Strategic Communication in Mexico*. Cambridge: Cambridge University Press.

Staton, Jeffrey K. 2017. 'Judicial Independence Research Beyond the Crossroads'. In *Routledge Handbook of Judicial Behavior*, 355–69. London: Routledge.

Staton, Jeffrey K., Drew A. Linzer, Christopher Reenock, and Jordan Holsinger. 2019. 'Update, A Global Measure of Judicial Independence, 1900–2015'. https://doi.org/10.7910/DVN/NFXWUO.

Stephenson, Matthew C. 2003. '"When the Devil Turns ...": The Political Foundations of Independent Judicial Review'. *The Journal of Legal Studies* 32 (1): 59–89.

Stone Sweet, Alec. 2000. *Governing with Judges: Constitutional Politics in Europe*. Oxford: Oxford University Press.

Svolik, Milan. 2012. *The Politics of Authoritarian Rule*. Cambridge: Cambridge University Press.

Tate, C. Neal, and Torbjörn Vallinder. 1997. *The Global Expansion of Judicial Power*. New York: New York University Press.

Vanberg, Georg. 2005. *The Politics of Constitutional Review in Germany*. Cambridge: Cambridge University Press.

Vanberg, Georg. 2015. 'Constitutional Courts in Comparative Perspective: A Theoretical Assessment'. *Annual Review of Political Science* 18 (1): 167–85.

VonDoepp, Peter, and Rachel Ellett. 2011. 'Reworking Strategic Models of Executive-Judicial Relations: Insights from New African Democracies'. *Comparative Politics* 43 (2): 147–65.

Ward, Damian, and Igor Filatotchev. 2010. 'Principal–Principal–Agency Relationships and the Role of External Governance'. *Managerial and Decision Economics* 31 (4): 249–61.

CHAPTER 35

CONCEPTUALIZING AND MEASURING JUDICIAL INDEPENDENCE

FRANS VAN DIJK

1. Introduction

Intuitively, independence is a straightforward notion. If I go to court, I want a judge who examines and decides my case only by being led by the law and who is not beholden to any public or private interests. I also want a judge with an independent state of mind who does not necessarily follow vested opinion. These wishes concern not only high-profile cases of citizens against powerful parties such as government and big business but also the myriad disputes among ordinary people and ordinary businesses. This intuitive understanding of judicial independence seems justification for surveys that ask citizens to what extent the judiciary is independent in their country.

Unsurprisingly, when examining the literature, the concept becomes more complicated. These complications are particularly acute if the intention is to measure judicial independence quantitatively, beyond the just mentioned perception surveys. To measure, one needs to be specific. Conceptualization for measurement, in particular with regard to level of abstraction, depends on the context in which it takes place and its purpose. In political science, the interaction of the judiciary with the other state powers and the level of independence granted to the judiciary are important research areas. In economics, the impact of the rule of law and, in particular, the independence of the judiciary on economic growth is an important theme. To test theories in both areas, much use is made of cross-national models. These cross-national models include judicial independence as—generally but not necessarily—an independent variable and often try to capture independence in a single metric which allows the ranking of as many as possible countries of the world. A substantial number of measurements are available and these have been combined to arrive at a best estimate of independence (Rios-Figueroa and Staton 2014).

At the other side of the spectrum of abstraction, there is the multi-dimensional perspective of the institutional design of judicial systems. In the previous decennia, the governance of the judiciary has undergone changes in many countries, for instance leading to the establishment of councils for the judiciary. Where governance structures were changed, new bodies had to make arrangements for the external and internal independence of the judiciary. Requirements had to be drawn up for independence and related subjects such as accountability and judicial self-governance. In Europe, this was done by judicial networks and, in particular, the European Network of Councils for the Judiciary (ENCJ).[1] This cooperation has led to the development of (minimum) standards for key areas of independence such as appointment, promotion, and discipline of judges and funding of the judiciary (ENCJ 2017). The follow-up question was then to what extent judiciaries are actually measuring up to these standards. This approach is inherently multi-dimensional, and single metrics are of no use. Obviously, what is sufficient detail for one purpose is inadequate for another purpose. These approaches—and what falls in between—differ not only in abstraction, but also in scope. In the single metric approach it seems of particular interest how the highest courts are behaving. In the multi-dimensional approach all courts are relevant. Furthermore, in this approach independence is not exogenously given, but subject to legal and societal forces as well as policy interventions.

This review gives an overview of conceptualizations of independence in the single-metric approach and in the multi-dimensional approach towards measurement and of measurement itself. The review has limitations. The sole focus is on measuring independence in a cross-country context, encompassing worldwide studies and regional studies. The regional studies are confined to Europe, where due to the legal and judicial development of the European Union much attention is given to the independence of the judiciary, the standards that should apply, and the measurement thereof. Another limitation is that the outcomes of studies that use measures of independence are not reviewed. This review is solely about the definition and measurement of independence.

Section 2 addresses the conceptualization of independence. In section 3, the available measures of independence and their constituent parts are examined. In section 4, the development that single metrics underwent is discussed, while in section 5 the multi-dimensional measurement of independence for institutional design is examined. Section 6 concludes.

2. Conceptualization of Independence

2.1 Intuitive Understanding of Independence

The independence of the judiciary is apparently something people care about. In the EU, a yearly survey among the general public and among companies is conducted specifically on this topic (EC 2022a, 2022b). The main question is: 'From what you know, how would you rate the justice system in your country in terms of the independence of courts and judges? Would you say it is very good, fairly good, fairly bad, very bad?' There is no attempt at definition. Most respondents have an opinion. On average in 2022, 11 per cent of the respondents do not know or give no answer. The differences in outcomes among countries are very large, ranging from 83 per cent in Austria and Finland, rating independence as good, to 29 per cent in Poland, 28 per cent in Slovakia, and even only 17 per cent in Croatia. In follow-up questions, the survey asks about reasons for a positive or negative opinion. Respondents are given three (not exclusive) options: interference or pressure from government and politicians, interference or pressure from economic or special interests, and the status and position of judges that are insufficient to guarantee their independence. From the answers, it is clear that respondents do not confine independence to the political sphere. The survey shows that people have—often strong—opinions about judicial independence.

2.2 Independence as Professional Attitude

Within the judicial profession, thought has been given, of course, to what independence means. The Bangalore principles of judicial conduct give an implicit definition of judicial independence: 'A judge shall exercise the judicial function independently on the basis of the judge's assessment of the facts and in accordance with a conscientious understanding of the law, free of any extraneous influences, inducements, pressures, threats or interference, direct or indirect, from any quarter or for any reason' (Judicial Group on Strengthening Judicial Integrity 2002, Article 1.1). To put it more succinctly, judges are only bound by the law (e.g. Van Dijk and Vos 2018).

Similar definitions can be found in the literature on measurement of independence. For example, 'a judge is independent when she does not respond to undue pressures to resolve cases in particular ways' (Rios-Figueroa and Staton 2014, 107). For later reference, I follow these authors by reserving the term 'autonomy' for this type of independence. The Bangalore definition is similar to that proposed by Becker, assuming the terms 'court' and 'judge' are interchangeable: 'the extent to which a court may adjudicate free from institutional controls, incentives, and impediments imposed or intimidated by force, money, or other extralegal, corrupt methods by individuals or institutions outside the judiciary, whether within or outside of government' (Becker 1970 as cited by Howard and Carey 2004, 286). A more restricted view can be found in Melton and Ginsburg (2014, 190): 'at its core it involves the ability and willingness of courts to decide cases in light of the law without undue regard to the views of other governmental actors'. It is the same idea but confined to governmental actors.

The Bangalore principles provide more detail. According to the principles, '[a] Judge shall be free from inappropriate connections and influence by the executive and legislative branches of government but must also appear to a reasonable observer to be free therefrom' (Article 1.3). Thus, appearance and perception play a role. One may wonder what a reasonable observer is. The Court of Justice of the European Union (CJEU) has a broader view: it extends reasonable observers to 'individuals' in general (CJEU, C-216/18, paragraph 66). The Bangalore principles also address internal independence in a rather tautological way: 'A judge shall be independent of judicial colleagues in respect of decisions which the judge is obliged to make independently' (Article 1.4).

2.2.1 *Connection with the Independence of the Judiciary as a Whole*

The definitions discussed above focus exclusively on the independence of the judge. The Bangalore principles recognize the institutional and operational independence of the judiciary to which judges are expected to contribute in order to uphold safeguards for the discharge of judicial duties (Article 1.5). The independence of the judiciary as a whole is logically a requirement for the independence of the judge. This is reflected in the case law of, for instance, the CJEU which defines organizational requirements for judicial independence, in particular with regard to selection and appointment as well as the discipline of judges. These requirements set standards for the governance of the judiciary, for instance on what constitutes a council for the judiciary that can be responsible for the selection of judges. In addition, diverse sources argue that sufficient (financial) resources are a necessity to allow judges to conduct procedures in the way and time they deem necessary for a fair trial (see section 3.4). The indicators for independence developed by the ENCJ provide an overview of the connections between the independence of the judge and the independence of the judiciary (see Table 35.2).

2.3 Independence as a State of Mind

It has been pointed out that a judge may be fully autonomous but still not act independently (Rios-Figueroa and Staton 2014; Van Dijk and Vos 2018). Without any pressure, judges may make decisions that are in line with vested opinion and current but obsolete case law, and they may be uncritical about current government or business thinking. This may stem from a shared cultural background. Climate change cases in several countries show the opposite (Setzer and Vanhala 2019; Smith 2019). In these cases, governments are held to account for not keeping their commitments under international treaties. There are also examples of conforming behaviour, where judges fail to protect citizens against government, despite the absence of undue pressure (Brenninkmeijer and Bish 2021). This is not only an issue for the highest courts. First instance and appeal courts may unquestioningly apply decisions of the highest courts despite flaws or changing circumstances.

2.4 Independence as Influence

There is an important strand of literature that views independence not only in the above sense as autonomy but also as influence, in the absence in general of the means of the judiciary to physically enforce decisions (e.g. Rios-Figueroa and Staton 2014). If parties can ignore judicial decisions or delay implementation, independence in the sense of autonomy does not have much meaning. Government agencies play an important role in enforcing court judgments regarding private parties in all areas of law. In addition, government is required to implement court decisions regarding itself, also when these decisions go against its interests. Apart from outright non-implementation, continued litigation without a purpose other than to frustrate inevitable implementation and procrastination of implementation after a final decision is rendered can and do occur regularly in many countries. The extension of independence to influence, therefore, is practically relevant.

It should be noted, however, that the extension to influence leads to a merging of concepts. For instance, the legitimacy of the judiciary is often defined as the legal and moral authority awarded to it in society to make decisions (e.g. Gibson, Caldeira, and Spence 2003). Authority implies that decisions are implemented. Conceptually, independence and legitimacy seem to merge. While there is a strong causal relationship between the two in the sense that only an autonomous judiciary is likely to gain legitimacy in the eyes of the population, the concepts are not the same. To keep the two concepts apart is consistent with legal thinking and judicial practice, as reflected for instance in the CJEU case law. As Prechal, a judge of the CJEU, argues in a recent discussion of developments in the case law of the Court, both the compliance with court decisions and the independence of the judiciary, in the sense of autonomy, belong to the core of effective judicial protection, a concept that has been developed by the court as legal doctrine (Prechal 2020). The cases that she describes with respect to independence as autonomy deal with other (material) matters than those with regard to the (non-)implementation of judicial decisions which may lead to the disabling of national laws and financial penalties.

2.5 Interaction between Concepts

A reason to measure independence as influence or power is that autonomy is not likely to exist without authority (Rios-Figueroa and Staton 2014). When judgments are not implemented by the government or other powerful actors such as 'big business', if they do not like them, it is conceivable that courts are reluctant to deliver judgments that they can expect will be ignored and/or lead to retaliation. It has been suggested—and empirically supported—that courts may have an incentive to dismiss or indefinitely delay such cases, and thereby avoid a confrontation that they may not be able to win (e.g. Ginsburg 2003; Herron and Randazzo 2003; Simmons 2009). If such strategic considerations affect judicial decisions, judges are evidently not independent in the sense of the definitions in section 2.2. It should be noted that for a court as a whole to act strategically, the judges must coordinate their decisions or the management (president of the court) must be able to influence the decisions of the judges. In both instances, the internal independence of the judges is breached (see section 2.2). In practice, different behaviours of judges are likely to occur at the same time, as developments in Hungary and Poland show (see ENCJ 2022 on Hungary). Some judges avoid confrontation, while others exhibit high standards of judicial conduct for reasons of principle, but they may also do so in order to reinforce public confidence in and, thereby, support for the judiciary. Under political pressure, it becomes visible that judges do not share the same values.

If strategic behaviour occurs, the measurement of independence as autonomy and influence is affected (Rios-Figueroa and Staton 2014). Implementation of judicial decisions by government does not signify judicial influence anymore, as the courts do not pass judgments that go against major interests of the government. The judiciary looks stronger than it is. Thus, one would observe a relatively low level of autonomy and, falsely, a high level of influence. It seems that these considerations support keeping both interpretations of independence separate.

2.6 Independence or Effective Judicial Protection?

Even broader (implicit) definitions of independence can be found, for instance, incorporating access to justice. Feld and Voigt (2003, 502) argue that without adequate access to justice a court is not effective in keeping government in check, and include access to justice as an indicator in their measure of (*de jure*) independence (see below). If ordinary citizens are not allowed to bring cases to court or, by extension, time and costs make it impossible for many citizens who seek judicial protection to actually bring cases, independence as autonomy, as well as influence, is of little use. Sufficient funding of the judiciary to keep court fees at an affordable level and provide for adequate legal representation would then become part of the definition of independence.

In this definition, judicial independence drifts further towards effective judicial protection. Again, according to the CJEU, effective judicial protection includes the rights of defence, the principle of equality of arms, the right of access to a tribunal, and the right to be advised, defended, and represented (C-348/16, paragraph 32).

2.7 Conclusion

Generalizing, the definition of independence differs between political science and economics, on the one hand, and law and legal practice, on the other hand. This is not an entirely satisfactory situation. Instead of stretching the definition of independence, the concept of effective judicial protection may capture better what many researchers want to measure when they measure independence. In the following, the type of independence (autonomy, influence) is specified, where necessary.

An unresolved complication is furthermore that, even when fully independent in all respects, judges may not display independent behaviour by uncritically following current opinion out of habit, cultural background, or deference to the highest court.

3. Measuring Independence

3.1 Motivation for Measuring Independence

As noted in the introduction, the way independence is measured depends on the purpose of measurement. Two major strands can be distinguished in the literature.

(1) Judicial independence is measured in a single metric for inclusion in statistical models. Judicial independence plays a role in diverse theories in political science and economics. In political science, the roles of the judiciary in a democracy (e.g. Howard and Carey 2004; Staton, Reenock and Holsinger 2022) and in ensuring human rights (e.g. Camp Keith 2012) are important themes. In economics, the interest in the link between institutions and economic development (North 1990) triggered economic growth theories in which the protection of property rights by an independent judiciary is an important factor (La Porta et al. 2004). To test such theories statistically, use is often made of worldwide cross-national comparisons, for which judicial independence has to be measured. The attempt at worldwide coverage limits the type of data that can be used. A number of measures have been developed, in the beginning for specific research and later on as part of a broader enterprise in political science (V-Dem) and access to justice in a broad sense (Rule of Law index). The availability of a number of single metric estimates of independence has led to a sophisticated aggregation of these measures into a best-estimate of independence, taking into account, for instance, missing variables (Rios-Figueroa and Staton 2014; Linzer and Staton 2015). In cross-national models, this aggregate measure is now often used.

(2) Judicial independence is captured in a multi-dimensional profile to assess the performance of judicial systems. Judiciaries, governments, and non-governmental organizations (NGOs) display the need for a multi-dimensional insight in the independence of judiciaries, often in a regional context (ABA 2022; EC 2022; ENCJ 2023). This need follows from the development of standards for independence, for instance with regard to appointments, discipline, case allocation, but also governance and funding. The next step is then to measure the attainment of these standards which in Europe has resulted in country profiles of independence that are regularly updated (most recently ENCJ 2023). Country profiles serve as a diagnostic tool by providing insight into weaknesses and strengths of the judiciary. The CJEU is increasingly playing a role here by setting and formalizing standards in many cases on issues about the independence of the judiciary stemming in particular from Poland and Hungary (i.e. C-619/18; C-83/19).

What stands somewhat apart is the Rule of Law index of the World Justice Project (WJP), which presents itself as the world's leading source for original, independent data on the rule of law (WJP 2021b). It takes the perspective of ordinary people and their experience with the rule of law. Judicial independence is not seen as a goal in itself. Still, several indicators are informative about independence as autonomy and as influence.

The differences between the two strands (and the Rule of Law Index) are not as large as they may seem, as in most single-metric studies the single metric is an aggregate of a set of factors. This set is smaller than in the second strain but covers some of the same key factors such as selection and appointment of judges. It is, therefore, of interest to compare the diverse operationalizations at the level of the underlying factors.

3.2 Object of Measurement

Judicial independence in the definitions discussed in section 2 and, in particular, in the sense of the mindset of judges, is not directly observable. Even apart from personal motivations, actual judicial decisions are often difficult to classify in terms of the underlying level of independence, making it not practical to gather data worldwide. This holds true a fortiori for independence in the sense of authority. To what extent judgments are implemented is often hard to determine (Kapiszewski and Taylor 2013). In statistical terms, independence is a latent variable that can be estimated by aggregating independence-related variables that can be measured. I am not going to discuss the methods available for aggregation. These methods have been explained and implemented by Rios-Figueroa and Staton (2014). Here, I am interested in the diverse aspects and manifestations of independence that have been measured. Figure 35.1 categorizes the objects that have been measured.

A classic distinction is between *de jure* and *de facto* independence (e.g. Feld and Voigt 2003). *De jure* independence concerns the legal design of the judicial system and its safeguards to guarantee and protect independence, as laid down in the constitution, law and/or court regulations. Countries differ in their use of these legal instruments. *De jure* independence can be used as an approximation of real (*de facto*) independence, if it is assumed that a higher level of *de jure* independence leads to a higher level of *de facto* independence. This assumption is regularly made. For instance, Hayo and Voigt put it this way: 'we suggest that providing broader de jure support for [judicial independence] in the constitution may enhance de facto [judicial independence]' (2016, 6). While this is a sensible assumption, the relation between *de jure* and *de facto* independence is tenuous in practice (see below).

De jure independence	*De facto* independence			
Legal design and safeguards	Actual implementation of design/safeguards	Independent behaviour observable in court	Independent decisions	Societal outcomes made possible by independence

FIGURE 35.1 Object of measurement of independence.

De facto independence has been researched in several ways. In relation to *de jure* protections, it has been tried to measure the actual implementation of these protections and whether this implementation had any effect on the subject of the protections. This approach has been pioneered by Voigt and collaborators. It does not assess whether judges actually behave independently.

The dominant approach to *de facto* independence is to assess independent behaviour of judges directly by means of questionnaires among experts and surveys among the population. This has been done in more or less detail, in one question or in a batch of questions, dealing with different aspects of independence.

Finally, independence can be measured in principle by means of societal outcomes that can only be achieved when an independent judiciary is in place. This requires irrefutable proof of a link between such phenomena and judicial independence. Next the different types of measurement will be discussed in some detail, but first the scope of measurement will be addressed in general.

3.3 Scope of Measurement

The judiciary consists of several levels. Independence is relevant at all levels, from first instance courts to Supreme Courts and, where these exist, Constitutional Courts. Except for the measurement of independence by societal outcome, all methods require a choice as to the courts that are considered. In most studies to test theories, for theoretical and for practical reasons the focus is on the highest courts, often interpreted as the court that reviews the constitutionality of laws. An argument is that the independence of the court that interprets the constitution is of primary importance for the interaction of the state powers. Another argument is that the judiciary is hierarchical: the higher courts are able to overrule the sentences of the lower courts (Feld and Voigt 2003) or, more broadly, the Supreme Court sets the standards and the lower courts follow (Melton and Ginsburg 2014). There are also practical arguments. It is much easier to gather data on the highest court than on all courts. In the words of Melton and Ginsburg (2014, 191), a focus on the highest courts makes the analysis 'manageable'.

Within this approach, a question is which is the highest court when a Constitutional Court and a Supreme Court coexist. The tendency is to see the Constitutional Court as such (Feld and Voigt 2003; Linzer and Staton 2015). Feld and Voigt, however, note that it can be argued that private law courts are more relevant for the security of property rights and investment behaviour than Constitutional Courts. Consequently, a single focus on Constitutional Courts seems problematic.

Multi-dimensional studies including the Rule of Law index, choose a broader scope, reasoning that the role of the highest courts is confined to a small number of cases and focuses on legal aspects rather than factual aspects. For citizens, their interaction with the first instance courts is generally their only interaction with the judiciary. In a court user-oriented approach, ignoring the independence of the lower courts is not meaningful.

As to scope, it should also be noted that studies generally ignore supranational courts such as the CJEU. This is a serious limitation. For instance, in the member states of the EU, the Treaty on the European Union overrides national constitutions and the judgments of the CJEU overrule those of Supreme and Constitutional courts, at least in the case law of CJEU. As a result, in countries where, for instance, constitutional review of laws by the judiciary is not allowed, laws can be reviewed against the treaty which contains many of the fundamental human rights protected by a constitution. The implication is that for a substantial group of countries (twenty-seven) the measurements, based on purely national characteristics of the judicial system, does not reflect independence accurately. This may well be the case for other regional groupings as well.

3.4 *De Jure* Independence: Design and Safeguards

Several operationalizations of *de jure* independence exist. Table 35.1 gives an overview of exemplary studies. As was already noted, studies differ in their scope by either focusing on the highest court or addressing the whole judiciary. Four studies consider only constitutional safeguards. While constitutions can be changed, in most countries it is much easier to change laws, let alone court regulations (Feld and Voigt 2003; Melton and Ginsburg 2014). This, however, does not mean that protections in law are irrelevant. In the ENCJ indicators, this is explicitly addressed by giving lower scores to safeguards in law than in the constitution. Obviously, this is easier to do in a regional study than globally.

As Table 35.1 shows, there are important common aspects in these studies. The presence of a guarantee of independence in the constitution is a recurring aspect, as well as tenure, appointment and removal of judges, the protection of their salaries, and the budgets of the court(s). On these aspects questions are, however, not the same. For instance, Melton and Ginsburg consider the appointment for life as essential, while Camp Keith is interested in guaranteed terms of office, whether judges are appointed or elected. Not surprisingly, normative considerations are reflected in the design of the indicators. As to appointments, an issue is who should select and appoint judges. This links with the governance of the judiciary. For instance, Melton and Ginsburg assume that appointment procedures that involve a judicial council (or multiple institutions) improve independence. The implication is that, also for the common aspects, the score of a judiciary does not need to be the same.

Then there are less common aspects. Some of these follow from a more comprehensive examination of court processes that affect independence, and are primarily relevant in studies that concern the whole judiciary (Camp Keith and ENCJ). The governance and management of the judiciary, case allocation, internal independence, and evaluation of judges fall into this category. Other aspects stem from a broader interpretation of independence. The two studies by Voigt and colleagues extend the definition to access to justice, transparency (publishing of judgments, including dissenting opinions), and

Table 35.1 Measurement of *de jure* independence

	CK 2002	F&V 2003	M&G 2014	H&V 2016/19	ENCJ 2023
Scope	Judiciary	Highest Court	Highest Court	Highest Court	Judiciary
Formal arrangements, guaranteed in	Constitution	Constitution	Constitution	Constitution	All legal documents
Method	Analysis of constitutions	Analysis by country experts of constitutions	Analysis of constitutions	Analysis of constitutions	Analysis by judiciaries with external validation
Single/multiple metric	Multiple	Single, average	Multiple	Single, factor analysis	Multiple
Number of countries	54–58	71	167	87	23
Aspects captured by indicators					
Court founded in constitution, combined with difficulty to change the constitution		x			
Guarantee of independence in constitution (including finality of decisions)	x		x	x	x
Tenure of judges (appointment for life, fixed term, no renewable term)	x	x	x	x	x
Appointment of judges (by whom, criteria, procedure)	x	x	x	x	x
Removal of judges (by whom, criteria, procedure)		x	x	x	x
Salary and/or budget protection	x	x	x	x	x
Governance (separate branch of government)	x				x
Ban on exceptional and military courts	x				

(continued)

Table 35.1 Continued

	CK 2002	F&V 2003	M&G 2014	H&V 2016/19	ENCJ 2023
Accessibility of the court		x			
Case allocation		x			x
Publishing of judgments		x		x	
Constitutional review		x		x	
Internal independence					x
Evaluation of judges					x

Notes: CK 2002: Camp Keith (2002), F&V 2003: Feld and Voigt (2003), M&G 2014: Melton and Ginsburg (2014), H&V 2016/19: Hayo and Voigt (2016) and Hayo and Voigt (2019); ENCJ 2023: ENCJ (2023).

reach of the judiciary (constitutional review). The link with independence is not always obvious.

Several topics are of interest to note.

(1) Research questions of *de jure* studies

The research in this field has its own dynamic. The earlier studies mentioned in Table 35.1 concern the impact of independence on societal outcomes. Camp Keith examines the relevance of judicial independence for human rights protection, where her hypothesis is that 'a truly independent judiciary is expected to be able to counter incursions upon individual rights by other branches of government' (Camp Keith 2002, 195). In their ground-breaking study, Feld and Voigt (2003) explore the link between economic growth and (*de jure* and *de facto*) judicial independence. However, two later studies are follow-up studies that address whether *de jure* independence has a (positive) impact on *de facto* independence (Melton and Ginsburg 2014; Hayo and Voigt 2019). This question has become a major discussion. The ENCJ approach is different as it concerns the institutional design of the judiciary.

(2) Choice and operationalization of *de jure* aspects

The selection of relevant aspects and the operationalization of these aspects in observable phenomena, for instance in constitutions, and determining what is good or bad for independence has been approached differently. Melton and Ginsburg describe the process as follows: 'we introduce six aspects of formal constitutions that we expect may enhance judicial independence in practice, explain how we operationalize those concepts, and provide some data on the prevalence of those aspects in constitutions written around the world since 1789' (Melton and Ginsburg 2014, 189). There seems to be a strong subjective element, perhaps less in the choice of indicators, but certainly in the operationalization. Hayo and Voigt present their choices without much argument.

Camp Keith has a different approach as she applies UN principles directly (UN 1985). Still, in the operationalization subjectivity is present. The ENCJ indicators are also based on international principles that were developed by a range of supranational (governmental and judicial) bodies over the years (Van Dijk and Vos 2018). Furthermore, principles were elaborated into standards, thereby reducing but not eliminating subjectivity. Subjectivity is problematic, in particular, if one wants to confront *de jure* and *de facto* independence. Research can easily become divorced from reality. As Feld and Voigt themselves remark, the ranking of countries on their *de jure* scale contains more than one surprise (see Feld and Voigt 2003, 523 for the ranking).

A related issue is whether it is advisable to aggregate the various aspects in one variable to measure *de jure* independence. Feld and Voigt and Hayo and Voigt do this, while this is not done in the other studies. Melton and Ginsburg note that 'those who wish to interfere with courts need only find one hole in the judicial armour' (Melton and Ginsburg 2014, 194). The implication is that a 'good' score on one aspect cannot compensate for a 'bad' score on another aspect. This point of view is shared by others (see also Rios-Figueroa and Staton 2014, 129).

(3) **Limitations of constitutional analysis**

Databases of constitutions offer important possibilities for multi-country research. It must be recognized, however, that constitutions are a function of the societies from which they stem, and of the times in which they were written. Democratic countries with the highest level of *de facto* independence tend to be countries with older constitutions. These older constitutions tend to have weaker *de jure* protection of judicial independence (Melton and Ginsburg 2014, 208). An alternative reasoning to reach a similar conclusion is that the length of constitutions is negatively associated with national levels of trust (Bjørnskov and Voigt 2014). Generally, a short constitution will also have a short text on the judiciary. For these countries, the focus on constitutions results in a low score on *de jure* independence combined with a high score on *de facto* independence.

(4) **Devil in the details**

The most comprehensive and detailed inventory of aspects of independence in the sense of autonomy has thus far been drawn up by the ENCJ. See Table 35.2. Obviously, these aspects need not be equally important. However, they are also interlinked. The allocation of cases among judges is a case in point. The standard is the random allocation of cases to judges, without back doors to intervene for instance by court presidents. If this standard

Table 35.2 Aspects of formal independence.

	JUDICIARY AS A WHOLE
1.	Legal basis of independence (formal guarantee of independence, formal assurance that judges are only bound by the law, methods for determination and adjustment of judges' salaries, involvement in legal reform)
2.	Organizational autonomy of the judiciary (governance structure, such as an independent Council for the judiciary or mechanisms for influence of judges in a ministry of justice model)
3.	Financial independence (funding system, budgetary arrangements, conflict resolution)
4.	Management of the court system (judiciary itself or Ministry of Justice)
	INDIVIDUAL JUDGE
5.	Human resource decisions about judges and court presidents (selection, appointment, dismissal, promotion, evaluation, training). Differentiation by type of court
6.	Disciplinary measures against judges
7.	Non-transferability of judges
8.	Allocation of cases (content of the mechanism in use)
9.	Internal independence (influence of higher ranked judges and of management, use of guidelines)

Source: ENCJ (2023).

is not met, discretionary allocation may lead to management determining the outcome of a case by giving it to a specific judge. The judiciary becomes easier to manipulate: most judges can be honest but the court corrupt, if management can allocate sensitive cases to a few corrupt judges. Without considering case allocation, a judiciary in which this happens can show a high level of independence. Also, the mere presence of a potentially favourable arrangement, such as a council for the judiciary, is not sufficient. A council has to be independent, that is not appointed or indirectly controlled by government or parliament. Poland offers probably the most disturbing example of a council that has been taken over by the government. The methodological problem is that small details can have major consequences for independence. Such detail is often not contained in constitutions.

3.4.1 *Conclusion*

The measurement of *de jure* independence is complicated, conceptually and practically. The ENCJ taxonomy suggests that in the available measures aspects are missing and that measurements are imprecise, due to the impact of difficult to observe but essential details and due to the heavy reliance on constitutions.

It should also be noted that nearly all aspects of independence in Tables 35.1 and 35.2 concern the autonomy of the judiciary. The authority of judges is either not addressed in these studies or there are no safeguards in constitutions and law.

3.5 *De Facto* Independence: Implementation of Design/Safeguards

An interesting operationalization of *de facto* independence is by Feld and Voigt (2003) with robust outcomes (see Voigt, Gutmann, and Feld 2015 for a validation of their *de jure* and *de facto* indicators twelve years later). It is one of the few efforts to establish whether *de jure* safeguards are actually put into practice. This seminal study uses eight indicators, with respect to the highest ordinary court, that are, in principle, objectively measurable, thus without having to take recourse to perceptions. The indicators are well conceived and cover the following five topics.

(1) Term of office of the judges, consisting of the effective average length of office, actual deviations from the legal term, and incidence of removal of judges from office before the end of their term.
(2) Number of judges that have been replaced since 1960.
(3) Financial matters: whether or not the income of judges has remained at least constant over time in real terms. Same regarding the budget of the court.
(4) Stability of the legal basis of the highest court: frequency of changes of the legal rules. High frequency of change is thought to signal a lack of independence.
(5) Dependence of the court on the actions of the other branches of government to implement its decisions. The more frequent outside actions are needed, the less independent is the court.

The data has been collected by national experts. As in most countries, data is not available from official sources such as court statistics, these experts seem to have had to make assessments based on personal observation. The ranking of countries is again surprising (see Feld and Voigt 2003, 525). A general criticism on this intermediate type of *de facto* independence is that it is not proven that positive outcomes actually lead to independent behaviour of the judges (Rios-Figueroa and Staton 2014, 108). It remains open whether the safeguards create such incentives that their realization actually improves *de facto* independence in the sense of behaviour.

A second source of data for this type of indicators is the database on human rights by Cingranelli and Richards (e.g. 2014). While this data is not easy to classify as it also contain aspects of perceptions of judicial behaviour (next section), the database provides insight into the realization of specific safeguards, such as the actual tenure of judges. Data are derived from the country reports of the US State Department. This method is followed by other studies as well, as will be discussed below.

3.6 Independent Behaviour and Independent Decisions

Whether judges are only led by the law and not by political or economic interests should show in court by the way judges treat the parties, their procedural decisions, and final judgments. Judges should be free from any improper influence, and they should appear so to a reasonable observer (Bangalore principles, see section 35.2) and, more generally, to the parties/society in general (CJEU). Independence in the sense of authority should show by the actual implementation of (final) judgments by the parties. The common approach to measurement is surveying the perceptions in society on these matters, either of the general population or of specific groups (such as court users), or of experts. In recent years much progress has been made in this area. Earlier studies collected data to answer specific research questions. Emphasis has shifted to structural data gathering, often in broader data bases. Also, surveys are held on a regular basis. I will discuss these efforts in some detail below.

Illustrative of the earlier studies is research by Howard and Carey which addresses whether an independent judiciary is necessary for democracy (Howard and Carey 2004). It uses the US State Department assessments of the independence of the judiciary, with a focus on the highest courts. The study uses a coding in three categories, based on broad assessments of the degree to which (i) the judiciary functions in practice independent of the executive and legislature, (ii) is free from corruption and bribery, and (iii) affords basic criminal due process protections to criminal defendants. To offer meaningful answers to these questions, the reports of the State Department need to be based on extensive knowledge about the actual functioning of the judicial system in a country. For a broad categorization, this method seems to be sufficiently reliable, but it cannot be used for more precise measurement. More precise measurements can be derived from the structural gathering of data that is taking place in several contexts.

(1) **Rule of Law index of the WJP**: the largest undertaking about the functioning of the legal and judicial systems of countries is the Rule of Law Index (WJP 2021b). Its focus is strictly on final outcomes and not on intermediate results, such as the realization of safeguards discussed in the previous section. It is based on by far the most detailed questions to experts and to the general public. It does not give an aggregate measure of judicial independence, but it measures essential components.

One of these components is whether government powers are effectively limited by the judiciary. The scoring is based on questions to experts and to the general public. These questions address the freedom of the courts from political influence and the government's compliance with the decisions of the courts. To give an impression, the population poll contains the following questions: (i) 'Assume that the President [of the country concerned] decides to adopt a policy that is clearly against the Constitution: how likely are the courts to be able to stop the President's illegal actions?' (ii) 'In your opinion, most judges decide cases according to (a) What the government tells them to do; (b) What powerful private interests tell them to do; (c) What the law says' (WJP 2021a, 2). A second relevant component concerns the use of office for private gain (WJP 2021a, 10). Subjects of questions are bribery/corruption and the influence on final decisions of undue pressure from parties, criminal organizations, and government.

Results are given for the judiciary as a whole, and civil and criminal justice separately. In the aggregation process, autonomy and authority dimensions of independence are mixed up, but the database leaves room for other aggregations.

The index for 2021 is based on thirty so-called qualified respondents (in-country practitioners and academics) per country, surveyed between October 2020 and May 2021. The poll among citizens has a sample size of 1,000 respondents per country. Not all countries are surveyed in the same year, but over a number of years from 2011 until 2021 with most countries in 2017 and 2018. While impressive, the data does not provide precise time series and precise information about the current situation.

(2) **Varieties of democracy (V-Dem) database:** the database contains information about the political systems of the democracies of the world. It contains also data on the judiciary. The statements by which this data is solicited concern independence as autonomy ('… it [the high court] makes decisions that merely reflect government wishes regardless of its sincere view of the legal record') and independence as authority ('… the government complies with important decisions of the court with which it disagrees'). See the detailed codebook (Coppedge et al. 2023, 172). These questions are primarily about the 'high court' and about the judiciary as a whole. The high court is defined as the constitutional court, if it exists. In addition, data has been collected on judicial review, purges and attacks on the judiciary, court packing, and corruption. These questions partly overlap with the Rule of Law Index and are partly complementary. As to the methodology, countries are coded by country experts, guided by the above-mentioned code book. A minimum of five coders for each question is aimed for. V-Dem puts a lot of effort in selecting high-quality country experts for the coding. However, the empirical basis is much smaller than that of the Rule of Law Index.

(3) **Regional surveys on independence:** the discussion is limited here to Europe. As discussed in section 2.1, perceptions of citizens and companies about the independence of the judiciary are surveyed annually in EU countries (EC 2022a, 2022b). Importantly, these surveys also gather data on some characteristics of the respondents, including their experience with the courts. The sample size for the citizens survey is 500 and for large countries 1,000 (250 for very small countries). The large advantage of these surveys is that they are conducted annually and thus generate time series.

In addition, the ENCJ organizes regularly (currently every three years) a survey among the judges of Europe about their independence (ENCJ 2022). It contains questions on how they rate their own independence and that of all judges in their country, their perception of the implementation of judicial decisions by government that are against its interests, and asks judges about the respect for judicial independence of political actors, parties/lawyers in procedures, and the leadership of the judiciary. In addition, it addresses intermediate results, such as whether judges are appointed solely based on knowledge and experience (see Table 35.2 for the main categories). These surveys are restricted to the professional judges. A separate survey has been conducted about the perceptions of independence of lay judges (ENCJ 2018). The perceptions of professional and lay judges proved similar. The ENCJ has also organized surveys among lawyers, together with the Council of Bars and Law Societies of Europe (ENCJ/CCBE 2019). It proved, however, problematic to get a high participation of lawyers.

The comparison of the perceptions of these groups provides insight in the accuracy of perceptions. Van Dijk (2021) shows that the outcomes of the surveys for all groups are highly correlated, but that the means differ substantially. Judges are more positive about their own independence than about the independence of all judges in their country, judges are more positive about independence than lawyers and lawyers are more positive than citizens and companies. The differences among groups are larger, the lower perceived independence is by any of the groups. There are strong indications that judges are too positive and citizens too negative about independence. Lawyers occupy the middle ground, and are probably the best informed and least biased observers.

3.6.1 *Discussion*

It seems possible to get a much deeper and differentiated insight into independence than was possible until recently. There is a development towards more and better data about *de facto* judicial independence at a worldwide and regional scale. At worldwide level, data is getting a more solid foundation, by means of large surveys and experts that are carefully selected. Still, it would be valuable to conduct in more parts of the world regional surveys, in particular, to build time series that allow studying the development of the perceptions of independence over time.

3.7 Societal Outcomes Made Possible by Judicial Independence

A study frequently referred to is by Clague, Keefer, Knack, and Olson (1999). This economic study concerns the extent to which, globally, judicial systems ensure that contracts are enforceable and property rights secure. The study does not explicitly address judicial independence, but under the assumption that independence is the dominant factor to guarantee these rights, the degree to which rights are enforced is informative about actual independence. The study hypothesizes that better contract enforcement in general facilitates the use of sophisticated forms of money. As data is available about the latter, an approximation of the strength of the institutions of contract and property rights enforcement can be derived. For this purpose, they coin the term 'contract-intensive money' which is defined as the total money supply minus currency, relative to the total money supply. A high value of this ratio reflects that legal institutions are effective. The authors recognize that there are alternative explanations of different levels of contract-intensive money, but, according to the authors, these other explanations are not dominant. The study finds a positive relationship between investment and economic growth rates, on the one hand, and contract-intense money on the other hand, by means of a cross-national analysis.

3.7.1 *Discussion*

Studies of societal outcomes are very valuable. However, given the abstract level of analysis and the many factors that play a role, it is questionable whether such studies can deliver an accurate measurement of judicial independence as such.

4. Single-Metric Approaches

While *de jure* independence does not lend itself well for aggregation in a single metric due to the non-additivity of its components, this is less of an issue for *de facto* independence. Several of the studies discussed in sections 3.5 to 3.8 result in a single metric for *de facto* independence. Rios Figuera and Staton (2014) have combined thirteen cross-national measures of judicial independence, three of which concern (also) *de jure* independence and the other ten *de facto* independence, including the above study of Clague et al., to arrive at a best estimate of independence, taking into account that the underlying studies cover different sets of countries and different years. This methodology has been further developed by Linzer and Staton (2015) who use eight measures to scale judicial independence. The data covers the period from 1948 to 2012. An update has one more data source (V-Dem) and covers the period from 1900 to 2015 (Staton et al. 2019). The most relevant of the constituent measures have been discussed above. This single aggregate metric has become the standard for including *de facto* judicial independence in multi-country models. For instance, Hayo and Voigt, and Melton and Ginsburg, discussed above, relate these estimates with their measures on *de jure* independence.

It should be noted that the constituent measures are a somewhat mixed bag, in terms of definition (autonomy and/or authority), scope (highest courts versus whole judiciary), and relevance. The emphasis is on the highest courts and on independence as authority. Given the strong correlations between variables, this is not likely to be a large issue, when comparing dissimilar countries. For countries that are similar, the rank order is likely not to be precise. The conceptual diversity limits the value of this aggregate measure.

Given the improved data availability, it would be feasible to measure independence more specifically and differentiate between highest courts and the whole judiciary and between autonomy and authority. In particular, the Rule of Law and V-Dem databases allow a study of the relationship between these concepts of independence.

5. Country Profiles

A multi-dimensional approach to independence can be used to detect weak and strong points of judiciaries by measuring against standards and in comparison with other countries. While the Rule of Law Index presents country profiles of the whole legal and judicial system, profiles for the judiciary itself are provided by the ENCJ but only for (most) European countries. These profiles address independence in combination with accountability, based on the premise that in the long run the judiciary will not be granted independence if it is not accountable to society. Focusing here on independence, the profiles consist of the formal safeguards discussed earlier and, for *de facto* independence, of the perceptions of court users, citizens in general and judges. In addition, perceptions of corruption within the judiciary and trust in the judiciary, relative to other state powers are included. Figure 35.2 presents two country profiles with typical patterns. Previous editions were for the years 2017/2018 and 2019/2020. The profile illustrates for the example of Ireland that in countries where the judiciary has a tradition of independence formal safeguards are often weak, while perceptions of independence are positive and relatively equal among groups. Especially, in Central Europe, here Slovakia, it is the other way round. Formal safeguards have been adopted by a desire to improve real independence but in particular by strong pressure from the EU. Perceptions of independence by citizens are unfavourable and show a large gap with those of judges. Thus, strong *de jure* independence has not (yet) led to strong *de facto* independence. It should be noted that, in contrast, the steep decline of *de jure* independence in Poland has immediately led to a sharp decline of *de facto* independence, as measured by the perceptions of citizens (EU 2022a). This asymmetry seems to be caused, in particular, by the composition of the judges: 'good' judges have been replaced by 'loyal' judges at high speed in that country, while the reverse process would be complicated, if not impossible, by considerations of judicial independence.

A similar approach has been developed recently by the American Bar Association (ABA) for use by civil society organizations (ABA 2022). Its monitor covers comparable ground, but uses a broader definition, for instance by extending independence to the presence of appellate review and incorporating accountability and transparency. Its focus is on *de jure* independence but it includes threats and attacks on judges. The aim of the monitor is to find the 'pressure points' in a judiciary. It does not aim at quantification.

Each topic covered in the country profiles can be analysed deeper. For instance, Sipulova et al. (2022) explores judicial self-governance. Its indicators show in more detail than the ENCJ indicators that in judiciaries that have no independent governance institutions judges can still have influence in procedures that are relevant for independence such as appointment of judges.

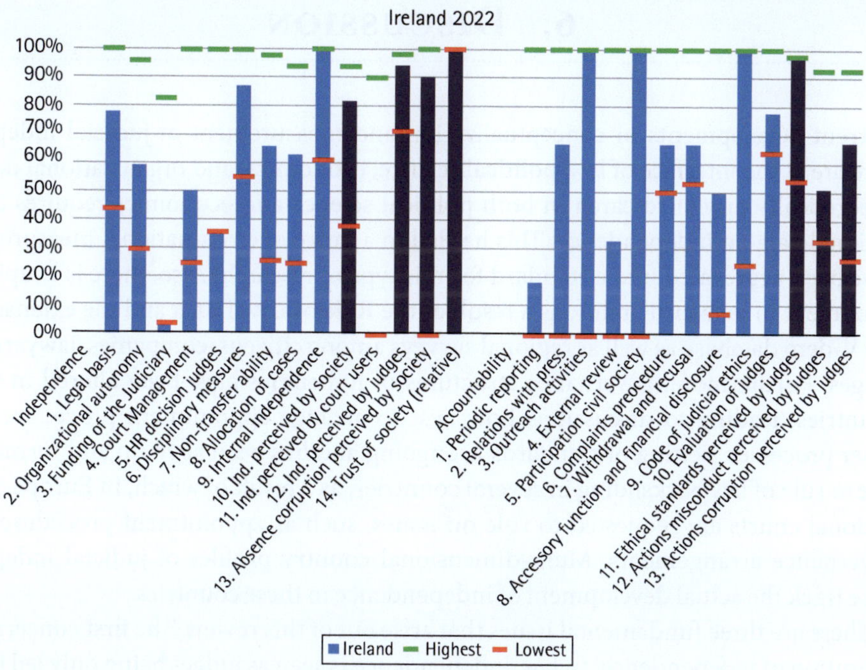

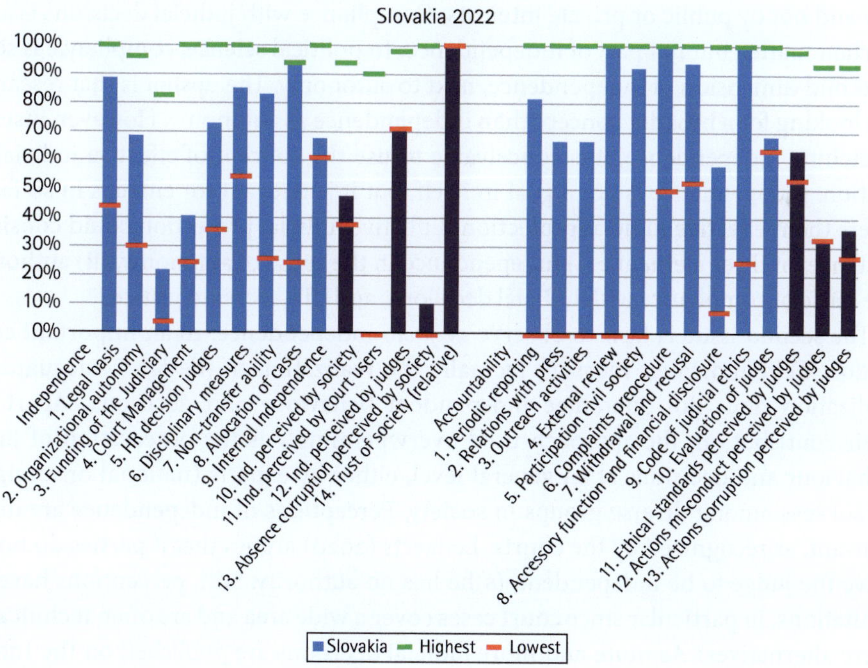

FIGURE 35.2 Examples of country profiles of judicial independence and accountability.

Source: ENCJ (2023).

Note: Formal arrangements of independence and accountability are denoted light blue and perceived independence and accountability in dark blue. Scores are between 0 and 100 per cent of the maximum score. Zero scores on perceived independence by court users is caused by the absence of court user surveys.

6. Discussion

Current developments in conceptualization and measurement of judicial independence are at the interface of law, political science, economics, and organizational design. Theoretically driven research in both political science and economics requires cross-national data on independence. This has led to a range of cross-national measures that have been aggregated into a standard for this type of research. Also, there is a rapid development in data availability, as a result of the Rule of Law Index and the extension of the V-dem database as well as regional surveys among citizens, companies, lawyers, and judges. Furthermore, governance structures of judiciaries have been altered in many countries, leading to discussions how best to arrange appointment procedures and other processes. Setting of standards is ongoing and has been sped up and formalized due to rule of law backsliding in several countries, as a result of which, in Europe, supra national courts are requested to rule on issues, such as appointment procedures and governance arrangements. Multi-dimensional country profiles of judicial independence track the actual development of independence in these countries.

There are three fundamental issues that arise out of this review. The first concerns the definition of independence. In law, independence is seen as judges being only led by the law and not by public or private interests. Compliance with judicial decisions is an important matter, but not part of independence. In political science, compliance is seen as a second dimension of independence, next to autonomy. The upshot is that researchers are looking for a broader concept than independence as autonomy. However, instead of stretching independence, it is conceivable to use the concept of effective judicial protection. Independence is not a goal in itself, but it is relevant for citizens in so far as it offers them effective judicial protection. Effective judicial protection could consist, for instance, of three elements: (i) independence in the sense of autonomy, (ii) authority in the sense of compliance with judicial decisions, and (iii) access to justice.

The second issue is how to observe *de facto* independence. In an important contribution, Feld and Voigt measure factually the realization of (*de jure*) safeguards, but realization does not guarantee independent behaviour and decisions. Apart from their contribution, the approach used overwhelmingly is the observation of judicial behaviour and decisions at an general level, either by experts (national or foreign) or by surveys among diverse groups in society. Perceptions of independence are directly relevant, as recognized by the courts. Lenaerts (2020) argues that if parties do not perceive the judge to be independent, (s)he has no authority. Still, perceptions have their limitations, in particular since court cases cover a wide area and are often technical. Are there alternatives? As more and more judicial decisions are published on the Internet, actual judgments may offer insight in important questions. Do judges rule against powerful parties, whether public or private, and what is the impact of these decisions? Are judicial decisions implemented, or are there many procedures for lack of compliance? The observation of these matters requires legal detail but brings independence closer to the actual behaviour of judges. While probably not applicable on a global scale, regional application could be feasible to bring independence to life.

Finally, purely national measurement does not suffice anymore, as, for instance, in Europe supranational arrangements and courts supplement national protections and have a direct impact on *de jure* and *de facto* independence. While supranational protections are far from absolute, they can also not be ignored.

Note

1. The ENCJ has been founded by councils for the judiciary which are its members. Countries with other governance structures such as Austria and Germany participate as observers. See Jackson (2023) for a detailed description of its working methods.

References

ABA. 2022. *The Judicial Independence Monitor. A Toolkit Developed by the American Bar Association Rule of Law Initiative*. Chicago: American Bar Association.

Becker, Theodore L. 1970. *Comparative Judicial Politics. The Political Functioning of Courts.* Lanham: University Press of America.

Bjørnskov Christian, and Stefan Voigt. 2014. 'Constitutional Verbosity and Social Trust'. *Public Choice* 161: 91–112.

Brenninkmeijer, Alex, and Bish Didel. 2021. 'Professional Ethics for Judges—Lessons Learned from the Past. Dialogue as Didactics to Develop Moral Leadership for Judges'. *Law and Method*. doi:10.5553/REM/.000057.

Cingranelli, David L., David L. Richards, and K. Chad Clay. 2014. 'The CIRI Human Rights Dataset'. http://www.humanrightsdata.com, accessed 11 December 2023.

Clague, Christopher, Philip Keefer, Stephen Knack, and Mancur Olson. 1999. 'Contract-Intensive Money: Contract Enforcement, Property Rights, and Economic Performance'. *Journal of Economic Growth* 4: 185–211.

Coppedge Michael, John Gerring, Carl Henrik Knutsen, Staffan I. Lindberg, Jan Teorell, David Altman, Michael Berhard, et al. 2023. *Codebook v13-March 2023*, V-Dem Varieties of Democracy. www.v-dem.net/documents/24/codebook_v13.pdf, accessed 11 December 2023.

Dijk, Frans van. 2021. *Perceptions of the Independence of Judges—Congruence of Society and Judiciary*. London: Palgrave Macmillan.

ENCJ. 2018. *Data ENCJ Survey on the Independence of Lay Judges, 2017–2018*. http://www.encj.eu, accessed 11 December 2023.

ENCJ. 2017. *Distillation of ENCJ principles, Recommendations and Guidelines 2004–2017*. http://www.encj.eu, accessed 11 December 2023.

ENCJ. 2022. *ENCJ Survey on the Independence of Judges 2022*. http://www.encj.eu, accessed 11 December 2023.

ENCJ. 2023. *Indicators Independence, Accountability and Quality of the Judiciary; Reenforcing Judicial Protection. ENCJ Report 2022–2023*. http://www.encj.eu, accessed 11 December 2023.

ENCJ/CCBE. 2019. *ENCJ/CCBE Survey among Lawyers on the Independence of Judges 2018–2019*. http://www.encj.eu, accessed 11 December 2023.

European Commission (EC). 2022. *The 2022 EU Justice Scoreboard.* COM(2022) 234.

European Commission (EC). 2022a. *Perceived Independence of the National Justice Systems in the EU among the General Public.* Flash Eurobarometer 503, https://europa.eu/eurobarometer. doi: 10.2838/685657.

European Commission (EC). 2022b. *Perceived Independence of the National Justice Systems in the EU among Companies.* Flash Eurobarometer 504. https://europa.eu//eurobarometer. doi: 2838/084544.

Feld, Lars P., and Stefan Voigt. 2003. 'Economic Growth and Judicial Independence: Cross-country Evidence Using a New Set of Indicators'. *European Journal of Political Economy* 19: 497.

Gibson James L., Gregory A. Caldeira, and Lester K. Spence. 2003. 'The Supreme Court and the US Presidential Election of 2000: Wounds, Self-Inflicted or Otherwise?' *British Journal of Political Science* 33: 535.

Ginsburg, Tom. 2003. *Judicial Review in New Democracies: Constitutional Courts in Asian Cases.* Cambridge: Cambridge University Press.

Hayo, Bernd, and Stefan Voigt. 2016. 'Explaining Constitutional Change: The Case of Judicial Independence'. *International Review of Law and Economics* 48: 1.

Hayo, Bernd, and Stefan Voigt. 2019. 'The Long-Term Relationship between De Jure and De Facto Judicial Independence'. *Economics Letters* 183: 1

Herron, Eric S., and Kirk A. Randazzo, 2003. 'The Relationship between Independence and Judicial Review in Post-Communist Courts' *The Journal of Politics* 65: 422.

Howard, Robert M., and Henry F. Carey. 2004. 'Is an Independent Judiciary Necessary for Democracy?' *Judicature* 87: 284.

Jackson, Erin. 2023. 'Inside European Judicial Networks. A Qualitative Study of Judges' Cross-Border Interactions and the Role of Networks from a Judicial Culture Perspective'. PhD diss., Utrecht University.

Judicial Group on Strengthening Judicial Integrity. 2002. 'Bangalore principles of Judicial Conduct'. Annex to ECOSOC. 2006. *Strengthening Basic Principles of Judicial Conduct.* ECOSOC 2006/23.

Kapiszewski, Diana, and Matthew M. Taylor. 2013. 'Compliance: Conceptualizing, Measuring, and Explaining Adherence to Judicial Rulings'. *Law and Social Inquiry* 38 (4): 803–35.

Keith, Linda Camp. 2002. 'Judicial independence and human rights protection around the world'. *Judicature* 85 (4): 195–200.

Keith, Linda Camp. 2012. *Political Repression: Courts and the Law.* Pittsburgh: University of Pennsylvania Press.

La Porta, Rafael, Florencio Lopez de Silanes, Cristian Pop-Eleches, and Andrei Shleifer. 2004. 'Judicial Checks and Balances'. *Journal of Political Economy* 112: 445–70.

Lenaerts, Koen. 2020. 'New Horizons for the Rule of Law within the EU'. *German Law Journal* 21: 29–34.

Linzer, Drew, and Jeffrey K. Staton. 2015. 'A Global Measure of Judicial Independence, 1948–2012'. *Journal of Law and Courts* 3: 223.

Melton, James, and Tom Ginsburg. 2014. 'Does De Jure Judicial Independence Really Matter: a reevaluation of explanations for judicial independence'. *Journal of Law and Courts* 2 (2): 187.

North, Douglas C. 1990. *Institutions, Institutional Change and Economic Performance.* Cambridge: Cambridge University Press.

Prechal, Sacha. 2020. 'Effective Judicial Protection: some recent developments – moving to the essence'. *Review of European Administrative Law* 13 (2): 175.

Ríos-Figueroa, Julio, and Jeffrey K. Staton. 2014. 'An Evaluation of Cross-National Measures of Judicial Independence'. *Journal of Law, Economics, and Organization* 30: 104–34.

Setzer, Joana, and Lisa C. Vanhala. 2019. 'Climate Change Litigation: A Review of Research on Courts and Litigants in Climate Governance'. *WIREs Climate Change* 10 (3): e580. doi:10.1002/wcc.580.

Simmons, Beth. 2009. *Mobilizing for Human Rights: International Law in Domestic Politics*. Cambridge: Cambridge University Press.

Sipulova, Katarina, Samuel Spac, David Kosar, and Tereza Papouskova. 2022. 'Judicial Self-Governance Index: Towards Better Understanding of the Role of Judges in Governing the Judiciary'. *Regulation and Governance*. doi:10.1111/rego.12453.

Smith, Don C. 2019. 'Landmark Climate Change-Related Judicial Decisions Handed Down in the Netherlands and Australia: A Preview of What's to Come?' *Journal of Energy & Natural Resources Law* 37 (2): 145–47.

Staton, Jeffrey, Drew Linzer, Christopher Reenock, and Jordan Holsinger. 2019. 'Update, A Global Measure of Judicial Independence, 1900–2015'. https://doi.org/10.7910/DVN/NFXWUO, accessed 29 November 2023.

Staton Jeffrey K., Christopher Reenock, and Jordan Holsinger. 2022. *Can Courts be Bulwarks of Democracy?* Cambridge: Cambridge University Press.

United Nations Department of Public Information. 1985. *Basic Principles on the Independence of the Judiciary*. New York: United Nations Department for Public Information.

Van Dijk, Frans, and Geoffrey Vos. 2018. 'A Method for Assessment of the Independence and Accountability of the Judiciary'. *International Journal of Court Administration* 9 (3): 1–21.

Voigt Stefan, Jerg Gutmann, and Lars P. Feld. 2015. 'Economic Growth and Judicial Independence, A Dozen Years On: Cross-Country Evidence Using an Updated Set of Indicators'. *European Journal of Political Economy* 38: 197–211.

WJP. 2021a. *Variables Used to Construct the WJP Rule of Law Index 2021*. Washington: World Justice Project.

WJP. 2021b. *World Justice Project Rule of Law Index 2021*. Washington: World Justice Project.

PART IX

COURTS AND SOCIETY

CHAPTER 36

PUBLIC OPINION AND LEGITIMACY

RUSSELL SMYTH

1. Introduction

Judicial legitimacy is fundamental to ensuring that the public accept the decisions of courts, which is expressly pressing for the courts given that, with few exceptions, they lack a direct electoral mandate.[1] Judicial legitimacy is generally equated with the courts having diffuse support, which, in traditional theorizing about legitimacy, is sharply delineated from specific support (Gibson 2017). Specific support is dependent on whether one agrees with the specific outcome in a given case, while diffuse support depends on a reservoir of goodwill that remains intact irrespective of whether one agrees with the specific decision (Scheb and Lyons 1999). Hence, one might not agree with the Court's ruling in a specific case, but still accept the decision because one fundamentally respects the right of the Court to make it. In this sense, it is often said that 'legitimacy is for losers' (Gibson 2015).

For a long period of time, the accepted wisdom, largely based on studies of the US Supreme Court, was that diffuse support was generally deep and durable and that it did not depend on ideological dissatisfaction with the outcome (Caldeira and Gibson 1992). This accepted wisdom has been questioned by a series of studies beginning with Bartels and Johnson (2013) that suggest diffuse and specific support are much more closely linked than previously thought and that diffuse support ebbs and flows with performance satisfaction.

The implications of these different perspectives are incredibly important. As Nelson and Gibson (2020, 76) put it, in the context of the US Supreme Court:

> The stakes of this debate are high. If the linkage between ideological disagreement and judicial legitimacy is tight, then the Court's likely rightward turn in the coming years could provide the basis for a steep, persistent, and substantively important

> decline in diffuse support. At the same time, if the Court's policymaking has only a tenuous connection with its legitimacy, then we should expect the Court's legitimacy to continue to remain relatively high and steady.

Gibson and Nelson (2016, 623) note the implications for judicial behaviour:

> A fragile Court is likely to act differently from a secure Court; or, more precisely, justices with heightened concerns about institutional legitimacy might even shape their votes in highly salient cases so as to protect their institution.

In this chapter I seek to provide an overview of the current state of the literature on public opinion and legitimacy of the courts. I first outline the competing theoretical perspectives and the courts and countries that have been studied. Following this, I consider the main data and methodological issues, outline the main findings, and provide a discussion of the challenges facing the literature and suggestions for future research.

A major conclusion that emerges is that the competing theoretical perspectives have produced conflicting results, leaving the literature somewhat in a state of flux on key issues such as the stability of legitimacy over time, the importance of policy disagreement and the relationship between diffuse and specific support. One of the main difficulties is that the findings seem to depend, at least to a certain extent, on the research design and how legitimacy is measured. Another issue with the literature is that much of what we know about public opinion and legitimacy of the courts is for the United States. While there are studies for other countries, the research designs and way in which legitimacy is measured are often lacking, making it difficult to draw reliable conclusions (Driscoll and Nelson 2020).

2. Theoretical Foundations of Public Opinion and Legitimacy

The traditional theory of legitimacy of the courts is couched in terms of positivity bias (Gibson and Caldeira 2009). Positivity bias states that diffuse support for courts is maintained through exposure to judicial imagery and symbolism, such as honorific forms of address, judicial robes, and majestic court buildings. In periods in which courts are salient, this imagery is heavily featured, activating pre-existing loyalties to the court and reinforcing the notion that decisions are made fairly, even if one does not agree with the outcome in a specific case (Gibson and Caldeira 2009). Hence, to know more about the courts is to love them more (Gibson and Nelson 2017). A key prediction of positivity bias is that exposure to legitimizing symbols will create a stock of goodwill that protects courts from attacks, meaning that diffuse support for the courts will be high and will remain stable over time. Positivity bias indicates that specific support, at best, should only be moderately related to diffuse support and that satisfaction with how the courts perform will be less important than more fundamental values about democracy (Gibson and Nelson 2015). Positivity bias also suggests that there will be little, or no, correlation, between individuals' ideological or partisan outlook and their perception of whether the courts are legitimate.

An alternative theory of legitimacy of the courts is subjective ideological disagreement (Bartels and Johnson 2013). Subjective ideological disagreement proffers that when the perceived ideological or policy distance between an individual and the court is high and the court hands down a decision with which the individual disagrees, the individual will view the court as being less legitimate. Hence, this theoretical perspective suggests that the relationship between specific support, measured in terms of subjective ideological dissatisfaction or policy disagreement, and diffuse support is much stronger than positivity bias would suggest and that the legitimacy of the courts is closely connected with their rulings (Bartels and Johnson 2013). The mechanism underpinning subjective ideological disagreement is motivated reasoning (Badas 2016). If an individual agrees with a decision, he or she tends to perceive that the court acted legalistically; however, if an individual disagrees with a decision, they perceive that the court was motivated by extra-legal political factors and that this undermines the court's legitimacy in the eyes of the individual. An important feature of subjective ideological disagreement is the argument that people do not pay close attention to the decisions of courts and that people form global views about the ideological disposition of the court on the basis of a few well-publicized decisions.

3. Breadth of Coverage

These competing theories of public opinion and legitimacy have been tested for myriad courts. Many of the seminal studies in the literature have focused on the United States Supreme Court (see e.g. Caldeira and Gibson 1992; Gibson, Caldeira, and Spence 2003; Gibson and Caldeira 2009a; Bartels and Johnson 2013; Christenson and Glick 2015a, 2019). Several studies also exist for the US state Supreme courts, examining the moderating role of judicial elections and campaign financing on the relationship between public opinion and legitimacy (see e.g. Gibson 2008, 2009, 2011, 2012; Gibson et al. 2011; Woodson 2017; Nelson 2018; Barwick and Dawkins 2020). There are also a few studies on public opinion and legitimacy for the Supreme Court of Canada (see e.g. Hausegger and Riddell 2004; Goodyear-Grant, Matthews, and Hiebert 2013).

Outside North America, a number of studies exist for courts in Europe. Using public opinion surveys, Gibson, Caldeira, and Baird (1998) examine the legitimacy of seventeen high courts in Europe. In related studies, Garoupa and Maghalaes (2020, 2021) examine public trust in the courts across thirty-two European countries, while Navarrete and Castillo-Oritz (2020) consider how constitutional courts in Europe affect public perception of judicial fairness and judicial independence. Multiple studies have examined the relationship between public opinion and legitimacy of the European Court of Justice (Caldeira and Gibson 1995, Gibson and Caldeira 1998; Voeten 2013) and the European Court of Human Rights (Cali, Koch, and Bruch 2013; Dinas and Gonzalez-Ocantos 2021). Other studies have examined diffuse support for courts in specific European countries, namely Germany (Cheruvu 2020), Norway (Bentsen 2019), and the United Kingdom (Gonzalez-Ocantos and Dinas 2019). The latter studies diffuse support for the UK Supreme Court following its Brexit decision.

There are a few studies for countries in Africa. Bartels and Kramon (2020) test subjective ideological disagreement by examining the extent to which support for judicial power depends on who is in power using survey evidence from thirty-four African countries. Bartels, Horowitz, and Kramon (2023) examine public reaction to the Kenyan Supreme Court's role in the 2017 election crisis. Multiple studies have examined the relationship between public opinion and the legitimacy of the South African Constitutional Court using the theoretical lens of positivity bias (Gibson and Caldeira 2003; Gibson 2008a, 2016).

Driscoll and Nelson (2020) examine public support, and institutional trust, in the courts across several countries in Latin America. Salzman and Ramsey (2013) examine public confidence in the judiciary in ten Latin American countries. Other studies consider public confidence, or trust, in courts in specific Latin American countries (Bergoglio 2012; Gonzalez-Ocantos 2016; Huebert and Liu 2017). There are related studies for Asian countries, including China (Chen and Li 2020), Japan (Shigemura et al. 2021), and the Philippines (Deinla 2014). There are also studies for Australia (Krebs, Nielsen, and Smyth 2019; Nielsen and Smyth 2019; Nielsen, Robinson, and Smyth 2020). Dotan, Sulitzeanu-Kenan, and Yair (2015) consider support for the Israeli High Court of Justice.

There a few related studies for international courts, such as the International Criminal Court and the International Court of Justice (Ford 2012; Voeten 2013; Hehir 2019; Zvobgo 2019).

4. Data and Measurement Issues

Most studies have employed publicly available cross-sectional surveys of a representative sample of the relevant population. Chen and Li (2020) survey university students in China because of the sensitivity of examining judicial legitimacy in that country. Some US studies have used the Amazon Mechanical Turk (MTurk) platform (Loeffler and Menounou 2020; Zilis 2022; Black et al. 2023). Evidence on the reliability of MTurk samples is mixed. On the one hand, Coppock (2019) finds a very high degree of replicability using MTurk samples, but other studies have found that data quality on MTurk has declined over time (Chmielewski and Kucker 2020). Other studies have employed macro-level cross-country surveys, such as the European Social Survey (Garoupa and Magalhães 2020, 2021; Navarrete and Castillo-Ortiz 2020), Afrobarometer, the Americas

Barometer, or Eurobarometer (Gibson, Caldeira, and Baird 1998; Voeten 2013; Bartels and Kramon 2020; Driscoll and Nelson 2020). A limitation of using cross-sectional data is that it is likely that key right-hand-side variables, such as political knowledge, support for the rule of law, and confidence in public institutions are endogenous, reflecting reverse causality, measurement error, and omitted variable bias. Cross-sectional studies are similarly unable to measure whether legitimacy is stable over time, which is a key prediction of positivity bias (Nelson and Smith 2014; Nelson and Tucker 2021).

One approach to addressing the limitation of cross-sectional designs has been to employ longitudinal data to capture individual-level temporal dynamics (Gibson 2011; Christenson and Glick 2015a, 2015b; Humphries Ginn, Searles, and Jones 2015; Bartels and Kramon 2020; Krewson, Schroedel, and Immormino 2020; Bartels, Horowitz, and Kramon 2023). Among US studies to employ longitudinal data, many have used The American Panel Survey (TAPS) (see e.g. Nelson and Smith 2014; Gibson, Pereira, and Ziegler 2017; Woodson 2018; Nelson and Tucker 2021). The use of panel data, together with fixed effects estimation, can control for time-specific factors affecting support for courts as in Bartels and Kramon (2020). A limitation of many of these studies, though, is that some panels only have two waves, which is the shortest possible. Also, the use of panel data per se does not address potential reverse causality (Leszczensky and Wolbring 2022). Another approach to realize causal inference is to use an experimental design embedded in a survey. Such studies often use an experimental vignette to manipulate the information treatment(s) (see e.g. Gibson 2009; Bentsen 2019; Barwick and Dawkins 2020; Loeffler and Menounou 2020; Nielsen, Robinson, and Smyth 2020; Shigemura et al. 2021; Black et al. 2023). Experimental designs, however, also have limitations (Gibson and Nelson 2018b). Potential disadvantages of hypothetical vignettes include that the hypothetical nature of the statements may lower participant's effort or cause experimenter demand effects. It may also be cognitively challenging for participants to think in terms of hypotheticals that might introduce measurement error or impair external validity (Haaland, Roth, and Wohlfart 2020).

An important point of difference between proponents of the competing theories of legitimacy is how it is measured. Gibson and Nelson (2017, 613–14) suggest: 'Our view is that one reason why the literature on institutional support is in a bit of disarray has to do with measurement. Only a small proportion of the research in the field addresses basic issues of validity and reliability.' Gibson (2017) and Gibson and Nelson (2015) argue that support for subjective ideological disagreement turns, in part, on how that literature measures legitimacy and that many of the studies are measuring specific support or performance evaluation, rather than diffuse support, which is fundamentally a multi-item construct.

Most studies that have been couched in terms of positivity bias have measured legitimacy using the Gibson, Gibson, Caldeira, and Spence (2003) index, which asks participants if the Court should be done away with altogether, whether the Court can be trusted, whether the Court's jurisdiction should be limited, whether the Court's ability to exercise judicial review should be limited, and whether the Court favours some groups over others. Recently, Badas (2019) criticized the Gibson, Gibson, Caldeira, and Spenc (2003) index and proposes, in lieu, an applied legitimacy index, which he estimates using TAPS. He finds that the Gibson, Gibson, Caldeira, and Spence (2003) index is biased in favour of the predictions of positivity bias, while the applied legitimacy index produces results more consistent with the predictions of subjective ideological disagreement.

With a few exceptions, such as Krebs, Nielsen, and Smyth (2019), studies that examined the relationship between public opinion and legitimacy for courts outside the United States have typically used confidence or trust to measure legitimacy (see Salzman and Ramsey 2013; Voeten 2013; Deinla 2014; Huebert and Liu 2017). The reason is such studies generally use publicly available surveys and these are the only available proxies. As such, 'cross-national researchers often cite constraints of data availability, and then interpret institutional confidence measures as valid measures of legitimacy' (Driscoll and Nelson 2020, 8). However, this interpretation is problematic. Gibson, Gibson, Caldeira, and Spence (2003) show that single item indicators of confidence or trust in courts equate better with specific support, rather than diffuse support for the courts. Hence, the main difficulty is that most of the cross-national research that employs observational data is not measuring legitimacy as the term is usually understood.

Bartels and Johnson (2020) and Bartels and Kramon (2020) argue that legitimacy is difficult to evaluate and prefer, instead, citizen support for judicial power. Using judicial power to test for legitimacy directly facilitates testing the predictions of subjective ideological disagreement. As Bartels and Kramon (2020, 146) describe the relationship between judicial power and legitimacy:

> If people support judicial power only when they agree with a ruling or foresee partisan political advantage and they withhold power otherwise, that is a detriment to legitimacy. Legitimacy can therefore be evaluated on the basis of whether partisan or policy/ideological considerations influence support for judicial power.

5. Main Findings and Controversies

5.1 Is Legitimacy Stable over Time?

The traditional finding in the literature is that 'legitimacy is basically obdurate and determined chiefly by the public's core democratic values' (Nelson and Smith 2014, 4). This finding is consistent with positivity bias creating a reservoir of goodwill that buffets the courts from unpopular decisions. This result conforms with diffuse support for courts being persistent or 'sticky' (Gibson 2015, 85). According to this conventional wisdom, unpopular decisions, or controversies concerning the courts, affect specific support for the courts. Changes in specific support represent structural breaks in diffuse support, but, for the most part, diffuse support will revert to its mean. As Gibson (2015,

84) puts it, performance dissatisfaction leading to changes in specific support are 'short term detours that do not last very long'. To claim that legitimacy is obdurate, here means resistant, and not impervious, to change (Gibson 2015). The mean of diffuse support can be lowered 'if there is a sustained series of performance disappointments' (Gibson 2015, 85). For example, Gibson and Caldeira (1992) suggest that diffuse support among African-Americans for the US Supreme Court was reduced because of a series of accumulated grievances.

The traditional finding that diffuse support is persistent over time has been challenged by those proposing subjective ideological disagreement as the theoretical framework (Bartels and Johnson 2013; Nicholson and Hansford 2014; Christenson and Glick 2015a, 2019; Clark and Kastellec 2020; Badas 2019a).[2] Subjective ideological disagreement posits a much closer relationship between specific and diffuse support. Bartels and Johnson (2013) find that in an experimental setting *one* unfavourable decision can decrease legitimacy evaluations. The mechanism underpinning these results is ideological updating. As Christenson and Glick (2015a) describe it, each 'decision provides new information that people can use to update their assessment of the Court's ideology, and these updates affect assessments of legitimacy'. Thus, rather than being mean reverting, Bartels and Johnson (2013) and Christenson and Glick (2015a) find that diffuse support resembles a random walk, in which legitimacy of the courts depends on perceived ideological dissatisfaction or policy disagreement at a point in time. This result implies that individual-level performance dissatisfaction translates directly and simultaneously into a decrease in diffuse support and that diffuse support for the courts should ebb and flow with their rulings (Gibson and Nelson 2014, 2015).

The revisionist perspective on stability of legitimacy has been questioned by Gibson and Nelson (2014, 2015, 2017). They (2015) criticize Bartels and Johnson (2013) and Christenson and Glick (2015a) for not controlling for democratic values or measures of specific support. They show that when these factors are controlled for, the relationship between specific and diffuse support is more muted. Gibson and Nelson (2015) also advance criticisms about the experimental treatments used in Bartels and Johnson (2013). Nelson and Gibson (2020) find that several common measures of subjective ideological disagreement suffer from systematic measurement error, making the results unreliable.

Using a relatively long panel from TAPS—eleven waves spanning May 2012 to July 2016—Nelson and Tucker (2021) find that diffuse support for the US Supreme Court is durable and stable. As they put it, 'the timeline for a meaningful aggregate shift in the Court's support is one of *years* rather than *weeks*. This finding stands in stark contrast to the results of single-shot studies that suggest fairly large changes in diffuse support' (emphasis in original). This said, consistent with the revisionist perspective, while they conclude that the Court's support has been remarkably stable in the aggregate, they find that there has been systematic change at the individual level, which are related to respondents' satisfaction with the Court's performance and their political orientations. Moreover, a limitation of Nelson and Tucker (2021) is that TAPS does not specifically measure subjective ideological disagreement.

5.2 Does Legitimacy Reflect Policy Disagreement and/or Ideological Dissatisfaction?

Positivity bias rests on the public recognizing that the courts are not just another political institution. As Gibson and Caldeira (2009, 119–20) observe:

> The driving mechanism for change in institutional support has to do with whether the Supreme Court is seen as an ordinary political institution or whether it is judged to be distinctive. To the extent that people believe the Court is a relatively non-political institution, support for it is more easily generated. Anything that drags the Court into ordinary politics damages the esteem of the institution.

However, as Gibson and Nelson (2017) emphasize, seen through the lens of positivity bias, the extent to which people see courts as ordinary political institution is not the same thing as recognizing that judges rely on their own ideologies or values when making decisions. Nor does it depend on a subjective calculus of the extent to which the ideological values of the justices differ from one's own ideological position. Studies such as Gibson and Caldeira (2011) and Gibson and Nelson (2017), using the theoretical lens of positivity bias, show that the US public are legal realists, but that legal realism poses no threat to legitimacy. Relatedly, studies in the positivity bias tradition find that ideological or policy disagreement has no effect on legitimacy (Gibson and Nelson 2015, 2017). Gibson (2007, 2017) finds that even in light of increasing polarization in the United States (Hasen 2019), when legitimacy is measured using a multi-item indicator, rather than in terms of public approval, there is little ideological variation in respondents' respect for the US Supreme Court. Gibson (2012) reaches the same conclusion for the Kentucky Supreme Court. Rather, what matters is the extent to which decisions are perceived to be fair or judicious (Gibson and Caldeira 2009). Gibson and Nelson (2014) suggest this result could reflect that the public values procedural considerations over policy disagreements or that the US Supreme Court roughly decides cases in a liberal versus conservative direction about 50 per cent of the time, so that both conservatives and liberals are happy with the Court's decision about half of the time, cancelling each other out.

But for adherents to subjective ideological disagreement, subjective policy disagreement or ideological dissatisfaction with the courts has a direct effect on reducing legitimacy. Moreover, contrary to findings in studies such as Gibson (2007), increasing polarization in the United States has the effect of reinforcing ideological and policy disagreement and reducing legitimacy further (Bartels and Johnson 2020). In the context of the US Supreme Court, Bartels and Johnson (2013, 2020), Nicholson and Hansford (2014), Christenson and Glick (2015a, 2015b, 2019), Clark and Kastellec (2020), Badas (2019a), and Zilis (2022) present a mixture of observational and experimental evidence consistent with the idea that policy disagreement leads people to view the Court as being less legitimate. For instance, Badas (2019a) finds that support for the New Deal predicts support for the 1937 Court packing plan, a desire to see Congress pass the plan and limitations on the Supreme Court's ability to invalidate acts of Congress. Barwick and Dawkins (2020) presents observational and experimental evidence to the same effect for the US State Supreme courts.

Beyond the United States, Bartels and Kramon (2020) find that partisan alignment with the executive shapes support for judicial power in their study of thirty-four African countries, while Bartels, Horowitz, and Kramon (2023) find strong partisan responses to the Kenyan Supreme Court's role in the 2017 election crisis, consistent with subjective ideological disagreement.

The response of proponents of the traditional positivity bias position has been largely to criticize these studies on methodological grounds. Gibson (2015), for instance, criticizes Bartels and Johnson (2013) for failing to distinguish between ideological and policy disagreement and show that respondents in the Bartels and Johnson (2013) study had difficulty mapping their ideological preferences to policy preferences and vice versa. Gibson, Pereira, and Ziegler (2017) argue that ideological updating places unreasonable information demands on the public. As they (2017, 982) put it: 'One must have an ideology, perceive the Court in ideological terms and understand the ideological location, judge policies by ideological criteria, hold attitudes toward the institution; and update those attitudes continuously.' Employing TAPS, Gibson, Pereira, and Ziegler (2017) find that the basic assumptions underpinning ideological updating are not plausible for the vast majority of Americans.

5.3 Do Landmark Rulings Affect Legitimacy?

Conceptually positivity bias predicts that blockbuster rulings in highly politicized cases could contribute to courts appearing to be like other political institutions and, hence, undermining their reservoir of goodwill (Gibson, Pereira, and Ziegler 2017). However, studies of landmark rulings, which have clear political winners, that are couched in terms of positivity bias have found no evidence that they affect diffuse support. Most notably, Gibson, Caldeira, and Spence (2003a) examine the effect of the US Supreme Court decision in *Bush v Gore* on diffuse support for the Court, finding that it did not undermine legitimacy. They concluded (at 553) 'even an enormously controversial decision like *Bush v Gore* has little influence on institutional loyalty' because the Court's reservoir of goodwill runs deep. It would most likely take a series of unpopular landmark decisions, generating accumulated grievances, for diffuse support to fall below a threshold, before re-establishing at a new lower mean level of diffuse support (Gibson 2015).

Subjective ideological disagreement predicts that each salient decision has the potential to contribute to a change in perceived legitimacy, depending on whether the individual agrees with the outcome and the perceived ideological distance between the individual and the Court. Given that the public do not hear about most decisions that courts make (Gibson, Pereira, and Ziegler 2017), people tend to make their subjective assessments about ideological distance on the basis of well-publicized cases which, of course, include blockbuster decisions. Johnston, Hillygus, and Bartels (2014), Christenson and Glick (2015a), and Woodson (2018) found that the US Supreme Court's decision in the Affordable Care Act (Obamacare) case affected diffuse support for the Court. Similarly, Christenson and Glick (2019) found that the US Supreme Court's decisions in high profile cases on the Voting Rights Act and same-sex marriage affected diffuse support for the Court. At the state level, Humphries Ginn, Searles, and Jones (2015) found that a decision of the Supreme Court on Ohio School vouchers affected diffuse support for the Court in Ohio among those directly vested in the outcome of the case.

There are few studies outside of the United States. Dotan, Dotan, Sulitzeanu-Kenan, and Yair (2015) find that one decision of the High Court of Justice pertaining to the 2013 municipal elections in Israel influenced diffuse support for the Court in cities affected by the decision. Bartels, Horowitz, and Kramon (2023) find that, in contrast to Gibson, Caldeira, and Spence's (2003a) findings for *Bush v Gore,* a highly partisan decision of the Kenyan Supreme Court to overturn the decision of the 2017 election in Kenya reduced support for judicial power. There are some methodological differences between the two studies—for example, Bartels, Horowitz, and Kramon (2023) measure the outcome variable in terms of judicial power, rather than legitimacy and employ panel data, while Gibson et al. measure legitimacy in the conventional way and use cross-sectional data. The study by Bartels, Horowitz, and Kramon (2023) is also for an emerging democracy in which the reservoir of goodwill may not run so deep.[3]

Another reason for the difference in results between Gibson, Caldeira, and Spence (2003a) and later studies is that aggregate stability in legitimacy orientations following landmark decisions may be masking considerable offsetting movements in individual legitimacy orientations. Christenson and Glick (2015a) and Nelson and Smith (2014) provide some evidence that this is what happened following the US Supreme Court ruling in the 2012 Affordable Care Act (Obamacare) decision. Bartels and Johnson (2020) conjecture that the same dynamic is likely to have occurred following the US Supreme Court decision in *Bush v Gore.*

Another study outside the United States is Gonzlez-Ocantos and Dinas (2019), who examine public response to the UK Supreme Court's Brexit decision. This study differs from the others in that it focuses on compliance and compensation effects. The main findings were that the UK Supreme Court's attempt to compensate losers increased public acceptance of the decision, as did compliance pledges from both major political parties.

5.4 Do Attacks from Politicians Affect Legitimacy?

Positivity bias predicts that attacks on the courts from politicians could potentially reduce diffuse support by making courts look more like ordinary political institutions. As Gibson and Nelson (2018, 35) describe it, from a positivity bias perspective: 'Citizens do not penalize courts for making ideological decisions.... But, when citizens believe that judicial behaviour crosses the line from principled to politicized, they no longer extend high levels of support to courts.' For example, when Donald Trump characterizes judges who ruled against his Muslim travel ban as 'incompetent' and 'so political' (Revesz 2017), this depicts their decisions as being politicized, rather than principled. Given that the public frequently relies on source cues when forming judgments (Clark and Kastellec 2020; Sen 2017), they may rely on characterizations from political elites to form views of the courts.

Gibson and Nelson (2018) and Nelson and Gibson (2019) examine the effect of Trump's attacks on the courts on legitimacy and compare their effects with statements by law professors. They find that Trump's attacks have no effect on lowering legitimacy, but if law professors describe the courts as politicized this does lower legitimacy. The most likely explanation for this finding is that law professors are credible source cues (Nicholson and Hansford 2014), but Trump is not. According to Gibson and Nelson (2018, 39):

> President Trump's criticisms have become so ubiquitous in everyday life in America as to be rendered 'cheap talk' by the American public. On the other hand, the views of law professors—whose views ordinary Americans may not hear every day—represent professionals making judgments in their area of expertise.

In a very similar study, Kromphardt and Salamone (2021) examine the effect of Trump's criticism of the federal judiciary on Twitter on diffuse support for the federal courts. They find that specific, but not diffuse, support for the courts changes in response to the attacks.

A related study is Armaly (2018), who uses an experimental design to test whether Donald Trump and Hilary Clinton, when Presidential candidates, were capable of altering diffuse support for the US Supreme Court by making statements that were critical of the Court. In contrast to Gibson and Nelson (2018), Nelson and Gibson (2019), and Kromphardt and Salamone (2021), Armaly (2018) finds that statements by both Clinton and Trump do affect diffuse support for the Court. Specifically, individuals who dislike Clinton/Trump increase their diffuse support for the Court after exposure to their negative statements and vice versa. This result is consistent with Badas' (2019a) findings for the effect of Roosevelt's Court packing plan on diffuse support for the Court. One way to reconcile the findings in Armaly (2018) for Trump as a candidate with those studies that have examined the effect of Trump's statements as President is that Trump's statements as a candidate had more source credibility. As President, Trump's hyperpoliticized rhetoric has muted his effect on diffuse support for the courts because he is not viewed as a credible source cue (Nelson and Gibson 2019).

5.5 Do Politicized Nominations Affect Legitimacy?

Positivity bias represents a frame through which events are perceived and evaluated. Confirmation hearings are an example of competing frames, in which legality, or what Gibson and Caldeira (2009a) term 'judiciousness', is advanced by proponents of the nominee, and political considerations, such as ideology and policy preferences, are advanced by opponents of the nomination. In highly politicized nominations, the legitimizing symbols upon which courts rely—such as impartiality and strict adherence to the law—are potentially compromised. If so, this may undermine diffuse support for the Court. The alternative hypothesis is that positivity frames may override attempts to politicize the nomination process, so that diffuse support for the Court is unaltered (Gibson and Caldeira 2009a).

Subjective ideological disagreement offers a different lens through which to view nominations. It posits that controversial nominations will polarize views of the nomination along partisan lines—increasing (decreasing) diffuse support for the Court among those who see the nomination as making the Court less (more) ideologically distant.

Gibson and Caldeira (2009a) examine the effect of George W. Bush's nomination of Samuel Alito on diffuse support for the US Supreme Court. They find that positivity frames override attempts to politicize nominations, consistent with legitimacy of the Court being high and persistent. Krewson and Schroedel (2020) reach similar conclusions in a study of the effect of Trump's appointment of Brett Kavanaugh. In a related study, using an experimental design embedded with a cross-section, Armaly (2018a) finds that positivity frames were enhanced by exposure to the legitimizing symbols of the Court following the vacancy on the Court created by Antonio Scalia's death. However, Rogowski and Stone (2021) find that Trump's nomination of Neil Gorsuch polarized partisan views of the nomination—increasing perceptions of legitimacy among conservatives and reduced perceptions of legitimacy among liberals, consistent with subjective ideological disagreement. This is further supported by polls following Amy Coney Barett's nomination (see e.g. Gross 2020).

5.6 Do Judicial Elections and Campaign Financing Affect Legitimacy?

Judicial elections potentially have competing effects on legitimacy. Elections per se make judges more accountable, which one would expect to increase legitimacy. At the same time, elections typically involve advertising and campaign financing which detract from the myth of legality which underpins positivity bias and make courts appear like ordinary political institutions. A growing number of studies have examined whether judicial elections and campaign financing undermine the legitimacy of state courts in the United States. Their main conclusion is that elections generally increase the legitimacy of state courts in the United States (Gibson et al. 2011; Gibson 2012; Woodson 2017; Crabtree and Nelson 2019).

With respect to political advertising, Gibson et al. (2011) found that both attack ads and conventional, non-attacking, endorsement ads reduce legitimacy, but the negative effects of advertising are outweighed by the legitimacy conferring effects of having judicial elections. Gibson (2012) also emphasizes the importance of the public's expectations on the effect of ads on legitimacy; specifically, exposure to partisan ads only has a negative effect on legitimacy for those who expect courts to be apolitical, but for those who fully expect the courts to be political, partisan ads have no effect on legitimacy.

In terms of the effects of campaigning, several studies have found that exposure to campaign speeches or policy views does not affect court legitimacy, but campaign contributions reduce legitimacy because they imply a conflict of interest or even a quid pro quo relationship between donor and judge (Cann and Yates 2008; Gibson 2008, 2009; Gibson and Caldeira 2012, 2013). Gibson and Caldeira (2012, 2013) found that recusals help restore legitimacy but not to the level that existed when no conflict of interest existed. Woodson (2017) found the legitimacy of elected judges is only higher than appointed judges in states with little campaign activity, but in states with high amounts of campaign activity the negative effects of campaigning outweigh the benefit of having elections per se on conferring legitimacy on courts. Other studies have examined heterogeneity in the effects on legitimacy of donations from different groups. For example, Nelson (2018) found that donations from known litigants reduced legitimacy by a larger amount than donations from dark money groups—that is, untraceable political donations routed through opaque not-for-profit associations.

In addition to the United States, the only other countries with popular judicial elections are Bolivia (Driscoll and Nelson 2012, 2015) and Japan (Law 2008). Driscoll and Nelson (2015) examine the effect of the 2011 judicial elections in Bolivia on confidence in the courts. Features of this election were that candidates were not able to list their partisan affiliation on the ballot and media coverage of the election was limited. Some candidates, though, were touted as being affiliated with the government. Driscoll and Nelson (2015) found that confidence in the courts increased among government supporters and those who shared similar demographic characteristics with elected judges, but decreased overall.

5.7 How Do the Internal Arrangements of the Court Affect Legitimacy?

One strand of literature examines perceptions of the legitimacy of the courts' opinions. Boddery, Moyer, and Yates (2019) use an experimental design to examine whether delivering an opinion of the Court or seriatim opinion writing affects the legitimacy of the US Supreme Court. They find that when a Supreme Court outcome is ascribed to the institution as a whole, rather than to a particular Justice, it enhances the legitimacy of the Court.

Other studies examine the effect of how the opinion is written on public acceptance of the decision. Hansford and Coe (2019) find that complex language decreases acceptance of the decision by reducing processing fluency, but the use of legalistic terminology increases acceptance. Consistent with positivity bias, the use of legal language is a form of legal symbolism that sets it apart from ordinary political institutions. Relatedly, Zink, Spriggs, and Scott (2009) also find that when the public is told that the decision follows precedent, suggesting a legalistic approach, this increases public acceptance, consistent with positivity bias. As Gibson, Caldeira, and Spence (2005, 188) put it, 'the court profits when it grounds its decisions in law'. The effect of utilizing extra-legal reasons, such as public opinion, personal beliefs, and religious texts, in support of a reason on diffuse support for the US Supreme Court is mixed. Some studies find that providing extra-legal reasons reduces the legitimacy of the Court (see e.g. Farganis 2012), although Bonneau et al. (2017) find that it has no effect, consistent with diffuse support being persistent.

Yet other studies examine the effect of dissent on public support for the courts. Findings for studies for the US Supreme Court have been mixed. Overall, though, the results seem to suggest that unanimity fosters higher levels of acceptance, at least with issues of low salience (Peterson 1981; Marshall 1987; Gibson, Caldeira, and Spence 2005; Zink, Spriggs, and Scott 2009; Salamone 2014). Salamone (2014) suggests that dissent may foster higher levels of acceptance if the issues being desired are moderately salient to the individual by demonstrating procedural justice. Bentsen (2019) finds that dissent can increase support for the Supreme Court of Norway through demonstrating procedural justice in high salience cases.

5.8 Legitimacy in Settings with Weak Democratic Norms

As Bartels, Horowitz, and Kramon (2023) point out:

> Nearly all on the literature on public attitudes toward judicial power focuses on long-standing democracies. Scholars know less about whether the lessons learned from these settings hold in cases ... where democracy is newer, judiciaries have only begun to assert their authority after long periods of subservience to executives and where citizens may have good reason to doubt whether judiciaries can serve as independent actors in national affairs.

What we do know in such contexts is that high courts typically face a legitimacy deficit as they seek to assert themselves, particularly in politically charged disputes. In a study of public trust in courts in thirty-two European courts, Garoupa and Magalhães (2021) find that the notion 'to know the courts is to love them' is stronger in countries with high levels of accountability and independence. Gibson and Caldeira (2003) examine the legitimacy of the fledging Constitutional Court in South Africa. They 'conclude that theories of the legitimacy–acquiescence linkage do not work well in South Africa; the findings from research on stable democracies do not seem to be easily and directly generalizable to transitional regimes' (Gibson and Caldeira 2003, 23). Similarly, Bartels, Horowitz, and Kramon (2023) conclude that there is a strong political foundation to support for judicial power in Kenya, suggestive of a legitimacy deficit. Other studies for emerging democracies in Latin America, such as Bolivia and Peru, note that it will take time to build a reservoir of goodwill (Bergoglio 2012; Driscoll and Nelson 2015, 2020; Gonzalez-Octanes 2016). One-off high-profile cases, such as the 2017 election case in Kenya (Bartels, Horowitz, and Kramon 2023) or the Fujimori trial in Peru (Gonzalez-Octanes 2016), will not be sufficient. Rather, '[b]uilding a reservoir of goodwill among the public requires a series of salient decisions satisfying overlapping constituencies over time' (Gonzalez-Octanes 2016, 462). In their study of eighteen national high courts, Gibson, Gibson, Caldeira, and Baird (1998) find that older courts are more successful at establishing diffuse support, reflecting their ability to satisfy successive, overlapping constituencies. Overall, these results are consistent with studies for established democracies, such as Krebs, Nielsen, and Smyth (2019) who find perceived legitimacy is highly correlated with democratic values.

5.9 Judicial Attempts to Cultivate Public Opinion

Increasingly courts around the world are cultivating public opinion to increase support for their decisions (Staton 2010; Vanberg 2005). Most apex courts, for example, have websites containing biographies and speeches of the judges, electronic copies of their decisions, video recordings of hearings, and media releases of important decisions. Most courts now also maintain Twitter accounts on which important judgments are announced. Many also give tours of the court and some, such as the Supreme Courts of India and Israel, have dedicated museums.[4] Several of the chapters in Davis and Taras (2017) discuss how courts are reaching out to the public, sometimes with the help of the press. The purpose of cultivating public opinion is to build confidence in the courts and 'develop deep reservoirs of public support … offsetting the benefits of court bashing' (Epstein and Knight 2021, 283). One such example is the High Court of Australia in the late 1980s and early 1990s, in which judicial attempts to increase public understanding was a direct response to the perceived need to steel judicial independence in the light of the failure of the Attorney-General to support the Court following political attacks on controversial decisions. There are several other examples around the world. Staton (2010) documents that the Mexican Supreme Court has used an aggressive public relations campaign to increase understanding of its decisions and promote public confidence. Vanberg (2005) discusses how the Federal Constitutional Court in Germany has sought to garner public support as 'a shield for judicial independence' (Vanberg 2005, 177). Yet it is not totally clear that attempts to make themselves more accessible or promote understanding is the best way for judges to build diffuse support. Frishman (2017) notes that courts' attempts to cultivate a particular image can backfire if there is miscommunication or a specific audience is overlooked. More fundamentally, positivity theory posits that the courts rely on legitimizing symbols to evoke images of learning and pageantry. It could be that attempts to explain decisions and increase transparency have an adverse effect on the legitimacy of court by removing some of the mystique associated with the decision-making process (Nielsen, Robinson, and Smyth 2020).

Black et al. (2023) examine the effects of cameras on judicial legitimacy in US appellate courts. Their results are mixed, suggesting that although cameras might improve legitimacy in some circumstances, televising proceedings can impede legitimacy in other circumstances. Black et al. (2023) suggest that factors influencing the effect of cameras in the courtroom on judicial legitimacy are the degree of contentiousness of the footage being viewed, the camera angle at which the footage is shot and the interaction between these two factors.

6. Challenges and Directions for Future Research

The greatest challenge in this literature is that the findings on key issues, such as stability of legitimacy over time and the role of policy disagreement and ideological dissatisfaction on legitimacy, is in a state of flux. One cannot help but conclude that the main protagonists on both sides of the debate—Gibson and his colleagues as proponents of positivity bias and Bartels and his colleagues as advocates of subjective ideological disagreement—are firing off shots across each other's bows, but there is little real engagement with each other's perspective.[5] Both sides of the debate have criticized the assumptions underpinning each other's model (Bartel and Johnson 2013; Gibson and Nelson 2014) and how the other measures legitimacy (Gibson and Nelson 2017; Badas 2019). Nelson and Gibson (2020) purport to show that measuring subjective ideological disagreement contains systematic measurement errors, making conclusions unreliable. Beyond this, there is even disagreement about what we should be measuring, with Bartels, in recent studies, preferring the concept of judicial power, rather than legitimacy (Bartels and Kramon 2020; Bartels, Horowitz, and Kramon 2023).

One way to move beyond this impasse is for researchers on both sides of the debate to agree on what we should be measuring, as well as the meaning and significance of different dependent variables. Relatedly, future research needs to focus more on methodological differences between the two camps, including coming up with an appropriate measure of legitimacy. This is likely to involve a modified, or updated, measure of the Gibson, Gibson, Caldeira, and Spence (2003) index, whether it is termed judicial legitimacy or judicial power or something else (Badas 2019). An important component of doing this will be to differentiate clearly between specific and diffuse support and that when measuring diffuse support, employ models that clearly control for specific support (Gibson and Nelson 2015; Gibson 2017).

A related challenge is that most of what we know about the relationship between public opinion and legitimacy is for the United States and the US Supreme Court in particular. At the same time, though, this also represents an opportunity; studying legitimacy in courts outside the United States using cutting-edge methods and appropriate measures of legitimacy has the potential to shed light on the main points of difference between findings consistent with positivity bias and subjective ideological disagreement. For example, studying legitimacy in mature common law democracies such as Australia, New Zealand, or the United Kingdom, in which decision-making on their high courts is not as partisan political might help to clear up some of the disagreement about the role of ideology or at least clarify it (see Gonzalez-Ocantos and Dinas 2019; Krebs, Nielsen, and Smyth 2019; Nielsen, Robinson, and Smyth 2020). There is also much potential to study legitimacy in nascent democracies, taking advantage of specific decisions, such as the 2017 election crisis in Kenya, that see the judiciary assert itself against the executive (Bartels, Horowitz, and Kramon 2023). Studying these sorts of occurrences can extend, and enrich, what we know from US courts. There is also potential to study the effect of specific institutional arrangements, such as judicial elections, on legitimacy in Bolivia. Driscoll and Nelson (2015) represent a good starting point, but much can be learned from subsequent elections using appropriate methods. Such studies would complement the increasing number of studies on US state judicial elections.

A final opportunity to study legitimacy in courts outside the United States is to take advantage of different responses to COVID-19—for instance, governments have varied in the extent to which they have implemented lockdown measures—and how this may have affected perceptions of the legitimacy of the executive and judiciary. One such study using Japanese data is Shigemura et al. (2021), but studies in other contexts are needed.[6]

Another area in need of further research is the role of group identification as a moderator of the relationship between public opinion and legitimacy. Most studies have used demographic and human capital variables as controls. Few studies have made these factors the main focus. There are a few examples for ethnicity/race (Gibson and Caldeira 1992; Huebert and Liu 2017; Gibson and Nelson 2018a; O'Brien 2020), education (Cheruvu 2020), gender (Krewson, Schroedel, and Immormino 2020), and religion (Kromphardt, Smith, and Starling 2019). But more research is needed on the role of group identification, particularly in different contexts.

O'Brien (2020) examines the role of incarceration rates in the United States on differences in the perceptions of Whites and African-Americans on perceptions of courts. Yet we know little about the effect of macro variables more generally on legitimacy perceptions. This is another area for future research, particularly if it is coupled with an examination of the relationship between group identification and perceptions as in O'Brien (2020).

Gibson and Nelson (2018b) suggest that one potential reason why the legitimacy literature is confused is that it fails to take legal federalism seriously. As they (2018b) point out, a problem for legitimacy theory is that when appellate courts overturn the decisions of lower courts in the court hierarchy, those lower courts have their own reservoir of goodwill. In the United States, where most state judges are elected, that people have voted for them is a powerful source of legitimacy. Very little research exists on the relative legitimacy of different courts in the court hierarchy and the effect that an appellate court has in overturning the decision of a lower court on the relative legitimacy of the two courts. A few studies exist for the United States (Gibson and Nelson 2018b; Groves 2021), but we could learn more from studying courts in other federal structures as well. There is also a further dynamic at play—the role of final courts of appeal in accepting appeals for a full hearing or dismissing them. By way of example, the High Court of Australia almost always has an oral hearing of special leave for applications that meet various criteria. The US Supreme Court, though, does not and often dismisses appeals without any reason. Each process has gained acceptance, but the US case remains mysterious. Future research could tease out the effect of differences in special leave procedures on conferring relative legitimacy in federations.

Another avenue for further research is the mechanisms underpinning positivity theory and ideological updating. There are only a few studies that have used an experimental design to test the role of legitimizing symbols in reinforcing positivity bias (Woodson, Gibson, and Lodge 2011; Gibson, Lodge, and Woodson 2014; Gibson and Nelsen 2016; Nielsen, Robinson, and Smyth 2020). Gibson, Pereira, and Ziegler (2017) examine the mechanisms underpinning ideological updating that underpins subjective ideological disagreement. Again, different institutional settings provide the basis to explore the channels in more detail. For example, Nielsen, Robinson, and Smyth (2020) take advantage of changes in judicial dress on the High Court of Australia from robes, jabot, and wig to plain black robes in 1988 to examine the effect of change in judicial dress, as a legitimizing symbol, on public perceptions of the legitimacy of the Court. In other courts, such as the UK Supreme Court and Judicial Committee of the House of Lords before it, the judges do not wear robes. In the UK case this seems all the more striking given the pageantry of so much else about UK public life, such as the theatre of the opening of parliament. Judges of the UK Supreme Court, however, do receive titles, being made Peers (Lords and Ladies). It would be interesting to examine if this affects perceptions of legitimacy of the Court.

In addition to the attacks on the judiciary within the United States, attacks on the judiciary have occurred in Poland, Hungary, and Israel. We lack parallel surveys on public opinion on courts in these countries at the time of these various instances. But awareness of these attacks and their possible impact on legitimacy could be discussed and hypothesized in future studies when comparative scholars research how public opinion affects judicial legitimacy.

A final suggestion for future research is to make greater use of Twitter and other social media to assess diffuse support. Gibson and Nelson (2018), Nelson and Gibson (2019), and Kromphardt and Salamone (2021) each use social media to examine how political attacks affect diffuse support. Clark et al. (2018) propose a framework for using Twitter to study mass opinion discourse. They find that the US Supreme Court decisions on same-sex marriage had a significant effect on how the public discussed same-sex marriage on Twitter and a polarizing effect on public opinion.

7. Conclusion

The role of public opinion in informing legitimacy of the courts seems to be a universal concern, but there are relatively few non-US studies. I conclude with a few observations on why this might be the case. I suggest the main reason is that with a few notable exceptions, there is a lack of scholars working on this topic in countries outside the United States. This means that we are not seeing the institutional-relevant methods development in these countries or anywhere near the volume of studies needed to build robust conclusions.[7] Another reason is that the lack of non-US data impedes construction of appropriate measures of key constructs, such as legitimacy (Driscoll and Nelson 2020). Most studies outside the United States have not used appropriate multi-item constructs of legitimacy or used experiments to address causal inference. Rather, they have used 'proxies' for legitimacy, such as confidence or trust, that capture specific support in better ways (Gibson, Gibson, Caldeira, and Spence 2003). More generally, it might be argued, that measures of legitimacy have been developed to understand diffuse support for courts in the United States and that the concepts, and especially measures, are too US-centric. This last point needs to be explored more, but it depends on there being more scholars working in non-US settings and dedicated work carefully examining US measures in other institutional settings.

In this chapter, I have discussed some theories and tools to that could be adapted and employed in countries other than the United States to increase our comparative understanding of public opinion and judicial legitimacy, which will hopefully move the field forward.

Acknowledgements

I thank Lee Epstein, Nuno Garoupa, Gunnar Grendstad, Matthew Groves, Shiri Krebs, Michael Nelson, and Zoe Robinson for very helpful discussions, suggestions, and pointers on earlier versions of this chapter. I alone am responsible for the views expressed and any remaining errors.

Notes

1. For a discussion of the historical evolution of judicial legitimacy being conceived in terms of public support and the role of public opinion polling in this rise see Bassok (2021).
2. This literature has mainly focused on the United States. Non-US studies that find evidence consistent with subjective ideological disagreement on stability of legitimacy are Dotan et al. (2015) for Israel, and Bartels and Kramon (2020) and Bartels, Horowitz, and Kramon (2021) for Africa.
3. See also Gonzalez-Ocantos (2016) who examines the effect of the Fujimoro trial on confidence in judicial institutions in Peru, finding that the reservoir of goodwill is not as deep

in embryonic democracies. Given the outcome measure in Gonzalez-Ocantos (2016), it is likely that this study is really measuring specific support, rather than diffuse support, and it is not well placed to test the effects of landmark decisions on the reservoir of goodwill, which is inherently a long-run concept (see Gibson et al. 2003).

4. For a more general discussion of the many ways in which courts communicate with the public and, in so doing, seek to mould their intended image see Frishman (2017).
5. In recent studies, Gibson and Nelson typically mention studies such as Bartels and Johnson (2013) and Christenson and Glick (2015a), but note that in other studies (e.g. Gibson and Nelson 2015; Gibson 2017), they have challenged the assumptions of subjective ideological disagreement and point to a long list of studies in the tradition of positivity bias, suggesting legitimacy is high and persistent in stable democracies, such as the United States. Meanwhile, studies in the tradition of subjective ideological disagreement typically refer to the emerging challenge that it represents to the traditional perspective (see e.g. Badas 2019a).
6. For a related comparative study of differences in support for lockdown between Israel, Japan, and the United States, see Chilton et al. (2020). This study does not look at the relationship with legitimacy, but a similar approach to that employed in this study could be used to do so.
7. See also Smyth (2020), where I make this point more generally in the context of studies on comparative judicial behaviour in countries outside the United States, such as Australia and New Zealand.

References

Armaly, M. 2018. 'Extra-judicial Actor Induced Change in Supreme Court Legitimacy'. *Political Research Quarterly* 71: 600–13.

Armaly, M. 2018a. 'Politicized Nominations and Public Attitudes Toward the Supreme Court in the Polarization Era'. *Justice System Journal* 39: 193–209.

Badas, A. 2016. 'The Public's Motivated Response to Supreme Court Decision-Making'. *Justice System Journal* 37: 318–30.

Badas, A. 2019. 'The Applied Legitimacy Index: A New Approach to Measuring Judicial Legitimacy'. *Social Science Quarterly* 100: 1848–61.

Badas, A. 2019a. 'Policy Disagreement and Judicial Legitimacy: Evidence from the 1937 Court-Packing Plan'. *Journal of Legal Studies* 48: 377–408.

Bartels, B., J. Horowitz, and E. Kramon. 2023. 'Can Principles Protect High Courts from Partisan Backlash? Public Reactions to the Kenyan Supreme Court's Role in the 2017 Election Crisis'. *American Journal of Political Science* 67 (3): 790–807.

Bartels, B., and C. Johnson. 2013. 'On the Ideological Foundations of Supreme Court Legitimacy in the American Public'. *American Journal of Political Science* 57: 184–99.

Bartels, B., and C. Johnson. 2020. *Curbing the Court: Why the Public Constrains Judicial Independence*. New York: Cambridge University Press.

Bartels, B., and E. Kramon. 2020. 'Does Public Support for Judicial Power Depend on Who is in Political Power? Testing a Theory of Partisan Alignment in Africa'. *American Political Science Review* 114: 144–63.

Barwick, C., and R. Dawkins. 2020. 'Public Perceptions of State Court Impartiality and Court Legitimacy in an Era of Partisan Politics'. *State Politics and Policy Quarterly* 20: 54–80.

Bassok, O. 2021. 'Beyond the Horizons of the Harvard Forewords'. *Cleveland State Law Review* 70 (1): 1–45.

Bentsen, H. L. 2019. 'Dissent, Legitimacy, and Public Support for Court Decisions: Evidence from a Survey-Based Experiment'. *Law and Society Review* 53 (2): 588–610.

Bergoglio, M. I. 2012. 'Legitimacy of the Judicial System and Lay Participation in Judicial Decision-making Processes in Corboda, Argentina'. Paper presented at the 2012 Conference on Law and Society, 5–8 June, Honolulu, USA.

Black, R. C., T. R. Johnson, R. J. Owens, and J. Wedeking. 2023. 'Televised Oral Arguments and Judicial Legitimacy: An Initial Assessment'. *Political Behavior* 1–21. https://doi.org/10.1007/s11109-022-09848-5

Boddery, S., L. Moyer, and J. Yates. 2019. 'Naming Names: The Impact of Supreme Court Attribution on Citizen Assessment of Policy Outcomes'. *Law and Society Review* 53: 353–85.

Bonneau, C., J. Kelly, K. Pronin, S. Redman, and M. Zarit. 2017. 'Evaluating the Effects of Multiple Opinion Rationales on Supreme Court Legitimacy'. *American Politics Research* 45 (3): 335–65.

Caldeira, G., and J. Gibson. 1992. 'The Etiology of Public Support for the Supreme Court'. *American Journal of Political Science* 36: 635–64.

Caldeira, G., and J. Gibson. 1995. 'The Legitimacy of the Court of Justice in the European Union: Models of Institutional Support'. *American Political Science Review* 89: 356–76.

Cali, B., A. Koch, and N. Bruch. 2013. 'The Legitimacy of Human Rights Courts: A grounded Interpretivist Analysis of the European Court of Human Rights'. *Human Rights Quarterly* 35: 955–84.

Cann, D., and J. Yates. 2008. 'Homegrown Institutional Legitimacy: Assessing Diffuse Support for State Courts'. *American Politics Research* 36: 297–326.

Chen, B., and Z. Li. 2020. 'Judicial Legitimation in China'. *Cornell International Law Journal* 53 (2): 169–206.

Cheruvu, S. 2020. 'How Does Education Affect Public Support for Courts?' Manuscript. Department of Political Science, Emory University.

Chilton, A., K. L. Cope, C. Crabtree, and M. Versteeg. 2020. Support for Restricting Liberty for Safety: Evidence during the COVID-19 Pandemic from the United States, Japan, and Israel (2 May 2020). Available at SSRN: https://ssrn.com/abstract=3591270 or http://dx.doi.org/10.2139/ssrn.3591270

Chmielewski, M., and S. C. Kucker. 2020. 'An MTurk Crisis? Shifts in Data Quality and the Impact on Study Results'. *Social Psychological and Personality Science* 11 (4): 464–73.

Christenson, D. P., and D. M. Glick. 2015a. 'Chief Justice Robert's Health Care Decision Disrobed: The Microfoundations of the Supreme Court's Legitimacy'. *American Journal of Political Science* 59: 403–18.

Christenson, D. P., and D. M. Glick. 2015b. 'Issue Specific Opinion Change: The Supreme Court and Health Care Reform'. *Public Opinion Quarterly* 79 (4): 881–905.

Christenson, D. P., and D. M. Glick. 2019. 'Reassessing the Supreme Court: How Decisions and Negativity Bias Affect Legitimacy'. *Political Research Quarterly* 72: 637–52.

Clark, T., and J. Kastellec. 2020. 'Source Cues and Public Support for the Supreme Court'. *American Politics Research* 43: 504–35.

Clark, T., J. Staton, Y. Wang, and E. Aichtein. 2018. 'Using Twitter to Study Public Discourse in the Wake of Judicial Decisions: Public Reactions to the Supreme Court's Same Sex Marriage Cases'. *Journal of Law and Courts* 6 (1): 93–126.

Coppock, A. 2019. 'Generalizing from Survey Experiments Conducted on Mechanical Turk: A Replication Approach'. *Political Science Research and Methods* 7 (3): 613–28.

Crabtree, C., and M. Nelson. 2019. 'Judging Judicial Review in the American States'. *State Politics and Policy Quarterly* 19: 287–311.

Davis, R., and D. Taras, eds. 2017. *Justices and Journalists: The Global Perspective*. Cambridge: Cambridge University Press.

Deinla, I. 2014. 'Support and Judicial Empowerment of the Philippine Supreme Court'. *Contemporary Southeast Asia* 36: 128–58.

Dinas, E., and E. Gonzalez-Ocantos. 2021. 'Defending the European Court of Human Rights: Experimental Evidence from Britain'. *European Journal of Political Research* 60 (2): 397–417.

Dotan, Y., R. Sulitzeanu-Kenan, and O. Yair. 2015. 'When Court Legitimacy is Updated: The Moderating Effect of Content Relevance on the Relationship Between Specific and Diffuse Support of the Judiciary'. Paper presented at the CELS annual meeting St Louis, 30–31 October.

Driscoll, A., and M. Nelson. 2012. 'The 2011 Judicial Elections in Bolivia'. *Electoral Studies* 3 (31): 628–32.

Driscoll, A., and M. J. Nelson. 2015. 'Judicial Selection and the Democratization of Justice: Lessons from the Bolivian Judicial Elections'. *Journal of Law and Courts* 3 (1): 115–48.

Driscoll, A., and M. Nelson. 2020. 'Instrumentalism, Democratic Values, and Diffuse Support for Latin American High Courts'. Paper presented at the Latin American Public Opinion Project's Conference 'The Public and Democracy in The Americas', 22–23 October 2020, Lima, Peru (held virtually).

Epstein, L., and J. Knight. 2021. 'Efficacious Judging on Apex Courts'. In *Comparative Judicial Review*, edited by Rosalind Dixon and Erin Delaney. Cheltenham: Edward Elgar.

Farginis, D. 2012. 'Do Reasons Matter? The Impact of Opinion Content on Supreme Court Legitimacy'. *Political Research Quarterly* 65: 206–16.

Ford, S. 2012. 'A Social Psychology Model of the Perceived Legitimacy of International Criminal Courts: Implications for the Success of Transnational Justice Mechanisms'. *Vanderbilt Journal of Transnational Law* 45: 405–76.

Frishman, O. 2017. 'Court–Audience Relationships in the 21st Century'. *Mississippi Law Journal* 86 (2): 213–72.

Garoupa, N., and P. C. Magalhães. 2020. 'Judicial Performance and Trust in Legal Systems: Findings from a Decade of Surveys in over 20 European Countries'. *Social Science Quarterly* 101 (5): 1743–60.

Garoupa, N., and P. C. Magalhães. 2021. 'Public Trust in the European Legal Systems: Independence, Accountability and Awareness'. *West European Politics* 44 (3): 690–713.

Gibson, J. 2007. 'The Legitimacy of the United States Supreme Court in a Polarized Polity'. *Journal of Empirical Legal Studies* 4: 507–38.

Gibson, J. 2008. 'Challenges to the Impartiality of State Supreme Courts: Legitimacy Theory and "New Style" Judicial Campaigns'. *American Political Science Review* 102: 59–75.

Gibson, J. 2008a. 'The Evolving Legitimacy of the South African Constitutional Court'. In *Justice and Reconciliation in Post-Apartheid South Africa*, edited by F. du Bois and A. du Bois-Pedain, 229–66. New York: Cambridge University Press.

Gibson, J. 2009. '"New Style" Judicial Campaigns and the Legitimacy of the State High Courts'. *Journal of Politics* 71: 1285–304.

Gibson, J. 2011. 'Judges, Elections and the American Mass Public: The *Net* Effects of Judicial Campaigns on the Legitimacy of Courts'. Paper presented at the sixth annual CELS conference, Northwestern University Law School, 4–5 November.

Gibson, J. 2012. *Electing Judges: The Surprising Effects of Campaigning on Judicial Legitimacy*. Chicago: University of Chicago Press.

Gibson, J. 2015. 'Legitimacy is for Losers. The Interconnections of Institutional Legitimacy, Performance Evaluations and the Symbols of Judicial Authority'. In *Motivating Cooperation and Compliance with Authority*, edited by B. H. Bornstein and A. J. Tomkins, 81–115. New York: Springer International Publishing.

Gibson, J. 2016. 'Reassessing the Institutional Legitimacy of the South African Constitutional Court: New Evidence, Revised Theory'. *Politikon: South African Journal of Political Studies* 43: 53–77.

Gibson, J. 2017. 'Performance Evaluations Are Not Legitimacy Judgments: A Caution About Interpreting Public Opinions toward the United States Supreme Court'. *Washington University Journal of Law & Policy* 54: 71–88.

Gibson, J., and G. Caldeira. 1992. 'Blacks and the United States Supreme Court: Models of Diffuse Support'. *Journal of Politics* 54: 1120–45.

Gibson, J., and G. Caldeira. 1998. 'Changes in the Legitimacy of the European Court of Justice: A Post-Maastricht Analysis'. *British Journal of Political Science* 28: 63–91.

Gibson, J., and G. Caldeira. 2003. 'Defenders of Democracy? Legitimacy, Popular Acceptance and the South African Constitutional Court'. *Journal of Politics* 65: 1–30.

Gibson, J., and G. Caldeira. 2009. *Citizens, Courts and Confirmation: Positivity Theory and the Judgments of the American People*. Princeton: Princeton University Press.

Gibson, J., and G. Caldeira. 2009a. 'Confirmation Politics and the Legitimacy of the U.S. Supreme Court: Institutional Loyalty, Positivity Bias and the Alito Nomination'. *American Journal of Political Science* 53: 139–55.

Gibson, J., and G. Caldeira. 2011. 'Has Legal Realism Damaged the Legitimacy of the US Supreme Court?' *Law & Society Review* 45: 195–219.

Gibson, J., and G. Caldeira. 2012. 'Campaign Support, Conflicts of Interest, and Judicial Impartiality: Can Recusals Rescue the Legitimacy of Courts?' *Journal of Politics* 74 (1): 18–34.

Gibson, J., and G. Caldeira. 2013. 'Judicial Impartiality, Campaign Contributions and Recusals: Results from a National Survey'. *Journal of Empirical Legal Studies* 10: 76–103.

Gibson, J. L., G. A. Caldeira, and V. A. Baird. 1998. 'On the Legitimacy of National High Courts'. *American Political Science Review* 92 (2): 343–58.

Gibson, J., G. Caldeira, and L. Spence. 2003. 'Measuring Attitudes Towards the United States Supreme Court'. *American Journal of Political Science* 47: 354–67.

Gibson, J., G. Caldeira, and L. Spence. 2003a. 'The Supreme Court and the US Presidential Election of 2000: Wounds, Self-inflicted or Otherwise?' *British Journal of Political Science* 33 (4): 535–56.

Gibson, J., G. Caldeira, and L. Spence. 2005. 'Why Do People Accept Public Policies they Oppose? Testing Legitimacy Theory with a Survey Based Experiment'. *Political Research Quarterly* 58: 187–201.

Gibson, J., J. Gottfried, M. Delli Carpini, and K. Hall Jamieson. 2011. 'The Effects of Judicial Campaign Activity on the Legitimacy of Courts: A Survey-based Experiment'. *Political Research Quarterly* 64: 545–58.

Gibson, J., M. Lodge, and B. Woodson. 2014. 'Losing but Accepting, Positivity Theory and the Symbols of Judicial Authority'. *Law & Society Review* 48 (4): 837–66.

Gibson, J., and M. Nelson. 2014. 'The Legitimacy of the US Supreme Court: Conventional Wisdoms and Recent Challenges Thereto'. *Annual Review of Law and Social Science* 10: 201–19.

Gibson, J., and M. Nelson. 2015. 'Is the Supreme Court's Legitimacy Grounded in Performance Satisfaction and Ideology?' *American Journal of Political Science* 59: 162–74.

Gibson, J., and M. Nelson. 2016. 'Change in Institutional Support for the US Supreme Court: Is the Court's Legitimacy Impeded by the Decisions it Makes'. *Public Opinion Quarterly* 80: 622–41.

Gibson, J., and M. Nelson. 2017. 'Reconsidering Positivity Theory: What Roles Do Politicization, Ideological Disagreement and Legal Realism Play in Shaping U.S. Supreme Court Legitimacy?' *Journal of Empirical Legal Studies* 14: 592–617.

Gibson, J., and M. Nelson. 2018. 'Has Trump Trumped the Courts?' *New York University Law Review* 93: 32–40.

Gibson, J., and M. Nelson. 2018a. *Blacks and Blue. How African Americans Judge the US Legal System*. New York: Oxford University Press.

Gibson, J., and M. Nelson. 2018b. 'De-Conferring Judicial Legitimacy'. Manuscript, Department of Political Science, Washington University in St Louis.

Gibson J., M. Pereira, and J. Ziegler. 2017. 'Updating Supreme Court Legitimacy: Testing the "Rule, Learn, Update" Model of Political Communication'. *American Politics Research* 45 (6): 980–1002.

Gonzalez-Ocantos, E. 2016. 'Evaluation of Human Rights Trials and Trust in Judicial Institutions: Evidence from Fujimori's Trial in Peru'. *International Journal of Human Rights* 20: 445–70.

Gonzalez-Ocantos, E., and E. Dinas. 2019. 'Compensation and Compliance: Sources of Public Acceptance of the UK Supreme Court's Brexit Decision'. *Law & Society Review* 53 (3): 889–919.

Goodyear-Grant, E., J. S. Matthews, and J. Hiebert. 2013. 'The Courts/Parliament Trade-off: Canadian Attitudes on Judicial Influence in Public Policy'. *Commonwealth & Comparative Politics* 51 (3): 377–97.

Gross, E. L. 2020. 'Poll: 51% Of Voters Support Amy Coney Barrett's Confirmation'. *Forbes*, 20 October. https://www.forbes.com/sites/elanagross/2020/10/20/poll-51-of-voters-support-amy-coney-barretts-confirmation/?sh=e3e596147243, accessed 8 January 2021.

Groves, T. L. 2021. 'Sacrificing Legitimacy in a Hierarchical Judiciary'. *Columbia Law Review* 121 (5): 1555–615.

Haaland, I. K., C. Roth, and J. Wohlfart. 2020. 'Designing Information Provision Experiments'. CESifo Working Paper, No. 8406. Munich: CESifo.

Hansford, T. G., and C. Coe. 2019. 'Linguistic Complexity, Information Processing, and Public Acceptance of Supreme Court Decisions'. *Political Psychology* 40 (2): 395–412.

Hasen, R. 2019. 'Polarization and the Judiciary'. *Annual Review of Political Science* 22: 261–76.

Hausegger, L., and T. Riddell. 2004. 'The Changing Nature of Public Support for the Supreme Court of Canada'. *Canadian Journal of Political Science/Revue canadienne de science politique* 37 (1): 23–50

Hehir, A. 2019. 'Lessons Learned? The Kosovo Specialist Chambers' Lack of Local Legitimacy and Its Implications'. *Human Rights Review* 20: 267–87.

Huebert, E., and A. Liu. 2017. 'Ethnic Identity and Attitudes Toward State Institutions: Evidence of Judicial Legitimacy Among the Indigenous in Latin America'. *Politics, Groups and Identities* 5: 561–79.

Humphries Ginn, M., K. Searles, and A. Jones. 2015. 'Vouching for the Court? How High Stakes Affect Knowledge and Support of the Supreme Court'. *Justice System Journal* 36: 163–79.

Johnston, C., D. Hillygus, and B. Bartels. 2014. 'Ideology, the Affordable Care Act Ruling and Supreme Court Legitimacy'. *Public Opinion Quarterly* 78: 963–73.

Krebs, S., I. Nielsen, and R. Smyth. 2019. 'What Determines the Institutional Legitimacy of the High Court of Australia?' *Melbourne University Law Review* 45: 605–53.

Krewson, C., and J. Schroedel. 2020. 'Public Views of the U.S. Supreme Court in the Aftermath of the Kavanaugh Confirmation'. *Social Science Quarterly* 101: 1431–41.

Krewson, C., J. Schroedel, and J. Immormino. 2020. 'Supreme Court Legitimacy and the Gender Gap. Survey Evidence from a Two-wave Panel'. Manuscript, Brigham Young University.

Kromphardt, C., and M. Salamone. 2021. '"Unpresidented!" Or What Happens When the President Attacks the Federal Judiciary on Twitter'. *Journal of Information Technology & Politics* 18 (1): 84–100.

Kromphardt, C., J. Smith, and A. Starling. 2019. 'Group Identification and Support for the Supreme Court: Evidence from Evangelical Protestants'. *Journal for the Scientific Study of Religion* 58 (4): 854–73.

Law, D. S. (2008). 'The Anatomy of a Conservative Court: Judicial Review in Japan'. *Texas Law Review* 87: 1545.

Leszczensky, L., and T. Wolbring. 2022. 'How to Deal with Reverse Causality Using Panel Data? Recommendations for Researchers Based on a Simulation Study'. *Sociological Methods & Research* 51 (2): 837–65.

Loeffler, M., and E. Menounou. 2020. 'The Effect of Median Judges on Supreme Court Legitimacy'. Manuscript, California Polytechnic State University, Pomona.

Marshall, T. 1987. 'The Supreme Court as an Opinion Leader: Court Decisions and the Mass Public'. *American Politics Quarterly* 15 (1): 147–68.

Navarrete, R., and P. Castillo-Oritz. 2020. 'Constitutional Courts and Citizens' Perceptions of Judicial Systems in Europe'. *Comparative European Politics* 18: 128–50.

Nelson, M. 2018. 'Is There a Silver Lining? Dark Money and the Support for State Courts'. *De Paul Law Review* 67: 187–218.

Nelson, M., and J. Gibson. 2019. 'How Does Hyperpoliticized Rhetoric Affect the US Supreme Court's Legitimacy?' *Journal of Politics* 81: 1512–16.

Nelson, M., and J. Gibson. 2020. 'Measuring Subjective Ideological Disagreement with the United States Supreme Court'. *Journal of Law and Courts* 8 (1): 75–94.

Nelson, M., and S. Smith. 2014. 'Change and Stability in Diffuse Support for the Supreme Court'. Manuscript, Department of Political Science, Pennsylvania State University.

Nelson, M., and P. Tucker. 2021. 'The Stability and Durability of the U.S. Supreme Court's Legitimacy'. *Journal of Politics* 83 (2): 767–71.

Nicholson, S. P., and T. G. Hansford. 2014. 'Partisans in Robes: Party Cues and Public Acceptance of Supreme Court Decisions'. *American Journal of Political Science* 58 (3): 620–36.

Nielsen, I., Z. Robinson, and R. Smyth. 2020. 'Keep Your (Horse) Hair On? Experimental Evidence on the Effect of Exposure to Legitimizing Symbols on Diffuse Support for the High Court'. *Federal Law Review* 48: 382–400.

Nielsen, I., and R. Smyth. 2019. 'What the Australian Public Knows About the High Court'. *Federal Law Review* 47: 31–63.

O'Brien, T. 2020. 'Racing Justice: Mass Incarceration and Perceptions of Courts'. *Social Science Research* 90: 1–14, Article 102443.

Peterson, S. 1981. 'Dissent in American Courts'. *Journal of Politics* 43 (2): 412–34.

Revesz, R. 2017. 'Donald Trump Says Federal Judges Ruling Against His Muslim Ban are Political'. *The Independent* (London, 8 February). https://www.independent.co.uk/news/

world/americas/donald-trump-muslim-ban-federal-judges-political-ruling-immigration-travel-restrictions-a7569341.html, accessed 28 December 2020.

Rogowski, J., and A. Stone. 2021. 'How Political Contestation Over Nominations Polarizes Americans' Attitudes Toward the Supreme Court'. *British Journal of Political Science* 51 (3): 1251–69.

Salamone, M. F. 2014. 'Judicial Consensus and Public Opinion: Conditional Response to Supreme Court Majority Size'. *Political Research Quarterly* 67 (2): 320–34.

Salzman, R., and A. Ramsey. 2013. 'Judging the Judiciary: Understanding Public Confidence in Latin American Courts'. *Latin American Politics and Society* 55 (1): 73–95.

Scheb, J. M., and W. Lyons. 1999. 'Diffuse Support, Specific Support and Attentiveness: Components of the Public's Assessment of the Supreme Court'. *Politics & Policy* 27: 765–80.

Sen, M. 2017. 'How Political Signals Affect Public Support for Judicial Nominations: Evidence from a Conjoint Experiment'. *Political Research Quarterly* 70: 374–93.

Shigemura, S., T. Iseki, S. Ikeda, and H. Ishima. 2021. 'Public Support for the Judicial Branches under the COVID-19 Pandemic'. *Journal of Elections, Public Opinion and Parties* 31: 348–60.

Smyth, R. 2020. 'Empirical Studies of Judicial Behaviour and Decision-making in Australian and New Zealand Courts'. In *High Courts in Global Perspective: Evidence, Methodologies, and Findings*, edited by Nuno Garoupa, Lydia Tiede, and Rebecca D. Gill, 108–28. Charlottesville: University of Virginia Press.

Staton, J. K. 2010. *Judicial Power and Strategic Communication in Mexico*. New York: Cambridge University Press.

Vanberg, G. 2005. *The Politics of Constitutional Review in Germany*. Cambridge: Cambridge University Press.

Voeten, E. 2013. 'Public Opinion and the Legitimacy of International Courts'. *Theoretical Inquiries in Law* 14: 411–36.

Woodson, B. 2017. 'The Two Opposing Effects of Judicial Elections on Legitimacy Perceptions'. *State Politics & Policy Quarterly* 17: 24–46.

Woodson, B. 2018. 'The Dynamics of Legitimacy Change for the U.S. Supreme Court'. *Justice System Journal* 39: 75–94.

Woodson, B., J. Gibson, and M. Lodge. 2011. 'Judicial Symbols and the Link Between Institutional Legitimacy and Acquiescence'. Paper presented at the Annual Meeting of the American Political Science Association, Seattle.

Zilis M. A. 2022. 'How Identity Politics Polarizes Rule of Law Opinions'. *Political Behavior* 44: 179–99.

Zink, J. R., J. F. Spriggs, and J. T. Scott. 2009. 'Courting the Public: The Influence of Decision Attributes on Individuals' Views of Court Opinions'. *Journal of Politics* 71 (3): 909–25.

Zvobgo, K. 2019. 'Human Rights Versus National Interests: Shifting US Public Attitudes on the International Criminal Court'. *International Studies Quarterly* 63: 1065–78.

CHAPTER 37

COURTS AND TRANSITIONAL JUSTICE

ELIN SKAAR

1. Introduction

In October 2021, a trial started in a regional court in the northern town of Itzehoe in Germany against a ninety-six-year-old woman for her alleged involvement in the Holocaust. A French news channel reported that '[t]he first woman to be prosecuted for Nazi-era crimes in decades, Irmgard Furchner is charged with complicity in the killing or attempted killing of more than 11,000 people at the Stutthof camp in occupied Poland'.[1] Furchner is likely to have been one of the last defendants to be on trial for crimes against humanity committed during the Second World War. Trials for crimes committed during the Second World War were conducted first and foremost in two international courts, the Nuremberg and the Tokyo tribunals. Subsequently, trials were also conducted in national courts in a number of countries in Western Europe (such as Germany,[2] France, Belgium, and Norway), as well as Central and Eastern Europe (such as Czechoslovakia, Yugoslavia, and the Soviet Union).[3] These trials laid the foundations of modern international criminal law. They also marked the start of what scholars and practitioners much later came to refer to as 'transitional justice',[4] which essentially refers to how societies respond to the legacies of massive and serious human rights violations.[5]

More than seven decades after the Second World War ended, there is a lingering fear in Europe (indeed, in the world) that the Russian full-scale invasion of Ukraine from February 2022 may trigger a third world war. Jurists, victims organizations, and more than forty states have referred the situation in Ukraine to the International Criminal Court (ICC) for investigations. The Pre-Trial Chamber II of the ICC responded in 2023 by issuing arrest warrants for President Vladimir Putin and Lvova-Belova, the Commissioner for Children's Rights in the Office of the President of the Russian

Federation.[6] Proposals have also been made for the creation of an international ad hoc tribunal to specifically investigate and prosecute the crime of aggression against Ukraine.[7] International courts are today increasingly more active in cases involving large-scale international crimes in charged political situations. Recent examples include the ongoing South African genocide case against Israel before the International Court of Justice (ICJ), and the ICC Prosecutor's applications in May 2024 for arrest warrants against three Hamas leaders and Israel's President Benjamin Netanyahu and Minister of Defense, Yoav Gallant.[8] The attempts at setting in motion different kinds of accountability measures for the crimes committed in Ukraine, Israel, and Gaza follow a long historical development in how the international community may respond in international conflicts.[9] There is also a long list of within-nation conflicts where transitional justice is employed domestically.

While the transitional justice literature often deals with courts and trials at the aggregate level, it is, ultimately, judges' choices and actions that determine whether trials of alleged human rights perpetrators lead to conviction and justice. Exploring the role of judges in a transitional justice context sheds light on how judicial behaviour in politically sensitive cases is conditioned by a series of factors that go well beyond the 'normal' working environment in which judges usually operate in well-established, stable democracies.

The aim of this chapter is therefore twofold. First I show that, although the 'toolbox' of transitional justice has been vastly expanded over the last few decades to include a wide range of institutional and non-institutional measures, criminal accountability continues to constitute one of the core pillars of transitional justice. Second, I offer a tentative explanation for how and why claims for criminal justice rarely translate into successful trials, despite the general consensus that trials are considered vital to re-establishing the rule of law, and hence contribute to a transition to peace and democracy, after violent conflict. The contentious nature of such political transitions places multiple restrictions on judicial behaviour in so-called transitional justice cases.[10] For judges to exercise judicial independence and reach fair verdicts in these types of cases, a series of conditions must be in place. This chapter explores some of the enabling factors that account for the increasing number of trials, as well as identifies obstacles, that prevent judges from holding alleged human rights perpetrators to account.

The rest of this chapter proceeds in five sections. After next providing an overview of how courts feature in the broader literature on transitional justice (section 2), section 3 examines scholarly claims regarding how trials contribute (or not) to enhancing peace and democracy. Section 4 provides selected historical examples of how courts have constituted an important part of the transitional justice development. Section 5 zooms in on the role of judges and the choices they make. It identifies some of the conditions that must be in place for human rights trials to take place, while also identifying some of the obstacles that prevent judges from acting in such cases. Section 6 offers summary comments on the role of courts and judges in transitional justice and points out possible avenues for further research.

2. How Courts Feature in the Scholarly Transitional Justice Literature

The scholarly field of transitional justice has evolved from narrowly focusing on criminal accountability to taking on a much broader approach to how to deal with past systematic and gross human rights violations.

At the turn of the century, Ruti Teitel defined transitional justice as '*the conception of justice* associated with periods of political change, *characterized by legal responses* to confront the wrongdoings of repressive predecessor regimes' (Teitel 2003, 69, emphasis mine). Much later, the International Center for Transitional Justice (ICTJ), the world-leading non-governmental organization (NGO) in the transitional justice field, defined transitional justice as

> *a range of approaches* that societies undertake to reckon with legacies of widespread or systematic human rights abuse as they move from a period of violent conflict or oppression toward peace, democracy, the rule of law, and respect for individual and collective rights. In making such a transition, societies must confront the past in order to *achieve a holistic sense of justice for all citizens*, to establish or renew civic trust, to reconcile people and communities, and to prevent future abuses. (emphasis mine)

The United Nations Human Rights Office of the High Commissioner (OHCHR) has adopted an even more comprehensive approach, defining transitional justice as

> the *full range of processes and mechanisms* associated with a society's attempt to come to terms with a legacy of large-scale past conflict, repression, violations and abuses, in order to ensure accountability, serve justice and achieve reconciliation (explained further in S/2004/616). These processes may include *both judicial and non-judicial mechanisms*, including truth-seeking, prosecution initiatives, reparations, and various measures to prevent the recurrence of new violations, including constitutional, legal and institutional reform, the strengthening of civil society, memorialization efforts, cultural initiatives, the preservation of archives, and the reform of history education. Transitional justice aims to provide recognition to victims, enhance the trust of individuals in State institutions, reinforce respect for human rights and promote the rule of law, as a step towards reconciliation and the prevention of new violations.[11] (emphasis mine)

To sum up briefly: while transitional justice (TJ) in the early days was principally, though not exclusively, understood as criminal justice, TJ has been substantially broadened to include a range of non-judicial measures. The TJ 'toolbox', then, contains much more than criminal procedures to settle the past. This expanding toolbox reflects empirical developments. The main focus in the part of the transitional justice literature dealing with justice for human rights violations has been on courts as institutions, rather than on the central actors—like judges—within these institutions.

2.1 The Three Phases of Transitional Justice—Moving into a Fourth

Following Ruti Teitel's genealogy, one may distinguish between three major phases of transitional justice. The first phase, covering the few years between the end of the Second World War and the onset of the Cold War, was characterized by interstate cooperation, war crimes trials, and sanctions, as seen in the Nuremberg and Tokyo trials. The second phase, starting with the end of the Cold War, coincided with the 'third wave of democratization' (Huntington 1991). This period saw diversification of the formal mechanisms employed to bring about transitional justice, including a series of non-legal mechanisms such as truth commissions.[12] The TJ discourse expanded from an almost exclusive focus on legal responses intended primarily to ensure the rule of law,[13] to a more diverse focus on 'truth' and 'justice', with reconciliation as a desired outcome. In the third phase, TJ became an established component of post-authoritarian and post-conflict processes (Teitel 2003). In more recent years, we have seen that transitional justice may begin even before a conflict has ended (as in the case of the peace talks in Colombia or the peace process in Sudan, or during the ongoing wars in Ukraine and Gaza/Palestine), thus challenging the *post*-conflict, *post*-authoritarian assumptions. A particular feature of the third phase of TJ is an increased interest in local or traditional processes of justice and reconciliation (Shaw and Hazan 2010; Viaene 2010). Another feature is the diversification of actors. In addition to local actors, including ordinary citizens at the grassroots level, there has been a proliferation of donors eager to contribute to the so-called justice cascade (Lutz and Sikkink 2001). Human rights and international legal norms have become more firmly ingrained in the international political agenda and are increasingly invoked by scholars as well as practitioners.

A fourth phase of transitional justice is currently unfolding, as TJ mechanisms adopted and developed in post-authoritarian and post-conflict settings to deal with atrocities committed by a previous non-democratic regime are increasingly being adopted in contexts of mature democracies to address historical wrongs committed against Indigenous people and national minorities (Skaar 2023). Although the main TJ mechanisms employed to address these kinds of historical harms are first and foremost truth commissions and reparations, it is not unthinkable that some of the findings made by these non-transitional truth commissions may later lead to criminal prosecutions.

The TJ literature was initially dominated by legal scholars and political scientists, who tended to take a narrow approach to the topic. More recent contributions from philosophers, anthropologists, criminologists, sociologists, historians, and psychologists, amongst others, have made the field truly interdisciplinary. The debate has, as a result, become increasingly complex. From a focus on retributive justice and the rule of law, the discussion of transitional justice has broadened to include other elements, such as discussing the meaning of key concepts (e.g. 'truth', 'justice', 'peace', and 'reconciliation') as well as methodological and qualitative issues in the evaluation of their societal impact (e.g. defining and measuring impact, including the question of whether some aims are inherently contradictory). Although courts are first and foremost associated with 'justice', they arguably also contribute to 'truth', though a narrower kind of truth than what truth commissions are expected to bring about. Some consider 'justice'[14] to be a premise for reconciliation (Skaar 2013). Despite this expanding and broadening scholarly approach to the concept of 'justice', criminal trials for gross human rights violations remain one of the core pillars of transitional justice, principally due to their multiple aims.

3. What Are Trials in a TJ Context Expected to Achieve?

Trials in a transitional justice context are first and foremost expected to mete out punishment to alleged human rights perpetrators, when found guilty; yet their societal aims are much broader. By trials I mean criminal prosecution for human rights violations. By prosecution I mean processes that include indictments, arrests, extraditions, detentions, as well as trials for violations of core human rights by state officials.[15] There are four main kinds of formal courts in which such TJ trials may take place: national courts, international ad hoc tribunals, mixed courts (so-called hybrid courts) and, as of recent years, the International Criminal Court (ICC) and the International Court of Justice (ICJ).[16] In addition to these formal courts there are also situations where justice procedures can take place in sub-national local courts, such as the famous *gacaca* courts in Rwanda.[17]

In transitions from authoritarian rule, guarantees for impunity through formal amnesties have often been considered vital to holding elections or facilitating transfers of power to democratically elected new governments (Freeman 2009). Similarly, the most frequently used argument for introducing amnesties for gross human rights violations in post-conflict countries or when conflict is still ongoing, is that formal guarantees for immunity is the only tool that will make warring parties sit down at the negotiation table and hence secure peace.

3.1 The Impact of Trials on Democracy and Peace: Claims and Evidence

Beyond placing individual guilt and punishing individuals for violations of domestic and international law, transitional justice trials are important because they are believed to contribute to much broader societal goals, such as establishing 'peace' and 'democracy' after violent conflict. Scholars and practitioners who support trials for gross human rights violations consider criminal accountability to be necessary or desirable for complex moral, legal, and institutional reasons. Supposedly, punishment creates accountability, restores justice and dignity to the victims of abuse, establishes a clear break with past regimes, contributes to reconciliation, demonstrates respect for democratic institutions (particularly the judiciary), and (re-)establishes the rule of law, thereby helping to ensure that similar atrocities will never happen again. If hideous crimes go unpunished, it is claimed, people in newly established or re-established democracies will be unable to trust the state in general and the legal system in particular. At worst, a new civil war could erupt.

In post-authoritarian settings, gross human rights violations committed or permitted by the state or its agents during the period of dictatorship are particularly serious crimes because they are committed by those whose responsibility it is to enforce the law. In Latin America, which was largely dominated by military dictatorships in the 1970s and 1980s, the state apparatus typically committed, supported, or tolerated such violations. Moreover, the state, specifically the police and judiciary, failed to investigate the crimes at the time they occurred. Given that the governments established after the transitions to democracy were supposed to guarantee the human rights of all their citizens, their responses to past human rights violations were arguably of utmost importance for democratic consolidation and for (re)establishment of the rule of law.

Much of the early TJ scholarship is based on the Latin American experience of transitions from authoritarian rule to democracy. This may explain why a general scholarly pessimism prevailed in the 1980s and early 1990s regarding the impact of human rights trials on the prospects for democratic consolidation. In part based on the Argentine experience with several attempted, but ultimately unsuccessful, military coups, after judges in Argentina pushed for large scale trials of human rights perpetrators following the 'Dirty War' of the juntas in 1985, some scholars started to argue that pushing for trials would have a destabilizing effect and threaten democracy (O'Donnell and Schmitter 1986; Huntington 1991; Zalaquett 1992). Years later, when democracies had proven durable in Latin America, the main claim was that trials would have a positive effect on democracy by serving as a deterrent and by strengthening the rule of law (McAdams 1997; Méndez 1997).

The challenge of establishing the rule of law and democracy may be even greater after prolonged armed conflict, where violations ordered or encouraged by the state have left the justice system in shambles and where civilians or rebel groups rather than state representatives have carried out extensive abuses against civilians. In these situations, trials may strengthen democracy by engaging people in civic behaviour—as in the case of massive popular participation in the *gacaca* trials in Rwanda (Wierzynska 2004). The failure to pursue criminal accountability for these crimes would undermine the rule of law and the legitimacy of the post-transition government (Huyse 2001). In contrast to the pessimism regarding trials following dictatorship, in the early years of transitional justice some scholars argued that post-war trials were both legally and ethically desirable: they would deter future violations and thus would contribute to a lasting peace (Méndez 1997; Roht-Arriaza 1995). Specifically, trials would remove peace spoilers from positions of power (Meernik, Nichols, and King 2010, 311). A typical early mantra was 'no peace without justice', suggesting that public accounting for wartime crimes was necessary for peace and stability (Mendeloff 2004, 357).

However, striking a balance between consolidating democracy and simultaneously addressing past wrongs in a politically unstable condition is considered hard. Indeed, there is the possibility that in situations of internal armed conflict, human rights prosecutions will exacerbate human rights violations and thereby negatively affect peace (Kim and Sikkink 2010). Trial sceptics have argued that prosecutions may serve to sustain or even worsen the already deep social divisions between hostile parties emerging from civil war (Waldorf 2006). Mani (2005, 515) makes a similar observation, citing the 'danger of a backlash and relapse into violence' as one of many problems associated with war crimes trials.

Where national states have failed to prosecute those responsible for mass atrocity, the United Nations has in several cases set up special tribunals to deal with specific conflicts.[18] The assumed benefits are many. According to Mendeloff (2004, 361), 'deterrence of future war crimes is the primary claim of advocates of international criminal law'. This is done through public shaming and by physically removing from their positions power holders with blood on their hands. Advocates of international criminal trials for perpetrators of mass violence also believe that besides punishing the perpetrators and directly responding to the needs of victims, trials also 'promote the rule of law in emerging democracies' and 'promote reconciliation' (Fletcher and Weinstein 2002, 586). Disclosing the truth about those responsible for atrocities may also have a positive impact on democracy. For instance, Akhavan (2001) argues that truth-telling through the International Criminal Tribunal for the former Yugoslavia (ICTY) led directly to the ostracizing of extremist political leaders and hence strengthened democratic institutions by shaming and discrediting undemocratic leaders.

Not all scholars agree. Trial sceptics have argued that pushing for prosecutions according to universal standards in a politically and social fragile environment 'risks causing more atrocities than it would prevent' if insufficient attention is paid to political realities—and might thereby undermine peace and lead to an increase in repression (Snyder and Vinjamuri 2003/4, 5). Vinjamuri (2010, 206) questions what is at stake when the expectations outlined for international justice are set so high that justice is expected not only to spread the rule of law but also to deter crimes and bring peace. She argues that indicting individual leaders or rebels who are crucial to negotiations may increase pressures to use military force to resolve conflict. Postponing justice, not avoiding it altogether, may be a solution, Vinjamuri suggests, thus raising an important debate on the timing of justice.

Kitagawa and Bell (2022) take a middle position, suggesting that war crime prosecutions addressing war crimes generate uneven effects across domestic human rights practice. They argue that while holding trials may have a deterrent effect on committing certain kind of abuses, especially more visible abuses like torture, trials may encourage governments to continue.

In sum, the anticipated/expected contributions of human rights trials in achieving broad societal post-conflict goals like 'peace' and 'justice' are mixed. Trials are typically expected to positively contribute to the rule of law—and hence strengthen democracy. However, trials under certain circumstances can undermine democracy and lead to military coups.

Likewise, the anticipated impact of trials on peace is also mixed. Whereas some scholars contend that human rights trials are both legally and ethically desirable and practically useful in deterring future violations (Méndez 1997; Roht-Arriaza 1995), others argue that trials may undermine peace and lead to renewed violence (Meernik, Nichols, and King 2010) or an increase in repression (Snyder and Vinjamuri 2003/4). Other scholars contend that under situations of civil conflict and war, human rights prosecutions will exacerbate human rights violations (Kim and Sikkink 2010).

Empirical evidence supporting these in part contradictory claims is—not surprisingly—inconclusive. While some scholars find the positive effect of trials on peace is negligible (Lie, Binningsbø, and Gates 2007), others go even further, pointing to the danger of backlash and relapse into violence as one of the many problems associated with war crimes trials (Mani 2005). Sikkink and Walling's (2007) research shows that human rights trials have *not* undermined democracy or led to an increase in human rights violations or exacerbated conflict in Latin America. However, the authors make no claims as to the *positive* effects of trials. In a later study, Kim and Sikkink (2010) conclude that countries that record more 'trial years' are less repressive than countries that record fewer trial years. In contrast to the studies by Sikkink and Walling (2007) and Kim and Sikkink (2010), Olsen, Payne, and Reiter (2010) find that while single TJ mechanisms do not have statistically significant and positive effects on democracy and human rights, specific combinations of mechanisms—trials and amnesties or trials, amnesties, and truth commissions—can explain improvements in those two political goals. In a more recent study, Kitagawa and Bell (2022) test the premise that trials addressing wartime abuses deter future human rights violations. Using global data for the period 1982 to 2011, they find that while trials significantly reduce reliance on political imprisonment and extrajudicial killings (relatively visible abuses), gains for less visible physical integrity rights are limited. An additional important finding is that post-conflict governments sometimes use trials of regime opponent as a direct substitute for political imprisonment. Human rights prosecutions therefore can be part of a government's repressive toolkit.

Evidently, prosecutions and trials in a transitional justice context may have societal implications way beyond proving individual accountability for a committed crime. Importantly, most of these large-*N* comparative studies operate at the aggregate level, counting trials as observations and trial years as units of analysis. There is surprisingly little focus in the transitional justice literature on the institutions and people who ultimately make trials happen (or not), such as judges, but also other non-court and in-court actors like the police and prosecutors. The next section therefore zooms in on the importance of judges and the quality of their work in the discussion of transitional justice.

4. Courts and Accountability for Human Rights Violations

Against this scholarly scenario of contradicting claims and mixed empirical findings, this section tries to stake stock briefly of what has been achieved by courts in holding human rights perpetrators to account.

Returning again to the beginning of modern times 'transitional justice', the Nuremberg and Tokyo trials and the trials of Nazi criminals and their collaborators conducted in several European courts in the years following the end of the Second World War were the most comprehensive international efforts to get to grips with war crimes and human suffering on an unprecedented scale. This was made possible by a joint response from the world community; yet the number of alleged culprits who were tried and found guilty in the most famous trials in human history was dismal compared to the many millions of victims. Some of those who were found guilty were later pardoned after the onset of the Cold War.[19]

After these trials followed a long period of judicial inaction, principally due to antagonism between the five permanent members and veto powers of the UN Security Council (UNSC).[20] During the Cold War period, no international attempts and only two national attempts were made at prosecuting large-scale human rights violations: the trial of the juntas in Greece in 1975 after the end of the military dictatorship (where three military junta members were found guilty and sentenced to death for high treason) and then Argentina's famous trials of the generals (*Los Juntas*) a decade after the military dictatorship collapsed when Argentina lost the Falklands war against Great Britain.[21] Most countries refrained from even trying to prosecute the military, or the guerillas, after the end of military dictatorships. This falls into a pattern found at the end of the 1990s: courts were generally unwilling to take action against former military leaders or power holders responsible for human rights violations. More typically, countries undergoing transitions to peace or democracy established truth commissions to document human rights violations. Truth commissions were usually accompanied by amnesty laws which precluded prosecution from the human rights violations documented in the truth commission reports (Skaar 1999). Hence, criminal justice for past atrocities has been the exception rather than the rule, though the transitional justice scene is slowly changing.

When the Cold War ended with the collapse of the Berlin War in 1989 and the subsequent dismantling of the former Soviet Union, a new wave of democratization swept across the world, bringing about important changes for the pursuit of transitional justice. Scholars working on global data documented what is popularly referred to as 'the justice cascade' (Lutz and Sikkink 2001; Sikkink 2011). The general trend was clear: more perpetrators were held to account at the end of the twentieth century than in preceding decades. However, these efforts at criminal prosecutions were not even across the world. Latin America was again the region that paved the way (Skaar, García-Godos, and Collins 2016). This included the prosecution of the masterminds of repression. Former dictator Augusto Pinochet's arrest in London and subsequent extradition to Chile where he faced prosecution in domestic courts set a new precedent in universal jurisdiction (Roht-Arriaza 2000). Rios Montt in Guatemala was the first former head of state to be prosecuted by a domestic court for genocide and crimes against humanity (Burt 2016). Finally, former president of Peru, Alberto Fujimori, was held to account by the Peruvian Supreme Court for human rights abuses committed during his government (Burt 2009). Though relatively rare events, there has been a positive trend in holding power holders to account. Lutz and Reiger (2009 foreword) found that '[s]ince 1990, at least sixty-seven former heads of state or government have been prosecuted for serious human rights or financial crimes. Most of these leaders were brought to trial in free and fair judicial processes, and some served time in prison as a result'. Yet, at least for the Latin America region, it has proven easier to prosecute (former) heads of state for corruption than for human rights violations (Roht-Arriaza 2009).

Parallel to these domestic efforts of prosecuting human rights in national courts across the world[22] there have also been international efforts to establish some form of accountability for the worst crimes. The ICTY and the ICTR were UN responses to genocides committed in the former Yugoslavia and Rwanda respectively—made possible with the end of the Cold War. Ad-hoc mixed tribunals were also established for Cambodia and Sierra Leone. Important as these efforts were, very few persons were found guilty in the end. In search for a more permanent solution to international crimes, the ICC was established in 2000. This was yet a global attempt to put in place a more permanent institutional structure that could respond to the worst crimes committed globally and thus demonstrate that the world cannot remain passive when atrocities are committed. Its deterrent effects, though, have been questioned (Cronin-Furman 2013). More than two decades later, the track record of the ICC is not very impressive. Only a handful of people tried by the ICC have served jail sentences. The ICC's first issuance of an arrest warrant for a sitting head of state—then-President Omar al-Bashir of Sudan—in 2009 for genocide was considered an important milestone. However, the case remains at the pre-trial stage since Bashir is still (as of July 2024) at large. African countries, spearheaded by the African Union, has accused the ICC of being biased towards African countries, leaving crimes committed elsewhere in the world go unchallenged. One speaks of 'politicised justice'.[23] There is some reason to this critique, though part of the problems rests with African countries' reluctancies—either the states are unable or unwilling or both—to deal with human rights crimes in domestic courts. As long as the ICC remains under-financed and does not have the backing of the United States, judges at the Court are likely to continue to meet obstacles, making their quest for justice a slow process. This includes the arrest warrants against sitting heads-of-state Putin and Netanjahu mentioned earlier in this chapter.

5. Judicial Behaviour in Transitional Justice Cases

Tracing the history of transitional justice back to the end of the Second World War, we note, on the one hand, an increase in prosecutions and trials over time. On the other hand, there is a huge discrepancy between the scale and scope of human rights violations committed every year—in wars, internal armed conflicts, and in repressive regimes across the globe—and the number of people held accountable for these atrocities in national or international courts. In this section I offer some reflections on why this may be so. What has been the role of the judges? How have the judges contributed positively or negatively to accountability when presented with the opportunity to contribute to justice?

On a positive note, there has been a steep increase in judicial action to address human rights violations since the mid-1980s, especially since the turn of the millennium. This trend has been particularly noticeable in Latin America, where (as noted in the previous section), even heads of state have been held accountable for crimes against humanity and genocide in national courts. Many of these trials are so-called late trials, held well after the political transition or peace process has taken place. I have explored this phenomenon of post-transitional justice in earlier work, where I concluded that the observed increase in judicial independence (partly as a result of constitutional and structural reforms) was a chief explanation for the increased tendency of judges to take on cases of human rights violations (Skaar 2011; see also van Djik in this volume, and Epperly in this volume).[24] Other scholars have stressed the importance of deep transformations of the legal preferences of judges and prosecutors when accounting for how some judiciaries (in Latin America) have evolved from unresponsive bureaucracies into protectors of human rights (González-Ocantos 2016). Changes in the composition of the courts can make a difference. Appointment procedures and judicial tenure matter. Appointing pro-human rights judges to a court can make a positive difference in outcomes of cases dealing with gross human rights violations (see Brashear Tiede in this volume).[25] Likewise, the retirement or death of staunchly anti-human rights judges (often appointed by authoritarian leaders or with close ties to past non-democratic regimes) can make a difference.[26] Changes in court composition can be a result of deliberate political decision making, like changing appointment procedures, retirement requirements, or expanding the number of judges on a court to gain political control (so-called court packing; Perez-Liñán and Castagnola 2009). Changes in court composition can also be due simply to the passage of time. Comparative in-depth analysis of transitional justice trajectories in Latin America demonstrates that human rights trials are more likely to be held when some time had passed after the political transition (Skaar, García-Godos, and Collins 2016). A more enabling international institutional and legal framework has no doubt contributed to this development. International conventions against torture and rape have defined important crimes as violations against international law, providing judges pursuing transitional justice cases with new legal tools. Likewise, the establishment of the Inter-American

Commission and Inter-American Court of Justice have had an important impact in bringing about justice for past human rights violations in Latin America (Goldman 2009; Skaar, García-Godos, and Collins 2016).[27]

Despite this positive trajectory, we should also acknowledge that very few cases of human rights violations end up in court; even fewer are heard, and only a fraction of cases heard end in conviction. May I also add that of the few perpetrators who are convicted, many end up spending reduced sentences in jail, or serve jail sentences in comfortable surroundings, or are pardoned (by presidents) and never end up serving or completing their sentences.[28]

In this section I would like to reflect a bit on why this is so. What explains judicial (in)action in transitional justice cases? I would argue, that to have 'successful' trials of alleged human rights perpetrators, there are four necessary, though not sufficient, factors that must be present: (i) the case must be investigated and brought before a judge; (ii) the legal framework must enable the judge to hear the case; (iii) there must be sufficient evidence to prove guilt; and (iv) the judge must be able and willing to hear in the case and come to an unbiased, independent conclusion in the case—where conviction is a real possibility if the defendant is guilty.

When is this possible? First, the police and prosecutors must do their investigative work and bring the criminal case before a judge.[29] Second, once the judge is presented with the case, the judge must determine whether the legal framework allows the judge to act in the case. This means that the crime must violate either national law or international law. It also means that the crime must not be subject to statutes of limitation.[30] Finally, the crime should not be exempted from prosecution by the existence of an amnesty law. As mentioned above, transitions to democracy are frequently accompanied by amnesty laws, precisely to provide the outgoing regime protection from prosecution.

Third, as conflicts are often characterized by silencing crimes and repression, lack of reliable evidence can often be a problem. Especially where a long time has passed between the crime committed and the actual court hearings, assembling sufficient documentation and/or reliable witnesses can be very challenging—for example in the documentation of physical or psychological torture, or in cases trying to prove the crime of forced disappearances.

Fourth, and most importantly for the sake of this volume, the judge must be able and willing to give the case a fair hearing. This, in turn, requires judicial independence—both structural independence but also *de facto* individual independence. We know that the lack of judicial independence has been an obstacle to prosecution after many conflicts. This is so for many different reasons. First, in many conflict-ridden states, courts are weak (sometimes barely functioning, as after protracted civil war) and politically controlled by presidents. So, if there is no political will to have human rights perpetrators prosecuted, trials simply do not happen (Skaar 2011). Court packing in authoritarian systems is a well-known way to gain political control of the courts.[31] In some contexts, judges who have been appointed under military rule continue in office after transitions to democracy (as in the case of Chile) and have no incentives to prosecute the military for human rights violations. This is where the ideology of the judge matters:

close links to power holders (whether civilian or military) who disfavour trials are likely to incline judges not to prosecute.[32] Only in the cases where judges enjoy *de facto* independence from executives and superior judges in the judicial hierarchy, and where the judge is ideologically in favour of prosecuting human rights violations, can we expect fair trials to take place. Note, however, this can be expected only when the judge has sufficient evidence and the necessary legal tools. We know that judges who are committed to fair trials and justice have bypassed amnesty laws by declaring them unconstitutional or have bypassed statutes of limitations by reinterpreting the crime of disappearance for an ongoing crime etc., as in the cases of Chile and Argentina (Skaar 2011). Judges who are willing to prosecute have also been greatly aided by human rights activists and NGOs pushing for trials and presenting important documentation of human rights violations. Some judges pursue justice at high personal costs. Removal from judgeship, transfer to other courts, death threats inside and outside the court room, are just some of the things with which judges who conduct politically contentious human rights cases can be met. In sum, judges have to jump many political and legal hurdles as well as be personally disposed to act on cases of alleged human rights violations before justice can be done.

6. Concluding Remarks

This chapter has provided a snapshot of the role of courts in bringing about justice for gross and systematic human rights violations committed during violent conflict since the end of the Second World War up to the present. I have shown that although there has been an increase in human rights trials over time—especially within the Latin American region—it is still very challenging for judges to act in these often very politically contentious cases. Judges refrain from acting on these types of cases for numerous reasons, including insufficient evidence, lack of adequate legal frameworks, lack of resources, lack of judicial independence, and exposure to various types of threats and sanctions. These are all external factors that shape and help explain judicial behaviour in cases of human rights violations.

However, as this chapter also has shown, where there is a will, there is, at least sometimes, a way. There are stories in the transitional justice field of brave and courageous judges who are bent on overcoming obstacles, like finding loopholes in amnesty laws and applying international law where national law hinders prosecution. A judge's ideological outlook and attitude to human rights violations, in the end, can affect not only the judge's willingness to prosecute but also his/her ability to prosecute.

The boundaries for judicial action in human rights cases in national courts takes place not only within a national context but increasingly in dialogue with regional and global institutions, norms, and legal frameworks. Future research could explore these connections more thoroughly.

Here are three proposals for future research on judicial behaviour in a transitional justice context. First, there is a geographical knowledge gap in that much of existing TJ literature focussing on criminal prosecutions is based on the Latin American experience. Exploring TJ processes in the under-researched African and Asian regions (to the extent that they exist) could bring in new contextual knowledge regarding the influence of, for example, regional bodies (like the equivalent of the Inter-American Court and Commission) in shaping judicial behaviour. In-depth comparative cross-regional research of judicial behaviour in TJ processes/cases could also provide new knowledge on the importance of different legal traditions in shaping judicial behaviour.

A second venue for future research (not mentioned in this chapter for reasons of time and space) is how the influx of women judges in courts at all levels in countries that have suffered violent conflict may help shape the future transitional justice trajectory.[33] Women are making it to the highest courts in countries across the world (Dawuni and Kang 2015; Escobar-Lemmon et al. 2021) and are increasingly being appointed as both prosecutors and judges in regional and international courts. How, or if, the changing gender balance in these courts will alter the future role of judges in transitional justice cases and the judicial outcomes remains to be seen. It may be worth exploring this further, especially since violence against women and children is often part of the picture, and there is an—unproven—assumption in parts of the courts and gender literature that women judges tend to rule differently from male judges in gender-sensitive cases.

Third, and last, comparative analysis of the behaviour of judges in 'normal' criminal court cases under democracy versus judicial behaviour in cases of gross human rights violations in transitional justice contexts could help us tease out even further how politics can shape the outcomes in these cases and what judges can do to withstand political pressure where this pressure goes against free and fair trials.

Acknowledgements

A draft of this chapter was presented online at 'Conference on Judicial Behaviour', Hebrew University, Jerusalem, 14–16 December 2022. I thank the editors of this volume for constructive comments. Part of section 2 builds on Skaar, Malca, and Eide (2015) and section 3 expands on that work also.

Notes

1. 'Trial begins in Germany for 96-year-old former Nazi death camp secretary', by NEWS WIRES, France 24, 19 October 2021. france24.com (accessed 4 December 2023).
2. As Germany at the time was occupied by the Allied forces and divided into four zones, separate trials were conducted in each zone by the Americans, British, French, and possibly also Russians, respectively.

3. There is a vast literature on the post-Second World War trials. See, for example, Taylor (2012), Totani (2008), and also Biess and Moeller (2010) and Bílková (2014).
4. Note that the 'transition' part of 'transitional justice' (TJ) is currently debated as political transition seems to no longer be a prerequisite for transitional justice to take place. TJ may take place a long time after the conflict ended, as in the case of Brazil, in which case we speak of *post*-transitional justice (Collins 2010; Skaar 2011). As the current examples of the wars in the Ukraine and Gaza show, TJ may also start before the conflict has ended.
5. Massive and serious human rights violations refer to war crimes and crimes against humanity, including arbitrary arrest, political imprisonment, torture, forced disappearance, rape, and genocide.
6. https://www.icc-cpi.int/news/statement-prosecutor-karim-khan-kc-issuance-arrest-warrants-against-president-vladimir-putin
7. The crime of aggression cannot currently in practice be prosecuted by the ICC.
8. https://www.icc-cpi.int/news/statement-icc-prosecutor-karim-aa-khan-kc-applications-arrest-warrants-situation-state
9. Note that war crimes prosecutions of alleged criminal acts committed by Russian forces were taking place within the Ukraine legal system on a fairly massive scale as at September 2023.
10. 'Judicial behaviour' is here understood as the choices that justices make, and the implications of those choices for the society.
11. OHCHR. 'Transitional justice and human rights' at https://www.ohchr.org/en/transitional-justice, accessed 2 October 2023.
12. One of the most widely used definitions of a truth commission in the scholarship on transitional justice is that of Priscilla Hayner: a mechanism that is '(1) focused on past, rather than ongoing, events; (2) investigates a pattern of events that took place over a period of time; (3) engages directly and broadly with the affected population, gathering information on their experiences; (4) is a temporary body, with the aim of concluding with a final report; and (5) is officially authorized or empowered by the state under review' (Hayner 2011, 11).
13. Rule of law is a widely contested concept. For a useful discussion, see e.g. Bingham (2011).
14. The concept of 'justice' in the TJ literature has generated an expansive set of subcategories: forward-looking justice, backward-looking justice, retributive justice, restorative justice, retroactive justice, reparatory justice, administrative justice, local justice, traditional justice, historical justice, and more. Each term has different content and connotations.
15. Here I follow the definition of Kim and Sikkink (2010).
16. The permanent international criminal tribunal, the ICC, can only investigate cases of human rights violations of the most severe kind (such as genocide, crimes against humanity, and war crimes) if the state where the violations have taken place is unable and/or unwilling to prosecute.
17. Rwanda is one of the post-conflict countries that has generated the most scholarly attention in the TJ field. See e.g. Clark (2010).
18. This includes the International Criminal Tribunal for the former Yugoslavia (ICTYJ), the International Criminal Tribunal for Rwanda (ICTR), and a few UN-assisted hybrid criminal courts (with national and international judges), like the Extraordinary Chambers in the Courts of Cambodia, the Special Tribunal for Lebanon and the Special Court, and the Residual Special Court for Sierra Leone. For more information, see United Nations, 'International and Hybrid Criminal Courts and Tribunals' at https://www.un.org/ruleof

law/thematic-areas/international-law-courts-tribunals/international-hybrid-criminal-courts-tribunals/, accessed 2 October 2023.

19. Note also that many of those who were found guilty had their sentences reduced—like converting death sentences to jail sentences. In some cases, those serving jail sentences were pardoned and let out of jail for political reasons after the start of the Cold War. An example was the trial of twenty-four Nazis for the extermination of about 1 million people in the Einsatzgruppen Trial (officially, *The United States of America v Otto Ohlendorf, et al.*) held by the United States in its occupation zone in Nuremberg. All were pardoned in the end.
20. The United Nations was established in 1945, with the UN Security Council (UNSC) counting five permanent members: the Republic of China, the Provisional Government of the French Republic, the Soviet Union, the United Kingdom, and the United States—all with veto powers. When the Cold War started, united action in situations of war or violent conflict became impossible.
21. Twelve thousand people had 'disappeared', thousands more had been tortured. Nine generals and former Junta members were accused of atrocities like child abduction, torture, and disappearances. Only five were found guilty. All five were pardoned by the next president, Carlos Menem, in the name of 'reconciliation' (Skaar 2005). Yet Argentina is considered the success story of the Latin American continent; the protagonist of transitional justice (Skaar, García-Godos, and Collins 2016). The parallel to the Einsatzgruppen Trial is striking (see note 17).
22. For reasons of space, and because much, if not most, of the transition literature comes out of the Latin American experience, the focus here has been on Latin America. Note, however, that there have been human rights trials in other parts of the world too, such as in several Asian countries. See e.g. Sellars (2016).
23. For a review of three recent books dealing with the ICC in Africa, see Rubin (2020).
24. 'Judicial independence' has many meanings. We speak of *de jure* versus *de facto* independence, individual v structural independence, etc. For a more thorough conceptualization of judicial independence, see van Dijk in this volume. Judicial independence is usually considered desirable for numerous reasons. For a discussion of the concept and its development, see Epperly in this volume.
25. On the importance of judicial selection in general, not specifically transitional justice contexts, see Brashear Tiede in this volume.
26. For a general discussion of the importance of judicial tenure and retirements, see Aníbal Pérez-Liñán and Castagnola in this volume.
27. For a critical analysis of compliance with IACtHR judgements, see Pérez-Liñán, Schenoni, and Morrison (2023).
28. An excellent example is Argentine president Carlos Menem pardoning the generals who were convicted in the junta trials under the Alfonsín government in the 1980s (Skaar 2005, 164–66). See also note 19.
29. In the civil law tradition, some judges, called investigative judges, can also open investigations into alleged human rights violations. This was the case for example in Italy (Illuminati 2005) and in many Latin American countries (Brinks 2008), prior to the judicial reforms in the 1990s and 2000s, which shifted from inquisitorial to adversarial procedure. The work formerly carried out by investigative judges has been transferred to the police and prosecutors.

30. Some crimes, like homicide, are usually subject to statutes of limitation (typically fifteen to twenty years) in most national jurisdictions. This means that when there is a large time span between when a crime has been committed and when it is investigated (which is often the case in situations of long-term dictatorships or armed conflicts), statutes of limitation can constitute legal impediments to prosecute the crime. Note, however, that certain universal crimes, such as genocide, war crimes, and torture, are not subject to statutes of limitations.
31. On court packing and executive control of courts in Latin America, see e.g. Helmke (2005) and Perez-Liñán and Castagnola (2009). However, court packing is not peculiar to the Global South, nor is it always done for executive egoistic reasons of political control. For a more nuanced discussion of the negative and potential positive consequences of court packing, see e.g. Kosař and Šipulová (2023).
32. As argued elsewhere in this volume, judges tend to favour litigants of their own group over outsiders. See Epstein and Weinshall in this volume.
33. Research shows that women constitute an increasingly larger proportion of judges in post-conflict and transitional developing countries. See Skaar et al. (under review).

References

Akhavan, Payam. 2001. 'Beyond Impunity: Can International Criminal Justice Prevent Future Atrocities?' *American Journal of International Law* 95: 7–31.

Biess, Frank, and Robert G. Moeller. 2010. *Histories of the Aftermath: The Legacies of the Second World War in Europe*. New York: Berghahn Books.

Bílková, Veronika. 2014. 'Post-Second World War Trials in Central and Eastern Europe'. In *Historical Origins of International Criminal Law*, Vol. 2, edited by Cheah Wui Ling, Morten Bergsmo, and YI Ping, 697–733. Brussels: Torkel Opsahl Academic EPublisher.

Bingham, Tom. 2011. *The Rule of Law*: London: Penguin.

Brinks, Daniel M. 2008. *The Judicial Response to Police Killings in Latin America: Inequality and the Rule of Law*. New York: Cambridge University Press.

Burt, Jo-Marie. 2009. 'Guilty as Charged: The Trial of Former Peruvian President Alberto Fujimori for Human Rights Violations'. *International Journal of Transitional Justice* 3 (3): 384–405.

Burt, Jo-Marie. 2016. 'From Heaven to Hell in Ten Days: The Genocide Trial in Guatemala'. *Journal of Genocide Research* 18 (2–3): 143–69.

Clark, Phil. 2010. *The Gacaca Courts, Post-Genocide Justice and Reconciliation in Rwanda: Justice Without Lawyers*, Vol. XII. Cambridge: Cambridge University Press.

Collins, Cath. 2010. *Post-Transitional Justice: Human Rights Trials in Chile and El Salvador* University Park, PA: Pennsylvania State University Press.

Cronin-Furman, Kate. 2013. 'Managing Expectations: International Criminal Trials and the Prospects for Deterrence of Mass Atrocity'. *International Journal of Transitional Justice* 7 (3): 434–54. doi:10.1093/ijtj/ijt016.

Dawuni, Josephine, and Alice Kang. 2015. 'Her Ladyship Chief Justice: The Rise of Female Leaders in the Judiciary in Africa'. *Africa Today* 62 (2): 45–69.

Escobar-Lemmon, Maria C., Valerie J. Hoekstra, Alice J. Kang, and Miki Caul Kittilson. 2021. 'Breaking the Judicial Glass Ceiling: The Appointment of Women to High Courts Worldwide'. *The Journal of Politics* 83 (2): 662–74.

Fletcher, Laurel E., and Harvey M. Weinstein. 2002. 'Violence and Social Repair: Rethinking the Contribution of Justice to Reconciliation'. *Human Rights Quarterly* 24 (3): 573–639.

Freeman, Mark. 2009. *Necessary Evils. Amnesties and the Search for Justice*. New York: Cambridge University Press.

Goldman, Robert K. 2009. 'History and Action: The Inter-American Human Rights System and the Role of the Inter-American Commission on Human Rights'. *Human Rights Quarterly* 31: 856–87.

González-Ocantos, Ezequiel A. 2016. *Shifting Legal Visions: Judicial Change and Human Rights Trials in Latin America*. Cambridge: Cambridge University Press.

Hayner, Priscilla B. 2011. *Unspeakable Truths: Transitional Justice and the Challenge of Truth Commissions*, 2nd ed. London and New York: Routledge.

Helmke, Gretchen. 2005. *Courts Under Constraints: Judges, Generals and Presidents in Argentina*. Cambridge, UK: Cambridge University Press.

Huntington, Samuel P. 1991. *The Third Wave: Democratization in the Late Twentieth Century*. New York and London: Cambridge University Press.

Huyse, Luc. 2001. 'Amnesty, Truth or Prosecution'. In *Peace-building, A Field Guide*, edited by Luc Reychler and Thania Paffenholtz, 322–29. Boulder: Lynne Rienner.

Illuminati, Giulio. 2005. 'The Frustrated Turn to Adversarial Procedure in Italy (Italian Criminal Procedure Code of 1988)'. *Washington University Global Studies and Law Review* 4: 567–81.

Kim, Hunjoon, and Kathryn Sikkink. 2010. 'Explaining the Deterrence Effect of Human Rights Prosecutions for Transitional Countries'. *International Studies Quarterly* 54 (4): 939–63.

Kitagawa, Risa, and Sam R Bell. 2022. 'The Logic of Transitional Justice and State Repression: The Effects of Human Rights Prosecutions in Post-Conflict States'. *Journal of Conflict Resolution* 66 (6): 1091–1118.

Kosař, David, and Katarína Šipulová. 2023. 'Comparative Court-Packing'. *International Journal of Constitutional Law* 21 (1): 80–126.

Lie, Tove Grete, Helga Malmin Binningsbø, and Scott Gates. 2007. 'Post-Conflict Justice and Sustainable Peace'. World Bank Policy Research Working Paper 4191, April 2007 WPS4191: 1–24.

Lutz, Ellen, and Caitlin Reiger, eds. 2009. *Prosecuting Heads of State*. New York: Cambridge University Press.

Lutz, Ellen, and Kathryn Sikkink. 2001. 'The Justice Cascade: The Evolution and Impact of Foreign Human Rights Trials'. *Chicago Journal of International Law* 2 (1): 1–33.

Mani, Rama. 2005. 'Rebuilding an Inclusive Political Community After War'. *Security Dialogue* 36 (4): 511–26.

McAdams, A. James, ed. 1997. *Transitional Justice and the Rule of Law in New Democracies*. Notre Dame, IN: University of Notre Dame Press.

Meernik, James D., Angela Nichols, and Kimi L. King. 2010. 'The Impact of International Tribunals and Domestic Trials on Peace and Human Rights After Civil War'. *International Studies Perspectives* 11 (4): 309–34.

Mendeloff, David. 2004. 'Truth-Seeking, Truth-Telling, and Postconflict Peacebuilding: Curb the Enthusiasm?' *International Studies Review* 6 (3): 355–80.

Méndez, Juan E. 1997. 'Accountability for Past Abuses'. *Human Rights Quarterly* 19 (2): 255–82.

O'Donnell, Guillermo, and Philippe C. Schmitter, eds. 1986. *Transitions from Authoritarian Rule. Tentative Conclusions about Uncertain Democracies*, Vol. 4. Baltimore and London: The Johns Hopkins University Press.

Olsen, Tricia D., Leigh A. Payne, and Andrew G. Reiter. 2010. *Transitional Justice in Balance: Comparing Processes, Weighing Efficacy*. Washington DC: United States Institute of Peace Press.

Perez-Liñán, Aníbal, and Andrea Castagnola. 2009. 'Presidential Control of High Courts in Latin America: A Long-Term View (1904–2006)'. *Journal of Politics in Latin America* 1 (2): 87–114.

Pérez-Liñán, Aníbal, Luis Schenoni, and Kelly Morrison. 2023. 'Compliance in Time: Lessons from the Inter-American Court of Human Rights'. *International Studies Review* 25 (1): viac067.

Roht-Arriaza, Naomi, ed. 1995. *Impunity and Human Rights in International Law and Practice*. New York & Oxford: Oxford University Press.

Roht-Arriaza, Naomi. 2000. 'The Pinochet Precedent and Universal Jurisdiction'. *New England Law Review* 35: 311.

Roht-Arriaza, Naomi. 2009. 'Prosecutions of Heads of State in Latin America'. In *Prosecuting Heads of State*, edited by Ellen Lutz and Caitlin Reiger, 46–76. New York: Cambridge University Press.

Rubin, Maxine. 2020. 'Politicized Justice: Africa and the International Criminal Court'. *International Journal of Transitional Justice* 14 (2): 401–11. doi:10.1093/ijtj/ijaa007.

Sellars, Kirsten. 2016. *Trials for International Crimes in Asia*. Cambridge: Cambridge University Press.

Shaw, Rosalind, and Lars Waldorf with Pierre Hazan, eds. 2010. *Localizing Transitional Justice: Justice Interventions and Priorities after Mass Violence*. Stanford, California: Stanford University Press.

Sikkink, Kathryn. 2011. *The Justice Cascade: How Human Rights Prosecutions Are Changing World Politics*. New York: W. W. Norton & Co.

Sikkink, Kathryn, and Carrie Booth Walling. 2007. 'The Impact of Human Rights Trials in Latin America'. *Journal of Peace Research* 44 (4): 427–45.

Skaar, Elin. 1999. 'Truth Commissions, Trials—Or Nothing? Policy Options in Democratic Transitions'. *Third World Quarterly* 20 (6): 1109–28.

Skaar, Elin. 2005. 'Argentina: Truth, Justice, and Reconciliation'. In *Roads to Reconciliation*, edited by Elin Skaar, Siri Gloppen, and Astri Suhrke, 157–75. Lanham, MD: Lexington Books.

Skaar, Elin. 2011. *Judicial Independence and Human Rights in Latin-America: Violations, Politics and Prosecution*. New York: Palgrave Macmillan.

Skaar, Elin. 2013. 'Reconciliation in a Transitional Justice Perspective'. *Transitional Justice Review* 1 (1, Article 10): 53–103. http://dx.doi.org/10.5206/tjr.2012.1.1.4.

Skaar, Elin. 2023. 'When Truth Commission Models Travel: Explaining the Norwegian Case'. *International Journal of Transitional Justice* 17 (1): 123–40.

Skaar, Elin, Pilar Domingo, Siri Gloppen, and Marianne Tøraasen (guest editors). 'Women on the Bench: On Access, Experiences, and the Roles of Women Judges in Fragile States' (Special Issue proposal under review with *European Journal of Politics and Gender*).

Skaar, Elin, Jemima García-Godos, and Cath Collins. 2016. *Transitional Justice in Latin America: The Uneven Road from Impunity towards Accountability*. London: Routledge.

Skaar, Elin, Camila Gianella Malca, and Trine Eide. 2015. 'Transitional Justice Alternatives: Claims and Counterclaims'. In *After Violence: Transitional Justice, Peace and Democracy*, 15–42. London: Routledge.

Snyder, Jack, and Leslie Vinjamuri. 2003/4. 'Trials and Errors: Principle and Pragmatism in Strategies of International Justice'. *International Security* 28 (3): 5–44.

Taylor, Telford. 2012. *The Anatomy of the Nuremberg Trials: A Personal Memoir*. New York: Knopf.

Teitel, Ruti. 2003. 'Transitional Justice Genealogy'. *Harvard Human Rights Journal* 16 (Spring): 69–94.
Totani, Yuma. 2008. *The Tokyo War Crimes Trial: The Pursuit of Justice in the Wake of World War II*, Vol. 299. Cambridge: Harvard University Asia Center.
Viaene, Lieselotte. 2010. 'Dealing with the Legacy of Gross Human Rights Violations in Guatemala: Grasping the Mismatch between Macro Level Policies and Micro Level Processes'. *The International Journal of Human Rights* 15 (30 September): 1160–1181.
Vinjamuri, Leslie. 2010. 'Deterrence, Democracy, and the Pursuit of International Justice'. *Ethics & International Affairs* 24 (2): 191–211.
Waldorf, Lars. 2006. 'Mass Justice for Mass Atrocity: Rethinking Local Justice as Transitional Justice'. *Temple Law Review* 79 (1): 1–88.
Wierzynska, Aneta. 2004. 'Consolidating Democracy through Transitional Justice: Rwanda's Gacaca Courts'. *New York University Law Review* 79: 1934–70.
Zalaquett, José. 1992. 'Balancing Ethical Imperatives and Political Constraints: The Dilemma of New Democracies Confronting Past Human Rights Violations'. *Hastings Law Journal* 42 (6): 1425–38.

CHAPTER 38

COMPLIANCE WITH JUDICIAL DECISIONS

COURTNEY HILLEBRECHT

1. Introduction

Understanding compliance with judicial decisions provides key insights into how and why courts function, how public authorities respond to court decisions, and how decisions can transform policy and practice. Generating compliance with their decisions is perhaps the most effective tool courts have in shaping law, politics, and social norms. Getting to compliance, however, is difficult. Compliance with judicial decisions is almost never rote and almost always political.

The study of compliance with judicial decisions is an inherently comparative endeavour. Research on compliance with judicial decisions poses questions about why some countries comply more often with (international) judicial rulings than others; why different courts hand down different kinds of judicial decisions and how that influences compliance; and how different judges anticipate (non-)compliance. While single-case studies are not uncommon, much of the literature that has advanced the study of compliance is comparative in nature, either working across cases, across countries, or across courts.

International courts occupy much of the attention of compliance scholars. In their chapter earlier in this volume, Naurin and Voeten (2023) argue that despite calls for unifying the literature on domestic and international courts, scholars working on judicial behaviour continue to operate in their respective silos. They highlight compliance as one area which has received substantial attention from scholars of international courts and comparatively little attention from scholars of domestic courts.

One reason for international relations and international law scholars' focus on international courts for understanding compliance lies in the key difference between international courts and their domestic counterparts. Unlike domestic courts, which operate within a broader enforcement system composed of other national and sub-national courts, as well as a set of political institutions, international courts lack any higher enforcement. That is, there is no high(er) court to enforce the decisions of international courts, and the political bodies that created these courts are ill-equipped to enforce the courts' rulings. Compliance with these courts' decisions can only be generated through institutional capacity for and political commitment to compliance. Compliance becomes a 'least likely' scenario, and if the factors that contribute to compliance can succeed in this hostile environment, then presumably they can transfer to other, less difficult contexts as well.

While much of the theorizing about compliance has centred on the experience of international courts, there are, of course, also areas in which scholars of international courts borrow from the literature on domestic courts. One particularly important area of convergence is in judicial strategy, and particularly judges' strategic decision-making to avoid non-compliance, which this chapter addresses in more detail below (Staton and Moore 2011; Naurin and Voeten 2023).

Like much of the compliance literature, this chapter focuses on the experience of international courts, but the theoretical framework it examines is broadly comparative and generalizable. The factors that contribute to compliance can be evaluated across courts, across cases, across countries and over time. In the chapter that follows, I suggest that while the academic literature on compliance has laid essential groundwork by focusing on the role and importance of institutional capacity for facilitating compliance, institutional capacity must be taken into consideration alongside two other factors: political agency and commitment and the nature of the decisions themselves. To build on this argument, the chapter proceeds in five parts. First, it considers core definitional issues regarding compliance. The chapter then turns to discussing the current literature on institutional capacity. The chapter then pivots to the role of political commitment and actors' agency for—or against—compliance and, subsequently, the agency of judges and the nature of judicial decisions as it relates to compliance. The chapter then offers a brief discussion of non-compliance as an area for future research before concluding.

2. What Is Compliance and Why Does It Matter?

Compliance with judicial decisions is both the outcome and the process that emerges when public authorities align their policies and practices with a court's decisions. Compliance is an inherently state-based process, whereby a variety of state actors and public authorities engage with a court decision. While civil society and non-state actors can help to facilitate compliance, public authorities are the key recipients of judicial decisions and those most responsible for compliance.

2.1 Compliance and Effectiveness

Compliance plays a central role in amplifying the impact of courts' decisions. Facilitating compliance with their judicial decisions is one of the primary ways that courts can influence policy and regulatory outcomes, alter political behaviour, promote the development of socio-legal norms, and shape subsequent legal decision-making (Kapiszewski and Taylor 2013). In other words, compliance is critical to connecting courts with the broader socio-legal environments in which they work. Understanding how and why compliance unfolds, then, is central to improving the efficacy of courts and their relationship with other actors.

Although some scholars argue that compliance is conceptually and empirically distinct from effectiveness (e.g. Raustiala and Slaughter 2002; Gilligan 2006; Martin 2013; Shany 2014), in this chapter I conceive of compliance as a component of courts' effectiveness but not the sum total of effectiveness. That is, courts can have an impact through means other than compliance, but accounts of effectiveness that exclude compliance miss the main mechanisms through which courts can exert their influence.

This statement comes with caveats, of course. Judicial decisions can go unheeded, and thus have very little effect on state practice. Moreover, even full compliance with a court's decisions does not necessarily equate to transformative change, particularly in situations in which courts repeatedly hand down the same decisions to the same public authorities. Consider, for example, Italy's caseload before the European Court of Human Rights (ECtHR). As of early 2022, over 64 per cent of the ECtHR decisions in Italian cases in which they found a violation pertained to the right to a fair trial, particularly with respect to the incredible slowness of Italy's judicial system (European Court of Human Rights 2022). If Italy were to comply with *all* these decisions, then, yes, the impact would be transformative. The impact of any one decision, however, is likely quite small (Bossi 2012).

Beyond compliance, courts' effectiveness can derive from the communicative effect of their decisions as well as their normative import as adjudicators of the law (Shany 2014, 2009). Moreover, many courts, particularly international courts, engage in quasi-judicial work, ranging from training to outreach programmes to *in situ* visits. This work can amplify courts' effectiveness and, in the long-term, improve compliance. In fact, compliance and effectiveness are endogenously related, and understanding their relationship requires not only a clear definition of compliance but also an understanding of who and what drives compliance and how.

2.2 Conceptualizing Compliance

When (international) courts hand down their decisions, they often set out a list of compliance obligations that state authorities need to meet, a process that lends itself to the study of compliance. While some types of domestic courts also can engage in this practice, for example, family courts, this practice is not as consistent or widespread as in international courts. Moreover, subsequent litigation on court compliance orders is possible, but not common on the international stage, while appellate adjudication is very common within the domestic sphere. This means that deciphering compliance with international courts is an implicitly political process, which has generated a variety of approaches to measuring and conceptualizing compliance.

Early conceptualizations understood compliance as a dichotomy. For example, public authorities either comply with a legal obligation or they do not, although all research on compliance has evolved to recast compliance in more nuanced ways (Chayes and Chayes 1993; Downs et al. 1996). One of the first shifts towards considering the nuances of compliance was considering the phenomenon of partial compliance. Scholars and stakeholders, such as the Inter-American Commission on Human Rights (IACtHR), recognized that compliance outcomes rarely fell neatly into zero-sum typologies. Instead, state actors often complied with some parts of a judicial decision but not others. Scholars and judicial institutions called this phenomenon partial compliance (Inter-American Commission on Human Rights 2009, 2021; Hawkins and Jacoby 2010). The challenge with this approach, however, is that partial compliance includes all compliance outcomes that fall between no compliance at all and full compliance. Partial compliance thus becomes a meaningless designator (Hillebrecht 2009).

To address the shortcomings of the partial compliance approach to conceptualizing and measuring compliance, the subsequent wave of compliance research recast compliance as a typology, broken down not by the degree of completion but rather by the types of actions required of state actors (Hillebrecht 2009; Hillebrecht 2014; Murray and Long 2015; Haglund 2020; Haglund and Welch 2021). Some categories include, but are not limited to, financial reparations; individual measures, such as providing medical care for victims; measures of non-repetition, such as changing laws and regulatory practices; judicial proceedings, including holding perpetrators accountable; symbolic measures, such as public apologies; and more (Hillebrecht 2014). This approach allows for the disaggregation of compliance into the discrete obligations that, taken together, amount to compliance with judicial decisions.

Compliance is not just an outcome, however. It is also a process, and more recent scholarship has focused on the dynamics of the compliance process (Murray and Long 2015; Hillebrecht 2017; Haglund et al. 2022). This research centres on the understanding that meeting a court's demands entails significant political, legal, and socio-cultural work. By focusing only on the outcome of compliance, the scholarship misses the rich and nuanced political processes that can connect a judicial decision with the broader environment of state behaviour and practice. Only by untangling the process of compliance can scholars and stakeholders alike capture the wide range of political decisions involved in the compliance process.

Practically speaking, achieving compliance can rarely be achieved with one action by one actor (Murray and De Vos 2020). Instead, the compliance process requires that states must first consider the requirements of any given judicial decision and then delegate the responsibility for addressing those obligations to the relevant public authorities who, in turn, must fulfil those obligations (Haglund et al. 2022). Compliance, then, requires institutional capacity. Executives, judges, legislators, and bureaucrats can all be called upon to facilitate compliance with judicial decision. Their institutional capacity, however, only tells part of the story. Institutional capacity must be paired with political commitments and tempered by the judges' own strategic decision-making and the quality of the judicial decision in question.

3. Institutional Capacity, Democratic Institutions, and Compliance

The academic literature on compliance generally stresses the importance of democratic institutions for facilitating compliance with judicial decisions, and one feature of comparative compliance studies has been a focus on the relative capacity of domestic institutions across countries for facilitating compliance. These institutions, which include but are not limited to executives, legislatures, judiciaries, the media, and civil society, provide the needed capacity for compliance, as well as the checks and balances that hold state actors accountable for their compliance obligations (Sims 2004; Viljoen and Louw 2007; Keller and Stone-Sweet 2008; Powell and Staton 2009; Hawkins and Jacoby 2010; Hillebrecht 2012; Huneeus 2013; Anagnostou and Mungiu-Pippidi 2014; Stiansen 2019; Murray and De Vos 2020; Haglund 2020). Unlike compliance with treaties, which can be self-executing, compliance with judicial decisions demands the participation of a variety of state agents and public authorities.

To illustrate the multiple obligations—and thus multiple stakeholders—involved in compliance with judicial decisions, consider the following example. In 2021, the IACtHR issued a decision regarding the murder of Mexican human rights defender, Digna Ochoa y Plácido. In its judgment, the IACtHR found the state responsible for the lack of due diligence in the investigation of Ms. Ochoa's death. The Court proceeded to enumerate the steps that the state needed to take to comply with the judgment. These steps were plentiful and included over twenty discrete obligations, ranging from naming a street in honour of the victim to creating a federal programme on the investigation of attacks on human rights defenders, to paying pecuniary and non-pecuniary damages (*Case of Digna Ochoa and Family Members v Mexico* 2021).

No single institution or state agency could address all these obligations. Each obligation requires state capacity, ranging from small and localized, such as renaming a street in the victim's honour, to nationally important, such as creating new federal programmes and amending the constitution. Although the scope of the tasks required by the IACtHR in this case is exceptionally broad and far-reaching, it illustrates a central truth about compliance with judicial decisions: compliance requires state capacity and, beyond that, delegation and coordination among public authorities.

3.1 Institutional Capacity and Compliance

To successfully comply with judicial decisions, executives, legislatures, and judiciaries must not only fulfil the compliance obligations for which they have the authority but they also must coordinate with other actors. This is difficult and politically charged work, and each institution has its own limitations and political orientation. In this section, I consider the role different actors—judiciaries, legislatures, and executives—play in the compliance process.

3.1.1 *Judiciaries*

Let us consider the above example from the IACtHR. When the IACtHR issued its decisions on the reparations in the *Digna Ochoa* case, it ordered the state to create a series of laws, practices, and procedures to protect witnesses participating in criminal proceedings, including but not limited to revising the current witness protection programmes, creating training programmes, and increasing the autonomy of the state's forensic services (*Case of Digna Ochoa and Family Members v Mexico* 2021). In this case, the domestic judicial system was asked to reflect on and change its own practices.

Judges and judiciaries are linchpins to the compliance process. Long-standing explanations of compliance by lower courts point to a number of hypotheses as to why lower courts comply with higher court decisions, including fear of having non-compliance decisions subsequently overturned, a commitment to upholding precedent, and a desire to be as legally accurate as possible (Klein and Hume 2003). Moreover, not only are courts often asked to make changes of their own but they also can oversee and evaluate the compliance processes undertaken by other state actors. Given the opportunity, some courts have expanded their oversight powers regarding compliance, particularly as a way to push back against the expansion of executive authority (Ahdout 2022).

This is not to suggest that domestic courts are always willing compliance partners (Huneeus 2011). Instead, domestic courts can view international courts' decisions as intrusive, incompatible with domestic laws and norms, or otherwise 'optional' (Klein and Hume 2003). The above-mentioned case of the Polish Constitutional Tribunal's rejection of the European Court of Justice's (ECJ) interim measures is a clear illustration of courts resisting compliance with higher or international courts. It is not a lone example. In perhaps the most egregious case of domestic courts undermining compliance with international courts, in 2017, the Russian Constitutional Court declared that it would only comply with ECtHR decisions that were consistent with the Russian Constitution. That is, rather than the ECtHR evaluating the viability of Russian rights protections and domestic courts responding accordingly, the Russian Constitutional Court would evaluate the ECtHR's decisions against its own constitution (Marchuk 2017). Compliance is inherently political, and the role of courts in the compliance process is no exception.

Examining the role of national courts in facilitating compliance, both with international court rulings and with their own judgments, opens the door to many rich comparisons. Consider, for example, the role of constitutional courts, which can both decide to implement—or not—international court rulings *and* evaluate the constitutionality of domestic legislation in light of both domestic and international law. As Engst et al. (2020, 3) suggest, 'highest courts do not play alone'. In the same way that international courts cannot automatically guarantee compliance with their rulings, national courts, too, interface with other domestic institutions to facilitate compliance. While national courts have more institutional power than their international counterparts, they still face the challenges of relying on other actors, including legislatures and executives, to fully execute their judgments.

3.1.2 *Legislatures*

When judicial decisions demand changes in existing laws or the creation of new laws, legislatures are brought into the compliance process and can be key compliance partners (Donald 2017). Legislative bodies can complicate the compliance process, however. Divided legislatures can delay compliance, as complying with judicial decisions requires forging sufficient consensus to pass new laws (Stiansen 2019). Moreover, legislatures can take different, and perhaps contradictory, views on if and how they should comply with judicial decisions (Macfarlane 2013; Butt and Murharjanti 2022). While research suggests that legislatures, particularly those that are divided along party lines and with multiple veto points, can delay compliance, these actors also can provide important accountability for compliance and promote compliance with judicial decisions, even if that means the compliance process unfolds at a slower pace (Voeten 2014; Stiansen 2019). Legislative compliance can have profoundly important impacts, ranging from providing new laws to hold perpetrators accountable to disarming paramilitary forces (Hillebrecht 2012).

3.1.3 *Executives*

While judges and legislatures provide critical institutional capacity for compliance with judicial decisions, it is executives that typically sit at the centre of the compliance process. In the case of international courts' decisions, the executive branch is the first and most formidable gatekeeper to compliance (Haglund 2020). A state's foreign service, which is typically under the executive branch, receives international courts' decisions and then must decide on if and how to disseminate the decision and delegate authority for the obligations embedded in it. This gives executives an incredible amount of latitude and power to sway the compliance agenda (Hillebrecht 2014; Haglund 2020). While other actors, such as legislatures and judiciaries, can hold executives accountable for their compliance responsibilities, executives have agenda-setting power, as well as the authority to delegate and coordinate the execution of compliance mandates by other public authorities.

Consider, again, the case of *Digna Ochoa v Mexico*. In its reparations order, the IACtHR required the state of Mexico to, in addition to those listed above: create an annual award for human rights defenders in Digna Ochoa's memory, design an outreach campaign to showcase the role of human rights defenders; create, execute, and support a programme to protect human rights defenders; implement a witness protection mechanisms; and 'elaborate, present and expedite, through the Office of the Legal counsel of the Federal Executive Branch, a proposed constitutional amendment to provide autonomy and independence to the Forensic Services'. (*Case of Digna Ochoa and Family Members v Mexico* 2021, 50). Executing these obligations requires that the state prioritize which obligations are at the top of the agenda—and which are not—and delegate authority for fulfilling them. These are not simple tasks, particularly when we consider that this is only one decision among many others, from both domestic and international courts alike. These organizational and logistical challenges are only amplified when executives ideologically and politically disagree with the decisions and the role of (international) courts in domestic politics.

As should now be clear, any one democratic institution alone is unlikely to provide the capacity needed to comply fully with judicial decisions. Instead, compliance with judicial decisions requires a coalition of actors, comprised of executives, legislatures, and civil society actors (Dai 2005; Cardenas 2007; Hillebrecht 2014). That said, as the example of Poland and the ECJ discussed below illustrates, even fully capable institutions are not in and of themselves enough to guarantee compliance. Compliance requires agency, and while institutionalist accounts of compliance tell part of the story, they elide the importance of political mobilization for—and against—compliance.

4. Commitment and Compliance

Institutional capacity alone is not sufficient to facilitate compliance processes. Compliance also requires agency. The institutions charged with facilitating compliance with judicial decisions must leverage their agency through political and legal commitments and through mobilization around judicial decisions. Democratically oriented institutions can do some of this work on their own. By their very nature, democratic institutions can hold state agencies—each other—to account. In democratic settings, executives cannot simply file away those court decisions with which they are disinclined to comply. While executives can set the agenda on compliance, legislatures, judiciaries and civil society can hold them accountable for their international commitments (Hillebrecht 2014; Haglund 2020). Even within democracies, however, compliance rates with international judicial decisions vary dramatically. While democracies comply *more* than non-democracies, they do not necessarily *always* comply (Haglund et al. 2022). Compliance should not be taken for granted even in the most robust democracies or in response to the most rigorous regulatory or enforcement regimes (Carrubba 2005). This is because compliance is a political process that is facilitated by institutional capacity but sparked by political commitment and forged through actors' agency and advocacy. To understand the role that political commitment and agency play in compliance, consider the following example.

In April 2018, Poland passed a new law that lowered the retirement age of Polish Supreme Court Justices from seventy to sixty-five years of age. This new law resulted in the immediate, forced retirement of nearly one-third of the seventy-two sitting justices on the Polish Supreme Court (European Commission 2019). The European Union (EU) swiftly condemned the new law as it coincided with a bevy of other anti-democratic measures that the nationalist Law and Justice Party (PiS) had been implementing since its election in 2015 (Cameron 2021).

With the view that this new law negatively impacted judicial independence, the European Commission began infringement proceedings against the government of Poland and referred the case to the ECJ in September 2018. In December 2018, the ECJ issued an interim measure to stop the implementation of the new age limits (European Commission 2019). Over the following two years, the European Commission launched two additional infringement procedures concerning judicial independence in Poland. The first pertained to Poland's newly established Disciplinary Chamber of the Supreme Court, which left the Supreme Court justices vulnerable to political usurpation, particularly as each of the Chamber members were selected by political appointees. This proceeding wound its way to the ECJ, which decided that Poland needed to suspend the disciplinary process. The second infringement process, in 2020, contended that a new body of Polish laws eroded judicial independence by preventing Polish judges from applying EU law (Cameron 2021).

Poland's Constitutional Tribunal did not, at the time of writing, agree with the ECJ's decisions, and it has ruled that the Tribunal does not need to comply with the ECJ's interim measures. Justice Minister Zbigniew Ziobro responded to the Constitutional Tribunal's decision by saying, '[f]ortunately the constitution and normality prevail over an attempt to interfere in the internal affairs of a member state' (Cameron 2021). Amidst continued non-compliance, the Commission asked for the ECJ to leverage financial penalties against Poland, which Poland's deputy justice minister referred to as 'an act of aggression' (Tilles 2021). In October, 2021, the ECJ issued its decision, placing a penalty of €1 million per day on Poland's non-compliance ('Poland Must Pay €1 Million Daily over Judiciary Reforms, ECJ Rules' 2021). By December, Polish authorities had offered a compromise on the Disciplinary Chamber, but the other issues of judicial independence remain untouched and concerns over the independence of the judiciary and the rule of law persist (Shotter and Fleming 2022).

Haglund, Hillebrecht, and Read (2022) set out a typology of the stages of compliance, which include (i) consideration, (ii) delegation, (iii) execution, and (iv) compliance. Each stage of this compliance process requires both institutional capacity and political commitment. Let us examine the first stage: consideration. Recalling that compliance is not simply an outcome but also a process, public authorities must first decide if they will pursue compliance with a judicial decision at all. This is important to highlight because even though both international and domestic judicial decisions are legally binding, public authorities will debate the extent to which they must abide by a judicial decision, or if they will engage with a judicial decision at all. These questions are particularly pertinent with respect to international judicial decisions.

The second stage of the compliance process, delegation, is the stage in which agency becomes critical. As highlighted in the IACtHR example above, compliance with court decisions, particularly international court decisions, requires many discrete actions. There is no single action that will satisfy the totality of compliance with a judicial decision. As such, even in instances in which institutions are acting with agency and are committed to the compliance process, compliance requires that the subsidiary tasks are delegated to various state agencies. This is a massive coordination effort that requires both the institutional capacity to fulfil the obligations and the political commitment necessary to continue to advocate for compliance amidst competing interests and demands. It is quite easy to imagine a scenario in which one state agency lets a particular task languish or in which an agency lacks the political commitment necessary to execute its compliance-related tasks. Delegation also implies some degree of prioritization. When public authorities are trying to manage multiple incentives and demands, not all compliance-related tasks will take top billing. Beyond that, delegation should not presume execution, which is the third stage of the compliance process. Even when state agents view compliance with a judicial decision as a priority and delegate responsibility for compliance with that decision, they need to do the work of executing those responsibilities before compliance, the fourth and final stage, is achieved.

Mobilization around and for compliance with judicial decisions, then, is critical. The research in this area suggests that several different stakeholders can help to galvanize sufficient political commitment to compliance. While these stakeholders can be advocates for a cause within state agencies, compliance proponents also can come from civil society. When confronted with the challenges implicit in eliciting compliance with judicial decisions, engaged civil society actors can help to move compliance issues into the public sphere and force executive, legislative, and judicial action (McCann 2008; Cichowski 2013; van der Vet 2014; Vanhala 2018). Of course, as the ECJ example above also illustrates, public authorities who are mobilized *against* compliance can grind the compliance process to a halt.

While institutional capacity is necessary for compliance with judicial decisions, it is not sufficient. Black-box understandings of how institutions work cannot explain nuanced variations in compliance, such as why democracies might comply with some judicial decisions and not others. To understand these important variations in compliance outcomes, scholars must consider the agency of the actors working within and beyond those institutions. They also must account for the quality and character of the judicial decisions themselves.

5. The Quality of Judgments and Agency of Judges

Chapters 9 through 16 in this volume provide more insight into judges and their decision-making. For this chapter, it is important to identify the connections between judicial decision-making and compliance processes. The previous section suggested that understanding compliance with judicial decisions requires a theoretical framework that invokes both the capacity and agency of those institutions tasked with discharging the obligations handed down by a court. A comprehensive view of compliance with judicial decisions also requires that scholars and stakeholders account for both the quality of judgements and the agency and strategy of judges. Judicial decisions invoke various moral interpretations of the law and also vary in terms of clarity and the degree of difficulty of the compliance orders they mandate (e.g. see Hawkins and Jacoby 2010; Haglund et al. 2022). Beyond the level of difficulty of judicial decisions, some might be clear and concise while others are vague and ambiguous. Moreover, the judges themselves are not empty vessels that blindly apply the law but rather strategic actors who behave accordingly. They can adjust their own behaviour based on how much they value compliance and their assumptions about how best to promote compliance with their decisions.

One important area of research considers if and how judges shape their decisions to anticipate compliance or, perhaps more accurately, non-compliance. At the broadest level, courts—and the individual judges that sit on them—are responsive to public opinion and the threat of their decisions being ignored or overridden. One line of argumentation suggests that judges also anticipate non-compliance or legislative override and generate decisions in a such a way as to either avoid the largest points of resistance and/or to facilitate compliance (Carrubba 2005; Harvey and Friedman 2006; Carrubba et al. 2008). Judges also anticipate potential backlash more broadly, becoming more deferential when the threat of backlash grows (Staton and Vanberg 2008; Shany 2014; Stiansen and Voeten 2020).

Examining how judges anticipate and respond to backlash is one area of convergence across international and domestic court scholarship and remains an area of productive inquiry. The existing scholarship suggests that judges on both international and national courts can circumnavigate restraints and anticipated non-compliance and backlash in several ways (Hillebrecht 2021). For example, they could make their decisions more achievable, avoiding more contentious issues (Shany 2014). Alternatively, they also could issue decisions that are more ambiguous, leaving state actors to their own devices to decide how to achieve compliance. With particularly ambiguous decisions, it would be difficult for the public or other stakeholders to discern non-compliance, thereby protecting the court from high rates of non-compliance with its decision (Staton and Vanberg 2008). This is because ambiguous decisions are less likely to provide a clear path towards compliance, which itself can invite criticism.

Staton and Romero (2019) find that judges leverage ambiguity in their language to allow on-the-ground stakeholders the flexibility they need to promote compliance with judicial decisions. This is consistent with broader arguments about the importance of the margin of appreciation and subsidiarity doctrines (e.g. Carozza 2003; Shany 2005; Letsas 2006). Both doctrines suggest that states need policy-making latitude to implement judicial decisions in a way that is consistent with domestic policies and practices. The margin of appreciation doctrine, which is central to the ECtHR, implies that while all states need to comply with the ECtHR's decisions, they have some flexibility to comply with ECtHR decisions in a way that makes the most sense given the domestic landscape (Letsas 2006; McGoldrick 2016). Of course, states and sub-state actors also push for expanding the margin of appreciation as a way to undermine the ECtHR's decisions and avoid any meaningful change as the result of the compliance process (Fikfak 2018; Follesdal and Ulfstein 2018; Aldao 2019).

The choices judges make about how directive to be in their decisions are related to how well the judges understand the social and political environment in which their decisions will be interpreted and how much they trust the authorities responsible for complying with their decisions to take this obligation seriously. In contrast to the argument that judges provide more ambiguity to allow for better compliance, recent scholarship suggests that more incisive decisions that take into account the context of compliance are likely to see better—and faster—compliance outcomes (Stiansen 2021). In other words, judges might try to facilitate compliance by offering very clear directions. While this approach might yield more resistance, it also mitigates uncertainty about the expectations for compliance.

The discussion thus far has assumed that judiciaries are speaking with one voice, although, of course, judges sharing a bench often have decidedly different ideological orientations, understandings of their roles, and positions within the decision-making process.

As such, scholars also need to consider judges' relationships with *other* judges. For example, Westerland et al. (2010) argue that judges on lower courts in the United States will be less bound to precedent set by the US Supreme Court when the current court is ideologically divorced from the court that handed down the precedent. The reverse is also true. That is, judges care about maintaining a strong relationship with their superiors and, as such, they will follow precedent and comply with higher court decisions in order to maintain those relationships (Westerland et al. 2010).

Of course, any given court is unlikely to work as a cohesive whole. Judges have their own preferences regarding the rule of law, as well as the content of any given decision. They seek particular policy goals based on their individual normative preferences and experiences (Voeten 2008). Individual judges will have differing opinions on the merits and reparations of a case and generating cohesion on the bench is a difficult task. Cohesion can be wrought by attrition, or the gradual wearing down of judges' individual preferences to meet the group's norms, or by collegiality (Cardozo 1921, as cited in Edwards 2003). Cohesion, in turn, can lead to judicial decisions sending a stronger signal about the court's intent and interpretation of the law, and thus creating more demand for compliance. Dissent, on the other hand, can negatively affect compliance outcomes (Naurin and Stiansen 2020). At the same time, others argue judging by consensus can generate 'bland, disjointed judgments ... that lack clarity and persuasion' (Pierce 2008, 319).

When judges face dissent on the bench or disagree with public authorities about a particular policy, they can reach out directly to constituents through interviews with the media, press releases and other mechanisms. This can help to bolster their reputation and help them circumnavigate challenges associated with the separation of powers typically required to generate compliance with their decisions. That is, when judges decide in ways that typically go against a consensus wrought by the public authorities, they can engage directly with the public to sway those same authorities, thus generating compliance (Staton 2006).

A comprehensive view of compliance with judicial decisions cannot treat the decisions themselves as value-neutral, nor can it treat the judges as empty vessels. The production of judicial decisions is endogenous to the compliance process, and the more that scholars and stakeholders embrace this complicated relationship, the more nuanced our understanding of compliance will become.

6. A Word on Non-Compliance

The literature on compliance is rich, nuanced, and constantly evolving. In addition to the extant lines of inquiry around the role of institutional capacity, political commitment, judicial quality, and the strategic planning of judges, I would like to advance one additional theme for consideration, which is a deep interrogation into systemic non-compliance. Examining only the outcome of non-compliance obscures the various mechanisms that can contribute to this result. Returning to thinking of compliance as a process and examining where compliance stalls or stops along that process—consideration, delegation, execution, or compliance—is critical for understanding non-compliance. For instance, non-compliance can be the result of domestic institutions' lack of institutional capacity and their inability to hold states accountable for judicial decisions. Alternatively, non-compliance can be a function of a lack of political commitment, or even an intentional strategy to undermine the judicial institution in question. Both processes would yield the same outcome—non-compliance—but they require different theoretical frameworks to understand and different policy interventions to alter. A comparative lens can shed light on why some courts struggle more with non-compliance than others, and also help scholars understand why the same court can have both radically different non-compliance rates across countries or issue areas.

Let us consider again Italy's case load before the ECtHR. Italy has thousands of cases pertaining to the long duration of judicial proceedings. The sheer quantity of these cases is largely caused by systemic non-compliance, failure to comply with the general measures of one of these decisions subsequently leads to hundreds more. What drives this systemic non-compliance? One might argue that this non-compliance is largely wrought by both insufficient capacity and political commitment. Addressing these compliance mandates would require that the country completely overhaul its entire judicial system. It lacks both the capacity and the political commitment to undertake such a monumental task (Bossi 2012).

In contrast, non-compliance also can be an intentional strategy. Recall Russia's contentious relationship with the ECtHR. Although no longer an ECtHR member, Russia has long made non-compliance a key part of its strategy in dealing with the ECtHR. In the early 2000s, Russia's non-compliance flooded the ECtHR, bogging the court down in repeat cases. By overloading the system, Russia ensured that the ECtHR could not decide on too many new cases or new issues. In fact, the Kremlin even worked to stop the implementation of Protocol 14, which was devised to give the Court the authority to rule more expeditiously on repeat cases through three-judge panels. This new approach, which ultimately was approved despite Russian resistance, would have an incredible impact on the rapidity with which the ECtHR could address new cases, including those against Russia (Council of Europe 2004; Caflisch 2006; Buyse 2009; Bowring 2010).

Systemic non-compliance is an effective strategy for backlash against judicial bodies because it undermines the courts' authority and makes the courts appear illegitimate in the eyes of stakeholders. Perhaps courts cannot facilitate compliance because their decisions are too ambitious, too ambiguous, or, alternatively, too specific, or too divorced from the socio-political context in which they will be implemented. If the courts cannot foster compliance, then, supporters and critics alike must ask, what *can* they accomplish? Systemic non-compliance draws attention to the courts' shortcomings and can be part of a broader—and dangerous—strategy of backlash against judicial institutions (Staton and Vanberg 2008; Alter et al. 2015; Stiansen and Voeten 2020; Hillebrecht 2021).

Systemic non-compliance, whether driven by a lack of institutional capacity or a failure of political commitment, is just as much of a political process as compliance. To put it differently, non-compliance is not simply the absence of compliance but rather a process in its own right that demands more attention.

7. Conclusion

The study of compliance with judicial decisions has experienced a significant revolution over the past three decades. This revolution has been prompted, in part, by better and more nuanced data. While early conceptualizations and operationalizations of compliance regarded compliance as a dichotomous outcome, more recent research has embraced the nuances and complexities of compliance with judicial decisions, highlighting variations in the types of compliance obligations public authorities must manage, the process of compliance, and the role that judicial authorities have in facilitating or thwarting compliance. These changes in both the conceptualization and operationalization of compliance have been transformative. Not only have they helped scholars and practitioners alike begin to draw more nuanced conclusions about how and when judicial decisions prompt compliance, but they also have opened the door to incorporate a broader range of actors into models of compliance. Large data collection efforts focused on national courts, and particularly constitutional courts, also has facilitated this revolution in our understanding of compliance. Efforts such as the German Constitutional Court Database (Engst et al. 2020), the US Supreme Court Database, and the Israeli Supreme Court Database (Weinshall et al. 2018) all facilitate comparative compliance analyses across court cases within national contexts. This volume is also a call to action for more cross-national datasets on judicial decisions and compliance with them.

While democracies comply more often and more readily with judicial decisions than non-democracies, this chapter suggests that the story of compliance is far more complicated. This is not to suggest that capacity is not important. To the contrary, capacity is hugely important. Compliance with judicial decisions demands that multiple actors engage with the compliance process and execute a wide range of legal, social, and political tasks. But institutions alone are insufficient. They need political commitment and agency to bring them to life. This is particularly true because facilitating compliance is inevitably a political task. Not only must public authorities delegate the different compliance tasks to a range of state actors but if they are serious about compliance, they also need to overcome various points of political resistance and lethargy. Without public authorities or civil society to actively champion the cause of compliance with judicial decisions, compliance orders can lay dormant and unfilled.

It is not just state actors that matter, of course. As this chapter has demonstrated, judges play an important, and perhaps underspecified, role in the compliance process. Judges make important choices about the clarity and quality of judicial decisions. While on the one hand, clearer decisions provide a blueprint for compliance, they also do not leave much 'wriggle room'. Judges can err on the side of ambiguity, thereby eliding some of the biggest compliance challenges. At the same time, ambiguous and overly broad decisions do little shore up courts' own legitimacy.

What these current and future research avenues all suggest is that compliance is an inherently political process. It is not purely an outcome, nor can it be accomplished by institutions alone. Compliance requires political commitment as well as institutional capacity. It also hinges on judicial behaviour and judges' strategic decision-making in their decisions. As such, academics, activists, and stakeholders alike must come to appreciate the nuanced and complicated patterns that can contribute to public authorities' compliance with judicial decisions and the long-term effects compliance with those decisions can have on policy, politics, and state practice.

References

Ahdout, Z. Payvand. 2022. 'Enforcement Lawmaking and Judicial Review'. *Harvard Law Review* 135 (4): 940–1006.

Aldao, Martin. 2019. 'Entre La Deferencia y La Indiferencia: Margen de Apreciación, Democracia y Situaciones de Vulnerabilidad En La Jurisprudencia Del Tribunal de Derechos Humanos (Between Deference and Indifference: Margin of Appreciation, Democracy and Vulnerability Situations in the Caselaw of the European Courts of Human Rights)'. SSRN Scholarly Paper ID 3444287. Rochester: Social Science Research Network. https://papers.ssrn.com/abstract=3444287.

Alter, Karen J., James Thuo Gathii, and Laurence R. Helfer. 2015. 'Backlash Against International Courts in West, East and Southern Africa: Causes and Consequences'. SSRN

Scholarly Paper ID 2591837. Rochester Social Science Research Network. http://papers.ssrn.com/abstract=2591837.

Anagnostou, Dia, and Alina Mungiu-Pippidi. 2014. 'Domestic Implementation of Human Rights Judgments in Europe: Legal Infrastructure and Government Effectiveness Matter—EJIL'. *European Journal of International Law* 25 (1): 205–27.

Bossi, Elena. 2012. 'The Execution of the European Court of Human Rights' Judgments in Italy: Measures to Reduce Domestic Excessive Length of Proceedings'. Netherlands, Helsinki Human Rights Commission.

Bowring, Bill. 2010. 'The Russian Federation, Protocol No. 14 (and 14bis), and the Battle for the Soul of the ECHR'. *Goettingen Journal of International Law* 2 (2): 589–617.

Butt, Simon, and Prayekti Murharjanti. 2022. 'What Constitutes Compliance? Legislative Responses to Constitutional Court Decisions in Indonesia'. *International Journal of Constitutional Law* 20 (1): 428–53. https://doi.org/10.1093/icon/moac014.

Buyse, Antoine. 2009. 'ECHR BLOG: Protocol 14 Bis—The Interim Solution'. *ECHR Blog*. 4 May 2009. http://echrblog.blogspot.com/2009/05/protocol-14-bis-interim-solution.html.

Caflisch, Lucius. 2006. 'The Reform of the European Court of Human Rights: Protocol No. 14 and Beyond'. *Human Rights Law Review* 6 (2): 403–15. https://doi.org/10.1093/hrlr/ngl007.

Cameron, David R. 2021. 'After the EU Demands Compliance with ECJ Decisions, Poland Says It Will Replace Judges' Disciplinary Chamber'. The MacMillan Center. 17 August 2021. https://macmillan.yale.edu/news/after-eu-demands-compliance-ecj-decisions-poland-says-it-will-replace-judges-disciplinary.

Cardenas, Sonia. 2007. *Conflict and Compliance: State Responses to International Human Rights Pressure*. Philadelphia: University of Pennsylvania Press.

Cardozo, Benjamin Nathan. 1921. *The Nature of the Judicial Process*. New Haven: Yale University Press.

Carozza, Paolo. 2003. 'Subsidiarity as a Structural Principle of International Human Rights Law'. *American Journal of International Law* 97 (1): 38–79.

Carrubba, Clifford J. 2005. 'Courts and Compliance in International Regulatory Regimes'. *Journal of Politics* 67 (3): 669–89. https://doi.org/10.1111/j.1468-2508.2005.00334.x.

Carrubba, Clifford J., Matthew Gabel, and Charles Hankla. 2008. 'Judicial Behavior under Political Constraints: Evidence from the European Court of Justice'. *The American Political Science Review* 102 (4): 435–52.

Case of Digna Ochoa and Family Members v Mexico. 2021. Inter-American Court of Human Rights (I/A Court H.R.). Preliminary Objections, Merits, Reparations and Costs. Judgment of 25 November 2021. Series C No. 447.

Chayes, Abram, and Antonia Handler Chayes. 1993. 'On Compliance'. *International Organization* 47 (2): 175–205.

Cichowski, Rachel A. 2013. 'Legal Mobilization, Transnational Activism, and Gender Equality in the EU'. *Canadian Journal of Law & Society / La Revue Canadienne Droit et Société* 28 (2): 209–27. https://doi.org/10.1017/cls.2013.22.

Council of Europe. 2004. *Protocol No. 14 to the Convention for the Protection of Human Rights and Fundamental Freedoms, Amending the Control System of the Convention*. Council of Europe Treaty Series No. 194. Council of Europe, Strasbourg, France.

Dai, Xinyuan. 2005. 'Why Comply? The Domestic Constituency Mechanism'. *International Organization* 59 (2): 363–98.

Donald, Alice. 2017. 'Parliaments as Compliance Partners in the European Convention on Human Rights System'. In *The International Human Rights Judiciary and National*

Parliaments: Europe and Beyond, edited by Andreas Follesdal, Geir Ulfstein, and Matthew Saul, 75–109. Cambridge: Cambridge University Press. https://doi.org/10.1017/9781316874820.005.

Downs, George W., David M. Rocke, and Peter N. Barsoom. 1996. 'Is the Good News about Compliance Good News about Cooperation?' *International Organization* 50 (3): 379–406.

Edwards, Harry. 2003. 'The Effects of Collegiality on Judicial Decision Making'. *University of Pennsylvania Law Review* 151 (5): 1639–90.

Emmett Macfarlane. 2013. 'Dialogue or Compliance? Measuring Legislatures' Policy Responses to Court Rulings on Rights'. *International Political Science Review* 34 (1): 39–56. https://doi.org/10.1177/0192512111432565.

Engst, Benjamin G., Thomas Gschwend, Christoph Hönnige, and Caroline E. Wittig. 2020. 'The Constitutional Court Database: Conceptualizing a Relational Database'. Working Paper. https://ccdb.eu/.

European Commission. 2019. 'EC statement on the judgment of the ECJ on Poland's SC law'. Text. European Commission - European Commission. 24 June 2019. https://ec.europa.eu/commission/presscorner/detail/mt/statement_19_3376.

European Court of Human Rights. 2022. 'The ECHR and Italy: Facts and Figures'. https://www.echr.coe.int/Documents/Facts_Figures_Italy_ENG.pdf.

Fikfak, Veronika. 2018. 'Changing State Behaviour: Damages before the European Court of Human Rights'. *European Journal of International Law* 29 (4): 1091–125. https://doi.org/10.1093/ejil/chy064.

Shotter, James, and Sam Fleming. 2022. 'Poland Offers Compromise in Rule of Law Dispute with EU'. *Financial Times*, 12 February 2022.

Follesdal, Andreas, and Geir Ulfstein. 2018. 'EJIL: Talk!—The Draft Copenhagen Declaration: Whose Responsibility and Dialogue?' 22 February 2018. https://www.ejiltalk.org/the-draft-copenhagen-declaration-whose-responsibility-and-dialogue/.

Gilligan, Michael J. 2006. 'Is Enforcement Necessary for Effectiveness? A Model of the International Criminal Regime'. *International Organization* 60 (04): 935–67. https://doi.org/10.1017/S0020818306060310.

Haglund, Jillienne. 2020. *Regional Courts, Domestic Politics, and the Struggle for Human Rights*. Cambridge: Cambridge University Press.

Haglund, Jillienne, Courtney Hillebrecht, and Hannah Roesch Read. 2022. 'International Human Rights Recommendations at Home: Introducing the Women's Rights Compliance Database (WRCD)'. *International Interactions* 45 (5): 1070–87. https://doi.org/10.1080/03050629.2022.2090935.

Haglund, Jillienne, and Ryan M Welch. 2021. 'From Litigation to Rights: The Case of the European Court of Human Rights'. *International Studies Quarterly* 65 (1): 210–22. https://doi.org/10.1093/isq/sqaa089.

Harvey, Anna, and Barry Friedman. 2006. 'Pulling Punches: Congressional Constraints on the Supreme Court's Constitutional Rulings, 1987–2000'. *Legislative Studies Quarterly* 31 (4): 533–62. https://doi.org/10.3162/036298006X201922.

Hawkins, Darren, and Wade Jacoby. 2010. 'Partial Compliance: A Comparison of the European and Inter-American Courts for Human Rights'. *Journal of International Law and International Relations* 6 (1): 35–85.

Hillebrecht, Courtney. 2009. 'Rethinking Compliance: The Challenges and Prospects of Measuring Compliance with International Human Rights Tribunals'. *Journal of Human Rights Practice* 1 (3): 362–79. https://doi.org/10.1093/jhuman/hup018.

Hillebrecht, Courtney. 2012. 'The Domestic Mechanisms of Compliance with International Law: Case Studies from the Inter-American Human Rights System'. *Human Rights Quarterly* 34 (4): 959–85.

Hillebrecht, Courtney. 2014. *Domestic Politics and International Human Rights Tribunals: The Problem of Compliance*. Cambridge Studies in International and Comparative Law. Cambridge: Cambridge University Press.

Hillebrecht, Courtney. 2017. 'Compliance: Actors, Context and Causal Processes'. *Research Handbook on the Politics of International Law*, February. Cheltenham, UK. https://www.elgaronline.com/view/edcoll/9781783473977/9781783473977.00010.xml.

Hillebrecht, Courtney. 2021. *Saving the International Justice Regime: Beyond Backlash Politics*. Cambridge: Cambridge University Press.

Huneeus, Alexandra. 2011. 'Courts Resisting Courts: Lessons from the Inter-American Court's Struggle to Enforce Human Rights'. *Cornell International Law Journal* 44 (3): 493–533.

Huneeus, Alexandra Valeria. 2013. 'Compliance with International Court Judgments and Decisions'. SSRN Scholarly Paper ID 2198595. Rochester: Social Science Research Network. http://papers.ssrn.com/abstract=2198595.

Inter-American Commission on Human Rights. 2009. 'Annual Report of the Inter-American Commission on Human Rights 2009'. OEA/Ser.L/V/II. Doc. 51, corr. 1. Washington, DC: Organization of American States. http://www.cidh.oas.org/annualrep/2009eng/TOC.htm.

Inter-American Commission on Human Rights. 2021. 'Effects of Total Compliance with Structural Recommendations: Cases with Published Merits Report'. Organization of American States. https://www.oas.org/es/cidh/Publicaciones/2021/01_cuadernillo_seguimiento_EN.pdf.

Kapiszewski, Diana, and Matthew M. Taylor. 2013. 'Compliance: Conceptualizing, Measuring, and Explaining Adherence to Judicial Rulings'. *Law & Social Inquiry* 38 (4): 803–35. https://doi.org/10.1111/j.1747-4469.2012.01320.x.

Keller, Helen, and Alec Stone-Sweet. 2008. *A Europe of Rights: The Impact of the ECHR on National Legal Systems*. New York: Oxford University Press.

Klein, David E., and Robert J. Hume. 2003. 'Fear of Reversal as an Explanation of Lower Court Compliance'. *Law & Society Review* 37 (3): 579–606.

Letsas, George. 2006. 'Two Concepts of the Margin of Appreciation'. *Oxford Journal of Legal Studies* 26 (4): 705–32.

Marchuk, Iryna. 2017. 'Flexing Muscles (Yet Again): The Russian Constitutional Court's Defiance of the Authority of the ECtHR in the Yukos Case'. *EJIL: Talk!* (blog). 13 February 2017. https://www.ejiltalk.org/flexing-muscles-yet-again-the-russian-constitutional-courts-defiance-of-the-authority-of-the-ecthr-in-the-yukos-case/.

Martin, Lisa. 2013. 'Against Compliance'. In *International Law and International Relations: Synthesizing Insights from Interdisciplinary Scholarship*, edited by Jeffrey L. Dunoff and Mark Pollack, 591–610. New York: Cambridge University Press.

McCann, Michael. 2008. 'Litigation and Legal Mobilization'. In *The Oxford Handbook of Law and Politics*, edited by Gregory A. Caldeira, R. Daniel Kelemen, and Keith E. Whittington, 522–40. Oxford Academic. http://www.oxfordhandbooks.com/view/10.1093/oxfordhb/9780199208425.001.0001/oxfordhb-9780199208425-e-30.

McGoldrick, Dominic. 2016. 'A Defence of the Margin of Appreciation and an Argument for Its Application by the Human Rights Committee'. *International & Comparative Law Quarterly* 65 (1): 21–60. https://doi.org/10.1017/S0020589315000457.

Murray, Rachel, and Christian De Vos. 2020. 'Behind the State: Domestic Mechanisms and Procedures for the Implementation of Human Rights Judgments and Decisions'. *Journal of Human Rights Practice* 12 (1): 22–47. https://doi.org/10.1093/jhuman/huaa004.

Murray, Rachel, and Debra Long. 2015. *The Implementation of the Findings of the African Commission on Human and Peoples' Rights*. Cambridge: Cambridge University Press.

Naurin, Daniel, and Øyvind Stiansen. 2020. 'The Dilemma of Dissent: Split Judicial Decisions and Compliance with Judgments from the International Human Rights Judiciary'. *Comparative Political Studies* 53 (6): 959–91. https://doi.org/10.1177/0010414019879944.

Naurin, Daniel, and Erik Voeten. 2023. 'Transcending the Domestic-International Divide'. In *Oxford Handbook of Comparative Judicial Behavior*, edited by Lee Epstein, Gunnar Grendstad, Urška Šadl, and Keren Weinshall. Oxford: Oxford University Press.

Pierce, Jason. 2008. 'Institutional Cohesion in the High Court of Australia: Do American Theories Travel Well Down Under?' *Commonwealth & Comparative Politics* 46 (3): 318–40. https://doi.org/10.1080/14662040802176582.

'Poland Must Pay €1 Million Daily over Judiciary Reforms, ECJ Rules'. 2021. *Euronews*. 27 October 2021. https://www.euronews.com/my-europe/2021/10/27/poland-must-pay-daily-fines-of-1-million-over-its-controversial-judiciary-reforms-ecj-rule.

Powell, Emilia Justyna, and Jeffrey K. Staton. 2009. 'Domestic Judicial Institutions and Human Rights Treaty Violation'. *International Studies Quarterly* 53 (1): 149–74. https://doi.org/10.1111/j.1468-2478.2008.01527.x.

Raustiala, Kal, and Ann-Marie Slaughter. 2002. 'International Law, International Relations, and Compliance'. In *Handbook of International Relations*, edited by Walter Carlnaes, Beth Simmons, and Thomas Risse, 538–58. New York: Sage.

Shany, Yuval. 2005. 'Toward a General Margin of Appreciation Doctrine in International Law?' *European Journal of International Law* 16 (5): 907–40. https://doi.org/10.1093/ejil/chi149.

Shany, Yuval. 2009. 'No Longer a Weak Department of Power? Reflections on the Emergence of a New International Judiciary'. *European Journal of International Law* 20 (1): 73–91. https://doi.org/10.1093/ejil/chn081.

Shany, Yuval. 2014. *Assessing the Effectiveness of International Courts*. Oxford: Oxford University Press.

Sims, John Cary. 2004. 'Compliance without Remands: The Experience under the European Convention on Human Rights'. *Arizona State Law Journal* 36 (2): 639–60.

Staton, Jeffrey K. 2006. 'Constitutional Review and the Selective Promotion of Case Results'. *American Journal of Political Science* 50 (1): 98–112.

Staton, Jeffrey K., and Will H. Moore. 2011. 'Judicial Power in Domestic and International Politics'. *International Organization* 65 (3): 553–87.

Staton, Jeffrey K, and Alexia Romero. 2019. 'Rational Remedies: The Role of Opinion Clarity in the Inter-American Human Rights System'. *International Studies Quarterly* 63 (3): 477–91. https://doi.org/10.1093/isq/sqz031.

Staton, Jeffrey K., and Georg Vanberg. 2008. 'The Value of Vagueness: Delegation, Defiance, and Judicial Opinions'. *American Journal of Political Science* 52 (3): 504–19. https://doi.org/10.1111/j.1540-5907.2008.00326.x.

Stiansen, Øyvind. 2019. 'Delayed but Not Derailed: Legislative Compliance with European Court of Human Rights Judgments'. *The International Journal of Human Rights* 23 (8): 1221–47. https://doi.org/10.1080/13642987.2019.1593153.

Stiansen, Øyvind. 2021. 'Directing Compliance? Remedial Approach and Compliance with European Court of Human Rights Judgments'. *British Journal of Political Science* 51 (2): 899–907. https://doi.org/10.1017/S0007123419000292.

Stiansen, Øyvind, and Erik Voeten. 2020. 'Backlash and Judicial Restraint: Evidence from the European Court of Human Rights'. *International Studies Quarterly* 64 (4): 770–84. https://doi.org/10.1093/isq/sqaa047.

Tilles, Daniel. 2021. 'EU Seeks Daily Fines for Poland over Non-Compliance with ECJ Ruling'. *Notes from Poland* (blog). 7 September 2021. https://notesfrompoland.com/2021/09/07/eu-seeks-financial-penalties-for-poland-over-non-compliance-with-ecj-rulings/.

Vanhala, Lisa. 2018. 'Is Legal Mobilization for the Birds? Legal Opportunity Structures and Environmental Nongovernmental Organizations in the United Kingdom, France, Finland, and Italy'. *Comparative Political Studies*, 51 (3): 380–412. https://doi.org/10.1177/0010414017710257.

Vet, Freek van der. 2014. 'Holding on to Legalism: The Politics of Russian Litigation on Torture and Discrimination Before the European Court of Human Rights'. *Social & Legal Studies* 23 (3): 361–81. https://doi.org/10.1177/0964663914530420.

Viljoen, Frans, and Lirette Louw. 2007. 'State Compliance with the Recommendations of the African Commission on Human and Peoples' Rights, 1994–2004'. *American Journal of International Law* 101 (1): 1–34.

Voeten, Erik. 2008. 'The Impartiality of International Judges: Evidence from the European Court of Human Rights'. *American Political Science Review* 102 (04): 417–33. https://doi.org/10.1017/S0003055408080398.

Voeten, Erik. 2014. 'Domestic Implementation of European Court of Human Rights Judgments: Legal Infrastructure and Government Effectiveness Matter: A Reply to Dia Anagnostou and Alina Mungiu-Pippidi'. *European Journal of International Law* 25 (1): 229–38. https://doi.org/10.1093/ejil/chu004.

Weinshall, Keren, Lee Epstein, and Andy Worms. 2018. 'The Israeli Supreme Court Database'. 2018. https://iscd.huji.ac.il/data.

Westerland, Chad, Jeffrey A. Segal, Lee Epstein, Charles M. Cameron, and Scott Comparato. 2010. 'Strategic Defiance and Compliance in the U.S. Courts of Appeals'. *American Journal of Political Science* 54 (4): 891–905. https://doi.org/10.1111/j.1540-5907.2010.00465.x.

CHAPTER 39

COURTS AS AGENTS OF CHANGE

GERALD N. ROSENBERG

1. Introduction

As of the end of 2022 the United Nations recognized 193 countries. While they differ in many aspects, all of them have courts with varying degrees of power and influence. Some courts, including, for example, those in Columbia, India, Israel, South Africa, and the United States, are generally seen as powerful and important. Other courts, particularly those in authoritarian or failed political systems such as Afghanistan, China, the Central African Republic, the Democratic Republic of Congo, Myanmar, and North Korea are usually seen as less influential. And courts in some countries such as Hungary and Russia, once seen as powerful, have lost influence. At first glance it appears to be an act of supreme hubris to generalize about the comparative role of courts as agents of change, yet to the extent that courts share features in common it may be possible to gain some insight into their ability to promote social change. With such a vast universe of courts, generalization will necessarily glide over important differences between them, let alone subtle nuances.

It would be impossible to discuss all 193 judicial systems in a single chapter, let alone a book. There is too much variation among political and judicial systems. Choices have to be made. For the purpose of this chapter, I will focus on the seventy-four countries included on the list of full and partial democratic regimes compiled in 2021 by *The Economist* Intelligence Unit. While courts in authoritarian regimes can sometimes produce change,[1] they rarely enjoy independence from central governmental authority. Judicial decisions promoting social change in authoritarian countries generally simply second the acts of governmental and party leaders. Policy-making remains in the hands of political leadership, not courts. As Tate notes, it is 'unlikely that one will encounter the judicialization of politics outside democratic polities' (1995, 28).

Tate's reference to 'judicialization' points to the involvement of courts in policy-making. There are a growing number of courts in democratic countries that are not only hearing cases about social change, but also, and importantly, issuing decisions requiring it. 'The late 20th and early 21st centuries', Delaney and Dixon write, 'may well be marked as the Judicial Era. Courts have burgeoned across the globe' (2018, 1). There has been enormous growth in the number of courts with the power of judicial review: the power to invalidate acts of the other branches of government on the ground that those acts violate constitutional rights. Exploring the growing worldwide importance of courts and judges in making policy decisions, Hirschl sees it as 'one of the most significant developments in late-20th and early-21st century government' (Hirschl, in this volume). This is a new phenomenon. Calabresi notes that

> almost all written constitutions in the 19th century—and really up until 1945—did not provide for enforcement of constitutional texts against the legislature by judicial review. The only pre-1945 exceptions were the four federal regimes in the United States, Canada, Australia and, to some extent, in Switzerland.
>
> (Calabresi 2018, 83)

However, by the second decade of the twenty-first century judicial review existed 'in some form in more than two-thirds of countries worldwide' (Delaney and Dixon 2018, 1). In addition, courts around the world are doing more than telling governments they can't act in certain ways. They are also issuing decisions that require governments to take certain actions. Hirschl even coined a word for the growing involvement of courts in policy-making: 'Juristocracy' (Hirschl 2004).

Narrowing the list to seventy-four partial and full democratic countries still includes too many political and judicial systems for detailed analysis. Again, choices must be made. This chapter will lay out what appear to be key factors in the comparative relationship of courts to social change among democratic countries. The factors will be illustrated by examples drawn from multiple countries.

What do I mean by social change? Courts affect social change in myriad ways. In a mundane sense, every judicial decision changes the relationship between the parties before the court. However, when scholars and lay people alike talk about courts making social change they typically mean 'progressive' judicial decisions that protect and further the rights of large groups of historically disadvantaged people such as the poor, ethnic and racial minorities, women, gay men and lesbians, immigrants, political dissidents, etc. Courts interact with change when they order governments to extend benefits to groups of people being denied them and to create programmes to help the disadvantaged. Courts in democratic polities can also issue decisions aimed at preventing overreach by one part of government, for example telling a president or prime minister that she can't take an action she wants to do. While this might not necessarily further the interests of the relatively disadvantaged in the short run, it does maintain the rule of law which is essential to protecting everyone's rights.

There is a danger that focusing on court decisions ordering progressive social change rather than on the effects of those decisions overstates the importance of courts. The challenge all courts face, everywhere, is that they lack the power to implement their decisions. As Albert asks, when courts speak, 'will the wrongdoer listen'? (Albert 2023, 15). The call to rights may be noble and heart-warming but it doesn't necessarily produce change. Under limited conditions that are likely to vary by country and context, courts may sometimes be effective in furthering the interests of the relatively disadvantaged (see Hillebrecht, in this volume).[2] Investigating the actual effects of progressive court decisions on social change requires in-depth, detailed, and intensive examination of 'facts on the ground' that is beyond the scope of this chapter.

It must be remembered, too, that judicial decisions requiring progressive social change are neither necessary nor sufficient for that change to occur. In her comparative study of courts and economic and social rights, Young notes that 'aspirational principles can be realized without the direct protection of the judiciary, or even without the dim prospect of judicial review' (Young 2012, 212). The reader needs to be careful not to assume that decisions ordering progressive social change are implemented or that any change that occurs is the result of judicial action. But if courts sometimes decide cases on behalf of the relatively disadvantaged, I want to know the factors that make it more or less likely they will do so. The focus of this chapter, then, is on the factors that lead courts in democratic countries to issue decisions in favour of the relatively disadvantaged and protect the rule of law.

It is important to acknowledge that courts can be opponents of social change. Indeed, in many countries courts are an obstacle to change, committed to protecting the status quo unequal distributions of power, privilege, and wealth.[3] For example, in its 1992 *Australian Capital Television* decision, the High Court of Australia invalidated the Political Broadcasts and Political Disclosures Act 1991 which regulated campaign advertising. The result was to return campaign finance to a playing field which benefitted the wealthy (Rosenberg and Williams 1998). Similarly, in the United States, in cases like *Citizens United* (2010) and *Shelby County* (2013), the Supreme Court made it easier for the wealthy to spend unlimited funds on political campaigns and weakened the 1965 Voting Rights Act which protected the voting rights of minorities, respectively. And as the 2022 US Supreme Court's *Dobbs* decision rescinding women's constitutional right to reproductive autonomy illustrates, courts can take away rights, too, Indeed, Hirschl, illustrating his argument with case studies from Canada, Israel, New Zealand, and South Africa, argues that the creation of judicial review and the adoption of judicially enforced constitutional bills of rights in new democracies are designed not to further the interests of the relatively disadvantaged but rather to protect business elites and political leaders and to empower lawyers and judges (Hirschl 2004). Although I focus in this chapter on the role of courts in producing progressive social change, history is replete with examples of courts around the world doing just the opposite.

When courts become involved in policy-making, their actions are sometimes labelled 'judicial activism'.[4] Writing about 'judicial activism', Urbano notes that it is 'a very complex and multifaceted phenomenon, influenced by multiple factors' (2015, 170).

Delaney and Dixon list some of the factors involved: 'the distribution of political power, the presence of religious and political cleavages, the role of individual members of the political elite, the nature of political parties and the dynamics of civil society, as well as the concerns of judges, lawyers' (2018, 1). Other factors include public opinion, the perceived legitimacy of courts, the nature of constitutional rights and the constitutions that grant them, the independence of the courts from other governmental institutions, the legal rules of jurisdiction, and so forth.

In pages that follow I identify key factors that make it more or less likely that courts will issue decisions ordering progressive social change. In section 2 I focus on the characteristics of judges and legal systems that influence judges' ability to act. These include the four factors of judicial independence, the rules and procedures governing jurisdiction and access to courts, the willingness of judges to act, and the breath of rights, both constitutional and statutory, available to judges. In section 3 I turn to the political and social factors that influence progressive judicial decision-making. I highlight six factors: history and legitimacy, public opinion, government inaction, allies and support structures, resource constraints and expertise, and the importance of strategic thinking in judicial decision-making. Putting these ten factors together suggests that judicial decision-making designed to produce progressive social change is highly contextual, varying from country to country. In section 4 I suggest some potential approaches for future research. Section 5 concludes.

2. Judicial Factors That Make It More or Less Likely That Courts Will Issue Decisions

2.1 Furthering the Interests of the Relatively Disadvantaged

2.1.1 *Independence*

There are a number of prerequisites that make it more or less likely that courts will act to promote social change. One is that courts need to have at least some institutional independence from the other institutions of government. Independence allows judges to decide cases without being subservient to the preferences of other governmental actors. Of course, if those other governmental actors act to promote change on their own, a subservient, non-independent, court is likely to act as well. However, its decisions won't add much to the change process initiated by other governmental institutions. Factors that influence judicial independence include term length, secure budgets and salaries, and broad public support. Judges with short terms may worry about reappointment or post-judicial employment and may consequently refrain from making decisions that will anger their appointers. Similarly, if judicial salaries and budgets are not guaranteed, judges are likely to be reticent to act. Public support for courts can also support independence by constraining other governmental actors from attacking them. Independence is not an either/or variable but rather a continuum. The more independent a court is, the more it has the potential to act as an agent of social change. Commenting on the decisions of the Columbian Constitutional Court promoting social change, former Justice Cepeda-Espinoza highlighted the Court's independence: 'one of the specific features of the Colombian situation is the degree of independence of the constitutional court in the political system. We have a very strong tradition of judicial independence, and the court has built on this independence' (2011, 1669).

2.1.2 *Jurisdiction and Judicial Access*

For courts to promote social change they need to be able to hear cases that request it. For the most part, judges are dependent on litigants filing cases. Different legal systems make it easier or harder for litigants to do so. In the United States, for example, in order for a court to hear a case litigants must demonstrate that they have suffered an actual injury that violates a legally protected right. They must also show that the injury is the fault of the defendant and that the remedy they seek is likely to redress the injury (*Lujan v Defenders of Wildlife* 1992). Contrast this with India where the justices of the Supreme Court can act on their own initiative (*sua sponte*) to start a case (Galanter and Ram 2019). In Columbia, there is a remarkable legal practice called the *tutela*, created in the 1991 Constitution and similar to the *amparo* found in many South American legal systems. It allows Columbians to lodge a complaint with any court in the country that has jurisdiction asserting that their rights are being violated. Complaints can be written or verbal and may be filed without the aid of lawyers. Examples of *tutelas* include complaints that medical care, education, housing, pensions, and other socio-economic rights guaranteed in the Columbian Constitution are being withheld. Judges are required to respond quickly. All *tutela* decisions must be sent to the Constitutional Court which has discretionary authority to select those it wishes to hear (Cepeda-Espinoza 2011, 1699). Young reports that over the first two decades of the introduction of *tutelas*, the Constitutional Court received a stunning 1.4 million of them (out of a population of 44 million) (Young 2012, 197). This means, according to former Justice Cepeda-Espinoza of the Columbian Court, that 'the court has had a lot of opportunities to intervene in the enforcement of social rights' (Cepeda-Espinoza 2011, 1669).

Courts in many democracies have procedures by which they can decline to hear cases. In the United States these include, in addition to standing requirements, the requirement that the claim presented is a 'Case or Controversy' as described in Article III of the US Constitution, doctrines of mootness and ripeness, the political question doctrine, and the legislatively created procedure of *certiorari* which gives the Court the authority in almost all cases brought to it to decline to hear the case. Procedures differ from country to country but all courts have ways, some informal, to avoid making some decisions. For example, while European constitutional courts lack a formal political question doctrine, European 'courts have devised approaches that yield a roughly similar result' (Epstein and Knight 2018, 282). In Germany, for example, the Constitutional Court has a practice of returning to the Bundestag 'a question that it believes to be the exclusive competence of politically accountable branches of government' (Pasquino, quoted in Epstein and Knight 2018, 282). As Delaney puts it, 'avoidance is everywhere' (Delaney 2016, 3).

There are also variations in the extent of judicial review. A key distinction is between abstract and concrete review. In the United States, for example, courts can only hear challenges to laws in operation. This 'concrete' review is designed to limit judicial involvement in governance. In many other countries, including most European countries, courts also have the power of abstract review. Under the abstract review procedure, courts can examine legislation before it takes effect. Abstract review gives courts greater opportunities to promote social change. In the view of former Justice Cepeda-Espinoza, the Columbian Constitutional Court is powerful in part because it has a 'very broad jurisdiction that permanently involves the court in structural problems because the court not only decides on concrete cases but has to face judicial review in the abstract of all kind of statutes approved by congress' (Cepeda-Espinoza 2011, 1669).

2.1.3 *Judicial Willingness to Act*

As the preceding discussion suggests, judges have varying degrees of latitude to decide whether or not to hear a case. For courts to make decisions furthering social change, judges have to be interested in, able to, and willing to do so (see Epstein and Knight, in this volume, and Hartmann and Arguelhes, in this volume).[5] This is not always the case. Unsurprisingly, on courts that have made progressive decisions in support of the relatively disadvantaged, justices have expressed their commitment to acting. In his 'surprising, controversial even' (Mathebe 2021, 24) opinion for the South African Constitutional Court overturning the death penalty in *S v Makwanyane and Another* (1995), Chief Justice Chaskalson wrote:

> The very reason for establishing the new legal order, and for vesting the power of judicial review of all legislation in the courts, was to protect the rights of minorities and others who cannot protect their rights adequately through the democratic process. Those who are entitled to claim this protection include the social outcasts and marginalised people of our society. It is only if there is a willingness to protect the worst and the weakest amongst us, that all of us can be secure that our own rights will be protected.
>
> (Chaskalson 1995, 59)

Ten years later, in 2005, reflecting on the fiftieth anniversary of the US Supreme Court's *Brown* decision, Chaskalson, wrote of the challenge to 'create a society in which the basic needs of all our people are met, a society in which there is social justice, a society in which we can live together in harmony respect and concern for each other' (Chaskalson 2005, 512). Similarly, in Israel, Justice Aharon Barak, whose decisions 'transformed private, public, and criminal law' (Weill 2020, 230), wrote that it is the 'task of the judge to protect and uphold human rights' (Barak 2002, 42). Courts have the potential to make decisions ordering social change when the justices that serve on them are willing to act. It is no surprise that the Constitutional Court of South Africa has been one of the world's leaders in trying to further social justice, and the Israeli Supreme Court has at times issued controversial decisions protecting minority rights.

2.1.4 *Rights, Constitutional and Statutory*

Rights provide the resources with which justices can work to write opinions supporting progressive social change. Typically they are found in domestic constitutions and international treaties. On the international side, the Ad Hoc Committee for the Establishment of an International Constitutional Court points to nine such treaties:

> [T]he Universal Declaration of Human Rights, the International Covenant on Civil and Political Rights, the Treaty on European Union, the European Convention on Human Rights, the Charter of the Organization of American States, the American Convention on Human Rights, the Inter-American Democratic Charter, the Constitutive Act of the African Union, as well the 'Harare Principles'.
>
> (cited in Albert 2023, 20)

Landau (2012, 193) adds the International Covenant on Economic, Social and Cultural Rights to the list as well. These treaties provide a rich source of rights for judges who wish to act. Indeed, Tate writes that 'the European Convention and Court of Human Rights in Strasbourg have been of great importance in spreading the gospel of judicialization' (Tate 1995, 3).

Rights are embedded in domestic constitutions as well. Here, of course, there is great variation with some constitutions providing a well-developed set of positive rights and obligations while others contain only limitations on government power. The classic example of the latter is the US Constitution which provides no substantive obligation to provide rights nor a list of socio-economic rights it protects. In the nineteenth century, Landau notes, it served as a 'very influential model' for other constitutions. However, Landau points out, 'the force of the U.S. model began to cede ground to competing ideologies and newer models in the twentieth century'. He points to the inclusion of social rights in both the Mexican constitution of 1917 and the German constitution of the Weimar Republic as the start of the inclusion of positive socio-economic rights in constitutions (Landau 2012, 193).

In the post-Second World War era, many constitutions have included social and economic rights. For example, the Indian Constitution obliges the government to protect and enhance a variety of civil and political rights. In addition, Part IV of the Indian Constitution, dealing with Directive Principles, lays out a number of positive socio-economic goals of state action. Although formally non-justiciable, some justices of the Indian Supreme Court have been willing to use them to hold that the positive obligations they set forth supply the substantive content of the civil and political rights the Constitution protects. The Constitution of South Africa also contains socio-economic rights. Under Chapter 2 of the Constitution, the 'Bill of Rights', Article 26 protects the 'right to have access to adequate housing'. Article 27 states that '[e]veryone has the right to have access to health care services, including reproductive health care; sufficient food and water; and social security'. The state 'must respect, protect, promote and fulfil these rights' (Section 7(2)). Under Section 39, 'Interpretation of Bill of Rights', the Constitution stresses that '[w]hen interpreting the Bill of Rights, a court, tribunal or forum ... must promote the values that underlie an open and democratic society based on human dignity, equality and freedom ... [and] must promote the spirit, purport and objects of the Bill of Rights' (South Africa's Constitution of 1996, 2022). The inclusion of such language in constitutions gives courts an array of rights with which to work.

The exclusion of certain rights in constitutions constrains the ability of courts to further the interests of the relatively disadvantaged. There is no language in the US Constitution, for example, guaranteeing such basic rights as the right to housing, employment, health care, food, a safe environment, etc. When such rights are absent it is more challenging for judges to create and develop them to help the relatively disadvantaged. At the same time, the absence of language can also constrain courts from acting to stymie government action on behalf of the relatively disadvantaged. Versteeg and Zackin note that the drafters of both the Canadian Charter of Rights and Freedoms and the Indian Constitution 'deliberately avoided the term "due process of law," for fear that it would provide overly broad discretion to the judiciary', as it has in the United States (Versteeg and Zackin 2018, 292). Rather, they chose both more specific language about rights and language directing that those rights be interpreted, in the words of the Canadian Charter, 'subject only to such reasonable limits prescribed by law as can be demonstrably justified in a free and democratic society' (Canadian Charter of Rights and Freedoms 2017 [1982], Section 1) and, in the Indian Constitution, that the 'State shall, in particular, strive to minimise the inequalities in income, and endeavour to eliminate inequalities in status, facilities and opportunities' (Constitution of India 2022 [1949], Section 38 (2)).

Domestic legislation can also provide courts with resources with which to work. 'The growth of the Welfare State with the concomitant implementation of an extensive social security system and the strengthening of social rights (such as food, health care, housing and social security)' (Urbano 2015, 164) can be an alternative source of rights for both litigants and judges. Sometimes, too, legislatures provide courts with an opportunity to act by enacting such ambiguous and vague statutes as virtually to insure that their interpretation will be litigated. Legislators around the world often find it in their electoral interests to avoid controversial actions, in effect 'passing the buck' to judges. If judges interpret the laws in popular ways, then legislators claim credit for them. On the other hand, if judges interpret the laws in unpopular ways, then legislators criticize them for 'judicial activism', for acting to further their own goals, not those of the legislature. Buck-passing to courts is a win-win for legislators who can take credit and escape blame. But it does give courts an opportunity to issue opinions in support of social change. Finally, particularly in newly emerging democracies, empowering courts can be a form of 'insurance' for governmental officials that the incoming government won't easily be able to reverse their actions (Ginsburg 2003; Dixon and Ginsburg 2018).

3. Political and Social Factors That Make It More or Less Likely That Courts Will Issue

3.1 Decisions Furthering the Interests of the Relatively Disadvantaged

As important as these four judicial factors are, independent courts, with jurisdiction to hear cases asking for social change and the procedural rules to hear them, with the willingness to act, and the rights on which to base their decisions, still face a host of challenges and choices. These are largely the result of courts lacking power and consequently needing to take account of the broader political, cultural, and economic setting in which they operate. Albert puts the point this way:

> It matters also how well the judgment reflects the history, practices, and political dynamics of the local jurisdiction. The more familiar, the better—and the more likely the ruling is to be seen as relevant in that jurisdiction. This is a point about specificity. Local specificities matter, and the Court's ruling, in order to be effective, should reflect its awareness of those local specificities.
>
> (Albert 2023, 23)

This section examines some of these factors.

3.1.1 *History and Legitimacy*

Historical practice can create societal understanding and acceptance of a broad role for courts. It can create a foundation of legitimacy on which courts can build. For example, the Columbian Constitutional Court is seen as one of the most powerful in the world. Justice Cepeda-Espinoza, who served on the Court from 2001 to 2009, believes it 'enjoys a great deal of legitimacy' because 'Columbia had a century old tradition of active uninterrupted judicial review at the moment the constitutional court was created in 1991' (Cepeda-Espinoza 2011, 700). The Israeli Supreme Court, also known for decisions promoting social change, has historically been held in high regard by Israelis. According to Edelman, 'the Israeli public plainly trusts the judgments of the civil courts' (Edelman 1995, 407). The US Supreme Court had sufficient legitimacy in effect to decide the contested presidential election of 2000. Newer courts can be garlanded with legitimacy, too. The South African Constitutional Court emerged out of the successful democratic revolution and carried with it the aspirations of a newly democratic people. In Canada, Russell suggests that the very limited use of the notwithstanding clause (which allows both the federal Parliament and the provincial legislatures to enforce legislation declared unconstitutional by the High Court) highlights the societal acceptance of the role of the Court (Russell 1995, 141). As Dixon puts it, '[c]ourts in some cases clearly enjoy a general "reservoir of public support" that can allow them to engage in successful forms of strong review even in the face of quite real public opposition to a specific ruling' (Dixon 2021, 361–62).

3.1.2 *Public Opinion*

Closely related to judicial legitimacy is public opinion (see Smyth, in this volume).[6] Courts need public support. When they lack it, they face two challenges. First, citizens may resist implementing judicial decisions requiring social change. Second, if public support is lacking then legislators and executives opposed to decisions may perceive little risk in defying the courts and, perhaps, attacking them. The more public support a court has, the more leeway it has to act. A good example is judicial action to expand the right of marriage to gay and lesbian couples. While much attention is focused on the 2015 *Obergefell* decision of the US Supreme Court, the United States was a comparative laggard, being the twenty-second democratic county to adopt marriage equality. Even Catholic Ireland adopted marriage equality before the United States, albeit only a month before, when 62 per cent of voters approved amending the Irish Constitution to permit same-sex couples to marry! Public support for marriage equality around the world made it easier for judges, as well as legislators, to support it.

3.1.3 *Government Inaction*

The capacity of governments to act influences the role of courts. When legislatures and/or executives are seen as corrupt, inefficient, and unable to act, courts may be able to step into the political vacuum. Public opinion also comes into play in such situations.

> When the public and the leaders of interest groups and major economic and social institutions view the majoritarian institutions as immobilized, self-serving, or even corrupt, it is hardly surprising that they would accord the policy-making of judiciaries . . . as much or more legitimacy as that of executives and legislatures.
>
> (Tate 1995, 31)

In Columbia, for example, Justice Cepeda-Espinoza summarized the views the justices held of the Columbian Congress this way: 'we had such a bad Congress that we had no choice but to try and do something' (quoted in Young 2012, 198). In India, many activists believe that political in-fighting, corruption, ossified bureaucracies, and a traditionalist cultural system render the political system incapable of enacting progressive social change, leaving courts as the only hope. It is also the case that when government is immobilized, and parties are weak, 'judges will pay a lower price for defying political movements and may score points for acting as "political entrepreneurs" that gain popular reputations' (Landau 2018, 234). In Pakistan, for example, although the High Court repeatedly failed in its attempts to hold corrupt officials accountable, it gained a lot of popular support for at least trying, support that helped it enforce other decisions (Qazi 2018). In Israel, Edelman writes that the 'partisanship and immobilism besetting Israel's elected institutions explains the judiciary's increasingly important role' (Edelman 1995, 409). In the United States, a gridlocked Congress has meant that the Court would be unlikely to face legislative pushback for even controversial decisions such as *Dobbs* rescinding the constitutional right to reproductive autonomy. Similarly, during the presidency of George W. Bush, slim Republican majorities in Congress and then a divided government allowed the Court repeatedly to invalidate the Bush administration's procedures for tribunals in the War on Terror despite two attempts by Congress to strip the courts of jurisdiction to hear such cases. And in a number of South American countries including Argentina, Brazil, Columbia, and Mexico, Ruibal finds that the 'judiciary can be a favourable venue for feminist activism ... when other institutional sites are blocked' (Ruibal 2021, 579).

3.1.4 *Allies and Support Structures*

As noted repeatedly in this chapter, courts lack power to implement their decisions. They also have few institutional tools to protect themselves from attack. Most judges around the world are conscious of their lack of power. They know that if they wish to issue decisions supporting progressive social change, they need help. Where might that help come from? Delaney and Dixon suggest that judges 'must look to the distribution of political power, the presence of religious and political cleavages, the role of individual members of the political elite, the nature of political parties and the dynamics of civil society, as well as the concerns of judges [and] lawyers' (Delaney and Dixon 2018, 1). Landau concurs, writing that '[h]igh courts everywhere ... would seem to be reliant on the support of external actors of some kind'. He suggests they can be 'political parties, ordinary court judges, domestic civil society groups of different types, international NGOs or various slices of the public' (Landau 2018, 230). In particular, where courts issue 'structural remedies, the aid of social movements may be indispensable in order to achieve progress from recalcitrant bureaucracies' (Landau 2018, 229). Ideally, of course, decisions furthering the interests of the relatively disadvantaged will be implemented by responsible governmental authorities and bureaucracies. The political reality, however, is often different.

In a path-breaking study of judicial decisions furthering rights in Canada, India, the United Kingdom, and the United States, Charles Epp focuses on the involvement of interest groups and organizations. He argues that in order for high courts to be able to make civil liberties and civil rights decisions, they need a dense array of groups and organizations that bring a steady stream of cases to court (Epp 1998). Building on Epp's insight, Landau argues that on some, perhaps many issues, 'the aid of social movements may be indispensable in order to achieve progress from recalcitrant bureaucracies' (Landau 2018, 229). The importance of a robust support structure for courts to make decisions furthering social change can be illustrated in a number of countries.

The Indian Supreme Court is one of the world's most active in issuing decisions requiring progressive social change (Rosenberg, Krishnaswamy, and Bail 2019). Among its most well-known are a series of decisions about providing meals to school children (*PUCL* 2001). The initial so-called *Midday Meal* decision was issued in 2001 and required state governments to provide every child attending a public or public-supported schools a free cooked midday meal. The litigation has continued over several decades. Part of the challenge the Court faced was the inability of some Indian states to implement the decision due to lack of bureaucratic capacity, lack of commitment, and corruption. However, both Dixon and Chowdury (2019) and Brierley (2019) find that a collection of organizations, operating under the umbrella of the 'Right to Food Campaign', organized to pressure state governments to act and help implement the decision. Identifying itself as 'an informal network of individuals and organisations committed to the realisation of the right to food in India' (Right to Food Campaign 2022), these organizations provided the help the Court needed to see its decision at least partially implemented.

One of the most famous decisions of the US Supreme Court is *Brown v Board of Education* (1954) which invalidated racial segregation in elementary and secondary school in the United States. Aimed largely at the eleven southern states of the former Confederacy in which slavery was practiced prior to the Civil War and the adoption of the 13th Amendment, *Brown* was singularly ineffective in those states until the civil rights movement pressured Congress and the President to act a decade later. By the 1963–1964 school year, a decade after the decision, barely one in 100 Black schoolchildren in those states was in a school with Whites. But within just a few years of congressional action in the mid-1960s over 90 per cent of those children were in integrated schools (Rosenberg 2023, 60). The civil rights movement, and the political pressure it created, made rights real.

In 2004 the Columbian Constitutional Court issued a decision requiring government aid to persons internally displaced by Columbia's civil war (Corte Constitutional *Sentencia* T-025/04). Four years later, in 2008, it essentially took over the entire healthcare system (Corte Constitutional *Sentencia* T-760/08). Both decisions were written by Justice Manuel José Cepeda Espinoza whom I have quoted several times in this chapter. Landau finds that there was more progress implementing the displaced persons case than the healthcare decision because of the support provided by civil society organizations. In the case of displaced persons, Landau writes that the Court 'received support from a strong and fairly cohesive civil society group' (Landau 2012, 227). In addition, there was support from the state bureaucracy, and President Uribe 'managed to find a way to fit support for displaced persons into his broader political program' (Landau 2012, 228). In contrast, in healthcare, where Landau found little implementation, he writes that 'there is little organized support or shared vision for the Court's work in this area' (Landau 2012, 229).

The necessity of support from civil society organizations is found in South Africa, too. One of the most famous cases of the South African Constitutional Court, the *Grootboom* case (2001), dealt with housing and evictions. In *Grootboom* the Court held that the government had failed to devise a housing plan that would meet the needs of the poorest South Africans and held that the government needed to do so. While the results of the decision are mixed, at best, 'a number of South African non-governmental organizations have focused on evictions, including the Centre for Applied Legal Studies, the Legal Resources Centre, and the Socio-Economic Rights Institute of South Africa'

(Williams 2014, 820). Without the support and activities of these organizations, the Court would have accomplished little.

Additional examples of the importance of support structures for court decisions furthering social change come from Pakistan and South America. In Pakistan Qazi finds that the judiciary has relied upon the army to protect its institutional independence, allowing it to act. In return, he finds, the Court has never really threatened the military's core prerogatives (Qazi 2018). Ruibal, in her study of judicial involvement in abortion policy in a number of countries including Argentina, Brazil, Columbia, and Mexico, finds that abortion rights organizations played a key role. Courts 'expanded abortion law', she writes, in 'response to feminist strategic litigation' (Ruibal 2021, 581). Writing in the *New York Times* in the spring of 2022, with the then recent decriminalization of abortion in Mexico, Argentina, and Columbia in mind, the senior regional director of the Center for Reproductive Rights in Latin America and the Caribbean pointed to the crucial role of support structures: 'The hard-fought gains in Latin America are the result of decades of organizing, mobilizing, working to shift the conversation around abortion and, most importantly, working together to bring about change' (Coral 2022). Arguably, it was the lack of such efforts in the United States that made it possible for the Supreme Court to rescind the constitutional right to abortion access in 2022.

Judges are not entirely at the mercy of civil society groups. Landau points out that 'judges have some ability to shape their external support structures' (Landau 2018, 226). In deciding which cases to hear, and in their opinions, judges signal their interests. This in turn can invite subsequent litigation, particularly from civil society groups. For example, the development of the Public Interest Litigation (PIL) docket by the Indian Supreme Court was aimed at bringing marginalized litigants, and their concerns, to the Court. Savvy judges with a developed sense of the political landscape, can aim decisions at catalysing and mobilizing the support groups that will be necessary for change to occur. Justice Cepeda-Espinoza of the Columbian Constitutional Court well understood this: 'judicial intervention is a way to mobilize the political process ... [and] promote a broader participation in the decision making that will lead to the fulfillment of the orders of the court' (Cepeda-Espinoza 2011, 1704). One result of the Indian Supreme Court's *PUCL* decision discussed above, whether intended or not, was the development of the Right to Food campaign which was crucial in bringing the decision to life (Brierley 2019). And Landau reports that through their decisions high courts in Brazil and Columbia have 'created the middle class as a constituency for social rights' (Landau 2018, 239).

A challenge that judges face in ordering social change on behalf of the relatively disadvantaged is that without the intervention and support of strong and well-organized civil society groups, the intended beneficiaries may lack the knowledge and resources to act. In all too many cases, decisions that order the extension of rights mostly benefit middle-class litigants and not the relatively disadvantaged at whom the decisions are aimed. In India, for example, the creation of the PIL docket opened the courts to disadvantaged individuals and groups who had historically lacked access. However, Chitalkar and Gauri find that it was elite and vested interests that most successfully made use of the procedure (Chitalkar and Gauri 2019). Based on field work in Columbia, along with evidence from other countries including Brazil, Argentina, Hungary, South Africa, and India, Landau finds that 'most social rights enforcement has benefitted middle- or upper-class groups, rather than the poor'. Courts, he finds, 'are far more likely to protect pension rights for civil servants or housing subsidies for the middle class than they are to transform the lives of marginalized groups' (Landau 2012, 190; see also Young 2012, 199). Focusing on the Columbian healthcare case, Landau finds the 'main claimants in these cases have been relatively wealthy groups' (Landau 2012, 209). In Brazil, where courts have 'aggressively protected the right to health ... most of this litigation is being filed by middle-class petitioners rather than the poor' (Landau 2012, 232).

At perhaps the other extreme, courts sometimes overreach, deciding cases without sufficient support from either the public, political leaders, or civil society groups. The poster child for this kind of overreach is the Hungarian Constitutional Court whose decisions on social benefits in the 1990s angered political leaders. The result was the appointment of many new justices in 1999 when the terms of the original justices expired (Landau 2018, 274; 2012, 235). In addition, the Court was 'reengineered, after the adoption of a new Constitution, into a position of deference' (Young 2012, 200). In 2023, in Israel, after decades of decisions that conservatives viewed as too progressive, the recently elected conservative government introduced legislation to limit the independence of the Supreme Court. Although as of the end of 2023 the legislation had not been enacted, the Court was on notice that its position was precarious.

3.1.5 *Resource Constraints and Expertise*

Rights only get courts so far. To find a constitutional right to housing or healthcare or a clean environment, for example, is one thing. To develop, organize, and fund programmes to fulfil these rights is something entirely different. In a world of complete knowledge and unlimited resources, this would not be a problem. Alas, that is not the world in which any of us live, or in which courts operate. Judges are generalists and seldom have the expertise necessary to make effective policy (Horowitz 1977). Focusing on socio-economic rights in Latin America, Rodriguez-Garavito writes, 'One does not have to be a legal formalist to concede that courts lack the technical knowledge, personnel, and resources (let alone the legitimacy) to find and implement solutions to problems as complicated as forceful displacement or lack of access to essential medicines' (Rodriguez-Garavito 2011, 1696). Discussing the role of the South African Constitutional Court in protecting the broad constitutional rights of access to basic necessitates, Williams points out that the rights 'cannot tell us much about how to design and finance social welfare policies that incorporate and deliver on the rights to housing, social assistance, water, education, health care and universal social assistance' (Williams 2014, 844). Nor is this challenge unique to South Africa. 'Courts and legislatures in countries with constitutions containing progressive social and economic rights provisions face difficult decisions about how to stretch limited resources to build housing, deliver water, provide medical care, construct schools, and so on', Williams notes. She continues, pointing out that rights discourse 'gives little guidance on how to set priorities, make the inevitable trade-offs among the panoply of social and economic rights, or establish institutional systems that will produce results on the ground' (Williams 2014, 844).

3.1.6 *Strategic Action*

In the preceding pages I have discussed a multiplicity of factors that influence whether judges will make progressive decisions in support of the relatively disadvantaged. They can be brought together under the concept of strategic action, introduced by Walter F. Murphy in 1964 in the *Elements of Judicial Strategy* and elaborated by Lee Epstein and Jack Knight in 1998 in *The Choices Justices Make*. The underlying insight of the strategic actor model of judicial decision-making is that judges who wish to see their opinions become law must look not only at the law and the facts of the case before them but also at the views of their colleagues and, importantly, at the views and potential responses of other actors. These include political elites, government bureaucrats, administrators, civil society groups, the public, the press, and others whose cooperation is necessary for decisions to be implemented. This means that the timing of decisions matters. If support from key actors is lacking, and if necessary resources are likely to be unavailable, a strategic court will refrain from acting. It may do so by finding ways not to decide cases as discussed earlier, by writing vague opinions that don't clearly require action, and by avoiding struggles with other governmental institutions that it can't win. Rather than create struggles with other governmental actors, successful strategic courts, Dixon suggests, can write decisions that aim for 'engagement with government and civil society actors as partners' (Dixon 2021, 302). They can also avoid antagonizing other governmental actors. Writing in 1995, Russell suggests that the lack of use of the notwithstanding clause in Canada is due not only to the public acceptance of the role of the Court but also to the fact that 'the Charter, as it was being interpreted and applied by the courts, did not threaten their ["Canadian governments' "] vital policy interests' (Russell 1995, 141).

Justices on strategic courts can attempt to cultivate public opinion and, as suggested above, create and cultivate supportive constituencies. One example comes from Hungary where, following a controversial 1995 decision, one of the justices 'gave a number of interviews to Hungarian magazines and newspapers defending the Court' (Dixon 2021, 358). An unusual attempt at cultivating public opinion comes from Indonesia where soon after the creation of the Constitutional Court, a justice 'created a weekly program on national television and radio designed to explain the workings of the Constitutional Court and particular decisions'. He also 'gave numerous press conferences after controversial decisions' (Dixon 2021, 358, 359). Even in the United States justices sometimes cultivate public opinion. A favourite example is the appearance of US Supreme Court Justice Sonya Sotomayor on the children's television show 'Sesame Street' in February and November 2012. In February she resolved a dispute between the characters 'Baby Bear' and 'Goldilocks' and in November she gave career advice to the character 'Abby Cadabby'. Cultivating public opinion can start at an early age! This suggests that strategic judges may employ both short-term and long-term strategies to further social change (see Dothan, in this volume).[7]

The most direct way to create supportive constituencies is to write opinions protecting or enlarging rights that are likely to be popular. Epstein and Knight provide examples from India, South Africa, and Singapore where high courts took this approach (Epstein and Knight 2018, 285). In building popular support, courts hope both to ease implementation of their social change decisions and to make it harder for political opponents to challenge them. Indeed, Landau claims that 'courts are actually pro-majoritarian actors in many circumstances' (Landau 2012, 191). One of the reasons the US Supreme Court has been successful over several centuries, McCloskey suggests, is that it seldom issues opinions that stray far for mainstream views (McCloskey 2016). And when it does it can count on its well-developed legitimacy to protect it from retribution.

Strategic courts that wish to make social change but are aware of the constraints under which they are operating at a given time may take a dialogic approach to their decisions. That is, rather than issuing decisions requiring governments to create or expand programmes and expend resources, the court orders the government and the parties to negotiate or engage in dialogue. 'Dialogic rulings', Rodriguez-Garavito explains, 'set broad goals and clear implementation paths through deadlines and progress reports, while leaving substantive decisions and detailed outcomes to government agencies' (Rodriguez-Garavito 2011, 1676). According to Landau, the South African Constitutional Court has moved towards this dialogic approach. 'The core of the engagement remedy', Landau writes, 'is that the Court orders the state to negotiate with the plaintiffs so that a satisfactory agreement can hopefully be reached' (Landau 2012, 198). Reviewing judicial action in South America aimed at expanding socio-economic rights, Rodriguez-Garavito argues that 'impact is likely to be higher when courts engage in "dialogic activism"' (Rodriguez-Garavito 2011, 1676). The challenge of dialogic rulings, however, is that dialogue requires two parties to engage. As discussed above, courts have limited tools to incentivize other governmental institutions to engage in dialogue.

Bringing strategic action and dialogic decision-making together, former Justice Cepeda-Espinoza of the Columbian Constitutional Court writes of 'prudent activism'. Under prudent activism,

> [the] court does not try to fix the problem, it leaves the fixing of the problem to the competent agencies. It does not go into the details of the remedies. It respects the competence and the processes involved, and it values financial restrictions. And finally, it is aware of the political dynamics derived from the judicial intervention. So there is an element of prudence in this activism.
>
> (Cepeda-Espinoza 2011, 1704–05)

It may well be that prudent activism is the most likely path for courts to follow to promote social change.

It might be suggested that one result of judges acting strategically will be to fail to protect the least popular and most vulnerable populations. A 2005 article in the Toronto

Globe and Mail highlights the strengths and weaknesses of a strategic approach to decisions furthering the rights of the relatively disadvantaged. The article reports that when Beverley McLachlin became Chief Justice of the Canadian Supreme Court, it was 'under sustained attack from a common front of critics'. In response she spent 'years of tremendous effort in explaining the role of judges in the Charter of Rights era' and countering criticisms of 'judicial activism'. In addition, according to some legal scholars, under her leadership the 'court picks its battles strategically', 'exercises its power in a pragmatic, shrewd way', and shows 'deference to the wishes of legislators'. Critics allege that as a result the Court has become 'overly cautious' and 'shies away from granting leave to appeal in cases with explosive potential'. One critic described the Court's approach to the rights of criminal defendants as 'abdication'. Overall, critics complain, the 'Court is paying a high price for appeasing critics' (Makin 2005).

Strategic courts and judges aren't necessarily weak. They are just careful. Justice Aharon Barak, a justice of the Israeli Supreme Court for twenty-eight years, eleven of which he served as President of the Court, has been seen as 'a worldwide renowned jurist' (Weill 2020, 229). In an analysis of his decisions, Weill labels him 'a strategic judge' (Weill 2020, 232), carefully attuned to social and political realities. Another example of strategic action is two decisions of the Supreme Court of the United Kingdom. Created in 2005, and situated in a political culture in which 'parliamentary sovereignty retains a powerful conceptual hold on judges, politicians, and academics' (Delaney 2014, 605), the Court appears to be precariously placed. However, given divided public opinion, and an effectively immobilized parliament, the Court was able to issue two major decisions in 2017 and 2019 on government overreach. In the first decision, *Miller & Anor, R (on the application of) v Secretary of State for Exiting the European Union* (2017), the Court invalidated the attempt by the government to initiate the UK's withdrawal from the European Union without an act of parliament. The government acquiesced and brought a bill to parliament. In the second case, *Miller, R (on the application of) v The Prime Minister* (2019), also known as *Miller II*, the Court unanimously invalidated the attempt by Prime Minister Boris Johnson to prorogue Parliament in the run-up to the UK's withdrawal from the European Union. Again, the government acquiesced and parliament was not prorogued. Understanding the politics of the UK's withdrawal for the European Union, the Supreme Court was able to assert itself.

4. Future Research

Over the course of the last decade of the twentieth century and the first few decades of the twenty-first century, scholars have suggested a number the factors that influence justices and courts to make decisions in support of social change. These are the factors that have been discussed in this chapter. This research is largely based on observations from afar, more often than not ad hoc. To better understand the role of courts as agents of change we need a reliable baseline of in-depth, focused, country studies. Such studies would include both qualitative work and empirical work. Unfortunately, these studies are time-consuming, making comparative work a challenge. However, once there is a collection of such studies then there would be a strong foundation for comparative analysis.

Qualitatively, our understanding of these factors would be greatly enhanced if scholars interviewed the justices themselves. Several of the most interesting and revealing insights in this chapter came from former Justice Cepeda-Espinoza of the Columbian Constitutional Court. Are his views idiosyncratic? Unique to the Columbian Court? Time bound? In the United States, justices don't allow themselves to be interviewed outside formal and constrained settings such as visits to academic institutions. This reluctance may not be shared everywhere. If sitting justices around the world decline to be interviewed, it's possible that retired justices will be more forthcoming. Learning from those who have served on courts faced with questions of social change will enhance scholarly understandings.

Scholars believe that the factors identified in this chapter play an important role in how justices and courts think about social change. Although I suspect that the applicability of these factors is likely to vary from country to county and time to time, we know little about whether, and under what conditions these decisions actually produce the change required. As Rodriguez-Garavito notes, 'we do not have systematic studies on the fate of activist decisions after they are issued' (Rodriguez-Garavito 2011, 2674). One path for future scholarship is to examine the actual impact of decisions in support of the relatively disadvantaged. Are they implemented? What factors, under what conditions, play a prominent role in implementation? Are some factors more important than others? In work I have done on the US Supreme Court I lay out three hypothesized constraints that limit the ability of courts to make progressive decisions furthering the rights of the relatively disadvantaged and suggest four conditions under which those constraints can be overcome and decisions can improve lives (Rosenberg 2023). Building on these constraints and conditions I joined with a group of scholars to examine the same questions in India (Rosenberg, Krishnaswamy, and Bail 2019). Perhaps surprisingly, my colleagues and I discovered that in some cases the Indian Supreme Court is less constrained and more effective in helping the relatively disadvantaged than is the US Supreme Court. We identify the rights guaranteed in the Indian Constitution, the flexibility of judicial procedures, and the weakness of state capacity as key factors in explaining how some Indian Supreme Court cases such as the Right to Food cases have contributed to improving the lives of the poorest Indian children. Here, too, more intensive, in-depth, empirical studies of the implementation of court decisions requiring social change would greatly improve our understanding.

In addition, comparative work on courts and social change would benefit from compiling a database such as the Supreme Court Database in the United States which includes over 200 pieces of information about each case.[8] Although the task is daunting, a database on courts and social change would highlight key variables. Such a database would allow scholars to examine the same variables to highlight both the similarities and differences between legal systems. Similarly, scholars could make fuller use of the

Comparative Constitutions Project[9] to identify key constitutional rights that are most used in judicial decisions requiring progressive social change.

5. Conclusion

In his famous 1960 book, now in its sixth edition, Robert McCloskey credits the strength and legitimacy of the US Supreme Court to the fact that it 'learned to be a political institution and to behave accordingly' (McCloskey 2016, 292). By a 'political institution' McCloskey meant that most of the time a majority of the justices have been aware of the constraints under which they operate and the factors that, when present, empower them to further social change. When the Court was successful, McCloskey argued, it acted strategically, with a 'lively sense of its own limitations', not trying to do too much and avoiding clashes with the other branches of government and with popular opinion (McCloskey 2016, 60). 'The Court's greatest successes', McCloskey concluded, 'have been achieved when it has operated near the margins rather than in the center of political controversy, when it has nudged and gently tugged the nation, instead of trying to rule it' (McCloskey 2016, 295). When the Court overreached, as in the early years of the New Deal, its legitimacy was threatened and its power diminished.

McCloskey's argument is probably not unique to the Supreme Court of the United States. At its most foundational level, courts everywhere lack power. They depend on others to carry out their decisions and take the actions those decisions require. Judges need to act strategically both to further social change and protect themselves from attacks. The factors discussed in this chapter highlight the resources justices can use, and the constraints they face, in making decisions furthering progressive rights. While both the presence and strength of these factors and constraints vary from country to country and time to time, scholars suggest they are crucial to the ability of courts to issue decisions furthering social change. Empirical investigation of the conditions under which decisions requiring social change and furthering the rights of the relatively disadvantaged improves their lives holds the promise of deepening our understanding of the role of courts and social change.

Notes

1. See e.g. Helmke (2004).
2. For a study of the constraints on, and the conditions under which, the US Supreme Court can produce progressive social change, see Rosenberg (2023). For a comparative study, see Hillebrecht, 'Compliance with Judicial Decisions', Chapter 40 of this *Handbook*.
3. For an argument that this is the main role of the US Supreme Court, see Rosenberg (2017).
4. Throughout this chapter I avoid using the term 'judicial activism' because it carries with it a normative critique of judicial action. The aim of this chapter is to explore the factors that make judicial action furthering progressive change possible, not to analyse whether courts

doing so is normatively problematic. For thought-provoking essays on judicial activism in comparative perspective, see Coutinho, La Torre, and Smith (2015).

5. For an in-depth analysis of judicial motivations, see Epstein and Knight, 'Personal Motivations', Chapter 10 of this *Handbook*. For a comparative analysis of the ability of judges to decide what cases to hear, see Hartmann and Arguelhes, 'Agenda Setting', Chapter 24 of this *Handbook*.
6. For a comparative study of public opinion and judicial legitimacy, see Smyth, 'Public Opinion and Legitimacy', Chapter 38 of this *Handbook*.
7. For examination of the differences between short-term and long-term strategic action by judges, see Chapter 9 of the *Handbook*.
8. http://scdb.wustl.edu/, accessed 11 December 2023.
9. https://comparativeconstitutionsproject.org/, accessed 11 December 2023.

References

Albert, Richard. 2023. 'Does the World Need an International Constitutional Court?' *Rutgers International Law and Human Rights Journal* 3: 1–25.

Barak, Aharon. 2022. 'A Judge on Judging: The Role of a Supreme Court in a Democracy'. *Harvard Law Review* 116 (1): 19–162.

Brierley, Alyssa. 2019. '*PUCL v. Union of India*: Political Mobilization and the Right to Food'. In *A Qualified Hope: The Indian Supreme Court and Progressive Social Change*, edited by Gerald N. Rosenberg, Sudhir Krishnaswamy and Shishir Bail, 212–40. New York: Cambridge University Press.

Calabresi, Steven Gow. 2018. 'The Origins and Growth of Judicial Enforcement'. In *Comparative Judicial Review*, edited by Erin F. Delaney and Rosalind Dixon, 83–97. Northampton: Edward Elgar.

Canadian Charter of Rights and Freedoms. 2017 (1982). https://publications.gc.ca/collections/Collection/CH37-4-3-2002E.pdf, accessed 11 December 2023.

Cepeda-Espinoza, Manuel Jose. 2011. 'Transcript: Social and Economic Rights and the Colombian Constitutional Court'. *Texas Law Review* 89: 1699–705.

Chaskalson, Arthur. 2005. '*Brown v. Board of Education*: Fifty Years Later'. *Columbia Human Rights Law Review* 36: 503–12.

Chitalkar, Poorvi and Varun Gauri. 2019. 'The Recent Evolution of Public Interest Litigation in the Indian Supreme Court'. In *A Qualified Hope: The Indian Supreme Court and Progressive Social Change*, edited by Gerald N. Rosenberg, Sudhir Krishnaswamy, and Shishir Bail, 77–91. New York: Cambridge University Press.

Constitution of India. 2022 (1949). https://legislative.gov.in/constitution-of-india/, accessed 11 December 2023.

Coral, Catalina Martine. 2022. 'The Key Argument on Abortion That Changed Everything in Colombia'. *New York Times* (New York, 14 March). https://www.nytimes.com/2022/03/14/opinion/latin-america-colombia-abortion.html?smid=url-share, accessed 11 December 2023.

Coutinho, Louis Pereira, Massimo La Torre, and Steve D. Smith, eds. 2015. *Judicial Activism: An Interdisciplinary Approach to the American and European Experiences*. New York: Springer.

Delaney, Erin F. 2014. 'Judiciary Rising: Constitutional Change in the United Kingdom'. *Northwestern University Law Review* 108: 543–605.

Delaney, Erin F. 2016. 'Analyzing Avoidance: Judicial Strategy in Comparative Perspective'. *Duke Law Journal* 66: 1–68.

Delaney, Erin F., and Rosalind Dixon. 2018. 'Introduction'. In *Comparative Judicial Review*, edited by Erin F. Delaney and Rosalind Dixon, 1–11. Northampton: Edward Elgar.

Dixon, Rosalind. 2021. 'Strong Courts: Judicial Statecraft in Aid of Constitutional Change'. *Columbia Journal of Transnational Law* 59: 298–363.

Dixon, Rosalind, and Tom Ginsburg. 2018. 'The Forms and Limits of Constitutions as Political Insurance'. *International Journal of Constitutional Law* 15 (4): 988–1012.

Dixon, Rosalind, and Rishad Chowdhury. 2019. 'A Case for Qualified Hope? The Supreme Court of India & the Midday Meal'. In *A Qualified Hope: The Indian Supreme Court and Progressive Social Change*, edited by Gerald N. Rosenberg, Sudhir Krishnaswamy, and Shishir Bail, 243–68. New York: Cambridge University Press.

Edelman, Martin. 1995. 'Israel'. In *The Global Expansion of Judicial Power*, edited by C. Neal Tate and Torbjorn Vallinder, 403–15. New York: New York University Press.

Epp, Charles R. 1998. *The Rights Revolution: Lawyers, Activists, and Supreme Courts in Comparative Perspective*. Chicago: University of Chicago Press.

Epstein, Lee, and Jack Knight. 1998. *The Choices Justices Make*. Washington: Congressional Quarterly Press.

Epstein, Lee, and Jack Knight. 2018. 'Efficacious Judging on Apex Courts'. In *Comparative Judicial Review*, edited by Erin F. Delaney and Rosalind Dixon, 272–89. Northampton: Edward Elgar.

Galanter, Marc, and Vasujith Ram. 2019. '*Suo Motu* Intervention and the Indian Judiciary'. In *A Qualified Hope: The Indian Supreme Court and Progressive Social Change*, edited by Gerald N. Rosenberg, Sudhir Krishnaswamy, and Shishir Bail, 92–122. New York: Cambridge University Press.

Ginsburg, Tom. 2003. *Judicial Review in New Democracies: Constitutional Courts in Asian Cases*. New York: Cambridge University Press.

Helmke, Gretchen. 2004. *Courts under Constraints: Judges, Generals, and Presidents in Argentina*. New York: Cambridge University Press.

Hirschl, Ran. 2004. *Towards Juristocracy: The Origins and Consequences of the New Constitutionalism*. Harvard University Press.

Horowitz, Donald L. 1977. *The Courts and Social Policy*. Washington: Brookings.

Landau, David. 2012. 'The Reality of Social Rights Enforcement'. *Harvard International Law Journal* 53: 189–247.

Landau, David. 2018. 'Courts and Support Structures: Beyond the Classic Narrative'. In *Comparative Judicial Review*, edited by Erin F. Delaney and Rosalind Dixon, 226–43. Northampton: Edward Elgar.

Makin, Kirk. 2005. 'Judicial Activism Debate on Decline'. *Globe and Mail* (Toronto, 8 January).

Mathebe, Lucky. 2021. 'The Constitutional Court of South Africa: Thoughts on its 25-Year-Long Legacy of Judicial Activism'. *Journal of Asian and African Studies* 56 (1): 18–33.

McCloskey, Robert G. 2016 (1960). *The American Supreme Court*, 6th edn. Chicago: University of Chicago Press.

Murphy, Walter F. 1964. *Elements of Judicial Strategy*. Chicago: University of Chicago Press.

Qazi, Asher Asif. 2018. *A Government of Judges: A Story of the Pakistani Supreme Court's Strategic Expansion*. JSD Dissertation, University of Chicago.

Right to Food Campaign. 2022. http://www.righttofoodcampaign.in/, accessed 11 December 2023.

Rodriguez-Garavito, Cesar. 2011. 'Beyond the Courtroom: The Impact of Judicial Activism on Socioeconomic Rights in Latin America'. *Texas Law Review* 89: 1669–98.

Rosenberg, Gerald N. 2017. 'Protecting Privilege: The Historic Role of the U.S. Supreme Court and the Great Progressive Misunderstanding'. In *Judicial Power and the Left*, edited by Richard Elkins and Graham Gee, 76–88. London: Policy Exchange.

Rosenberg, Gerald N. 2023. *The Hollow Hope: Can Courts Bring About Social Change?* 3rd edn. Chicago: University of Chicago Press.

Rosenberg, Gerald N., Sudhir Krishnaswamy, and Shishir Bail, eds. 2019. *A Qualified Hope: The Indian Supreme Court and Progressive Social Change*. New York: Cambridge University Press.

Rosenberg, Gerald N., and John Williams. 1998. 'Do Not Go Gently into that Good Right: The First Amendment in the High Court of Australia'. *1997 Supreme Court Review* 439–95.

Ruibal, Alba. 2021. 'Using Constitutional Courts to Advance Abortion Rights in Latin America'. *International Feminist Journal of Politics* 23 (4): 579–99. https://www.tandfonline.com/doi/abs/10.1080/14616742.2021.1947148, accessed 11 December 2023.

Russell, Peter H. 1995. 'Canadian Constraints on Judicialization from Without'. In *The Global Expansion of Judicial Power*, edited by C. Neal Tate and Torbjorn Vallinder, 137–50. New York: New York University Press.

The Economist Intelligence Unit. 2022. 'South Africa's Constitution of 1996 with Amendments through 2012'. ConstituteProject.org. https://www.constituteproject.org/constitution/South_Africa_2012.pdf?lang=en, accessed 11 December 2023.

Tate, C. Neal. 1995. 'Why the Expansion of Judicial Power?' In *The Global Expansion of Judicial Power*, edited by C. Neal Tate and Torbjorn Vallinder, 27–37. New York: New York University Press.

Urbano, Maria Benedita. 2015. 'Politics and the Judiciary: A Naive Step Towards the End of Judicial Policy-Making'. In *Judicial Activism: An Interdisciplinary Approach to the American and European Experiences*, edited by Louis Pereira Coutinho, Massimo La Torre, and Steve D. Smith, 161–71. New York: Springer.

Versteeg, Mila, and Emily Zackin. 2018. 'Limiting Judicial Discretion'. In *Comparative Judicial Review*, edited by Erin F. Delaney and Rosalind Dixon, 290–316. Northampton: Edward Elgar.

Weill, Rivka. 2020. 'The Strategic Common Law Court of Aharon Barak and its Aftermath: On Judicially-Led Constitutional Revolutions and Democratic Backsliding'. *Law & Ethics of Human Rights* 14 (2): 227–72.

Williams, Lucy A. 2014. 'The Right to Housing in South Africa: An Evolving Jurisprudence'. *Columbia Human Rights Law Review* 45: 816–45.

Young, Katharine G. 2012. *Constituting Economic and Social Rights*. Oxford: Oxford University Press.

Case References

Australian Capital Television Pty. Ltd. v The Commonwealth (1992) 177 CLR 106 (Austl.).

Brown v Board of Education, 347 US 483 (1954).

Citizens United v Federal Election Commission, 558 US 310 (2010).

Corte Constitutional [C.C.] [Constitutional Court], enero 22, 2004, Sentencia T-025/04, M.P: M. Espinosa (Colom.).

Corte Constitutional [C.C.] [Constitutional Court], julio 31, 2008, Sentencia T-760/08, M.P: M. Espinosa (Colom.).

Dobbs v Jackson Women's Health Organization, 597 US ___ (2022).

Government of the Republic of South Africa v Grootboom 2001 (1) SA 46 (CC).

Lujan v Defenders of Wildlife, 504 US 555 (1992).
Miller & Anor, R (on the application of) v Secretary of State for Exiting the European Union (Rev 3) [2017] UKSC 5. http://www.bailii.org/uk/cases/UKSC/2017/5.html, accessed 11 December 2023.
Miller, R (on the application of) v The Prime Minister [2019] UKSC 41. https://www.bailii.org/uk/cases/UKSC/2019/41.html, accessed 11 December 2023.
Obergefell v Hodges, 576 US 644 (2015).
PUCL v Union of India & Ors. WRIT PETITION (Civil) No. 96 of 2001, Supreme Court of India.
S v Makwanyane and Another 1995 (3) SA 391 (CC) (S. Afr.) http://www.saflii.org/za/cases/ZACC/1995/3.html, accessed 11 December 2023.
Shelby County v Holder, 570 US 529 (2013).

PART X

ON THE FRONTIERS OF COMPARATIVE JUDICIAL BEHAVIOUR

CHAPTER 40

THE CONCEPTUAL CHALLENGE TO MEASURING IDEOLOGY

KEVIN L. COPE

1. Introduction

MANY courts scholars now agree that "judicial ideology" drives much of judicial behaviour, but few agree on exactly what that term means. A substantial fraction of the judicial behaviour literature of the last several decades has—explicitly or implicitly—attempted to capture ideology in some form. For good reason: a valid measure of judicial ideology would enable systematic comparisons between judges and allow us to improve predictions and our understanding of how judges decide. But a concept cannot be measured unless some consensus exists on what exactly that thing is. In part because most empirical researchers give the question little attention, such a consensus has thus far eluded us.

The lack of conceptual clarity on this front has likewise prevented consensus on how best to capture the concept empirically. Judging is a complex, mainly qualitative process that involves philosophy, subjectivity, and intuition—things that are not easily captured on a numerical scale. Moreover, as a latent concept, judicial ideology cannot be directly observed. Instead, it must be inferred from the statements, opinions, and other conduct of judges. And judges in different domains—for example, countries and jurisdictions, levels in the hierarchy, and periods in time—consider cases on different issues using different rules.

The numerous innovative methods that have been devised to measure and quantify ideology each have unique strengths and advantages. But they might be put to even better use, and new and even better ones more readily devised, if we had greater clarity on what it is we wish to measure.

This chapter examines how and why the concept of judicial ideology eludes both intra- and inter-country consensus. The lack of consensus among experts on this matter underscores why developing valid measures of ideology (especially across different systems) is so difficult. I therefore develop a broad, functional definition of judicial ideology, which I use to synthesize the existing theories of judicial decision-making into a two-dimensional space. I then review the broad existing approaches to measuring judicial ideology—vote counting, proxy, and third party—and consider the implicit assumptions about the nature of judicial ideology that each makes, as well as their relative strengths and weaknesses. In doing so, I give special attention to one barely explored method for measuring ideology: using the opinions of legal experts to derive quantitative estimates of ideology. I argue that using such expert-based evaluations—inferring ideology from the statements, opinions, and other conduct of judges—can in many cases overcome the limitations presented by other existing approaches. The chapter concludes by urging researchers to consider carefully the underlying assumptions behind the choice of any measure, and in doing so, to make those implicit assumptions more explicit.

2. The Meaning of Judicial Ideology

2.1 Comparative Concepts of Judicial Ideology

All judges and jurists in every system have a *judicial ideology*, yet there exists no consensus on just what that term means. This is true not just in the judicial politics literature but also in the minds of legal practitioners. As Fischman and Law (2009) note, '[s]cholars have used the term "ideology" in a bewildering variety of ways, often without even attempting to define it'. Rather, 'ideology is in the eye of the beholder'.

To get a sense of the variety of ways that judicial ideology is conceived, I surveyed over three-dozen leading experts of judicial behaviour—including many of the contributors to this volume—from fourteen different countries covering five continents.[1] The experts were asked, 'How would you define the concept of "judicial ideology" (as understood in [your country of expertise]) in one sentence or phrase?' Some responses, mainly from continental European civil law countries, implied that the concept was not commonly understood or was otherwise unmeaningful: 'I would think no equivalent concept is used in Germany'; 'I don't think it is well defined. Judges simply decide the law' (Netherlands); 'There is no concept' (Spain); 'The term is not used' (Norway).

Others, largely from the Americas and Asia, implied that ideology has a negative connotation, or applies only to extra-legal considerations, as in policy preferences. For example, 'Judges seek to have their policy preferences reflected in decisional outcomes' (United States); 'Judicial ideology is associated with partisan ideology of judges and justices' (Argentina); 'The ideas and reasoning frameworks guiding judge decision-making, especially those that convince judges not to follow precedent' (United States); 'Something to be avoided' (Japan).

Finally, some gave more normatively neutral descriptions. The sample of those below implies that judicial ideology constitutes an underlying set of beliefs about the proper role of courts and how best to pursue the act of judging: 'A judge's broader views about justice and the rule of law, and the role of courts and judges in promoting those views' (Brazil); 'Judicial ideology describes a judge's approach to interpreting the law' (Mexico); 'As a dimension describing differences in judicial philosophies among judges in the courts' (Norway); 'A set of beliefs about how to interpret the Constitution and statutes' (United States). For their part, Fischman and Law (2009, 142) note that empirical researchers assume that a judge's ideology—that is, 'a set of related ideas, preferences, or beliefs that are at least arguably political in character'—leads him to decide cases in a certain way.

Thus, there is significant expert disagreement, especially between judicial systems but even within a given country, about the meaning of judicial ideology. To measure something, however, we must reach at least some consensus on what that thing is.

Keeping this variety of conceptions of judicial ideology in mind, in this chapter I define judicial ideology most similarly to the last set: as *an underlying set of normative beliefs about the appropriate aims and functions of law and courts, which are applied to adjudicate a legal issue*. Let me elaborate on this definition. Given any set of legal problems requiring judicial resolution, any two trained jurists may reach different results. I assert that, assuming these two judges have access to the same set of facts and body of law on which to base their decisions, any systematic variation in outcomes is, by definition, a function of variation in their judicial ideology. Granted, the amount of discretion that judges enjoy in this regard varies significantly between national judicial systems, between levels in the judicial hierarchy, and even between cases and issues. Yet, so long as a legal problem is capable of multiple possible resolutions, the above definition is broad enough to capture the concept of judicial ideology in any such system.

I will call this definition the 'functional' definition because functionality is its primary advantage. The key reason jurists and courts scholars wish to measure judicial ideology is to better understand why courts decide cases as they do. I ascribe to judicial ideology all variation in outcome produced by similarly situated judges, because variation in outcomes (both dichotomous votes and holdings) is the main thing that jurists and legal/political researchers are interested in learning about. (How individuals make decisions given their backgrounds, values, biases, and available information, certainly interests, say, psychologists and neuroscientists, but is generally of secondary interest to most lawyers and political scientists.) An ideology measure is therefore useful only to the extent that it accurately predicts judicial outcomes. Indeed, as described below, some measures that purport to capture ideology, like vote counting, implicitly equate ideology with *all* variation in case voting.

In this vein, this definition differs from some others (including those from my cross-national survey) in at least two ways. First, while the notion of a judge's being 'ideological' or an 'ideologue' has a pejorative stigma in most legal circles, the functional definition above has no such connotation; all jurists have such a set of beliefs, even those who are considered moderates or formalists. Second, although the literature has reached no consensus on the meaning of judicial ideology and it is rarely formally defined, where its meaning is stated or implied, the term is often narrower than the definition just given. In contrast, the functional definition above is broad enough to encompass a wide variety of beliefs that affect case outcomes, including interpretive philosophies (like originalism and purposivism) and the degree of deference that courts should afford the political branches. In other words, it includes attitudes and behaviours that most jurists would likely consider not only legitimate but inevitable.

2.2 The Judicial Ideology Trichotomy

Different implicit understandings of judicial ideology affect how it is measured. To understand how and why, it is useful now to review the three leading models of judicial decision-making. These theories each purport to provide a competing explanation for the forces that shape judges'—conscious or subconscious—legal decision-making. Those three models are legalism, attitudinalism (or politics), and strategy (or rational choice). First, *legalism* stresses doctrinal interpretative approaches and the complexity of legal analysis in case outcomes. Traditional legal scholarship typifies the legalist perspective, and it tends to relegate the role of politics in judicial decision-making. Though this research has rarely claimed that law is fully determinate, its approach implies that rules, together with the choice of interpretive approach, are the *most important* determinant of judicial outcomes. The late US federal appellate judge Patricia Wald wrote that 'it would certainly be cause for acute concern that federal judges, constitutionally designed to be apolitical, appeared be deciding cases based on political motivations. I do not think that is the reality' (Wald 1999). Indeed, recent empirical research provides support for legalism in some contexts (e.g. Gilbert 2011). And yet, political scientists have increasingly rejected the legalism model, as the field now widely believes 'that judges do not perceive the facts and the law as they are, plug them into a logical formula, and deduct the one single correct outcome of the case' (see Morell's chapter in this volume).

With the decline of legalism among social scientists over the last few decades came the rise of *attitudinalism*, now the 'dominant model among social scientists' (Bonica and Sen 2021, 97). Adherents to the attitudinal model believe that judges' pre-existing ideologies are the 'key component' to their decisions (Bonica and Sen 2021, 97). Rohde and Spaeth (1976) argue that, due to the institutional incentives associated with having life tenure on a court of last resort, US Supreme Court justices' decisions 'largely reflect their attitudes, values, or personal policy preferences' (Segal and Cover 1989), or even that justices 'base their decisions *solely* upon personal policy preferences' (Rohde and Spaeth 1976, emphasis added). Other political scientists have found widespread evidence of attitude-driven judging, including in the courts of Spain and Portugal (Hanretty 2012), Italy (Pellegrina and Garoupa 2013), the

European Court of Justice (Malecki 2012), and the EU General Court (Wijtvliet and Dyevre 2021), among others.

Finally, the *strategic* account of judicial decision-making has been part of the judicial behaviour conversation for decades (Murphy 1964) but more recently enjoyed a resurgence (Epstein and Knight 2013). Strategic theories posit that judges vote and write opinions in ways that maximize their or their institutions' influence, prestige, power, career stability, or even leisure time (Epstein and Weinshall 2021). One example is aversion to dissent, in which the political costs of alienating colleagues and/or the time and effort of writing a separate opinion push judges to join case outcomes with which they disagree. Evidence of dissent aversion has been found in numerous settings, including the Brazilian Supreme Court (de Mendonça 2019) and the US appellate courts (Epstein et al. 2011; Fischman 2015).

This legalistic/attitudinal/strategic trichotomy has been extensively theorized, debated, honed, and, increasingly, tested empirically, yet conceptual murkiness persists in some corners. This is in part because many of the applied models are derived from models designed by political scientists to measure legislatures, along with the rational-choice assumptions about strategic voting, policy preferences, and utility-maximizing that accompany them. Some of those assumptions are justified as applied to some courts, but some others are not.

Consider four examples. First, while ideology and partisanship are sometimes considered distinct, they are more often conflated. As Epstein and Knight (2013) observe, 'the political science literature tends to treat political goals, policy goals, ideological goals, and partisan goals as interchangeable terms'. Before noting the shortcomings of the practice, Solberg and Waltenburg note in this volume that '[o]ne of the most common operationalizations of judicial attitudes is to associate ideology with party identification' (cf Fischman and Law 2009). This may make more sense in a legislature, in which members are often chosen via a partisan process and rewarded for producing policies preferred by the median voter or party's electorate. But though they often correlate empirically to some degree, political ideology and judicial ideology are distinct concepts; one can, and many do, believe that a particular policy would be ideal under no constraints, and yet also believe that a court case should be decided to produce a different policy (perhaps because one believes it would better serve society to have the issue decided via democratic politics). Indeed, legal issues can produce ideological coalitions within an apex court that bear little resemblance to the coalitions produced by political issues in that same society (see e.g. Hanretty 2015, on Estonia).

Second and relatedly, judges are often seen as expressing their attitudes through 'policy seeking', but with little detailed inquiry into the nature of the 'policies' allegedly being sought. A judge's seeking a particular case outcome regardless of the law (uncommon and, surely, professionally unethical) is too often implicitly lumped together as 'policy seeking' with a judge's implementing her preferred legal-interpretive technique, like originalism (inevitable).

Third, when judicial decision-making is presented as a 'law vs politics' dichotomy (as with Judge Wald's reaction to attitudinalism above), partisanship and politics are sometimes rolled into one concept, standing as the rival to legalism. But politics is broader than political partisanship; judges might 'play politics' for myriad reasons that serve their personal or institutional interests, rather than those of their political party.

Finally, in suggesting that legalism has been 'refuted' (e.g. Morell's chapter in this volume),[2] that model is sometimes straw-manned, likened to a mathematical syllogism with only one correct answer, such that if two competent judges reach different results, it must be that one or both were 'policy seeking' and thus behaving non-legalistically. But even among those jurists like Judge Wald who balk at attitudinalism's claims, virtually none would insist that judges who decide cases with purely legal or jurisprudential considerations must all reach a single result. Rather, it is plausible that they were simply using different, outcome-blind interpretative legal methods, a practice entirely consistent with legalism. This becomes even truer when moving down the judicial hierarchy, where judges' policy-making discretion is usually more constrained.

A more parsimonious and more useful understanding of judicial ideology, then, recognizes it as a different and broader concept than either politics/strategy, partisanship, or policy seeking. Indeed, as a threshold matter, the functional definition of ideology determines the relative weight that a judge tends to give each of the three schools of decision-making. Suppose an issue has a clear doctrinal legal resolution that would produce obviously bad policy, and all judges agree on both counts. A judge considered legalist under the functional definition would be more willing to produce the bad policy outcome, perhaps because she believes that courts' strictly adhering to positive law produces rule-of-law benefits that outweigh that one bad policy. But a judge who acts strategically in his own interests might hesitate to issue that ruling for fear of reputational damage to his institution.

In addition to influencing which school(s) a judge initially gives weight to, judicial ideology also plays a role in how each of the three schools of judicial decision-making operate. First, ideology can affect what legalistic interpretive method a judge believes is most appropriate (legalism), *ex ante* to any particular case or controversy: purposivism, intentionalism, textualism, dynamic interpretation, etc., and the sub-schools of each, which in turn can determine a legal outcome.

Second, ideology can affect how judges weigh external considerations such as their own or the judicial institution's interests (strategy) relative to other considerations internal to a given issue presented. For instance, is it appropriate to sign on and not dissent from a poorly reasoned decision in an effort to curry favour with the opinion's authoring colleague whose vote a judge expects to need in an important future case? Or would doing so violate the integrity of the judicial institution?

Third, and most classically, ideology affects what outcome a judge thinks is desirable purely as a matter of policy (attitudinalism); like all people, judges differ on issues such as how much power should be centralized in a supra-national or federal government, whether harsher or more lenient criminal sentences better serve justice, and whether mothers or fathers are generally more fit guardians, to name a few. Two judges, both using attitudinalist approaches to a case, but who sit at opposite poles of some policy spectrum, are perhaps most likely to disagree on a case's outcome most vehemently.

With these observations in mind, I have attempted to synthesize the theories of decision-making by modelling their relationships in two-dimensional space. Figure 40.1 has two dimensions. First, the horizontal (x) axis captures the variation in the influence of Policy and/or Preferences; it indicates the degree to which a decision-making exercise is more rule driven vs more outcome driven. Where a decision is highly rule driven, I call it *legalism*. Legalism is defined as decision-making driven by objective, result-blind interpretative techniques, such as the law's plain meaning or the apparent intent of the law-maker. In contrast, where a decision is highly outcome driven, I call it *activism*. Activist decisions, which rely highly on policy preferences, are driven by how the case outcome will affect the parties or society generally. Note that, per the discussion above, an activist judge can produce decisions preferred by the traditional political left or right, or something else. Highly legalist judges can also produce such diverging results via opposing legal interpretive approaches, though, being more constrained by rules, the average variation is likely to be somewhat smaller.

The vertical (y) axis captures the variation in the influence of political and/or strategic concerns; it indicates the degree to which the decision weighs considerations internal to the formal issue presented vs. those external to that formal issue. Where a decision

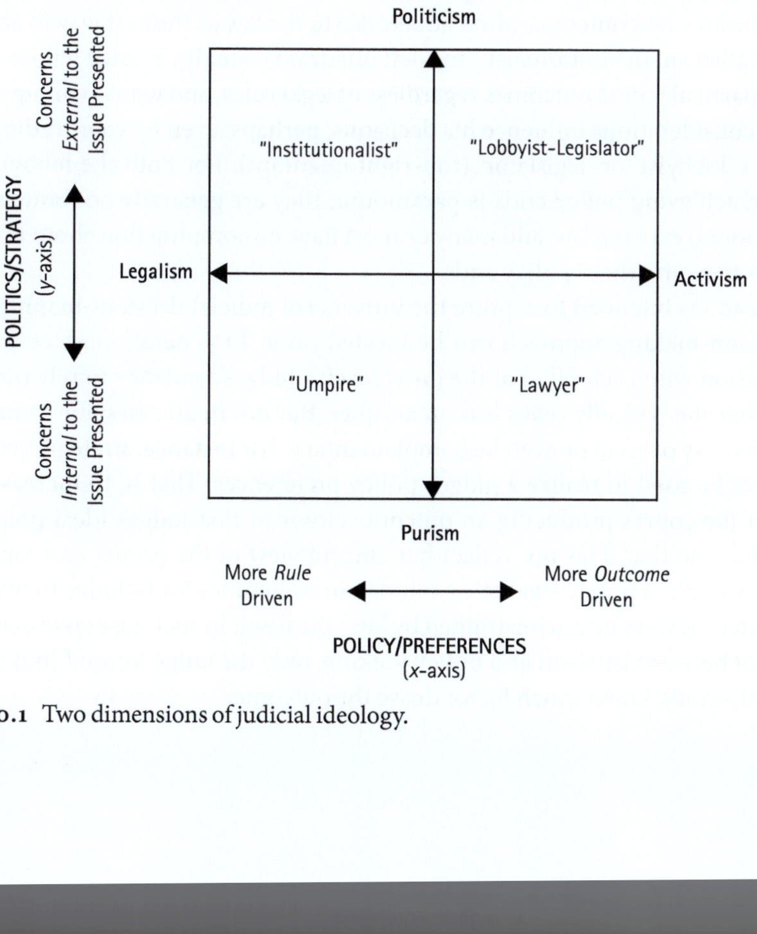

FIGURE 40.1 Two dimensions of judicial ideology.

is highly internally focused (little consideration of politics or strategy), I call it *purism*. Such a process will reach the optimal decision given the law and facts (including any legal policy considerations of the decision), without consideration for political factors such as how the decisions will affect the judge or the court's reputation, or how it will be enforced. Where a decision is highly externally focused (much consideration of politics or strategy), I call it *politicism*. Political decisions are driven by judges' desire to maximize their or their court's power, influence, prestige, or position, or by other professional or personal objectives. Such a process will be highly attuned to how the decision will resonate externally: outside the judge's chambers, with the public, and with other branches of government (for example, concern about legislative court-curbing), or even with other governments.

Since these two dimensions are distinct, any combination of the four traits is possible. First, a theoretical judge who is blind to outcome and indifferent to external political considerations, using legal rules alone to decide issues, is perhaps described as an 'umpire' (bottom-left quadrant), US Supreme Court Justice John Roberts's mere caller of 'balls and strikes'. Second, the judge who is indifferent to external, political considerations but who is principally driven to achieve a particular case outcome for the litigants or society regardless of law, is called a 'lawyer' (bottom-right quadrant). Consider how an actual legal advocate is motivated, not mainly to achieve a 'just' outcome but to achieve (within the ethical rules) a particular result for her client; moreover, she must confine her arguments to the facts, law, and policy of the case before the court. Third, a highly political judge, concerned with the institution's power and influence, but who views outcome-blind adherence to the law as the best way to achieve that result is called an 'institutionalist' (top-left quadrant). Finally, a judge who is motivated to reach particular case outcomes regardless of legal rules, and who is willing to let case-external considerations influence his decisions, perhaps, even by vote-trading between cases, is a 'lobbyist' or 'legislator' (top-right quadrant). For both the lobbyist and the legislator, achieving policy ends is paramount; they are generally not bound by (non-constitutional) existing law, and many or most have no compunction about making outside deals to realize those policy ends.

Figure 40.1 is intended to capture the universe of judicial decision-making such that any decision-making approach can be located on it. In general, these considerations are in tension with each other at the jurist level; a judge's tendency to rely more on one implies that she typically relies less on another. But not in all cases; for some disputes, the factors may overlap or even be complementary. For instance, strategic voting might sometimes be used to realize a judge's policy preferences. That is, to increase the likelihood of the court's producing an outcome closer to that judge's ideal point, a judge may cast a vote that does not reflect her sincere view of the proper case outcome. As another example, a purely legalistic analysis can sometimes lead a judge to his preferred policy outcome were he unconstrained by law. The result in such cases is observationally equivalent between legalism and policy seeking; only the judge himself (but maybe not even him!) would know which factor drove the outcome.

3. Measuring Judicial Ideology

Since the early to mid-twentieth century, researchers have been trying to use quantitative measures to measure judicial behaviour (see e.g. Gaudet et al. 1933; Schubert 1960; Nagel 1961). In an effort to predict and/or explain judges' rulings, and inspired partly by the insights of the attitudinal model, social scientists have developed a variety of quantitative measures that purport to capture judges' ideology.

But if, as we just saw, simply defining judicial ideology is difficult, then measuring it validly is even more so (Fischman and Law 2009). And given the inter-national disagreement, this is especially true if we want to accomplish any meaningful comparative analysis. Equally important, because each method for measuring ideology measures something different, each implicitly assumes something about what judicial ideology is, even if few make those assumptions explicit. But if we are to make progress in designing new and better measures and improving on old ones, we must keep working to improve our understanding of exactly what is being measured.

To do so, I first divide the existing methods into three categories: vote counting, proxy, and third party (cf Fischman and Law 2009).[3] I then review their leading applications, discuss their respective strengths and weaknesses, and explore the different theoretical assumptions underlying each.

3.1 Vote Counting

The most widely used judicial ideology measurement method involves an approach known as *vote counting*. Vote counting was one of the first methods used to understand ideology (Gaudet et al. 1933), and it has grown increasingly popular in recent years with advances in computing power. This method varies from more rudimentary 'per cent conservative/liberal' vote counting, to multidimensional scaling (Robertson 1982, United Kingdom House of Lords), and Bayesian Markov chain Monte Carlo estimations (e.g. Windett et al. 2015, US state supreme courts; Martin and Quinn 2002, US Supreme Court). Most vote counting methods quantify judicial decisions by transforming each judge's preference into a binary score. There are two broad approaches to vote counting: guided and agnostic.

3.1.1 *Guided Vote Counting*

Under a *guided* approach, the researcher assigns some substantive value to each vote: either (i) a substantive, case type-specific result (e.g. grant/deny an asylum petition, rule for an employer/employee, uphold/strike down a regulation) (see e.g. Law 2004b, US asylum petitions; Coroado et al. 2017, Portuguese Constitutional Court); or (ii) an ideological (e.g. liberal/conservative, centre/periphery) result (see Fischman 2011, US Courts of Appeal, Pellegrina and Garoupa 2013, Italian Constitutional Court; Cope and

Fischman 2017, 2018, appellate votes of US Supreme Court nominees). The most widely used guided approach is perhaps the US Supreme Court Database, which covers the entire history of the Court (Spaeth et al. 2017).

Unfortunately for measurement purposes, in many national and supra-national systems, the decisions of appellate panels are announced in a single opinion, with no public dissents permitted. Though this makes vote counting of individual judges impossible, where the panel varies from case to case and the panel's composition is public, researchers have used the characteristics of the panel's (or chamber's) mean or median judge to explore the relationship between outcome and judge identity (e.g. Pellegrina et al. 2017, Belgian Constitutional Court; see also Malecki 2012, European Court of Justice).

3.1.2 *Agnostic Vote Counting*

An alternative to the guided approach, *agnostic* vote counting, indicates only whether the judge voted with the majority or the minority, regardless of the legal content or implication underlying the vote. Using statistical scaling tools, the researcher can then orient the members of a court relative to each other on one or more dimensions, but she must use her qualitative knowledge of the court and its issues to assign substantive meaning to those dimensions. Such studies include the US Supreme Court (Martin and Quinn 2002); Supreme Court of Canada (Ostberg and Wetstein 2007; Alarie and Green 2009); high courts of the United States, Canada, India, Philippines, and Israel (Weinshall et al. 2018); small chambers generally (Peress 2009); and the European Court of Human Rights (Voeten 2007).

One advantage of both forms of vote counting is their sensitivity. A measure's *sensitivity* is how it responds to small variations in the attribute it is trying to measure, including both differences between judges in a given period, and changes in a given judge's ideology over time. By their nature, judicial vote counting measures are generally quite sensitive in both respects; the addition of a single case vote can affect a judge's score, differentiating her from others who did not vote similarly, and changing her score over time. Indeed, Martin and Quinn's approach (and the studies of national apex courts based on it) are innovative in part because of this dynamic capability.

With this in mind, what do guided and agnostic vote counting approaches assume about the nature of judicial ideology and decision-making? By coding each decision on some pre-determined scale related to policy outcomes (e.g. liberal–conservative), most guided approaches assume that judges' decisions are largely driven by their policy attitudes. But assuming, as I argue, that ideology comprises other elements beside policy preferences, then guided vote-counting captures only that one component of ideology. And relatedly, because the method *assumes* a policy-salient outcome, the method's power to tell us to what extent judges do in fact act based on their attitudes, is, at a minimum, blunted.

In contrast, by basing a judge's ideology entirely on the votes she casts and recognizing a theoretically unlimited number of defining dimensions, agnostic vote counting approaches implicitly use the functional definition of judicial ideology introduced above. That is, they allow a judge's ideology to vary based on any criterion that causes judges to decide cases differently, be it their legalistic interpretive methods, their policy outcome preferences, or their rational strategizing. Relatedly, by remaining agnostic about the substantive nature of dimensions until they are observed, agnostic vote counting methods are also agnostic about which theory of judicial decision-making has the most explanatory power.

This theoretical agnosticism matters, because where a researcher using agnostic vote counting observes significant variation on a dimension, she may be tempted to attribute it to outcome-driven, policy seeking behaviour. But per the discussions in section 2 above, it could also be a sign that judges are using different, outcome-blind legal interpretive techniques that lead them to diverging results. That pattern might not be obvious to the empirical researcher who considers only the most superficial case characteristics; she would need to study carefully the different opinions to see that different legalistic approaches lie behind the observed variation in ideology.

Construct validity is the degree to which a measure captures an underlying theoretical construct. Where a judicial ideology measure suffers from weak construct validity, the measure usually either conflates political and judicial ideology, or fails to capture the nuance of judicial reasoning. Binary vote counting methods do not conflate judicial and political ideology, because they are based on the judge's own behaviour as a judge. But they feature a different construct validity-related limitation: they capture only the most superficial aspects of a judicial outcome—majority or minority, affirm or reverse—and not the content of the opinion. For this reason, Professor Mark Tushnet derides most of the vote counting methods as 'suffering from an unbearable simple-mindedness' (Tushnet 1980). Likewise, US federal Circuit Judge Patricia Wald characterizes judging as 'a complex, case-specific, and subtle task that defies single-factor analysis' (Wald 1999). And as Professor Carolyn Shapiro notes in critiquing Spaeth's binary outcome-oriented approach, '[t]his focus on outcome to the exclusion of law can reach extremes that, to a lawyer, are mind-boggling' (Shapiro 2009).

While vote counting is probably the best available method to measure legislative ideology, judicial and legislative outcomes differ in one key way. A 'legislative outcome' comprises the text of the bill, whether the bill was enacted or defeated, and perhaps, the vote margin. All legislators either support or oppose the version of the bill as considered, and no legislator may unilaterally (without majority support) insert terms or provisions into a bill.[4] Influenced by this model, judicial vote counting methods consider only the judges' votes.[5] But from a law-making or policy standpoint, the most important aspect of a typical (published) common law appellate case is not its effect on the parties before the court, but how the judges' words affect precedent. As such, the most valuable clues to judicial ideology are not in the panel's vote count, but in the written decision announcing and explaining the holding, as well as the content of any concurrences and dissents. Overlooking the language of opinions therefore leaves out perhaps the most significant component of judicial behaviour.

To illustrate, consider US Chief Justice Roberts's vote in *National Federation of Independent Business v. Sebelius* (2012) to preserve much of the Affordable Care Act under Congress's taxing power. That vote aligned him with the liberal wing of the Court and would be considered a liberal vote under either a guided or agnostic approach. But that vote masked his important opinion holding that Congress had exceeded its power under the Commerce Clause, a quintessentially conservative legal view.

As another example, consider *Bond v United States*, a 2014 Supreme Court criminal case. Carol Ann Bond's offence was rubbing an abrasive chemical on a neighbour's mailbox. The question before the Court was whether the Constitution's treaty power and *necessary and proper* clause allowed prosecutions under the Chemical Weapons Convention Implementation Act (which implemented the Chemical Weapons Convention) for conduct like Ms Bond's. How would one code this case's possible outcomes? Consider that a traditional conservative view might (i) take a narrow view of Congress's power to legislate pursuant to treaties (favouring the defendant); (ii) take an originalist view of the Constitution (favouring the defendant); (iii) oppose the (Obama-led) Justice Department's expansion of federal power (favouring the defendant); (iv) defer to the government's prosecution decisions (favouring the government); and (v) defer to the executive in its conduct of foreign relations (favouring the government). The traditional liberal positions might take the opposite view on each of these five. Should a decision favouring the government be coded as liberal or conservative? As it turns out, the justices decided unanimously for Bond, though on statutory interpretation grounds. But the justices generally considered most conservative—Alito, Thomas, and Scalia—wrote or endorsed separate opinions most hostile to the government position, based mostly on constitutional limits on government power. These justices' views about the limits of federal power to legislate pursuant to treaties are typically libertarian/conservative judicial ones. They clash with liberal views promoting expansive federal authority (often to curtail US state authority) and promoting internationalism to facilitate international cooperation.

Bond provides a treasure-trove of information about each of the justices' ideologies. But the Supreme Court Database codes all cases ruling for defendants as 'liberal', so it would code *Bond* as a liberal decision, even though it apparently disappointed most liberal jurists. Because the decision was a unanimous reversal, it would provide no useful information for an agnostic vote counting model,[6] which is sensitive only to judges' positions vis-a-vis other judges. While *Bond* is more ideologically complex than many cases, it is not terribly unusual in that sense. Criminal cases, cases involving the scope of government power, cases involving constitutional interpretation, cases involving traditional party politics, and (as mentioned above) cases involving statutory pre-emption, often mix traditional politics in interesting and ideologically confounding ways. The difficulty with the binary, left–right coding approach, then, is that cases like *Bond* must be coded some way and added to the dataset. However that decision is made, it will obscure important nuance in a mix of legal issues. More importantly for the purpose of social science, the coding errors are unlikely to be random, tending to err systematically in one direction.

3.2 Proxy

Proxy measures use some alternative, observable trait as a stand-in for judicial ideology. The chosen measure is theoretically distinct from judicial ideology, but it must be sufficiently theoretically related that we should expect the two to be empirically correlated. Early versions of this technique considered judges' self-identified party affiliation (Schubert 1960; Nagel 1961). Recently developed proxy methods select a political actor connected to the judge, measure that actor's political ideology, and use it as a stand-in indicator for the judge's judicial ideology. The appointing party or executive's party (Hanretty 2013, UK House of Lords; Pinello 1999; Cross 2007; Sunstein et al. 2004) has been used as a proxy in dozens of articles over the last several decades.[7] More complex proxy measures of ideology incorporate the ideal points of other political actors. For instance, the Common Space scores (Giles et al. 2001) and the Judicial Common Space (JCS) (Epstein et al. 2007) incorporate the Poole and Rosenthal (2000) NOMINATE ideal points of the US senators who were involved in an appellate judge's nomination and who share the president's party.[8] By incorporating political actors more closely connected to the appointment process, the JCS represents a refinement of the appointing president's party method. Of course, this method can apply only in those systems in which a judicial appointer has an observable and measurable ideology themselves and that appointer varies by judge, which limits its application to many systems, in which the only selector is a head of government or judicial council.

A recently developed proxy method is Bonica et al.'s (2017) Clerk-Based Ideology (CBI) scores. The method assumes that US federal judges generally prefer to hire clerks who share their judicial ideology, and thus, it estimates the political ideology of US federal law clerks based on their publicly available campaign contributions. The average of a judge's clerks' ideology scores thus serves as the proxy for the judge's own judicial ideology. While useful for understanding US federal judicial ideology, the collection of institutions that make such a proxy method possible—delegation of significant responsibility to short-term judicial clerks, a system of partly privately funded campaign finance, and availability of both types of data—are, collectively, probably unique among national systems. As a result, the CBI ideology measure may not be replicable outside the US federal system. More broadly, this fact underscores the notion that proxy methods are often idiosyncratic, dependent on the particular structures of the selection process and judiciary, making cross-national comparisons challenging.

The sensitivity of proxy measures varies considerably. On one extreme, party of the appointing president is the least sensitive, as it treats all judges appointed over a four- or eight-year administration as identical. The JCS should allow for somewhat more sensitivity, considering the ideology of the senators involved in the appointment (though not for the DC Circuit and some other judges). But JCS is insensitive to change over time, because the scores are frozen at the time of nomination.[9] The CBI scores' sensitivity is similar to that of most vote counting methods; every campaign contribution and new clerk hire can shift a judge's score marginally.

The theoretical assumptions behind proxy methods also vary by the type of proxy used. Where that proxy is a political actor and judicial ideology is inferred from the political behaviour of those actors, the method assumes that the same thing that drives the political actor—implementing preferred policies, and institutional preservation—also drives the judge in his judicial decision-making. That is, judicial ideology is implicitly *defined as* (another's) policy preferences. It therefore assumes that, at least to some degree, the judge is the lobbyist legislator in the top-right quadrant of Figure 40.1 above. If this assumption is violated, a proxy method may still have predictive power, but we would not expect it to have much. For the same reason, the method by itself may be of limited use in attempting to determine to what extent attitudes or values motivate judicial behaviour.

Granted, political and judicial ideology may correlate well for some courts and types of cases, but they are also susceptible to considerable error. By necessity, most proxy methods measure the political behaviour of people connected to the judge, because most sitting judges cannot vote on bills or make public campaign endorsements. An assumption implicit in the JCS is that the political ideology that drives US congressional behaviour is often a reasonably good proxy for the ideology that drives judges' decisions (an assumption that, at least in some contexts, is backed by evidence). CBI implicitly makes a similar assumption about the behaviour that leads lawyers to contribute to political candidates. But even assuming that senators' or clerks' *political* views perfectly match those of their judge counterparts, that does not imply that their *judicial* ideologies match. This is especially true in the US circuit and district courts, where many important decisions turn on complex procedural rules, and where cases producing a clear left–right dimension are less common. A large fraction of cases turns on the appropriate level of deference to the political branches and lower courts, or on the proper theory of statutory or regulatory interpretation, issues that often do not divide neatly along left–right political lines. In essence, two judges may have similar policy preferences on multiple dimensions, but different preferred formal legalistic approaches (e.g. the relative weight to give text vs legislative history) which can produce different case outcomes.

Even if political and judicial ideology were perfectly correlated, it is unclear to what extent the actors selected for the proxies are good stand-ins for the judges' ideologies. For JCS, senators selecting a judicial appointee probably prefer a judge who, all else equal, shares their views of the law. But they also have other important incentives in that choice (cf Law 2004a). They may use the appointment in part to appease one particularly important interest group. A senator may also want to use the carrot of judicial appointment to elicit financial and other support from nominee hopefuls.[10]

3.3 Third Party

Finally, *third-party* measures consist of observers' judgment or predictions about a judge's ideology. Whereas proxy measures derive from personal political behaviour of actors in some way connected to the judge, third-party measures purport to observe and evaluate judicial ideology itself (past or anticipated).

3.3.1 *Editorial-Based Third Party*

Segal and Cover (1989)'s scores of US Supreme Court justices' ideology have served as a model for similar measures of national apex courts and judges. Segal and Cover derive their scores from textual analysis of media editorials about judicial nominees written after their nomination but before their confirmation. They measure the relative liberal–conservative tenor of the editorials, placing each justice on a scale from −1 (unanimously conservative) to +1 (unanimously liberal). The Segal–Cover scores were the most-used measure of US Supreme Court ideology during the 1990s (Sheehan et al. 1992; Bailey 2016). Studies of the high courts in Australia and Canada (Weiden 2011) have since used comparable approaches.

Such third-party approaches have the advantage of being quite sensitive between judges: commentators can consider nuances in their case decisions or legal writings. However, under existing pre-appointment editorial-based approaches, the scores are locked-in before the judge decides her first case, so they cannot detect evolution in ideology. For instance, the locked-in approach can sometimes produce a very odd ideology result, such as that for US Associate Justice John Paul Stevens. A 2003 study of Stevens's Court voting record made him the most liberal member of the Court at the time (Sirovich 2003). But his Segal–Cover score, recorded at his nomination in 1975, placed him on the Court's conservative wing, just between Anthony Kennedy and Clarence Thomas.

By treating expectations about a judge's performance at the time of nomination, editorial-based methods have the power to take a broad view of the concept of ideology. That is, the editorials can and do draw on any aspect of a nominee's background that the commentator deems relevant to how he will perform as a judge, including any past judicial behaviour, legal writings, or other legal experience. Likewise, the commentators might write about not just their policy positions, but their jurisprudence, reputation for (lack of) integrity, or anything else. Yet most approaches then coerce this *n*-dimensional information into one a single, predetermined, left–right political dimension. Doing so is useful for many research questions, but, as with guided vote counting, it prevents us from saying much about the factors behind judicial decision-making. If we were using this method to gauge the impact of judges' attitudes on cases, it would essentially beg the question.

Yet Segal and Cover (1989) claim that their findings provide 'exceptional support for the attitudinal model', which the authors define as 'votes [being] strongly dependent upon [judges'] attitudes, values, or personal policy preferences' (562). Specifically, they base their conclusion on the .80 correlation they observe between ideology predicted from editorials and actual votes in civil rights cases. It is unclear, however, how this finding supports the attitudinal model. It seems to establish only that legal commentators were able to predict with fair accuracy how judges would later vote. It does not establish the cause of those votes, or why the justices' votes differ. Under the theory of attitudinalism described above in the discussion surrounding Figure 40.1 (to which Segal and Cover's definition is similar), attitudinal voting is outcome-driven, activist legal behaviour. But showing that people can predict that judges will disagree, and how, does not preclude the possibility that they are disagreeing at least in part for strategic—or, more likely, legalistic reasons.

3.3.2 *Expert-Based Third Party*

One especially promising but as of yet barely explored method for measuring ideology is a form of third-party measurement: using the opinions of legal experts to derive quantitative estimates of ideology (and perhaps, other traits). Like other methods, this approach presents several logistical challenges, but it also has the potential to overcome many of the shortcomings of past and existing approaches discussed above. To my knowledge, Grendstad et al.'s (2012, 2015) analysis of the Norwegian Supreme Court is the only existing use of expert surveys to estimate ideology for an apex national court. The authors asked members of the Norwegian Supreme Court bar to rate the current justices along a radical–conservative/left–right scale. Perhaps surprisingly, the measure correlated poorly with a proxy measure of their political ideology as determined by the appointing party coalition, that is social democratic vs non-socialist (Grendstad et al. 2012). This discrepancy illustrates how political expectations of judges can differ, sometimes significantly, from their performance once they take the bench.

Wijtvliet and Dyevre's (2021) analysis of economic cases for judges on the General Court of the European Union is another innovative example of using expert surveys to estimate judicial ideology. Wijtvliet and Dyevre surveyed forty-six competition-law experts, asking them to rate the ideology of fifty-one judges who had served on the General Court. They find that the pro-business score of a panel's median judge significantly predicts competition and state aid case outcomes, but that 'Europhilia' has less predictive power.

Like editorial-based methods, an expert-based method is amenable to the broad, functional concept of judicial ideology; so long as an expert can observe it, that expert can incorporate it into the ideology score. To do so, the researcher must be able to ask the experts about different traits beyond traditional left-right ideology or other policy orientations. Wijtvliet and Dyevre's (2021)'s General Court study did just that; it asked experts about traits about not just policy but also expertise and personal traits, including attitude toward European integration and common-law expertise. An even more dimensionally agnostic method might involve asking open-ended questions and using a form of unguided content analysis, like topic modelling, to determine what traits the experts thought most motivated the judges' decision-making.

One assumption unique to expert-based evaluations is that legal practitioners have special insight into how judges decide cases—insight that neither the judicial appointment process, nor judges' political behaviour, nor judicial case votes can fully capture. While ideology is a latent trait and therefore not directly observable, we can assume that a judge's 'underlying set of normative beliefs about the appropriate aims and functions of law and courts, which are applied to adjudicate a legal issue' directly cause him or her to apply the law in certain ways in written opinions and oral decisions. This judicial behaviour—for example written orders and opinions, private settlement discussions in chambers, and comments made from the bench—is therefore a direct manifestation of the judge's ideology, and it is the closest thing to ideology itself that can be observed. Lawyers and judicial participants directly observe all of this behaviour.

As to sensitivity, expert evaluations can also be sensitive to minor variations between judges and to change over time. Indeed, because well-designed evaluator sampling would produce a sample that roughly represents the theoretical population of all potential evaluators, one could estimate standard errors and confidence intervals for each point estimate of an observed trait, revealing just how confident we can be in the estimate.

Expert surveys can also address potential threats to validity that can affect any measure of judicial ideology in two ways. First, expert surveys derive from the observed judicial behaviour of the judges themselves rather than political actors connected to the judges. They therefore require (at least) one fewer inferential leap about how judges manifest their ideologies. Whatever judicial ideology is, most would agree that it is conceptually closer to the actions of judges themselves than to the actions of others. Second, while judicial 'votes' are probative of judicial ideology, a judge's judicial reasoning in her written opinions, orders, and analysis from the bench provides clearer insight into her judicial ideology than her decision to simply affirm or reverse. Expert surveys might capture that nuance, albeit indirectly, by drawing on the experiences of legal experts who have studied their opinions and interacted with them in person over time. In this limited sense, the technique is similar to editorial-based methods (e.g. Segal and Cover 1989; Weiden 2011) which, for nominees with judicial experience, draw on the judge's previous opinions. But unlike editorial-based methods' source material, which is written before the judge is confirmed, expert evaluations reviews are based on the judge's past conduct in that judicial position.

For these reasons, expert evaluations could, in many cases, come reasonably close to observing the latent trait of judicial ideology. At a minimum, expert-sourced evaluations might relate more closely to ideology than the observations underlying current measurement approaches.

Of course, expert evaluations are not flawless. One possible limitation is the evaluators' structural or categorical biases. There may be systemic conscious or unconscious bias based on region or location; or against members of certain demographic groups, based on ethnicity, gender, or age, for example (see e.g. Sen 2014a, 2014b). For instance, if lawyers were systematically and unfairly to evaluate female judges as more liberal than male judges, middle-aged judges as more able than elderly judges, or Hindu judges as more tolerant than Muslim judges, those biases would bias the scores. Researchers might check for this form of bias by comparing variation across demographics to that contained in more objective measures.

Unlike other evaluation systems such as online product ratings and student course evaluations, this method can overcome survey limitations. Systems like Trip Advisor and Amazon ratings are rightfully criticized for their reliance on self-selected, nonrepresentative samples and the lack of meaningful curation or guidance in evaluations. For instance, Trip Advisor reviewers may have never visited the reviewed venue, and even experienced reviewers are self-selected, leading to biased results. Moreover, these systems lack a standardized framework for evaluating specific aspects. Different reviewers cover various topics, making it challenging to determine the distribution of considerations that influenced their final ratings. Similarly, in online product reviews, negative feedback can stem from unrelated factors like disliking a book's content or delivery issues. The opaque nature of these evaluations makes it difficult to discern the underlying factors contributing to the overall evaluation. In contrast, a well-designed evaluator selection process would effectively address these flaws. It would involve verified legal experts who possess substantial experience with the judge(s) under review. The evaluations would be focused on specific aspects of the judge's behaviour, facilitating a fair and direct comparison.

Expert evaluations face another challenge, though. Identifying and surveying experts is an extraordinarily time-consuming and resource-intensive enterprise. Thus, such survey initiatives are feasible for a small set of courts and perhaps for smaller jurisdictions, but producing such scores on a larger, system-wide scale would thus likely require an independent, pre-existing survey system.

To my knowledge, the only such large-scale initiative is the Jurist-Derived Judicial Ideology Scores (JuDJIS) (Cope 2024[11]; see also Cope 2018; Cope and Zhang 2024), an initiative designed to potentially cover every non-Supreme-Court Article III judge in the United States on one ideological scale. When complete, the dataset will comprise dynamic, interval-level, and potentially multidimensional data of essentially every federal district and appellate judge serving since 1991. It uses text analysis of expert lawyer evaluations collected over a period of thirty-plus years. The computational method involves some relatively new text-analysis techniques, but the approach itself is conceptually simple: it quantifies thirty-plus years of evaluations drawn from tens of thousands of experts. The experts comprise lawyers and ex-law clerks with professional experience with each of the judges, including the judges' written opinions, judging style, and courtroom/chambers demeanour. In response to prompts, the experts use their own words to evaluate the judges' ideologies, written opinions, judging styles, and courtroom/chambers demeanour. The evaluations are compiled by academic publisher Wolters Kluwer's *Almanac of the Federal Judiciary*, a periodical which, since the 1980s, has surveyed a stratified sample of the pool of qualified experts for each judge. As mentioned, one limitation in applying the JuDJIS method elsewhere is that the initiative covers thousands of judges on different courts and multiple levels over three decades. As a result, the underlying data collection involves tens-of-thousands of hours of survey and response-processing in total, making it largely dependent on a pre-existing, commercial survey enterprise.

4. Conclusion

The field of judicial behaviour has made great strides over the past decades, both in theorizing the reasons for judges' behaviour, and in finding innovative ways to measure it, yet there is still opportunity for progress in integrating these two domains. These efforts have been and will be synergetic undertakings: greater clarity on the thing we are trying to measure—judicial ideology—will facilitate sharper empirical research and the development of new and better empirical methods. And new empirical findings will undoubtedly lead to conceptual and theoretical breakthroughs.

In this chapter, I have attempted to make explicit the implicit theoretical assumptions behind the leading existing approaches, and I have considered the assumptions that might underlie potential future initiatives, especially expert-based evaluations. I hope that future theoretical and empirical judicial behaviour initiatives will use this discussion as a starting point for achieving even greater conceptual clarity about judicial ideology, and more valid and useful measures thereof.

Acknowledgements

I thank Josh Fischman, Michael Gilbert, and the Handbook editors, especially Gunnar Grendstad, for helpful feedback.

Notes

1. The sample was based partly on convenience; I contacted all the contributors to this *Handbook*, which presumably represent some of the world's leading experts across dozens of systems.
2. 'Legalism is a refuted descriptive theory of judicial behavior ... [S]ocial scientists see clearly that judges do not perceive the facts and the law as they are, plug them into a logical formula, and deduct the one single correct outcome of the case.'
3. This typology is inspired by that described by Fischman and Law (2009), but I have modified it to reflect my sense of how the categories have evolved in light of methodological developments over the last fifteen years.
4. Legislators' and committees' comments on the legislation create a legislative history, but (except for certain statutory interpretation cases), those comments have little bearing on the law's substance.
5. Defending this practice, Spaeth argues that he 'focus[es] upon [judges'] votes' rather than 'upon their opinions', because, he says, 'I find the key to judicial behavior in what justices do' rather than 'in what they say' (Spaeth 1965). Spaeth overlooks the fact that what judges say is perhaps the most important thing that they do (Tiller and Cross 2006).
6. Though an agnostic vote-counting method could in theory take account of concurrence coalitions.
7. That measure has been shown to correlate highly with many outcomes on the courts of appeals. This effect is far less significant for the district courts (Ashenfelter et al. 1995), though that effect appears to have changed over time (Rowland and Carp 1980).
8. A senator's ideology is a plausible proxy for that of the appointed judge because of a custom called 'senatorial courtesy', which gives senators of the president's party the prerogative to recommend a judicial nominee from their state for nomination.
9. The data developed by Tate and Handberg (1991), who record background characteristics of the justices, are similar in this respect.
10. As to the CBI scores, Bonica et al. (2017) acknowledge the equivalent shortcoming in their method: that judicial ideology is a small or non-existent factor in many clerkship hiring and acceptance decisions. Some judges seek political sycophants as clerks, but others seek an ideological mix of clerks to 'keep them honest'. For instance, the late Justice Scalia

was known to hire one liberal clerk each year. Other judges are mostly indifferent to their clerks' politics, so they simply seek the best resumes or personality fit.

11. See the Jurist-Derived Judicial Ideology Scores (JuDJIS), at https://judjis.org.

References

Alarie, Benjamin, and Andrew Green. 2009. 'Policy Preference Change and Appointments to the Supreme Court of Canada'. *Osgoode Hall Law Journal* 47: 1.

Ashenfelter, Orley, Theodore Eisenberg and Stewart J Schwab. 1995. 'Politics and the Judiciary: The Influence of Judicial Background on Case Outcomes'. *The Journal of Legal Studies* 24 (2): 257–81.

Bailey, Michael. 2016. Measuring Ideology on the Courts. Technical report Working Paper.

Bonica, Adam, Adam S. Chilton, Jacob Goldin, Kyle Rozema, and Maya Sen. 2017. 'The Political Ideologies of Law Clerks'. *American Law and Economics Review* 19 (1): 96–128.

Bonica, Adam, and Maya Sen. 2021. 'Estimating Judicial Ideology'. *Journal of Economic Perspectives* 35 (1): 97–118.

Cope, Kevin L. 2024. 'An Expert-Sourced Measure of Judicial Ideology' (working paper).

Cope, Kevin L., and Joshua B. Fischman. 2017. 'For A Trump Nominee, Neil Gorsuch's Record is Surprisingly Moderate on Immigration and Employment Discrimination'. https://fivethirtyeight.com/features/for-a-trump-nominee-neil-gorsuchs-record-is-surprisingly-moderate-on-immigration/.

Cope, Kevin L., and Joshua B. Fischman. 2018. 'It's hard to find a federal judge more conservative than Brett Kavanaugh'. https://www.washingtonpost.com/news/monkey-cage/wp/2018/09/05/its-hard-to-find-a-federal-judge-more-conservative-than-brett-kavanaugh/.

Cope, Kevin L., 'Exactly How Conservative are the Judges on Trump's Short List for the Supreme Court? Take a Look at This One Chart.' *The Washington Post* Monkey Cage (7 July 2018). https://www.washingtonpost.com/news/monkey-cage/wp/2018/07/07/exactly-how-conservative-are-the-judges-on-trumps-short-list-for-the-supreme-court-take-a-look-at-this-one-chart/?utm_term=.c92b9f7b198d.

Cope, Kevin L. and Li Zhang. 2024. 'Applications of a Hierarchical Dictionary Method for Analyzing Legal and Political Texts Via Nested Ngrams' (working paper).

Coroado, Susana, Nuno Garoupa, and Pedro C. Magalhães. 2017. 'Judicial Behavior Under Austerity: An Empirical Analysis of Behavioral Changes in the Portuguese Constitutional Court, 2002–2016'. *Journal of Law and Courts* 5 (2): 289–311.

Cross, Frank B. 2007. *Decision Making in the US Courts of Appeals*. Stanford: Stanford University Press.

de Mendonça Lopes, Felipe. 2019. 'Dissent Aversion and Sequential Voting in the Brazilian Supreme Court'. *Journal of Empirical Legal Studies* 16 (4): 933–54.

Epstein, Lee, William M. Landes, and Richard A. Posner. 2011. 'Why (and When) Judges Dissent: A Theoretical and Empirical Analysis'. *Journal of Legal Analysis* 3 (1): 101–37.

Epstein, Lee, and Jack Knight. 2013. 'Reconsidering Judicial Preferences'. *Annual Review of Political Science* 16: 11–31.

Epstein, Lee, Andrew D. Martin, Jeffrey A. Segal, and Chad Westerland. 2007. 'The Judicial Common Space'. *The Journal of Law, Economics, & Organization* 23

Epstein, Lee, and Keren Weinshall. 2021. *The Strategic Analysis of Judicial Behavior: A Comparative Perspective*. Cambridge University Press.

Fischman, Joshua B. 2011. 'Estimating Preferences of Circuit Judges: A Model of Consensus Voting'. *The Journal of Law and Economics* 54 (4): 781–809.

Fischman, Joshua B. 2015. 'Do the Justices Vote Like Policy Makers? Evidence From Scaling the Supreme Court with Interest Groups'. *The Journal of Legal Studies* 44 (1): 269–93.

Fischman, Joshua B., and David S. Law. 2009. 'What Is Judicial Ideology, and How Should We Measure It'. *Washington University Journal of Law and Policy* 29: 133.

Gaudet, Frederick, J., George S. Harris, and Charles W. St. John. 1933. 'Individual Differences in the Sentencing Tendencies of Judges'. *Journal of Criminal Law and Criminology* 23 (5): 811–18.

Gilbert, Michael D. 2011. 'Does Law Matter? Theory and Evidence From Single-Subject Adjudication'. *Journal of Legal Studies* 40 (2): 333–65.

Giles, Micheal W., Virginia A. Hettinger, and Todd Peppers. 2001. 'Picking Federal Judges: A Note on Policy and Partisan Selection Agendas'. *Political Research Quarterly* 54 (3): 623–41.

Grendstad, Gunnar, William R. Shaffer, and Eric N. Waltenburg. 2015. *Policy Making in an Independent Judiciary: The Norwegian Supreme Court*. Colchester, UK: ECPR Press.

Grendstad, Gunnar, William R. Shaffer, and Eric N. Waltenburg. 2012. 'Ideologi Og Grunnholdninger Hos Dommerne I Norges Høyesterett'. *Lov og rett* 51 (4): 240–53.

Hanretty, Chris. 2012. 'Dissent in Iberia: The Ideal Points of Justices on the Spanish and Portuguese Constitutional Tribunals'. *European Journal of Political Research* 51 (5): 671–92.

Hanretty, Chris. 2013. 'The Decisions and Ideal Points of British Law Lords'. *British Journal of Political Science* 43 (3): 703–16.

Hanretty, Chris. 2015. 'Judicial Disagreement Need Not Be Political: Dissent on the Estonian Supreme Court'. *Europe-Asia Studies* 67 (6): 970–88.

Law, David S. 2004a. 'Appointing Federal Judges: The President, the Senate, and the Prisoner's Dilemma'. *Cardozo Law Review* 26: 479.

Law, David S. 2004b. 'Strategic Judicial Lawmaking: Ideology, Publication, and Asylum Law in the Ninth Circuit'. *University of Cincinnati Law Review* 73: 817.

Malecki, Michael. 2012. 'Do ECJ Judges All Speak With the Same Voice? Evidence of Divergent Preferences From the Judgments of Chambers'. In *The Power of the European Court of Justice*. Routledge.

Martin, Andrew D., and Kevin M. Quinn. 2002. 'Dynamic Ideal Point Estimation via Markov Chain Monte Carlo for the US Supreme Court, 1953–1999'. *Political Analysis* 10 (2): 134–53.

Murphy Walter F. 1964. *Elements of Judicial Strategy*. Chicago: University of Chicago Press.

Nagel, Stuart S. 1961. 'Political Party Affiliation and Judges' Decisions'. *American Political Science Review* 55 (4): 843–50.

Ostberg, C. L., and Matthew E. Wetstein. 2007. 'In a Different Voice: Sex Difference in Economic Cases Decided by the Canadian Supreme Court'. In *Annual Meeting of the Canadian Political Science Association. Saskatoon, Saskatchewan*.

Pellegrina, Lucia Dalla, and Nuno Garoupa. 2013. Choosing Between the Government and the Regions: An Empirical Analysis of the Italian Constitutional Court Decisions'. *European Journal of Political Research* 52 (4): 558–80.

Pellegrina, Lucia Dalla, Jef De Mot, Michael Faure, and Nuno Garoupa. 2017. 'Litigating Federalism: An Empirical Analysis of Decisions of the Belgian Constitutional Court'. *European Constitutional Law Review* 13 (2): 305–46.

Peress, Michael. 2009. 'Small Chamber Ideal Point Estimation'. *Political Analysis* 17 (3): 276–90.

Pinello, Daniel R. 1999. 'Linking Party to Judicial Ideology in American Courts: A Meta-Analysis'. *The Justice System Journal* 20 (3): 219–54.

Poole, Keith T., and Howard Rosenthal. 2000. *Congress: A Political-Economic History of Roll Call Voting*. Oxford: Oxford University Press on Demand.
Rohde, David W., and Harold J. Spaeth. 1976. *Supreme Court Decision Making*. New York: W. H. Freeman.
Robertson, David. 1982. 'Judicial Ideology in the House of Lords: A Jurimetric Analysis'. *British Journal of Political Science* 12 (1): 1–25.
Rowland, C. K., and Robert A. Carp. 1980. 'A Longitudinal Study of Party Effects on Federal District Court Policy Propensities'. *American Journal of Political* Science 24 (2): 291–305.
Schubert, Glendon A. 1960. *Quantitative Analysis of Judicial Behavior*. New York: Free Press.
Segal, Jeffrey A., and Albert D. Cover. 1989. 'Ideological Values and the Votes of US Supreme Court Justices'. *American Political Science Review* 83 (2): 557–65.
Sen, Maya. 2014a. 'How Judicial Qualification Ratings May Disadvantage Minority and Female Candidates'. *Journal of Law and Courts* 2 (1): 33–65.
Sen, Maya. 2014b. 'Minority Judicial Candidates Have Changed: The ABA Ratings Gap Has Not'. *Judicature* 98: 46.
Shapiro, Carolyn. 2009. 'Coding Complexity Bringing Law to the Empirical Analysis of the Supreme Court'. *Hastings Law Journal* 60 (3): 477–540.
Sheehan, Reginald S., William Mishler, and Donald R. Songer. 1992. 'Ideology, Status, and the Differential Success of Direct Parties before the Supreme Court'. *American Political Science Review* 86 (2): 464–71.
Sirovich, Lawrence. 2003. 'A Pattern Analysis of the Second Rehnquist US Supreme Court'. *Proceedings of the National Academy of Sciences* 100 (13): 7432–37.
Spaeth, Harold J. 1965. 'Jurimetrics and Professor Mendelson: A troubled relationship'. *The Journal of Politics* 27 (4): 875–80.
Spaeth, Harold J., Lee Epstein, Andrew D. Martin, Jeffrey A. Segal, Theodore J. Ruger, and Sara C. Benesh. 2017. '2017 Supreme Court Database'. http://Supremecourtdatabase.org
Sunstein, Cass R., David Schkade, and Lisa Michelle Ellman. 2004. 'Ideological Voting on Federal Courts of Appeals: A Preliminary Investigation'. *Virginia Law Review* 90 (1): 301–54.
Tate, C. Neal, and Roger Handberg. 1991. 'Time Binding and Theory Building in Personal Attribute Models of Supreme Court Voting Behavior, 1916–88'. *American Journal of Political Science* 35 (2): 460–80.
Tiller, Emerson H., and Frank B. Cross. 2006. 'What is Legal Doctrine'. *Northwestern University Law Review* 100: 517.
Tushnet, Mark. 1980. 'Post-Realist Legal Scholarship'. *Wisconsin Law Review* 1980 (6): 1383–1401.
Voeten, Erik. 2007. 'The Politics of International Judicial Appointments: Evidence From the European Court of Human Rights'. *International Organization* 61 (4): 669–701.
Wald, Patricia M. 1999. 'A Response to Tiller and Cross'. *Columbia Law Review* 99 (1): 235–61.
Weiden, David L. 2011. 'Judicial Politicization, Ideology, and Activism at the High Courts of the United States, Canada, and Australia'. *Political Research Quarterly* 64 (2): 335–47.
Weinshall, Keren, Udi Sommer, and Ya'acov Ritov. 2018. 'Ideological Influences on Governance and Regulation: The Comparative Case of Supreme Courts'. *Regulation & Governance* 12 (3): 334–52.
Wijtvliet, Wessel, and Arthur Dyevre. 2021. 'Judicial Ideology in Economic Cases: Evidence from the General Court of the European Union'. *European Union Politics* 22 (1): 25–45.
Windett, Jason H., Jeffrey J. Harden, and Matthew EK Hall. 2015. 'Estimating Dynamic Ideal Points for State Supreme Courts'. *Political Analysis* 23 (3): 461–69.

CHAPTER 41

RESEARCH COMMUNITIES AND THE COLLECTIVE INVESTMENT IN DATA INFRASTRUCTURE

JEFFREY K. STATON

1. Introduction

The comparative law and politics research community has grown considerably over the past twenty years. Where once it was a challenge to put together a conference panel on the subject, the challenge now is how to fit all the papers onto a single schedule. This has followed no doubt from a commitment among comparativists, legal academics, and an international network of social scientists studying law to train a new generation of judicial scholars with the necessary skillset to investigate the politics of law globally. The discipline's leading journals now commonly publish articles in comparative law and politics. A quick glance at the subfield's own journal suggests that comparative work is being both recognized and featured.[1] The field is also rewarding new scholars. Until 1999, a single comparative dissertation won the American Political Science Association's Corwin Award for best doctoral work in the field of public law (Charles Epp's in 1996). Since 2000 roughly 50 per cent of the award winners have been recognized for contributions to the comparative study of law and politics. Although the COVID-19 disrupted academic research that relies on field-based methods involving considerable travel, it also created opportunities to bring together global communities linked together by the same concerns. This was surely true of law and politics where scholars held multiple virtual workshops for scholars at different stages of their careers.[2]

Despite its growth, a number of features of the community raise important questions about how to enrich the inquiry our field supports. Key concepts like judicial independence, rule of law, judicial quality, efficiency, fairness, etc., are contested conceptually and raise difficult challenges of measurement. Although there are multiple databases of judicial decisions for particular countries, cross-national databases of decisions are less common and far from complete. Many of our theoretical models directly imply that observed samples of judicial orders will be far from random.[3] Like the social sciences more generally, the set of methodological tools required to tackle the most interesting questions are highly varied from ethnographic techniques, historical processes of archival research, machine-learning applications to text data, as well as statistical methods for analysing quantitative data. All of this is happening in the context of the credibility revolution in the social sciences, which has focused attention on the challenges of drawing causal inferences in all types of empirical designs as well as community-based problems associated with the failure to correct for multiple comparisons and the pressures to place null results in the file drawer (e.g. Ho and Rubin 2011; Keele 2015; Nyhan 2015).

At the risk of unfairly characterizing the subfield, it is worth considering what these claims could imply. Suppose that members of our community simply disagree about definitions of our key concepts, and in so far as we agree, the concepts are unclear and possibly unmeasurable even if they were clarified. Suppose that scholars employ a limited set of research designs, failing to identify creative strategies for valid descriptive and causal inference. Suppose further that data sources are limited and that data sharing is so rare that even if a new scholar was prepared to improve on an old design, she would have to reconstruct the data collection exercise from scratch. In so far as this is true, the best-case scenario is that we are organized in a highly inefficient manner and that we lack an appropriate self-consciousness about the limitations in our approach to science. The worst-case scenario is that our theoretical arguments rest on extremely weak theoretical and empirical footing, so weak as to call into question fundamentally many of our knowledge claims. No matter where the field lies on the spectrum between the best- and worst-case scenarios, we clearly can do better.

Consider the possibility in light of the discipline's debate over the Data Access and Research Transparency (DA-RT) initiative.[4] DA-RT's primary goal was to promote greater research openness through a community-based approach to standards construction (Lupia and Elman 2014, 22). The point of greater openness was to assist in the communication of knowledge claims within and across scientific communities. The entire enterprise rested on the assumption that there were sets of research communities prepared to contribute to the conversation and ultimately shape the institutionalization of shared understandings of appropriate research standards. If the best-case scenario is correct, it will take more than simple data transparency in order to leverage the information and talent in the field. Under the worst-case scenario, we would be left questioning whether there is a viable research community in comparative law and politics with which the larger community might converse.

Of course, the subfield has produced profitable research exchanges about contested concepts (Bergman 2012; Carlin and Sarsfield 2012; Rios-Fígueroa 2012). Scholars have in fact used a variety of data-analytic techniques from comparative historical analysis to network analysis and text analysis (e.g. Alter 2009; Kapiszewski 2012; Ríos-Figueroa

2016). The chapters developed by Hirschl, Martin, Quinn, and Epstein, Livermore, and Chau, among others in this volume, offer clear illustrations of a diverse conceptual and methodological landscape. Scholars are, in fact, leveraging stronger designs for causal inference than the field commonly supported in the past (e.g. Wang 2016). There are publication outlets for findings that rely on descriptive inference alone (e.g. Linzer and Staton 2015; Basabe-Serrano 2016).

There is a viable research community in this field. I nevertheless believe that it is worth assuming for the moment that an extreme and ultimately distorted characterization of the field is true for two reasons. First, though we can find counterexamples it would still seem readily apparent that there is much room for improvement in the way that our community conducts its science. Second, even if the characterization is ultimately too extreme it helps us focus on what it means to build a more complete, stimulating, and ultimately useful scientific community. In this chapter, I assume that our community could be better and more usefully connected. I will then ask how these connections might be built via the promotion of a large-scale collaborative project aimed at the production of data resources intended to promote research coordination in the field.

2. Challenges and Opportunities in Community Building

If our goal is to build a more connected scientific community, it is important to remember what a scientific community is and what it is not. A scientific community is an interconnected group of scholars working in parallel on shared problems (Kornfeld and Hewitt 1981). This definition does not necessarily imply collaboration in every sense. Working in parallel means working separately on the same problems. It certainly does not imply that members of the community need to be in agreement about everything. A healthy scientific community, especially one that is in its relative infancy, will involve heated argumentation over substance and process, including I suspect over the very standards under which we are supposed to operate. This is especially likely in a field like ours, which is drawn from so many rich research traditions. But of course we have to collaborate. At a minimum, we have to share information with each other. We have to make it possible for others to succeed where we fail. And we cannot disagree about all aspects of our enterprise for all time. We have to be making progress towards some kind of consensus, certainly over standards but probably also over a set of knowledge claims. As we think about what might be improved it will be helpful to distinguish the features of our community that are actually problematic from those that are just the result of a growing discipline. My first goal in this chapter is to highlight the challenges we confront in building and nurturing a dynamic scientific community.

That we disagree about how to measure judicial independence or whether process tracing provides a more useful picture of causal mechanisms than a statistical analysis of observational data, a lab experiment or an analytic narrative is not necessarily problematic. We do not need a uniform group of process tracers or formal theorists or political statisticians, and I am sceptical about the prospects of constructing a field made up of scholars who are comfortable using all these approaches (see Gehlbach 2015). Our field can continue without trouble as a multi-methodological space. Our disagreements may foster inspiration and innovation. Results from different approaches may even inform each other. Of greater concern are features of our field that fundamentally undermine our ability to work in parallel on shared problems. Again we need not prioritize collaboration over all other goals but research in parallel means that we have to be able to communicate our results effectively. Ineffective communication is our primary problem. There are several aspects to the problem.

First, effective communication requires that scholars understand each other's knowledge claims or be prepared to learn how to understand them. If scholars operating via different traditions are disinterested or incapable of evaluating each other's work because of the nature of the methodological structure within which the claims are made it is here that communication challenges interact with methodological training. Our field must have a minimum set of standards for productive professional engagement. Being prepared to understand does not imply being prepared to act. It does imply having a basic familiarity with the advantages and disadvantages of particular approaches. Scholars must be familiar with some of the basic features of research across the traditions. For example, a scholar who primarily relies on statistical methods should be able to articulate the value of a hoop test in the context of a process analysis. She should have some idea of the standards for evaluating the results of this test. Similarly the scholar who traces processes must understand what it means to say that while we cannot identify unit-level causal effects, we can identify average causal effects. She should understand the basic standards used for evaluating statistical evidence. I do not mean to imply that we all have to be competent methodological reviewers of all designs, but we should attempt to build a basic competency. At a minimum, we need an open mind and a willingness to engage in a conversation meant to clarify results that rely on foreign procedures. This engagement, in addition to helping to promote multiple types of research, is a core element of a field-wise effort to actually built competency in core elements of the science used by others in the field. Becoming conversant in the basic languages of our field does require a minimal level of training. Ideally, much of this can be done at the undergraduate level and perfected at the PhD level; however, we need a field whose members are prepared for a career of learning new skills and new techniques as well as infrastructure to help make that possible.

Effective communication also depends on data openness and data sharing. Part of what allows me to understand what you have said is my ability to reproduce your claim. Part of what allows us to advance our field quickly is our commitment to making our data available as soon as possible. I am not aware of a subfield-level commitment to a particular approach to data openness and sharing. My own experiences have been quite varied. Some scholars now make their work available via a personal website immediately upon producing a result, well prior to submitting the study for peer review.

Other scholars commonly post to repositories like Dataverse, some as a condition for publishing an article and some simply because they believe it to be good practice. This approach commonly ensure that procedures are clear. Of course, this makes replication possible, but the more important point is that the practice promotes the communication of knowledge. Still other scholars provide some combination of data access upon request and replication material that is incomplete or otherwise unclear about what procedures were used. Worst of all, some members of the community still claim data embargoes, even after they have published results relying on the requested data. This is particularly vexing in contexts where the data sources are relatively easy to collect (and measure) with sufficient resources so that the only effect of the embargo is to render inefficient our field's work. Solving the data openness problem is an obvious high priority.

A third and significant communication problem involves the restricted nature of data sources. There really are tremendous gaps in the simple empirical record around which our field seems to revolve. Elkins and Ginsburg's (2012) Comparative Constitutions Project has offered an incredible resource, but so much of what matters to what we care about takes place at the level of statutory law or in the informal practices that animate constitutional politics. For example, consider questions regarding the appointment of constitutional judges. The German Basic Law tells us that eight members of the Federal Constitutional Court are appointed by the Bundestag and eight members are appointed by the Bundesrat, but that is it. Given the proportionality of the German electoral system and a political cultural commitment to grand coalitions when necessary, an understanding of the appointment politics in Germany requires a strong account of sub-constitutional information (see e.g. Collings 2015). It is not that the constitutional information will be unhelpful to all research tasks. Some tasks might only require the knowledge two legislative chambers appoint members of the constitutional court. Yet other tasks might require information about sub-constitutional norms and rules. Similarly, the Haynie et al.'s (2007) National High Courts Database and Carrubba et al.'s (n.d.) Comparative Law Project have provided information on judicial opinions on supreme and constitutional courts globally. The IUROPA Project (https://www.iuropa.pol.gu.se) provides a comprehensive database for decisions of the Court of the European Union. Unfortunately, the field is still very far from having a resource like the Spaeth Database which might provide common ground for shared research across all regions of the world. A fourth, related concern of communication, follows from our data practices. It is possible that there are too few of us working on too many problems. There are not too few scholars. There are not too many questions. We just do not have enough people working on the same problems. How many scholars really are working on the same aspect of judicialization or judicial independence, or the problem of mobilizing advocacy in the context of social and economic rights? How many scholars are working on the problem of judicial corruption or the politicization of prosecutors or the link between formal institutions, legal actors, and development? How many actual replications can we point to? Answering this question naturally leads to a focus not just on theme but on place. We are led to ask who works on which problem in which country? That only fractures our field further. At our best, we have rough groups of studies conducted in diverse research settings (i.e. states or cities or regions), which are broadly comparable, but require a large set of assumptions to really place results in context. Many of us may have become bored with research on who controls policy making in the US Congress, on the determinants of inter-state war, or on decision-making on the US Supreme Court, but those parallel research endeavours built productive communities which have evolved in new directions after the original set of questions grew stale.

A final communication challenge centres on our beliefs about what makes for good scholarship. It is best revealed by considering how we think about (if we do at all) the relationship between mere description, descriptive inference, theory, and causal inference. Political science seems ever more focused on producing designs for causal inference. Indeed, the old quantitative-qualitative cleavage is profitably bridged through a shared interest in identifying the precise way through which concept A causes concept B, if at all. This attention to causation and stronger designs for causal inference should be welcomed, but it seems to have been accompanied by a deemphasis on research that is purely descriptive or purely theoretical. A healthy scientific community should embrace both designs for causal inference as well as descriptive inference. There ought to be a space for mere description as well (Gerring 2012). In light of the fact that we are extremely far from a situation in which the world's legal systems have been mapped, much less deeply described, we really do require simple descriptive information. Without good description it is hard to imagine how we are going meaningfully to advance theory or even identify good opportunity for strong causal designs. Identifying this challenge is fine, but disciplinary challenges make solving it challenging. Can you publish a purely descriptive paper in the *American Political Science Review*? The *American Journal of Political Science*? How about *World Politics*, *International Organization*, or the *Journal of Politics*? It would be one thing if the editors of these journals took a position against the publication of descriptive work but my sense is that collectively we are part of the problem. I suspect that as reviewers we reserve the top journals for causal claims. The argument for this, I suppose, is that they are general journals, and so a person in field X will only care about a causal claim in field Y whereas a person in field Y would be interested in both causation and description. I am frankly sceptical of whether this is a sensible position to take, but whether it is defensible or not it seems consistent with reserving the general journals for ideas that are of general interest. In any event, we can promote studies that are primarily descriptive at general journals via our role as reviewers. What is more, we can and certainly should do this in our field journals, most obviously in the *Journal of Law and Courts*. We might even propose a new journal (e.g. the *Journal of Comparative Judicial Behaviour*) in which we are willing to publish a wider variety of studies.

What I have discussed so far are challenges that any field confronts. Our field couples these challenges with the routine concerns that emerge from interdisciplinary work. The field of comparative law and politics spans multiple disciplines. Within disciplines it spans subfields. The nature of the subject leads naturally to these facts. Consider one example from substantive focus from the field: the protection of individual rights in Latin American political systems. To study this problem is to study overlapping domestic and international legal obligations, interpreted by judges at both the domestic and international levels, and promoted by international advocacy networks (e.g. Sikkink 2005; Brewer-Carías 2009; Huneeus 2011; Binder 2012; Dulitzky 2015). Even constraining oneself to political science, this implies that a scholar working in this area will be working simultaneously in comparative politics and international relations, speaking to scholars of judicial politics and to scholars of social movements, to scholars of legislatures, and to scholars of the bureaucracy. Of course, the subject matter also implies that you are communicating with scholars of comparative law, international law, as well as legal history and sociology, among others.

Two further implications follow, both of which have significant implications for how our field ought to develop. The subject matter is likely to be too diverse for any one scholar to be an expert in all aspects of the processes under analysis. In addition, although it will be possible to be conversant in the methods developed and deepened by particular fields (in part because many fields share methodological emphases) it is likely to be impossible to be an expert in all of the methods that might prove useful in answering shared research questions.

2.1 What Should We Do About It?

There are a number of potential solutions to these challenges. Unfortunately, some will follow from disciplinary coordination. Most obviously, the DA-RT initiative itself as well as Joint Editors Transparency Statement (JETS) (http://www.dartstatement.org/#!blank/c22sl) will affect some aspects of the data sharing problem, especially the issue of unreasonable embargoes. They will do it by requiring increasing levels of data openness in exchange for the ability to publish in peer-reviewed outlets. Other solutions depend on departmental coordination across all of the discipline. PhD-granting departments provide the training of future scholars, at the graduate and undergraduate levels. The varied approaches our departments take will be the primary determinant of their ability to effectively communicate results across research traditions. Members of our community will be part of these developments, but we will just be one voice among many. The point is that these are problems that we can influence at best; we cannot solve them without help.

There are some steps that can be taken as a subfield. There are some problems that can be addressed immediately. Small conferences are designed to promote debate and encourage the identification of and shared solutions to our common problems. They almost always accomplish the former task. But we need concrete solutions. Rather than working in the abstract, I want to suggest a project-based approach to building a more robust subfield. We need to encourage the construction of research teams. A team-based approach follows immediately if we recognize that no single scholar can be an expert in all, or even most, of the areas of research that will be useful to answering our questions. This is true on both substantive and methodological grounds. We ought not to try to construct new scholars who are such experts but we should also avoid splintering into ever more specialized research silos. We ought to be training scholars who are experts in particular areas of research but nevertheless ready to work in teams.

What kind of team might we attempt to build? There are many options. Here I develop how we (perhaps different groups of 'we') might build a team centred around a collaborative effort to build data infrastructure for the field. The field does not lack core infrastructure for storing and sharing data. There are multiple repositories for the safe and efficient storage of all types of data, such as Dataverse or The Qualitative Data Repository. What we lack are shared resources that help the field coordinate research around shared questions. A single location for the investigation of peak court opinions (or perhaps key elements of jurisprudence) over a long time series and for a large set of countries is an obvious candidate. But every state's judicial system is hierarchical, so the target of measurement need not be restricted to peak courts, assuming there was a viable set of research interests. We need not focus on judicial opinions at all. Another possible candidate would be information on the legal support community across the globe. At a very broad level, we might imagine a general project aimed at producing data infrastructure for a robust research programme on law and politics. At a slightly more specific level, we might build infrastructure around the issue of constitutionalism, a concept that would link the subfield to other vibrant research communities in the social sciences. Such a project might focus on a variety of data sources, which would be useful to a large set of researchers inside and outside our field. Likely, any project of significant breadth will be too complicated and resource-consuming for any one small group of scholars to tackle alone. Even if we can automate some of the data collection tasks through web scraping, named entity recognition, topics models, and classification techniques, there will be a massive role for human expertise on a global scale.

Building a large team of scholars from diverse research traditions may seem an unconventional way to tackle this problem. What I wish to argue is that by attacking the problem in a large, diverse team, we will also be helping resolve the communication problems I described above. Scholars from different traditions will be forced to articulate shared data needs but will be encouraged to think about designs that suit their own preferences and skills. They will be encouraged to try to answer similar questions with different approaches, sometimes using identical data sources and sometimes not. Doing this well will require the resolution of several challenges, some obvious and some subtle.

In what follows, I discuss some of the experiences of the Varieties of Democracy Project (V-Dem) (https://v-dem.net/), a project that reflects something like what I have in mind, albeit one in a distinct research context. I discuss features of the V-Dem organizational project that have helped overcome the core challenges it confronted. I also consider the ways in which these features might have undermined some potential project goals. Building a research community ultimately involves making trade-offs and V-Dem certainly has privileged some kinds of work over others.

3. Building a Collaborative Project

Detailed information about the Varieties of Democracy Project, including a summary of project goals, organizational structure, freely available data and research papers, can be found at https://www.v-dem.net. V-Dem's primary goal was to produce multiple measures of democracy drawing on several conceptual definitions. The measurement of democracy cross-nationally had been limited to a relatively small set of concepts, mostly focusing on the provision of free and fair elections and the extent to which there were effective mechanisms of constraining the state. Yet democratic theorists had developed concepts of democracy emphasizing a wider set of ideas including popular participation, high-quality deliberation, and socio-economic equality (Munck 2009; Coppedge et al. 2011; Coppedge et al. 2015). V-Dem set about making it possible to study democracy empirically from these more diverse perspectives. V-Dem has produced hundreds of indicators of democratic features of countries (and some colonies) from 1900 to the present. A related piece of the project has provided similar measures dating back to 1789.

Although the provision of new data on democracy drove much of the discussion on the V-Dem team, the ultimate goal of the project was to help encourage the development of international teams of researchers on subjects related to regimes. To date, the project has produced well over 200 articles and working papers (https://www.v-dem.net/publications/), as well as several books (Altman 2019; Coppedge et al. 2020; Staton et al. 2022) on topics as diverse as vote buying, colonial networks, the role of civil society and parties in democratic stability, gender balance on high courts, non-compliance with judicial orders and regime survival, corruption, human development, parties and economic growth, direct democracy, and the sequencing of rights and democratization, among many others. Research partnerships have developed between methodologically oriented scholars and scholars with a passion for historical comparisons, between scholars who are at home with cross-national research and scholars who typically work on particular cases. Through its international network, V-Dem has also supported the development of regional centres of scholarship, the first of which is in Estonia and directed by Vello Pettai. It has conducted capacity-building seminars in many parts of the world, designed to help activists and policy-makers best ascertain and verify the data. It conducts yearly conferences, sponsors panels at academic conferences and encourages scholarship from within and without the V-Dem team. Finally, V-Dem has been responsible for thematic and country reports designed for use by government agencies, international organizations (IOs) and non-governmental organizations (NGOs) in international conversations about democracy.

3.1 Challenges of Collaboration

The question V-Dem leadership confronted was how to produce information on this scale given their own expertise. At the start, the principal investigators (PIs) were Michael Coppedge of the University of Notre Dame, Staffan Lindberg of the University of Gothenburg, John Gerring of Boston University, and Svend-Erik Skaaning of Aarhus University.[5] The PIs judged that it was not possible to achieve their goals alone, even though collectively they possessed deep and general knowledge about politics globally. Getting the project done would require the participation of many scholars with diverse interests and at diverse stages of their careers.

The PIs dramatically increased their capacity by building an international, interdisciplinary team of connected researchers. The first step was to divide the concept of democracy into thematic categories led by scholars associated with work in that area. V-Dem's work is divided into thirteen thematic areas, each of which is directed by an academic project manager. The areas include Executives, Legislatures, Judiciaries, Parties and Party Systems, Media, Civil Society, Civil Liberties, Sovereignty, Subnational Government, Direct Democracy, Democratization, Evolutionary Theory, and Methodology.[6] V-Dem is also divided regionally and by country. Helping manage the workflow are six staff members, two full time post-doctoral fellows, thirty-two regional coordinators, and nearly 200 country coordinators (https://www.v-dem.net).

The size of the team raised a number of challenges, which manifested in a number of ways. The overarching problem was how to align individual interests with group goals. This problem affected the group's ability to obtain the financial investment necessary to get the project off the ground, as well as its ability to execute.

The first challenge in aligning interests was *substantive*. Although PIs Coppedge, Gerring, and Lindberg had long-run interests in working on questions of democracy and democratization, their commitment to build data infrastructure from a disaggregated perspective meant that they would have to work with scholars whose substantive expertise pushed them in research areas not necessarily tied to democracy research per se, much less to a project of massive historical and global scope. For scholars of this volume, this would be like asking a scholar working on problems of judicial citation networks to contribute to a project designed to measures of legal systems. There are surely connections but if the literature to which we contribute has not already constructed natural ways of articulating the importance of comparing citation patterns across legal traditions, it may prove difficult to guild the collaboration.

Related to this issue, the V-Dem project itself became interested in measuring high-level concepts of democracy. V-Dem currently offers indices of electoral democracy, liberal democracy, participatory democracy, deliberative democracy, and egalitarian democracy. In addition, it offers some thirty 'mid-level' indices including *inter alia* freedom of association, alternative sources of information, suffrage, civil society participation, women's civil liberties, and political corruption. Importantly, many of the individual V-Dem contributors had no interest in measurement at these levels. Indeed, many were drawn to the project initially precisely because of its disaggregated approach. Yet their expertise would be useful to the development of sensible strategies for creating indices.[7] Part of the changed interest in measuring higher-level concepts was driven by funding imperatives and the interests of the advocacy community; however, part of it derived from the PI's sincere interests in developing multiple alternatives to Polity IV or Freedom House and many other regime indicators. The bottom line is that very quickly there emerged a tension between the interests of the project's leaders and many of its contributors.

The second set of challenges were *conceptual and theoretical*. Project members were bound to differ about the meaning of particular concepts. What does it mean for a legislature to be powerful, for an election to be clean, or for a judge to be autonomous? Should a deliberative concept of democracy be developed without regard to the electoral dimension? How should the project approach the aggregation challenges that every project faces when measuring democracy? Further, there were disagreements about whether it was possible to pursue a sensible measurement strategy absent the specification of particular theoretical models. To take an example from our field, whether a constitutional court decision striking down an act of parliament can be treated as a manifestation of judicial autonomy really does require a theoretical model of the process linking judges and politicians in the policy-making process (compare the logic in Ríos-Figueroa (2007) and Rodríguez-Raga (2011) to that in Whittington (2005)). Recognizing this issue invited conversations about theoretical models and the process of modelling itself. To say the least, the project made precisely no progress toward anything that could be called a project-level model of political processes, that is, a model that would guide all of the work of members of the team.

My own experience illustrates some of the tensions that can emerge in a project like this. In 2009 I began work on a series of empirical studies of compliance with judicial orders, a project that would require considerable time in the field and attention to the very particular in very particular states (in many cases municipalities). The V-Dem Project's focus on the state-year, on many states and many years was in tension with my other goal and my other commitments. Similarly, key members of the V-Dem team turn commonly to sociological and psychological mechanisms whereas I am an institutionally oriented scholar guided in many cases by rationalist models which I often formalize. So, finding natural research partnerships was challenging, if only because the way that we approach problems was just a bit different. I was ultimately attracted by the possibility of measuring features of judicial politics, which I believed might reveal unique information, for example measures of court purging and packing, attacks on key institutions, verbal attacks, and compliance with decisions at multiple levels of the judiciary. But I was not particularly interested in helping to conceptualize and measure 'participatory' or 'deliberative democracy', in addition to many of the other targets of the project. What I hoped to be, at a minimum, was a source of intellectual support to scholars working on related but distinct problems, doing so the way that scholars typically do: by sharing thoughts on working papers.

The third set of challenges were *organizational*. From the beginning, V-Dem's primary organizational structure was, unsurprisingly, democratic! PIs attempted to promote deliberation among project managers on nearly every major issue related to the project. This included, among many others, the conceptualization of democracy, the precise items that would make it onto the expert survey, the requirements of a database management system, the right assumptions to make about the prior distribution for the latent variable in the measurement model and the right way to keep track of the scholarship that team members were producing. The initial commitment to democratic deliberation interacted powerfully with the conceptual and theoretical challenges. In many ways, while helpful for building a shared set of purposes also risked tearing the project apart for a lack of consensus.

In addition to this fundamental set of problems, it was clear that a project of V-Dem's size was going to require significant resources and time developed to organization and management. That meant that some member or members of the team was going to give up time publishing, at least for a time. This was a significant question for the PIs but it has affected project managers as well. Michael Coppedge and Staffan Lindberg in particular made tremendous sacrifices to ensure that the project moved to completion. How would team members be rewarded for providing this kind of infrastructure? In many ways, V-Dem project members took a risk that their time invested would pay off in the end. At this point, every member of the original team has produced work of which they are proud and placed that work in high-quality outlets. Still, it is important to recognize that in some cases the ideal substantive expert for the team was an untenured professor, a post-doctoral fellow, or a graduate student. In addition to the challenges of incentivizing such a scholar to participate, the project itself confronted an important ethical question about whether it was appropriate to try to include a scholar at stage of their career.

The fourth challenge concerned *funding* and the relationship between funding sources and project goals. To date, the project has spent millions of dollars in pursuit of its goals. Given the scale of the project, the appropriate programs of the National Science Foundation were not appropriate funders.Initial funding for the project came from the Kellogg Institute at Notre Dame University and the University of Gothenburg. Ultimately the project has been funded by the Riksbankkens Jubileumsfond; the Swedish and Danish Ministries of Foreign Affairs; the European Commission; Vetenskapsradet; the Portuguese Ministry of Science, Technology and Higher Education; the US National Science Foundation; and International IDEA, among others. Steffan Lindberg is to be greatly credited from the incredible success in organizing these efforts. But it is worth noting that as the number and diversity of funders increased, so too did the pressure to produce higher level democracy indices, putting the work in tension with the project's original goal of providing disaggregated indicators.

A fifth set of challenges derived from key *disciplinary incentives* that undermine infrastructure development. Despite a short period in the latter half of the 2000s, political science, in the United States at least, has been far more concerned with issues of causal inference than with measurement. Understanding that this would be an issue,

V-Dem recruited Adam Glynn, a political statistician with particular expertise in causal inference in observational studies. Glynn and Blackwell produced an important paper on making causal inferences in time series, cross-sectional data (Blackwell and Glynn 2018). Yet, even with members of the team working on this issue, the basic fact is that the primary V-Dem deliverables are a series of cross-sectional, time series datasets. Although there were opportunities to do other kinds of research in the project, much of the work was influenced by this basic data structure.

3.2 Addressing These Challenges

V-Dem made several adjustments to its structure and plans in response, if not necessarily in anticipation, of these challenges. V-Dem centralized some aspects of its approach while simultaneously decentralizing other aspects.

First, PIs centralized broad authority for the project. PIs simply took charge of core decision-making, including most critically the construction of high- and mid-level democracy indices. Since they are a group as well, fundamental problems of collective decision making still complicated their work; however, they greatly simplified the challenges they were confronting in seeking conceptual consensus from nearly twenty academics. Instead of playing active roles in important project choices, project managers were asked to take on advisory roles. Given the cooperative nature of the project, when a project manager holds particularly strong views on an issue in her project, her view is commonly adopted. Yet the project manager is not asked to join in every important project discussion. Rather she is pulled in for advice when appropriate.

At the same time, the PIs delegated considerable policy-making power to project managers in individual projects. Since project managers were better situated to understand what might be a useful contribution to their own fields and would ultimately be able to use the data collected to advance long-run intellectual interests, each member faced strong incentives to work on pieces of the project that might not have been attractive in a centralized system.

In my case, at the beginning of the project, I was most interested tracing institutional variation in appointment and removal institutions for constitutional judges. I was authorized to use V-Dem resources to pursue this goal, an effort that resulted in a study of institutional causes of the appointment of the first female justice to a peak court Arrington et al. (2021). Still, I was strongly encouraged to think about whether the expert survey might offer the subfield important, new sources of information. I sought advice from members of the field and returned to suggest that we attempt to measure court curbing activities of various sorts as well as questions of compliance. All that was required to be included was a strong argument for why these various features were related to some concept of democracy. Doing this was not a problem, with respect to nearly all of the concepts. This delegation was particularly important in the field of methodology. In short, members of the group working on methodology were encouraged to work with all V-Dem members in order to build appropriate solutions to critical measurement issues.

The PIs also centralized the effort to build collaborative research projects but did so in a way that allowed for diverse relationships to bloom. To ensure credit as best as possible for the considerable work put into infrastructural development and to ensure that Michael Coppedge and Staffan Lindberg were especially recognized for their considerable effort, V-Dem developed a project-level author agreement. All project managers and PIs would be authors on key, general articles introducing the project as well as the project's codebook and datasets. V-Dem data were embargoed for one year prior to the completion of the first dataset. This permitted some empirical papers to be started prior to the public release of the data. Team members were required to invite project managers to co-author papers should data from their project be used in the study, but project managers need not accept the invitation. The result of this rule was largely to encourage but not force co-authoring partnerships (see https://v-dem.net).

To promote synergies and improve communication across the project, V-Dem also hosted an annual conference in Gothenburg. At the beginning, the conference was designed to evaluate the validity and reliability of measures being developed; to discuss conceptual, theoretical, and methodological concerns; and to seek coordination on research studies. Over time, the project began to invite scholars from outside the project to comment on early drafts of papers or research designs. A key element of the strategy was to host break-out, brain-storming sessions for project and non-project members alike. This format has been particularly useful in helping to link substantive to methodologically oriented scholars for the purpose of solving technical problems in a substantively important setting (see Arrington et al. 2015 and Lindenfors et al. (2015). It has also promoted collaborations among scholars with diverse substantive interests (see e.eg. Sundstrom et al. 2015).

4. Infrastructure Development in Comparative Law and Politics

Above I have suggested that the field of comparative law and politics might develop a collaborative project aimed at building core infrastructure in our field. I have something like the V-Dem project in mind, though I do not believe that its precise structure, goals, or time frame are essential to duplicate in our context. The scope and scale of V-Dem may be too large. We need not attempt to measure key concepts at the country-year level or attempt to take our work back into the nineteenth century, at least not for all places. Having said that, it seems fairly obvious that the field is in need of significant infrastructural investments, which seem unlikely to be provided by any one research group.

How might we proceed? There are two related approaches, one that starts from the ground and seeks the organic identification of a shared project. The second would start with a precise project. Under the first approach, we should immediately seek to coordinate among programmes with strong law and courts faculties. The aim is to create a series of conferences that promote four types of activities. The rationale for this approach is that we might find an agreement on a shared project if we pursue it organically, in the context of our regular production of research. I imagine conferences that are restricted to perhaps two days. The activities include the following.

4.1 Design-Based Activities

Our typical conference opportunities involve the presentation of completed research projects. We should provide space for scholars to pitch and develop research designs or theoretical models. A fully developed community would not need such an event but if our field is still far from fully formed then devoting time to collective discussion of research ideas will promote the construction of shared standards. It will also help us to identify opportunities for building infrastructure. Critically, workshop activity should be focused on design or early theoretical work. We should not be reading half-baked descriptions of studies that have been conducted, something we often do at regional conferences like the Midwest Political Science Association or Southern Political Science Association. Instead, we should devote at least some time to evaluating high quality research designs or simply to theoretical accounts.

4.2 Exemplars

We should have space for the presentation of completed studies. I suggest that we prioritize published papers. Scholars in our field are almost never in a position to present the best, most complete version of their papers, as workshop norms push us toward presenting works in progress.[8] Published papers are 'presented' in seminars and reading groups in graduate programmes around the world, but unless an author happens to be visiting, they are not present to clarify their work. Exemplar presentations mean that authors are available to speak about the various choices they made or how they were inspired to conduct the study.[9] Ultimately, exemplar presentations will serve to expose participants to new and exciting studies, which serve to benchmark top research in the field.

4.3 Skill Building

If we are going to ask our community to improve the quality of their analytical skills we should provide training. Within the context of a two-day conference, we could feature one or two sessions simply designed to introduce and demonstrate the effectiveness of a new skill. This approach can be paired with a commitment to offer skills sessions on the days immediately preceding the American Political Science Association (APSA) meetings.

4.4 Project Discussion/Brainstorming

We should set aside time for scholars simply to discuss potential projects and opportunities for collaboration. I am suggesting institutionalizing the brainstorming that we typically do at conferences, but linking it to the other three activities our conferences support.

The costs of this kind of approach should not be significant. I would anticipate asking scholars to pay for their own travel, and ask that the host institution provides space and perhaps a meal.

We can seek funding from obvious sources, but I do not wish to wait on this. We should just move forward with what we can actually do.

A second approach is to attempt to identify a shared project from the start. There are many general themes around which an infrastructure project could begin to be developed. I am not wedded to one in particular, but for the sake of starting the conversation, let me propose a focus on constitutionalism. A theme of this scope, like 'democracy', focuses the effort on some obvious and familiar ideas while still inviting considerable innovation with respect to particular lines of thought as well as conceptualization that might even allow for a considerable broadening of the theme. For example, in so far as constitutions establish general structures for governance, a scholar who can articulate a reason to focus on aspects of the law that are not, strictly speaking, part of constitutional law could persuasively add to the project.

Like V-Dem's expert survey on features of democracy, I would propose framing the project around a core piece of infrastructure. Having been involved in a pilot study designed to learn about the potential for building a global database for opinions of constitutional courts or supreme courts with constitutional jurisdiction (for a summary of CompLaw see Carrubba et al. n.d.), I am drawn to building infrastructure around high court opinions in their constitutional jurisdiction. This is naturally connected to the work of Engst and Gschwend in this volume.

Many questions would still need to be answered about precisely what to compile. Critically, data collection need not end at features of the opinions, judges, parties, and laws involved in the decisions. Instead, this type of database might serve to frame a larger effort, where the ultimate goal would be to build capacity in multiple areas of interest. Quite obviously, the exact nature of the project would depend on those involved. It seems to me that such a project could support multiple thematic sub-projects. For example, one might envision projects on Opinion Quality; Citation Practices; Judicial Policy Implementation, or a broader project on impact; Litigants and the litigation process; International Law; Networks; Law and Social Media; Political Conflict; Economic Development; and, more generally, Methodology. Methodologically, it seems clear that we would want to include a scholar specializing in textual analysis, probably multiple scholars given the variety of potential topics of text research.

The constitutionalism frame would naturally link together many existing efforts to build infrastructure in comparative law and politics, including the Comparative Constitutions Project (http://comparativeconstitutionsproject.org/); CompLaw (http://complaw.wustl.edu/); the National High Courts Database (http://artsandsciences.sc.edu/poli/juri/highcts.htm); iCourts (http://jura.ku.dk/icourts/); the World Justice Project (https://worldjusticeproject.org); the European Consortium of Political Research section Law, Courts, and Judicial Politics; V-Dem; and potentially many others.

Linking such a large number of projects together is a useful place to begin because it affords an opportunity to take an inventory of what exactly we have and what we might need in particular contexts. More simply, it draw on existing interest.

5. Conclusion: Coordination and Collaboration in Shared Projects

Above I have reviewed several challenges that must be met to succeed in producing a collaborative project. The fundamental problem is really quite familiar: how can you organize the project's practices and aims such that individuals are incentivized to contribute to the project's overall deliverables, which we might naturally conceptualize as a public good. Solving this problem requires promoting coordination and generating incentives for group members to contribute at what is sometimes a quite high cost. At the very least, social scientists are familiar with challenges of public goods provision. This is, in the end, what the task is all about.

V-Dem's leaders addressed their problem in several ways, which might prove useful now to frame in more familiar terms. Many of the project's structures were designed to create focal solutions for deep coordination problems. The annual conference in a single location (Gothenburg), paired with a yearly gathering at the APSA were obvious attempts to create focal locations for collaboration. The author agreement can be considered in precisely the same way—it clarified in a fairly simple way a natural way to coordinate around potentially shared research interests. The PIs decision simply to centralize authority over many broad aspects of the project solved several coordination problems by effectively eliminating the need to coordinate.

Just as the meetings and the author agreements served to coordinate members they also addressed the issue of free-riding. The author agreement offered benefits to project team members, which could only be enjoyed by participation in the project. The agreement dramatically expanded the number of publications that a scholar could produce in a fixed time frame. Coupled with the meeting structure, it made it possible to work more efficiently and on a wider set of problem than it would have been without the agreement. The annual conferences themselves offered project members precious time to think away and brainstorm, away from one's day to day service and teaching obligations.

A final aspect of the V-Dem structure was its leaders' ability to create a real sense of a research community among very diverse scholars. By telling stories about why it was important, by reminding each other about the interesting and valuable work of every team member, and by linking what we were doing to a global effort to promote democracy, the team build camaraderie. The feeling that you are part of something really does go a long way to connecting you to group members and to offsetting the costs of contribution.

The key lesson of V-Dem lies in the way that it organized itself to produce a public good. In thinking about a new research collaboration, we ought to be guided by that key idea. As between the group-up and the top-down approach, my inclination is to draw on both approaches. We ought to begin with quite particular conceptual and theoretical goals. This will take off the table many of the most contested problems that undermine coordination. I doubt that this will be feasible if we are committed to starting with a large and diverse group of partners for exactly the same reason that this was impossible for V-Dem. This project made the most progress when it reduced the number of top-level decision-makers to a few. At the same time, if the project needs to draw on multiple perspectives, it will need activities that benefit diverse scholars in small and sometimes surprising ways. Thus, the conferencing and skill-building structures are essential as they will jointly promote focal solutions to our varied coordination problems and promote contributions to the public good by offering collaborate activities that difficult to creat acting alone.

Notes

1. The first issue of the *Journal of Law and Courts* featured papers on law and economic development, the judicialization of international legal regimes and the cross-national measurement of the rule of law (Hadfield and Weingast 2013; Nardulli et al. 2013; Sweet and Brunell 2013). Together these papers reflected one-half of the content. Since then the journal has continued to actively support comparative and international research.
2. For two notable examples, see International and Comparative Law and Courts Collaborative and the Junior Law and Politics Research Community.
3. Fox and Stephenson (2011).
4. Information about DA-RT can be found at http://www.dartstatement.org/.
5. Jan Teorell of Lund University, an original principal investigator is now responsible for V-Dem's historical arm, taking democracy measurement back to the nineteenth century.
6. The project managers include Kelly McMann (Subnational Government), Pamela Paxton (Formal and Descriptive Representation), David Altman (Direct Democracy), Michael Bernhard (Civil Society and Sovereignty), Steve Fish (Legislatures), Allen Hicken (Parties and Party Systems), Carl Henrik Knutsen (Historical Data), Patrik Lindenfors (Evolutionary Theory), Jan Teorell (Executives), and Jeffrey Staton (Judiciaries). Megan Reif has also worked as a project manager on electoral violence and fraud. The Methodology

project has three managers. Adam Glynn focuses on questions of causal inference. Dan Pemstein is chiefly responsible for measurement theory. Brigitte Zimmerman manages experimental components.

7. For example, the PIs' interest in measuring 'constraints on the executive' suggested the involvement of scholars working on the judicial, legislative, civil society projects and media projects.
8. To be fair, by the time a paper is published, authors are typically exhausted by the study, having moved on to other things. Events would not feature many of these talks—they would serve in lieu of keynote speeches, and the benefit to the author will come from the collective celebration and focus on their work.
9. Of course there is room for critical review even though the paper cannot be edited for publication further. This is true in precisely the same way that we critique work in seminar.

References

Alter, Karen J. 2009. *The European Court's Political Power: Selected Essays*. New York: Oxford University Press.

Altman, David. 2019. *Citizenship and Contemporary Direct Democracy*. Cambridge: Cambridge University Press.

Arrington, Nancy, Leeann Bass, Adam Glynn, Jeffrey K. Staton, Brian Delgado, and Staffan Lindberg. 2015. 'Gender Diversity on High Courts'. Paper presented at the American Political Science Association Meetings.

Arrington, Nancy, Leeann Bass, Adam Glynn, Jeffrey K Staton, Brian Delgado, and Staffan I. Lindberg. 2021. 'Constitutional Reform and the Gender Diversification of Peak Courts'. *American Political Science Review* 115 (3): 851–68.

Basabe-Serrano, Santiago. 2016. 'The Quality Of Judicial Decisions In Supreme Courts: A Conceptual Definition And Index Applied To Eleven Latin American Countries'. *Justice System Journal* 37 (4): 331–47.

Bergman, Marcelo. 2012. 'The Rule, the Law, and the Rule of Law: Improving Measurement and Content Validity'. *Justice System Journal* 33 (2):174–93.

Binder, Christina. 2012. 'The prohibition of amnesties by the Inter-American Court of Human Rights'. *International Judicial Lawmaking* 12 (5): 295–328.

Blackwell, Matthew, and Adam N Glynn. 2018. 'How to Make Causal Inferences with Timeseries Cross-Sectional Data under Selection on Observables'. *American Political Science Review* 112 (4): 1067–82.

Brewer-Carías, Allan. 2009. *Constitutional Protection of Human Rights in Latin America: A Comparative Study of Amparo Proceedings*. Cambridge: Cambridge University Press.

Carlin, Ryan E., and Rodolfo Sarsfield. 2012. 'Rethinking the Rule of Law: Concepts, Measures, and Theory'. *Justice System Journal* 33 (2): 125–30.

Carrubba, Clifford J., Matthew Gabel, Gretchen Helmke, Andrew D. Martin, and Jeffrey K. Staton. n.d. 'CompLaw: A Coding Protocol and Database for the Comparative Study of Judicial Review'. Working Paper.'.

Collings, Justin. 2015. *Democracy's Guardians: A History of the German Federal Constitutional Court, 1951–2001*. Oxford: Oxford University Press.

Coppedge, Michael, John Gerring, David Altman, Michael Bernhard, Steven Fish, Allen Hicken, Matthew Kroenig, Staffan I. Lindberg, Kelly McMann, Pamela Paxton, et al. 2011.

'Conceptualizing and Measuring Democracy: A New Approach'. *Perspectives on Politics* 9 (02): 247–67.

Coppedge, Michael, John Gerring, Adam Glynn, Carl Henrik Knutsen, Staffan I. Lindberg, Daniel Pemstein, Brigitte Seim, Svend-Erik Skaaning, Jan Teorell, David Altman, et al. 2020. *Varieties of Democracy: Measuring Two Centuries of Political Change*. Cambridge: Cambridge University Press.

Coppedge, Michael, Staffan Lindberg, Svend-Erik Skaaning, and Jan Teorell. 2015. 'Measuring High Level Democratic Principles Using the V-Dem Data'. *International Political Science Review* 50: 45.

Dulitzky, Ariel E. 2015. 'An Inter-American Constitutional Court—The Invention of the Conventionality Control by the Inter-American Court of Human Rights'. *Texas International Law Journal* 50: 45.

Elkins, Zachary, and Tom Ginsburg. 2012. 'Comparative Constitutions Project'. http://www.comparativeconstitutionsproject.org.

Fox, Justin, and Matthew C. Stephenson. 2011. 'Judicial Review as a Response to Political Posturing.' *American Political Science Review* 105 (2): 397–414.

Gehlbach, Scott. 2015. 'The Fallacy of Multiple Methods.' *Comparative Politics Newsletter*, Fall 2015. https://www.comparativepoliticsnewsletter.org/wp-content/uploads/2021/04/2015_fall.pdf

Gerring, John. 2012. 'Mere Description'. *British Journal of Political Science* 42 (4): 721–46.

Hadfield, Gillian K., and Barry R. Weingast. 2013. 'Law Without the State: Legal Attributes and the Coordination of Decentralized Collective Punishment'. *Journal of Law and Courts* 1 (1): 3–34.

Haynie, Stacia L., Reginald S. Sheehan, Donald R. Songer, and C. Neal Tate. 2007. *National High Courts Database*. http://artsandsciences.sc.edu/poli/juri/highcts.htm.

Ho, Daniel E., and Donald B. Rubin. 2011. 'Credible Causal Inference for Empirical Legal Studies'. *Annual Review of Law and Social Science* 7: 17–40.

Huneeus, Alexandra. 2011. 'Courts Resisting Courts: Lessons from the Inter-American Court's Struggle to Enforce Human Rights'. *Cornell International Law Journal* 44: 493.

Kapiszewski, Diana. 2012. *High Courts and Economic Governance in Argentina and Brazil*. Cambridge: Cambridge University Press.

Keele, Luke. 2015. 'The Statistics of Causal Inference: A View from Political Methodology'. *Political Analysis* 23 (3): 313–35.

Kornfeld, William A., and Carl E. Hewitt. 1981. 'The Scientific Community Metaphor'. *IEEE Transactions on Systems, Man and Cybernetics* 11 (1): 24–33.

Lindenfors, Patrik, Fredirk Jansson, Yi tin Wang, and Staffan I. Lindberg. 2015. 'Investigating Sequences in Ordinal Data: A New Approach with Adapted Evolutionary Models'. V-Dem Working Paper 2015.18. https://www.v-dem.net/wp.html

Linzer, Drew A., and Jeffrey K. Staton. 2015. 'A Global Measure of Judicial Independence, 1948–2012'. *Journal of Law and Courts* 3 (2): 223–56.

Lupia, Arthur, and Colin Elman. 2014. 'Openness in Political Science: Data Access and Research Transparency'. *PS: Political Science & Politics* 47 (01): 19–42.

Munck, Gerardo L. 2009. *Measuring Democracy: A Bridge Between Scholarship and Politics*. Baltimore: Johns Hopkins University Press.

Nardulli, Peter F., Buddy Peyton, and Joseph Bajjalieh. 2013. 'Conceptualizing and Measuring Rule of Law Constructs, 1850–2010'. *Journal of Law and Courts* 1 (1): 139–92.

Nyhan, Brendan. 2015. 'Increasing the Credibility of Political Science Research: A Proposal F= for Journal Reforms'. *PS: Political Science & Politics* 48 (S1): 78–83.

Ríos-Figueroa, J. 2007. 'Fragmentation of Power and the Emergence of an Effective Judiciary in Mexico, 1994–2002'. *Latin American Politics & Society* 49: 31–57.

Rios-Fígueroa, Julio. 2012. 'Justice System Institutions and Corruption Control: Evidence from Latin America'. *Justice System Journal* 33 (2): 195–214.

Ríos-Figueroa, Julio. 2016. *Constitutional Courts as Mediators: Armed Conflict, Civil-military Relations, and the Rule of Law in Latin America*. Cambridge: Cambridge University Press.

Rodríguez-Raga, Juan Carlos. 2011. 'Strategic Deference in the Colombian Constitutional Court'. In *Courts in Latin America*, edited by Gretchen Helmke and Julio Ríos Figueroa, 81–98. Cambridge: Cambridge University Press.

Sikkink, Kathryn. 2005. 'The Transnational Dimension of the Judicialization f Politics in Latin America'. In *The Judicialization of Politics in Latin America*, edited by Rachel Sieder, Line Schjolden, and Alan Angela, 263–92. New York: Springer.

Staton, Jeffrey K., Christopher Reenock, and Jordan Holsinger. 2022. *Can Courts be Bulwarks of Democracy? Judges and the Politics of Prudence*. Cambridge: Cambridge University Press.

Sundstrom, Aksel, Yi-ting Wang, Pamel Paxton, and Staffan I. Lindberg. 2015. 'Women's Political Empowerment: A New Global Index, 1900–2012'. V-Dem Working Paper 2015.19. https://www.v-dem.net/wp.html

Sweet, Alec Stone, and Thomas L. Brunell. 2013. 'Trustee Courts and the Judicialization of International Regimes: The Politics of Majoritarian Activism in the European Convention on Human Rights, the European Union, and the World Trade Organization'. *Journal of Law and Courts* 1 (1): 61–88.

Wang, Yuhua. 2016. 'Relative Capture in the Judiciary: Evidence from Corporate Lawsuits in China'. Working Paper, Harvard University.

Whittington, Keith E. 2005. 'Interpose Your Friendly Hand: Political Supports for the Exercise of Judicial Review by the United States Supreme Court'. *American Political Science Review* 99 (4): 583–96.

CHAPTER 42

ARTIFICIAL INTELLIGENCE AND JUDGING

ANTHONY NIBLETT

1. Introduction

Artificial intelligence (AI) is a hot topic. Stories in the popular media marvel at the ability of AI tools to perform tasks that were thought to be the exclusive domain of humans. AI has the capacity to revolutionize and disrupt professions. Could AI revolutionize and disrupt the profession of judging? A futurist literature, both in popular media and scholarship, has explored the concept of 'robot lawyers' and 'robot judges' (D'Amato 1976; Remus and Levy 2017; Casey and Niblett 2020; Chen, Stremitzer, and Tobia 2023). Concepts such as 'legal singularity' have entered the vernacular (Alarie 2016; Aidid and Alarie 2023). Could the future really bring 'the death of judging' (Casey and Niblett 2017)?

The promise of justice with AI is clear. Human judges are fallible. Their decisions are noisy (Kahneman, Sibony, and Sunstein 2022) and inconsistent (Niblett 2013; Fischman 2014). Their decisions are tainted by political preferences and bias (Sawicki et al. 2006; Abrams, Bertrand, and Mullainathan 2012; Posner 2008). And human judges take a long time to decide cases. There is enormous backlog in cases. In Ontario, Canada, for example, nearly 15 per cent of filed civil court cases take over two years to resolve. Even for small claims, the average case takes over nine months to be resolved (Niblett and Yoon 2017). The situation is worse in other countries. In 2020, the average disposition of a civil law dispute in France was 637 days; in Italy it was 674 days (CEPEJ 2022). This delay is costly for litigants.

An optimistic strand of literature has explored how AI algorithms can improve judging. AI can analyse vast amounts of data, identify patterns, and make predictions with a high degree of accuracy. This capability could be leveraged to support judges in their decision-making process by providing them with relevant data and insights to make informed decisions. These algorithms are consistent. They do not tire. They can used to identify and reduce disparities and discrimination. Algorithms offer the promise of faster, more consistent, and less biased justice.

But the use of AI in the justice system is enormously controversial. Critics argue that relying on AI could lead to biased outcomes, perpetuate existing societal inequalities, and undermine human judgment (see e.g. Howard and Borenstein 2018; Pasquale 2020; Rodrigues 2020). Moreover, there are concerns around the accountability and transparency of AI algorithms, particularly in cases where the decisions made by AI systems are not easily explainable (Pasquale 2015). The past decade has seen an explosion of legal research exploring the fears and risks associated with AI (Goanta, van Dijck, and Spanakis 2019; Kolt, forthcoming).

Although AI is very much at the 'frontier' of research in comparative judicial behaviour, the literature is already voluminous. In this short chapter, I will not attempt to cover all aspects of AI and judging. Rather, I will touch on four major topics:

(1) **The definition of AI**: What exactly is artificial intelligence? Here, I will discuss the breadth of the field of AI. Much of the focus of this chapter is on supervised machine learning, a subfield of AI that deals with prediction. Much of the judicial behaviour literature using AI to analyse data has used supervised machine learning techniques. Courts that have already adopted some form of AI have turned to supervised machine learning predictions.
(2) **The use of AI by academics researching judicial behaviour**: How have academics employed AI to predict how judges behave? How have they used AI to show that machine learning predictions can outperform human judges? Here, I discuss how machine learning tools have been used to help predict outcomes, damages, and risk of committing crime. Predictions of judicial outcomes have been made of courts in several different countries across most continents. I illustrate how machine learning has been used not just to predict what the law is (i.e. predict what a judge will do) but also show how machine predictions can improve upon human decision-making (i.e. predict what a judge should do).
(3) **The (current) use of AI in courts**: How do courts and judges around the world currently use AI tools to assist with their decision-making? Here, I will discuss how Brazil is using AI to triage caseload, the United States uses AI to predict the risk of releasing criminal defendants, and how China is using AI to detect deviations from other judicial decisions.
(4) **The use of AI predictions to assist (or even replace) judges**: Looking ahead, it is likely that the use of AI predictions by the judiciary will become more prevalent in coming years. Here, I explore some of the main concerns that have been raised: algorithmic bias, transparency and explainable AI, prediction error, and reduction in dynamism in the law. Further, important and interesting questions looking at how human judges behave when they interact with algorithms are being explored.

The literature on AI and judging is growing apace, but these four topics provide an overview of where the literature on AI and judicial behaviour currently lies. The first topic defines the bounds of the literature discussed in the chapter. The second topic explores how machine learning methods can be used by academics to shine a light on judicial behaviour. The third topic looks at how some courts around the world are already adopting AI, and the fourth explores some of the contemporary concerns with greater adoption of AI in the courtroom.

As we forge ahead into the world increasingly infused with AI, different countries will move at varying speeds in their adoption of AI in the courtroom. And different courts around the world will use AI in different ways. This variation will present scholars with ample opportunity to study how human judges and AI predictions interact—and empirically identify the benefits and costs of such interactions.

2. Defining AI

2.1 An Overview of AI

AI is a notoriously difficult to define. It is 'still a surprisingly fuzzy concept' (Kaplan and Haenlein 2019, 15). What we mean when we say AI seems to change with every passing year and every innovation in the field. For example, some may balk at the idea that computers playing chess or simple calculators are 'artificial intelligence', but it was not so long ago that these belonged in the realm of science fiction. A broad overview of AI may be helpful, describing how research in the field has changed over time and narrowed the definition of what we mean by AI. Excellent overviews of the development of the field can be found in Haenlein (2019) and Portinale (2022).

Broadly, AI is a multidisciplinary field of computer science that aims to create systems that can perform tasks that would typically require human intelligence (see Wang 2019). These tasks may include learning, reasoning, problem-solving, perception, language understanding, and decision-making. AI systems can be classified into two categories: narrow or weak AI, which is designed for specific tasks, and general or strong AI, which is intended to possess the broad cognitive abilities of a human being. The field of AI draws on various disciplines such as mathematics, psychology, linguistics, philosophy, and neuroscience (Russell and Norvig 2010; Kaplan 2016).

Early research in AI focused largely on symbolic AI, which attempted to represent human knowledge through symbols and logical rules. Symbolic AI systems were effective in solving well-defined problems within a limited domain but struggled with real-world complexity and ambiguity (Newell and Simon 1972; Winograd 1972).

Much of the focus of new applications in AI in recent years has been on data-driven AI. Machine learning, a subset of AI that involves the development of algorithms that can learn from and make predictions or decisions based on data. Machine learning has gained prominence due to its ability to analyse vast amounts of data and adapt to changing environments, making it a valuable tool for various applications. Machine learning techniques can be categorized into three primary types: supervised learning, unsupervised learning, and reinforcement learning (Mitchell 1997; Kaplan 2016). Much of the discussion of AI in this chapter will focus on supervised machine learning. Deep learning, a subfield of machine learning, has gained significant attention in recent years. Deep learning algorithms are inspired by the structure and function of the human brain. The 'depth' in deep learning refers to multiple layers that progressively extract more predictive features from 'big' data. These algorithms are capable of automatically discovering hierarchical representations of data, which enables them to solve complex problems with minimal human intervention (LeCun, Bengio, and Hinton 2015).

Other important areas of AI are knowledge representation and reasoning (which involves organizing, structuring, and manipulating information to enable reasoning and decision-making) (Brachman and Levesque 2004) and natural language processing (NLP) (Jurafsky and Martin 2019). In this chapter, I will not focus heavily on NLP because this topic is covered in other chapters of this *Handbook* (see especially Livermore and Bao Kham Chau, discussing text analysis, and Ash on judicial language choice).

2.2 Supervised Machine Learning

Supervised machine learning is a type of machine learning in which an algorithm is trained on labelled data, meaning that each data point is associated with a known output or target variable. The goal of supervised machine learning is to learn a function that can accurately predict the output variable for new, unseen inputs (see Varian 2014; Jordan and Mitchell 2015; Athey and Imbens 2019). Supervised machine learning methods such as support vector machines (Cortes and Vapnik 1995), decision trees (Quinlan 1986), random forests (Breiman 2001), *k*-nearest neighbours (Cover and Hart 1967), and neural networks (Haykin 1998) can all be used for predicting outputs. There are two main types of problems: classification and regression.

With classification problems, the goal is to predict a discrete class label. Examples include email spam detection, image recognition, or sentiment analysis. These algorithms are used to sort classes such as 'face' and 'not face', or 'cat' and 'dog' (Alpaydin 2020). Take, for example, a spam email detector. The machine learning model is fed (many) examples of spam messages and not-spam messages. The model is trained on a portion of the data (training set). The model seeks to identify those features or combinations of features of a message that predict whether the message is spam. The model is then tested on the portion of the data that was not used in the training set. That is, the predictions are evaluated on out-of-sample messages. The probability of a message being spam is determined by fitting different types of machine learning algorithms to the training data. Given a new out-of-sample message, the algorithm can predict the most probable class (i.e. spam or not spam) based on the predicted probabilities. With regression problems, the goal is to predict a continuous numerical value. Examples include predicting housing prices or sales forecasts (Mullainathan and Spiess 2017). The accuracy of predictions depends on the quality and representativeness of the training data, the choice of algorithm, and the algorithm's ability to generalize well to new, unseen data.

Readers may see similarities between machine learning techniques and those of statistics and econometrics (Berk 2008). As Kleinberg et al. (2018, 238) note, modern machine learning builds on older statistical insights of prediction. While both machine learning and statistics involve the analysis of data, they differ in their assumptions, goals, and approaches. Statistics typically relies on assumptions about the underlying data distributions, whereas machine learning often uses algorithmic models that do not require explicit distributional assumptions. Statistics emphasizes inference, hypothesis testing, and understanding relationships between variables. Machine learning focuses on prediction and the ability to perform well on unseen data. Evaluation metrics also vary. In statistics, common metrics include *p*-values, confidence intervals, and goodness-of-fit tests. In machine learning, metrics like accuracy, precision, recall, F1-score, and area under the receiver operating characteristic (ROC) curve are used to assess model performance.

2.3 An Emphasis on Prediction

Applications of supervised machine learning techniques have been described as 'prediction machines' (Agarwal, Gans, and Goldfarb 2018). For example, these algorithms are developed to predict stock prices based on historical data (Dixon, Klabjan, and Bang 2017). By feeding historical stock prices and other relevant financial indicators as input features, a supervised learning model can learn to predict future stock prices. This can be useful for investors and traders who wish to make informed decisions about their investments. Predictions are also important in healthcare, particularly in disease diagnosis. By training a model with patient data (e.g. age, gender, genetic information, and medical history) and corresponding disease outcomes, the model can predict the likelihood of a disease in a new patient. This can help healthcare professionals to make better decisions regarding treatment and interventions (Esteva et al. 2019).

Recommendation engines, like those used by YouTube and Netflix, are prediction machines based on supervised machine learning algorithms. The engines use data to predict what the viewer will want to watch next. Similarly, facial recognition software offers a prediction. Here, the machine learning algorithm uses the underlying data of an image to predict its similarity to the underlying data in the images contained in a training set.

Prediction is, of course, not the same as causation. The emphasis on prediction can lead to obvious errors. For example, a supervised machine learning tool was highly accurate in predicting which skin lesions were malignant and which were benign. For the purposes of prediction, the most important feature in the images was the presence of a ruler. Medical images of malignant lesions included an image of a ruler, images of benign lesions did not (Narla et al. 2018). A predictive tool based on this machine learning algorithm would generate obvious false negatives where new images of malignant lesions were not accompanied by a ruler.

Government agencies face prediction problems (Kleinberg et al. 2015). Resource-constrained tax agencies, for example, wish to predict which taxpayers are most likely to be evading paying their taxes. The authorities wish to concentrate their efforts on those taxpayers who are high risk rather than auditing those who are low risk (Alarie, Niblett, and Yoon 2020). Supervised machine learning techniques can help assess the risk and make predictions of who should be audited (see e.g. Alarie, Niblett, and Yoon 2020; Engstrom et al. 2020). Coglianese and Lehr (2017) outline a number of fields where the administrative state has turned to machine learning to help with their data analysis and solving prediction problems. They refer to this as 'regulation by robot'. Regulatory agencies charged with environmental protection, food and drug administration, and competition and consumer protection have all leveraged machine learning to help with their prediction problems (see also Alarie, Niblett, and Yoon 2016a; Niblett 2018, 2021). Municipalities use machine learning to allocate fire inspectors or to determine which restaurants to audit for health and sanitation violations (Athey 2017).

Lawyers face a multitude of prediction problems. For example, lawyers need to predict whether their client's case has merit, what the likely damages are if liability will be found, whether a particular law is relevant to their client's situation, whether including a contract clause will be beneficial, and whether a particular fact will be helpful to bring up in court. There are many more. A large legal technology industry has emerged in recent years to help lawyers solve some of these prediction problems (see e.g. Alarie, Niblett, and Yoon 2018; Engstrom and Gelbach 2021). Some of these solutions are based on supervised machine learning tools. Judges and arbitrators also face prediction problems. In section 3, I discuss how some courts around the world are turning to AI to help solve these prediction problems. But first, in section 2, I demonstrate how scholars of judicial behaviour have started using machine learning predictions when analysing the decisions of human judges.

3. Use of AI by Academics Researching Judicial Behaviour

Over the past decade or so, academics studying judicial behaviour have turned to machine learning techniques to help predict the outcomes of legal cases. Authors have employed various machine learning techniques to construct models to predict binary outputs, such as the verdict of the court (e.g. whether the court will find that a defendant violated the law or not), and also predict continuous outputs, such as damages awards. Academics have also turned to machine learning techniques to expose biases in human judgments.

3.1 Using Machine Learning to Predict Outcomes

Most of the legal scholarship exploring the machine learning, prediction, and judicial behaviour has focused on predicting binary outcomes (e.g. liable or not liable). Supervised machine learning tools can be used to analyse past cases and identify patterns that can be used to predict the likely outcome of a future case. Kastellec (2010) explained how classification trees can be used to be describe the content of the law of search and seizure in the United States. Alarie, Niblett, and Yoon (2016b) develop a hand-coded dataset to describe the relevant facts of over 600 cases in the Tax Court of Canada. The authors confine their analysis to one legal issue only: whether the taxpayer is an independent contractor or an employee. Simple machine learning algorithms in this dataset can predict the outcome in over 95 per cent of out-of-sample cases. This compares favourably with simple linear regression techniques in this dataset, where the outcomes of about 88 per cent of out-of-sample cases can be predicted correctly (see Niblett 2020b, using the same dataset). Further work has demonstrated that tax cases are a good environment for using machine learning to predict outcomes (Aidid and Alarie 2020).

In a prominent paper, Katz, Bommarito, and Blackman (2017) developed a machine learning model to predict the behaviour of the Supreme Court of the United States. Based on data available before a decision, their model was able to predict the overall outcome of the case (i.e. whether the Court will affirm or reverse the lower court's decision) and the votes of individual Justices (i.e. will each justice vote to affirm or reverse the decision) from 1816 to 2015. These techniques have been extended to lower courts (Agrawal et al., 2017). Machine learning and natural language processing tools have also been used by scholars to predict the outcomes of European Court of Human Rights (ECtHR) decisions. Aletras et al. (2016) and Medvedeva et al. (2020) developed models to predict if a case was decided to be a violation of a European Convention on Human Rights article or not. The accuracy of these models was in the range of 75 per cent to 79 per cent. Chalkidis, Androutsopoulos, and Aletras (2019) developed a method to make numerous legal predictions regarding ECtHR decisions (e.g. to predict if any article was violated, the specific article violated, and the case's importance based on its contribution to the development of case law).

Asylum cases in United States have proved to be a rich lode of data for predicting outcomes. These cases are voluminous, and the outcomes and features of these cases can be easily identified. A number of authors have developed algorithms to predict whether an asylum application will be granted or denied. Dunn et al. (2017) constructed a model to predict such decisions based on the features of an asylum case. These features include the nationality of and language spoken by the applicant, the date of the notice to appear, the regional immigration court to which the applicant is assigned, the hearing location, whether the applicant was represented by an attorney, the case type (i.e. whether the application was triggered by a removal order), and judge features (including features unique to the individual judge and general features about the judge like gender). The predictive accuracy of this model was 80 per cent. Additionally, the model predicted whether an applicant would be granted or denied asylum with 71 per cent accuracy from only the identity of the presiding judge. Chen and Engels (2017) also found that a judge's identity (namely trends in that judge's decisions) carried significant weight in predicting the outcome of an asylum application. Ash et al. (2020) developed a method to predict the decisions of the appeals board of the US Asylum Courts. A tuned random forest model correctly predicts just over 80 per cent of appeals. Ash et al. find that the nationality of the asylum seeker is a strong predictor of the decision. The identity of the lower court judge in the original hearing offers some additional predictive power, potentially indicating that some lower court judges are more likely to be offered deference by the appeals court.

Academic work in this sphere has illustrated how machine learning techniques are used to predict the outcomes of the French Supreme Court (Sulea et al. 2017), the UK's highest court of appeal (Strickson and De La Iglesia 2020), the Philippine Supreme Court (Virtucio et al. 2018), Turkish higher courts (Mumcuoğlua et al. 2021), Brazilian State higher courts (Lage-Freitas et al. 2022) and lower courts (Bertalan and Ruiz 2020), and German appellant courts (Waltl et al. 2017). Additionally, Niklaus, Chalkidis, and Stürmer (2021) developed multilingual (i.e. trained across German, French, and Italian) and native (i.e. pre-trained in the respective language of the case) models to predict the verdict of a case tried at the Federal Supreme Court of Switzerland. Further, the style of speech in a courtroom has been explored as a predictive factor of outcomes. Vunikili et al. (2018) used machine learning techniques to examine if vocal intonations and the masculine/feminine style of speakers (i.e. the judges and lawyers) at the Supreme Court of the United States could be used to predict the outcome of a case. Using datasets of cases tried by Chinese courts, many authors have created models aimed at predicting the charges, applicable law articles, and prison term of a criminal law case from the textual description of its facts (e.g. Li et al. 2018; Zhong et al. 2018; Yang et al. 2019). These types of studies may provide interesting sources for scholars of comparative judicial behaviour wishing to study the predictability of different courts around the world.

There are some common themes that have emerged from this literature using machine learning to predict legal outcomes. First, typically, the better structured the dataset of inputs, the higher the accuracy. Judicial opinions, and other legal documents, are typically unstructured. By transforming unstructured data into structured data that describes the cases, the predictive accuracy can be greatly improved. The more detail about the facts that can be described in the structured dataset, the better the predictions. Second, the accuracy is higher when authors focus on specific legal issues that have been the subject of much litigation. Third, and somewhat obviously, the predictive accuracy of these algorithms is higher when the facts of the different legal cases in the dataset are similar and with legal issues where the judges are more consistent.

3.2 Using Machine Learning to Predict Damages Awards

Machine learning tools can also be used to predict damages. Such techniques have been discussed in the context of personal injury law. For example, Haidar et al. (2022) illustrate the use case of predicting compensation level for plaintiffs in accident cases in Morocco. Dahan et al. (2020) explore the limitations of using various machine learning techniques to predict the damages awarded in wrongful dismissal cases in Canada. Dahan et al. hand-code data from nearly 1,400 cases. The data describes outcomes and important variables. A well-constructed linear regression model predicts outcomes with high error. This can be improved upon with boosted decision trees and random forest models, but the improvement is confined to about a 10 per cent reduction in prediction error.

3.3 Using Machine Learning to Understand Risk of Recidivism and Flight Risk

Machine learning tools have been used to study judicial behaviour in ways other than predicting decisions. The decisions of human judges, particularly in the context of bail decisions and sentencing, have been shown to be racially biased (Arnold, Dobbie, and Hull 2022). Machine learning tools have helped expose biases in human judging. Scholars have sought to use machine learning tools to illustrate the benefits of more accurate predictions (Lin et al. 2020). The seminal work of Richard Berk and co-authors has explored the benefits and limitations of using machine learning tools in making assessments of recidivism, both generally (Berk and Hyatt 2015; Berk 2019b) and in specific contexts, such as parole decisions (Berk 2017), juvenile offenders (Berk 2019a), and in forecasting domestic violence (Berk et al. 2016).

In a seminal paper, Kleinberg et al. (2018) develop a machine learning model that analyses data from over 750,000 New York bail decisions. The authors show that machine learning techniques do a much better job of forecasting a defendant's flight risk compared to human judges. That is, the prediction problem here is that the judge needs to make a prediction whether the defendant will flee and not return for their trial, or will they commit a crime while out on bail. One type of judicial error is easily observed, when the defendant is released but they commit a crime. The other type of error, however, is not observed. The authors cannot easily observe whether a judge erred by detaining a defendant who is low risk. But the authors take advantage of the fact that defendants are as good as randomly assigned to judges, and these judges differ in their leniency. The machine learning algorithm prediction is compared against lenient judges and against stringent judges. Using this methodology, the authors simulate what would happen if the machine learning algorithm were used to make bail decisions. There are real life consequences from poor predictions on the part of human judges. By correcting these errors, fewer people can be denied bail. The authors' simulations suggest that the jail population could be reduced by nearly 42 per cent with no increase in crime. Alternatively, the crime level could be reduced by about 25 per cent with no increase in the jail population. Further, the authors' simulations suggest that racial disparities in the law could also be reduced. The decisions of human judges are infected with racial bias, which leads to errors in assessing the flight risk of some racialized defendants. Kleinberg et al. argue that if flight risk is predicted with higher accuracy using their machine learning simulations, a court could simultaneously reduce the jail population, lower the crime level, and reduce racial disparities.

4. Current Use of AI by Courts around the World

AI has the potential to improve efficiency and accuracy of courts. But AI algorithms are not currently used widely by the judiciary in courts around the world. There are examples of countries around the world to support judicial decision-making in different applications. But the dreams and nightmares of 'robot judges' seem a long way off. It has been claimed that some countries are moving in the direction of using AI in the courtroom, but for many of these claims, it can be difficult to separate the hype from the substance. For other claims, it can be difficult to distinguish whether these tools are operational or whether they are aspirational (Penney 2019; Sourdin and Cornes 2018; Brkan, Claes, and Rauchegger 2020). I will highlight some examples from Brazil, the United States, and China where AI is being employed by courts. Some commentators have also noted the use of AI in courts in India (Jauhar et al. 2021) and Estonia (Heller 2017; Niiler 2019; although see Tuulik 2022), for example, but little academic research explaining these tools exists at time of writing.

4.1 Brazil

Brazilian courts appear to have been an early adopter of AI technology to assist with judging. The most noteworthy application is VICTOR, an application used to help triage extraordinary appeals to the Brazilian Supreme Court (STF). According to Becker and Ferrari (2020), VICTOR uses a convolutional neural network trained to identify certain themes in the litigation materials. This prediction helps to determine whether the case deals with issues of 'general repercussion', which in turn informs the decision of whether the STF will hear the appeal. Since VICTOR is used in triaging cases, it is solely used to support decision-making in the more procedural aspects of the court, contributing to the work of civil servants working at the STF, rather than that of judges.

VICTOR is not the only AI system employed by the Brazilian judiciary (De Sanctis 2021). Salomao (2020) explores a variety of other machine learning systems used by other Brazilian courts to support the court's research and clerical activities. Salomao lists twenty-seven AI projects currently in production in Brazilian courts, while a further thirty-six projects are in development or pilot stages. For example, Athos is a tool developed and employed by the Superior Court of Justice to identify repetitive claims that are based on legal controversies that have already been decided. Athos also helps to identify relevant precedents that the court should consider in its decisions. The Justice Court of Alagoas uses a tool named Hercules to group similar petitions to the court into a specific queue. Many of the systems described were developed in-house at the various Brazilian courts, while others, like LEIA, were built by private companies. LEIA, which analyses cases to identify relevant higher court precedents, is used by five different State Justice Courts.

4.2 United States

As noted in section 2, courts in the United States have used AI algorithms to assist with criminal sentencing (Berk 2019b). These algorithms are used to predict the likelihood of defendants reoffending or failing to appear in court. The algorithms analyse data such as criminal history, demographic information, and social factors, and generate a risk score that judges can use to inform their decisions on bail and sentencing. The use of algorithmic risk assessment is not new. But the use of machine learning to make the predictions is a more recent phenomenon. For many of these risk assessments, it is difficult to determine whether there is any machine learning prediction behind the assessment, or whether the predictions were developed in a cruder fashion. The use of AI in this way has generated much controversy and attracted the attention of academics studying how judges decide (Starr 2014; Berk 2019b; Stevenson 2018).

One prominent example is the use of a tool called Compas (Correctional Offender Management Profiling for Alternative Sanctions). Compas was developed by a private company and has been adopted by courts in many jurisdictions to support sentencing decisions. In short, the judge inputs information about the offender's personal and criminal profile, and the algorithm returns an assessment of recidivism, violent recidivism, and pre-trial risks. These risks have been used by courts to inform decisions on pre-trial detention, type of sentence imposed, and early release (Reiling 2020). Given the proprietary nature of Compas, the techniques used to derive the prediction are not disclosed. However, the developer's own documentation indicates that it uses methods 'described in various books on regression modelling and machine learning' (Northpointe 2015).

Compas has been challenged both in courts and in the public forum. It has been shown that the tool generated results that disproportionately overpredict risk of recidivism by Black offenders as compared to the risk by White offenders (Angwin et al. 2016; Larson et al. 2016). This bias is likely to arise in part from using past data which is itself biased. In *Wisconsin v Loomis*, the Wisconsin Court of Appeal held that using tools such as Compas to support sentencing decisions does not violate an offender's due process rights.

4.3 China

Zou (2020) indicates that Chinese courts are incorporating 'AI judges' in personal injury cases. Zou describes these 'smart court' systems as allowing judges to submit the details of a case, and the system will return similar cases that have been previously decided. Zou notes that some courts employ systems that can conduct deviation analysis on a judge's drafted opinion to determine whether it departs from those earlier decisions. Stern et al. (2021) describe the use of predictive systems used in Chinese courts that allow judges to input certain facts about a case and the system will return data about the sentences imposed in cases with similar facts.

Here I have provided three of the more prominent examples of how different countries' courts have begun to adopt AI in both the process and substance of judicial decision-making. At time of writing, there is only limited use of machine learning tools by courts around the world, but this is likely to change in the coming years as good data becomes increasingly available, predictions improve, and our comfort level with AI decisions increases. Different countries will adopt the technology at different rates. Different judges will use the algorithmic predictions in different ways. This variation will present a fascinating opportunity for comparative judicial behaviour scholars to compare the use of such tools in different countries.

5. Machine Predictions, Human Judgments, or Both?

Suppose there were AI systems that could predict the outcome of a case with high accuracy, would we need the expense and time of a costly trial? Could we simply use a machine to resolve the dispute? Such algorithmic decisions are likely to be more consistent than human judgments. If they are simulated replicas of previous decisions, then adopting the predictions of an AI system would be akin to a strong version of the doctrine of precedent. In some sense, it would be an algorithmic version of the legalism discussed in Morell's chapter in this *Handbook*.

But many legal commentators have written much about the concerns of using machine learning in the courtroom and have raised objections to the substitution of machine decision-making for human judgment. In this section, I will outline some of the main concerns and limitations with the use of AI predictions in this way.

5.1 Concerns about Machine Learning Algorithms

5.1.1 *Algorithmic Bias*

A major concern with courts using AI is algorithmic bias. Algorithmic bias refers to situations where machine learning algorithms produce results that are systematically skewed towards certain groups of people or outcomes due to the biased data used to train them. In the context of legal decision-making, algorithmic bias can result in decisions that unfairly disadvantage certain individuals or groups, such as people of colour, women, or people with disabilities (Sacks, Sainato, and Ackerman 2014; Arnold, Dobbie, and Yang 2018; Dastin 2018; Bartlett et al. 2022). For example, if a machine learning algorithm is trained on historical court data that is biased against a particular group, the algorithm may learn to make decisions that perpetuate this bias. This could result in unfair or discriminatory outcomes in legal proceedings. Using machine learning tools to replicate the existing law will entrench the existing bias. For example, the history of wrongful dismissal case law in Canada has shown a bias against women (Niblett 2020a).

On the other hand, machine learning can be valuable in helping expose bias in human judging and decision-making (Goel et al. 2016; Kleinberg et al. 2018), which in turn can help improve the fairness and accuracy of the legal system (Huq 2020, forthcoming; Chen et al. 2023). Further, if we are not simply replicating the law from past legal decisions but we instead employ machine learning algorithms to achieve some given objective (e.g. minimize flight risk in bail decisions), then there is the possibility that machine predictions may be less biased than human judgments (Sunstein 2019, 2022). Of course, this requires a clear understanding of what the specific, translatable objective that the law is trying to optimize (Casey and Niblett 2019, 2021).

5.1.2 *Transparency and Explainable AI*

Another key concern is the lack of transparency in the decision-making process of AI systems. Machine learning algorithms can be very complex. It can be difficult for users—and even for the developers—to parse reasons why a particular output was generated. This can make it difficult to identify and correct biases. If the decision-making process of an AI system is opaque or difficult to understand, it can be difficult to determine whether the system is making fair and unbiased decisions. There is a large literature in AI discussing the need for explainable AI (XAI) (see Hofman, Sharma, and Watts 2017; Miller 2019; Arrieta et al. 2020; O'Hara 2020).

This problem has given rise to a burgeoning literature in legal scholarship discussing the problem of a black-box algorithms and the degree to which explanations of AI systems are required (Pasquale 2015; Edwards and Veale 2017; Ananny and Crawford 2018; Selbst and Barcoas 2018). This literature has grown in response to legislative changes in Europe, with the GDPR (Goodman and Flaxman 2017; Selbst and Powles 2017; Wachter et al. 2017; Sovrano et al. 2020). The literature has explored the differences between (and the relative merits of) explanation and justification (Biran and McKeown 2017; Gillis and Simons 2019; Schubbach 2019).

Transparency and explanation are of paramount importance in legal decision-making (Akehurst 1970; Flick 1978; Raz 1979; Craig 1994). Transparency and explanation can help ensure that legal decisions are made fairly and in accordance with the law and help build trust in the legal system (Coglianese and Lehr 2017; Kroll et al. 2017; Walmsley 2021). Transparency and explanation can also provide insight into the underlying data and factors that are driving the algorithm's decision-making process. This can help judges improve their understanding of the utility of the algorithm's output and question it. While some literature has explored whether XAI may be asking more of algorithms than we expect or obtain from human decision-makers (Zerilli et al. 2018; Gunther and Kasirzadeh 2022).

Proposed solutions to the problems of transparency and explanation have been explored in the literature (Edwards and Veale 2017; Wachter, Mittelstadt, and Floridi 2017). There are subject-centric solutions that provide post hoc explanations of why the AI output made a specific decision. A notable example of this is the use of counterfactuals to explain what the output would have been if the case had different features or inputs (Pearl 2013; Wachter, Mittelstadt, and Russell 2018). Counterfactuals can be a powerful way of explaining the important or even dispositive features of a litigant's case. Another way to use counterfactuals is to demonstrate what would need to be different in order to get a different result. There are also more general solutions, that are model-centric, providing an *ex ante* explanation that speaks the functionality of the system as a whole, explaining what data was used, what model was used, and how the algorithm optimizes.

5.1.3 *Errors in Prediction*

Algorithms can help reduce errors but they cannot eliminate them. Prediction errors are still made. How much machine error are we willing to accept in the judiciary? Are we willing to accept more human error than machine error? A literature on algorithm aversion has explored this question more generally (see Jussupow, Benbasat, and Heinzl 2020).

There are many reasons for predictive errors. An obvious concern is the quality of data. It is somewhat trite to say 'garbage in, garbage out', but the concern is real, and the effects are corrosive. If algorithms rely on poor-quality data then the outputs will suffer. Take the example of using of algorithms to triage caseload by replicating what previous judges have done in similar cases. Here there is a potential concern of selection bias. Selection bias is a type of bias that occurs when the selection of data used to train a machine learning model is not representative of the population or phenomenon being studied. The types of cases that have been litigated in the past may not be representative of the types of new cases that would come before a court (see Engstrom and Gelbach 2021; Niblett 2021b). The data do not reflect the full picture of cases. If the training data do not reflect real life cases, then prediction errors will be made. As noted in section 3, the predictions of legal outcomes typically work well in areas of law where there is a large volume of data, the legal issue is appropriately confined, and the facts of cases, both past and future, are not too heterogeneous.

Even with good quality data that accurately represents what is sought to be measured, there will be procedural justice questions about which algorithms are used to make decisions. The different types of machine learning algorithm may rank and classify situations differently. For example, a complex neural network algorithm may classify a criminal defendant as high risk, while a less complex algorithm, such as a random forest model, may predict low risk. Algorithms are fragile and the outputs sensitive to the choice of model (Ludwig and Mullainathan 2021). Which algorithm should we use and why? There may be good reasons to use simpler algorithms that may generate slightly lower accuracy where the predictions comport with common sense and the outputs are more easily explainable.

5.1.4 *Reduced Dynamism in the Law*

Another concern with using algorithms using prior decisions as the basis of future decisions is that the law becomes static. Aidid (2023) describes this as 'calcification' of the law. Machine learning algorithms that simply replicate past legal decisions without taking into account changing social, economic, or political conditions will not account for emerging legal trends or new legal issues that have not been seen in the historical data. This can limit their ability to provide useful insights into new or rapidly evolving legal areas, such as free speech.

5.2 Concerns about the Implementation by Judges

5.2.1 *Human Judges in the Loop*

A fertile source of future research will be investigating the interaction between human judges and algorithmic predictions. The question of machine predictions or human judgments is sometimes posed as a binary choice. But this is obviously a false dichotomy. One can think of a spectrum of decision-making, where humans take more or less of a role in the process. Consider the following taxonomy, based loosely on the levels of autonomy of self-driving cars:

- *Level 0*—Full human decision-making.
- *Level 1*—Judges have access to descriptive data only.
- *Level 2*—Judges have access to algorithmic predictions.
- *Level 3*—Judges are given a suggested decision; judges are free to override.
- *Level 4*—Judges are given a recommended decision; a judge needs to issue written reasons should they wish to depart from the recommendation.
- *Level 5*—A preliminary decision is based on an algorithmic prediction, but the human judge can override with written reasons.
- *Level 6*—Full 'algorithmic decision-making', no human judge can override.

Many legal scholars have argued that machine learning algorithms should only be used to complement, rather than replace, human expertise in legal decision-making (Pasquale 2020). Scholars have explored whether we have a 'right' to a human decision in law (Huq 2020). In each of the levels between levels 2 and 5 there is a 'human in the loop' in addition to the prediction of the algorithm. Exciting research at the frontier of judicial behaviour is likely to address the following questions: How exactly do human judges interact with and use algorithms? When should a human judge be afforded the discretion to override the predictions of an algorithm? When should that discretion be exercised?

The nascent empirical literature in this area has shown that human judges frequently override the recommendations of predictive algorithms in practice (Stevenson 2018; Albright 2019; Anwar, Bushway, and Engberg 2022). Engel's chapter on experimental data in this *Handbook* provides examples of experimental work where decision-makers elect not to adopt the recommendations of an algorithm. Empiricists studying the judiciary have shown that human judges may exercise their discretion in ways that exacerbate racial biases, rather than reduce disparities. Stevenson (2018) shows that a policy change in Kentucky, introducing a recommended bail bond, led to an increase in racial disparities. Albright (2019) shows that this increase is not simply due to differences in risk scores by race. The differences emerge because the recommended default was more likely to be overridden for Black defendants than similar White defendants; that is, the discretion to override favourable recommended bond conditions, and impose harsher conditions, was more likely to be used with Black defendants. Stevenson and Doleac (2023), using data from sexual assault and rape cases in Virginia, show how judges may use risk assessments as a shield that implicitly justifies leniency for low-risk offenders. The assessment provides a 'second opinion' that can mitigate blame or guilt should a low-risk offender go on to reoffend.

5.2.2 *Converting Probabilities into Binary Outcomes*

Another area for new research will be how judges convert probabilistic predictions (e.g. 80 per cent likelihood of liability) into binary outcomes (liable or not liable). Casey and Niblett (2020, 2023) show that using the usual balance of probabilities approach will impact litigation outcomes and perhaps more importantly, dramatically affect settlement outcomes. For example, if a plaintiff seeks $1 million in compensation and the parties agree that the plaintiff has an 80 per cent likelihood of success, under the usual theoretical models of litigation and settlement we would assume that the parties would settle in the neighbourhood of $800,000. But in a world where the algorithmic prediction (80 per cent) is converting into liability using a balance of probabilities approach, the case will now settle in the neighbourhood of $1 million. Casey and Niblett (2020, 2023) show that there is no obvious or dominant way of converting probabilities without having an impact on the law or settlement outcomes. All options of converting probabilities each come with costs and benefits.

6. Conclusion

The role AI plays in our justice system will continue to spark fervent debate. AI has immense potential to revolutionize and streamline judging, particularly at the trial level. The ability of AI to analyse vast quantities of data and make accurate, consistent predictions presents a compelling vision of faster, more equitable justice, devoid of human bias, inconsistency, and fatigue. But the adoption of AI in the justice system is accompanied by significant controversy. Concerns around the potential for AI to perpetuate societal inequalities, bias, and undermine human judgment are valid and must be taken into account. Transparency and accountability in AI algorithms remain crucial, especially when the decisions made by AI systems can have life-altering consequences and may not be easily explainable.

The topics discussed in this chapter are very much at the frontier of research in comparative judicial behaviour. As we move towards an AI-assisted future, there will be a push to leverage the power of AI to improve the efficiency and consistency of our justice system, while ensuring we retain what is 'good' about human judging. In exploring 'how and why judges make the choices they do and what effect those choices have on society', research will continue to explore the degree to which AI can make those choices and decisions. Given what we know about the fallibility, inconsistency, and ponderous nature of human judging, we then must ask whether it is in our interests to have human judges to making these choices and decisions at all.

Acknowledgments

I wish to thank the organizers of the conference (Lee Epstein, Gunnar Grendstad, Urška Šadl, and Keren Weinshall) for their hard work and stewardship of this tremendous project. I also wish to extend my enormous gratitude to Gordon Milne and Samson An for their excellent research assistance. I wish to acknowledge funding from SSHRC (Grant: "Algorithms as Legal Decisions") and from the Canada Research Chair Program (funding ref. no. 950-232818.)

References

Abrams, David S., Marianne Bertrand, and Sendhil Mullainathan. 2012. 'Do Judges Vary in Their Treatment of Race?' *The Journal of Legal Studies* 41 (2): 347–83. https://doi.org/10.1086/666006.

Agarwal, Ajay, Joshua Gans, and Avi Goldfarb. 2018. *Prediction Machines: The Simple Economics of Artificial Intelligence*. Boston, MA: Harvard Business Review Press.

Agrawal, Sharan, Elliott Ash, Daniel Chen, Simranjyot S. Gill, Amanpreet Singh, and Karthik Venkatesan. 2017. 'Affirm or Reverse? Using Machine Learning to Help Judges Write Opinions'. National Bureau of Economic Research Working Paper. https://users.nber.org/~dlchen/papers/Affirm_or_Reverse.pdf.

Aidid, Abdi. 2023. 'Legal Prediction and the Calcification Problem'. Unpublished manuscript, University of Toronto Faculty of Law.

Aidid, Abdi, and Benjamin Alarie. 2020. 'Predicting Economic Substance Cases with Machine Learning'. *Journal of Tax Practice & Procedure* 22: 27–38. https://ssrn.com/abstract=3628421.

Aidid, Abdi, and Benjamin Alarie. 2023. *The Legal Singularity: How Artificial Intelligence Can Make Law Radically Better*. Toronto: University of Toronto Press.

Akehurst, Michael. 1970. 'Statements of Reasons for Judicial and Administrative Decisions'. *The Modern Law Review* 33 (2): 154–69. https://doi.org/10.1111/j.1468-2230.1970.tb01262.x.

Alarie, Benjamin. 2016. 'The Path of the Law: Towards Legal Singularity'. *University of Toronto Law Journal* 66 (4): 443–55. https://doi.org/10.3138/utlj.4008.

Alarie, Benjamin, Anthony Niblett, and Albert Yoon. 2016a. 'Regulation by Machine'. In *NIPS'16: Proceedings of the 30th Conference on Neural Information Processing Systems*, 7. Barcelona, Spain: IEEE. https://doi.org/10.2139/ssrn.2878950.

Alarie, Benjamin, Anthony Niblett, and Albert Yoon. 2016b. 'Using Machine Learning to Predict Outcomes in Tax Law'. *Canadian Business Law Journal* 58 (3): 231–54.

Alarie, Benjamin, Anthony Niblett, and Albert Yoon. 2018. 'How Artificial Intelligence Will Affect the Practice of Law'. *University of Toronto Law Journal* 68 (1): 106–24. https://doi.org/10.3138/utlj.2017-0052.

Alarie, Benjamin, Anthony Niblett, and Albert Yoon. 2020. 'Data Analytics and Tax Law'. In *Research Handbook in Big Data and Law*, edited by Roland Vogl, 135–49. Cheltenham: Edward Elgar.

Albright, Alex. 2019. 'If You Give a Judge a Risk Score: Evidence from Kentucky Bail Decisions'. Harvard John M. Olin for Law, Economics, and Business Fellow's Discussion Paper 85. http://www.law.harvard.edu/programs/olin_center/Prizes/2019-1.pdf.

Aletras, Nikolaos, Dimitrios Tsarapatsanis, Daniel Preotiuc-Pietro, and Vasileios Lampos. 2016. 'Predicting Judicial Decisions of the European Court of Human Rights: A Natural Language Processing Perspective'. *Peer Journal of Computer Science* 2 (1): e93. https://doi.org/10.7717/peerj-cs.93.

Alpaydin, Ethem. 2020. *Introduction to Machine Learning*. Cambridge: The MIT Press.

Ananny, Mike, and Kate Crawford. 2018. 'Seeing Without Knowing: Limitation of the Transparency Ideal and Its Application to Algorithmic Accountability'. *New Media & Society* 20 (3): 973–89. https://doi.org/10.1177/1461444816676645.

Angwin, Julia, Jeff Larson, Surya Mattu, and Lauren Kirchner. 2016. 'Machine Bias'. ProPublica. https://www.propublica.org/article/machine-bias-risk-assessments-in-criminal-sentencing.

Anwar, Shamena, Shawn D. Bushway, and John Engberg. 2022. 'The Impact of Defense Counsel at Bail Hearings'. RAND Working Paper No WR-A1960-1. https://www.rand.org/pubs/research_briefs/RBA1960-1.html.

Arnold, David, Will Dobbie, and Peter Hull. 2022. 'Measuring Racial Discrimination in Bail Decisions'. *American Economic Review* 112 (9): 2992–3038. https://doi.org/10.1257/aer.20201653.

Arnold, David, Will Dobbie, and Crystal S. Yang. 2018. 'Racial Bias in Bail Decisions'. *The Quarterly Journal of Economics* 133 (4): 1885–932. https://doi.org/10.1093/qje/qjy012.

Arrieta, Alejandro Barredo, Natalia Diaz-Rodriguez, Javier Del Ser, Adrien Bennetot, Siham Tabik, Alberto Barbado, and Salvador Garcia, et al. 2020. 'Explainable Artificial Intelligence (XAI): Concepts, Taxonomies, Opportunities and Challenges toward Responsible AI'. *Information Fusion* 58 (1): 82–115. https://doi.org/10.1016/j.inffus.2019.12.012.

Ash, Elliott, Daniel Chen, Colin Andrus, Dustin Godevais, and Gary Ng. 2020. 'Machine Prediction of Appeal Success in U.S. Asylum Courts'. National Bureau of Economic Research Working Paper. https://users.nber.org/~dlchen/papers/Machine_Prediction_of_Appeal_Success_in_US_Asylum_Courts.pdf.

Athey, Susan. 2017. 'Beyond Prediction: Using Big Data for Policy Problems'. *Science* 355 (6324): 483–85. https://doi.org/10.1126/science.aal4321.

Athey, Susan, and Guido W. Imbens. 2019. 'Machine Learning Methods That Economists Should Know About'. *Annual Review of Economics* 11 (1): 685–725. https://doi.org/10.1146/annurev-economics-080217-053433.

Bartlett, Robert P., Adair Morse, Nancy Wallace, and Richard Stanton. 2022. 'Algorithmic Discrimination and Input Accountability under the Civil Rights Acts'. *Berkeley Technology Law Journal* 36 (2): 675–736. https://doi.org/10.15779/Z381N7XN5B.

Becker, Daniel, and Isabela Ferrari. 2020. 'VICTOR, the Brazilian Supreme Court's Artificial Intelligence: A Beauty or a Beast?' In *Regulacao 4.0: Desafios da Regulacao Diante de Um*

Novo Paradigma Cientifico, edited by Daniel Becker and Isabela Ferrari. Sao Paulo: Editora Revista dos Tribunais. https://www.jusbrasil.com.br/doutrina/secao/victor-the-brazilian-supreme-court-s-artificial-intelligence-a-beauty-or-a-beast-regulacao-40-desafios-da-regulacao-diante-de-um-novo-paradigma-cientifico/1198075998#a-249557352.

Berk, Richard A. 2008. *Statistical Learning from a Regression Perspective. Springer Series in Statistics*. New York: Springer New York. https://doi.org/10.1007/978-0-387-77501-2.

Berk, Richard A. 2017. 'An Impact Assessment of Machine Learning Risk Forecasts on Parole Board Decisions and Recidivism'. *Journal of Experimental Criminology* 13 (2): 193–216. https://doi.org/10.1007/s11292-017-9286-2.

Berk, Richard A. 2019a. 'Accuracy and Fairness for Juvenile Justice Risk Assessments'. *Journal of Empirical Legal Studies* 16 (1): 175–94. https://doi.org/10.1111/jels.12206.

Berk, Richard A. 2019b. *Machine Learning Risk Assessments in Criminal Justice Settings*. New York: Springer.

Berk, Richard A., Susan B. Sorenson, and Geoffrey Barnes. 2016. 'Forecasting Domestic Violence: A Machine Learning Approach to Help Inform Arraignment Decisions'. *Journal of Empirical Legal Studies* 13 (1): 94–115. https://doi.org/10.1111/jels.12098.

Berk, Richard A., and Jordan Hyatt. 2015. 'Machine Learning Forecasts of Risk to Inform Sentencing Decisions'. *Federal Sentencing Reporter* 27 (4): 222–28. https://doi.org/10.1525/fsr.2015.27.4.222.

Bertalan, Vithor Gomes, and Evandro E. S. Ruiz. 2020. 'Predicting Judicial Outcomes in the Brazilian Legal System Using Textual Features'. *CEUR Workshop Proceedings: Digital Humanities and Natural Language Processing*. https://ceur-ws.org/Vol-2607/paper3.pdf.

Biran, Or, and Kathleen McKeown. 2017. 'Human-Centric Justification of Machine Learning Predictions'. In *IJCAI'17: Proceedings of the 26th International Joint Conference on Artificial Intelligence*, 19–26 August 2017. 6. IJCAI. https://doi.org/10.24963/ijcai.2017/202.

Brachman, Ronald J., and Hector J. Levesque. 2004. *Knowledge Representation and Reasoning*. Amsterdam: Elsevier.

Breiman, Leo. 2001. 'Random Forests'. *Machine Learning* 45 (1): 5–32. https://doi.org/10.1023/A:1010933404324.

Brkan, Maja, Monica Claes, and Clara Rauchegger. 2020. 'European Fundamental Rights and Digitalization'. *Maastricht Journal of European and Comparative Law* 27 (6): 697–704. https://doi.org/10.1177/1023263X20983778.

Casey, Anthony J., and Anthony Niblett. 2017. 'The Death of Rules and Standards'. *Indiana Law Journal* 92 (4): 1401–28. https://www.repository.law.indiana.edu/ilj/vol92/iss4/3.

Casey, Anthony J., and Anthony Niblett. 2019. 'A Framework for the New Personalization of Law'. *University of Chicago Law Review* 86 (2): 333–61. https://chicagounbound.uchicago.edu/uclrev/vol86/iss2/8.

Casey, Anthony J., and Anthony Niblett. 2020. 'Will Robot Judges Change Litigation and Settlement Outcomes? A First Look at the Algorithmic Replication of Prior Cases'. *MIT Computational Law Report 2.0*. https://law.mit.edu/pub/willrobotjudgeschangelitigationandsettlementoutcomes.

Casey, Anthony J., and Anthony Niblett. 2021. 'Micro-directives and Computational Merger Review'. *Stanford Journal of Computational Antitrust* 1: 132–49. https://ssrn.com/abstract=4007518.

Casey, Anthony J., and Anthony Niblett. 2023. 'Problems with Probability'. *University of Toronto Law Journal* 73 (1): 92–104. https://doi.org/10.3138/utlj-2023-0006.

CEPEJ. 2022. 'CEPEJ Indicators on Efficiency'. European Commission for the Efficiency of Justice. https://public.tableau.com/app/profile/cepej/viz/EfficiencyEN/Efficiency, accessed 12 May 2023.

Chalkidis, Ilias, Ion Androutsopoulos, and Nikolaos Aletras. 2019. 'Neutral Legal Judgment Prediction in English'. In *ACL'19: Proceedings of the 57th Annual Meeting of the Association for Computational Linguistics*, Florence, Italy, July 2019, 6. Cedarville, OH: Association for Computational Linguistics. https://doi.org/10.18653/v1/P19-1424.

Chen, Benjamin Minhao, Alexander Stremitzer, and Kevin Tobia. 2023. 'Having Your Day in Robot Court'. *Harvard Journal of Law & Technology* 36 (1): 128–69. https://jolt.law.harvard.edu/assets/articlePDFs/v36/Chen-Stremitzer-Tobia-Having-Your-Day-in-Robot-Court.pdf.

Chen, Daniel L., and Jess Eagel. 2017. 'Can Machine Learning Help Predict the Outcome of Asylum Adjudications?' In *ICAIL '17: Proceeding of the 16th edition of the International Conference on Artificial Intelligence and Law*, London, UK, 12–16 June 2017, 3. New York: Association of Computing Machinery. https://doi.org/10.1145/3086512.3086538.

Coglianese, Cary, and David Lehr. 2017. 'Regulating by Robot: Administrative Decision Making in the Machine-Learning Era'. *Georgetown Law Journal* 105: 1147.

Cortes, Corinna, and Vladimir Vapnik. 1995. 'Support-Vector Networks'. *Machine Learning* 20 (3): 273–97. https://doi.org.10.1007/bf00994018.

Cover, Thomas, and Peter E. Hart. 1967. 'Nearest Neighbor Pattern Classification'. *IEEE Transactions on Information Theory* 13 (1): 21–27. https://doi.org.10.1109/TIT.1967.1053964.

Craig, P. P. 1994. 'The Common Law, Reasons and Administrative Justice'. *The Cambridge Law Journal*, 53 (2): 282–302.

Dahan, Samuel, Jonathan Touboul, Jason Lam, and Dan Sfedj. 2020. 'Predicting Employment Notice Period with Machine Learning: Promises and Limitations'. *McGill Law Journal* 65 (4): 711–53. https://doi.org/10.7202/1076909ar.

D'Amato, Anthony. 1976. 'Can/Should Computers Replace Judges?' *Georgia Law Review* 11:1277–301.

Dastin, Jeffrey. 2018. 'Amazon Scraps Secret AI Recruiting Tool that Showed Bias Against Women'. https://www.reuters.com/article/us-amazon-com-jobs-automation-insight-idUSKCN1MK08G.

De Sanctis, Fausto Martin. 2021. 'Artificial Intelligence and Innovation in Brazilian Justice'. *International Annals of Criminology* 59 (1): 1–10. https://doi.org/10.1017/cri.2021.4.

Dixon, Matthews, Diego Klabjan, and Jin Hoon Bang. 2017. 'Classification-Based Financial Markets Prediction Using Deep Neural Networks'. *Algorithmic Finance* 6 (3-4): 67–77. https://arxiv.org/abs/1603.08604.

Dunn, Matthew, Levent Sagun, Hale Sirin, and Daniel Chen. 2017. 'Early Predictability of Asylum Court Decisions'. In *ICAIL'17: Proceedings of the 16th edition of the International Conference on Artificial Intelligence and Law*, London, 12–16 June 2017, 3. New York: Association of Computing Machinery.https://doi.org/10.1145/3086512.3086537.

Edwards, Lilian, and Michael Veale. 2017. 'Slave to the Algorithm? Why a "Right to an Explanation" Is Probably Not the Remedy You're Looking For'. *Duke Law & Technology Review* 16: 18–84. https://doi.org/10.2139/ssrn.2972855.

Engstrom, David F., and Jonah B. Gelbach. 2021. 'Legal Tech, Civil Procedure, and the Future of Adversarialism'. *University of Pennsylvania Law Review* 169 (4): 1001–80. https://scholarship.law.upenn.edu/penn_law_review/vol169/iss4/2.

Engstrom, David F., Daniel E. Ho, Catherine M. Sharkey, and Mariano-Florentino Cuellar. 2020. *Government by Algorithm: Artificial Intelligence in Federal Administrative Agencies*,

Report Submitted to The Administrative Conference of the United States, Washington, DC, February 2020, 122. https://www.acus.gov/sites/default/files/documents/Government%20by%20Algorithm.pdf.

Esteva, Andre, Alexandre Robicquet, Bharath Ramsundar, Volodymyr Kuleshov, Mark DePristo, Katherine Chou, Claire Cui, Greg Corrado, Sebastian Thrun, and Jeff Dean. 2019. 'A Guide to Deep Learning in Healthcare'. *Nature Medicine* 25 (1): 24–29. https://doi.org/10.1038/s41591-018-0316-z.

Fischman, Joshua B. 2014. 'Measuring Inconsistency, Indeterminacy, and Error in Adjudication'. *American Law and Economics Review* 16 (1): 40–85. https://doi.org/10.1093/aler/aht011.

Flick, G. A. 1978. 'Administrative Adjudication and the Duty to Give Reasons'. *Public Law* 16: 56–73.

Gillis, Talia B., and Josh Simons. 2019. 'Explanation < Justification: GDPR and the Perils of Privacy'. *University of Pennsylvania Journal of Law & Innovation* 2 (1):71–99. https://dx.doi.org/10.2139/ssrn.3374668.

Goanta, Catalina, Gijs van Dijck, and Gerasimos Spanakis. 2019. 'Back to the Future: Waves of Legal Scholarship on Artificial Intelligence'. In *Time, Law and Change: An Interdisciplinary Study*, edited by Sofia Ranchordás and Yaniv Roznai, 327–46. Oxford: Hart Publishing. https://dx.doi.org/10.2139/ssrn.3402676.

Goel, Sharad, Justin M. Rao, and Ravi Shroff. 2016. 'Personalized Risk Assessments in the Criminal Justice System'. *American Economic Review* 106 (5): 119–23. https://doi.org/10.1257/aer.p20161028.

Goodman, Bryce, and Seth Flaxman. 2017. 'European Union Regulation on Algorithmic Decision-Making and a "Right to Explanation"'. *AI Magazine* 38 (3): 50–57. https://doi.org/10.1609/aimag.v38i3.2741.

Gunther, Mario, and Atoosa Kasirzadeh. 2022. 'Algorithmic and Human Decision Making: For a Double Standard of Transparency'. *AI & Society* 37 (1): 375–81. https://doi.org/10.1007/s00146-021-01200-5.

Haidar, Aissa, Tarik Ahajjam, Imad Zerousal, and Yousef Farhaoui. 2022. 'Application of Machine Learning Algorithms for Predicting Outcomes of Accident Cases in Moroccan Courts'. *Indonesian Journal of Electrical Engineering and Computer Science* 26 (2): 1103–08.

Haykin, Simon S. 1998. *Neural Networks: A Comprehensive Foundation*, 2nd edn. New Jersey: Prentice Hall.

Haenlein, Michael. 2019. 'A Brief History of Artificial Intelligence: On the Past, Present, and Future of Artificial Intelligence'. *California Management Review* 61 (4): 5–14.

Heller, Nathan. 2017. 'Estonia, The Digital Republic'. *New Yorker Magazine*. 18 December 2017. https://www.newyorker.com/magazine/2017/12/18/estonia-the-digital-republic.

Hofman, Jake M., Amit Sharma, and Duncan J. Watts. 2017. 'Prediction and Explanation in Social Systems'. *Science* 355 (6324): 486–88. https://doi.org/10.1126/science.aal3856.

Howard, Ayanna, and Jason Borenstein. 2018. 'The Ugly Truth About Ourselves and Our Robot Creations: The Problem of Bias and Social Inequity'. *Science and Engineering Ethics* 24: 1521–36.

Huq, Aziz Z. 2020. 'A Right to a Human Decision'. *Virginia Law Review* 106 (3): 611–688. https://chicagounbound.uchicago.edu/cgi/viewcontent.cgi?article=14060&context=journal_articles.

Huq, Aziz Z. Forthcoming. 'Artificial Intelligence and the Rule of Law'. In *The Routledge Handbook of the Rule of Law*, Michael Sevel edn. London: Routledge.

Jauhar, Ameen, Vaidehi Misra, Arghya Sengupta, Partha P. Chakrabarti, Saptarishi Ghosh, and Kripabandhu Ghosh. 2021. 'Responsible AI in the Indian Justice System: A Strategy Paper'. *Vidhi Centre for Legal Policy*, April, 31. https://vidhilegalpolicy.in/wp-content/uploads/2021/04/Responsible-AI-in-the-Indian-Justice-System-A-Strategy-Paper.pdf.

Jordan, Michael I., and Tom M. Mitchell. 2015. 'Machine Learning: Trends, Perspectives, and Prospects'. *Science* 349 (6245): 255–60. https://doi.org/10.1126/science.aaa8415.

Jurafsky, Daniel, and James H. Martin. 2019. *Speech and Language Processing*, 3rd edn. New Jersey: Prentice Hall.

Jussupow, Ekaterina, Izak Benbasat, and Armin Heinzl. 2020. 'Why Are We Averse Towards Algorithms? A Comprehensive Literature Review on Algorithm Aversion'. In *ECIS'20: Proceeding of the 28th European Conference on Information Systems*. Marrakech, Morocco, 15–17 June 2020. Dagstuhl, Germany: DBLP.https://aisel.aisnet.org/ecis2020_rp/168.

Kahneman, Daniel, Olivier Sibony, and Cass R. Sunstein. 2022. *Noise: A Flaw in Human Judgment*. New York: Little, Browns Spark.

Kaplan, Andreas, and Michael Haenlein. 2019. 'Siri, Siri, In My Hand: Who's the Fairest in the Land? On the Interpretations, Illustrations, and Implications of Artificial Intelligence'. *Business Horizons* 62 (1): 15–25.

Kaplan, Jerry. 2016. *Artificial Intelligence: What Everyone Needs to Know*. Oxford: Oxford University Press.

Kastellec, Jonathan P. 2010. 'The Statistical Analysis of Judicial Decisions and Legal Rules with Classification Trees'. *Journal of Empirical Legal Studies* 7 (2): 202–30. https://doi.org/10.1111/j.1740-1461.2010.01176.x/.

Katz, Daniel Martin, Michael J. Bommarito, and Josh Blackman. 2017. 'A General Approach for Predicting the Behavior of the Supreme Court of the United States'. Edited by Luis A. Nunes Amaral. *PLoS One* 12 (4): e0174698. https://doi.org/10.1371/journal.pone.0174698/.

Kleinberg, Jon, Himabindu Lakkaraju, Jure Leskovec, Jens Ludwig, and Sendhil Mullainathan. 2018. 'Human Decisions and Machine Predictions'. *The Quarterly Journal of Economics* 133 (1): 237–93. https://doi.org/10.1093/qje/qjx032

Kleinberg, Jon, Jens Ludwig, Sendhil Mullainathan, and Ziad Obermeyer. 2015. 'Prediction Policy Problems'. *American Economic Review* 105 (5): 491–495. https://doi.org/10.1257/aer.p20151023.

Kolt, Noam. forthcoming. 'Algorithmic Black Swans'. In *Washington University Law Review* 99. https://ssrn.com/abstract=4370566.

Kroll, Joshua A., Joanna Huey, Solon Barocas, Edward W. Felten, Joel R. Reidenberg, David G. Robinson, and Harlan Yu. 2017. 'Accountable Algorithms'. *University of Pennsylvania Law Review* 165: 633–705.

Lage-Freitas, Andre, Hector Allende-Cid, Orivaldo Santana, and Livia de Oliverira-Lage. 2022. 'Predicting Brazilian Court Decisions'. *Peer Journal of Computer Science* 8: e904–4. https://doi.org/10.7717/peerj-cs.904.

Larson, Jeff, Surya Mattu, Lauren Kirchner, and Julia Angwin. 2016. 'How We Analyzed the COMPAS Recidivism Algorithm'. ProPublica. 23 May. https://www.propublica.org/article/how-we-analyzed-the-compas-recidivism-algorithm.

LeCun, Yann, Yoshua Bengio, and Geoffrey Hinton. 2015. 'Deep Learning'. *Nature* 521 (7553): 436–44. https://doi.org/10.1038/nature14539.

Li, Shang, Hongli Zhang, Lin Ye, Xiaoding Guo, and Binxing Fang. 2018. In 2018 *IEEE Third International Conference on Data Science in Cyberspace (DSC)*, Guangzhou, China, 18–21

June, 5. Washington DC: IEEE Computer Society. https://ieeexplore.ieee.org/document/8411884.

Lin, Zhiyuan 'Jerry', Jongbin Jung, Sharad Goel, and Jennifer Skeem. 2020. 'The Limits of Human Predictions of Recidivism'. *Science Advances* 6 (7): eaaz0652. https://doi.org/10.1126/sciadv.aaz0652.

Ludwig, Jens, and Sendhil Mullainathan. 2021. 'Fragile Algorithms and Fallible Decision-Makers: Lessons from the Justice System'. *Journal of Economic Perspectives* 35 (4): 71–96. https://doi.org/10.1257/jep.35.4.71.

Medvedeva, Masha, Michel Vols, and Martijn Wieling. 2020. 'Using Machine Learning to Predict Decisions of the European Court of Human Rights'. *Artificial Intelligence and Law* 28 (2): 237–66. https//doi.org/10.1007/s10506-019-09255-y.

Miller, Tim. 2019. 'Explanation in Artificial Intelligence: Insights from the Social Sciences'. *Artificial Intelligence* 267: 1–38. https://doi.org/10.1016/j.artint.2018.07.007.

Mitchell, Tom M. 1997. *Machine Learning*. New York: McGraw-Hill.

Mullainathan, Sendhil, and Jann Spiess. 2017. 'Machine Learning: An Applied Econometric Approach'. *Journal of Economic Perspectives* 31 (2): 87–106. https://doi.org/10.1257/jep.31.2.87.

Mumcuoğlu, Emre, Ceyhun E. Öztürk, Haldun M. Ozaktas, and Aykut Koç. 2021. 'Natural Language Processing in Law: Prediction of Outcomes in the Higher Courts of Turkey'. *Information Processing & Management* 58 (5): 102684. https://doi.org/10.1016/j.ipm.2021.102684.

Narla, Akhila, Brett Kuprel, Kavita Sarin, Roberto Novoa, and Justin Ko. 2018. 'Automated Classification of Skin Lesions: From Pixels to Practice'. *Journal of Investigative Dermatology* 138 (10): 2108–10.

Newell, Allen, and Herbert A. Simon. 1972. *Human Problem Solving*. New Jersey: Prentice Hall.

Niblett, Anthony. 2013. 'Tracking Inconsistent Judicial Behaviour'. *International Review of Law & Economics* 34: 9–20.

Niblett, Anthony. 2018. 'Regulation Reform in Ontario: Machine Learning and Regulation'. *C.D. Howe Institute Commentary* 43 (3): 507–20. https://www.cdhowe.org/sites/default/files/2021-12/March%2027%20Commentary_507.pdf.

Niblett, Anthony. 2020a. 'Algorithms as Legal Decisions: Gender Gaps and Canadian Employment Law in the 21st Century'. *University of New Brunswick Law Journal* 71: 112–28. http://dx.doi.org/10.2139/ssrn.3702495.

Niblett, Anthony. 2020b. 'How Lower Courts Respond to a Change in a Legal Rule'. In *Selection and Decision in Judicial Process Around the World: Empirical Inquiries*, edited by Yun-chien Chang, 110–131. Cambridge: Cambridge University Press.

Niblett, Anthony. 2021. 'Artificial Intelligence and Regulation'. In *Leading Legal Disruption: Artificial Intelligence and a Toolkit for Lawyers and the Law*, edited by Giuseppina D'Agostino, Aviv Gaon, and Carole Piovesan, 315–28. Toronto: Thomson Reuters.

Niblett, Anthony, and Albert H. Yoon. 2017. 'Unintended Consequences: The Regressive Effects of Increased Access to Courts'. *Journal of Empirical Legal Studies* 14 (1): 5–30. https://doi.org/10.1111/jels.12140.

Niller, Eric. 2019. 'Can AI Be a Fair Judge in Court? Estonia Thinks So'. Wired. https://www.wired.com/story/can-ai-be-fair-judge-court-estonia-thinks-so.

Niklaus, Joel, Ilias Chalkidis, and Matthias Stürmer. 2021. 'Swiss-Judgment-Prediction: A Multilingual Legal Judgment Prediction Benchmark'. In *Proceedings of the Natural Legal Language Processing Workshop 2021*, Punta Cana, Dominican Republic, November 2021,

18. New York: Association for Computational Linguistics. https://aclanthology.org/2021.nllp-1.3.

Northpointe. 2015. 'Practitioner's Guide to COMPAS Core'. 19 March 2015. https://s3.documentcloud.org/documents/2840784/Practitioner-s-Guide-to-COMPAS-Core.pdf.

O'Hara, Kieron. 2020. 'Explainable AI and the Philosophy and Practice of Explanation'. *Computer Law & Security Review* 39 (1): 1–17. https://doi.org/10.1016/j.clsr.2020.105474.

Pasquale, Frank. 2015. *The Black Box Society*. Cambridge: Harvard University Press.

Pasquale, Frank. 2020. *New Laws of Robotics: Defending Human Expertise in the Age of AI*. Cambridge: Harvard University Press.

Pearl, Judea. 2013. 'Structural Counterfactuals: A Brief Introduction'. *Cognitive Science* 37 (6): 977–985. https://doi.org/10.1111/cogs.12065.

Penney, Jonathon. W. 2019. 'Privacy and Legal Automation: The DMCA as a Case Study'. *Stanford Technology Law Review* 22 (1): 412–86. https://law.stanford.edu/wp-content/uploads/2019/09/Penney_20190923_Clean.pdf.

Portinale, Luigi. 2022. 'Mapping Artificial Intelligence: Perspectives from Computer Science'. In *Contracting and Contract Law in the Age of Artificial Intelligence*, edited by Martin Ebers, Cristina Poncibò, and Mimi Zou, 3–18. Oxford: Hart Publishing.

Posner, Richard A. 2008. *How Judges Think*. Cambridge: Harvard University Press.

Quinlan, John Ross. 1986. 'Induction of Decision Trees'. *Machine Learning* 1 (1): 81–106. https://doi.org/10.1007/BF00116251.

Raz, Joseph. 1979. *The Authority of Law: Essays on Law and Morality*. Oxford: Oxford University Press.

Reiling, A.D. (Dory). 2020. 'Courts and Artificial Intelligence'. *International Journal for Court Administration* 11 (2): 8–18. https://doi.org/10.36745/ijca.343.

Remus, Dana A., and Frank Levy. 2017. 'Can Robots Be Lawyers? Computers, Lawyers, and the Practice of Law'. *Georgetown Journal of Legal Ethics* 30 (3): 501–58. http://dx.doi.org/10.2139/ssrn.2701092.

Rodrigues, Rowena. 2020. 'Legal and Human Rights Issues of AI: Gaps, Challenges, and Vulnerabilities'. *Journal of Responsible Technology* 4: 10005.

Russell, Stuart J., and Peter Norvig. 2010. *Artificial Intelligence: A Modern Approach*, 3rd edn. New Jersey: Prentice Hall.

Sacks, Meaghan, Vincenzo A. Sainato, and Alissa R. Ackerman. 2014. 'Sentenced to Pre-trial Detention: A Study of Bail Decisions and Outcomes'. *American Journal of Criminal Justice* 40 (1): 661–81. https://doi.org/10.1007/s12103-014-9268-0.

Salomao, Luis Felipe. 2020. 'Artificial Intelligence Applied to Conflict Management in the Judiciary Scope'. *First Forum on Law and Technology–Centro de Inovacao, Administracao e Pesquisa do Judiciario*, FGV Conhecimento, Brasilia, Brazil, 29 June–2 July 2020, 94.

Sawicki, Andres, Cass R. Sunstein, David Schkade, and Lisa M. Ellman. 2006. *Are Judges Political? An Empirical Analysis of the Federal Judiciary*. Washington: Brookings Institution Press.

Schubbach, Arno. 2019. 'Judging Machines: Philosophical Aspects of Deep Learning'. *Synthese* 198: 1807–27. https://doi.org/10.1007/s11229-019-02167-z.

Selbst, Andrew D, and Solon Barocas. 2018. 'The Intuitive Appeal of Explainable Machines'. *Fordham Law Review* 87 (3): 1085–139. https://ir.lawnet.fordham.edu/flr/vol87/iss3/11.

Selbst, Andew D, and Julia Powles. 2017. 'Meaningful Information and the Right to Explanation'. *International Data Privacy Law* 7 (4): 233–42. https://doi.org/10.1093/idpl/ipx022.

Sourdin, Tania, and Richard Cornes. 2018. 'Do Judges Need to Be Human? The Implications of Technology for Responsive Judging'. In *The Responsive Judge*, edited by Tania Sourdin and Archie Zariski, 87–119. Singapore: Springer.

Sovrano, Francesco, Fabio Vitali, and Monica Palmirani. 2020. 'Modeling GDPR-Compliant Explanations for Trustworthy AI'. In *EGOVIS'20: Proceedings of the 9th International Conference on Electronic Government and the Information Systems Perspective*, Bratislava Slovakia, 14–17 September 2020, 14. Dagstuhl, Germany:DBLP. https://doi.or g/10.1007/978-3-030-58957-8_16.

Starr, Sonja B. 2014. 'Evidence-Based Sentencing and the Scientific Rationalization of Discrimination'. *Stanford Law Review* 66 (4): 803–72. https://ssrn.com/abstract=2318940.

Stern, Rachel E., Benjamin L. Liebman, Margaret E. Roberts, and Alice Z. Wang. 2021. 'Automating Fairness? Artificial Intelligence in the Chinese Courts'. *Columbia Journal of Transnational Law* 59: 526–53. https://ssrn.com/abstract=4026798.

Stevenson, Megan T. 2018. 'Assessing Risk Assessment in Action'. *Minnesota Law Review* 103: 303–83. https://dx.doi.org/10.2139/ssrn.3016088.

Stevenson, Megan T., and Jennifer L. Doleac. 2023. 'The Counterintuitive Consequences of Sex Offender Risk Assessments at Sentencing'. *University of Toronto Law Journal* 73 (1): 59–72. https://doi.org/10.3138/utlj-2023-0014.

Strickson, Benjamin, and Beatriz De La Iglesia. 2020. 'Legal Judgments Predictions for UK Courts'. In *ICISS'20: Proceedings of the 3rd International Conference on Information Science and Systems*, New York, 19–22 March 2020, 5. New York: Association for Computing Machinery. https://doi.org/10.1145/3388176.3388183.

Şulea, Octavia-Maria, Marcos Zampieri, Mihaela Vela, and Josef van Genabith. 2017. 'Predicting the Law Area and Decisions of French Supreme Court Cases'. In *RANLP'17: Proceedings of the International Conference Recent Advances in Natural Language Processing*, Varna, Bulgaria. September 2017, 6. Shuman, Bulgaria: INCOMA Ltd. https://doi.org/10.26615/978-954-452-049-6_092.

Sunstein, Cass R. 2019. 'Algorithms, Correcting Biases'. *Social Research: An International Quarterly* 86 (2): 499–511. https://doi.org/10.1353/sor.2019.0024.

Sunstein, Cass R. 2022. 'Governing by Algorithm? No Noise and (Potentially) Less Bias'. *Duke Law Journal* 71 (6): 1175–205. https://dx.doi.org/10.2139/ssrn.3925240.

Tuulik, Maria-Elisa. 2022. 'Estonia does not develop AI Judge'. 19 May 2022. https://www.just.ee/en/news/estonia-does-not-develop-ai-judge.

Varian, Hal R. 2014. 'Big Data: New Tricks for Econometrics'. *Journal of Economic Perspectives* 28 (2): 3–28. https://doi.org/10.1257/jep.28.2.3.

Virtucio, Michael Benedict L., Jeffrey A. Aborot, John Kevin C. Abonita, Roxanne S. Avinante, Rother Jay B. Copino, Michelle P. Neverida, Vanessa O. Osiana, Elmer C. Peramo, Joanna G. Syjuco, and Glenn Brian A. Tan. 2018. 'Predicting Decisions of the Philippine Supreme Court Using Natural Language Processing and Machine Learning'. In *2018 IEEE 42nd Annual Computer Software and Applications Conference (COMPSAC)*, Tokyo, Japan, 23–27 July 2018, 5. Washington, DC: IEEE. https://ieeexplore.ieee.org/document/8377844.

Vunikili, Ramya, Hitesh Ochani, Divisha Jaiswal, Richa Deshmukh, Daniel L. Chen, and Elliott Ash. 2018. 'Analysis of Vocal Implicit Bias in Scotus Decisions Through Predictive Modelling'. In *Proceedings of Experimental Linguistics*, 4. https://exlingsociety.com/wp-content/uploads/proceedings/exling-2018/09_0029_000362.pdf.

Wachter, Sandra, Brent Mittelstadt, and Luciano Floridi. 2017. 'Why a Right to Explanation of Automated Decision-Making Does Not Exist in the General Data Protection Regulation'. *International Data Privacy Law* 7 (2): 76–99. https://doi.org/10.1093/idpl/ipx005.

Wachter, Sandra, Brent Mittelstadt, and Chris Russell. 2018. 'Counterfactual Explanations without Opening the Black Box: Automated Decisions and the GDPR'. *Harvard Journal of Law & Technology* 31 (2): 841–87. https://dx.doi.org/10.2139/ssrn.3063289.

Walmsley, Joel. 2021. 'Artificial Intelligence and the Value of Transparency'. *AI & Society* 36 (2): 585–95. https://doi.org/10.1007/s00146-020-01066-z.

Waltl, Bernhard, Georg Bonczek, Elena Scepankova, Jorg Landthaler, and Florian Matthes. 2017. 'Predicting the Outcome of Appeal Decisions in Germany's Tax Law'. In *International Conference on Electronic Participation 2017*, St. Petersburg, Russia, 4-7 September, 10. New York: Springer Press.

Wang, Pei. 2019. 'On Defining Artificial Intelligence'. *Journal of Artificial General Intelligence* 10 (2): 1–37. https://doi.org/10.2478/jagi-2019-0002.

Winograd, Terry. 1972. 'Understanding Natural Language'. *Cognitive Psychology* 3 (1): 1–191. https://doi.org/10.1016/0010-0285 (72)90002-3.

Yang, Wenmian, Weijia Jia, Xiaojie Zhou, and Yutao Luo. 2019. 'Legal Judgment Prediction via Multi-Perspective Bi-Feedback Network'. In *IJCAI'19: Proceedings of the 28th International Joint Conference on Artificial Intelligence*, Macao, China, 10–16 August 2019, 7. Washington, DC: AAAI Press. https://doi.org/10.24963/ijcai.2019/567.

Zhong, Haoxi, Zhipeng Guo, Cunchao Tu, Chaojun Xiao, Zhiyuan Liu, and Maosong Sun. 2018. 'Legal Judgment Prediction via Topological Learning'. In *EMNLP'18: Proceedings of the 2018 Conference on Empirical Methods in Natural Language Processing*, Brussels, Belgium, October–November 2018, 9. Cedarville, OH: Association for Computational Linguistics. https://doi.org/10.18653/v1/d18-1390.

Zerilli, John, Alistair Knott, James Maclaurin, and Colin Gavaghan. 2018. 'Transparency in Algorithmic and Human Decision-Making: Is There a Double Standard?' *Philosophy & Technology* 32 (4): 661–83. https://doi.org/10.1007/s13347-018-0330-6.

Zou, Mimi. 2020. '"Smart Courts" in China and the Future of Personal Injury Litigation'. *Journal of Personal Injury Law* 1: 5–11. https://ssrn.com/abstract=3552895.

Index

Introductory Note

References such as '178–9' indicate (not necessarily continuous) discussion of a topic across a range of pages. Wherever possible in the case of topics with many references, these have either been divided into sub-topics or only the most significant discussions of the topic are listed. Because the entire work is about 'judicial behaviour', the use of this term (and certain others which occur constantly throughout the book) as an entry point has been restricted. Information will be found under the corresponding detailed topics. Entries in a form such as 'supreme courts, *see also individual countries*' refer to a class of entries (in this case, 'United Kingdom, Supreme Court') rather than a specific 'individual countries' entry.

For the benefit of digital users, indexed terms that span two pages (e.g., 52–53) may, on occasion, appear on only one of those pages.